System and Software Requirements Engineering

Edited by: Richard H. Thayer and Merlin Dorfman

Foreword by: Raymond T. Yeh

System and Software Requirements Engineering

IEEE Computer Society Press Tutorial

Richard H. Thayer
Merlin Dorfman

Foreword by: Raymond T. Yeh

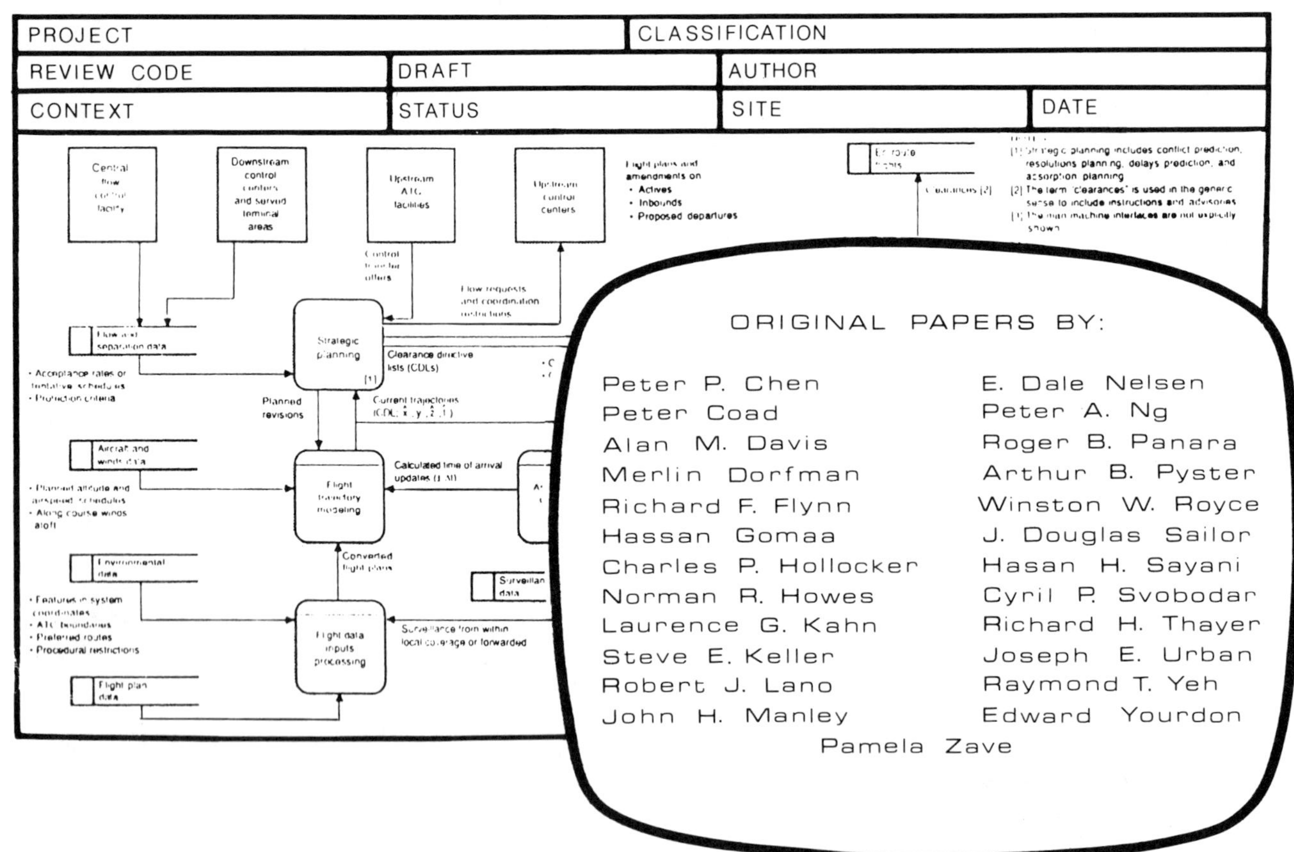

System and Software Requirements Engineering

Edited by: Richard H. Thayer and Merlin Dorfman

Foreword by: Raymond T. Yeh

IEEE Computer Society Press
Los Alamitos, California

Washington ● Brussels ● Tokyo

Published by

IEEE Computer Society Press
10662 Los Vaqueros Circle
P.O. Box 3014
Los Alamitos, CA 90720-1264

Cover designed by Jon Digerness

Printed in United States of America

IEEE Computer Society Order Number 1921
IEEE Catalog Number EH0304-6
ISBN 0-8186-8921-8 (case)
ISBN 0-8186-5921-1 (microfiche)
SAN 264-620-X

Additional copies may be ordered from:

IEEE Computer Society
10662 Los Vaqueros Circle
P.O. Box 3014
Los Alamitos CA 90720-1264

IEEE Service Center
445 Hoes Lane
P.O. Box 1331
Piscataway, NJ 08855-1331

IEEE Computer Society
13, Avenue de l'Aquilon
B-1200 Brussels
BELGIUM

IEEE Computer Society
Ooshima Building
2-19-1 Minami-Aoyama,
Minato-Ku
Tokyo 107 JAPAN

THE INSTITUTE OF ELECTRICAL AND ELECTRONICS ENGINEERS, INC.

Contributors of Original Papers

Dr. Peter P. Chen, Chen & Associates, Inc., 4884 Constitution Avenue, Suite 1E, Baton Rouge, LA 70808

Mr. Peter Coad, Object International Inc., 6304 Sprucewood Cove, Austin, TX 78731

Dr. Alan M. Davis, School of Information Systems, George Mason University, 4400 University Drive, Fairfax, VA 22030-4444

Dr. Merlin Dorfman, Lockheed Missiles & Space Company, Inc., P.O. Box 3504, Sunnyvale, CA 94088-3504

Mr. Richard F. Flynn, Lockheed Missiles & Space Company, Inc., P.O. Box 3504, Sunnyvale, CA 94088-3504

Dr. Hassan Gomaa, School of Information Systems, George Mason University, 4400 University Drive, Fairfax, VA 22030-4444

Mr. Charles P. Hollocker, Northern Telecom, Inc., 2435 North Central Express, Richardson, TX 75080

Dr. Norman R. Howes, Institute for Defense Analyses, 1801 N. Beauregard, Alexandria, VA 22311

Mr. Steve E. Keller, Dynamics Research Corporation, 60 Frontage Road, Andover, MA 01810

Mr. Laurence G. Kahn, Dynamics Research Corporation, 60 Frontage Road, Andover, MA 01810

Mr. Robert J. Lano, Lano Enterprises, 46 Malaga Way, Manhattan Beach, CA 90266

Dr. John H. Manley, Department of Industrial Engineering, University of Pittsburgh, 1044 Benedum Hall, Pittsburgh, PA 15261

Mr. E. Dale Nelsen, Lockheed Missiles & Space Company, P.O. Box 3504, Sunnyvale, CA 94088-3504

Dr. Peter A. Ng, Department of Computer and Information Science, New Jersey Institute of Technology, Newark, NJ 07102

Mr. Roger B. Panara, Command and Control Division, Rome Air Development Center, Griffiss AFB, NY 13441-5700

Dr. Arthur B. Pyster, Software Productivity Consortium, 2214 Rock Hill Road, Herndon, VA 22070

Dr. Winston W. Royce, SoftwareFirst, 22534 Paul Revere Drive, Woodland Hills, CA 91364

Mr. J. Douglas Sailor, Lockheed Missiles & Space Company, P.O. Box 3504, Sunnyvale, CA 94088-3504

Dr. Hasan Sayani, Advanced Systems Technology Corporation, 9111 Edmonston Road #404, Greenbelt, MD 20770

Dr. Cyril P. Svoboda, Advanced Systems Technology Corporation, 9111 Edmonston Road #404, Greenbelt, MD 20770

Dr. Richard H. Thayer, Department of Computer Science, California State University at Sacramento, Sacramento, CA 95819

Dr. Joseph E. Urban, Department of Computer Science, Arizona State University, Tempe, AZ 85287

Dr. Raymond T. Yeh, Syscorp International, Suite 200, 9420 Research Boulevard, Austin, TX 78759

Mr. Edward Yourdon, 161 West 86th Street, New York, NY 10024

Dr. Pamela Zave, AT&T Bell Laboratories, 600 Mountain Avenue, Murray Hill, NJ 07974-2070

Foreword

This tutorial on System and Software Requirements Engineering edited by Richard H. Thayer and Merlin Dorfman is a very timely and helpful book.

It is timely because requirements engineering is one of the most important and yet least understood subdisciplines of system engineering. Lack of good requirements has caused the failures of multimillion dollar projects, has impeded development productivity, and has been a major contributor to the rise of software maintenance costs.

There are two major reasons why it is difficult to have good requirements. First of all, requirements are supposed to bound the solution space but not provide solutions. However, it is sometimes necessary, especially for one-of-a-kind systems, to do prototyping to explore the limits of the solution space to validate the requirements. Lack of prototyping in the requirements engineering process leads to inadequate requirements that are costly to correct later in the development phases. Secondly, the customer often does not really know what the requirements are or is unable to express the requirements. Consequently, requirements change often during the development life cycle.

While there are numerous articles and books written on requirements engineering, I have not seen a comprehensive treatment of this subject. In my opinion, such a treatment would consist of a discussion of the process model and various related subjects such as language, methodology, tools, and management support. Furthermore, it needs to be recognized that no methodology, language, or tool is universally applicable to all systems. It is with this perspective that I am delighted to see Thayer and Dorfman's collection. Not only does this book touch on all subjects just mentioned, it also provides different approaches for different applications. Furthermore, the section on CASE studies is an excellent way to bring real-world experience to the usage of various tools and techniques. If you are managing a large project and are contemplating its requirements or just want to understand this field, this book can help you.

To make a collection of papers cohesive is sometimes more difficult than writing a book. Thayer and Dorfman should be congratulated for this excellent volume which reflects well on their thoughts and efforts.

Raymond T. Yeh
SYSCORP International, Inc.
Austin, Texas

Preface

The purpose of this tutorial is to assemble under one cover a comprehensive body of knowledge about systems and software requirements engineering. Emphasis is on software requirements analysis and specifications, system engineering and its interface with software engineering, as well as information on subjects that are affected by system and software requirements, such as verification and validation, management, and configuration management. An additional volume, *Standards, Guidelines, and Examples: System and Software Requirements Engineering,* edited by Merlin Dorfman and Richard H. Thayer and published by the IEEE Computer Society Press, contains material that may be considered as an appendix to this tutorial.

This tutorial contains 44 original papers and reprints on system and software requirements engineering, a glossary of over 1400 system/software engineering terms applicable to requirements engineering, an "Annotated Bibliography" of books and reports with over 50 entries, and a list of "Selected References and Other Readings" with over 300 entries.

This tutorial is intended for:

- *Managers:* The tutorial provides an overview of system and software requirements issues and describes many of the "popular" software requirement methodologies and tools. Included are descriptions of software requirements specifications and methodologies, descriptions of several "new" software process models and their relationships to requirements engineering, discussions on software requirements reviews and verification, and approaches to managing the requirements activities. Several case studies are provided.
- *System and software system engineers:* The tutorial describes the front end of the software lifecycle and the difficulties interfacing with the system specifications. It also presents a basic understanding of system and software system engineering: partitioning, allocation, and flowdown of system requirements to software; software requirements analysis; and specification writing.
- *Software engineers, programmers, analysts, and other computer personnel:* The tutorial contains a general description of procedures and techniques for analyzing and specifying system and software requirements, and for writing a good requirements specifications, as well as descriptions of a number of state-of-the-art methodologies, representation methods, tools, and techniques.
- *Hardware engineers:* The tutorial describes how system specifications are partitioned and allocated to software, the techniques and tools for analyzing and describing software specifications, and how software interfaces with hardware.
- *College-level students and their teachers:* The tutorial offers sufficient background and instructional material to serve as a main or supplementary text for a course in system/software requirements analysis and specifications, in other words, requirements engineering.

This tutorial takes the view that system and software requirements engineering is the technical "center" of any system and/or software development project. Papers were selected that either describe this technical center or describe activities that interact with it (e.g., project management, configuration management, and reviews and walkthroughs). This approach provided a framework for selecting appropriate papers and assembling original material. This tutorial also takes the view that the techniques, tools, and procedures used for system engineering are similar, if not identical, to those used for software engineering.

Both original and reprinted papers are organized into chapters according to their impact on system and software requirements. Chapter 1 starts with a paper that introduces system and software engineering. Other papers in the chapter define and describe software engineering and the effect requirements have on the engineering process. Terminology and issues are also discussed.

Chapter 2 contains papers describing system engineering, operational concepts, methods for deriving software requirements from system requirements, and the application of system engineering principles to software called software system engineering.

Chapter 3 contains papers on "classic" software requirements analysis and the five types of requirements—functional, performance, external interfaces, design constraints, and quality metrics—as well as an approach to representing a software requirements specification by a users' manual. Chapter 3 also includes the most popular standard in software engineering, the IEEE *Guide to Software Requirements Specifications.*

Chapter 4 contains papers on ways to analyze and document software requirements. The papers deal with the classic (non-realtime) and modern (realtime) approaches to structured analysis, data-structured approaches, object-oriented methods, a method based on interface analysis, and formal (mathematically based) approaches to requirements engineering.

Chapter 5 contains papers on automated approaches to software requirements analysis (called requirements tools or computer-aided software engineering (CASE) tools). Classic tools such as SREM (Software Requirements Engineering Methodology) are described as well as innovative, experimental tools such as the knowledge-based system called *Requirement Apprentice.* Requirements analysis and documentation tools for personal computers are also presented, as well as some general purpose tools, such as Fourth Generation Languages (4GLs) and automated traceability tools.

Chapter 6 is concerned with managing the software requirements engineering activity and with testing and verification of system and software requirements. Papers describe a management view of requirements; the verification, validation, walkthrough/inspection, and review of requirements; and the part configuration management plays in the requirements phase.

Chapter 7 begins with three papers that provide different perspectives on the overall strategy of software development. It continues with detailed discussion of two new software development paradigms—reuse and prototyping—and their impact on software requirements.

Chapter 8 is devoted to case studies. Four case studies highlight the application of information hiding, realtime structured analysis, prototyping, and formal specification methods.

All papers, whether original or reprinted, are tutorial in nature and are intended to explain some aspects of system and/or software requirements engineering. Every attempt was made to use the latest information. However, recent papers that present the latest (as yet unproven) technology were, as a rule, excluded. The papers in this tutorial explain the best state-of-the-practice in specifying and documenting system and software requirements.

In order to fill gaps in the published literature, the authors of this tutorial contacted experienced, seasoned authors and practitioners in the areas of system and software engineering and asked them to write or revise papers for the tutorial. Each of these original papers has been independently refereed through the IEEE Computer Society peer review process. The following authors, listed alphabetically, have contributed original or revised papers to this tutorial:

- Dr. Peter P. Chen (Chen & Associates) describes the Entity-Relationship approach to data modeling that he pioneered.
- Mr. Peter Coad (Object International, Inc.) and Mr. Edward Yourdon have written about a new, but rapidly growing, approach, Object-Oriented Analysis, and its advantages over conventional methods.
- Dr. Alan M. Davis (George Mason University), chair of the IEEE working group for a "Guide for Software Requirements Specifications," has written a paper on software requirements analysis and specifications that is based on the IEEE standard.
- Dr. Merlin Dorfman (Lockheed Missiles & Space Company, Inc.) has written an introductory paper on system and software requirements and the application of allocation, partitioning, flowdown, and traceability to system engineering.
- Mr. Richard F. Flynn (Lockheed Missiles & Space Company, Inc.) and Dr. Merlin Dorfman have updated their 1984 paper, "ARTS: An Automated Requirements Traceability System," to reflect recent improvements in ARTS and to relate their experiences in supporting the system.
- Dr. Hassan Gomaa (George Mason University) has written a paper that emphasizes the difference between rapid and evolutionary prototyping.
- Mr. Charles P. Hollocker (Northern Telecom, Inc.), chair of the IEEE working group for a "Standard for Software Reviews and Audits," has prepared a paper on requirements reviews, walkthroughs, and inspections.

- Dr. Norman R. Howes (Institute for Defense Analyses) has rewritten his paper on the procedure for substituting a user manual for a requirements specification.
- Mr. Steven E. Keller and Mr. Laurence G. Kahn (Dynamics Research Corporation) and Mr. Roger B. Panara (Rome Air Development Center) have written a paper on quality metrics for software requirements. This paper incorporates the R&D work done at RADC on Software Quality Attributes. There were no existing papers on software quality metrics as applied to software requirements.
- Mr. Robert J. Lano (Lano Enterprises) has written a paper on the operations concept document. The operations concept document is one of the most valuable tools in system engineering today and is required on most government contracts. There is no other existing public paper on the subject.
- Dr. John H. Manley (University of Pittsburgh) has contributed a paper on a new software development lifecycle strategy. Manley's two-track lifecycle model separates and shows the interrelationships between the management lifecycle and the technical lifecycle. The impact of system and software requirements on this model is highlighted.
- Mr. E. Dale Nelsen (Lockheed Missiles & Space Company, Inc.) has contributed an original paper on requirements allocation and flowdown, entitled "System Engineering and Requirement Allocation." One of the most important issues in system engineering today is how to properly partition, allocate, flowdown, and trace system requirements to software implementation.
- Dr. Arthur Pyster (Software Productivity Consortium) has prepared a paper on a new software development strategy called the *Synthesis Process.* This new process acknowledges and uses iteration, prototyping, and incremental development. It is specifically intended to promote the reuse of software.
- Mr. J. Douglas Sailor (Lockheed Missiles & Space Company, Inc.) has written a paper on system engineering patterned after the Defense Systems Management College textbook, *Systems Engineering Management Guide.* Sailor was the author of the first edition of the text. There were no existing papers that provided a view of system engineering to the necessary breadth and depth.
- Dr. Hasan Sayani (Advanced Systems Technology Corporation) has written a history and current status report on the Problem Statement Language/Problem Statement Analyzer (PSL/PSA).
- Dr. Cyril P. Svoboda (Advanced Systems Technology Corporation) has written on realtime and non-realtime structured analysis, consolidating the research and implementation activities in structured analysis over the past 13 years.
- Dr. Richard H. Thayer (California State University, Sacramento) and Dr. Winston W. Royce (SoftwareFirst) have written a paper on software system engineering that outlines and describes the system engineering approach to developing software.
- Dr. Joseph E. Urban (Arizona State University) has contributed a new paper on formal requirements analysis methods and executable specifications.
- Dr. Raymond T. Yeh (Syscorp International) and Dr. Peter A. Ng (New Jersey Institute of Technology) have contributed a general description of software requirements analysis and specifications from a management perspective. Dr. Yeh also wrote the foreword to the tutorial.
- Dr. Pamela Zave (AT&T Bell Laboratories) has modified her paper on "Assessments," which shows a taxonomy of the various software requirements analysis methods and techniques.

No successful endeavor has ever been carried through by one person alone. This is one of the measures of management, and this tutorial is no exception. The authors would like to thank the people and organizations that supported us in this effort, including:

- Ms. Margaret Brown, Managing Editor, IEEE Computer Society Press, for removing much of the drudgery in writing a book.
- Dr. Garry Kampen and his editors, for their review and comments.
- Ms. Barbara Dietrich of California State University, Sacramento, California, for her part in writing the glossary.
- Mr. Joseph Kramer of the library of California State University at Sacramento, for his research help.

- California State University at Sacramento, Computer Science Graduate Class in *Advanced Software Requirements Analysis* (Fall 1988), for reviewing all the papers in this tutorial and providing their frank opinions.
- Mr. Jon Digerness of Carmichael, California, for providing the illustrations that accompany the introductions to each chapter.

Richard H. Thayer
California State University, Sacramento

Merlin Dorfman
Lockheed Missiles & Space Company, Inc.

Table of Contents

Chapter 1: Introductions, Issues, and Terminology

1: Introduction

Requirements engineering is the science and discipline concerned with analyzing and documenting requirements, including needs analysis, requirements analysis, and requirements specification. It also provides the appropriate mechanisms to facilitate the analysis, documentation, and verification activities. Requirements engineering can also be defined as a combination of requirements analysis and the documentation of the requirements into the form called requirements specifications.

In turn, *system requirements engineering* is the science and discipline concerned with analyzing and documenting system requirements. It involves transforming an operational need into a system description, system performance parameters, and a system configuration through the use of an iterative process of analysis, design, trade-off studies, and prototyping.

Software requirements engineering has a similar definition as the science and discipline concerned with analyzing and documenting software requirements. It involves partitioning system requirements into major subsystems and tasks, allocating those subsystems or tasks to software, and transforming these allocated system requirements into a description of software requirements and performance parameters through use of an iterative process of analysis, design, trade-off studies, and prototyping.

And, last, a *system* can be considered a collection of hardware, software, data, people, facilities, and procedures organized to accomplish some common objectives. In software engineering, a system is a set of software programs that provides the cohesiveness and control of data that enable the system to solve the problem.

The major difference between system requirements engineering and software requirements engineering is that the origin of system requirements lies in user needs while the origin of software requirements lies in the system requirements and/or specifications. Thus, the system requirements engineer works with users and customers, eliciting their needs, schedules, and available resources, and must pro-

EHO304-6/90/0000/0001$01.00

duce documents that can be understood by them as well as by management, software requirements engineers, and other system requirements engineers. The software requirements engineer works with the system requirements documents and engineers, translating system documentation into software requirements that must be understood by management and software designers, as well as by software and system requirements engineers. When there is effectively no hardware component, and the system is all or almost all software, the software engineer effectively becomes the system engineer and works directly with the customer and/or user. Accurate and timely communication must be ensured all along this chain if the software designers are to begin with a valid set of requirements.

The purpose of Chapter 1 is to establish the environment of system and software engineering activities within the software engineering life cycle, to define terms used in and around system and software engineering, and to identify some of the major issues. The problems in writing good, correct, complete, and measurable system and software specifications are a major issue in software development today.

Other major issues in the requirements area concern

- engineers' inability to write a correct software requirements specification
- managers' desire to truncate requirements activity with the view that the major effort in any software development is programming and testing
- customers' failure to cooperate in verifying that the software requirements are correct, and the lack of software requirements documentation customers can understand
- the failure to understand that system requirements are essential to the development of good software requirements, or the unwillingness to act in accordance with that fact
- systems engineers' lack of training on how to partition and allocate system functions to software
- the desire of senior management in many large corporations to place personnel with little software knowledge or experience in positions of responsibility over what is essentially a major software project

Many problems concern terminology. Because the fields of computer science and software engineering are so new, many terms do not have universally accepted definitions. Computer scientists and software development groups define things in different ways. One of the purposes of this tutorial is to provide a common set of definitions that can be used in system and software requirements engineering.

The three papers in this chapter were selected to introduce the tutorial, to provide definitions, and to establish the requirements engineering issues and problems.

2: Description of Papers

The first paper, "System and Software Requirements Engineering" by Merlin Dorfman, is an overview of this tutorial. Dorfman discusses the value of good requirements and specifications, the place of requirements analysis in the lifecycle, and the framework for developing system requirements. The paper introduces the concepts of architectural design, allocation, flowdown, and traceability, and explains the application of configuration management, interface definition, and verification and validation to the requirements activity. The paper briefly introduces some of the tools and methods discussed in detail later in the tutorial.

"Pinpointing Requirements" by Laura Scharer defines the major issues involved in writing a software requirements specification. The paper points out that analysts and users harbor grave doubts about each other. The origins of these attitudes are obvious—failure encourages blame. Users are disenchanted because developers constantly bungle new system developments, and developers are disenchanted because they alone are blamed for the failures.

This paper is about software development for an in-house user; in other words, the user belongs to the same parent company as the software development team. In this environment, the relationship between the developer and user is much closer than in a contract situation. Scharer points out the problems that exist between experienced and inexperienced users and experienced and inexperienced software developers. She goes on to discuss some realistic goals and how to improve the relationship between the developer and the user. The paper also points out 12 different environmental factors that influence the software development process.

The Scharer paper goes on to define methods of controlling the system, how to select a user for the project team, methods of training the user, and a well-defined approach to developing a software system.

The last paper in the chapter, "A Taxonomy of Current Issues in Requirements Engineering" by Gruia-Catalin Roman, came from the April 1985 issue of *Computer,* which was devoted to "Requirements Engineering Environments: Software Tools for Modeling User Needs." Roman begins by pointing out that requirements specifications are critical because to a large extent they determine what is produced in a software project.

Roman divides requirements into two categories: functional and non-functional. The functional requirements deal with what a product should do, while the non-functional requirements deal with how the product should go about accomplishing this task given the constraints of a non-ideal world. Typical non-functional requirements might include performance constraints, interface constraints, operating constraints, and political constraints.

These constraints, it is pointed out, are often difficult to define.

Roman discusses the contents of a software requirements specification and brings up a number of requirements engineering issues. The paper presents a list of desirable requirements specification properties. The major thrust of the paper is to identify and classify the key issues facing the requirements engineering field today.

Readers interested in an overview of software engineering are referred to References 1, 2, and 3.

3: References

[1] Ramamoorthy, C.V., Atul Prakash, Wei-Tek Tsai, and Yutaka Usuda, "Software Engineering: Problems and Perspectives," *Computer,* Vol. 17, No. 10, Oct. 1984.

[2] Goldberg, R., "Software Engineering: An Emerging Discipline," *IBM Systems Journal,* Vol. 25, Nos. 3 and 4, 1986.

[3] Musa, John D., "Software Engineering: The Future of a Profession," *IEEE Software,* Vol. 2, No. 1, Jan. 1985.

System and Software Requirements Engineering

Merlin Dorfman
Lockheed Missiles and Space Company, Inc.

Abstract: Requirements engineering is presented and discussed as a part of systems engineering. The need for good requirements engineering and the consequences of a lack of it are most apparent in systems that are all or mostly software. Requirements engineering approaches are closely tied to the lifecycle or process model used. A distinction is made between requirements engineering at the system level and at lower levels (e.g., software elements). The fundamentals of requirements engineering are defined and presented; these are decomposition and abstraction; allocation, flowdown, and traceability; the role of prototyping; and validation and verification. Requirements development approaches, tools, and methods, as well as their capabilities and limitations, are briefly discussed.

Introduction

When the "software crisis"[1] was discovered and named in the 1960s, much effort was directed at finding the causes of the now-familiar syndrome of problems. The investigations determined that requirements deficiencies are among the most important contributors to the problem:

> In nearly every software project which fails to meet performance and cost goals, requirements inadequacies play a major and expensive role in project failure.[2]
>
> Development of the requirements specification "in many cases seems trivial, but it is probably the part of the process which leads to more failures than any other."[3]

The investigations determined that the benefits of good requirements include

1. Agreement among developers, customers, and users on the job to be done and the acceptance criteria for the delivered system
2. A sound basis for resource estimation (cost, personnel quantity and skills, equipment, and time)
3. Improved system usability, maintainability, and other quality attributes
4. The achievement of goals with minimum resources (less rework and fewer omissions and misunderstandings)

It was also observed that the value of good requirements and the criticality of doing them well increased dramatically with the size and complexity of the system being developed. Additionally, software-intensive systems seemed to have more inherent complexity (i.e., they were more difficult to understand) than systems that did not contain a great deal of software; thus these systems were more sensitive to the quality of their requirements. The bankruptcy courts are full of companies that were successful in developing small software products but that ran out of money before achieving a marketable result when the companies attempted to develop a larger, more complex product.

The products of a good requirements analysis include not only definition but also proper documentation of the functions, performance, internal and external interfaces, and quality attributes of the system under development, as well as any valid constraints on the system design or on the development process.

As the value of good requirements became clear, the focus of investigation shifted to the requirements themselves: How should they be developed? How can developers know when a set of requirements is good? What standards, tools, and methods can help; do they exist, or must they be developed? These investigations are by no means complete: Not only are new tools and methods appearing almost daily, but overall approaches to requirements and how they fit into the system lifecycle are evolving rapidly. As a result, requirements engineering has been well established as a part of systems engineering. Requirements engineers perform requirements analysis and definition on specific projects, as well as investigate in the abstract how requirements should be developed.

Requirements Engineering and the Development Lifecycle

Many models exist for the system and/or software lifecycle, the series of steps a system goes through from first realization of need through construction, operation, and retirement.[4] (Reference 5 provides a good overview of many existing models and presents a new, risk-driven approach that includes many other models as subsets. Reference 6 describes conditions under which various models might be used.) Almost all models include one or more phases variously named "requirements analysis" or "user needs development." Many models require generation of a document called, or serving the function of, a requirements specification. Even those that do not call for such a document have a product such as a diagram or diagrams that incorporates or expresses the user's needs and the development objectives, for example, Jackson System Development (JSD).[7]

A few of the better-known lifecycle models will be briefly discussed, and the way requirements engineering fits into them will be presented.

Baseline Management

Among the most extensively used models are baseline management[8, 9] and the waterfall upon which it is based.[10] (Baseline management differs from the waterfall in that it specifically requires each lifecycle phase to generate defined products that must pass a review and be placed under configuration control before the next phase begins.) In these models, as shown in Figure 1, determination of requirements should be complete, or nearly so, before any implementation begins. Baseline management, which provides a high degree of management visibility and control, has been found suitable for developments of very large size in which less complex methods often fail, and is required under many military standards and commercial contracts. This model, however, has been called into question[11] when it is difficult to determine the user's needs without some form of operational system to review (i.e., when the use of an a priori set of requirements presents an unacceptable risk).

Prototyping

The prototyping lifecycle (Figure 2) is one approach to the use of an operational system to help determine require-

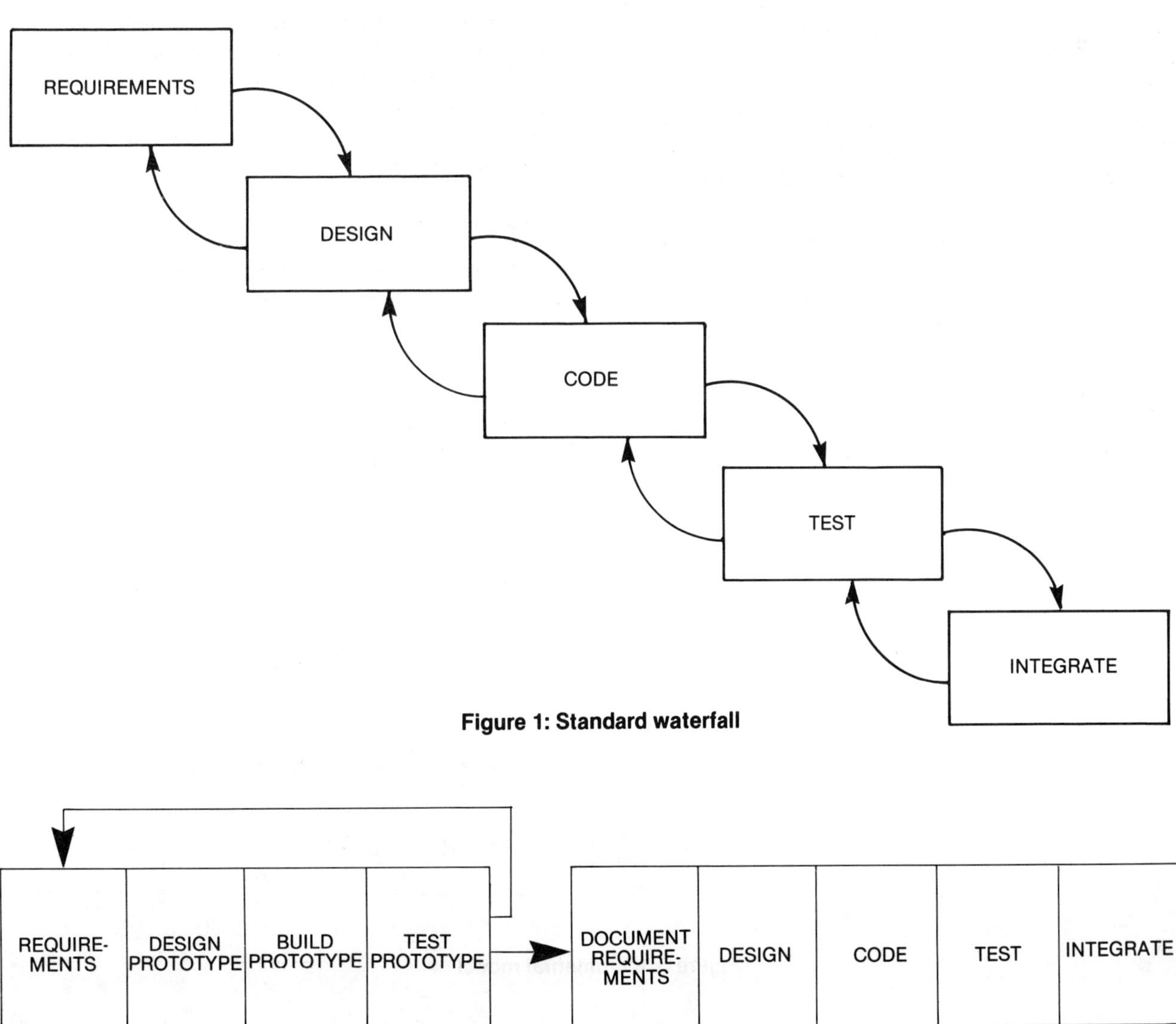

Figure 1: Standard waterfall

Figure 2: Prototyping model

ments.[12] In this model, some system capability is built with minimum formality and control to be run for or by the user, so that requirements can be determined accurately. Several successive prototypes will usually be built. The amount of requirements analysis that precedes prototyping depends on the specifics of the problem. It is normally recommended that the prototype should be used only to help generate a valid set of requirements. After the requirements are available, they should be documented, and development should proceed as in the baseline management model. If this recommendation is followed, the prototyping portion of the lifecycle may be considered as a tool or method supporting requirements analysis, and baseline management may be used as a model without loss of generality.

Many tools and methods are available to help support prototyping. The term "rapid prototyping" is associated with some of them to distinguish them from other forms, such as the development of high-risk hardware and software components, which is a slow, expensive process. Much of rapid prototyping is concentrated in two application areas, user interfaces and database operations. In these areas, a distinction can be made between prototyping tools and approaches that provide only "mock-ups" (simulations of the system's response to user actions) and those that actually perform the operations requested by the user. In this latter category are the so-called fourth-generation languages (4GLs),[13] which provide methods of generating code for user operations included within the 4GL's capability. Such tools provide the option of retaining the prototype as (part of) the final system. Considerations of execution time and efficiency of memory usage are weighed against the time and cost of building a system using the baseline management model and requirements determined by the rapid prototyping effort.

Incremental Development

The incremental development lifecycle calls for a series of development efforts, each of which leads to a delivered product to be used in the operational environment over an extended period of time (Figure 3). In contrast to the prototyping model, in which the purpose of each early product is to help determine requirements, each delivered increment provides some needed operational capability. Each increment is developed according to good software engineering practice (i.e., configuration management, reviews, and documentation are carried out). However, feedback from users of the operational systems may affect requirements for later increments.

Each increment in this model represents a full development cycle, including requirements analysis. The product of each requirements analysis phase is an addition or improvement to the product(s) of the requirements analysis phase of the previous increment. Similarly the implementation portions of each increment may add to, or upgrade, products of earlier increments. With this understanding, each increment may be looked at as a small example of a baseline management lifecycle.

The Spiral Model

Reference 5 describes the spiral model, an innovation that permits combinations of the conventional (baseline

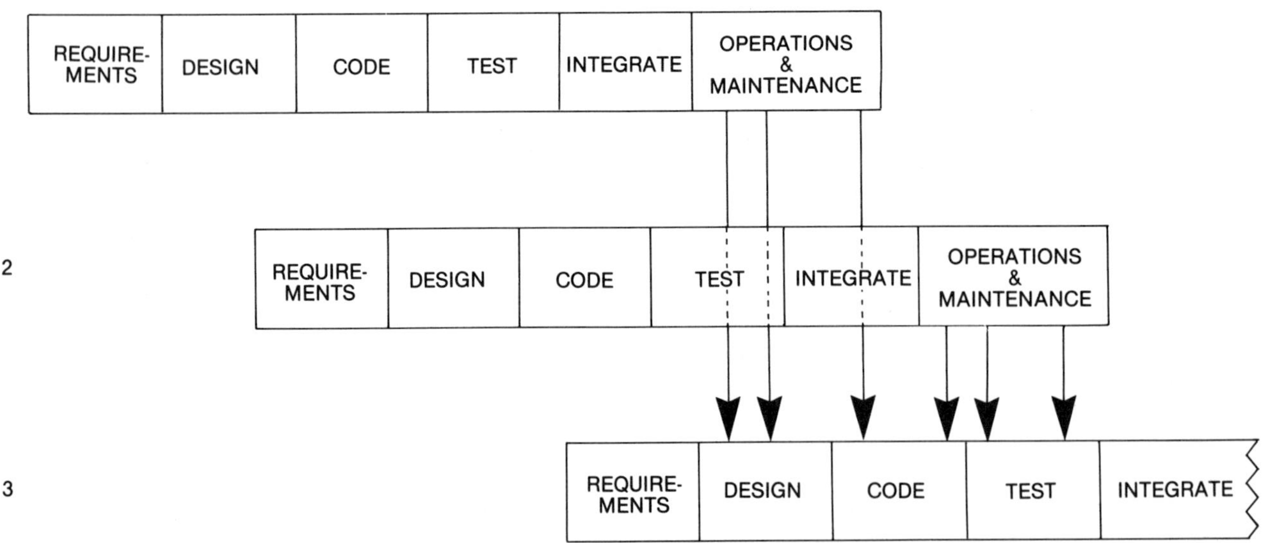

Figure 3: Incremental model

management), prototyping, and incremental models to be used for various portions of a development. It shifts the managment emphasis from developmental products to risk and explicitly calls for evaluations as to whether a project should be terminated. Figure 4 summarizes the spiral model.

The radial coordinate in Figure 4 represents total costs incurred to date. Each loop of the spiral, from the (– x) axis clockwise through 360 degrees, represents one phase of the development. A phase may be specification oriented, prototyping oriented, an evolutionary development step, or one of other variants; the decision on which form to use (or whether to discontinue the project) is made at each crossing of the (– x) axis by evaluating objectives, constraints, alternatives, and status (particularly risk).

System and Software Requirements

System and software requirements are often treated together because the tools and methods used to derive them and the techniques of documenting them are similar. Most of the tools and methods originated with software developers and were later found to be appropriate for system use as well. However, some important differences between system and software requirements should be pointed out.

System requirements describe the behavior of the system as seen from the outside (e.g., by the user). Although requirements documents and specifications cannot easily be read by users,[14] the system requirements serve at least as a partial communications vehicle to the more technically inclined users, or to a purchasing organization, as well as to analysts and designers who are concerned with the development of system elements or components.

Requirements for elements below the system level, whether they are for elements that are all hardware, all software, or a composite of hardware and software, are normally of minimal interest to users. These requirements serve to communicate with the developers, who need to know what is expected of the elements for which they are responsible and who also need information about those elements with which they must interface.

This distinction is important for several reasons. First, like any communication vehicle, a requirements document should be written with its intended audience in mind. The degree to which nontechnical users must read and understand a requirements document is a factor in how it is written. Second, and perhaps more importantly, the skills and experience of the requirements developers must be considered. All too frequently, systems engineers with limited software knowledge are responsible for software-intensive systems. They not only write system-level requirements, which demands knowledge of what functions and performance a software-intensive system can be expected to meet; they also allocate functions and requirements to hardware and software. Thus the software developers are asked to develop designs to meet requirements that may be highly unrealistic or infeasible. Software developers seem to be reluctant to get involved in systems engineering. One of the results of this reluctance is that the development of software elements often starts with poor requirements.

The next section will describe further the distinction between system and software requirements as it outlines the approach to generating requirements for all elements.

Fundamentals of Requirements Engineering

This section presents the overall framework within which requirements engineering takes place. Information about tools and methods is not presented here; at this point we are concerned with the sequence of events.

A system of any but the smallest size will be decomposed into a hierarchy of elements (Figure 5). Several approaches are available for development of the hierarchy (e.g., functional or physical decomposition), but all produce definitions of elements at all levels of the hierarchy. After the lowest-level elements ("Units" in Figure 5) are defined, they are separately developed and then integrated to form the next-larger elements ("Programs" in Figure 5). These elements are then integrated into larger-size elements at higher levels, back up to the full system. Thus the lifecycle models we presented earlier can be seen to be oversimplified in that they do not account for the development and integration of the various elements that compose the system. The requirements engineer needs to be concerned with all the requirements work that takes place. As described above, this includes requirements for the entire system, for composite (hardware and software) elements at lower levels, and for all-hardware and all-software elements. It should be noted at this point that references to "the requirements specification" are meaningless for any but the smallest systems; there will be several or many requirements specifications.

System Requirements

Ignoring for the time being the question of how the requirements for the various elements are developed and documented, we will describe the mechanics of filling out the system hierarchy with requirements.[15] Early in the system development process, as the system-level requirements are being generated (in itself an iterative process), requirements engineers and others begin to consider what elements should be defined in the hierarchy. By the time the system requirements are compelte in draft form, a tentative definition of at least one and possibly two levels should be available. This definition will include names and general functions of the elements. Definition of the system hierarchy is often referred to as "partitioning."

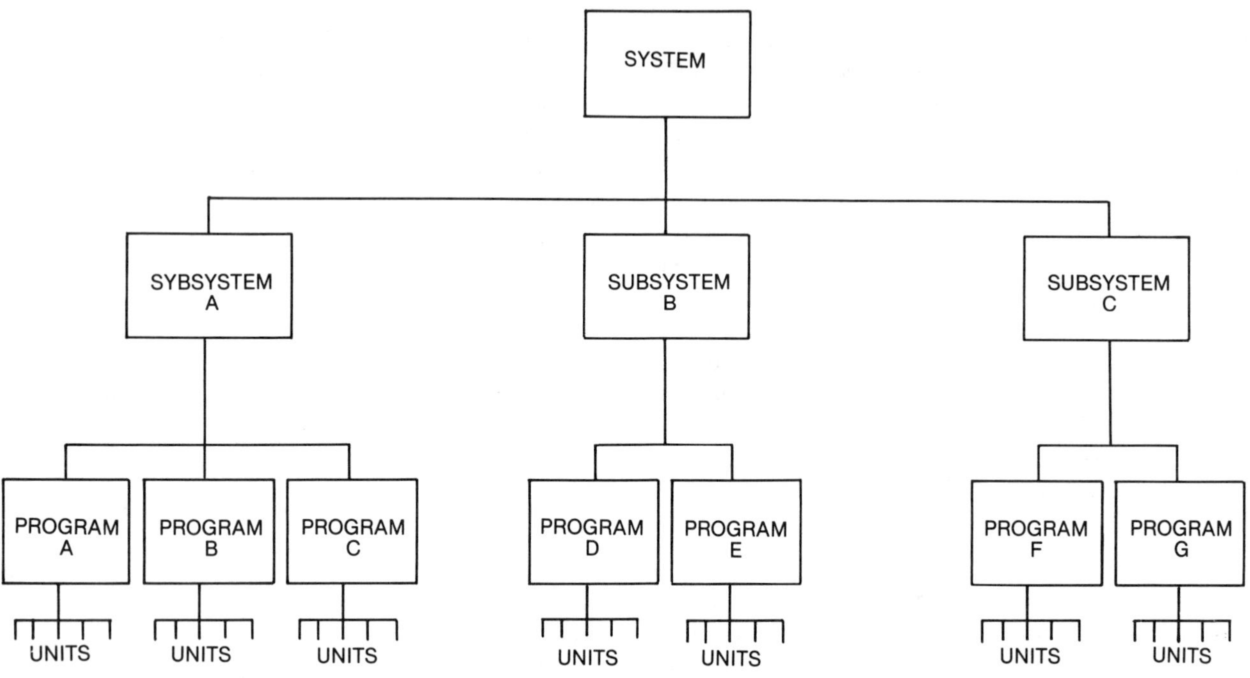

Figure 5: Hierarchy

Allocation

The next step is usually called "allocation." Each system-level requirement is allocated to one or more elements at the next level (i.e., it is determined which elements will participate in meeting the requirement). In performing the allocation, it will become apparent that (a) the system requirements need to be changed (additions, deletions, and corrections) and (b) the definitions of the elements are not correct. The allocation process therefore is iterative, leading eventually to a complete allocation of the system requirements, as shown in Figure 6. The table shows which element or elements will meet each system requirement; all requirements must be allocated to at least one element at the next level. In this example, we have called the level below system the subsystem level; in practice, the names are arbitrary, depending on the number of levels in the entire hierarchy and the conventions in use by the systems engineering organization. Figure 6 shows that the system-level requirement denoted as SYS 001 is allocated to subsystems A and B, SYS 002 is allocated to A and C, and so forth.

Flowdown

The next step is referred to as "flowdown." (The reader should be aware that this nomenclature is not universal.) Flowdown consists of writing requirements for the lower-level elements in response to the allocation. When a system requirement is allocated to a subsystem, the subsystem must have at least one requirement that responds to the allocation. Usually more than one requirement will be written. The lower-level requirement(s) may closely resemble the higher-level one, or may be very different if the system engineers recognize a capability that the lower-level element must have to meet the higher-level requirement. In the latter case, the lower-level requirements are often refered to as "derived."

The level of detail increases as we move down in the hierarchy. That is, system-level requirements are general in nature, while requirements at low levels in the hierarchy are very specific. A key part of the systems engineering approach to system development is decomposition and abstraction: The system is partitioned (decomposed) into finer and finer elements, while the requirements start at a highly abstract (general) level and become more specific for the lower-level elements. Large software-intensive systems are among the most logically complex of human artifacts, and decomposition and abstraction are essential to the successful managment of this complexity.

When flowdown is done, errors may be found in the allocation, the hierarchy definition, and the system requirements; thus the flowdown process is also iterative and may cause parts of previous processes to be repeated.

Figure 7 shows the first level of flowdown. System-level requirements SYS001 was allocated to subsystems A and B; subsystem requirements (in this example, SSA001, SSA002, and SSB001) are written in response to the allocation.

SYSTEM REQUIREMENTS	SUBSYSTEM A	SUBSYSTEM B	SUBSYSTEM C
SYS 001	X	X	
SYS 002	X		X
SYS 003		X	
SYS 004	X	X	X
SYS 005			X
SYS 006		X	
SYS 007	X	X	

Figure 6: Allocation

SYSTEM REQUIREMENT	SYSTEM A REQUIREMENT	SYSTEM B REQUIREMENT	SYSTEM C REQUIREMENT
SYS 001	SSA 001 SSA 002	SSB 001	—
SYS 002	SSA 003 SSA 004 SSA 005	—	SSC 001 SSC 002
SYS 003	—	SSB 002 SSB 003	—
SYS 004	SSA 006 SSA 007	SSB 004 SSB 005 SSB 006	SSC 003
SYS 005	—	—	SSC 004 SSC 005
SYS 006	—	SSB 007 SSB 008	—
SYS 007	SSA 008 SSA 009	SSB 009	—

Figure 7: Flowdown

Similarly, SYS002 was allocated to subsystems A and C; the subsystem requirements SSA003, SSA004, SSA005, SSC001, and SSC002 are the flowdown of SYS002 to subsystem level. The result is a complete set of requirements for each of the subsystems. After completion of this level of flowdown, allocation of the subsystem requirements is carried out to the next level, followed by flowdown to that level. Again, the processes are iterative and changes may be needed to higher-level hierarchy definition, allocation, or flowdown.

The process of partitioning, allocation, and flowdown is then repeated to as low a level as needed for this particular system; for software elements, this is often to the module level. Figure 8 emphasizes the iterative nature of this process at each level in the many levels of partitioning, allocation, and flowdown.

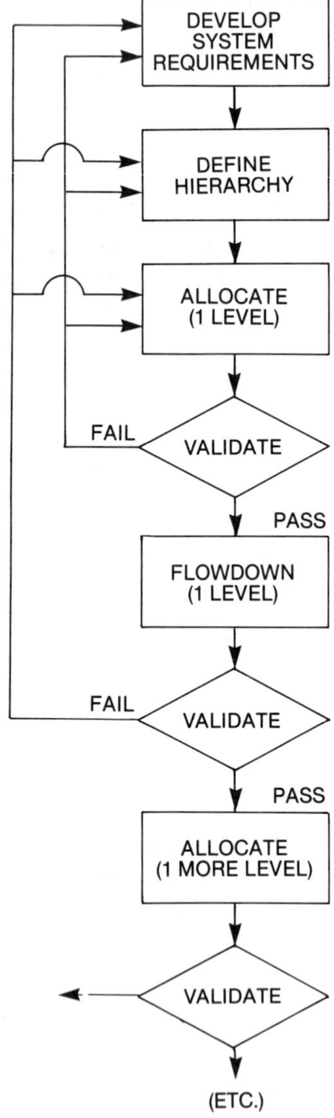

Figure 8: Iteration in partitioning, allocation, and flowdown

Traceability

The number of requirements proliferates rapidly during the allocation and flowdown process. If we assume that there are four levels in the hierarchy, that each element partitions to four at the next level, that each requirement is allocated to two of the four, and that each flowdown results in three requirements per allocated element (all reasonable assumptions), there will be over 250 requirements in the hierarchy for each system-level requirement. Keeping track of all these requirements is essential to make sure that all requirements are properly flowed down to all levels with no requirements lost and no "extras" thrown in. Reading and understanding the requirements to answer these questions is difficult enough; without a way to keep track of the flowdown path in a hierarchy of thousands of requirements, it becomes impossible. Traceability is the concept that implements the necessary bookkeeping.[15] Establishment of traceability as allocation and flowdown are done helps assure the validity of the process. Then, if changes are needed (e.g., a system-level requirement because of user input, or a lower-level requirement due to a problem with allocation or flowdown), traceability enables the engineer to locate the related requirements, at higher and lower levels, that must be reviewed to see if they need to be changed.

Figure 9 shows the traceability path corresponding to the allocation and flowdown in Figures 6 and 7. System requirement SYS001 traces downward to SSA001, which in turn traces downward to PGA001, PGA002, and PGB001. SYS001 also traces to SSA002, which further traces to PGA003, PGC001, and PGC002. Upward traceability also exists (e.g., PGB001 to SSA001 to SYS001). Other formats such as trees and indented tables can be used to illustrate tracebility, as in reference 15.

Note that while allocation and flowdown are technical tasks, traceability is not strictly an engineering function: it is a part of requirements management. A case can be made that more of the requirements problems observed in system development are due to failures in requirements management than in the technical functions.

Interfaces

An additional step is interface definition. Before development of system requirements can begin, the system's external interfaces (the interfaces between the system and the outside world) must be known. As each level of partitioning, allocation, and flowdown takes place, the interfaces of each element to the rest of the system must be specified. This definition has two parts. First, interfaces defined at higher levels are made more specific, i.e., the external interfaces to the entire system are identified as to

SYSTEM REQUIREMENT	SUBSYSTEM A REQUIREMENT	PROGRAM A REQUIREMENT	PROGRAM B REQUIREMENT	PROGRAM C REQUIREMENT
SYS 001	SSA 001	PGA 001 PGA 002	PGB 001	—
	SSA 002	PGA 003	—	PGC 001 PGC 002
SYS 002	SSA 003		PGB 002 PGB 003	—
	SSA 004	PGA 004	PCB 004	PGC 003
	SSA 005	PGA 005	PCB 005 PCB 006	PGC 004 PGC 005

Figure 9: Requirements traceability

which subsystem(s) actually perform the interface. Second, internal interfaces at that level are defined, i.e., the subsystem-to-subsystem interfaces needed to enable each subsystem to meet the requirements allocated to it.

Figure 10 illustrates this concept. In the top diagram, "A" represents an external interface to the system. When subsystems 1, 2, 3, and 4 are defined, as shown in the lower diagram, "A" is identified to subsystem 1, and internal interfaces, such as "B" between 3 and 4, are found to be necessary. This process continues throughout development of the hierarchy.

It is also possible that errors in partitioning, allocation, and flowdown will be discovered when interface definition is taking place, leading to iteration in those earlier steps.

The Refined Lifecycle Model

We will next examine the implications of the above processes for the lifecycle models discussed earlier. It should now be apparent that the single "requirements analysis" phase, even if extended to "system requirements analysis" and "software requirements analysis," is inadequate. The lifecycle model should account for the multiplicity of levels in the hierarchy, and furthermore should recognize that the various subsystems and other elements at any level do not need to be synchronized. That is, if we are willing to accept the risk that flowdown to the last subsystem will surface some errors in partitioning or allocation, we can phase the subsystems and, of course, the lower-level elements as well.

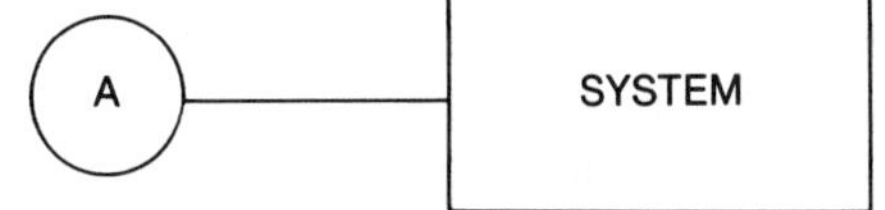

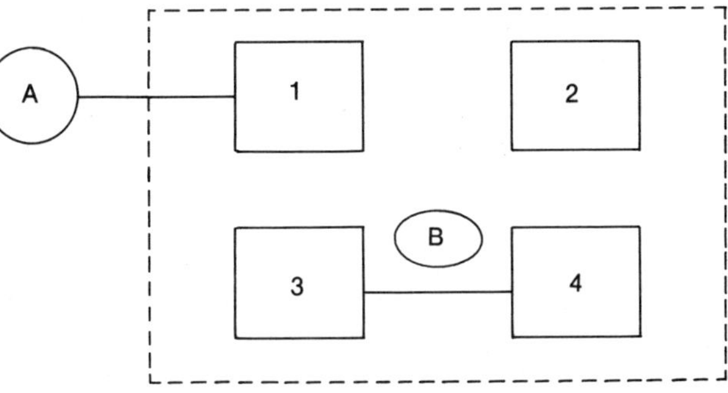

Figure 10: Increasing detail of interface definition

Plate 1 is the more realistic and more complicated lifecycle chart that results from the above considerations. Although it builds on a baseline management approach, the nesting and phasing shown will apply to any of the models discussed earlier or to combinations. Two features of the figure are particularly significant. First, for all but the lowest level of the hierarchy, the implementation phase of its lifecycle becomes the entire development cycle for the next lower elements. Thus the subsystems have their development cycle shown as a phase of the system lifecycle. Second, elements at any level may be phased. Thus the subsystems are shown as starting and finishing their development cycles at different times.

Validation and Verification

A final point in the framework of fundamentals relates to another requirements management task, the review of the developed products.[16] Validation and verification of the partitioning, allocation, flowdown, and interfaces are as important as their generation. It has been shown repeatedly that it is much more expensive to fix requirements errors found late in the development cycle than those found before the requirements phase is completed.[17] The baseline management model mandates that the requirements be fully and properly reviewed before design and implementation begin, and adequate review should be part of any requirements development.

Requirements Engineering and Architectural Design

The previous section presented an overview of the process of partitioning, allocation, and flowdown. The result of this process (a definition of the hierarchy down to some level, generation of the requirements for all elements, and determination of the interfaces between them) is known as the "architectural design" or "top-level design" of the system. Although it is called a design, requirements engineering is involved throughout the process. What, then, is the distinction between requirements analysis and design in this process?

Requirements analysis is often defined as the "what" of a problem: It is implemenation-free and contains objectives, not methods. Design, then, is the "how:" it describes the implementation that will meet the requirements. The two are supposed to be kept distinct although, of course, the feasibility of meeting a requirement must always be considered. However, if we look closely at the process of generating the architectural design, we will see that both requirements analysis and design are involved.

The generation of system-level requirements is, to the extent possible, a pure "what," addressing the desired characteristics of the complete system. The next steps, determining the next level of the hierarchy and allocating system requirements to the elements, are in fact a "how." They do not address objectives beyond the system requirements, but they define a subsystem structure that enables the requirements to be met. Flowdown is again a "what," determining what each element should do (functions, performance, etc.).

Development of the architectural design is, then, a process in which the steps of requirements analysis and design alternate, with more detail brought out at each cycle. The output of requirements analysis is input to the next state of design, and the output of design is input to the next stage of requirements analysis.[18]

Pure requirements analysis, like pure design, can only go so far. Both disciplines are needed to achieve the desired result, a system that meets its users' needs. Note that the character of requirements analysis, like that of design, changes as we move down in the hierarchy: requirements analysis for a low-level element is much more detailed and involves knowledge of previous design decisions. The tools and methods used for "analysis" do, in fact, support all aspects of architectural design development: partitioning, allocation, and flowdown. They are useful, therefore, in both the requirements analysis and design stages of the process.

Requirements Engineering Practices

Requirements engineering practices may be divided into three levels: overall, general approaches that will be referred to as methodologies; more specific, detailed approaches that will be called methods; and step-by-step formalized, manual or automated processes that will be called tools. While the categorization of some individual items may be slightly blurred, the distinction is nevertheless useful. The application of methodologies, methods, and tools to the development of system and software requirements will be outlined in this section.

Methodologies

In the category of broad, general approaches we find the lifecycle models presented above (baseline management, prototyping, incremental development, and spiral). The applicability of these models, for an entire development or one phase, has already been discussed. Also worth mentioning at the methodology level are the following approaches.

As pointed out by Davis,[19] precision and ease of understanding are conflicting objectives. Developers need a precise requirements document, in terminology with which they are familiar, as a basis for system development, while users cannot be expected to review and comment on such a document. Lano[14] proposes an operational concept document, written by the developers before requirements are generated, which is understandable by both parties. Howes[20] proposes the user manual as an approach to solving the user-developer communication problem. Lavi-Loeb[21] proposes an overall approach to software engineering based on the principles of system engineering. Papers by

Ramamoorthy et al.,[22] Roman,[23] Sailor,[24] and Nelsen[25] provide overviews of various aspects of system and software engineering as related to requirements.

Methods

The number of requirements engineering methods, like the number of tools, is proliferating rapidly. For this tutorial, it was not possible to print articles on all available methods. Only instructive descriptive articles about methods in extensive use or regarded as technologically significant could be printed. It was also desired to describe methods compatible with the lifecycle and methodologies discussed here. References are provided to additional articles beyond what could be described here.

Requirements analysis methods may be roughly divided into four categories, as shown in Figure 11. The categorizations should not be regarded as absolute: most methods have some of the characteristics of all the categories, but usually one viewpoint is primary.

Process-oriented methods take the primary viewpoint of the way the system transforms inputs into outputs, with less emphasis on the data itself and control aspects. Classical structured analysis (SA)[26, 27] fits into this category, as do Structured Analysis and Design Technique (SADT),[28] operational/executable models such as PAISLey[29] and Descartes,[30] and formal methods such as Vienna Design Method (VDM)[31] and Z.[32]

Data-oriented methods emphasize the system state as a data structure. While SA and SADT have secondary aspects of the data viewpont, JSD[7] and entity-relationship modeling[33] are primarily data oriented.

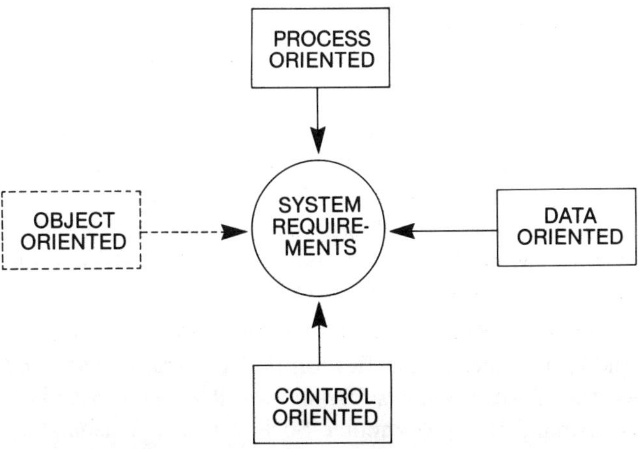

Figure 11: Categories of requirements analysis methods

Control-oriented methods emphasize synchronization, deadlock, exclusion, concurrency, and process activation and deactivation. SADT and the realtime extensions to SA[34, 35] are secondarily control oriented. Flowcharting is primarily control oriented.

Finally, object-oriented methods, which have come into prominence in recent years for software design,[36] are being extended to include requirements analysis.[37] These methods base analysis on classes of objects of the system and their interactions. Figure 11 shows object-oriented methods in dotted lines, because they may be considered as either a major enhancement of data-oriented methods or a separate approach.

Tools

Tools may support one or more methods. The number of tools that provide support for requirements engineering has also been proliferating rapidly, and this tutorial could print material on only a few. Software Requirement Engineering Methodology (SREM)[38] is both a tool and a method, important as the first to use an approach combining graphics and a requirements language, and still in development after 12 years. Problem Statement Language/Problem Statement Analyzer (PSL/PSA) is also a tool with a long history that is still being upgraded—it supports a wide range of methods.[39] Software through Pictures[40] is representative of a large number of integrated environments that support much of the system and software development cycle; these tools typically provide extensive support for SA with one or both realtime enhancements, and some also support analysis methods such as entity-relationship modeling and design methods such as Warnier-Orr.

Fourth generation languages[41] are an important class of tool, primarily used, as mentioned above, for user interface modeling and for applications involving access to databases and operations and reporting on the data.

Knowledge-based requirements generation, while far from practical application, is an important technology for the future. The article by Rich, Waters, and Reubenstein[42] describes progress and prospects for this goal.

Traceability, interface definition, and configuration management do not directly contribute to requirements analysis but are indispensable support functions. Tools that deal with traceability and interface definition are described in References 15 and 43. The Automated Requirements Traceability System (ARTS) automates the establishment and maintenance of traceability within the requirements hierarchy and to design and test. N^2 charts are a highly capable tool for description of interfaces, deserving of much wider knowledge and use than they have today. The principles of configuration management are presented clearly, concisely, and completely in Reference 44.

The Role of Tools and Methods

In conclusion, a few words are in order about the role of tools and methods in requirements engineering and indeed across the full scope of software and systems engineering. It has been established that the proper use of tools and methods appropriate to a problem can significantly increase productivity and quality.[45] It has equally been shown that developers cannot adopt or purchase methods and tools and just throw them at the problem. Selection of tools and methods requires study of their applicability and compatibility with the organization's practices. Commitment, training, and the time to make the transition are essential. Tools and methods are not a panacea: if selected and used correctly, they can provide great benefits; if regarded as magic solutions or otherwise misused, they will prove to be an expensive failure.

References

(1) Naur, P. and B. Randell, eds., "Software Engineering: report on a Conference Sponsored by the NATO Science Commission, Garmisch, Germany, 7-11 October 1968." Scientific Affairs Division, NATO, Brussels, Belgium, January 1969.

(2) Alford, M.W. and J.T. Lawson, "Software Requirements Engineering Methodology (Development)." *RADC-TR-79-168,* U.S. Air Force Rome Air Development Center, Griffiss AFB, N.Y., June 1979 (DDC-AD-A073132).

(3) Schwartz, J.I., "Construction of Software, Problems and Practicalities," *Practical Strategies for Developing Large Software Systems,* E. Horowitz, ed. Addison-Wesley, Reading, Mass., 1975.

(4) IEEE Standard 729, *Glossary of Software Engineering Terminology.* IEEE, New York, 1983.

(5) Boehm, Barry W., "A Spiral Model of Software Development and Enhancement." *IEEE Computer,* Vol 21, No. 5, May 1988. Reprinted in *Tutorial: System and Software Requirements Engineering,* R.H. Thayer and M. Dorfman, IEEE Computer Society Press, Washington, D.C., 1990.

(6) Davis, Alan M., Edward H. Bersoff, and Edward R. Comer, "A Strategy for Comparing Alternative Software Development Life Cycle Models." *IEEE Transactions on Software Engineering,* Vol. SE-14, No. 10, October 1988. Reprinted in *Tutorial: System and Software Requirements Engineering,* R.H. Thayer and M. Dorfman, IEEE Computer Society Press, Washington, D.C., 1990.

(7) Cameron, John R., "An Overview of JSD." *IEEE Transactions on Software Engineering,* Vol. SE-12, No. 2, February 1986.

(8) Mangold, E.R. et al., "TRW Software Development and Configuration Management Manual." *TRW-SS-73-07.* TRW, Inc., Redondo Beach, Calif., 1973.

(9) Metzger, Philip W., *Managing a Programming Project.* 2nd ed., Prentice-Hall, Englewood, Cliffs, N.J., 1981.

(10) Royce, Winston W., "Managing the Development of Large Software Systems." *Proceedings, IEEE Wescon,* IEEE, New York, August 1970. Reprinted in *Proceedings, Ninth International Conference on Software Engineering,* IEEE Computer Society Press, Washington, D.C., 1987.

(11) Brooks, Frederick P., Jr., Chairman, *Report of the Defense Science Board Task Force on Military Software.* Office of the Under Secretary of Defense for Acquisition, U.S. Department of Defense, Washington, D.C., September 1987.

(12) Gomaa, Hassan and D.B.H. Scott, "Prototyping as a Tool in the Specification of User Requirements." *Proceedings, Fifth International Conference on Software Engineering,* IEEE Computer Society Press, Washington, D.C., 1981.

(13) Verner, June and Graham Tate, "Third-Generation versus Fourth-Generation Software Development." *IEEE Software,* Vol. 5 No. 4, July 1988.

(14) Lano, Robert J., "A Structured Approach for Operational Concept Formulation." *Tutorial: System and Software Requirements Engineering,* R.H. Thayer and M. Dorfman, IEEE Computer Society Press, Washington, D.C., 1990.

(15) Dorfman, Merlin and Richard F. Flynn, "ARTS—an Automated Requirements Traceability System." *Journal of Systems and Software,* Vol. 4, No. 1, 1984.

(16) Boehm, Barry W., "Verifying and Validating Software Requirements and Design Specifications," *IEEE Software,* Vol. 1, No. 1, January 1984. Reprinted in *Tutorial: System and Software Requirements Engineering,* R.H. Thayer and M. Dorfman, IEEE Computer Society Press, Washington, D.C., 1990.

(17) Boehm, Barry W., *Software Engineering Economics.* Prentice-Hall, Englewood Cliffs, N.J., 1981.

(18) Hatley, Derek J. and Imtiaz A. Pirbhai, *Strategies for Real-Time System Specification.* Dorset House, N.Y., 1987.

(19) Davis, Alan M., "A Comparison of Techniques for the Specification of External System Behavior." *Communications of the ACM,* Vol 31, No. 9, September 1988. Reprinted in *Tutorial: System and Software Requirements Engineering,* R.H. Thayer and M. Dorfman, IEEE Computer Society Press, Washington, D.C., 1990.

(20) Howes, Norman R., "On Using the Users Manual as the Requirements Specification II." *Tutorial: System and Software Requirements Engineering,* R.H. Thayer and M. Dorfman, IEEE Computer Society Press, Washington, D.C., 1990.

(21) Lavi (Loeb), Jonah Z., "A System Engineering Approach to Software Engineering." *Proceedings, The Soft-*

ware Process Workshop, IEEE Computer Society Press, Washington, D.C., 1984.

(22) Ramamoorthy, C.V. et al., "Software Engineering: Problems and Perspectives." *IEEE Computer,* Vol. 17, No. 10, October 1984. Corrected copy printed in *Tutorial: System and Software Requirements Engineering,* R.H. Thayer and M. Dorfman, IEEE Computer Society Press, Washington, D.C., 1990.

(23) Roman, Gruia-Catalin, "A Taxonomy of Current Issues in Requirements Engineering." *IEEE Computer,* Vol. 18, No. 5, April 1985. Reprinted in *Tutorial: System and Software Requirements Engineering,* R.H. Thayer and M. Dorfman, IEEE Computer Society Press, Washington, D.C., 1990.

(24) Sailor, J. Douglas, "System Engineering Overview." *Tutorial: System and Software Requirements Engineering,* R.H. Thayer and M. Dorfman, IEEE Computer Society Press, Washington, D.C., 1990.

(25) Nelsen, E. Dale, "System Engineering and Requirements Allocation," *Tutorial: System and Software Requirements Engineering,* R.H. Thayer and M. Dorfman, IEEE Computer Society Press, Washington, D.C., 1990.

(26) DeMarco, Tom, *Structured Analysis and System Specification.* Prentice-Hall, Englewood Cliffs, N.J., 1979.

(27) Svoboda, Cyril P., "Structured Analysis: A Tutorial." *Tutorial: System and Software Requirements Engineering,* R.H. Thayer and M. Dorfman, IEEE Computer Society Press, Washington, D.C., 1990.

(28) Ross, Douglas T., "Structured Analysis (SA): A Language for Communicating Ideas." *IEEE Transactions on Software Engineering,* Vol. SE-3, No. 1, Janaury 1977.

(29) Zave, Pamela, "The Operational Versus the Conventional Approach to Software Development." *Communications of the ACM,* Vol. 27, No. 2, February 1984. Reprinted in *Tutorial: System and Software Requirements Engineering,* R.H. Thayer and M. Dorfman, IEEE Computer Society Press, Washington, D.C., 1990.

(30) Urban, Joseph E., "The Descartes Specification Language." *Tutorial: System and Software Requirements Engineering,* R.H. Thayer and M. Dorfman, IEEE Computer Society Press, Washington, D.C., 1990.

(31) Bjoerner, Dines, "On the Use of Formal Methods in Software Development." *Proceedings, Ninth International Conference on Software Engineering,* IEEE Computer Society Press, Washington, D.C., 1989.

(32) Norris, M., "Z (A Formal Specification Method). A Debrief Report." STARTS, National Computing Centre Ltd., 1986. Reprinted in *Tutorial: System and Software Requirements Engineering,* R.H. Thayer and M. Dorfman, IEEE Computer Society Press, Washington, D.C., 1990.

(33) Chen, Peter, "Entity-Relationship Approach to Data Modeling." *Tutorial: System and Software Requirements Engineering,* R.H. Thayer and M. Dorfman, IEEE Computer Society Press, Washington, D.C., 1990.

(34) Ward, Paul T. and Stephen J. Mellor, *Structured Development Techniques for Real-Time Systems,* (3 vols). Prentice-Hall, Englewood Cliffs, N.J., 1985.

(35) Hatley, Derek J., "The Use of Structured Methods in the Development of Large Software-Based Avionics Systems." *AIAA Paper 84-2592, Sixth Digital Avionics Systems Conference,* AIAA, Baltimore, MD., 1984.

(36) Booch, E. Grady, "Object Oriented Development." *IEEE Transactions on Software Engineering,* Vol. SE-12, No. 2, February 1986.

(37) Coad, Peter and Edward Yourdon, "An Introduction to OOA—Object-Oriented Analysis." *Tutorial: System and Software Requirements Engineering,* R.H. Thayer and M. Dorfman, IEEE Computer Society Press, Washington, D.C., 1990.

(38) Alford, Mack W., "SREM at the Age of Eight: The Distributed Computing Design System." *IEEE Computer,* Vol. 18, No. 4, April 1985. Reprinted in *Tutorial: System and Software Requirements Engineering,* R.H. Thayer and M. Dorfman, IEEE Computer Society Press, Washington, D.C., 1990.

(39) Sayani, Hasan, "PSL/PSA at the Age of Fifteen." *Tutorial: System and Software Requirements Engineering,* R.H. Thayer and M. Dorfman, IEEE Computer Society Press, Washington, D.C., 1990.

(40) Wasserman, Anthony I. and P.A. Pircher, "A Graphic, Extensible Integrated Environment for Software Development." *ACM SIGPLAN Notices,* ACM, Inc., New York, January 1987. Reprinted in *Tutorial: System and Software Requirements Engineering,* R.H. Thayer and M. Dorfman, IEEE Computer Society Press, Washington, D.C., 1990.

(41) Cobb, R.H., "In Praise of 4GLs." *Datamation,* July 15, 1985. Reprinted in *Tutorial: System and Software Requirements Engineering,* R.H. Thayer and M. Dorfman, IEEE Computer Society Press, Washington, D.C., 1990.

(42) Rich, C., R.C. Waters, and H.B. Reubenstein, "Toward a Requirements Apprentice." *Proceedings, Fourth International Workshop on Software Specifications and Design,* IEEE Computer Society Press, Washington, D.C., 1987. Reprinted in *Tutorial: System and Software Requirements Engineering,* R.H. Thayer and M. Dorfman, IEEE Computer Society Press, Washington, D.C., 1990.

(43) Lano, Robert J., "N^2 Charts." Extracted from TRW Defense and Space Systems Group, *TRW-SS-77-04,* TRW, Inc., Redondo Beach, Calif., 1987. Reprinted in *Tutorial: System and Software Requirements Engineering,* R.H. Thayer and M. Dorfman, IEEE Computer Society Press, Washington, D.C., 1990.

(44) Bersoff, Edward H., "Elements of Software Configuration Managment." *IEEE Transactions on Software Engineering,* Vol. SE-10, No. 1, January 1984. Reprinted in *Tutorial: System and Software Requirements Engineering,* R.H. Thayer and M. Dorfman, IEEE Computer Society Press, Washington, D.C., 1990.

(45) Boehm, Barry W., Maria H. Penedo, E. Don Stuckle, Robert D. Williams, and Arthur B. Pyster, "A Software Development Environment for Improving Productivity." *IEEE Computer,* Vol. 17, No. 6, June 1984.

-Cycle
ery Model

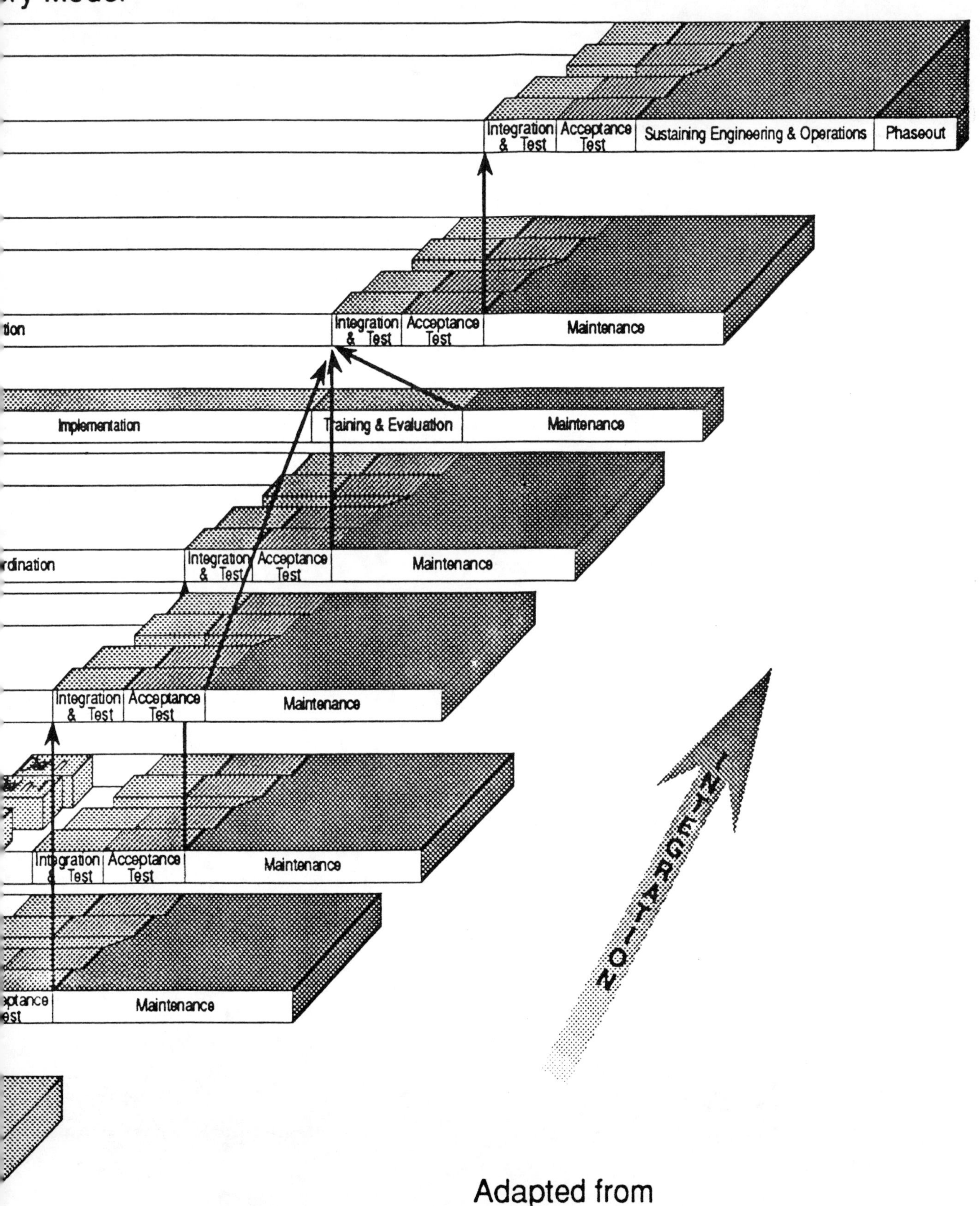

Adapted from
NASA Software Management and Assurance Program

System Life

A Phased-Deliv

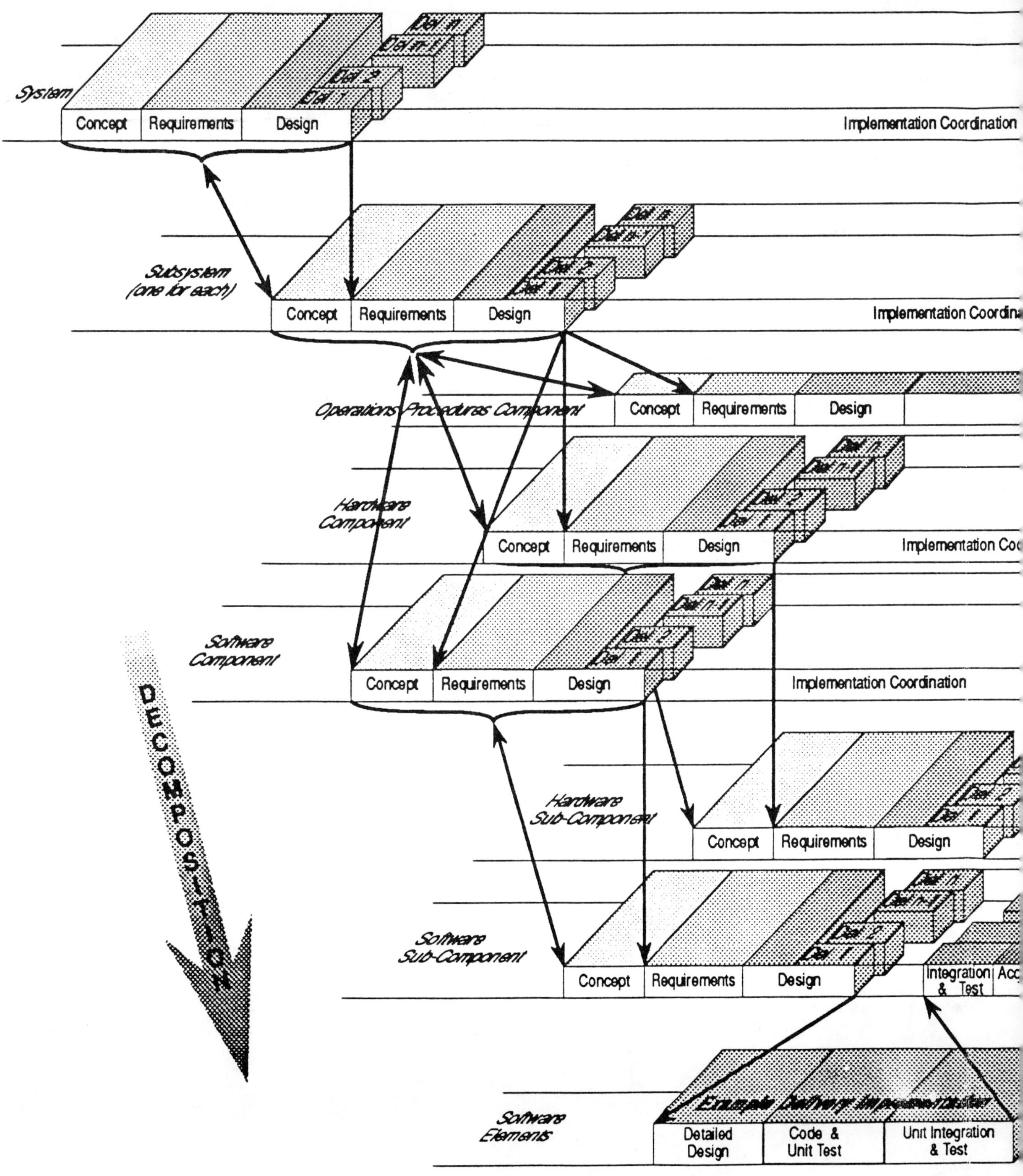

Good requirements definition can be an important factor in the success of a system development project.

Reprinted from *Datamation*, April 1981, © 1981 by Cahners Publishing Company.

PINPOINTING REQUIREMENTS

by Laura Scharer

One of the most common reasons systems fail is because the definition of system requirements is bad.

Why are we consistently unable to produce a good statement of requirements? Because it is difficult; we have a poor attitude about working with users (and vice versa); our expectations for this phase of systems design is different from the users' expectations; we let the situation control us; and we don't always use the techniques that are most appropriate.

More specifically:

- Sophisticated problem solving is required to produce good statements of requirements. Problems must be translated into corrective goals, which must be translated into solutions, which must in turn be reduced to functional terms. There is no guarantee that the functions will create the desired results.
- The articulation of requirements is unusually difficult. Functions and processes are not easily described.
- System requirements change, and the definition must be able to absorb these changes.
- Tools and techniques for optimizing the definition process are not generally available.
- Heavy user involvement can introduce interpersonal and project management problems.
- User motivation is difficult because reinforcement for their work is traditionally postponed until the implementation stage, by which time they have learned to expect disappointment.
- The definition process can become highly political.
- Definition is mentally taxing.
- Compromises which will eventually disenchant some of the users and analysts are required.
- We have no real yardstick other than the ultimate success or failure of the system; there is no way to judge the quality of our definition.

While we can't expect these difficulties to disappear, we can minimize their impact.

Analysts and users harbor grave doubts about each other (Table I), and the origins of these attitudes are obvious. Failure encourages blame. Users are disenchanted because we consistently bungle new system development; we are disenchanted because we alone are blamed for the failures. Somehow, even when users participate heavily in the definition process, they succeed with the help of unquestioned corporate mores in abdicating responsibility for system results. In other words, users provide the system definition but the systems people are responsible for it.

However, we should not expect users to metamorphose into analysts just because they are sitting on a project team. Remember:

- Assume that the user is trained in his own functional field but not necessarily in systems skills. Give him work assignments involving existing system education and new system definition—work that he can perform better than an analyst just because he is a user.
- The user's primary objective on the project is to protect his own interests. Let him.
- If you have recruited good users for the project team, they are usually good workers who receive recognition in the company and have confidence in their own abilities. In other words, they have delicate egos. It is very easy to insult users' intelligence by appropriate work assignments: we can't give them all the dirty work.
- The systems group, although responsible for project management, has no real organizational authority over users on the project team. The users can't be forced to do anything for the project.
- Users need periodic, if not constant, attention. After we've received all their input, we can't leave them hanging. Provide written status reports on a regular schedule and contact them personally whenever possible.

Another problem is that users and analysts don't even share a common goal for the definition process. Certainly both groups would agree that the objective of requirements definition is to produce a specification of what the system will do.

ANALYSTS DEFINE SYSTEM

Let's define what the system will do from the analyst's point of view. We are to produce this definition, but we impose some conditions on it. For one thing, the definition must be translatable into a system design. This requires that it be a functional specification, expressed in terms of processes, outputs, inputs, and data structures. We want the definition to be precise, clear and not open to misinterpretation. Quite understandably, we hope that the definition will be complete, because design is optimized when all features are known and can thus be integrated neatly into databases and programs. In the best of situations, the specification is frozen so that design, coding, and testing will never have to be reworked.

Now, two important time constraints surface which affect the definition of the system and the system itself. Because the systems group is responsible for the project, we ask that the definition be produced within the time allotted to this project phase. The specification activity to do this must have a definite beginning and end, and the end of this phase must precede the beginning of the design phase. Additionally, we must insist that the system thus defined can be implemented within project schedules and budget, both of which are usually preset before definition begins and thus before the real size and complexity of the system are known.

Finally, analysts are interested in developing a definition for a good system. We want to specify a system that is not only technically feasible but also elegant. We want integrated functions, clean and simple databases, efficient computer runs, and economical output.

Now, let's start again, this time from the user's point of view.

The users seem to be more satisfied with a qualitative definition which, in many

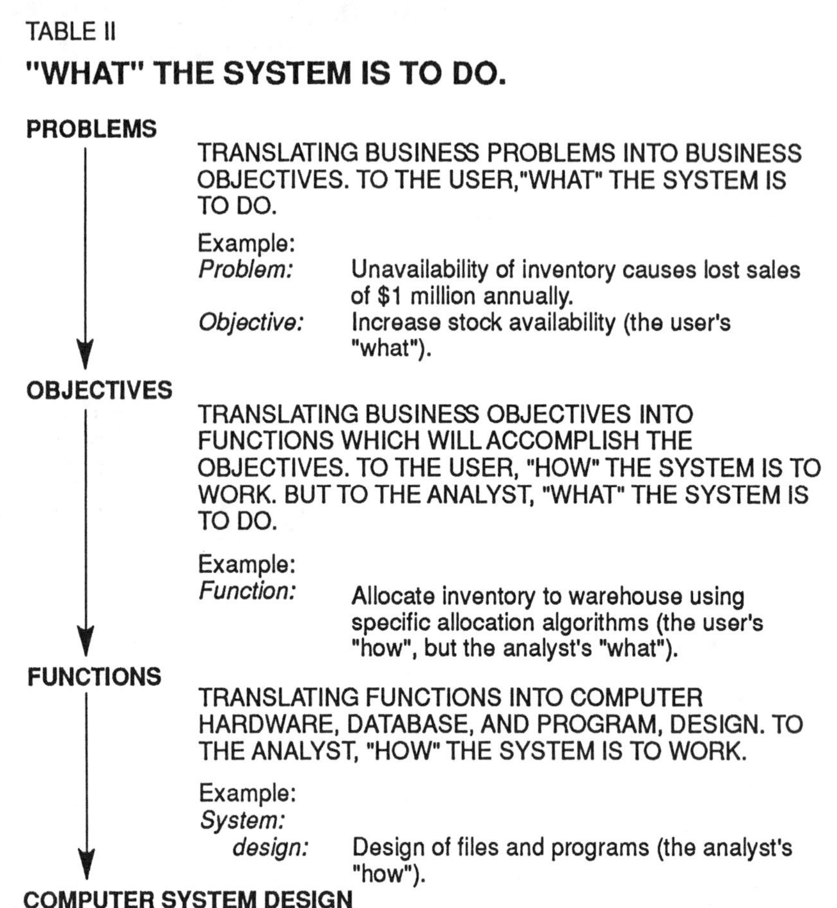

TABLE II

"WHAT" THE SYSTEM IS TO DO.

PROBLEMS

TRANSLATING BUSINESS PROBLEMS INTO BUSINESS OBJECTIVES. TO THE USER,"WHAT" THE SYSTEM IS TO DO.

Example:

Problem: Unavailability of inventory causes lost sales of $1 million annually.

Objective: Increase stock availability (the user's "what").

OBJECTIVES

TRANSLATING BUSINESS OBJECTIVES INTO FUNCTIONS WHICH WILL ACCOMPLISH THE OBJECTIVES. TO THE USER, "HOW" THE SYSTEM IS TO WORK. BUT TO THE ANALYST, "WHAT" THE SYSTEM IS TO DO.

Example:

Function: Allocate inventory to warehouse using specific allocation algorithms (the user's "how", but the analyst's "what").

FUNCTIONS

TRANSLATING FUNCTIONS INTO COMPUTER HARDWARE, DATABASE, AND PROGRAM, DESIGN. TO THE ANALYST, "HOW" THE SYSTEM IS TO WORK.

Example:

System: design: Design of files and programs (the analyst's "how").

COMPUTER SYSTEM DESIGN

TABLE III

THE OBJECTIVE OF REQUIREMENTS DEFINITION

Objective: To define what the system will do.

ANALYSTS	USERS
Functional definition	Qualitative definition
Precise	Interpretation to be expected
Complete	All requests to be met
Frozen	Flexible definition
Definition produced within alloted time	Definition an ongoing process
Resulting system implemented within project schedule and budget	Favorable impact of system on departmental budgets
Good system	System will work

cases, specifies the system in generalities and in terms of benefits to be derived. To reach the level of detail that analysts desire, the users must actually enter what they consider to be problem solving, or design (how) mode: they must arrive at functions that will solve their problems. They can't quite understand us when we distinguish our whats and hows: we're usually thinking a step ahead of them (Table II).

The qualitative nature of the user's definition suggests that it is to be interpreted, to be fleshed out in greater detail, at a later time. But the users, since you are asking them what they want and since they're telling you, expect that all requests will be met in the new system. They are often sincerely puzzled by arguments of technical feasibility or advisability, especially because they usually believe firmly that they need all requested features in order to achieve their stated goals.

Flexibility is a key consideration for the users. The system specification must be changeable with their needs, as must be the system after it is developed. This emphasis on flexibility also suggests that the users do not consider system definition to be a front-end activity with a definite ending point; it becomes, in essence, an ongoing process.

Finally, users are simply interested in defining a system that will work. They are not as interested in the project budget as they are in the impact of the system on their individual budgets. They want the system to perform specified functions without flaw, to be operationally efficient for their people, and to achieve the subjective goals.

USERS DEFINE SYSTEMS

Users who try to define a system with the analysts' goals in mind can find themselves in a predicament, particularly when one of the following is true:

- The system in question is just not definable by traditional means.
- The system can be defined but the user doesn't really know what he wants.
- The user knows what he wants but can't articulate it.

To defend themselves—to produce a system specification that will satisfy the analysts despite the above conditions—users have developed strategies which by now are classic.

The Kitchen Sink. This strategy, employed by users who throw everything into their system definition, has as its outstanding characteristics exaggeration and a protective overstatement of needs. An overabundance of reports, exception processing, and politically motivated system features are also symptomatic. The Kitchen Sink also provides a marvelous cover-up for the user who doesn't know what he wants but who can bury that fact in the sheer volume of his requests.

Smoking: Known also by its full name, "Smoke Gets in Your Eyes," this strategy is practiced by the user who sets up a smokescreen by requesting 10 system features, knowing that he really wants only one of them. The nine extra requests give him bargaining power. The Smoker is usually a rather experienced user who is consciously manipulating the definition process (as contrasted to the Kitchen Sink user, who is usually naive in believing that he really needs everything he asks for). In both cases, the full set of system requirements submitted by the users must be reduced to one that is necessary, sufficient, manageable, and achievable Surprisingly, despite his premeditation, the Smoker is easier to work with because he has a realistic idea of what he really wants.

The Same Thing. Sometimes a euphemism for the embarrassing words, "I don't know," sometimes a sign of laziness, the Same Thing is manifest by the statement: "Just give me the same thing I'm getting

Users provide the system definition, but the systems people are responsible for it.

now." The statement may be qualified in many ways, such as, "... but more accurately," or "... more timely," or "... but computerize it." The user who employs the Same Thing is often quite satisfied he has told the analysts everything they need to know to proceed. The only thing the analysts really know, however, is that the user probably isn't aware of what his current system does, and that he doesn't want to take the time for an introspective review of his own functions and problems. Here, the systems group has little chance of succeeding because only the user can fully discover his own needs and problems.

Each time we witness one of these syndromes, we are reminded that despite our prodding and despite users' (usually) good intentions, they just don't seem to produce the kind of system specification we envision. It would be easy to play the blame game here and conclude that users are not capable of system definition, but it would be more productive to reexamine our goals for the definition process and to ask if our objective is possible to achieve.

A concept known as definability can help us answer that question.

TABLE I

THE USER - ANALYST RELATIONSHIP

HOW WE SEE USERS	HOW USERS SEE US
They...	We...
Don't really know *what* they want.	Don't understand "the business."
Can't articulate what they want.	Handle company politics awkwardly.
Have too many "needs" which are politically motivated.	Try to tell them how to do their jobs.
Want everything right now.	Can't translate a system definition into a successful system.
Can't prioritize needs.	Say no all the time.
Want "me first," not company first.	Place too much emphasis on technicalities.
Refuse responsibility for the system.	Are always over budget.
Are unable to provide a definition for a system that will work.	Are always late.
Are not committed to system development projects.	Ask users for time and effort even to the detriment of their primary duties.
Are unwilling to compromise.	Set unrealistic standards for requirements definition.
Can't remain on schedule.	Are unable to respond quickly to legitimately changing needs.

CAN WE DEFINE IT?

Definability is the ability of a system to be defined; it is not a repeat of the "feasibility" question (can a computerized solution to this problem be developed at all?). Rather, it assesses the relative ease or difficulty of defining this system in this environment, and is assigned a loose value on a scale from "low" to "high." By assessing definability, you have an opportunity to establish more realistic goals for the definition process and to select definition techniques that are most appropriate to your situation.

Definability is affected by characteristics of the system itself. For example:

Type of system. Transaction processors and reporting systems—with very traditional accounting systems at one extreme—are functionally specific, finite, and quite tangible, and hence highly definable. At the other extreme, management support systems, decision support systems, simulators, and other systems that may be lumped together as "management information systems" are by nature less definable, because their purpose is to support a dynamic and changing management environment.

Size of system. Size is measured in several ways, including:

- number of functions performed
- number of departments affected
- number of individuals contributing to the definition
- number of subsystems
- number of system interfaces

As size increases, definability decreases and the possibility for error and omission is greater. There is also a hesitancy to attack each element of a very large system with the thoroughness that is possible with smaller systems.

Complexity of system. Complexity decreases the definability of a system. It is determined by:

- number of variables
- degree of interdependence of the variables
- number of databases accessed and updated
- difficulty of logic
- degree of flexibility
- need for specialized knowledge (e.g., mathematical, statistical, forecasting)

Similarity to existing systems. Definability is enhanced when experience data for similar systems is available.

Environmental factors can also have an overriding influence on the definition process. These include:

1. *Users' understanding of their own needs*. Definability is positively affected by users who know what they want, or who at least can work with analysts to discover what they want.

2. *Consensus among users*. Definability is increased when each user department makes an effort to gain a consensus opinion before going to the systems group with requests.

3. *Systems' understanding of user needs*. Analysts who know the business application favorably impact definability.

4. *Ability to communicate ideas*. Definability often suffers because users and analysts cannot communicate with each other. Development of system models, or use of a structured documentation format which uses an unambiguous language, can help.

5. *Accessibility to all affected users*. "Representative" user participation is usually mandatory because of the size of the user community affected by a new system. But definability is enhanced by direct user contact, so analysts should make an effort to talk to as many users as possible.

6. *Systems development experience*. Definability increases when analysts and users have experience in new systems development. Experienced participants have more realistic expectations as well as the knowledge and skills that contribute to successful definition.

7. *Personalities*. Good users improve definability. A good user is willing to make decisions, sticks by his decisions, cooper-

Definability is enhanced when experience data for similar systems is available.

ates, and thinks positively and aggressively.

8. *Availability of human resources*. Project staffing that places appropriate emphasis on front-end definition by including users and analysts with specification skills is important. More often, however, there are a disproportionate number of programmers on the project team.

9. *Project length*. The longer project minimizes definability because it gives the users more time to change their mind and the environment more time to change around the system.

10. *Schedule*. Definability decreases when inadequate time is allowed for the definition process.

11. *Budget*. Monies allocated to a project translate into available man hours; time for consulting, training, and software aids; and proportion of time assigned to front-end work.

12. *Corporate stress*. Corporate pressure, project visibility, reasonableness of expectations for system results, and the time and budget allowed for a system all influence definability. Unreasonable stress leads to fear, frustration, defeatism, and mistakes, but some degree of stress and attention, some feeling of high-level support and of accountability for results, can enhance the quality of the definition process.

CONTROL THE SYSTEM

Our goal should be to control the system before it controls us. Reduction of the system is accomplished by examining each proposed feature to determine whether it is valid and necessary.

1. Before definition begins, develop a precise scope document which clearly demarcates project boundaries. Obtain written acceptance of project scope from the users, then utilize the scope document to weed out requests that do not belong with this system.

2. Break the system into smaller pieces to be attacked separately. This may increase interface considerations, but it will also increase the possibility for understanding completely each part of the system.

3. Separate transaction-oriented portions of the system from management support sections so they can be considered as distinct entities.

4. Require users to justify each requested feature, in terms of either decisions, supported, benefits derived, or money saved.

5. Ask the users to assign a relative priority to each of their requests. This is helpful because it takes the pressure of saying no off the systems group and it provides a framework for partitioning the system into smaller pieces.

6. Find a similar system in another organization and learn as much as you can from their experiences.

7. Reduce the number of variables and of databases affected by the system.

8. Eliminate flexibility that users cannot realistically control. Determine whether flexibility is needed to support changing conditions of normal operations or if it is requested only to handle rare exceptions.

9. Reject a system feature if your equipment or your personnel do not possess the required technical capabilities for implementing it (the technical veto).

10. Reject a system feature if it will consume computer time, disk storage, printer time, or other machine resources out of proportion to its potential benefits (the operations veto).

11. Reject a system feature (or features, taken together) if they cannot be implemented with available manpower within imposed time constraints (the manpower veto)

In other words, if you recognize that the system is getting out of hand, speak up. Go formally on record with your recommendations for reduction. Submit amendments to the official project documents describing scope, feasibility, and cost justification, and require user approval of these changes. Because the system may be altered significantly by reduction, the corporate view of the system and the time and money allocated to it may also change, hopefully so that expectations are more realistic than in earlier project phases.

We also have an opportunity to control the external factors. Our goals in controlling the environment should be to surround ourselves with good users, to strengthen the base of knowledge upon which the users and the analysts are building, and to place realistic constraints on the project.

Users heavily influence the atmosphere of a project, so they should be chosen for the project team very carefully. Be sure that every area impacted by the system is represented. Balance the team so that users are equally represented, not only in numbers, but also in rank, authority, and seniority. Select users who can and will truly function as representatives. As representatives, a user must:

- provide regular status reports to his constituents
- give everyone a chance to contribute to the definition and to review formal definition documents
- present consensus opnions to the systems group
- favorably influence his constituents toward the project
- relate well to persons above and below him in his area
- have authority to commit his area in matters such as policy, budget, and interdepartmental procedures
- be accountable for his performance as a representative

Select users who have a thorough knowledge of their functional areas and of corporate policies, procedures, and organizational nuances which could affect definition. Look for users who enjoy being busy, are positively motivated to work on the project, and are organized, flexible, realistic, decisive, responsible, and able to express themselves.

TRAINING THE USERS

You undoubtedly are reading this list with a growing smile on your face because such users don't exist. We can strengthen the background knowledge of project participants by conducting a thorough existing system review with heavy user participation; providing books, seminars, or coursework in this particular business application; and providing formal training in the requirements definition technique which will be used in the project.

All these considerations—from getting good users assigned to the project to training them well—require time, money, and corporate commitment, which lead us to our final opportunity for controlling the environment. We must do two things for ourselves. First, we must take the time to make realistic project estimates for time, manpower, and money. Then, we must be honest when communicating these constraints to corporate management. In this way we can establish a realistic schedule which gives us time to do things right; work with a budget that is adequate for staffing the project and educating participants; gain some credibility with management by sticking to budget and schedule; reduce undue stress.

When confronted by an undefinable system, the users are faced with the impossible task of deciding what they want without knowing if what they want will work. They must perform some very difficult activities, such as reducing problem solutions to functional terms, visualizing system components and their interaction and effect on everyday operations, and discriminating between alternative approaches.

Unfortunately, the only sure way to determine if a system will work is to try it. Often users find themselves in the frustrating position of defining and building a system, only to realize that the system they really need will have to come next time.

Our goal should be to control the system before it controls us.

We must realize that in many cases the users need to try a system before they can define it. Prototyping addresses this problem. With prototyping, construction of a quick and dirty system begins after the bare minimum of a specification has been prepared. This quick and dirty system has one purpose, and that is to show the users what they are asking for, giving them some working knowledge of the results that can be achieved by the system they have defined. There is no attempt to create a good system from the technical or operational point of view, but rather to build a working, scaled model of the critical and most difficult portions of the system. After definition is complete, the prototype will be discarded and replaced by the operating version of the system.

Prototyping is relatively untried, so we don't have a great deal of experience data available. Examination of the concept reveals several potential benefits:

- The prototype system provides a concrete frame of reference for the users and analysts. Most important, the users can see how their definition has been interpreted by the systems group. The understanding of the analysts is evident by what they do rather than by what they say.
- The time lag between system definition and system demonstration is minimized. System demonstration and implementation are different, but they have traditionally occurred at the same time. This time lag has been very expensive to development projects, since changes are not discovered until considerable time and effort have already been invested in design and coding.
- Definitional changes can be incorporated into the model rather rapidly, encouraging active user participation and enthusiastic feedback.
- Prototyping is more attuned to the normal style and work habits of the users—usually managers—who sit on the project team. Emphasis is placed on active, hands-on evaluation of a working system rather than passive study and review of written documents.
- The technique provides at least some programmers—the ones working on the prototype—with closer user contact and longer project involvement, resulting in greater understanding of the permanent system.
- Experience data gained during prototyping can favorably influence the design of the permanent system.

There are, of course, potential drawbacks. Prototyping may be overkill for very simple systems and yet too involved for the whole of an extremely large system. Prototyping is unproven, quite different, and potentially expensive, so management support for the technique can be lacking. In addition, prototyping is not an academically pleasing technique. Distinctly bounded project phases are absent, and the prototype itself replaces the formal documentation which traditionally evolves during the definition stage. Finally, prototyping is so new that the high-level programming tools and the personnel skills required to perform prototyping are not generally available.

WELL-DEFINED APPROACH

Systems that promise to be difficult to define require an orderly, methodical approach to needs analysis and requirements definition. In these instances, functional definition will occur in a more traditional mode, as a bounded, front-end project phase, with development of an official written specification for the system.

In selecting a definition technique for these cases, we will want one which is repeatable (based on general concepts which can be applied to many situations), productive (efficient use of analyst and user time), and which, of course, produces a high-quality system definition.

We have several formal methodologies available. The characteristics which these techniques have in common are:

1. strict separation of functional specification (what the system is to do) from system design (how the system is to work)
2. development of a definition that is, however, easily translated into a physical system design
3. orderly decomposition of system requirements from the highest to the lowest level
4. representation of system requirements as a logical model expressed in graphic terms, using a minimum of textual explanation
5. active participation of the user groups, with emphasis on the user's role as a review agent
6. strict attention to system boundaries
7. separation of activities analysis from data analysis
8. documentation technique that is relatively easy to change and that records the evolution of the system definition
9. procedure for using the methodology is well defined and training materials are available

Traditional definition, despite its drawbacks, still has its place for one very simple reason: it is familiar, so users feel comfortable with it.

Characteristics of traditional definition are:

1. Textual description is the predominant definition tool, resulting in a specification document that is lengthy, ambiguous, and boring.
2. Top-down decomposition is not a requirement, and as a result, functions are described to inconsistent levels of detail.
3. Requirements are presented in list form rather than modeled; dynamic system flows and relationships are lost in the static, piece-by-piece specification.
4. Data analysis is deemphasized, if performed at all.

Traditional definition is also relatively inexpensive, if we consider its cost alone and not the costs incurred during design and coding to make up for inadequate specifications. Also, there is little or no learning curve involved with traditional definition in most organizations.

So, because it is comfortable, and perhaps not always by choice, it appears that we will be performing requirements definition using traditional techniques for some time to come. Rather than resigning ourselves to failure, we can borrow some of the important principles of prototyping and the well-defined methods to improve the results of definition activity. And rather than perpetuating the traditional methodologies without improvement, we can subtly begin to change common practice so that we accomplish a transition toward more structured techniques without unduly alienating the users or our managers.

We can begin by placing renewed emphasis on illustration of the functional specifications. Illustration may be in the form of charts or graphs, but should also include visitations to other companies with similar systems, walk-throughs of the proposed system with the users, and simulations of everyday procedures using newly defined functions and reports. And after coding begins, we can provide sample output to users as it becomes available, rather than waiting for official system implementation. Results of incremental testing can thus be used almost as a prototype, providing a concrete point of reference and eliciting comments from users much earlier than under normal circumstances.

We should also encourage use of a systematic approach to definition. We can use top-down decomposition to assure that all functions have been discovered and explored. We can also make a conscious effort to perform data analysis in addition to function analysis, thus providing at least external data needs to the design team.

The initiative for improving requirements definition must be ours, but it is an effort which is sure to be repaid with increased success. ✻

Unfortunately, the only sure way to determine if a system will work is to try it.

Laura L. Scharer is a senior systems analyst with O.M. Scott & Sons, Inc., Marysville, Ohio. Her responsibilities include project management, feasibility studies, requirements definition, and user support and training.

Reprinted from *Computer*, April 1985, pages 14-22.

A Taxonomy of Current Issues in Requirements Engineering

Gruia-Catalin Roman
Washington University, St. Louis

The growing area of requirements specification still needs a broader formal foundation, more automation, new development methods, and a higher level of integration into the overall design process.

In the simplest terms, the design process consists of three activities: the identification of a need, the development of a solution, and the implementation of the solution. Requirements and design specifications describe the engineer's perception of a need and his understanding of the solution. Requirements specifications state the desired functional and performance characteristics of some component independent of any actual realization, while design specifications describe the component's real internal structure and behavior. While requirements specifications facilitate understanding, design specifications faithfully render physical and logical structures that implement the requirements.

A component's design is not necessarily an implicit statement of its requirements. Even for simple and well understood functions, for example, sorting, the design can turn out to be unexpectedly complex when demanding design constraints are applied, for example, sorting in linear time. The ensuing loss of requirements traceability and separability can cause serious maintenance problems—one cannot tell if a particular function is essential or if it is simply a consequence of some design constraint that is no longer significant. Furthermore, without the requirements specification's explicit statement of purpose the designer may solve the wrong problem, a state of affairs that often leads to disastrous consequences.

The economic realities of large systems development, in particular, are such that discrepancies between the delivered system and the needs it must fulfill may cost in excess of 100 times what would have been required if the errors were discovered during the initial problem definition; in some extreme cases, discrepancies may make the entire system useless.[1] For this reason, recent years have been marked by an increased general interest in requirements specification.

The purpose of this article is to increase awareness of several requirements specifications issues: (1) the role they play in the full system development life cycle, (2) the diversity of forms they assume, and (3) the problems we continue to face. The article concentrates on ways of expressing requirements rather than ways of generating them. A discussion of various classification criteria for existing requirements specification techniques follows a brief review of requirements specification contents and concerns.

Requirements specification contents

As shown by Yeh,[2] among others, requirements fall into two general categories: functional and non-functional (the latter are also called constraints). The functional requirements capture the nature of the interaction between the component and its environment. The non-functional requirements restrict the types of solutions one might consider. Certain kinds of information ought to be included in a requirements specification document independently of the nature of the component for which the requirements are written. The component may be a whole system, a software package, or a hardware device.

Functional requirements. The construction of the functional requirements involves modeling the relevant internal states and behavior of both the component and its environment. Balzer and Goldman[3] have noted that the model, often called a *conceptual model,* must be cognitive in nature, that is, its concepts are relevant to the milieu in which the component is used and not related to its design or implementation. Aside from defining the functional validation criterion for the component design, the conceptual model also helps designers communicate among themselves and with users.

The conceptual model is incomplete unless the environment with which the component interacts is also modeled. If the environment is not well understood, it is unlikely that the requirements, as specified, will reflect the actual needs the component must fulfill. Moreover, since the environment affects the complexity of the component design, constraining the environment can reduce component complexity.

Non-functional requirements. Design complexity is also determined by the nature of the non-functional requirements. A constraint such as high reliability, for instance, may raise significantly both the cost of the system and the level of effort associated with its design and testing. Unfortunately, formally specifying the non-functional requirements is difficult. Some constraints (e.g., response to failure) are related to design solutions that are not known at the time the requirements are written. Others (e.g., human factors) may be determined only after complex empirical evaluations. Many constraints (e.g., maintainability) are not formalizable given the current state of the art, and many others are not explicit. Finally, there is a great diversity of types of non-functional requirements, as the following taxonomy shows.

Interface constraints define the ways the component and its environment interact. In some application programs, for instance, the environment may consist of the system users, the operating system, the hardware, and the software packages. The functional requirements for these programs must capture the demands and services associated with each one of these environmental entities, but not the syntax of the procedure invocations, the interrupt addresses, or the screen format. These latter details are interface constraints that should not affect what the program does, but the way it does it.

Performance constraints cover a broad range of issues dealing with time/space bounds, reliability, security, and survivability. The first category covers response time, workload, throughput, and available storage space; we expect that user-oriented measures such as productivity will also become increasingly important in the definition of requirements for systems that provide direct production support. Reliability constraints deal with both the availability of physical components and the integrity of the information maintained or supplied by some component. Similarly, security constraints span physical considerations such as emission standards and logical issues such as permissible information flows (e.g., for secure operating systems) and information inference (e.g., from statistical summaries about the database contents). Survivability is a requirement associated not only with defense systems but also with every day processing where off-site copies of the database prevent loss in case of fire.

Operating constraints include physical constraints (e.g., size, weight, power, etc.), personnel availability, skill level considerations, accessibility for maintenance, environmental conditions (e.g., temperature, radiation, etc.), and spatial distribution of components.

Life-cycle constraints fall into two broad categories: those that pertain to qualities of the design and those that limit the development, maintenance, and enhancement process. In the first group we include maintainability, enhanceability, portability, flexibility, reusability of components, expected market or production life span, upward compatibility, integration into a family of products, etc. Failure to satisfy any of these constraints may not compromise the initial, delivered component, but may result in increased life cycle costs and an overall shorter life for the component. In the second group we place development time limitations, resource availability, and methodological standards. The latter include design techniques, tool usage, quality assurance programs, programming standards, etc.

Even for simple and well understood functions, the design can turn out to be unexpectedly complex.

Economic constraints represent considerations relating to immediate and long term costs. They may be limited in scope to the component at hand (e.g., development cost), but, most often, they involve global marketing and production objectives. A high life-cycle cost may be accepted in exchange for some other tangible or intangible benefits.

Political constraints deal with policy and legal issues. A company's unwillingness to use a competitor's device or its obligation to use a certain percentage of equipment indigenous to some foreign country illustrate issues falling in this category of nonfunctional constraints.

Requirements specification concerns

Growing interest in requirements specification has been accompanied by the emergence of general guidelines regarding the properties of a good specification. Our own attempt to organize and evaluate these guidelines led us to adopt a functionalist viewpoint: *a property of a requirements specification is desirable if it satisfies some identifiable need of the design process.* This approach suggests that the way requirements are used determines the kind of properties they ought to have. Some properties are needed because the requirements must be read, others because designs must be checked against the requirements, yet others because requirements change with time during development and enhancement. Aspects that contribute to having a good requirements specification today may lose their significance in the future if the design process changes its character due to increased levels of automation or other factors.

We provide below a list of desirable requirements specification properties. The list is compiled from several sources[3,4] and is annotated from a functionalist perspective.

Appropriateness refers to the ability of the specification to capture, in a manner that is straightforward and free of implementation considerations, those concepts that are germane to the component's role in the environment for which it is intended (business data processing, process control, communication hardware, etc.). An inappropriate specification technique makes requirements operation cumbersome or impossible.

A related property is *conceptual cleanliness.* It covers notions such as simplicity, clarity, and ease of understanding. It is needed above all because people are involved in developing and using the requirements. When the requirements are generated and used by tools alone, conceptual cleanliness is often sacrificed for the sake of enhancing the *computational efficiency* of the automation tools.

Constructability deals with the existence of a systematic (potentially computer-assisted) approach to formulating the requirements. This property recognizes that the mere availability of a requirements specification formalism is not sufficient to make it useful, particularly on large problems.

Both humans and tools that have to examine the requirements benefit from *structuring* that emphasizes separation of concerns and from *ease of access* to frequently needed information.

Precision, lack of ambiguity, completeness, and *consistency* are important because the requirements represent the criteria against which the component acceptability is judged. Lack of precision (e.g., "large main memory") is defined as the impossibility to develop a procedure for determining if some realization does or does not meet some particular requirement. Lack of ambiguity is present whenever two or more interpretations cannot be attached to a particular requirement—this is different from the case when several possible realizations are equally acceptable. A requirements specification is complete if some relevant aspect has not been left out and is consistent if parts of the specification do not contradict one another. Both completeness and consistency require the existence of criteria against which one may evaluate the specification. While some of them may be included in the semantics of the requirements specification language, others may not. Formal definition of completeness and consistency is especially difficult to accomplish when multiple related specifications such as a human interface prototype and a dataflow model of the functionality are involved.

Completeness and consistency checks, the verification of the design against requirements, and other analytic activities presuppose the *analyzability* of the requirements by mechanical or other means. The higher the degree of *formality* the more likely it is that requirements may be analyzed by some mechanical means, thus opening the way to the use of tools.

When the requirements are generated and used by tools alone, conceptual cleanliness is often sacrificed for the sake of enhancing the computational efficiency of the automation tools.

Testability is defined as the availability of cost-effective procedures that allow one to verify if the design and/or realization of some component satisfies its functional and nonfunctional requirements. This property is probably the most important one, and, at the same time, the most difficult one to achieve. To illustrate the complexity involved in guaranteeing testability, one may want to think of the difficulties associated with program verification where the code is checked against a set of assertions stated in predicate calculus.

Traceability of the requirements is often used as a substitute for testability. Traceability refers to the ability to cross-reference items in the requirements specification with items in the design specification. Without assuring testability, some help is thus provided to the designer in his effort to check that all requirements have been considered.

Executability is the extent functional simulations of the component can be constructed from its requirements specification prior to starting the design or implementation; it plays an important role in requirements validation.

Finally, in recognition that requirements are built gradually over long periods of time and continue to evolve throughout the component's life cycle, the specifications must be *tolerant of temporary incompleteness* and *adaptable* to changes in the nature of the needs being satisfied by the component; they must exhibit *economy of expression,* and they must be easily *modifiable.*

Classification criteria

The main objective of this section is to identify the key issues facing the requirements engineering field today. To help organize the presentation, we separate the discussion into five parts, each corresponding to a criterion that can be used to classify existing requirements specification techniques. The selected criteria have engineering relevance leading to meaningful technical comparisons. We illustrate each criterion by discussing how it might be applied to current specification techniques. For a complete survey of the area, we recommend Ramamoorthy and So's paper on the subject.[5] (The classification criteria below are a superset of those used by Ramamoorthy and So.)

(1) *Formal foundation.* The theory that forms the basis for the particular technique (e.g., dataflow, logic, etc.);

(2) *Scope.* The type of requirements addressed by the technique (e.g., functionality, reliability constraints, etc.);

(3) *Level of formality.* The extent to which the specification could be understood by a machine without need for human interpretation;

(4) *Degree of specialization.* The size of the class of problems for which the application of the technique is appropriate;

(5) *Specialization area.* The class of components whose requirements may be conveniently specified through the use of the technique; and

(6) *Development method.* The approach used to construct the specification.

We now discuss the relevance of each criterion and the requirements engineering issues pertaining to it.

Formal foundation. Significant advances in the requirements field are determined by the strength of its theoretical foundation, which is the basis for subsequent automation, and by the extent to which the theoretical results make their way into engineering practice. Efforts to develop practical tools for the specification of system-level requirements, for instance, have exploited a number of alternative formal foundations, including the use of finite-state machines, dataflow, stimulus-response paths, communicating concurrent processes, functional composition, and data-oriented models.

Finite-state machines. The use of finite-state machines offers elegance and a great degree of analyzability. Requirements Language Processor,[6] for example, treats system processing as a mapping that takes the current system state and an incoming stimulus and produces a new system state and a response. Redundancy, incompleteness, and inconsistency in the definition of the finite-state machine are related to corresponding problems in the requirements specification.

Dataflow. Dataflow models are among the most popular in use today. The typical dataflow model consists of processing activities and data arcs showing the flow of data between the activities. Processing is triggered by the presence of data in the input queues associated with each activity. SADT[7] and PSL/PSA[8] illustrate two distinct uses of dataflow. SADT is a requirements "blueprint language" that stresses accurate communication of ideas by graphical means; while PSL/PSA stresses the use of a requirements database and automated tools for the development and analysis of dataflow type requirements. What makes dataflow attractive is that it is very well suited for modeling the structure and behavior of most human organizations. For this reason, new dataflow-based methods, for example, CORE,[9] are still being proposed and evaluated.

Stimulus-response paths. Techniques using stimulus-response paths decompose the requirements with respect to the processing that must be carried out subsequent to the receipt of each stimulus. The approach, rooted in the needs of the real-time processing, is widely known primarily due to the development of SREM.[10]

Efforts to develop practical tools for the specification of system-level requirements have relied on a number of formal devices.

Communicating concurrent processes. The activities identified in both dataflow and stimulus-response models may be easily simulated by using communicating concurrent processes. Formally, a process is represented by a set of states and by a state transition mapping. This view is shared by all the techniques that use communities of processes to model requirements. Fundamental differences occur mostly in the manner in which communication is being defined. In PAISLey, asynchronous interactions are specified by means of function applications.[11] (Pairs of "exchange functions" return as values each others arguments.) Jackson uses unbounded queues defined such that only one process may "write" to each queue and only one process may "read" from each queue.[12] IORL provides a set of eight communication primitives that permit the establishment of communication paths and the exchange of data.[13]

Functional composition. The functional composition approach has been promulgated by the Higher Order Software methodology,[14] and is now supported by a tool called USE.IT that allows one to define (graphically) the system's functionality as a composition of mathematical functions.

Data-oriented models. Data-oriented techniques concentrate on the specification of the system state represented by the data that needs to be maintained. The Conceptual Schema Definition Language for instance, helps structure one's knowledge of the application area.[15] Based on semantic network modeling and other techniques proven successful in the artificial intelligence field, CSDL provides highly abstract and intuitive representations of knowledge. While in CSDL the system functionality is defined in terms of built-in data manipulation primitives, other techniques (e.g., see work by Greenspan et al.[16]) provide the means to define system activities in a manner similar to that of defining data objects.

Transferring techniques among different fields shows that important benefits can be derived from evaluating proven techniques in new contexts. There are other similar success stories. Modular programming, for instance, has benefited greatly from the work on programming language semantics.

Compilers and interpreters represent a class of components for which formal functional requirements are routinely built. Their requirements are given by the syntax and semantics of the language for which they are constructed. Standard methods are available today for the definition of both syntax and semantics.[17] Of particular interest to the broader area of requirements specification are the three types of semantic models currently in use: *denotational* (the meaning of a program is stated as a mathematical function), *axiomatic* (the meaning of a program is stated by providing the axioms and inference rules needed to prove programs correct), and *operational* (the meaning of the program is given by the result of executing it on an abstract machine).

These models are expected to play an increasingly important role in the field. To date, they clearly influenced the work on the specification of functional requirements for individual programs.[18] For pure procedures, axiomatic specifications take the form of input/output assertions, and operational specifications are represented by simple and clear algorithms that perform the same function as the intended program but ignore any performance issues. (These algorithms are not intended for use by the actual program.) Abstract objects (appearing in object-oriented design) may be specified by sets of axioms relating the operations permissible over each object or, operationally, by showing how each operation uses and modifies some abstract representation of the object.

There is a wealth of formal models that have not yet made their way into requirements engineering practice.

New system requirements specification techniques have been successfully based on programming language semantic models, but the full potential of the new techniques has not yet been established. However, a good grasp of the principles behind the semantic models for programming languages is important in any type of design activity that involves writing or interpreting requirements. In general, designers can benefit from being trained how to exploit existing theoretical results in an engineering setting. A designer documenting an Ada package specification, for instance, can benefit from some knowledge of how to specify abstract objects. Similarly, a designer, by not understanding the operational specification concept, will be more likely to misinterpret requirements written in a language such as RSL (used by SREM), which has an operational nature.

The problem of applying existing theory to practice is by no means solely an education issue. As past surveys of the area show, there is a wealth of formal models that have not yet made their way into requirements engineering practice. It is clear, for instance, that probabilistic concepts have not received appropriate attention, that logic-based models are just beginning to be exploited, that most distributed processing models are still a primarily theoretical concern, etc. The single most important reason why this situation continues to prevail is the high investment required for developing and evaluating a production-version tool. Even for older tools, systematic empirical evaluation such as the one to which SREM was recently subjected[19] are more the exception than the rule.

Finally, we must point out that despite the broad body of formal knowledge that is not being applied, there is still a need to expand the formal foundation of the requirements area. No technique is equally appropriate for all applications or comprehensive in its coverage of the requirements issues. In our own work, for instance, we are currently exploring the use of formal logic in the specification of geographic data-processing requirements, a highly specialized area that, by and large, has been ignored as far as requirements specification techniques are concerned.

Scope. Scope is defined by the type of requirements the specification technique attempts to express. Some techniques limit themselves to functional requirements, others are concerned solely with particular nonfunctional requirements (e.g., reliability), while others cover functionality and a selected subset of the non-functional requirements. SREM, for instance, falls in the last category. By employing stimulus-response paths to model the system functionality, SREM makes the formal specification of processing time constraints relatively easy.

There are two major difficulties in attempting to expand the scope of current specification techniques. First, despite progress in the ability to express adequately the functionality, there are still major difficulties with the establishment of a formal foundation for most of the non-functional requirements. Second, broad integration of functional and non-functional requirements has not been accomplished. We should remember that the severity of the constraints determines the complexity of the design and that much of the design evaluation effort is invested in checking whether the constraints are met.

Level of formality. The level of formality is the extent to which a specification language may be understood by some machine. The typical user manual for a software package has a certain degree of structure, but lacks formality because it is written in a natural language. PSL/PSA represents a next step toward formality. Relationships between arbitrary entities (e.g., "Inputs *A* and *B* generate output *C*") may be formally captured without any concern as to their meaning. Interpreting the meaning of the entities (e.g., *A, B,* and *C*) and of the relationships (e.g., "generate") depends on some consensus among designers. Completely formal specification techniques do exist but they are for highly specialized classes of problems. We need to reach increasing levels of formality. However, without proper automated tools, the designer's ability to be more formal is limited.

A dramatic illustration of the advantages of formal specifications comes from the database area where a number of models have been proposed,[20] with the relational model being the simplest and the cleanest among them. These models are in fact requirements specifications for the class of components we call databases; they describe the desired functionality and not the way the database is implemented.

Degree of specialization. Specilization of the requirements technique to a particular type of component increases the technique's analyzability and makes the designer's concepts more susceptible to direct representation. The former helps to increase the potential for automation, while the latter makes the technique easy to use.

Broad integration of functional and non-functional requirements has not been accomplished.

Current techniques cover the entire spectrum from domain specific, to domain sensitive, and, finally, to domain independent. An extreme case of specialization is represented by requirements techniques that address such a small class of components that automatic generation of the component from the requirements becomes possible. Problem-oriented languages can be viewed as part of this category. Most system requirements specification techniques tend to fall into the category we call domain sensitive. Both RSL and PSL, for instance, are adequate for problems that fall outside their primary domains of applicability and adapt to the specifics of particular problems by means of designer-defined extensions. The SADT notation is representative of the domain-independent techniques. So is the use of formal logic in the definition of requirements.

Because there are merits associated with both specialization and generality, the developer of a requirements engineering environment must evaluate carefully the tradeoffs between the two. The ideal technique is general enough to be useful for a large number of problems (e.g., real-time control, data processing, databases, etc.) and, at the same time, capable of defining the problem-specific concepts needed (or convenient to use) in each case (e.g., internal and external events, report formats, relations, etc.) To achieve this, the environment would have to provide the designer with a user-expandable language suitable for the definition of problem-specific concepts and semantic constraints and a tool set sharing a single unified formal foundation and a single human interface style.

Specialization area. To understand fully the opportunities for specialization and the diversity of needs that requirements specification techniques must satisfy at different points in the development life cycle, one simply has to consider what is involved in the development of a complete system, that is, a software/hardware aggregate. The Total System Design framework proposed by Roman et al.[21] separates the development of such systems into six stages:

- Problem definition,
- System design,
- Software design,
- Machine design,
- Circuit design, and
- Firmware design.

Among the stages of the TSD framework the problem-definition stage is distinguished in two ways: it is application oriented and it involves no design activities. Its sole purpose is to assure that a clear understanding of the problem has been achieved and a statement of the system requirements has been generated prior to the start of the system design. Because of the large number of applications that are exploiting the use of computer systems, specialized requirements specification techniques have been developed for use with this stage. Some are aimed at large classes of applications sharing some common feature (e.g., real-time processing), while others address the needs of specific application domains (e.g., geographic data processing). The growing interest in expert systems for requirements specification will, most likely, increase the pressure toward specialization.

Requirements work is often assumed to be limited to the problem-definition stage. This kind of narrow definition may be a convenient simplifying assumption if one is interested in the problem-definition stage alone, but, if taken seriously, it may suggest a fundamental lack of understanding of the very essence of the design process. The design of each component entails the specification of both functional and non-functional requirements for a set of subcomponents from which the component will be eventually assembled. Variability in the nature of the requirements techniques occurs along the development life cycle due to changes in the nature of the components involved. Because a distributed system may be viewed as a set of processing nodes and communication lines, the system-design stage is tasked with the development of the software and hardware requirements for each node and communication line. These requirements are subsequently used by the software and machine design stages, respectively. The same paradigm occurs also within a stage, even though (unfortunately) the requirements for some components (e.g., input/output assertions for procedures) are not always formally generated.

The key to across-life-cycle integration of design activities rests with the ability to relate design and requirements specifications.

This state of affairs suggests that any attempt to separate requirements and design specifications is counter productive when one deals with the design stages. The key to across-life-cycle integration of design activities rests with the ability to relate design and requirements specifications. Since the design of a component (e.g., system) must satisfy all the functional and non-functional requirements specified for it, this means that, at design time, one needs to show that the component's requirements are satisfied as long as the subcomponents (e.g., subsystems) will meet their requirements. When the subcomponent requirements are not included as part of the design, this is impossible to do.

Consequently, design languages must have the ability to specify the requirements for the types of subcomponents they identify, and they must overcome the current emphasis on functionality alone by incorporating formally an increasing number of non-functional requirements. In the case of a software design language, for instance, it is not sufficient to have the ability to state the logic of a procedure using pseudo-code. One must also be able to state its requirements using pre- and post-assertions, say. For, otherwise, little may be said of the design's correctness until all procedures are designed, and, for a large system, this is a major drawback.

The TSD framework goes one step further. It suggests that, for very high performance systems where the design of the software and of the hardware must be tightly coordinated, the designer must have the ability to define the interdependency between software and hardware requirements. In a recently published paper, we provide an example of how this might be accomplished.[22]

Development method. Recent years brought about a new distinguishing factor among requirements specification techniques: the development method. While the prevailing approach is to state the requirements completely before proceeding with the design, rapid prototyping has made significant gains in popularity. As recent studies show, both methods have advantages and disadvantages.[23] Rapid prototyping seems to lead to less code, less effort, and ease of use, while the traditional approach is characterized by better coherence, more functionality, higher robustness, and ease of integration. More importantly, these results could be interpreted as suggesting the need to use a mixed approach where one uses a subset of the requirements to develop rapid prototypes that in turn lead to further clarification and refinement of the original requirements. (Note: We consider that even pure rapid prototyping does lead to a statement of requirements. While written requirements specifications may never be generated, product documentation is still needed.)

Within these two broad categories further distinctions may be considered. They would have to include the type of human interface (e.g., linguistic versus graphic), the degree of automation, the problem decomposition or composition rules employed in order to control complexity, etc. Although space limitations do not permit us to discuss these issues in any detail, it must be said that the industrial success of a specification technique is heavily dependent upon its treatment of human factors, that is, the concepts it makes available and the interface style it supports.

Two more exotic methods are also making their beginnings in the requirements field. The first one is represented by efforts to introduce expert knowledge-based systems into the process of developing the requirements. (The Seventh International Conference on Software Engineering in March 1984, for instance, included one session on this topic.) The second method defines requirements for situations where the problem is extremely ill specified (e.g., a medical diagnosis system). This situation is very common in the artificial intelligence community and the usual solution is not to specify the "functionality" but an evaluation procedure and a set of related acceptance criteria (e.g., 90 percent agreement with some group of experts on a predefined set of cases).

Many of the shortcomings we see in today's approaches are due to the underlying assumptions being made about how requirements ought to be developed. While current strategies tend to structure the requirements specification process, future requirements development strategies might provide instead a milieu for reasoning about the problem at hand. However, the systematic investigation of new requirements development strategies has just been started, and its full impact remains still to be determined.

Despite significant growth, the requirements area still faces a number of important unresolved issues and suffers from a lack of crystalization. The formal foundation of the field must be broadened by evaluating the capabilities of different types of formalisms (e.g., logic, probability theory, etc.). A theoretical foundation for the specification of non-functional requirements still needs to be established. The degree of formality must be increased in order to reach greater levels of automation. The designer's abilities to deal with formality must be enhanced through proper training and new forms of automation that take into consideration the human factor and incorporate more domain-specific concepts in the requirements. New methods for developing requirements specifications must be considered. A major integration effort must be undertaken for the purpose of establishing a unified formal foundation that could bring together application- and design-oriented specifications, functional and non-functional requirements, the life-cycle phases, and requirements definition and design activities.

Work on requirements specification techniques must overcome the current conceptual fragmentation of the field. This requires the emergence of a consensus on what is to be expected from the use of a particular technique in a given set of circumstances, the refinement of current evaluation methods, and the development of highly integrated design/requirements engineering facilities. □

References

1. B. W. Boehm, *Software Engineering Economics,* Prentice-Hall, Inc., 1981.
2. R. T. Yeh, "Requirements Analysis—A Management Perspective," *Proc. COMPSAC '82,* Nov. 1982, pp. 410-416.
3. R. Balzer and N. Goldman, "Principles of Good Software Specification and Their Implications for Specification Languages," *Proc. Spec. Reliable Software Conf.,* Apr. 1979, pp. 58-67.
4. B. Liskov and S. Zilles, "An Introduction to Formal Specifications of Data Abstractions," *Current Trends in Programming Methodology—Vol. I: Software Specification and Design,* R. T. Yeh, ed., Prentice-Hall, 1977, pp. 1-32.
5. C. V. Ramamoorthy and H. H. So, "Software Requirements and Specifications: Status and Perspectives," *Tutorial: Software Methodology,* C. V. Ramamoorthy and R. T. Yeh, eds., IEEE Computer Society, 1978, pp. 43-164.
6. A. M. Davis and T. G. Rauscher, "Formal Techniques and Automatic Processing to Ensure Correctness in Requirements Specifications," *Proc. Spec. Reliable Software Conf.,* Apr. 1979, pp. 15-35.
7. D. T. Ross, "Structured Analysis (SA): A Language for Communicating Ideas," *IEEE Trans. Soft. Eng.,* SE-3, No. 1, Jan. 1977, pp. 16-34.
8. D. Teichroew and E. A. Hershey III, "PSL/PSA: A Computer-Aided Technique for Structured Documentation and Analysis of Information Processing Systems," *IEEE Trans. Soft. Eng.,* SE-3, No. 1, Jan. 1977, pp. 41-48.
9. G. P. Mullery, "CORE—A Method for Controlled Requirements Specification," *Proc. Fourth Int'l Conf. Soft. Eng.,* Sept. 1979, pp. 126-135.
10. M. Alford, "Requirements for Distributed Data Processing Design," *Proc. First Int'l Conf. Distributed Computing Systems,* Oct. 1979, pp. 1-14.
11. P. Zave and R. T. Yeh, "Executable Requirements for Embedded Systems," *Proc. Fifth Int'l Conf. Soft. Eng.,* Mar. 1981, pp. 295-304.
12. M. A. Jackson, "Information Systems: Modeling, Sequencing and Transformations," *Proc. Third Int'l Conf. Soft. Eng.,* May 1978, pp. 72-81.
13. "IORL Version 2—Language Reference Manual," Teledyne Brown Engineering, Dec. 1982.
14. M. Hamilton and S. Zeldin, "Higher Order Software—A Methodology for Defining Software," *IEEE Trans. Soft. Eng.,* SE-2, No. 1, Mar. 1976, pp. 9-32.
15. N. Roussopoulos, "CSDL: A Conceptual Schema Definition Language for the Design of Data Base Applications," *IEEE Trans. Soft. Eng.,* SE-5, No. 5, Sept. 1979, pp. 481-496.
16. S. J. Greenspan, J. Mylopoulos, and A. Borgida, "Capturing More World Knowledge in the Requirements Specification," *Proc. Sixth Int'l Conf. Soft. Eng.,* Sept. 1982, pp. 225-234.
17. F. G. Pagan, *Formal Specification of Programming Languages: A Panoramic Primer,* Prentice-Hall, Inc., 1982.
18. B. Liskov and V. Berzins, "An Appraisal of Program Specifications," *Research Directions in Software Technology,* P. Wegner, ed., MIT Press, 1979, pp. 276-301.

19. P. A. Scheffer, A. H. Stone III, and W. E. Rzepka, "A Large System Evaluation of SREM," *Proc. Seventh Int'l Conf. Soft. Eng.*, Mar. 1984, pp. 172-180.

20. D. C. Tsichritzis and F. H. Lochovsky, *Data Models,* Prentice-Hall, Inc., 1982.

21. G.-C. Roman, M. J. Stucki, W. E. Ball, and W. D. Gillett, "A Total System Design Framework," *Computer,* Vol. 17, No. 5, May 1984, pp. 15-26.

22. G.-C. Roman and M. S. Day, "Multifaceted Distributed Systems Specification Using Processes and Event Synchronization," *Proc. Seventh Int'l Conf. Soft. Eng.*, Mar. 1984, pp. 44-55.

23. B. W. Boehm, T. E. Gray, and T. Seewaldt, "Prototyping vs. Specifying: A Multi-Project Experiment," *Proc. Seventh Int'l Conf. on Soft. Eng.*, Mar. 1984, pp. 473-484.

Gruia-Catalin Roman has been on the faculty of Washington University in Saint Louis since 1976; he is an associate professor in the Department of Computer Science. He is also a software engineering consultant for several firms, and he has developed custom methodologies for both private and government organizations.

His current research deals with formal specification of geographic data-processing requirements, distributed-system design models and methodologies, and the dynamics of software development environments. His previous research has been primarily in the area of methodology development and assessment. Other areas in which he has worked include formal languages, biomedical simulations, computer graphics, and distributed databases.

Roman was a Fulbright Scholar at the University of Pennsylvania, where he received a BS degree (1973), an MS degree (1974), and a PhD degree (1976), all in computer science. He is a member of Tau Beta Pi, ACM, and IEEE Computer Society. His address is Department of Computer Science, Washington University, Box 1045, Saint Louis, MO 63130.

Chapter 2: System and Software System Engineering

1: Introduction

System and software system engineering are the first steps in the development of any software-intensive system. *System engineering* is the application of scientific and engineering efforts to (1) transform an operational need into a description of system performance parameters and a system configuration through the use of an iterative process of definition, synthesis, analysis, design, test, and evaluation; (2) integrate related technical parameters and ensure compatibility of all related functional and program interfaces in a manner that optimizes the total system definition and design; and (3) integrate reliability maintainability, safety, survivability, human, and other such factors into the total engineering effort to meet cost, schedule, and technical performance objectives. [1]

Software system engineering is likewise both a technical and a management process. The technical process is the analytical effort necessary to transform an operational need into a software design of the proper size and configuration, and its documentation in requirements and design specifications. The management process involves assessing the risk and cost, integrating the engineering specialties and design groups, maintaining configuration control, and continuously auditing the effort to ensure that cost, schedule, and technical performance objectives are satisfied to meet the original operational need. [2]

The purpose of this chapter is to introduce the concept of system engineering and to present a view of the major system engineering activities: partitioning, allocation, flowdown, and traceability. It starts with a paper on system engineering and then examines the interfacing document between the customer and the developer called an "operations concept document." The chapter then looks at the method of deriving software requirements from system requirements called "allocation." Last, it considers how to apply system engineering principles to software.

2: Description of Papers

"System Engineering Overview" by Doug Sailor is the only self-contained paper on system engineering of which

EHO304-6/90/0000/0033$01.00

the tutorial authors are aware. Sailor wrote the first edition of the Defense Systems Management College textbook, *System Engineering Management Guide* [3], and has incorporated many of its ideas into his paper. System engineering has a major impact on software engineering. The proper use of the system engineering procedures of partitioning, allocation, flowdown, and derivation of requirements will identify those parts of the system that can be most effectively and economically implemented in software. Sailor defines system engineering and identifies the system engineering process, describes a system engineering organization, defines the major system engineering tools, and discusses how to write requirements statements.

"A Structured Approach for Operational Concept Formulation" by Bob Lano represents the only existing paper that describes the operations concept document (CONOPS). The CONOPS is a valuable system engineering document that forms "bridge" between the users' needs/wants and the more formal system/software requirements specifications. A CONOPS document is required for all Department of Defense contracts and should be included in requirements traceability (see [4]). This paper is derived from Lano's 1980 TRW publication [5].

Lano describes the operations concept formulation process as a means of producing the operations concept document. This paper provides background concerning the operations concept formulation process, the audiences for which the CONOPS is intended, problems, lessons learned, the prerequisites for developing the document, and recommended approaches.

The paper by Dale Nelsen, "System Engineering and Requirement Allocation," describes the allocation process, which is essential in all system developments but which is often done poorly and ineffectively. Too many system engineers regard allocation as a mystery to be solved at the inception of each new project, rather than as a repeatable process. Unfortunately as the author points out, the mystery is not solved soon enough or often enough to get the task performed properly.

The paper discusses top-down analysis as well as the difficulties encountered in applying the methodology. It describes how requirements analysis and the allocation process should be performed, in contrast to the way they typically are performed. The paper uses a series of dataflow diagrams to define and illustrate the allocation process from top-level requirements to third-level allocation. The paper also explains the use of the term "derived requirements."

Nelsen discusses the four ways the product can be verified: test, demonstration, analysis, and examination (sometimes called inspection). Nelsen provides a case study to illustrate requirements flowdown, allocation, and traceability.

The last paper, "Software System Engineering," by Dick Thayer and Win Royce, applies the concepts of system engineering to software. This paper describes the application of system engineering principles, activities, tasks, and procedures to the development of a software system. This application, called software system engineering, is the overall integrating concept encompassing the managerial and technical activity that controls the cost, schedule, and technical achievement of the developing software system. This paper recognizes the difference between software systems engineering and software engineering, just as system engineering is recognized as being different from hardware engineering of all types. The Royce-Thayer paper partitions the software development process into five general phases, and each phase is partitioned into a number of software system engineering processes. The activities and tasks associated with each process are described.

3: References

[1] MIL-STD-499A, Engineering Management (USAF), 1974.

[2] Adapted from Sailor, J. Douglas, "System Engineering Overview," *Tutorial: System and Software Requirements Engineering,* edited by R.H. Thayer and M. Dorfman, IEEE Computer Society, Washington, DC, 1989.

[3] Sailor, J.D., Lockheed Missiles & Space Co., Systems Engineering Management Guide, Defense Systems Management College, 1983. (The second edition of this book can be obtained from the Superintendent of Documents, Government Printing Office, Washington, DC. The cost is $17.00.)

[4] Flynn, R.F. and M. Dorfman, "ARTS: An Automated Requirements Traceability System," *Journal of Systems and Software,* Vol. 4, 1984, pp. 63-74.

[5] Lano, R.J., "A Structured Approach for Operational Concept Formulation," *TRW Software Series, TRW-SS-80-02,* Jan. 1980.

System Engineering: An Introduction

J. Douglas Sailor

The terms "system" and "system engineering" are widely applied in many technical fields and areas, but no generally agreed-upon definition exists for system engineering and the boundaries within which it operates. This lack may exist because only in recent years has system engineering become a generally recognized discipline, such as mechanical engineering or electrical engineering. Another factor may be that virtually any grouping of items that function together can be (and usually are) identified as a system. Indeed, there are often systems within a system. Thus we have computer systems, communication systems, and aircraft systems; aircraft systems contain both communication and computer systems. To provide a common understanding for the discussions that follow, let us define some basic terminology.

System: a set of functional elements organized to satisfy specified objectives. These elements include hardware, software, people, facilities, material, and data.

System engineering: both a technical and management process. The technical process is the analytical effort necessary to transform an operational need into a system design of the proper size and configuration and to document requirements in specifications. The management process involves assessing the risk and cost, integrating the engineering specialties and design groups, maintaining configuration control, and continuously auditing the effort to ensure that cost, schedule, and technical performance objectives are satisfied to meet the original operational need.

The technical process is primarily a "front-end" process; it is concentrated at the beginning of the development phase. The management process is present at the beginning of the development phase and increases in scope as the design evolves. The need for thorough and complete system engineering in the earliest program phases is shown in Figure 1, which shows that approximately 90 percent of the program costs are committed when only 10 percent of the program cost has been expended.

System engineering process: the means by which a set of objectives is transformed into an operational system. This process is an iterative one in which requirements are developed and allocated to succeedingly lower levels. Design activities begin before requirements allocation trades are complete and serve to "test" the allocation of requirements against what may be really achieved. The objective of system engineering is to completely define the necessary capability that will satisfy mission objectives while minimizing cost and risk.

Hierarchy: Systems are organized into a hierarchy to aid in their development and management. A hierarchy is the organizational structure established by dividing the system into functional areas at succeedingly lower levels until the component level is reached. A component performs a specific function and is manufactured and tested as an identifiable entity.

Requirements: identifiable capabilities expressed as performance measurables or functions that the system must possess to meet the mission objectives. They are defined in abstract terms (they do not define implementation) and are contained in specifications.

Allocation: the process of assigning portions of a requirement among its supporting functional areas throughout succeedingly lower levels of the system hierarchy. When a requirement changes form, it becomes a derived requirement, usually through the process of analysis, which translates user requirements into parameters that a designer can relate to, such as power and weight.

Verification: the assessment of a system's capability against the requirements of its specification. It is accomplished by one of four methods: test (using precision instrumentation), demonstration (a functional test), analysis (or simulation), or examination (of documentation).

Definitions

The Department of Defense (DoD) has been very active in developing and employing the system engineering process in the acquisition of large military and aerospace systems. Because of their complexity and the use of advanced technology, these systems require a highly structured approach to system engineering to reduce the development risk and thereby ensure that cost and schedule goals are achieved. The terminology and approach generally applied to DoD programs is therefore used herein to illustrate the development of large systems. However, the methodology described applies equally well to civilian systems.

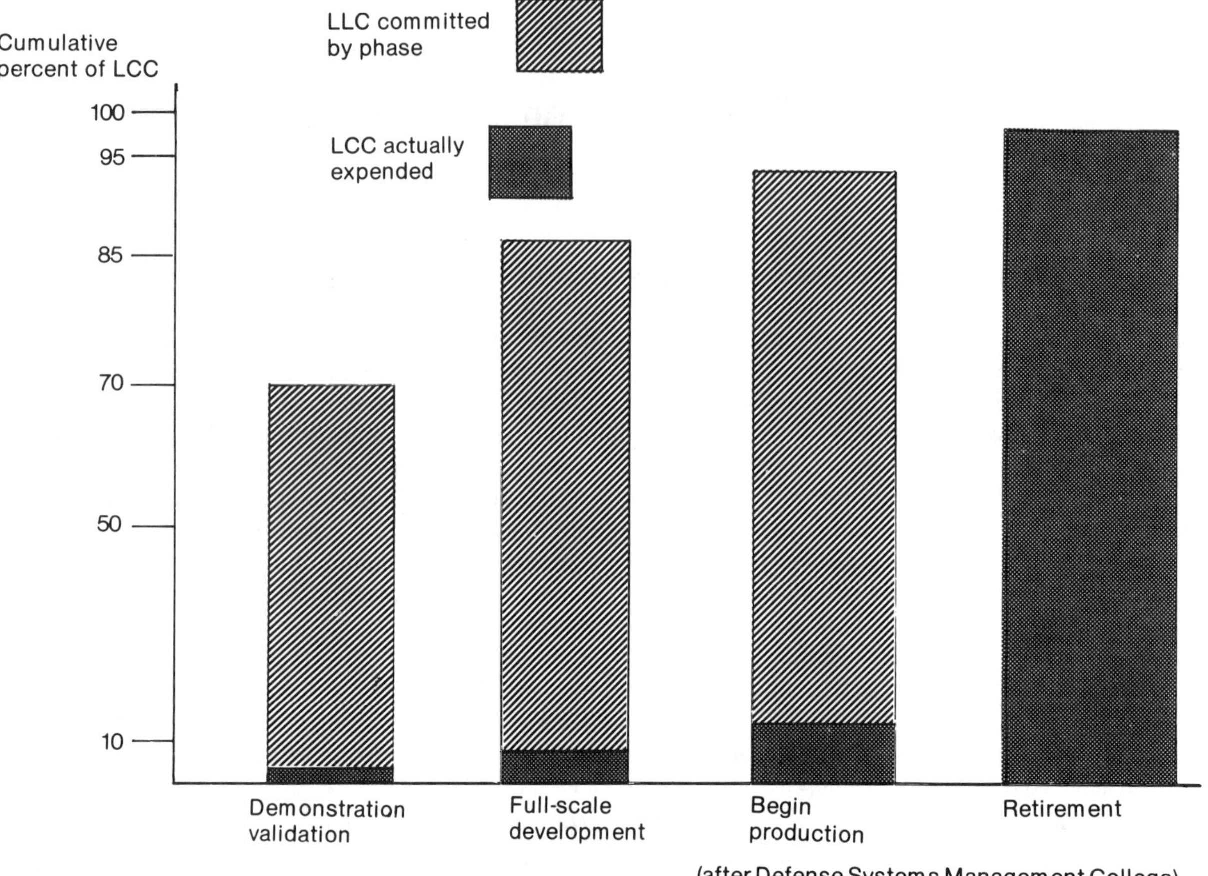

Figure 1: System life-cycle cost expenditure versus commitment

System Life Cycle

The system life cycle is generally divided into seven phases in the DoD acquisition process, as shown in Figure 2. The first phase, *need determination,* involves studies by planning organizations and potential users of the system to establish the technical objectives of a new system. Part of this process is establishing the status of technology that might be applied to the proposed endeavor.

The *concept exploration phase* is generally conducted by a small group organized to form a program office within the contracting agency. This group may draw on outside contractor or consultant support to provide expertise in areas where it is lacking. It evaluates broad concepts that may be capable of satisfying the mission need. It attempts to quantify user requirements and assess the capability of technology to meet the conceptual requirements. If current technology is not adequately developed, contracts may be awarded to bring hardware and software from the laboratory stage to an operational state.

The *demonstration and validation* (DEM/VAL) *phase* involves several contractors in a competition. The effort in this phase is to establish a firm set of system performance specifications and to allocate them to lower levels. Concurrently, a design is defined in enough detail that its performance can be analyzed to establish its capability to meet system level requirements. Trade studies are conducted to optimize (balance) the design in regard to cost, performance, schedule, and operational support goals. During this phase, requirements are allocated from the system level to the hardware and software.

The *full-scale development* (FSD) *phase* is usually performed by a single contractor, although several contractors may be selected to build prototypes and to engage in a demonstration before selection. During FSD, the system proceeds into the detailed design state, followed by fabrication, assembly, and test of the first article. Several major reviews are held during this period. A *preliminary design review* (PDR) and a *critical design review* (CDR) are held in the design phase to examine how well the design meets re-

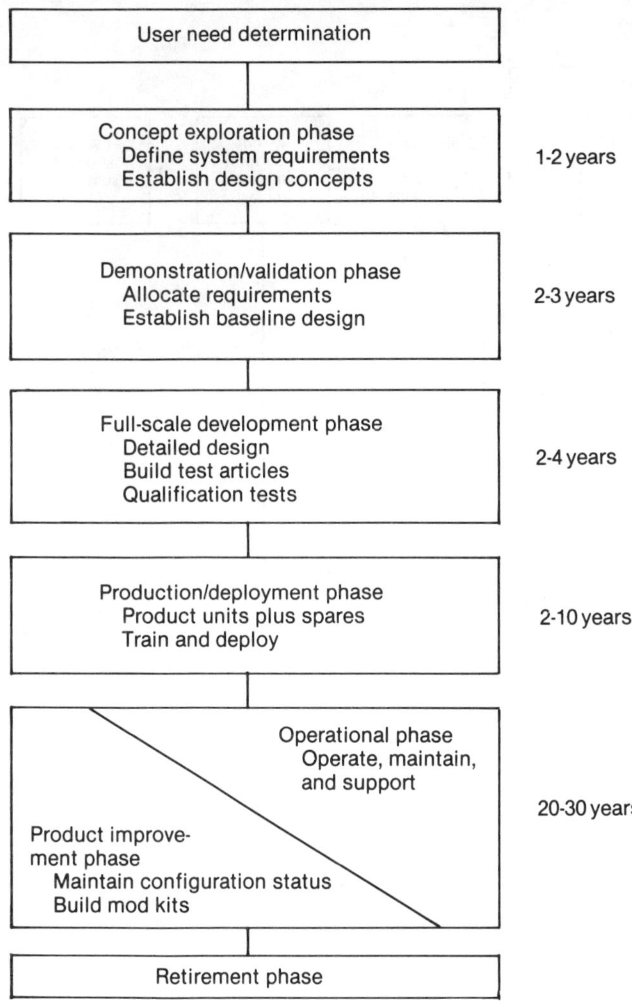

Figure 2: System life cycle

quirements, based on simulation and analysis. Following the testing period, a *formal qualification review* is held to certify that the system has demonstrated its capability to meet operational requirements. The detailed software requirements specifications are developed and completed before PDR. The software design is completed before CDR, and it then proceeds into coding and checkout.

The *production deployment phase* generally begins with a *production readiness review* to insure that all production paper is in place, the machinery available, and the work force assembled and trained. Production is initiated at a low rate, and a *physical configuration audit* held on the first production article to verify that it conforms to specifications and drawings. Production is then built up to a peak rate after it has been determined that changes resulting from initial operational use, testing, production tooling, and manufacturing are incorporated.

The *operational phase* begins when there has been sufficient production to establish interim operational capability. An example of sufficient production might be the first squadron of a new fighter aircraft. In this phase, logistics comes into full operation. Personnel must be trained, manuals and procedures to operate and maintain the system must be produced, and material and spares must be supplied. Because the operational phase can require 50 to 60 percent of the total program life-cycle cost (LCC), logistics planning must be accomplished early to ensure that personnel and maintenance costs are minimized through proper design requirements.

As systems mature, the need arises to accommodate new mission requirements on a changing environment, or to prevent obsolescence. Modification of the system to accommodate these changes is called the *product improvement phase,* which may begin shortly after the start of the operational phase. Improvements that are developed along with the system but integrated at a later date because of schedule differences are termed *planned product improvement.* Improvements that will be added to the system later but for which provisions are made in the basic system design (space, electrical power, wiring, cooling, memory, and processor capacity) are known as *pre-planned product improvement.*

The retirement phase comes at the end of the system's useful life—when it is replaced by a new system with greatly extended capabilities, when its mission is fulfilled or no longer needed, or when it wears out. Although this phase is often not considered in the planning phases, it may be critical as in the case of a nuclear power plant that has a limited life because of materials considerations. In this case, the cost of dismantling the plant and disposal of the parts can be several times the original plant cost and require a number of years to complete.

The System Engineering Process

The system engineering process begins with the definition of user objectives and results in a complete set of requirements for the system together with a system configuration of the proper size and capability to meet those requirements. The process (shown in Figure 3) is iterative, with individual steps repeated several times as additional, more detailed data are developed and fed back to optimize the design.

The user objectives are first developed into quantitative mission requirements. The first step is gathering (or developing) data related to the mission and analyzing those data to extract meaningful parameters that define required system capability. Various system concepts can then be postulated and an operational concept can be developed. When the potential capability of various systems is examined against the desired capability, a rational and realizable set of mission parameters can be established.

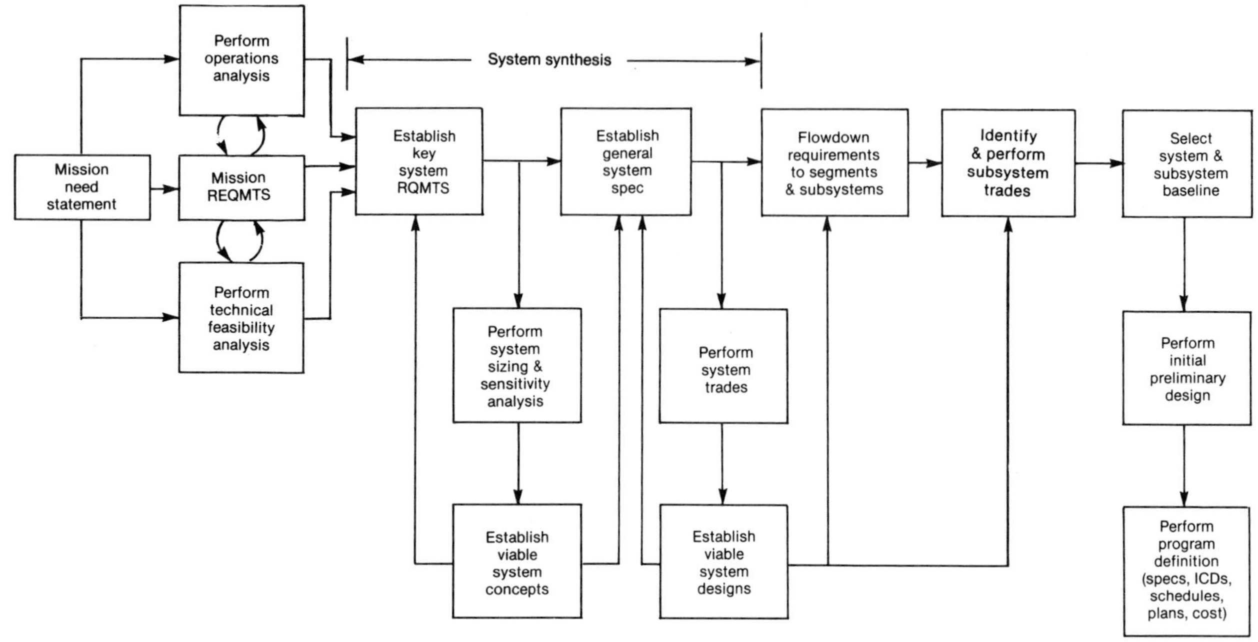

Figure 3: The system engineering process

When the mission-related requirements have been defined, requirements can be placed on the supporting areas that make up the total system. These include areas such as communications, control, power, structures, and facilities. These areas, combined with the mission requirements, become the total set of system requirements. The initial system concepts can then be refined and developed and a system sizing and sensitivity analysis can be performed. The purpose of this analysis is to ensure that all elements are of proper size or adequate capacity to meet system needs (including growth) at minimum cost. The sensitivity analysis exposes those items that are drivers, that is, areas in which small change in capability of the item would cause a large change in total system performance or cost.

Trade studies are then performed to select the concept that best satisfies the total system requirements. Several alternative candidates are defined that could satisfy requirements. Data are then gathered on performance and on other factors. The selection is made on a set of objective criteria such as performance, cost, schedule, and reliability. Requirements are allocated to succeedingly lower levels as the design progresses. Trades are also performed at succeedingly lower levels until finally a *baseline design* is selected. This baseline is analyzed to evaluate its predicted capability to meet specified requirements and to establish the system cost. The end result of this process is (1) a documented set of requirements and (2) a system configuration that meets those requirements and assures that a relative balance is achieved among performance, cost, risk, schedule, reliability, and other factors deemed critical to satisfying the original mission need.

The System Engineering Organization

There is no typical system engineering organization; its composition will vary with the size and nature of the project, management's approach to system engineering, and the customer's view of the role of system engineering. However, a system engineering organization that includes all the elements usually found in most system engineering functions is shown in Figure 4. On large programs typical of DoD, the manager of System Engineering is the final technical authority on the program. The role of this organization is to develop and allocate requirements upon which the design is based, and then to audit the design throughout the development phase to ensure that it complies with the requirements. System Engineering defines the the overall configuration and sizing of the system but does not produce any design drawings or software code. It performs its function by preparing documentation in the form of specifications, plans, and *interface control documents* (ICDs), and by conducting periodic reviews of the evolving design. The functions and responsibilities of the various groups within System Engineering are described in the following paragraphs.

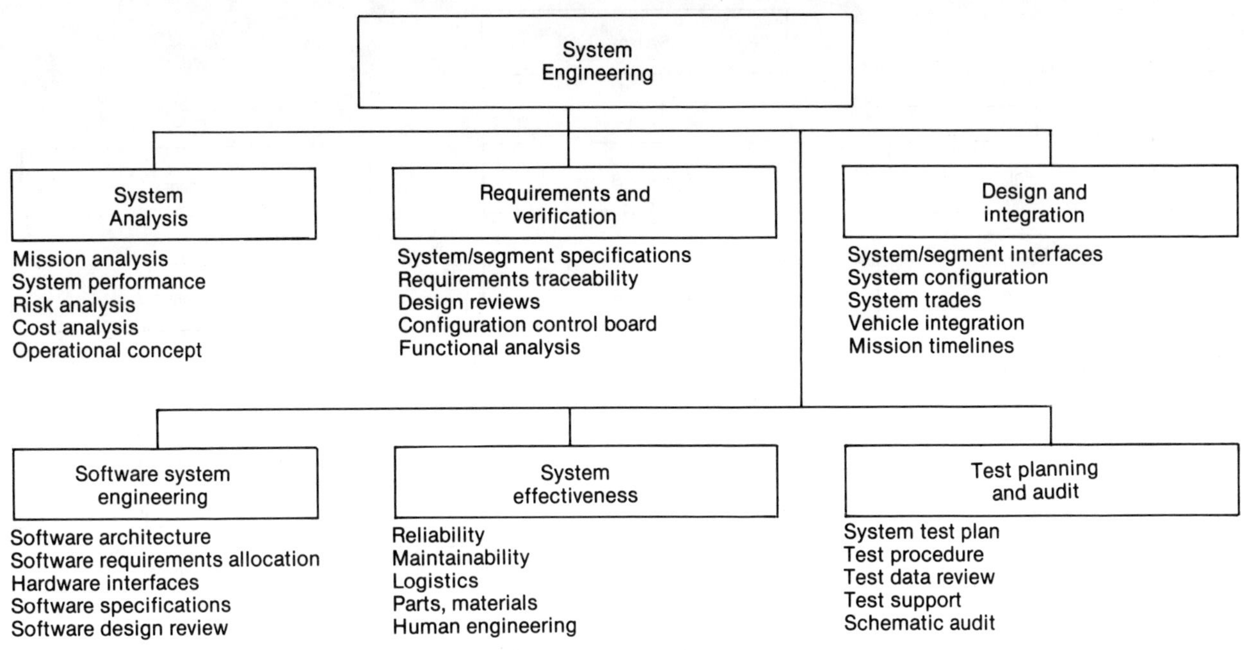

Figure 4: System engineering organization

The *system analysis group* is responsible for all simulation and functional analysis done at the system level, including a full simulation of the operation of the system. This simulation is used first to size the system. The outcome of these studies, in the form of performance parameters, are placed in the system specifications. As design and test data are developed, they are input to the simulation to ascertain the expected performance capability of the system. In the design area, system trade studies are performed to optimize the configuration with regard to cost and risk. This results in a definition of the system configuration and its sizing. Risk evaluation is also performed by this group to identify those items posing the greatest risk to the program. This evaluation is often accomplished by assigning numerical values to the likelihood of failure and the consequence of failure and then combining these values to establish high-, medium-, and low-risk categories. Proposed means for mitigating high and medium risks are also defined. Risk areas are then monitored and alternate activities are initiated or terminated to minimize risk and cost to the program.

The *requirements and verification group* prepares and maintains the specification tree that identifies all specifications on the program and prepares the *system* and *segment specifications.* They also manage the preparation of all lower-level box and computer program specifications, and prepare "fill-in guides" for those documents to ensure uniformity of document format and common requirements. This function also establishes the traceability of requirements throughout all specifications and maintains the automated traceability system. A primary function of this group is the operation of the *configuration control board* (CCB). This group prepares a *design review and audit plan* that identifies and schedules all design reviews and audits to be conducted and defines the format, content, and responsibilities for preparation. They prepare system-level design reviews and they follow up on resulting action items.

The *design and integration group* defines the system configuration and sizing and identifies interface requirements. It organizes and manages the *interface working groups* and prepares ICDs that define all interfaces. They also provide a hardware integration function and perform trade studies to establish the best configuration with respect to cost, risk, and performance. They audit hardware schematics against the system logic diagram (which they prepare), and they establish weight, power, telemetry, and command *control boards* to ensure that the design remains within system capabilities.

The *software system engineering group* supports the functional analysis to allocate functions to hardware, software, and personnel. They prepare the software requirements specification and the *hardware/software interface document,* and they establish software standards and practices. They perform timing and sizing analyses and define the software system architecture to allocate the functions

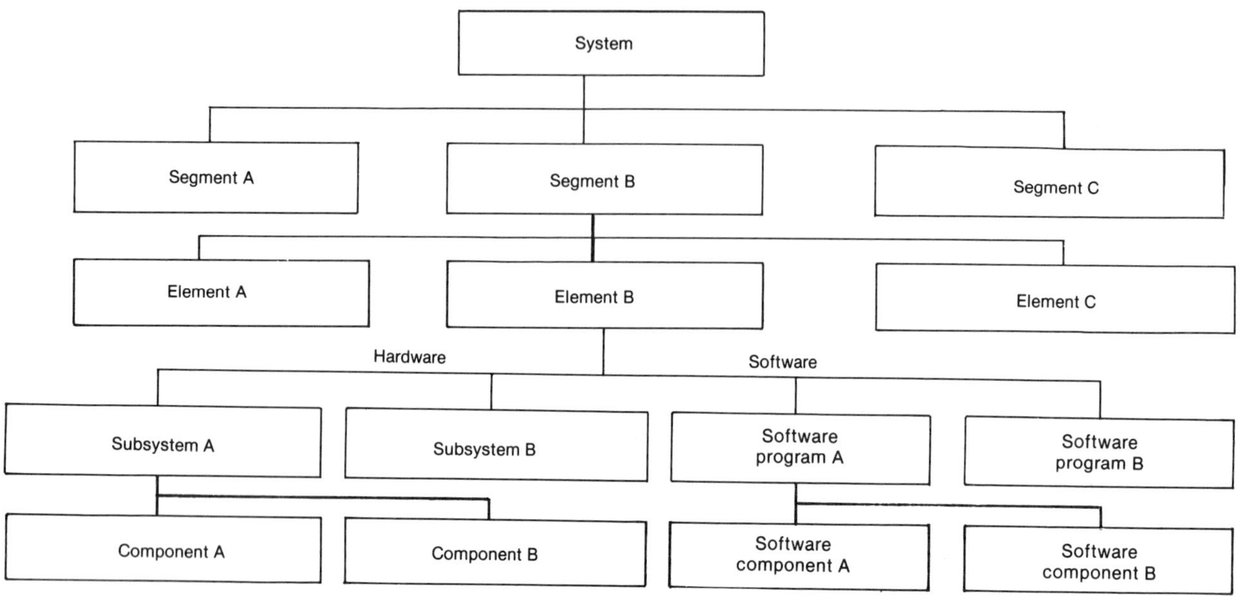

Figure 5: Generic system hierarchy

among the various computer program components. They review the design by periodically auditing the software requirements, design data, functional capabilities, source code, test plan, test procedures, and test data. They also serve as the design review team for all software design reviews and audits, and they analyze system test data to ensure that the software capability satisfies requirements.

The *test planning and audit group* prepares the *program verification plan* that identifies all development, qualification, and reliability tests together with analyses and simulations needed for total verification of capability to meet requirements. The objective is to minimize the testing required while providing adequate proof of capability. They also define the test articles and test flow for all system tests, prepare the system test plan, and review the system test procedures. They audit the test set-up before testing begins, review the test data as they are produced, and give approval for final disconnect and test tear-down.

The *system effectiveness group* consists of specialists in reliability; maintainability; logistics; human factors; safety; producibility; electromagnetic compatibility; and parts, materials, and processes. These individuals are placed in System Engineering because they prepare requirements that are documented in specifications. However, they also work directly with the designers, reviewing drawings and proposing changes to incorporate their requirements. They prepare plans and perform failure modes and effects analyses, hazards analyses, electromagnetic interference analyses, and maintainability timeline analysis. On large systems with wide deployment the logistics portion usually becomes a separate organization after CDR.

A *cost analysis group* may also be part of System Engineering; it is responsible for establishing the LCC of the program and updating it periodically. It uses the equipment list and software estimates on lines of code to establish system costs. An automated pricing program is generally used to rapidly evaluate changes in cost or equipment. This group supports trade studies by providing the relative cost data for design alternatives. The cost analysis includes the total LCC, which covers operational and logistics costs in addition to development costs.

Organizing the System

To maintain proper management the system must be structured into a hierarchy. The generic system hierarchy shown in Figure 5 follows the commonly used terminology in major DoD programs for the various levels. Definitions of the levels below system follow.

Segment: a grouping of items that perform a major function of the system and are physically closely related. They are often produced by several contractors and integrated by a prime contractor.

Element: an integrated set of items that performs a significant operational role, usually produced by a single contractor.

Subsystem: a grouping of items that performs a major function within an element, such as providing electrical power.

Component: a functional unit viewed as an entity for purposes of manufacturing, testing, or record keeping, such as an electronic box or batteries.

Software program: an independent unit of software code that performs a major function, such as the executive in an operating system.

Software program component: software code that performs a subfunction. A computer program component is composed of independent modules, which in turn employ procedures to accomplish specific functions and routines to accomplish repeatedly used functions.

The number of areas at each level is somewhat arbitrary but should not exceed six to eight for best management. Considerations in dividing the functional areas at each level include the planned physical location of items, the complexity of interface, and the contractural responsibility for the items. The number of levels is also somewhat arbitrary, depending on the size and complexity of the system. For example, the element level may be omitted on less complex systems.

The system hierarchy guides the development of the entire system. It is used to develop the specification tree, which in turn identifies the flow-down path for all requirements and forms the basis for requirements analysis. It also forms the basis for the *work breakdown structure* (WBS), which identifies all tasks that must be accomplished on the program.

The development of the specification tree follows the system hierarchy, although specifications may not appear at all levels. For example, subsystem requirements may be in element specifications rather than being separately specified. However, if a subsystem is being separately procured from another contractor, a specification for that subsystem would be mandatory. The tree identifies all hardware and software items that must be produced to implement the system. It does not identify personnel, management, data, material, or other types of items, and it does not indicate the total number of items making up the system. It provides the basis for all requirements documents on the program in order that they can be scheduled and produced. It is therefore done very early in the program.

When the system has been organized, the tasks that must be performed to implement it can also be organized. This organizing is accomplished through the WBS. The WBS is also organized according to the system hierarchy, and it contains within it the specification tree. In addition to hardware and software items, it contains services (such as management, system engineering, and testing) needed to bring the system into operation. Each item is given a number indicating its level in the hierarchy and relating it to a specific development item. These numbers are used to track costs of development of each item and also to specify task descriptions given in the *WBS dictionary,* which contains written descriptions of all tasks on the program with the specific items to be developed, documentation to be prepared, or services to be performed.

System Requirements Tools

The early development phase of a system needs three elements: a set of requirements, a design concept, and an operational description. A number of tools are available to the system engineer for developing the system requirements. The system hierarchy described earlier is useful in organizing the system and establishing the functional areas. Closely related to the system hierarchy is the *functional block diagram* (FBD) that not only identifies the functional areas but also shows the data flowing between them. This diagram is subject to the process of functional decomposition. That is, each block can be broken up into elements at the next lower level, again showing the data flowing between the elements, and continuing until the lowest (box) level is reached. As the design progresses, the FBD develops into system schematics and logic diagrams. Although this tool identifies the functional areas such as receivers, transmitters, and computers and can be used to illustrate the flow of data throughout the system, it does not evaluate the interfaces rigorously.

Use of the N-squared chart developed by Lano[3] ensures a thorough examination of all interfaces at each level. It can also be functionally decomposed. An $N \times N$ matrix is developed (where $N =$ number of elements at any level) with the elements located along one diagonal. Each opposing pair of squares represents the input to and feedback from the two elements located at their intersection on the matrix. Specific data crossing the interface are identified in each box. Where no data are present (i.e., there is no interface), the box is left empty. This process assures that all potential interfaces will be examined.

One of the earliest and still most commonly used methods is the *functional flow diagram* (FFD). Rather than the static functional area relationship of the FBD, the FFD is a time-sequenced diagram that shows all of the functions to be performed to complete a mission. Like the other diagrams, it is subject to decomposition until each action to be performed by either hardware or software components is identified. Because the FFD itself does not indicate the exact time involved in the function's occurrence, a separate *timeline analysis* is necessary for time-critical events.

Another tool more closely related to software is the *data/control flow diagram.* This diagram shows the software processes, the data files, the inputs and outputs, and the named data flows between them. It also shows the control actions as dashed lines. These diagrams form the basis for *structured analysis,* which is a more formal methodology for developing lower-level requirements. The essential elements of structured analysis are as follows.

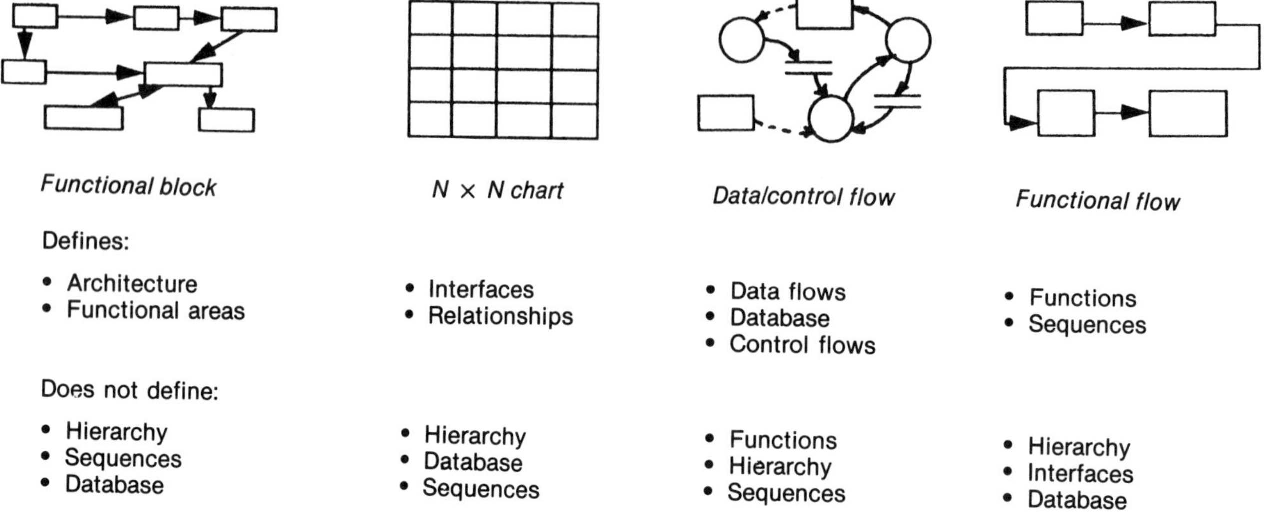

Figure 6: Summary of system requirements tools

- Data/control flow diagrams
- Data dictionary (defining composition of the data flows)
- Data models (defining files and their interaction)
- Process specification (in the form of structured English and decision trees or decision tables)
- State transition diagrams (showing modes of operation)

Various approaches to structured analysis are discussed in greater detail elsewhere in this tutorial.

In summary, no single functional analysis tool is best or sufficient to establish requirements. They all have advantages and drawbacks, as shown inFigure 6. It is necessary to select those that best serve the need.

The *operations concept document* describes the system engineer's understanding of how a system works, and the interactions both within the system and to the external environment. It defines the role of personnel in operating the system, and defines the allocation of functions to hardware, software, personnel and facilities. It too is a structured document, related to the other documentation and tools employed, such as FFDs (4).

In arriving at a design concept, planners must perform a number of trades to arrive at the "best" solution. An optimum solution is usually not possible, because time, budget, or contract constraints may force the use of existing hardware, software, or facilities. Usually a number of possible solutions exist for any specific problem. A *trade tree* is an useful means for organizing this effort. The trade tree begins with major decision areas and proceeds into areas of finer detail. At each decision point, several alternative candidates designs are developed and evaluated by using a *decision analysis* process. Criteria are defined, based on the objectives of the trade study, such as performance, cost, and weight, against which the candidate designs can be evaluated. These criteria are then weighted by System Engineering from the most important (10) to the least important (1). The candidate designs that meet minimum performance requirements are then analyzed and scored by the design engineering organizations (without knowledge of the weights), based on data developed by them. The totals of the weighted scores of all candidates are then compared, and the one with the highest score is selected (providing it exceeds the next lower one by 10 percent). A sensitivity analysis is then conducted to evaluate the sensitivity of results to the small change in weight or score. Is there an unacceptable score of one alternative against one criterion? Any adverse consequences resulting from these analyses are then examined, and the scores are adjusted if necessary.

This same principle can be applied to the system as a whole by using a *system effectiveness model,* as shown in Figure 7. This model examines the items considered most critical to the development of a system, such as cost, schedule, availability, performance, and produceability, to establish a measure of total system effectiveness. The major measures are broken down to lower levels and allocated a portion of the total 100 points as shown. Scoring may be done by using *utility curves,* which are derived before the scoring process by discussions with a number of experts, and by combining their inputs. Risk is introduced through the shape of the curve; the higher score is for a better performance.

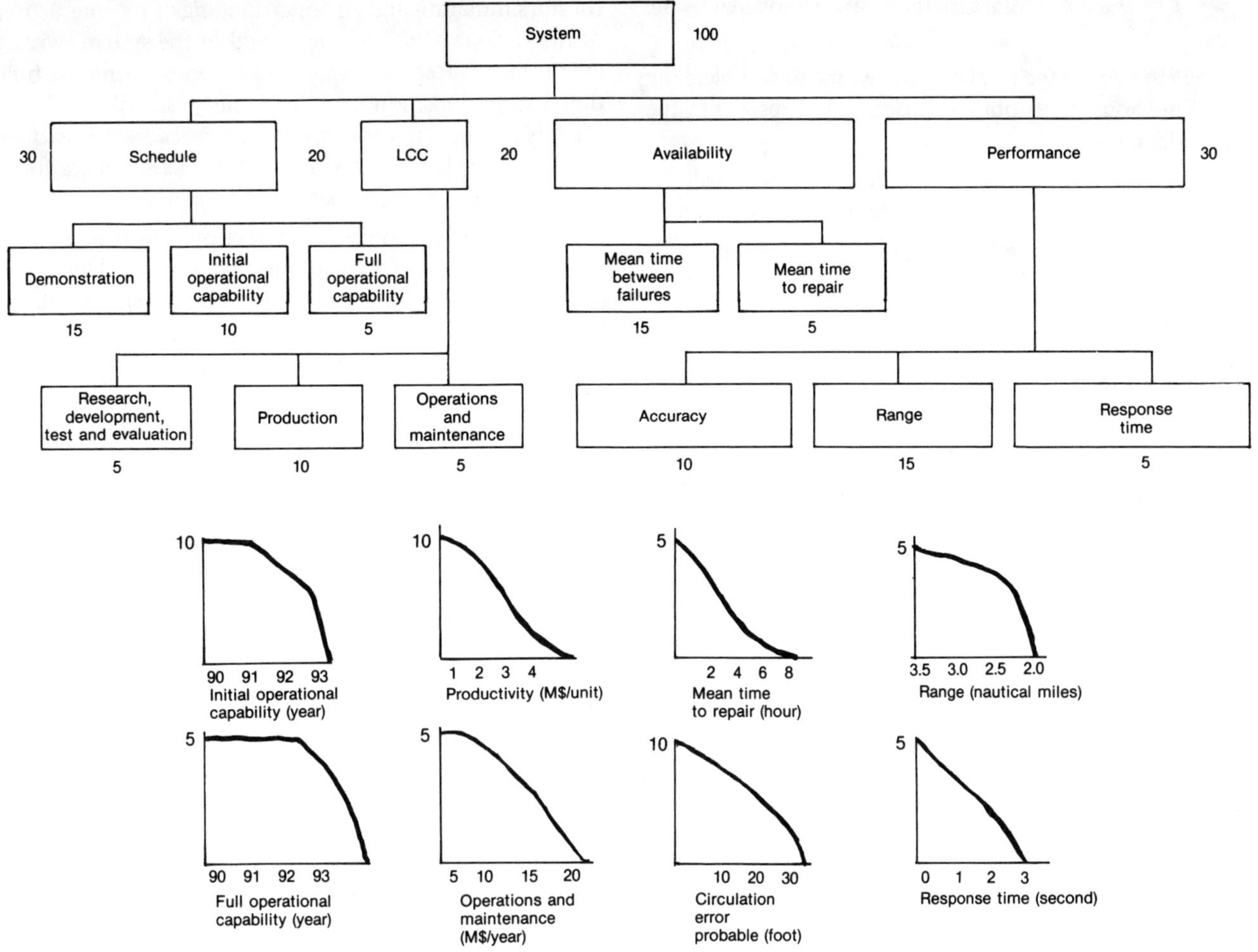

Figure 7: System effectiveness model, with utility curves

Requirements Development

The development of requirements from mission objectives identified in the conceptual phase is an iterative process that comprises the following steps.

- Establish system objectives
- Identify system functions
- Specify performance measurables
- Define candidate concepts
- Describe the operational concept
- Establish interactions
- Perform parametric analysis
- Evaluate candidates with regard to performance, cost, and risk
- Reallocate requirements and update candidate concepts if necessary.
- Select a baseline configuration
- Document and flowdown all requirements

The process begins by examining the desired objectives of the system by discussions with the users. These may be formalized in a needs statement and then developed as a set of functional requirements (i.e., data to be gathered, transmitted, and processed) that characterize the system. To provide the designer with parameters such as size and accuracy that can be used to evolve a design, it is necessary to translate these functional requirements into quantitative or measurable values. Some basic measurable parameters that have been found to characterize most large systems and examples of specific parameters are as follows.

- *Quantity:* the amount of data being produced or capacity of the system
- *Quality:* the precision of the data being produced or the accuracy of the system

- *Coverage:* the total geographical area covered by the system
- *Timeliness:* the total allowable time to complete the mission, or to obtain, process, and distribute the data
- *Availability:* probability that the system will be ready for use when needed (defined as a function of reliability and maintainability)

The use of these measurables for various types of large systems is shown in Figure 8. Although their application may not be universal, they provide a starting point for developing quantitative requirements. Usually a number of requirements can be identified for each measurable. In addition, other mission-unique requirements can be developed, such as the operating modes, responses, and outputs.

Mission requirements relate primarily to the payload. For the system to be complete and viable, support must be provided in a number of areas. These may include communications, security, power, propulsion, command and control, data processing and routing, attitude determination and control, and protection from the operating environment. The requirements for these areas can be developed by using the tools described in the "Systems Requirements Tools" section. The complexity of modern systems requires that the system engineer understand the interactions between elements of the system that must function together. To accomplish this end, it is usually necessary that a large-scale simulation be developed to model the system to simulate its operation and to develop performance parameters. The operational concept must be developed early to provide a basis for the simulation and an understanding of the interactions of the various system elements and of the system, with its environment. Requirements are derived by using the functional decomposition tools previously described. As the process proceeds to lower levels, interfaces are exposed and requirements developed to ensure satisfactory operation of the system when its elements are interconnected.

Inherent in the requirements development process is the definition of the system configuration and size. This definition provides the framework for the requirements allocation process and ensures that the system has sufficient capacity to meet mission requirements. The defined system functions and the system hierarchy are used together to establish the functional areas that provide a top-level definition of the configuration. The system physical configuration is established through trade studies that analyze various candidates for each functional area and select those that best satisfy requirements. The sizing of the design is established through parametric analysis that examines a range of values over which the system and its functional areas could operate and selects the operating points (or size) that provide the best balance for the total system. This avoids the "point design" solution, which is often done based on experience but which may result in mismatched elements within the system. Candidate designs are exercised against operational scenarios to determine which one best meets performance objectives. The LCCs are defined for the configurations, and the risks associated with the designs are identified. Candidates are then evaluated with regard to performance, cost, and risk. Once a configuration is established, it should be identified as the "baseline" and defined in a formal *design description document.*

Attribute	Measurable			
	Earth obervation satellite	Communication satellite	Rapid transit	Aircraft
Quantity	Frames/day, Sq mi/day	Number of throughput (BPS), or no. of channels	Number of passengers	Number of passengers, payload (lb)
Quality	Resolution (ft)	Signal/noise, bit error rate	Ride comfort	Navigation accuracy (ft)
Coverage	Geographical access area	Geographical access area	Area served (sq mi)	Range (mi)
Timeliness	Revisit time, proceess and delivery time	Channel availability on demand (sec)	Travel time between points (min)	Load/unload time (min)
Availability	Available for use (%)	99.88/(CCIR regulation)	Time between trains (min)	Flight readiness

Figure 8: Requirements measurables

Another important source of requirements is the area of engineering specialties: reliability, maintainability, human factors, parts, materials, processes, logistics, and safety. The standards applied in these areas are developed from data taken from previous experiments, tests, analyses, and operational experience of similar systems. The specialists apply knowledge gained from many programs over many years to establish design requirements that will ensure a durable, operable, and supportable system.

Requirements Flowdown, Allocation, and Traceability

When a complete set of top-level system requirements has been defined, they must be flowed down through lower and lower levels of the hierarchy until the hardware and software component levels are reached. This is known as "top-down" analysis and is the preferred method because (in theory) it produces a system in which all elements are completely balanced or "optimized." In the real world, complete balance is seldom achieved, because fiscal, schedule, and technological constraints result in some "flow-up" of requirements. However, the system engineer attempts to flow down all requirements in the process shown in Figure 9.

Requirements are either allocable or nonallocable. Nonallocable requirements are items such as environments, operational life, and design standards, which apply unchanged across all elements of the system or its segments.

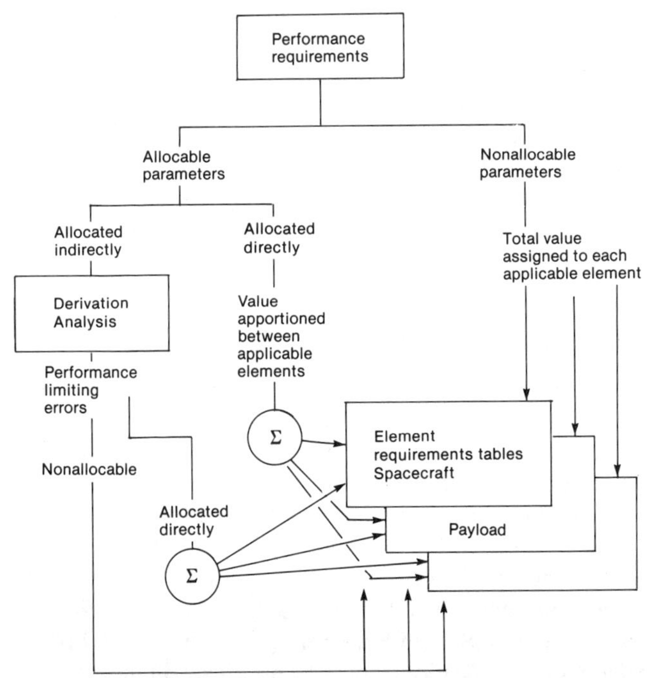

Figure 9: Requirements flow-down process

Allocable parameters can be allocated either directly or indirectly. Those allocated directly do not change form but are simply divided (in a technical budget) among several lower-level elements. This would be the case for a pointing error expressed in degrees, which might be allocated among the payload, structure, computer, and attitude control subsystem. At the next lower level the subsystem error, still in degrees, could be allocated to the star tracker and gyros. Indirectly allocated parameters means that the parameter must change its form through a derivation analysis. A system requirement of targets per orbit pass, for example, means little to the hardware or software designer who is interested in the output power required from the transmitter or the processing speed of the computer. The derivation process transforms mission requirements into requirements against which designers can produce and test their equipment and software.

An example of the requirements flow-down process for the power subsystem of an earth satellite is shown in Figure 10.

Requirements Documentation

The sole product of system engineering is documentation, not hardware drawings or software code. It is through this documentation that we communicate within the System Engineering organization, with others involved in developing the system, and with the future to establish the system configuration, size, and performance. The requirements process is of no value unless the requirements are placed in formal documents of recognized authority and maintained under configuration control throughout their life. These documents, called specifications, are written in a standard format by using a unique requirements statement language. The rationale for arriving at the requirements is also documented in *engineering analysis reports.*

The specifications are defined in a specification tree that follows the system hierarchy. Each deliverable item (or assembly of items) should have a specification. The acceptance test of an item is performed against its specification.

A specification is a listing of requirements. It is not a novel, a statement of work, a plan, or an operational description. Its primary purpose is to define the performance required of an item. The basic elements of a specification as defined in MIL-STD-490 and DOD-STD-2167 are its scope, the applicable documents, a functional description of the item, the performance and physical characteristics, the design standards being applied, the requirements allocation to the next lower level, and the verification methods to be used. The performance requirements have a standard format and should exhibit the following attributes.

- *Abstract:* does not define design implementation
- *Achieveable:* within cost and technology constraints

System: Provide coverage of Atlantic and Pacific Oceans between lat. 10° N and 60° N

Orbit coverage analysis

Segment: Provide payload operation of 4 hr/day

Spacecraft conceptual design
Payload design analysis

Vehicle: Provide 1000 W average power with 2000 W peak for 4 hr/day

Subsystem conceptual design study and equipment survey

Component: Solar arrays: Provide 250 W per panel
Batteries: Provide 60 amp-hours storage with 50% depth-of-discharge
Charge controller: Allow battery to achieve 0.95 full charge

Figure 10: Requirements derivation example

- *Allocated:* through an identifiable, documented analysis
- *Concise:* specifies only the input, output, and process or action to be taken. Does not provide rationale, definitions, or ultimate usage
- *Complete:* stands alone when separated from other requirement statements
- *Integrated:* consistent with other requirement statements
- *Proper level:* of the system hierarchy
- *Traceable:* to a higher-level requirement
- *Understandable:* clear and unambiguous
- *Unique:* not redundant or overlapping
- *Verifiable:* within a single test or analysis

A typical example of a requirement statement is:

"Upon operator request, the telemetry process shall retrieve the last ten specified measurands from the database, convert them to engineering units, format them as defined in ICD 1234, and route them to the display unit."

Note the use of the word "shall," the specification of the input, process, and output, and the reference to the ICD. The ICD defines the design implementation of this requirement and is traceable to it.

Requirements Change Control

When the flow-down process and trade studies are complete, a baseline design is established (usually in the DEM/VAL phase). At that time, it is essential that all requirements be placed under formal control. This is accomplished by CCB, which is usually chaired by the program manager. The function of the CCB is to review all proposed changes to baseline documentation, including specifications. Changes nearly always result in a cost increase or schedule delay that has an adverse impact on the program. This impact increases as the system proceeds through the development cycle. For this reason, a review by senior program personnel is required to ensure that the change is necessary and that the proposed solution is the most economical one. System Engineering is responsible for preparing or reviewing all changes brought before the CCB to ensure that all potential impacts on documentation, hardware, and software have been defined; that alternative methods of solution have been identified and evaluated; and that the proposed solution has been fully evaluated in terms of performance, cost, schedule, and risk.

Requirements Verification

As the hardware and software are designed, produced, and tested, System Engineering has the responsibility to verify that the capabilities demonstrated do in fact meet the requirements of the system as documented in its specifications. This is a continuing process, starting with design reviews in the early portion of the FSD phase and ending with review of data from the all-up system tests before the system becomes operational. A *design verification plan* that is prepared by System Engineering early in the FSD phase defines all verification data to be produced on the program and identifies the time of its availability. The data produced become the basis for the design review data packages. As data are produced by the hardware and software organizations, they are audited against specified requirements by System Engineering.

System Engineering organizes and schedules all formal design reviews and defines the content and format, which follows the outline of the specification. It serves as the *design review team* for the lower-level reviews, and prepares the system-level reviews. Included in these reviews are the results of analyses and simulations that predict component, subsystem, and system performance. Where engineering models or prototypes have been produced to reduce risk, development test results may also be included in the review. As qualification and system-level tests are completed, System Engineering reviews the data and gives final certification that the system is ready for production and deployment.

Summary

The system engineering process is iterative, using a structured approach to ensure that the system, when developed, will meet specified objectives. It must consider the elements of performance, cost, risk, schedule, and operational complexity to ensure that a balanced design is achieved. The system engineer must have the broadest possible outlook, and continually question the data presented against his/her knowledge and experience to surface discontinuities and erroneous implementation of requirements.

References

1. J.D. Sailor, Lockheed Missiles and Space Company: *System Engineering Management Guide,* Defense Systems Management College, 1983. (The second edition of this book can be obtained from the Superintendent of Documents, Government Printing Office, Washington, D.C. The cost is $17.00).

2. A. Frager, et al. *Integrated Logistics Support—A Guide for Acquisition Managers* (Draft), Defense Systems Management College, Fort Belvoir, Va., 1985.

3. R.J. Lano, *A Technique for Software and Systems Design,* North-Holland Publishing Co., Amsterdam, The Netherlands, 1979.

4. R.J. Lano, "A Structured Approach for Operational Concept Formulation," *Tutorial: System and Software Requirements Engineering,* edited by R.H. Thayer and M. Dorfman, IEEE Computer Society Press, Washington, D.C., 1990.

A Structured Approach for Operational Concept Formulation

Robert J. Lano

1: Introduction

One significant problem encountered in the development, deployment, and utilization of today's complex systems is the accurate and timely definition of the desired system requirements, operations, characteristics, and constraints.

System engineering is the term most often used to describe the activities associated with this "front-end" definition process. The initial point of departure for this overall process should be provided by the operational concept formulation activity, which defines the general system goals, missions, functions, and components in a document called the "operational concept document" (OCD or CONOPS). This document forms the basis for all subsequent system design, planning, coordination, analysis, definition, and development activities. The leverage exerted by this document can, therefore, have a significant impact on the overall system design and development process. The effectiveness of the operational concept formulation activity greatly influences the quality of the resultant system performance, cost, schedule, and overall usability parameters. The material presented in this paper is, therefore, focused on improving this front-end operational concept formulation process.

Subsection 2 of this paper provides a brief background concerning the operational concept formulation process. Subsection 3 points out the problems and lessons learned from present-day activities in this area. Subsection 4 summarizes the requirements for the resultant product(s). Subsections 5 through 7 recommend a suggested approach (concepts, processes, and products). Subsection 8 recommends detailed outlying guidance, and Subsection 9 concludes with a summary of the results of using the approach described in this document.

2: Background

The operational concept document (OCD) is usually produced as the first step in the system definition phase of a given program. The purpose of the OCD is to describe the overall desired system characteristics from an operational viewpoint. The document is used to coordinate the overall non-quantatative system goals with the users, the buyers, the contractors, and the other system interfacing organizations (e.g., training, facilities, staffing, interfacing, and maintenance elements).

The OCD forms the basis for long-range operational planning activities and provides guidance for the development of the subsequent system definition documentation, (i.e., functional system specifications, deployment plans, long-term budgeting, interface control drawings, etc.). The fact that this document is not a legally binding "test to" specification (except as individually referenced to in later specifications) provides a freedom of approval that allows this document to be produced, modified, and distributed in a timely and efficient manner.

Many major program efforts have been either cancelled or started in a disastrous manner in the early program phases because of a lack of the overall sponsor and user coordination afforded by a well constructed operational concept formulation process. The importance of the OCD cannot be overly stressed in the overall system lifecycle acquisition, development, deployment, and support process.

The primary ingredients of the OCD consists of the higher-level definitions of the missions, mission objectives, system goals, organizational involvements, and general operational philosophies to be employed. These definitions should be accompanied by summary descriptions of the system components, physical locations, operational sequences, organizational and physical interfaces, and basic functions performed. The OCD is conceptual in nature, and therefore, does not contain specific implementation nor design-dependent constraints. This conceptual characteristic usually results in the production of an informally structured document that does not follow the rules and disciplines of the specification type documents that are generated later in the system definition process. The resulting document, however, is usually maintained as a controlled system definition document, and therefore places traceability requirements on all subsequent system documentation definition activities.

The activities following the operational concept formulation process normally consist of mission analysis and tradeoffs, program planning (system engineering management plan), requirements analysis and specification (system specification), and/or preliminary design studies and tradeoff analysis (preliminary system design). These activities are greatly influenced by the quality and rigor associated with the OCD. The OCD is, therefore, a primary system definition tool and should be developed with as much attention to detail and structure as the remaining system level documents.

3: Current Problems and Lessons Learned

The current method for generating an OCD consists of assembling a set of experienced individuals, who agree on a basic document outline, assign authors to specific sections, write a preliminary document, restructure the outline, rewrite the document, edit the document, integrate the document, and produce the final OCD.

The individuals assembled are of various disciplines, come from a variety of skill centers, have various experiences, possess various writing styles, and are accustomed to different document formats. The initial writing process is usually very rapid because each participant writes about his or her specific interests, experiences, and concerns. Completeness and accuracy characteristics are then abandoned to meet the imposed deadline. The resulting document is then edited, integrated, produced, and delivered to meet the schedule milestones imposed.

The problems associated with this approach are summarized as follows:

- *lack of planning:* distributed authority implies distributed planning. Each author plans his/her own section in outline, content, format, and writing style. This produces a totally non-integrated document
  - *lessons learned:* contralized planning and control
- *lack of direction:* distributed authority also results in distributed direction. Each section author provides his/her own direction as to outline, contents, style, and format of the section. This produces an even more non-integrated document
  - *lessons learned:* centralized program direction
- *lack of coordination:* each section author is transparent to all other sections, since he/she is totally dedicated to his/her specific section. This produces a totally inconsistent document
  - *lesson learned:* total coordination at all levels
- *slow start:* the lack of detailed planning in the early program phases results in low productivity and definer frustrations, which further decreases the efficiency of the normal "start-up" process
  - *lessons learned:* detailed planning increases "start-up" efficiency
- *lack of early review:* the lack of immediate OCD product review milestones results in constraining the review process to a total product review instead of to a sequential review methodology. This process leads to a totally unreviewed higher-level concept with totally reviewed lower-level typing and grammar corrections
  - *lessons learned:* top-down progressive design review and freeze
- *lack of integrated reviews:* the document production process is normally so disorganized that the total picture is never presented at one time to the reviewers. This results in partial (module) reviews instead of in a total integrated system concept review
  - *lessons learned:* reviews should be held at each level of abstraction, whether or not the complete text/write-up is present
- *continual rewrite/retype:* the unstructured nature of the regular OCD process causes a great deal of rewriting and retyping activity. All sentences are judged on their individual merit before their need or applicability are evaluated. Much of the correction process is therefore wasted on sentences that are eventually discarded because of their non-applicability to the subject
  - *lessons learned:* approve the applicability of the thought before correcting the grammar and spelling errors
- *wasted artwork:* a great quantity of artwork (more than 40 percent) is usually abandoned during the concept formulation process because of the unstructured nature of its development. A slower, more structured approach, could have decreased this art waste significantly with a small effort on the part of the top-level system designers. A simple disciplined (top-down) approach could have been adopted that would have released artwork as a function of the level of design freeze activity
  - *lessons learned:* produce artwork in a hierarchical manner consistent with the approved level of design freeze
- *excessive reproduction services:* the bulk reproduction of every version of every section is common in the past operational concept formulation processes. If successive levels of detail have been defined, agreed to, and frozen, there would be no reason to reproduce these levels for each revision of the publication. Therefore, the emphasis should be directed toward the structure and upper levels, rather than downward to the grammar and spelling corrections in the individual detailed sentences
  - *lessons learned:* structure the OCD documentation in a manner that reduces breakage and excess reproduction at the higher levels

The quality of the OCD documents produced by the normal process defined above suffers from at least formality and discipline, if not from structure, completeness, consistency, and rational detail. It is, therefore, the intent of this paper to suggest activities that will improve the quality of the OCD and decrease the inherent waste in the production of these documents.

4: The Basic OCD Requirements

The OCD must satisfy the needs of four types of audiences: users, buyers, builders, and interfacing organization. The "system users" primary interest is in the planning, operational, organizational, and support aspects of the system, and their secondary interest is in the more detailed technical attributes such as components, locations, sequences, interfaces, functions, and detailed requirements. The "buyers" primary interest is to accomplish the mission objectives within the imposed cost and schedule constraints. The "builders" primary interest is to accurately define what they are contracting to build rather than in the overall system needs, objectives, and support characteristics. The lower echelons of all organizations are additionally interested in various component details rather than in system level architectural philosophies. The "interfacing organizations" interests are normally restricted to the direct physical interfaces to their systems, the resultant impacts imposed, and the support characteristics required. All of these audiences must be accommodated to the appropriate level of detail within the OCD.

The OCD must additionally satisfy the needs of four different types of readers: the "generalist," the "system thinker," the "component thinker," and the "item thinker." The generalist requires an overview presentation, and usually does not have enough time to digest the entire document. The system thinker is interested in the overall system philosophies and structures rather than in the component details. The component thinker is only responsible for a given part of the system and requires a general overview, followed by an easily accessible detailed discussion of the individual component that he/she is associated with. The item thinker is oriented either toward a discipline (i.e., logistics, facilities, and availability), or a characteristic of the system (i.e., system interfaces, standards, and communications). All of these reader types must be accommodated to their required level of detail within the same OCD.

Some of the standard rules for the development of any specification type document should also apply to the OCD if it is to be structured. These rules are summarized as follows:

- *complete:* every subject is identified, defined, and described to the appropriate level of detail
- *concise:* every subject is treated in a direct manner without requiring excessive verbiage, experience, or referencing
- *clear:* every subject is stated with a direct approach—that is, only a small possibility of error in reader interpretation
- *simple:* every subject is defined with simple language and sentence structure. All acronyms, assumptions, and prerequisites are defined
- *understandable:* every subject is stated in common language and in common form. Minimum assumptions are made with regard to reader comprehension
- *unambiguous:* every subject is stated in a manner that cannot be misinterpreted by any reasonable level of discipline, organization, training, experience, or educational background
- *specific:* every subject is oriented toward a single thought, requirement, instance, condition, component, interface, or attribute
- *consistent:* every reference, allocation, interface, relationship, and structure is consistent throughout the document
- *referenceable:* every subject is uniquely identifiable by a numerical, positional, or special connotation. The simpler the identification, the simpler the reference
- *traceable:* every subject is related horizontally or vertically to a reference in another document
- *implementation-free:* every subject is stated so that various implementations could satisfy the directed requirement ("what" not "how")
- *feasible:* every subject is evaluated for practicability within the economy of effort and available utilization resources
- *maintainable:* every subject is structured for flexibility and modularity of change and redirection
- *manageable:* subjects are selected to satisfy the detail level required without imposing excessive management expenditures

Implementing these rules while enforcing the operational concept importance in the overall system design philosophy will result in an OCD that is an integral part of the system definition process. Evolving and updating these concept philosophies will also carry the operational system goals through the development process and will have a positive effect on the total system product utilization.

The bottom line in operational concept formulation is, therefore, to produce an OCD that does all things for all people, and at the same time obeys various logical constraints and formats. In the end, the OCD must show the "how" of system operation. This "how" is initially described by defining the "what," "where," "when," "who," and sometimes "why" of the concept formulated. A summary of the contents of each of these definition "questions" is provided below:

- *what:* defines the components, modules, elements, and requirements that are necessary (at the highest level of abstraction) to perform the tasks at hand

- *where:* defines the components and interfaces (geographical, physical, or functional) that accomplish each required function or activity
- *when:* defines the event sequences (tasks, activities, and flows) that are required to complete the mission goals and requirements in a sequence or time-oriented fashion
- *who:* defines the operators/systems and operator interactions required to accomplish the basic mission tasks
- *why:* defines the reasoning for partitioning the mission tasks to the components, requirements, operators, interfaces, and sequences presented in the OCD

The "how" of the system operations is then constructed by integrating the "W's" of operations and by applying the constraints presented (cost/schedule/performance). The operational concept document becomes the integrated presentation of these results.

5: The Suggested Approach Concepts

The major concepts employed in the approach suggested include "top-down," "structured design," "hierarchical decomposition," "multiple tool set utilization," "disciplined coordination," "detailed traceability," and "structured documentation."

The top-down concept requires that the definers view the system from the top and continually limit their depth of field to the level of detail under study. The system structure at the higher levels becomes more important than the associated technical descriptions. Each level of definition must be complete at a uniform level of detail and must encompass all possible system additions before proceeding to the next lower level. Emphasis is placed on constructing a logical organization of modules at each successive level of detail (a place for everything, and everything in its place) to minimize structure breakage and, therefore, prevent major top-level reorganization activities. "Stub" modules are inserted in areas that cannot be defined at a given time to serve as a reminder to everyone concerned that additional requirements will be defined as more information becomes available. The major structures generated at the highest level of an operational concept include the definition of the basic system components, the primary external and internal interfaces, the functional mission modes and phases, and the higher-level organizational structures. All definers, with this concept, are forced to complete the definition of all co-elements at each level before proceeding to the following, and possibly more familiar, levels of the definition process. The discipline inherent in this approach assures a complete and consistent definition activity in terms of all of the functions, components, requirements, interfaces, operational characteristics, and sequences involved.

The structured design concept employed in the suggested approach is based upon well known partitioning and decomposition principles. The simple definition of partitioning or decomposition is the process of dividing a system, function, module, area, requirement, or activity into multiple elements that collectively accomplish the desired results. The purpose of the partitioning activity is to segregate specific analysis, definition, development, implementation, test, and documentation tasks into pieces that are understandable and implementable by a given number of management, implementation, test, documentation, and operational personnel and equipments.

The basic premise of structured design is that simplicity can be enhanced by dividing a system into separate parts so that any given part can be considered, implemented, eliminated, and/or changed with minimal consideration or effect on the other parts of the system. Using this concept forces the definers to perform the partitioning process based on simplicity, modularity, and flexibility guidelines. The resultant process is therefore more efficient in terms of its generation, application, modification, and overall lifecycle cost characteristics.

The hierarchical decomposition concept, when coupled with a level of abstraction philosophy, is used throughout this operational concept formulation approach. This concept is applied not only to the functional partitioning activities, but also to the interface, sequence, and organizational definition tasks. Every component, interface, operational position, and operational sequence is hierarchically related to its higher-level "parent." All defined entities are described at their highest level of abstraction to incorporate new and changing requirements through the definition process. All detailed charts, figures, and tables are subsets of some higher-level set of definitions arranged in a Dewey Decimal accounting system. This hierarchical decomposition concept implementation guarantees direct traceability from each lower-level system subject through the various levels of the system structures.

The multiple tool set utilization concept acknowledges the fact that no single tool and/or philosophy can produce an optimized conceptual design. A multiple tool set is therefore proposed that examines all dimensions of a system (structure, interfaces, people, and sequences), rather than tilting the process toward one particular influence (e.g., timeline, functional purity, or minimum interfaces). The multiple tool sets recommended are the following:

- *the structure chart:* hierarchical structuring of components and requirements. This is the primary tool used to define the functional structure of the system. The structure chart answers the "what" questions of system definition. The final requirements tabulation and compliance outlines are also provided by the structure chart

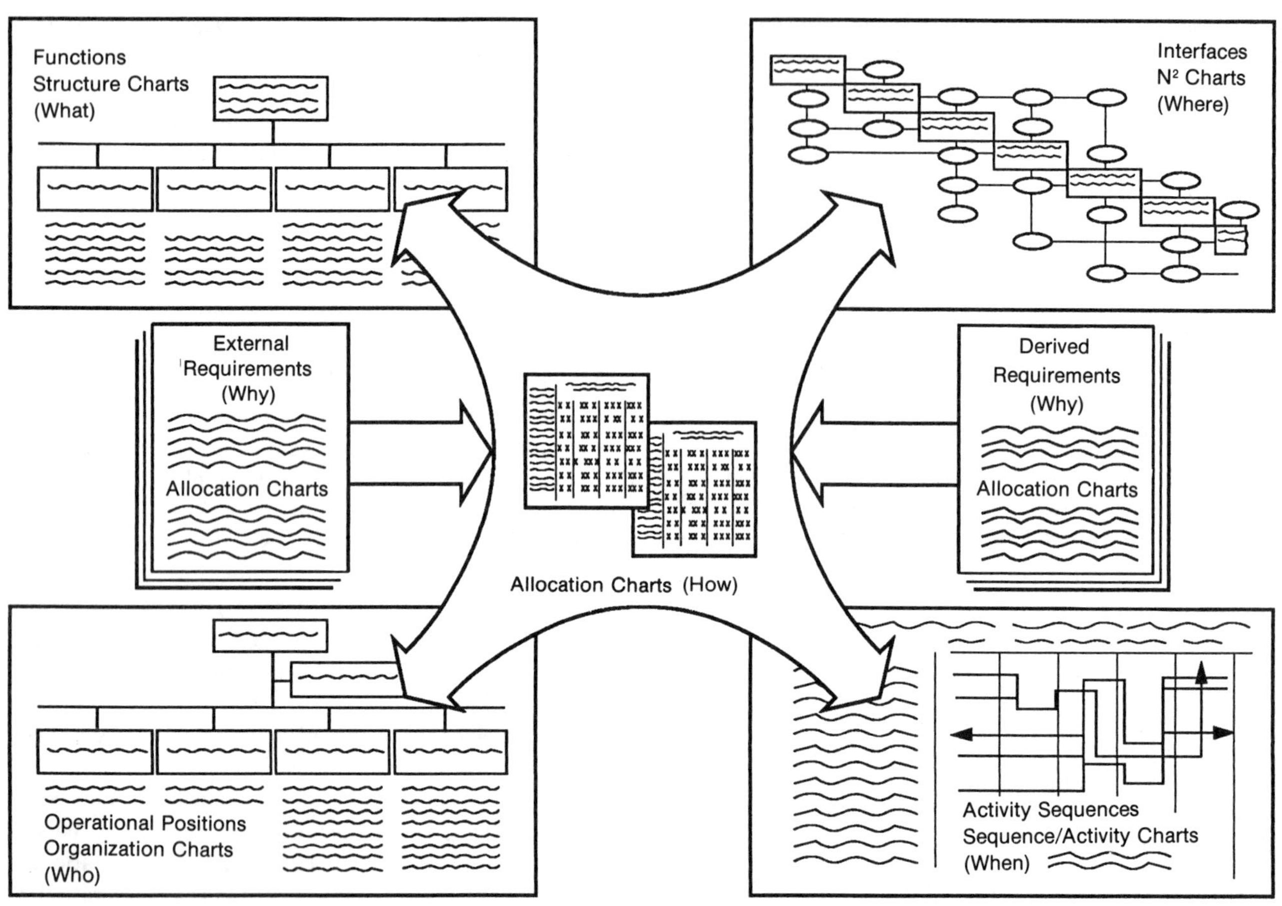

Figure 1: Tool relationships

- *the interface definition chart:* structured identification and definition of external and internal system interfaces. This is the primary tool used to define the functional interfaces and operational relationships of the system. The interface definition chart answers the "where" questions of system definition. The N Squared Chart (N2 Chart) is the recommended tool for this definition activity (it is defined elsewhere in this book)
- *the sequence chart:* flow definitions of major system modes and sequences. This is the primary tool used to formally define the basic phases, modes, and sequences of the overall mission. The sequence chart helps to answer the "when" question of system definition
- *the activity chart:* timing definitions for individual system activities. This tool is used to define the more detailed timing relationships of the lower-level operational tasks performed. The activity chart completes the answer to the "when" question of system definition
- *the organization chart:* structured definition of system operations and organizational relationships. This is the tool used to define the organizations involved with the system, the organizational structure of the system, and the operators and operator positions required to conduct system operations. The organization chart answers the "who" question of system definition
- *the allocation chart:* integrating matrix for the correlation and allocation of function, interface, sequence, activity, and organizational elements. This tool is used for both external and internal traceability purposes. External traceability is accomplished by allocating and tabulating all requirement references to applicable top-level external documentation. This usage helps to answer the "why" question of system definition. Internal traceability and allocations are also provided by the matrix capability of the allocation chart. This type of usage helps to answer the "how" question of system definition.

Figure 1 summarizes these tools and their interrelationships. The definition features of this multiple tool set approach enhance the conceptual definition process by focusing attention on all of the primary aspects of the system design.

The disciplined coordination concept is used to enforce definer communications and the effective implementation of the concepts previously described. All tasks, processes, and products are accomplished under a strict set of rules and constraints. Definers are required to conform to a well-defined and structured set of process rules, rather than to perform their tasks in a non-integrated haphazard manner. Progress is monitored at each level of detail throughout the process to rapidly correct any direction misunderstandings, definition inconsistencies, or completeness errors. System operations, structures, interfaces, and sequences are continually reviewed and approved at every level of detail, thereby minimizing product breakages and maximizing the definition efficiency.

The detailed traceability concept is accomplished both by the hierarchical nature of the tools used and by the discipline imposed in the conceptual formulation process. All requirements, functions, and components are directly traceable through the structure chart definition process. All interfaces are hierarchically defined and are directly related to individual system components and functions through the interface definition chart. Every entity (function, interface, operator, sequence, or activity) is vertically traceable to the higher levels of the system requirements because of the hierarchical nature of the tools employed. Operator actions and system activities are additionally traceable to components, interfaces, and sequences with the use of the allocation chart. External documentation traceability is ensured by the discipline of the process.

The structured documentation concept not only improves the operational concept formulation process, but also improves the overall usefulness of the resulting OCD. The document structuring approach employed is designed to aid the readability of the output product by segmenting the information in a manner satisfying the needs of the various reader audiences and types. This segmentation additionally improves the overall definition process, because the writers and definers are also usually divided into these distinct interest types. The documentation structure in the suggested approach is therefore designed to satisfy the following guidelines:

- *audience:* user, buyer, builder, interfacer, supporter
- *types:* generalists, system, component, and item thinkers
- *rules:* complete, concise, clear, simple, understandable, unambiguous, specific, consistent, referenceable, traceable, nonimplementing, feasible, maintainable, and manageable
- *contents:* structured, segmented, top-down, hierarchical, modular, flexible, traceable, and disciplined

6: The Suggested Approach Process

The major activities associated with the development of any system throughout its lifecycle include: establishing the need for the system, obtaining the support and resources necessary to develop and operate the system, defining the basic goals and requirements for the system, acquiring the system, deploying the system, operating the system, maintaining the system, and improving the system. The primary communications areas involved include user, buyer, builder, interfacer, and support coordination and approval tasks. The builder tasks are normally composed of the management, definition, design, development, testing, and deployment activities. The operational concept formulation process occurs early in such a program and, therefore, has a significant impact on the successful outcome of the overall program objectives.

The basic operational concept formulation activities consist of planning, defining, describing, integrating, and producing the OCD and related project database materials that are discussed next.

The planning activity associated with the operational concept formulation process includes the definition of all documents, procedures, tasks, facilities, formats, and products related to the project. These definitions should be provided clearly and unambiguously early in the program to maximize the efficiency of the "start-up" process. Definition items should include, but not be limited to, the following:

- applicable documents (RFP, concepts, studies, and existing operations)
- applicable specifications (system, interface, and development)
- applicable standards (military, industry, customer, and contractor)
- applicable experience (projects, concepts, and components)
- applicable data (technology, techniques, and processes)
- facilities (locations, allocations, and characteristics)
- assignments (names, titles, locations, and tasks)
- procedures (definition, writing, review, and reproduction)
- schedules (definition, description, integration, and production)
- tasks (inputs, contents, outputs, and interfaces)
- formats (style, structure, type, and composition)
- nomenclature (names, references, terms, and acronyms)
- reviews (what, where, when, who, why, and how)

- history (mission, customer, project, etc.)
- status (activities, dates, and assignments)
- key issues (organizational, procedural, and functional)
- product outlines (volumes, sections, contents, sizes, etc.)

Proper planning greatly reduces the integration and production efforts by enforcing uniformity and minimizing description overlaps. Timely planning greatly influences the efficiency of the start-up process by providing each participant with the needed information, assignment, and tasking data to begin the job. Structured planning reduces the overall effort required by minimizing breakage and major reorganization exercises. The planning activity develops the foundation for the disciplined management and control functions that must be performed throughout the entire process to guarantee a truly effective overall program effort.

The defining activity is involved with describing the overall mission goals and the development of the major system structures. This approach structure includes a set of hierarchical charts that define the system components, functions, and requirements; external and internal interfaces; operational sequences and activities; and organizational configurations. All of these structure charts are, furthermore, cross-correlated through the use of the allocation chart.

The defining activity is performed by "system definers," "component definers," and "item definers." The system definers, which are the major participants in the formulation activity, generates the overview material, the system missions, the basic operations, the overall sequences, and the top-level system structure. The structure defined at this point includes a structure chart illustrating the major components and functions, an interface definition chart illustrating the external and component-to-component interfaces, sequence charts showing the major mission phases and modes, an organizational chart defining the major organizational entities and functional positions involved, and an allocation matrix cross-correlating the entries on each of the other charts. This structure definition is reviewed, clarified, approved, and controlled before proceeding to the next level of definition detail. The component definers now continue the structure definition to the next level of detail for their individual components. The resulting lower-level structure is again reviewed, clarified, approved, and controlled by the system definers. The development of this lower-level structure completes the definition activity.

The material generated is used by the system definers to describe the system concepts and by the component definers to structure their description of the individual component concepts. The item definers support the entire process by establishing viewpoints that are perpendicular to the process used by both the system and component level definers. These "horizontal" opinions provide the additional inputs required to balance the operational concept formulation process.

The "describing activity" includes those processes involved with the actual writing of the textual information. This activity is unstructured in nature and varies in content and format as a function of the addressed subjects. The approach suggested does not attempt to discipline this activity, but rather tries to house it within a uniform structure and outline. The description activity encompasses several levels of detail within the output product document. The system definers are responsible for summarizing and describing this information in the overview and system-general information. They are also tasked to describe the system at the higher levels of abstraction to satisfy the system thinker-level readers. This requirement can be effectively satisfied by presenting an annotated version of the system structures data previously discussed. This presentation, to a given level of detail, should accommodate the system reader and provide a sufficient background for the component and item readers. The item thinkers have a major role in this portion of the output document, because this is the last time they will have the opportunity to describe their item characteristics at the system level. The next document level accommodates the component and item thinkers with a detailed description of each component/item to a structured and uniform outline. These sections of the document should also be hierarchically formatted to satisfy the reading needs of both the system-level buyers and the component-level buyers and builders. The last level of the document contains detailed appendix information that should include an index, glossary, bibliography, correlation, traceability, allocation, and detailed analysis information.

The "integrating activity" consists of collecting all of the description data and modifying these inputs to form a complete, concise, and uniform document. This activity is unnecessary for a properly planned and managed project. It is usually, however, one of the most important activities in the process because of the lack of disciplined planning in most operational concept formulation activities. It is the last level of management influence on the scope, technical content, and uniformity of the documentation. The only functions performed by this activity in a well-planned program should be that of detailed correlation, allocation and traceability reporting, and production coordination for the final product. Correlation and allocation information should be presented by the allocation chart. This chart correlates each activity with the associated sequences, functions, operational positions, interfaces, etc. Traceability information should be presented in a tabular format that associates each subject of the final document with either a paragraph reference to an external document, or a reference to an internally derived requirement, component, sequence, or operational position. The integration activity should also include the tasks required to identify, store, and manage the project database that has been acquired throughout the process. The integration activity concludes the technical tasks associated with the operational concept formulation process.

The producing activity is normally the last task in the process and is accomplished by the reproduction organization in a panic mode. The approach recommended encourages a progressive release of final materials (rather than a bulk release of the total document) to reduce the final production costs and time requirements. Art and textual material are released in top-down stages after the appropriate review/approval cycle. The order of release of this operational concept data is summarized next:

- planning data (outline, estimates, and schedules)
- introduction and history text
- overview text and art
- mission and operations text and art
- system requirements text and art
- system structure charts (text and art)
- updates and corrections to the above
- system description sections
- component/item description sections
- updates and corrections to the above
- appendix sections
- cover letter and signoff information
- database reproduction item definitions

7: The Suggested Approach Product

The OCD is the major product of the operational concept formulation process. Other process products include supporting studies and data, referenced documentation, and all of the materials used or generated during the process. These materials should be used to form a project database. The following paragraphs will be limited to the discussion of the output OCD product.

The OCD should conform to the basic requirements defined in subsection 4 of this paper. The structure of the document should be as disciplined as possible within the constraints of the outline imposed by the customer organization and/or by the referenced standards (i.e., DoD-STD-2167A). The top level of this structure should contain the following ingredients:

- introduction (scope, objectives, and contents)
- applicable documents (MIL-STDs, customer, project, and other)
- overview (background, objectives, and summary)
- system requirements (missions, characteristics, interfaces, etc.)
- system description (components, relationships, sequences, and operations)
- system structure (functions, interfaces, operators, and operations)
- component descriptions (functions, interfaces, activities, and operations)
- appendix material (index, correlation, traceability, and detailed analysis)

The following paragraphs summarize the desired contents for each of these major elements.

The introduction section should clearly and succinctly state the name and objectives of the system, the constraints and interfaces imposed on the system, the scope of the document, and a summary of the contents of the document. Change, review, and approval procedures should also be included if the document is to be distributed to a large audience. Unique terms and/or acronyms should also be defined, either by inclusion or by reference to an appropriate appendix section.

The applicable documents section should list the current version of every document referenced or included within the OCD. Document priorities should be clearly established to resolve conflicts between the contents of any two documents. Detailed information should additionally be provided as to the scope of applicability of each document (i.e., "to the extent specified herein," or "Section xxx," or "as guidance," etc.).

The overview section should summarize the history, needs, requirements, constraints, interfaces, characteristics, and general composition of the conceptual system. This section should provide the necessary background to make an objective evaluation of the operational concept proposed. The section should be "stand-alone" in nature, and should not require excessive references to other materials. Top-level mission phases, functions, interfaces, sequences, and organizational structures should additionally be described in an undisciplined and simplified manner to rapidly communicate with the generalist readers. A more detailed roadmap of the document's contents should be presented to direct each reader to specific subjects.

The system requirements section should contain concise statements of the missions and characteristics of the system. These statements should be as quantitative as possible, and not be directive in a specific implementation approach. The type of requirements presented in this section should include the following:

- system missions (operations, phases, modes, and activities)
- system functional characteristics

- system physical characteristics
- system performance characteristics
- system interfaces and interrelationships
- system environment (physical, functional, and operational)
- system operational constraints and manning
- system operations requirements, goals, and desires
- system RAM (reliability, availability, and maintainability)
- system efficiency (lifecycle cost versus accomplishments)
- system design and construction standards
- system support (logistics, personnel, training, etc.)

This section, if properly approached, can serve as the foundation for the system-level requirements generated in the next major project task (requirements analysis and definition). Defining these requirements here (at a high level of abstraction) not only will provide a smooth transition to the next task, but it will also initiate a top-down review and approval mechanism for the remainder of the development effort. Early agreement on top-level requirements is essential for an efficiently managed development program.

The system description section should introduce the system structure at the next level of detail. System components and functions should be tabulated, summarized, and integrated to provide an overall understanding of the system level concepts. Major operational activities and flows should be described with emphasis placed on concept-unique attributes. Operational positions should be categorized and defined in relation to tasks performed and organizational associations. External interfaces should be defined in detail including the type of interface, the operational timeframe of the interface, the data transferred over the interface, the preliminary bandwidth and sizing estimates, and the standards applicable. The level of detail included should be sufficient to completely satisfy the more detailed generalist and interfacer readers, and to provide a clear baseline for the system, component, and item level readers.

The system structure section should provide the details of the operational concept from the system viewpoint. This section should consist of five primary subsections: functions, interfaces, operators, operations, and allocations.

The functions subsection should present a hierarchical structure chart of all of the system functions. This chart not only serves as the detailed system level definition product but also defines the outline for the following component level definition sections. The structure chart is probably the most important item contained in the document. If this chart is constructed properly, it will be the outline for the subsequent system specifications and continue throughout the program as the basis for the development organizational structure, the work breakdown structure, and the definition of configured items.

The interface subsection should define the major internal system interfaces to one level of detail below the major system components. This section, together with the external interface definitions previously defined, provides the foundation for the subsequent interface requirements definition activities and the development of the associated interface control documents (ICDs). Interface data is therefore maintained by a smooth flow of approvals from the operational concept formulation activity, through the system requirements analysis and definition tasks, down to the component design and test activities.

The operators subsection should provide detailed definitions of all operator positions. This definition should include the position names, the position operator requirements (i.e., skill levels), each operator's functions and tasks, and the overall system control and reporting structure. All descriptions in this section should be hierarchically related to the descriptions previously presented. The operator-oriented "item thinkers" should be able to obtain the information they need from this section to evaluate the staffing concepts and to begin their staffing planning activities.

The operations subsection should provide the detailed sequence and activity diagrams required to define the participation of all components in each major system level operational flow. System level "timeline" information should be incorporated within this section.

The allocations subsection should contain the system level allocation charts required to correlate the functions, interfaces, operators, and operations of the concept. Each entity contained in a section discussed above should be chart-correlated with the associated entities in all other subsections. This correlation process provides the cross-checking and integrating activities necessary to complete the integrated concept description.

The component description section of the document should provide a complete higher-level definition of each major component of the system. These descriptions should follow the outlines established by the system structure section and include information on the functions, interfaces, operators, and operations involved. The contents and levels of detail provided for each of these subsections will vary as a function of component type, critically, complexity, operational significance, and experience.

The appendix section should contain the detailed information that substantiates, clarifies, and further defines the system concepts. This information should consist of the raw data, rather than narrative textual descriptions. Detailed allocation charts and traceability tables should be included to demonstrate the completeness and consistency of the proposed concept. Detailed subsystem level analysis data should be included as appropriate to provide justification information for the concepts generated. Tradeoff material may also be included as specified by the customer.

The OCD, if constructed as defined above, will not only meet the requirements defined in subsection 4 of this paper but will also play a significant role in the total system definition process. The approach proposed places the operational concept formulation activity in the mainstream of the system requirements definition process. The structure, discipline, and content requirements of the resulting OCD document elevates its usefulness to a living system definition document that can be used and maintained throughout the program's life.

8: The Suggested Approach Detailed OCD Outline

The OCD is the primary output of the operational concept formulation process and is also an extremely important system level definition document that can greatly influence the efficiency and quality of the overall system development and deployment process. The content, format, and outline characteristics of this document should, therefore, be highly structured and disciplined in nature. The OCD should meet all of the requirements defined in subsection 4 of this paper to provide the overall (user, buyer, builder, and interfacer) communications required at this critical phase of the program.

Table 1 displays an abstract and detailed listing of a typical OCD outline that is presented as a "check list" for individual tailoring to your specific project needs.

9: Approach Results

The approach defined by this paper has been implemented on several different project types with excellent results. Major improvements were experienced in the start-up, breakage, review, product, cost, and transition characteristics of the programs involved. The start-up process was greatly accelerated because of the timely generation of the OCD and the structured nature of the tools and techniques used. All definers involved with the project knew their exact assignments and the form of the expected short-term products. Project resources were applied to the top-level structure definition tasks rather than the lower-level component or item definition tasks. Start-up manpower loading requirements were also reduced because of the hierarchical nature of the involved definition process.

Product breakages were significantly reduced because of the top-down design and approval concepts employed. Top-level definition charts were reviewed, approved, and frozen early in the process. This design freeze caused the top-level decisions to be made by the top-level people in a timely manner that greatly reduced the wasteful restructuring and redrawing activities normally associated with a conceptual definition activity. The hierarchical definitions accomplished at each lower level had little effect on higher-level definition and description material. Level of abstraction, completeness testing, and the documentation discipline played major roles in minimizing product breakage throughout the formulation process.

Table 1

1: Introduction

1.1: Purpose
1.2: Scope
1.3: Change Procedures
1.4: Document Contents (RoadMaps)

2: Applicable Documents

2.1: Government Documents	(Specifications, Standards, Drawings, etc.)
2.2: Industry Documents	(Specifications, Standards, Drawings, etc.)
2.3: Program Documents	(Specifications, Standards, Drawings, etc.)
2.4: Other Documents	(Specifications, Standards, Drawings, etc.)

3: Overview

3.1: Program Background (Objectives, History, Existing Systems, Present Status, New Requirements, etc.)
3.2: System Objectives (Missions, Goals, Constraints, Functions, Characteristics, Resources, and Risks)
3.3: System Environment
- 3.3.1: Organizational Environment (Acquisition Organization, Operating Organization, User Organizations, Maintenance Organizations, Support Organizations, Organizational Constraints, and Organizational Desires)
- 3.3.2: Physical Environment (Geographical Deployment, Facility Locations, Physical Configurations, Environmental Conditions, Physical Constraints, and Special Physical Characteristics)
- 3.3.3: External Interfaces (Organizational Interfaces, Functional Interfaces, Physical Interfaces, Facility Interfaces, Operational Interfaces, and Interface Constraints)
- 3.3.4: Schedule (Development, Integration and Test, Deployment, Operations, Follow-on Phasing, and Schedule Constraints)
- 3.3.5: Other Constraints (Operational, Maintenance, Personnel, Training, Design and Construction, Performance, Security, Activation, and Support)

3.4: System Overview

3.4.1: System Modes	(Mode 1 through Mode N)
3.4.2: System Phases	(Phase 1 through Phase N)
3.4.3: System Operations	(Operation 1 through Operation N)
3.4.4: System Architecture	(Philosophy, Structure, and Interfaces)
3.4.5: Major System Components	(Component 1 through Component N)
3.4.6: Requirements Compliance	(Functions, Performance, Operability, Effectivity, and Resources)

3.5: Document Roadmap
- 3.5.1: System Concepts (Structure, Interface, Operations, Operators, Allocations)
- 3.5.2: Component Descriptions (Component 1 through Component N)
- 3.5.3: Supporting Characteristics (Reliability, Availability, Maintainability, Integrated Logistics Support, Safety, Security, Human Factors, etc.)
- 3.5.4: Supporting Material (Traceability Documentation, Analysis Study Results, Tradeoff Analysis Results, Bibliography, Glossary, and Reference Data)

4: System Definition

4.1: System Requirements
- 4.1.1: Missions
- 4.1.2: Functional Characteristics
- 4.1.3: Physical Characteristics
- 4.1.4: Performance Characteristics
- 4.1.5: Interface Characteristics

Table 1 continued

- 4.1.6: Reliability, Availability, Maintainability (RAM) Characteristics
- 4.1.7: Design and Construction Standards
- 4.1.8: Integrated Logistics Support
- 4.1.9: Quality Assurance Provisions

4.2: System Description

- 4.2.1: System Configuration
- 4.2.2: Key Features and Capabilities
- 4.2.3: Major Function Description
- 4.2.4: Major Activity Description
- 4.2.5: Hardware
- 4.2.6: Data Processing Equipment
- 4.2.7: Software
- 4.2.8: Integration and Support
- 4.2.9: Personnel and Man-Machine Interface (MMI) Characteristics

4.3: System Structure

- 4.3.1: Components and Functions
- 4.3.2: Interfaces
- 4.3.3: Operators
- 4.3.4: Operations
- 4.3.5: Allocations

5: Component Definitions (Component 1 through Component N)

6: Item Definition Summary (Items 1 through Item N)

A: Appendix Material

- A.1: Glossary of Acronyms and Terms
- A.2: Bibliography and References
- A.3: Reference Material
- A.4: Analysis Results
- A.5: Tradeoff Study Results
- A.6: Allocation Charts
- A.7: Traceability Tables
- A.8: Other (As Required)

System Engineering and Requirement Allocation

E. Dale Nelsen

Introduction and Summary

There are some nagging questions heard again and again as engineers review requirements. They are heard during all phases of a program, from early studies through proposal preparation, to development and deployment of the systems. Virtually every program, in any phase, raised the following questions.

- "How do we get requirements out of the customer's documents and into specs?"
- "How do we separate software requirements from hardware?"
- "Now that we've written the specs, how do we provide traceability of requirements through the spec tree?"
- "How on earth can I test this requirement? It's in the design, but I can't test it."
- "Where do we get one of those exotic computer programs to do this for us with a push of a button?"

Well, there is no magic computer, and no one button to push that will give you instant answers. However, there is a fairly uncomplicated, logical process that can answer most of these questions, or at least point you in the right direction. Quite a few papers discuss individual facets of the process, but the end-to-end system engineering process from the customer's requirements through the system design, test, and installation are not discussed in totality.

This paper attempts to show that, when taken in its entirety, the system engineering process need be neither mysterious nor mythical. The following subjects are covered in detail:

- The problem definition
- The solution to the mystery
- The source documentation
- The allocation process in detail
- Requirement validation methods
- Requirement traceability
- Additional system engineering aspects

The paper concludes with an example of the total process by designing a hypothetical freeway traffic control system design. The example uses the described process to analyze the customers request and to perform the top-down allocation and derivation of requirements through several levels of system hierarchy. It puts the process to practice and shows that the system engineering process is neither mysterious nor mythical.

The Problem

The mystery of requirement allocation prevails at the inception of nearly every new program. Unfortunately, this mystery usually does not get solved soon enough and, in some cases, it never gets solved. The key to the mystery is well touted in many proposals and programs with phrases such as "top-down design" and "structured analysis is performed." Yet the true meaning of the well intentioned phrases and the implementation thereof, often remains elusive. It may be difficult to find anything "top-down" or "structured" about some of the final requirements that are allocated or derived.

The Solution

Top-Down, Structured Analysis

The key to the requirement definition process is the understanding and implementation of "top-down, structured analysis."

"Top-down" simply means that the requirements are decomposed from the top, or system level, and allocated down through subsystems, hardware equipments, and software programs in an orderly fashion. System level requirements should be kept to the system level and should be concerned with system interfaces from and to other systems; and those transforms required to the input interface data to provide the required output interface data. The decomposition of these requirements to the lower levels is the continuation of the top-down process, and requires the same thought processes. The requirements are decomposed down to the level at which the requirement can be designed to and tested. The purpose is to provide the level of detail necessary to allow all levels of system designers to perform their tasks.

Determining the proper stopping point in this decomposition process requires the same discipline as the highest level. We are all aware that too much decomposition can begin to smell. It applies to a system design also.

"Structured" means that the analysis is logical in nature and is documented and implemented in a consistent manner throughout all levels of the system. There are a variety of sophisticated tools and processes available in the literature to aid in the accomplishment of this analysis. Many of these are computer-based tools that present the results very nicely, once they are fed all the necessary information. However, the thought process needed for allocation and derivation of requirements has yet to be automated. It's still a sit down, grind it out, manual process. The methodology discussed here is a fairly straightforward procedure to accomplish the initial allocation and derivation. Understanding the concept and a methodology for getting the requirements down on paper are of utmost importance.

Top-Down Implementation Difficulties

Top-down structured analysis is not an overly complex concept. The most difficulty is encountered in convincing people that it will save time in the long run and that it will result in a better understood, better documented program. Consider a program manager's point of view. Assuming they have been trying for many months to land a given contract, and when it is finally awarded, they are anxious to get under way. He would have to explain to his management why he had only a few personnel on the job for the first few months rather than a full design crew. It is too often expeditious to take the customer's initial documentation, jump into the middle of it, and begin writing requirement specifications. It certainly provides the impression that the program is off to a good start for budget and schedule tracking, although this may be a false impression.

This approach usually results in a set of specifications that do not necessarily cover all directed and implied customer requirements. It also necessitates a frantic effort to resolve requirement flow from the bottom up and side to side to generate a final set of specifications and test plans. This is a much more difficult and is often a more expensive and time consuming process than a true top-down approach from the beginning. A structured design will permit similar functions to be resolved with a common solution rather than with a "reinvention of the wheel." Large systems will inherently have many more subsystems and personnel involved, and an independent design structured will be more prone to multiple versions of a similar design solution.

Requirement Analysis Disciplines

The requirement analysis function is a system engineering function and ideally would be accomplished by a team of system engineers. Practically, however, this is seldom the case. Usually, personnel from specific hardware or software disciplines are gathered to perform this function under the direction of system engineering. These specifically disciplined personnel must be made to think on a system level rather than to consider only their own specific field of expertise. Some of the literature states that, to keep the requirements strictly on a functional level, there must be no design implications whatsoever. Ideally, this is true. However, human nature, being what it is, will steer the design toward that implementation which is best understood by the author of that portion of the system. It can easily be understood why some of the requirements are written in such a manner that the design is assumed to be frozen already. While specific design detail can and should be excluded, unless it is customer dictated, the general system design should be allowed to evolve as part of the requirement analysis process and associated trade studies.

Iterative Process

True requirement analysis and system design are a combined, iterative process. The necessary iterations are often down-played by pressure from a combination of schedule and technical vanity. These factors often prevent a designer or analyst from admitting that the original concept may be improved on by further analysis or by a different design approach. As each system requirement is isolated and understood, it will tend to fall into one of several functional categories. As more requirements are added, the review and iteration process will begin to bound the system into functional groups. These groupings of requirements provide the first cut at subsystems. Iterations may well end up moving a functional requirement from one group to another where the implementation may be in software rather than in hardware, as was originally envisioned.

Understanding the Documentation Provided

Precontractural documentation comes in a variety of forms. Some customers supply a first cut at a top-system specification, some provide a system functional description, and some provide a study request document. All of these documents contain essentially the same type of information, but the degree to which "wants" and "musts" are detailed will differ, not so much by document type as by customer type. Some customers provide overall, general requirements and allow the bidders to do the system design, and some provide considerable design detail, leaving the bidders the task of providing the implementation. This usually is determined by the number and level of precontractural studies that have been accomplished, and whether or not the program is a follow-on to an existing program or a new system concept. The complexity of the system engineering tasks differ somewhat for these two extremes, but the same general methodology can result in the same end: a well structured, well documented system.

Requirement Isolation

One of the best methods of understanding the requirements documentation is to isolate individual requirements. There are often many individual requirements in a given paragraph of the source document. A major system engineering task is to isolate these individual requirements. Long, complex paragraph requirements are difficult to verify throughout the entire process of design, documentation, implementation, and test. In addition, these individual requirements extracted from a given paragraph might be best implemented by allocating them to different subsystems. The requirement isolation reduces the verification problem and reduces the potential for some specific requirements to be overlooked and not be satisfied in the design. The analysis of the isolated requirements and allocations and their associated iterations should assure that all requirements have the proper home in the design.

Up to this point, there has been only the isolation of the top-level documented requirements and no overt derivation of requirements. There have undoubtedly been implications of additional requirements in the minds of the analysts, but they are not truly part of the process as yet. The derivation of lower-level, associated requirements will be a significant part of the analysis and allocation below the system level. The system level requirements should be quite explicitly stated in the customer's documents. Where they are not, it is up to the system designers to define the system requirement and to derive the lower-level requirements in the next step of the process.

In some cases, customer documentation is quite explicit in detail that would normally appear three or four hierarchical levels lower in the system. This comes about because customers, as well as contractor personnel, come from various disciplines. There are hardware and software specialists, as well as system engineers, generating requirements documents, and they may suffer from the same human nature. They tend to drift toward their field of expertise with a preconceived design implementation in mind. In specifying the system requirements, these design oriented details sometimes manage to creep into the system requirements. They should be put aside temporarily, but identified in such a way that they can be retrieved when the design reaches that level of detail. Preconceived design can upset the orderly, top-down process.

During the requirement isolation process, these detailed, design-oriented requirements may have to be extrapolated to a system level. For example, there may be specifications of signal characteristics between two stages of processing functions within the system, because the author is familiar with a particular manufacturer's equipment to perform this function. Since this particular equipment is not dictated, nor is it the only method of performing this function, the system requirement should be written more generally, such as:

> Signal characteristics from (processing function B) shall be of sufficient amplitude, data rate, impedance, and frequency range such as to introduce no additional errors to those introduced by (processing function A).

This type of requirement provides some constraint on the interface without unduly limiting the design freedom of the system designers. Detail designers may consider it so vague that it doesn't say anything. At this point in the analysis, it really isn't vague, it simply doesn't try to complete the entire design of the specific interface. All of the parameters are identified and can be quantified as the design progresses, and the trade studies are completed. Seldom are the specifics known at this stage to the extent they can be written with assurance. It is more difficult to "undo" a requirement than it is to "enhance" it later on in the process.

Often there is an assumed system architecture in the minds of the customer and/or the designers that is thought to be the final configuration for the system. This is true even though trade studies may not have been performed. The analysis may prove this preconceived architecture to be correct or incorrect, but the trade studies should be given a fair chance. They have shown some well founded assumptions to be quite invalid. If the design process begins too soon, there may be sufficient effort completed by the time the analysis is completed. It is then that pressures may come to bear regarding the final design decisions.

The Allocation Process

One analysis method which has been used effectively, is based on structured analysis, which defines the system one step at a time from the top. This is a multi-level process whereby the first step is to take the system as a whole and to define the total system transfer function. All of the external inputs and outputs associated with the system are generally defined, including their source and destination. A tubular listing, a diagram, or any means of recording the element name, the inputs and the outputs along with the sources and destinations would accomplish this purpose. It is a matter for the analyst to decide the method providing the most assurance that all functions and all interfaces are accounted for. These inputs and outputs are reviewed and iterated as necessary against the requirements to assure completeness and validity. All of the overall system requirements are defined that would apply to this single transfer function. The thought process of understanding what each requirement means is a major part of the functional system design.

Second-Level Allocation

This second level of allocation is the decomposition of that single system transfer function into major elements. By using the functional requirements isolated from the customer's documentation by the system engineers, the requirements are categorized and grouped according to these general functions. We are now at the second level of the system and have the second-level functions enclosed as separate elements. All inputs and outputs from the first level will be included at this level, but rather than go into or out of one element, they must be directed toward that element to which they apply.

At this point the derivation of additional requirements begins to come into play. There are additional interfaces required between these second-level elements, which are not explicit system level requirements, but are requirements derived from the system decomposition into the major functional areas that must communicate with one another. These elements are still functional and may or may not result in subsystems in the final architecture. It is still too early in the process for the final architecture to begin solidifying.

A significant point should be made regarding these inputs and outputs. It is necessary to account for each and every one of them. This must be done at this and at each subsequent level of allocation. This assures that all of the interfaces are accounted for through the total design process; if any functions are moved or split into multiple other functional areas, all of the interfaces get moved accordingly. If this process is faithfully performed, the result will be the first cut at all of the interfaces for the Interface Control Document, which can be detailed as the specific interface design proceeds.

The initial requirements are reviewed once again, both for completeness and to derive any additional requirements at this level. Care must be taken to prevent deriving requirements at a lower level than that being analyzed at the time. The overriding tendency to get down to the nuts and bolts level quickly is one major reason that many requirement analysis programs become disjointed and confused.

Third-Level Allocation

For level 3 allocation, each level 2 element is individually decomposed into the next lower-level functions. Level 3 allocations are those elements that will functionally satisfy all the requirements associated with one of the level 2 elements and that will include all of the interfaces of that element. These elements may not be the lowest level, but may still be able to be decomposed further at the next level. As the process continues to lower functional levels, the derivation of requirements becomes a more significant part of the process and calls upon the expertise at the more detailed design level. As each function becomes more defined, more implied requirements are exposed. The design detail requirements in the customer's documentation, which were put aside and compressed into the generalized system requirements earlier, must be recovered and extracted at the proper functional level.

Apportionment of Requirements

The allocation of requirements to functional elements also includes the proper apportionment of overall system requirements to these functional elements. These usually show up as overall system capabilities such as system timing requirements. Assume a system requirement to perform some function within a specified amount of time. It may be the amount of time specified for the receipt of an input signal to the resulting processed data being output. Each system element—the receiver, the processor, and the transmitter—will need an apportionment of the time requirement to complete its function. Each requirement will require some range of time measurement tolerance, depending on the dynamics of each element. The design criteria of each element will have a range of performance times for all of the specific conditions of that element. The worst case conditions for all elements will rarely, if ever, occur simultaneously. This is especially true if the individual element errors are not dependent errors: that is, if the conditions causing the worse case errors in one element are not the same conditions causing the worse case errors in another element. The overall system time will not usually be the sum of the individual times, but a statistically valid combination of those individual times, depending on the interdependency of the errors in each element.

Each designer assumes that his element is the most important and deserves most of the tolerance. These values usually cannot be finalized until more detailed design has been completed, but the requirement should be generated with a "to be determined" (TBD) value. The follow-up process to validate these tolerance apportionments and changing the TBDs to realistic values is another important task for the system engineer. It is difficult to convince the designer of one element that a tighter tolerance is required in a particular design application because another element cannot achieve the tolerance apportioned to it and the system requirement cannot be met otherwise. The system engineer must also be able to arrive at the realistic apportionment of these requirements—evaluating performance, costs, and schedules.

Allocation and Iteration

During the review of each step of the process, consideration should be given to the function being performed by each element, in what can be called a design iteration. Questions concerning the appropriateness of this function being performed in a given function, rather than in conjunction with some other function, should be considered in this review. This is not to imply that the analysis stops and design takes over, but, as previously stated, the functional analysis and design are interactive and iterative.

Total functional analysis can result in redundant functions being generated at lower levels which should properly be combined into a common function. An example of this could be a networked system of computer subsystems that require communications between each other. If each subsystem designer were to develop the method of handling this communication, there would be as many versions of the design as there were subsystems. The schedule and budget problems caused by this redundancy can be eliminated with adequate iterative review of the requirements. This type of design redundancy should be found in the iteration process. The basic design task should be allocated to a single subsystem with the remaining subsystems referring to that design to satisfy their requirement.

A combination of redundant functions can be accomplished after the fact, but may require a fair amount of reconstruction of the functional elements, and usually at the expense of budget and schedule. This is one more system engineering function that requires management support. The iterative process should be performed before the lower-level element design moves very far ahead. This will result in a more controllable design schedule in the long run.

Some sage once asked, "Why is there never enough time to do it right, but always enough time to do it over?" This holds true in the system design and requirement allocation process as well. The first time through, the system design will have some holes in it. If the "first cut" is assumed to be the final design, there will definitely be time needed to "do it over." The final system design must be the result of an interactive and iterative process. Iteration must be part of the design, and cannot be construed as re-design. Time must be allocated for the iteration, with due consideration for the fact that the design must be frozen at some time to produce a product.

There is a distinct tendency for engineers to "never quit engineering." Determining the fine line between completed design and over-design is one of the tasks that makes the Chief Systems Engineer earn his pay. Allowing engineers to drag one more fraction of a dB, or one more microsecond from a design may cause the costs and schedule to become real threats. It may also permit the system to meet that last, questionable system performance criteria performance. Proper weight must be given to each one at each level to allow the proper amount of design without becoming completely design driven. This also keeps the budget and schedule managers from becoming too violent.

Allocation Flowdown

Another significant operation to take place in this continuing review process is the verification that each requirement of a given level has been flowed down properly to the actual level where the function will be performed. The requirements for each functional area, or element of the system, which has a subordinate element requires that those requirements be allocated to the next lower level. While it may appear that a requirement at a subsystem level may stand alone, this is seldom the case. The subsystem may have a requirement to perform some function in that subsystem alone, and it may appear that this requirement will not be performed in a lower-level assembly or program. There must necessarily be requirements at some lower level to provide some hardware or software, which will allow the subsystem to perform its designated function. Only at the lowest hierarchical level where the requirement can actually be validated and documented should the allocation process stop.

Verifiable Requirements

All requirements, whether allocated or derived, should be written in such a manner that they are verifiable. The author must keep in mind a method of verification for each isolated requirement. The group responsible for the testing and validation of the system now has the task of preparing the test planning documents, and one of our infamous questions arises. "How can this requirement be tested?" The requirement is clear enough to the designer for implementation, but is so imbedded in the design that there is no way to prove that capability really exists in the design. Had the requirement been allocated to a lower-level element, it could have been tested and validated at the lower level, possibly when the assembly was tested.

There have been many discussions concerning the validation of a requirement that can not be proven by positive actions, but only through the lack of negative reactions. Now that the system element has been designed and incorporated into the next higher level of implementation, there is no way to clearly show the capability. A common answer at this point is, "It must be there, or it wouldn't work this well." That may be true for the specific test conditions, but for extremely dynamic systems, the range of operating conditions may be so large that all of them can not be duplicated without very costly, time-consuming system test methods. At the lower level, where the input parameters are readily controlled, is where the requirement must be validated. This is true for software as well as hardware requirements. For a hardware assembly, there may be sufficiently variable test equipment available for covering the entire range of conditions for that assembly. In a software system, a program, module, or routine is usually tested with some test code that can simulate the entire range of input parameters and timing at a level that cannot be readily simulated in a subsystem or system configuration. It is very important to consider verification methods during the allocation process. Allocation to the proper level will result in a test program that satisfies the validation requirements. Many schedule delays occur near the end of a program redesigning the tests to validate those requirements that are not readily proven at the higher level.

Validation Methods

There are several methods used for validating requirements. The most common means and the preferred order of precedence are test, demonstration, analysis, and examination.

Test

The most desirable method of validation of the functional performance requirements is by test. Tests result in documented proof that the requirement was met, or can be repeated to dispel any questions on the test. The resulting data can be reviewed by all concerned for confirmation of capabilities. Tests are performed with a controlled set of conditions and stimuli that may be repeated at any time. An example of validation by test would be a TV receiver tested with a signal generator whose output characteristics are readily adjusted and measured. The test can detect and record very specific signal voltages at specific stages of the TV receiver. This test can be repeated at any time, since the test conditions are available in a test procedure.

Demonstration

Demonstration should apply to those requirements that must be verified by utilizing an uncontrolled source of stimuli for which the results cannot be entirely predicted. By using controlled stimuli, the requirement would be testable, but some uncontrolled data source, which may be statistically equivalent to the simulation, would only permit demonstration of the requirement satisfaction under those specific conditions of the uncontrollable stimuli. An example of validation by demonstration would be the same TV receiver with the input signal source being the commercially transmitted TV signal. Since the parameters of the signal are not easily controlled or measured, the validation of the receiver performance is by visual demonstration of the picture quality compared to the viewers personal criteria. It is not a quantitative measurement, but the viewer will be convinced that the receiver works. This type of validation would be used if a controlled signal source was not available, or possibly in the case where a sample of a production lot were thoroughly tested, and the remainder of the production lot were demonstrated with a similar, less rigorous procedure.

Analysis

Analysis should be used only for those items for which no reasonable test or demonstration can be defined, and can be shown to be verified by some analysis based on a combination of data from various levels of test, along with theoretical calculations. An example of validating by analysis would be a statistically derived requirement such as performance with 95 percent effectiveness over a range of conditions. It is not usually practical, nor cost effective to attempt a test over all range limits of the controlling parameters such as environmental conditions. Test data taken over some specific sets of the controlling conditions can be interpolated or extrapolated over the remaining extremes.

Examination

Some requirements will undoubtedly be verified by examination, such as size, weight, color, and any other physical attributes. While the size and weight can be measured, it is considered more of an examination than a test. Quality Control inspections would be another example of an examination.

Traceability of Requirements

It should be fairly obvious by now that a considerable amount of documentation is being generated, depending on the complexity of the system. We have made functional logic charts for each element, the number of which increases considerably from one level to the next. We also have listed all of the individual requirements at each step of the process, so there is a separate list of requirements for each functional element. There are documentation requirements to be generated for deliverable specifications, verification and validation plans, and test procedures. All of these are going to require some means of associating requirements to each other from level to level in a manner that will allow these tasks to be accomplished thoroughly and efficiently.

Traceability of requirements is an area that should be considered for automating. This is a critical capability, not only during the requirement allocation effort, but throughout the life cycle of the program. Often times, after a system has become operational, design modifications are requested. The specifications are reviewed for necessary changes, the drawings are reviewed and the cost of the modification is proposed. As the effort gets underway, some original capability is found to be incompatible with the modification. Unfortunately, without traceability it was not recognized as a required change and results in increased cost and schedule from the proposed modification plan. This incompatibility could have been planned for, had there been a clear cut method of reviewing all related requirements. Assume that each requirement, either allocated or derived, was identified at any level as being related to a specific source requirement in a computer database. It would be a simple matter to request a sorted listing of that database to show all requirements related to the system requirement which was being changed by the proposed modification. Since interfaces are functionally specified in the allocation process as well as performance requirements, the interfaces affected by the modification will also be retrieved by this sort. If the traceability is complete, the modification costs and schedule can be determined more accurately than by hoping the engineer or programmer can remember all the affected areas.

How is this traceability performed, and is it necessary to computerize this function? It need not be computerized but it would be a wise investment to do so. In fact, the first part of the task is necessarily manual, and if the project is not too large, it can be used in that form quite adequately. There have been many cases where it appeared, at the outset, that it would be an easy task to keep track of this traceability, but when the system design is complete, and the customer is trying to understand whether all the test data really satisfies the original requirements they wrote, the automated traceability would be "worth its weight in gold."

There are a variety of methods of identifying requirements so the association and traceability can be performed. One effective method is a combination of alpha and numeric characters, with a fixed number of alpha characters denoting the functional area or element, and a number of numeric characters identifying the specific requirement of that element. In an extremely large system, more alpha characters may be desirable so the alpha designators can have a mnemonic relationship to the element involved. The numeric characters of the requirements are usually numbered in a sequence that has an inherent functional flow to it, such as inputs, followed by process or transform, followed by outputs. If the numbering is done in a sequence such as 10, 20, 30. . . , it will allow the creation of an insertion of new requirements during the iteration process into that sequence, as 11, 12, 21. . . , without disturbing the functional flow nature of the requirement list. This has been shown to be very beneficial to the review and iteration of the requirement allocations process through the entire system. Automation of the traceability can have many degrees of sophistication. The simplest is a tabulated list that can be sorted by the ID of the requirement. This list can be edited as needed to support the analysis and iteration process. Additional complexities can be added by use of a database program that has the flexibility to identify any desired para meters of the requirement, from the full text to the method and date of validation.

The traceability should not be confused with the specification tree. The traceability of requirements is essentially a tool to follow a requirement from one element to another through the tree of specifications. it will work in either direction; upward from the lowest level, or "children," to determine the highest-level system requirement, or "parent," that led to this detail of the design; or from the parent to all of the lower-level children.

The traceability should include such things as:

- The requirement ID
- The source of the requirement, such as the customer's document paragraph number
- An abbreviated summary of the requirement
- A pointer to the full text of the requirement
- For allocated or derived requirements, a pointer to the requirement from which it was derived, or parent requirement
- A pointer to the next lower-level requirements that this requirement was allocated to during the allocation process

More sophisticated database routines can include any additional information that the size and complexity of the system warrant. The amount of information included is only limited by the capability of the database being used. Some additional features may be such things as:

- The system configuration level at the time of validation
- The document name controlling the validation
- The date of the final validation
- The name of the responsible engineer

With the completion of specifying the requirements for a functional area that include the unique requirement designator, the requirement text, the source requirement designator, the next lower allocation designator, and the logical function charts, the entire system can be reviewed in a logical manner. This can assure that all system requirements are allocation and traceable to some function, and that all lower-level requirements can be traced upward to a parent, and ultimately to a source requirement.

This set of documentation can be used manually to trace all requirements. It also can form the basis for a database program input from which searches and sorts can be listed for any specific, or functional group of requirements, either upward or downward. The sample system described at the end of this article provides a clear picture of this traceability.

Hardware versus Software Requirements

It is purely intentional that there has been no discussion of the delineation of hardware vs. software requirements. The reason is that there is no difference between them on a functional level. A large number of the sophisticated tools and processes, which were alluded to earlier, are found in papers that describe how to analyze and document software requirements. It is not clear why these tools and processes consider software as being different from hardware and as such need a different methodology. When defining a function to be performed, it makes no difference what the final implementation may be. Many functions, which ultimately end up in a software program, could be performed in a hardware assembly, although possibly not optimally, and vice-versa. The design iteration and trade study analysis is expected to result in the optimum implementation. Too often these decisions are made too early in the process, and are forced by preconceived ideas of the implementation.

The major cause of this attempt at isolating hardware and software seems to be that hardware engineering has been around for a long time and there has not been a dedicated effort to integrate the emerging software system engineering discipline into overall system engineering. This isolationist syndrome is created by hardware engineers who think a computer is a magic box that is bought with the functions built in, by software engineers who are convinced that anything worth doing can be better done with bits and bytes, and by management who builds hardware organizations and software organizations and ignores system engineering, hoping the first two organizations will eventually work out their differences.

This attitude is evident in the entire industry, including many customers who often prescribe that requirement documentation be prepared in that same functionally separated form. This is evidenced by the variety of separate and distinct hardware and software specification format requirements that are levied. It almost appears that they are trying to find some optimum means of system documentation, but are ignoring the obvious, which is not to separate the two. Obviously some of the wording will be different, but, for example, the transfer of a digital software file from one element to another is essentially the same as transferring an analog signal from one element to another. The software file has a specified format, a specified content and data rate, and some control protocol while the analog signal has a specified impedance, amplitude, bandwidth, and a physical interface. As long as these characteristics are properly delineated in each case, the requirement description can be essentially the same. Usually the best system is one designed by a contractor with a multi-disciplined team of personnel with software and hardware expertise. That is a unique mix of talents, not often found, and also requires the good judgment of a qualified referee when these disciplines become undisciplined.

Additional Aspects of System Design

Trade Studies

A large part of the system design is actually completed by the time the allocation and decomposition of all functional area requirements is completed. All the requirements have been allocated, derived, and collected into functional groupings. The iterations through these processes have resulted in a basic system design concept being formulated. The design continues with the analysis of each functional grouping with respect to how this function can best be performed. Trade studies should be performed for each function. Sometimes these trades get conducted mentally because the designer has a perfectly valid rationale for his decision, but fails to document this rationale. It then becomes difficult for anyone in the review process to understand why it was done as it was, or what other options were considered. All trade decisions should be documented, even the obvious ones.

Trade study documentation consists of verifying that each possible option, whether it be a particular vendor's equipments or a hardware or software implementation, will satisfy all of the "must" requirements. Then a set of criteria is developed for each trade consisting of such things as cost, risk, capability to meet all requirements, and reliability. Each of the criteria is given a weight based on its importance to the program and each option is scored against each criterion. The sum of the weighted scores shows which option best suits the system.

The trade decisions are, like the requirement analysis, an iterative process. For example, assume that a trade decision at functional level 2 resulted in the selection of a computer implementation. The trade analysis at level 3 may show that one or more of those functions is best performed in an available hardware design. This may result in a design iteration, which would isolate these level 3 hardware functions from the computer element for manageability of the system implementation.

Final system design elements must consider functional relationships, implementation manageability, and logical documentation flow. Unrelated functions should be delegated to separate design elements so that each element can be managed properly throughout the program life cycle. Manageability of a design element means the element can be considered singularly in terms of cost, schedule, personnel, documentation, and validation.

Specifications

Documentation flow relates to the functional tree that was created by the collection of the functional logic charts created during the decomposition of system requirements. This tree will essentially be a system documentation tree or specification tree, whereby each defined functional area will require a specification to be written. A case has been seen in which a subsystem was defined merely as a collection point for three unrelated functions. A specification was not meaningful because the functions at that level were unrelated, but were thought to be too small to be considered as subsystems by themselves. Other cases have been seen in which requirements at a given level did not flow smoothly from the previous level without an intermediate specification. In both cases further analysis allowed the functions to be expanded and/or reallocated to adjust to a more manageable, well flowing system. This system hierarchy tree also provides the proper structure for the technical portion of the Work Breakdown Structure (WBS). The WBS is a method of defining responsibility to the appropriate work group. This is necessary when the budget and task definitions are split between organizations. With the addition of the management and support elements, the basis for the entire system has been defined and all aspects of the program are on a solid, consistent foundation. This total system concept, whereby the logical requirement flow, the system design elements, and the specification tree are all essentially synonymous, is in conflict with some existing specification standards, but it is felt that this process results in a more easily understood and manageable system.

The previously mentioned conflicts with existing standards refer to a statement in one company's standard that said "Specifications should not be prepared for subsystems,... Subsystems usually are not complete until they are assembled as part of an integrated vehicle. As such, the individual subsystems do not operate independently and therefore cannot be specified separately." This seems to be a case where the functional requirement allocation was not performed properly. If there are no functional requirements to be defined and validated at this level, then this is a poor choice of subsystem definition. It is perfectly conceivable that some specific subsystem requirements can better be validated at the system level. This can be true at any level in the hierarchy. If the cost and schedule impacts to develop the necessary interface simulators for testing at the subsystem level are prohibitive, then the subsystems requirement can justifiably be validated at the system level. However, it is more conceivable that the interface simulation and stimulation can be created much more easily and inexpensively at the lower level than at the system level.

In come cases, these consequences are implied direction from the customer, but in many cases they result from the program management fear of having to generate so many specifications in such a short time with so few people. These fears are unfounded if the top-down, structured process is used.

The system design process and subsequent documentation will fit any program. This described process results in a very easy method of formatting the specification. The functional requirements have all been defined, and can be copied directly into the applicable paragraph of the specification. The validating method, defined in the design allocation process, forms the basis for the test section of the specification.

Government Specifications

Many large programs are related to Government contracts, and require the use of Military Standards (MIL-STDs). MIL-STDs have been written for nearly any process, material, or function that can be imagined, including how to write a specification. In many cases, they are written in generalized form to apply to as many possible situations as the authors can think of. They also go through a wide range of review to be sure that everything is covered for all potential applications. Sometimes this leads to a document that is so generalized that is is difficult to find the direct applicability to the system being designed. The MIL-STDs for the documentation of specifications in most cases require that the specifications be written just as stated, with no deviation. There are sometimes a different set of standards for specifying hardware and software elements. This is another example of singularly disciplined authors creating generalized documentation. Government contracting agencies require that MIL-STDs be followed by contractors and they are listed in a procurement document.

However, it has been found that some Government customers will permit minor deviations, when they can be shown the validity of the deviations which can usually result in cost and schedule savings. For example, the paragraphs defining the functional requirements of the element to be constructed may be able to be copied from the list of individual requirements written as part of the system design process. One such customer was approached with a proposal to wait for the specifications to be written until all of the requirement allocation and review process was completed. The specifications had been revised several times by this time, but the customer was very receptive to conducting the design reviews with the requirements list on the next procurement. With all of the requirements in a database, the changes to any requirement would be quite easy and the impact on any other requirements could be easily determined by use of the traceability tree that had been generated in the same database. All of the initial reviews with the customer were conducted through the family of specifications to see that all requirements were met. Any changes to a requirement at one level usually meant the modification and republishing of an entire family of documents.

The customer acknowledged that this process of reviewing the requirements of the entire system for completeness, testability, and flowdown from a database file that was easily changed and reported would be very cost effective. It has been noted that the traceability of requirements from one element to the others is a requirements of many Government contracts. The database method described will accomplish this requirement as well as be a great aid in the design process.

Example of the Total Process

How does it all work? The example to demonstrate this total system concept will be a hypothetical traffic control system requested for a specific section of freeway. It is not intended, in this brief space, to complete the entire system design and documentation, but rather to isolate some paragraph of the requirements document and make a vertical cut through the system with examples of each phase of the process.

The system, in summary, requires that the volume and rate of traffic flow be measured at a number of places; the cause of congestion be determined; a method be provided to indicate rerouting information; and time-oriented historical data be maintained for reporting. The paragraph to be analyzed and allocated reads as follows:

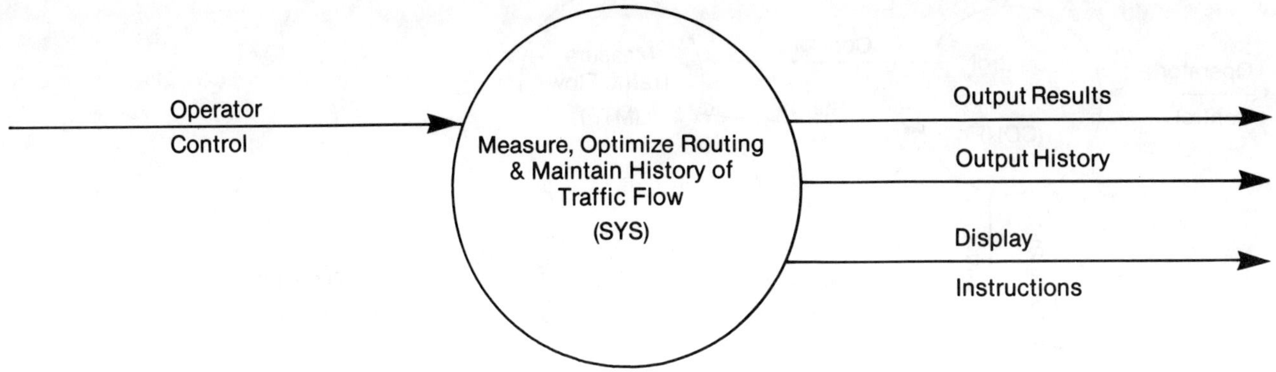

Figure 1: Level 1—Overall System Function

Table 1: System Level Requirements

SYS0060	The system shall provide the necessary sensors to allow determination of traffic volume and rate in each lane of Highway 710 between Exits 12 and 15 with an accuracy of plus or minus 5%.
SYS0070	The system shall provide a time standard with resolution adequate to separate vehicle moving at a maximum of (TBD) mph with a minimum separation of (TBD) feet.
SYS0080	All on-ramps in this section of Highway 710 shall be instrumented to detect the volume and rate of traffic entering the highway system.
SYS0090	Indicators shall be provided to instruct drivers as to actions required on their part to alleviate problems encountered and maintain optimum traffic flow.
SYS0100	The system shall include the capability to determine the set of instruction changes to be displayed to drivers. The instructions shall be clear and concise and shall include recommended speeds, lane changes and weather conditions. Additional types of information may be recommended.
SYS0110	The system shall be capable of displaying to an operator, the data and results of any or all processing necessary to generate the driver instructions. This shall include as a minimum, the instructions displayed at any given time, the location, cause and description of the condition requiring a change in these instructions.

3.7 The section of Highway 710 between Exits 12 and 15 shall be instrumented with measurement devices whose output can be used to provide a display of clear and concise information to the drivers to maintain the flow of traffic with minimum manual intervention. The conditions under which the flow is to be maintained are listed in the following sub-paragraphs. The instrumentation must be able to provide data from which traffic volume and rate can be determined to plus or minus 5% accuracy.

Figure 1 shows the top-level system function. It simply indicates the general function to be performed and the system external interfaces. The system level requirements, which are expressed or derived from this paragraph, are shown in Table 1. The requirement identifier selected for the system requirements are SYSXXXX. The numbering sequence is immaterial, but it has been found constructive to delineate requirements in an input, transform function, output sequence. In addition, it is helpful in the review process to be able to see all the requirements concerned with a specific function in one collective grouping, rather than scattered

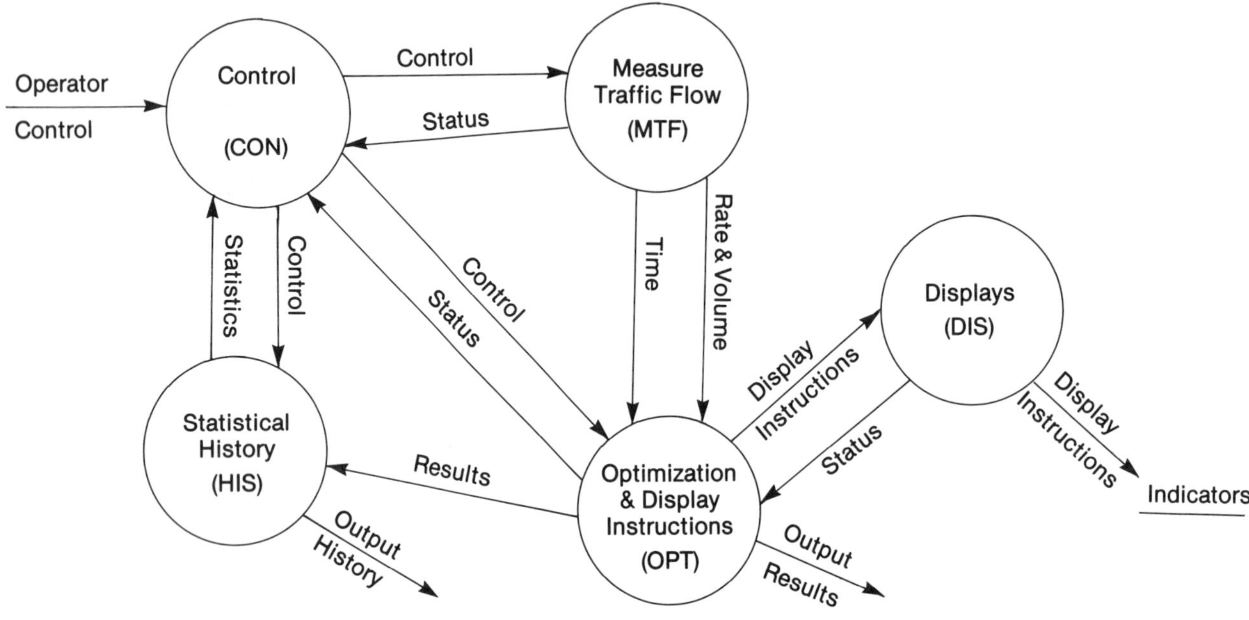

Figure 2: Level 2—Major Functional Areas

throughout the documentation. It also minimizes the possibility of a requirement being missed in the allocation process. Requirement traceability, either manual or automatic, will not help if the initial customer's requirement is lost in the allocation process. Depending on the system, it may be advantageous to assign blocks of numbers to specific functions, such as SYS1XXX for control functions, SYS2XXX for interfaces, etc. Regardless of the method used to assign numbers, the most important part of the process is to list the source requirement identification for each specific requirement generated so that the traceability can be compiled.

Those system level requirements, which are explicit or implicit in paragraph 3.7, are listed in Table 1. SYS0060 is allocated directly from paragraph 3.7, and SYS0070 is an example of a derived requirement. The requirement to provide time tags to the sensor data is implied by the necessity to compute traffic rate. The TBD values in SYS0070 are used at this point to await the results of a study to determine these limits, such that they are neither overspecified to cause system overdesign, nor underspecified to the point where the system fails when someone exceeds the maximum speed or tailgates too close. SYS0080 is derived from the fact that to control the flow of traffic, there must also be control of the access ramps. SYS0090 is allocated directly and SYS0100 is a derived extension of SYS0090. SYS0110 is derived from the fact that, while minimum manual intervention is required, provision should be made for operator interaction as well as for system testing.

Allocation to the Second Level

The logical breakdown of the system of Figure 1 is shown in Figure 2. The breakdown is accomplished through a review of the customer requirements and the system level requirements of Table 1. The functional breakdown includes a control function, a measurement function, a display function, an optimization function, and a statistical history function. All of the external interfaces shown on Figure 1 also show up on Figure 2 with the additional functional interfaces being provided between these five functions. There are no quantitative values attached to any of these functions as yet since there were none specified in paragraph 3.7, which is the source of these requirements. The quantitative values will begin to surface as requirements are allocated to these functions or as trade studies are completed, which result in quantitative values.

Second-Level Requirements

The "Measure Traffic Flow" function (MTF) contains those elements necessary to sense the traffic flow, determine volume and rate, and provide the status of these functions to the control function. The requirements resulting from the review and allocation process of the system requirements are shown in Table 2. The requirement to provide traffic rate implies the need for a time source. The interfaces to and from MTF are arrived at by reviewing the functions performed in the other elements. Either automatic or manual control will be provided and the operating status will be fed back to the control function. Volume and rate data will be passed to the optimization function where the proper display instructions will be generated.

There are several studies to be performed to resolve the TBDs in MTF0015 and MTF0040. These parameters are a function of vehicle size, vehicle spacing, and vehicle speed. These studies should really be completed prior to defining requirements for DET and VAR, as part of the design iteration process, which was mentioned earlier. Obviously a millimeter wave-length radar system, with picosecond timing is overkill for a highway traffic problem, but it cannot be limited to a design for a minimum sized car similar to full size sedan, travelling at 55 mph or the system will not function as it's supposed to. There are large semi-trailer trucks as well as motorcycles to be considered. Often times, the customer has had these studies completed and the limiting parameters are provided initially. If they are not supplied, the analyst must inject a little design concept into the allocation procedure to keep the functional requirements from becoming completely meaningless at the lower levels.

It should be noted that the functional interfaces are included in the MTF requirements, MTF0025, 0030 and 0032. While the specifics of these interfaces are not available at this point, they will be developed in detail as the design progresses and will not be forgotten.

The requirement traceability table up to this point is quite simple since all requirements trace back to a single paragraph and no further breakdown has been accomplished yet. Table 3 shows the system requirement traceability table to this point. The "allocated to" column will be filled in after the allocation to the next lower level has been completed. The verification level is the level at which this requirement is to be verified such as qualification, development test of an element, integration of multiple elements, or acceptance of an element or system. While system level requirements will all be verified by some test at the system level, this column becomes more useful at lower levels where, for either technical or cost reasons, the requirement is best verified at a higher level. This identification of verification level aids in assuring that all requirements will be

Table 2: Second-Level Requirement Allocation and Derivation

Measure Traffic Flow (MTF) Requirements	
MTF0010	The MTF shall provide sensors capable of indicating individual vehicle speed and spacing in each lane of the highway and each entrance and exit ramp.
MTF0015	The sensors shall be spaced such that the number of vehicles in each lane, moving less that (TBD) mph and greater that (TBD) ft apart can be determined relative to those in the other lanes. All measurements shall be accurate to + − 5%.
MFT0020	The sensors shall be capable of performing 95% of the time for all weather conditions typical of the area.
MFT0025	The MTF sensors shall provide the capability to determine the rate of flow of traffic consistent with the volume measurements of MTF0015 and transfer the rate to OPT.
MTF0030	The MTF sensors shall provide operability status to CON.
MTF0032	The MTF shall accept control information from CON.
MTF0035	The MTF shall be capable of calculating the rate of flow from the data provided by MTF 0025. The calculations shall include both the number of vehicles between any two sensors on any given lane over a period of time to be prescribed by the operator, and the average speed of traffic in any given lane between any two sensors.
MTF0040	The MTF shall include a timing system such that a time tag with a resolution of (TBD) sec can be assigned to each vehicle sensed in each lane.

Table 3: System Requirements Traceability—Top Level

REQ	REQ SOURCE	ALLOCATED TO	VERIF METHOD	VERIF LEVEL	VERIF DOC
SYS0060	3.7	MTF0010 MTF0020 MTF0030 MTF0032 MTF0035	TEST		
SYS0070	3.7	MTF0015 MTF0025 MTF0035 MTF0040	ANALYSIS		
SYS0080	3.7	MTF0010	TEST		
SYS0090	3.7	DISXXXX OPTXXXX	TEST		
SYS0100	3.7	OPTXXXX DISXXXX	TEST		
SYS0110	3.7	CONXXXX DISXXXX	TEST		

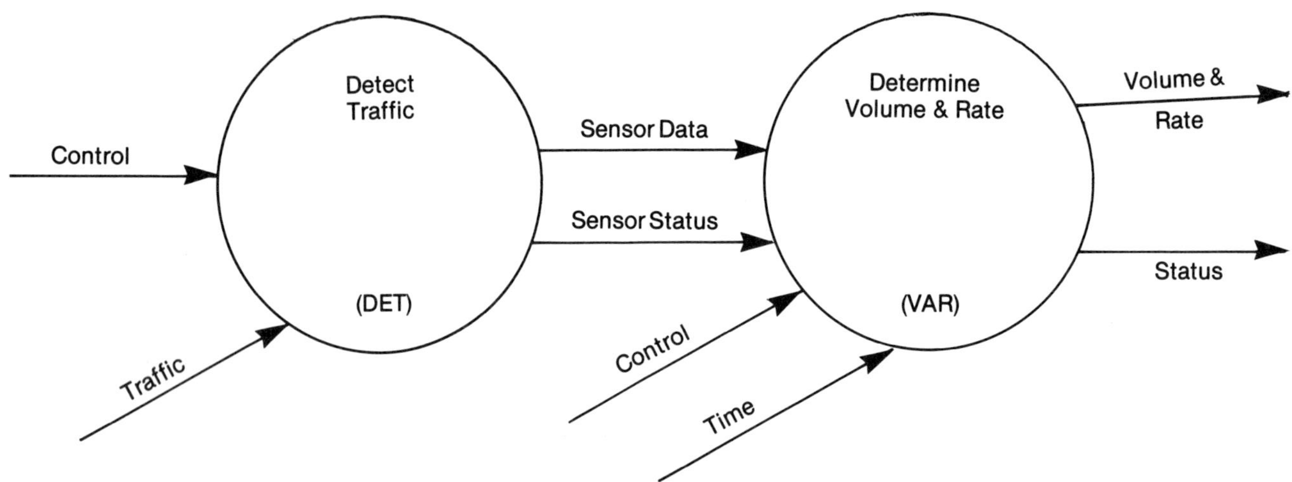

Figure 3: Level 3—Measure Traffic Flow

verified at the proper level. The final column, "verification document," will be completed when the procedures are generated, and includes the document and paragraph numbers of the test procedure, which will be used for verification of each requirement. This information is the basic traceability data which, even if traceability were to be automated, must be manually provided.

Third-Level Allocation

It is assumed that a map has been provided or is available showing the details of Highway 710 between Exits 12 and 15, and that the system engineers have visited and become familiar with that section of the highway. They now know the number of lanes, the type of terrain, and such things as the spacing between exits from which they can generate a set of measurement requirements and define some studies to be conducted or trade-offs to be performed. With this information and the MTF requirements, it is possible to continue the process. The breakdown of MTF into third-level elements is shown in Figure 3.

Tables 4 and 5 contain the requirements for the two functional areas of MTF. They are the detector function (DET)

Table 4: Third-Level Requirement Allocation and Derivation

Detect Traffic (DET) Requirements	
DET0010	The DET shall accept control from CON to enable or disable sensors in any given lane.
DET0015	The DET shall provide operability status to VAR indicating the health of the sensors to prevent VAR from responding to malfunctioning sensors.
DET0020	The sensors shall be configured such that they do not impede traffic in any way. That is, they shall not be mounted above ground between lanes. Any above-ground sensors shall be outside the shoulder limitations or higher than the lowest obstruction on the highway.
DET0025	The spacing of the sensors shall be no more than (TBD) feet apart nor no closer than (TBD) feet.
DET0030	The sensors shall include the capability to provide a unique identifier to each detected vehicle. This may be in the form of a time measurement in the field of view of the sensor. This unique identifier will be used to determine speed between sensors and to account for lane changes between sensors.
DET0035	The sensors shall be capable of performing 95% of the time for all weather conditions typical of the area.
DET0040	The DET shall provide the output of each sensor to VAR continuously.
DET0045	The DET shall provide a time source with an accuracy of (TBD) and a resolution of (TBD).

Table 5: Additional Third-Level Requirement Allocation and Derivation

Determine Volume and Rate (VAR) Requirements	
VAR0010	The VAR shall accept the output of each sensor from DET.
VAR0015	The VAR shall accept the status of all sensors.
VAR0017	The VAR shall accept a time input from CON.
VAR0020	The VAR shall be capable of accepting control from CON.
VAR0025	The VAR shall include the capability to calculate traffic volume and rate from sensors associated with each lane of traffic to an accuracy of (TBD) vehicles per unit time and (TBD) mph.
VAR0030	The calculated speed shall be sufficient to operate with (TBD) vehicles on all lanes moving at up to (TBD) mph.
VAR0035	The VAR shall provide volume and rate data for each traffic lane to OPT.
VAR0040	The VAR shall calculate traffic volume in each lane over variable time periods which can be stored and updated by an operator.
VAR0045	The VAR shall be capable of outputting the volume and rate data either in accordance with a preplanned schedule, upon request by the operator, or upon change of value beyond some preset limits.
VAR0050	The VAR shall be capable of providing the status of the sensors and the VAR element to CON.

and the volume and rate measuring function (VAR). These requirements remain functional and point out the need for a trade study to determine the optimum sensors. They may be TV cameras, light beams, magnetic strips in the roadbed, or some other radar or laser device. Items such as cost, complexity, ability to meet requirements, reliability, and maintainability must be considered before a selection can be made.

The calculation requirements in VAR imply a trade study to determine the best implementation. It may be accomplished in hardware, in a microprocessor, or in a minicomputer. The earlier studies for sensor indications and resolution, along with the number of sensors will be necessary inputs to this study.

Now that the third-level allocation process is complete, the database can be updated to include the "allocation" data. This is seen in Table 6. The first two columns show which system requirement or requirements are the immediate source for each MTF requirement. Columns 3 and 4 show what element and what requirement the MTF requirements of column 1 were allocated to, and how the MTF requirements are to be verified. The last 3 columns will be provided later in the design phase of the program, after the basic architecture is established.

Table 6: MTF Requirements Traceability—Second Level

REQ	REQ SOURCE	ALLOCATED TO	VERIF METHOD	VERIF LEVEL	VERIF DOC
MTF0010	SYS0060 SYS0080	DET0020	TEST		
MTF0015	SYS0060	DET0025 DET0030 VAR0030	TEST		
MTF0020	SYS0060	DET0035	ANALYSIS		
MTF0025	SYS0070	DET0040 VAR0030 VAR0035 VAR0040	TEST		
MTF0030	SYS0060	DET0015 VAR0015 VAR0050	TEST		
MTF0032	SYS0060	DET0010 VAR0020	TEST		
MTF0035	SYS0060 SYS0070	VAR0010 VAR0025 VAR0040	TEST		
MTF0040	SYS0070	DET0030 DET0045 VAR0017 VAR0025	TEST		

Tables 7 and 8 show the traceability of the DET and VAR requirements, and the method of validation for each. The "allocated to" column is not filled out at this time since there is no obvious functional breakdown until the type of sensor is selected. This may be the lowest documented element level, the next being specification control drawings. If this is the case, the "allocated to" column becomes "not applicable," although it may be desirable to put the drawing numbers in that column.

Generally the "verification level" will be the acceptance test for that element, but there may be some exceptions whereby the verification is delayed until a later, more in-

Table 7: DET Requirements Traceability—Third Level

REQ	REQ SOURCE	ALLOCATED TO	VERIF METHOD	VERIF LEVEL	VERIF DOC
DET0010	MTF0032		TEST		
DET0015	MTF0030		TEST		
DET0020	MTF0010		TEST		
DET0025	MTF0015		TEST		
DET0030	MTF0015 MTF0040		TEST		
DET0035	MTF0020		ANALYSIS		
DET0040	MTF0025		TEST		
DET0045	MTF0040		TEST		

Table 8: VAR Requirements Traceability—Third Level

REQ	REQ SOURCE	ALLOCATED TO	VERIF METHOD	VERIF LEVEL	VERIF DOC
VAR0010	MFT0035		TEST		
VAR0015	MFT0030		TEST		
VAR0017	MFT0040		TEST		
VAR0020	MFT0032		TEST		
VAR0030	MFT0035 MFT0040		ANALYSIS		
VAR0035	MFT0025		TEST		
VAR0040	MFT0035		TEST		
VAR0045	MFT0025		TEST		
VAR0050	MFT0030		TEST		

tegrated test because of cost or simulation complexity factors.

At this point, the requirements are of the same functional nature even though they may eventually be satisfied in a software system. The design details will not change the functional requirements nor the method of verification. As the design progresses and a specification is written for the next lower level, the details will describe the computer architecture and a software design, but it is not necessary to rewrite this set of requirements after the design is completed, as is often done.

This example, with very little specific data supplied by the customer, shows the interaction and iteration of the requirement analysis and allocation with the design architecture. Granted, the more specific the parameters and limits defined by the customer are the less studying must be performed during this process.

Assuming the process has been completed for all elements, and the requirements and traceability has been generated for them, we now have a specification tree as seen inFigure 4, the first two or three levels of which are also the technical portion of the WBS. These two items should be essentially identical in a well organized program since the functional breakdown in both cases is based on the concept of well bounded, manageable, and controllable functions.

We have also completed the hard part of generating the system specification and sub-system specification. All of the functional requirements have been defined for all levels of the system, and the "boiler-plate" portions of the specification can be added. The detailing of the actual physical interfaces will be performed as the lower-level designs progress from this point. Test plans can begin to be prepared since there was some thought given to validation methods during the allocation process. There will be a minimum of changes required to the elements because the system engineering crew consisted of multiply-disciplined individuals that could assure the feasibility of the design concept as they iterated the requirement definitions and allocations.

The top-down analysis, performed in accordance with the process described in this paper, provides the basis for a well-structured system. The methodology espoused here in no way conflicts with the desire of many to automate and computerize the cross checking and traceability of requirement allocation and analysis. It does stress the fact that the systems analysis must be performed by multi-disciplined individuals and must be complete before any automation can be considered. As shown by this example, the effort spent in the initial analysis and allocation of requirements can save time in the long run by providing the basic inputs for a considerable amount of documentation, easing the actual document production effort, which often seems insurmountable at first sight.

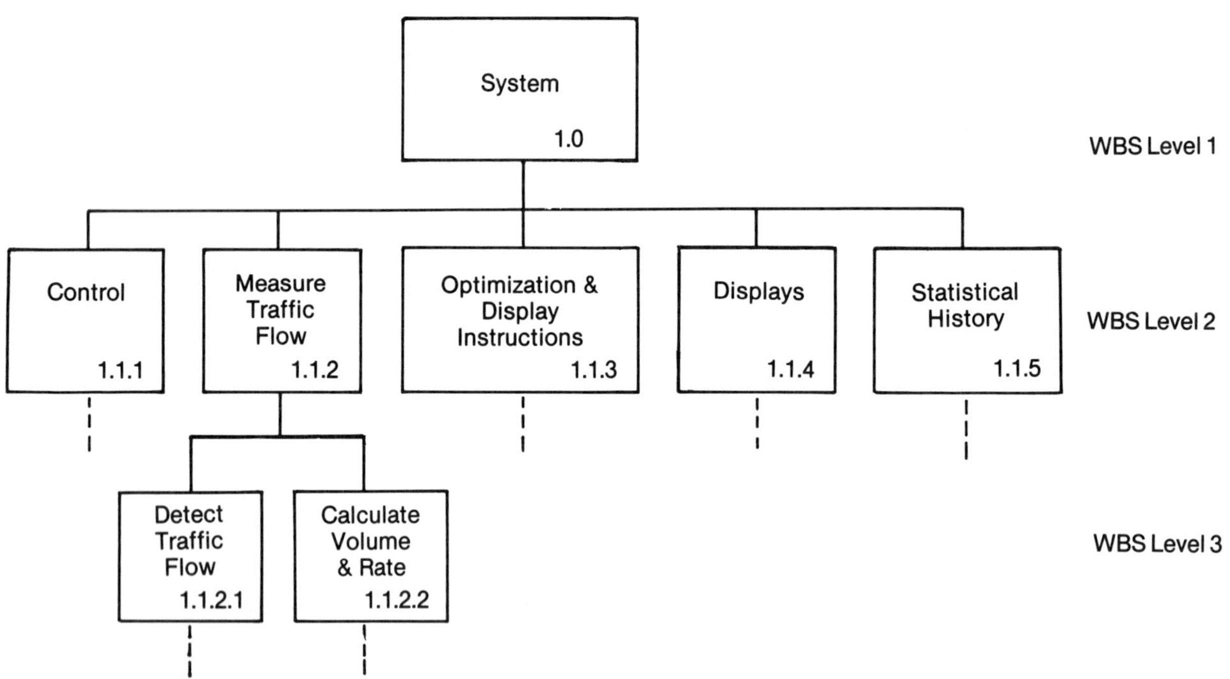

Figure 4: Specification Tree/Work Breakdown Structure

SOFTWARE SYSTEM ENGINEERING

Richard H. Thayer
California State University, Sacramento

Winston W. Royce
SoftwareFirst

Abstract — This paper describes the application of system engineering principles, activities, tasks, and procedures to the development of a software system. This application, called software system engineering, is the overall concept that integrates the managerial and technical activity that controls the cost, schedule, and technical achievement of the developing software system. This paper recognizes the difference between software system engineering and software engineering, just as system engineering is recognized as being different from hardware engineering (all types).

In this paper, the software development process is partitioned into five general phases, and each phase is partitioned into a number of software system engineering processes. The activities and tasks associated with each process are described.

Key Words — system engineering, software system engineering, system definition, software requirements generation, software design, code and component testing, software integration, software system testing

1. Introduction

This paper describes the application of system engineering principles, activities, tasks, and procedures to the development of a computer software system. This resulting system engineering process is called software system engineering. The purpose of this paper is to identify and separate those processes that are properly system engineering processes from those processes that are software engineering in order that the principles and procedures of system engineering can be applied to software development.

Software system engineering (SwSE) is the technical management of a software development. It is the overall concept that integrates the managerial and technical activity that controls the cost, schedule, and technical achievement of the software system. SwSE applies the procedures, practices, technologies, and know-how of system engineering which, together with the technical process of software engineering, ensures the highest quality software product produced within cost and schedule constraints. *Know-how,* in this case, means the skill, background, and wisdom to apply knowledge effectively in practice.

This paper recognizes the difference between SwSE and software engineering, just as system engineering is recognized as being different from hardware engineering (all types). SwSE supports the premise that the quality of a software product depends on the quality of the process used to create it. *The products of both system engineering and SwSE are documents.* This is in contrast to hardware (component) engineering, in which the products are the devices or components being produced, and software engineering, in which the products are computer programs (software) and, in both cases, the documentation necessary to use, operate, and maintain them.

SwSE is not a job description; it is a process. SwSE can be done by many organizations and people: system engineers, managers, software engineers, programmers, and, not to be ignored, customers and users. *Many consider SwSE to be a special case of system engineering. Others consider SwSE to be the dominant discipline for computer-based systems.*

System engineering and SwSE are often overlooked in a software development project. Systems that are all software and/or run on commercial, off-the-shelf computers are often considered just software projects, not system projects, and no effort is expended to develop a system engineering approach. Ignoring the systems aspects of the project often results in software that will not run on or with the hardware selected, will not integrate with hardware and other software systems, and frequently contributes to the so-called "software crisis."

1.1 The Software System Engineering Challenge.

The dominate SwSE challenge is to ensure that the most effective and efficient software system is delivered and to provide the proper balance of:

- System functionality and performance
- Development (or lifecycle) costs
- Development schedule
- Managerial and technical risks

1.2 The Role of Software in Systems.

The dominant technology in many technical systems is software. *Software often provides the cohesiveness and control of data that enable the system to solve problems.* Software also provides the flexibility to work around hardware or other problems, particularly those discovered late in the development cycle.

Software is part of the U.S. commitment to a high-technology defense. The Institute for Defense Analyses recently reported that 80 percent of the weapons systems currently being built depend significantly on software. [1] In 1986, the Pentagon spent $11.4 billion on mission-critical software for weapons systems, communications, and intelligence gathering. This was 80 percent of the total computer resources budget. The Electronic Industries Association projected that by 1990 this amount will more than double and will account for 20 percent of the Pentagon's total spending on weapons. Furthermore, by 1995, Department of Defense software costs will have escalated to an estimated $35.6 billion. [2]

Thus, highly reliable software is crucial to the success of the U.S. military commitment. Modern U.S. Army command and control systems depend on software to collect, reduce, and display information to battlefield commanders for decision making. The modern Navy depends on software to direct and launch weapons accurately at an often unseen enemy. The new fighter aircraft proposed by the Air Force cannot be flown by a human alone but requires on-board computer software to perform the millions of calculations that will allow it to maintain its stability and perform effectively.

Software has also been called the biggest block to the Strategic Defense Initiative (SDI). [3] In a 1986 issue of *Fortune* magazine, Edward Lieblein, Director of Computer Software and Systems, Department of Defense, said, "We are definitely facing a software crisis." [4]

Many commercial products also depend on software. For many companies, using software is a cost-effective way of producing a product. In fact, many commercial companies are as dependent as the U.S. military on software for a successful product. For instance, software systems provide an economical way for automobile manufacturers to meet stringent emission controls while at the same time aiding them in designing cars that are more attractive to the consumer. Electronic and communication equipment firms use software to reconfigure general-purpose electronic components to perform special purposes, thereby saving the cost of tooling for the more expensive special purpose devices.

In a different realm, automatic teller machines would not be possible without telecommunication systems, computer networking, and realtime, embedded software systems. The intelligent point-of-sales systems that are expected to be a boon to retailers could not exist without software to track the transactions. Software supports industry in everything from talking spelling checkers for children to automated prosthetics for the handicapped.

1.3 Scope of Software System Engineering.

SwSE is a necessary activity regardless of the type of software that is being developed. SwSE can be applied to commercial, scientific, or military software projects, both realtime and batch systems; applicability is not restricted by the size, complexity, or criticality of the software product. SwSE covers the total lifecycle.

SwSE is applicable in system development under a number of different hardware/software configurations:

1. Systems in which software is not a technical challenge. Software engineering and production costs are small in comparison with hardware engineering and hardware production costs.
2. Systems in which software is the technical challenge and dominant technical feature of the system. However, the cost of software engineering and production is minor in comparison with hardware production costs.
3. Systems in which software is the technical challenge and dominant cost of the system.

SwSE is most valuable under configurations 2 and 3 above. Under Configuration 1, SwSE plays a very minor role (once it has been determined that software is not dominant). In Configuration 2, system engineering and SwSE should work together with full recognition that many crucial decisions fall under SwSE. *Unfortunately, the dominant cost of hardware components focuses management's attention on hardware rather than software.* This often results in:

- Selection of hardware (which turns out to be inappropriate for the software) too early in the development cycle
- Poor cost and schedule estimates for software
- Inappropriate hardware-software allocation
- Software development started late in the development cycle

- Software cost and schedule overruns
- Software problems being ignored until they become a crisis

Equally important (from a software engineering viewpoint) is Configuration 3 where SwSE is the system engineering discipline.

1.4 Why Is Software System Engineering Necessary?

More and more new systems are being developed today, and many of these new systems are totally or almost totally functionally dependent on properly operating software systems. *Thus software is larger and more complex now than at anytime in history*. This trend is caused by:

- The availability of cheap hardware which motivates system requirements
- More and more system solutions being provided by software rather than hardware
- Increased software complexity caused by increased system complexity
- Customers who want more reliable and usable software systems
- Customers who want the capability and flexibility of software

As a result software development costs are growing and software takes much longer to build. These extremely large and complex systems require the technical system management and the oversight of system engineering. Without this system engineering approach the following problems often result:

- Complex software systems become unmanageable.
- Costs are overrun and schedules are missed.
- Unacceptable risks are sometimes taken.
- Unacceptable system engineering procedures (or none at all) are sometime used.
- Erroneous decisions are made early in the lifecycle that prove very costly in the end.
- Subsystems and components that are developed independently do not integrate properly.
- Parts and components never get built or requirements are not met.
- The delivered system fails to work properly.
- Parts of the system must be reworked after delivery (called maintenance).

SwSE is necessary in order to build the "new order" of computer dependent systems now being sought by government and industry.

1.5 Definitions.

A *system* is a collection of elements related in such a way that allows the accomplishment of some tangible objective. A *manmade system* is a collection of hardware, software, people, facilities, procedures, and other factors organized to accomplish some common objective. A *software system* is, therefore, a manmade system that consists of a collection of software and documents that relate in such a way as to allow the accomplishment of some set of requirements with software.

System engineering (SE) is the application of scientific and engineering efforts to (1) transform an operational need into a system description and performance parameters through the use of an iterative process of definition, analysis, synthesis, design, test, and evaluation; (2) integrate related technical parameters and ensure compatibility of all related functional and program interfaces in a manner that optimizes the total system definition and design; and (3) integrate reliability, maintainability, safety, survivability, human, and other such factors into the total engineering effort to meet cost, schedule, and technical performance objectives. [5]

SwSE is related to SE and is likewise both a technical and management process. The *technical process* of SwSE is the analytical effort necessary to transform an operational need into a description of a software system; a software design of the proper size, configuration, and quality; its documentation in requirements and design specifications; the procedures necessary to verify, test, and accept the finished product; and the documentation necessary to use, operate, and maintain the system.

The *management process* involves assessing the risks and costs of the software system, establishing a master schedule, integrating the various engineering specialties and design groups, maintaining configuration control, and continuously auditing the effort to ensure that cost and schedule are met and technical requirements objectives are satisfied. [6]

And, last, *software engineering* is (1) the practical application of computer science, management, and other sciences to the analysis, design, construction, and maintenance of software and its associated documentation; (2) an engineering science that applies the concepts of analysis, design, coding, testing, documentation, and management to the successful completion of large, custom-built computer programs; or (3) the systematic application of methods, tools, and techniques to achieve a stated requirement or objective for an effective and efficient software system.

1.6 Role of Software System Engineering.

SwSE is responsible for the overall technical management of the system and the verification of the final system products. It is responsible for the activities and tasks listed in Table 1.

Table 1: Activities and tasks of software system engineering

Activities and tasks
Interface technically with the customer
Determine project cost and schedule
Determine technical risk
Define and document requirements
Perform requirements functional analysis and flowdown
Determine system data throughput and storage
Perform tradeoff studies and timeline analysis
Develop prototypes
Design and document top-level system architecture
Define and document technical interfaces
Manage interface control working group
Develop verification and validation procedures and plans
Develop testing plans, procedures, and cases
Establish standards, practices, and methodologies
Conduct external and internal reviews
Verify and audit technical products
Manage software system configuration and change
Identify technology needs
Manage subcontractor technical direction

1.7 Overview of Paper.

As discussed in paragraph 1.3 above, SwSE can be used in a number of different circumstances and hardware/software configurations. The principal viewpoint of this paper is the application of SE to hardware/software systems in which software is the technical challenge (Configuration 2). However, many of the SwSE procedures can be applied to Configuration 1, and most of them can be applied to Configuration 3.

The paper provides guidance for project managers, software engineers, analysts, or students in the steps, activities, tasks, and documentation necessary to accomplish the SwSE process in software development. It separates the necessary activities that must be done and optional activities that may or may not be done, depending on the requirements, environment, and/or circumstances surrounding the project.

This paper uses a simplified lifecycle development process (model), called a waterfall chart [7], as the framework to discuss the activities and tasks of SwSE. These activities and tasks are identified as a series of individual processes in each phase of the software development process. The characteristic activities and tasks for each process are analyzed and defined.

2. The Software System Engineering Process

The SwSE process is a series of management and engineering activities and tasks necessary to complete a software project. These activities and tasks have been grouped into a series of processes which in turn have been grouped into a series of phases. This overall process is frequently called a lifecycle model or a lifecycle development model. The lifecycle model includes the installation and maintenance phase; the lifecycle development model does not.

Some of these processes must be done sequentially; for example, the software requirements specification must be accomplished before the developer and customer can agree upon the software requirements baseline. Other processes can be, in fact must be, done in parallel. For example, trade studies, which are necessary for SwSE to make the correct technical decisions, are made throughout the software development process.

It is also important to note that every SwSE process can be iterated with the previous process. In other words, process "n" can be iterated with process "n-1," in which each process "n-1" is reaccomplished in part or whole based on information that was determined during process "n."

For simplicity sake, this paper assumes a five-phase, waterfall model of the system software development process. This model is illustrated in Figure 1.

Please note there are other accepted development processes. Processes exist which emphasize reusability [8], prototyping [9], risk analysis [10], incremental development, and top-down development. See Reference 11 for an excellent overview of alternative software development lifecycle models. We take the position that the activities and tasks of SwSE are generally the same; only the emphasis and arrangements are different.

2.1 Common Attributes for Each Phase of the Lifecycle.

All phases of the software system process have many activities and tasks in common. This commonality is caused by the close interactions between phases and the common project goals of delivering a software system that satisfies the technical requirements on time and within costs.

Specifically, each phase of the five-part software system lifecycle:

- Has specific goals
- Has a characteristic set of activities and tasks
- Produces a specific set of documentation
- Verifies and audits the products of the phase
- Establishes necessary technical baselines
- Terminates with one or more reviews by customers, users, and developers

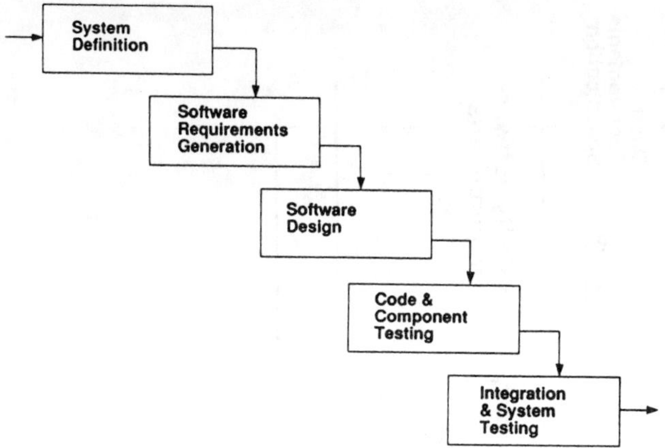

Figure 1: Software system development lifecycle model

Despite their common activities and tasks, each lifecycle phase requires different management and personnel skills. For example, the software requirements generation phase requires highly skilled analysts and applications specialists, while the code and component test phase requires a preponderance of programmers or often less experienced software engineers.

Management is also different. Managing and controlling the system definition phase requires a high degree of application knowledge and decision-making skills. The design phases require a high degree of software engineering and programming knowledge.

2.2 Software System Phases in the Software Development Process.

The SwSE process can be described as a series of tasks and activities accomplished by managers and engineers who have responsibility for developing the software system. Each one of these activities or tasks (called processes) takes place during one or more of the five phases of the software process. This paper has identified thirty-six processes that make up the SwSE process. The processes are listed and described in the paragraphs to come.

3. System Definition Phase

The first phase is concerned with determining what is to be built and delivered, how fast it must operate, how good it must be, with what will it interface, how much it will cost and, most important, what part will the software perform.

This phase essentially has two parts: system analysis and system design. *System analysis* is the activity of determining and collecting the diverse and sometimes conflicting customer/user software system needs into a cohesive whole. *System design* will determine how to best implement the system requirements from a very top-level architectural viewpoint. SE/SwSE will perform trade studies and timeline analysis to determine the best combination of hardware and software subsystems to deliver the system effectively and at least risk.

Also in this phase the major management and technical plans will be formulated such as system/software engineering management plans; verification, validation, and test plans; configuration management plans; software quality assurance plans; and others, as necessary. The phase will end with a formally agreed upon baseline that will describe the deliverable hardware and software requirements.

The following sections will describe each of the processes in the system definition phase. See Figure 2 for an overview model of the major activities, major documents and baselines created, and milestones met in this phase.

(1) Determine the system needs and/or requirements. Develop external interface requirements.

The first step in any system activity is to investigate, determine, and document the system requirements. A *system requirement* is (1) a system capability needed by a user to solve a problem or achieve an objective, and/or (2) a system capability that must be met or possessed by a system or system component to satisfy a contract, standard, specification, or other formally imposed document. [12]

Regardless of the mix of hardware, software, or manual procedures, the resulting document is usually called a system requirements specification.

A *system requirements specification* (SRS) is frequently the initial document prepared in a technical development—software or nonsoftware—that sets forth the requirements for a system or portion of the system (sometimes called a system segment). It is a written document that describes in detail the system that will satisfy the customers' and users' needs. Typically included are functional requirements and external interfaces, as well as performance requirements (sometimes called mission requirements), design constraints, and quality attributes of the finished system. System requirements specifications are sometimes referred to simply as *system specifications*.

External interface requirements are system requirements that specify a hardware, software, or manual entity with which a system or component must interface, or that set forth constraints on formats, timing, or other factors determined by such an interface. Interface requirements specifications are documented in *interface control documents* (called ICDs) that are used to define all interface requirements within and between hardware/software systems, or between hardware/software developers. The ICD consti-

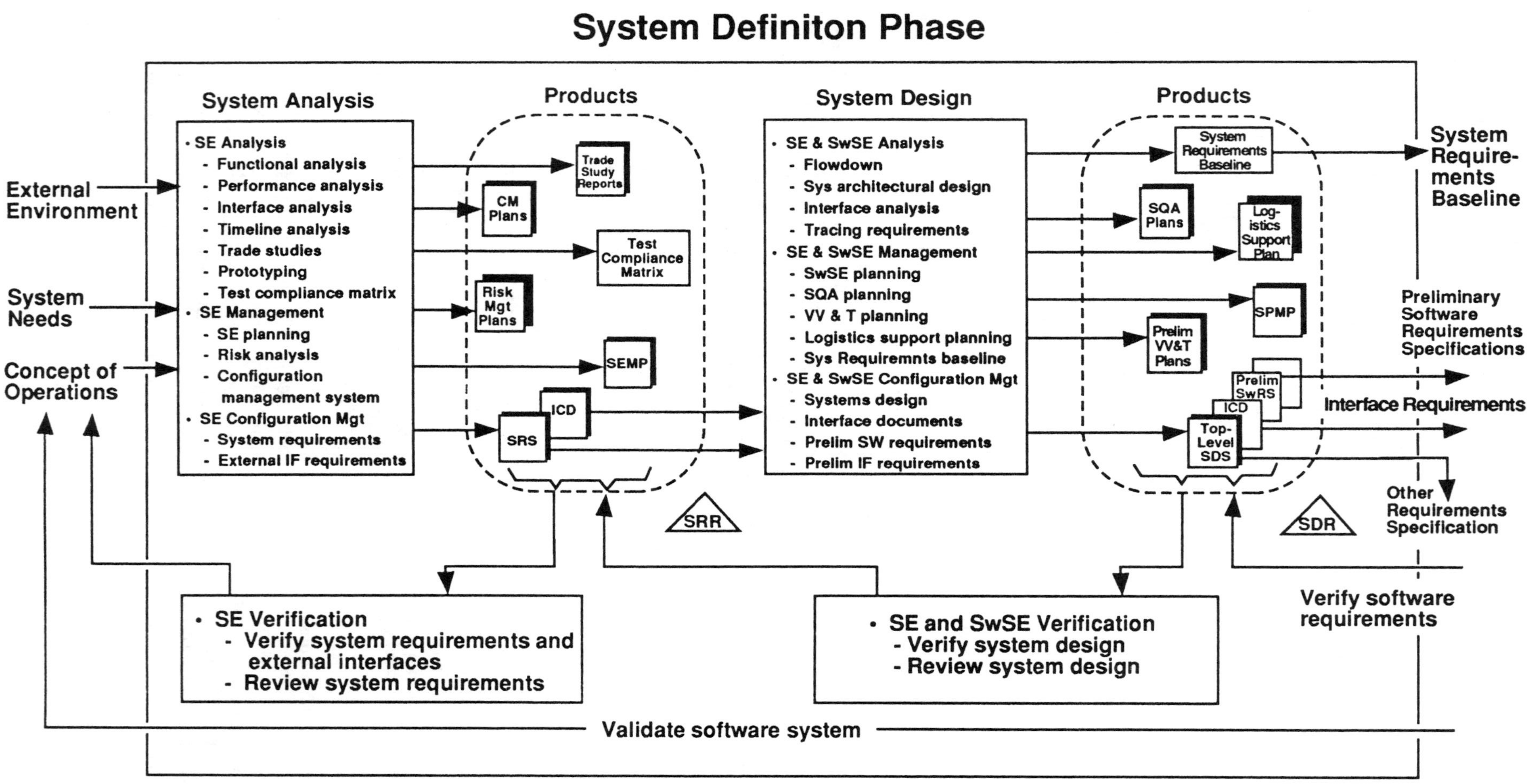

System Definiton Phase

External Environment

System Needs

Concept of Operations

System Analysis

- SE Analysis
  - Functional analysis
  - Performance analysis
  - Interface analysis
  - Timeline analysis
  - Trade studies
  - Prototyping
  - Test compliance matrix
- SE Management
  - SE planning
  - Risk analysis
  - Configuration management system
- SE Configuration Mgt
  - System requirements
  - External IF requirements

Products

Trade Study Reports

CM Plans

Test Compliance Matrix

Risk Mgt Plans

SEMP

ICD

SRS

SRR

System Design

- SE & SwSE Analysis
  - Flowdown
  - Sys architectural design
  - Interface analysis
  - Tracing requirements
- SE & SwSE Management
  - SwSE planning
  - SQA planning
  - VV & T planning
  - Logistics support planning
  - Sys Requiremnts baseline
- SE & SwSE Configuration Mgt
  - Systems design
  - Interface documents
  - Prelim SW requirements
  - Prelim IF requirements

Products

System Requirements Baseline

SQA Plans

Log-istics Support Plan

SPMP

Prelim VV&T Plans

Prelim SwRS

ICD

Top-Level SDS

SDR

System Require-ments Baseline

Preliminary Software Requirements Specifications

Interface Requirements

Other Requirements Specification

Verify software requirements

- SE Verification
  - Verify system requirements and external interfaces
  - Review system requirements

- SE and SwSE Verification
  - Verify system design
  - Review system design

Validate software system

Figure 2: Overview model of the system definition phase

tutes a bilateral technical and administrative agreement between affected agencies and/or developers.

System requirements are usually based on or obtained from one or more of the following documents or sources:

- Marketing surveys, competitive analysis, and customer comments
- Customer-prepared procurement specifications and statements of work
- Customer-prepared needs documents
- Concept of operations (CONOPS) documents
- Observations and measures of the current system
- Interviews with the customers and users
- Current system documentation
- Models and prototypes

SE must be especially aware of the external factors and environments that influence a systems development. These external factors influence the system requirements and external interface specifications. Some of the technical, physical, and social interfaces to consider are:

- Existing systems that will receive or send data
- National, government, or company development standards
- State of the current technology
- Environment, either natural or manmade
- Trends in both the application and computer science technology
- Competition and business environment
- Social environment and human factors

One of the most important sources of system requirements is the concept of operations (CONOPS) document. In SE/SwSE, the CONOPS document is normally produced as the first step in the system definition phase of a given program. The CONOPS document should be (but is not always) prepared by the customer or buyer.

The purpose of the CONOPS is to describe the overall system characteristics from an operational (users') viewpoint, as apposed to the more technically oriented requirements specification. The CONOPS document is also used to coordinate overall nonquantitative system goals for the users, buyers, developers, and other system-interfacing organizations (e.g., training, facilities, staffing, interfacing contractors, and maintenance elements). The CONOPS also forms the basis for long-range user planning activities and provides guidance for the development of subsequent system definition documents (e.g., functional system specifications, employment plans, long-term budgeting, interface control drawings, etc.). The CONOPS therefore satisfies and integrates the needs of four types of audiences: users, buyers, builders, and interfacing organizations. [13]

Some of the tools used to assist SE in establishing and representing system requirements are:

- *Work breakdown structure* (WBS) to illustrate and represent the relationships between components of a system. See Figure 3 for an example of a product WBS. Each level represents the system being delivered. Each subsystem represented by a "box" can be partitioned into smaller subsubsystems. Top levels of the WBS tend to be logical components, and low levels of the WBS tend to be physical components.
- *Functional flow block diagrams* (FFBDs) to "rough out" the major functions and their interfaces. See Figure 4, a *FFBD* of an Area Control Center, for an example of a FFBD. The figure illustrates a second level FFBD. The first level would be the top-level Air Traffic System. Conventionally data or materiel flows from left to right. The input/output blocks, "Flight Plan Data," "Other ATC Areas," and "Other Terminals/Towers," are outside the second level FFBD and are shown with a broken border.
- *Data flow diagrams,* borrowed from software engineering, to aid in partitioning, allocating, and representing system requirements. Data flow diagrams illustrate and represent dependencies between processes. See Figure 5 for an example of a data flow diagram used at the systems level. [14]
- *Prototyping models* to demonstrate potential requirements (and sometimes design) to the user in order to obtain agreement on the functionality and performance of the system.
- *N-squared* (N^2) *charts* to aid in establishing and representing system and subsystem interfaces. See Figure 6 for example of an N^2 chart. The small oval indicates that an interface exists between the functions connected to it. The number in the oval references a paragraph or section in the interface control document (ICD) that describes the interface. A N^2 chart can be used at any level of the system design.

(2) Perform trade studies and timeline analysis. Determine how best to implement the requirements.

Trade studies, prototyping, functional analysis, simulation, and timeline analysis are some of the design tools and methods used by SE in determining how best to implement the system requirements and in determining which requirements can best be solved through hardware, which by software, and how will they integrate with each other. *This is the SE decision-making process.*

A *trade study* (sometime called tradeoff analysis) is a formal decision analysis method that can be used to solve any complex problem having more than one solution. A good tradeoff analysis requires a formal methodology (ap-

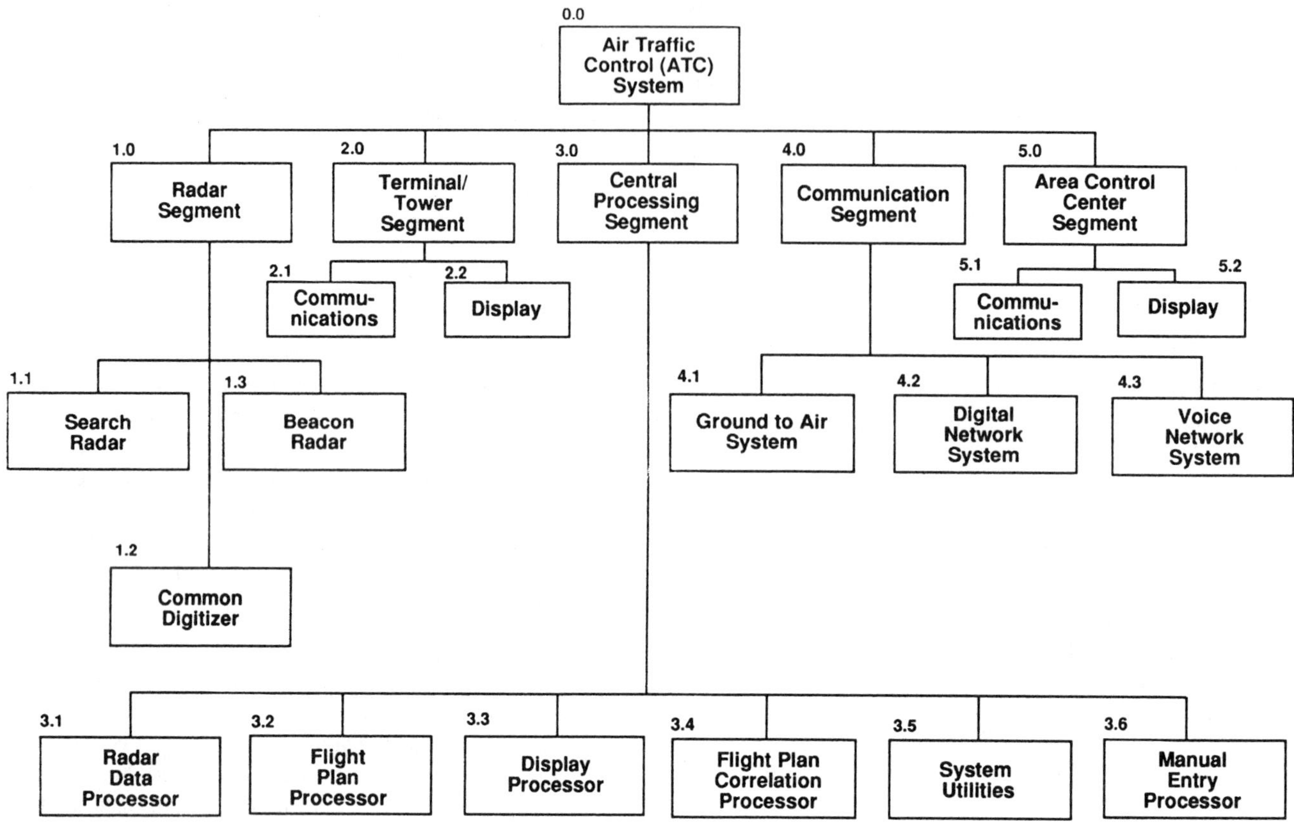

Figure 3: Example of a work breakdown structure (WBS)

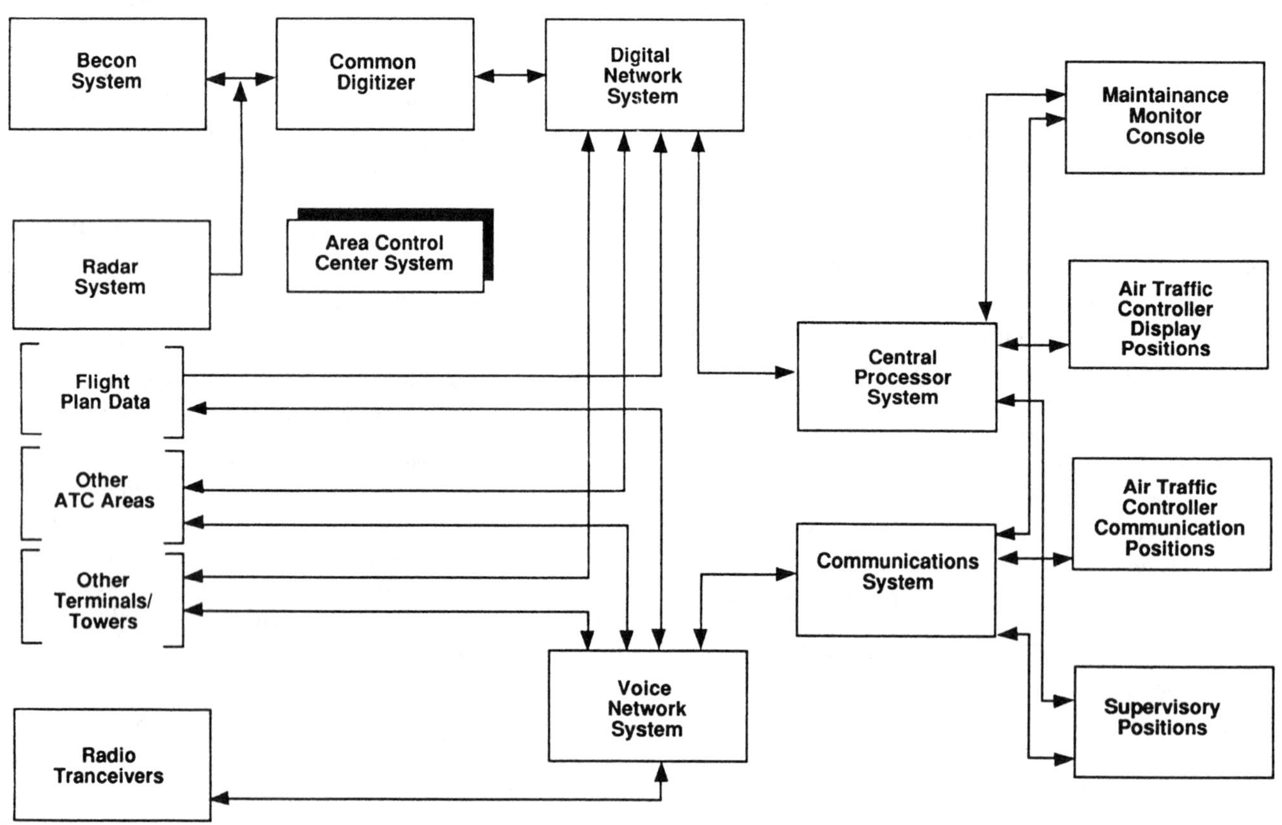

Figure 4: Example of a functional flow block diagram

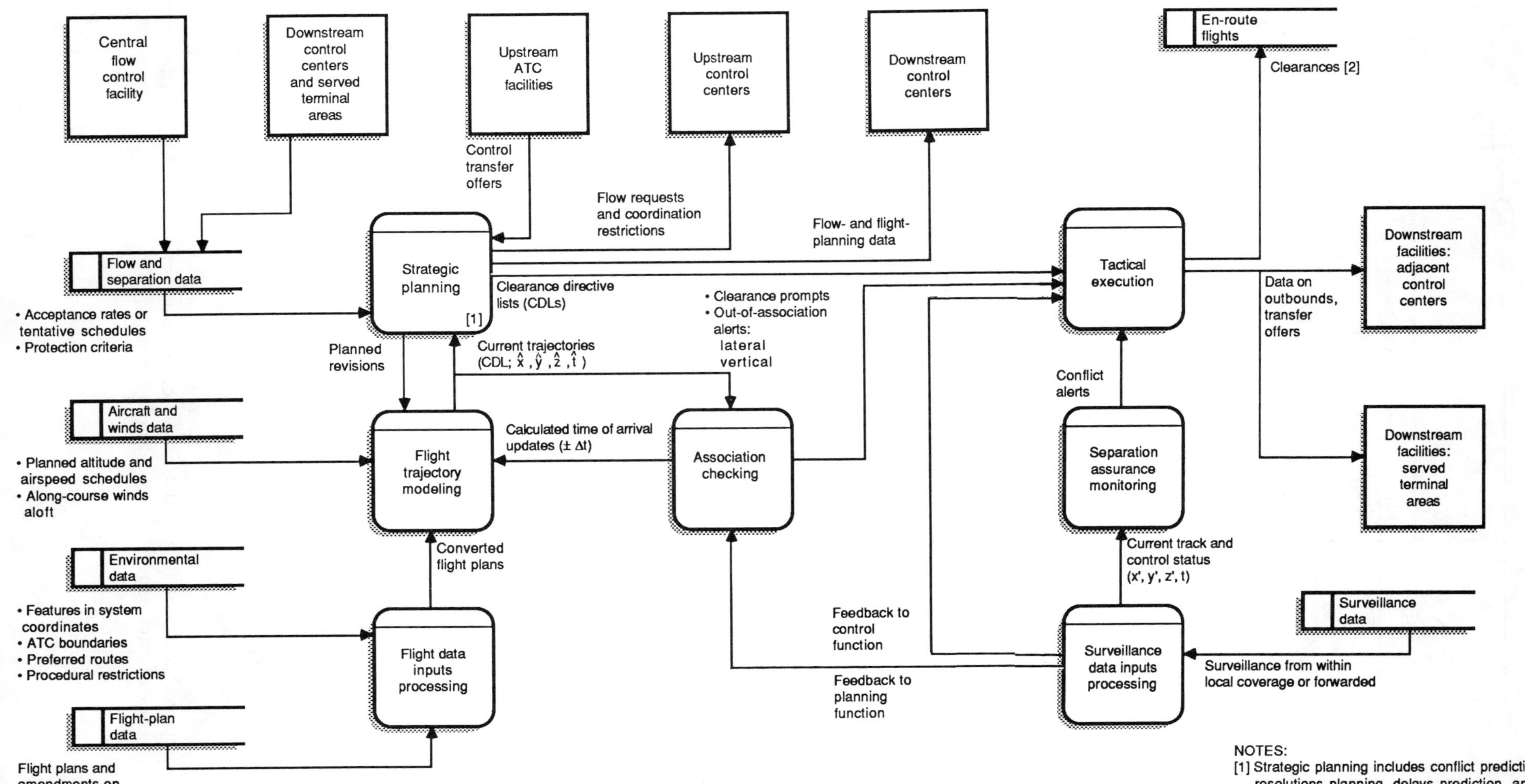

Figure 5: Example of a data flow diagram

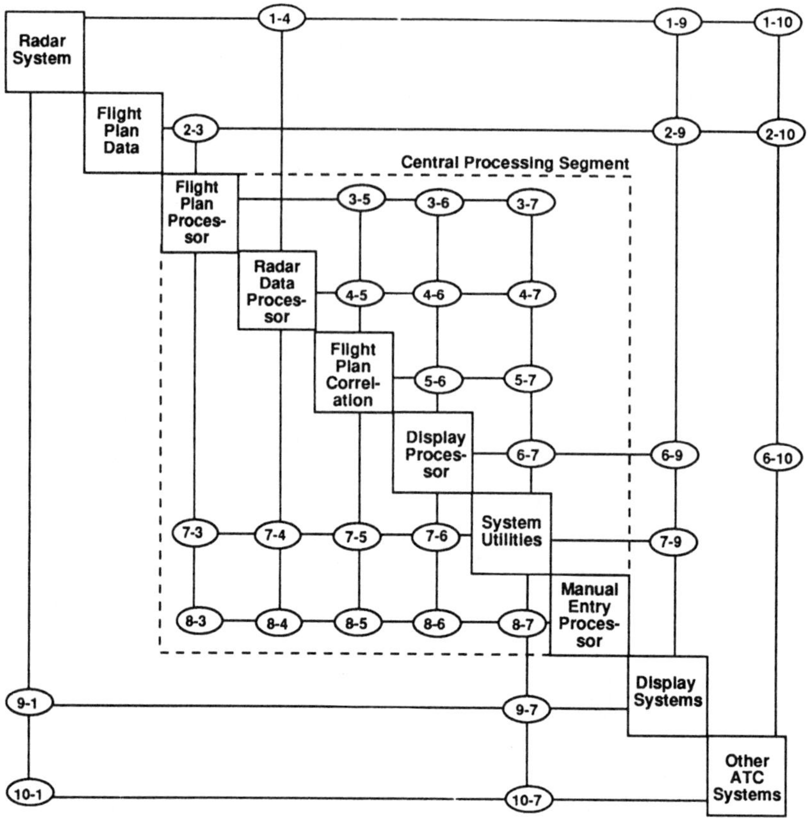

Figure 6: Example of a N^2 chart

proach) for organizing data and the decision-making process (see Figure 7). Beginning with a need or requirement to be implemented or designed, evaluation criteria are established, and competing concepts (usually designs) are identified. These competing concepts are compared and evaluated against the evaluation criteria (sometimes through prototyping, simulation, and other types of analysis), sensitivity analysis is performed, adverse effects are examined, and a decision is made. Competing decisions for consideration can either be predetermined or can be developed specifically for the trade study. The evaluation criteria must be expressed in precise, explicit, measurable terms in order for the criteria to serve accurately as the basis of decision making.

Sensitivity analysis must be performed to determine the value of results to the decision makers. An evaluation criterion is considered sensitive if a small change in the criterion makes a large change in the results. [15] If the evaluation criterion is too sensitive the criterion must be redesigned.

Some technical and management constraints to be considered in determining a design evaluation criteria are:

- Cost and schedule
- Verified customers' needs
- Operational concepts
- Political constraints
- Technical limits
- Risk limits

A common decision analysis technique involves separating the evaluation criterion into a "must have" part and a "want" part. Any alternative solution that does not meet *every* "must have" characteristic is eliminated. Each of the surviving alternative solutions is scored according to *how well* it satisfies each of the "want" characteristics. These scores are then weighted according to their value in meeting the customer's requirements. The alternative solutions and their scores are then evaluated, and the best solution picked. This is sometime called the Kepner-Tregoe (K-T) analysis technique after the developers. [16] See Figure 8 to show how the techniques could work for a simple system with three alternatives. [17]

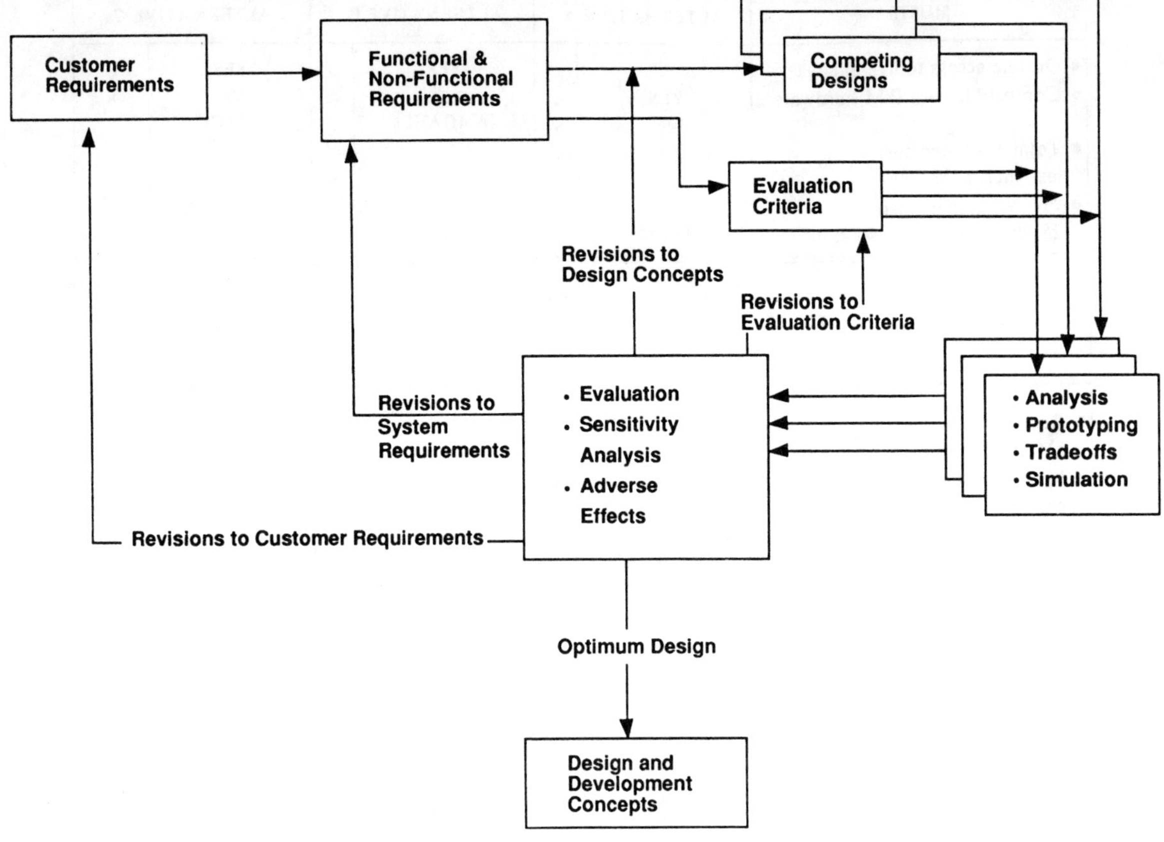

Figure 7: System tradeoff cycle

As a result of this decision-making process, major analysis and design decisions can now be made to efficiently and effectively design the system at least risk. The trade studies will continue in parallel throughout the early part of the software development process.

A prototype is a useful trade-study tool. In engineering, a prototype is a full-scale model and functional form of a new system or subsystem. (A prototype does not have to be the complete system, only the parts of interest.) The process of building the prototype will expose and eliminate a number of the ambiguities, inconsistencies, incorrect assumptions, and misunderstandings incorporated in the specifications. Operating or running the prototype will provide requirements and design information that can be used in the decision-making process.

Timeline analysis depicts the concurrency, overlap, and sequential relationship of functions and related tasks and helps identify time-critical functions (see Figure 9). [18] Time-critical functions are those that affect reaction time, down time, availability, or other time-dependent features. Timeline analysis can be used to support trade studies which in turn support decision making at the system level.

(3) Develop top-level system design specifications and interface requirements. Partition the system into effective hardware and software subsystems. Develop preliminary software system requirements and interface specifications.

The balance of the system definition task is to determine how the system requirements will be organized into a top-level system design specifications (SDS). This is sometimes called an architectural design. An architectural system design determines which part of the system can or should be done with software, which with hardware, which are better left to manual procedures, and what are the interfaces between them.

Architectural system design is concerned with making global decisions, rather than local ones, for determining the overall hardware-software architecture, data structure, and interfaces between the hardware-software products, along with other necessary components such as a draft users' manual and test plans. [19]

Some of the decisions are easy. For example, every commercial software system needs a computer (hardware) to run on. This commercial computer is then one (or more) of the subsystems of the overall system.

MUSTS	ALTERNATIVE A		ALTERNATIVE B		ALTERNATIVE C	
• On-line access to live data	YES	√	YES	√	YES	√
• Compatible with IBM hardware	YES	√	YES	√	NO	×
	(IBM)	√	(AMDAHL)	√	(DEC)	
• Total estimated cost less than $200,000	$180,000	√	$160,000	√		
• Process greater than 25,000 transactions per hour	35,000	√	40,000	√		NO GO

WANTS	WEIGHT	DETAILS	SCORE	WT x SC	DETAIL	SCORE	WT x SC	DETAIL	SCORE	WT x SC
• Requires less than 5Mbytes core	10	4.8	7	70	4.0	10	100			
• Maximum transaction processing rate	10	35K	8	80	40K	10	100			
• Written in COBOL	9	COBOL	10	90	FORTRAN	0	0			
• Documented to QA standards	8	YES	10	80	PARTLY	6	48			
• Uses Jackson design method	8	NO	0	0	YES	10	80			
• Meets all security requirements	7	PARTLY	5	35	PARTLY	7	49			
• Uses latest DBMS technology	7	NO	0	0	SOME	6	42			
• Is designed for expandability	7	YES	10	70	YES	10	70			
• Package needs no modifications	5	NO	0	0	YES	10	50			
• Package meets all editing requirements	1	NO	0	0	YES	10	10			
PERFORMANCE TOTAL				425			549			

Figure 8: Example of the Kepner-Tregoe evaluation technique

Some of the system methods and techniques used in determining the top-level design and software requirements are:

- *Flowdown* — A method for the systematic decomposition of system requirements into allocated and derived requirements, appropriately assigned to low-level functional components. In other words, generating a lower level requirements structure from the (system-supplied) top level. (The FFBD or data flow diagram can be used as a tool for this activity.)
- *Allocation* — The assignment or budgeting of top-level functional or performance requirements among the lower level partitioned functions for accomplishments. In this manner, the elements of a system that perform specific requirements and that contribute partially to performing others are identified. The result of the allocation process is an allocated requirement.
- *Derivation* — The changing or translation of a requirement through analysis in order to change top-level requirements into a form that are suitable for low-level analysis or design. The result of the derivation process is a derived requirement.
- *Interface analysis* — An approach to identifying and representing functional and physical interfaces between the system and external entities or constraints or between components within the system. The results of the interface analysis is an interface requirement.
- *Tracing* — A procedure for providing an auditable track from the requirements through design to the completed and tested product and back. As a result the allocated, derived, and interface requirements can be traced to their original system requirement

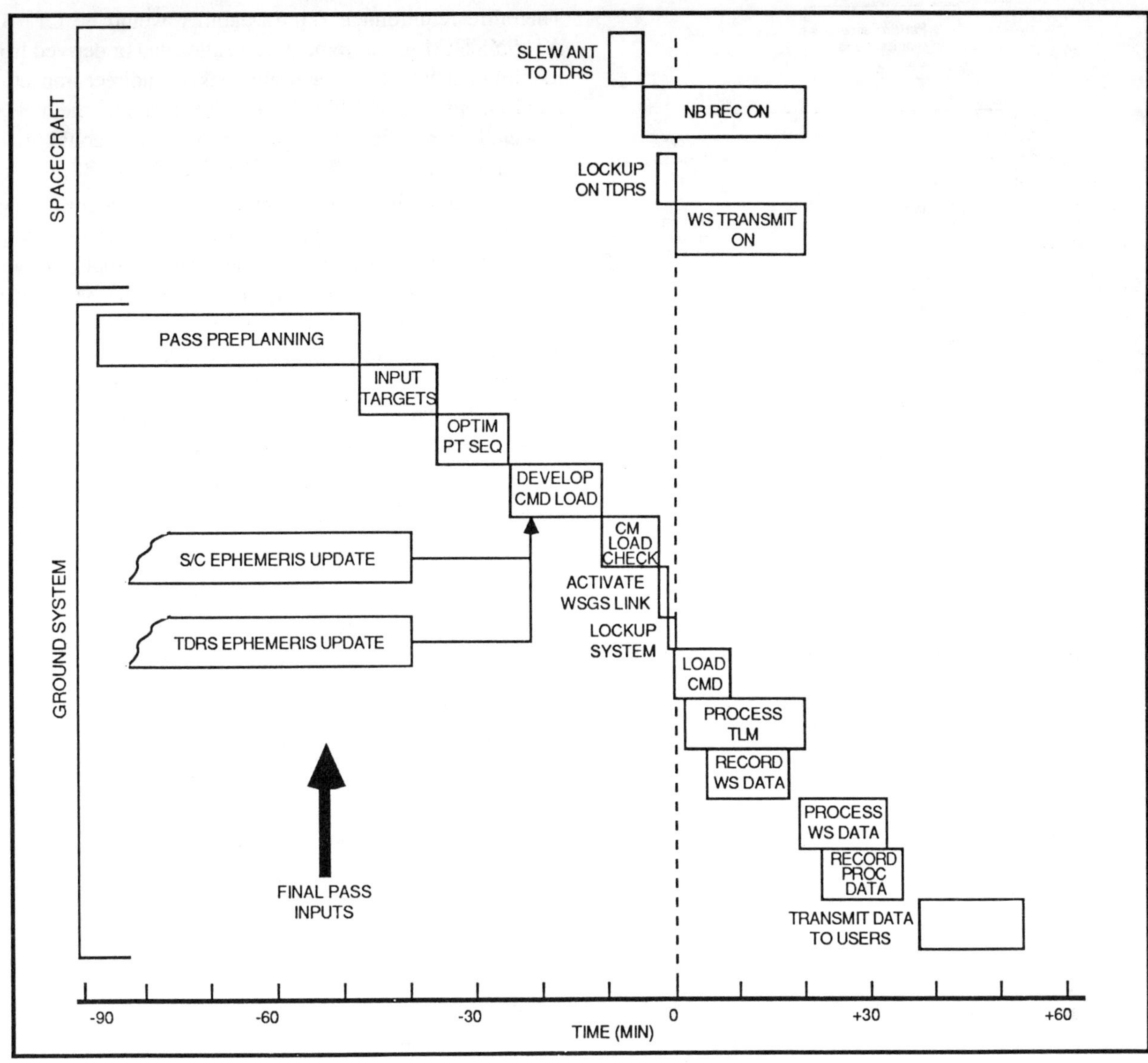

Figure 9: Example of a timeline analysis diagram

Sailor [20] states that requirements are either allocable or nonallocable (see Figure 10). Allocation assigns portions of a system requirement among its supporting functional areas throughout succeedingly lower levels of the system hierarchy. Nonallocable requirements are items such as environments, operational life, and design standards that apply unchanged across all elements of the system or its segments.

Allocable parameters can be allocated either directiy or indirectly. Those allocated directly do not change form, but are simply divided up (called a budget) among several lower level elements. This would be the case for a "pointing error" expressed in degrees, which might be allocated among the payload, structure, computer, and attitude control elements of a spacecraft subsystem, but still in degrees, or a reliability metric, which might be apportioned across several subsystems in series.

Indirect allocation of parameters means that the parameter must change its form through a derivation analysis. When a requirement changes form, it becomes a derived requirement. This usually occurs through the process of analysis, which translates user requirements into parameters to which a designer can relate such as power, weight, etc. For example, a system requirement of targets-per-orbit-pass means little to the hardware or software designer who is interested in the output power required from the transmitter or the processing speed of the computer. The derivation

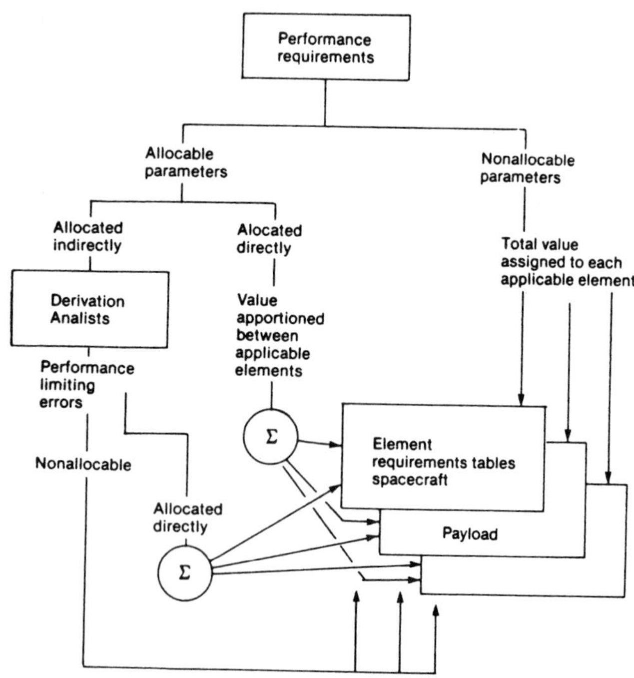

Figure 10: System flowdown and allocation tree

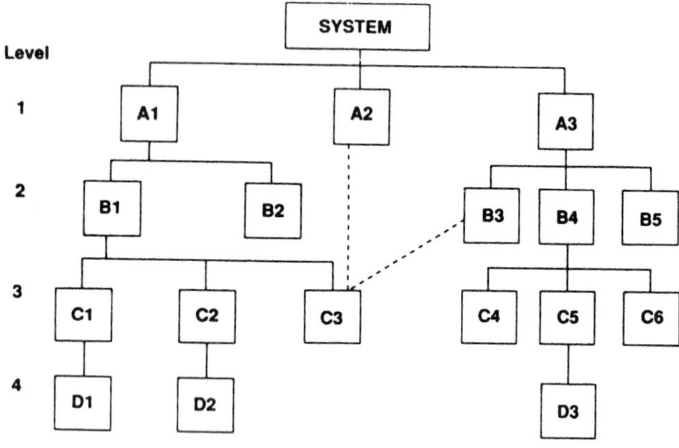

Figure 11: Traceability in a system engineering project

process transforms system requirements into requirements that designers can produce and against which they can test their equipment and software.

Tracing is a mechanism (either manual or automated) for identifying and documenting the derivation path (upward) and allocation/flowdown path (downward) of requirements in the system development hierarchy (see Figure 11). In the example, requirements B1 and B2 are both allocated or derived from A1. Requirements B3, B4, and B5 are all allocated or derived from requirement A3, and so forth. Therefore requirement D1 traceability would be C1, B1, A1, SYSTEM. Requirement C3 is allocated or derived from requirement B1; however it also has an indirect impact on requirements A2 and B3. As a result, if requirement B1 is canceled or modified the impact of the change could be felt on requirements C1, C2, C3, D1, D2, A2, and B3.

The partitioning of the system requirements into groups of similar functions (to be implemented in software), as well as into the external interfaces and new internal interfaces between these groups of functions, forms the basis of the software subsystems. Each system function that is to be implemented through software is allocated or assigned to one or more of the software subsystems. Performance requirements and constraints are then allocated and/or assigned to one or more of the functional requirements.

Some functions that might be candidates for allocation to the software subsystem are:

- Control concepts that are undefined
- Functions in which change is anticipated often during the life of the system
- Functions that integrate the entire system
- Functions too fast for humans to perform
- Functions too tedious for humans to perform
- Functions that would be performed less expensively in software
- Process that will tailor hardware that was designed for one purpose to perform another
- Functions with a low bandwidth and high accuracy requirements
- Hardware functions that were forgotten in an earlier design

The result of this process is the top-level design of each of the major software, hardware, and manual subsystems. From this top-level design, preliminary (draft) software requirements and interface specifications are written. Each one of these subsystems is a complete or almost complete system in its own right.

(4) Generate and document the management and technical plans and strategies. Perform risk management.

Concurrently with the development of the software architectural design, management plans are generated and documented. The system/software management plans provide the management and control of the project from the project beginning through product delivery and sign-off.

The three main functions of a management plan are to determine (1) the tasks to be performed that will lead to the successful accomplishment of the system, (2) a schedule for accomplishing these tasks, and (3) the cost of developing each task and the entire system.

The *system engineering management plan* (SEMP) is a document accomplished by the software developer that identifies the organizational configuration, functions and responsibilities, management techniques, analysis, simulations, technical performance measurement parameters, and schedules that will be initiated, tracked, or employed on the program. The SEMP is supported by a number of specialty plans that describe activities in specific critical areas, and, together with these plans, serves as a top-level technical management master plan. [21]

One of those specialty plans, the *software project management plan* (sometimes called software development plan or software engineering project plan) is the controlling document for managing a software project. [22] A software project management plan (SPMP) defines the technical and managerial functions, activities, and tasks necessary to satisfy the requirements of a software project, as defined in the project agreement. All other management plans (configuration management plan, software quality assurance plan, and so forth) are considered to be part of the software project management plan.

The software project management plan is the primary means of communicating between the software project manager, the project, and outside agencies. The plan informs project personnel and interfacing agencies what the manager expects to do and what is expected of them. SwSE is responsible for developing the tasks, schedule, and costs for the software project plan, as well as for preparing other documents, such as the quality assurance plan, configuration management plan, and test plans.

In a software development project, the SEMP and software project management plan are usually combined into one document. The contents, style, and format of the software project management plan usually dominate.

Typically, SwSE is required to determine:

- The *tasks* that need to be performed in order to deliver the final software product. This usually requires the partitioning of the project product or project activities into short, measurable tasks. A useful tool for representing the partitioned process/product is the work breakdown structure (WBS).
- The *software cost and resources* necessary to accomplish the project. The cost and schedule estimation method used most widely in the aerospace industry today is the COCOMO cost-estimation model developed by Dr. Barry Boehm. [23,24] COCOMO is an acronym for Constructive Cost Model.
- The project *schedule,* by determining priorities of actions, establishing milestones, deciding when and how the milestones are to be met, and creating the detailed schedule necessary to reach the milestones and to accomplish the objectives of the project. (For a further discussion on scheduling see References 23 and 24.)

Other specific plans required of most large software development projects are the *configuration management* (CM) and *software quality assurance* (SQA) plans. The configuration management plan is a program for carrying out the project, design, or schedule for hardware/software configuration. The configuration management plan is sometimes included in the SQA plans. (Configuration management will be discussed in a later section.)

Software quality assurance is the planned and systematic pattern of all actions necessary to provide adequate confidence that the software and the delivered documentation conform to established technical requirements. [25] A software quality assurance plan is a plan for implementing a software quality assurance program within a company, organization, or project. The plan should include the following sections:

- Purpose of the SQA plan
- Other documents referenced in the SQA plan
- Management (organization, tasks, and responsibilities of SQA)
- Minimum documentation required in the project
- Standards, practices, conventions, and metrics to be applied in the project
- Reviews and audits to be conducted
- Problem reporting and corrective action practices and procedures
- Tools, techniques, and methodologies to be used in developing the product
- Documentation and code control methods to be used during development (configuration management)
- Supplier control
- Record collection, maintenance, and retention of SQA documents
- Training for SQA personnel [26]

SwSE also might develop the following plans, among others:

- Integration and test plan
- Data management plan
- Data conversion plan
- Documentation plan
- Safety plan
- Logistics support plan

SE/SwSE is also responsible both for determining risk and for developing a risk management plan. *Risk* is defined as the potential for occurrences that would be detrimental to the project. Risk is measured as the combined effect of the likelihood of the occurrence and a measured or assessed consequence given that occurrence. See Figure 12 for a mathematical model for risk assessment. [27]

$$(1)\ \text{Risk Factor} = P_f + C_f - P_f \cdot C_f$$

$$(2)\ P_f = a \cdot P_{M_{hw}} + b \cdot P_{M_{sw}} + c \cdot P_{C_{hw}} + d \cdot P_{C_{sw}} + e \cdot P_D$$

where:

$P_{M_{hw}}$ = Probability of failure due to degree of hardware maturity

$P_{M_{sw}}$ = Probability of failure due to degree of software maturity

$P_{C_{hw}}$ = Probability of failure due to degree of hardware complexity

$P_{C_{sw}}$ = Probability of failure due to degree of software complexity

P_D = Probability of failure due to dependency on other items

and where: a, b, c, d, and e are weighting factors whose sum equals one.

$$(3)\ C_f = f \cdot C_t + g \cdot C_c + h \cdot C_s$$

where:

C_t = Consequence of failure due to technical factors

C_c = Consequence of failure due to changes in cost

C_s = Consequence of failure due to changes in schedule

and where: f, g, and h are weighting factors whose sum equals one.

Magnitude	Maturity Factor (P_M)		Complexity Factor (P_C)		Dependency Factor (P_D)
	Hardware $P_{M_{hw}}$	Software $P_{M_{sw}}$	Hardware $P_{C_{hw}}$	Software $P_{C_{sw}}$	
0.1	Existing	Existing	Simple Design	Simple Design	Independent of existing system, facility, or associate contractor
0.3	Minor Redesign	Minor Redesign	Minor Increases in Complexity	Minor Increases in Complexity	Schedule dependent on existing system, facility, or associate contractor
0.5	Major Change Feasible	Major Change Feasible	Moderate Increase	Moderate Increase	Performance dependent on existing system performance, facility, or associate contractor
0.7	Technology Available, Complex Design	New Software, Similar to Existing	Significant Increase	Significant Increase/Major Increase in # of Modules	Schedule dependent on new system schedule, facility, or associate contractor
0.9	State of Art Some Research Complete	State of Art Never Done Before	Extremely Complex	Extremely Complex	Performance dependent on new system schedule, facility, or associate contractor

Magnitude	Technical Factor (C_t)	Cost Factor (C_c)	Schedule Factor (C_s)
0.1 (low)	Minimal or no consequences, unimportant	Budget estimates not exceeded, some transfer of money	Negligible impact on program, slight development schedule change compensated by available schedule slack
0.3 (minor)	Small reduction in technical performance	Cost estimates exceed budget by 1 to 5 percent	Minor slip in schedule (less than 1 month), some adjustment in milestones required
0.5 (moderate)	Some reduction in technical performance	Cost estimates increased by 5 to 20 percent	Small slip in schedule
0.7 (significant)	Significant degradation in technical performance	Cost estimates increased by 20 to 50 percent	Development schedule slip in excess of 3 months
0.9 (high)	Technical goals cannot be achieved	Cost estimates increased in excess of 50 percent	Large schedule slip that affects segment milestones or has possible effect on system milestones

Figure 12: Mathematical model for risk assessment

The *risk management plan* describes programmatic aspects of risk identification, risk assessment, risk reduction, and risk management to be performed by the developer. The risk management plan outlines the developer's approach to handling risk: avoidance, prevention, assumption, transfer, knowledge and research [28]:

- *Avoidance* — Selecting a course of action that minimizes risk. (Avoiding one risk may transfer the risk to another area.)
- *Prevention (control)* — Continually sensing the condition of a program and developing options and fall-back positions that permit alternative lower risk solutions.
- *Assumption (retention)* — Acknowledging of the existence of the risk and decision to accept the consequences if failure occurs.
- *Transfer* — Passing the risk on to another organization or entity, usually with some compensation.
- *Knowledge* — Using engineering and technology approaches to obtain knowledge that may reduce risk. For example, rapid prototyping would provide advanced information on potential risks (and frequently solutions).
- *Research* — Continuously examining ways to reduce risk in high risk situations.

(5) Develop preliminary verification, validation, and test documentation for the system. Generate test compliance matrix.

Verification and validation (popularly called "V&V") is a group term for a set of system and software system tools that is used to continually monitor the processes and products of a software development. V&V ensures that the software performs its intended functions correctly, that it will perform no unintended functions, that it will work within the total system, and that it will meet its required performance, external interfaces, design constraints, and quality attributes. V&V will assist in the allocation of system functions to hardware subsystems, software subsystems, and manual activities. The V&V activity can also do preliminary studies on system performance of early system architecture decisions and man-machine interface designs. V&V is an SwSE discipline that evaluates the software in the context of the overall system. [29]

Verification is the process of determining whether or not the products of a given phase of the software development cycle fulfill the requirements established during the previous phase. *Validation* is the process of ensuring that what is intended to be build corresponds to what is actually required; it is concerned with the completeness, consistency, and correctness of the requirements. See Figure 13 for a pictorial description of the V&V cycle. [30]

V&V tasks include testing. However, because of the importance of testing in the overall development and the acknowledgement that testing is frequently discussed independently of V&V, the term "VV&T" (verification, validation, and testing) is sometimes used. [31] This paper discusses testing independent of V&V and uses the convention "V&V testing" or "testing" with the acknowledgement that testing is part of V&V.

V&V is typically performed by a group independent of the developer (called independent verification and validation or IV&V). It can be a separate organization within the developer's parent organization, or it can be a separate company. Separate companies (called IV&V contractors) are used to perform V&V on high-cost, extremely critical software systems, such as electronic funds transfer, manrated systems, and medical monitoring systems.

SwSE generally plans the V&V process, coordinates and interprets the performance and quality results obtained from V&V activities, reports discrepancies in a timely manner to the software development organizations, identifies early problems trends, and focuses V&V activities to address those problems. V&V provides a technical evaluation of the software performance and quality at each major program review and assesses the full impact of proposed software changes on the system. [32]

Some of the early tasks in V&V are planning (for the entire lifecycle), developing system testing documents, and verifying the early system requirements and design.

The V&V plan defines the V&V activities and tasks at each software lifecycle phase, identifies the development products necessary to verify the ongoing process, and establishes criteria for starting and stopping each V&V activity. (See Figure 14, extracted from ANSI/IEEE Standard 1012-1986, *Standard for Software Verification and Validation Plans*, which summarizes a minimum set of V&V activities. [33]) In addition, V&V planning includes selecting the most cost-effective V&V tools and techniques for each phase and developing an organization and staff to accomplish the plan.

One of the tools used in determining "testing requirements" for a hardware/software system is a *test compliance matrix*. A test compliance matrix is a representation method for displaying which methods will be used to verify ("test") each system requirement. Figure 15 illustrates a test compliance matrix generated by the ARTS (Automatic Requirements Traceability System). [34] The information in Column 7, "verif method," establishes how the requirement identified in Column 1, "REQID," will be verified.

In general, the five types of verification methods are:

- *Testing* — A verification method which applies a controlled set of conditions and stimuli for the purpose of

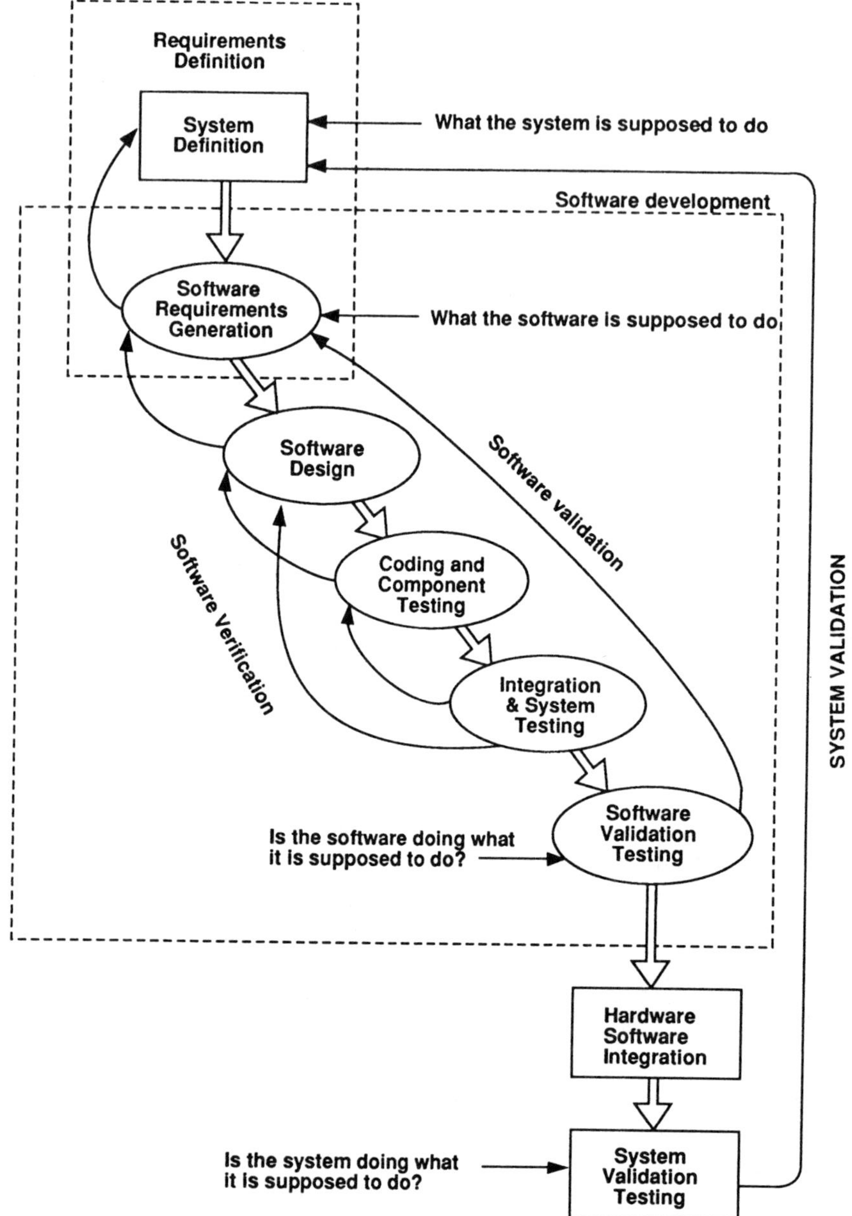

Figure 13: Verification and validation (V&V) cycle

finding errors. This is the most desirable method of verifying the functional and performance requirements. Tests result in documented proof that the requirements were met and can be repeated. The resulting data can be reviewed by all concerned for confirmation of capabilities.

- *Demonstration* — A verification method which applies to those requirements that must be verified using an uncontrolled source of stimuli for which the results cannot be entirely predicted.

- *Analysis* — A verification method which is used for items for which no reasonable test or demonstration can be defined. A system/software product can be shown to be verified with analysis based on a combination of data from various levels of tests, along with numerical calculations. [35]

- *Similarity* — A verification method which compares an item already tested to a item yet to be tested. If there is sufficient similarity between the items and an analysis of the verification methods indicates that a second test

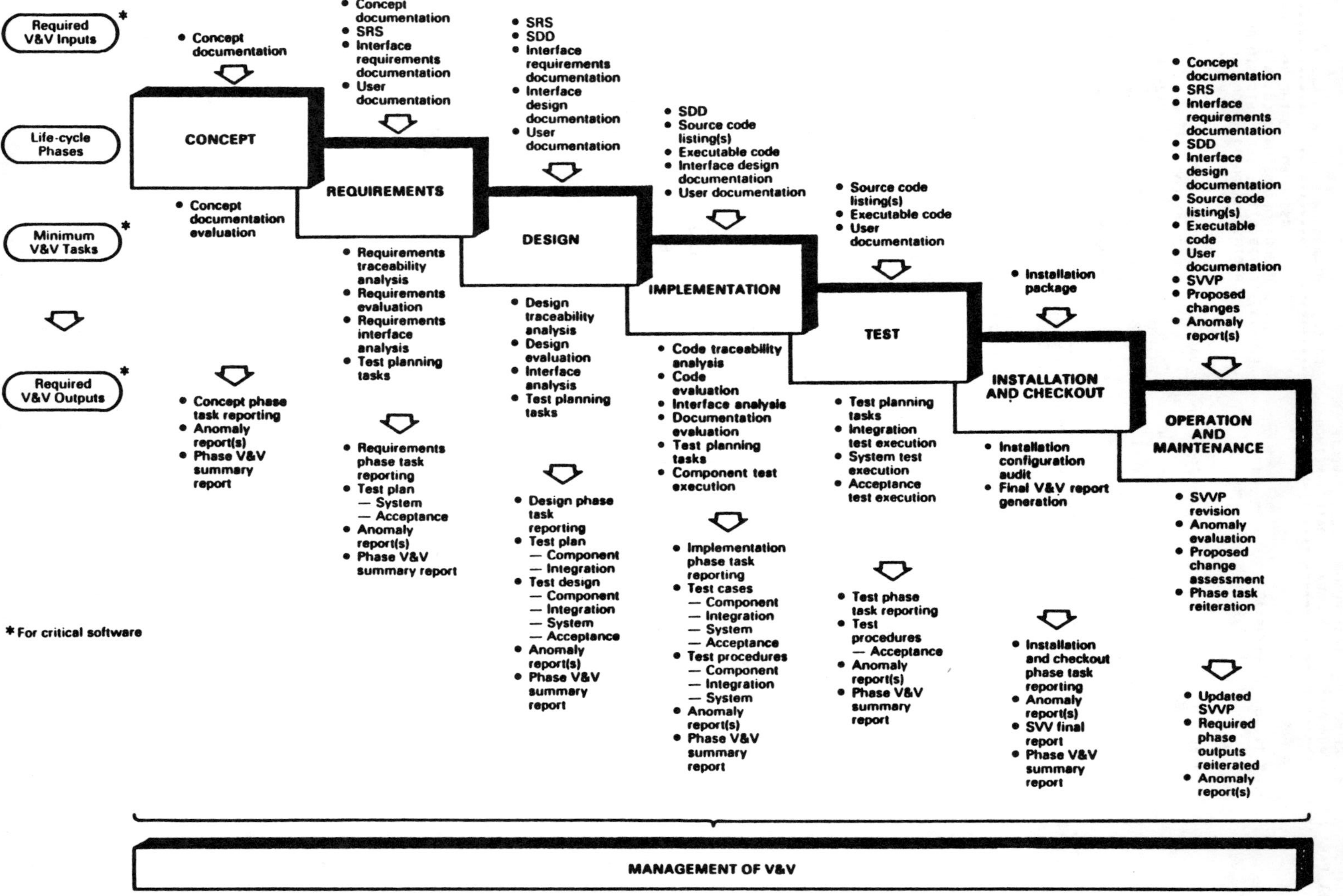

Figure 14: V&V test tasks and documentation

SCTS REQUIREMENTS TRACEABILITY, TEST AND VERIFACATION MATRIX

VERIFICATION LEGEND: INSPECTION (I), DEMONSTRATION (D), FUNCTIONAL TESTING (F), ANALYSIS (A), & LOAD TEST (L)

REQID	LEVEL	SCT PARA NO	REQMT PARA NO	TEST PLAN TEST PARA	TEST DATE	VERIF METHOD	DATE	REMARKS	SUMMARY
GSE01632	02		3.12.1c	F173517 4.3c & REM		IDF	FEB-18	... , GSE00380, GSE00450, GSE00470 F173518/7.0; SEE REQIDS: GSE00072, ... , GSE00302, GSE00342, GSE01432	THE 45K # P-L WT & CGs & I-Fs OF P-Ls STS SIM BE USED TO SUPT SCTS TSTNG & DEVLP & PROVE P-L HNDLG PROCDS
PLI01630	02		3.1.1.1a	F110212 4.14		IDFA	JAN-20	INFO ONLY, SEE REQIDS:PLI00040	SCT CA ACOMDTS P-L WITH MAX THML-DYN SIZE AS INDCTD IN FIG 3-1
TRA01630	02		3.1.2k	F173504 8.4		IDFA	JAN-20	SEE REQID: TRA0000240, TRA00250	PHYSICAL INTERFACE BETWN P-Ls & TRANSPTR BE IAW CA -P-L ICD
SCT01640	01	3.2.2.2a				ID	JAN-20		SCTS TOTAL MAX WEIGHT IS 216,000 lb (INCLUDES 45,000 P-L)
GFI01640	02		3.4.2.1b	N-T		ID	JAN-20	NO ROAD TEST OF 165,000-LB LOADING	THE SCTS ROADS BE ABLE TO ACCOMODATE A GROSS WEIGHT OF 165,000-LB
SCM01640	02		3.3a	F110212 1.3.5		IDF	JAN-20	SEE REQID: SCM00020	WIEGHT OF SCTS CARGO NOT EXCEED 216,000 LB
TRA01640	02		3.1.2e	F110212 4.21		IDFAL	JAN-20	SEE REQID: 00020	DEAD WT OF TRANSPTR COMPONENTS NOT TO EXCEED 62,500 LBS
TRA01641	02		3.1.2f	F110212 4.20		IDFAL	JAN-20	SEE REQID: TRA0021	TARGET WT OF FWD HEIGHT ADJ SYS IS 2910 LB
TRA01642	02		3.1.2g	F110212 4.20		IDFAL	JAN-20	SEE REQID: TRA00022	TARGET WT OF ECS IS 7346 LB
TRA01643	02		3.1.2h	F110212 4.20		IDFAL	JAN-20	SEE REQID: TRA00023	TARGET WT FOR EPDS PLUS MARS IS 1950 LB
TRA01644	02		3.1.2i	F110212 4.20 ,		IDFAL	JAN-20	SEE REQID: TRA00024	TARGET WT FOR BASE +COVER, ETC. IS 50,284 LB
TRA01645	02		3.1.2j	F110212 4.17		IDFAL	JAN-20	SEE REQID: TRA00025	TARGET WT FOR AFT SUSPENSION SYS ID 30,000 LB
SCT01650	01	3.2.2.2b				ID	JAN-20		SCTS WHEN LOADED SATISFIES C-5A SCM CENTR OF GRAV LIMITS IAW FIG 3-10

Figure 15: Example of a test compliance matrix using ARTS

is unlikely to identify additional errors, the second item can be shown to be verified through similarity.

- *Examination* — A verification method which is used to verify the physical attributes of a system, such as code, documentation, storage media, etc.

(6) Verify the system requirements and design documents.

Verification, as in V&V, is the process of determining whether or not the products of a given phase of the software development cycle fulfill the requirements established during the previous phase. The first V&V task is to verify the system requirements specifications.

The system definition phase V&V activities include evaluating the source documents for the project, for example, concept documents (CONOPS) and customer's/user's operational procedures, and comparing them with the system specifications in order to determine if the system requirements specifications properly implemented the customer's requirements. Later in the lifecycle phases, V&V will compare the system/software design documents to the system requirements specifications to determine if the design documents properly implemented the system requirements.

System definition phase V&V tasks include:

- Evaluating the project source documents to determine whether the proposed system will satisfy the customer's/user's needs
- Identifying major constraints of interfacing systems
- Verifying the proposed design against the requirements
- Identifying the risks in the proposed top-level design
- Identifying major problems and noncompliances.

The V&V activity would then report the discrepancy between these levels of lifecycle documents and other major problems and noncompliances to the technical management authority.

(7) Produce the system requirements baseline. Establish configuration management system.

The system requirements and the top-level software system design are maintained (i.e., change is controlled) through an approved *baseline management system*. The methodology that is used to control change is called *configuration management*. A formal *baseline* is hardware/software work products (usually documents) that have been formally reviewed and agreed upon by the customer, user, and developer, which then serve as the basis for further development. Such a baseline can only be changed through formal change control procedures.

Baselines can also be informal. These are called development baselines, and are managed by SwSE to maintain control of the internal development configuration.

Each baseline must specify documents and products that form the baseline (for example, software requirements specifications, design documentation, deliverable source code, and so forth), the review and approval mechanisms, the acceptance criteria associated with the baseline, and the customer and project organization that participated in establishing the baseline.

Baselines, plus approved changes to those baselines, constitute the current hardware/software configuration identification of a product. The formal baseline is maintained by the configuration control board. The informal development baselines are maintained by the SwSE and are administered by the *program support librarian*.

A *configuration management system* is the mechanisms (both formal and informal) for maintaining the various baselines. The configuration management system identifies and defines the hardware/software configuration items in a system, controlling the release and change of these items throughout the system lifecycle, recording and reporting the status of configuration items and change requests, and verifying the completeness and correctness of configuration items. Elements of the configuration management system for maintaining a *formal* baseline are:

- *Configuration identification* — The process of designating the hardware/software configuration items in a system and recording their characteristics
- *Configuration control* — The process of evaluating, approving or disapproving, and coordinating changes to hardware/software configuration items after formal establishment of their configuration identification
- *Configuration control board* (CCB)— The authority responsible for evaluating and approving or disapproving proposed engineering changes to the hardware/software configuration that are under formal configuration control, and ensuring implementation of the approved changes
- *Configuration status accounting* — The recording and reporting of the information that is needed to manage a hardware/software configuration effectively, including a listing of the approved configuration identification, the status of proposed changes to configuration, and the implementation status of approved changes
- *Configuration auditing* — The process of verifying that all required hardware/software configuration items have been produced, that the current version agrees with specified requirements, that the technical documentation completely and accurately describes the configuration items, and that all change requests have been resolved [36]

Elements of the configuration management system to maintaining an *informal* baseline are:

- *Project manager* — The authority responsible for evaluating and approving or disapproving proposed engineering changes to the hardware/software configuration that are under informal (development) configuration control, and ensuring implementation of the approved changes
- *Product support library* — Maintains configuration control for software products under development (not formal) control, e.g., plans, specifications, software versions, test procedures and test results, deliverable (but not yet delivered) documents

See Figure 16 for a graphic representation of a configuration management system. [37]

The *system requirements baseline* is the agreed upon system/software requirements established towards the end of the system definition phase. In Department of Defense (DoD) usage, this baseline is called the *functional baseline,* established at the end of the requirements definition activity, and the *allocated baseline*, established at the end of the system design activity and is documented in the system design documents. The software allocated baseline is sometimes not established until the end of the software requirements analysis phase. [38]

(8) Review the products of the phase and obtain joint concurrence among developers, customers, and users.

Product reviews (sometimes called milestone reviews) are formal evaluations of the products of a software development phase by a qualified review team. This review team is normally headed by a senior individual from the staff of either the customer or developer. The review team members are qualified system engineers, software system engineers, analysts, and other experts from the developer, customer, and user organizations.

A review consists of two stages: the premeeting stage and the meeting stage. Approximately 45 to 60 days prior to the

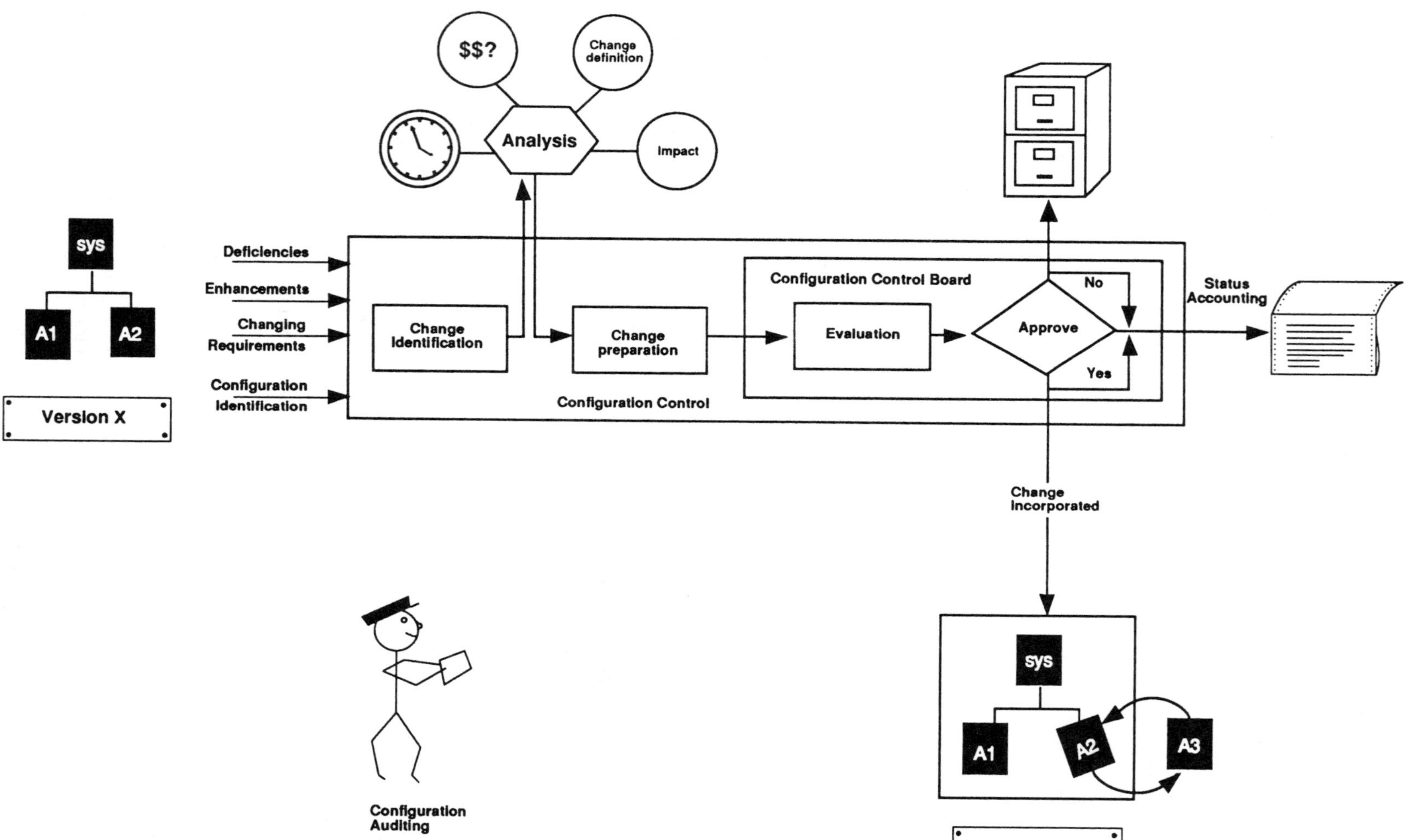

Figure 16: Configuration management (CM) system

scheduled review, technical documents are forwarded from the developer to the reviewers. During the premeeting stage, the documents are reviewed to answer such questions as:

- Do the phase products produced conform to their specifications?
- Is the software development being done according to plan, standards, and guidelines?
- Is the project on schedule and within cost?
- Are risks properly identified and risk avoidance/reduction properly carried out?

During the meeting, status, problems, and potential solutions are brought out and recorded in the minutes of the meeting. The minutes will record:

- Agreement on the work accomplished to date
- Identification of problem areas and actions needed to solve or reduce the problems
- Agreement on who will accomplish the action items and by what time
- Establishment of the appropriate baseline
- Signatures of the representative customers, users, and developers, which signify their agreements

A successful review results in the developer being allowed to proceed to the next phase.

There may be more than one review during the system definition phase. The *system requirements review* (SRR) is a system milestone review that ascertains the adequacy of the system developer's efforts in defining system requirements. It will be conducted when a significant portion of the system functional and performance requirements has been established. In turn, the *system design review* (SDR) is a system milestone review conducted when the definition effort has proceeded to the point where system requirements and the design approach are defined. The SDR reviews the alternative designs, reviews the decision-making process that selected the design, ensures that the corresponding test documents have been considered, and confirms that the developer has defined and selected the required equipment, logistic support, personnel, procedural data, and facilities.

These reviews should be detailed enough to ensure a technical understanding between the system developer and customer. The software subsystems are identified in the system design specification.

4. Software Requirements Generation

The software requirements generation is the activity of determining what functions the software will perform and documenting those functions and other requirements in a software requirement specification. This phase is therefore concerned with determining what the software will do.

Through the system mechanism of flowdown, allocation, and derivation, a software requirements specification will be established for each software subsystem, software configuration item, or component. A requirements traceability mechanism will be established that will generate an audit trail between the system/software requirements and final tested code. A preliminary users' manual and test documents will be developed from the software requirements specifications. The phase will end with a formal agreed-upon baseline as to the deliverable software requirements. See Figure 17 for an overview model of the major activities, major documents and baselines created, and milestones met in this phase.

The following sections describe each of the processes in the software requirements generation phase.

(9) Establish a software requirements specification for each software subsystem. Develop external software interfaces. Continue to perform trade studies.

This process establishes a software requirements specification (SRS) for each of the *software configuration items* (CI). A software configuration item can be a software subsystem and/or computer programs established in the system definition phase.

A *software requirement* is a software capability needed by a user to solve a problem or to achieve an objective. The set of all software requirements forms the basis for subsequent development of the software or software component. Software requirements engineering (sometimes called software requirements analysis) involves transforming system requirements into a description of software requirements and performance parameters and a system configuration through the use of an iterative process of definition, analysis, tradeoff studies, and prototyping.

A *configuration item* (CI) is an aggregation of hardware/software, or any of its discrete portions, which satisfies an end-user function and is designated by the customer or senior management for configuration management. CIs may vary widely in complexity, size, and type, from an aircraft, electronic or ship system to a test meter, circuit board, or bicycle. [39] A *software configuration item* (SCI) is a CI for software. A software subsystem, computer program, and/or any piece of software can be designated a software configuration item. Regardless of the size of the software CI, a subdivision of the CI is called a *software component*.

Some of the system requirements methods and procedures that were described in Processes (1) and (3) are used in the SwSE requirements engineering process. However, SwSE frequently will use different tools in applying the methods and procedures:

- *Partitioning* — The separation or decomposing of a top-level requirement or design into succeedingly low-

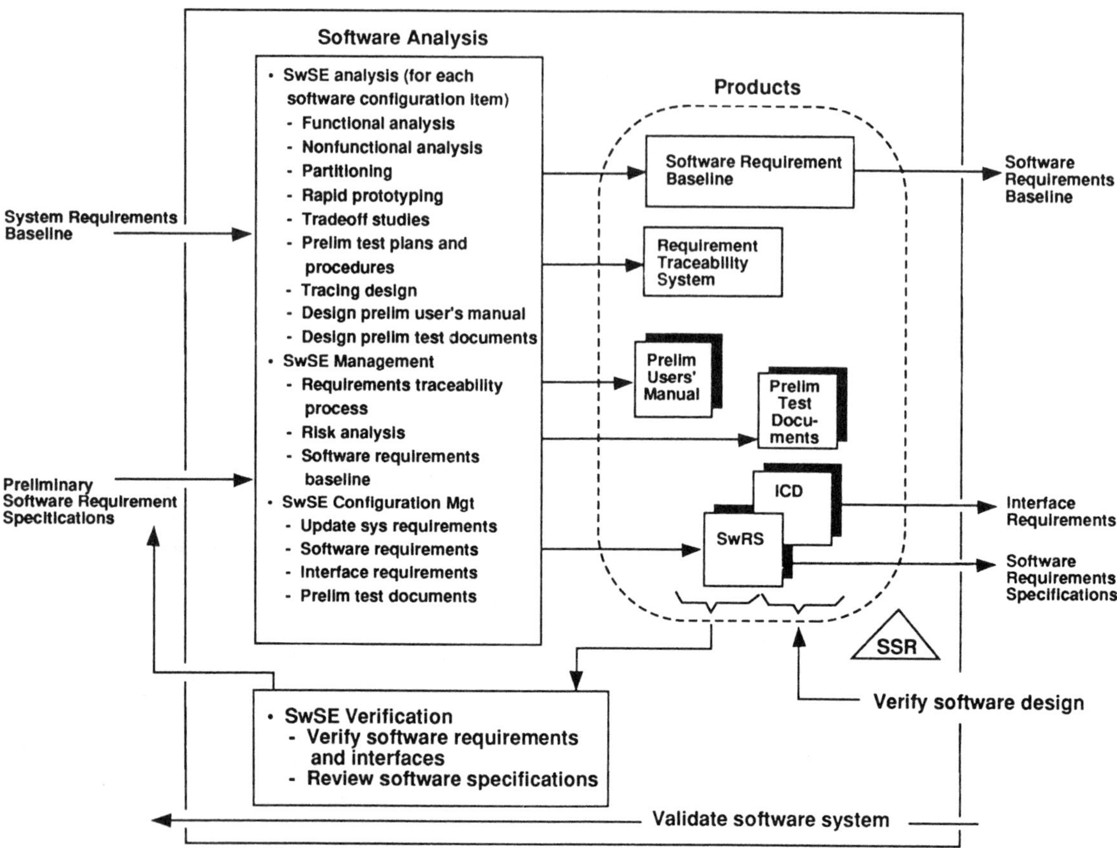

Figure 17: Overview model of the software requirements generation phase

level detailed requirements or design. The separation (decomposition) of a system into its logical or physical parts. Figure 18 illustrates the use of a dataflow diagram (DFD) in this activity. Each process in a dataflow diagram can be partitioned into a lower lever DFD.

- *Allocation* — The assignment or budgeting of top-level functional or nonfunctional requirements among the low-level partitioned functions for accomplishment. In this manner, the elements of a system that perform specific requirements and that contribute partially to performing others are identified. Work breakdown structures are sometimes used to represent the allocated functions. Figure 19 illustrates this process. The functions at the top level of the WBS are allocated (assigned) to the next level, which in turn are partitioned and assigned to the next level.
- *Derivation* — The changing or translation of software requirement through analysis in order to change top-level requirements into a form that are suitable for low-level analysis or design.
- *Interface analysis* — An approach to identifying and representing data interfaces between the system and external entities or constraints or between components within the system. A structure chart is sometime used to represent data interfaces (see Figure 20).
- *Tracing* — A procedure for providing an auditable track from the requirements through design to the completed and tested code and back.
- *Rapid prototyping* — The rapid development of some parts of a software system in order to determine the software requirements.

Requirements engineering is used either to allocate or to derive the detailed requirements for each software subsystem. Once determined, a set of top-level software requirements must be partitioned and allocated down through lower and lower levels of the hierarchy until a complete understanding of the software component levels is reached (see Figure 21).

A rapid prototyping system can be used to assist in defining requirements or, in this case, to assist in evaluating

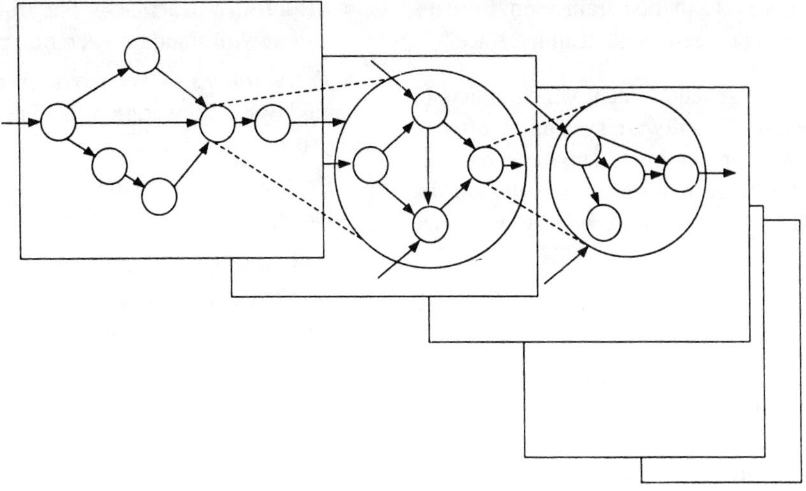

Figure 18: The partitioning of a software system using a data flow diagram

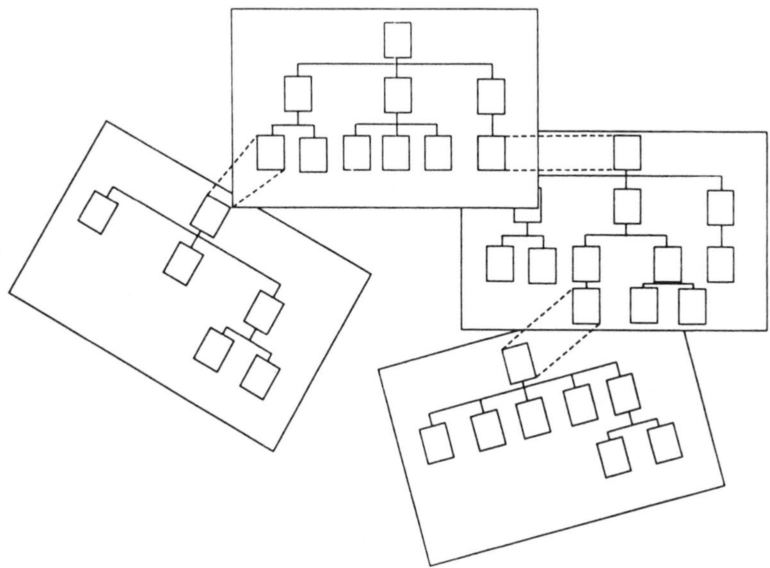

Figure 19: Representing the allocation of a software system with a work breakdown structure (WBS)

alternatives. A software prototype is a computer program that implements some parts of the system requirements. *Rapid prototyping* [40] is a software development strategy that rapidly develops a prototype of some part of a software system to enable customers to assess and recommend changes to the requirements definition. Examples include determining how to obtain the required computational accuracy, how to develop a user-friendly system, and so forth.

Software requirements can be identified as belonging to one of several different categories:

- *Functional requirements* — A requirement which specifies functions that a system or system component must be capable of performing
- *Performance requirements* — A requirement which specifies performance characteristics that a system or system component must possess, e.g., speed, accuracy, frequency.
- *External interface requirements* — A requirement which specifies hardware, software, or database elements with which a system or system component must

interface, or that sets forth constraints on formats, timing or other factors caused by such an interface.

- *Design constraints* — A requirement which affects or constrains the design of a software system or software system component, for example, language requirements, physical hardware requirements, software development standards, and software quality assurance standards.

- *Quality attributes* — A requirement which specifies the degree to which software possesses of attributes that affects quality; e.g., correctness, reliability, maintainability, portability. [41]

Software requirements are governed and/or justified by one or more of the following guides:

- *System axioms* — For requirements that are either unprovable or clear-cut and understandable
- *Functional analysis* — For requirements that can establish logical relationships among operating elements that are not amenable to mathematical analysis
- *Established practice* — For requirements that are consistent with standard operation procedures
- *Trade studies* — For requirements governed by physical laws, engineering principles, or mathematical analysis
- *Prototyping* — For requirements that are provable by testing or that need demonstration

Quality attributes (sometime called quality metrics, performance requirements, or design constraints) are one of the nonfunctional requirements. A software quality attribute is a quantitative measure of the degree to which software possesses a given attribute that affects quality or its perceived value, for example, correctness, reliability, maintainability, and portability. Software quality metrics are different than the other requirements in that they are difficult to measure and/or test. Many quality metrics are treated as goals rather than requirements. Additional information can be found in Reference [42].

The completed software requirements analysis is documented in a software requirements specification (SRS). Zave [43] defines a requirements specification as

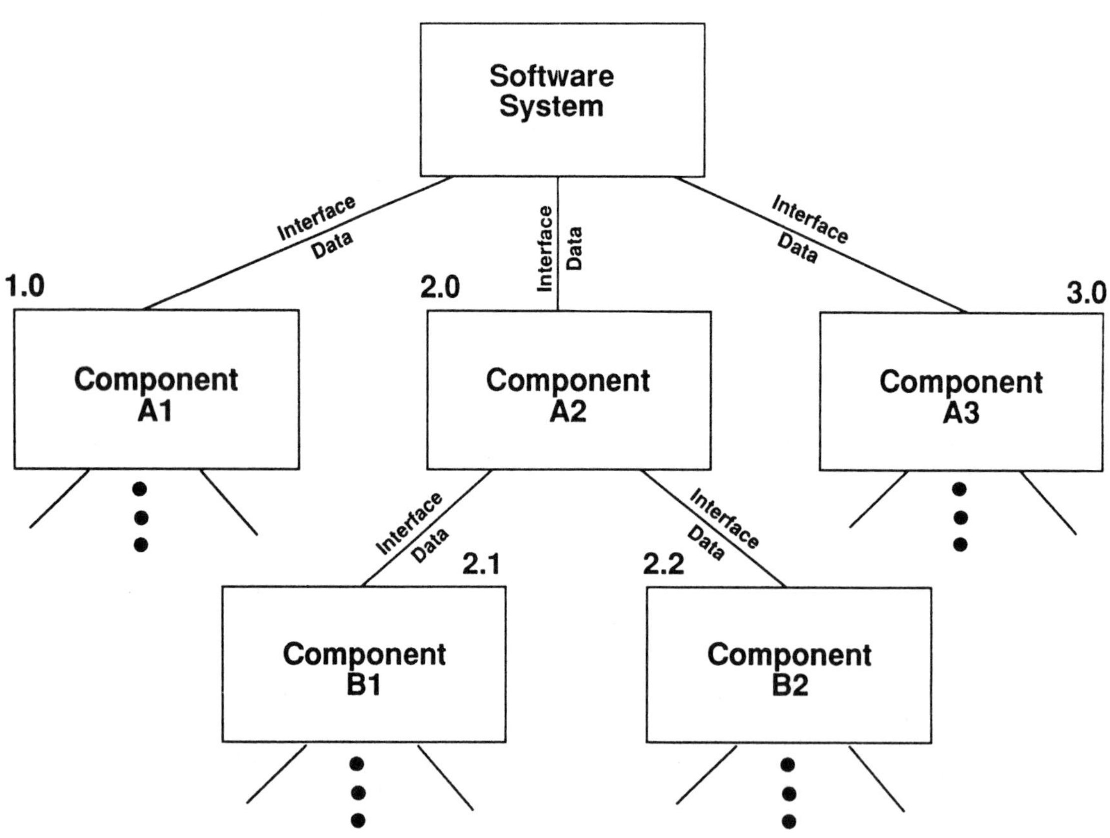

Figure 20: Structure chart to illustrate data interfaces between software components

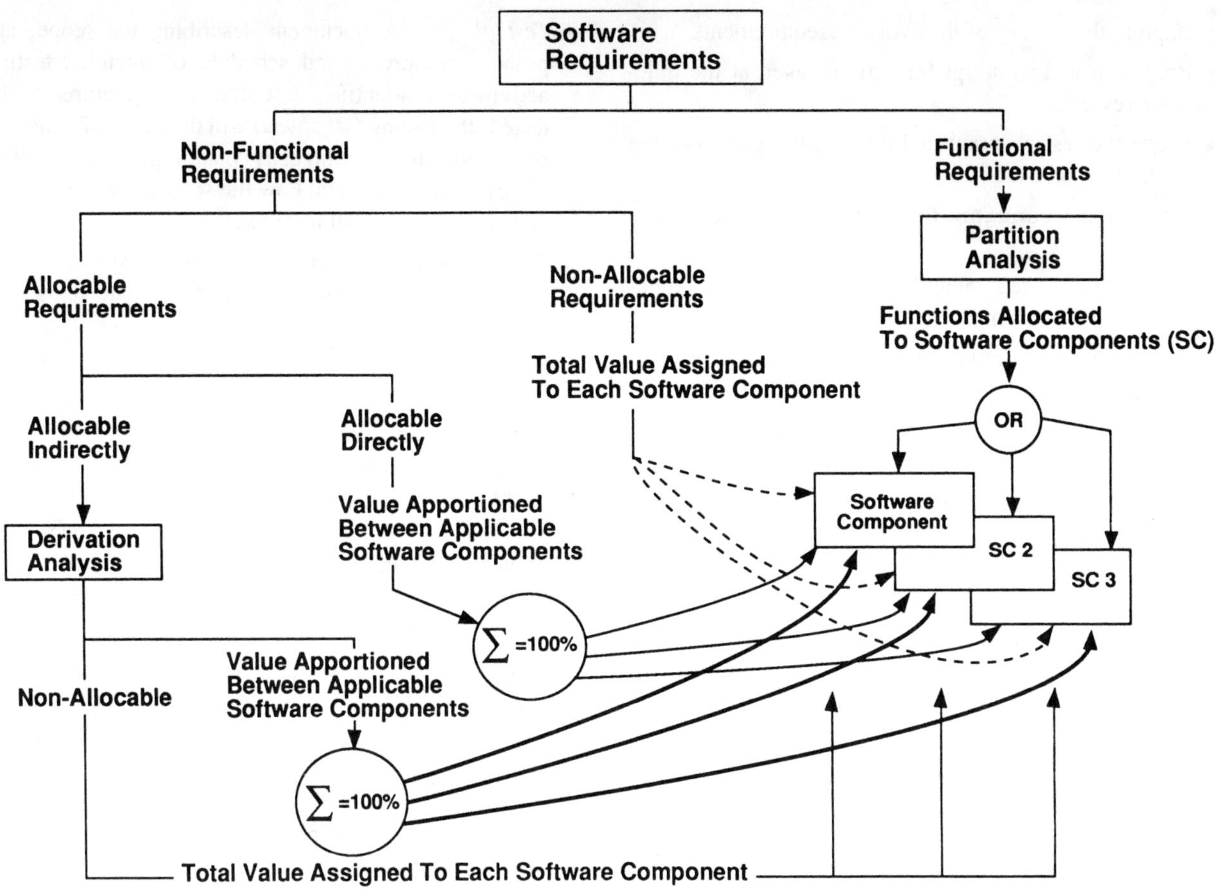

Figure 21: Software partitioning and allocation tree

A representation of a proposed or existing computer system. It can serve as the basis for a contract between a developer and a customer to produce the proposed system. The specification is intended to describe all the required properties of the system while leaving all other properties unconstrained. A specification is generally understood to be simpler, more comprehensive, and easier to modify than the actual hardware and software used to implement the specified system.

Trade studies should be continued through the requirements and design phases to ensure that proper engineering decisions are being made.

(10) Establish requirements traceability between top-level requirements and software requirements. (This will eventually be extended to the lowest level of code.)

A requirements traceability system is a mechanism for identifying and documenting the flowdown/partitioning/allocation path (downward) and the derivation path (upward) of requirements in the system development hierarchy. The system development hierarchy starts with system requirements and ends with tested and delivered source code and its supporting documentation.

In the requirements generation phase, the requirements traceability system is concerned with establishing requirements traceability between top-level requirements and software requirements. In subsequent phases, the requirements traceability system will be extended to top-level design, detailed design modules, and finally to tested code.

The requirements traceability system provides upward/downward traceability among many of the software system artifacts, for example, requirements source documents, statement of work (SOW), WBS, schedule of events, deliverables, organizations and people, code, test cases, and many others.

Many requirements traceability systems are automated. [44] These automated requirements traceability systems can:

- Capture the history of the evolving requirements.

- Capture the history of the evolving requirements.
- Provide principal script for actions taken at the milestone reviews
- Scope the test program and document the verification methods to be used
- Support the configuration management accounting function
- Provide automated capability to process tens of thousands of requirements
- Expose missing, redundant, and conflicting requirements

See Figure 15 again for a product of the ARTS system.

(11) Write a preliminary software users' manual.

The users' manual (UM) is a document prepared by the developer and used to provide customer and/or user personnel with the necessary instructions on how to use and operate the software system. The manual content and format are specifically designed to meet the needs of the intended users.

The preliminary users' manual is developed early in the software development process for the following reasons:

- It provides a description of the software system in the users' own terms. (This is only applicable to software systems that are not transparent to the user. In other words, the user is aware that the software system is performing its functions.)
- It provides one means of verifying the software requirements. The users' manual is prepared from the software requirements specifications because the requirements specifications describe the finished system. If the software requirements specifications contain errors of omission, incompleteness, or incorrectness, these errors will likely be discovered by the users during their review of the users' manual. [45]
- It provides guidance to designers on how to make a system usable and assists in writing test documents.

(12) Develop preliminary test documentation for the software system.

The software V&V test plan and procedures started during the system definition phase are completed during the software requirements generation phase. Plans and procedures are added on how to verify many of the nonfunctional requirements, such as performance, external interfaces, design constraints, and quality attributes.

Preliminary V&V test documents like those described below are developed for each software subsystem identified by a separate software requirement specification:

- *Test plan* — A document describing the scope, approach, resources, and schedule of intended testing activities. It identifies test items, the features to be tested, the testing tasks, who will do each task, and any risks requiring contingency planning. It also determines what, when, and how the software will be tested and defines the pass/fail criteria.
- *Test design specification* — A document specifying the details of the test approach for a software feature or combination of software features and identifying the associated tests. It shows in detail what items will be tested.
- *Test procedure specification* — A document specifying a sequence of actions for the execution of a test. It is a step-by-step description of the process of testing.
- *Test case specification* — A document specifying inputs, predicted results, and a set of execution conditions for a test item. It defines the input and output data used in the test. [46]

This form of testing that is based only on the software requirements specifications is called "black-box testing" (also called functional testing). Black-box testing is a software test strategy which derives its test specifications and case data from the external specifications and requirements of the system. This is in contrast to "white-box testing" in which the internals of the code are specifically exercised. Methods for black-box testing include nominal testing (expected values), random testing, and testing at boundary values (both inside and outside the boundaries). It verifies the end results at the system level but does not check on how the system is implemented. It also does not assume that all statements in the program are executed. A good test document should include both black-box and white-box testing.

The preliminary test documents are developed early in the software development process to accomplish several things:

- It provides one means of verifying the software requirements. The test documents are prepared from the requirements specifications because the requirements specifications describe the finished system. In the event the software requirements specifications contain errors of omission, incompleteness, or incorrectness, this will likely be discovered by the test developers early in the lifecycle. No requirement is complete until its testability has been demonstrated in a test planning document.
- The engineering exercise that goes into developing a test suite is similar to the exercise that goes into engineering the software requirements (see Table 2). When the system testers are independent of the software developers, a fresh examination of the software requirements can frequently uncover overlooked requirements, ambiguous statements, and other errors.

Table 2: Similarities between development and testing documents

Development documents	Testing documents
Project management plan	Test plan
Requirements specifications	Test design specifications
Design specifications	Test procedure specifications
Coding	Testing
Applications data	Test case specifications

(13) Verify the software requirements and interface documents.

In this phase, the software requirement specifications are verified against the system requirements and the architectural design. The verification function looks for bad software requirements—incorrect, incomplete, ambiguous or untestable—and noncompliance with the system functional and nonfunctional requirements.

Some of the tools and procedures used by V&V in this phase include requirements traceability analysis, requirements evaluation, requirements interface analysis, and test planning. [47] Some additional tools are control flow analysis, data flow analysis, algorithm analysis, simulation analysis, in-process audits, and requirements walkthroughs.

(14) Produce the software requirements baseline and place under configuration control.

The *software requirements baseline* is the initial software configuration identification established at the end of the software requirements generation phase. This baseline is established by an approved software requirements and interface specification and placed under formal configuration control by joint agreement between the developer and the customer. Department of Defense developers would call this the *software allocated baseline*.

(15) Review the products of the phase and obtain joint concurrence among developers, customers, and users.

A *software specification review* (SSR) is a milestone review conducted to finalize software requirements so that the software developer can initiate top-level software design. The SSR is conducted when software requirements have been sufficiently defined so as to evaluate the developer's responsiveness to and interpretation of the system/segments level technical requirements. A successful SSR will be predicated upon the customer's and/or developer's determination that the software requirements specification and interface specifications form a satisfactory basis for proceeding into top-level design phase. [48]

5. Software Design

This phase is concerned with determining how to implement the software requirements in the most effective and efficient manner. It will determine the contents and organization of the software system and its supporting documentation.

Design is the activity of determining a pattern or plan; or a sketch to work from. Design represents satisfying requirements with a specific solution. Software design is the activity of planning the software system.

This phase can also be in two parts—top-level software design (sometime called architectural design) and detailed software design (sometimes called low-level design or critical design). The top-level design lays out the architecture of the software system. The detailed (low-level) design provides the details of the software design, usually down to module description levels. The software test documents are updated and a unit development folder is initiated. The phase ends with the definition of a product development baseline. See Figure 22 for an overview model of the major activities, major documents and baselines created, and milestones met in this phase.

The following sections describe each of the processes in the software design phase.

(16) Design the top-level (architecture) of the software system. Develop software internal interface requirements. Complete the final system trade studies.

Software design is the process of designing a system by identifying its major components, decomposing them into their low-level components, and iterating until the desired level of detail is achieved. Top-level design (sometimes called architectural design or preliminary design) typically includes definition and structuring of computer program components and data, definition of the interfaces, and preparation of timing and sizing estimates.

The product of top-level design is the top-level design specifications (sometimes call architectural specifications or preliminary design specifications). Top-level design specifications include such information as the:

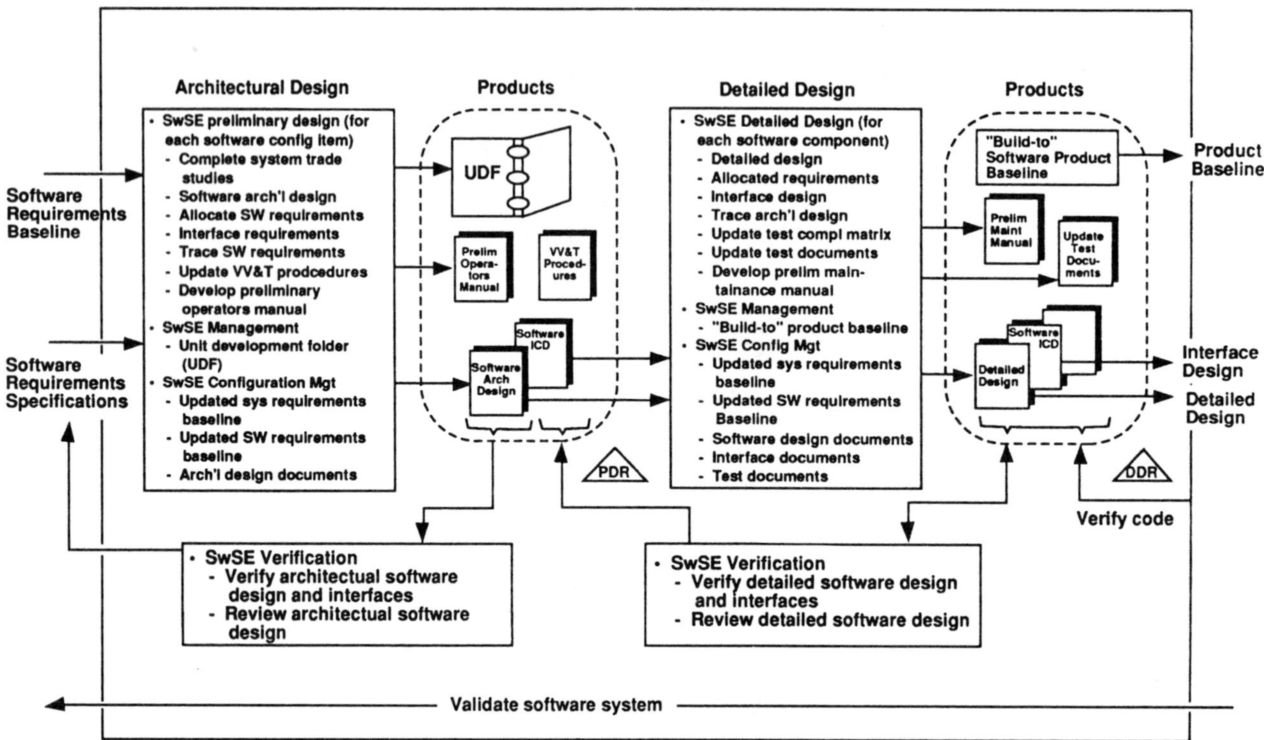

Figure 22: Overview model of the software design phase

- Overall processing architecture
- Allocated functions to lowest level (but not described in detail)
- Data flow, database, and associated processors
- Control of processing
- System utilities and operating system interfaces
- External and internal interfaces
- Allocated storage and throughput

The design represents a logical satisfaction of the requirements by a specific approach. Two software engineering tools useful in determining where and how to partition top-level descriptions into lower level descriptions are cohesion and coupling. See Table 3 for an overview of coupling and cohesion.

Coupling is a measure of the interdependence among subsystem, program, or modules in a computer program. A good software design will try to maintain a *low* degree of coupling. *Cohesion* is the degree to which the tasks performed by a subsystem, program, or module are functionally related. A good software design will try to maintain a *high* degree of cohesion.

The design solution can be represented at the top level by data flow diagrams, flowcharts, structure charts, program design language (PDL), Warnier-Orr charts, and many of the modern computer-aided software engineering (CASE) tools. A good software design methodology systematically forces each design attribute to be exposed, selected, and documented.

The final system trade studies are completed during the design phase. Examples of some of the decisions that can be made are:

- Distributed versus single processor
- Functional allocation to microprocessor
- Approach to database processing
- Approach to operating system control, system utilities
- Response to hardware failures
- Establishment of throughput margins

(17) Initiate a unit development folder (UDF).

The *unit development folder* (UDF), sometimes called software development file, is a management control tool. It is a project management technique for monitoring software

Table 3: Overview of coupling and cohesion

Overview of coupling
• Coupling is the measure of the strength of association between modules • The best designs strive for loose coupling • Measures of coupling (best to worst design) 1. *Data coupling* — Communication by parameters 2. *Stamp coupling* — Refers to the same data structure 3. *Control coupling* — Control information is passed 4. *Common coupling* — Refers to the same global data area 5. *Contents coupling* — Refers to the insides of another module • Best coupling method is data coupling [49]
Overview of cohesiveness
• Binding is the measure of cohesiveness • The best designs strive for high cohesion • Measure of binding (best to worse design) 1. *Functional* — All elements related to a single function 2. *Sequential* — Output of one activity is input to another 3. *Communication* — Use same set of input or output data 4. *Temporal* — Related by time 5. *Logical* — Logical relationship between elements 6. *Coincidental* — No meaningful relationship • Best binding method is functional, sequential, and communication [50]

work accomplished. It is a central repository for recording the progress that has been made toward a "unit's" objectives. A unit can be a product developed by a single project member or a small (5 to 7 person) project team. Initial development of the UDF is credited to Frank Ingrassia. [51]

The UDF will contain:

- Unit requirements
- Design considerations and constraints
- Design documents and data
- Cost, schedule, and status information
- Unit test plans, test procedures, test cases, and test results
- Unit configuration control and identification
- Important correspondence
- Any other information that would have a bearing on developing the unit

The UDF also contains a section for project leaders and management sign-off signifying that the manager has read and approved the work done as represented by the UDF.

The UDF is one of the most widely used and effective management tools today. Many companies have automated the UDF, creating an electronic unit development folder (EUDF).

(18) Design the detailed-level software system. Maintain the interfaces and traceability.

Detailed design (frequently called low-level design) is the process of refining and expanding the software top-level designs to contain more detailed descriptions of the processing logic, data structures, and data definitions, to the extent that the design is complete enough to be implemented (coded).

The product of the detailed design is the detailed design specifications which describe the exact detailed configuration of a computer program. Each entity (sometimes called module) identified by the architectural design will contain the following information:

- *Identification* — The name of the entity. Two entities shall not have the same name.
- *Type* — A description of the kind of entity. For example, subprogram, module, procedure, process, or data store.
- *Purpose* — A description of why the entity exists. Describe the specific functional and performance requirements for which the entity exists.
- *Function* — A statement of what the entity does. For example, a functional attribute shall state the transformation applied by the entity to inputs to produce the desired outputs.
- *Subordinates* — The identification of all entities composing this entity. Used to identify parent/child structural relationships.
- *Dependencies* — A description of the relationships of this entity with other entities. Describe the other entities and conditions under which they either use or are used by the subject entity.
- *Interface* — A description of how other entities interact with this entity. Describes the methods of interaction and the rules governing those interactions.
- *Resources* — A description of the elements used by the entity that are external to the design. Identifies and describes all the resources external to the design that are needed to perform its function, for example, physical devices, software services, and processing resources.
- *Processing* — A description of the rules used by the entity to achieve its function. A refinement of the functional attribute. Describe the algorithm to perform a specific task and contingencies when necessary.
- *Data* — A description of the data elements internal to the entity. Describe the method of representing initial values, use, format, and acceptable values. [52]

The design can be represented by a continuation of the methodologies started in the top-level design (data flow diagrams, flowcharts, structure charts, PDL, Warnier-Orr charts, and many of the modern CASE tools). Another popular detailed design tool is pseudocode to describe the individual software modules.

(19) Write preliminary operator's manual and software maintenance manual.

The preliminary operator's manuals and preliminary maintenance manuals are preliminary versions of two of the three deliverable documents used to support a software system. (The other one is the users' manual which was discussed in Process 11.)

An *operator's manual* is a document used by the operators of a system (in contrast to the users) to enable them to support the users and to operate the system. On many systems, particularly modern desk-top computers, the operator and the user are the same, and, as a result, the operator's manual and the users' manual are combined.

The *maintenance manual* is the legacy the software developers leave to aid future software engineers in maintaining the system. A maintenance manual (sometimes called a software maintenance document) is a software engineering project deliverable document that is used to describe the software system to software engineers and programmers who are responsible for maintaining the software in the operation and maintenance phase of the lifecycle. *Software maintenance* is the performance of those activities required to keep a software system operational and responsive after it is accepted and placed into production. [53] Maintenance includes the modification of the software after delivery to correct faults, improve performance or other quality attributes, or to adapt the product to a changed environment.

(20) Update the software verification, validation, and test documents.

The VV&T documents are reviewed and updated where necessary. Test procedures and test case descriptions should be added to test any new capabilities added to the system.

The test procedures developed in the preliminary test documents were concerned primarily with black-box testing. Not all system attributes can be tested completely in that manner. Another method that tests the internal workings of a system is called "white-box testing" (also called structural testing), which can be developed after the design is complete.

White-box testing is a software test methodology at the module level in which test procedures and test cases are derived from the internal structure of the program. It may execute all the statements or branches in the program to check on how the system is implemented. Some methods of white-box testing are statement coverage, branch coverage, and path coverage.

Other items that must be updated or developed are the test compliance matrix, which must be updated to account for the "as-designed" configuration, and additional computer systems and hardware needed for checkout.

(21) Verify the software design documents.

In this phase, the software design specifications are verified against the software requirements and the top-level design. The verification function looks for incomplete or incorrect design, inefficient and unmaintainable design, poor user interfaces, and poor documentation.

The minimum V&V tasks are design traceability analysis, design evaluation, interface analysis, and updating the V&V test plan and test design specifications for component testing, integration testing, system testing, and acceptance testing. [54] The V&V activity then reports the discrepancies found between these levels of lifecycle documents and other major problems.

(22) Update the software requirements baselines; produce the "build-to" software product baseline and place under development control.

The software requirements baseline is the initial configuration of the software architecture. The *product baseline* is the final delivered configuration of the system. To distinguish between the product baseline that exists before the product is built and the product baseline after the product is built, the former is called the "build-to" baseline and the later the "as-built" baseline. The "build-to" baseline is not placed under formal configuration control but under development control—a local control maintained by SwSE and administered by the program support librarian.

(23) Review the products of the phase and obtain joint concurrence among developers, customers, and users.

The software design products are reviewed jointly by the developers, customers, and users. The purpose of these reviews is to obtain concurrence on the top-level and detailed design. The reviews can be conducted in two or more stages. The early reviews are called preliminary design reviews. The later reviews are called detailed design reviews (sometimes called critical design reviews).

A *software design review* is a milestone review at which the preliminary or detailed design of a system is presented to the user, customer, or other interested parties for comment and approval. The schedule and plan for conduct of software design reviews should be included in the developer's program plan and master schedule.

A software *preliminary design review* (PDR) evaluates the progress and technical adequacy of the selected top-level design approach, determines its compatibility with the functional and performance requirements of the requirements specification, and establishes the existence and compatibility of the physical and functional interfaces between the software subsystems and computer programs and other items of equipment or facilities.

A software *detailed design review* (DDR) is a milestone review conducted for each software subsystem or computer program to determine if the detail design properly implemented the preliminary software design and is sufficiently complete to commence coding.

6. Code and Component Testing

This phase is concerned with implementing the detailed software design in machine-readable code and conducting tests on independent parts of the system. The smallest independent part is called a unit; larger parts are called components, programs, or subsystems. Component testing includes low-level integration testing.

Programming (sometime called coding) is the activity of implementing a software design in executable machine instructions. Testing is the controlled exercise of the program code in order to expose errors. Component testing is the exercising of self-contained components of the software system. The components can be units (sometimes called modules) or much larger pieces created by combining smaller units of code. The formal system test documentation is completed during this phase. The baselines (system and software requirements baselines) are updated if necessary and a new baseline called the "as-built" product baseline is established and approved. See Figure 23 for an overview model of the major activities, major documents and baselines created, and milestones met in this phase.

The following sections describe each of the processes in the code and component testing phase.

(24) Implement (code) the software design.

The detailed design is turned into machine-readable code. Programming is performed in accordance with the standards and procedures contained in the software project management plan. Progress and quality are monitored by code walkthroughs. A *code walkthrough* (sometimes called inspection or peer review) is a software engineering quality assurance procedure in which a designer or programmer leads one or more members of the development team through a segment of design or code that he or she has written, while other members ask questions and make comments about technique, style, possible errors, violation of development standards, and other problems.

(25) Test and debug the individual components of the system.

The basic component of a software system is a module or unit. The testing of a unit is normally done by the developer (programmer) of the unit. Unit testing is the process of ensuring that the unit executes as intended. It usually involves testing all statements and branch possibilities (white-box testing). Some of the errors found could be missing design features, design features added but not required, programs that do not handle the proper input data, and unfriendly and difficult user interfaces. Formal testing (sometimes with informal test procedures) is called unit testing. Informal unit testing by the programmer is called debugging.

Code and Component Testing Phase

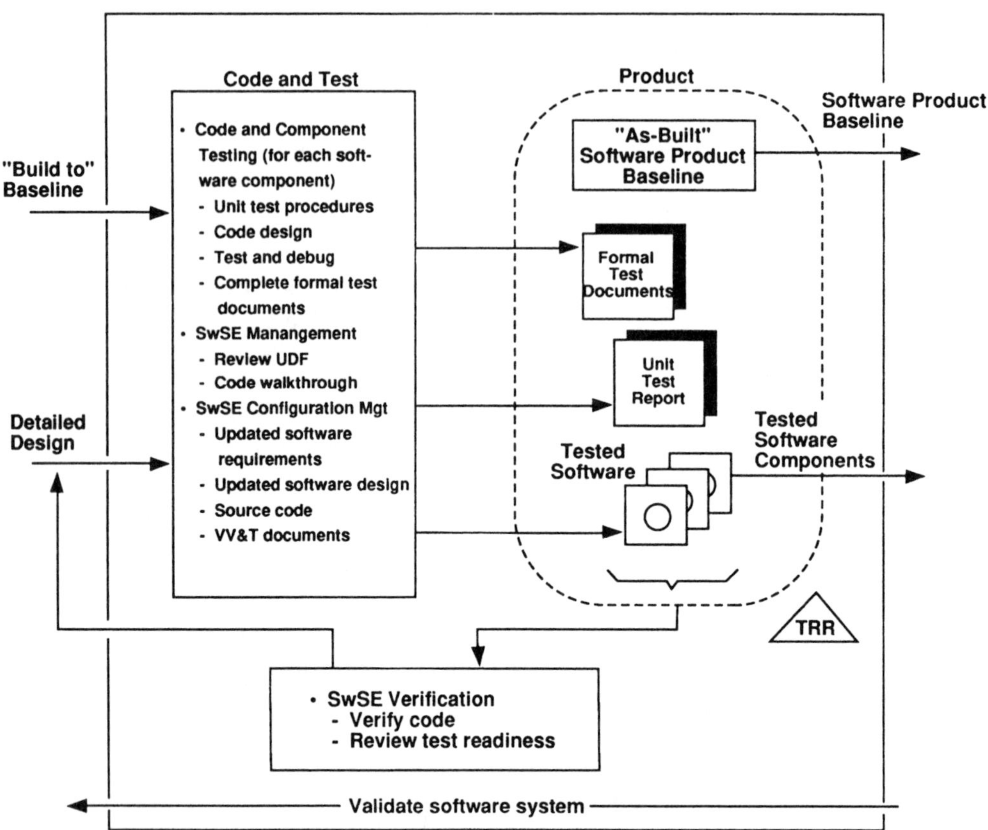

Figure 23: Overview model of code and component testing phase

Component testing would involve testing larger programs of the system, but would not typically involve integration testing.

(26) Complete the validation and test documentation and prepare for formal testing.

The VV&T documentation is updated to account for the changes in the system made during the implementation phase. V&V and testing procedures are maintained under configuration control, as are software products. The programming support librarian keeps the approved completed copy of the plans, procedures, test data and test results that have been developed by the project.

(27) Verify the code and other products.

In this phase, the software code is verified against the software top-level and detailed design. The V&V function looks for incomplete or incorrect code, inefficient and unmaintainable implementation, poor user interfaces, and poor documentation.

The minimum V&V tasks are source code traceability analysis, source code evaluation, software code interface analysis, source code documentation evaluation, continue test case development, and continue test procedure specifications. [55] The V&V activity then reports the discrepancies found between these levels of lifecycle documents and other major problems or noncompliances to *SwSE*.

(28) Update the requirements and product ("as-built") baseline.

The requirements and product baselines are updated to account for the changes in the system during the implementation phase. The resulting baseline is called the "as-built" product baseline as distinguished from the "build-to" product baseline. The "as-built" product baseline is placed under formal configuration control.

(29) Conduct the test readiness review and obtain concurrence among developers, customers, and users.

A *test readiness review* (TRR) is a milestone review to determine if the software test procedures are complete and to ensure that the software developer is prepared for formal software system testing. The results of any informal testing will also be reviewed. The TRR will be attended by developer, customer, and user representatives. With their concurrence, the developers can proceed to performing integration and testing of the system.

7. Integration and Testing Phase

This phase is concerned with integrating the independent parts of the system that have been component tested, testing the completed system, and integrating the final software system with its hardware components.

System integration is the act of merging a software component or components with another software component; merging a hardware component or components with another, merging software CIs with hardware CIs, in order to produce a total system that satisfies customer requirements.

As stated earlier, *testing* is the controlled exercise of the program code in order to expose errors; testing cannot prove the absence of errors. System testing is the activity of testing the completed system with either artificial data built by the developers or sample real data furnished by the prospective customer.

This phase can also be accomplished in two parts: software integration testing and, where necessary, system integration testing. Software testing integrates and tests the software component of the system. In systems that are almost totally software, this is the major part of the system testing. In those systems that have a hardware component, defined during the system definition phase, the software will be integrated with and tested on the appropriate hardware. If the customer/user contractually requires it, an acceptance test can be run in order to "sell off" the system. The phase ends with a formal agreed on baseline that describes the final delivered product. See Figure 24 for an overview model of the major activities, major documents and baselines created, and milestones met in this phase.

The following sections describe each of the processes in the software system testing phase.

(30) Integrate the software units and components into larger components and perform integration testing.

Software integration testing involves integrating (putting together) the components of the software system and testing the integrated system to determine if the system works as required. Integration testing can be either incremental or

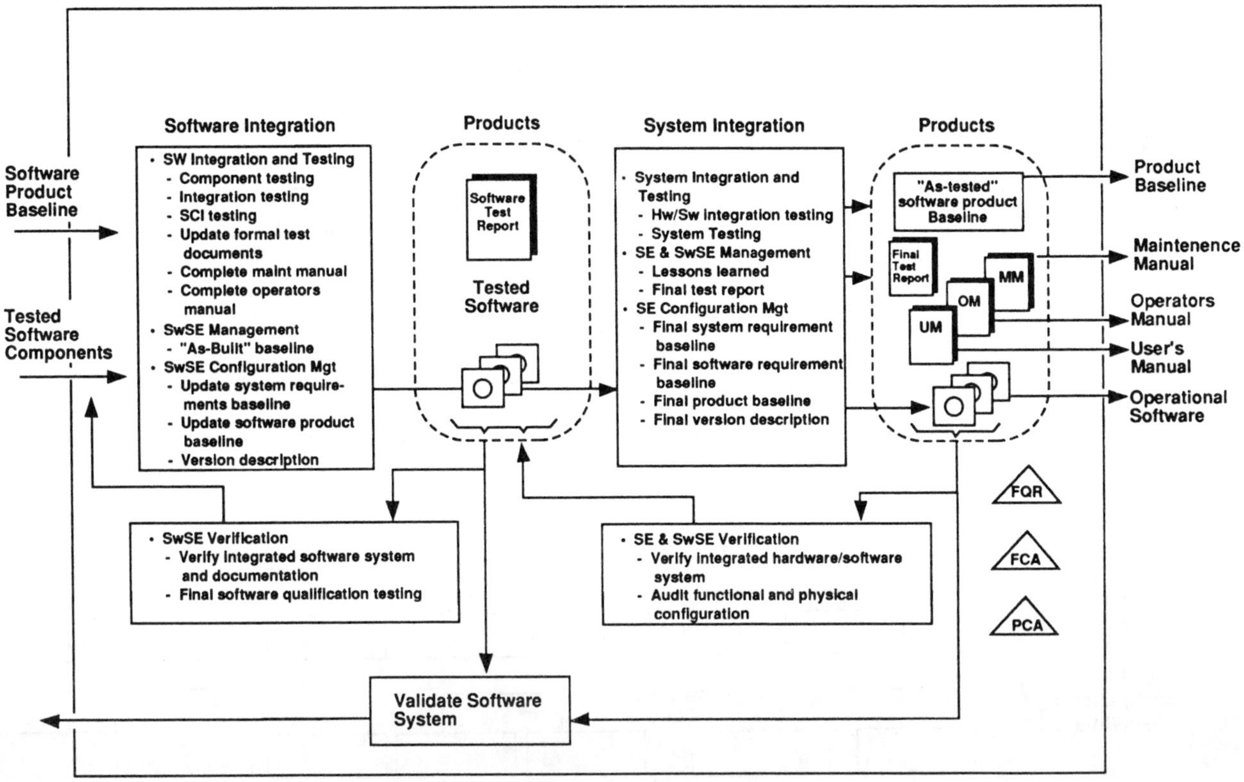

Figure 24: Overview model of integration and testing phase

nonincremental. Incremental testing involves testing a small part of the system and then incrementing the configuration of the system-under-test one component at a time—testing after each increment. Nonincremental testing involves assembling all the components of the system and testing them all at once. Hardware engineers call this the "smoke test," i.e., "let's test it all at once and see where the smoke rises." Since software failures don't smoke, it is often difficult to tell where a system has failed when all the components are being tested at one time. Incremental testing has proven to be a more successful approach.

There are two separate strategies to incremental testing: top-down testing and bottom-up testing (see Figure 25). *Top-down testing* is the process of integrating the system-under-test, progressively, from top to bottom, using simulations of low-level components (called stubs) during testing to complete the system. This is in contrast to *bottom-up testing*, which is the process of incrementing the system-under-test, progressively, from bottom to top, using software drivers to simulate top-level components during testing.

Each of these strategies has a number of different advantages and disadvantages. Some of these advantages and disadvantages are listed in Table 4.

At first glance, bottom-up testing appears to have the most advantages and the least disadvantages. However, Advantage 3 under top-down testing and Disadvantage 2 under bottom-up testing provide significant management advantages through increased customer satisfaction and visibility of progress, so that top-down testing is often the preferred method.

(31) Conduct software validation and testing in conformance with formal software verification, validation, and testing documents.

In this process, the completed software system is verified against the design and validated against the system and software requirements. Tests are conducted in conformance with formal test documents and the test compliance matrix. As described earlier, *verification* is the process of determining whether or not the products of a given phase of the software development cycle fulfill the requirements established during the previous phase. *Validation* is the process of ensuring that what is built corresponds to what was actually required; it is concerned with the completeness, consistency, and correctness of the requirements.

During the software system testing phase, the software system is verified against the "build-to" baseline to deter-

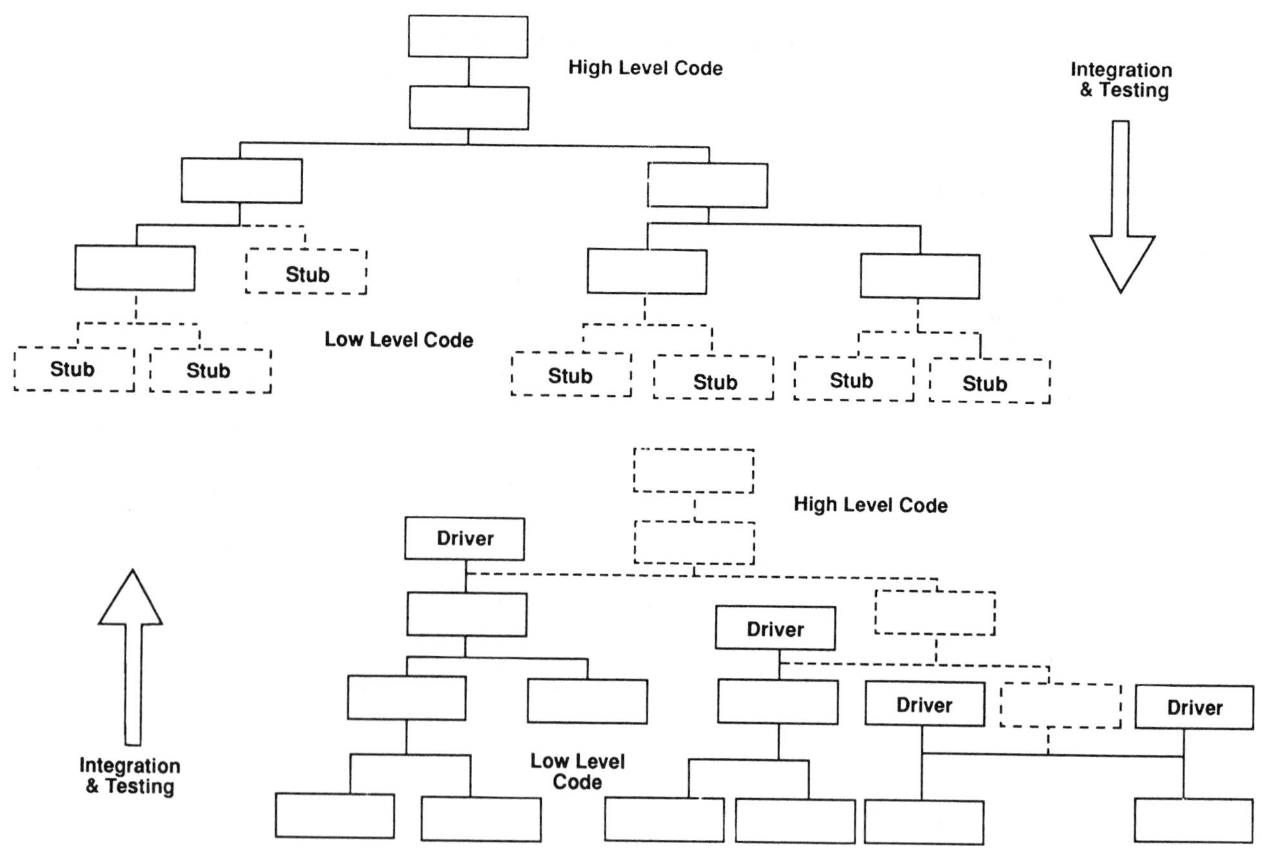

Figure 25: Top-down testing vs. bottom up testing

Table 4: Comparison of top-down vs. bottom-up testing [56]

Advantages	Disadvantages
Top-down testing	
1. More productive if major flaws occur toward the top of the program.	1. Stub modules must be produced.
2. Representation of test cases is easier.	2. Stub modules are often complicated.
3. Earlier skeletal programs allow demonstration (and improve morale)	3. The representation of test cases in stubs can be difficult.
	4. Observation of test output is more difficult.
Bottom-up testing	
1. More productive if major flaws occur toward the bottom of the program.	1. Driver modules must be produced.
2. Test conditions are easier to create.	2. The program as an entity does not exist until the last module is added.
3. Observation of test results is easier.	

mine if the final program properly implements the design. At roughly the same time, the software system is tested and validated against the original system and software requirements specification to see if the product was built correctly.

(32) Integrate the software system with the hardware components and conduct system validation in conformance with formal system verification, validation, and test documents.

In this process, the software system is integrated with the hardware components and system integration testing is conducted. This phase does not include acceptance testing unless requested and contracted for. System testing validates the entire software system against system and performance requirements using a simulated environment and contrived data. (Contrived data are better than "real" data for system testing. They provide "stress" data that might not be received from real sources except in the most unusual circumstances.)

When required, qualification or acceptance testing can be conducted by the customer, or by the developer for the customer, to demonstrate that the software meets its specified requirements. Acceptance testing validates the software against acceptance criteria in the users' environment with the final hardware-software configuration.

(33) Complete the users' manual, operator's manual, and maintenance manual.

The users' manual, operator's manual, and maintenance manual are also the products of the software development process. The users carry out the system functions; the operators are responsible for facility operation, recovery, periodic backup, and so forth.

The users' manual, described earlier, communicates with the users of the system and tells them how to use the software system. The users' manual would also include positional handbooks. The operator's manual provides instructions on how to operate the system. Operator's and users' manuals are frequently combined, particularly when intended for use with personal computers.

The users' manual is initiated during the software requirements generation phase primarily as a check on the software requirements specifications. The operator's and maintenance manuals are initiated during the software design phase. These manuals are reviewed, audited for accuracy, corrected where necessary, and delivered to the customer along with the finished software.

(34) Update the software product ("as-tested") baseline and place under configuration control.

During the software system testing phase, the requirements baselines and product baselines are updated to account for the changes in the system during the implementation and integration phases. The final product baseline is called the "as-tested" product baseline and placed under formal configuration control. This is the baseline that is carried forward to the operation and maintenance phase of the lifecycle.

(35) Review the products of the phase and obtain joint concurrence among developers, customers, and users.

The *formal qualification review* (FQR) is the test, inspection, or analytical process by which hardware/software products at the end-item level are verified to have met contractual performance requirements.

(36) Conduct final audits and reviews and "sell off" the product.

The *functional configuration audit* (FCA) is a formal examination of functional characteristics from test data for a hardware/software system prior to acceptance to verify that the item has achieved the performance specified in its requirements baselines. The *physical configuration audit* (PCA) is a formal examination of the configuration of a hardware/software system against its technical documentation in order to establish the product or operational baseline.

Functional and physical configuration audits are performed on all items of software and hardware. The functional configuration audit is conducted on the software at the completion of formal software testing. The physical configuration audit may be conducted at the completion of the formal software testing or after system integration and testing.

Upon concurrence of the customer, the final system is turned over to the customer for future installation and operation.

8. Summary and Conclusions

Conducting software engineering without conducting system engineering puts a project in jeopardy of not being able to be completed or the components not working together, and exceeding its cost and scheduled budget.

SE and SwSE are primarily disciplines used in the front end of the system lifecycle for technical planning and at the very late part of the lifecycle to verify if the plans have been met. A review of the emphasis in this paper will show that much of the work of planning and SE is done during the top-level requirements analysis and top-level design phases. The other major activity of SwSE is the final validation and testing of the completed system.

SE principles, activities, tasks, and procedures can be applied to software development. This paper summarizes, in broad steps, what is necessary to implement SwSE on either a hardware-software system (that is primarily software) or on an almost totally software system. SwSE is not cheap, but it is cost effective.

9. Additional Background Material

Additional background in SE and SwSE can be obtained from the following guides:

- *Military Standard: Defense System Software Development*, DOD-STD-2167A, Department of Defense, 29 February 1988
- DOD-STD-2167A, Data Item Descriptions, Department of Defense, 29 February 1988
- *System Engineering Management Guide*, 2nd edition, Defense Systems Management College, Technical Management Department, Fort Belvoir, VA, 1986

10. Acknowledgements

This paper was based on the *software systems engineering seminar*, given by Dr. Winston W. Royce to the "Management of Software Acquisition" course, Defense Systems Management College, Fort Belvoir, Virginia, during 1981–1988.

We would like to thank Dr. Kevin Forsberg for his contribution of system engineering lore to this paper, Dr. Merlin Dorfman for his reviews and contributions, Mr. J. Douglas Sailor (Lockheed) who provided insight into SE through his paper, and Ms. Kathy Tillett who did all the original figures. We also acknowledge the use of the *System Engineering Management Guide* as a major source of system engineering illustrations.

References

1. J.P. Newport, Jr., "A Growing Gap in Software," *Fortune*, 28 April 1986, pp. 132–142.
2. *DOD Computing Activities and Programs: Ten Year Market Forecast Issues 1985–1995*, Electronic Industries Association, 1985.
3. D.L. Parnas, "Software Aspects of Strategic Defense Systems," *American Scientist*, Vol. 73, September-October 1985, pp. 432–440.
4. J.P. Newport, Jr., "A Growing Gap in Software," *Fortune*, 28 April 1986, pp. 132–142.
5. MIL-STD-499A, *Engineering Management* (USAF), Department of Defense, May 1, 1974.
6. Adapted from J.D. Sailor, "System Engineering Overview," in *Tutorial: System and Software Requirements Engineering* , edited by R.H. Thayer and M. Dorfman, IEEE Computer Society Press, Washington DC, 1990.

7. W.W. Royce, "Managing the Development of Large Software Systems," *Proceedings, IEEE WESCON*, August 1970, pp. 1–9. Reprinted in *Tutorial: Software Engineering Project Management*, edited by R.H. Thayer, IEEE Computer Society Press, Washington DC, 1988.
8. P.C. Grabow and W.B. Noble, "Reusable Software Concepts and Software Development Methodology," *Proceedings, AIAA Computers in Aerospace V Conference,* 1985, pages 140–147. Reprinted in *Tutorial: Systems and Software Requirements Engineering,* edited by R.H. Thayer and M. Dorfman, IEEE Computer Society Press, Washington DC, 1990.
9. H. Gomaa, "The Impact of Prototyping on Software System Engineering," in *Tutorial: System and Software Requirements Engineering,* edited by R.H. Thayer and M. Dorfman, IEEE Computer Society Press, Washington DC, 1990.
10. B.W. Boehm, "A Spiral Model of Software Development and Enhancement," in *Tutorial: Software Engineering Project Management,* edited by R.H. Thayer, IEEE Computer Society Press, Washington DC, 1988. Also published in IEEE *Computer,* Vol. 21, No. 5, April 1988, pp. 61–72.
11. A.M. Davis, E.H. Bersoff, and E.R. Comer, "A Strategy for Comparing Alternative Software Development Lifecycle Models," *IEEE Transactions on Software Engineering,* Vol. 14, No. 10, October 1988, pp. 1453–1461. Reprinted in *Tutorial: System and Software Requirements Engineering,* edited by R.H. Thayer and M. Dorfman, IEEE Computer Society Press, 1990.
12. Adapted from *IEEE Standard Glossary of Software Engineering Terminology,* ANSI/IEEE Std 729–1983, IEEE, Inc., NY, 1983.
13. R.J. Lano, "A Structured Approach for Operational Concept Formulation," in *Tutorial: System and Software Requirements Engineering,* edited by R.H. Thayer and M. Dorfman, IEEE Computer Society Press, Washington DC, 1990.
14. J-M. Garot, D. Weathers, and T. Hawker, "Evaluating Proposed Architectures for the FAA's Advanced Automation System," *Computer*, Vol. 20, No. 2, February 1987.
15. *System Engineering Management Guide,* second edition, Defense Systems Management College, Technical Management Department, Fort Belvoir, VA, 1986.
16. C.H. Kepner and B.B. Tregoe, *The Rational Manager,* McGraw-Hill Book Company, NY, 1965.
17. D. King, *Current Practices in Software Development,* Yourdon Press, NY, 1984, p. 110.
18. *System Engineering Management Guide,* second edition, Defense Systems Management College, Technical Management Department, Fort Belvoir, VA, 1986.
19. *The STARTS Guide,* The National Computing Centre, Oxford, England, 1987.
20. J.D. Sailor, "System Engineering Overview," in *Tutorial: System and Software Requirements Engineering,* edited by R.H. Thayer and M. Dorfman, IEEE Computer Society Press, Washington DC, 1990.
21. *System Engineering Management Guide,* second edition, Defense Systems Management College, Technical Management Department, Fort Belvoir, VA, 1986.
22. R.E. Fairley, "A Guide for Preparing Software Project Management Plans," in *Tutorial: Software Engineering Project Management,* edited by R.H. Thayer, IEEE Computer Society Press, Washington DC, 1988.
23. B.W. Boehm, "Software Engineering Economics," *IEEE Transactions on Software Engineering,* Vol. SE-10, No. 1, January 1984, pp. 4–21. Reprinted in *Tutorial: Software Engineering Project Management,* edited by R.H. Thayer, IEEE Computer Society Press, Washington DC, 1988.
24. B.W. Boehm, *Software Engineering Economics*, Prentice-Hall, Inc., Englewood Cliffs, NJ, 1981.
25. ANSI/IEEE Std 729–1983, *IEEE Standard Glossary of Software Engineering Terminology,* IEEE, Inc., NY, 1983.
26. Adapted from *IEEE Standard for Software Quality Assurance Plans* (Draft), IEEE, Inc., NY, 1989.
27. *System Engineering Management Guide,* second edition, Defense Systems Management College, Technical Management Department, Fort Belvoir, VA, 1986.
28. *System Engineering Management Guide,* second edition, Defense Systems Management College, Technical Management Department, Fort Belvoir, VA, 1986.
29. D.R. Wallace and R.U. Fujii, *Software Verification and Validation: Its Role in Computer Assurance and Its Relationship with Software Project Management Standards,* National Institute of Standards and Technology (NIST) Special Publication 500–165, May 1989.
30. Adapted from J.M. Bunyard and J.M Coward, "Today's Risks in Software Development—Can They Be Significantly Reduced?" *Concepts: Journal of Defense Systems Acquisition Management,* Vol. 5, No. 4, August 1982, pages 73–94. Reprinted in *Tutorial: Software Engineering Project Management*, edited by R.H. Thayer, IEEE Computer Society Press, Washington D.C., 1988.
31. *Guideline for Lifecycle Validation, Verification, and Testing of Computer Software,* Federal Information

Processing Standards Publication 101, U.S. Government Printing Office, Washington DC, June 6, 1983.

32. D.R. Wallace and R.U. Fujii, *Software Verification and Validation: Its Role in Computer Assurance and Its Relationship with Software Project Management Standards,* National Institute of Standards and Technology (NIST) Special Publication 500–165, May 1989.

33. ANSI/IEEE Std 830–1984, *IEEE Guide for Software Requirements Specifications,* IEEE, Inc., NY, 1984.

34. AFR 800–14, *Lifecycle Management of Computer Resources in Systems,* U.S. Air Force, 14 September 1987.

35. E.D. Nelsen, "System Engineering and Requirement Allocation" in R.H. Thayer and M. Dorfman (eds,) *Tutorial: System and Software Engineering Requirements,* IEEE Computer Society Press, Washington, DC, 1990.

36. DOD Directive 5010.19, *Configuration Management,* U.S. Department of Defense, October 28, 1987.

37. E.H. Bersoff, "Elements of Software Configuration Management," *IEEE Transactions on Software Engineering,* Vol. SE-10, No. 1, January 1984, pp. 79–87. Reprinted in *Tutorial: System and Software Requirements Engineering,* edited by R.H. Thayer and M. Dorfman, IEEE Computer Society Press, Washington DC, 1990.

38. *System Engineering Management Guide,* second edition, Defense Systems Management College, Technical Management Department, Fort Belvoir, VA, 1986.

39. DOD Directive 5010.19, *Configuration Management,* U.S. Department of Defense, October 28, 1987.

40. H. Gomaa, "The Impact of Prototyping on Software System Engineering," in *Tutorial: System and Software Requirements Engineering,* edited by R.H. Thayer and M. Dorfman, IEEE Computer Society Press, Washington DC, 1990.

41. ANSI/IEEE Std 830–1984, *IEEE Guide for Software Requirements Specifications,* IEEE, Inc., NY, 1984.

42. S.E. Keller, L.G. Kahn, and R.B. Panara, "Specifying Software Quality Requirements with Metrics. " in *Tutorial: Systems and Software Requirements Engineering,* edited by R.H. Thayer and M. Dorfman, IEEE Computer Society Press, Washington DC, 1990.

43. P. Zave, "A Comparison of the Major Approaches to Software Specifications and Design," in *Tutorial: System and Software Requirements Engineering,* edited by R.H. Thayer and M. Dorfman, IEEE Computer Society Press, Washington DC, 1990.

44. R.F. Flynn and M. Dorfman, "The Automated Requirements Traceability System (ARTS): An Experience of 8 Years," in *Tutorial: System and Software Requirements Engineering,* edited by R.H. Thayer and M. Dorfman, IEEE Computer Society Press, Washington DC, 1990.

45. N.R. Howes, "On Using the Users' Manual as the Requirements Specification II," in *Tutorial: System and Software Requirements Engineering,* edited by R.H. Thayer and M. Dorfman, IEEE Computer Society Press, Washington DC, 1990.

46. ANSI/IEEE STD-829–1983, *IEEE Standard for Software Test Documents,* IEEE, Inc., NY, 1983.

47. ANSI/IEEE STD-1012–1986, *Standard for Software Verification and Validation Plans,* IEEE, Inc., NY, 1986.

48. MIL-STD 1521B (USAF), *Technical Reviews and Audits for Systems, Equipment, and Computer Programs (proposed revision), Joint Policy Coordination Group on Computer Resource Management,* 1985.

49. M. Page-Jones, *The Practical Guide to Structured Systems Design,* Yourdon Press, NY, 1980.

50. W.P. Stevens, G.L. Myers, and L.L. Constantine, "Structured Design," *IBM Systems Journal,* Vol. 13, No. 2, 1974, pp. 115–139.

51. F.S. Ingrassia, "The Unit Development Folder (UDF): A Ten-Year Perspective," in *Tutorial: Software Engineering Project Management,* edited by R.H. Thayer, IEEE Computer Society Press, Washington DC, 1988.

52. ANSI/IEEE STD 1016–1987, *IEEE Recommended Practices for Software Design Description.* IEEE, Inc., NY, 1987.

53. R.J. Martin and W.M. Osborne, *Guidance on Software Maintenance,* National Bureau of Standards Reports on Computer Science and Technology, NBS Special Publication 500–106, U.S. Government Printing Office, Washington DC, December 1983.

54. ANSI/IEEE STD-1012–1986, *Standard for Software Verification and Validation Plans,* IEEE, Inc., NY, 1986.

55. ANSI/IEEE STD-1012–1986, *Standard for Software Verification and Validation Plans,* IEEE, Inc., NY, 1986.

56. G.J. Myers, *The Art of Software Testing,* John Wiley & Sons, NY, 1979.

Chapter 3: Software Requirements Analysis and Specifications

1: Introduction

Software requirements can be defined in a number of different ways [1]:

- a software capability needed by a user to solve a problem or achieve an objective
- a software capability that must be met or possessed by a system or system component to satisfy a contract, standard, specification, or other formally imposed document
- a short description sometimes used in place of the term "software requirements specifications"

Software requirements analysis is the process of studying user needs to arrive at a definition of software requirements. A *software requirements specification* is the document that clearly and precisely describes each of the essential requirements (functions, performance, design constraints, and quality attributes) of the software and its external interfaces. Each requirement should be defined in such a way that its achievement is capable of being objectively verified by a prescribed method, for example, by test, demonstration, analysis, or inspection. [2]

Chapter 3 contains papers on "classic" software requirements analysis and the five types of requirements—functional, performance, external interfaces, design constraints, and quality metrics—as well as an approach to representing a software requirements specification by a users' manual. The chapter also contains the most popular standard in software engineering: the IEEE/ANSI *Guide to Software Requirements Specifications.* This chapter looks at software requirements from the basic premise that the analysis determines what the customer needs, and specifications document these needs. This view holds regardless of the tools and methodology used to arrive at the needs and specifications.

2: Description of Papers

The first paper in this chapter is "The Analysis and Specification of System and Software Requirements" by Al Davis. Davis, a prolific writer and lecturer in software requirements and chair of the IEEE Working Group for the *"Guide to Software Requirements Specifications,"* prepared the paper especially for this tutorial. He excerpted

some of this material from his forthcoming book, *Software Requirements: Analysis and Specification.* [3]

Davis's paper:

- defines the difference between requirements and design
- resolves the "what versus how" dilemma
- defines and shows how to put into practice the system engineering concepts of partitioning, abstraction, and projection
- describes the analysis tools and methods of structured requirements definition, Structured Analysis and Design Technique (SADT™), structured analysis and system specification (also called the Yourdon technique or the DeMarco technique), and PSL/PSA (Problem Statement Language/Problem Statement Analyzer). [4]
- describes how to write a "good" requirements specification

The second paper, "Specifying Software Quality Requirements with Metrics" by Steven Keller, Laurence Kahn, and Roger Panara, defines and gives an excellent example of software requirements quality metrics. The paper defines the many overlapping and sometimes apparently contradictory terms used in the area of software quality metrics. It describes direct and indirect metrics as a means of measuring quality. The paper also provides, in an appendix, an overview and example of the U.S. Air Force Rome Air Development Center (RADC) [5] methodology for specifying software quality requirements. The appendix illustrates the considerations and decisions involved in defining and measuring software quality.

The third paper, "On Using the Users' Manual as the Requirements' Specification" by Norm Howes, also concerns software requirements specifications and takes a unique approach to determining the project's objectives. Howes recommends preparing a users' manual as a substitute for the software requirements specifications, as he did in this case study for a NASA application. The reader may wish to compare Howes's approach with Lano's CONOPS, described in the preceding chapter. Both approaches seek to communicate with the user by means of a document that is easier for the user to understand than a requirements specification.

The last paper is a copy of ANSI/IEEE Standard 830-1984, *IEEE Guide to Software Requirements Specifications.* This guide is an outstanding thesis on what a software requirement specification should contain. This guide was written by the Working Group for Software Requirements Specifications, Software Engineering Standards Subcommittee of the Technical Committee on Software Engineering of the IEEE Computer Society, chaired by Al Davis. Its purpose was to provide an outline for a software requirements specification and to describe a "good" software requirements specification. The Guide describes several alternative approaches to specifying software requirements. The Guide is general in nature and does not suggest the hierarchy of software requirements specifications.

The Guide contains criteria that may be used in evaluating a software requirements specification. The criteria are based on the concept that a specification should be unambiguous, complete, verifiable, consistent, modifiable, traceable, and usable during operations and maintenance.

3: References

[1] Adapted from *IEEE Standard Glossary of Software Engineering Terminology,* ANSI/IEEE Std 729-1983, IEEE, Inc., NY, 1983.

[2] ANSI/IEEE Std 830-1984, *IEEE Guide to Software Requirements Specifications,* IEEE, Inc., NY, 1984. Reprinted in *Tutorial: System and Software Requirements Engineering,* edited by R.H. Thayer and M. Dorfman, IEEE Computer Society, Washington, DC, 1989.

[3] Davis, A.M., *Software Requirements: Analysis and Specification,* Prentice-Hall, Englewood Cliffs, NJ, 1989.

[4] Papers devoted to the details of some of these techniques can be found elsewhere in this tutorial.

[5] Bowen, T.P., G.B. Wigle, and J.T. Tsai, *Specification of Software Quality Attributes, Final Technical Report.* Volume I; *Software Quality Specifications Guidebook,* Volume II; *Software Quality Evaluation Guidebook,* Volume III; *RADC-TR-85-37,* prepared by Boeing Aerospace Company for Rome Air Development Center, Griffiss AFB, NY, Feb. 1985.

The Analysis and Specification of Systems and Software Requirements*

Alan M. Davis

1: Introduction

1.1: Role of Requirements in the Lifecycle

There is general agreement among software engineers and researchers that an early stage of the software development lifecycle called "requirements" exists. Furthermore, most people would define the requirements stage as when developers or analysts define *what* the system should do without describing *how* it should do it. Unfortunately, there is little agreement beyond this concerning what requirements are. For the purpose of this paper, the term "requirements" will refer to all project activities occurring before the decomposition of a system into its actual constituent components (i.e., prior to what most people call "design"). Within this so-called requirements stage, there are four distinct types of activities.

1. *Problem analysis,* during which one tries to understand fully *what* the problem being solved is without defining *how* it will be solved;
2. *External product description,* during which one fully documents *what* the expected external behavior of the product to be built is, without defining *how* it will work internally;
3. *System design,* during which the major hardware subsystems and their interrelationships are defined;
4. *Software requirements specification,* which is performed independently for each of the software-bearing major subsystems defined during system design. This activity includes the complete documentation of *what* the software does externally without regard to *how* it works internally.

As described by Davis, there is little uniformity in terminology for these activities [Davis 1988a]. For example, "problem analysis" is also called analysis [Freeman 1983], requirements analysis [Charette 1986, Pressman 1982, Wasserman et al. 1986], problem definition [Roman 1984], requirements definition [Berzins and Gray 1985], and the pragmatic phase [Kerola and Freeman 1981]. The description of the product's external behavior is also called requirements [Alford 1977, Boehm 1976, Searle 1981], system design [Roman 1984], functional specification [Berzins and Gray 1985], external design [Wasserman et al. 1986], system segment specification [DoD 1988], and the input/output perspective [Kerola and Freeman 1981]. "System design" is also called system/software design documentation [DoD 1988]. "Software requirements specification" [IEEE 1984, Pressman 1982] is also called specification [Charette 1986], requirements [Glaseman and Davis 1980], and software requirements analysis [DoD 1988].

The purpose of this paper is to survey the issues, techniques, and tools that relate to the first, second, and fourth of the above four activities (the third is excluded because it is generally considered a design activity rather than a requirements activity. However, interested readers may want to refer to any of a number of recent extensions to requirements techniques to accommodate system design [Alford 1985, Sutcliffe 1988, Zave 1982]).

So far, Section 1 has introduced terminology and has defined the scope of this paper. The remainder of Section 1 will explore the problem of understanding why it is so difficult to reach agreement on what the *requirements* phase includes. Section 2 will explore the problem analysis domain. Section 3 will explore the domain of describing external behavior of either systems or software. Section 4 is a summary.

1.2: The Requirements of Definition Problem

As previously mentioned, most people agree that the requirements stage defines *what* a system should do without describing *how* it should do it. This sounds like an easy, unambiguous definition; however, it is fraught with ambiguity, which stems from the fact that system development is an iterative process in which every step defines the "requirements" for the next step. As a result, our selection of where the software lifecycle phase "requirements" ends and the next one begins is quite fuzzy. There are three factors to consider when determining what the scope of "requirements" will be for any particular project or standard:

*Much of the material in this paper has been excerpted from a book by the author titled *Software Requirements: Analysis and Specification,* Prentice-Hall, Englewood Cliffs, New Jersey, 1990. The original material was supported by the Commonwealth of Virginia Center for Innovative Technology Grant #STC-87-002.

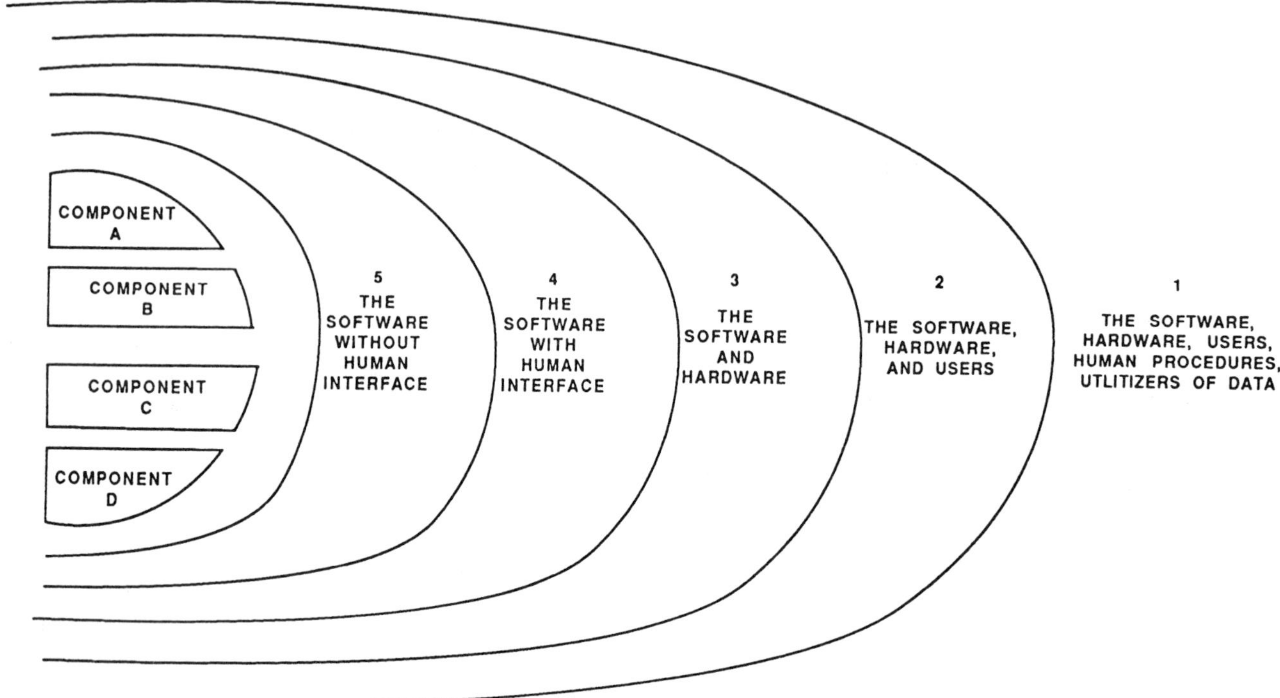

Figure 1: What is the system?

- definition of the "system"
- level of abstraction
- the *what* versus *how* dilemma

These three factors are discussed in the following paragraphs.

The first factor is the use of the term "system," or the thing that we are analyzing or specifying. Figure 1 shows a number of levels at which we can define the "system." If the system is defined as level 1, then the requirements analysis and specification of that system deals with the general information flow between that system (including software, hardware, users, and human procedures) and its environment. For example, if dealing with a payroll system, then those information flows might include:

- paychecks
- terminations
- new hirings
- system user functions
- raises
- promotions
- employee status changes

Notice that is this case, the "users" are actually the paycheck recipients. If the system is defined as level 2, then the requirements analysis and specification deals with the interface between the physical (i.e., software and hardware) system and its users (i.e., the people who operate the payroll system). In the case of the payroll system, the relevant information flows might include:

- size of screens
- size of keyboard
- educational level of users
- variety of user experience
- need to perform certain actions in certain orders
- illegal sequences of actions
- meaning of particular keyboard key presses

If the system is defined at level 3, the interface to the environment (i.e., the hardware) includes:

- software commands to manipulate the hardware (e.g., erase screen and define window)
- timing considerations
- screen formats
- error messages
- command formats and sequences

If the system is defined at level 4, the relevant interfaces include:

- standard graphics package interfaces
- operating system interfaces
- message buffering protocols.

Thus, depending on where you define your system to be, you will end up with very different results. The most common use of the term "system requirements" is to connote levels 1 or 2; the most common use of the term "software requirements" is to connote level 3.

The second factor deals with differences in levels of abstraction. For example, when defining a telephone system, we could define the requirements very abstractly:

- to provide a means for voice communication

or we could define them less abstractly:

- provide local calls, long distance calls, call forwarding, etc.

We could define them even less abstractly as the following:

- Provide long distance calls via the following sequence: 9-1-area code-exchange-phone #
- provide call forwarding via . . . .

or less abstractly yet for a long distance call:

- lift phone
- hear dial-tone within 5 seconds
- dial 9
- hear distinctive dial-tone within 5 seconds
- dial 1
- remove tones
- dial 10-digit phone #
- IF called party is busy
  - — THEN hear busy-tone
  - — ELSE hear ring-back-tone

or even less abstractly:

- phone is idle
- IF calling-party lifts phone
- THEN IF no tone generator available
  - — THEN reorder tone
- ELSE dial-tone within 5 seconds
  - — IF calling party dials 9
  - — THEN .

.

.

As you can readily see, all of the above levels of abstraction remain at the level of the external view of the system but their level of abstraction differ.

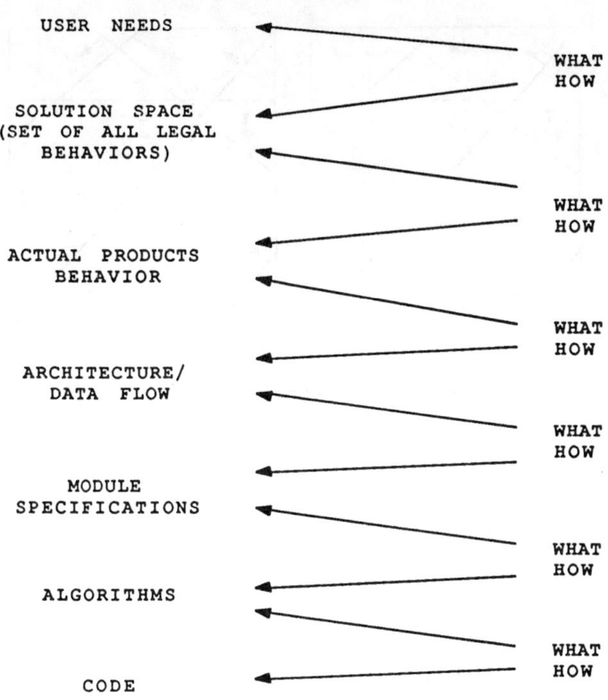

Figure 2: The "what vs. the how" dilemma

The third factor relates to what has been called the "what versus how" dilemma [Davis 1988a] and is characterized as "Each person's *how* is the next person's *what*." As shown in Figure 2 [Davis 1988a], user needs definition establishes the overall mission to be automated. The product space definition establishes the range of all possible solutions to the problem of satisfying the user needs. Next, we must define the desired external behavior of the desired system to be built or otherwise obtained. It is only after all of these have been defined that we can venture into defining the actual constituent components of the design of the real system.

It is because of the above three dimensions of acceptable flexibility in the definition of "requirements" that there is so little agreement among practitioners or researchers concerning what "requirements" really are.

2: Problem Analysis

2.1: Introduction

During the early stages of the "requirements" stage (regardless of definition), it is a necessity to analyze, and thus begin to understand, the problem to be solved. At this early stage, we often may not know if the eventual solution will be realized in hardware, software, or a combination.

Problem analysis is the activity that encompasses learning about the problem to be solved (often through brainstorming

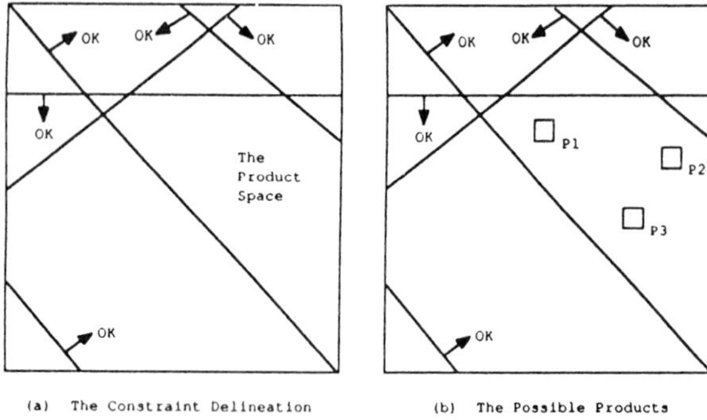

Figure 3: The product space

and/or questioning), understanding the needs of the potential users, trying to find out who the user really is, and understanding all the constraints upon the solution. Problem analysis can be thought of as defining the product space (i.e., the range of all possible solutions). The product space is that range of problem solutions that meets all known constraints. The sources of constraints might include users, customers, developers, technology, laws, and standards [Cronhjort and Gallmo 1982].

Figure 3a shows the goal of problem analysis; namely, to define the product space, where the product space defines the range of products that would satisfy all of the constraints (in this case, five) upon the solution. Within this range, any product P_i (see Figure 3b) would be an acceptable product; each might exhibit a different external behavior but each would satisfy all constraints.

2.2: Principles of Partitioning, Abstraction and Projection

There are at least two contrasting schools of thought on how to approach problem analysis, the functional and the object oriented. In the functional world, the problem domain is analyzed from the perspective of functions that must be provided to solve those problems. Most of the analysis deals with functions (or processes) and data or control flows between and among those functions. In the object-oriented world, the problem domain is analyzed from the perspective of objects in the application domain. Most of the analysis deals with objects; classes of objects; attributes of objects; information passed between objects; relationships between objects; and services provided by, or for, objects. In either world, any of the subjects of analysis can be described at many levels of detail. For example, functions can be described at any level from the very abstract (e.g., provide voice communications) to the very specific (e.g., the local call shall be operated by pressing the "X" button). Data items can be described at any level from the very abstract (e.g., payroll data) to the very specific (e.g., John Doe's annual salary for 1990). Objects can be described at any level from the very abstract (e.g., vehicles) to the very specific (e.g., 1990 BMW 750iL).

Because there are so many relationships that can exist between items under analysis and so many levels of possible detail, analysts need techniques to organize the plethora of information that surfaces. In particular, what is needed is a *knowledge structure,* which is just a structured collection of concepts and their interrelationships.

To provide a better understanding of this "knowledge structure," let us look at an example: an elevator control system for a 20-story building. During the early discussions, somebody may make the comment, "The ergonomics of the control system are important." Later, somebody else may say, "It is important for passengers restricted to wheel chairs to be able to reach the control panel," and "The buttons should be labeled with the floor numbers." The latter two comments are subordinate to the former or are at a lower level of abstraction. Thus, what we have is an information tree such as that shown in Figure 4a. Later, two additional comments are made: "We must address the handling of emergencies," and "The software shall control the temperature." These are then added to the tree (see Figure 4b). By using such a tree, we can easily locate underspecified areas of the software requirements (in this case, details of emergency handling), potentially overspecified areas (subtrees with many more small branches than other subtrees), and failures to raise sufficiently abstract concepts (in this case, environmental control is a missing main branch between the trunk and the temperature control). As particular sections of the problem become well understood, it is often time to define the specific behavior of that aspect of the software solution in the software requirements specification (SRS).

Yeh and Zave [Yeh and Zave 1980] were the first to isolate partitioning, abstraction, and projection as three underlying principles of structuring used during problem analysis. Usually analysts are no more aware of their use than speakers are consciously aware that they are using a noun or a verb. Just as speakers simply speak, analysts simply analyze.

Partitioning captures the "aggregation/part of" structural relation among entities or problems in the real world. It is used when it is difficult or impossible to describe a problem or its solution any way except in terms of its parts. For example, let's say we want to understand the problem of defending a nation against ballistic missiles. It is quite difficult to comprehend the entire problem, so instead we describe it in terms of its parts, which might be target detection, communication, intelligence gathering and resolution, defensive weapon launch, and defensive weapon

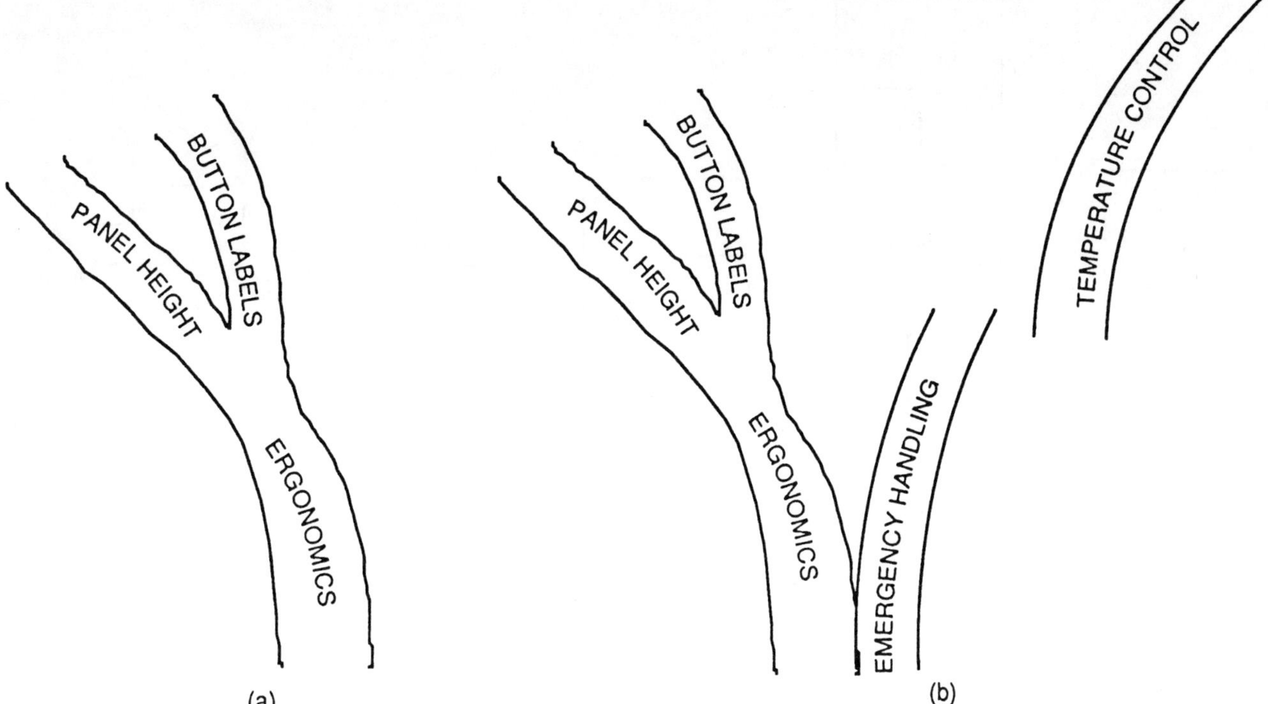

Figure 4: The knowledge tree of the elevator

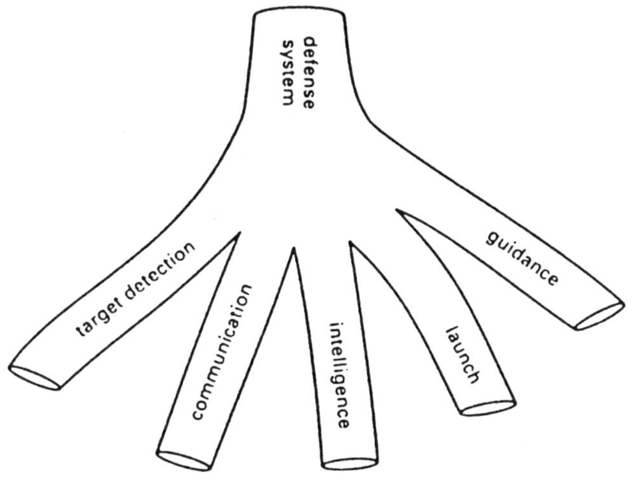

Figure 5: Partitioning example

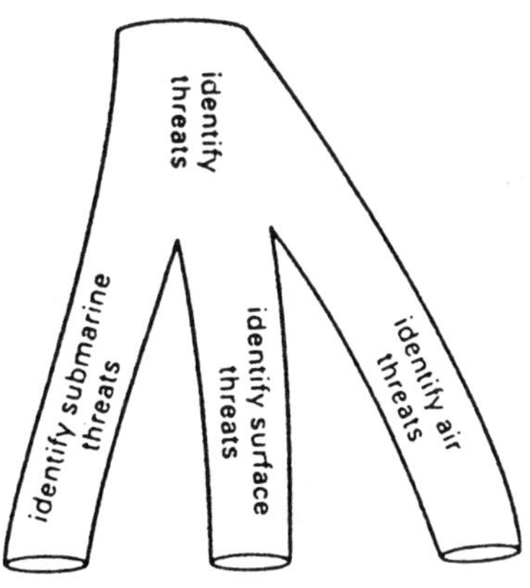

Figure 6: Abstraction example

guidance. Note that this is not a design; we have simply decomposed the problem into five subproblems for analysis. When the real system is finally built, it could be composed of any number of subcomponents with little or no relationship to these subproblems. If we had analyzed each of the parts separately, we could then extrapolate and conclude that the entire problem is the union of the five subproblems, as shown in Figure 5.

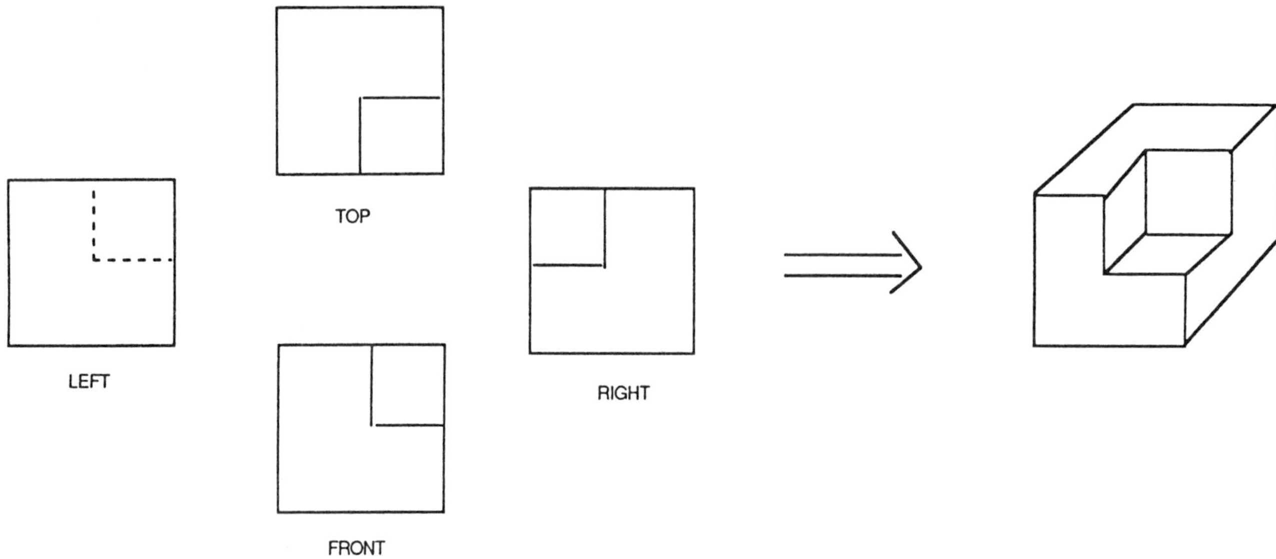

Figure 7: Analogy for projection

Abstraction captures the "general/specific" structural relation among entities or problems in the real world. When using abstraction, we define some aspect of the problem in abstract terms, and provide more details in association with particular instances of that abstract concept. For example, we may define the function of identifying threats and recognize that there are three kinds: identifying submarine threats, identifying surface threats, and identifying air threats, as shown in Figure 6.

Projection is yet another approach to structuring aspects of some problems and is defined as describing the system from multiple viewpoints. It is analogous to using two-dimensional diagrams to specify an object, as in Figure 7. One example of using it during analysis is when the analyst for an elevator control system system steps back and says, "Let's look at the elevator from the perspectives of the passenger, the maintenance person, and the fireperson." Another example occurs during the analysis of the external behavior of a telephone switching system for the "call waiting" feature. This is the feature for which subscribing parties would be notified by a clicking sound in their receiver during a phone call whenever another party tries to call them. Trying to describe the complete external behavior from a global viewpoint is quite tedious and error prone. On the other hand, describing the desired behavior from the perspectives of each of the three involved parties is much more straightforward, as shown in Figure 8. In this figure, assume parties A and B are having a conversation, and party A receives another incoming call from party C. The behavior of call waiting in Figure 8 is shown in the style of the system definition language (SDL) [Rockstrom and Saracco 1982].

In summary, partitioning, abstraction, and projection can each be used in a top-down or a bottom-up manner. All define structural relationships between objects, tasks, functions, or data. Recording the fact that *A* is subordinate to *B* means different things when using the three techniques. In partitioning, it means *A* is a part of *B*; in abstraction, it means that *A* is an example of *B* and thus inherits all of *B*'s attributes; in projection, it means that *A* is one view of *B*.

2.3: Evaluation Criteria

Many analysts simply analyze a problem randomly by asking questions, writing down the answers, asking other questions, etc. The primary advantage of applying a technique to problem analysis is that it simplifies the task. But analysts do not need simplification of the easy parts of their job; they need simplification of the following difficult parts:

- organizing all the information
- relating different people's perspectives
- surfacing and resolving conflicts
- avoiding design

Organizational aids are important because, during the analysis of a nontrivial problem, reams of information about the problem are generated. During problem analysis, different people may have very different views of the problem. It is important to be able to track these different perspectives and to relate them to one another. When these perspectives

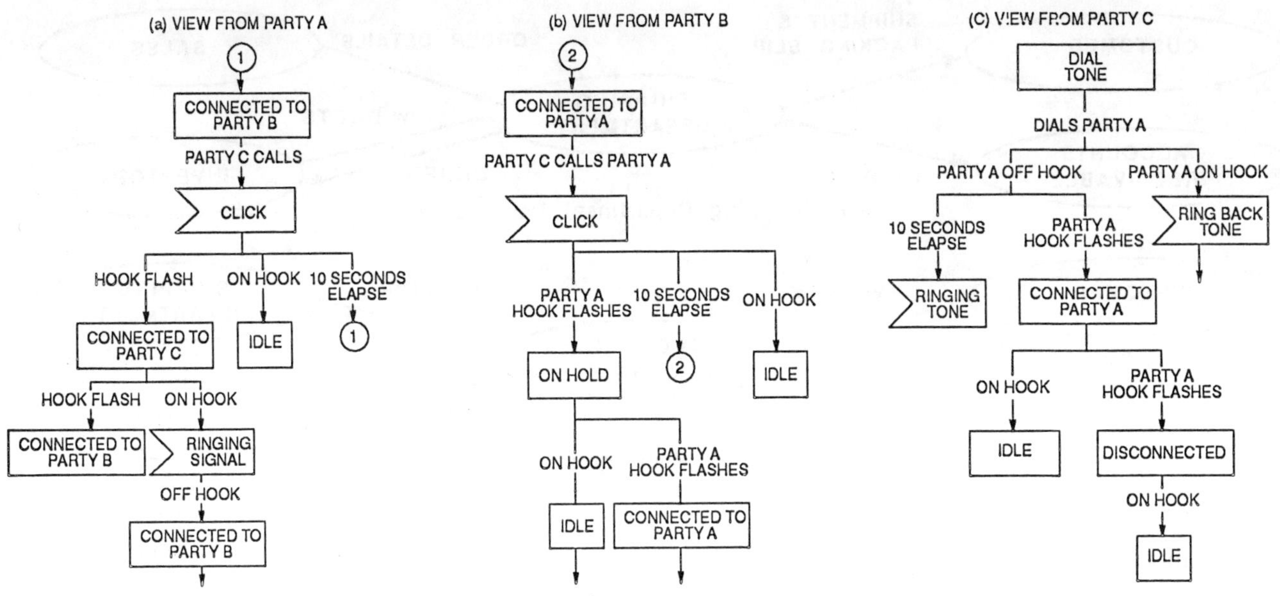

Figure 8: Projection example

Stage		Aspect	Primary Activity		Primary Goal
System Requirements	<	Problem Analysis	Decomposition	>	Understanding
		Writing an SSS	Behavior Description		
System Design	—	Defining System Components	Decomposition	—	Optimization
Software Requirements	—	Writing the SRS	Behavior Description	—	Understanding
Software Design	<	Preliminary Design	Decomposition	>	Optimization
		Detailed Design	Behavior Description		

Figure 9: Similarities between requirements and design

are in conflict, a quality problem analysis technique will surface the conflict to resolve it rather than to bury it.

Perhaps the most difficult aspects of problem analysis is avoiding falling into design. If we examine the requirements and design stages of the system development lifecycle as shown in Figure 9, we see that problem analysis is primarily a decomposition process: decomposing problems into subproblems to understand the entire problem at hand. System design is also primarily a decomposition process: decomposing the overall system into its primary hardware subsystems. Preliminary design is also primarily a decomposition process: decomposing software components into smaller software components to generate an optimal design that meets all the software requirements. From a technique or tool point of view, decomposition is decomposition regardless of the "material" being decomposed. As a result, most problem analysis techniques and tools are equally effective during system and preliminary design. There is, however, a very good reason for performing them each independently and not mixing the three. Remember that the problem analysis goal is understanding, and the system design and preliminary design goals are optimization (e.g., of perform-

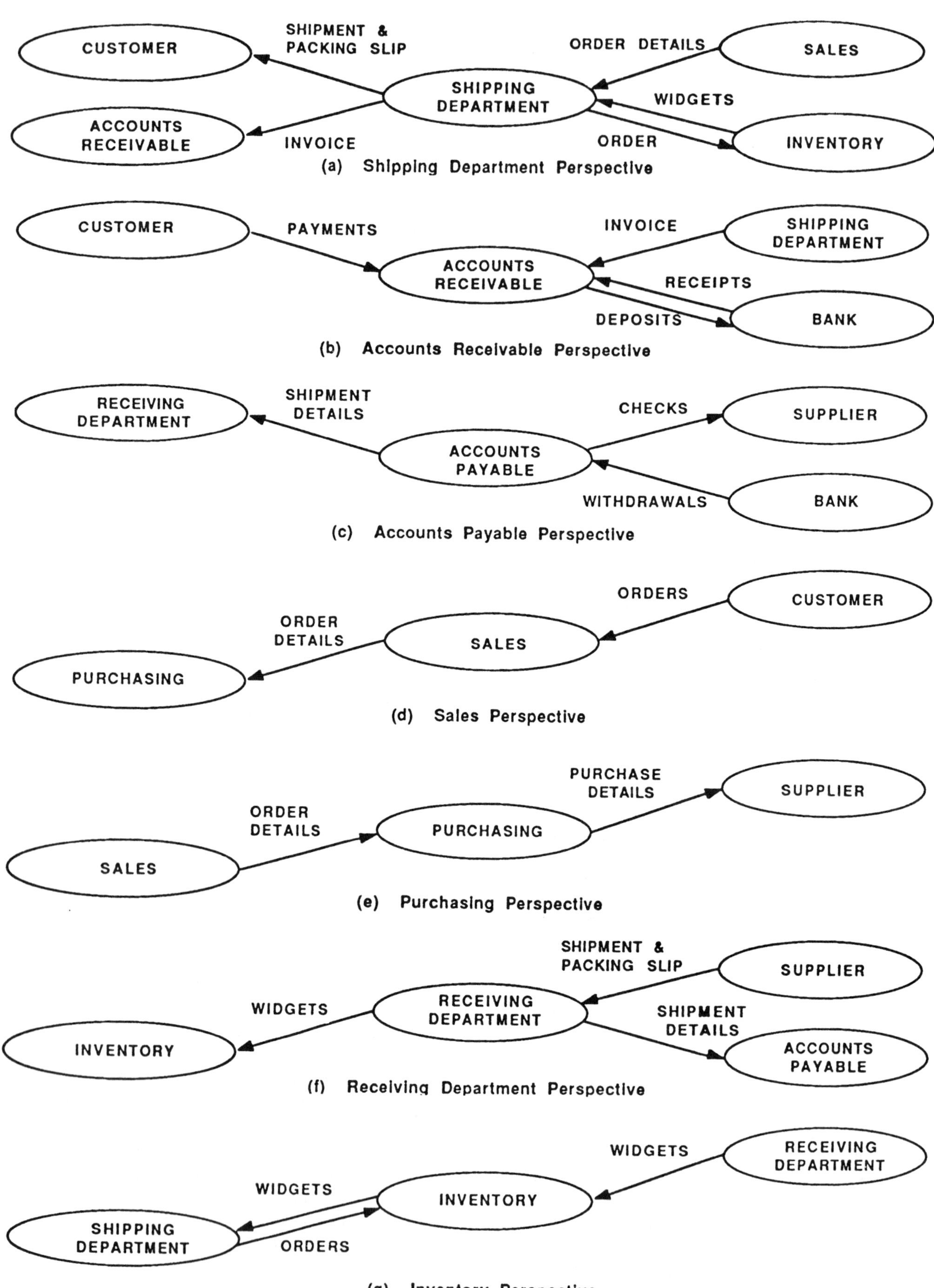

Figure 10: Sample entity diagrams

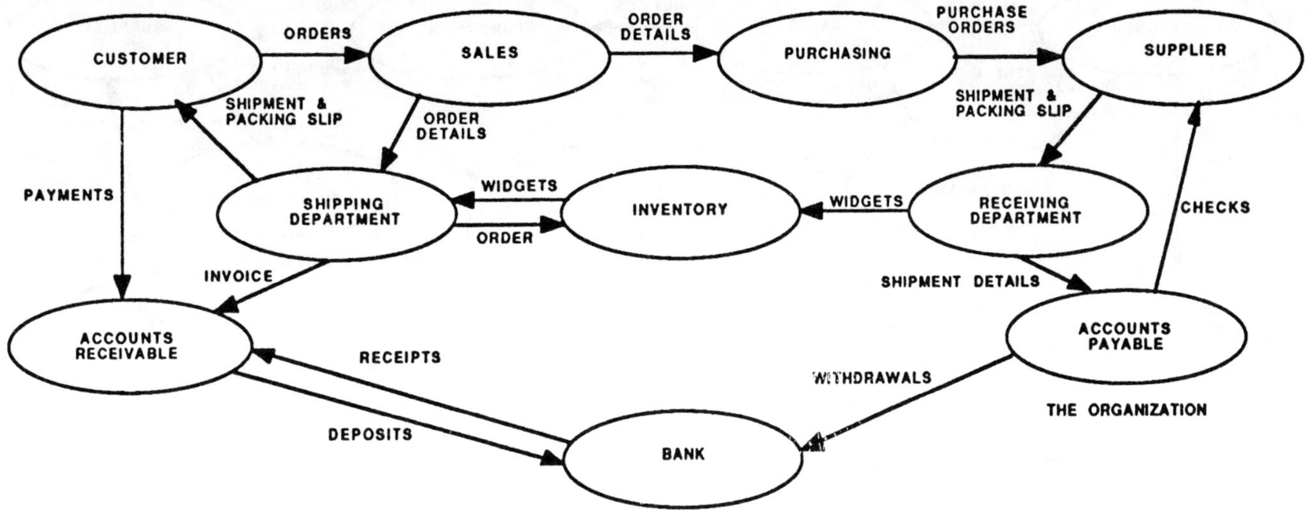

Figure 11: The integrated entity diagram

ance or maintainability). For critical applications, system and preliminary design might consume 25 to 30 percent of the total project resources. A project team certainly cannot afford to spend so much money during the requirements stage—especially not before the team even knows what system it is going to build (i.e., there are no requirements specifications yet).

The traits that we would like to see a problem analysis technique exhibit are the following:

1. facilitate communication (probably via an easy-to-understand language)
2. provide a means of defining the system boundary (as defined in subsection 1.2)
3. provide a means of defining partitions, abstractions, and projections
4. encourage the analyst to think and document the problem (i.e., the application) rather than the solution (i.e., the hardware and/or software)
5. allow for opposing alternatives but alert the analyst to their presence.
6. make it easy to modify the knowledge structure

As you read the following sections of this paper, remember the following points:

- different kinds of problems require different kinds of techniques
- different aspects of any particular problem may require different kinds of techniques
- there are no panaceas

This means that to be effective, we need to know when and how to apply the appropriate technique at the correct time.

2.4: Brief Survey of Techniques

In this section, the five following techniques are briefly described:

- structured requirements definition
- structured analysis by Ross
- structured analysis by DeMarco
- PSL/PSA™ by Teichroew.
- object–oriented analysis by Coad

2.4.1: Structured Requirements Definition (SRD)

In his book on requirements definition, Orr describes a methodology to learn the complete set of inputs and outputs [Orr 1981]. He calls the methodology "defining the application context." It is a multistep process as follows:

Step 1. *Define a user-level entity diagram:* This step requires the analyst to interview each individual who is currently performing some task within an organization and thus to learn what that individual receives as inputs and generates as outputs. Record the inputs and outputs for each individual in an entity diagram, an example of which appears in Figure 10.

Step 2. *Define a combined user-level entity diagram:* Merge all like bubbles in the individual entity diagrams to create one integrated diagram. As this is done, inconsistencies in perspectives will likely be detected. After resolving such differences of opinion, create the single integrated entity diagram, as shown in Figure 11.

PSL/PSA™ is a trademark of Meta Systems, Inc.

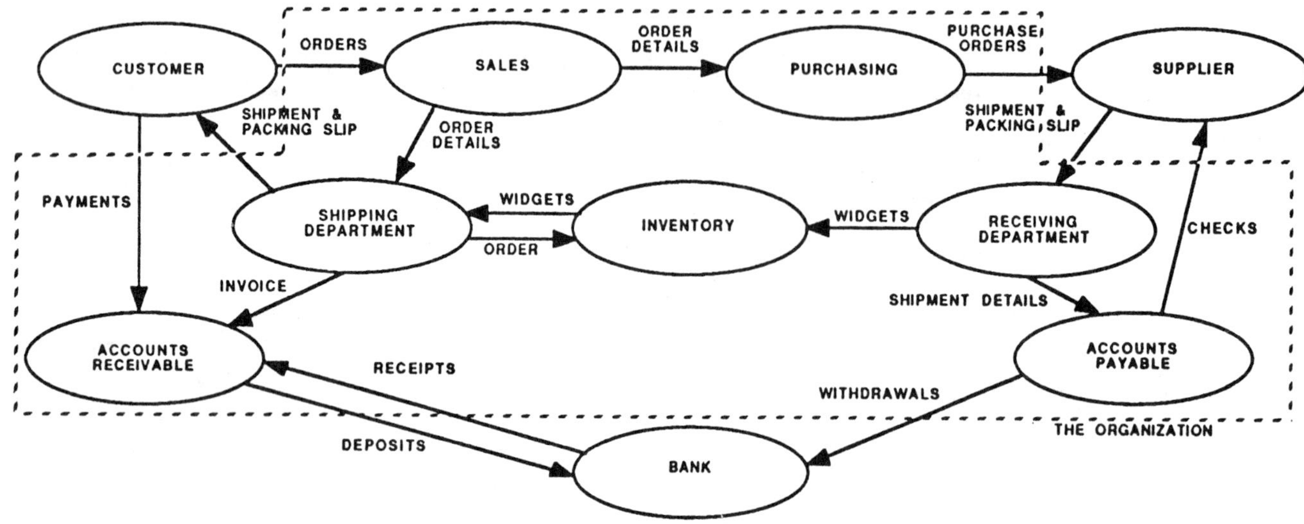

(a) Draw a Dotted Line Around the Organization

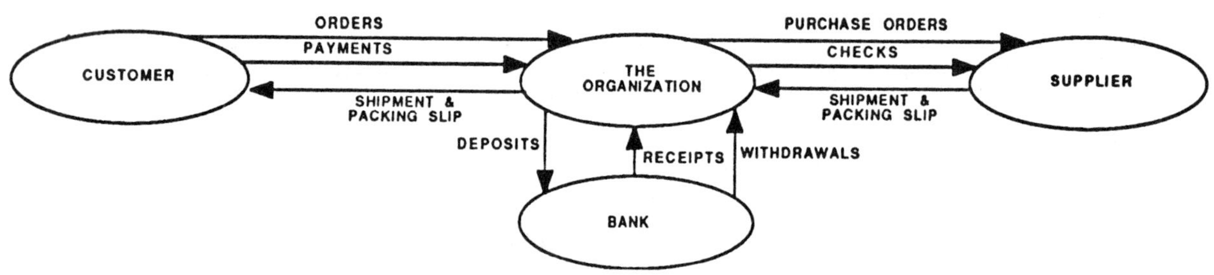

(b) Collapse the Dotted Area Down into One Ellipse

Figure 12: Defining the application using SRD

Step 3. *Define the application-level entity diagram:* Draw a dotted line around that part of the diagram that corresponds to the "organization" or "system" under analysis. Then, collapse the area surrounded by the dotted line into a single ellipse, as shown in Figures 12a and 12b. This results in a definition of all external system inputs and outputs.

2.4.2: Structured Analysis and Design Technique

The Structured Analysis and Design Technique (SADT)™ was developed in the early 1970s by Doug Ross at SofTech, Inc. [Ross 1977]. The most popular aspects of SADT have been thoroughly described by Marca and McGowan [Marca and McGowan 1988]. It is Ross's view that nature by itself has no problems; that a problem is only that which a human understands is a problem. The only way to express a problem (and of course any solution to that problem) is in terms of natural language, for by definition natural language *is* the language that is natural for humans (who *are* the only parties who perceive the problem). However, since natural language is inherently ambiguous it might be necessary but it is certainly not sufficient. Therefore, SADT uses a non-ambiguous graphical notation in which natural language is embedded. The graphical notation provides for projection, abstraction, and partitioning.

Using, SADT, a model of the problem is constructed. The model is composed of a hierarchy of diagrams. Each diagram is composed of boxes and arrows. The uppermost diagram, called the *context diagram* defines the problem

---

SADT™ is a registered trademark of SofTech, Inc.

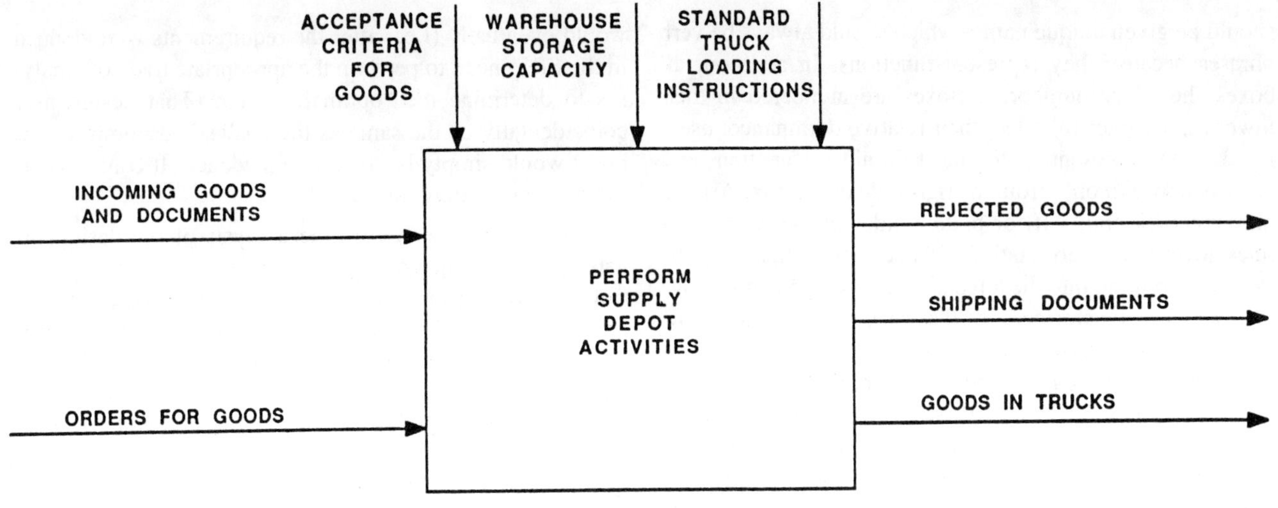

Figure 13: An SADT example

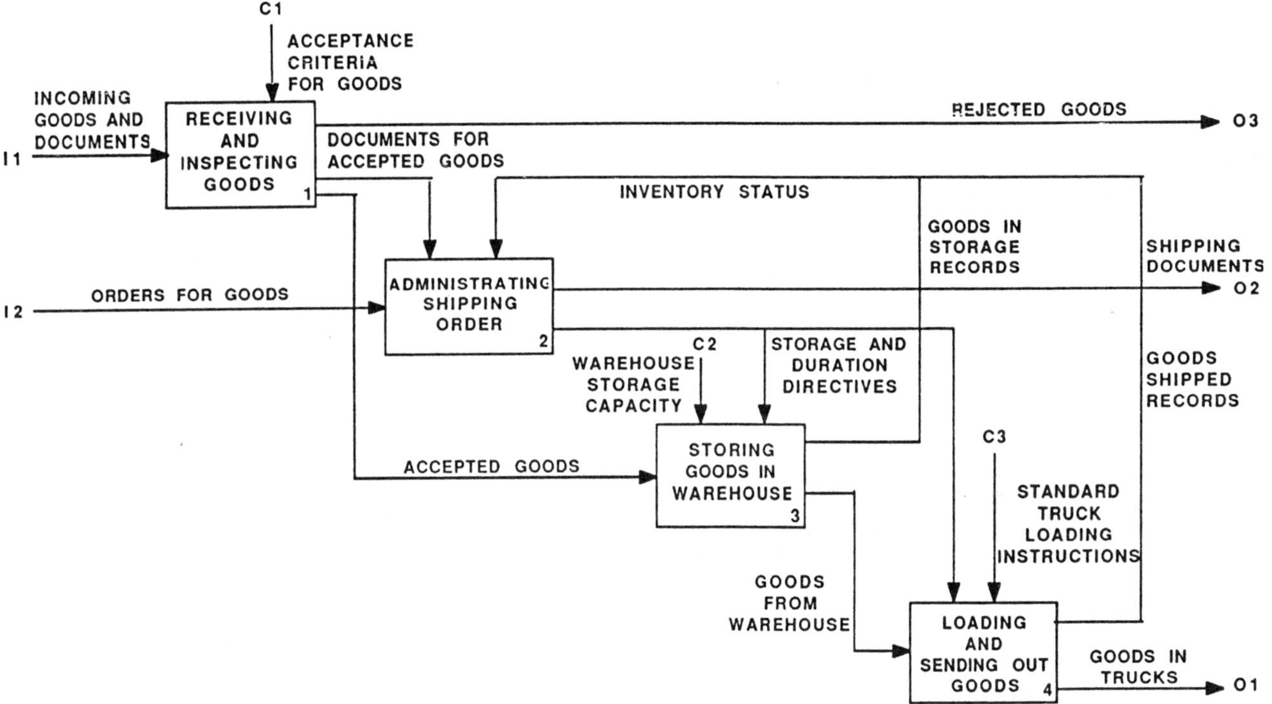

Figure 14: An SADT example continued

most abstractly. See Figure 13 for an example of a context diagram for an Army supply depot [McGowan 1982]. It captures the main inputs, outputs, and functions of the depot as follows:

- "incoming goods and documents" enter from supply lines. Based on the "acceptance criteria for goods" and the "warehouse storage capacity," the goods are either stored for future use or returned as "rejected goods"
- meanwhile, as truck convoys arrive with supply needs, they have "orders for goods." Based on the "standard truck loading instructions" (which state maximum allowable weight per truck type and per truck axle), the "goods in trucks" are generated along with appropriate "shipping documents" to record the delivery of the goods

Our understanding of the problem is now refined and that refinement is documented in another diagram, as shown in Figure 14, in which each box represents one well-defined piece of the whole problem.

Generally, boxes in any diagram are arranged along the diagonal, with arrows interconnecting the boxes. Boxes should be given unique names which should always be verb phrases because they represent functions. In addition, all boxes should be numbered. Boxes are numbered in their lower right corner to reflect their relative dominance; use 1 for the box representing the most dominant function, etc. Arrows may exit only from the right side of the box. Arrows may enter the top, left, or bottom sides of the box. Strict rules govern the interpretation of those arrows. In particular, an arrow pointing into the left side of a box represents things that will be transformed by the box, whereas an arrow pointing down into the top of a box represents *control* that affects how the box transforms the things entering the left side [Marca and McGowan 1988]. Arrows entering into the bottom of a box represent *mechanism* and provide the analyst with the ability to document how the function will operate, who will perform it, or what physical resources are needed to perform the function.

Figure 14 shows the documentation using SADT of the supply depot problem as four subproblems: receive and inspect the goods, administer the shipping order, store the goods in the warehouse, and load and send the goods out on trucks. Notice that the number and types of arrows in Figures 13 and 14 have been preserved; in particular, there were two inputs into the left on Figure 13 and there are two inputs into the left on Figure 14; there were three inputs into the top on Figure 13 and there are three inputs into the top on Figure 14; and there were two outputs out the right-hand side in Figure 13 and there are two outputs out the right-hand side in Figure 14. This situation will *usually* be the case, although there are exceptions (see Chapter 3 of Marca and McGowan [Marca and McGowan 1988]).

The next step in the analysis is to define any and all information flows between the four subproblems of the supply depot, as shown in Figure 14. Now each of the boxes at this level is further decomposed into its subproblems in the same manner until the resulting hierarchy of diagrams provide a level of detail sufficient to define the entire problem domain for the analyst.

It is important to note that this decomposition is not a software design; we are simply analyzing the problem by using repetitive decomposition. Each box corresponds to an aspect of the problem rather than a component of the solution. Once the analysis is completed, it is necessary to make the decision of what will be automated. When looking at Figure 14, we might decide to solve the problem by automating all of the boxes, but not any of the arrows; or to automate all of the arrows but not any of the boxes; or to automate only one of the boxes; or to automate the entire "system." Even if the latter strategy were to be selected, the diagram of Figure 14 still is not a design. The designers would eventually (i.e., after the requirements were defined in the SRS) need to perform the appropriate trade off analyses to determine the "optimal" design. That design may coincidentally be the same as the analyst's decomposition, but it would simply be that, a coincidence. It could just as easily be an entirely different design.

SADT's first use was in the analysis of the design, finance, QA/QC, marketing, manufacturing, inventory control, and product support functions of the aerospace industry in support of the U.S. Air Force Computer Aided Manufacturing (AFCAM) Program. It was used to define both how the aerospace industry is today as well as how it should be [Air Force 1974]. SADT has also been used by ITT Europe since 1974 for training personnel on telephone switches [Ross and Schuman 1977]. The status of SADT as of 1985 was reported by Ross [Ross 1985].

2.4.3: Structured Analysis and System Specification

Structured analysis and system specification (SASS), developed by Tom DeMarco, is a spinoff of the early requirements work of Ross and it is closely related to the design work of Yourdon and Constantine [Yourdon and Constantine 1977; DeMarco 1978; Ross 1977]. Like SADT, the SASS approach is a pure top-down technique in which the analyst starts by representing the system in a context diagram showing all system inputs and outputs and repeatedly refines the system while representing each refinement as a more detailed diagram.

Fundamental to the entire lifecycle is the concept of a data flow diagram (DFD), which shows the logical flow of data through a "system." The "system" can be a company, an organization, or a set of procedures, or it can be a computer (hardware) system, or a software system, or any combination of these. DFDs are composed of data on the move, shown as an arrow; transformations of data into other data, shown as bubbles; sources and destinations (external to the "system") of data, shown as rectangles; and data in static storage (i.e., databases), shown as two parallel lines. Figure 15 is an example of a DFD (adapted from [Gane and Sarson 1979]). The following observations about DFDs are important:

1. *All names should be unique*: This is to make it easier to refer to items in the DFD. Without unique names, you might be forced to say things such as, "The big circle just to the right of the smallest circle just above the double parallel arrows coming out of the database."
2. *Remember that a DFD is not a flow chart*: The arrows in a flow chart represent order of events; the arrows in

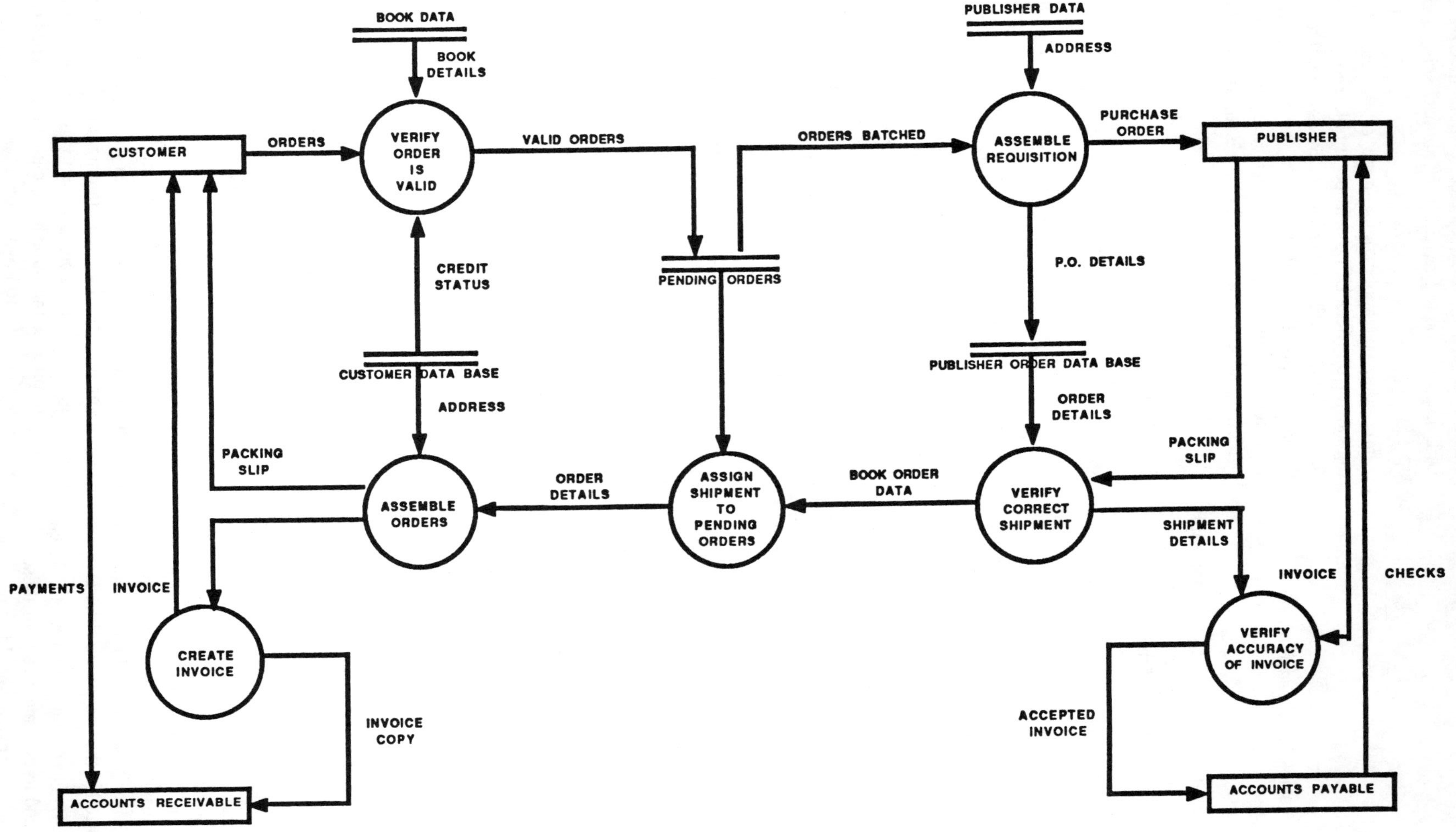

BOOK DATA
BOOK DETAILS
CUSTOMER
ORDERS
VERIFY ORDER IS VALID
VALID ORDERS
CREDIT STATUS
CUSTOMER DATA BASE
ADDRESS
PENDING ORDERS
ORDERS BATCHED
PUBLISHER DATA
ADDRESS
ASSEMBLE REQUISITION
PURCHASE ORDER
PUBLISHER
P.O. DETAILS
PUBLISHER ORDER DATA BASE
ORDER DETAILS
PACKING SLIP
VERIFY CORRECT SHIPMENT
BOOK ORDER DATA
ASSIGN SHIPMENT TO PENDING ORDERS
ORDER DETAILS
ASSEMBLE ORDERS
PACKING SLIP
SHIPMENT DETAILS
INVOICE
CHECKS
VERIFY ACCURACY OF INVOICE
ACCEPTED INVOICE
ACCOUNTS PAYABLE
PAYMENTS
INVOICE
CREATE INVOICE
INVOICE COPY
ACCOUNTS RECEIVABLE

ALS-305-AMD-1

Figure 15: A sample data flow diagram

Chris Gane/Trish Sarson, Structured Systems Analysis: Tools and Techniques, © 1979, p. 12; adapted by permission of Prentice Hall, Englewood Cliffs, New Jersey.

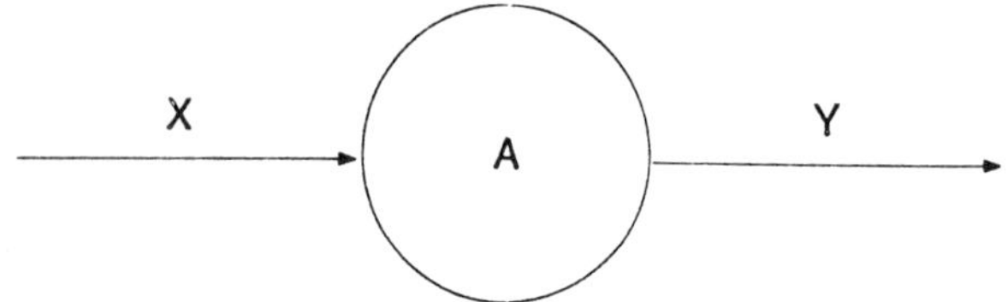

Figure 16: A single DFD transform

a DFD represent flowing data. A DFD does not imply any order of events. Thus, Figure 16 does not imply anything about the relative order of the arrival of X at A or the departure of Y from A: they might occur simultaneously, or independently, or Y may get generated each time X arrives, or X may arrive as soon as Y departs.

3. *Suppress logical decisions*: If you ever have the urge to draw a diamond-shaped box in a DFD, suppress the urge! A diamond-shaped box is used in flow charts to represent decision points with multiple exit paths of which only one is "taken." That implies an ordering of events and makes no sense in DFDs.
4. *Don't get bogged down in details*: Defer error conditions and error handling to the end of the analysis (unless, of course, the purpose of the "system" is to find errors, for example, hardware diagnostics or patient monitoring).

Figure 17 shows the structured analysis stages as defined by DeMarco [DeMarco 1978]. According to SASS, the first activity of structured analysis is to study the current environment (Step 2.1). During this activity, a DFD is drawn that shows how information flows through the current nonautomated organization. The bubbles should be labeled with names of organizational units and/or individuals within those units. This DFD is called the "current physical DFD."

The second activity (Step 2.2) of structured analysis is called "deriving logical equivalents." During this activity, action verbs replace people's and organizational units' names and define the activity they perform. Once the customer reviews and verifies this "current logical DFD," it is time to start defining the effect of automation on the organization.

During Step 2.3, the new logical system is modeled. During this stage, we modify the current logical DFD to reflect how information will move through the organization *after* the automated system is in place. However, no attempt is made to differentiate between those activities that will eventually be automated and those that will remain manual. The result of this step is called the "new logical DFD."

The next step (Step 2.4) is to define a number of different automation alternatives and to document each of these as a "new physical DFD." Each alternative should show clearly what will and what will not be automated. Step 2.5 analyzes each of these alternatives with the customers through a series of cost/benefit analyses. Finally, at Step 2.6, one of the new physical DFDs is selected for implementation. That DFD is passed on to Step 2.7 for final packaging and clean up.

For nontrivial applications, none of the current, new, logical, or physical DFDs will be simple enough to represent as a single DFD and still have enough detail to analyze the current problem sufficiently. In these cases, a DFD is written at the highest (most abstract) level; then each bubble (which now serves as a "parent") is decomposed into a complete DFD (unveiling its "children") of its own. This process may be repeated for as many levels as necessary until the problem is well understood.

When do you stop decomposing bubbles into sub-bubbles? DeMarco's recommendation is as follows:

- when the specification for a process can be written on one page
- when a bubble has only one input and one output

The problem with this advice is that a specification for a process can *always* be written on one page if written abstractly enough. Much better advice is that when the nouns and verbs used in the names and descriptions of the bubbles and data flows are no longer able to be seen, felt, smelled, heard, or tasted, you have gone too far. Remember, the purpose of analysis is to analyze the problem and not to design the system.

Throughout this process, all DFDs are augmented with data dictionaries (DD), which are simply repositories in which to store information about all the data items defined in the DFDs. Typical stored information includes the following:

- name of data item
- aliases (other names for item)
- description/purpose
- related data elements
- range of values
- data flows
- data structure definition

With the relatively recent introduction of low-priced graphics terminals and workstations, structured analysis has become an extremely popular technique to "automate." The tools (1) permit the analyst to "draw" DFDs easily on a graphics terminal, (2) manage the large collection of DFDs and their interrelationships, and (3) create a skeleton of a data dictionary. I put the word "automate" in quotations because the tools simply unburden the analyst's librarian from the manual chore of maintaining all of the DFDs; the tools in no way "automate" the analysis process. Most of these tools provide the same basic capabilities. They enable users to perform the following functions:

- request that a bubble be drawn at any particular place on the screen (usually with a mouse, rollerball, or joy stick)

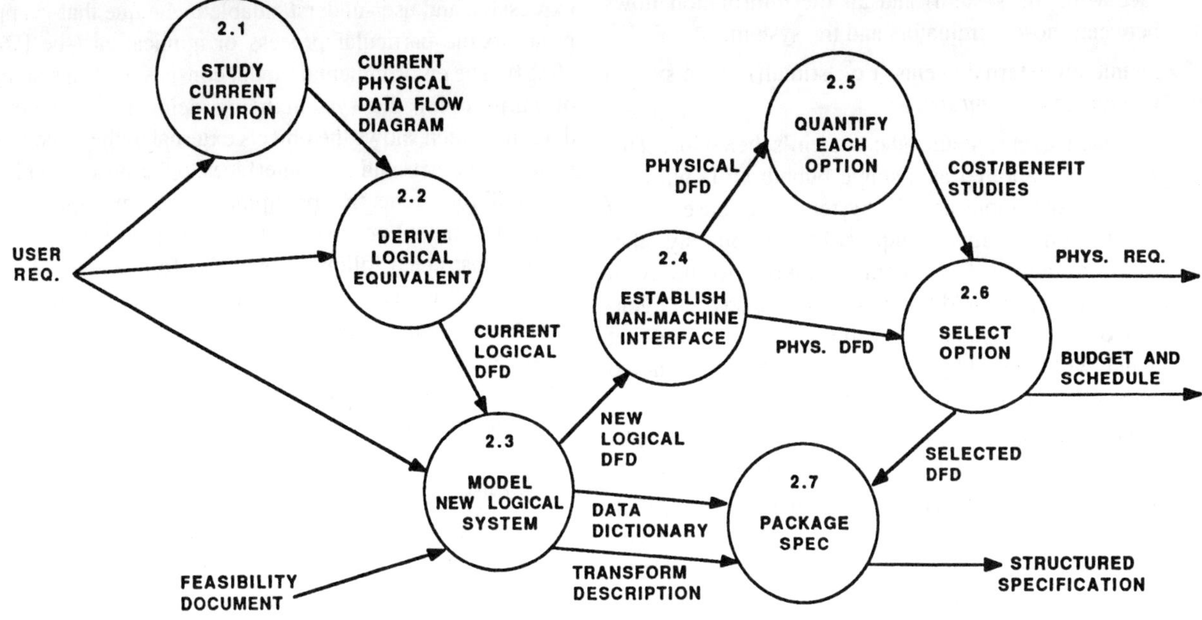

Figure 17: Structured analysis stages

- request that a database be drawn at any particular place on the screen
- request that arrows be drawn interconnecting bubbles (and/or databases)
- name all items
- retrieve and edit previously created DFDs
- enter lower levels of abstraction (i.e., while pointing to any particular bubble, that bubble would be expanded on the screen revealing the next level of underlying detail)
- enter higher levels of abstraction (i.e., while the user is looking at any DFD, the entire DFD would contract down to just one bubble revealing all the aunt and uncle bubbles)
- examine an automatically generated data dictionary
- request the tool to check for completeness. In this case, completeness means that all bubbles, arrows, and databases are labeled, and that all arrows have sources and destinations. Note that the really good tools simply prevent these violations in real time rather than offering an after-the-fact check
- request a check by the tool for consistency. In this case, consistency means that all bubbles, arrows, and databases have unique names, and that a DFD that is the expansion of a parent bubble exhibits the same number of inputs and outputs as its parent (i.e., "leveling"). Note that the really good tools simply prevent these violations in real time rather than offering an after-the-fact check
- perform analysis or design (but, unfortunately, few make the distinction)

By the late 1980s, structured analysis had been applied to a wide variety of problems with mixed success. Based on pioneering work by McMenamin and Palmer [McMenamin and Palmer 1984] on essential modeling, Paul Ward and Stephen Mellor [Ward and Mellor 1985] proposed a set of modifications to the development methodology originally proposed by DeMarco. Ed Yourdon [Yourdon 1989] later expanded on these changes. These changes recognized that:

- full-scale development of both a current physical and a current logical model could easily induce "paralysis through analysis"
- pure top-down approaches to analysis (1) do not necessarily make sense for very complex systems, and (2) may tempt the analyst to perform a real design prematurely
- entity-relationship diagrams are extremely valuable capturing the complexities of objects and their relationships.

Ward and Mellor's extensions eliminate the current physical model, and include a specific methodology for defining either a current or a new logical model. Their methodology can be summarized as follows:

1. Define the system context. This means define all the terminators (i.e., objects external to the system under specification which communicate or otherwise inter-

face with the system) and all the information flows between those terminators and the system.

2. Define all external events (i.e., stimuli) to the system in a narrative *event list*.
3. For each event, define the system's behavior. This should be captured as a single-bubble DFD with the event as one input and the system's response to that event as one (or more) outputs. In addition, any other data required by the system to respond to the event should appear as additional inputs, and any data generated by the system in response to the event but which will be used by other parts of the system should appear as outputs to data stores.
4. Perform upward leveling to create what Yourdon calls the *behavioral model*. Because the result of step 3 is potentially a large quantity of disjoint diagrams, group these together into successively more abstract models. This should be performed in such a way as to preserve the spirit of the environment's structure in the model's structure. Ward presents a number of useful guidelines for the selection of this grouping:
   a. minimize interfaces
   b. identify hierarchies of control
   c. group common responses
   d. group processes which share common data stores
   e. group common terminators
   f. group to ensure that names can be given to the abstract groups (i.e., avoid the requirements-equivalent of design's coincidental cohesion [Yourdon and Constantine 1979]).

   Yourdon's advice is simpler: group diagrams that share common data, and group diagrams that can hide information from the rest of the system.

Note that the result of the above process is a hierarchy of DFDs that capture the structure of the environment and whose lowest most detailed level is still a pure external view of the system under specification. This solves one of structured analysis's biggest problems, namely that the model constructed in a top-down manner often implied a design to the reader.

Yourdon's *Modern Structured Analysis* [Yourdon 1989] is an excellent compilation of all the wisdom and experience collected during two decades of structured analysis in practice. Yourdon defines systems analysis to include the development of two models: the environmental model and the behavioral model, which together are called the *essential model*. All of the models are composed of data flow diagrams, data dictionaries, entity relationship diagrams, and process specifications which should be thoroughly analyzed for consistency. Using Ward's real-time notational extensions [Ward 1986], the data flow diagrams may include control flows and data flows, and control processes can be further defined in terms of finite-state machines. Primitive bubbles in a data flow diagram can be defined using any expressive and user-understandable technique that is appropriate to the particular process or application (see [Davis 1988]). The environmental model consists of (1) a statement of purpose for the system being defined, (2) a context diagram which shows the objects external to the system with which it interacts and their interfaces to the system, and (3) a list of all the events that precipitate a system response. The behavioral model consists of (1) a complete set of leveled DFDs constructed following Ward's aforementioned methodology, (2) entity relationship diagrams to capture all the objects manipulated by the system, their attributes and interrelationships, (3) state-transition diagrams for all the control processes, (4) a data dictionary, and (5) process specifications for each lower-level process.

2.4.4: PSL/PSA

The problem statement language/problem statement analyzer (PSL/PSA) was originally developed during the early 1970s by Dan Teichroew and the ISDOS project at the University of Michigan, and it is now marketed by Meta Systems, Inc. [Teichroew and Hershey 1977]. One of the earliest requirements analysis tools, PSA predates the availability of inexpensive, widely available graphics terminals. Since Teichroew knew that analysis was primarily an iterative decomposition process but that graphics terminals were not practical, he did the only thing possible: he developed PSL, a completely text (nongraphical) language to describe processes, information flow between processes, and hierarchical decomposition of process and data. Using PSL/PSA is similar to using any of the SASS-type automated tools except that the input is entirely text. For example, the data flow diagram shown in Figure 18 can be described in PSL by using the text shown in Figure 19 (adapted from [Teichroew and Hershey 1977]).

Although the problem statement analyzer has an out-of-date input style, it does have extensive error analysis and reporting capabilities. PSA generates a wide variety of reports, including the following:

- DDs
- DFDs
- data flow inconsistency reports (e.g., information generated but not used or information used but not generated)
- database modification reports (e.g., who modified the requirements database when)
- reference reports (e.g., summaries of all processes referencing an item of information)
- hierarchical summary reports showing the superordinate/subordinate relationships between information items or processes
- analysis reports (e.g., process chain or data/process interaction)

PSL/PSA has been augmented with additional abilities over time so that it goes beyond simple data flow. In particular, PSL/PSA can be used to show system-level

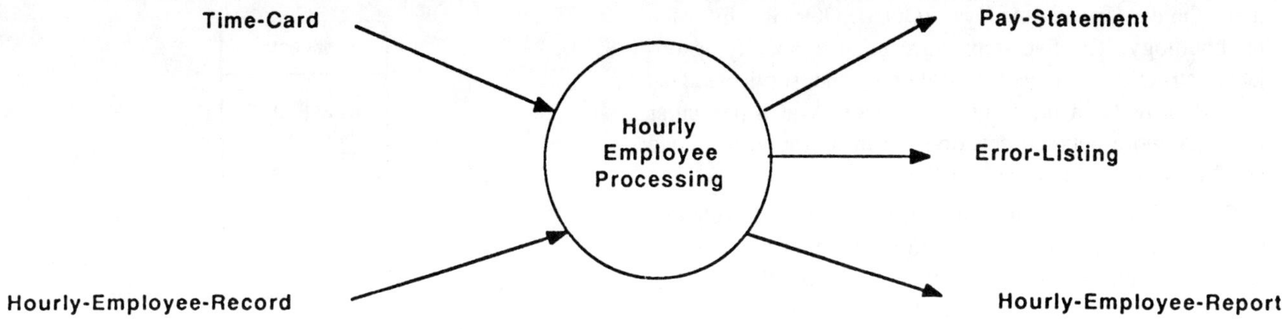

Figure 18: A parent node in a DFD

```
PROCESS
  - hourly-employee-processing:
  DESCRIPTION:
        this process performs those actions needed to
        interpret time cards to produce a pay statement for
        each hourly employee.;
  ATTRIBUTES ARE:
        complexity-level
                          high;
  GENERATES:        pay-statement, error-listing,
                    hourly-employee-report;
  RECEIVES:         time-card, hourly-employee-record;
  SUBPARTS ARE:     hourly-pay check-validation,
                    hourly-emp-update,
                    h-report-entry-generation,
                    hourly-paycheck-production;
  PART OF:          payroll-processing;
  DERIVES:          pay-statement
  USING:            time-card, hourly-employee-record;
  DERIVES:          hourly-employee-report
  USING:            time-card, hourly-employee-record;
  DERIVES:          error-listing
  USING:            time-card, hourly-employee-record;
  PROCEDURE:
      1. compute gross pay from time card data.
      2. compute tax from gross pay.
      3. subtract tax from gross pay to obtain net pay.
      4. update hourly employee record accordingly.
      5. update department record accordingly.
      6. generate paycheck.
      Note: If status code specifies that the employee
      did not work this wook, no processing will be done
      for this employee.;
  HAPPENS:
      number-of-payment TMES-PER pay-period;
  TRIGGERED BY:
      hourly-emp-processing-event;
  TERMINATION-CAUSES:
      new-employee-processing-event;
  SECURITY IS:
      company-only;
```

Figure 19: A parent node specification in PSL

input/output (i.e., interaction between the system being analyzed and its environment), decomposition of the problem into subproblems, the actual system's design (not appropriate for the problem analysis phase), data structure, data and program sizing, system behavioral dynamics, attributes of the system, and project management functions such as personnel, schedules, and resources. More recently, Meta Systems has produced an interactive front end called the structured architect,™ which provides capabilities similar to the "automated" tools described in Section 2.4.3.

To date, PSL/PSA has been used on more than 140 projects including numerous large systems for the Department of Defense. Although it *can* be used for problem analysis effectively, it has often been used only for the *design* of the software into its actual subcomponents.

2.4.5: Object-Oriented Analysis

The concept of object-orientation in software development has its roots in the language Smalltalk. Rentsch [Rentsch 1982] provides an excellent historic perspective of object-oriented *programming*. Booch [Booch 1986] discusses the effect of object-orientation on *design*. Finally, Bailin [Bailin 1989] and Coad [Coad and Yourdon 1989] discuss the effect of object-orientation on problem analysis.

All object-oriented approaches stress the definition and refinement of *objects* in the real world and classes of objects in the real world. A *class* of objects can be thought of as an abstraction that represents one or more objects or other classes of objects. Thus, if we have objects called manufacturers, wholesalers, and retailers, they might all be members of the class of objects called companies. Also, in any object-oriented approach, objects (and classes of objects) possess *attributes* and all objects *inherit* the attributes of the classes to which they are members. Since problem analysis is the analysis and description of the real world, its entities, their attributes and their relationships, it makes sense to use object-oriented concepts in problem analysis. The primary motivation for object-orientation is that as a system evolves, its functions tend to change, but its objects tend to remain unchanged. Thus, a system built using object-oriented techniques may be inherently more maintainable than one built using more conventional functional approaches.

By far the most thorough methodology for using an object-orientation during problem analysis has been put forth by Peter Coad [Coad and Yourdon 1989] under the

---

Structured Architect is a trademark of Meta Systems, Inc.

name Object-Oriented Analysis (OOA). OOA is a five-step methodology. The five steps correspond to specifying objects, structures, subjects, attributes, and services. This section provides a brief summary of OOA at a particular point. A more detailed description can be found in [Coad and Yourdon 1989] and [Coad 1989].

Objects are "an encapsulation of attributes and exclusive services; an abstraction of something in the problem space, with some number of occurrences in the problem space" [Coad and Yourdon 1989]. Unlike other authors, Coad provides explicit guidance on how to identify objects. His advice is to examine structure in the real world (e.g., nurses and physicians are members of the medical profession), identify other systems with which the current or proposed system will interact (e.g., Blue Cross/Blue Shield), identify those things in the real world that need to be remembered for later retrieval (e.g., patient's blood pressure), identify specific roles played by individuals (e.g., physician, patient), identify physical locations that need to be known (e.g., physician's office address), identify organizations that humans belong to (e.g., AMA, HMOs), identify catalogs that need to record quantities of repetitive, static, information about things (e.g., patient medical history).

The identification of *structure* is one of the most important steps in OOA. It is fundamental to the definition of objects and to the minimization of the complexity of the analysis. There are two types of structure: *classification* and *assembly*. They enable you to utilize abstraction and partitioning respectively, in describing objects. Classification enables you to define one class of objects that captures common attributes and services and enables all objects that are members to inherit those attributes and services. Figure 20 shows how in-patients and out-patients are both members of the class patients. This structure can be realized both top-down and bottom-up. For example, in the medical example, we may be analyzing in-patients separately from out-patients, and then realize that they have much in common and that it would be useful to define the more abstract concept of patient. On the other hand, we might be analyzing in-patients when we realize that the attributes and services associated with cardiac-care patients are different than those associated with psych patients, so that it would be useful to define two less abstract objects, cardiac-care and psych, which would be subordinate to the class of in-patients. The other type of structure is assembly. It captures the concept of "what is a part (or component) of what." For example, hearts, kidneys, and eyes may be parts of a patient, as shown in Figure 21. As in the case of classification, you can create these in practice in both a top-down and bottom-up fashion.

At this point in the process, the model starts to become somewhat complex. To simplify the understanding of the model, the next step is to examine the objects and their underlying structures to arrive at a less complex, more abstract view. This view is called the *subject* view and entails the definition of subjects. Each classification structure and assembly structure becomes one subject. Accord-

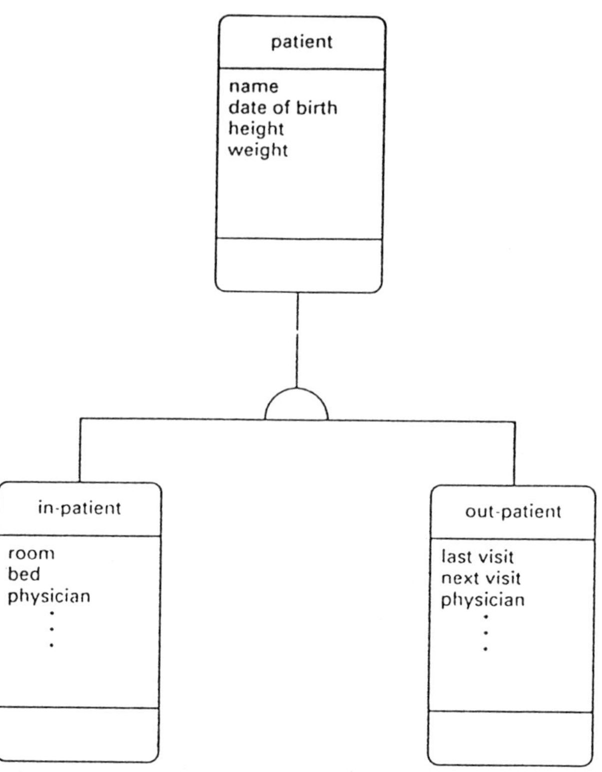

Figure 20: Classification structure in OOA

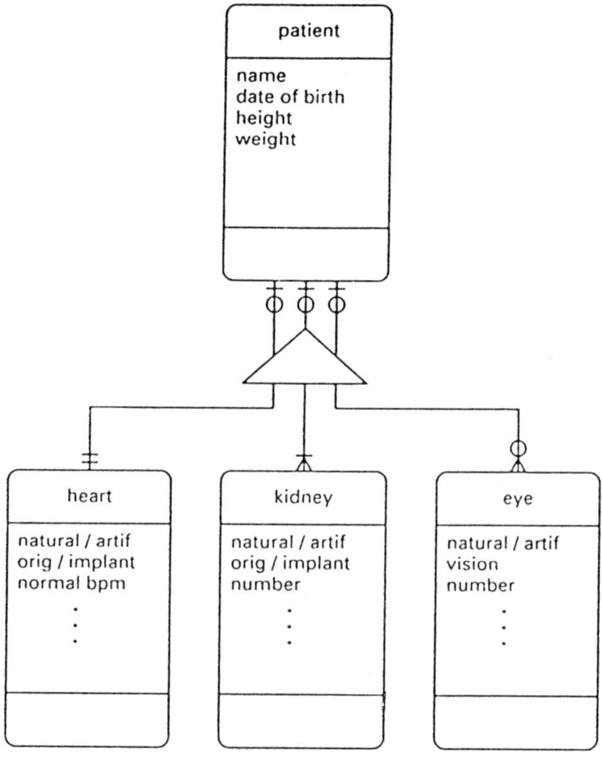

Figure 21: Assembly structure in OOA

ing to Coad, each remaining object also becomes a subject, although if there are a considerable number of these, I would recommend that you search the problem space for additional candidate structures among the remaining objects, in order to reduce the number of subjects. Once the subjects are defined, a subject diagram is constructed. It looks just like an object diagram except that its contents are limited to the names of the subjects. When the next two steps are completed, you will augment the subject diagram to reflect any instance connections or message connections that result from defining attributes and services, respectively.

The next step is the definition of attributes associated with objects. From the real-world perspective, these express some aspect of the object. From the computer perspective, these represent some value or aspect that needs to be stored for all instances of the object. Thus, for example, if the object is patient, then some of the attributes may be height, weight, name, social security number, date of birth, etc. The definition of attributes must be made hand-in-hand with the definition of structures. As sets of objects evolve to have attributes in common (for good reason, not coincidental), you might consider defining a class of objects to "hold" the common attributes. Every object that is a member of a class of objects possesses all attributes unique to that object as well as those of its class. This is called *inheritance*. During the process of defining attributes, a situation often occurs where the attribute of one object *is* another object. For example, in an elevator control system, one possible attribute of an elevator is the current floor, or one possible attribute of a floor is the number of elevators currently present on that floor. When this occurs, it is far easier not to include these attributes, but instead to add instance connections between these related objects. *Instance connections* define one-to-one, one-to-many, and many-to-many relations that exist in the real world between instances of objects, as shown in Figure 22.

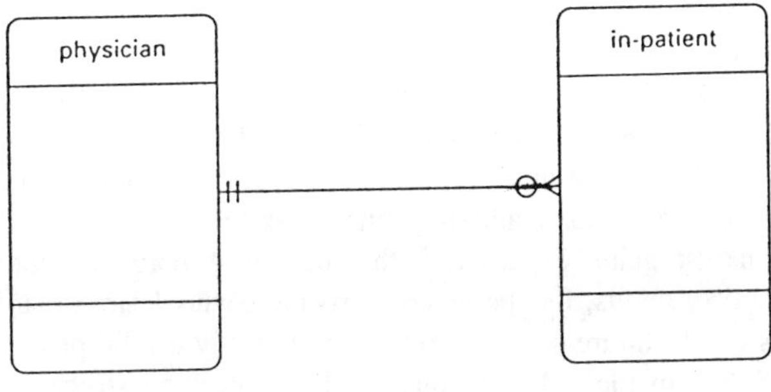

Figure 22: Instance connection in OOA

The last step is the specification of the services performed by each object (see Figure 23). According to Coad, there are three types of services: occur, calculate, and monitor. *Occurrence services* are those that relate to the creation, deletion and modification of instances of the object. Rather than specifying add, delete, change, test, and select services for every object, Coad suggests using a single abstract service type called "Occur," which is omitted from the model due to its omnipresence. *Calculate services* are used when one objects needs the calculated result from another object. Each calculate service is explicitly placed in the model. *Monitor services* are those where instances of an object monitor some other process for a condition, an event, etc. For every service, you must specify its external behavior in a *service specification*. These should be as short and focused as possible, and most importantly, should use terminology from the problem domain.

Finally, the entire problem analysis is documented in three packages: the OOA model itself (which includes the diagrams), a dictionary (with definitions of all attributes), and service specifications (one for each object).

2.5: Comparison of Techniques

In subsection 2.3, the following six ideal traits of a problem analysis technique were given:

1. facilitate communication
2. provide a means of defining the system boundary
3. provide a means of defining partitions, abstractions, and projections
4. encourage the analyst to think and document the problem rather than the solution
5. allow for opposing alternatives but alert the analyst to their presence
6. make it easy to modify the knowledge structure

The following paragraphs discuss to what extent Structured Requirements Definition, SADT, SASS, PSL/PSA, and OOA exhibit these traits.

Facilitate communication: Seven years ago, I would have claimed that SRD, SADT, and SASS were nonfriendly, and that the data flow diagrams they employed were difficult for noncomputer-oriented personnel to understand. However, I have now worked with hundreds of individuals who are specialists in medicine, weapons, telephony, manufacturing, logistics, aviation, construction, and management who have little understanding or appreciation for computers, and I have found that with very few exceptions they can understand a set of well-written (i.e., using the customers' terminology) problem analysis data flow diagrams. The same is probably true for OOA, but there exists much less experience to verify it.

Define system boundary: For a tool or technique to enable the analyst to define the system boundary, there should be an explicit way to say that *this* entity belongs to the system or to its environment and that *that* attribute describes the system or describes its environment. Although none of the techniques provide that specific function overtly, SADT, SASS, and PSL/PSA all permit the analyst either to separately model the system from its environment or to start the analysis with two bubbles: the system and its environment. From that point on, it becomes quite clear what is in the system and what is not. Of course, be aware that during much of the problem analysis activities, we may not know (or care) what the system boundary is. However, by the time the entire requirements phase is complete, we must know. OOA appears to discourage the early definition of the system boundary. This is not a problem because the software solution's structure will so well parallel the real world.

Define partitions, abstractions, and projections: SRD appears to provide no real means to define partitions or abstractions. At first glance, it appears to be perfect for defining projections. After all, SRD is little more than a process of asking people for their perspectives of a "system." However, I do not believe that SRD has much in common with projections because a projection is a set of contrasting views of the "system" from external viewpoints, just as in Figures 7 and 8; the people interviewed during SRD are all internal viewpoints—in effect, they are part of the system (see Figure 24). This is not meant as a criticism of SRD, which works very well when automating tasks that are currently performed manually, but it does not offer the projection trait. SASS, SADT, PSL/PSA and OOA all provide abstraction and partitioning as basic aspects; however, only OOA provides unique notation to differentiate them. Only SADT specifically recognizes and encourages multiple external viewpoints [Ross 1977], i.e., projection.

Document in terms of problem, not solution: This trait is probably the most important trait of any problem analysis technique—it should encourage the analyst to think and document the problem rather than the solution (i.e., it should help the analyst avoid falling into design). Unfortunately, most of the techniques fare poorly in this category. DeMarco's original SA, SADT, and PSL/PSA are all notoriously poor in this regard. The explanation for this is simple: these techniques have been developed as both problem analysis *and* design techniques (after all, decomposing items into subitems is independent of the item). In contrast, users of SRD and OOA rarely fall into design. In the case of SRD, the methodology is limited to interviewing working personnel and recording their observations on paper in their own terminology, thus keeping the problem analysis in the problem domain. However, subsequent stages of SRD (not explained here) strongly discourage the analyst from remaining in the problem domain. In the case of OOA, it appears relatively straightforward to ensure that your objects, attributes, connections and structures remain in the problem domain. However, regardless of which technique you use, human discipline is the best way of guaranteeing that you stay out of the design domain.

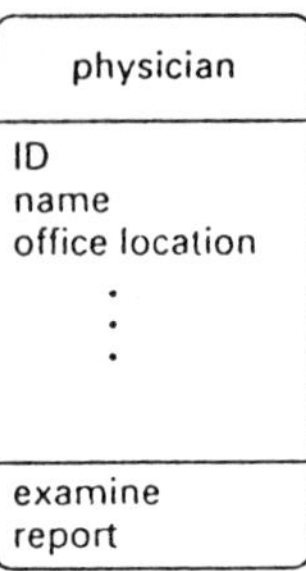

Figure 23: Services in OOA

Allow opposing alternatives: Opposing alternatives should be recordable during a problem analysis session; a user-oriented technique would permit this conflict but alert you to its presence. This trait is more a function of the particular tool implementation than is the raw technique itself. Most of the automated tools for SASS, SADT, or PSL/PSA have consistency checking capabilities. It is obviously impossible for a tool to differentiate between an intentional inconsistency (used to record a tentative disagreement between individuals) and an unintentional inconsistency (caused by error). PSL/PSA does deserve special points here for its extensive reporting capability and flexibility.

Easily modifiable: Finally, the ease of modifying problem analysis information is directly related to the user orientation of the automated tools. As mentioned earlier, SADT, SASS, and PSL/PSA have all been automated.

2.6: Summary

This section has discussed a variety of representative problem analysis techniques, most of which have been automated. Each fills a particular niche in the world of problem analysis; none is a panacea. The most important item to remember is this: use the right tool for the right job. While using any technique or tool, be constantly aware and driven by your goal: understanding a real problem. Do not get so hung up with the intricacies of a technique or tool that you lose sight of that goal. If you are spending more time analyzing the technique than analyzing your problem, you may be using the wrong technique. When you have completed your goal and understand the problem, stop! Just because the technique says, "Follow these 26 steps," don't get lured into displacing your goal (i.e., understanding the problem) with another (i.e., following the technique).

A beginning analyst needs to decide consciously which tools are needed and how they should be used. As the analyst gains experience, this becomes more and more subconscious. Inexperienced carpenters who desire to build some furniture discover that they can't buy a solid piece of 8′ × 4′ maple and must consciously decide to construct it out of four pieces of 8′ × 1′ lumber. They may try to align the four strips of wood only to discover that the wood is not

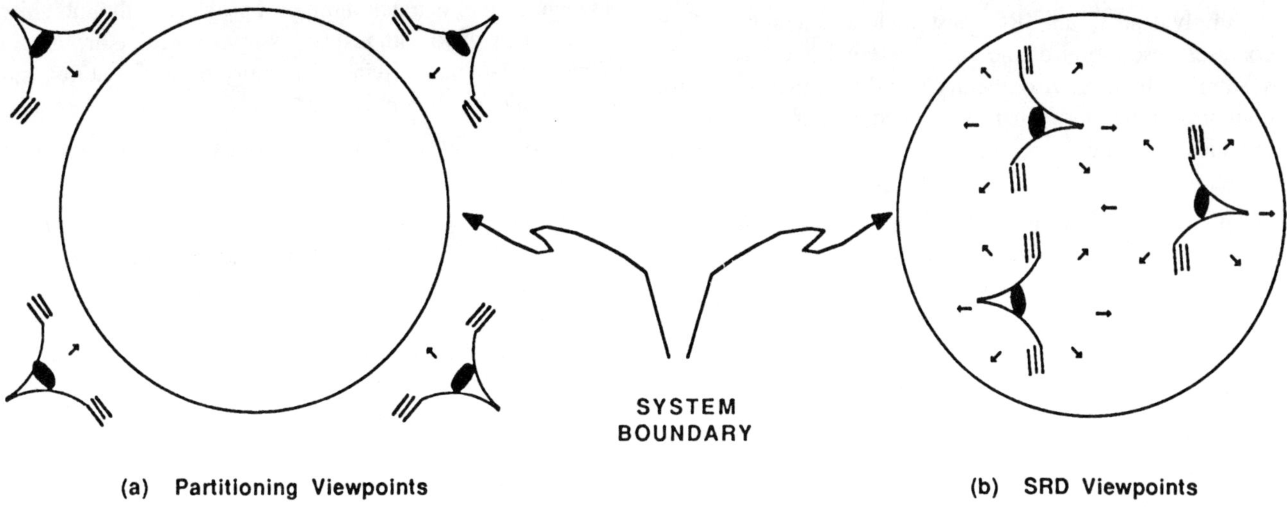

Figure 24: Partitioning vs SRD

smooth and even; they must read about what tool is needed (a jointer/planer) and how to use it. After learning how to use it by reading, the tool is purchased and used, then they read about types of glues, and so on. Everything that is done is done consciously. Experienced carpenters who desire to build such a table, simply build it: they buy the proper wood, smooth the surfaces, glue and clamp it, and so on. They don't have to think about it any more than an automobile driver has to think about how to make a vehicle turn left.

When an experienced analyst is faced with a new problem, the right tools and techniques are simply selected and used, often completely subconsciously. Just as the carpenter maintains a rich set of tools to ensure that the right tool is available at the right time, the analyst must also do so.

3: Writing an SRS

3.1: Introduction

During problem analysis, we repeatedly decompose the problem until it is finally understood thoroughly. However, the software requirements phase is not complete until the SRS is written. The SRS contains a complete description of the external behavior of the software system. It *is* possible to complete the entire problem analysis before writing the SRS. However, what is more likely is that as the problem analysis decomposition process spawns aspects of the problem that are well understood, the corresponding section of the SRS is written.

The SRS can serve a variety of purposes depending on who is writing it: (1) The SRS could be written by a potential system user (or customer) and (2) the SRS could be written by a system developer. The two scenarios induce entirely different situations and establish entirely different purposes for the document. In the former case, the primary purpose of the SRS is to define the need. This document sometimes serves as a basis of a competitive bidding process among companies who desire to satisfy that need. To encourage competition (which potentially helps the customer receive the best product for the least money), the SRS should be as general as possible. Let us say, for example, that a building owner wishes to buy an elevator control system. The SRS should be general enough to enable a variety of elevator companies (each with a different dispatch algorithm and each with a different elevator flight path) to respond, but should be specific enough to clearly eliminate from the competition a company offering a series of ramps connecting the floors and a parade of elephants walking up and down the ramps transporting people on their backs! Ideally, the SRS should carve the universe of systems into two independent sets: a set containing all the systems which would satisfy the users' real needs and one containing all those that would not.

On the other hand, an SRS written by a development organization as the first step of the software development process must be far more specific. This type of SRS is the subject of this section and performs an entirely different set of functions from the so-called SRS of the previous paragraph. Its purpose is to provide a means of the following:

- communicating among customers, users, analysts, and designers
- supporting the system testing activities
- controlling the evolution of the system

3.2: What Should Be Included in an SRS?

Simply stated, an SRS must include a complete, yet concise, description of the entire external interface of the system with its environment, including other software, communication ports, hardware, and human users. This includes two types of requirements: behavioral and nonbehavioral.

The behavioral requirements define the functions of the system. They describe all the inputs and outputs to and from the system as well as information concerning how the inputs and outputs interrelate. In other words, we need to define completely the transform function of the system software being specified. This description of how inputs map into outputs are typically called "behavioral description" or "operational specifications." The nonbehavioral requirements define the attributes of the system as it performs its job. They include a complete description of the system's required levels of efficiency, reliability, security, maintainability, portability, visibility, capacity, and standard compliance, for example.

3.3: Attributes of a Well-Written SRS

If a "perfect" SRS could exist it would exhibit the following qualities:

- correct
- nonambiguous
- complete
- verifiable
- consistent
- understandable by noncomputer specialists
- modifiable
- traceable
- annotated

Each of these is briefly explained in the following paragraphs.

An SRS is *correct* if and only if every requirement stated therein represents something that is required of the system to be built. There is no real way to teach this quality since it totally depends on the application at hand. If the need is for the software to respond to all button presses within 5 seconds and the SRS states that "the software shall respond to all button presses within 10 seconds," then that requirement is incorrect.

An SRS is *nonambiguous* if and only if every requirement stated therein has only one interpretation [IEEE 1984]. Imagine that a sentence is extracted from an SRS, given to 10 people and they are asked for their interpretation of the sentence. If there is more than one such interpretation then that sentence is probably ambiguous. At a minimum, all terms with multiple meanings must appear in a glossary. However, there is much more of a problem with ambiguity than can be solved with just a glossary. In particular, the use of natural language invites ambiguity because natural language is inherently ambiguous.

An SRS is *complete* if it possesses the following four qualities:

1. *Everything that the software is supposed to do is included in the SRS.* This is the most difficult of the attributes to define or detect violations for. The reason why a violation is so difficult to detect is because it implies that something is not in the SRS; it is obviously difficult to find something that is not present by examining what is present. The only people who could detect such an oversight or omission are those who have the problem which is to be solved by the software. Prototyping is one technique to address this problem.
2. *Definitions of the responses of the software to all realizable classes of input data in all realizable classes of situations is included. Note that it is important to specify the responses to both valid and invalid inputs* [IEEE 1984]. This implies that for every system input mentioned in the SRS, the SRS specifies what the appropriate output will be. However, the appropriate output may be a function of more than just the input; it may also be a function of the current state of the system. For example, in a telephone switching system, the software's response to detection of the user dialing 9 is a function of the state of the system which, in turn, is a function of what the user did previously. Thus, if the user's phone handset is in its cradle, no system output is generated (i.e., the input is ignored); if the user is listening to a dial tone, the system output might be a distinctive dial tone; and if the user has already started dialing a phone number, the "9" is collected as one more digit of the phone number. In other words, the SRS must establish a complete mapping from the cross product of the input domain (I) and state domain (S) into the cross product of the output domain (O) and the state domain (S), i.e.,

$$\text{SRS}: I \times S \rightarrow O \times S.$$

3. *All pages are numbered, all figures and tables are numbered, named, and referenced, all terms and units of measure are provided, and all referenced material and sections are present* [IEEE 1984]. This is "completeness" from a word processing perspective.
4. *No sections are marked "to be determined (TBD)."* Inserting the three letters "TBD" in a section of an SRS should be avoided whenever possible. When

included, the TBD should be appended with a notation of *who* has responsibility for determining the contents and *when* the section will be completed. This approach ensures that the TBD is not interpreted carte blanche as an excuse to delay the completion of the SRS indefinitely as if the TBD meant "to be done tomorrow" and, of course, tomorrow never occurs!

An SRS is *verifiable* if and only if every requirement stated therein is verifiable. A requirement is *verifiable* if and only if there exists some finite cost-effective process with which a person or machine can check that the actual as-built software product meets the requirement [IEEE 1984]. It is important to realize that verifiability is a function of the way the SRS is written (many people think it is purely a function of the product as-built). There are a number of reasons why a requirement may be non-verifiable. First, any ambiguity would certainly lead to non-verifiability; obviously, there is no way to verify that the software exhibits a trait if that trait is defined ambiguously. Second, use of non-measurable quantities such as "usually" or "often" imply the absence of a finite test process and these imply non-verifiability. Third, any requirement that is equivalent to a statement of the halting problem ([Turing 1936] or read any textbook on computability or automata theory) cannot be verified.

An SRS is *consistent* if and only if no subset of individual requirements stated therein conflicts. This may be manifested in a number of ways [IEEE 1984]. The following are examples of this:

1. *Conflicting terms*: Two terms are used in different contexts to mean the same thing.
2. *Conflicting characteristics*: Two parts of the SRS demand that the product exhibit contradictory traits.
3. *Temporal inconsistency*: Two parts of the SRS demand that the product obey contradictory timing characteristics.

In an attempt to make an SRS less ambiguous, more verifiable, complete, and consistent, we might be tempted to resort to extremely formal notations. Unfortunately, most such notations make it impossible for the SRS to be *understood by noncomputer specialists*. The customer or user is a primary reader of the SRS in many cases. Customers and users tend to be experts in an application area but are not necessarily trained in computer science. Perhaps one way of achieving the goal is to utilize formal notations for the development of a tool to automatically translate the resulting formal SRS into equivalent easy-to-understand prose. However, I question why the formal version is needed at all. If a complete non-ambiguous mapping between the formal and informal representations exists, then the informal representation would satisfy all of the required attributes including understandability by the noncomputer specialist.

An SRS is *modifiable* if its structure and style are such that any necessary changes to the requirements can be made easily, completely, and consistently [IEEE 1984]. Modifiability implies that a table of contents, an index, and cross references exist where necessary. Thus, if a requirement needs to be modified at a future date, we can check and easily locate the section of the SRS that needs modification.

An SRS is *traceable* if the origin of each of its requirements is clear and if it facilitates the referencing of each requirement in future development or enhancement documentation [IEEE 1984].

The following are four types of traceability (see Figure 25):

1. *Backward from requirements traceability* implies that we know why every requirement in the SRS exists. It implies that each requirement explicitly references its source in previous documents.
2. *Forward from requirements traceability* implies that we understand which components of the software satisfy each requirement. It demands that each requirement in the SRS explicitly reference a design component.
3. *Backward to requirements traceability* implies that every software component explicitly references those requirements that it helps to satisfy. It implies that each requirement in the SRS has a unique name or reference number.
4. *Forward to requirements traceability* implies that all documents that preceded the SRS can reference the SRS. Like "backward to requirements" traceability, this implies that each requirement in the SRS has a unique name or reference number.

The purpose of *annotating* the requirements contained in an SRS is to provide guidance to the development organization. The two types of annotations that are of most help are relative necessity and relative stability.

Occasionally, a development organization might spend an inordinate amount of time trying to satisfy a particular requirement, only to discover afterwards that the customer would have preferred to have the product on time with an unsatisfied particular requirement than to have the product six months late with a satisfied requirement. This scenario would have been prevented had the relative necessities of the individual requirements been specifically stated. One way to do this is to append to every individual requirement in the SRS, an E, D, or O in parentheses to indicate essential, desireable, or optional. Of course, the concept of an "optional requirement" is oxymoronic, but the fact is that there *are* relative importances of requirements. In addition, annotating each requirement with an indicator of the impor-

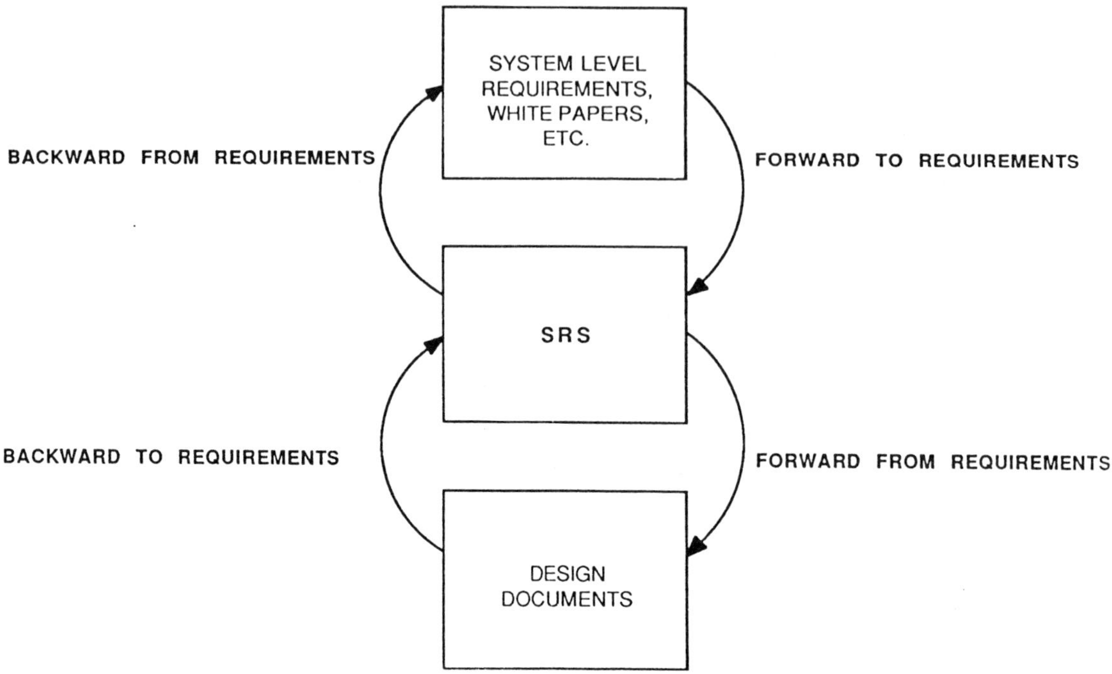

Figure 25: Traceability expectations of an SRS

tance of the requirement provides the development organization with guidance concerning design flexibility.

Achieving all of the above attributes in any SRS is impossible. For example, as we attempt to eliminate all traces of inconsistency and ambiguity (usually by moving away from natural language as the language in which the SRS is written), the SRS tends to get less understandable to the noncomputer specialist. As we attempt to be absolutely complete, costs of the SRS skyrocket and the document gets extremely unwieldy. If we try to increase modifiability by eliminating all redundancy, the SRS becomes quite choppy and hard to follow. The only conclusion we can reach from this is **THERE IS NO SUCH THING AS A PERFECT SOFTWARE REQUIREMENTS SPECIFICATION!**

3.4: SRS Techniques

An earlier paper [Davis 1988] provides a detailed description of a variety of tools and techniques for the writing of a software requirements specification. Included in that paper are discussions of the following items:

- finite state machines
- decision tables and trees
- program design languages
- structured analysis/real time
- statecharts
- Requirements Engineering Validation System
- Requirements Language Processor
- Specification and Description Language
- PAISLey
- Petri nets

All of these techniques can augment or replace selected portions of an SRS to decrease ambiguity and to increase consistency and completeness. The key to using them to improve the SRS is the careful selection of the right tool for the right job and the knowledge of the pro's and con's of the tool. A full description of these pro's and con's of appropriate applications for each tool is given in [Davis 1988]. The criterion by which each is evaluated are the following:

- understanding by computer-naive personnel
- basis for design and test
- automatic consistency/ambiguity checking
- external not internal view
- organizational assistance
- automatic prototype and test generator
- appropriateness to applications

4: Summary of Paper

This paper has explored the key issues that surround understanding a problem (i.e., uncovering the needs) and the writing of a software requirements specification (i.e., defining the requirements). It has surveyed a variety of tools and techniques that place some order in the process and that help to reduce the inherent ambiguity, inconsistency, and incompleteness present in an SRS.

5: References

[Air Force 1974] Air Force Materials Laboratory, *Air Force Computer-Aided Manufacturing Master Plan,* Vol. II., Appendix A, and Vol. III, Report #AFML-TR-74-104, Wright Patterson Air Force Base, Ohio, 1974.

[Alford 1977] Alford, M., "A Requirements Engineering Methodology for Real-Time Processing Requirements," *IEEE Transactions on Software Engineering,* Vol. SE-3, No. 1, January 1977, pp. 60–69.

[Alford 1985] Alford, M., "SREM at the Age of Eight, the Distributed Computing Design System," *Computer,* Vol. 18, No. 4, April 1985, pp. 36–46.

[Bailin 1989] Bailin, S., "An Object-Oriented Requirements Specification Method," *Communications of the ACM,* Vol. 32, No. 5, May 1989, pp. 608–623.

[Berzins and Gray 1985] Berzins, V. and M. Gray, "Analysis and Design in MSG.84: Formalizing Functional Specifications," *IEEE Transactions on Software Engineering,* Vol. SE-11, No. 8, August 1985, pp. 657–670.

[Boehm 1976] Boehm, B., "Software Engineering," *IEEE Transactions on Computers,* Vol. C-25, No. 12, December 1976, pp. 1226–1241.

[Booch 1986] Booch, G., "Object-Oriented Development," *IEEE Transactions on Software Engineering,* Vol. SE-12, No. 2, February 1986, pp. 211–221.

[Celko et al. 1983] Celko, J., et al., "A Demonstration of Three Requirements Language Systems," *SIGPLAN Notices,* Vol. 18, No. 1, January 1983, pp. 9–14.

[Charette 1986] Charette, R., *Software Engineering Environments,* McGraw Hill, New York, 1986.

[Coad 1989] Coad, P., "Object-Oriented Analysis," appears elsewhere in this tutorial.

[Coad and Yourdon 1989] Coad, P. and E. Yourdon, *OOA—Object-Oriented Analysis,* Prentice-Hall, Englewood Cliffs, N.J., 1989

[Cronhjort and Gallmo 1982] Cronhjort, B. and B. Gallmo, *A Model of the Industrial Product Development Process,* Report #1982-09-01-C-TB-BG-82010, L.M. Ericsson Information Systems, Bromma, Sweden, 1982.

[Davis 1988] Davis, A., "A Comparison of Techniques for the Specification of External System Behavior," *Communications of the ACM,* Vol. 31, No. 9, September 1988, pp. 1098–1115; reprinted elsewhere in this tutorial.

[Davis 1988a] Davis, A., "A Taxonomy for the Early Stages of the Software Development Life Cycle," *The Journal of Systems and Software,* Vol. 8, No. 4, September 1988, pp. 297–311.

[DeMarco 1978] DeMarco, T., *Structured Analysis and System Specification,* Prentice Hall, Englewood Cliffs, N.J., 1978.

[DoD 1988] Department of Defense, *Military Standard: Defense System Software Development, DOD-STD-2167A,* Department of Defense, Washington, D.C., 1988.

[Freeman 1983] Freeman, P., "Fundamentals of Design," *IEEE Tutorial on Software Design Techniques,* Fourth Edition, edited by P. Freeman and A. Wasserman, IEEE Computer Society Press, Washington, D.C., 1983, pp. 2–22.

[Gane and Sarson 1979] Gane, C. and T. Sarson, *Structured Systems Analysis,* Prentice-Hall, Englewood Cliffs, N.J., 1979.

[Glaseman and Davis 1980] Glaseman, S. and M. Davis, *Software Requirements for Embedded Computers: A Preliminary Report,* Report #R-2567-AF, U.S. Air Force, Washington, D.C., March 1980.

[IEEE 1984] The Institute of Electrical and Electronics Engineers, Inc., *IEEE Guide to Software Requirements Specifications,* ANSI/IEEE Standard #830-1984, The Institute of Electrical and Electronics Engineers, Inc., New York, 1984.

[Kerola and Freeman 1981] Kerola, P. and P. Freeman, "A Comparison of Life Cycle Models," *IEEE 5th International Conference on Software Engineering,* IEEE Computer Society Press, Washington, D.C., 1981, pp. 90–99.

[Marca and McGowan 1988] Marca, D. and C. McGowan, *Structured Analysis and Design Technique,* McGraw Hill, New York, 1988.

[McGowan 1982] McGowan, C., private correspondence, Waltham, Mass., 1982.

[McMenamin and Palmer 1984] McMenamin, S. and J. Palmer, *Essential Systems Analysis,* Prentice-Hall, Englewood Cliffs, N.J., 1984.

[Orr 1981] Orr, K., *Structured Requirements Definition,* Ken Orr and Associates, Topeka, Kan., 1981.

[Pressman 1982] Pressman, R., *Software Engineering: A Practitioner's Approach,* McGraw-Hill, New York, 1982.

[Rentsch 1982] Rentsch, T., "Object-Oriented Programming, *ACM SIGPLAN Notices,* Vol. 17, No. 9, September 1982, pp. 51–59.

[Rockstrom and Saracco 1982] Rockstrom, A. and R. Saracco, "SDL—CCITT Specification and Description Language," *IEEE Transactions on Communications,* Vol. SE-30, No. 6, June 1982, pp. 1310–1317.

[Roman 1984] Roman, G.-C. et al., "A Total System Design Framework," *IEEE Computer,* Vol. 17, No. 5, May 1984, pp. 15–26.

[Ross 1977] Ross, D., "Structured Analysis (SA): A Language for Communicating Ideas," *IEEE Transactions on Software Engineering,* Vol. SE-3, No. 1, January 1977, pp. 16–34.

[Ross 1985] Ross, D., "Applications and Extensions of SADT," *Computer,* Vol. 18, No. 4, April 1985, pp. 25–34.

[Ross and Schuman 1977] Ross, D. and K. Schuman, Jr., "Structured Analysis for Requirements Definition," *IEEE Transactions on Software Engineering,* Vol. SE-3, No. 1, January 1977, pp. 6–15.

[Searle 1981] Searle, L., *An Air Force Guide to the System Specification,* Report #TM-5772/010/00, ESD-TR-

81-128, U.S. Air Force, Washington, D.C., January 1981.

[Sutcliffe 1988] Sutcliffe, A., *Jackson System Development,* Prentice-Hall, Englewood Cliffs, N.J., 1988.

[Teichroew and Hershey 1977] Teichroew, D. and E.A. Hershey, III, "PSL/PSA: A Computer-Aided Technique for Structured Documentation and Analysis of Information Processing Systems," *IEEE Transactions on Software Engineering,* Vol. SE-3, No. 1, January 1977, pp. 41–48.

[Turing 1936] Turing, A., "On Computable Numbers, with an Application to the Entscheidungs problem," *Proceedings of the London Mathematical Society,* Vol. 2, No. 42, 1936, pp. 230–265.

[Ward 1986] Ward, P., "The Transformation Schema: An Extension of the Data Flow Diagram to Represent Control and Timing," *IEEE Transactions on Software Engineering,* Vol. SE-12, No. 2, February 1986, pp. 198–210.

[Ward and Mellor 1985] Ward, P. and S. Mellor, *Structured Development for Real-Time Systems,* Prentice-Hall, Englewood Cliffs, N.J. 1985.

[Wasserman et al. 1986] Wasserman, A. et al., "Developing Interactive Information Systems with the User Software Engineering Methodology," *IEEE Transactions on Software Engineering,* Vol. SE-12, No. 2, February 1986, pp. 326–345.

[Yeh and Zave 1980] Yeh, R. and P. Zave, "Specifying Software Requirements," *Proceedings of the IEEE,* Vol. 68, No. 9, September 1980, pp. 1077–1085.

[Yourdon 1989] Yourdon, E., *Modern Structured Analysis,* Prentice-Hall, Englewood Cliffs, N.J., 1989.

[Yourdon and Constantine 1979] Yourdon, E. and L. Constantine, *Structured Design,* Prentice-Hall, Englewood Cliffs, N.J., 1979.

[Zave 1982] Zave, P., "An Operational Approach to Requirements Specification for Embedded Systems," *IEEE Transactions on Software Engineering,* Vol. SE-8, No. 3, May 1982, pp. 250–269.

Biography

Alan M. Davis received a B.S. degree in Mathematics from the State University of New York at Albany, and M.S. and Ph.D. degrees in Computer Science from the University of Illinois at Urbana-Champaign in 1973 and 1975, respectively. He is currently a Visiting Professor of Software Systems Engineering at George Mason University and an internal consultant at BTG, Inc. From 1984 to 1986 and during 1988, he was Vice President and Director of Engineering Services at BTG, Inc. In this position, he was responsible for all aspects of BTG's $4 million services business. This business included providing systems engineering, product assurance, program management support, consulting and training services, mostly to the Federal Government. During 1987, Dr. Davis was Vice President and Director of Research for BTG, Inc. In this role, he was responsible for all aspects of corporate research, especially software engineering research. Prior to joining BTG, he was a Director of R&D for GTE Communication Systems, and the Director of the Software Technology Center at GTE Laboratories. In the former role, he managed 140 software and hardware engineers developing large commercial telephone switching systems. In the latter role, he was responsible for all GTE corporate-wide research in software engineering and electronic computer-aided design; this included a staff of 40 research professionals. Dr. Davis was also an Assistant Professor of Computer Science at the University of Tennessee, a Visiting Assistant Professor at the University of Illinois and an Adjunct Instructor at Boston University.

Dr. Davis is the author or co-author of over 30 papers on software engineering, has written a new book titled *Software Requirements: Analysis and Specification* (Prentice Hall, 1990), has contributed chapters to three other books, and has been invited to speak at 30 different companies or universities in 12 countries. He is a senior member of the IEEE, and a member of the American Management Association (AMA), the Armed Services Communication and Electronic Association (AFCEA), the Association for Computing Machinery (ACM), and Sigma Xi. Dr. Davis was a 1983 IEEE International Distinguished Lecturer, a recipient of the IEEE Computer Society Certificate of Appreciation Award in 1984, and the General Chairman of IEEE's COMPSAC '86 Conference. He is on the editorial board of the *Journal of Systems and Software,* a member of ACM's Computing Practices Advisory Panel, a member of the executive committee of the IEEE Computer Society's Technical Committee on Software Engineering, and chair of the IEEE working group responsible for the creation and revision of *IEEE/ANSI Standard 830—A Guide for Software Requirements Specification.* His current research interests include software engineering methodology, software management, software development tools/environments, and requirements specification techniques.

Specifying Software Quality Requirements with Metrics

Steven E. Keller
Laurence G. Kahn

Dynamics Research Corporation
Systems Division
60 Frontage Rd.
Andover, MA 08180
(508) 475-9090

Roger B. Panara

Rome Air Development Center
RADC/COEE
Griffiss Air Force Base,
Rome, NY 13441-5700

1: Introduction

This paper provides an overview of the use of software quality metrics to specify testable software quality requirements in a software requirement specification. "Software quality is the degree to which software possesses a desired combination of attributes" [1]. With the increasing cost of software, software consumers—those who use, evaluate, or acquire software products—are increasingly concerned with software quality and want a product that will satisfy their needs.

Software consumers often express their needs in general, qualitative terms, such as reliability, maintainability, portability, efficiency, etc. To affect the outcome of a development effort or to determine objectively whether a given product is satisfactory, they need to define precisely the specific attributes they want the software to possess.

This paper examines techniques for identifying and specifying the desired attributes of a software system. Software quality metrics play an important role in this process because they provide a way to measure the degree to which software exhibits a given attribute. The techniques described in this paper provide a basis for formulating testable requirements for the quality attributes of software systems.

Software quality attributes are discussed in Section 2. The notion of software quality requirements and the reasons they are needed are described in Section 3. Background on software quality metrics is provided in Section 4. Section 5 introduces the software quality metrics framework, which organizes metrics into metric-aggregates with the intention of representing more general attributes of software quality. Section 6 discusses the use of metrics to formulate software quality metrics requirements and a methodology for specifying software quality goals, with a detailed description and example provided in Appendix A. Section 7 summarizes the key concepts. Appendix B offers guidelines for constructing software quality metric requirements.

2: Software Quality Attributes

Software engineers concerned with improving software quality have identified general attributes that apply across different application areas, operational environments, and development methodologies. The Rome Air Development Center (RADC) has invested over 10 years in the development of a methodology for specifying and evaluating software quality attributes [2]. This work incorporates the application experience of many corporations involved in large-scale software and systems development. RADC described thirteen general attributes of software that are of interest to software consumers. They are shown in Figure 1 [3].

Although the terms shown in the figure are widely used, they are not industry standard terminology. Software quality specification is a young and evolving discipline, and its terminology is not universally standardized. The IEEE Quality Metrics Standards Committee (P1061) is developing a standard for a software quality metrics methodology [1]. The sample attributes listed there differ somewhat from the RADC attributes (e.g., testability is used instead of verifiability, and the attributes evolutionary stability, manageability, resource quality, and responsiveness are added).

EH0304-6/90/0000/0145$01.00

Acquisition Concern	User Concern	Quality Attribute
Performance—How Well Does It Function?	How well does it utilize a resource?	Efficiency
	How secure is it?	Integrity
	What confidence can be placed in what it does?	Reliability
	How well will it perform under adverse conditions?	Survivability
	How easy is it to use?	Usability
Design—How Valid Is the Design?	How well does it conform to the Requirements?	Correctness
	How easy is it to repair?	Maintainability
	How easy is it to verify its performance?	Verifiability
Adaptation—How Adaptable Is It?	How easy is it to expand or upgrade its capability or performance?	Expandability
	How easy is it to change?	Flexibility
	How easy is it to interface with another system?	Interoperability
	How easy is it to transport?	Portability
	How easy is it to convert for use in another application?	Reusability

Figure 1: The RADC software quality consumer-oriented attributes

Software quality researchers have attempted to decompose consumer-oriented attributes into technically oriented attributes that are more meaningful to software producers (e.g., analysts, designers, programmers, testers, and maintainers). Identifying relationships between consumer-oriented attributes and technically oriented attributes of software facilitates objective communication between consumers and producers.

RADC described twenty-six general technically oriented attributes, such as accuracy, anomaly management, generality, modularity, and simplicity. Figure 2 shows relationships between consumer-oriented attributes and technically oriented attributes identified in the RADC work [4]. The general consumer-oriented attributes are known as "software quality factors" in both the RADC and IEEE work. The technically oriented attributes are referred to as "criteria" in the RADC work and "sub-factors" in the IEEE work. The sample technically oriented attributes listed by the IEEE Quality Metrics Standards Committee differ somewhat from the RADC attributes.

3: Software Quality Requirements

Software quality requirements are engineering requirements that address the degree to which software possesses desired quality attributes. To attain desired levels of reliability, maintainability, portability, usability, efficiency or any other software quality attribute in a large system development, many people, perhaps even from different organizations, must cooperate in building individual software components that contribute to meeting the overall objective. Software quality requirements provide the essential formal communications needed to coordinate the many activities of a large-scale project.

For example, achieving high system availability in an avionics flight control system requires that each component in the software perform its function reliably. Definitions of software reliability and the required degree of reliability guide people, teams, and organizations to build software components in a way that supports the objective of availability.

Unfortunately, high-level software quality terms have different meanings to different people in different environments. This is partly because of their lack of familiarity with standardized terminology, but also because different projects and organizations have widely varying needs and characteristics. The meaning of a term such as "portability" is affected by project circumstances, such as planned contingencies for future host and target environments. For example, if the plan calls for porting the software within a family of upwards compatible computers with the same in-

Acquisition Concern	Criterion/Acronym		Performance					Design			Adaptation				
	Factor/Acronym		Efficiency EF	Integrity IG	Reliability RL	Survivability SV	Usability US	Correctness CR	Maintainability MA	Verifiability VE	Expandability EX	Flexibility FX	Interoperability IP	Portability PO	Reusability RU
PERFORMANCE	Accuracy	AC			X										
	Anomaly management	AM			X	X									
	Autonomy	AU				X									
	Distributedness	DI				X									
	Effectiveness communication	EC	X												
	Effectiveness processing	EP	X												
	Effectiveness storage	ES	X												
	Operability	OP					X								
	Inconfigurability	IN				X									
	System accessability	SS		X											
	Training	TN					X								
DESIGN	Completeness	CP						X							
	Consistency	CS						X	X						
	Traceability	TC						X							
	Visibility	VS							X	X					
ADAPTATION	Application independence	AP													X
	Augmentability	AT									X				
	Commonality	CL											X		
	Document accessibility	DO													X
	Functional overlap	FO											X		
	Functional scope	FS													X
	Generality	GE									X	X			X
	Independence	ID											X	X	X
	System clarity	ST													X
	System compatibility	SY											X		
	Virtuality	VR									X				
GENERAL	Modularity	MO				X			X	X	X	X	X	X	X
	Self-descriptiveness	SD							X	X	X	X		X	X
	Simplicity	SI			X				X	X	X	X			X

Figure 2: Software quality factors and criteria

put/output subsystem, then input/output portability is less important than timing portability.

Different kinds of software reliability can also result in confusion over definitions. Error recovery introduces the possibility that erroneous results are produced from operations on incorrect data. However, in many real-time systems, error recovery is essential (e.g., a flight control system in an airplane that requires computer support to fly). In other systems, the concern for accurate detection of errors often overrides the possible advantages of recovery (e.g., compilers often limit the scope of error recovery in order to avoid producing incorrect results).

Since, development of large software systems involves a substantial financial investment, such systems tend to be used and modified over a long period of time to amortize the investment. In the largest systems, the operation and maintenance phase often is the most significant cost element. In this context, supportability attributes, such as maintainability, flexibility, and portability, are particularly important. Careful planning of supportability requirements and success in meeting them have a substantial impact on overall life-cycle costs.

For the reasons outlined above, software quality requirements are an important part of a requirements specification. The U.S. Department of Defense (DoD), recognizing the importance of software quality requirements, includes them in the DoD standard for software development (DOD-STD-2167A) [5]. Software quality metrics, described in the next section, provide a way to develop quantitative, testable software quality requirements.

4: Software Quality Metrics

A metric is a number indicating amount. The IEEE draft metrics standard defines a software quality metric as follows: "A software quality metric is a function whose inputs are software data and whose output is a single (numerical) value that can be interpreted as the degree to which software possesses a given attribute that affects its quality" [6]. For example, the proportion of execution paths that have been tested is a single numerical value for the degree of test coverage that affects the quality of verification for a computer software unit during the code and test phases [7].

A data item is a unit of data necessary to compute a metric value. For example, the number of execution paths in a computer software unit is a data item.

Metrics may be characterized by the type of input data. A product metric is used to measure the characteristics of the documentation and code [8]. A process metric is used to measure characteristics of the methods, techniques, and tools employed in acquiring, developing, verifying, and operating the software [9]. This paper focuses on product metrics.

Software quality metrics have been developed and used for a variety of purposes [10-21]. Metrics should be developed and used for a specific, well-defined, and well-documented purpose. Applying metrics without a clear purpose muddles the metrics discipline, just as misuse of statistical information confounds other disciplines. Metrics are used to provide visibility to engineers and managers; to assess adherence to standards, guidelines, and principles; to estimate and predict; and to accept the product. Each of these uses is described briefly in Sections 4.1-4.4. Section 4.5 describes software quality metrics validation.

4.1: Visibility

Metrics can provide visibility and insight to decision-makers. In large projects, the total amount of inherent information is often much more than a decision-maker can digest and understand. Therefore, to make an informed decision, a decision-maker needs summary information. Quantitative metrics can be used to summarize information needed to make distinctions, to identify outlying software characteristics, or to detect trends.

4.1.1: Example—Number of Branches

This metric provides visibility into the amount of branching in the executable part of the software. A well-defined metric for the number of branches must provide an objective definition of a branch. It can be used in the following ways:

1. *To make distinctions:* Based on experience in a project or application area, a component with a greater number of branches typically requires a greater effort to test; this information may be helpful in planning the testing effort.
2. *To identify outlying software characteristics:* Based on experience in a project or application area, an inordinately large number of branches in a component (in comparison to other components or a baseline estimate) may warrant further investigation of why the number of branches is so large.
3. *To detect trends:* Based on experience in a project or application area, a trend of growth in the number of branches in a component may indicate the need to re-examine the algorithms and data structures used to determine whether other choices would provide a more appropriate solution.

4.2: Adherence

Metrics can be used to assess adherence to a well-defined and documented standard, guideline, or principle. Adherence metrics can be employed to measure deviations, which can be used in a management feedback loop to recover to an acceptable level. Adherence metrics provide a mechanism for assessing adherence to guidelines or principles that are difficult or impossible to express and establish as a standard [23, 24].

4.2.1: Example—Communication Formats

An example of a metric that assesses adherence to standards is the proportion of communication data objects that adhere to an established standard for communication data formats. Non-adherence can be a technical as well as a management issue. For example, non-adherence may result when the standard must be violated in order to achieve program-specific requirements (e.g., efficiency). Quantitative information provides a mechanism for isolating problem areas within the system and over time.

4.3: Estimation/Prediction

Metrics can be used as input into a model designed to estimate software parameters, such as timing, number of errors, effort, or utilization of a resource.

4.3.1: Example—Software Error Rate

The methodology for software reliability prediction [25] describes one approach to predicting and estimating software error rates. During the early stages of software development, software metrics and characteristics are used to calculate a figure of merit, which makes a quantitative statement about future error rates. During testing and later phases, error rates are estimated based on a mathematical model that incorporates the predictive figure of merit. In most previous efforts, model parameters were fitted to the data obtained from a particular project. Poor results were generally observed when the models were applied to data from other environments [26]. The above technique provided estimations within 30 percent of actuals [27]. The accuracy of estimation techniques can be improved as more data become available.

4.4: Acceptance

Metrics can be used as a standard for acceptance of a software product produced under a contractual agreement. Adopting a metric as an acceptance criterion implies that the procurer has a very high degree of confidence based on past experience in the relationship between the metric and desired properties of the system. Very few metrics are so well understood. However, it is possible to integrate weaker metrics into a meaningful metrics policy, as described in Section 6.

4.5: Validation

Validation is the process of building objective evidence that a metric is effective in meeting its stated purpose. For example, validation could involve determining that a visibility metric is useful to decision-makers; that an adherence metric accurately reflects adherence to the stated standard, guideline, or principle; or that the underlying standard, guideline, or principle is beneficial to the project in the intended manner. For estimation models, validation involves determining the accuracy of the model as compared to observed data. Good validation incorporates application of a metric for its stated purpose on real projects.

5: Software Quality Metrics Framework

A software quality metrics framework is a hierarchical structure in which metrics are organized into metric-aggregates. A metric-aggregate is a metric whose inputs are other metrics. (Metrics that are not metric-aggregates, i.e., that are not computed from other metrics, are often referred to as metric-elements.) The metric-aggregates in a software quality metrics framework are designed to provide a quantitative representation of general attributes of software quality, such as those described in Section 2.

Figure 3 shows an example of a framework. The RADC framework has three layers of metric-aggregates: metric-aggregates designed to represent factors (e.g., reliability, maintainability, portability, etc.) at the top level, metric-aggregates designed to represent criteria at the second level, and metric-aggregates made up of metric-elements at the third level [28].

The concept of a software quality metrics framework grew out of attempts to develop quantitative representations of general software quality attributes. Two kinds of metrics are used to quantify software quality attributes: direct metrics and indirect metrics. A direct metric is a rating expressed in terms of timing, number of errors, effort, or utilization of a resource. Examples are efficiency expressed in terms of actual utilization of a resource, correctness expressed in terms of errors in conformance to specifications, and portability expressed in terms of effort to port the system. The IEEE draft introduced the term "direct metric" [29]. An example of a direct metric for maintainability is "the ease of effort for locating and fixing a software failure within a specified time period," with the following rating formula: 1-0.1 * (average-labor-days-to-fix) [30].

An indirect metric is a quantity representing software characteristics that may influence a direct metric score. An advantage of indirect metrics is that they can be used early in the software development life cycle, before resource, timing, error, or effort data are available. A software quality metrics framework is really a tool for defining indirect met-

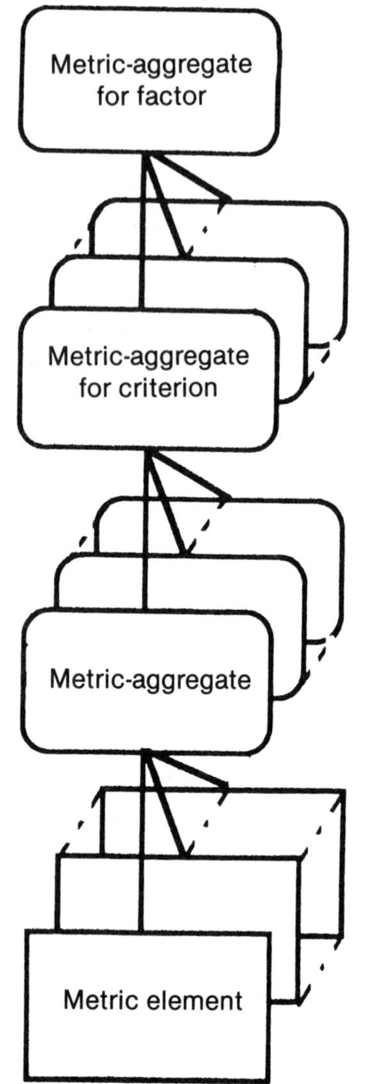

Figure 3: Structure of a software quality metrics framework

rics. A metric-aggregate designed to represent a factor is decomposed into metric-aggregates designed to represent criteria, which in turn are decomposed into metric-aggregates designed to represent more detailed attributes, and so on.

Figure 4 shows how a metric-aggregate corresponding to the factor maintainability is decomposed into metrics for criteria [31]. The criteria metric-aggregates measure the application of software characteristics that influence consistency, modularity, self-descriptiveness, simplicity, and visibility, which in turn influence maintainability. For example, the metric-aggregate for consistency is a measure of "those characteristics of the software which provide for uniform design and implementation techniques and notation" [32]. The item CS.1 shown in the figure is an abbreviation for a metric that addressed characteristics of consistency between procedures (as opposed to consistency of data, addressed by metric CS.2) [33]. Aspects of procedure consistency measured by CS.1 include standardization of design representations, external input/output protocols, error handling, and naming.

A well-defined scoring technique is an important part of a framework definition. One scoring technique is the weighted average of the component framework elements [34].

To be effective, a metrics framework must be tailored to the characteristics and needs of the project. Tailoring is applied at each layer of the framework from factors through data items. In order for a framework element to be included in a project specific framework, it should meet the following criteria: (1) The element measures characteristics that are within the scope of the project, (2) the element measures characteristics that are consistent with the performance and supportability objectives and the chosen design approach, and (3) the element provides sufficient benefits with respect to its purpose to warrant the cost of collection.

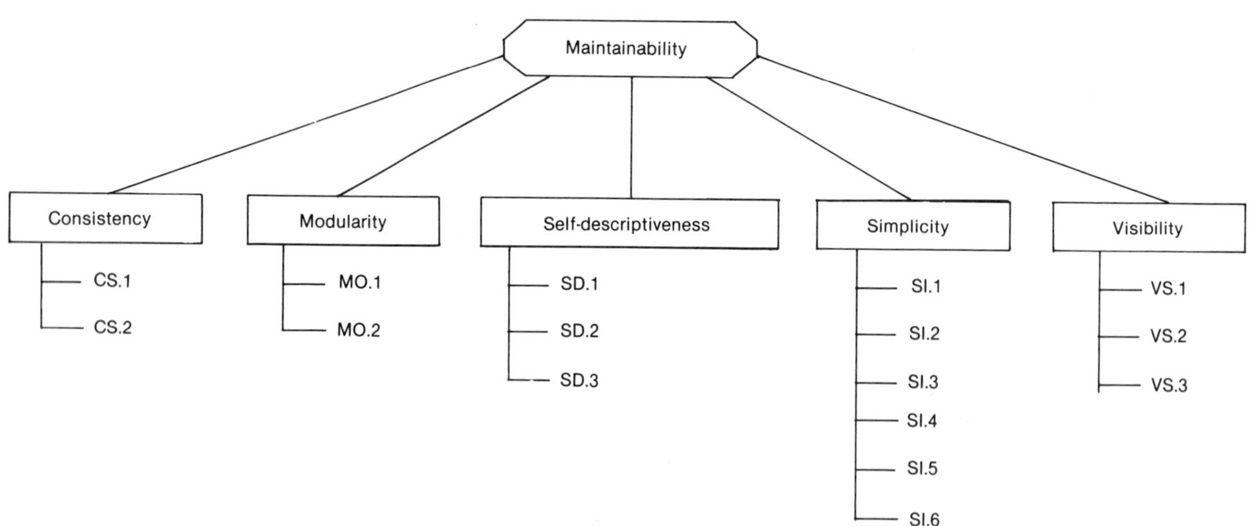

Figure 4: Definition of the factor maintainability

Table 1 shows tailoring considerations for layers of a software quality framework.

6: Software Quality Metric Goals and Requirements

A software quality metric goal is a score for a software quality metric (or a condition or set of conditions on the score) that one hopes to achieve. Experience gathered through previous attempts to apply a software quality framework to actual software products has shown that establishing goals is an important aspect of applying metrics [35-37].

The RADC software quality specification methodology provides a technique for establishing goals and is divided into three main components: (1) ranking factors and criteria according to their relative importance to the project ("Rank Factors and Criteria"), (2) establishing goals for factor metric-aggregates ("Quantify Factors"), and (3) assessing differences between the evaluation results (achieved metric scores) and the established goals ("Assess Compliance"). These components are time-dependent, in the Step 1 must be performed before Step 2, and Step 3 occurs much later, after evaluation of the product(s)/process. Figure 5 graphically shows the main components of the methodology. Appendix A illuminates the considerations and decisions involved in specifying quality goals and illustrates the methodology by applying it to the specification of quality goals for a hypothetical software engineering environment.

Once appropriate metrics have been identified and goals established, one can specify software quality metric requirements. A software quality metric requirement is a condition or set of conditions defined in terms of software quality metrics that must be met to satisfy the requirement. These are all examples of software quality metrics requirements: (1) The scores for each computer software component for reliability and its metric constituents shall be made available for design and code reviews four weeks prior to review, (2) an explanation shall be required at reviews for all components of the network software with less than 80 percent adherence to procedure consistency metrics, and (3) a written waiver shall be required for acceptance of any computer software configuration item in which more than 10 percent of the modules attain a portability score below 0.4. Notice that goals are often an important part of a software quality metrics requirement (e.g., 80 percent adherence in requirement two, less than 10 percent of the modules below 0.4 in requirement three).

The specification of testable software quality metric requirements is not widely practiced in industry today, although it is becoming more common. For the most part, organizations lack experience with the benefits, costs, and behavior of software quality metrics in the context of different application areas, environments, and development methodologies. This lack of experience often prevents organizations from identifying rigid requirements for the software product, and rightly so. However, it is possible and often appropriate to specify meaningful software quality requirements in the context of the software development *process*. With this approach, requirements specify an action that is triggered when a condition on a metric value holds. The actions are activities of the software development process. The previous examples are of this nature. Appendix B suggests how to construct software quality metric requirements in this manner.

Table 1: Tailoring considerations

Framework layer	Tailoring information	Tailoring action
Factors	Project needs and characteristics	Applicable factors Priority
Criteria	Project needs and characteristics	Applicable criteria Weighting
Metrics	Cost of collection Benefits Languages and tools How used Development method	Applicable metrics Weighting Tailored definitions Tailored calculations
Data Items	Availability and validity of data Life-cycle phase Periodicity Languages and tools Development method	Tailored definition (unambiguous)

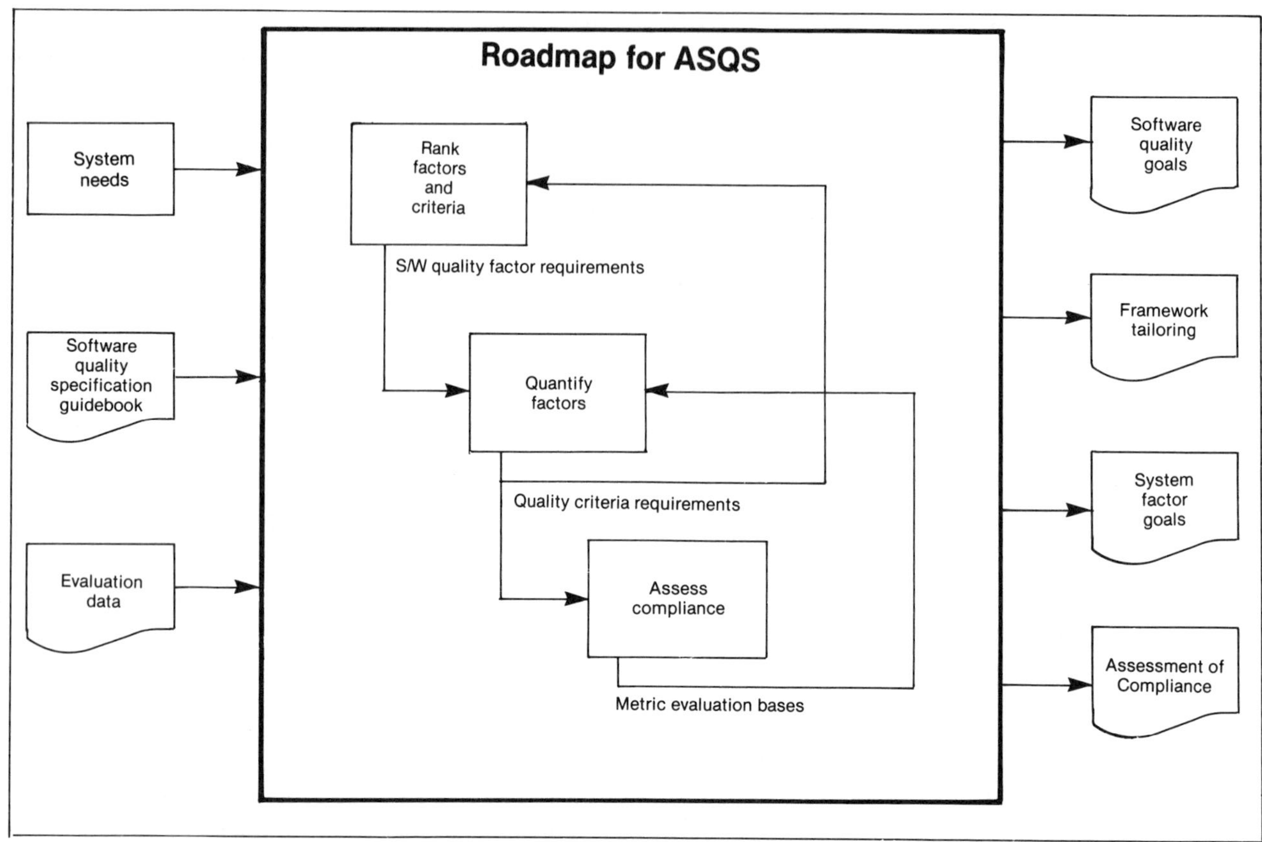

Figure 5: Main components of the RADC specification methodology and their interrelationships as displayed in the top-level roadmap of the assistant for specifying the quality of software (ASQS)

7: Summary

Since software systems are becoming larger, more complex, and more significant components of a system's overall functionality, specifying precise software quality requirements is increasingly important. Software quality requirements provide the formal communications essential to coordinate the many elements of a large-scale project. Supportability requirements are crucial to controlling operation and maintenance costs for very large systems, since they tend to be used over a long period to amortize the substantial investment in development.

Software quality metrics are a basis for establishing quantitative, testable software quality requirements. Metrics should be developed and used for a specific, well-defined, and well-documented purpose. A software quality metrics framework captures relationships between metrics and abstract quality attributes. To be effective, a metrics framework must be tailored to the characteristics and needs of the project.

The RADC software quality metrics methodology provides a starting point for anyone interested in establishing software quality goals and associated quality requirements. Because the field of software development is still young, no complete framework or methodology exists today. No existing framework could possibly address all the software attributes necessary for a high-quality system. However, as our experience in software development and quality grows, frameworks can be improved to measure more characteristics of documentation, code, and the development process necessary for high-quality software. By specifying quality goals and requirements and evaluating quality during development, deficiencies can be identified and located early, thereby reducing the risk of cost/schedule overruns or performance/supportability deficiencies associated with poor-quality systems.

8: References

1. IEEE Quality Metrics Standards Committee P1061, *Standard for a Software Quality Metrics Methodology,* Draft Version 13b, IEEE, New York, July 7, 1987.
2. Bowen, T.P., Wigle, G.B., and Tsai, J.T., "Specification of Software Quality Attributes," *RADC-TR-85-37,* Vol. I (Introduction), Vol. II, (Software Quality

Specification Guidebook), Vol. III, (Software Quality Evaluation Guidebook), Rome Air Development Center, Griffiss Air Force Base, N.Y., Feb. 1985.

3. *RADC-TR-85-37,* Vol. II (Software Quality Specification Guidebook), pp. 2-17.
4. *RADC-TR-85-37,* Vol. II (Software Quality Specification Guidebook), pp. 3-10.
5. *Data Item Descriptions for DoD-STD-2167A,* Rome Air Development Center, Griffiss Air Force Base, N.Y., Feb. 29, 1988, paragraph 10.1.5.2.5 (system quality factors), paragraph 10.1.5.10 (software quality factors).
6. IEEE Draft Version 13b, pp. 1.
7. *RADC-TR-85-37,* Vol. III (Software Quality Evaluation Guidebook), pp. A-179 (VS.1(1)).
8. IEEE Draft Version 13b, p. 3.
9. IEEE Draft Version 13b, p. 3.
10. Gannan, J.D., Katz, E.E., and Basili, V.R., "Metrics for Ada Packages: An Initial Study," *Communications of ACM,* Vol. 29, No. 7, July 1986.
11. Henry, S. and Kafura, D., "The Evaluation of Software Systems' Structure Using Quantitative Software Metrics," *Software-Practice and Experience,* Vol. 14 (6), June 1984.
12. Gordon, R.D., "A Qualitative Justification for a Measure of Program Clarity," *IEEE Transactions on Software Engineering,* Vol. SE-5, No. 2, March 1979.
13. Reynolds, R.G., "Metrics to Measure the Complexity of Partial Programs," *The Journal of Systems and Software,* Vol. 4, 1984.
14. Basili, V.R., "Metric Analysis and Data Validation Across FORTRAN Projects," *IEEE Transactions on Software Engineering,* Vol. SE-9, No. 6, Nov. 1983.
15. Basili, V.R., *Tutorials on Models and Metrics for Software Management and Engineering,* IEEE Computer Society Press, Washington, D.C., 1980.
16. Basili, V.R. and Perricone, B.T., "Software Errors and Complexity: An Empirical Investigation," *Communications of ACM,* Vol. 27, No. 1, Jan. 1984.
17. Behrens, C.A. "Measuring the Productivity of Computer Systems Development Activities with Function Points," *IEEE Transactions on Software Engineering,* Vol. SE-9, No. 6, Nov. 1983.
18. Boehm, B. et al., *Characteristics of Software Quality,* North-Holland Publishing Company, Amsterdam, The Netherlands, 1978.
19. Kafura, D. and Henry, S., "Software Structure Metrics Based on Information Flow," *IEEE Transactions on Software Engineering,* Vol. SE-7, No. 5, Sept. 1981.
20. Rombach, H.D. and Basili, V.R., "Quantitative Assessment of Maintenance: An Industrial Case Study," *Proceedings of the Conference on Software Maintenance,* IEEE Computer Society Press, Washington, D.C., Sept. 21-24, 1987.
21. McCabe, T.J., "A Complexity Measure," *IEEE Transactions on Software Engineering,* Vol. SE-2, No. 4, Dec. 1976.
22. *ADAMAT Reference Manual,* Dynamics Research Corporation, Andover, Mass.
23. Keller, S.E. and Perkins, J.A., "Ada Measurement Based on Software Quality Principles," *Washington Ada Symposium,* March 1985.
24. Anderson, J.D. and Perkins, J.A., "Experience Using an Automated Metrics Framework in the Review of Ada Source for WIS," *6th Annual National Conference on Ada Technology,* March 1988.
25. McCall, J. et al., "Methodology for Software Reliability Predicton," *RADC-TR-87-171,* Vol. I, Rome Air Development Center, Griffiss Air Force Base, N.Y., Nov. 1987.
26. Ibid., pp. 1-4.
27. Ibid., pp. 6-18.
28. *RADC-TR-85-37,* Vol. II (Software Quality Specification Guidebook), pp. 2-16.
29. IEEE Draft Version 13b, pp. 2, 12, 13.
30. *RADC-TR-85-37,* Vol. II (Software Quality Specification Guidebook), pp. 3-2, 3-6.
31. *RADC-TR-85-37,* Vol. II (Software Quality Specification Guidebook), pp. 2-19.
32. *RADC-TR-85-37,* Vol. II (Software Quality Specification Guidebook), pp. 3-12.
33. *RADC-TR-85-37,* Vol. II (Software Quality Specification Guidebook), pp. 3-13.
34. *RADC-TR-85-37,* Vol. II (Software Quality Specification Guidebook), pp. 4-63.
35. Technical Reports, *CDRL Sequence Number 105-109,* Contract No. F19628-84-D-0016, Task Number 80073, Rome Air Development Center, Griffiss Air Force Base, N.Y., Sept. 1986.
36. *Software Quality Measurement Demonstration Project I,* Rome Air Development Center, Griffiss Air Force Base, N.Y.
37. Software Quality Measurement Demonstration Project II, *RADC-TR-87-164,* Rome Air Development Center, Griffiss Air Force Base, N.Y., Oct. 1987.
38. *RADC-TR-85-37,* Vol. II (Software Quality Specification Guidebook), pp. 4-12—4-13.
39. *RADC-TR-85-37,* Vol. II (Software Quality Specification Guidebook), pp. 4-9.

40. *Technical Report Enhanced SQS Guidebooks,* CDRL Sequence Number 109, Contract No. F19628-84-D-0016, Task Number 80073, Rome Air Development Center, Griffiss Air Force Base, N.Y., Sept. 30, 1986.
41. *RADC-TR-85-37,* Vol. II (Software Quality Specification Guidebook), pp. 4-13.
42. *RADC-TR-85-37,* Vol. II (Software Quality Specification Guidebook), pp. 4-14.
43. *Documentation for the Assistant for Specifying the Quality Software (ASQS),* CDRL Sequence Numbers A002-A005, Contract No. F30602-86-C-0157, Rome Air Development Center, Griffiss Air Force Base, N.Y., Oct. 23, 1987.
44. Winston, Patrick Henry, *Artificial Intelligence,* Addison-Wesley, Reading, Mass., 1977, pp. 243-244.
45. *RADC-TR-85-37,* Vol. II (Software Quality Specification Guidebook), pp. 4-23.
46. *RADC-TR-85-37,* Vol. II (Software Quality Specification Guidebook), pp. 4-22.
47. *RADC-TR-85-37,* Vol. II (Software Quality Specification Guidebook), pp. 4-28—4-33.

9: Appendix A—Overview of the RADC Methodology for Specifying Software Quality Goals

9.1: Introduction

This appendix provides an overview and example of the RADC methodology for specifying software quality goals and illustrates the considerations and decisions involved in this process. The methodology is divided into three main components: (1) ranking factors and criteria, (2) quantifying factors, and (3) assessing compliance. Each of these components will be described next.

9.2: Rank Factors and Criteria

To rank factors and criteria and arrive at software quality goals, the following steps are performed: (1) the functions of the application are identified, (2) initial software quality rankings are assigned to each function, (3) rankings are revised based on factor interrelationships, and (4) the cost of achieving the rankings is considered. The following sections outline this process in greater detail.

9.2.1: Identify Application/Functions

Before specifying software quality goals, it is important to identify the application area and software functions of your system. These activities will be discussed next.

Identification of application area: The identification of the application area is important because characteristics of the application area affect typical software quality requirements. For instance, knowing that the application area is "flight critical avionics systems" implies that the system will process information in real-time. This fact alone affects software quality. For example, efficiency may play an important role.

Another reason to identify an application area is to facilitate reuse of information. After you have identified the application area for your project, give some time and thought to whether you can use any similar work that has been performed as a source of information. For example, if a similar project has already been completed, or if yours is an upgrade to an existing system, information may already be available that could save time and help the software quality specification process. You may be able to use an existing body of knowledge, such as Tables 4.1.2-1 and 4.1.2-2 of RADC Guidebook Volume II [38].

Identification of functions: It is important to identify those software functions that will have separate quality requirements [39]. During the early stages of project planning, a functional decomposition of the project may not exist. During this time, quality requirements are usually specified for the project as a whole. As more information emerges and as it becomes apparent that the system functions each have varying quality requirements, the system can be further decomposed into lower-level functions. Give careful thought to decomposing the system, because each new function increases the cost of software quality evaluation. Too few functions, however, may not provide enough resolution to differentiate functions adequately with regard to software quality. Figure 6 is a sample decomposition for a hypothetical software engineering environment.

9.2.2: Assign Factor and Criteria Rankings

Arriving at initial factor/criteria rankings is a three-step process. First, for each function a list is developed of system characteristics, needs, and/or requirements mapped to software quality-related terms from a software quality framework. Next, each characteristic/need/requirement is assigned a ranking based on importance. Finally, based on the strength and importance of the relationships between the characteristic/need/requirement and software-related terms, the initial factor and criteria rankings are determined. These steps are outlined in more detail in the following sections.

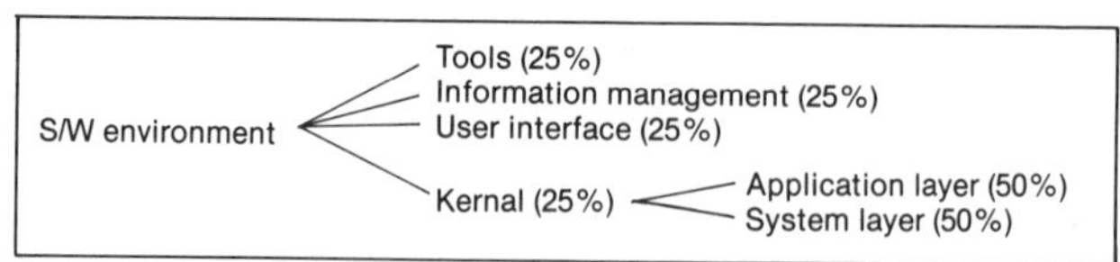

Figure 6: Sample decomposition of a hypothetical software engineering environment

Identify characteristics, needs, and/or requirements related to software quality: System characteristics, needs and/or requirements related to software quality should be identified and documented in table form. Each function of the system should have a separate list of characteristics/ needs/requirements. The list should also document quality-related terms for each entry. Table 2 is an example that shows characteristics/needs/requirements for two functions of a software engineering environment.

When completing a table of this kind, follow these guidelines:

1. The characteristic/need/requirement should appear in the left column of the table under each function name.
2. The right column of the table should contain the related software quality terms (i.e., factor, criterion, or metric-related term) and rationale.
3. If a characteristic/need/requirement does not imply all criteria contained in a factor but indicates only certain criteria, list the factor and the specific criterion.
4. If a characteristic/need requirement does not indicate a specific criterion of a factor, simply list the factor.
5. A rationale should be provided to record reasons for certain quality terms. Preserving the rationale facilitates updating software quality goals as a project characteristics or needs change. Later, if the quality goals are not being met, it will be important to know the reasons for requiring them in the first place. This information can also help acquaint new personnel with the quality aspects of the project.
6. Include all characteristics/needs/requirements related to software quality in the table, even those that you feel are not as important as others.
7. If documents (such as a system specification) are available, then the list of needs and requirements might include a phrase (with references) from the document that implies quality-related issues (see Table 2.4.1.2-1 of the Enhanced SQA Guidebook for assistance in mapping document references to software quality terms) [40].
8. Consider characteristics of the application, the deployment and maintenance environment, and the development plan, as well as functional characteristics (e.g., the function has a database or a network processing component).

The following list provides some examples of these characteristics and the implied quality-related term(s). The list is not meant to be comprehensive, but to suggest the type of characteristics that should be considered and to outline an appropriate thought process.

1. Application Characteristics
    a. Real-time application with short response requirements
        1. => Efficiency
        2. => Reliability (if failure to recognize sensory input data is unacceptable)
        3. => Correctness (Needed to achieve above two factors). See Table 4.1.2-2 from RADC Guidebook, Volume II [41]
    a. Large size/complexity
        1. => Modularity, self-descriptiveness, simplicity, consistency, visibility
2. Environment Characteristics
    a. Multiple maintenance sites
        1. => Maintainability among others
    b. Different environment for development and deployment
        1. => Maintainability
3. Development Characteristics
    a. Is it a prototype system with a short life-cycle (planned to be redeveloped if successful)
        1. => Less need for portability among other factors
    b. Examine software development plan standards, guidelines, and principles to determine appropriate metrics for assessing adherence e.g., standard for module prologue (proportion of modules that adhere to the standard).
4. Functional Characteristics
    a. Contains a database management system that stores classified data.
        1. => Integrity

The development of large systems often involves the early identification of system-level qualities, such as availability, safety, or transportability. Attaining these goals often implies a need for specific software quality goals. For example, high system availability may require high software reliability. Table 4.1.2-3 of the RADC Guidebook, Volume II, provides an example of how system quality factors relate to software quality factors. These system factor requirements (if any) should also appear in the table being constructed [42].

Survey results can also be used to help identify software quality characteristics/needs/requirements. Care to decide who will be surveyed and what background definitions of relevant software quality terminology (e.g., factors and criteria) to give them. Instruct those being surveyed to identify quality characteristics in the same tabular form used earlier. Stress the importance of including a rationale, since this is the primary piece of information that will be used to evaluate and rank their results. Along with each survey result, keep a current record of those who completed the

Table 2: Quality characteristics/needs/requirements and rationale

System/software characteristic/need and/or requirement	Quality-related terms (factor, criterion, metric)	Rationale
Function: Integration Framework		
• Performs DBMS functions		
• Stores classified data	Integrity	Prevent access of unauthorized personnel to classified data
• Required to record and report accesses	Integrity	
• Consistency of information after system failures	Reliability —Anomaly Management • Detection	Must detect failure in order to maintain consistency
	• Recovery	Ensure data integrity after failure
• Several different maintaining organizations	Maintainability —Self Descriptiveness —Consistency —Simplicity —Modularity	Ease of understanding needed for large staff
	Correctness —Completeness	Conformance to specifications needed so that documentation is accurate
• • •	Modularity	Ease distribution and inclusion of changes
Function: Kernal		
Subfunction: Kernal—application layer		
• Transportability across a single family of computers; Later transport to smaller scale systems	Portability —Wordsize —Capacity independence —system software independence is less important	
	Usability —Training	Training in use/operation needed for maintainers
Subfunction: Kernal—system layer • • •		

survey and their roles or jobs in relation to the project. (This information will be helpful when assigning rankings to the survey results.)

Although the given examples can help lead you in the right direction, there is no step-by-step algorithm for identifying quality requirements. The characteristics and cirsumstances of every system are different. The initial step is probably the most difficult and time consuming, but it is important to consider your system characteristics and the impact they have on software quality.

The Assistant for Specifying the Quality of Software (ASQS) currently under development for RADC is an expert system designed for this area [43]. ASQS helps the specifier identify important software quality issues by making inferences about software quality needs based on responses to questions about system characteristics, needs, and requirements. It organizes the many issues that the quality specifier must consider into a focused consultation, which is based on an underlying knowledge base.

Rank each requirement based on importance: Once all software quality characteristics/needs/requirements have been documented, each entry should be assigned a ranking or weighting based on its perceived importance. At this step, give careful thought to how important each requirement is to the overall success of the project. Hypothesize what would happen to the project if this requirement were not met or if the characteristic did not exist in the final system. If this analysis reveals that the effects could be disastrous, then the requirement/characteristic should be assigned a very high ranking. There is no single correct method for assigning rankings. One method is simply to assign a number between 1 and 5, with 1 indicating the least importance and 5 the most. Along with each ranking show a rationale or reason for the decision. If surveys are being used, then the requirements from each survey should also be assigned an importance ranking. When assigning rankings to survey results, keep in mind the roles within the organization of those you surveyed. For instance, an eventual maintainer of the system may naturally inflate the ratings for factors such as maintainability, flexibility, etc. Table 3 shows the rankings assigned for a portion of a software engineering environment.

Aggregate rankings by criteria and factor: After assigning each entry a relative ranking, reorganize the list accord-

Table 3: Quality characteristics/needs/requirements and ranking

System/software characteristics/needs/ and/or requirement	Quality-related terms (factor, criterion, metric)	Ranking
Function: Integration Framework		
• Performs DBMS functions Stores classified	Integrity	5
Required to record and report accesses	Integrity	4
• Consistency of information after system failures	Reliability	
	—Anomaly Management	
	• Detection	3
	• Recovery	3
• Several different maintaining organizations	Maintainability	
	—Self Descriptiveness	3
	—Consistency	3
	—Simplicity	3
	—Modularity	3
	Correctness	
	—Completeness	3
	Modularity	4
•		
•		
•		
Function: Kernal		
Subfunction: Kernal—application layer		
• Transportability across a single family of computers; Later transport to smaller scale systems	Portability	
	• Wordsize	5
	• Capacity independence	5
	• System software indep. is less important	2
	Usability	
	• Training	3
Subfunction: Kernal—system layer		
•		
•		
•		

ing to the function and the associated software quality-related terms. For each function, order the requirements by factor, then by criterion, and so on. Organizing the list in this way simplifies the aggregation of results to calculate an overall ranking for each criterion and factor by function. The output of this step is a relative ranking (prioritizing) of the factors and criteria by function: the most important factors and criteria are assigned a higher ranking than those that are less important. One method for doing this is to assign an H, M, L, or N/A to each factor and criterion: H for high; M, medium; L, low; and N/A, not applicable. The exact method used to perform this step is not important, as long as the output ranks each factor and criterion in relative terms for each system function for which you desire to specify and evaluate software quality goals. Note that assigning an H to a factor—for example, reliability—at this time does not necessarily mean that software reliability must be .999, but that in relation to the other factors that have *not* been assigned a ranking of H, reliability is more important. This indicates that your system needs software reliability very much in order to succeed and meet all its requirements. It also indicates that you are willing to spend more money and effort to achieve the desired reliability than to achieve lower priority factor/criterion goals.

Many different methods can be used to accumulate the amount or strength of evidence reflecting the need for a certain factor/criterion. ASQS uses a simplified Bayesian approach for accumulating evidence [44]. Figure 7 is an example set of initial software quality factor rankings for the software engineering environment.

Rank Factors and Criteria

Assign Factor and Criteria Rankings

Software Quality Factor Identification Form—Initial Goals

Software Quality Factor / System or Software Unique Function	Performance					Design			Adaptation				
	Efficiency	Integrity	Reliability	Survivability	Usability	Correctness	Maintainability	Verifiability	Expandability	Flexibility	Interoperability	Portability	Reusability
Tools		G	E		E	A	G	E	E	E	G	G	
Information Management	G	E	E	E		E	G	G	G				
User Interface	E	A	E	E	E	G	G	E	E	E			
Application Layer	G		E	E		E		G	G		E		
System Layer	E		E	E		E		E	E		E		

Figure 7: Initial software quality factor rankings

9.3: Revise Rankings Based on Interrelationships

The next step in the methodology is to evaluate whether the initial set of software factor rankings or goals for each function can be achieved [45]. This step involves exploring complementary software quality factors and their interrelationships.

9.3.1: Consider Complementary Factors

Four quality factors are complementary to most other factors and should be considered when choosing important factors. They are reliability, correctness, maintainability, and verifiability. Section 4.1.2.4 of the RADC Guidebook, Volume II, provides a table of complementary relationships of these factors to others [46]. It may be difficult or impossible to achieve high *direct* factor scores [29] without a high *indirect* score for the appropriate complementary factors. For example, high reusability is usually not achieved when the specifications are incorrect or incomplete (i.e., low correctness), or when the system was not tested thoroughly (i.e., low verifiability). High correctness and verifiability are also needed for high reusability.

9.3.2: Factor Interrelationships

In addition to complementary factors, other types of relationships can exist between the factors and criteria. A high goal for one factor/criterion may have a negative influence on another. For instance, a high maintainability goal has a negative impact on efficiency. For example, the most efficient systems are typically developed in assembly language, which reduces maintainability. There are also positive relationships between the factors. For example, building expandable software by making the system general (generality) often makes the system easier to interface with other systems (interoperability). Specific factor interrelationships may or may not apply, depending on the exact circumstances of a system. Candidate positive and negative factor interrelationships are documented in Tables 4.1.3-2 and 4.1.3-3 of the RADC Guidebook, Volume II [47].

9.3.3: Update Rankings and Requirements

Careful thought should be given to the rankings and set of software quality factors, assigned to each function carefully. Based on positive interrelationships or complementary factors, it may be appropriate to raise one or more factor goals. Based on negative interrelationships, it may not be possible to achieve the set of goals assigned to one or more functions, or it may cost a great deal to achieve the goals. Examine the goals and any relationships that affect your system and, if necessary, modify the underlying needs/requirements/characteristics that caused you to specify a certain set of factor goals. For example, simply because a negative factor relationship exists between maintainability and efficiency and you have specified high goals for each, do not immediately lower one of the goals. Instead, reevaluate the system characteristics that are the underlying reason for the goals. Figure 8 shows updated software quality factor rankings based on factor interrelationships for our hypothetical software engineering environment.

9.4: Cost Considerations

Factor interrelationships affect the cost of achieving the set of factor goals. Positive factor interrelationships may make it easier to achieve the required goals at less expense. Shared criteria, which are common across more than one factor, affect cost. For instance, the criterion visibility is a component of both maintainability and verifiability. When specifying goals for one or more factors, you may be able to raise the requirements for related factors that have shared criteria or other positive factor interrelationships without an increase in cost. Factor goals with negative interrelationships can also have a great affect on cost. It may be possible to build software that is both highly maintainable and highly efficient, but the cost of such an effort would increase. Never specify perfect scores for all metrics, criteria, and factors, because the achievement of such scores is costly and unattainable.

Based on an analysis of the cost of achieving the required factor and criteria goals for each function, it may be appropriate to raise one or more of the factor goals. Lowering any of the goals, however, requires extreme caution. Reevaluate the underlying requirements/characteristics/needs that initially caused you to require the goal(s). If cost becomes a driving issue, reevaluate the requirements for any that were unnecessary or overly stringent. Because a system is costly to achieve in terms of quality requirements is not a reason in itself to lower your requirements. Some systems are implicitly very costly to build. Therefore, the lack of availability of data on the cost of building software quality into a system during development makes this step difficult to perform. If analysis indicates that cost is a problem, monitor the cost during development closely. In our software engineering environment sample, no goals were changed as a result of this analysis.

9.5: Quantify Factors and Criteria

Quantifying factors and criteria entails setting a numerical goal for factors/criteria for each function that is based on the actual framework or method that will be used to measure quality during evaluation. This is a two-step process: (1) Determine the framework that will be used during evaluation and tailor this framework to each function of your system and each software development phase and (2) determine the desired range of scores for the tailored framework. These two steps are detailed in the following sections.

Rank Factors and Criteria

Assign Factor and Criteria Rankings

Software Quality Factor Identification Form—Initial Goals

Software Quality Factor / System or Software Unique Function	Performance					Design			Adaptation				
	Efficiency	Integrity	Reliability	Survivability	Usability	Correctness	Maintainability	Verifiability	Expandability	Flexibility	Interoperability	Portability	Reusability
Tools	−5	G	E+6		E	E+9	G	E	E	E	G	G	
Information Management	G−2	E	E	E+2		E+8	G	G	G				
User Interface	E−5	A	E+6	E+2	E	E+8	G	E	E	E			
Application Layer	G−2		E	E		E		G	G		E		
System Layer	E−3		E	E		E		E	E		E		

Figure 8: Updated software quality factor rankings (based on factor interrelationships)

9.5.1: Qualify Metrics, Criteria, and Factors

Qualifying the metrics involves tailoring the desired evaluation framework for each development phase and system function. Evaluate each metric to decide if the issue it measures is applicable and desirable for your project. This evaluation enables you to determine which components of the selected evaluation framework are or are not applicable. For instance, your project may not have any concurrent processing, which makes an entire set of anomaly management metrics inapplicable. Tailor these metrics out of the framework so as not to confuse evaluators or to skew evaluation results. The final output of this step is a tailored framework for each factor, function, and development phase. Figure 9 is an example output of the ASQS showing a tailored framework for reliability during one phase of the software development cycle. Items shown in lighter type are not applicable and have been tailored out. This step results in a list of metrics, criteria, and factors for each function, factor, and phase of your project.

9.5.2: Quantify Metrics

Quantifying the framework links evaluation results to goals. One approach is to identify desired ranges for metrics

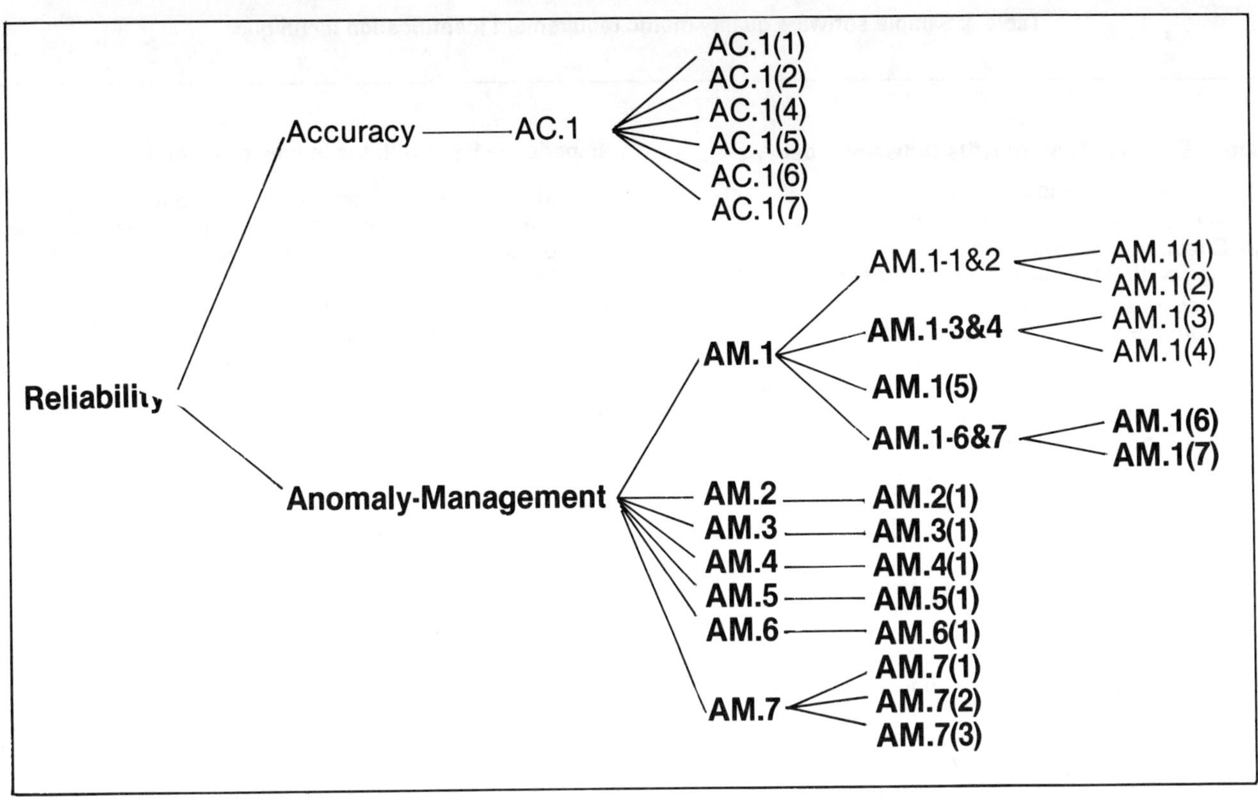

Figure 9: Tailored framework for reliability

as a basis for determining quantitative criteria and factor scores. Proceeding from the bottom up, examine each metric with regard to project characteristics and project experience to determine an appropriate range. The ranges for criteria and factors are determined based on the ranges for their constituents. In some cases, known project characteristics contribute to knowledge of expected metric scores. For instance, the use of Ada as the development language immediately causes the scores of certain metrics to attain a guaranteed value of 1.

This step is one of the most difficult in the methodology. In many cases it may only be possible to estimate a wide range of scores for each metric. However, this step is valuable because it provides a baseline for comparing evaluation results. Establishing quantitative goals will become easier and more effective as data from actual software development projects become available.

9.6: Compare Goals with Project Data

Compare your specified goals with data available from similar past projects. If you find that the achieved quality (e.g., as measured by indirect metric scores) for these projects is inconsistent with the desired levels for your project, reconsider your goals. If, for example, 90 percent of similar projects with goals comparable to yours had an actual reliability rate much lower than you desire, then you may want to reevaluate your reliability goals. As the size of the database of specification and evaluation experience grows, this step becomes increasingly useful.

9.7: Assess Compliance

Perform this step after you have completed quality specification and when evaluation results from each phase of development are available. During the evaluation, calculate factor, criterion, and metric scores for each component of your system. To assess compliance, compare these evaluation results to your original goals. There are two possible reasons for discrepancies: (1) Your original goals were unreasonable, impossible, or inappropriate and should be reevaluted or (2) the software quality is either too low or too high. Scores above the goal can in some cases indicate that unnecessary effort has been spent to build in quality that is not required. Such effort might have been better spent elsewhere to improve another aspect of quality. Establishing quality goals is a process that needs continual refinement. As evaluation results become available, never rule out the possibility that the goals should be refined.

Table 4: Sample software quality metric requirement identification technique

Type of Evidence That Benefits Outweigh Cost

(T1) Scientific Evidence
e.g., gathered in a controlled experiment.

(T2) Circumstantial evidence
e.g., statistical correlation on a past project.

(T3) Anecdotal evidence
Examples where low scores caused problems and techniques for improving scores are known.

(T4) Logical evidence
A logical argument for why the costs outweigh the benefits is documented.

Conditions Based on a Threshold (T)

(C1) $X < T$
The condition is true for any component with a metric value X that is less than T. Applicable only if investigation of the experience base indicates that no component obtained a metric value less than T.

(C2) (Percent With $X < T$) > Z%
The condition is true when more than Z percent of the components have a metric value X that is less than T. Applicable only if investigation of the experience base indicates that no more than Z% of the components obtained a metric value less than T.

(C3) $X < T - Y$
The threshold T is derived from the metric values for all of the components (e.g., mean, median). The condition is true for any component with a metric value X that is less than $T - Y$. Applicable only if investigation of the experience base indicates that no component with a metric value less than T deviated from T by more than Y.

Experience Base with the Values of a Metric

(E1) Metric values for same kind of system
Metric values are known for a system with the same application, environment, and development plan characteristics.

(E2) Metric values for similar system
Metric values are known for a system with similar characteristics, and differences are expected to have a minor or no impact on metric values.

(E3) Metric values for different system
Metric values are known for a system with different characteristics.

(E4) No past experience

Requirements

(A1) A waiver is required for acceptance of any component for which condition C1 holds.

(A2) A waiver is required for acceptance of the system if condition C2 holds.

(A3) The metric value for any component for which condition C1 holds shall be reported to a review or oversight organization.

(A4) If condition C2 holds for the system, then the metric values for all noncompliant component shall be reported to a review or oversight organization.

(A5) The metric value for any component for which condition C3 holds shall be reported to a review or oversight organization.

(A6) A written justification is required for any component for which condition C1 holds.

(A7) If condition C2 holds for the system, then a written justification is required.

(A8) A written justification shall be required for any component for which condition C3 holds.

(A9) Metric values shall be made available N days prior to formal reviews (e.g., requirements, design, or code reviews).

Sample Software Quality Metric Requirements Identification Matrix

Experience Base

Type of Evidence

	E1	E2	E3	E4
T1	A1	A2	A5	NA
T2	A1	A3	A5	NA
T3	A3	A4	A8	NA
T4	A6	A7	A8	A9

10: Appendix B—Suggestions for Constructing Software Quality Metric Requirements

This appendix offers suggestions on how to construct software quality metric requirements. Table 4 provides a sample matrix and supporting elements that can be helpful in identifying an appropriate requirement. The table is not intended to be used as an algorithm for identifying requirements, but merely to stimulate ideas. In practice, an organization will need to develop its own techniques for identifying software quality metric requirements, based on its own experiences with metrics.

Experience with a metric is the most important prerequisite to specifying metric requirements. Therefore, the technique illustrated in Table 4 begins by informally characterizing the experience. First is the type of evidence that can be added to show that benefits of applying a metric outweigh its costs (T1-T4). Examples of such benefits are reduced effort to develop or maintain; fewer errors; and better utilization of resources. Costs include the cost of collecting, reporting, and analyzing the metric values and the effort to improve the software to raise metric values. (Within this table, we assume higher metric values are more desirable than lower values.) Within categories T1-T4, it is assumed that each category subsumes the next one on the list (i.e., if circumstantial evidence was gathered, then anecdotal evidence was also gathered).

The base of experience with values that have been obtained for a metric is also very important (E1-E4). For categories E1 through E3, it is assumed that the experience includes an acquired understanding by the organization of how to improve the software to raise a metric value.

C1 through C3 are conditions and A1 through A9 are sample requirements based on those conditions. The individual parameters of a particular condition for a metric requirement should be determined based on actual experience. In general, the requirements shown here tend to be somewhat conservative (i.e., less demanding). Requirements A1-A9 specify an action that is triggered when one of the various conditions holds. The actions are activities of the software development process. Without exhaustive evidence about the benefits, cost, and behavior of a metric, it is usually inappropriate to specify a software quality metric requirement on the software product alone. Although this kind of evidence is not available for most metrics, it is still possible to specify meaningful software quality requirements in the context of the software development process.

Finally, the matrix provides a recommended type of requirement (A1-A9) for a given type of evidence (T1-T4) and a given amount of experience with metric values (E1-E4). Depending on an organization's own experience with metrics in a given domain, it may very well be that a more or less demanding requirement is appropriate, for example, a higher threshold (T), a lower percent allowed to fall below the threshold (Z), a smaller deviation from the derived threshold (Y), or a different requirement.

On Using the Users' Manual as the Requirements Specification II

Norman R. Howes
Computer and Software Engineering Division
Institute for Defense Analyses
Alexandria, Virginia
and
Department of Computer Science
George Mason University
Fairfax, Virginia

This paper continues the discussion begun in the author's previous paper that appeared in the 1988 IEEE Computer Society Press Tutorial: *Software Engineering Project Management* under the title "On Using the Users' Manual as the Requirements Specification." The purpose of the paper is to clarify the advantages and the limitations of this widely applicable technique. There are three major sections, labeled advantages, limitations, and experience. The author argues that even when it is inappropriate to use the users' manual as the requirements specification, it is often advantageous to produce a draft version of the users' manual as part of the requirements analysis process.

Introduction

In a paper with almost the same title that appeared in the 1988 IEEE Computer Society Press Tutorial: *Software Engineering Project Management,* the author discussed his experience with using the users' manual as the requirements specification on two rather dissimilar projects. The first was a PC-based project management system, and the other was a prototype version of the Space Station Data Management System. In the latter case, the requirements specification was titled *Users' Manual for the Data Management System (DMS) Test Bed,* published as NASA/JSC Document No. 22161, April 1986.

This paper continues the discussion and presents another example. The intent of this paper is to clarify the advantages and limitations of this technique. The need for such clarification became evident when the technique was used to specify the software engineering project for the senior software engineering course at George Mason University. For example, during a lecture on formal specification techniques, a student asked how the users' manual approach could be used in the case where a formal proof of correctness is required. Clearly, the users' manual technique is not suitable as a replacement for a formal specification, but then the vast majority of application software does not require one.

The advantages and limitations with using the users' manual as the requirements specification reported herein are based on the author's experience with only a small number of projects; consequently, the conclusions drawn are not supported by a large body of statistical evidence. However, in these cases, the technique worked so much better than other methods the author had tried, that it led him to reflect on how much better past requirements efforts could have been, had they been managed with this technique. From these reflections, the author conjectures that the technique has wide applicability. Furthermore, one of the requirements specifications developed in this manner was for a very large system, so the problem of whether or not the technique will scale up (i.e., be applicable for large systems) appears to have been resolved.

In fact, as the section on limitations of the system will attempt to show, the range of applicability of the technique does not depend so much on size of the project, but on whether or not the functions of the system are directly visible to the user.

Advantages of the Technique

As pointed out in reference HOW88, the users' manual is the only document to which most users of a system are exposed and from which they learn what the system does. The user's manual is often produced near the end of the development cycle, concurrently with the integration and acceptance testing of the new system. At this phase of product development, the system has already been designed and implemented, so the user of the system commonly does not understand clearly *how* the system will work (as opposed to what it will do) until after it is too late to do anything about it.

In most cases, even if the user had access to the requirements specification for the system before implementation, he or she could not understand it. One of the reasons users cannot understand conventional system specifications is that they are usually organized to support goals such as traceability, testability, functional allocation, etc., which have nothing to do with precisely communicating intent to the designers, programmers, testers, and managers involved in the development process. Often, the potential user of a new system is financing its development. In such cases the user does not have a clear understanding of what it is he or she is buying. Why does this happen?

In the acquisition of almost all products other than software, this situation would be considered intolerable. Many products that we purchase are *finished* products, such as automobiles or televisions, and we often buy them on the basis of trial usage or observation. In this case a specification is not needed. But when we have a house built (as opposed to buying one that has already been built), we want to know in advance exactly what it will look like, how many bedrooms it will have, how much storage space, etc. Floor plans, drawings, samples of materials, etc., serve as a form of specification that the buyer can understand. What is needed with respect to software is a specification the user can understand.

This is the first advantage of using the users' manual as the requirements specification. It serves as an excellent vehicle for communicating with the potential user. The user can read the manual and, although the system does not yet exist, the user can still *conceptualize* how the system will behave when it is available. With this level of understanding, the user is in a position to clarify likes and dislikes about the proposed system. How much better to discover these things before the system is implemented rather than after!

Another advantage of the users' manual technique is the potential for considerable savings in time and money. Producing documentation often takes from 30 percent to 40 percent of the resources of the project [BOE81, FAI85]. The requirements specification and the users' manual take a substantial portion of this amount. The author's experience is that these two efforts can consume 50 percent of the total documentation effort. Simple arithmetic leads one to the conclusion that combining these efforts could lead to savings in the range of 10 percent of total project resources. Exact savings are probably impossible to measure, because no project is going to be executed in two ways so that the costs can be compared.

Using the users' manual as the requirements specification can have significant advantages during the design phase of a system's development. It focuses attention on the *mode* in which a requirement is to be satisfied (which we sometimes refer to as the "mode of delivery" in what follows), as well as the requirement itself. Often, requirements specifications specify *what* the system will do without stating the mode in which it will be done. This practice is defended by stating that the requirements specification should not be so specific as to limit the creativity of the system's designers and that the design documentation will reflect *how* the requirement will be fulfilled.

If we return to the example of buying a house, we see that this approach would probably not be acceptable. Not many buyers of custom-built houses want to leave the details of how their requirements are to be fulfilled to the architect. The requirement that a house have four bedrooms or a fireplace can be fulfilled in infinitely many ways, many of which may be very undesirable to the prospective buyer. Why should we think that buyers of software are any different from buyers of other commodities? If, during the requirements analysis, the mode of satisfying the requirements is analyzed and specified, the designer is more likely to design something that the prospective user wants. When properly used, the technique of using the users' manual as the requirements specification should not interfere with the systems designer's creativity; rather, it should channel creativity in a direction that is acceptable to users.

Using the users' manual as the requirements specification can have a number of secondary advantages that stem from the fact that this technique makes the users' manual an integral part of the development process, not an after-the-fact creation. If the users' manual includes a tutorial that leads the user through the various functions that the system provides by means of a *model,* then this model can be used as the basis for test cases during integration testing. This results in the model being tested extensively during integration testing, which will ensure that the model works correctly in all situations. Many users' manuals that are created after the fact include examples that do not work. Nothing can be more irritating to a new user than examples in the users' manual that will not compile, will not execute, or which compute the wrong answer. This technique ensures that the users' manual is also *debugged.*

Developing a model for the tutorial part of the users' manual is an important part of the technique of using the users' manual as the requirements specification. This activity focuses on the *sequencing* of the system's capabilities and how the user interacts with them. Many systems provide a variety of related capabilities that the user employs in a number of different sequences (but not infinitely many different sequences). Understanding all the possible sequences in which the user can rationally be expected to employ the capabilities leads to the specification of user interfaces appropriate to the sequence in which the capabilities are exercised. For example, data entry can often be streamlined in certain special cases where some of the input data can be obtained implicitly, based on the sequence in which the user is employing the capabilities. Yet many systems with multiple capabilities reach the user-acceptance testing phase with inflexible input mechanisms used for all cases. Such systems are judged to be slow by users, because they are always required to enter data in all fields even when they can intuit that in certain special cases only a few data elements will suffice.

Taking the time to work through an *example scenario,* such as that needed for a users' manual tutorial, usually uncovers a variety of ways of interacting with the system that are suitable for the various ways in which the system will be used. This is especially true if the potential user it asked to review and approve the proposed tutorial part of the users' manual. These interfaces can be prototyped to give the user a more graphic understanding of just how to interface with the system.

Since modern computer systems are often highly interactive, the effect of the mode of delivery in fulfilling requirements cannot always be fully understood until the user gains some experience with the mode of interaction with the system. Often this interaction is of the utmost importance, as, for instance, in the case of real-time systems that interact with various sensors and human inputs to generate commands to effectors and other systems. Rapid prototyping is being used more and more in developing components of systems that present high technical risk or critical user interactions, to the extent that software development lifecycle models are being proposed based on prototyping [FAI85, GUN78]. Specification of the mode of delivery for fulfilling requirements provides a foundation on which to build these prototypes.

Once such a model scenario is developed, it can be employed in various forms for various levels of testing. Often system designers do not completely understand the application for which they are designing the system. It is as if they are viewing the application through a veil, namely, the requirements specification. Often the requirements specification reveals nothing about how to test the piece of the system they have designed. But if a users' manual with a tutorial is available, the designer can read it and can see clearly the various ways the system will be used, thereby learning how to formulate relevant test cases instead of the *coverage* and *stress* cases that are often used when the designer knows nothing better to use for a test.

The full example scenario from the tutorial can be used as a framework for integration testing. This has the double advantage of providing a relevant integration testing scenario, while at the same time debugging the tutorial for the final version of the users' manual. If the potential users have participated in the design of the example scenario, they will most likely use it or something similar for acceptance testing, which should facilitate this phase of the project (which is often hard to get through).

Finally, this approach improves control of a software development project. Not only are the clarity of the specification and communication with the customer (potential user) improved, but there is a natural flow of activity from the requirements specification into the high-level design of the system. Transition from the requirements phase of a project into the design phase has historically been a problem, especially when the requirements are developed by an organization different from the one responsible for the design and implementation. Specification of the mode of delivery of requirements *extends* the requirements analysis one step further toward design activity. This approach facilitates requirements traceability (for those projects that require such an activity), since the mode of delivery is easier to recognize and trace in the design and in the final code than an abstract statement of the capability itself. On large systems it is often difficult to understand how certain design features relate to the original requirements. Again, specification of the mode of delivery of the fulfillment of requirements facilitates the understanding of how the design proceeded from the requirements.

Limitations of the Technique

Let us explore the limitations of this technique by considering some examples of software products for which the users' manual alone will not suffice to specify the product for design purposes. Imagine a company whose business it is to develop cross-compilers that execute on a host computer but generate code for various microprocessors. These compiler suites include a downloading capability to the target microprocessors. The users' manual for a compiler is usually quite brief, explaining how to execute the compiler and what options are available for listings, optimization, etc. The user of such a cross-compiler product will probably not be interested in the downloading protocol, the buffering of data during the downloading process, etc. The user would only be interested in what commands were needed to accomplish the compilation, downloading, and execution of application programs.

Consequently, the users' manual by itself would not be adequate to characterize the system for design purposes in this case. However, it should be observed that although the users' manual by itself would be inadequate, it might still be appropriate to make development of the users' manual part of the requirements specification process.

Another example of a software product whose users' manual would be inadequate by itself for design purposes is a secure communications system, the messages of which were so sensitive, that the organization acquiring the system specified that a formal proof of correctness be produced to ensure that the program behaved precisely as designed. The user of such a system would be interested in the commands necessary to compose, edit, send, and receive messages. But the formal specification of protocols, security algorithms, encryption techniques, etc., upon which a formal proof could be based would be inappropriate for inclusion in a users' manual.

We observe that, in both of these examples, some requirements need to be part of the requirements specification, but are inappropriate for inclusion in the users' manual. This is not, however, a valid argument for not including the development of the users' manual as part of the requirements specification process. It is simply an observation that there are cases when more than the users' manual needs to be included in the requirements specification. Much of the applications software developed today does not fall in this category. Many systems can be specified adequately for design purposes merely by specifying how the system interfaces with the users. For example, most application systems built on the transaction processing paradigm (which constitutes the majority of business applications) fall into this category. The argument that the users' manual fails to characterize such things as the database side of the transaction processing architecture is to miss the point. Characterization of the data structures or the database organization is a design issue, not a requirements issue.

We conclude that the limitations of the technique of using the users' manual as the requirements specification do not necessarily preclude using the technique even when it is inadequate for a complete specification of the system. In such a case, it may still be appropriate to use the technique by supplementing the users' manual with additional requirements to produce the requirements specification.

The question arises, "When is it appropriate to use the technique?" Fairley [FAI85] suggests (page 16) that there are essentially three levels of software complexity: application programs, utility programs, and system-level programs. According to him, application programs include both scientific and data-processing routines written in high-level languages. Utility programs include compilers, assemblers, linkage editors, and loaders. These may be written in either high-level languages or assembly language. System programs include communication packages, real-time process control systems, and operating system routines.

Application systems have another property: They can usually be characterized by their interaction with the user(s) of the system. Application systems can often be characterized by their inputs (transaction entry formats, entry screen formats, etc.) and their outputs (reports, graphs, output screens, etc.). On the other hand, much of what utility programs and system level programs do is transparent to the user of the system. Consequently, the users' manual is usually not adequate for specifying this type of system.

Even when it is not appropriate to use the users' manual as the requirements specification, it is still a good idea to integrate the development of the requirements specification with the development of the users' manual. Having a users' manual available for user comment early in the project lifecycle (preferably before design) makes this worthwhile. Many of the benefits cited in the last section accrue from having the users' manual, or at least a fairly complete draft, available early on.

In the event the users' manual is not used as the requirements specification but is produced concurrently with the requirements specification, it can often be used as a verification tool for the requirements specification. Presumably, if the users' manual and the requirements specification are produced simultaineously as part of the requirements analysis phase, the users' manual will be consistent with the requirements specification and will be based on the same set of interpretations and assumptions used by the analysts in their development of the requirements specification. While the users may not be able to understand a conventional requirements specification, or may not feel it is their job to read and understand some technical document (which is their view of the requirements specification), they will read the users' manual. If the users' manual is given to the customer or user to approve, the customer or user will often return the users' manual with comments or criticisms, which often arise from misinterpretations or erroneous assumptions on the part of the analysts about the customers' needs or intents. This information can be used to correct both the requirements specification and the users' manual. This process can be repeated until the customer or user approves the users' manual, at which time the requirements specification should be much more in tune with what the customer or user wants.

Experience with the Technique

After using this technique on the two projects documented in reference HOW88, the author used it for the senior software engineering project at George Mason University in spring 1988. The purpose of the senior software engineering course is to acquaint students with what life is like in industry, working on a real software project, where they develop a product whose success depends on their ability to cooperate with one another and to integrate the pieces contributed by each class member into one consistent whole. Before this class, their programming projects are individual efforts that measure in the hundreds or perhaps a few thousand lines of code.

The software engineering project was to develop a software engineering management tool in Ada. The tool the students were to develop was essentially the PC-based project management system mentioned in reference HOW88. It consisted of approximately 20,000 to 25,000 lines of BASIC and assembler code. However, the students were to program the system in Ada on a VAX 8600 computer, by using the Verdix Ada Compiler. A users' manual already existed for this tool. The PC implementation of this tool was designed as a classical transaction processr (i.e., it was divided into programs that could be categorized as (1) programs that maintained the database and other supporting files, (2) the transaction processing programs, (3) programs that generated reports from the database, and (4) programs that generated graphical displays from the database).

The class (of 25 students) was divided into five teams, corresponding to the four categories of programs listed above, and an additional team called the "integration team." The integration team was responsible for verifying that the Ada specifications generated by the various teams were consistent (by developing the main program specification and compiling it together with the Ada specifications from the other teams) and for performing integration testing on the component packages as they were finished.

The teams were given the users' manual from the PC-based project management tool and were told that the hypothetical customer had determined, through an in-depth study by a hypothetical consulting firm, that it wanted a system that would do what the system described in the users' manual was supposed to do. Each team was instructed to choose a team leader, and the author acted in the capacity of project manager. The various teams developed proposed designs for those capabilities described in the users' manual that they interpreted were the responsibility of their team. The project manager met with the team leaders to resolve conflicting interpretations, to ensure that all of the capabilities were the responsibility of some team, and to resolve interface disputes arising largely out of design approach biases.

The Ada language greatly facilitated this approach, in that the discussions at this level concentrated on the Ada specifications being proposed by the various teams. This fact was beneficial in isolating design issues from interface issues and in assisting inexperienced students (whose basic impulse is to program) with conceptualizing how the whole system would work together before they tackled detailed design problems. Furthermore, the ability to compile these specifications provided an early check on consistency and completeness and provided all the students with a specification of all of the interfaces they needed by mid-semester. All the students could then work independently on the piece of the system for which they were responsible. The students were told that if one of the programs with which they needed to interface was not completed at the time they began testing, they would have to write a test driver to simulate the interface. In this way, each student could ensure that his or her own commitment was satisfied in the event another student did not deliver on time or at all.

Having the users' manual at the start allowed the students to understand, in a very short time, not only what their part of the system needed to do and how it needed to interface with a user, but also the intent, scope, and style of the entire system. These very real advantages are worth considering in any case where the system specification writers and the system implementors are separate organizations or companies.

The existing users' manual for the PC implementation of the tool contained a tutorial that a new user could follow. The tutorial started with a few pages of explanation of the mechanics of project management (in the event the new user did not understand the theoretical basis on which the tool was built) and then described a hypothetical project. The user was shown how the work of this *model project* could be subdivided into a work breakdown structure (WBS) and how this WBS could be entered into the system's database. After the new user entered the data and printed a report based on these data, the user was shown other features, such as how to enter estimating and scheduling data and how to use the scheduling data to time-phase the budget to produce a baseline. Thereafter, the user was shown how to get certain reports out of the system that summarized the data that were entered.

The next part of the tutorial showed the user how to manage a project on a day-to-day basis by means of *model project days*. Each model project day consisted of the data that might be gathered (in a day of the life of the project) by a hypothetical project manager and entered into the system. As the new user progressed from day to day through the model, the user became familiar with both the day-to-day mechanics of project management and the associated data that would be entered into the project management tool.

Not only did the tutorial assist the students in understanding the overall objectives of the system, how it was intended to be used on a day-to-day basis, and the features of the system, but it was helpful in integration testing. The students (wisely) decided to use the model from the tutorial as the basis for integration testing. As soon as the first database programs were ready for testing, they were used to create a database with the project data from the model project. Other programming teams were able to use this database for unit testing of their modules before submitting them for integration testing with the result that all the teams used test data that were interrelated in a logical way based on the model project.

The advantages of using test data related to real-world scenarios (even if from a hypothetical model project) can be seen as follows: the integration test team, which was not always familiar with the detailed operation of the other team's programs, could often spot errors readily, because in such cases the behavior of the system or the data output on a report did not correspond logically to the team's understanding of the operation of the model project. It is much easier to understand the model than the detailed operation of the system. Coverage and stress tests can, of course, also uncover error conditions, but they are often spotted less readily. Coverage and stress tests are important, but they tend to test the limits of the system, rather than its nominal behavior.

Conclusions

The experience discussed in this paper and those in reference HOW88 suggest that the development of the users' manual should be part of the requirements specification phase of most computer projects. Furthermore, it can be seen that the users' manual can often suffice for the requirements specification, and in many cases where it will not suffice, the requirements specification can be obtained by supplementing the users' manual with requirements that are not visible in the user interface.

Furthermore, even when it is not appropriate to use the users' manual as the requirements specification, it is still a good idea to integrate the development of the users' manual with the development of the requirements specification. Finally, this technique has many advantages in clarity, transition into design, project control, and project testing that will result in better use of resources, which in turn will result in cost savings.

References

[BOE81] B. Boehm, *Software Engineering Economics,* Prentice-Hall, Englewood Cliffs, N.J., 1981.

[FAI85] R. Fairley, *Software Engineernig Concepts,* McGraw-Hill, New York, 1985.

[GUN78] R. Gunther, *Management Methodology for Software Product Engineering,* Wiley Interscience, New York, 1978.

[HOW88] N. Howes, "On Using the Users' Manual as the Requirements Specification," *IEEE Tutorial on Software Engineering Project Management,* edited by R.H. Thayer, IEEE Computer Society Press, Washington D.C., 1988, pp. 172-177.

An American National Standard

IEEE Guide to Software Requirements Specifications

Sponsor

Software Engineering Technical Committee
of the
IEEE Computer Society

Approved September 30, 1983

IEEE Standards Board

Approved July 20, 1984

American National Standards Institute

IEEE standards are currently being reviewed and revised. They are updated periodically.

EH0304-6/90/0000/0170$01.00 © 1984 IEEE

EE **Standards** documents are developed within the Technical Com-
ees of the IEEE Societies and the Standards Coordinating Commit-
of the IEEE Standards Board. Members of the committees serve
ntarily and without compensation. They are not necessarily mem-
bers of the Institute. The standards developed within IEEE represent a consensus of the broad expertise on the subject within the Institute as well as those activities outside of IEEE which have expressed an interest in participating in the development of the standard.

Use of an IEEE Standard is wholly voluntary. The existence of an IEEE Standard does not imply that there are no other ways to produce, test, measure, purchase, market, or provide other goods and services related to the scope of the IEEE Standard. Furthermore, the viewpoint expressed at the time a standard is approved and issued is subject to change brought about through developments in the state of the art and comments received from users of the standard. Every IEEE Standard is subjected to review at least once every five years for revision or reaffirmation. When a document is more than five years old, and has not been reaffirmed, it is reasonable to conclude that its contents, although still of some value, do not wholly reflect the present state of the art. Users are cautioned to check to determine that they have the latest edition of any IEEE Standard.

Comments for revision of IEEE Standards are welcome from any interested party, regardless of membership affiliation with IEEE. Suggestions for changes in documents should be in the form of a proposed change of text, together with appropriate supporting comments.

Interpretations: Occasionally questions may arise regarding the meaning of portions of standards as they relate to specific applications. When the need for interpretations is brought to the attention of IEEE, the Institute will initiate action to prepare appropriate responses. Since IEEE Standards represent a consensus of all concerned interests, it is important to ensure that any interpretation has also received the concurrence of a balance of interests. For this reason IEEE and the members of its technical committees are not able to provide an instant response to interpretation requests except in those cases where the matter has previously received formal consideration.

Comments on standards and requests for interpretations should be addressed to:

Secretary, IEEE Standards Board
345 East 47th Street
New York, NY 10017
USA

Foreword

(This Foreword is not a part of IEEE Std 830-1984, IEEE Guide to Software Requirements Specifications.)

This guide describes alternate approaches to good practice in the specification of software requirements. The requirements may be explicitly stated by the user or they may be allocated to computer software (that is, programs) by the system requirements analysis process. This guide does not suggest that a hierarchy of software requirements specifications exists, of which each, in turn, defines a smaller subset of requirements.

As a guide, this document should help:

(1) Software customers to accurately describe what they wish to obtain.

(2) Software suppliers to understand exactly what the customer wants.

(3) Individuals to accomplish the following goals:

(a) Develop standard software requirements specifications (SRS) outline for their own organizations.

(b) Define the form and content of their specific software requirements specifications.

(c) Develop additional local supporting items such as an SRS quality checklist, or an SRS writer's handbook.

To the customers, suppliers and other individuals, a good SRS provides several specific benefits. It will accomplish the following goals:

(1) Establish the basis for agreement between the customers and the suppliers on what the software product is to do. The complete description of the functions to be performed by the software specified in the SRS will assist the potential user, to determine if the software specified meets their needs or how the software must be modified to meet their needs.

(2) Reduce the development effort. The preparation of the SRS forces the various concerned groups in the customer's organization to consider rigorously all of the requirements before design begins and reduces later redesign, recoding, and retesting. Careful review of the requirements in the SRS can reveal omissions, misunderstandings, and inconsistencies early in the development cycle when these problems are easier to correct.

(3) Provide a basis for estimating costs and schedules. The description of the product to be developed as given in the SRS is a realistic basis for estimating project costs and can be used to obtain approval for bids or price estimates. The SRS also provides a clear description of the required software and makes it easier to estimate and plan the necessary resources. The requirements which, together with a development plan, can be used to measure progress.

(4) Provide a baseline for validation and verification. Organizations can develop their validation and verification plans much more productively from a good SRS. As a part of the development contract, the SRS provides a baseline against which compliance can be measured. (However, that the converse is not true; a standard legal contract cannot be used as an SRS. Such documents rarely contain the detail required and are often incomplete.)

(5) Facilitate transfer. The SRS makes it easier to transfer the software product to new users or new machines. Customers thus find it easier to transfer the software to other parts of their organization, and suppliers find it easier to transfer it to new customers.

(6) Serves as a basis for enhancement. Because the SRS discusses the product but not the project that developed it, the SRS serves as a basis for later enhancement of the finished product. The SRS may need to be altered, but it does provide a solid foundation for continued production evolution.

This guide is based on a model in which the result of the software requirements specification process is an unambiguous and complete specification document. In principle, the SRS can be mechanically translated into the specified software program directly. As such, the resulting SRS document itself is the specified software, and the supplier's only duty (after completing the SRS) would be the mechanical compilation of the SRS into machine code for the target computer. The present state of the art does not support such a compiler with an optimizer of such efficiency to make it practical but this limitation need not, and should not, restrict the intermediate objective of an unambiguous SRS.

This guide is consistent with IEEE Std 729-1983, IEEE Standard Glossary of Software Engineering Terminology; ANSI/IEEE Std 730-1981, IEEE Standard for Software Quality Assurance Plans; and IEEE Std 829-1983, IEEE Standard for Software Test Documentation. This guide may be used in conjunction with those standards or separately.

This guide was prepared by the Software Requirements Working Group of the Software Engineering Standards Subcommittee of the Technical Committee on Software Engineering of the IEEE Computer Society.

At the time the guide was approved, the Software Requirements Working Group had the following membership:

A. M. Davis, *Chairperson*

M. Bariff
H. Berlack
F. Buckley
E. Byrne
F. Calm
K. Foster
S. Frankel
T. L. Hannan
P. W. Kendra
T. M. Kurinara
R. A. C. Lane
R. Lechner
E. Levinson
P. Lindemann
S. Mroczek
A. J. Neumann
W. Newson
D. Paster
B. Pope
P. B. Powell
G. R. Niedhart
J. Russell
A. Salwin
N. B. Schneidewind
D. Schultz
R. W. Szczech
A. Weigel
P. Willis
H. Willman
A. W. Yonda

At the time that it approved this guide, the Software Engineering Standards Subcommittee had the following membership:

F. J. Buckley, *Chairperson*

R. J. Abbott
A. F. Ackerman
L. Beltracchi
D. W. Bragg
D. W. Burt
E. R. Byrne
H. Carney
J. W. Center
A. M. Cicu
G. G. Cooke
A. J. Cote, Jr
P. W. Daggett
G. Darling
B. Dasarathy
A. M. Davis
P. A. Denny
J. A. Dobbins
M. L. Eads
J. D. Earls
L. G. Egan, Jr
D. W. Fife
J. Flournoy
J. J. Forman
F. K. Gardner
D. Gelperin
E. L. Gibbs
G. Gladden
S. A. Gloss-Soler
J. W. Grigsby
R. M. Gross
D. A. Gustafson
R. T. Gustin
T. L. Hannan
H. Hecht
L. R. Heselton, III
S. Horvitz
P. Howley
R. N. Hurwitz
S. Hwang
J. H. Ingram
J. P. Kalasky
R. Kessler
T. M. Kurinara
D. V. LaRosa
R. A. C. Lane
G. R. Lewis
F. C. Lim
G. S. Lindsay
M. Lipow
W. M. Lively
M. Lubofsky
D. Lindquist
A. K. Manhindru
P. C. Marriott
C. F. Martiny
M. McCollough
B. Menkus
B. Meyer
E. F. Miller, Jr
G. S. Morris
G. T. Morun
W. G. Murch
J. Nebb
G. R. Niedhart
M. A. Neighbors
J. O. Neilson
D. J. Ostrom
D. J. Pfeiffer
R. M. Poston
P. B. Powell
J. W. Radatz
J. C. Rault
S. T. Redwine
L. K. Reed
W. E. Riddle
C. W. Rutter, III
P. E. Schilling
N. F. Schniedewind
A. D. Schuman
L. W. Seagren
R. L. Skelton
W. Smith
H. M. Sneed
K. C. Tai
B. J. Taute
R. H. Thayer
G. D. Tice, Jr
T. L. Tillmans
W. S. Turner, III
E. A. Ulbrich, Jr
D. Usechak
U. Voges
R. Wachter
J. P. Walter
D. Webdale
A. H. Weigel
N. P. Wilburn
W. M. Wong
T. Workman
A. W. Yonda
P. F. Zoll

Special representatives to the software engineering standards subcommittee were:

J. Milandin: ANSI Z1
W. G. Perry: Data Processing Manufacturers Association
R. Pritchett: EDP Auditors Association
T. L. Regulinski: IEEE Reliability Society
N. C. Farr: Nuclear Power Engineering Committee, IEEE Power Engineering Society

Suggestions for improvement of this guide are welcome. They should be provided to:

The Secretary
IEEE Standards Board
345 East 47th St
New York, New York 10017

At the time the IEEE Standards Board approved this standard on September 20, 1983 it had the following members:

James H. Beall, *Chairman* **Edward Chelotti**, *Vice Chairman*

Sava I. Sherr, *Secretary*

J. J. Archambault
John T. Boettger
J. V. Bonucchi
Rene Castenschiold
Edward J. Cohen
Len S. Corey
Donald C. Fleckenstein
Jay Forster
Donald H. Heirman
Irvin N. Howell
Joseph L. Koepfinger*
Irving Kolodny
George Konomos
John E. May
Donald T. Michael*
John P. Riganati
Frank L. Rose
Robert W. Seelbach
Jay A. Stewart
Clifford O. Swanson
Robert E. Weiler
W. B. Wilkens
Charles J. Wylie

*Member emeritus

Contents

SECTION PAGE

FIGURES

TABLES

IEEE Guide to Software Requirements Specifications

1. Scope and Organization

1.1 Scope. This is a guide for writing software requirements specifications. It describes the necessary content and qualities of a good Software Requirements Specification (SRS) and presents a prototype SRS outline.

This guide does not specify industry-wide SRS standards nor state mandatory SRS requirements. This guide is written under the premise that the current state of the art does not warrant or support such a formal standards document.

This guide is applicable to in-house and commercial software products. Special care, however, should be used in its application because:

(1) This guide is aimed at specifying requirements of software to be developed. Application of this material to already-developed software is counter-productive.

(2) This guide does not cover the specification of requirements for software being developed using the techniques of rapid prototyping.

1.2 Organization. The remainder of this guide is organized as follows:

(1) Section 2 provides the references used throughout the guide.

(2) Section 3 provides definitions of specific terms used throughout the guide.

(3) Section 4 provides background information for writing a good SRS.

(4) Section 5 provides specific guidance for expressing software requirements.

(5) Section 6 discusses each of the essential parts of an SRS and provides alternate prototype outlines.

2. References

[1] ANSI/IEEE Std 100-1977, IEEE Standard Dictionary of Electrical and Electronics Terms.

[2] ANSI/IEEE Std 730-1981, IEEE Standard for Software Quality Assurance Plans.

[3] ANSI/IEEE Std 729-1983, IEEE Standard Glossary of Software Engineering Terminology.

[4] BRUSAW, C. T., ALRED, G. and OLIU, W., *Handbook of Technical Writing*, New York, St. Martin's Press, 1976.

[5] DASARATNY, B., *Timing Constraints of Real-Time Systems: Constructs for Expressing Them*, IEEE Real-Time Systems Symposium, Dec 1982.

[6] DAVIS, A., The Design of a Family of Applications-Oriented Requirements Languages, *IEEE Computer*, 15, 5 May 1982, pp 21–28.

[7] FREEDMAN, D. and WEINBERG, G., Handbook of Walkthroughs, *Inspections and Technical Reviews*, 3rd Ed, Little and Brown Publishers, New York.

[8] KAIN, R., Automata Theory: Machines and Languages, McGraw Hill, New York, 1972.

[9] KOHAVI, Z., Switching and Finite Automata Theory, McGraw Hill, New York, 1970.

[10] KRAMER, J., Editor, Application Oriented Specifications Glossary of Terms, *European Workshop on Industrial Computer Systems (EWICS)*, Imperial College, London, England, May 6, 1981.[1]

[1] Copies of this document are available from EWICS, c/o G. R. Koch, BIOMATIK Gmbh, Carl-Mez Str 81–83, D-7800 Freiburg, Federal Republic of Germany.

[11] MILLS, G., and WALTER, J., *Technical Writing*, New York, Holt, Rinehart and Winston, 4th Ed, 1978.

[12] PETERSON, J., *Petri Nets*, ACM Computing Surveys, 9, 4, Dec 1977, pp 223–252.

[13] RAMAMOORHY, C. and SO, H. H., *Software Requirements and Specifications: Status and Perspectives*, Tutorial: Software Methodology, RAMAMOORTHY, C. and YEH, R. T., Editors. IEEE Catalog no EHO 142-0, 1978, pp 43–164.

[14] TAGGART, W. M. Jr, and THARP, M. O., *A Survey of Information Requirements Analysis Techniques*, ACM Computing Surveys, 9, 4, Dec 1977, pp 273–290.

[15] TEICHROEW, D., *A Survey of Languages for Stating Requirements for Computer-Based Information Systems*, 1972 Fall Joint Computer Conference, 1972, pp 1203–1224.

3. Definitions

Except for the definitions listed below, the definitions of all terms used in this guide conform to the definitions provided in IEEE Std 729-1983 [3][2], for example, the terms requirement, requirements specification. If a term used in this guide does not appear in that Standard, then ANSI/IEEE Std 100-1977 [1], applies.

The terms listed in this section have been adopted from Section 2, [10].

contract. A legally binding document agreed upon by the customer and supplier. This includes the technical, organizational, cost and schedule requirements of a product.

customer. The person, or persons, who pay for the product and usually (but not necessarily) decides the requirements. In the context of this document the customer and the supplier may be members of the same organization.

language. A means of communication, with syntax and semantics, consisting of a set of representations, conventions and associated rules used to convey information.

partitioning. Decomposition; the separation of the whole into its parts.

[2]Numbers in brackets correspond to those of the references in Section 2.

supplier. The person, or persons, who produce a product for a customer. In the context of this document, the customer and the supplier may be members of the same organization.

user. The person, or persons, who operate or interact directly with the system. The user(s) and the customer(s) are often not the same person(s).

4. Background Information for Writing a Good SRS

This section provides background information necessary for writing an SRS. This includes:

(1) Examination of the nature of the SRS

(2) Environmental considerations surrounding the SRS

(3) Characteristics required for a good SRS

(4) Recommendations for joint preparation of an SRS

(5) Evolutionary aspects of the SRS

(6) The use of automated tools to develop an SRS

4.1 The SRS. The SRS is a specification for a particular software product, program, or set of programs that does certain things. See ANSI/IEEE Std 730-1981 [2], 3.4.2.1.

The description places two basic requirements on the SRS:

(1) It must say certain things. For example, software developed from an SRS that fails to specify that error messages will be provided, will probably fail to satisfy the customer.

(2) It must say those things in certain ways. For example, software developed from an SRS that fails to specify the format and content of error messages and instead is developed from a vague and non-quantifiable requirement such as *All error messages will be helpful*, will probably be unsatisfactory. What is *helpful* for one person can be a severe aggravation to another person.

For recommended contents of an SRS see Section 6.

4.2 Environment of the SRS. It is important to consider the part that the SRS plays in the total software project. The provisions in ANSI/IEEE Std 730-1981 [2], define the minimum required documents for a software project. See [2], 3.4.2.

ANSI/IEEE Std 730-1981 [2] also identifies the other useful documents. See [2], 3.4.3.

Since the SRS has a definite role to play in this documentation scheme, SRS writers should be careful not to go beyond the bounds of that role. This means the following requirements should be met:

(1) The SRS must correctly define all of the software requirements, but no more.

(2) The SRS should not describe any design, verification, or project management details, except for required design constraints.

Such a properly written SRS limits the range of valid solutions but does not specify any particular design and thus provides the supplier with maximum flexibility.

4.3 Characteristics of A Good SRS. The previous sections describe the types of information that should be contained in an SRS. The following concepts deal with particular characteristics. A good SRS is:

(1) Unambiguous
(2) Complete
(3) Verifiable
(4) Consistent
(5) Modifiable
(6) Traceable
(7) Usable during the Operation and Maintenance Phase

4.3.1 Unambiguous. An SRS is unambiguous if — and only if — every requirement stated therein has only one interpretation.

(1) As a minimum, this requires that each characteristic of the final product be described using a single unique term.

(2) In cases where a term used in a particular context could have multiple meanings, the term must be included in a glossary where its meaning is made more specific.

4.3.1.1 Natural Language Pitfalls. Requirements are often written in a natural language (for example, English). SRS writers who use a natural language must be especially careful to review their requirements for ambiguity. The following examples are taken from Section 2, [7].

(1) The specification *The data set will contain an end of file character*, might be read as:

(a) There will be one and only one end of file character

(b) Some character will be designated as an end of file character

(c) There will be at least one end of file character

(2) The specification *The control total is taken from the last record*, might be read as:

(a) The control total is taken from the record at the end of the file

(b) The control total is taken from the latest record

(c) The control total is taken from the previous record

(3) The specification *All customers have the same control field*, might be read as:

(a) All customers have the same value in their control field

(b) All customer control fields have the same format

(c) One control field is issued for all customers

(4) The specification *All files are controlled by a file control block*, might be read as:

(a) One control block controls the entire set of files

(b) Each file has its own block

(c) Each file is controlled by a control block, but one control block might control more than one file

4.3.1.2 Formal Requirements Specifications Languages. One way to avoid the ambiguity inherent in natural language is to write the SRS in a formal requirements specification language.[3]

(1) One major advantage in the use of such languages is the reduction of ambiguity. This occurs, in part, because the formal language processors automatically detect many lexical, syntactic, and semantic errors.

(2) One major disadvantage in the use of such languages is the length of time required to learn them.

4.3.2 Complete. An SRS is complete if it possesses the following qualities:

(1) Inclusion of all significant requirements, whether relating to functionality, performance, design constraints, attributes or external interfaces.

(2) Definition of the responses of the software to all realizable classes of input data in all realizable classes of situations. Note that it is important to specify the responses to valid and invalid input values.

(3) Conformity to any SRS standard that applies to it. If a particular section of the standard is not applicable, the SRS should

[3] For detailed discussion on this topic, suggested readings are [6], [13], [14], and [15].

include the section number and an explanation of why it is not applicable.

(4) Full labeling and referencing of all figures, tables, and diagrams in the SRS and definition of all terms and units of measure.

4.3.2.1 Use of TBDs. Any SRS that uses the phrase *to be determined* (TBD) is not a complete SRS.

(1) The TBD is, however, occasionally necessary and should be accompanied by:

(a) A description of the conditions causing the TBD (for example, why an answer is not known) so that the situation can be resolved.

(b) A description of what must be done to eliminate the TBD.

(2) Any project documents that are based on an SRS that contains TBDs, should:

(a) Identify the version or state the specific release number of the SRS associated with that particular document.

(b) Exclude any commitments dependent upon the sections of the SRS that are still identified as TBDs.

4.3.3 Verifiable. An SRS is verifiable if and only if every requirement stated therein is verifiable. A requirement is verifiable if and only if there exists some finite cost-effective process with which a person or machine can check that the software product meets the requirement.

(1) Examples of nonverifiable requirements include statements such as:

(a) *The product should work well*, or *The product should have a good human interface.* These requirements cannot be verified because it is impossible to define the terms *good* or *well.*

(b) *The program shall never enter an infinite loop.* This requirement is non-verifiable because the testing of this quality is theoretically impossible.

(c) *The output of the program shall usually be given within 10 s.* This requirement is non-verifiable because the term *usually* cannot be measured.

(2) An example of a verifiable statement is *The output of the program shall be given within 20 s of event* X, 60% *of the time; and shall be given within 30 s of event* X, 100% *of the time.* This statement can be verified because it uses concrete terms and measurable quantities.

(3) If a method cannot be devised to determine whether the software meets a particular requirement, then that requirement should be removed or revised.

(4) If a requirement is not expressible in verifiable terms at the time the SRS is prepared, then a point in the development cycle (review, test plan issue, etc) should be identified at which the requirement must be put into a verifiable form.

4.3.4 Consistent. An SRS is consistent if and only if no set of individual requirements described in it conflict. There are three types of likely conflicts in an SRS:

(1) Two or more requirements might describe the same real world object but use different terms for that object. For example, a program's request for a user input might be called a *prompt* in one requirement and a *cue* in another.

(2) The specified characteristics of real world objects might conflict. For example:

(a) The format of an output report might be described in one requirement as *tabular* but in another as *textual.*

(b) One requirement might state that all lights shall be green while another states that all lights shall be blue.

(3) There might be a logical or temporal conflict between two specified actions. For example:

(a) One requirement might specify that the program will add two inputs and another specify that the program will multiply them.

(b) One requirement might state that *A* must always follow *B*, while another requires that *A and B* occur simultaneously.

4.3.5 Modifiable. An SRS is modifiable if its structure and style are such that any necessary changes to the requirements can be made easily, completely, and consistently. Modifiability generally requires an SRS to:

(1) Have a coherent and easy-to-use organization, with a table of contents, an index and explicit cross-referencing.

(2) Not be redundant; that is, the same requirement should not appear in more than one place in the SRS.

(a) Redundancy itself is not an error, but it can easily lead to errors. Redundancy can occasionally help to make an SRS more readable, but a problem can arise when the redundant document is updated. Assume, for instance, that a certain requirement is stated in two places. At some later time, it is determined that the requirement should be altered, but the change is made in only one of the two locations. The SRS then becomes inconsistent.

(b) Whenever redundancy is necessary, the SRS should include explicit cross-references to make it modifiable.

4.3.6 Traceable. An SRS is traceable if the origin of each of its requirements is clear and if it facilitates the referencing of each requirement in future development or enhancement documentation. Two types of traceability are recommended:

(1) Backward traceability (that is, to previous stages of development) depends upon each requirement explicitly referencing its source in previous documents.

(2) Forward traceability (that is, to all documents spawned by the SRS) depends upon each requirement in the SRS having a unique name or reference number.

When a requirement in the SRS represents an apportionment or a derivative of another requirement, both forward and backward traceability should be provided. Examples include:

4.3.6.1 The allocation of response time to a data base function from the overall user response time requirement.

4.3.6.2 The identification of a report format with certain functional and user interface requirements.

4.3.6.3 A software product that supports legislative or administrative needs (for example, tax computations, reporting of an overhead ratio). In this case, the exact legislative or administrative document that is being supported should be identified.

The forward traceability of the SRS is especially important when the software product enters the operation and maintenance phase. As code and design documents are modified, it is essential to be able to ascertain the complete set of requirements that may be affected by those modifications.

4.3.7 Usable During the Operation and Maintenance Phase. The SRS must address the needs of the operation and maintenance phase, including the eventual replacement of the software.

(1) Maintenance is frequently carried out by personnel not associated with the original development. Local changes (corrections) can be implemented by means of a well-commented code. For changes of wider scope, however, the design and requirements documentation is essential. This implies two actions

(a) The SRS should be modifiable as indicated in 4.3.5.

(b) The SRS should contain a record of all special provisions that apply to individual components such as:

(i) Their criticality (for example, where failure could impact safety or cause large financial or social losses).

(ii) Their relation to only temporary needs (for example, to support a display that may be retired soon).

(iii) Their origin (for example, function X is to be copied from an existing software product in its entirety).

(2) Knowledge of this type is taken for granted in the developing organization but is frequently missing in the maintenance organization. If the reason for or origin of a function is not understood, it is frequently impossible to perform adequate software maintenance on it.

4.4 Joint Preparation of the SRS. The software development process begins with supplier and customer agreement on what the completed software must do. This agreement, in the form of an SRS, should be jointly prepared. This is important because usually neither the customer nor the supplier is qualified to write a good SRS by himself.

(1) Customers usually do not understand the software design and development process well enough to write a usable SRS.

(2) Suppliers usually do not understand the customer's problem and field of endeavor well enough to specify requirements for a satisfactory system.

The customer and the supplier need to work together to produce a well written and completely understood SRS.[4]

4.5 SRS Evolution. The SRS may need to evolve as the development of the software product progresses.

(1) It may be impossible to specify some details at the time the project is initiated. For example, it may be impossible to define during the Requirements Phase, all of the screen formats for an interactive program in a manner that guarantees that they will not be altered later.

(2) Additional changes may ensue as deficien-

---

[4]This guide does not specifically discuss style, language usage, or techniques of good writing. It is quite important, however, that an SRS be well written; for guidance, please refer to general technical writing guides such as [1] and [11].

cies, shortcomings, and inaccuracies are discovered in the SRS, as the product evolves.

Two major considerations in this process are:

4.5.1 The requirements should be specified as completely and thoroughly as possible, even if evolutionary revisions can be forseen as inevitable. For example, the desired screen formats should be specified as well as possible in the SRS as a basis for later design.

4.5.2 A formal change process should be initiated to identify, control, track, and report projected changes, as soon as they are initially identified. Approved changes in requirements should be incorporated in the SRS in such a way as to:

(1) Provide an accurate and complete audit trail of changes.

(2) Permit the review of current and superseded portions of the SRS.

4.6 Tools for Developing an SRS. The most obvious way to create an SRS is to write it in a natural language (for example, English). But because natural languages are rich, although imprecise, a number of more formal methods have been devised to assist SRS writers.

4.6.1 Formal Specification Methodologies. The degree to which such formal methodologies may be useful in preparing an SRS depends upon a number of factors:

(1) The size and complexity of the program

(2) Whether a customer contract requires it

(3) Whether the SRS is a vehicle for contracts or merely an internal document

(4) Whether the SRS document will become the top level of the design document

(5) What computer facilities are available to support such a methodology

No attempt is made here to describe or endorse any particular tool.[5]

4.6.2 Production Tools. A computer-based word processor is a most useful production aid. Usually, an SRS will have several authors, will undergo several revisions, and will have several reorganizations. A word processor that manages the text as a computer file facilitates this process.

Almost all computer systems have a word processor and often a document preparation package is associated with it. This automates paragraphing and referencing, the printing of headings and subheadings, the compilation of tables of contents and indexes, etc, all of which help in the production of a more readable SRS.

4.6.3 Representation Tools. Some words in the SRS, especially nouns and verbs, refer specifically to entities and actions in the system. There are several advantages to identifying them as such.

(1) It is possible to verify that an entity or action always has the same name everywhere in the SRS. Thus *calculate trajectory* would not co-exist with *determine flight path*.

(2) It is possible to identify every place in the specification where a particular entity or action is described.

In addition, it may be desirable to formalize the English structure in some way to allow automated processing of the content of the SRS. With such constraints it becomes possible to:

4.6.3.1 Display the requirements in some tabular or graphical way.

4.6.3.2 Automatically check the SRS requirements in hierarchical layers of detail, where each layer is complete in itself but may also be expanded upon in a lower hierarchical layer or be a constituent of an upper hierarchical layer.

4.6.3.3 Automatically check that the SRS possesses some or all of the characteristics described in 4.3.

5. Software Requirements

Each software requirement in an SRS is a statement of some essential capability of the software to be developed. The following subsections describe:

(1) Methods used to express software requirements

(2) Annotation of the software requirements

(3) Common pitfalls encountered in the process

5.1 Methods Used To Express Software Requirements. Requirements can be expressed in a number of ways:

(1) Through input/output specifications

(2) By use of a set of representative examples

(3) By the specification of models

5.1.1 Input/Output Specifications. It is often effective to specify the required behavior of a software product as a sequence of inputs and outputs.

[5] For detailed discussion on this topic, see, for example, [6], [13], [14], and [15].

5.1.1.1 Approaches. There are at least three different approaches based on the nature of the software being specified:

(1) Some software products (such as reporting systems) are best specified by focusing on required outputs. In general, output-focused systems operate primarily on data files. User input usually serves to provide control information and trigger data file processing.

(2) Others are best specified by focusing on input/output behavior. Input/output-focused systems operate primarily on the current input. They are required to generate the *matching* output (as with data conversion routines or a package of mathematical functions).

(3) Some systems (such as process control systems) are required to remember their behavior so that they can respond to an input based on that input and past inputs; that is, behave like a finite state machine. In this case the focus is on both input/output pairs and sequences of such pairs.

5.1.1.2 Difficulties. Most software products can receive an infinite number of sequences as input. Thus, to completely specify the behavior of the product through input/output sequences would require that the SRS contain an infinitely long set of sequences of inputs and required outputs. With this approach, therefore, it may be impossible to completely specify every conceivable behavior that is required of the software.

5.1.2 Representative Examples. One alternative is to indicate what behavior is required by using representative examples of that behavior. Suppose, for example, that the system is required to respond with a "1" every time it receives a "0". Clearly, a list of all possible sequences of inputs and outputs would be impossible. However, by using representative sequences one might be able to fully understand the system's behavior. This system's behavior might be described by using this representative set of four dialogues:[6]

0101
010101010101
01
010101

These dialogues provide a good idea of the required inputs and outputs but they do not specify the system's behavior completely.

5.1.3 Models. Another approach is to express the requirements in the form of a model.[7] This can be an accurate and efficient way to express complex requirements.

At least three generalized types of models are in common usage:

(1) Mathematical
(2) Functional
(3) Timing

Care should be taken to distinguish between the model for the application; that is, a linear programming model (with a set of linear inequalities and an objective function) and the model for the software which is required to implement the application model. See 5.1.3.5.

5.1.3.1 Mathematical Models. A mathematical model is a model that uses mathematical relations to describe the software's behavior. Mathematical models are especially useful for particular application areas, including navigation, linear programming, econometrics, signal processing and weather analysis.

A mathematical model might specify the response discussed in 5.1.2 like this:

(01)*

where * means that the parenthesized character string is repeated one or more times.

5.1.3.2 Functional Models. A functional model is a model that provides a mapping from inputs to outputs. Functional models, for example, finite state machines or Petri nets can help identify and define various features of the software or can demonstrate the intended operation of the system.

A functional model might specify the response, previously described by the mathematical model, in the form of a finite state machine as shown in Fig 1. In this figure, the incoming arrow points to the starting state. The double lined box represents the accepting state. The notation X/Y on the lines indicates that when X is accepted as an input, Y is produced as an output.

5.1.3.3 Timing Models. A timing model is a model that has been augmented with timing constraints. Timing models are quite useful for specifying the form and details of the software's behavior, particularly for real-time systems or for human factors of any system.

[6]Each of the four sample dialogues given here (one per line) represents a sequence of one-character user inputs and one-character system outputs.

[7]For details on using modeling techniques, see [5], [8], [9], and [12].

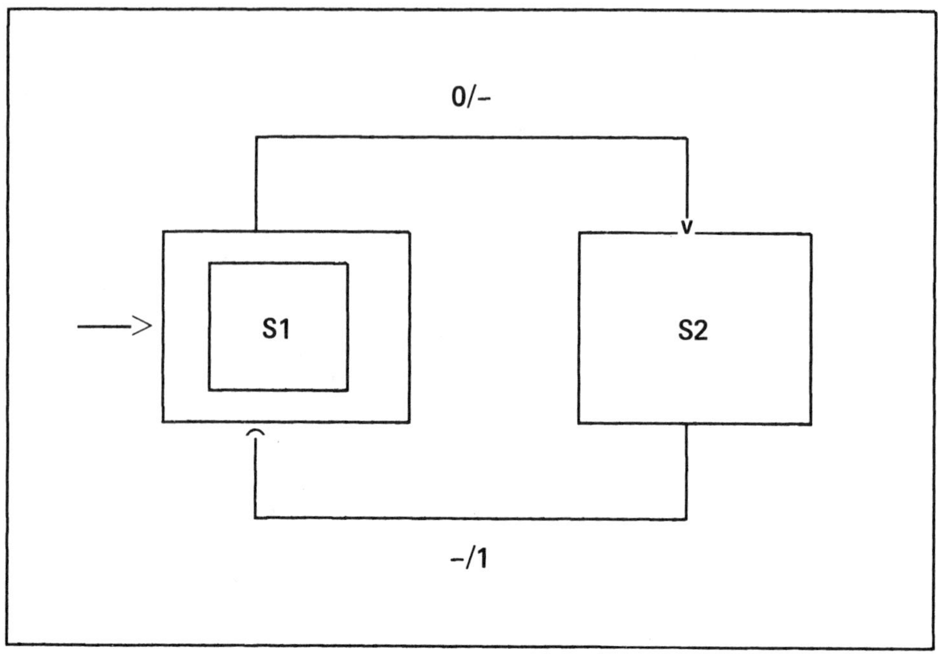

Fig 1
A Functional Model Specifying Any Sequence of Alternating 0s and 1s

A timing model might add these constraints to the model shown in Fig 1.

(1) The stimulus 0 will occur within 30 s of the arrival in state S1

(2) The response 1 will occur within 2 s of the arrival in state S2

5.1.3.4 Other Models. In addition to the aforementioned, specific applications have particularly helpful models. For example, a compiler specification might employ attribute grammars, or a payroll system might use tables. It is to be noted that the use of a formal requirements language for an SRS usually implies a need for the use of a particular model.

5.1.3.5 Cautions. Whatever type of model is used:

(1) It must be rigorously defined, either in the SRS or in a document referenced in the SRS. This definition should specify

(a) The required ranges of the model's parameters

(b) The values of constraints it uses

(c) The required accuracy of results

(d) The load capacity

(e) The required execution time

(f) Default or failure response

(2) Care must be taken to keep a model definition within the domain of requirements. Whenever an SRS uses a model:

(a) It means that the model provided an especially efficient and accurate way to specify the requirements

(b) It does not mean that the implementation of the software product must be based on that model.

A model that works effectively for explaining requirements in a written document may not be optimal for the actual software implementation.

5.2 Annotation of the Software Requirements. Typically, all of the requirements that relate to a software product are not equally important. Some requirements may be essential, especially for life-critical applications, while others may be just *nice to have.*

(1) Each requirement in the SRS should be annotated to make these differences in relative importance clear and explicit.

(2) Annotating the requirements in this manner, helps:

(a) Customers to give more careful consideration to each requirement, which often clarifies any hidden assumptions they may have.

(b) Developers to make correct design decisions and devote appropriate levels of effort to the different parts of the software product.

5.2.1 Stability. One method of annotating requirements uses the dimension of stability. A requirement may be considered *stable* when it is thought that the needs which it addresses will not change during the expected life of the software, or it may be considered *volatile* and subject to change.

5.2.2 Degree of Necessity. Another way to annotate is to distinguish classes of requirements as mandatory, desirable, and optional.

(1) Mandatory implies that the software will not be acceptable unless these requirements are provided in an agreed manner.

(2) Desirable implies that these are requirements that would enhance the software product, but would not make it unacceptable if they are absent.

(3) Optional implies a class of functions that may or may not be worthwhile, which gives the supplier the opportunity to propose something which exceeds the SRS.

5.2.3 Annotation Caution. Prior to annotating the requirements, a thorough understanding of the contractual implications of such annotations, should be obtained.

5.3 Common Pitfalls Encountered in Expressing Requirements. An essential point about the SRS is that it should specify the results that must be achieved by the software, not the means of obtaining those results.

(1) The basic issues that the requirements writer must address are these:

(a) *Functionality* — what the software is supposed to do

(b) *Performance* — the speed, availability, response time, recovery time of various software functions, etc

(c) *Design Constraints Imposed on an Implementation* —any required standards in effect, implementation language, policies for data base integrity, resource limits, operating environment(s), etc

(d) *Attributes* — considerations of portability, correctness, maintainability, security, etc

(e) *External Interfaces* — interactions with people, hardware, other software and other hardware

(2) The requirements writer should avoid placing either design or project requirements in the SRS. The requirements writer should clearly distinguish between identifying required design constraints and projecting a design.

5.3.1 Embedding Design in the SRS. Embedding design specifications in the SRS unduly constrains the software designs and artificially places potentially dangerous requirements in the SRS.

(1) The SRS must specify what functions are to be performed on what data to produce what results at what location for whom. The SRS should focus on the services to be performed. The SRS should not normally specify design items such as

(a) Partitioning the software into modules

(b) Allocating functions to the modules

(c) Describing the flow of information or control between modules

(d) Choosing data structures

(2) It is not always practical to consider the design as being completely isolated from the SRS. Security or safety considerations may impose requirements that reflect directly into design constraints; for example, the need to

(a) Keep certain functions in separate modules

(b) Permit only limited communication between some areas of the program

(c) Compute check sums for critical quantities

In general, it must be considered that the selection of an appropriate high-level design for the software may require vast amounts of resources (perhaps as much as 10% to 20% of the total product development cost). There are two alternatives:

(1) Ignore the warning in this guide and specify the design in the SRS. This will mean that either a potentially inadequate design is stated as a requirement (because insufficient time was spent in arriving at it), or an exorbitant amount of time is spent during the requirements phase (because an entire design analysis is performed before SRS completion).

(2) Use the advice in 5.1.3 of this guide. State the requirements using a *model* design used solely to assist in the description of the requirements and not intended to serve as the actual design.

5.3.2 Embedding Project Requirements in the SRS. The SRS should address the software product, not the process of producing the software product.

(1) Project requirements represent an understanding between a customer and a supplier about the contractual matters pertaining to the production of software (and thus should not be

included in the SRS). These normally include such items as:

(a) Cost
(b) Delivery schedules
(c) Reporting procedures
(d) Software development methods
(e) Quality assurance
(f) Validation and verification criteria
(g) Acceptance procedures

(2) Project requirements are specified in other documents, typically in a computer program development plan or a statement of work. The requirements for only the software product itself are given in the SRS.

6. An SRS Prototype Outline

This section discusses each of the essential parts of the SRS. These parts are arranged in Table 1 in an outline that can serve as a prototype for any SRS.

Software suppliers and customers should tailor the content requirements of this guide based on the particular package being specified, and individual companies might base their own SRS standards upon it. Remember that while an SRS does not have to follow this outline or use the names for its parts, any good SRS must include all of the information discussed here.

6.1 Introduction (Section 1 of the SRS). The following subsections of the SRS should provide an overview of the entire SRS.

Table 1
Prototype SRS Outline

Table of Contents
1. Introduction
    1.1 Purpose
    1.2 Scope
    1.3 Definitions, Acronyms, and Abbreviations
    1.4 References
    1.5 Overview
2. General Description
    2.1 Product Perspective
    2.2 Product Functions
    2.3 User Characteristics
    2.4 General Constraints
    2.5 Assumptions and Dependencies
3. Specific Requirements
    (See 6.3.2 of this guide for alternate organizations of this section of the SRS.)

Appendixes
Index

6.1.1 Purpose (1.1 of the SRS). This subsection should accomplish the following:

(1) Delineate the purpose of the particular SRS

(2) Specify the intended audience for the SRS

6.1.2 Scope (1.2 of the SRS). This subsection should:

(1) Identify the software product(s) to be produced by name; for example, Host DBMS, Report Generator, etc

(2) Explain what the software product(s) will, and, if necessary, will not do

(3) Describe the application of the software being specified. As a portion of this, it should:

(a) Describe all relevant benefits, objectives, and goals as precisely as possible. For example, to say that one goal is to provide *effective reporting capabilities* is not as good as saying *parameter-driven, user-definable reports with a 2 h turnaround and on-line entry of user parameters.*

(b) Be consistent with similar statements in higher-level specifications (for example, the System Requirement Specification), if they exist.

6.1.3 Definitions, Acronyms, and Abbreviations (1.3 of the SRS). This subsection should provide the definitions of all terms, acronyms, and abbreviations required to properly interpret the SRS. This information may be provided by reference to one or more appendixes in the SRS or by reference to other documents.

6.1.4 References (1.4 of the SRS). This subsection should:

(1) Provide a complete list of all documents referenced elsewhere in the SRS, or in a separate, specified document.

(2) Identify each document by title, report number — if applicable — date, and publishing organization.

(3) Specify the sources from which the references can be obtained.

This information may be provided by reference to an appendix or to another document.

6.1.5 Overview (1.5 of the SRS). This subsection should:

(1) Describe what the rest of the SRS contains

(2) Explain how the SRS is organized

6.2 The General Description (Section 2 of the SRS). This section of the SRS should describe the general factors that affect the product and its requirements.

This section usually consists of five subsections, as follows:

(1) Product Perspective
(2) Product Functions
(3) User Characteristics
(4) General Constraints
(5) Assumptions and Dependencies

It should be made clear that this section does not state specific requirements; it only makes those requirements easier to understand.

6.2.1 Product Perspective (2.1 of the SRS). This subsection of the SRS puts the product into perspective with other related products or projects.

(1) If the product is independent and totally self-contained, it should be stated here.

(2) If the SRS defines a product that is a component of a larger system or project — as frequently occurs — then this subsection should:

(a) Describe the functions of each component of the larger system or project, and identify interfaces

(b) Identify the principal external interfaces of this software product.

NOTE: This is not a detailed description of these interfaces; the detailed description is provided elsewhere in the SRS.

(c) Describe the computer hardware and peripheral equipment to be used.

NOTE: This is an overview description only.

A block diagram showing the major components of the larger system or project, interconnections, and external interfaces can be very helpful.

This subsection should not be used to impose a specific design solution or specific design constraints on the solution. This subsection should provide the reasons why certain design constraints are later specified as part of the Specific Requirements Section of the SRS.

6.2.2 Product Functions (2.2 of the SRS). This subsection of the SRS should provide a summary of the functions that the software will perform. For example, an SRS for an accounting program might use this part to address *customer account maintenance*, *customer statement and invoice preparation* without mentioning the vast amount of detail that each of those functions requires.

Sometimes the function summary that is necessary for this part can be taken directly from the section of the higher-level specification (if one exists) that allocates particular functions to the software product. Note that, for the sake of clarity:

(1) The functions should be organized in a way that makes the list of functions understandable to the customer or to anyone else reading the document for the first time.

(2) Block diagrams showing the different functions and their relationships can be helpful. Remember, however, that such a diagram is not a requirement on the design of a product itself; it is simply an effective explanatory tool.

This subsection should not be used to state specific requirements. This subsection should provide the reasons why certain specific requirements are later specified as part of the Specific Requirements Section(s) of the SRS.

6.2.3 User Characteristics (2.3 of the SRS). This subsection of the SRS should describe those general characteristics of the eventual users of the product that will affect the specific requirements.

Many people interact with a system during the operation and maintenance phase of the software life cycle. Some of these people are users, operators, and maintenance and systems personnel. Certain characteristics of these people, such as educational level, experience, and technical expertise impose important constraints on the system's operating environment.

If most users of the system are occasional users, a resulting specific requirement might be that the system contains reminders of how to perform essential functions rather than assuming that the user will remember these details from the last session or from reading the user's guide.

This subsection should not be used to state specific requirements or to impose specific design constraints on the solution. This subsection should provide the reasons why certain specific requirements or design constraints are later specified as part of the Specific Requirements Section(s) of the SRS.

6.2.4 General Constraints (2.4 of the SRS). This subsection of the SRS should provide a general description of any other items that will limit the developer's options for designing the system. These can include:

(1) Regulatory policies
(2) Hardware limitations; for example, signal timing requirements
(3) Interfaces to other applications
(4) Parallel operation
(5) Audit functions

(6) Control functions

(7) Higher-order language requirements

(8) Signal handshake protocols; for example, XON -XOFF, ACK - NACK.

(9) Criticality of the application

(10) Safety and security considerations

This subsection should not be used to impose specific requirements or specific design constraints on the solution. This subsection should provide the reasons why certain specific requirements or design constraints are later specified as part of the Specific Requirements Section of the SRS.

6.2.5 Assumptions and Dependencies (2.5 of the SRS). This subsection of the SRS should list each of the factors that affect the requirements stated in the SRS. These factors are not design constraints on the software but are, rather, any changes to them that can affect the requirements in the SRS. For example, an assumption might be that a specific operating system will be available on the hardware designated for the software product. If, in fact, the operating system is not available, the SRS would then have to change accordingly.

6.3 The Specific Requirements (Section 3 of the SRS). This section of the SRS should contain all the details the software developer needs to create a design. This is typically the largest and most important part of the SRS.

(1) The details within it should be defined as individual specific requirements, following the guidelines described in Section 3 of this guide (verifiable, unambiguous, etc)

(2) Background should be provided by cross-referencing each specific requirement to any related discussion in the Introduction, General Description, and Appendixes portions of the SRS, whenever possible.

(3) One way to classify the specific requirements is as follows:

(a) Functional Requirements

(b) Performance Requirements

(c) Design Constraints

(d) Attributes

(e) External Interface Requirements

The important points to be recognized are that:

(1) Specific requirements should be organized in a logical and readable fashion.

(2) Each requirement should be stated such that its achievement can be objectively verified by a prescribed method.

6.3.1 Information Required as Part of the Specific Requirements

6.3.1.1 Functional Requirements. This subsection of the SRS should specify how the inputs to the software product should be transformed into outputs. It describes the fundamental actions that must take place in the software.

For each class of function or sometimes for each individual function, it is necessary to specify requirements on inputs, processing, and outputs. These are usually organized with these four subparagraphs:

(1) Introduction. This subparagraph should provide a description of the purpose of the function and the approaches and techniques employed. It should contain any introductory or background material which might clarify the intent of the function.

(2) Inputs. This subparagraph should contain:

(a) A detailed description of all data input to this function to include:

(i) The sources of the inputs

(ii) Quantities

(iii) Units of measure

(iv) Timing

(v) The ranges of the valid inputs to include accuracies and tolerances.

(b) The details of operator control requirements should include names and descriptions of operator actions, and console or operator positions. For example, this might include required operator activities such as form alignment — when printing checks.

(c) References to interface specifications or interface control documents where appropriate.

(3) Processing. This subparagraph should define all of the operations to be performed on the input data and intermediate parameters to obtain the output. It includes specification of:

(a) Validity checks on the input data

(b) The exact sequence of operations to include timing of events

(c) Responses to *abnormal* situations, for example:

(i) Overflow

(ii) Communication failure

(iii) Error handling

(d) Parameters affected by the operations

(e) Requirements for degraded operation

(f) Any methods (for example, equations, mathematical algorithms, and logical operations) which must be used to transform the system inputs into corresponding outputs. For example, this might specify:

(i) The formula for computing the withholding tax in a payroll package

(ii) A least squares curve fitting technique for a plotting package

(iii) A meteorological model to be used for a weather forecasting package

(g) Validity checks on the output data

(4) Outputs. This subparagraph should contain:

(a) A detailed description of all data output from this function to include:

(i) Destinations of the outputs

(ii) Quantities

(iii) Units of measure

(iv) Timing

(v) The range of the valid outputs is to include accuracies and tolerances

(vi) Disposition of illegal values

(vii) Error messages

(b) References to interface specifications or interface control documents where appropriate

In addition, for those systems whose requirements focus on input/output behavior, the SRS should specify all of the significant input/output pairs and sequences of pairs. Sequences will be needed when a system is required to remember its behavior so that it can respond to an input based on that input and past behavior; that is, behave like a finite state machine.

6.3.1.2 Performance Requirements. This subsection should specify both the static and the dynamic numerical requirements placed on the software or on human interaction with the software, as a whole.

(1) Static numerical requirements may include:

(a) The number of terminals to be supported

(b) The number of simultaneous users to be supported

(c) Number of files and records to be handled

(d) Sizes of tables and files

Static numerical requirements are sometimes identified under a separate section entitled *capacity*.

(2) Dynamic numerical requirements may include, for example, the numbers of transactions and tasks and the amount of data to be processed within certain time periods for both normal and peak workload conditions.

All of these requirements should be stated in measurable terms, for example, *95% of the transactions shall be processed in less than 1 s*, rather than, *operator shall not have to wait for the transaction to complete.*

NOTE: Numerical limits applied to one specific function are normally specified as part of the processing subparagraph description of that function.

6.3.1.3 Design Constraints. Design constraints can be imposed by other standards, hardware limitations, etc.

6.3.1.3.1 Standards Compliance. This subsection should specify the requirements derived from existing standards or regulations. They might include:

(1) Report format

(2) Data naming

(3) Accounting procedures

(4) Audit Tracing. For example, this could specify the requirement for software to trace processing activity. Such traces are needed for some applications to meet minimum government or financial standards. An audit trace requirement might, for example, state that all changes to a payroll data base must be recorded in a trace file with before and after values.

6.3.1.3.2 Hardware Limitations. This subsection could include requirements for the software to operate inside various hardware constraints. For example, these could include:

(1) Hardware configuration characteristics (number of ports, instruction sets, etc)

(2) Limits on primary and secondary memory

6.3.1.4 Attributes. There are a number of attributes that can place specific requirements on the software. Some of these are indicated below. These should not be interpreted to be a complete list.

6.3.1.4.1 Availability. This could specify the factors required to guarantee a defined availability level for the entire system such as checkpoint, recovery and restart.

6.3.1.4.2 Security. This could specify the factors that would protect the software from accidental or malicious access, use, modification, destruction, or disclosure. Specific requirements in this area could include the need to:

(1) Utilize certain cryptographical techniques

(2) Keep specific log or history data sets

(3) Assign certain functions to different modules

(4) Restrict communications between some areas of a program

(5) Compute checksums for critical quantities

6.3.1.4.3 Maintainability. This could specify the requirements to ensure that the software could be maintained. For example, as a part of this,

(1) Specific coupling metrics for the software modules could be required

(2) Specific data/program partitioning requirements could be specified for micro-devices

6.3.1.4.4 Transferability/Conversion. This could specify the user procedures, user interface compatibility constraints (if any) etc, required to transport the software from one environment to another.

6.3.1.4.5 Caution. It is important that required attributes be specified so that their achievement can be objectively verified by a prescribed method.

6.3.1.5 External Interface Requirements

6.3.1.5.1 User Interfaces. This should specify:

(1) The characteristics that the software must support for each human interface to the software product. For example, if the user of the system operates through a display terminal, the following should be specified:

(a) Required screen formats

(b) Page layout and content of any reports or menus

(c) Relative timing of inputs and outputs

(d) Availability of some form of programmable function keys

(2) All the aspects of optimizing the interface with the person who must use the system. This may simply comprise a list of do's and don'ts on how the system will appear to the user. One example might be a requirement for the option of long or short error messages. Like all others, these requirements should be verifiable and for example, *a clerk typist grade 4 can do function X in Z min* after 1 h *of training* rather than *a typist can do function X.* (This might also be specified in the Attributes section under a section titled *Ease of Use.*)

6.3.1.5.2 Hardware Interfaces. This should specify the logical characteristics of each interface between the software product and the hardware components of the system. It also covers such matters as what devices are to be supported, how they are to be supported, and protocols. For example, terminal support might specify full screen support as opposed to line by line.

6.3.1.5.3 Software Interfaces. This should specify the use of other required software products (for example, a data management system, an operating system, or a mathematical package), and interfaces with other application systems (for example, the linkage between an accounts receivable system and a general ledger system).

For each required software product, the following should be provided:

(1) Name

(2) Mnemonic

(3) Specification number

(4) Version number

(5) Source

For each interface, this part should:

(1) Discuss the purpose of the interfacing software as related to this software product.

(2) Define the interface in terms of message content and format. It is not necessary to detail any well-documented interface, but a reference to the document defining the interface is required.

6.3.1.5.4 Communications Interfaces. This should specify the various interfaces to communications such as local network protocols, etc.

6.3.1.6 Other Requirements. Certain requirements may, due to the nature of the software, the user organization, etc, be placed in separate categories as indicated below.

6.3.1.6.1 Data Base. This could specify the requirements for any data base that is to be developed as part of the product. This might include:

(1) The types of information identified in 6.3.1.1

(2) Frequency of use

(3) Accessing capabilities

(4) Data element and file descriptors

(5) Relationship of data elements, records and files

(6) Static and dynamic organization

(7) Retention requirements for data

NOTE: If an existing data base package is to be used, this package should be named under *Interfaces to Software* and details of using it specified there.

6.3.1.6.2 Operations. This could specify the normal and special operations required by the user such as:

(1) The various modes of operations in the user organization; for example, user-initiated operations

(2) Periods of interactive operations and periods of unattended operations

(3) Data processing support functions

(4) Backup and recovery operations

NOTE: This is sometimes specified as part of the User Interfaces section.

6.3.1.6.3 Site Adaptation Requirements. This could:

(1) Define the requirements for any data or initialization sequences that are specific to a given site, mission, or operational mode, for example, grid values, safety limits, etc.

(2) Specify the site or mission-related features that should be modified to adapt the software to a particular installation.

6.3.2 Organizing The Specific Requirements. This subsection is often the largest and most complex of all the parts of the SRS.

(1) It may be necessary to organize this section into subdivisions according to the primary classes of functions to be performed by the software. For example, consider a large interactive accounting system. This may be broken down at the top level into operational software (which supports near-real-time transactions), support software (logging functions, disk backup, loading tapes, etc), and diagnostic software (primarily hardware and communications support), and at the next level into accounts receivable, accounts payable, etc.

(2) It should be remembered, however, that the purpose of this subdivided organization is to improve the readability of the SRS, not to define the high level design of the software being specified.

The best organization for Section 3, Specific Requirements, in an SRS, depends on the application area and the nature of the software product being specified. Tables 2 through 4 show four possible organizations.

(1) In Prototype Outline 1 (Table 2), all the Functional Requirements are specified, then the four types of interface requirements are specified, and then the rest of the requirements are specified.

(2) Prototype Outline 2 (Table 3) shows the four classes of interface requirements applied to each individual Functional Requirement. This is followed by the specification of the rest of the requirements.

(3) In Prototype Outline 3 (Table 4), all of the issues addressed by the Functional Requirements are specified, then the other requirements that apply to them are specified. This pattern is then repeated for each of the External Interface Requirement Classifications.

Table 2
Prototype Outline 1 for SRS Section 3

- 3. Specific Requirements
  - 3.1 Functional Requirements
    - 3.1.1 Functional Requirement 1
      - 3.1.1.1 Introduction
      - 3.1.1.2 Inputs
      - 3.1.1.3 Processing
      - 3.1.1.4 Outputs
    - 3.1.2 Functional Requirement 2
    - . . . .
    - 3.1.*n* Functional Requirement *n*
  - 3.2 External Interface Requirements
    - 3.2.1 User Interfaces
    - 3.2.2 Hardware Interfaces
    - 3.2.3 Software Interfaces
    - 3.2.4 Communications Interfaces
  - 3.3 Performance Requirements
  - 3.4 Design Constraints
    - 3.4.1 Standards Compliance
    - 3.4.2 Hardware Limitations
    - . . . .
  - 3.5 Attributes
    - 3.5.1 Security
    - 3.5.2 Maintainability
    - . . . .
  - 3.6 Other Requirements
    - 3.6.1 Data Base
    - 3.6.2 Operations
    - 3.6.3 Site Adaptation
    - . . . .

Table 3
Prototype Outline 2 for SRS Section 3

- 3. Specific Requirements
  - 3.1 Functional Requirements
    - 3.1.1 Functional Requirement 1
      - 3.1.1.1 Specification
        - 3.1.1.1.1 Introduction
        - 3.1.1.1.2 Inputs
        - 3.1.1.1.3 Processing
        - 3.1.1.1.4 Outputs
      - 3.1.1.2 External Interfaces
        - 3.1.1.2.1 User Interfaces
        - 3.1.1.2.2 Hardware Interfaces
        - 3.1.1.2.3 Software Interfaces
        - 3.1.1.2.4 Communication Interfaces
    - 3.1.2 Functional Requirement 2
    - . . . .
    - 3.1.*n* Functional Requirement *n*
  - 3.2 Performance Requirements
  - 3.3 Design Constraints
  - 3.4 Attributes
    - 3.4.1 Security
    - 3.4.2 Maintainability
    - . . . .
  - 3.5 Other Requirements
    - 3.5.1 Data Base
    - 3.5.2 Operations
    - 3.5.3 Site Adaption
    - . . . .

Table 4
Prototype Outline 3 for SRS Section 3

3.	Specific Requirements
3.1	Functional Requirements
3.1.1	Functional Requirement 1
3.1.1.1	Introduction
3.1.1.2	Inputs
3.1.1.3	Processing
3.1.1.4	Outputs
3.1.1.5	Performance Requirements
3.1.1.6	Design Constraints
3.1.1.4.1	Standards Compliance
3.1.1.4.2	Hardware Limitations
. . . .	
3.1.1.7	Attributes
3.1.1.7.1	Security
3.1.1.7.2	Maintainability
. . . .	
3.1.1.8	Other Requirements
3.1.1.8.1	Data Base
3.1.1.8.2	Operations
3.1.1.8.3	Site Adaption
. . . .	
3.1.2	Functional Requirement 2
. . . .	
3.1.*n*	Functional Requirement *n*
3.2	External Interface Requirements
3.2.1	User Interfaces
3.2.1.1	Performance Requirements
3.2.1.2	Design Constraints
3.2.1.2.1	Standards Compliance
3.2.1.2.2	Hardware Limitations
. . . .	
3.2.1.3	Attributes
3.2.1.3.1	Security
3.2.1.3.2	Maintainability
. . . .	
3.2.1.4	Other Requirements
3.2.1.4.1	Data Base
3.2.1.4.2	Operations
3.2.1.4.3	Site Adaption
. . . .	
3.2.2	Hardware Interfaces
3.2.3	Software Interfaces
3.2.4	Communications Interfaces

(4) In Prototype Outline 4 (Table 5), the interface requirements and the rest of the requirements are specified as they pertain to each Functional Requirement.

The organization of the Specific Requirements Section of the SRS should be chosen with the goal of properly specifying the requirements in the most readable manner.

6.4 Supporting Information. The supporting information; that is, the Table of Contents, the Appendixes, and the Index, make the SRS easier to use.

(1) The Table of Contents and Index are quite important and should follow the generally accepted rules for good documentation practices.[8]

(2) The Appendixes are not always considered part of the actual requirements specification and are not always necessary. They might include:

(a) Sample I/O formats, descriptions of cost analysis studies, or results of user surveys.

(b) Supporting or background information that can help the readers of the SRS.

(c) A description of the problems to be solved by the software.

(d) The history, background, experience and operational characteristics of the organization to be supported.

(e) A cross-reference list, arranged by milestone, of those incomplete software requirements that are to be completed by specified milestones. (See 4.3.2 and 4.3.3 (4).)

(f) Special packaging instructions for the code and the media to meet security, export, initial loading, or other requirements.

(3) When Appendixes are included, the SRS should explicitly state whether or not the Appendixes are to be considered part of the requirements.

Table 5
Prototype Outline 4 for SRS Section 3

3.	Specific Requirements
3.1	Functional Requirement 1
3.1.1	Introduction
3.1.2	Inputs
3.1.3	Processing
3.1.4	Outputs
3.1.5	External Interfaces
3.1.5.1	User Interfaces
3.1.5.2	Hardware Interfaces
3.1.5.3	Software Interfaces
3.1.5.4	Communication Interfaces
3.1.6	Performance Requirements
3.1.7	Design Constraints
3.1.8	Attributes
3.1.8.1	Security
3.1.8.2	Maintainability
. . . .	
3.1.9	Other Requirements
3.1.9.1	Data Base
3.1.9.2	Operations
3.1.9.3	Site Adaption
. . . .	
3.2	Functional Requirement 2
. . . .	
3.*n*	Functional Requirement *n*

[8] See, for example: [4] and [11].

Chapter 4: Software Requirements Methodologies and Representation Methods

1: Introduction

A software development methodology can be defined as (1) an integrated set of software engineering methods, policies, procedures, rules, standards, techniques, tools, languages, and other methodologies for analyzing, designing, implementing, and testing software and (2) a set of rules for selecting the correct methodology, process, or tools for use.

A major problem in the past was our inability to represent or write down what the requirements were; the only alternative was to represent the requirements for a software system with the code that was going to implement it. This problem fueled our desire to "rush into code."

In the last 15 years, numerous software requirements methodologies have been developed that can aid a software engineer in establishing and documenting the software requirements—in other words, representing the requirements. Many of these tools and techniques, such as structured analysis are widely used. Others, such as realtime structured analysis and formal specification methods, are relatively new and little used.

This large chapter is the first to contain papers on ways to analyze and document software requirements. It reflects the current interest in tools and methodologies. It examines "manual" software requirements methods and representations that can be used both to analyze requirements and to "document" them for the benefit of the customer and the designer. The chapter contains papers on both realtime and non-realtime structured analysis (the classic and modern approaches) as well as on data-structured analysis, object-oriented methods, and formal (mathematical) methods. Many of these methodologies can be used in system as well as software engineering.

2: Description of Papers

"A Comparison of the Major Approaches to Software Specifications" by Dr. Pamela Zave, the developer of PAISLey, was adapted from her notes from the Fourth International Workshop on Software Specifications and Design, Monterey, California, April 3-4, 1987. Zave's paper homes in on the differences between natural language specifications, operational specifications (execution semantics), and mathematical specifications (proof semantics). She also provides a short description of several specification techniques and defines the categories into which they fit.

"A Comparison of Techniques for the Specification of External System Behavior" by A.M. Davis, takes the position that natural language alone is an inadequate means of representation for the requirements specification of a large system. To avoid misunderstandings because of ambiguity, inconsistency, incompleteness, etc., other, more formal techniques must be used along with, or instead of, natural language. Davis describes the application of a number of methods of differing formality to some elementary problems.

The third paper, "Structured Analysis: A Tutorial" by Cyril Svoboda, is an up-to-date tutorial on structured analysis, including realtime (RT-SA) and non-realtime (SA) structured analysis methodologies. Most of the existing papers that describe structured analysis are old and in many cases outdated in that they do not reflect the way structured analysis is done today, do not present structured analysis the way the "standard" reference/text books do, or present only one way of doing structured analysis, for example SADT™ or Gane and Sarson.

Svoboda's paper:

- discusses and illustrates, through drawings, "conventional" SA
- discusses and compares the variations on SA: SADT [1], Gane and Sarson [2], and others
- discusses and illustrates RT-SA
- compares Hatley [3] and Ward-Mellor [4] as to methodologies and representation methods
- discusses some of the automated tools that implement SA and RT-SA
- discusses some of the changes on the horizon for SA and RT-SA

"Entity-Relationship Approach to Data Modeling" by Peter Chen provides a method for modeling data requirements. Entity-relationship models are extensively used in the development of systems whose data interactions are their dominant feature (e.g., database, transaction-oriented, financial, and management information systems) and are sometimes considered part of structured analysis [5].

The N^2 Charts defined in Robert Lano's paper of the same title are a single-function tool for the description of external and internal interfaces. This paper is the introductory chapter from Lano's TRW Software Series Report on N^2 Charts [6] and his book *A Technique for Software and System Design* [7]. Lano describes N^2 Charts as an implementation tool and methodology for the tabulation, definition, analysis, and description of functional interactions and interfaces. The N^2 Chart is, in effect, a tool for the integration of all the people, products, and paper that make up any given system. The paper describes the format of an N^2 Chart, gives examples of time sequence N^2 Chart and loop N^2 Chart, and provides information about what the N^2 Chart can show. The N^2 Chart is required on many Department of Defense and other government contracts.

In "Introduction to OOA: Object-Oriented Analysis," Peter Coad and Ed Yourdon describe a new, object-oriented approach to requirements analysis. They have observed that dataflow diagram analysis and database/data structure analysis are often conducted in parallel, leading to conflicting results that are never reconciled. They propose an approach that combines the advantages of functional decomposition, dataflow modeling, and information modeling; it starts with identifying the objects of the problem and proceeds to classify the structure of the objects, to define the attributes of the individual objects and classes, to identify the interfaces between the objects, and finally to define the services (functions and processes) that the objects require. Coad and Yourdon make the key observation that, in this sequence, the most stable characteristics of the problem are defined first and the most volatile last. Therefore the results of analysis are least likely to be disrupted when, inevitably, the problem (or the analyst's understanding of it) changes [8].

In "A Comparison of Object-Oriented and Structured Development Methods," Patrick Loy seeks a perspective on the two approaches. He summarizes the history and attributes of object-oriented methods, considers and rejects the idea that object-oriented is a more natural (or less natural) approach to system analysis than is a functional approach, and presents a plan for evaluating a transition to object-oriented development.

COntrolled Requirement Expression (CORE), a structured method for requirements specification, was developed by G.P. Mullery and is popular in the United Kingdom. Mullery's paper is entitled "CORE—A Method for Controlled Requirement Specifications." CORE is applicable to the description of the dynamic aspects of many systems, not just computer systems. CORE is supported by a diagram notation whose features are derived from several widely used specification and design diagram notations (structured analysis and Michael Jackson's design notation [9]).

CORE is supported by British Aerospace and by System Designers Limited, each organization producing a slightly different version. CORE has now been automated by using a tool also supported by Software Designers Limited. Mullery's original 1979 paper is reprinted here. CORE has evolved significantly in the past 10 years, but there is no short paper that can supplant the original. For a longer description and case studies, see the Debrief Reports of the Software Tools for Application to Large Realtime Systems (STARTS) project of the U.K. National Computing Centre, Ltd., in Manchester.

"SSADM—System Buildup Made Simple" by J. Williams discusses Structured System Analysis and Design Methodology (SSADM), a popular analysis technique used in the United Kingdom. SSADM was originally developed for the U.K. government by Learmonth and Burchett Management Systems (LBMS) and has a commercial counterpart called LBMS System Development Methodology (LSDM). It resembles structured analysis in many ways but has some extensions.

In "The Operational Versus the Conventional Approach to Software Development," Pamela Zave reports on PAISLey (Process-oriented, Applicative, Interpretable Specification Language). PAISLey is one of a class of executable specification languages. Zave tells us that this older paper is still the best description of PAISLey. This methodology, while not yet widely adopted in industry, is receiving support and interest as a teaching tool in graduate-level education. The executable specification is a form of prototyping tool. The developer specifies a system in the PAISLey language, according to his/her understanding of the user's needs, and executes the specification to observe the system's behavior. The user and developer then correct any misunderstandings and account for any changes in the user's views that result from observing the behavior. After some iteration, the final specification is used as the basis for system development. The executable specification cannot be the final system because it is very slow and inefficient in resource utilization. It should also be pointed out that PAISLey handles timing performance requirements by reporting the simulated system time; it does not execute in realtime.

"The Descartes Specification Language" by Joe Urban describes the language he developed. It is another abstract language that can be directly executed, shortening and improving the requirements analysis and preliminary design phases of the lifecycle. Descartes uses a data structure method suggested by Hoare [10, 11] to analyze program inputs into particular parts that are then used to synthesize a description of program output.

The next paper, "Z," by M. Norris of British Telecom, is concerned with a formal specification language called Z. Z was developed by the Programming Research Laboratory at Oxford University. The paper is one in a series of "debriefing" reports published by the STARTS program of the National Computing Centre Limited in Manchester, England. Norris reports that Z is a rigorous system specification technique. It uses set theory and logic to abstract essential features of a design. Subsequent analysis and development of the specification can be carried out on a well-founded mathematical basis. Z is very similar to the Vienna Design Method. [12] Both use set theory and logic to create abstract specifications that can be proven correct. The main difference lies in the presentation format and degree of standardization.

The final two papers of the chapter relate to the recent adoption by the British Ministry of Defence (MOD) of Defence Standard 00-55. This standard, still in the process of being defined and implemented, mandates the use of formal methods, formal verification, and approved tools in the development of safety-critical software for MOD.

In "Formal Methods: Set Piece," Darrel Ince briefly reviews the history of specification methods, beginning with natural language and moving through structured methods to formal methods; he expects that Standard 00-55 will bring about a radical change within the next few years in the way software is specified and developed.

Douglas Barrie in "Formal Methods: Might Is Right" contends that Standard 00-55 will encourage defense contractors in the United Kingdom to spend the time and money needed to adopt a formal methodology and tools and to train the software staff in their use.

3: References

[1] Ross, D.T., Applications and Extensions of SADT™, *Computer,* April 1985, pp. 25-34.

[2] Gane, C. and T. Sarson, *Structured Systems Analysis: Tools and Techniques,* Prentice-Hall, Inc., Englewood Cliffs, NJ, 1979.

[3] Hatley, D.J. and I.M. Pirbhai, *Strategies for Real-Time System Specification,* Dorset House Publishing, NY, 1987.

[4] Ward, P.T. and S.J. Mellor, *Structured Development for Real-Time Systems,* Volume 1: *Introduction & Tools;* Volume 2: *Essential Modeling Techniques;* Volume 3: *Implementation Modeling Techniques,* Yourdon Press, NY, 1986. (Note: the principal author for Volume 3 is S.J. Mellor.)

[5] Yourdon, Edward, "Modern Structured Analysis," Yourdon Press (Prentice-Hall), Englewood Cliffs, NJ, 1989.

[6] Lano, R.J., "The N^2 Chart," *TRW-SS-77-04,* TRW, Inc., Redondo Beach, CA, Nov. 1977.

[7] Lano, R.J., "A Technique for Software and System Design," *TRW Series on Software Technology,* Volume 3, North-Holland Publishing Company, NY, 1979.

[8] Coad, Peter and Edward Yourdon, "An Introduction to OOA—Object Oriented Analysis," Prentice-Hall, Englewood Cliffs, NJ, 1990.

[9] Cameron, John R., "An Overview of JSD," *IEEE Transactions on Software Engineering,* Feb. 1986.

[10] Hoare, C.A.R., "Notes on Data Structuring," in J. Dahl, E.W. Dijkstra, and C.A.R. Hoare, *Structured Programming,* Academic Press, NY, 1972, pp. 83-174.

[11] Hoare, C.A.R., "Data Reliability," *ACM SIGPLAN Notices,* Vol. 10, No. 6, June 1975, pp. 528-533.

[12] Austwick, M. and M. Norris, *STARTS Debrief Report,* "VDM (Vienna Development Method)," U.K. National Computing Centre, Ltd., Manchester, England, 1986.

A COMPARISON OF THE MAJOR APPROACHES
TO SOFTWARE SPECIFICATION AND DESIGN

Pamela Zave
AT&T Bell Laboratories
Murray Hill, New Jersey

1. What Is a Specification?

Sometimes it seems that everyone means something different by the word ''specification,'' and everyone assumes that his definition is the only one. The following definition seems to be the least common denominator, and therefore the only one safe to use under all circumstances:

> A *specification* is a representation of a proposed or existing computer system. It can serve as the basis for a contract between a developer and a customer to produce the proposed system. The specification is intended to describe all of the required properties of the system while leaving all other properties unconstrained. A specification is generally understood to be simpler, more comprehensible, and easier to modify than the actual hardware and software used to implement the specified system.

Some controversies never die, and the controversy over which system properties belong in a specification is one of the most venerable. I have participated in a protracted debate, for instance, over whether the specification of an elevator controller should include the scheduling algorithm or only the performance and fairness constraints on it. The fact is, however, that either answer is correct under some circumstances. The only rule that always works is the one used in the definition: a property belongs in the specification if and only if the customer requires it. Here are some other examples in which it is difficult to classify properties as requirements or nonrequirements on technical grounds alone:

> This undersea cable must not require more than two ship repairs in its 25-year lifetime.

> Here is a list of functions, in priority order. Provide as many of them as possible in 64K bytes of memory.

> This module replaces one in our existing system, and must therefore be compatible with the hardware and software design of our existing system in all respects.

2. The Three Approaches to Specification

Here, again, communication is often hampered by parochialism. There are several fundamentally different ways to approach the specification problem, as well as many opportunities for combining the approaches in various ways. The three corners of the triangle below represent three pure approaches, while the points in its interior exemplify some of the possible combinations.

A mathematical specification language has a semantics based in a proof system. Proofs are used to discover inconsistencies and to derive consequences of the specification; consequences are helpful for validation and checking completeness. The question of whether an implementation satisfies the specification reduces to the question of whether an assertion is provable in some mathematical system. Operational specifications have all these capabilities, but provide them in different ways: An operational specification language has semantics defined in terms of an execution model. It is reasoned about, checked for consistency, and validated by static analysis based on the execution model or by execution. The question of whether an implementation satisfies the specification reduces to the question of whether you could tell the implementation and the specification apart by testing them (not counting nonfunctional properties such as timing, reliability, or resource consumption).

It is important to note that, although mathematical and operational specification languages are very different with respect to semantic foundations and normal usage, they are not necessarily different as formal languages. There is no *a priori* reason that the same specification language could not be given both a proof semantics and an execution model—in fact, it is a good idea. Even purely mathematical specification languages are already executable according to a weak definition allowing exhaustive search: If a mathematical specification language allows you to declare a function on a finite set and to give a relation constraining the value in terms of the argument, for instance, then it is possible to compute the value of the function by searching through the argument set until a value is found that satisfies the constraint.

EH0304-6/90/0000/0197$01.00 © 1990 IEEE

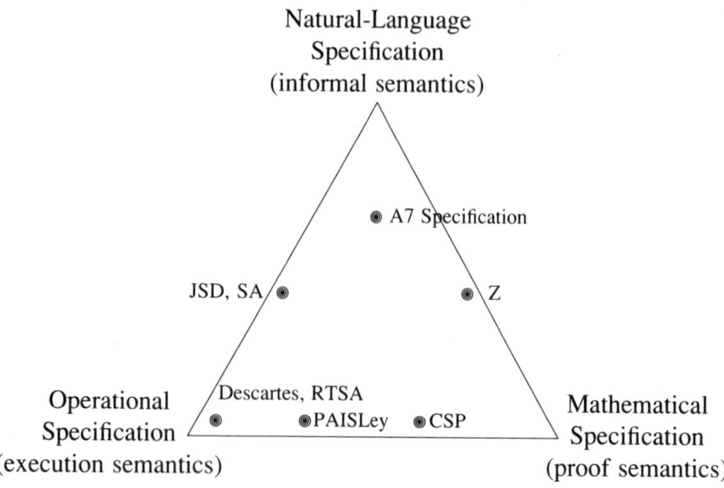

The A7 specification is in English, augmented by equations and finite-state machines. Both JSD and Structured Analysis represent some aspects of systems in an operational language, and the other aspects informally. A specification in Z has important components in both English and equations. Descartes and Real-Time Structured Analysis are strictly operational. PAISLey is primarily operational, but its timing constraints are mathematical. CSP has both proof and execution semantics, although validation by proof is stressed.

3. Evaluation Criteria for Specifications

The purpose of this essay is to evaluate, not individual specification languages, but whole approaches to specification. It seems that some characteristics of the approaches are inherently different, and act as limits on what can be achieved within each approach. We consider four classes of criteria:

> *Relation to the Requirements*: Can all required properties be specified? Must any nonrequired properties be specified? Does the approach help with exploring the solution space, *i.e.*, help distill vague needs into precise requirements?
>
> *Human Factors*: Are specifications comprehensible? (Comprehensibility is known to be improved by abstraction, multiple views, and notational flexibility, but is otherwise poorly understood.) How much intelligence, knowledge, experience, and effort are needed to write specifications? To read them? Is there guidance (usually in the form of procedures and heuristics) for constructing specifications? Do the specifications enhance communication with customers and users? Is there support for its adoption (case studies, statistics, reputation, *etc.*)? Is the approach mature (having stability, standards, *etc.*)?
>
> *Benefits for Quality and Productivity*: How are specifications checked for consistency? How are specifications validated? Is there help with modifying a specification? Is there help with exploring implementation strategies? Is there help with generating an implementation? Is there help with determining that an implementation is correct? Is there help with documentation? Keeping a project history?
>
> *Availability*: Are the necessary tools and techniques widely available now, mere speculations by researchers about what might be possible in the future, or somewhere in between?

4. Comparisons: The Conventional Wisdom

Many of the relationships among these approaches are quite obvious. There is a big difference between informal specifications and either type of formal specification. Informal specifications can specify all required properties, impose no inherent bias, and require no special training to read or write. Standards for these specifications exist, they are compatible with any organizational structure, and the necessary tools (word processors) are widely available. Formal specifications tend to be weak at specifying performance requirements and even weaker at specifying nonfunctional "-ility" requirements such as reliability and maintainability. They may impose implementation bias, and require knowledge and experience to write. They may be incompatible with existing ways of doing business, require specialized tools (which may not yet be available), and are (today) technically and methodologically immature.

On the other side of the coin, informal specifications have the major disadvantage that no automated processing is possible beyond the most superficial syntactic level. All of the major benefits for quality and productivity that specifications can offer—by means of browsing, consistency checking, static analysis, verification, simulation, and code generation—are possible only with formal specifications.

The differences between mathematical specifications and operational specifications are more subtle. It is widely believed that mathematical specifications present less implementation bias than operational specifications, because they describe the characteristics of a solution to a problem rather than stating how to compute the solution. It is also widely believed that the certainty provided by a proof of a mathematical specification is superior to the confidence provided by testing an operational specification. On the other hand, operational specifications are believed to be easier to use than mathematical specifications, and to provide an easier and more certain path to an implementation (because an operational specification *is* an implementation, and can even serve as the final implementation if its performance and resource characteristics are not too unsuitable).

All of these beliefs about operational *versus* mathematical specifications contain germs of truth, but the next section will show that they are less reliable than the conventional wisdom would indicate.

5. What Ain't Necessarily So

It is easy to leap to the conclusion that, because informal specifications can be read and written without specialized training, that they are easier to construct and to comprehend than formal specifications. It ain't necessarily so. Informal specifications are often nearly incomprehensible because of their size, ambiguity, incompleteness, and lack of structure. It is also extremely difficult to teach *how* to write a good specification in English, or to evaluate the result. There is also evidence that the content of a formal specification, which must in fact be written by someone with specialized knowledge, can be communicated effectively to less-trained personnel by such means as expert interpretation, highly simplified views, and automatically generated paraphrases in English.

Another piece of conventional wisdom deserving skepticism is the idea that formal specifications should not be adopted now because the technology is immature, and it is wiser to adopt a ''wait and see'' attitude. I am well aware of the cost of change in an established software-development process, but the software organizations I see are insufficiently aware of the cost of *not* changing, and insufficently worried about finding themselves lagging behind the competition in adopting productivity-enhancing formalizations. An organization caught in this position will find it difficult to catch up, because change cannot occur overnight: people who have never been exposed to formal methods will not adapt quickly to a formalized software-development process.

It may be true in many cases that mathematical specifications impose less implementation bias than operational specifications, but for *both* kinds of specification the most important factor in arriving at a high-level, implementation-independent specification is using the right set of primitives. These primitives should allow you to talk about the ''what'' and not the ''how'' for the current problem (in the world of mathematical specifications finding these primitives is called *building a theory of the domain*, while in the world of operational specifications we speak of *finding a language applicable to the problem*). In either approach, the wrong primitives will force you to simulate the right ones, *i.e.*, to implement the right primitives using the wrong ones.

One of the most powerful validation techniques applied to operational specifications is static analysis. Analysis algorithms range from type checking to protocol analysis (*e.g.*, establishing freedom from deadlock). Although more limited in scope than formal verification, static analysis provides the same certainty as a mathematical proof, and does so with relatively little effort on the part of the user.

Operational specifications are easy to implement if we are willing to settle for an implementation whose architecture is close to that of the specification; then simple transformations (manual or algorithmic) will quickly produce a correct implementation. In many cases this is a satisfactory and cost-effective approach. But if it is important to maintain the freedom to choose from a broad range of implementations, then an operational specification is no easier to implement than a mathematical one. In the operational case deriving a provably correct implementation means applying a sequence of equivalence-preserving transformations; in the mathematical case it means applying a sequence of refinement operations. Both transformations and refinements are based on the same underlying mathematics, and both are (equally) difficult.

Acknowledgment

This essay was motivated by a session I led at the Fourth International Workshop on Software Specification and Design. Preparation for the session led to many of these observations, but my understanding was deepened considerably by the discussion itself. Thanks to all of you who attended.

Edgar H. Sibley
Panel Editor

The elimination of ambiguity, inconsistency, and incompleteness in a Software Requirements Specification (SRS) document is inherently difficult, due to the use of natural language. The focus here is a survey of available techniques designed to reduce these negatives in the documentation of a software product's external behavior.

A COMPARISON OF TECHNIQUES FOR THE SPECIFICATION OF EXTERNAL SYSTEM BEHAVIOR

"A Comparison of Techniques for the Specification of External System Behavior" by A.M. Davis from *Communications of the ACM*, Volume 31, Number 9, September 1988, pages 1098-1115. Copyright 1988, Association for Computing Machinery, Inc., reprinted by permission.

ALAN M. DAVIS

During the requirements specification phase of the software development life cycle, it is necessary to describe in detail the expected external behavior of the system to be built. This behavior is recorded in a document commonly called the Software Requirements Specification (SRS). Currently, most SRSs are written in natural language. Unfortunately, natural language is inherently ambiguous, resulting in documents that are ambiguous, inconsistent, and incomplete. With software being used in more and more life-critical applications, it becomes increasingly important to find ways of reducing the ambiguity, inconsistency, and incompleteness in SRSs.

Software Engineering is the application of scientific principles to: (1) the orderly transformation of a problem into a working software solution, and (2) the subsequent maintenance of that software through the end of its useful life. People and projects that follow an engineered approach to software development generally pass through a series of phases. Royce [48] was the first to coin the phrase *waterfall model* to characterize the series of software engineering phases. Figure 1 shows the original model that Royce presented. This model, however, fails to show the symmetry that exists between the earlier and later phases of the development life cycle. For this reason, the symmetrical view of the development process, as shown in Figure 2, is generally more useful. In this model, the path indicated by a series of bold arrows is the primary path, consisting of the following steps:

- *Software Requirements.* The activity that includes analysis of the software problem at hand and concludes with a complete specification of the expected external behavior of the software system to be built.
- *Preliminary Design.* The activity that decomposes the software system into its actual constituent (architectural) components and then iteratively decomposes these components into successively smaller subcomponents.
- *Detailed Design.* The activity of defining and documenting algorithms for each component that will be realized as code.
- *Coding.* The activity of transforming the algorithms defined during the detailed design stage into a computer-understandable language.
- *Unit Testing.* The activity of checking each coded module for the presence of bugs.

Some of the material in this paper has been excepted from a forthcoming book by the author, entitled *Software Requirements: Analysis and Specification*, Prentice-Hall, Englewood Cliffs, New Jersey.

- *Integration Testing.* The activity that interconnects sets of previously tested modules to ensure that the sets behave as well as their independently tested module components did.
- *System Testing.* The activity of checking that the entire software system (i.e., fully integrated) embedded in its actual hardware environment behaves according to the SRS.
- *Delivery, Production, Deployment.* After final system testing, the software and its surrounding hardware become operational.
- *Maintenance and Enhancement.* Maintenance is the continued detection and repair of bugs after deployment, and enhancement is the addition of new capabilities.

The remaining three boxes in Figure 2 are present as it is best to figure out how you are going to test before the testing stage. Starting from the top and working down:

- *Software System Test Planning.* The activity whose primary purpose is to assess how the software system will be tested for conformity to the software requirements. Another purpose of software system test planning is the thorough examination of the SRS to determine whether it is verifiable, i.e., whether or not it is written in a manner that makes it possible to verify that the software meets the requirements.
- *Integration Test Planning.* The activity whose purpose is to generate and document plans and procedures to effect an orderly system integration.
- *Unit Test Planning.* The activity whose purpose is to generate and document plans and procedures to thoroughly test each module independently.

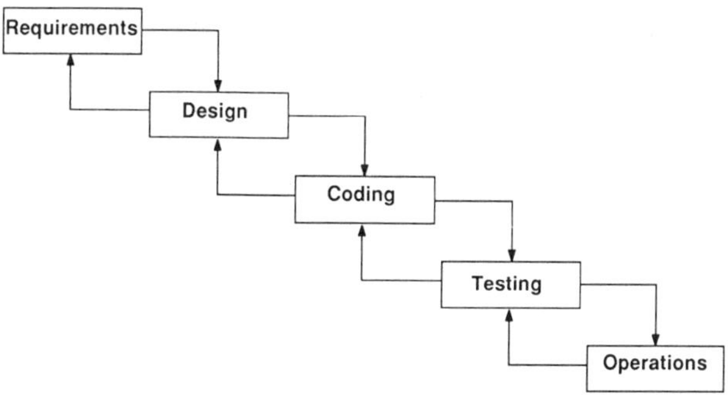

FIGURE 1. Standard Waterfall Life Cycle Model

As determined in Figure 1, the requirements phase is of extreme importance. During this phase, an SRS is written whose purpose is to:

- contain a complete description of *what* the software will do without describing *how* it will do it (i.e., it will contain a complete description of the software product's external behavior but not any information concerning the software product's internal structure).
- serve as *the* basis for all design activities; and
- serve as *the* basis for all system test planning.

Various terms are used to denote the writing of an SRS [25]: requirements [2, 9, 32, 49], specification [16], system design [47], functional specification [8], external design [56], software requirements specification [37, 45], and input/output perspective [39].

Errors in SRSs are common [5, 14], often not detected until after product delivery [10], and cost far more to fix the later they are detected [9, 18, 30]. Therefore, it is of extreme importance to find ways to reduce the most common types of errors in SRSs: incorrect facts, omissions, inconsistencies, and ambiguities [5]. The use of formal models to specify a product's external behavior reduces the number of errors that may remain latent in the SRS because the associated techniques and tools can alert the SRS writers to many potential errors.

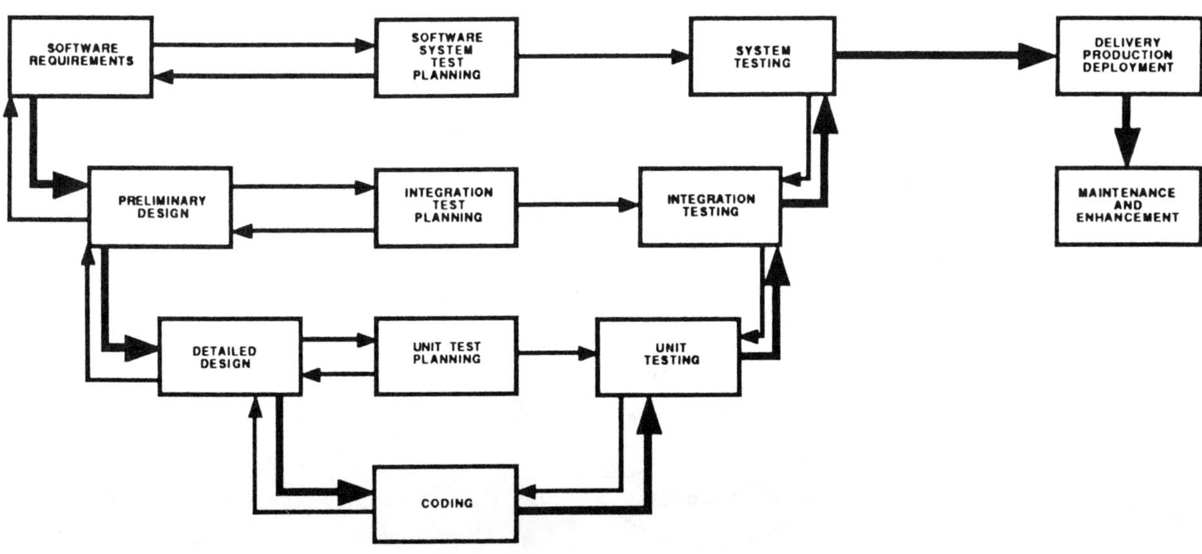

FIGURE 2. A Software Engineering Life Cycle

A SURVEY OF TECHNIQUES

Maintaining One's Perspective

Most requirements specifications today are written in natural language and range in length from a few pages to 5,000 pages or more. The size of the document rarely has any relationship to the complexity of the problem. The larger documents are usually created by organizations that are attempting more "completeness." In this attempt to create a comprehensive document, they often create monsters. The larger the natural language document becomes, the more impossible consistency and maintenance become. The fear of ruining a document becomes a major deterrent to the evolution of the product! While I am not opposed to large SRSs, I *am* opposed to large SRSs written in natural language. This is analogous to building a 100-story skyscraper. I am not opposed to 100-story office buildings, just to those constructed entirely of wood.

The solution to the skyscraper problem is simple: use steel. The solution to the SRS problem is also simple: use a formal technique. Nevertheless, wood does have its proper place, even in a 100-story building. And natural language does have its proper place in an SRS. Where do you apply a formal technique and where do you apply something else? The answer is: *use a formal technique when you cannot afford to have the requirement misunderstood.*

Criteria for Evaluating a Technique

The following subsections discuss a variety of behavioral requirements specification techniques and their underlying models. So they can be fairly judged, here are the traits that we would like to see a behaviorable specification technique exhibit:

(1) When the technique is properly used, the resulting SRS should be helpful and understandable to non-computer-oriented customers and users.
(2) When the technique is properly used, the resulting SRS should be able to serve effectively as the basis for design and testing.
(3) The technique should provide automated checks for ambiguity, incompleteness, and inconsistency.
(4) The technique should encourage the requirements writer to think and write in terms of external product behavior, not internal product components.
(5) The technique should help organize the information in the SRS.
(6) The technique should provide a basis for automated prototype generation.
(7) The technique should provide a basis for automated system test generation.
(8) The technique should be suitable to the particular application.

Finite State Machines

A *finite state machine* (FSM) is a hypothetical machine that can be in only one of a given number of states at any specific time. In response to an input, the machine generates an output and changes state. Both the output and the new state are purely functions of the current state and the input.

There are two notations commonly used to define FSMs: state transition diagrams (STD) and state transition matrices (STM). When STDs are used, a circle denotes a state, a directed arc connecting two states denotes the potential to transition between the two indicated states, and the label on the arc (which has two parts separated by a slash) denotes the input that triggers the transition and the output with which the sys-

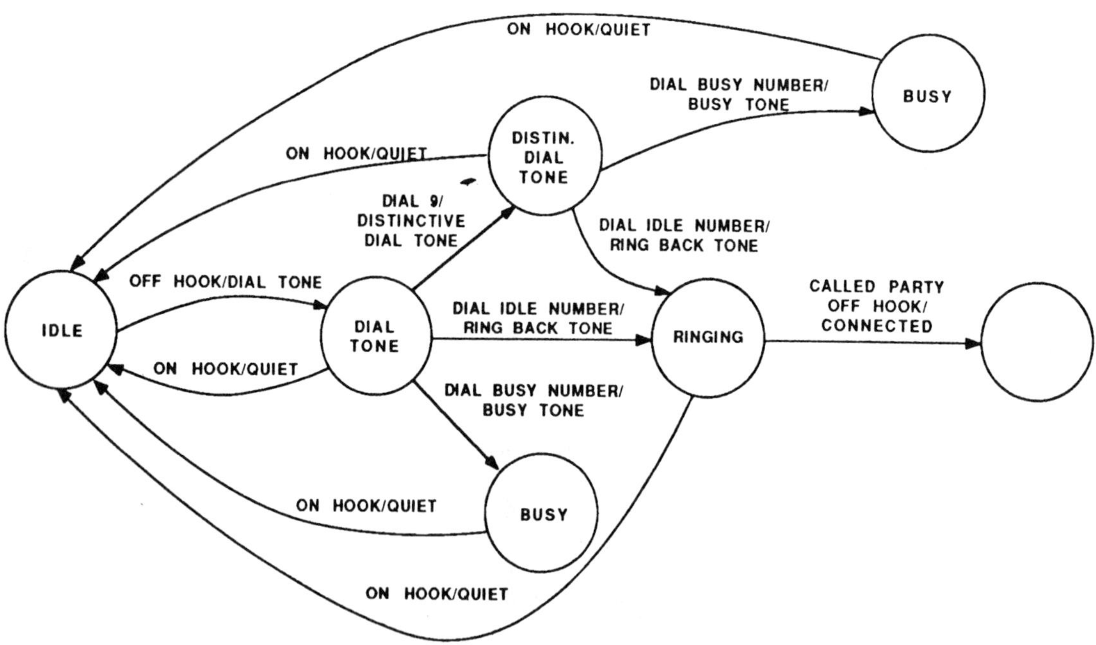

FIGURE 3. State Transition Diagram Example

One column for every combination of condition outcomes

List all conditions that influence decisions

List all the possible decisions

	RULE #1	RULE #2	RULE #3	RULE #4	RULE #5	RULE #6	RULE #7	RULE #8
CONDITION #1	Y	Y	Y	Y	N	N	N	N
CONDITION #2	Y	Y	N	N	Y	Y	N	N
CONDITION #3	Y	N	Y	N	Y	N	Y	N
ACTION #1	X	X	X				X	
ACTION #2		X	X	X				
ACTION #3						X		
ACTION #4	X			X	X			

All combinations of answers

Fill in with the actual required system behavior

FIGURE 5. Decision Table

decision table. Decision tables and decision trees have been known for decades. Their uses and capabilities were recently explored thoroughly by Chvalovsky [17] and Moret [41].

To construct a *decision table* (see Figure 5), first draw a row for each condition (or stimulus) that will be used in the process of making a decision. Next draw a column for every possible combination of outcomes of those conditions (if there are n conditions and each has a binary result, then there will be 2^n columns). Finally, add rows at the bottom of the table for each action (or response) that you may want the system to perform (or generate), and fill in the boxes to reflect which actions you want performed for each combination of conditions. Figure 6 shows a decision table for a software-controlled elevator door problem. Although it has 64 columns, it is easier to create and understand than an STD or STM and is considerably easier to understand than the corresponding English!

A *decision tree* captures the same information as a decision table but is graphical rather than tabular. Basically it is a flow chart without loops and without fan-in (i.e., two arrows pointing to the same node). The decision tree often takes up more room than the corresponding decision table because of the blank space required between the nodes, but because the decision tree captures the order of evaluating the conditions, it is possible to save considerable space on some problems due to the all-encompassing effect of some conditions. For example, the decision tree in Figure 7 shows the same behavior as the decision table in Figure 6.

Decision tables can easily be "automated" with any

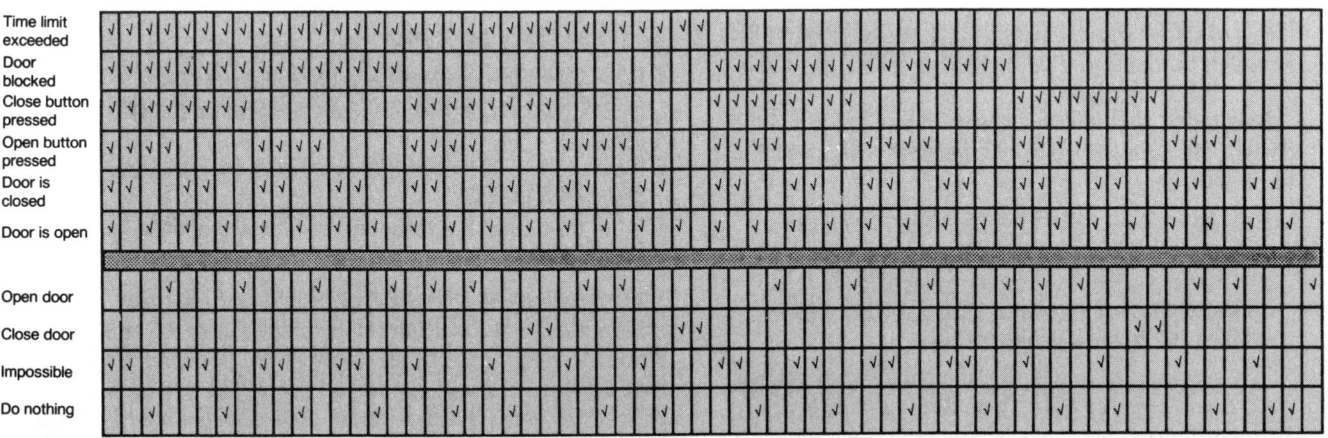

Time limit exceeded	√	√	√	√	√	√	√	√	√	√	√	√	√	√	√	√	√	√	√	√	√	√	√	√	√	√	√	√	√	√	√	√
Door blocked	√	√	√	√	√	√	√	√	√	√	√	√	√	√	√	√																
Close button pressed	√	√	√	√	√	√	√	√									√	√	√	√	√	√	√	√								
Open button pressed	√	√	√	√					√	√	√	√					√	√	√	√					√	√	√	√				
Door is closed	√	√			√	√			√	√			√	√			√	√			√	√			√	√			√	√		
Door is open	√		√		√		√		√		√		√		√		√		√		√		√		√		√		√		√	
Open door				√				√				√				√		√		√						√		√				
Close door																							√	√							√	√
Impossible	√	√			√	√			√	√			√	√			√				√				√				√			
Do nothing			√				√				√				√				√			√					√			√		

Time limit exceeded																																
Door blocked	√	√	√	√	√	√	√	√	√	√	√	√	√	√	√	√																
Close button pressed	√	√	√	√	√	√	√	√									√	√	√	√	√	√	√	√								
Open button pressed	√	√	√	√					√	√	√	√					√	√	√	√					√	√	√	√				
Door is closed	√	√			√	√			√	√			√	√			√	√			√	√			√	√			√	√		
Door is open	√		√		√		√		√		√		√		√		√		√		√		√		√		√		√		√	
Open door				√				√				√				√		√		√						√		√				√
Close door																							√	√								
Impossible	√	√			√	√			√	√			√	√			√				√				√				√			
Do nothing			√				√				√				√				√			√					√			√	√	

FIGURE 6. A Decision Table for an Elevator Door Control

STATE \ STIMULUS	LIFT PHONE	DIAL 9	DIAL 1-8	DIAL 0	HANG UP PHONE	SEVENTH DIGIT COLLECTED	OUTPUTS
IDLE	DIAL TONE STATE	—	—	—	—	—	QUIET
DIAL TONE STATE	—	DISTINCTIVE DIAL TONE	COLLECTING 7 DIGITS	OPERATOR	IDLE	—	DIAL TONE TO CALLING PARTY
DISTINCTIVE DIAL TONE STATE	—	COLLECTING 7 DIGITS	COLLECTING 7 DIGITS	OPERATOR	IDLE	—	DISTINCTIVE DIAL TONE TO CALLING PARTY
OPERATOR STATE	—	—	—	—	IDLE	—	CONNECT CALLING PARTY TO OPERATOR
COLLECTING 7 DIGITS STATE	—	COLLECTING 7 DIGITS	COLLECTING 7 DIGITS	COLLECTING 7 DIGITS	IDLE	IF CALLED PARTY BUSY, BUSY STATE; OTHERWISE, RINGING STATE	NO TONE TO CALLING PARTY
RINGING STATE	—	—	—	—	—	—	RINGING SIGNAL TO CALLED PARTY; RINGBACK TONE TO CALLING PARTY
BUSY STATE	—	—	—	—	—	—	BUSY TONE TO CALLING PARTY

FIGURE 4. Finite State Machine Telephony Example

tem responds. For example, Figure 3 shows a small fragment of the specification of the external behavior of a telephone switching system. Starting with the IDLE state on the left, there is exactly one arc emanating out of it. It is labeled "OFF HOOK/DIAL TONE" and terminates at the DIAL TONE state. That means that when the system is in IDLE and receives the stimulus OFF HOOK, it will generate a DIAL TONE and enter the DIAL TONE state. There are four arcs emanating from the DIAL TONE state, and the path taken will be a function of whether the system receives an ON HOOK (system will generate QUIET and return to the IDLE state), a "9" (system will generate a DISTINCTIVE DIAL TONE and enter the DISTINCTIVE DIAL TONE state), a DIAL IDLE NUMBER (system will generate a RING BACK TONE and enter the RINGING state), or a DIAL BUSY NUMBER (system will generate a BUSY TONE and enter the BUSY state). It *is* possible to describe the behavior shown in Figure 3 in natural language. We just have. As soon as you stop talking however, in terms of states, inputs, and outputs, the behavioral description becomes extremely hard to create or understand without ambiguity.

Remember that Figure 3 is part of an SRS; it is not a design. The implication to the designer reading Figure 3 in the SRS is:

> Dear Designer: I don't care how you design the system, but when it is all done and I observe it as a black box, I want it to behave externally as if it were designed as the finite state machine shown. Signed, the Requirements Writer.

The second way to describe the behavior of a finite state machine is the STM. In an STM, a table is drawn with all the possible states labeling the rows and all the possible stimuli labeling the columns. In the Mealy model, the next state and the required system response appear in each intersection. In the Moore model, the intersections of columns and rows contain only the name of the next state, and a separate column is drawn to indicate the system response associated with each state. The choice between Mealy and Moore should be guided by which one is most expressive and understandable for the particular application. Figure 4 shows a small subset of a telephone switching system's external behavior using a Moore STM.

Finite state machines have been used effectively for requirements specifications for telephony applications [38, 58]. They also serve as the underlying model of many of the techniques that follow.

Decision Tables and Decision Trees

Sometimes there is a need to describe the required external behavior of some aspect of a system when the FSM approach makes no sense. For example, if we want to specify the external behavior of a software-controlled elevator door on an elevator control system, we would easily agree that:

- If the elevator is stopped at a floor and the OPEN DOOR button is pressed, the elevator doors should open.
- If the CLOSE DOOR button is pressed, the elevator doors should close.
- If the time limit is exceeded, the elevator doors should close.

We would agree that the SRS should include these three statements, yet what if a combination of the conditions is true? For example, what do we do when the time limit is exceeded and the OPEN DOOR button is pressed? In general, the required system responses to all combinations of these stimuli are difficult to describe using a finite state machine, and even more difficult to describe in English. One simple solution is the

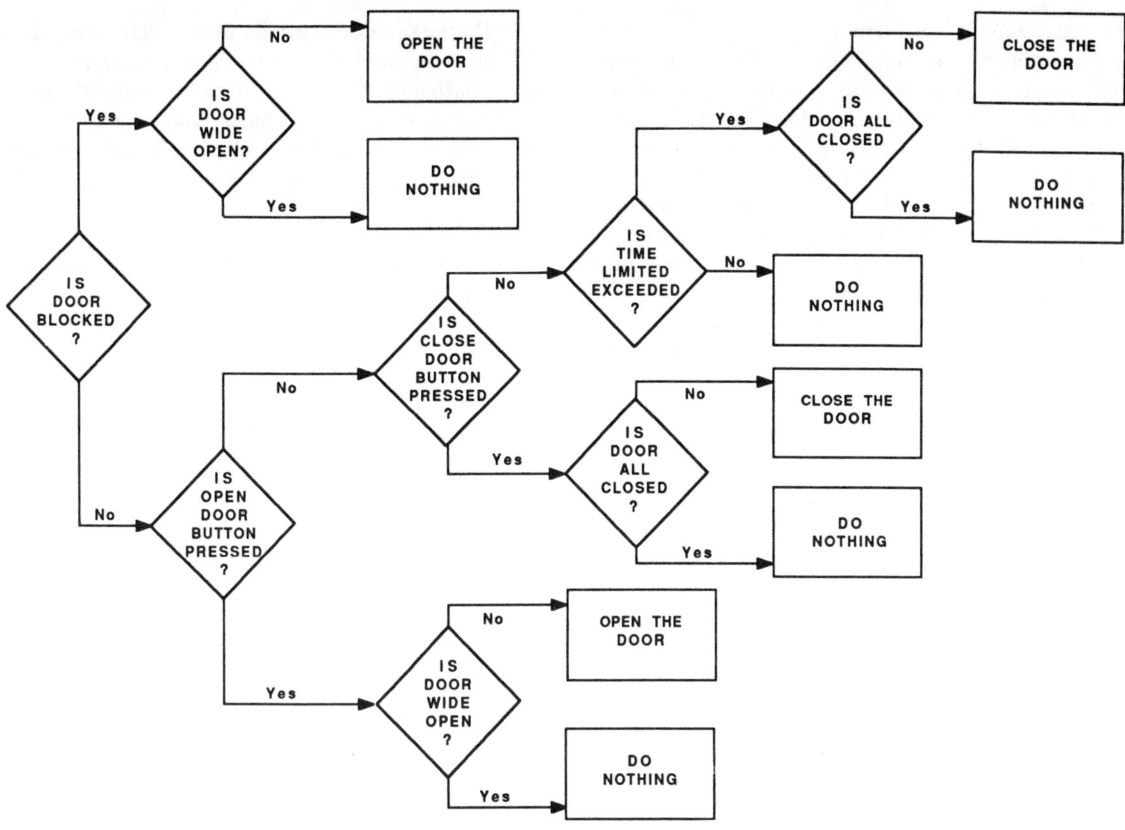

FIGURE 7. A Decision Tree for an Elevator Door Control

standard spreadsheet package. The external behavior of at least one large product was specified using decision tables [11].

Program Design Language

Program Design Language (PDL) is now the de facto standard for specifying detailed designs for software modules. PDL, also called structured English and pseudocode, is simply free-form English with special meanings for certain key words. The most commonly used PDL today is processed by a tool called PDL [12].

Many people who see PDL in SRSs claim that the requirements writers have overstepped their bounds and fallen into design. One reason for this may be that these people are voicing an objection because they are so familiar with seeing PDL during design that they may not even read the SRS PDL to find out what it says. It is not the format that makes something appropriate for the requirements or the design phase; it is the content.

For example, let us return to the elevator door control problem. We indicated that it is important during the requirements phase to specify completely the doors' desired *external* behavior resulting from all possible combinations of *external* stimuli that may be present. Figure 8 shows a PDL specification that exhibits the same behavior as Figures 6 and 7. One of the biggest problems with using PDL during the requirements phase is the incredible ease with which one can fall into design. The best advice to help one stay out of design is to initially select all the nouns, verbs, and adjectives to be used in the SRS to represent things that can be seen, smelled, felt, heard, or tasted by somebody who is an external observer of the final system. This approach of preselection was demonstrated for telephony by Casey [13] and Davis [27] and for a flight control application by Heninger [36].

```
IF door blocked
THEN IF door not wide-open
     THEN open door
     ENDIF
ELSE IF open_door_button pressed
     THEN IF door not wide-open
          THEN open door
          ENDIF
     ELSE IF close_door_button pressed
          THEN IF door not completely-closed
               THEN close door
               ENDIF
          ELSE IF time-limit exceeded
               THEN IF door not completely-closed
                    THEN close door
                    ENDIF
               ENDIF
          ENDIF
     ENDIF
ENDIF
```

FIGURE 8. A PDL for an Elevator Door Control

Structured Analysis/Real-Time

Two extensions of Structured Analysis (SA) [29] were recently proposed by Hatley [35] and Ward [54]. These extensions have been termed *Structured Analysis/Real-Time* (SA/RT). Hatley's extensions add control diagrams and control specs to their data counterparts. For example, in addition to the standard Data Flow Diagram (DFD), he adds the Control Flow Diagram (CFD). In addition to the process spec (DeMarco, et al., also called this the "mini-spec" [29]), he adds the control spec. Since Hatley appreciates the unique difference between requirements and design, he defines the requirements dictionary as the repository for all the processes, data, and controls present in the set of diagrams. The CFD looks just like a DFD but all arrows are drawn dotted, and the arrows denote control rather than data. Control implies either a command or a report of an occurrence of something happening. DFDs and CFDs are usually at the same level of abstraction. Thus, CFDs are associated with a corresponding DFD and are *slaves* (in the electrical engineering sense) of their DFD. Control specs are Mealy or Moore model state transition diagrams or matrices for finite state machines corresponding to a CFD. Hatley has applied his extensions to a commercial flight management computer system.

Ward's extensions are very similar to Hatley's. Rather than two types of diagrams, the DFD and the CFD, Ward allows the introduction of control information in the standard DFD. Thus, in addition to the usual processes (i.e., data transformations), data flows, and data stores (i.e., data bases) in a DFD, he allows for control transformations, event flows, and buffers. Furthermore, Ward differentiates between two types of data flows:

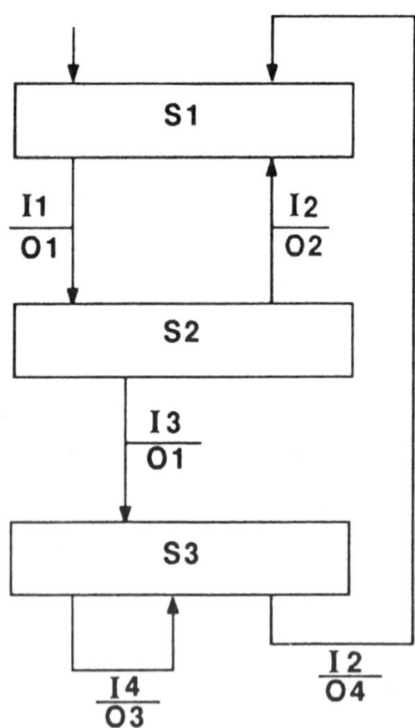

FIGURE 9. Ward-style State Transition Diagram

(1) *Discrete Data.* A single item of data (e.g., current floor in an elevator control example); and
(2) *Continuous Data.* A source of constantly available and perhaps continuously changing data (e.g., current position of doors where 0 is open and 1 is closed and all values in between are possible);

and three types of event flows:

(1) *Signal.* Reporting of an event (e.g., doors have reached their full open position);
(2) *Activation.* A direct overt action to initiate control process (e.g., the elevator control system activating the elevator door control process upon arrival at a floor); and
(3) *Deactivation.* A direct overt action to stop another process (e.g., the elevator control system deactivating the usual elevator dispatching process upon detecting a fire in the building).

In addition, Ward has given the SRS writer the ability to specify a Mealy model finite state machine description for each control transformer in the DFD. Notationally, rectangles are used for the states in the STD to prevent accidentally mistaking it for a DFD, as shown in Figure 9 [54]. Ward's final extension provides for the hierarchical definition of transformation schemas, that is, hierarchical finite state machines. His brief description falls far short of the elegance and rigor of statecharts, which we will discuss next.

Statecharts

Statecharts, extensions to Finite State Machines (FSM), were recently proposed by Harel [33]. Statecharts make it even easier to model complex real-time system behavior without ambiguity. The extensions provide a notation and set of conventions that facilitate the hierarchical decomposition of FSMs and a mechanism for communication between concurrent FSMs. The first extension to FSMs suggested by Harel allows a transition that is a function not only of an external stimulus but also of the truth of a particular condition. As shown in Figure 10, the condition becomes a convenient notation in telephony, for example, to specify that the new state (BUSY TONE or RING BACK TONE) is a function of whether or not the party being called (i.e., the CALLEE) is busy.

The next simple extension is the *superstate*. The superstate can be used to aggregate sets of states with common transitions. For example, let us assume that we have a situation in which two states, S_1 and S_2, both transition to state S_3 upon the same stimulus, *i*. Using regular STDs, Figure 11(a) would result. With the superstate concept, however, we can use the shorthand notation shown in Figure 11(b). Telephony, once again, provides an excellent example. In particular, the caller going on-hook causes a transition from most call states back to the idle state. Figure 12 demonstrates this application of the superstate. It is apparent that superstates can be conceptualized and defined before they are decomposed into subordinate states; thus superstates pro-

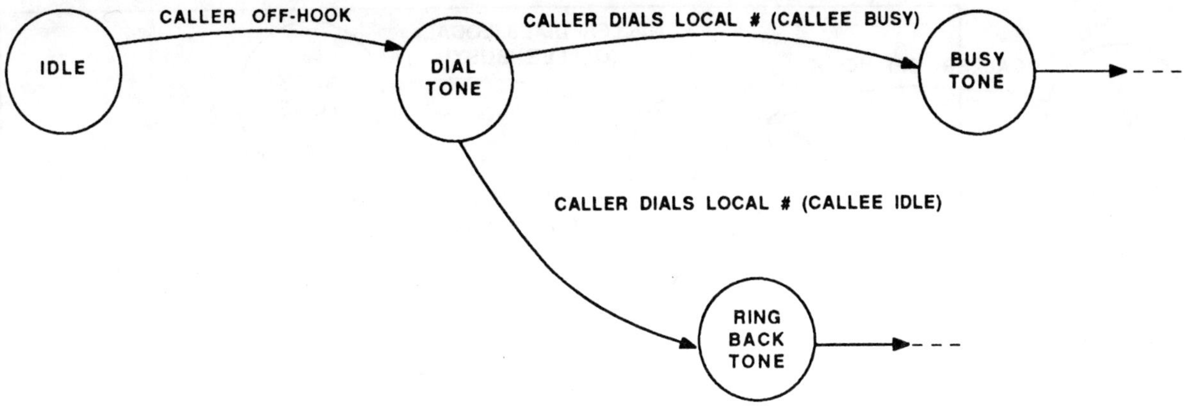

FIGURE 10. Using the Condition Transition Extension for a Local Telephone Call

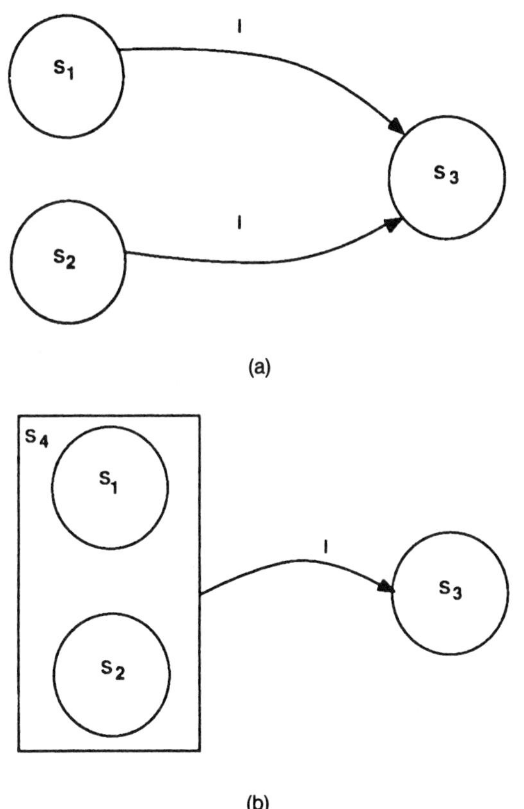

FIGURE 11. The Superstate Extension to FSMs

vide us with a formal basis for iterative refinement and successive decomposition of FSMs.

Harel also introduces the concept of the default entry state. This is the subordinate state of a superstate into which the FSM enters if no other subordinate state is specified as the next state. One specifies such a default entry state with a small arrow as shown in Figure 13. Thus, if state S_{21} were defined as the default entry state of state S_2, Figure 13 would imply that we move transitionally from state S_1 to state S_{21} in the event of stimulus, *i*.

Earlier, we described the process of decomposing a state (e.g., S_2) into subordinate states (e.g., S_{21} and S_{22}). The implied semantics of this refinement are that of an *or* function; namely, that when we are in state S_2 at the higher level of abstraction, we are really in either state S_{21} *or* state S_{22} at the lower level of abstraction. Harel also introduces a different type of state refinement: the *and* function. The *and* decomposition in statecharts is represented by splitting a box using dashed lines. For example, Figure 14(a) shows a simple STD. Figure 14(b) shows the refinement of state S_2 into its two subordinate states, S_{21} and S_{22}. The semantics behind this notation are well defined. In particular, when we are in state S_2, we are in states S_{21} *and* S_{22}. This becomes more meaningful when states S_{21} and S_{22} are further refined as shown in Figure 14(c). On receipt of stimulus i_1, in state S_1, we enter both states S_{211} and S_{222} simultaneously. If stimulus i_4 now arrives, we transition from states S_{211} *and* S_{222} simultaneously into states S_{212} *and* S_{223}. On the other hand, if stimulus i_6 arrives while we are in states S_{211} and S_{222}, only the S_{22} machine changes state from state S_{222} to S_{221}, leaving us in both S_{211} and S_{221}. Harel uses the term *orthogonal* to describe this type of decomposition and to emphasize the independence of state machines S_{21} and S_{22}. The simplicity, applicability, and elegance of Harel's orthogonal decomposition becomes most apparent when one compares equivalent behavioral descriptions using conventional state transition diagrams. Figure 15 shows the equivalent to Figure 14(c) using conventional STDs. Not only has the number of states increased (which makes STDs tenuous at best for describing complex system behavior), but also the monolithic structure of Figure 15 makes it extremely hard to understand in comparison to the statechart of Figure 14(c).

Earlier, we discussed the ability to specify the triggering of a transition not only on the arrival of a stimulus, but also on the truth of a condition. In concert with the orthogonality refinement, Harel has also defined the ability to specify a transition based on whether an FSM is in a particular state. For example, Figure 16 shows a modification of Figure 14(c) in order to specify that the

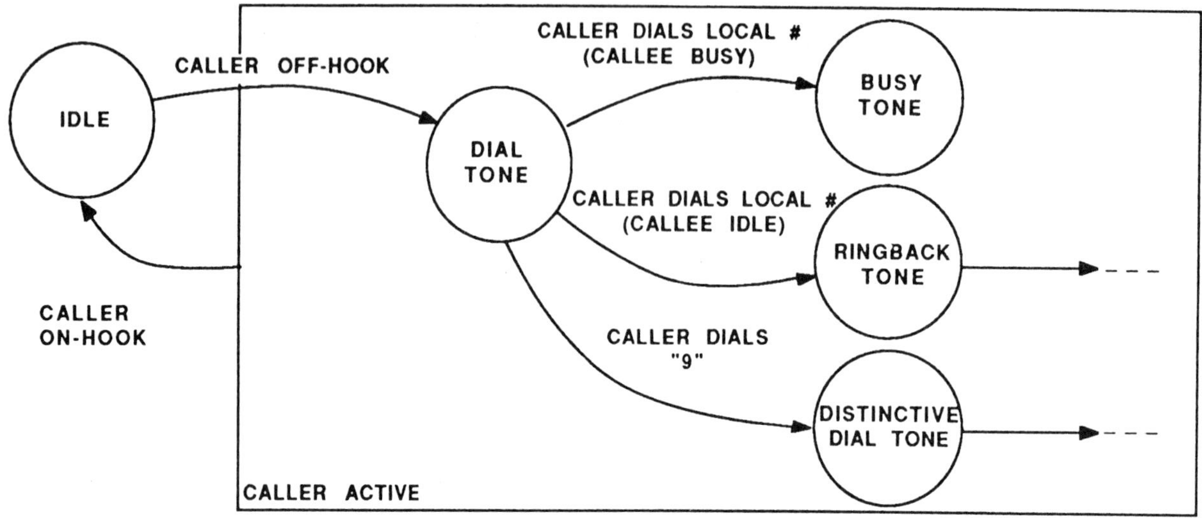

FIGURE 12. Using the Superstate Extension in Telephony

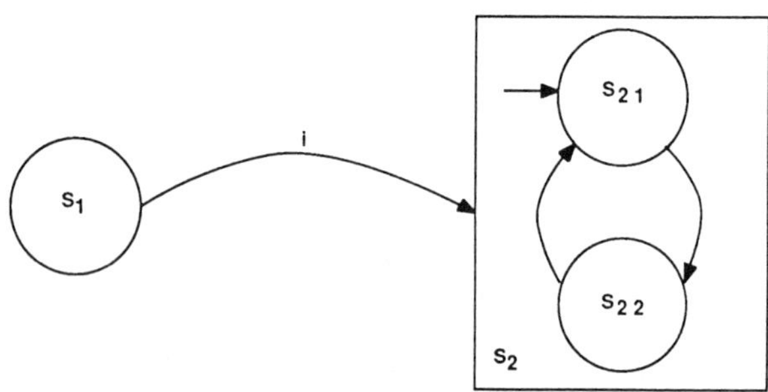

FIGURE 13. Default Entry State Example

transition from state S_{213} to state S_{211} will only occur if machine (superstate) S_{22} is in state S_{222}.

In summary, Harel's statecharts provide natural extensions to FSMs to make them more suitable for the specification of external behavior of real-time systems. These extensions provide for the hierarchical decomposition of states and the specification of transitions dependent on global conditions and on being in particular states.

Requirements Engineering Validation System

The *Requirements Engineering Validation System* (REVS) [28] is a set of tools that analyzes requirements written in the Requirements Statement Language (RSL) [6] developed using the Software Requirements Engineering Methodology (SREM) [2]. The tools, language, and methodology were developed by TRW, Inc., for the U.S. Army Ballistic Missile Defense (now called the Strategic Defense Command) Advanced Technology Center in Huntsville, Alabama. RSL and its corresponding graphical notation, R-nets [4], represent an extension to conventional FSMs. In particular, for some large, complex, real-time systems, it may not make sense to describe the external behavior of the entire system as one huge finite state machine.

As described earlier, Harel's extensions, which provide the hierarchical decomposition of FSMs, may not be easy or straightforward to apply. In particular, some applications are *stimulus rich*. Stimulus rich implies that customers view the system they want to buy or build in terms of its rich set of stimuli. For such systems, it is easier for customers to think of their requirements for the solution system's external behavior as organized into a set of units, each describing all required system responses to a single stimulus, R-nets. One can think of

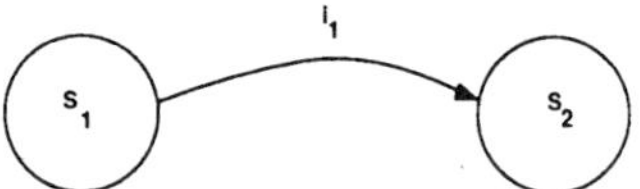

(a) The Highest Level Statechart

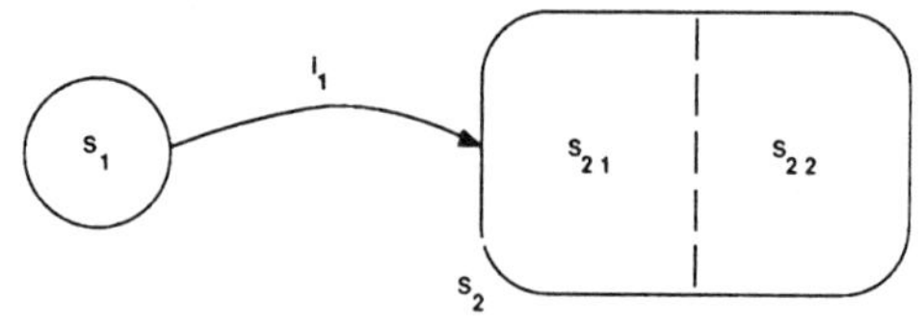

(b) The Refinement of State S_2

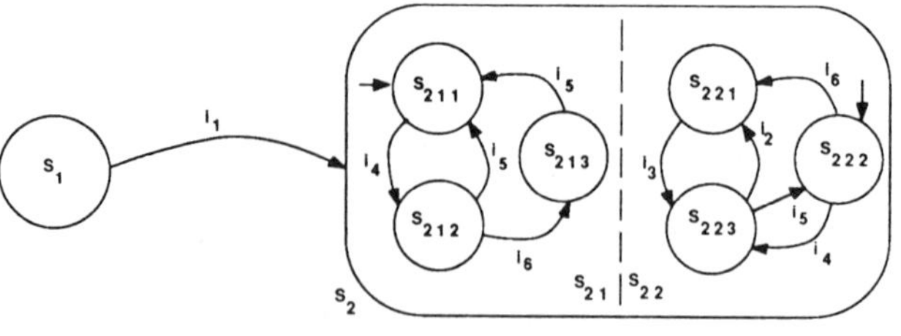

(c) The Refinement Of States S_{21} and S_{22}

FIGURE 14. Refinement Using the "And" Function

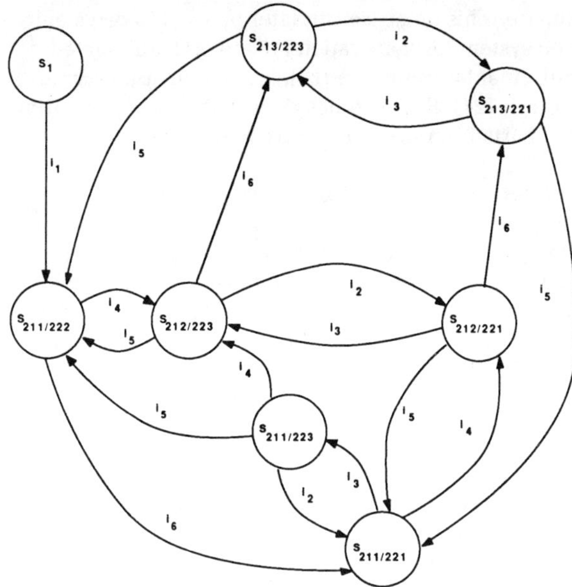

FIGURE 15. An Equivalent Conventional STD

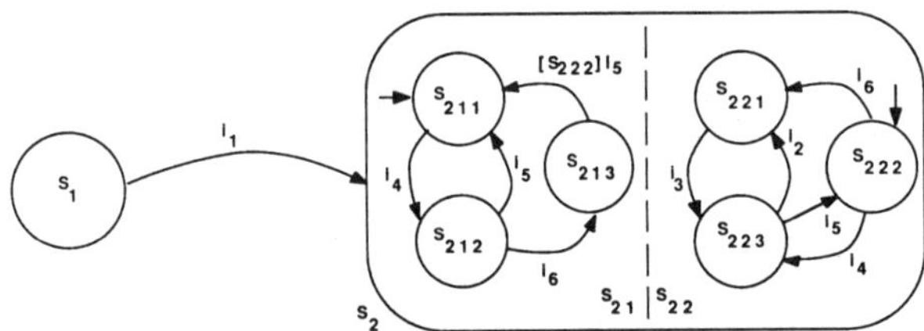

FIGURE 16. Specifying Transitions Dependent on States

an R-net as a column of the state transition matrix, and thus the R-net is simply an organizational piece of a full FSM. R-net notation is shown in Figure 17. Figure 18 shows an example of an R-net for the "Dial 9" column of Figure 4. Figure 19 defines the same behavior in RSL.

REVS has been operational since 1977. Originally hosted on a Texas Instruments Advanced Scientific Computer and on a CDC 7600, and later rewritten in PASCAL and rehosted on VAX, REVS has most recently been rewritten in Ada. TRW in Huntsville and Ascent Logic Corporation in San Jose have extended SREM and REVS to encompass earlier development phases, such as a system level requirements and system design. The new support tool is called the Distributed Computing Design System (DCDS), and the methodology is called the System Level Requirements Methodology (SYSREM) [3].

Requirements Language Processor

The Requirements Language Processor (RLP) [20, 26] is part of an overall Requirements Processing System (RPS) developed by GTE Laboratories in Waltham, Massachusetts. The motivation for developing RLP was similar to that of REVS: namely that monolithic FSMs seemed to be too unwieldy for the requirements specification of complex, real-time systems. Whereas REVS uses the R-net as the organizational unit of the SRS, RLP uses the *stimulus-response sequence*. In essence, a stimulus-response sequence is a trace of a two-way dialog between the system under specification and its environment. The selection of which sequences to use is simple: use sequences that define *typical* dialogs. These typical dialogs should correspond to actual user-oriented, user-known, external system features. Figure 20 shows a complete example of the external behavior of a local call [23].

The decision of whether or not to use RLP on a particular application should be based on the types of questions a typical customer or user would ask about

R-NET START

STIMULUS

VALIDATION POINT V (RESPONSE-TIME REQUIREMENTS)
AND &
OR +

ALPHA (AN "ACTION")
- GENERATE OUTPUT
- FOR EACH (FROM A SET)
- DO THIS
- SELECT DATA (FOR PROCESSING)

R-NET END

FIGURE 17. R-Net Notation

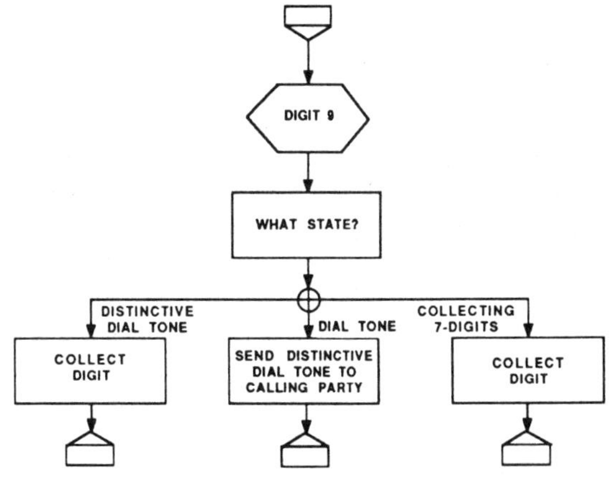

FIGURE 18. An R-Net Example

```
R Net: Process_digit_nine
  Structure:
        Input_interface digit_9_dialed_by_calling_party
        What_state
        Do (state = dial tone)
              Send_distinctive_dial_tone_to_calling_party
           (state = collecting 7 digits)
              Collect_digit
              Terminate
           (distinctive dial tone)
              Collect_digit
              Terminate
        End
  End
```

FIGURE 19. An RSL Example

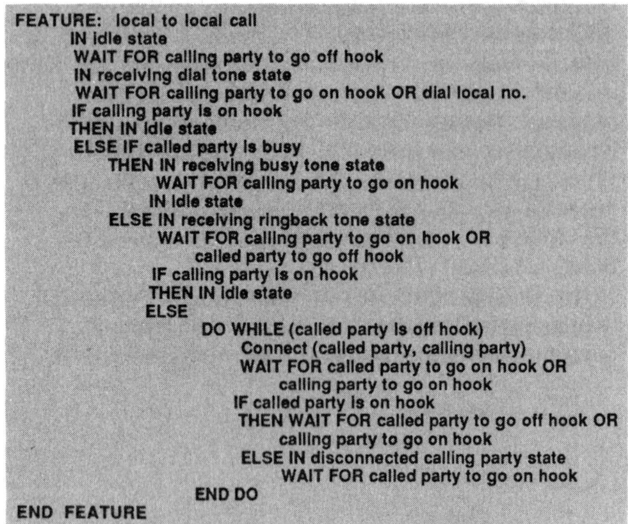
```
FEATURE: local to local call
    IN idle state
    WAIT FOR calling party to go off hook
    IN receiving dial tone state
    WAIT FOR calling party to go on hook OR dial local no.
    IF calling party is on hook
    THEN IN idle state
    ELSE IF called party is busy
        THEN IN receiving busy tone state
            WAIT FOR calling party to go on hook
            IN idle state
        ELSE IN receiving ringback tone state
            WAIT FOR calling party to go on hook OR
                called party to go off hook
            IF calling party is on hook
            THEN IN idle state
            ELSE
                DO WHILE (called party is off hook)
                    Connect (called party, calling party)
                    WAIT FOR called party to go on hook OR
                        calling party to go on hook
                    IF called party is on hook
                    THEN WAIT FOR called party to go off hook OR
                        calling party to go on hook
                    ELSE IN disconnected calling party state
                        WAIT FOR called party to go on hook
                END DO
END FEATURE
```

FIGURE 20. Stimulus-Response Sequence Example

the product. If the questions are about features (e.g., long-distance calls, call-forwarding) rather than particular stimuli (e.g., dialing 0, dialing 9), then RLP may be the answer.

Also, RLP is *multilingual* [23, 52], which means that it supports a wide variety of requirements languages, each tailored to a specific application. For example, it might be desirable to use RLP for four different applications: battlefield command and control, patient monitoring, ballistic missile defense, and nuclear reactor control. The four languages used would be defined in the "Language definition tables" as shown in Figure 21 (adapted from [21]). Once these tables existed, requirements writers would select an appropriate language, write requirements using that language, and run RLP. RLP would check the requirements for correct syntax and semantics; detect and report violations; detect and report any inconsistency, ambiguity, and incompleteness in the requirements; and generate a requirements

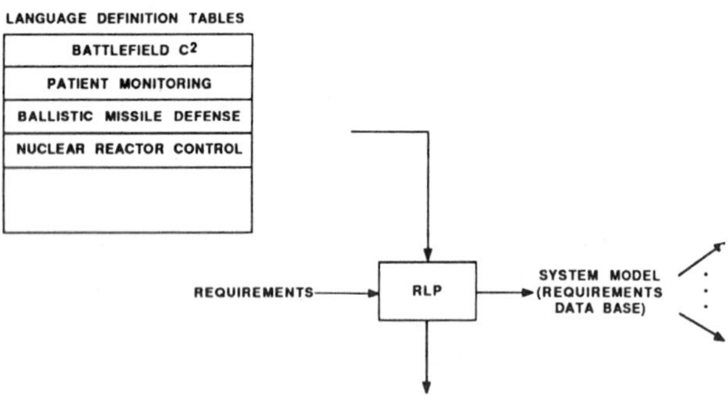

FIGURE 21. The Requirements Language Processor Architecture

database. This database can later be used to drive automatic system test generation [15, 19, 21], automated requirements simulation [22], and automatic program synthesis [24]. RLP also has the capability of generating SDL charts from textual requirements languages.

The Specification and Description Language

The *Specification and Description Language* (SDL) [46] was developed in the late 1970s by CCITT for the external behavior and internal design of telephone switching systems. SDL is a superset of STDs. Figure 22 shows the SDL for the identical segment of an SRS as was shown in Figure 20 using RLP.

PAISLey

The *Process-oriented, Applicative* and *Interpretable Specification Language* (PAISLey) was developed by Pamela Zave while at the University of Maryland and later at AT&T Bell Laboratories. PAISLey [60, 62] is a language for the requirements specification of embedded systems using an operational approach. *Operational* means that the resulting specification can be executed (or interpreted), and the resulting behavior would mimic the behavior required of the system to be built. From that perspective, statecharts, REVS, and RLP all provide operational approaches to requirements specification.

What makes PAISLey unique is that it is a simple language, with rigor and formality adopted from the disciplines of asynchronous processes and functional programming. *Asynchronous processes*, exemplified by the cooperating "and" FSMs of Harel, are independently operating autonomous abstractions of computations that usually communicate with each other via some protocol, such as interrupts, messages, handshakes, etc. *Functional programming* is a technique that describes behavior through the definition of functions that map inputs into outputs rather than through the definition of procedures that, when executed, transform inputs into outputs.

When using PAISLey, the requirements writer decomposes both the system under specification and its environment into sets of asynchronous interacting processes. For example, Figure 23 shows a decomposition of a patient monitoring system into five processes and its environment into four processes (adapted from [60]). Once this is accomplished, each process must be defined. This is accomplished by defining the range of possible states in which the process may enter (i.e., the state space) and by declaring and defining sets of functions that define how the processes change state (successor functions) and how the processes interact (exchange functions). Processes that are part of the environment are treated no differently than processes that are part of the system. Figure 24 shows a small subset of some of these definitions and declarations of processes and functions. Figure 24 is only a partial specification of the behavior of the patient monitoring system shown in Figure 23. Still necessary are descriptions of the update of the acceptable vital sign tolerances for

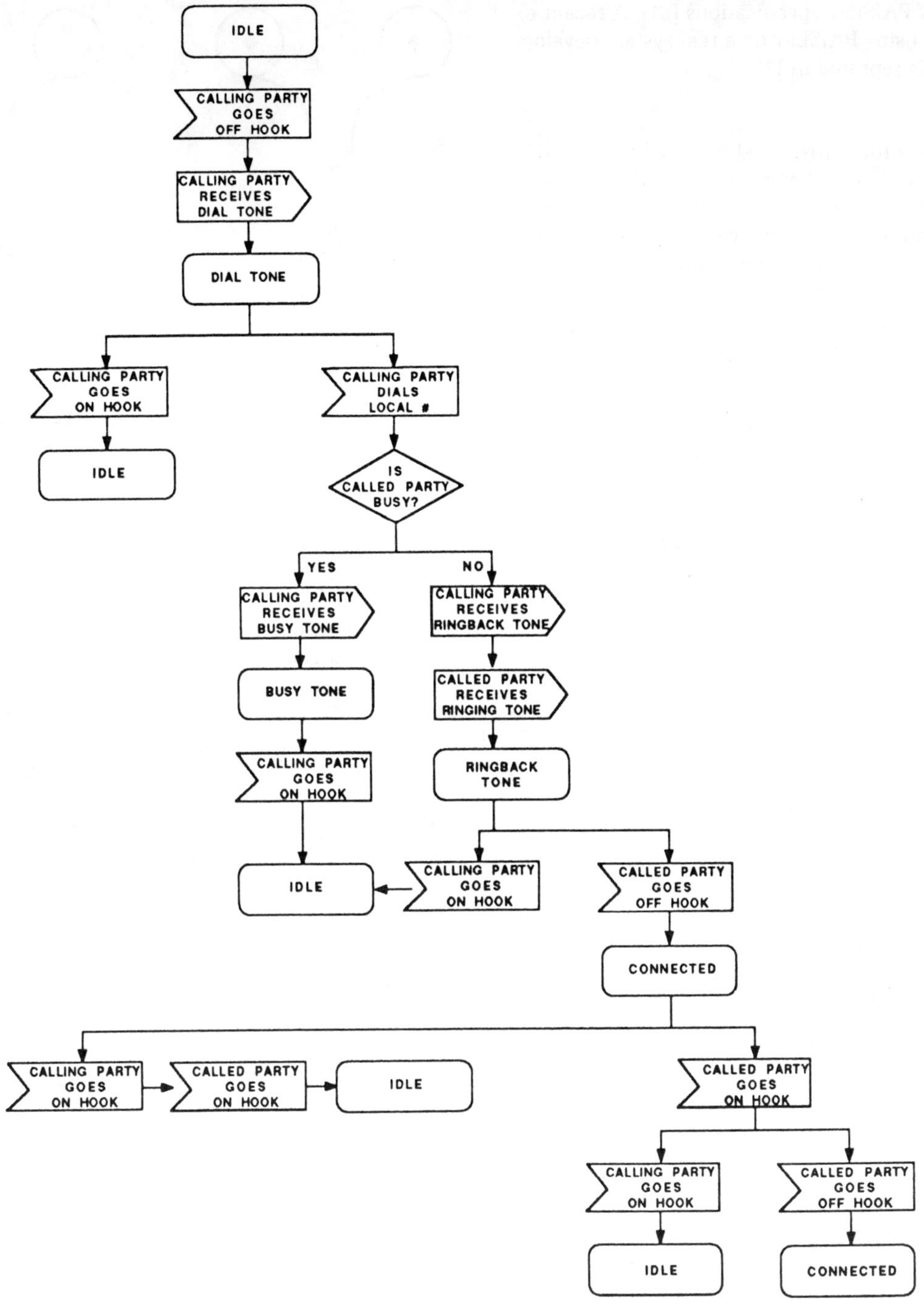

FIGURE 22. An SDL Example

patients, the action of the real-time clock as an initiator of the "patient-check-cycle" and as a source of the current time for the database storage, and many other functions.

Some critics of PAISLey claim that the resulting specification is a design specification, not a requirements specification. Two primary reasons for this claim are that the resulting specification is difficult, if not impossible, for the typical customer or user to understand, and that writing in PAISLey requires a lot of rigorous, detailed thought. Zave defends PAISLey against this claim [60] by saying that customers and users need not view the same representation of the requirements and that the difference between requirements and design is subtle. Further she claims that the software synthesis process is a series of iterations in which each level implies the requirements for the next level.

A set of PAISLey tools has recently been implemented to find and report syntactic or semantic violations, perform static analysis, and provide interactive execution of PAISLey specifications [61]. A recent experiment in using PAISLey on a real system development effort is reported in [7].

Petri-nets

Petri-nets were first introduced in 1962 by Petri [44] and later described by Peterson [43]. Like the finite state machines described earlier, Petri-nets are abstract virtual machines with a very well-defined behavior. They have been used for many years to specify process synchrony during the design phase of time-critical applications. There has only recently been interest in their application during the requirements phase.

Petri-nets are usually represented as a graph composed of two types of nodes: circles (called places) and lines (called transitions). Arrows (directed arcs) interconnect places and transitions. Black dots (called tokens) move from place to place according to a specific rule. The rule is that tokens may pass through a transition only when (a) a clock pulse has arrived (i.e., the Petri-net is synchronized) and (b) all the arrows entering that transition are emanating from places that contain tokens.

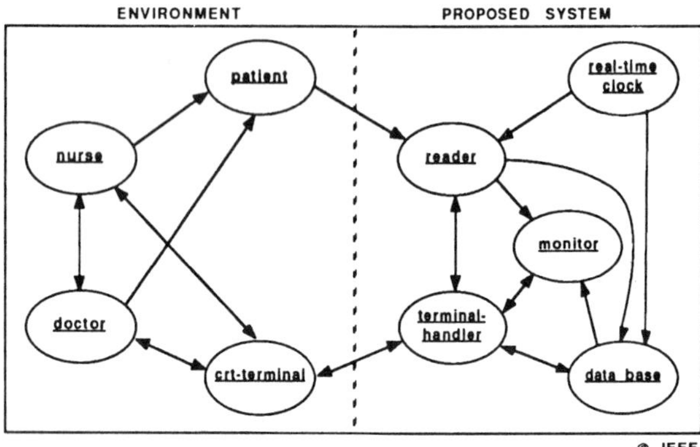

FIGURE 23. Asynchronous Processes for a System and Its Environment

```
(patient-cycle: PATIENT-STATE ——▶ PATIENT-STATE,
patient-check-cycle: ALERT-STATUS ——▶ ALERT-STATUS
retrieve: DATABASE x REQUEST ——▶ DATABASE x VITAL-SIGN-TOLERANCE
sense: PATIENT-STATE ——▶ ACTUAL-VITAL-SIGNS
check: VITAL-SIGN-TOLERANCE x ACTUAL-VITAL-SIGNS ——▶ ALERT-STATUS
update: DATABASE x ACTUAL-VITAL-SIGNS ——▶ DATABASE)
```

(a) Partial Declaration of Processes and their Successor Functions

```
patient-check-cycle[n] =

    proj-2-1[(check[(sense[n], retrieve[patient-database,n])],
        update[(patient-database, sense[n])])]
```

(b) Definition of the Primary Patient Monitoring System Function

FIGURE 24. Sample PAISLey Statements

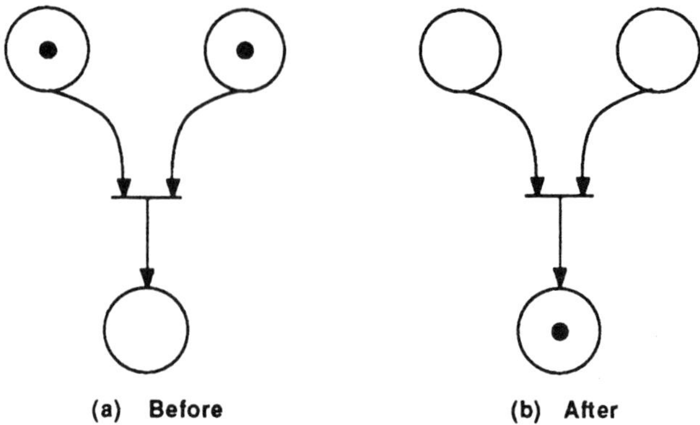

FIGURE 25. Token Merging in Petri Nets

Let us assume that only one token is permitted at any one place.[1] The arrival of a clock pulse at Figure 25(a) will result in Figure 25(b). Also, let us assume that, in the cases of a fan-out, the token will be replicated and a copy will follow every path that it can.

Let us now observe the behavior of a Petri-net through a series of clock pulses over a period of time. The initial state of the Petri-net is shown in Figure 26(a). Figures 26(b) through (e) show the movements of the tokens as each clock pulse is processed.

Let us now look at a specific application in which a Petri-net could be helpful during the requirements phase: the automation of a warehouse. Figure 27(a) shows a Petri-net that captures the timing requirements of this application. At place P_1, a truck arrives at the loading dock. At place P_2, the paperwork is processed and inventory is checked. At place P_3, all the conveyor belts are moving from the loading dock to the warehouse. The belts are transporting people, robots, and forklifts. At place P_4, the conveyor belts are moving from the warehouse to the loading dock with all the requisite merchandise. At place P_5, the goods are loaded onto the truck.

This is a fine use of a Petri-net and at first glance explicitly shows how more than one truck can be handled at a time. On closer examination, however, there is a problem: if one truck is being processed at P_4 and the next truck is being processed at P_3, the conveyor belts would need to be going in both directions at once—an obvious impossibility. The solution is to introduce three new places, as shown in Figure 27(b). In particular, place P_7 prevents P_3 and P_4 from being active simultaneously. I call the token in P_7 the *escort token*, because it escorts tokens representing trucks (i.e., those on the P_1 to P_5 track) along the critical region of P_3 and P_4. As soon as the conveyor belts have completed the return of all the merchandise to the loading dock, not only does the token at P_4 move to the next step, P_5, but P_7 becomes reactivated and ready to escort the next token through the critical region. P_6 and P_8

[1] This is not the case with pure Petri-nets, but is an extension put forth by Patil [59].

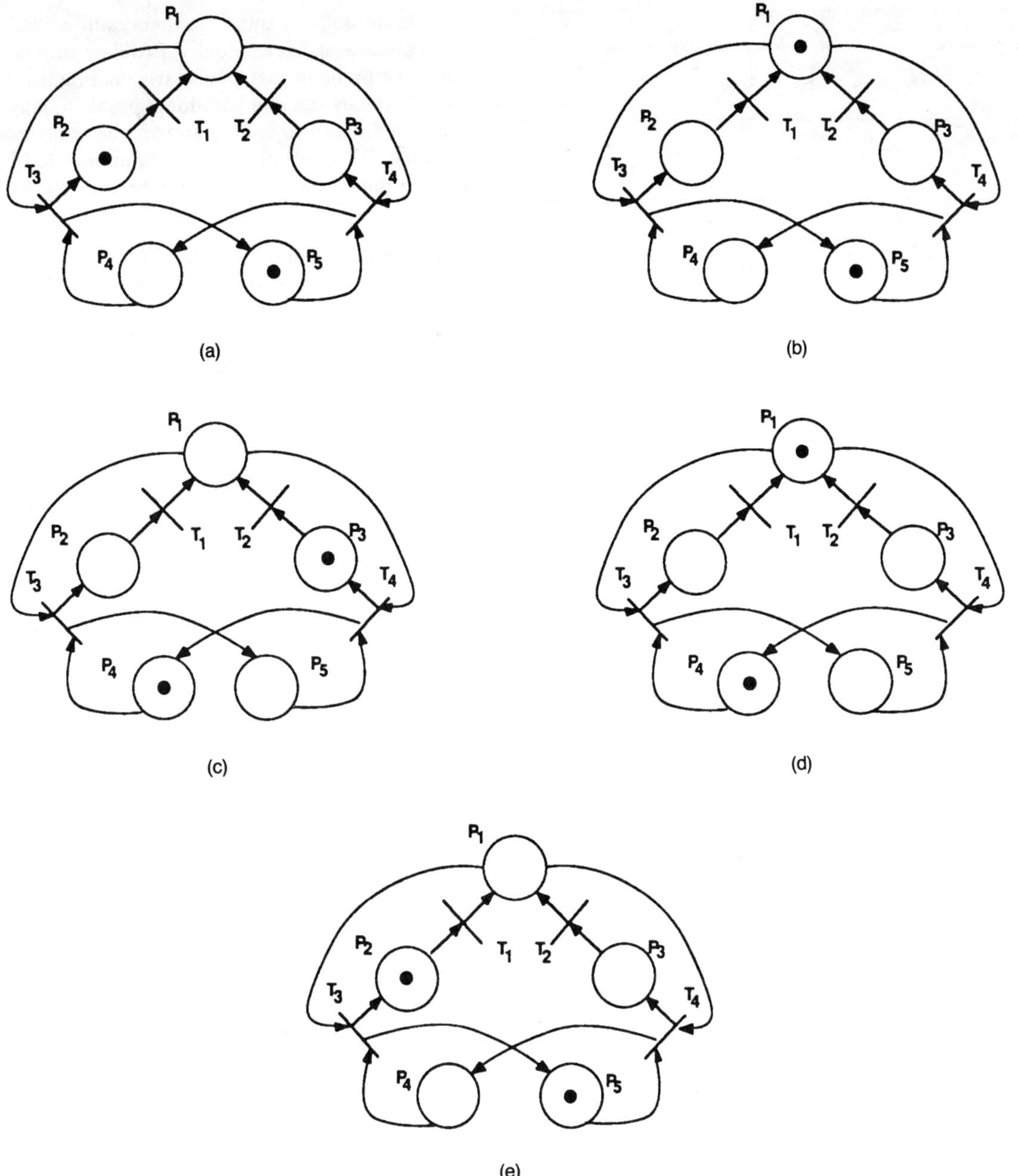

FIGURE 26. A Petri Net Sequence Example

serve similar functions for single steps; they prevent two tokens from accidentally falling into the same station.

Presumably, this entire Petri-net would also need places corresponding to physical buttons (see Figure 27(c)): the P_9 button would be pressed by the order taker when paperwork was complete, the P_{10} button would be pressed by the loaders when the conveyor belt was fully loaded with merchandise, and the P_{11} button would be pressed by the unloaders when the conveyor belt was completely unloaded.

Once again, Petri-nets are relatively simple to understand and are best used to describe pieces of intended system behavior where ambiguity cannot be tolerated and precise process synchrony is important. One of the best descriptions of how Petri-nets can be used for real applications is given in [1]. Extensive examples of applying Petri-nets for the requirements specification of real-time systems are found in [59].

COMPARISON OF TECHNIQUES

In an earlier section, eight criteria were defined for the evaluation of requirements specification techniques. The techniques will now be analyzed, compared, and contrasted using each of the eight criteria. Figure 28 summarizes the results and scores each approach and criteria on a scale from 0 (poor) to 10 (excellent).

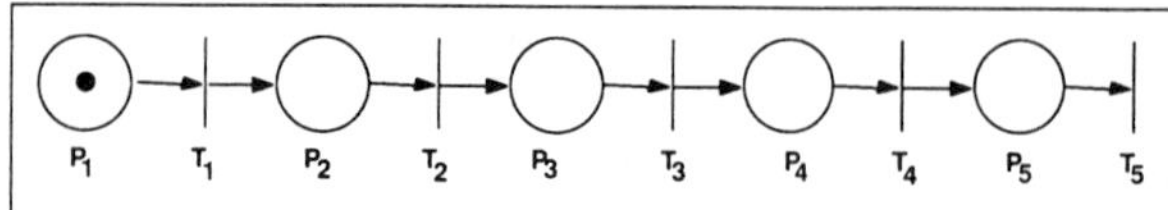

(a) Version 1

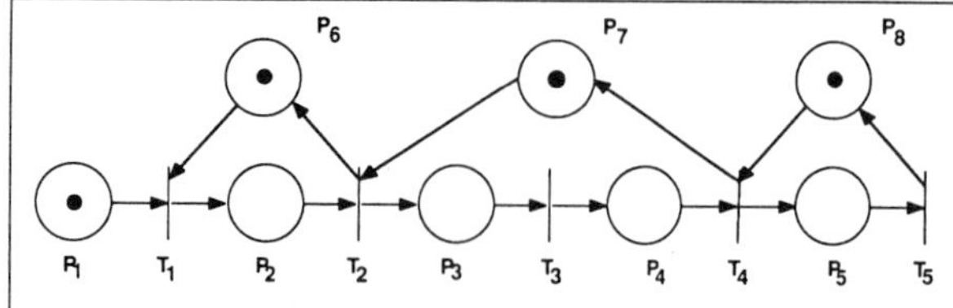

(b) Version 2

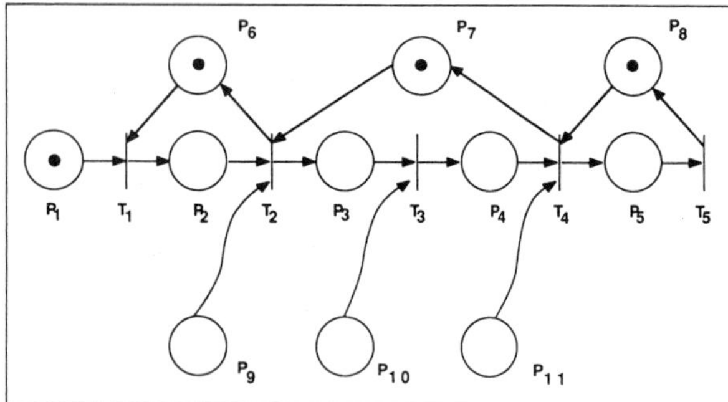

(c) Version 3

FIGURE 27. A Petri Net Example for a Warehouse

Understandable to Computer-naive Personnel

The ability of a computer-naive customer to understand an SRS is a subjective determination. On the other hand, understandability appears to be inversely proportional to the level of complexity and formality present [23]. Obviously, PDL, which is primarily natural language, is almost as easy to read as natural language. Decision trees appear in the non-technical literature regularly with no explanation, so they too are extremely understandable. Finite state machines, SA/RT, REVS, RLP, and SDL all require about the same amount of instruction to computer-naive people to enable them to read and comprehend SRS sections written using those approaches.

I have successfully taught hundreds of non-computer-oriented personnel to comprehend at least the basics of all these approaches in less than an hour per approach. Statecharts, PAISLey, and Petri-nets appear to be much more difficult to comprehend than the others for three unrelated reasons. In particular, statecharts are probably difficult because of their semantic richness. The concepts that statecharts add to basic FSMs provide expressive power and reduce the size of the resulting specification; many of the new concepts, however, are not intuitive to the non-computer scientist (albeit 100 percent intuitive to any computer scientist with even basic skills in automata theory and asynchronous processes). Conceptually, PAISLey suffers from the same problem that statecharts do. Practically, however, PAISLey has one additional problem: language that is a difficult to understand for the noncomputer scientist. Petri-nets are difficult to understand by an applications-oriented non-computer expert.

Basis for Design and Test

For a technique to make an SRS more useful to designers and system testers, its ambiguity level must be lowered and its understandability to the computer-oriented people who design and test must be increased. The former issue has already been discussed. For the latter issue, computer-oriented people prefer formal, precise documents. I contend that the very reasons why some techniques received low points for ambiguity are the same for why they received low points for understandability from testers and designers.

Automated Checking

Miller and Taylor [40] define three distinct levels of errors detectable in an SRS:

(1) *Static Structural.* Signals transmitted through inappropriate ports, or signals received by an entity but not sent by any entity;

(2) *Behavioral.* Two requirements conflict; a specification is ambiguous, incomplete, or redundant (see Davis [27] for further discussion of this class of error); and

(3) *Protocol.* Deadlocks between subsystems (see Sunshine [51] for further discussion of this class of error).

Natural language does not provide for automatic checking of any of these. PDL will be capable of detecting static structural errors. Finite state machines (using an automated tool, such as the Transition Diagram Editor [55–57]), SA/RT, REVS, and RLP all provide automatic checking of behavioral and static structural errors. Statecharts (using an automated tool such as STATEMATE1[2] [34, 50]) and PAISLey both provide full protocol error checking in addition to behavioral and static structural checking. Pure Petri-nets show synchrony very well, but one needs the Yoeli and Barzelai extensions [59] to fully specify protocols between asynchronous entities. Unfortunately, to my knowledge Petri-nets have not been automated, and thus suffer somewhat in their ability to automatically check for protocol violations. Decision trees and decision tables do not provide the ability to specify protocol and, although they are used to specify behavior, I do not know of any tools that automatically check for consistency. Finally, SDL can be used to specify protocol. To my knowledge, however, SDL has not been automated to any degree.

[2] STATEMATE1 is a trademark of I-Logix, Inc.

Criterion	Natural Language	FSM's	DT's	PDL	SA/RT	Statecharts	REVS	RLP	SDL	PAISLey	Petri-nets
1 Under-standable to computer-naive personnel	10 Obviously understandable to computer-naive personnel	10 Requires an hour of two of instruction to facilitate under-standing by computer-naive personnel	10 Appear in litera-ture regularly without explan-ation	10 Almost as easy to read as natural language because most of it is natural language	7 See FSM's	5 Many FSM extensions not intuitive to the noncomputer scientist	7 See FSM's	7 See FSM's	7 See FSM's	2 Many concepts are not intuitive to the noncomputer scientist; hard-to-understand language for same audience	4 Synchrony and Petri-nets appear to be difficult for noncomputer scientists to grasp
2 Basis For Design and Test	0 With no formality there is no basis	7 The formal model enables one to unambiguously define intended product behavior and thus serve as a basis for both design and test	7 See FSM's	2 Being little more than natural language, the lack of formality provides no basis	7 The static data-oriented view of a system is helpful for data-intensive applications. See also FSM's	9 With the addition-al expressive power over FSM's, there is less potential for ambiguity and thus a more formal basis for design and test	9 See statecharts	9 See statecharts	7 See FSM's	9 See statecharts	7 See FSM's
3 Automated Checking	0 No processor is available to perform any checking	7 Static structural and behavioral errors can be detected	0 See natural language	1 Static structural errors can be detected	7 See FSM's	9 Static structural, behavioral, and protocol errors can be detected	7 See FSM's	7 See FSM's	0 See natural language (potential exists for static structural and behavioral error checking)	9 See statecharts	0 See natural language (potential exists for protocol error checking)
4 External View, Not Internal View	0 No help provided	3 Needs human discipline in defining the external entities up front	3 See FSM's	0 No help provided	2 For many applications, the data flow view is the design of the software	5 Structural view provided explicitly and independent of behavioral views	7 Same as RLP, but slightly lower because R-Net is more design oriented than stim-ulus-response sequence	8 Once external entities are defined, specifier stays naturally in the requirements domain	8 See RLP	3 A common criticism of PAISLey is its design orientation. Zave is not concerned if design is performed during requirements	2 Very difficult to use Petri-nets in the applications domain. Many people versed in Petri-nets are designers
5 SRS Organizational Assistance	1 Paragraph and Chapter	2 The machine	2 The table or tree	2 The module	8 Hierarchical definition of transforms and machines	9 See SA/RT; plus more semantic richness of hierarchical alter-natives; multiple viewpoints	8 The R-Net plus hierarchies of alphas	7 The stimulus-response sequence; the feature	7 The stimulus-response sequence; the feature	9 See statecharts	2 The net
6 Prototype Generation	0 None	10 Yes, using IDE tools	0 None	0 None	0 None	10 Yes, using I-logix tools	7 Yes, using TRW tools plus auxiliary coding	2 Feasibility demon-strated, but not implemented	0 None	10 Yes, using Bell Labs tools	0 None
7 Automatic Test Generation	0 None	0 None	0 None	0 None	0 None	0 None	0 None	10 Yes, using GTE tools	0 None	0 None	0 None
8 Appropriate Applications	Any application where misinter-pretation of requirements is acceptable, or at least non-critical	Any real-time application that is small enough to not warrant statecharts, REVS or RLP. For example: small process-control applications	Those particular parts of any appli-cation which are decision-intensive	See natural language	Applications with strong data intensity or a need to identify cooperation between FSM's; for example: Most business applica-tions; many process-control applications	Any complex real-time application; especially those with sufficient complexity and criticality to warrant the multi-ple viewpoints and extra expressive power	Real-time applications that are stimulus-oriented; for example: many defense systems	Real-time applica-tions that are feature-oriented; for example: telephony	SDL was specific-ally developed for telephone switch-ing systems, but is probably applicable to all RLP applications	PAISLey was developed for complex real- time systems	Those particular parts of any application in which synchrony is critical to the specification of external behavior

FIGURE 28. A Comparison of SRS Approaches

External View, Not Internal View
PDL does not provide help for the requirements writer who needs to remain at the requirements level and not proceed into design. Due to its genealogy (i.e., structured analysis, which is one of the worst offenders in this regard), SA/RT, must also score low. Finite state machines, decision tables, and decision trees require a considerable amount of human discipline to first define the external entities and then use the approach to describe the attributes of and existent relationships between those entities. Statecharts are slightly better as they provide the structural viewpoint independent from the behavioral and data-flow viewpoints. The methodology, however, does not encourage one to specifically define the requirements for an entity before defining that entity's internal structure. Finally, REVS, RLP, and SDL provide much better assistance due to their requirement to deal only with previously defined explicit external signals, although all three can be easily misused. REVS probably scores slightly lower than RLP and SDL because the view of "what will the system do in response to this input signal" is somewhat more of an inside-out view than the "what do I have to do to make the system perform this function" view exhibited by RLP and SDL.

SRS Organizational Assistance
Finite state machines, decision tables, decision trees, PDL, and Petri-nets all provide rudimentary SRS organizational assistance. In particular, the FSM and Petri-net approaches offer the underlying machine model as the only organizational entity. Decision tables and trees provide the table and tree, respectively. PDL provides a module that can be used for anything. REVS enables SRS writers to organize the behavioral requirements into R-nets, each corresponding to a system stimulus. SDL and RLP enable SRS writers to organize the behavioral requirements into user-oriented features. SA/RT, statecharts, and PAISLey all provide at least two levels of organization because of their ability to separately model synchrony, data flow, and external behavior.

Automatic Prototype and Test Generation
Automatic generation of prototypes is possible with FSMs (e.g., when using TDE [55–57]), statecharts (e.g., when using STATEMATE1 [34, 50]), and PAISLey, without much intervention other than defining the requirements in their respective languages. REVS provides prototype generation capability, but it requires considerable auxiliary coding effort on the user's part [31]. The feasibility of automatic prototype generation using RLP has been explored but not implemented [22, 53]. None of the other approaches support prototype generation. RLP has the capability to automatically generate system-level tests directly from the requirements [15].

Appropriate Applications
Each technique is suitable to a particular subset of applications. The bottom row of Figure 28 describes the appropriate applications for each technique.

Acknowledgments. Dr. Edward Bersoff deserves special recognition for his faith, financial support, and moral support. Also, my thanks to Kathy Brown, Judy Israel, Marcia Lewis, Jere Milburn, and Lee Price for helping to make this a professional product.

REFERENCES

1. Agerwala, T. Putting Petri-nets to work. *IEEE Comput. 12*, 12 (Dec. 1979), 85–94.
2. Alford, M. A requirements engineering methodology for real-time processing requirements. *IEEE Trans. Softw. Eng. 3*, 1 (Jan. 1977), 60–69.
3. Alford, M. SREM at the age of eight; The distributed design system. *IEEE Comput. 18*, 4 (Apr. 1985), 36–46.
4. Alford, M., and Burns, I. R-nets: A graph model for real-time software requirements. In *Proceedings of the Symposium on Computer Software Engineering*. Polytechnic Press, New York, 1976, pp. 97–108.
5. Basili, V., and Weiss, D. Evaluation of a software requirements document by analysis of change data. In *Proceedings of the 5th International Conference on Software Engineering* (San Diego, CA, March 9–12). pp. 314–323, IEEE Press, Wash., D.C., 1981.
6. Bell, T., and Bixler, D. A flow oriented requirements statement language. In *Proceedings of the Symposium on Computer Software Engineering*. Polytechnic Press, New York, 1976, pp. 109–122.
7. Berliner, E., and Zave, P. An experiment in technology transfer: PAISLey specification of requirements for an undersea lightwave cable system. In *Proceedings of the 9th IEEE International Conference on Software Engineering* (Monterey, CA, March 30–April 2), pp. 42–50, IEEE Press, Wash., D.C., 1987.
8. Berzins, V., and Gray, M. Analysis and design in MSG 84: Formalizing functional specifications. *IEEE Trans. Softw. Eng. 11*, 8 (Aug. 1985), 657–670.
9. Boehm, B. Software engineering. *IEEE Trans. Comput. 25*, 12 (Dec. 1976), 1226–1241.
10. Boehm, B., et al. Some experience with automated aids to the design of large-scale reliable software. *ACM SIGPLAN Not. 10*, 6 (June 1975), 105–113.
11. Buhrke, R., et al. Design choices for a large PCM switch with multiprocessor control. In *Proceedings of the International Switching Symposium* (May 1979).
12. Caine, S., and Gordon, E. PDL—A tool for software design. In *Proceedings of the AFIPS National Computer Conference*, Vol. 44 (Anaheim, CA, 1975). AFIPS Press, Montvale, New Jersey, pp. 271–276.
13. Casey, B., and Taylor, B. Writing requirements in English: A natural alternative. In *Proceedings of the IEEE Software Engineering Standards Workshop* (San Francisco, California, August), IEEE Press, Wash., D.C., 1981. pp. 95–101.
14. Celko, J., et al. A demonstration of three requirements language systems. *SIGPLAN Not. 18*, 1 (Jan. 1983), 9–14.
15. Chandrasekharan, M., et al. Requirements-based testing of real-time systems: Modeling for testability. *IEEE Comput. 18*, 4 (Apr. 1985), 71–80.
16. Charette, R. *Software Engineering Environments*. McGraw Hill, New York, 1986.
17. Chvalovsky, V. Decision tables. *Softw. Pract. Exper.* 13 (1983), 423–429.
18. Daly, E. Management of software development. *IEEE Trans. Softw. Eng. 3*, 3 (May 1977), 230–242.
19. Dasarathy, B. Test plan generation for the requirements validati of real-time systems. In *Proceedings of the IEEE Workshop on Automatic Test Program Generation* (Philadelphia, PA, April), IEEE Press, Wash., D.C., 1986.
20. Davis, A. Requirements language processing for the effective testing of real-time software. *ACM Softw. Eng. Notes 3*, 5 (Nov. 1978), 61–66.
21. Davis, A. Automating the requirements phase: Benefits to later phases of the software life-cycle. In *Proceedings of IEEE COMPSAC '80* (Chicago, Ill., October 27–31), pp. 42–48, IEEE Press, Wash., D.C., 1980.
22. Davis, A. Rapid prototyping using executable requirements specifications. *ACM Softw. Eng. Notes 7*, 5 (Dec. 1982), 39–44.
23. Davis, A. The design of a family of applications-oriented requirements languages. *IEEE Comput. 15*, 5 (May 1982), 21–28.
24. Davis, A. The role of requirements in the software synthesis of real-time systems. In *Proceedings of the International Symposium on Current Issues in Requirements Engineering Environments* (Kyoto, Japan, Sept. 20–21) North-Holland, Amsterdam, The Netherlands, 1982, pp. 151–158.
25. Davis, A. A taxonomy for the early stages of the software development life cycle. *J. Syst. Softw. 8*, 4 (Sept. 1988).

26. Davis, A., et al. RLP: An automated tool for the processing of requirements. In *Proceedings of IEEE COMPSAC '79* (Chicago, Ill., November 5–8)), pp. 289–299, IEEE Press, Wash., D.C., 1979.
27. Davis, A., and Rauscher, T. Formal techniques and automatic processing to ensure correctness in requirements specifications. In *Proceedings of the IEEE Specifications of Reliable Software Conference* (Cambridge, Mass., April), pp. 15–35, IEEE Press, Wash., D.C., 1979.
28. Davis, C., and Vick, C. The software development system. *IEEE Trans. Softw. Eng. 3*, 1 (Jan. 1977), 69–84.
29. DeMarco, T. *Structured Analysis and System Specification*. Prentice Hall, Englewood Cliffs, New Jersey, 1979.
30. Fagan, M. Design and code inspections and process control in the development of programs. IBM Report IBM-SDD-TR-21.572. Dec. 1974, IBM, Bethesda, Maryland.
31. Furia, N. A comparative evaluation of RSL/REVS and PSL/PSA applied to a digital flight control system. In *Proceedings of the AIAA 2nd Computers in Aerospace Conference*, pp. 330–337, American Institute of Aeronautics and Astronautics, New York, NY, 1979.
32. Glaseman, S., and Davis, M. Software requirements for embedded computers: A preliminary report. U.S. Air Force Document R-2567-AF. Mar. 1980.
33. Harel, D. Statecharts: A visual formalism for complex systems. *Sci. Comput. Prog. 8* (1987).
34. Harel, D., et al. STATEMATE1: a working environment for the development of complex reactive systems. In *Proceedings of the Tenth International Conference on Software Engineering* (Singapore, April). IEEE Press, Wash. D.C., 1988.
35. Hatley, D. The use of structured methods in the development of large software-based avionics systems. In *Proceedings of the AIAA/IEEE 6th Digital Avionics Systems Conference* (Baltimore, MD), pp. 6–15, IEEE Press, Wash., D.C., 1984.
36. Heninger, K. Specifying software requirements for complex systems: New techniques and their application. *IEEE Trans. Softw. Eng. 6*, 1 (Jan. 1980), 2–13.
37. IEEE A guide for software requirements specifications. IEEE/ANSI Standard 830-1984. Institute of Electrical and Electronics Engineers, New York, 1984.
38. Kawashima, H., et al. Functional specification of call processing by state transition diagram. *IEEE Trans. Commun. 19*, 5 (Oct. 1971), 581–587.
39. Kerola, P., and Freeman, P. A comparison of life cycle models. In *Proceedings of the 5th International Conference on Software Engineering* (San Diego, CA, March 9–12), pp. 90–99, IEEE Press, Wash., D.C., 1981.
40. Miller, T., and Taylor, B. A system requirements methodology. In *Proceedings of the IEEE Electro '81 Conference* (New York, Apr.), pp. 18.5.1–18.5.5, IEEE Press, Wash., D.C. 1981.
41. Moret, B. Decision trees and diagrams. *ACM Comput. Surv. 14*, 4 (Dec. 1982), 593–623.
42. Patil, S. Coordination of asynchronous events. Ph.D. dissertation. MIT, Cambridge, Massachusetts, 1970.
43. Peterson, J. Petri-nets. *ACM Comput. Surv. 9*, 3 (Sept. 1977), 223–252.
44. Petri, C. Kommunikation mit automation. *Schriften des Reinsch-Westfalischen Inst. fur Instrumentelle Mathematik an der Universitat Bonn*, Bonn, West Germany, 1962.
45. Pressman, R. *Software Engineering: A Practitioner's Guide.* McGraw Hill, New York, 1982.
46. Rockstrom, A., and Saracco, R. SDL—CCITT specification and description language. *IEEE Trans. Commun. 30*, 6 (June 1982), 1310–1318.
47. Roman, G.-C., et al. A total system design framework. *IEEE Comput. 17*, 5 (May 1984), 15–26.
48. Royce, W. Managing the development of large software systems: Concepts and techniques. Reprinted in *Proceedings of the Ninth International Conference on Software Engineering* (Monterey, Calif., March 30–April 2), pp. 328–338, IEEE Press, Wash., D.C., 1987.
49. Searle, L. An air force guide to the system specification. U.S. Air Force Document TM-5772/010/00. Jan. 1981.
50. *STATEMATE1: The STATEMATE1 Working Environment for System Development.* AD CAD, Inc., Cambridge, Massachusetts, 1985.
51. Sunshine, C. Formal methods for communication protocol specification and verification. ARPA Order 3460/3681. Nov. 1979.
52. Taylor, B. A method for expressing functional requirements of real-time systems. In *Proceedings of the IFAC/IFIP Workshop on Real-Time Programming* (Leibnitz, Austria, April), Pergamon Press, New York, 1980.
53. Wang, Y. A distributed specification model and its prototyping. In *Proceedings of IEEE COMPSAC '86* (Chicago, Ill., October 8–10), pp. 130–137, IEEE Press, Wash., D.C., 1986.
54. Ward, P. The transformation schema: An extension of the data flow diagram to represent control and timing. *IEEE Trans. Softw. Eng. 12*, 2 (Feb. 1986), 198–210.
55. Wasserman, A. User software engineering and the design of interactive systems. In *Proceedings of the Fifth IEEE International Conference on Software Engineering* (San Diego, March 9–12). pp. 387–393, IEEE Press, Wash., D.C., 1981.
56. Wasserman, A. Extending state transition diagrams for the specification of human–computer interaction. *IEEE Trans. Softw. Eng. 11*, 8 (Aug. 1985), 699–713.
57. Wasserman, A., et al. Developing interactive information systems with the user software engineering methodology. *IEEE Trans. Softw. Eng. 12*, 2 (Feb. 1986), 326–345.
58. Whitis, V., and Chiang, W. A state machine development method for call processing software. In *Proceedings of the IEEE Electro 81* (Apr.) IEEE Press, Wash., D.C., 1981.
59. Yoeli, M., and Barzilai, Z. Behavioural descriptions of communication switching systems using extended Petri-nets. *Digital Processes 3*, 4 (1977), 307–320.
60. Zave, P. An operational approach to requirements specification for embedded systems. *IEEE Trans. Softw. Eng. 8*, 3 (May 1982), 250–269.
61. Zave, P., and Shell, W. Salient features of an executable specification language and its environment. *IEEE Trans. Softw. Eng. 12*, 2 (Feb. 1986), 312–325.
62. Zave, P., and Yeh, R. Executable requirements for embedded systems. In *Proceedings of the 5th IEEE International Conference on Software Engineering* (San Diego, CA, March 9–12), pp. 285–304, IEEE Press, Wash., D.C., 1981.

CR Categories and Subject Descriptors: D.2.1 [**Software Engineering**]: Requirements/Specifications; D.3.2 [**Programming Languages**]: Language Classifications

General Terms: Requirements Tools, Software Engineering Tools, Software Requirements Specifications

Additional Key Words and Phrases: Decision tables, decision trees, finite state machines, PAISLey, PDL, Petri nets, REVS, RPL, SDL, statecharts, structured analysis

Received 11/87; accepted 3/88

ABOUT THE AUTHOR:

ALAN M. DAVIS is vice president and director of engineering services at BTG, Incorporated, in Vienna, Virginia. He is also chair of the IEEE Computer Society's Working Group on Software Requirements Standards. He has authored numerous publications in the areas of software engineering tools, requirements specification techniques and languages. His current address is: Alan M. Davis, BTG, Inc., 1945 Old Gallows Road, Vienna, VA 22180.

Structured Analysis

Cyril P. Svoboda, Ph.D.
Advanced Systems Technology Corp. (ASTEC)
9111 Edmonston Road, Suite 404
Greenbelt, Maryland 20770
(301) 441-9036

1: Why a Methodology?

1.1: The Undisciplined Human Mind

Developing an information system can be considered a form of problem-solving. Someone has determined to move from a current state of affairs, i.e., the way a system is presently functioning, to some desired state of affairs, i.e., the way a system needs to function for the forseeable future. The gap between the two is closed by planning the project; analyzing the basic requirements for the system and incorporating desired new functionality; creating a design that uses pertinent new technology; and writing the programs that will implement the design. To solve such a complex problem, developers need to move carefully. The potential for costly errors is great.

Research in problem-solving shows that use of an appropriate strategy provides better solutions faster than use of no strategy. But use of a strategy assumes discipline: We have to expend the effort to plan for using a strategy and for staying with a strategy when we encounter difficulties. Yet philosophers have told us that the human mind is not by nature disciplined. Human beings do not come into this world gifted with a set of problem-solving strategies. Therefore, if we are faced with such a large, complex problem as building an information system, we need to adopt some disciplined, strategic method to guide our efforts. Without the help of some form of discipline, the human mind will approach the task of developing an information system in a random, reactive manner.

1.2: The Components of a Methodology

Those who want to develop an information system strategically, in a disciplined manner, employ a methodology, i.e., a body of rules, postulates, and procedures guiding their activity. Some of these methodologies support work in different phases of the system development life cycle, e.g., planning, analysis, design and programming. Others purport to cover the whole development life cycle.

Whatever its scope or application area, a methodology should contain at least four components: (1) a conceptual model of constructs essential to the problem, (2) a set of procedures suggesting the direction and order to proceed, (3) a series of guidelines identifying things to be avoided, and (4) a collection of evaluative criteria for assessing the quality of the product.

The conceptual model in a methodology should help developers distinguish things of importance from those that are irrelevant to the present activity. Without such guidance, developers may spend time and energy studying the wrong aspect of a system.

The set of procedures in a methodology lets both management and technicians know where the task should begin and what activities they need to follow. Without procedural direction, developers run the risk of "getting wrapped around the axle," suffering a series of "false starts," confusing different levels of detail, or decomposing only certain processes while stubbing others.

Evaluative criteria in a methodology give those involved in a system development project a handle on how well they are doing their jobs. Without such standards, developers have no way of knowing whether what they have done is complete, consistent, or traceable.

1.3: A History of System Development Methodologies

Methodologies to support information system development appeared in great number and variety in the 1970s. One of the earliest, "stepwise refinement" [1], covered the programming phase. Shortly thereafter, McGowan and Kelly [2] offered "structured programming," while Warnier [3] suggested the "logical construction of programs." Yourdon and Constantine [4] offered help with "structured design" and Jackson [5] proposed "principles of program design."

Eventually authors realized that something came before programming and design of programs. In quick succession

EH0304-6/90/0000/0218$01.00

they proposed some form of "structured analysis" for the development of business-oriented management information systems (MIS). These variants are discussed in more detail in Section 3. Doug Ross [6] and colleagues at SofTech, Inc. developed a composite: Structured Analysis and Design Technique (SADT). DeMarco [7] showed how "structured analysis" as practiced in Yourdon's firm could be used to produce a "system specification." Gane and Sarson [8] produced a variant of the Yourdon-DeMarco method with distinct graphic notation. Orr [9] adapted the ideas of Warnier and made available strategies for "structured systems development."

In 1971, Teichroew and Sayani [10] introduced the Problem Statement Language/Problem StatementAnalyzer (PSL/PSA™) as a tool for automating the system-building process. With PSL the system developer could capture information about the target system gathered during any phase of the life cycle. This formalized information could then be handed to PSA for examination (by means of display reports) and evaluation (by means of analysis reports). Later, Sayani [11] developed the Automated Documentation System (ADS) for incorporating PSA reports as part of documents that conform to any selected or mandated documentation standard.

Carnap [12] had shown that any system could be expressed in terms of its major components (objects), their distinctive characteristics (properties), and the associations (relationships) that link them systemically. In a similar vein, Chen [13] suggested that system analysts develop a "unified view of data" by identifying a system's data (entities), their distinctive properties (attributes), and the associations (relationships) that link any pairs of entities. Using the entity-relationship-attribute (ERA) model, system developers produce one or more ERA diagrams that show the major data components of a system, their data composition, and how they are linked to any other entities in the system. Flavin [14] built on these ideas to produce an analysis methodology called "information modeling." Following this approach, a study team examines the target system from the functional, data, and control points of view against the context of organization regulations and produces an extended ER diagram that forms the basis for a logical design of the system's database.

In 1977, Bell, Bixler, and Dyer [15] discussed a Software Requirements Engineering Methodology (SREM) which, though similar to PSL/PSA, bypassed system requirements to deal immediately at a much lower level with primitive processing requirements. For several years Alford [16] was intimately involved with the refinement of SREM and its technology. He has shown that, while SREM has a specification language and a software package for checking consistency and traceability (as does PSL/PSA), only with the introduction of SYSREM does the technique adequately address requirements at all levels of a system. Possibly because SREM is based on a finite-state-machine model of a system, it has proved most useful for the specification of real-time, embedded systems [17].

As methodologies and tools for handling requirements analysis were cropping up, authors inside IBM [18] turned to the planning phase, offering support for creating an information architecture of "business systems." This effort also gave birth to a number of variants. Since the introduction of Business Systems Planning, various authors have produced refinements of these different planning methodologies, and software vendors are beginning to offer automated support for them.

In the last few years authors [19, 20] have returned to the analysis phase and have offered extensions to structured analysis that make it applicable to the development of real-time, embedded information systems. Ward and Mellor [21] published the first set of strategies for the "structured development of real-time systems." Hatley and Pirbhai [22] followed that with their own approach for the development of a "real-time system specification." These four and other interested parties have lately banded together to produce a standard real-time system modeling language to be used by developers of real-time systems [23].

2: The Components of Structured Analysis

2.1: A Definition

Analysis is a development phase typically performed after planning and before design. The analyst assumes that the questions pertinent to the planning phase have been asked and seeks to begin analysis with the information contained in the answers to those questions. As a term, "structured analysis" applies to a number of methodological approaches that guide the practitioner in the analysis (i.e., identification of system requirements and phase of the development life cycle). Typically the structured analyst is concerned with answers to the question "What?": What must the system do? What must the system produce? What can the system expect as input? What are sources and destinations of the data with which the system interacts? What data must the system hold in storage? What is the structure and composition of data held in storage? What are the components of high-level system constructs? If the system is "real-time," what are the events to which the system must be responsive? What are the triggers that cause a transition from one operational phase to another? What are the resultant actions that must be carried out upon state transition?

While all systems have the three major construct-types of data, activity, and control, different types of systems will place different emphases on them. For data-oriented or activity-oriented systems, structured analysis proceeds in a top-down fashion. Attention is first focused on the system at its "top level" and then it is studied progressively through more detailed levels until a primitive level is reached. Since any lower level is an elaboration or explosion of its immediate superior, each "child" level must be balanced with its "parent" level. When analysts have completed this top-down, leveled analysis of a system, they will have created a hierarchy of system activities in which no activity has more than a single parent. For control-oriented systems, Hatley and Pirbhai also suggest a top-down, leveled, hierarchical approach. On the other hand, Ward and Mellor suggest that analysis begin at whatever level the system is responsive to the environment, proceeding to decompose further to the primitive level and, eventually, organizing the overall system into a hierarchical structure.

2.2: The Models of Structured Analysis

Analysis asks "What?"; design asks "How?" During analysis, the developer studies the different components of the system in varying levels of detail, *without trying to create any particular arrangement of these components.* Ideally, the analyst begins with a model of the "current physical" system (as it actually operates today) and proceeds to create models of the system free of any implementation constraints. Attaining this ideal requires intense discipline, because the human mind deals much more easily with the concrete, physical aspects of a problem than with its abstract, logical aspects.

The process of moving the system in its "current physical" state to the system in its "new physical" state is not direct. Beginning with the information describing the system as it now exists, the analyst must first build a "current logical" model of the system by abstracting from the "current physical" information what McMenamin and Palmer [24] call the system's "essential requirements." Then, taking into account the new objectives desired for the system and what new requirements these entail, the analyst builds a "new logical" model of the system under development. With this phase completed, the work of analysis is finished, and the "new logical" model can be turned over to the designers and programmers for implementation.

While this is the ideal path for redesigning a system (whether it is computer-based or not), it is not always chosen by organizations developing a system. As Yourdon [25] notes, political dynamics have killed many a development project that took too long to build a model of a system that was soon to be obsolete. Projects are likely to fall into this trap if the current system is poorly understood and documented within the organization. Information about the "current physical" system should not be an end in itself, but a means to develop by abstraction a model of the "current logical" system. Without this latter model, the analyst has to uncover for the first time both the essential requirements of the current system and those of the desired system, instead of working from the "current logical" model to the "new logical" model. The purpose of creating models is twofold: (1) to account for the functionality of the existing system and (2) to provide a means for making the transition from the current to the newly developed system.

2.3: MIS Constructs of the Structured Analysis Conceptual Model

After encountering several problems of the same type, the human mind forms a conceptual model of that type of problem. A conceptual model consists of three components: (1) major constructs (object-types) generic to the problem being modeled, (2) relationships that associate any one construct with others in the model, and (3) properties that either define or describe an object-type. Structured analysis methodologists, with the exception of Doug Ross, have identified six object-types of business-oriented MIS (not real-time) systems. These are the major constructs of importance to the structured analyst:

1. *Process:* Functions or activities in the system that transform or manipulate data in some way. Processes exchange data either with other processes, stores of data, or sources/destinations outside the boundaries of the system.
2. *Data flow:* Data that pass from some source, either internal or external to the system, to destinations, either internal or external to the system. Data flows relate not only to their sources and destinations, but also to data objects of which they are either a part or a composite.
3. *Data store:* A place where data are held for later transformation or for reference. Data stores relate to the data flows that are either stored within or drawn from them. Data stores can also relate to their components.
4. *External entity (alias, terminator) :* Some activity outside the boundary and control of the target system that interacts with the system by means of data. This object-type is of interest only insofar as it enables the analyst to identify specific sources and destinations of data with which the target system interacts. Externals, therefore, interact with processes by means of data, but never with data stores.
5. *Data group:* A cluster of data, identified as a component of one or more data flows. Data groups can be visualized as data flows, but are included in the data structure of higher-level data objects. A data group can consist of lower-level data groups or elemental units of data.
6. *Data element:* A basic unit of data which, with data group, forms the components of higher-level data

flows. Data elements are of interest only insofar as they help us to understand the elemental details of higher-level data objects.

The task of the structured analyst is to identify the many different instances of these six object-types and show how each relates to others within an MIS system. Section 4 shows the constructs that have been added to accommodate the analysis of real-time systems.

2.4: The Support Media of Structured Analysis

Traditional structured analysis (of business-oriented systems), with the exception of SADT, offers the practitioner four major tools to identify the requirements of the system under development. Each tool has a specific purpose and makes a specific contribution to the overall analysis of a system.

2.4.1: Data Flow Diagram

A data flow diagram (DFD) is a visualization of the data interaction that the overall system or some lower-level part of it has with other activities, whether internal or external to the system. On a DFD a reader will find graphic representations of external entities, processes, data flows, and data stores interconnected to show the progressive transformation of data. The disciplined analyst will create DFDs that are not overly cluttered, but are adequate representations of data interaction for the particular level of detail being visualized.

The first DFD to be created represents the target system at its context level. In a diagram such as that in Figure 1, the system is left as an unexplored "black box." The emphasis, instead, is on the types of data flows with which the system interacts: both those that enter the system from their source and those that travel from the system to their destination. The creation of the context level DFD permits the developer to sketch the boundaries of the target system, so that both client and developer can agree on the scope of the system to be developed. Not surprisingly, this first view of the system can take a disproportionately long time to complete because it exposes arguments of ownership, boundaries, rights, etc.

Once client and developer reach consensus on the scope of the target system, the developer can proceed to identify the data-process interaction in progressively finer detail. Each resulting DFD, at what are called the "intermediate levels," is an elaboration or explosion of data-process interaction at the prior level. For instance, the single process in the context level DFD shown in Figure 1, is now exploded into a diagram, such as that shown in Figure 2 that visualizes its inner workings. On this diagram the main functional areas of the system under development are represented as processes that accept or produce the data flows identified on the context level. Note that the external entities shown on the context level DFD are not repeated on lower-level diagrams, lest these become too cluttered. Instead, the reader is expected to read a child diagram in the context of its parent. In addition to data that flow from sources or to destinations external either to the diagram or to the system itself, processes on a diagram may produce data flows that they send to one or more of the other processes on the same diagram, and they may interact with one or more data stores as required.

Before proceeding with an explosion of each of these processes, the analyst must balance the child diagram against the parent. To do so, the analyst must make sure both that the "data in" at the child level (**Figure 2**) is identical with or adds up to the "data in" at the parent level (**Figure 1**) and

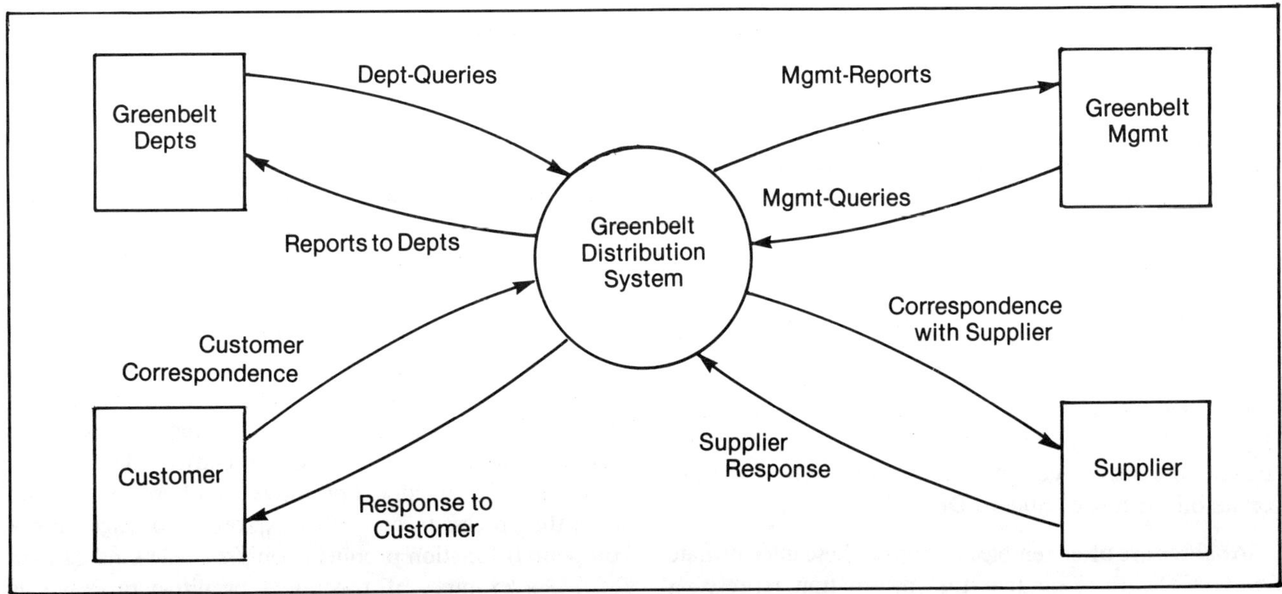

Figure 1: Context level data flow diagram

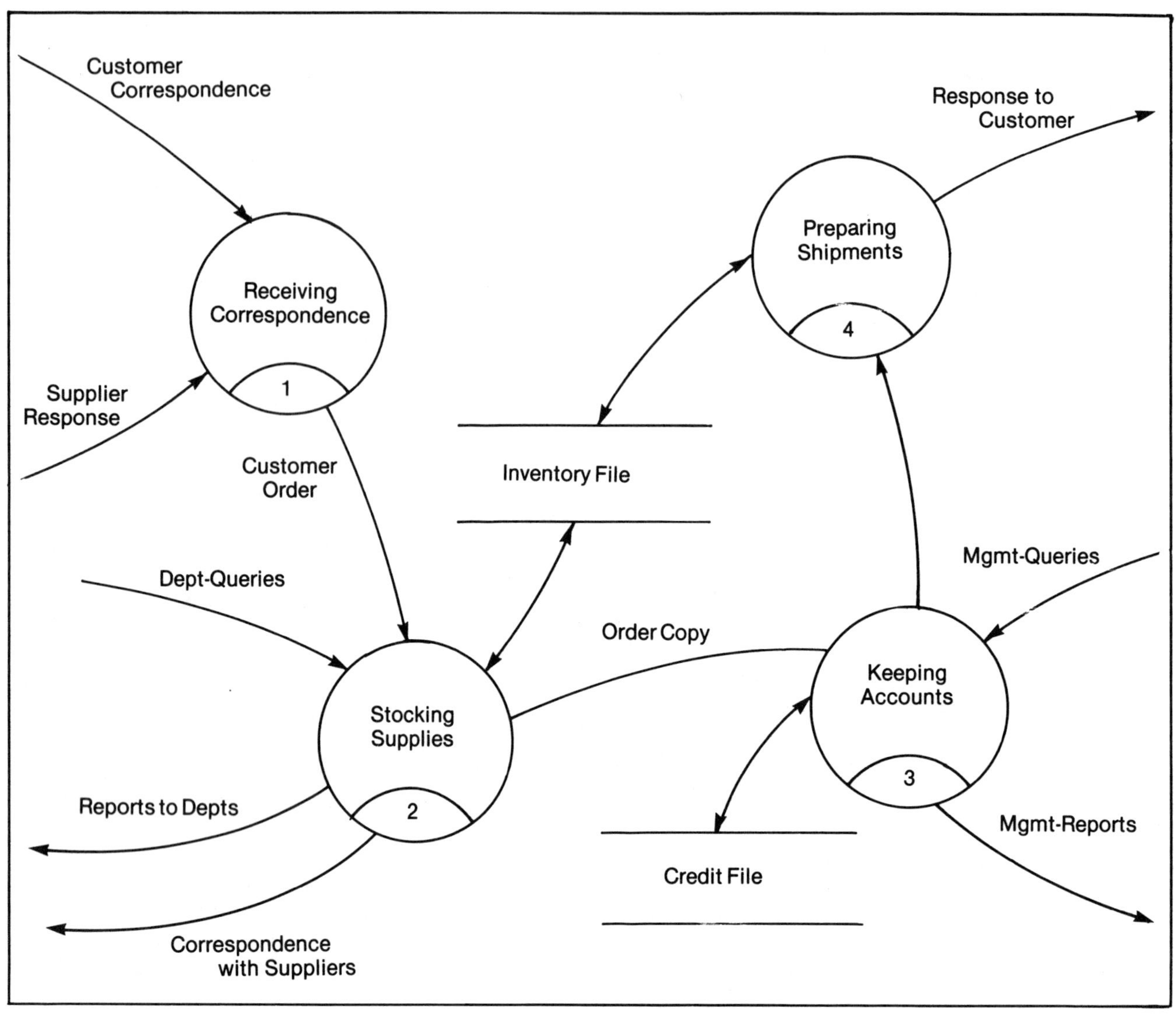

Figure 2: Level 0 data flow diagram

that the "data out" at the child level is identical with or adds up to the "data out" at the parent level. The data that pass between the processes on the child DFD do not enter into this evaluation because they were internal to the process at the parent level.

After completing "level balancing," the analyst explores each process on the balanced diagram into its own DFD, showing the inner workings of each. For instance, the process called "Receiving Correspondence" is explored in Figure 3. When any DFD is completed and balanced with its parent, the analyst continues to explore each of the processes on the just-completed DFD.

Analysts are often tempted to bypass these intermediate-level DFDs, thinking that the information represented thereon is trivial and merely gets in the way of the "good stuff," i.e., the information found on the lowest level of detail. However, without doing the intermediate-level DFDs, the analyst would have no way of ensuring that information has not been lost "through the cracks" or that spurious information has not entered the analysis.

Eventually the analyst reaches a level of detail at which it is no longer useful to decompose the functions and the data with which they interact. This level, called the "functional primitive," is not common across all system processes; the process hierarchy need not be symmetrical. The analyst knows that the functional primitive level has been reached when the process to be further explored is a single (not a compound) function producing only a single kind of data flow. An example of functional primitive processes is

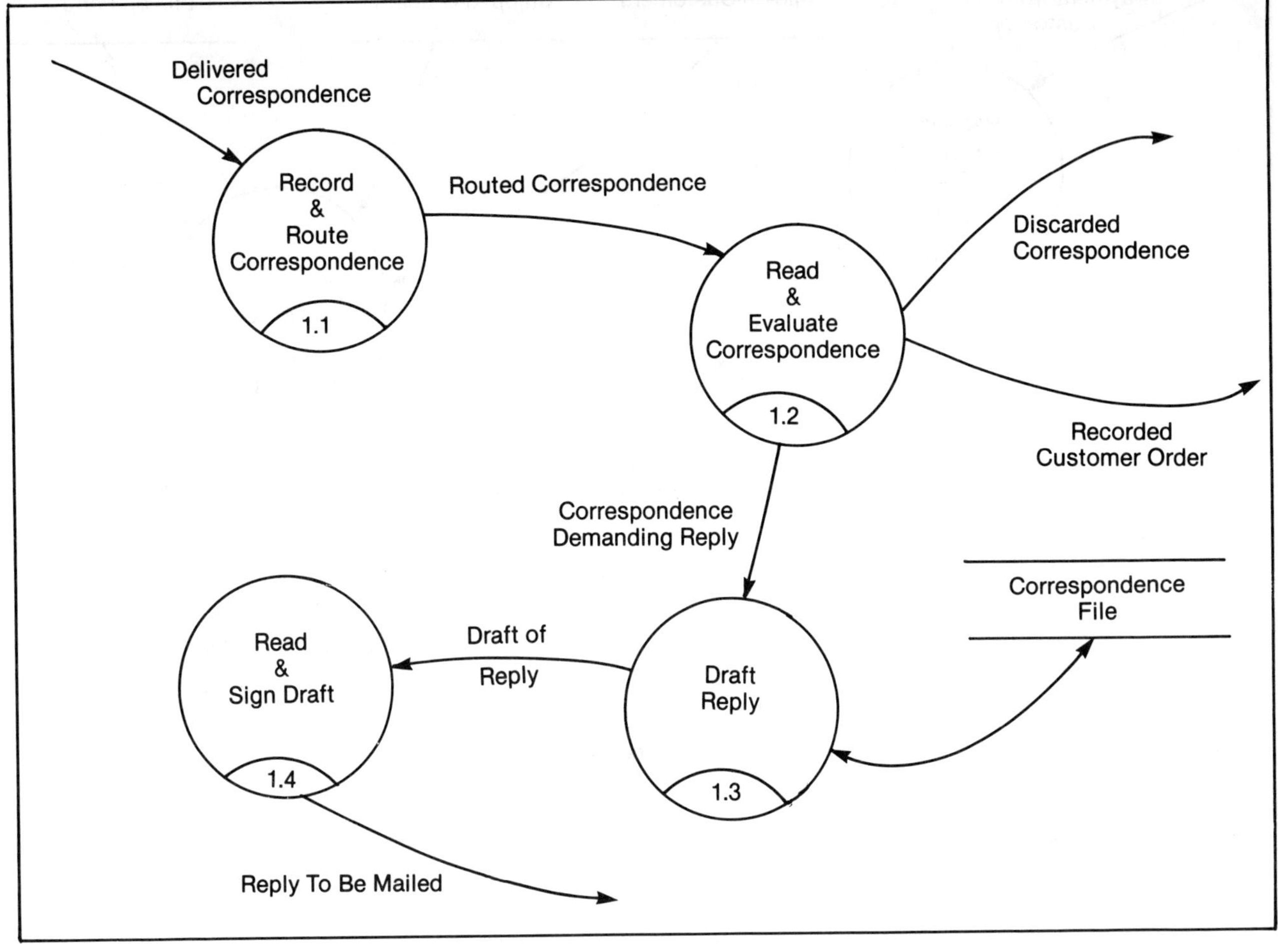

Figure 3: Intermediate-level DFD: Receiving correspondence

shown in Figure 4. When the analyst has explored all system processes to their functional primitive level and has completed level balancing, no further DFDs are needed.

2.4.2: Data Dictionary

As the analyst completes each data flow diagram, he/she should employ a second tool of structured analysis, the data dictionary. As envisioned by the original developers of structured analysis, the data dictionary is a repository, manual or computer-based, containing information about the various data objects appearing on each DFD. It should include an entry for each data object identified. For instance, for each data store there will be an entry that specifies its name, all of its aliases, narrative text describing it, its contents, and the names of all processes that access it. For each data flow there will be an entry, such as that in Figure 5, that specifies its name, all of its aliases, narrative text describing it, and its composition. When specifying the composition of a data flow, the analyst will show not only the names of its component data, but will indicate by means of Backus-Naur Form symbols whether any of the components are optional (surrounded by parentheses (. .)), alternates (surrounded by brackets [. .] with alternate components

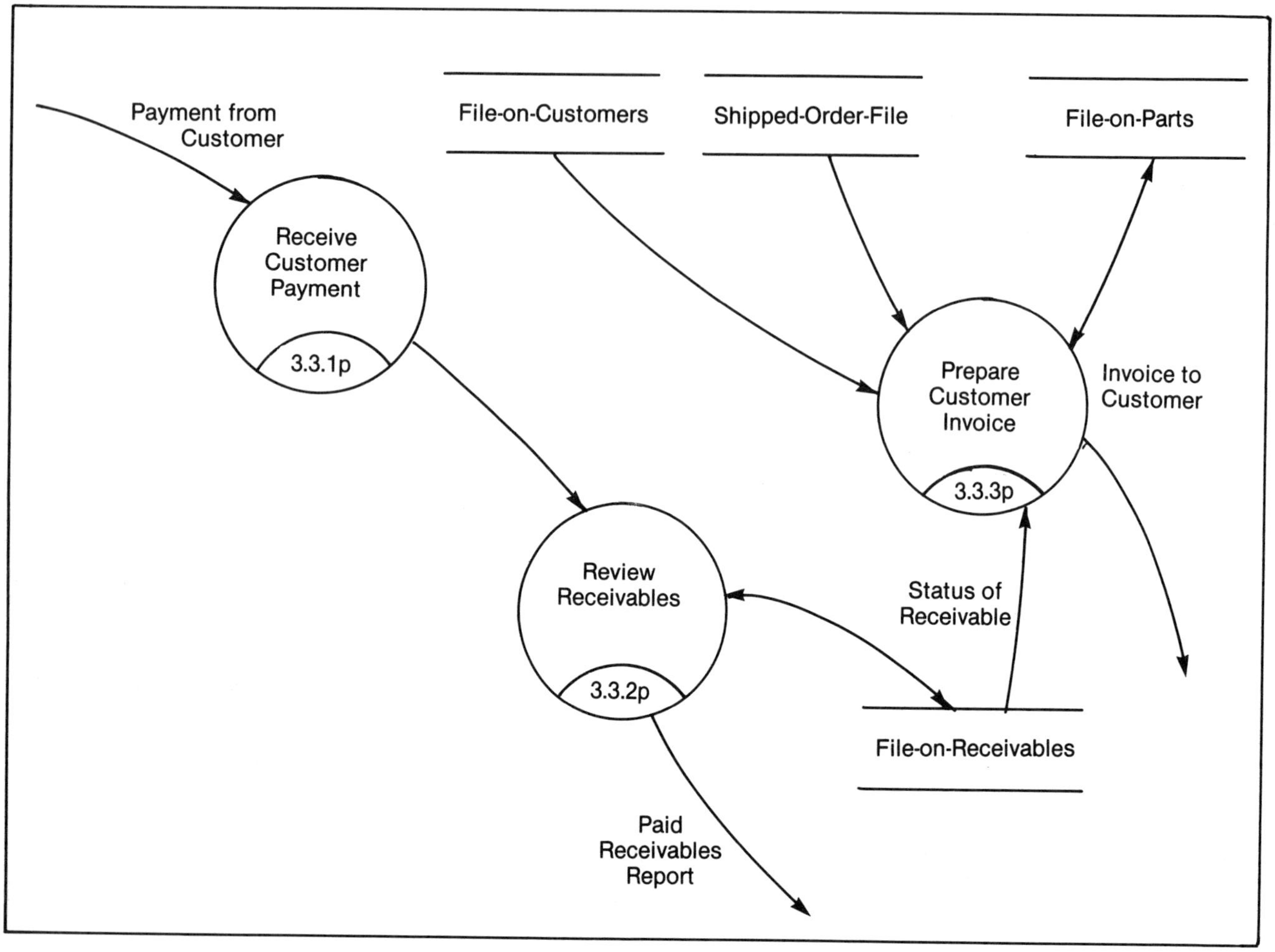

Payment from Customer

File-on-Customers

Shipped-Order-File

File-on-Parts

Receive Customer Payment

3.3.1p

Prepare Customer Invoice

3.3.3p

Invoice to Customer

Review Receivables

3.3.2p

Status of Receivable

File-on-Receivables

Paid Receivables Report

Figure 4: Functional primitive DFD: Accounts receivable

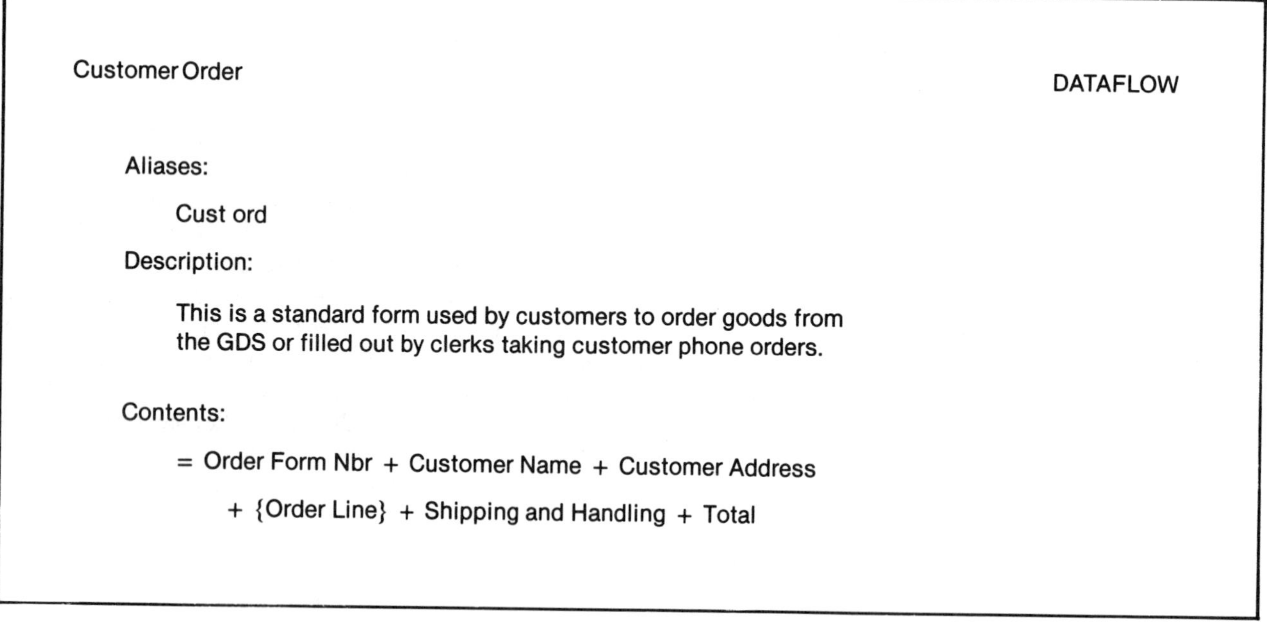

Customer Order

DATAFLOW

Aliases:

Cust ord

Description:

This is a standard form used by customers to order goods from the GDS or filled out by clerks taking customer phone orders.

Contents:

= Order Form Nbr + Customer Name + Customer Address

+ {Order Line} + Shipping and Handling + Total

Figure 5: Data dictionary entry for "Customer Order"

Table 1: Backus-Naur Form symbols

BNF

Symbol	Meaning
=	"is composed of"
+	"and," "as well as," "together with"
{name}	"repetitions of"
[name/name]	"choice between," "alternates are"
(name)	"optional," "may not be present"
{order-line}	"repetitions of order-line"
1 {order-line}n	"one-through-n repetitions of order-line"

```
Mailing Label Information                                   DATA GROUP
        = customer-name + customer-address
Customer-name                                               DATA GROUP
        = customer-last-name + customer-first-name
            + customer-middle-initial
Customer-Address                                            DATA GROUP
        = Local-address + community-address + zip-code
Local-address                                               DATA GROUP
        = House-number + street-name + (apt-number)
Community-address                                           DATA GROUP
        = city-name + [state-name/province-name]
```

Figure 6: Dictionary entries for data group

separated by a bar |), or repeating data (surrounded by braces {. .}). These symbols are explained in Table 1.

Data flows need not decompose immediately to data elements. Very often the components of a data flow may be what was called above a data group, i.e., named clusters of other data groups and/or data elements. Each data group will have an entry in the data dictionary showing its name, all of its aliases, narrative text describing it, and its composition.

For instance, a data flow called "Mailing Label Information" could decompose into such components as "Customer Name" and "Customer Address." "Customer Name" could be a data group consisting of "Last Name," "First Name," and "Middle Initial." "Customer Address," shown in Figure 6, might be modeled as a data group consisting of the data groups "Local Address" and "Community Address" and the data element "Zip Code." "Local Address" could consist of "House Number," "Street Name," and an optional "Apartment Number." "Community Address" could consist of "City Name" and either "State Name" or "Province Name."

Each data element identified will also have an entry in the data dictionary. In addition to its name, all of its aliases, and narrative text describing it, the data element entry might include any of its special characteristics (e.g., its format, type, length, etc.) and its set of legal values.

The pioneers of structured analysis suggested that each data dictionary entry be made on a separate 3 × 5 card kept in a box or on pages in a three-ring binder. These manual information storage means have been abandoned in favor of various computer-aided database management systems. Currently developers seem to feel that information about all system objects, not just the data objects, should reside in the dictionary.

This position is basic to the work done by the X3H4 technical committee of the American National Standards through the 1980s to provide the federal government with a data dictionary system standard that is flexible, user-friendly, and able to support all phases of the system development life cycle. In 1989, the Information Resource Dictionary System became a Federal Information Processing Standard and will likely become the criterion against which other dictionary systems will be judged.

2.4.3: The Primitive Process Specification ("MiniSpec")

As the analyst identifies functional primitive processes in any DFD, he/she can explore each, not into a lower-level DFD, but into its primitive process specification or "MiniSpec." This third tool of structured analysis is usually a linguistic statement of the essential procedural steps necessary to carry out the action of a primitive process. The information contained herein might be a narrative statement of relevant business policies or a formal listing of "condition-action" definitions. Ultimately a "MiniSpec" should express the actual component tasks required to carry out a function called for by some verifiable business policy; it should not be a collection of the "neat things" some developer could make it do. The process specification can be kept in the repository, as part of the description of the primitive process of which it is an explosion.

A "MiniSpec" may be expressed in various ways. During an interview with a client, an analyst may capture the steps of an identified primitive process in the client's English narrative. However, it is possible to use some formal notation, as shown in Figure 7, that expresses the same three major action types found in programming: sequence, decision, and iteration. Whether structured English, a decision tree, a decision table, or even some procedure definition language (PDL) is used, the emphasis in writing a process specification should be on *what* steps the process must carry out, not on *how* it will do them. The actual means of expression chosen should represent a compromise between the client's ease of understanding or expressing the steps and the rigor required for expressing them with precision. The choice will vary from organization to organization, from project to project, or from process to process.

2.4.4: Structured Walkthrough

A fourth tool of structured analysis is not so much a product as a process. The structured walkthrough is a formal meeting, ideally held periodically through the life of a development project, during which some part of the analysis is presented and critiqued. Participants are usually given formal roles (e.g., moderator, presenter, secretary, etc.) and responsibilities. For instance, the presenter has the responsibility of showing and explaining what and how the work being presented was done. The moderator has the responsibility of shepherding the communication processes and controlling the group dynamics active during the meeting. The secretary has the responsibility of documenting what items were called into question, what suggestions for change were made, and whether the moderator assigned any "action items" requiring resolution prior to final approval of that part of the analysis.

In addition to these participatory roles, other individuals ought to be invited to attend the structured walkthrough, at least as observers. If the emphasis of the analysis has been on the process side, someone involved in database design should bring a data orientation. Someone should represent the quality assurance department. A representative from the programming or maintenance team should be invited. In fact, any interested party in either the client or developer organization (if they are different) should be encouraged to attend.

There are various reasons for conducting structured walkthroughs:

- to gain as many perspectives on the target system as possible
- to elicit critical comments and suggestions to enhance the developing understanding of the target system
- to invest as many representatives from the organization as possible (to defuse an adversary atmosphere)

Development projects may call this step an inspection, in-process review, or milestone review.

3: Varieties of a Structured Approach to Analysis

Different individuals have suggested different ways to approach analysis in a structured manner. Common across these various approaches are the goals of improving understanding of the system under development and communication of that understanding to the client and others in the development process. Whichever structured analysis approach an organization adopts, it is encouraged to adapt the methodology to its own situation and culture.

3.1: Structured Analysis and Design Technique

Doug Ross and his colleagues at SofTech, Inc., proposed an early version called "Structured Analysis and Design

```
Prepare-Customer-Invoice                                        MINISPEC

        FOR EACH   Shipped-order-detail,
            GET customer-name + customer-address
            FOR EACH part-shipped,
                GET retail-price
                MULTIPLY retail-price by quantity-shipped
                    TO OBTAIN total-this-order

        CALCULATE shipping-and-handling
        ADD shipping-and-handling TO total-this-order
                    TO OBTAIN total-this-invoice

        PRINT INVOICE
```

Figure 7: Example of a process specification

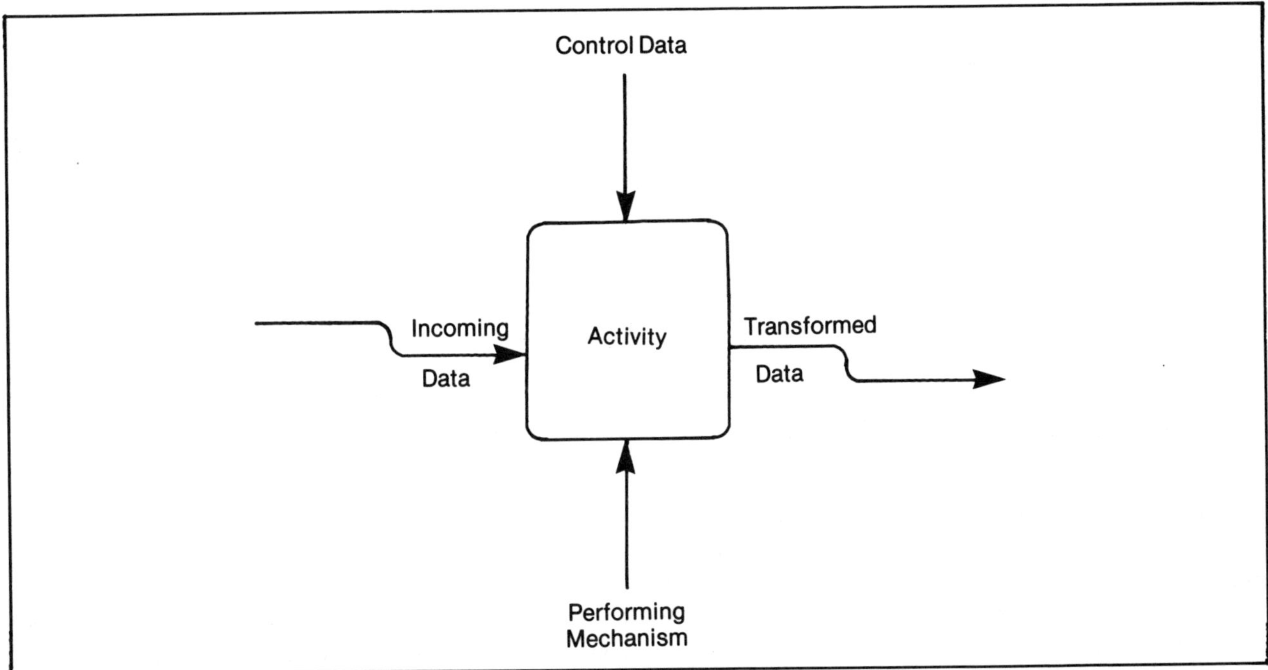

Figure 8: Constructs of a SADT activity diagram

Technique'' (SADT) [6] that encourages the analyst to begin by asking about the objectives of a system (the ''why?'' questions) before progressing to the major components of a system (the ''what?'' questions) and eventually determining the implementation techniques (the ''how?'' questions). This technique has been used for planning as well as for analysis and design.

Like all versions of structured analysis, SADT suggests that to understand a system you begin at the top and progress through the many layers from conceptual abstractions to concrete components. This top-down approach views data and activity as two sides of a coin. In a diagrammatic tool called the activity diagram, the analyst pictures the interaction of data and activities by means of the graphic symbols shown in Figure 8. Data are classified as ''consumed'' (i.e., data tranformed by the activity) and ''non-consumed'' (i.e., data that contol the activity but are not transformed). The analyst is also expected to identify the ''mechanism''

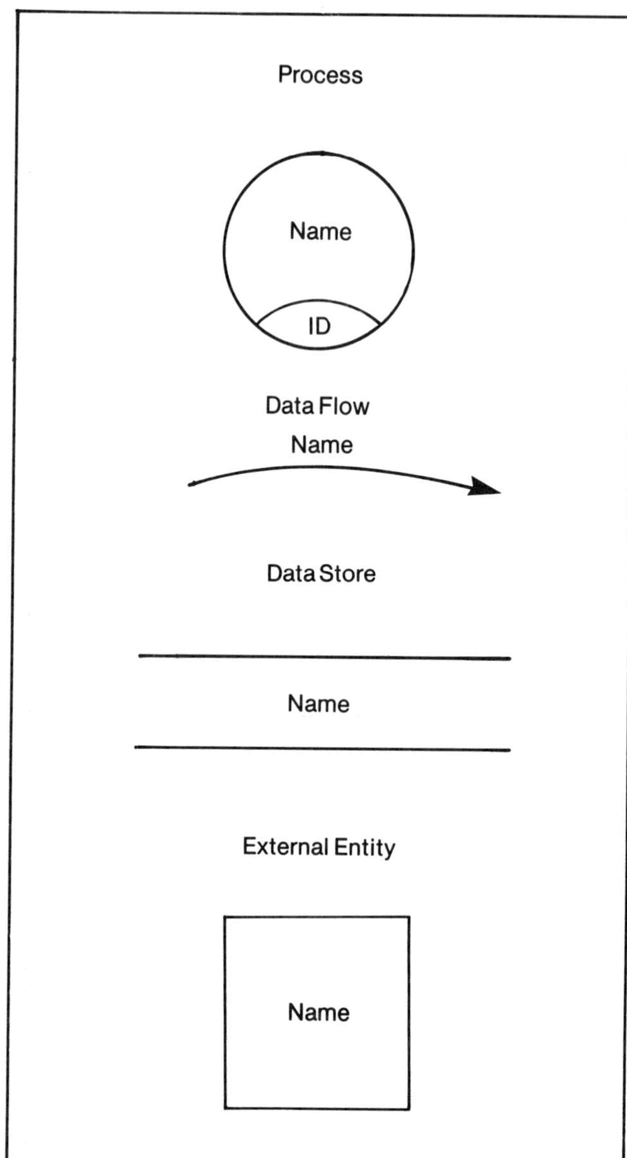

Figure 9: Constructs of Yourdon-DeMarco

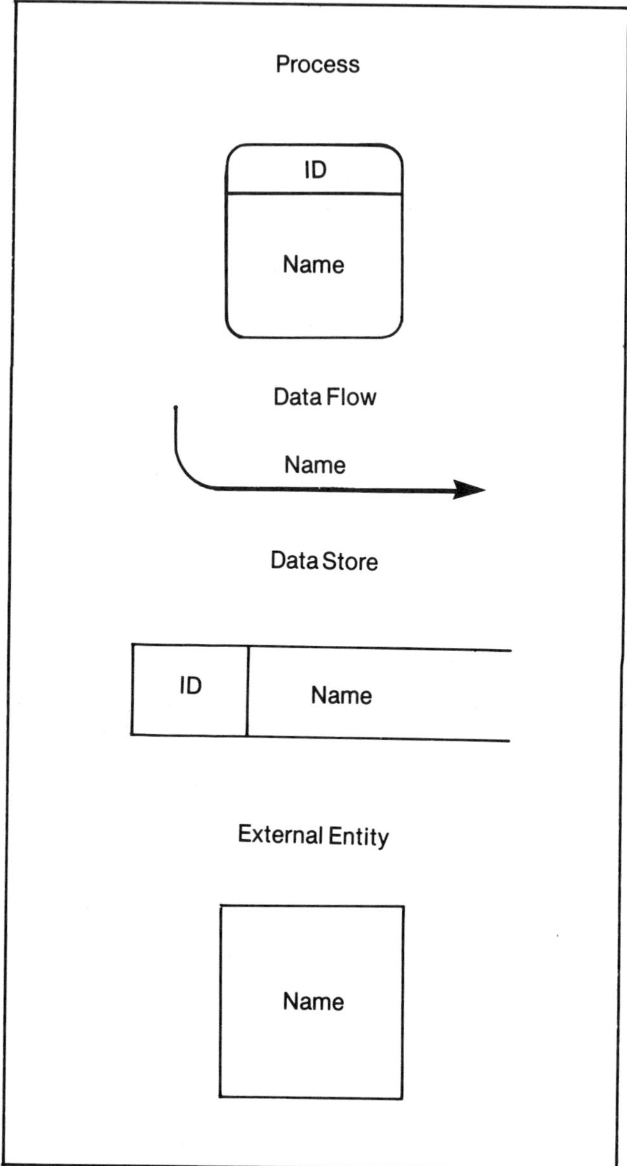

Figure 10: Constructs of Gane and Sarson

that will perform each activity. Using this approach at different milestones throughout a project, analysts are encouraged to develop "kits" of documents, such as activity diagrams, written records of decisions made and alternatives considered, etc., and present them to different individuals playing such roles as reader, commentator, technical expert, or project manager.

3.2: Yourdon-DeMarco

Yourdon founded a firm of consultants who developed and have taught a generic form of structured analysis to organizations throughout the world. DeMarco wrote one of the most popular books on their approach [7]. The technique advocates a top-down approach in which the analyst is led to decompose the system and its functions through levels of increasing detail. Other consultants of this firm have produced articles and books explaining and popularizing this approach.

The six object types discussed earlier and their graphic notation, presented in Figure 9, were first delineated by this approach, as were the four tools of structured analysis presented earlier. While it was initially process-oriented, more recent proponents [26] of this approach have introduced the technique of information modeling to provide a better balance between the aspects of data and activity.

3.3: Gane and Sarson

This pair co-wrote a study [8] of a version of structured analysis that suggests a slightly different emphasis from the Yourdon-DeMarco approach and a different graphic notation, shown in Figure 10, for the data flow diagram. This approach pays more attention than does the Yourdon-

DeMarco approach to the identification of the data components of a system. What we have called in this paper a data group, Gane and Sarson call a data structure. The two terms have the same meaning.

In addition to the four tools already presented, Gane and Sarson suggest the use of a data access diagram to describe the structure and contents of data stores in the system. Each data store is viewed as collecting several entity-types, each of which is related in some way to one or more of the other entities in the data store. The data access diagram pictorially presents the different entities in a data store and the access paths that link them.

4: Real-Time Extensions to Structured Analysis

Traditional structured analysis, with the exception of SADT, led practitioners to devote most of their energies to the identification of the activity and data aspects of the target system, to the exclusion of the control aspect. It was felt that the latter was actually a construct in the design phase and should not enter into analysis of a system. While this may have been true for MIS-type systems, it placed intolerable constraints on the analysis of systems in which process activation or deactivation, issues of deadlock, etc., are important. Recently methodologists have offered extensions to the traditional conceptual model of structured analysis that begin to fill that void.

4.1: Ward and Mellor

Ward and Mellor were the first to publish their techniques for the analysis of "real-time, embedded" systems [21]. To the six object-types presented in Section 2.3, they added the following constructs:

1. *Control transform:* An activity that coordinates the functioning of the processes (also called data transforms) in a real-time system. Such a process does not deal with value-bearing data, but only with signals declaring that important events have occurred or that monitored conditions have reached a critical point calling for determined action.
2. *Control flow:* Either a nonvalue-bearing signal denoting the occurrence of some event of importance to the system or a prompt given by a control transform commanding that other processes "turn on" or "turn off" their predefined activity.
3. *Control store:* A store for holding control flows for later sampling or polling. Data flows cannot be held in control stores, nor can control flows be held in data stores.
4. *State:* An operational mode in which some parts of the target system behave in a predetermined manner until triggered to change to a different state.
5. *Transition:* The actual movement or change from one operational mode to another.
6. *Condition:* A simple or compound stimulus that causes the transition from one state to another.
7. *Action:* A response made by some part of the target system as a result of a transition from one state to another.
8. *Entity:* A thing about which the system must keep information in memory. This thing can be a physical entity, such as an aircraft, or an informational entity, such as a flight plan.
9. *Relationship:* An association that links two or more entities. A relationship is often expressed as a verb with one of the entities playing the role of subject and the other playing the role of object.

Ward and Mellor advocate building a series of models during the analysis and design phases of real-time system development. Since real-time systems must be responsive to the environment, the analyst using their approach would first concentrate on building an essential model of the target system. This model consists of two subparts: the environmental model and the behavior model. The environmental model consists of a list of important events to which the target system must respond and a system context diagram that describes the high-level interaction of the target system with the outside world. The behavior model consists of three subparts: the information model, the process model, and the control model of the target system.

Ward and Mellor base their information model on a version of the ERA model, referenced in Section 1.3, and produce entity-relationship diagrams that identify the major entities about which information must be kept in the system and the associations that link any one entity with others in the model. A portion of such a model is shown in Figure 11.

Ward and Mellor's process model is visualized by means of a transformation schema, a data flow diagram that contains both traditional DFD constructs and real-time con-

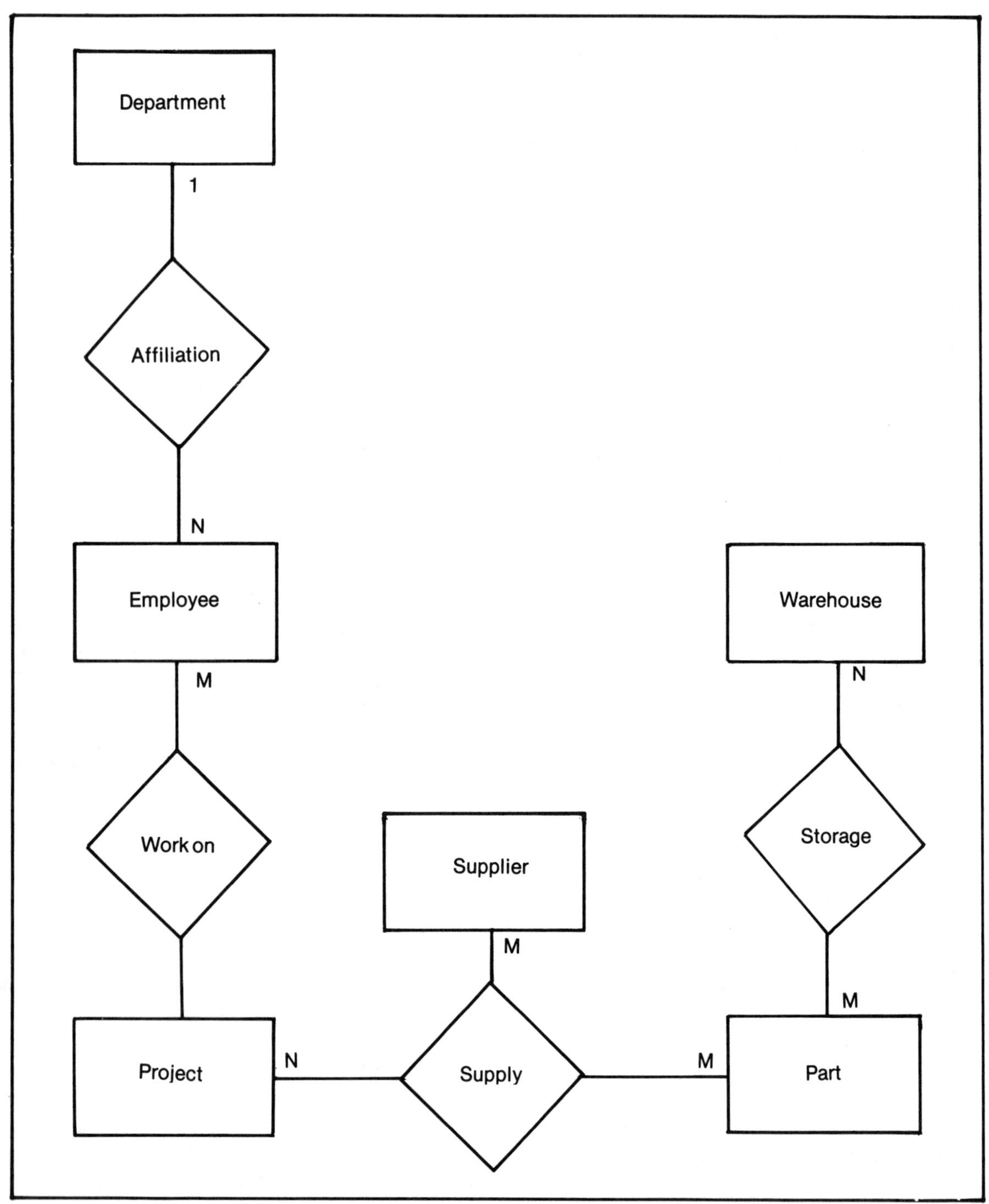

Figure 11: Portion of an information model

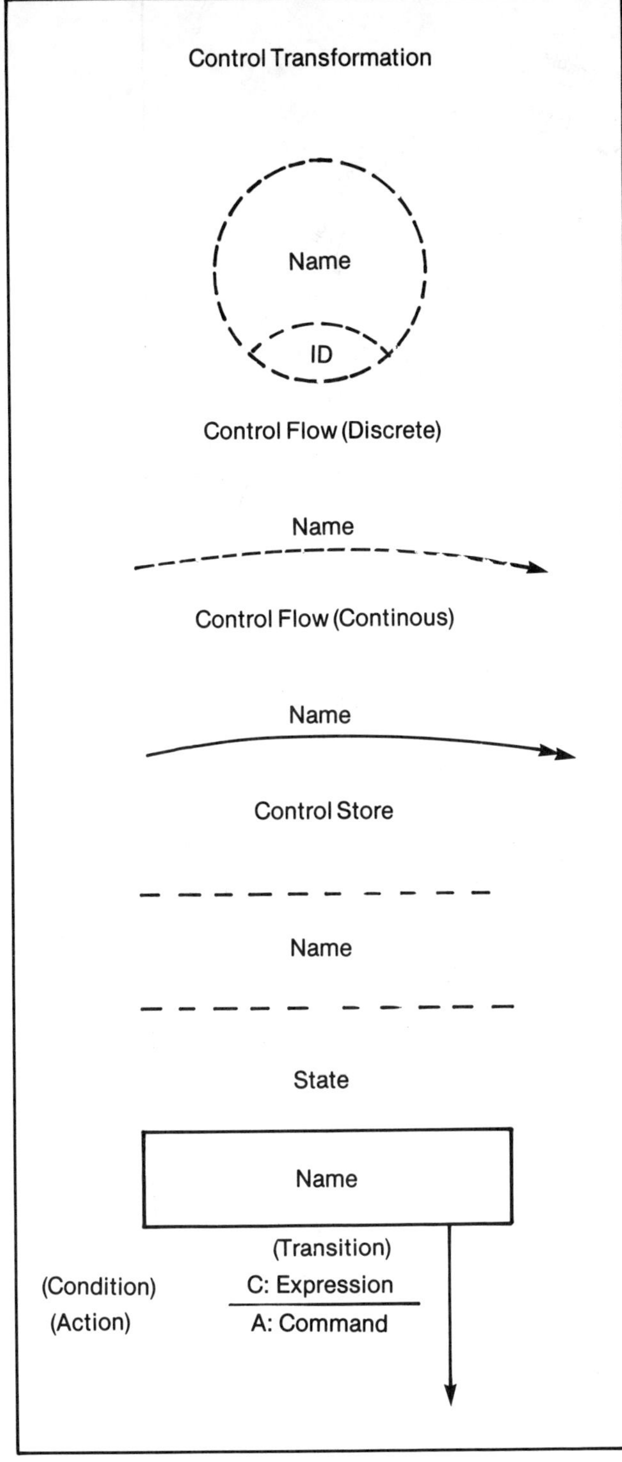

Figure 12: Real-time constructs (Ward and Mellor)

structs discussed earlier in 1-3, the graphic symbols of which are shown in Figure 12.

On the data flow diagram an analyst can show the interactions of both those processes that transform data and those that react to events in the environment and exercise control over other processes. Figure 13 presents an example of a transformation schema. Data processes explode to lower-level transformation schemas, which can contain both data and control objects.

However, the explosion of control processes contributes to the control model of the system under development. System developers visualize this model by means of either a state transition diagram (for sequential finite machines) or a state transition matrix (for combinational finite machines). Figure 14 is an example of a state transition diagram, showing states of an operation (oblong boxes), transitions from one state to another (vectors between boxes), conditions that trigger the transition ("C: <expression>"), and actions taken as a result of the transition ("A: <expression>").

Having completed the behavior model of the system, the designer following the Ward and Mellor technique proceeds to build an implementation model comprising a processor model, a task model, and a module model. The processor model captures the allocation of essential model constructs to different processors that will do the work. The task model determines the different activity units assigned to each processor identified in the processor model. The module model is built by designers employing Constantine and Yourdon's [4] structured design methodology. Designers translate the transformation schemas identified in the behavior model into structure charts that show the particular arrangement of modules required to carry out any task, as well as the data and status flags exchanged by the modules.

4.2: Hatley and Pirbhai

In 1987, Hatley and Pirbhai [22] published a study that presents a slightly different set of extensions for real-time system analysis and design. The constructs are much the same as those suggested by Ward and Mellor (see Figure 12); but the major difference is in the tools Hatley and Pirbhai suggest. The analyst uses not only the data flow diagrams of traditional structured analysis, but creates parallel control flow diagrams (CFDs) containing the processes of the DFD, devoid of data flows, but with control flows. Figure 15 presents an example of parallel data flow and control flow diagrams produced by following this approach.

Below the primitive-level DFD are process specifications or "MiniSpecs" (PSPECS). Any interaction between the DFDs and CFDs is captured in control specifications (CSPECS) which describe the logic of either sequential or combinational finite-state machines. These CSPECS can combine various diagrams (e.g., a state transition diagram), matrices (e.g., a state transition matrix), or tables (e.g., decision table, timing requirements table, or process activation tables). The authors advise against using CSPECS too liberally, lest analysts fall out of analysis and into design.

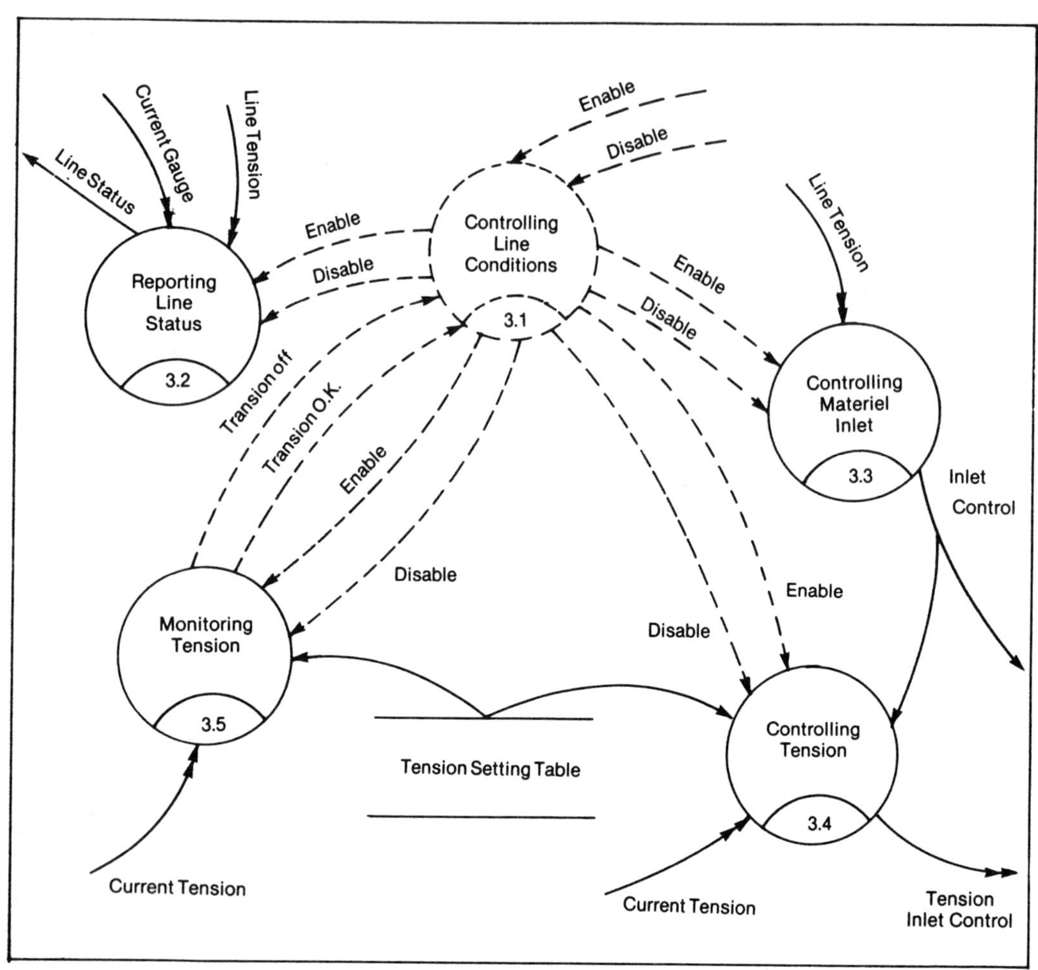

Figure 13: Example of transformation schema

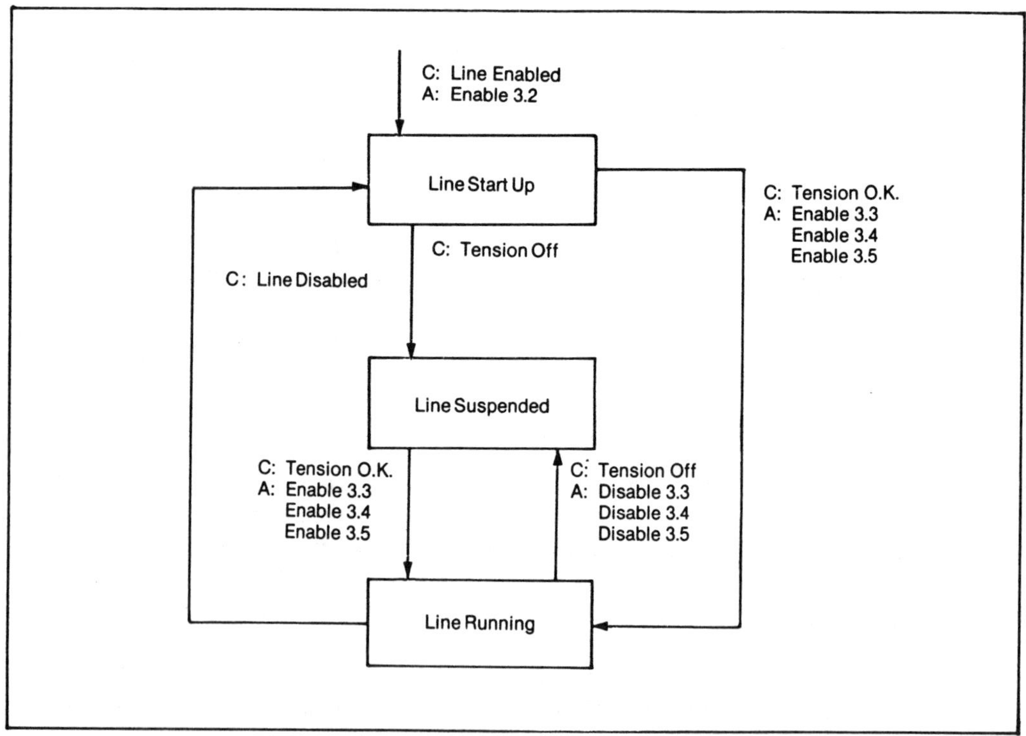

Figure 14: Example of state transition diagram

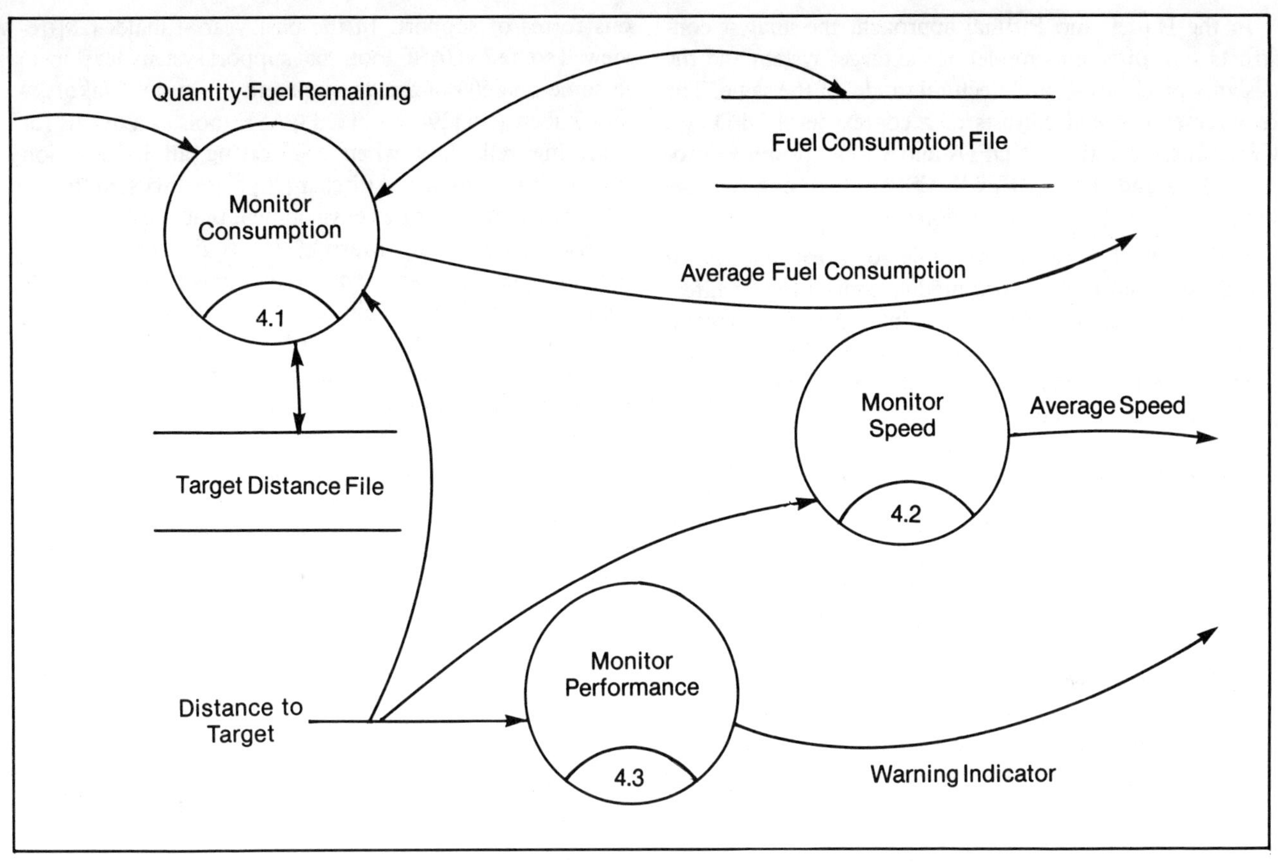

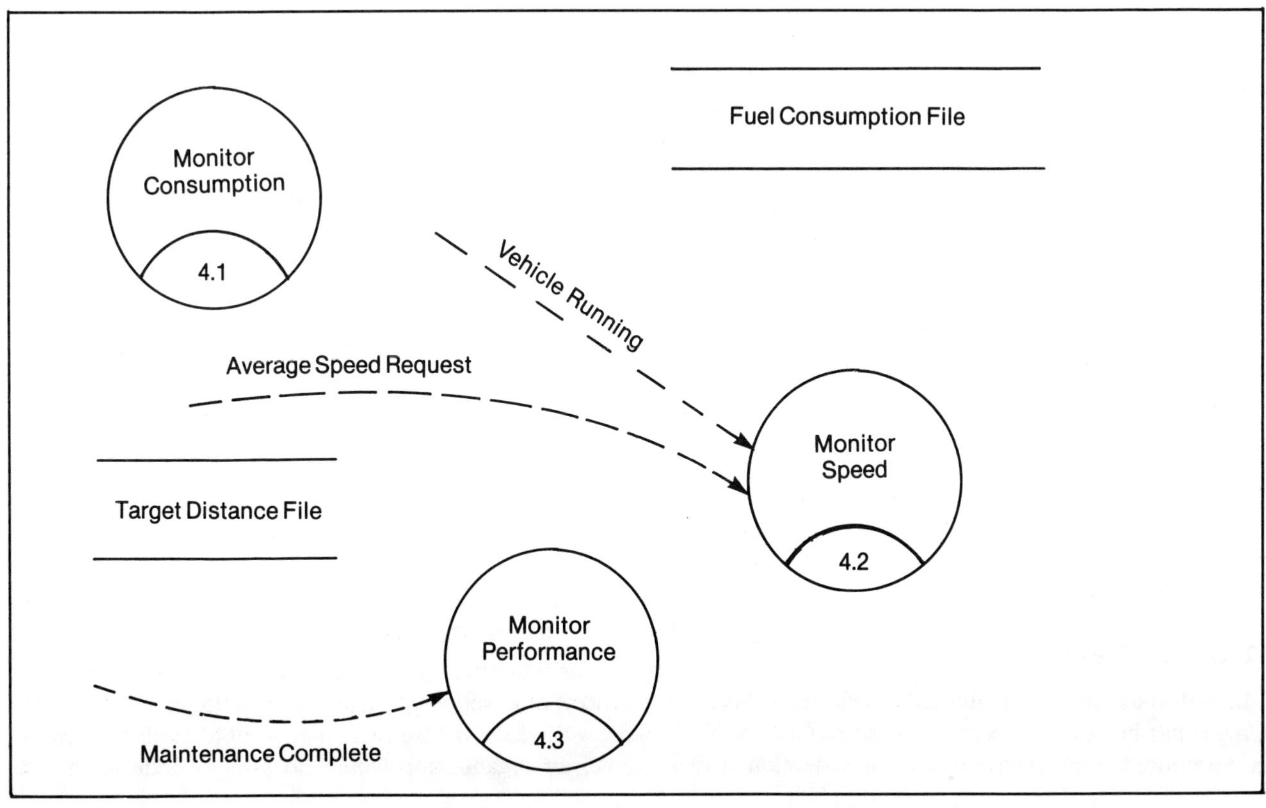

Figure 15: Examples of related data flow and control flow diagrams

In the Hatley and Pirbhai approach, the analyst constructs a requirements model of the target system and the designer produces an architectural model of the same. The requirements model consists of a context level DFD and CFD, intermediate-level DFDs and CFDs, primitive-process DFDs and their PSPECS, CSPECS, timing requirements, and a requirements dictionary.

In the view of these authors, design of a real-time system will produce an architecture model, comprising architectural flow diagrams, architectural interconnect diagrams, lower-level specifications of both, and an architectural dictionary showing the allocation of the requirements to implementation components.

4.3: Extended System Modeling Language

Ward and Hatley have worked with other methodologists to devise a compromise graphic notation for expressing components of a real-time system. Bruyn, Jensen, Keskar, and Ward [23] publicized an extended system modeling language (ESML) as having "a broad range of mechanisms for describing both combinatorial and sequential control logic." At present, the real-time constructs to be identified during the analysis phase have been agreed upon and are shown inFigure 16. Currently a committee is working on the constructs of the design phase.

5: Case Tools to Support Structured Analysis

The original creators of structured analysis presented developers with a strictly manual methodology. As practitioners found it increasingly cumbersome to maintain the mass of paper used to capture DFDs, MiniSpecs, and a data dictionary, they began to look for some automated support.

5.1: Linguistic Dictionaries

One of the first computer-aided tools to support structured analysis was PSL/PSA [27]. Commercial firms and government agencies have used PSL to capture the information on the DFDs, MiniSpecs, and in the data dictionary and then have entered it into the PSA database. From this database, these organizations have derived display reports for use in structured walkthroughs. They have used PSA's analysis reports to evaluate the quality of the information captured. By means of a related tool, the report specification interface, many of these organizations have been able to incorporate this information into documentation that conformed to mandated standards, such as Department of Defense (DoD) 7935.S or DoD 2167A.

5.2: Graphics Packages

In the last six years, computer-aided software engineering (CASE) has burst on the scene. Several different vendors have produced graphics packages that give developers various forms of support. In the past year, Rinaldi [28] reviewed some 75 CASE tools that support system developers in some phase(s) of the development life cycle. Chikofsky and Rubenstein [29] examined CASE tools as a means for achieving reliability when engineering an information system. Wasserman and Pircher [30] have discussed the capabilities of an integrated environment that assists software developers graphically. Martin [31] has diagnosed the less-than-complete acceptance of CASE tools by the development community. He maintains that these tools have certain inherent limits (e.g., lack of adaptability to different methodologies, a dearth of administrator tools, difficulty in producing user-formatted hard-copy documentation, and cumbersome diagram production).

Organizations are exploring the use of these graphics packages to draw DFDs, ER diagrams, structure charts, and state transition diagrams, as well as various forms of data model diagrams. Developers are able to store in the dictionary underlying any of these packages both information related to the visual icons on the diagrams and supplementary information. Most of these packages have both report writing and analysis capabilities to assist developers in reflecting on the information captured and evaluating it against various quality standards. In the last two years, several of these packages have added graphic support for the real-time extensions discussed above.

In the experience of the author, organizations enjoy the most success when adopting these tools if they view them as instruments or means to an end, not as solutions in themselves. Merely learning the mechanics of using these tools does not replace knowing the principles of the methodologies that they are intended to support. Knowing how to do something does not imply knowing what ought to be done or why.

6: Technology Transfer Issues

Organizations deciding to adopt some structured approach to analysis expose themselves to a number of problems bundled under the heading "technology transfer." Technology transfer refers both to the time that it takes for technology to be adopted and to the dynamics that militate against its effective adoption. Possibly because our business milieu focuses on the short term, we grow impatient with the learning curve that any new technology demands. The author has heard managers proclaim, "If my people can't become proficient with a tool in a day or two, it isn't worth it." This forces such individuals into "waiting for Godot," i.e., ignoring available technology while waiting for a technology that is cheap, painless, and universally applicable.

More important than the technology to be adopted is the process of introducing whatever technology is selected into the workplace. Before examining what technology is available, an organization would do well to understand the

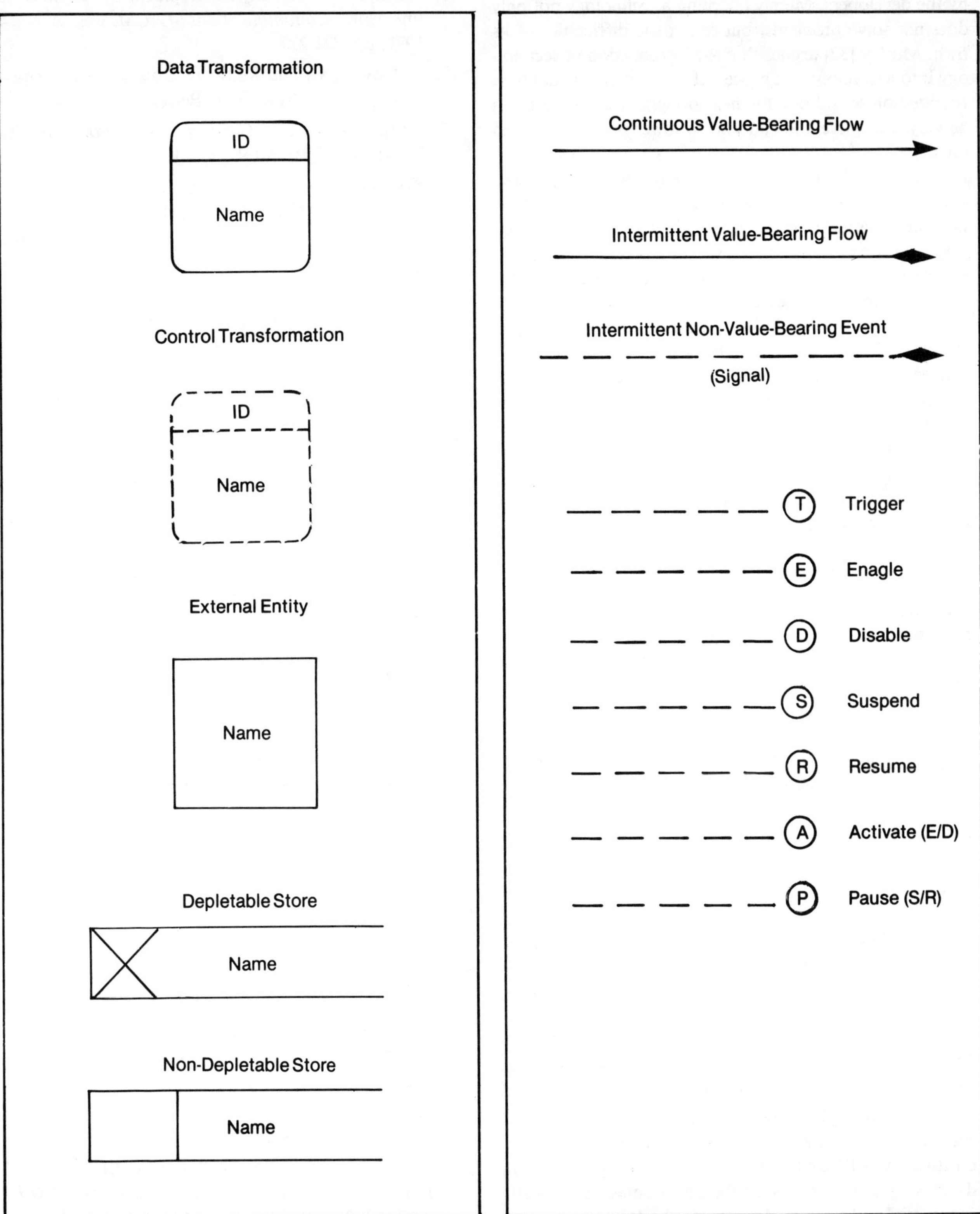

Figure 16: Real-time constructs (ESML)

specific characteristics of its business culture, lest it choose technology that runs counter to the culture and is rejected by the developers. Merely adopting a technology not only does not solve problems, but can create difficulties of its own. Mosley [32] argues that the introduction of technology into a development process that is not clearly defined, founded on sound development principles, or mature can be very disruptive and can lead to lower productivity and quality.

Two evaluative criteria have proved to be vital when considering the adoption of a methodology or support tool: (1) how well the technology can be adapted to the organization's culture or to a project's special situation and (2) how easily the products of the prior development phase can become the inputs for the subsequent phase. Having decided on some methodology and support tool, developers need to establish, disseminate, and enforce a set of standards and conventions as organizational guidelines for developing a system. Svoboda [33] has been arguing for several years that, without project standards and conventions, an organization has not "gotten its act together before putting the show on the road." The blame for the disaster that will follow should not be placed on the technology used, but on its improper introduction, usage, and support.

7: Conclusions and Future Directions

Human beings need methodologies to guide them in carrying out complex tasks on large problems. Structured analysis is a methodology that helps developers in the analysis phase of the system development life cycle. As computer support for this phase becomes not only available but increasingly sophisticated, more organizations will probably adopt computerized tools, thinking that they will automatically enforce a methodology. Eventually these organizations will discover that they need first to learn and commit to using the methodology, and then they may find that the tools can support their use and commitment quite well.

Organizations should examine the "real-time" extensions to structured analysis and realize that even their system includes some, admittedly limited, control aspect and that a complete analysis requires paying attention not only to activity, but to control. Finally, the work done on information (data) modeling should lead practitioners of structured analysis to complete the triad and build models for all three components of any information system: the data, the activities, and the controls.

Users of a methodology find that they have to make trade-offs: while the methodology does constrain their creativity, it will help to keep them from losing their way in developing a system. Use of the methodology can greatly reduce trial and error. Following a methodology requires an act of faith in its creator, but doing so guides technicians through a puzzling territory and enables managers to determine whether the work done is well done. To derive the full benefits of using a methodology, an organization must be able to adapt it to its own situation and culture.

8: References

[1] Wirth, N., "Program Development by Stepwise Refinement," *Communications of ACM,* Vol. 14, No. 4, 1971, pp. 221-227.

[2] McGowan, C. and Kelly, J., *Top Down Structured Programming.* New York: Petrocelli, 1975.

[3] Warnier, J., *Logical Construction of Programs.* New York: Van Nostrand Reinhold, 1974.

[4] Yourdon, E. and Constantine, L., *Structured Design.* Englewood Cliffs, N.J.: Prentice-Hall, 1979.

[5] Jackson, M., *Principles of Program Design.* London, England: Academic Press, 1975.

[6] Ross, D., "Structured Analysis (SA): A Language for Communicating Ideas," *IEEE Transactions on Software Engineering,* Vol. SE-3, No. 1, 1977.

[7] DeMarco, T., *Structured Analysis and System Specification.* New York: Yourdon Press, 1978.

[8] Gane, C. and Sarson, T., *Structured Systems Analysis: Tools and Techniques.* Englewood Cliffs, N.J.: Prentice-Hall, 1979.

[9] Orr, K., *Structured Systems Development.* New York: Yourdon Press, 1977.

[10] Teichroew, D. and Sayani, H., "Automation of System Building," *Datamation,* August 15, 1971, pp. 25-30.

[11] Sayani, H., "The Automated Documentation System," Paper presented at Seventeenth Annual Technical Symposium, National Bureau of Standards, Gaithersburg, Md., June 15, 1978.

[12] Carnap, R., *The Logical Structure of the World.* Berkeley, Cal.: University of California Press, 1967.

[13] Chen, P., "The Entity-Relationship Model—Toward a Unified View of Data," *ACM Transactions on Database Systems,* Vol. 1, No. 1, March 1976.

[14] Flavin, M., *Fundamental Concepts of Information Modeling.* Englewood Cliffs, N.J.: Prentice-Hall, 1981.

[15] Bell, T., Bixler, D., and Dyer, M., "An Extendable Approach to Computer-Aided Software Requirements Engineering," *IEEE Transactions on Software Engineering.* Vol. SE-3, No. 1, January 1977.

[16] Alford, M., "SREM at the Age of Eight: The Distributed Computing Design System," *IEEE Computer,* Vol. 18, No. 4, May 1985.

[17] Alford, M., "A Requirements Engineering Methodology for Real-Time Processing Requirements," *IEEE Transactions on Software Engineering,* Vol. SE-3, No. 1, January 1977.

[18] Staff, International Business Machines Corp., *Business Systems Planning—Information Systems Planning Guide,* 3rd ed., White Plains, N.Y.: IBM Corp., 1981.

[19] Hatley, D., "The Use of Structured Methods in the Development of Large Software-Based Avionics Systems," *AIAA/IEEE Sixth Digital Avionics Systems Conference,* 1984.

[20] Ward, P., "The Transformation Schema: An Extension of the Data Flow Diagram to Represent Control and Timing," *IEEE Transactions on Software Engineering,* Vol. SE-12, No. 2, February 1986.

[21] Ward, P. and Mellor, S., *Structured Development for Real-Time Systems.* Englewood Cliffs, N.J.: Prentice-Hall, 1985.

[22] Hatley, D. and Pirbhai, I., *Strategies for Real-Time System Specification.* New York: Dorset House, 1987.

[23] Bruyn, W., Jensen, R., Keskar, D., and Ward, P., "ESML: An Extended Systems Modeling Language Based on the Data Flow Diagram." *ACM SIGSOFT—Software Engineering Notes,* Vol. 13, No. 1, January 1988.

[24] McMenamin, S. and Palmer, J., *Essential Systems Analysis.* New York: Yourdon Press, 1984.

[25] Yourdon, E., "Whatever Happened to Structured Analysis?", *Datamation,* June 1, 1986, pp. 133-138.

[26] Stehle, G., "Data Modeling," paper presented at CASE Studies 1988, Ann Arbor, MI. Shows that data modeling is an integral part of structured systems analysis course given by Keith London Associates, Hertfordshire, Great Britain.

[27] Teichroew, D. and Heshey, A., "PSL/PSA: A Computer-Aided Technique for Structured Documentation and Analysis of Information Processing Systems," *IEEE Transactions on Software Engineering,* Vol. SE-3, No. 1, January 1977.

[28] Rinaldi, D., "Getting Beyond Drawings," *Software Magazine,* Vol. 8, No. 5, April 1988, pp. 51-58.

[29] Chikofsky, E. and Rubenstein, B., "CASE: Reliability Engineering for Information Systems," *IEEE Software,* Vol. 5, No. 2, March 1988.

[30] Wasserman, A. and Pircher, P., "A Graphic, Extensible Integrated Environment for Software Development," *ACM SIGPLAN Notices,* New York: Association for Computing Machinery, Inc., January 1987.

[31] Martin, C., "Second-Generation CASE Tools: A Challenge to Vendors," *IEEE Software,* March 1988, pp. 46-49.

[32] Mosley, D., "Are We Ready for CASE?," *American Programmer,* Vol. 2, No. 3, March 1989, pp. 20-25.

[33] Svoboda, C., "Setting Up Project Standards and Conventions," paper presented at Second Annual Excelerator Users Group Conference, San Diego, Calif., September 10, 1986.

Note: For a current, comprehensive view of this topic, read Yourdon, E., *Modern Structured Analysis.* Englewood Cliffs, N.J.: Prentice-Hall, 1989.

Entity-Relationship Approach to Data Modeling

Peter Chen

The entity-relationship (ER) model has been used successfully world-wide as a tool for communication between the system analysts/designers and the end user during the requirements analysis and conceptual design phases because of its simplicity, ease of understanding, and convenience of representation.

We will give a brief introduction to the ER diagrammatic technique. We discuss the advantages of the ER approach first, then define what entities and relationships are, and finally describe properties of entities and relationships.

1: Advantages of the Entity-Relationship Approach

The conventional approaches to logical database design usually have only one phase: mapping the information about objects in the real world directly to a user schema. The ER approach to logical database design consists of two major phases: (1) defining the enterprise schema by using the entity-relationship diagram and (2) translating the enterprise schema into a user schema. The advantages of the ER approach are:

1. The division of functionalities and labor into two phases makes the database design process simpler and better organized.
2. The enterprise schema is easier to design than the user schema because it does not need to be restricted by the capabilities of the database system and it is independent of storage and efficiency considerations.
3. The enterprise schema is more stable than the user schema. If one wants to change from one database system to another, one would probably have the user schema but not the enterprise schema, because the enterprise schema is independent of the database systems used. What needs to be done is to remap the enterprise schema to a user schema suitable for the new database system. Similarly, if one wants to change the user schema to optimize a new application program, one need not change the enterprise schema, but rather remap the enterprise schema to a new user schema.
4. The enterprise schema expressed by the ER diagram is more easily understood by non-EDP people.

2: Entities and Relationships

2.1: Entity Type

An entity is a "thing" that can be distinctly identified. Entities can be classified into different entity types, such as EMPLOYEE and COMPUTER. In the ER diagram, an entity type is represented by a rectangular-shaped box. A common *noun* in English corresponds to an entity type in an ER diagram.

An entity is the principal object about which information —usually denoting a person, place, thing, or event of informational interest—is to be collected. There are many "things" in the real world. Some of them are of interest to the enterprise, and the rest are not. It is the responsibility of the analyst/designer to select the entity types that are most suitable for his/her company.

2.2: Relationship Type

Relationships may exist between entities. For example, in Figure 1, MARRIED-TO is a relationship between the two person entities, man and woman.

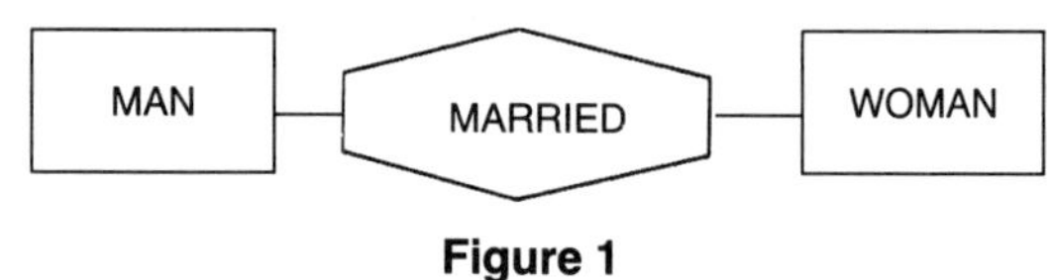

Figure 1

Relationships can be classified into different *relationship types*. For instance, WORKS-ON and MANAGE are two different relationship types between two entity types, PROJ (project) and EMP (employee) (see Figure 2).

In ER diagrammatic notation, a relationship type is represented by a diamond-shaped box with lines connected to related entity types. A *transitive verb* in English corresponds to a relationship type in the ER diagram.

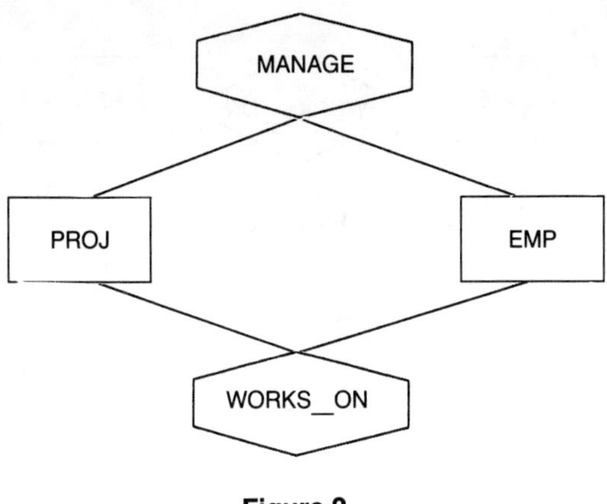

Figure 2

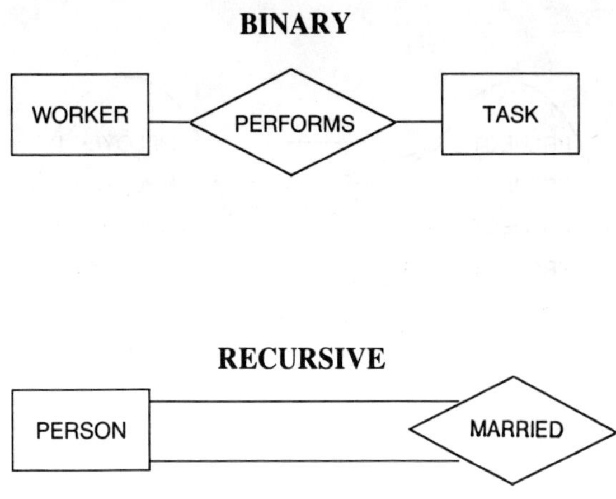

There are many types of relationships between entities, some of which are of interest to the enterprise; the database designer is responsible for the selection of the relationship types relevant to the enterprise. He should also specify the types of mapping of the relationship types (e.g., one-to-one, one-to-many, or many-to-many).

2.2.1: Degree of a Relationship

The degree of a relationship is the number of entities associated in the relationship. An n-ary relationship is of degree n. Unary, binary (including recursive), and ternary relationships are special cases where the degree is 1, 2, and 3 respectively (see Figure 3).

Recursive: In ER diagramming, it is sometimes convenient to form relationships from objects in an entity to other objects in the same entity. This type of relationship is called a recursive relationship. For example, one employee may manage many other employees.

It is possible to define a relationship type among more than two entity types. In the example above, SUPPLY is a relationship type defined on three entity types: PART, SUP, and PROJ. Note that a 3-way relationship usually cannot be replaced by three binary relationships. As an example, the 3-way relationship SUPPLY mentioned above may lose information if it is replaced by three binary relationships: PART-SUP, SUP-PROJ, and PROJ-PART. When we want to construct the 3-way relationship starting with these binary relationships, we get some "non-facts."

2.2.2: Connectivity of a Relationship

The connectivity of a relationship specifies the mapping of the associated entity occurrences in the relationship. Values for connectivity are either "one" or "many." The actual number associated with the term "many" is called the *cardinality* of the connectivity. The basic types of connectivity are as follows: one-to-one, one-to-many, and many-to-many.

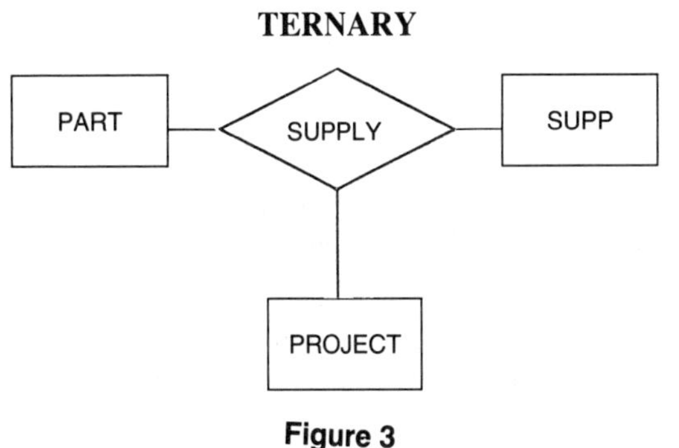

Figure 3

Although the term cardinality refers to the counting of some value, it is easier to think of cardinality in an ER diagram as a mapping of records between an Entity/Weak Entity pair. For example, the diagram segment shown in Figure 4 might look conceptually like Figure 5. Looking from the Relationship WORKS_ON to the Entity EMPLOYEE, the question which arises is "How many employees work on single project?"

Project one and Project six have more than one employee working on them. Therefore, the cardinality is one-to-many. Suppose this ER diagram comes from a company that has a rule stating that no more than 15 employees can work on the same project simultaneously. This would establish

Figure 4

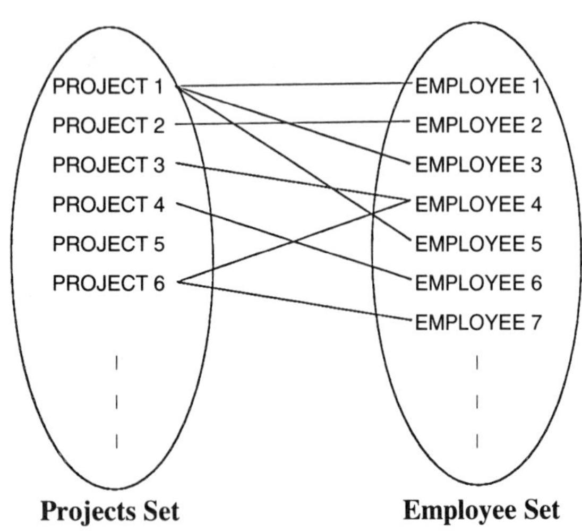

Figure 5

"15" as the value for "many." Often no value is established. In such cases, the value is assumed to be infinity.

Example of a one-to-one mapping: For each project there is only one employee. Each employee works on only one project as shown in Figure 6.

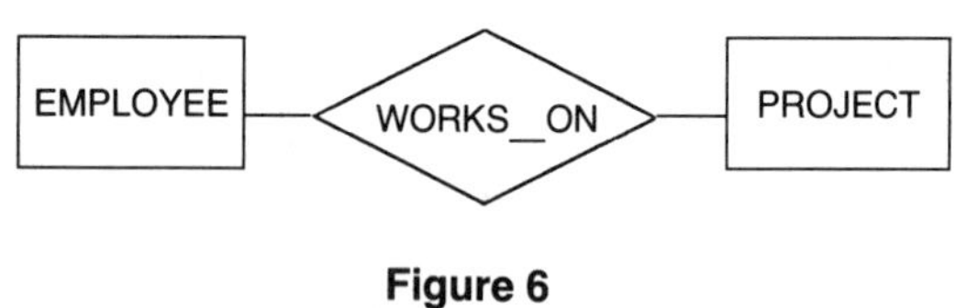

Figure 6

Example of a one-to-many mapping: Each project may consist of many employees. Only one project may be associated with each employee as shown in Figure 7.

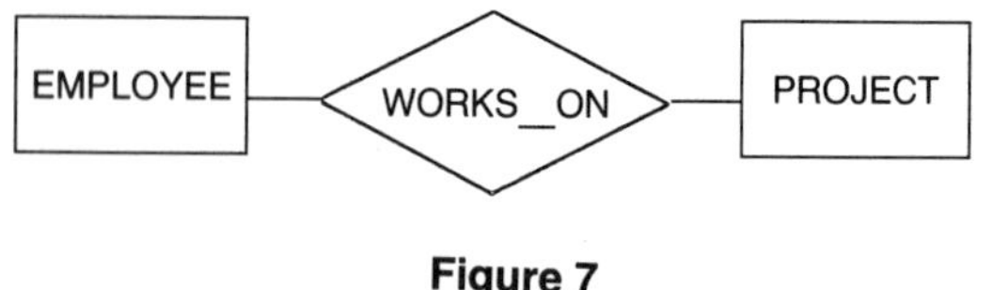

Figure 7

Example of a many-to-many mapping: Each project may consist of *many* employees, and each employee may be associated with *more than one project* as shown in Figure 8.

Figure 8

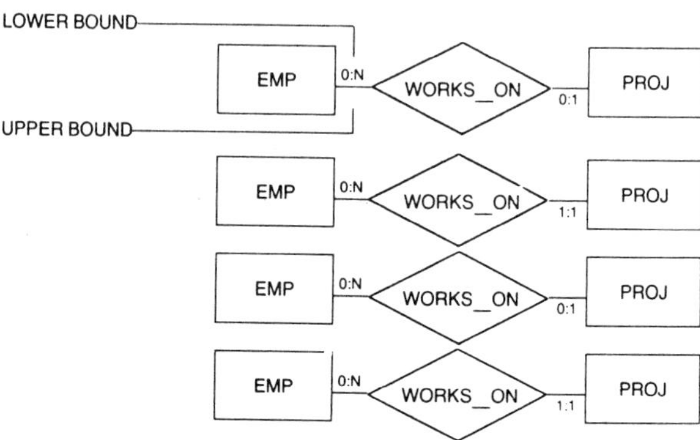

Figure 9

Upper bound or lower bound of connectivity: So far we have only considered the upper bound of the connectivity. When strictly considering only the upper bounds of cardinality, Figure 8 can be read as follows: Each project may consist of *at most* many employees and each employee may be associated with *at most* one project.

The lower bound of the connectivity can also be specified. When the lower bound is one or many, it is a *total* or *obligatory* relationship. When the lower bound is zero, it is a *partial relationship*. Using the example shown in Figure 7, we see Project five has no associated employees. Therefore the lower bound designator is "0" (zero).

Each project may consist of *at most* n employees and *at least* one employee. Each employee may be associated with *at most* one project and *some employee, may not be associated with any project*.

See Figure 9 for diagrammatic examples indicating lower bound and upper bound information.

The third line in this figure can be read as follows: There can be as few as one or as many as N employees working on each project. There can be as few as zero or as many as one project for each employee.

2.2.3: Generalization/specialization (or ISA) relationships

A generalization/specialization occurs when an entity is partitioned by different values of a common attribute. For example, STAFF is a generalization of SALARIED and HOURLY staff members. This is denoted by the ISA relationship, which is read STAFF is HOURLY. Both SALARIED and HOURLY share common attributes, such as employee identification and date hired, but both have distinct attributes associated only with that generalization/specialization. For example, SALARIED would have the attribute SALARY, while HOURLY would have the attribute PAY-PER-HOUR.

Therefore a STAFF member can be either SALARIED or HOURLY. If the STAFF member were SALARIED, he would have all the attributes of STAFF plus the attributes of SALARIED. Likewise, if he were HOURLY he would have all the attributes of STAFF plus the attributes of HOURLY.

To generalize, a STAFF member would have to be a member of either SALARIED or HOURLY. In a specialization, a STAFF member would have the option of being SALARIED, HOURLY, or neither. For example, a STAFF member could be temporary help and not be included in SALARIED or HOURLY.

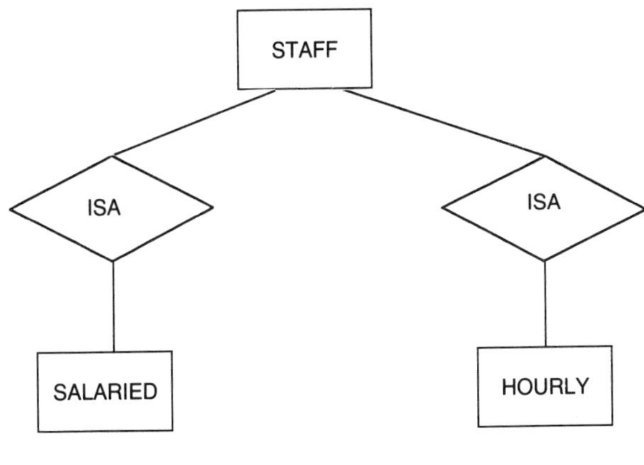

Figure 10

2.3: Weak Entity

The existence of an entity may depend on the existence of another entity type. For example, the existence of CHILDREN entities in the database depends on: the existence of the associated employees. In other words, if an employee leaves the company, we no longer keep track of his children. Figure 11 illustrates the ER diagram for this situation. A weak entity is represented by a double-rectangular-shaped box in the ER diagram.

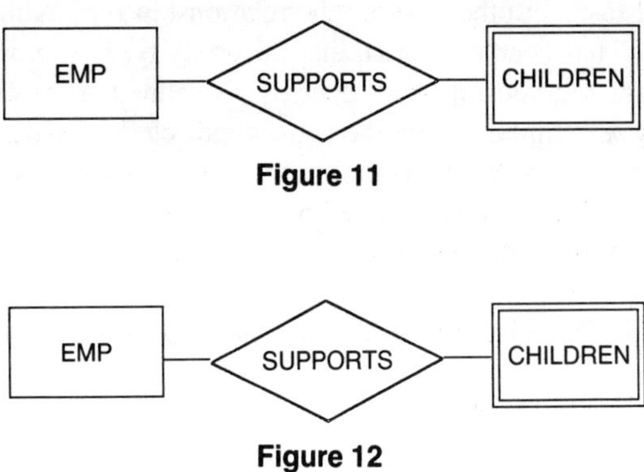

Figure 11

Figure 12

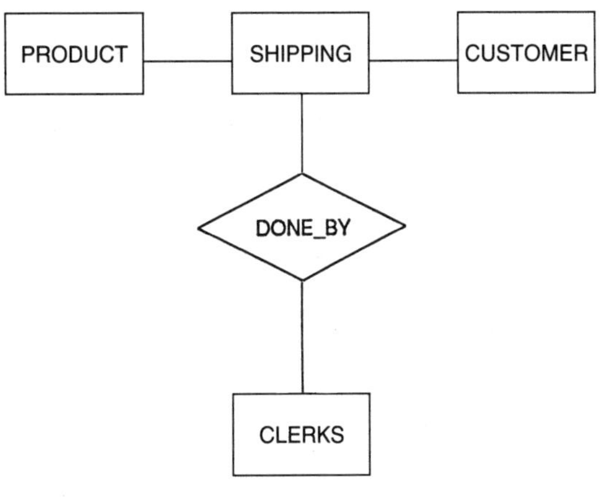

Figure 13

It is possible that the relationship between a weak entity and its associated entity is a many-to-many mapping. For example, if the father leaves the company, the CHILDREN entities may still exist if their mother is still an employee of the company. This situation is represented in the ER diagram shown in Figure 12.

2.4 Gerund

A gerund in English corresponds to a relationship-converted entity type in ER diagrams. Since a gerund is a noun converted from a verb, we may say that it corresponds to an entity type converted from a relationship type (see Figure 13).

English statement: Products are shipped to customers and the shipping is done by clerks.

> *Analysis:* Both "product" and "customer" are entity types, and "shipped to" is a relationship type between them. The verb "ship" is then converted to a gerund "shipping" in order to become the subject of the second

clause. In other words, the relationship type "shipped to" has been converted into the entity type "shipping." The relationship type "done by" is defined on the entity type "shipping" and the entity type "clerks." Note that we use a special symbol, a rectangular-shaped box on top of a diamond-shaped box, to represent a relationship-converted entity type.

3: Descriptions of Entities and Relationships

3.1: Attributes and Values

Entities and relationships have properties, which can be expressed in terms of attribute-value pairs. For example, in the statement "the AGE OF EMPLOYEE X is 24," "AGE" is an "attribute" of employee x, and "24" is the value of the attribute AGE. Values can be classified into different *value types* such as NO-OF-YEARS, QUANTITY, and COLOR.

An adjective in English refers to an entity attribute. In some cases, an attribute may have more than one value for a given entity. For instance, "PHONE-NO" of employee x may have two values: 253-6606 and 253-9999. However, many attributes, such as "AGE" and "SOC-SEC-NO," are single-valued.

So far, we have considered only the attributes of entities. Sometimes we are also interested in the properties of a relationship. For instance, we may want to know when employee x started working on a particular project. Using the EMP WORKS-ON PROJ relation mentioned earlier, STARTING-DATE is neither an attribute of EMP nor an attribute of PROJ because its value depends on both the particular employee and the project involved. Therefore, STARTING-DATE is an attribute of the relationship WORKS-ON. Another example of "attribute of relationship" is PERCENTAGE-OF-EFFORT, which is the percentage of time that an employee devotes to a particular project.

An adverb in English refers to a relationship attribute. The concept of "attribute of relationship" is important in understanding the semantics of data. The concept is similar to the "relationship data" in "network" (CODASYL) type database systems and is similar to the "intersection data" in hierarchical-type (IMS-type) database systems.

3.2 Entity Identifier

The entities discussed so far are those that exist in our minds or can be identified by pointing our finger at them. When someone asks, "What color is it?" "it" is either understood by both the speaker and the listener or it is identified by pointing a finger to the subject. This identification scheme can work for very few objects and we will run into difficulties when we want to communicate the information about a variety of objects to many different people. Therefore, in both daily conversation and computer data processing, we need another scheme to identify entities.

A commonly-used scheme is the use of attribute-value pairs to identify entities. Every entity has many attributes, but which ones should be chosen? The answer is that the attributes chosen should be able to absolutely identify the entities. For instance, we may use the attribute NAME to identify employees in a small company, but not in a large company. These chosen attributes of the entity are called the *entity identifiers*.

In some cases, it may be difficult or inconvenient to use available attributes as the entity identifiers. What we may do is create an artificial attribute that can positively identify the entities. Examples are "SOC-SEC-NO," "EMP-NO," "PART NO," and "PROJ-NO." The concept of "entity identifier" is similar to the concept of *primary key* in conventional data processing.

A weak entity is identified differently from a regular entity. It is identified by the identifier from the parent entity plus an identifier that uniquely identifies the weak entity. An example is shown in Figure 14.

Figure 14

The CHILDREN weak entity would have an identifier from EMP that identifies the parent of the child, plus an identifier to determine which child of that particular employee is being referenced.

3.3 Relationship Identifier

Relationships are identified by utilizing the identifiers of the entities involved in the relationship. For example, if a project is identified by its PROJ-NO and an employee is identified by EMP-NO, then the PROJ-EMP relationship is identified by *both* PROJ-NO and EMP-NO.

In some situations, a relationship type is defined between two occurrences of the same entity type. For instance, MARRIAGE is a relationship type defined between occurrences of the same entity type, PERSON. To positively identify such relationships, we not only use the entity identifier but also indicate what role the entity plays in the relationship. In the case of MARRIAGE, HUSBAND and WIFE are the "roles" they play in the relationship MARRIAGE.

To identify a n-ary relationship correctly, the identifiers from each associated entity must be present in the relationship. Therefore, a ternary relationship would have at least three relationship identifiers—one entity identifier from each associated entity.

To identify an ISA relationship, we use the identifier from the high-level entity (STAFF in the previous example), plus the identifier from whichever low-level entity. (SALARIED or HOURLY in the previous example) to which it belongs. For example, if a STAFF member were an HOURLY worker, then the identifiers would be the identifier from the high-level STAFF entity and the identifiers from the low-level HOURLY entity.

A gerund is also identified differently. Because a gerund is a relationship converted to an entity, it has identifiers like a relationship and an entity. It is identified by its own unique identifier, like an entity, plus the identifiers from any associated entities, like a relationship.

The steps to form a well-modeled entity-relationship diagram are the following:

1. Determine the entities (including weak entities or gerunds) together with the associated entity identifiers. All entities must have at least one identifier that uniquely identifies each entity.

2. Determine the relationships (including recursive and ISA) among the entities. Each relationship must have the identifier (or identifiers) from each of the associated entities. Each relationship also should have at least two entities associated with it, except that a recursive relationship only has one.

3. Determine mapping cardinality (upper bound) between each entity and relationship. Lower bound information about cardinality is optional.

TRW-SS-77-04

THE N^2 CHART

Prepared by
R. J. Lano

November 1977

SYSTEMS ENGINEERING AND INTEGRATION DIVISION
ONE SPACE PARK, REDONDO BEACH, CALIFORNIA 90278

ABSTRACT

One of the increasingly significant problems facing the system designers and master planners of today is the timely and accurate definition of system element interfaces and task or activity interrelationships.

The classical approach to requirements and/or activity definition and allocation consists of the subdivision of large functions into multiple, understandable, discipline-oriented modules or blocks. Each of these blocks is then defined or specified in terms of its inputs, outputs and transfer functions. The emphasis, unfortunately, is usually placed on transfer functions, while the inputs and outputs (interfaces) are all but ignored. Transfer function definitions are more readily understood and communicated than interface definitions since these functions are quantifiable, structured, close to the implementation design, and can be easily related to past experience. A structured technique or discipline must therefore be acquired by the effective system designer and master planner, which places equal weight on all of the definition and allocation parameters. Interfaces and activity relationships must be dealt with in a top-down, hierarchial manner which is as structured and timely as today's transfer function definition process. The implementation of an effective interface definition methodology has become essential due to the increasing relationship complexity of today's tasks, organizations and systems.

This paper describes the N^2 Chart, which is an implementation tool and methodology for the tabulation, definition, analysis and description of functional interactions and interfaces. The tool presented is not limited to any particular field, discipline, market area or system type. The N^2 Chart is simple and easy to understand, structured and methodical, top-down in nature, communicative of the design, and forces a uniform level of design consistency. The N^2 Chart is an effective tool for the integration of all of the people, products, and paper that make up any given system.

An initial N^2 Chart definition is provided, together with discussions relating to its various usages, formats and applications. Applications covered include interface tabulation, definition, design and analysis activities. Other non-obvious applications are additionally discussed which are concerned with design description, operational procedure analysis and schedule analysis activities. Examples are presented of actual N^2 Chart implementations on numerous TRW studies and proposal activities. Two examples are presented in detail which illustrate the applications of the N^2 Chart in interface problem solving and in top-down system design definition.

1. INTRODUCTION

This paper presents a detailed discussion of the N^2 Chart and its applications to interface and relational (or relationship) analysis. Relational analysis is a term used herein to define the broader spectrum of interfaces such as those that exist between people, organizations, procedures, activities, tasks, etc. The N^2 Chart is a visual aid which can be effectively employed to communicate functional or physical interface and interrelationship information to a large group and/or mixed discipline audience in a very short time period. The N^2 Chart additionally provides the user with an effective tool for the definition, tabulation, design and analysis of these interfaces. In this book, N^2 usage is explained largely through examples rather than text. There are many examples in the book. The reader need not dwell on further examples of the same type once he has grasped the principle.

The N^2 Chart is a fixed-format structure which graphically displays the total bidirectional interrelationships between the individual functions and/or components within a given system or structure. Interfaces external to the structure are also identified in a flexible format. In this book the emphasis is on how to represent information germane to problem solving – NOT on how to create solutions to problems (in general). Representation considerations dominate this paper.

Section 2 of this paper presents a detailed definition of the N^2 Chart characteristics, techniques, and format variations. Section 3 provides example applications of the N^2 Chart to interface tabulation, definition, design, analysis and description activities. Additional examples are also provided to illustrate the usage of the N^2 Chart in operational, planning and schedule analysis tasks. Many of the examples presented in these sections have been extracted from actual N^2 Charts used in various TRW proposals and presentations.

Sections 4 and 5 of this paper provide two detailed examples of the utilization of the N^2 Chart techniques for interface problem solving and overall system design activities. Section 6 presents the conclusion of the paper with respect to the application of N^2 Chart techniques.

The reader must be reminded, however, that the N^2 Chart is only a tool for interface definition and not an automatic solution to the problems at hand. The usage of the N^2 Chart gains benefits only if the user is diligent and methodical in his definition effort. The N^2 Chart has the potential of being a dangerous crutch which, if used improperly, conveys the feeling of user understanding to the reviewer who does not spend the energy to comprehend and study in detail this "lay it all out" visual presentation.

The N^2 Chart technique is new and not as yet fully developed. The formats and applications contained in this paper should, therefore, not be considered as final or limiting. The reader is encouraged to consider applications and formats not defined herein as an aid in the solution of his individual problem.

2. DEFINITION

2.1 GENERAL

The N^2 Chart provides a structured method for the definition of functional interactions and interfaces. The chart itself is a graphical presentation of all of the functions within a system (subsystem, task, etc.), together with the one-way interactions between each of these functions ordered in a fixed coordinate matrix format. The chart gets its name from the fact that for N functions there are N squared intersections or squares on the diagram, each of which may contain a function or function interface. The number of possible interfaces for the system is equal to $N^2 - N$, where N is the number of functions within the system. Since both functions and function interfaces occupy a square of the diagram, the total number of squares graphically illustrated is equal to the square of the number of functions involved.

Figure 2-1 illustrates a simplified N^2 Chart which contains all system functions (F_1 through F_4) on the diagonal axis and all system internal function interfaces in the remaining matrix locations ($N^2 - N$, where N is a 4, is equal to 12). Each interface square (dotted line) represents a one-way interface between two internal functions. The square labeled $F_1 \rightarrow F_4$, for example, represents the one-way interface between function 1 (output) and function 2 (input). All function outputs are defined in the squares which are in the horizontal row of the function, while all function inputs are defined in the squares which are in the vertical column of the function. External inputs and outputs are defined on the top and bottom areas and the side areas respectively. The system illustrated in Figure 2-1 has two external inputs (to F_1 and F_4) and two external outputs (from F_1 and F_4). One of the primary purposes of the N^2 Chart is to indicate where interactions and interfaces <u>do not exist</u>. In Figure 2-1, the squares below and to the right of function 3 are empty, indicating that there are no interfaces between functions F_3 and F_4. The table at the bottom of the figure defines the basic rules for the N^2 Chart.

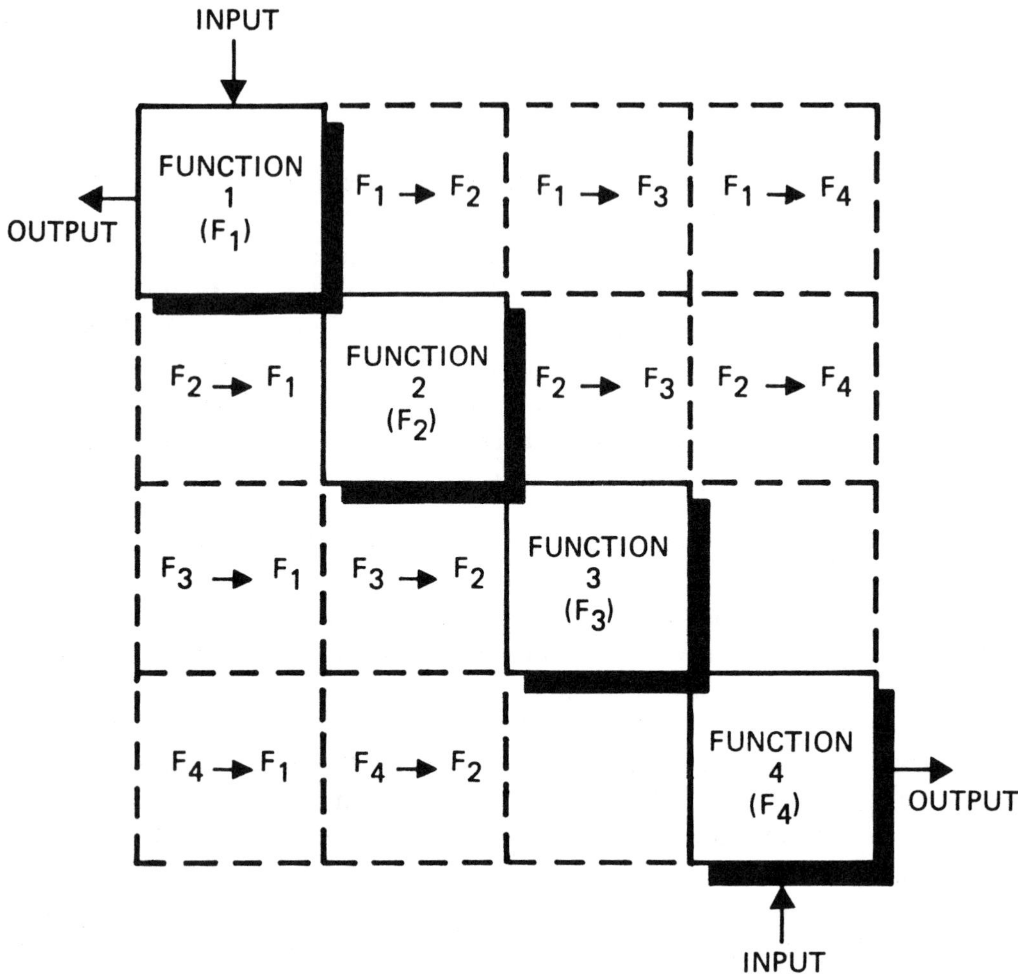

BASIC N^2 CHART RULES

- ALL FUNCTIONS ARE ON THE DIAGONAL
- ALL OUTPUTS ARE HORIZONTAL (LEFT OR RIGHT)
- ALL INPUTS ARE VERTICAL (UP OR DOWN)
- ALL NON-FUNCTION SQUARES DEFINE ONE-WAY INTERFACES BETWEEN THE ASSOCIATED FUNCTIONS

Figure 2-1. The N^2 Chart

Figure 2-2 illustrates an N^2 Chart of the functions and interfaces defined in the associated flowchart. The N^2 Chart resulting from this translation is rather simple since the functional elements in the flowchart are, in general, time sequenced and contain simple one-way interfaces from function to function. It can be observed from the N^2 Chart in Figure 2-2 that all inputs to functions F_2, F_3 and F_4 come from F_1, while all outputs from these functions go to F_5 which provides the eventual system or module output. Note that the chart dramatizes the interface simplicity by the intentional deletion of all other possible interfunction interfaces. Note also that the actual interface box can be used to tabulate the type of interface (or, in this case, action) which is provided to each of the associated functions ($<, >, =$).

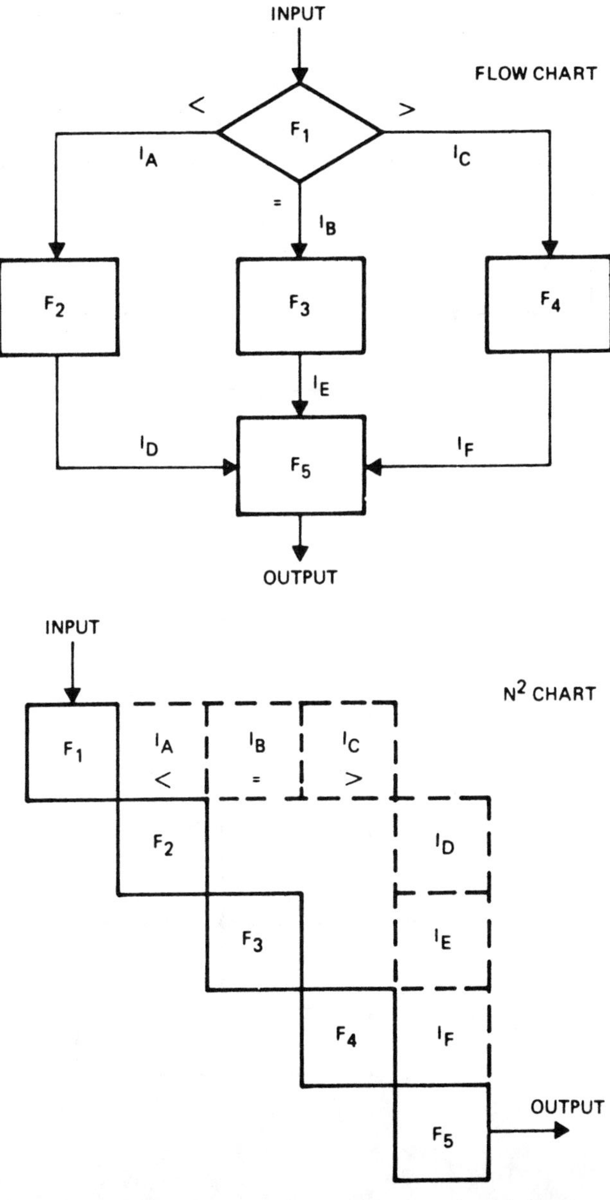

Figure 2-2. The N^2 Chart and the Flowchart

Figure 2–3 illustrates the correlation between the N^2 Chart and a simple functional block diagram. The N^2 Chart in the figure delineates all of the system functions and interfaces in an equally weighted manner, such that even the dual interface (I_B) is given appropriate definition emphasis. The N^2 Chart technique therefore places greater emphasis on definition consistency, since even the minor feedback or acknowledged interface paths must be exposed at the higher system levels. A system level block diagram may not show the minor "reverse" interfaces (such as may exist between 3 and 1 of the figure) for the sake of clarity, whereas the system level N^2 Chart demands that this interface be defined (i.e., fill in the interface box in the lower lefthand corner of the matrix).

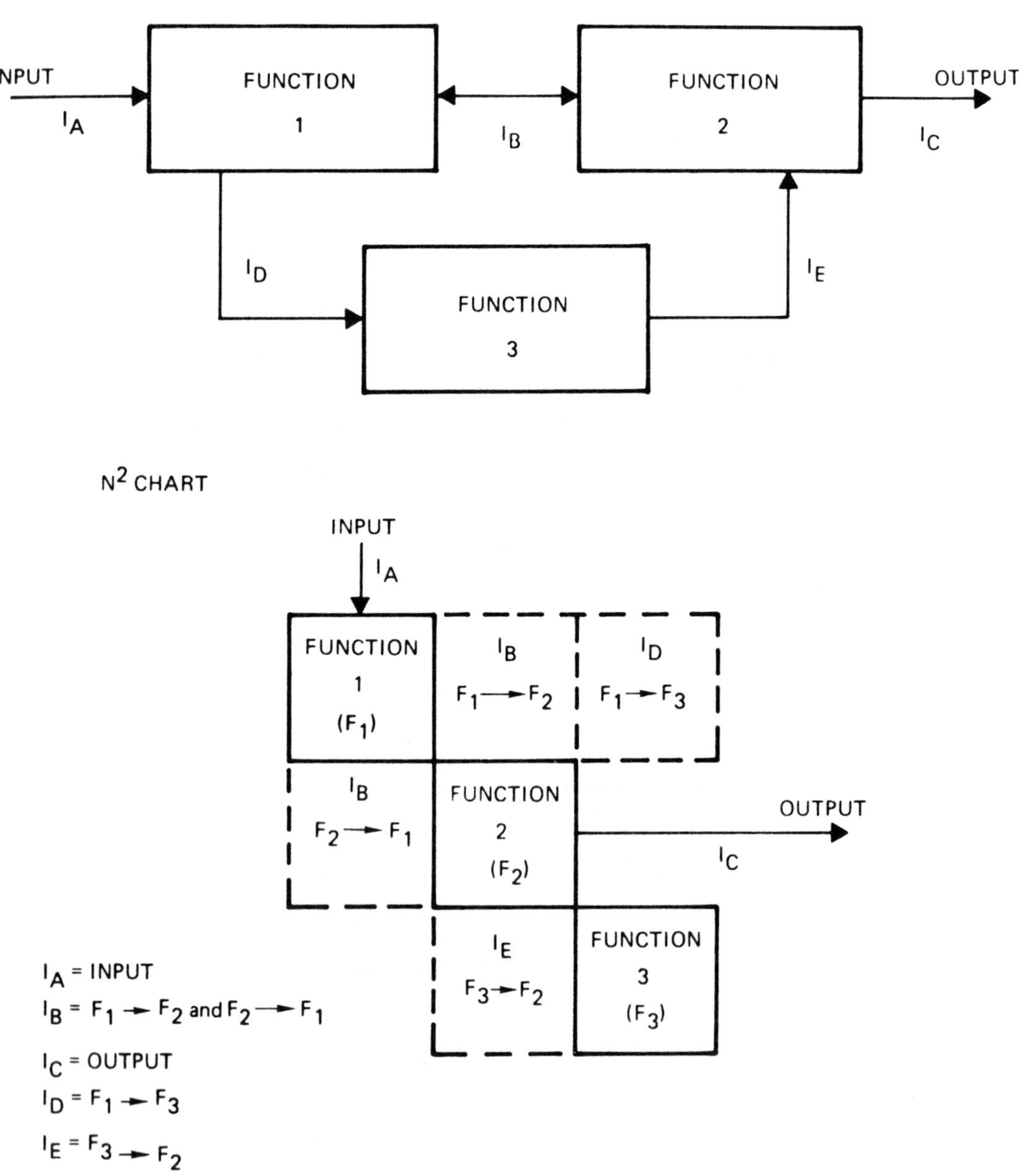

Figure 2–3. The N^2 Chart and the Block Diagram

Figure 2-3 also illustrates the fact that external interfaces may occur anywhere in the matrix and are not limited to the corner function boxes. Feedback and/or control/monitor loops (interface I_B in Figure 2-3) are emphasized in the N^2 Chart since the resultant return interfaces ($F_2 \rightarrow F_1$ in Figure 2-3) are illustrated to the left or bottom of the functions involved instead of the normal right or above positions

Figure 2-4 shows the correlation between the N^2 Chart and a simple PERT activity network. This example N^2 Chart immediately exposes the close relationship between tasks 1 and 2 (interfaces I_A and I_B fill in the quadrant around the task boxes) and the more independent relationship of task 3 (no feedback interface relationship). It is clear from the N^2 Chart that task 3 is dependent only on the completion of tasks 1 and 2 (I_D and I_E) and bears no complex relationship to either task. One of the advantages of the N^2 Chart is that I_D, for example, can define only the interfaces required for task 3 and does not necessarily assume that all of task 2 is completed (i.e., external document delivered).

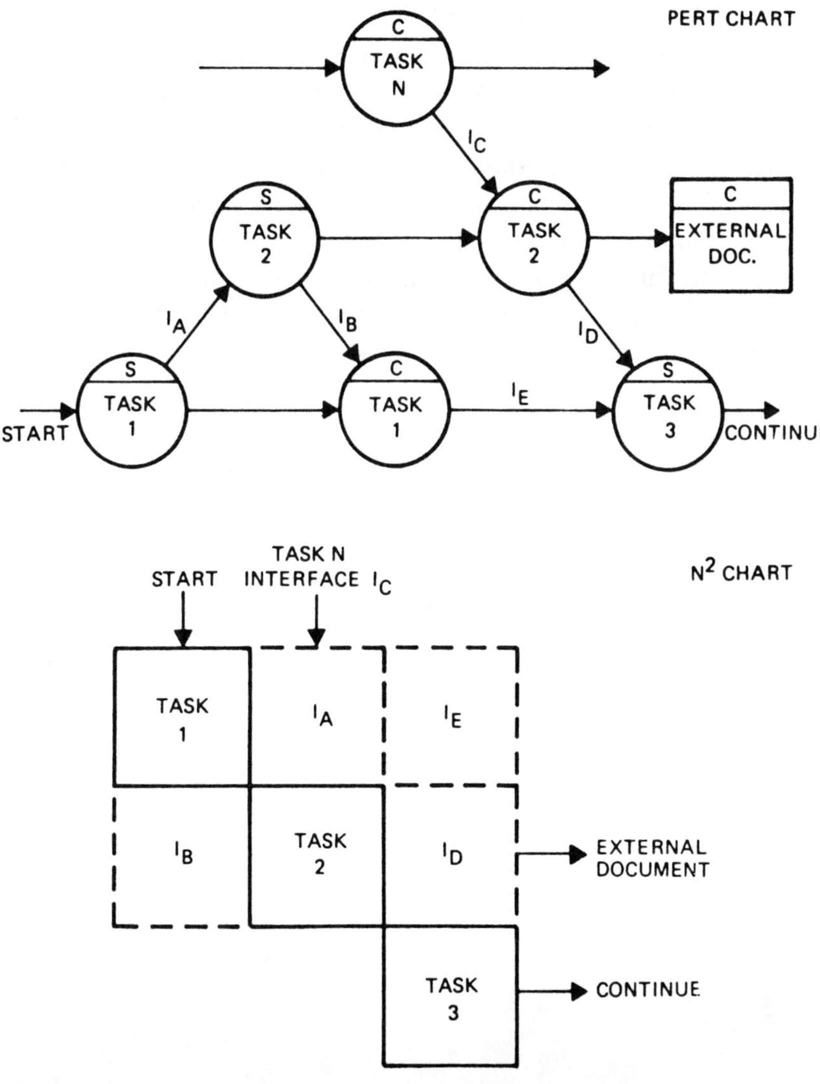

Figure 2-4. The N^2 Chart and the PERT Chart

Let us consider, as an example, that task 2 (Figure 2-4) is the development of a system specification and that task 3 is the definition of site facility requirements. Interface I_D would then define only the facility-related requirements which would be needed to start the facility definition activities. Task 3 could therefore start when these sections were approved (together with the inputs required from task 1) and would not be held pending the approval of insignificant, unrelated performance parameters which would have no effect on the facility definition activity.

Figure 2-5 shows the correlation between the N^2 Chart and a Gantt chart or program schedule. The N^2 Chart has the advantage of being able to define the external inputs required (vertical inputs above the matrix on the figure) and the external outputs provided (CDRLs on the right side and activities on the left side of Figure 2-5) in addition to providing a structured tool for the definition of all detailed task interrelationships (I_1 thru I_{12} on Figure 2-5). This example also serves to point out the external interface definition capability of the N^2 Chart even though the bottom of the matrix (external inputs) was not used.

Interface definition for I_1 through I_{12} of Figure 2-5 can be accomplished in an effective manner when using the N^2 Chart instead of a normal schedule. The operational concept definition activity, for example, has three distinct outputs in addition to the CDRL deliverable document output. Related activities need not be held up until the total document is approved and released. These activities, on the contrary, can start as soon as the task interface requirements have been met (I_1 for system specification, I_2 for conceptual design, and I_3 for detail design). The use of this technique would greatly expedite program schedule efficiency by identifying the critical interfacing element requirements instead of the CDRL product deliverable dates. Work schedules and program costs could be more effectively controlled by employing the N^2 Chart techniques.

SCHEDULE

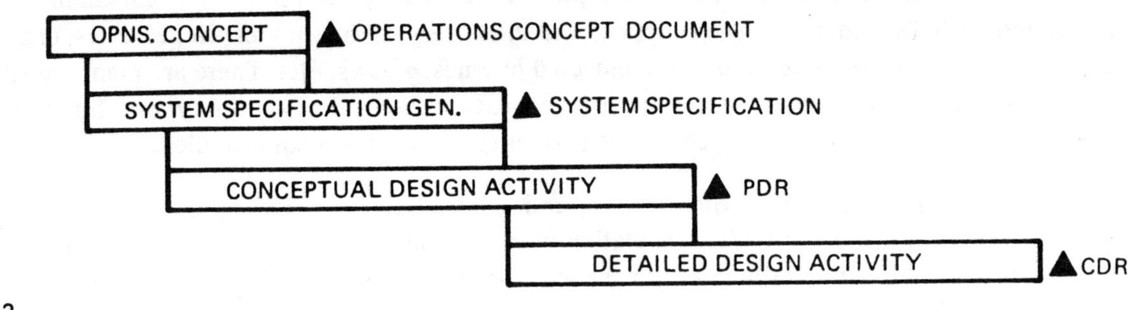

N^2 CHART

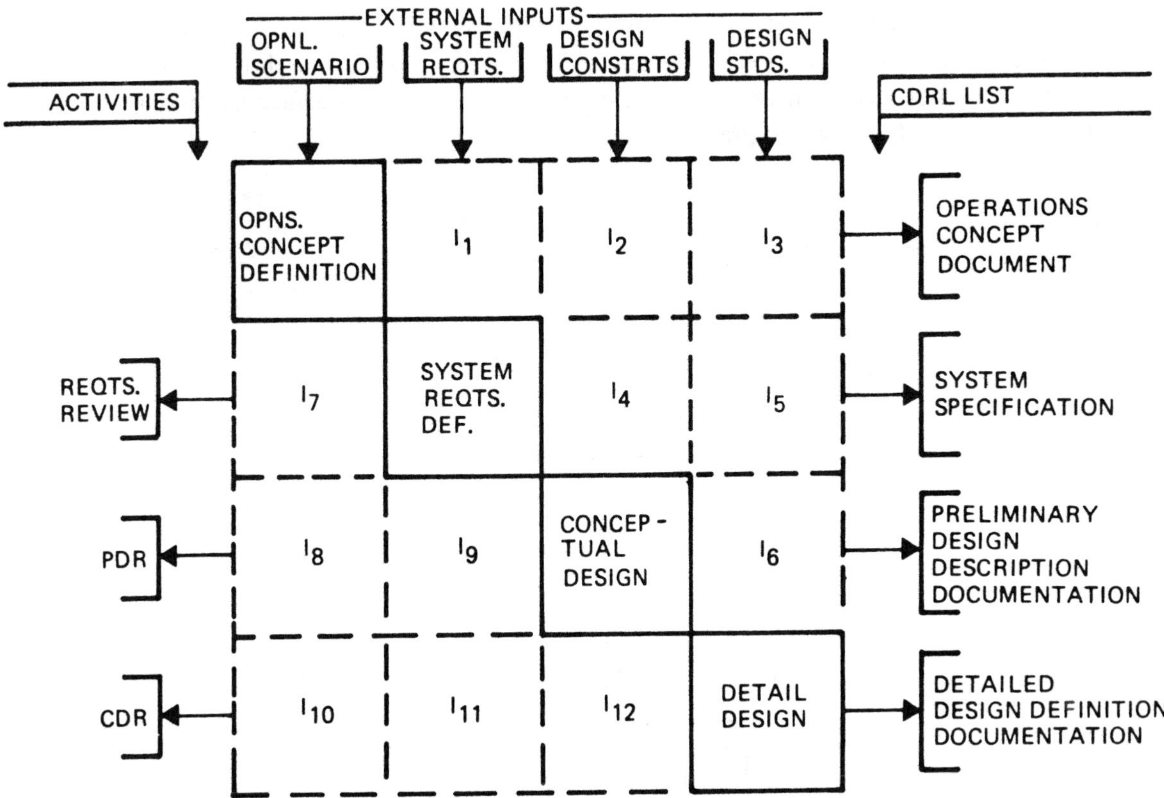

Figure 2-5. The N^2 Chart and the Schedule

2.2 FORMATS

The only rigid format requirements associated with using the N^2 Chart are that the functions occupy the center diagonal boxes, the output interfaces are placed in the horizontal row associated with the function, and the input interfaces are placed in the vertical column associated with the function. The functions and interfaces can be squares, circles, lines, etc., and may be of a stand-alone nature or connected by lines, arrows, etc. There are many possible variations of N^2 Chart formats, each having its advantages depending on the type of functions being defined, the purpose of the chart, the system type, and the reading audience.

Figure 2-6 illustrates the "square block" and "circle" formats. The square block format is the most useful tool for interface tabulation purposes, since the individual interface characteristics may be tabulated within each of the interface block figures. This format is, however, the most visually confusing to the casual reader since there is no simple visual indication of data flow. The circle format provides a more communicative picture of the interface characteristics but does not allow structured space for individual interface comments or notes. The circle format is very useful for detailed interface definition, wherein each numbered circle refers the reader to a detailed interface listing. The chart and list approach is a handy tool during the initial definition phases, since minor corrections to the interface list text do not affect the actual N^2 Chart visual presentation.

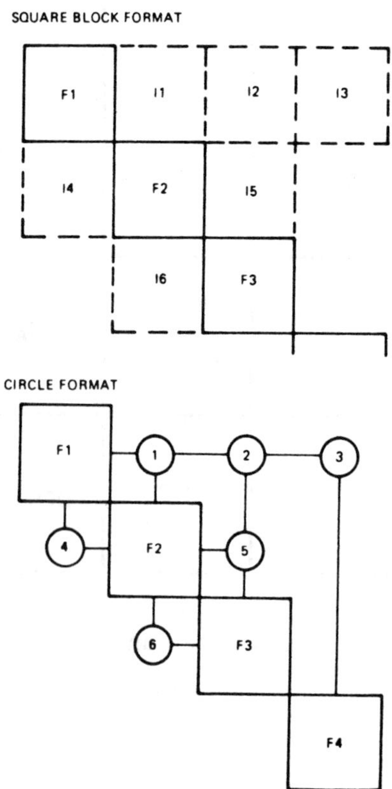

Figure 2–6. N^2 Chart Block and Circle Format

Figure 2-7 illustrates the "arrow" and "circle arrow" formats which provide a clearer visual presentation of interface direction and flow. These format types have been the most useful in the presentation of higher-level design descriptions to a general audience. Figures 2-8 and 2-9 show other possible variations to the N^2 Chart format. The actual format selected for any particular presentation or document depends on various factors, some of which are summarized below:

- Type of audience
- Level of detail required
- Points to be communicated
- Reproduction method
- Update requirements
- Presentation time
- Purpose
- Type of system
- Level of audience
- Chart size constraints
- Type of functions charted
- Presentation space

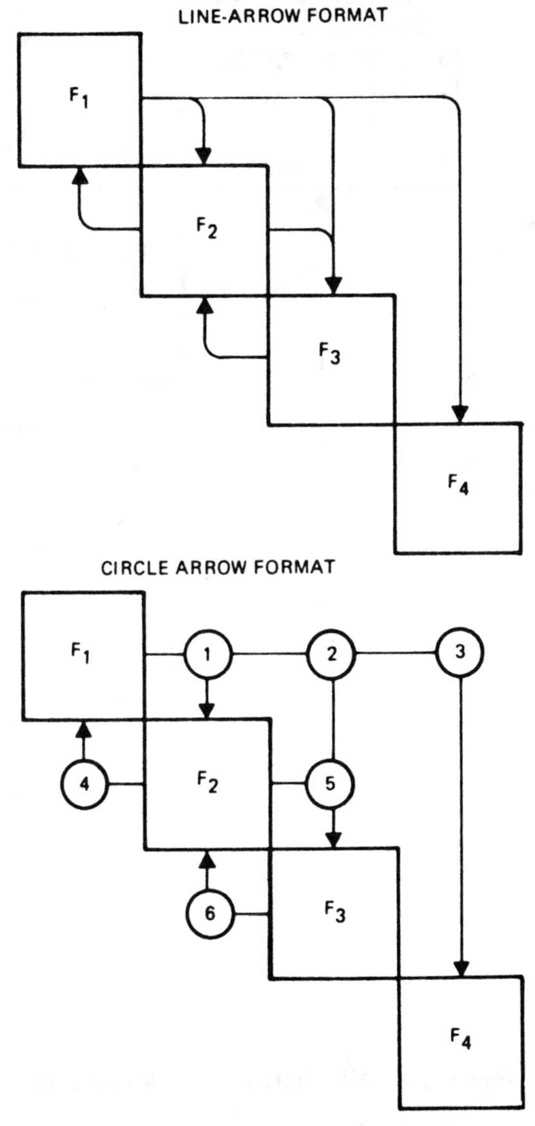

Figure 2-7. N^2 Chart Arrow Formats

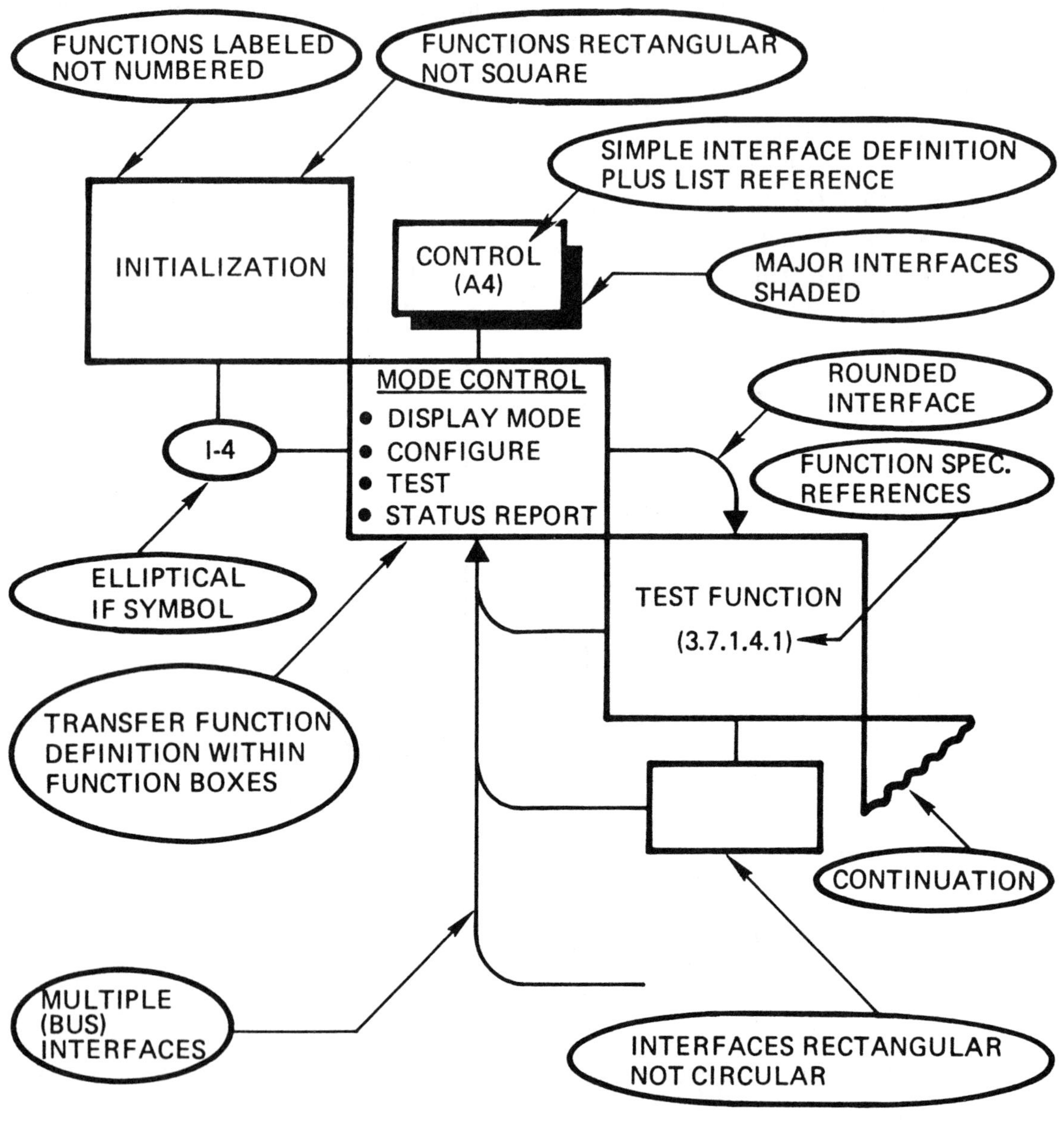

Figure 2-8. N^2 Chart Format Variations

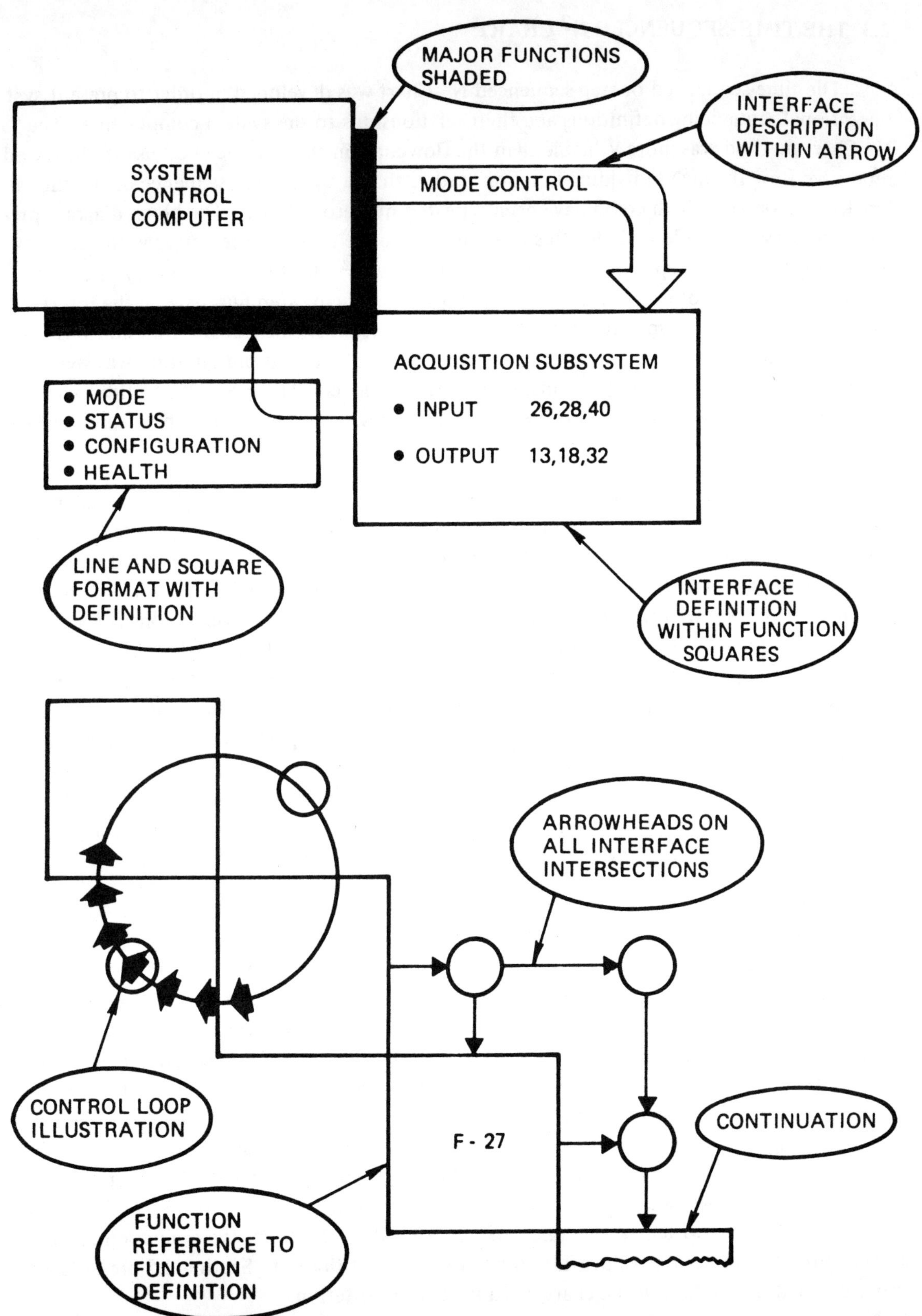

Figure 2-9. N^2 Chart Format Variations (Continued)

2.3 THE TIME-SEQUENCED N^2 CHART

The time-sequenced or step-sequenced N^2 Chart was developed in order to present system operational sequencing definitions and their relationships to the system components. The N^2 Chart method was more valuable than the flowchart in this instance because it illustrated repetitive flow through individual functions rather than a time-linear sequence of functional blocks, any one of which could have been repeated numerous times. The block diagram presentation was also inadequate for this task since there are no structured areas within a block diagram for time- or step-sequence connotations. The N^2 Chart method employed consisted of defining a sequence of events for a given operation by placing step numbers on the interfacing circles and defining the specific interface transfers rather than the transfer function variations at each step in the process. In one specific application, the resultant presentation was well received and thoroughly understood by the majority of the audience. The presentation time was therefore spent on discussing the real problems instead of trying to understand the meaning of the charts.

The presentation was constructed using viewgraphs to explain the high-level system components and operational functions to a rather general audience. The presentation started with the normal bullet charts and block diagrams. The system was then presented in an N^2 Chart fashion with all interfaces labeled and briefly explained. A series of charts was then presented which showed the progression of each of the major system operations through the system components as illustrated on the basic system N^2 Chart. Each of these charts dealt with a specific operation such as initialization, reconfiguration, test, function performance, etc. Each chart emphasized the interfaces involved and all but blanked out all other elements of the system. Step sequence notes were associated with each pertinent interface block (circle) in a space-random manner synchronous with the time or sequence relationships. Discussions were then held on specific operations with function participation in the design. Total emphasis was placed on the problems at hand since everyone in the room had a common clearly-defined basis for system understanding.

Figure 2-10 is an example of the kind of N^2 Chart used in this presentation. The figure shows the major system functions on the diagonal axis and the pertinent interfaces as circles in the matrix area. The interface points are not detailed or numbered in the figure since the definition of each interface was accomplished at the start of the presentation. The sequencing of events (interface functions in this case) is portrayed by a set of step numbers (and definitions) which are related to each individual interface. Each individual system operation (test, in the example) is described in toto on each successive chart (including all functions and interfaces involved). The example chart explains that the first two steps in the process are involved with the commanded setup and verification response for the particular test to be conducted. This initial action is then followed by the actual test configuration and mode setup (steps 3 and 4). Steps 5 through 7 then activate the test stimulus, which is monitored during steps 8 and 9 with detail status being reported as a function of step 10. Step 11 reports the evaluation results to the requestor while step 12 provides for termination of the test. Section 3.5 presents a more detailed illustration of the charts used in this presentation.

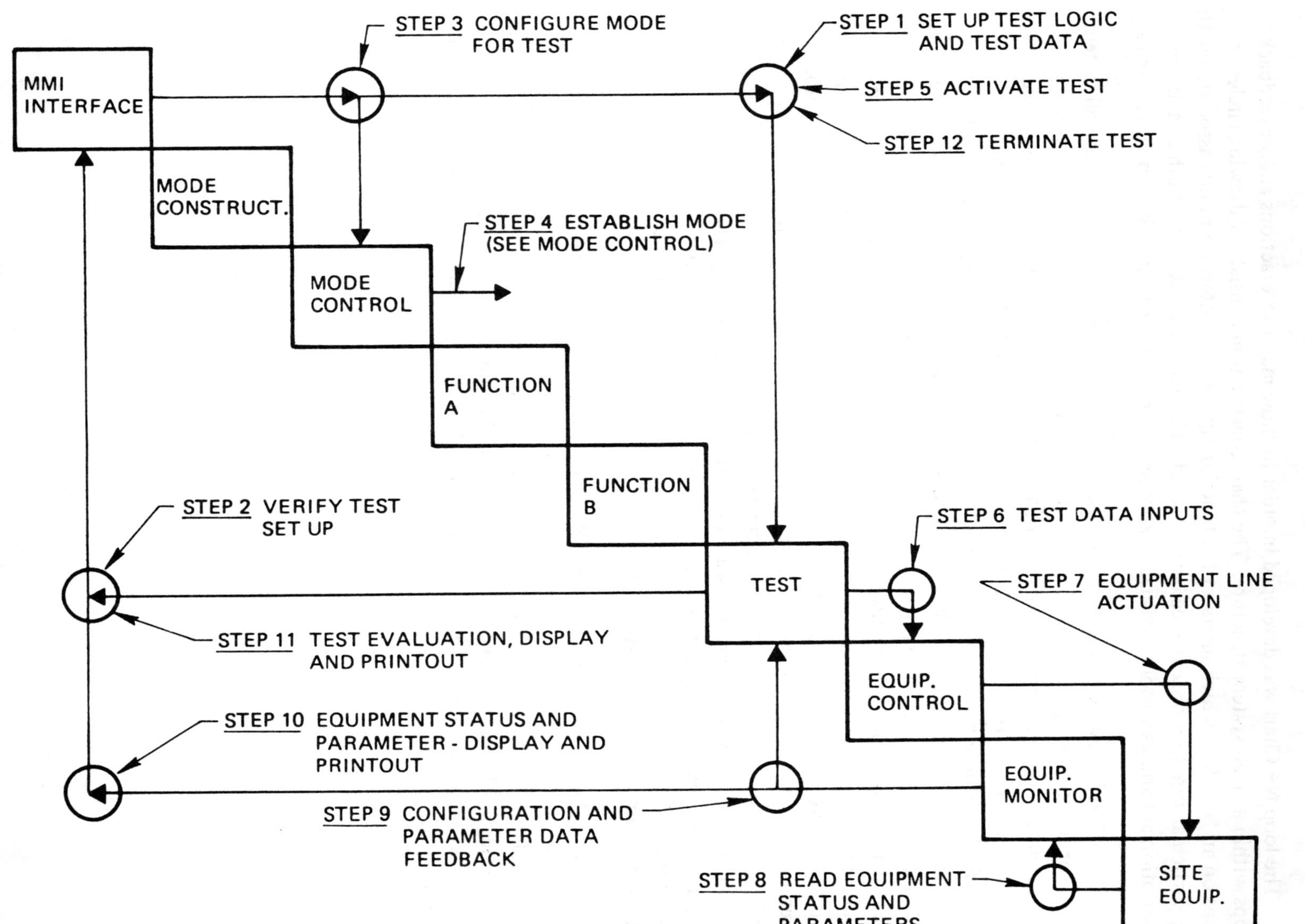

Figure 2-10. Example Step-sequenced N^2 Chart

2.4 THE LOOP N^2 CHART

The loop N^2 Chart was developed in order to show major interactions and/or feedback loops within a given system structure. The chart construction consists of drawing circles or loops on an N^2 Chart which intersect the function squares and interface points associated with the particular function or sequence being studied. This technique is useful both as a design description aid and as a tool for visually exposing control and/or feedback loop design conflicts.

Figure 2-11 shows an example of the usage of the loop N^2 Chart to show overall system control or function loop paths to a high-level general audience. The figure in this example pointed out the five major control loops and their major function interfaces. The mode construction loop, for example, illustrated the fact that only the MMI (Man Machine Interface) and mode construction functions were involved. It was further explained that this loop was active only in off-line time periods and had no real-time interfaces or conflicts with the other system control functions. The operator and automatic control loop illustration helped to explain the multistep interaction between the operator and the site equipment. This loop drawing pointed out the fact that the operator had no direct communication with the site equipment for control functions. It also pointed out that there was, however, a direct monitor loop which provided unprocessed equipment status and monitor information to the MMI function which was not dependent on most of the remaining system software. (The equipment monitor function was the only additional software required for this interface.) The general control loop illustrations of this drawing therefore aided in the general understanding of the system control architecture. An equivalent simplified illustration would be difficult to construct using either a block diagram or flowchart basic format.

Figure 2-12 shows an example loop N^2 Chart which was used as an aid in analyzing a particular system for control function conflicts. The multiple control loops intersecting the input interface and input processing functions were determined to be the major design problem in this example. These loops were all operational in the same time phase and all could simultaneously attempt to control the same parameters. The N^2 Chart served as an efficient visual aid in illustrating this control problem.

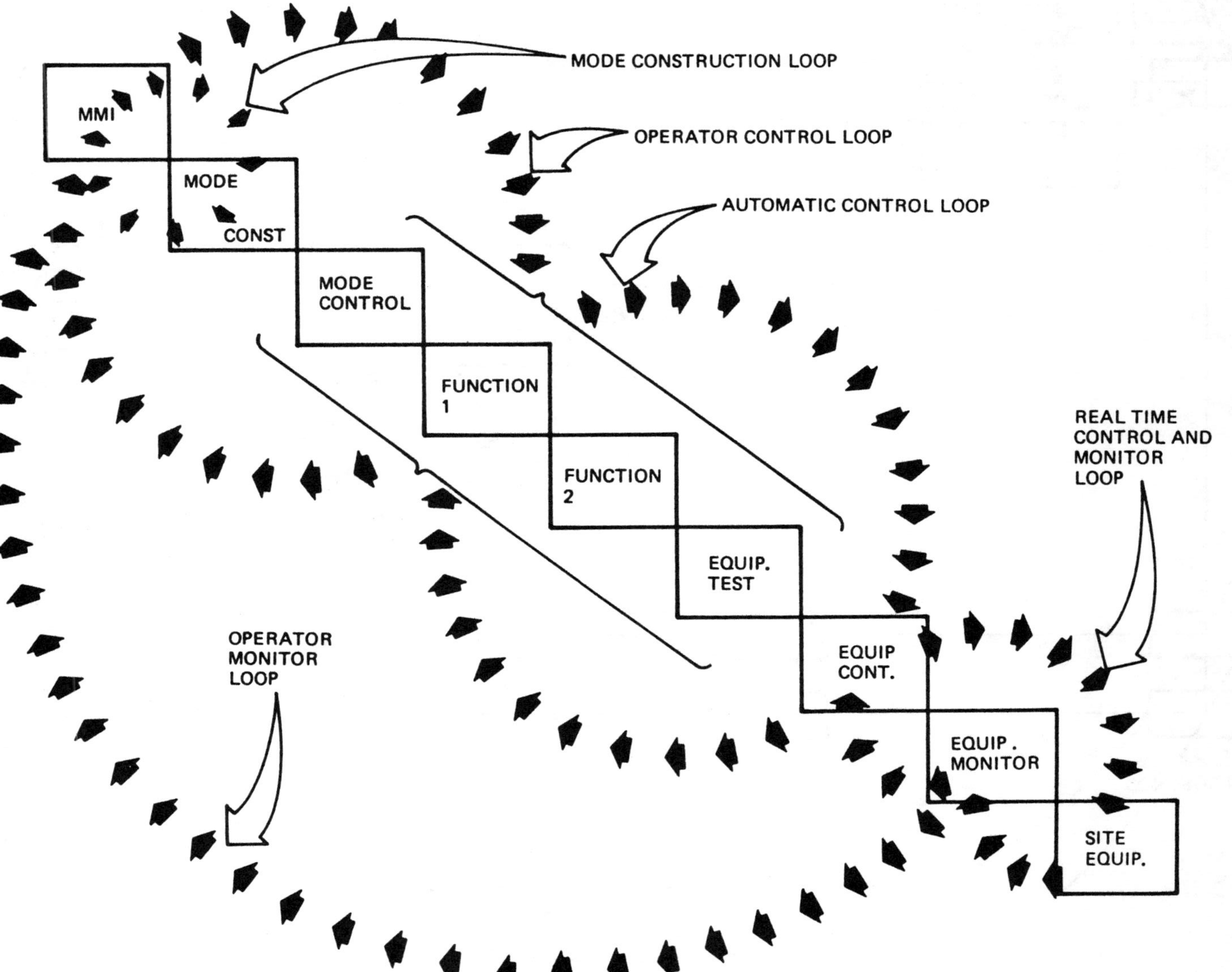

Figure 2-11. Example Loop N^2 Chart (Design Description)

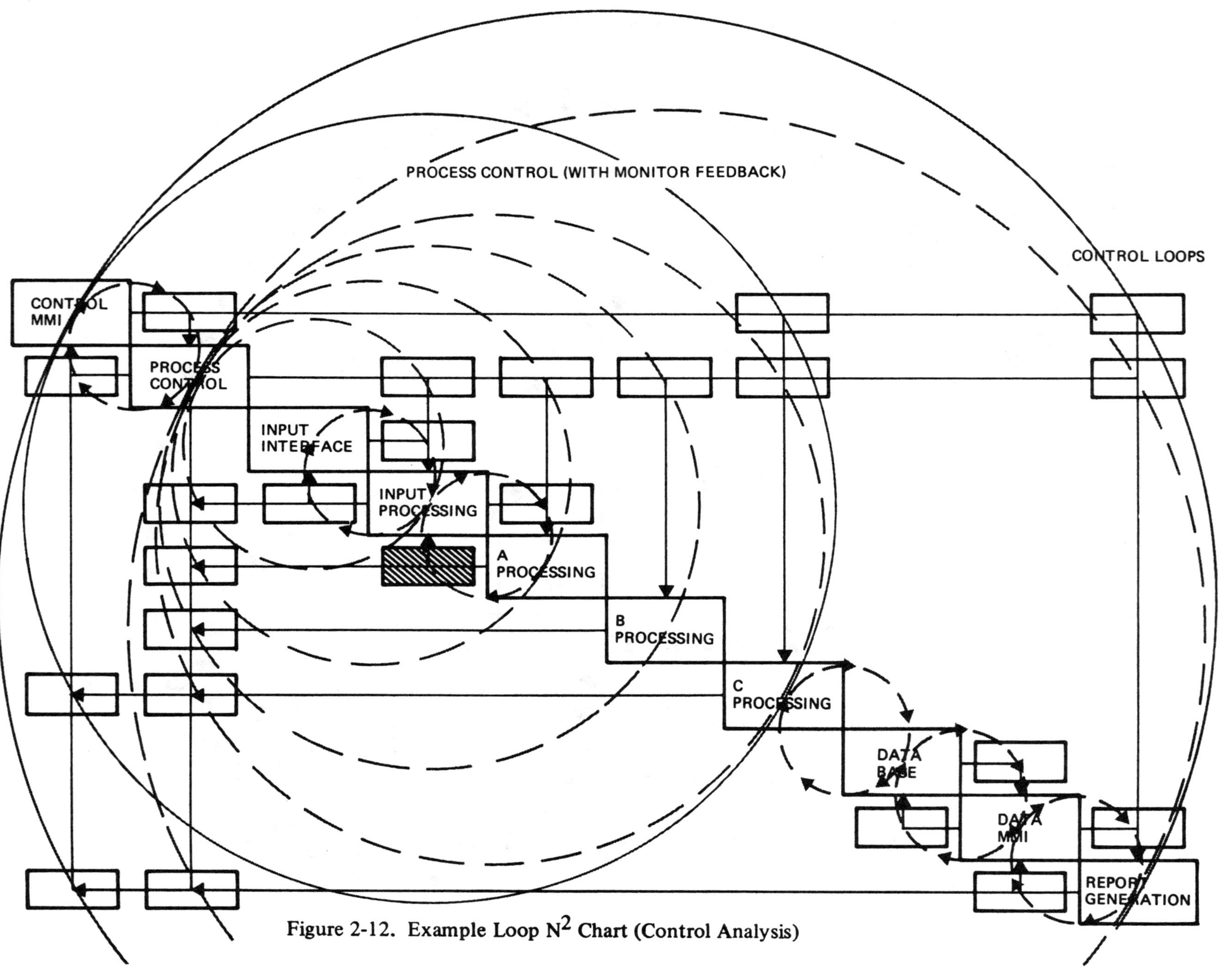

Figure 2-12. Example Loop N^2 Chart (Control Analysis)

2.5 WHAT THE N^2 CHART SHOWS

The N^2 Chart provides a visual presentation which differs from other visual presentation formats in that it exaggerates interfaces and underplays the transfer function information. The primary intelligence visually communicated by the chart is therefore concerned with interfaces and interrelationships between the functions involved. The N^2 Chart, first of all, shows all interface relationships to the level of detail desired (i.e., can be completely detailed as in the circle list format). The chart also exaggerates all noninterface intersections, thereby forcing an extra degree of thought for all "first level" noninterfacing relationships. External interfaces are also magnified by the chart technique. This magnification causes the system definer to reevaluate and fortify his position with regard to the true external interfaces required. The following paragraphs point out some primary characteristics to look for when examining an N^2 Chart. These examples are by no means all inclusive nor accurate for any given system application. They are merely discussed to awaken your visual perception capabilities.

Figure 2–13 is an illustration of the N^2 Chart used in the initial design of the TIPS system (Telemetry Integrated Processing System). The chart (simplified for this paper) shows the basic system components (within the dotted lines), together with the major external system functions and interfaces. The chart illustrates that the major signal flow is from left to right with the two primary inputs originating at the TDVS and VSM functions, while the two primary outputs are delivered to the RANGE SAFE and USER functions. The CONT function obviously provides some overall system control task, with switching control at the VSM (Video Switch Matrix), and TIPS control at the NBP (Near real-time Batch Processor). Note that the chart exposes the lack of completeness of this control task. The CONT function, for example, has no interface (and therefore no control) with the RANGE SAFE function and the TDVS function (test simulator). The CONT function additionally has no control output to the USER function, while the USER function seems to have a control loop interface with the TIPS system via the NBP function. The control processing within the TIPS system is also illustrated in a hierarchial implementation fashion with the TPP or QLSD functions exercising control over the PSD and APD functions as a result of higher-level direction from the NBP function. This seemingly inconsistent control philosophy is accurate and does meet the system requirements. The N^2 Chart, however, served to efficiently illustrate this design approach. Note also that the chart identifies the TPP and the QLSD functions as the main or critical functions within the TIPS system due to their extensive interface interactions.

Figure 2–14A illustrates an overly complex interface definition approach since functions F_5, F_6, and F_7 have a bidirectional interface with all of the other functions within the system. This system, if implemented, would be almost impossible to define let alone design and test. Figure 2–14B, on the other hand, describes a rather straightforward system design with the exception of the interfaces involved with function F_{13}. This design could be thoroughly adequate for any given system. The N^2 Chart, however, points out this multiple interface characteristic and thereby exposes F_{13} as the critical element of the system in terms of system interface definition, design and test difficulty.

Figure 2–15A illustrates the missing interface analysis aspect of the N^2 Chart. The chart forces a greater degree of thought concerning feedback loop interfaces. The designer of Figure 2–15A, for example, spends some time at reassuring himself that there is really no "mirror image"

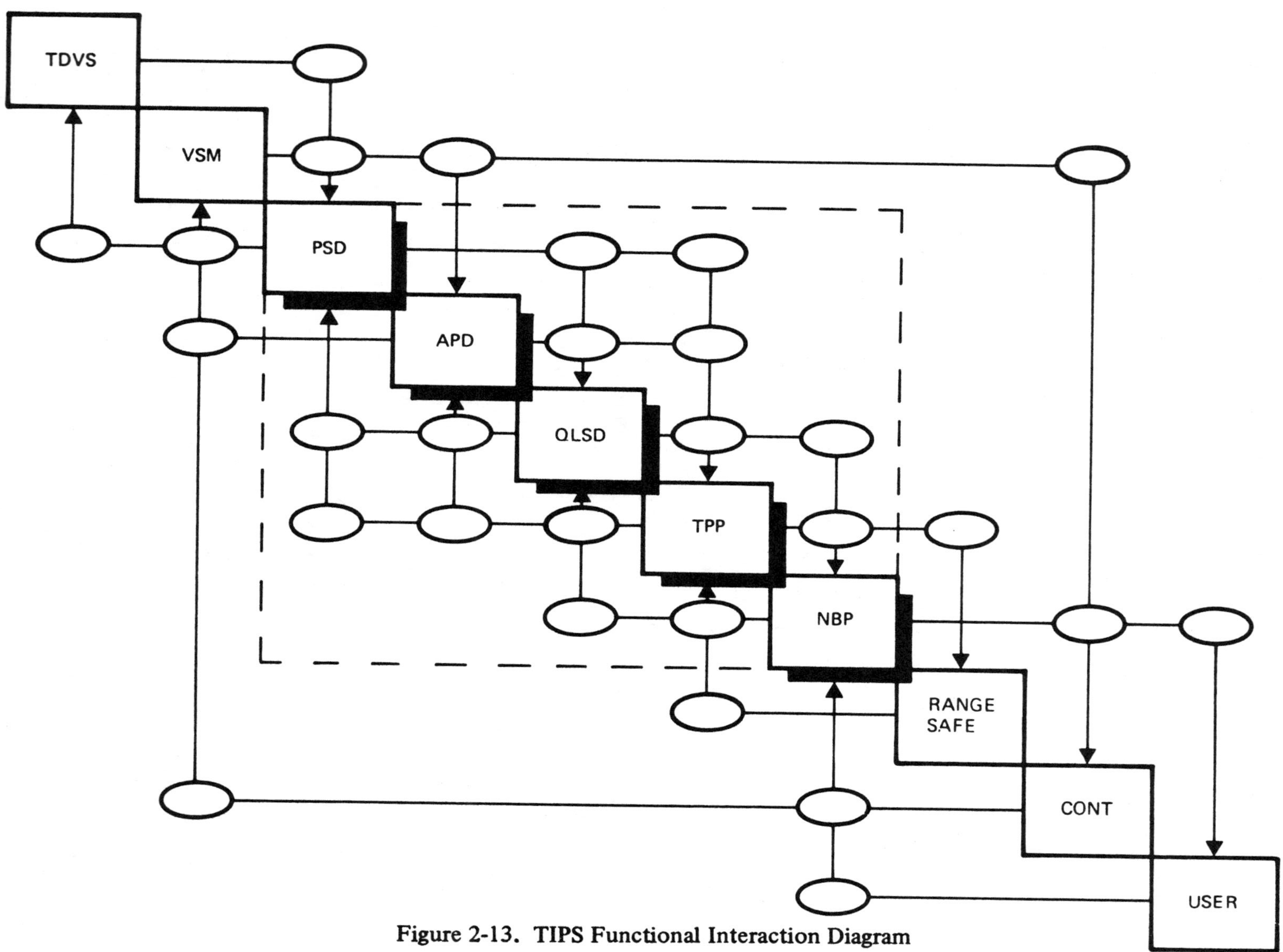

Figure 2-13. TIPS Functional Interaction Diagram

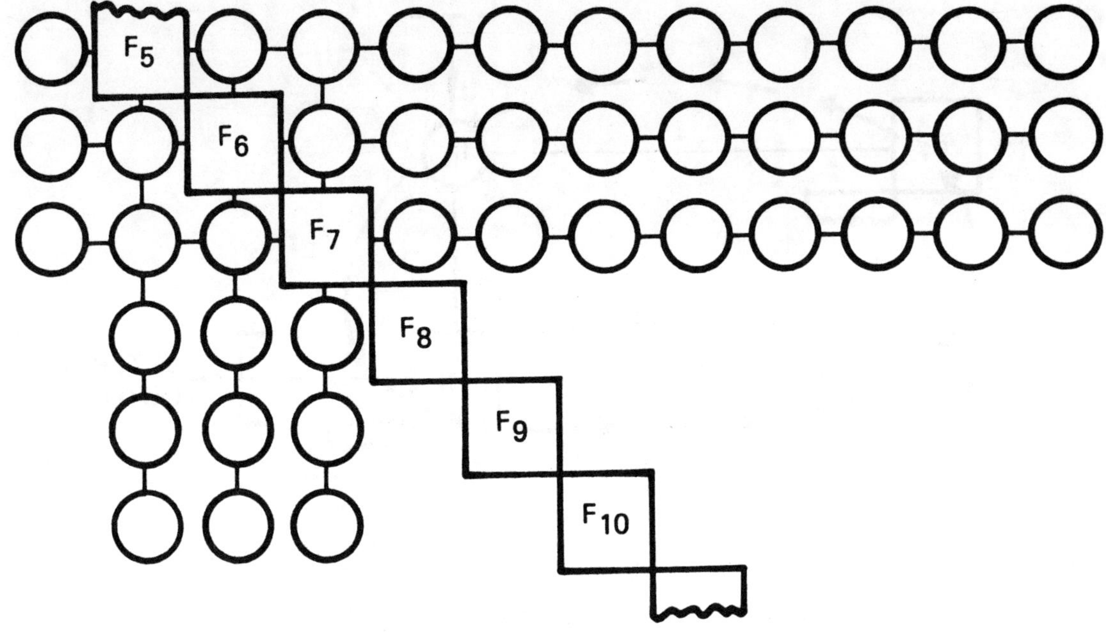

Figure 2-14A. Overly Complex Interfaces

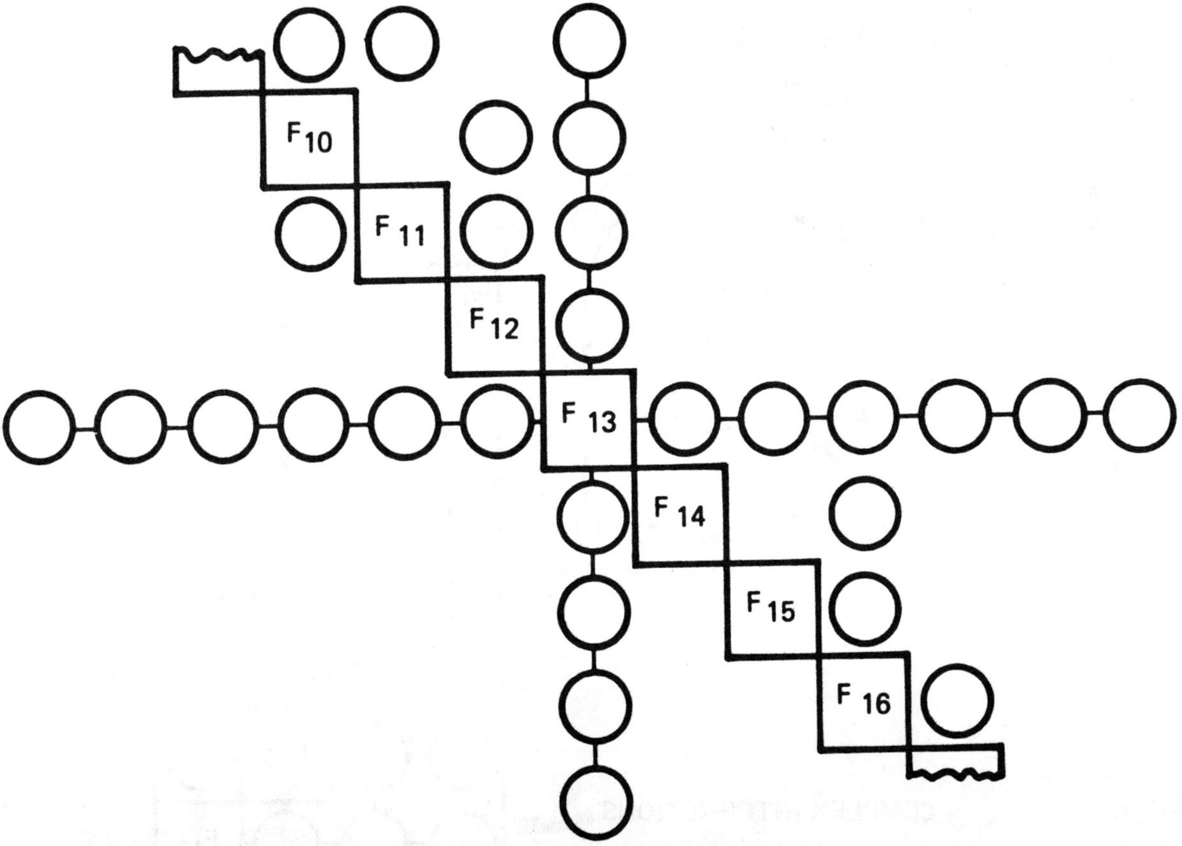

Figure 2-14B. Critical Element Illustration

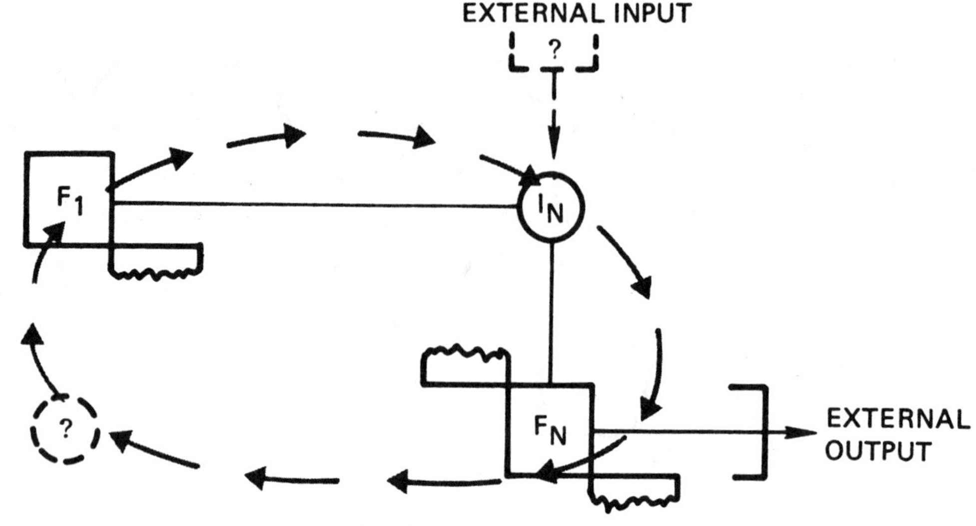

Figure 2-15A. Missing Interface Illustration

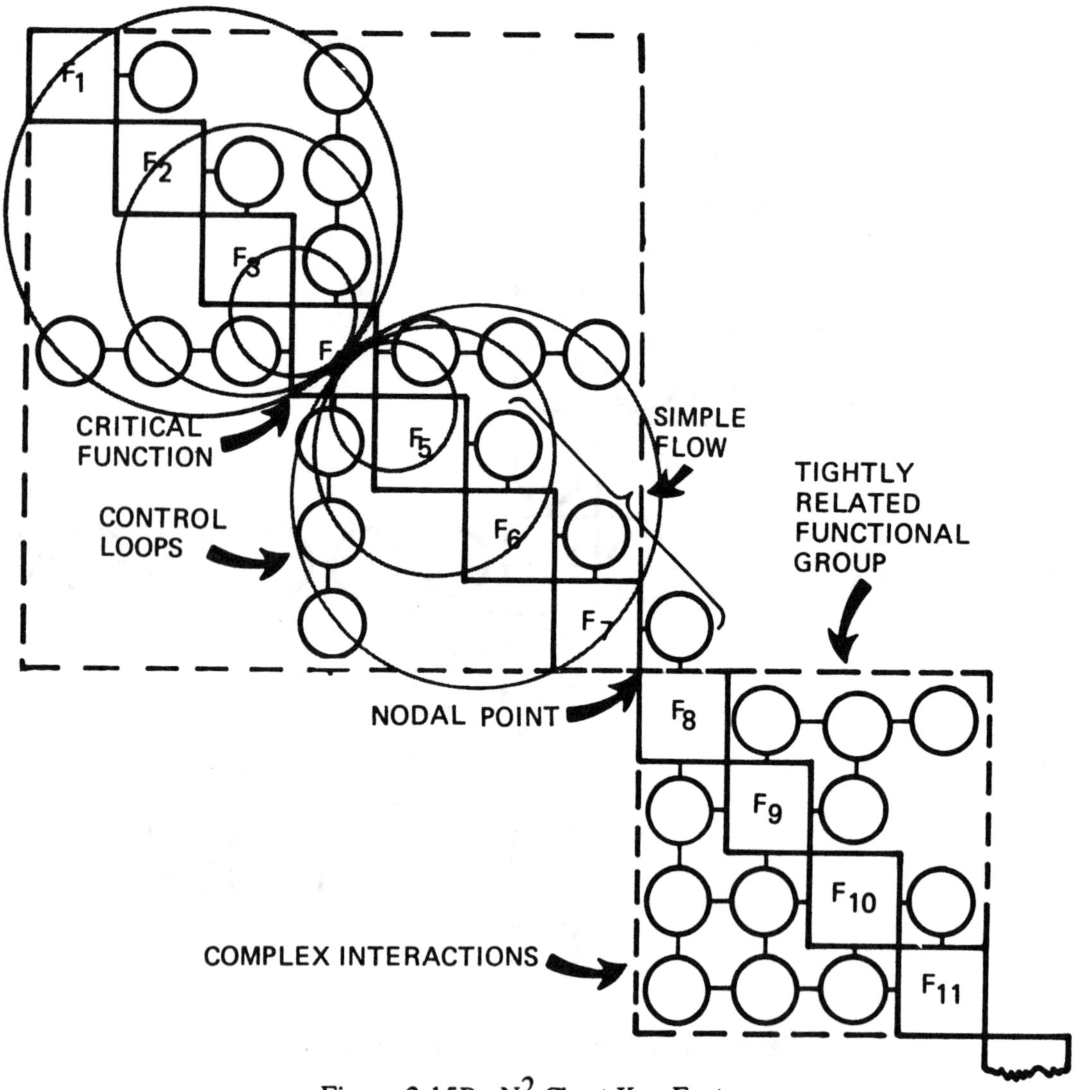

CRITICAL FUNCTION
CONTROL LOOPS
SIMPLE FLOW
TIGHTLY RELATED FUNCTIONAL GROUP
NODAL POINT
COMPLEX INTERACTIONS
F_1 F_2 F_3 F_4 F_5 F_6 F_7 F_8 F_9 F_{10} F_{11}

Figure 2-15B. N^2 Chart Key Features

or return loop feedback path corresponding to interface I_N. External input and output intersections are also double checked with this approach to assure that any asymmetry of interface intersections has been thoroughly justified. The external interface example is particularly applicable to schedule and/or activity charts, where external input data definition is extremely important to the definition of the task or work statement elements.

Figure 2–15B points out some of the major features to look for on any given system N^2 Chart. The critical functions are immediately exposed as being those with extensive horizontal and vertical interface intersections. The simple flow paths (and therefore simple interface design items) are exaggerated due to the fact that their interfacing intersections are close to the function diagonal and are above and to the right of the function line. Control loops (if included) define the major controlling functions (F_4 in the example) and illustrate the associated functions controlled. Functional groupings with near filled-in interface intersections illustrate "tightly related" functional groups which should be collocated in the implementation design of the system. Nodal points (i.e., F_8 in Figure 2–15B) are exposed, which are candidate spots for the system division in terms of physical location, subcontractor responsibilities, and/or unit or module implementation. Complex interface interactions (i.e., bottom of Figure 2–15B) expose possible problem areas in the definition, design, integration and test activities.

Figure 2–16 illustrates the function reorganization analytic power of the N^2 Chart. The functions in Figure A were initially laid out in a block diagram format and allocated to hardware or software implementation components. An "N^2 Chart analysis" was then performed which resulted in a reorganization of the functional grouping in order to simplify the interface characteristics. The new system organization, as viewed from the N^2 Chart (Figure B), is much more straightforward and should therefore be simpler to define, control and test. The new implementation was adopted immediately since the chart also provided an extremely valuable tool for the definition of the design options involved. The resultant implementation went very well since it was more understandable by a greater number of people than the original implementation. (This is not to say that the original implementation would not have succeeded.)

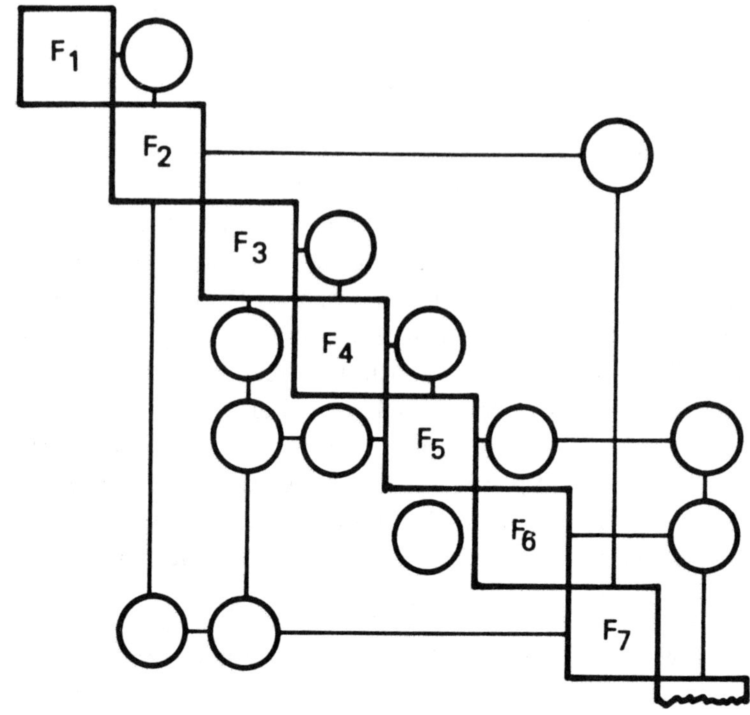

Figure 2-16A. Initial Function Organization

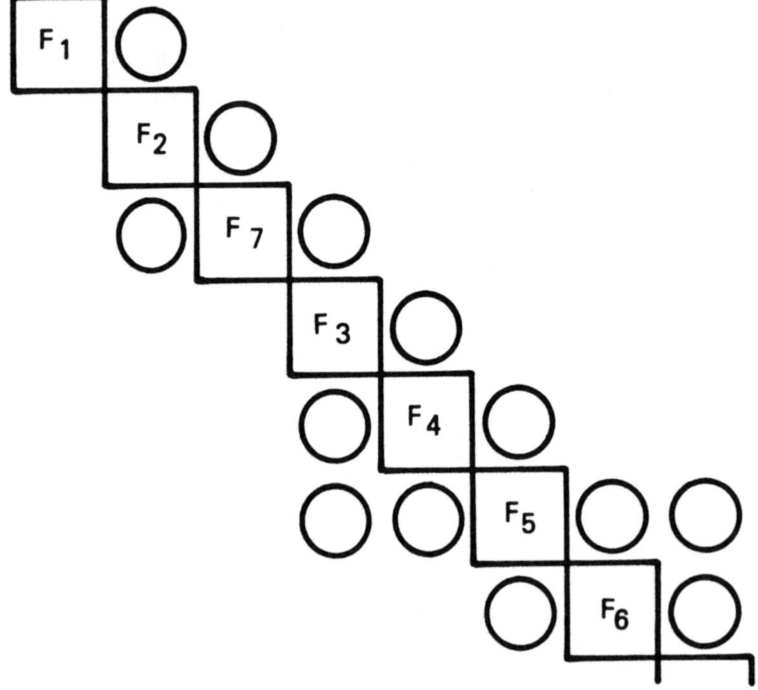

Figure 2-16B. Final Function Organization

The N^2 Chart can also be a helpful tool in functionally grouping a given system into easily implementable unit or program elements. Figure 2-17 provides an example of the use of an N^2 Chart to group detailed functions into effectively implementable hardware and/or software elements. Figure 2-17A shows the result of the detailed functional analysis activity. The dotted lines around the functional groupings of this figure show the initial function collection operation. Figure 2-17B shows the final implementation functional allocation, which follows the interface minimization grouping of the previous figure.

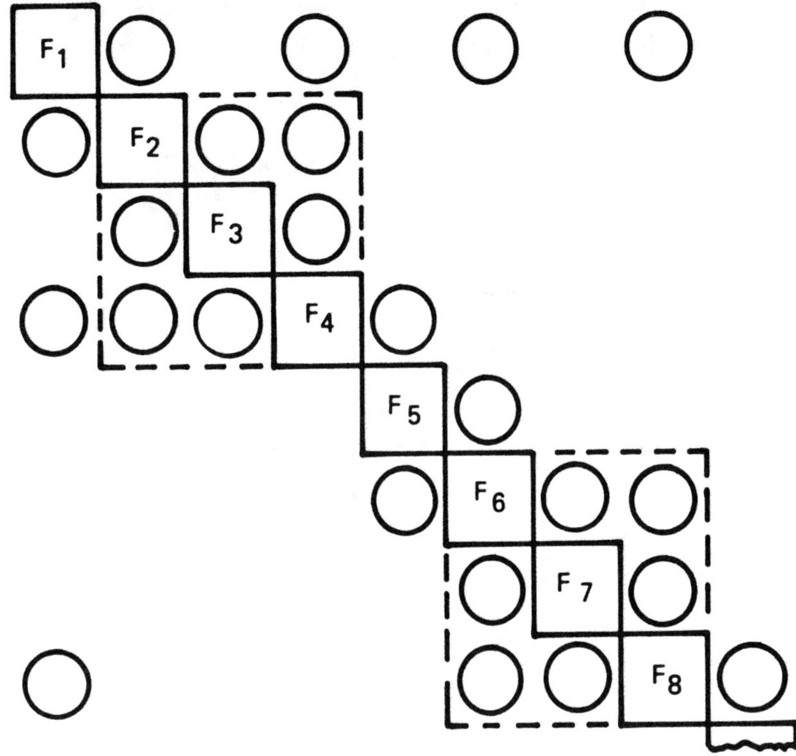

Figure 2-17A. Original Function Diagram

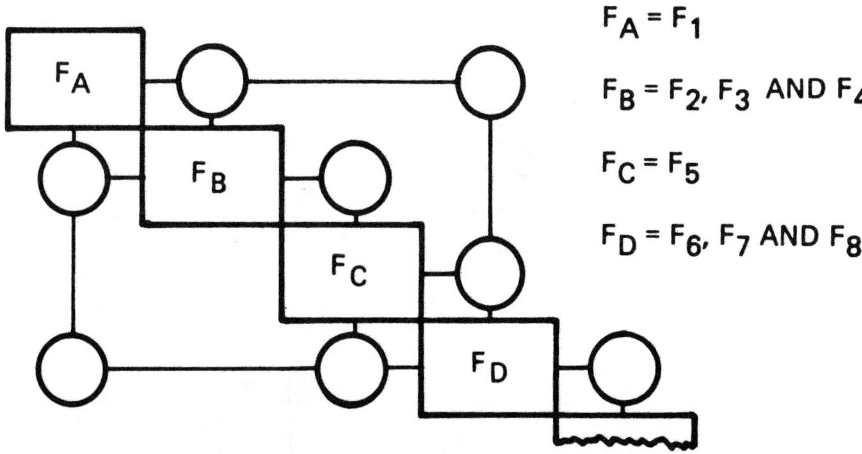

Figure 2-17B. Final Implementation Diagram

Figure 2–18 illustrates the signal flow analysis capabilities of the N^2 Chart. Figure 2-18A shows the signal flow for a monitor/display interface between functions F_4 and F_7. This design approach was not exaggerated with the block diagram or flowchart presentation methods and was, therefore, overlooked as a problem area until the detailed interface definition activity was started. The complexity of this interface was then recognized, since this one simple interface involved six of the seven subsystems within the system and additionally required definition effort in six subsystem interface sections. An N^2 Chart was used to expose this complexity and acted as a major tool for the restructuring of all of the system functions. The same interface is presented in Figure 2-18B mapped on the new system structure. The interface was now easily definable since it involves only two interfaces and three subsystems.

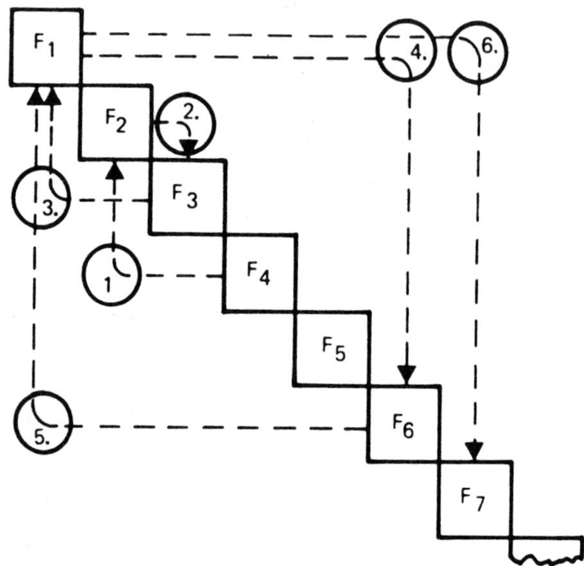

Figure 2–18A. Complex Signal Flow Illustration

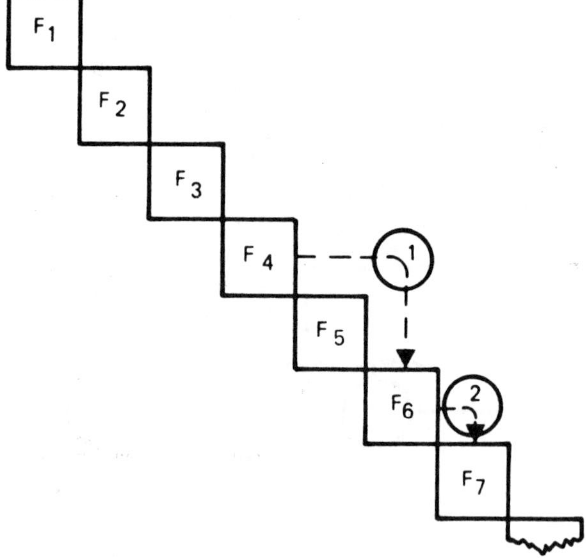

Figure 2–18B. Simple Signal Flow Illustration

Figure 2-19 illustrates a control loop N^2 Chart which was used during the initial design activity for the Tracking Data Relay Satellite (TDRS) program. This chart exposed the control loop conflicts involved with functions C&M and SCHED (dotted loops on the figure). The conflict occurred in this instance because several asynchronous real-time control directives could enter the same function at any given time and attempt to control the same parameters. Other control loop intersections (solid circles on the figure) caused no problems since the individual interface inputs either controlled different parameters or were active at different system time phases. The exposure of this conflict caused the system control philosophy to be changed. The resultant design is presented in more detail in Section 5 of this paper.

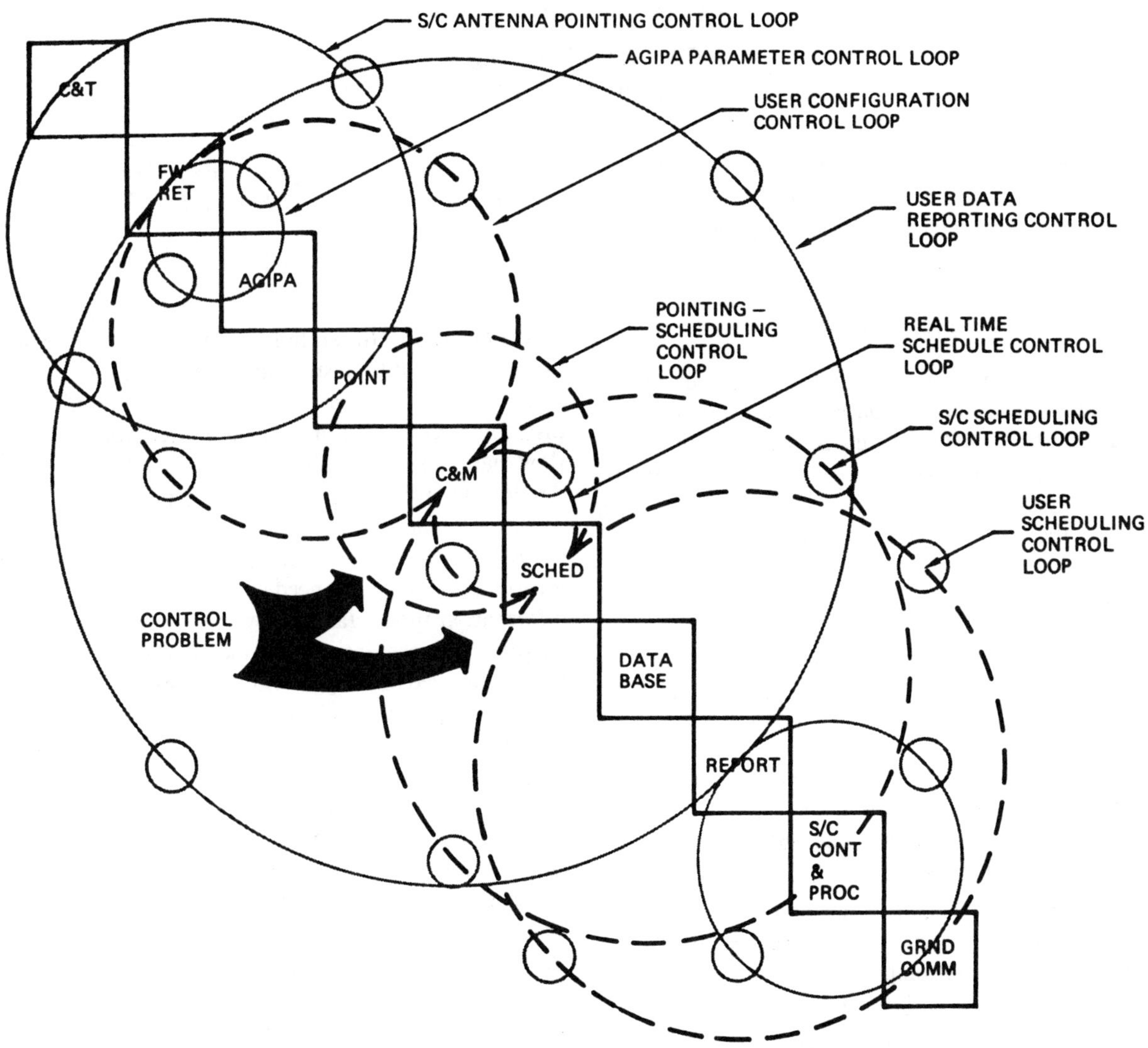

Figure 2-19. Control Loop Conflict Illustration

Object-Oriented Analysis

Peter Coad
Object International Inc.
3202 W. Anderson Lane, Suite 208-724
Austin, TX 78757-1022
(512) 343-6009

and

Edward Yourdon
161 West 86th Street
New York, NY 10024
(212) 769-9460

Abstract: *This article introduces the key motivations and rationale for object-oriented analysis (OOA). The article assesses more traditional analysis methods against principles for managing complexity. The article then introduces OOA notation and strategy.*

Introduction

OOA is based on concepts that we first learned in kindergarten: objects and attributes, classes and members, wholes and parts. Why it has taken us so long to apply these concepts to the analysis and specification of information systems is anyone's guess—perhaps we've been too busy "following the flow" during the heyday of structured analysis to consider the alternatives.

As the *Encyclopedia Britannia* points out:

> In apprehending the real world, men [people] constantly employ three methods of organization, which pervade all of their thinking:
>
> (1) the differentiation of experience into particular objects and their attributes—e.g., when they distinguish between a tree and its size or spatial relations to other objects,
>
> (2) the distinction between whole objects and their component parts—e.g., when they contrast a tree with its component branches, and
>
> (3) the formation of and the distinction between different classes of objects—e.g., when they form the class of all trees and the class of all stones and distinguish between them.
>
> *Encyclopedia Britannica,* "Classification Theory"

The notation and approach of OOA builds on these three constantly employed methods of organization.

In 1984, one of the authors consulted on the practical application of real-time structured analysis at a major aerospace company. He observed something interesting and yet disturbing. One team of analysts started out by using data flow diagrams (DFDs; this team is called the DFD team) to develop an overall functional decomposition as a framework for further specification. After a while, a second team of analysts (the database team) started out, focusing on the information the system needed to do its job and building an information model (also known as an entity-relationship diagram or a semantic data model). Over time, the DFD team continued to struggle with basic problem-space understanding (e.g., the details of what happens when one controller hands off responsibility for an aircraft to another controller). In contrast, the database team gained strong, in-depth understanding of air traffic control. Yet the results did not mesh, worse, they contradicted each other. In principle, these two models should have come together somehow. Yet under the pressure of schedule and budget, both products moved unresolved into preliminary design, with the hope of resolving the discrepancies at that time. Sadly, the database team were perceived as irksome, even somewhat as troublemakers; people (and their careers) paid the price for this major rift and its untidy resolution.

In 1987 and 1988, the same author saw this same pattern develop on projects at several government agencies. The DFD team marched on ahead in time and political power. The database team gained tremendous insight vital to analysis but were ignored. And again the database teams and their leaders were perceived as troublemakers.

Repeatedly, *in practice,* separate notations and strategies for process models and data models have kept them forever apart.

So the authors began to research and develop a method of notations and strategies that would help analysts to gain the much needed problem-space understanding first and then to add the processing requirements within the framework of that solid understanding. They put the method to work in practice, by refining and building the approach into a systematic method. Finally, one of the authors presented the method to top professionals throughout the United States, Canada, Israel, Italy, the Federal Republic of Germany, Sweden, and the United Kingdom and he received valuable feedback and insights from the participants. In applying OOA on actual projects, both clients and seminar participants contributed significantly to the development of this method.

Why do we need OOA? There are six prime reasons:

1. It allows us to define and communicate the requirements of a system within the framework of the *three basic methods of human organization (object and attributes, classification structure,* and *assembly structure).*
2. It focuses primarily on *problem-space understanding*—an understanding of the world the users live in and the nature of the system they want to automate.
3. It treats object attributes and exclusive services on those attributes as an *intrinsic whole*—in contrast to other analysis methods, which deal with these issues separately or incompletely.
4. It allows us to analyze and specify systems using *self-contained partitioning* (minimal dependency between one object and others).
5. It allows us to gain leverage through *explicit representation of commonality.*
6. It applies a *consistent, powerful underlying representation* for analysis (what is to be built) and design (how it is to be built this time).

We have aimed this article at practicing systems analysts and designers who have to tackle real-world systems development projects every day. We assume a fundamental understanding of computer technology and systems analysis concepts, and we expect that many of our readers will have some experience with such analysis tools as DFDs and entity-relationship diagrams. Managers, testers, standards-bearers, and users can read the article and expect to profit from the overall approach to improving requirements analysis.

Though it will become abundantly clear in this article, we stress here that our concern in this article is with OOA, not object-oriented programming (OOP) or object-oriented design (OOD). Systems analysts first must understand the problem domain at hand; it makes little sense to start writing air traffic control functional requirements—let alone think about design architectures or writing code—without first studying, expressing, and validating our understanding of what air traffic control is really all about. Objects as an abstraction of the real world provide a focus on gaining significant problem-space understanding; the ultimate result is a tangible, reviewable, and manageable collection of model layers (subject, object, structure, attribute, and service) produced during the five major steps of OOA.

We could argue that this perspective has *always* been important, even if it has not always been popular. Then why this article on OOA? Why has the "object paradigm" finally come of age now?

OOP was first discussed in the early 1970s by those working with the SIMULA language; by the late 1970s, it was an important part of the Smalltalk language developed at Xerox PARC. Meanwhile, the rest of the world bumbled along with languages like COBOL and FORTRAN and used functional decomposition methods (which we discuss later in more detail) to address problems of design and specification. There was little, if any, discussion of OOD and virtually none about OOA.

Three factors have changed over the past decade and are now key:

1. The underlying concepts of an object-oriented approach have had a decade to mature, and attention has gradually shifted from issues of coding, to issues of design, to issues of requirements analysis. The proponents of functional decomposition spent a decade progressing from structured programming to structured design to structured analysis; we should not be surprised to see the same progression in the object-oriented world.
2. The underlying technology for building systems has become much more powerful. Unfortunately, our way of thinking about systems analysis is influenced by our preconceived ideas of how we will design the system to meet its requirements; our ideas about design are influenced by our preconceived ideas about how we will write the code; and our ideas about coding are strongly influenced by the programming language we have available. It was difficult to think about structured programming (and thus difficult to think about structured design and structured analysis) when the customary languages were assembler, AUTOCODER, and FORTRAN; things became easier with Pascal, PL/1, ALGOL, FORTRAN-77, Structured BASIC, and newer versions of COBOL. Similarly, it was difficult to think about

coding in an object-oriented fashion with COBOL, FORTRAN, or plain-vanilla C; with coding has become easier with C++, Objective-C, Smalltalk, and Ada.

3. The systems we build today are different than they were ten or twenty years ago. In every respect, they are larger and more complex; they are also more volatile and subject to constant change. We will argue in sections that follow that an object-oriented approach to analysis (and design) is likely to lead to a more stable system. Also, we find that today's on-line, interactive systems devote much more attention to the *user interface* than did the text-oriented batch processing systems of the 1960s and 1970s. Some observers, such as Bill Joy of Sun Microsystems, argue that as much as 75 percent of the code in a modern system may be concerned with the user interface—e.g., manipulating windows, pull-down menus, icons, mouse movements, etc. Our experience has been that an object-oriented approach to such systems—from analysis through design and into coding—is a more natural way of dealing with such systems.

The Analysis Challenge

Requirements analysis exhilarates and aggravates those who fall prey to its siren song. What is so difficult about analysis? What is the challenge? We feel that three major difficulties plague systems analysts on all types of projects: problem-space understanding, person-to-person communication, and continual change.

The problem space

One of the biggest problems faced by analysts is studying the application domain and discovering things about it—the challenge of understanding the "problem space." As consultants, the authors usually experience this in an extreme form: we are dropped into a project for a week, a month, or a year. In most cases, we can't pretend to be subject-matter experts in the client's business or application. We need to grasp, to understand in depth, the problem space—and we need to do it as quickly as possible. Of course, the situation is less extreme for many systems analysts, but those who are subject-matter experts as well as analysts still need tools to effectively communicate their expertise to others on the team. For example, analysts who have been working with radar systems for the past twenty years probably have intimate knowledge of the problem space; when time comes to specify the requirements for yet another radar system, their primary problem may be communicating with other radar experts as well as with project members who can't distinguish a radar from a grapefruit.

Analysts must consider the problem space in which they work. For example, consider the problem of air traffic control. The analysts need to immerse themselves in that problem space, so deeply that they begin to discover nuances that even those who live with air traffic control every day have not yet fully considered. As another example, consider a business system that maintains information about motor vehicle registrations and titles; analysts working on such a system would need to study and assimilate all sorts of details—and many exceptions to the rules, resulting from special-interest-group demands and the statutes that follow.

Being an effective analysts means much more than just writing down some observable, measurable, functional requirements. Yes, analysts need to specify processing requirements, concisely packaged so that fellow human beings can read and understand what they believe those requirements are. But understanding the problem space is really the crux of requirements analysis.

If the analysts simply assume that they have subject-matter knowledge, they are likely to indulge in thinking that will lead to fuzzy requirements. One of the authors was recently involved in a large air traffic control project in which requirements analysts were still grappling with basic air traffic control concepts even after two years of specifying software requirements. Analysts need to understand and model the problem space *especially* for large, complex systems; with such understanding, the textual specifying of measurable requirements can be done fairly straightforwardly.

Communication

The analysis challenge also requires communication. Analysts need to communicate throughout the analysis effort. They must communicate just to extract the problem space and requirements from the client. They think about all these matters, refine their own thoughts, interact with their peers, and ultimately echo the problem-space understanding and subsequently requirements back to the client, to validate their understanding of the requirements. They also may need help in steering the client away from requirements that cannot be met within the budget and schedule constraints.

The term "software engineering" is ironic: though the words conjure up images of formulas, algorithms, and "hard" scientific approaches, software engineering is actually a people-oriented business. Recently, one of the authors spoke at a conference in Chicago and was asked if OOA (and/or other software methods) is the key to successful software development. The response? Yes, having a consistent technical approach is valuable. Yet software methods are effective only to the extent that they help people to communicate with one another. If the application of a software engineering method produces a monument of paper, then something is wrong—in the method, in the application of the method, or perhaps in both. If we lose sight of people and begin producing charts, diagrams, and piles of paper as an end in itself, we fail to communicate effectively. Software engineering is a people business. People make the problems; people solve the problems. We can solve our systems development problems only by interacting with each other.

At this same computer conference, the author then asked how many educators in the audience required some interpersonal communications training as part of their software engineering program. *No hands went up.* Yet effective communication—with management, peers, reviewers, standards bearers, and clients—is vital to successful requirements analysis.

Viable software methods must facilitate communication. Successful software methods build on human methods of organization, rather than on a contrived notation that works well for computation (e.g., "follow the flow") but not for humans.

Continual Change

Requirements continue to be in a state of flux. Management or clients may impose an artificial freezing of requirements at a particular point in time, but the true requirements, the needed system, will continue to evolve. Many forces affect this ever-changing requirements set: customers, competition, regulators, approvers, and technologists. As Gerhard Fischer [Fischer, 1989] pointed out, "We have to accept changing requirements as a fact of life, and not condemn them as a product of sloppy thinking."

Analysts endeavor to organize their notations and strategies so that the work can be resilient to change. They seek packaging of requirements that will remain stable over time. Explicit capture of commonality is a great help here, for both data and processing. As analysts find computer implementation issues and other design considerations, they file them away, deferring each added complexity until the requirements are put forth.

Managing Complexity

This section sets forth the four major principles for managing complexity through OOA: abstraction, information hiding, inheritance, and methods of organization.

Abstraction

> Abstraction. The principle of ignoring those aspects of a subject that are not relevant to the current purpose in order to concentrate more fully on those that are. [*Oxford, Dictionary of Computing,* 1986]

This definition means that even though analysts know about many things, they choose certain things over others.

Both authors have young children whose rooms are filled with a variety of toys, many of which are small-scale replicas of airplanes, cars, and exotic warriors. It's interesting to see how even little children deal with the concept of abstraction: a toy hook-and-ladder fire truck, for example, could have been built with a 100 pound hose hanging off its side, but the abstraction would be out of proportion and rendered useless for its intended user. Yet we know, and even the child knows, that the hose is there; we need its complexity in the real system, but it would be inappropriate for the abstraction our children play with on their bedroom floor.

Most of the things we deal with in the real world—people, places, objects, and systems—are intrinsically complex, far more complex than we can cope with at the first try. When we use the concept of abstraction, we admit that the thing we are considering is complex; rather than try to comprehend the whole thing, we select only part of it. We know there are additional details; we simply choose not to use them at this time. This is an important way of managing complexity.

Procedural abstraction is one form of abstraction used extensively by requirements analysts, as well as by designers and programmers. It's often characterized as "function/subfunction" abstraction. You may be familiar with diagramming methods such as structure charts, with the big box at the top—representing the entire system, or "thing" being considered—and the subordinate steps or subfunctions shown as boxes below the top-level box.

> Procedural Abstraction. The principle that any operation that achieves a well-defined effect can be treated by its users as a single entity, despite the fact that the operation may actually be achieved by some sequence of lower-level operations. [*Oxford Dictionary of Computing,* 1986]

Breaking processing (e.g., aircraft tracking) up into substeps is one basic method of handling complexity. But, as we will discuss in more detail below, using such a breakdown for organizing analysis and specification is somewhat arbitrary and highly volatile. Procedural abstraction is not the primary form of abstraction for OOA; however, it does come into play in OOA within the limited context of specifying and describing individual objects.

Another, more powerful, abstraction mechanism is data abstraction. This principle is at the core of object-oriented analysis. This principle forms the basis for the primary organization of thinking and specification.

> Data Abstraction. The principle of defining a data type in terms of the operations that apply

to objects of the type, with the constraint that the values of such objects can be modified and observed only by the use of operations. [*Oxford Dictionary of Computing*, 1986]

In OOA, analysts define "attributes" of "objects," and they define "services" that exclusively manipulate those attributes. The only way to get to the attributes is by means of a service. Attributes and the services on those attributes are treated as an intrinsic whole in the OOA approach. Indeed, Attributes, Objects, and Services are so important to the OOA approach that starting here, the words are capitalized whenever they are used in the rest of the article.

Information Hiding (Encapsulation)

> Information Hiding. A principle, used when developing an overall program structure, that each component of a program should encapsulate or hide a single design decision... The interface to each module is defined in such a way as to reveal as little as possible about its inner workings. [*Oxford Dictionary of Computing,* 1966]

This definition reflects the work of David Parnas, [Parnas, 1972] in design in the early 1970s.

The power and attractiveness of information hiding are that it helps minimize rework involved in developing a new system. If the parts of the requirements analysis effort that are most volatile are encapsulated, then the (inevitable) changing of requirements becomes less of a threat to the overall effort. Localizing volatility is essential: whether we like it or not, analysts live in an environment of continual change. *Encapsulation is done to separate the user of an Object from its author.*

Inheritance

> Inheritance: Properties or characterists received from an ancestor.

This principle forms the basis for a powerful technique of explicit expression of commonality. Inheritance allows us to specify common Attributes and Services *once*, along with specialization and extension of those Attributes and Services into specific cases. Thus, we might recognize automobiles and trucks as special cases in a transportation system: each of these special cases "inherits" common Attributes (e.g., vehicle identification number) of the generic Object "vehicle."

Using the concept of inheritance, a receiver (e.g., "automobile") acquires properties—Attributes and Services—from a giver (e.g., "vehicle"). In addition, the receiver can add to or extend those properties. Thus, a "truck" might have Attributes such as "number of axles" or "number of wheels," which might not be relevant or appropriate for the "automobile."

OOA uses inheritance to express commonality explicitly, beginning with the early activities of requirements analysis.

Methods of Organization

As authors, we would derive intellectual satisfaction from reporting that we studied philosophical ideas on methods of organization from Aristotle and Socrates to Descartes and Kant, and read and mused about their thoughts before writing this article. Then, based on the underlying methods human beings use, we could propose the basic constructs essential to a requirements analysis method, and in particular to OOA.

But in truth, we cannot say that, nor did we do it.

However, we approached the problem as practitioners and investigators. We researched and applied various software subjects, in particular semantic data modeling and OOP languages. We began to ferret out some of the embellishments, looking for the key principles that could be applied to organizing and representing requirements. We looked for the concepts that give the greatest leverage in understanding and expressing problem-space knowledge. Then we boiled our finding down to three key methods of organization.

Although we cannot claim to have made a comprehensive survey of classification theory and organizational methods proposed by philosphers and thinkers during the past three thousand years, we did check out *Encyclopedia Britannica,* to read about how people organize problem space. We found the quotation that appears at the beginning of this article, describing three constantly employed methods of organization.

The notation and approach of OOA are built on these three constantly employed methods of organization. In OOA, they'll be referred to, respectively, as Objects and Attributes, Assembly Structures, and Classification Structures.

Analysis Methods

This section surveys four major approaches to requirements analysis. These approaches are thinking tools, used to help in the formulation of requirements: functional decomposition, data flow (structured analysis), information modeling, and OOA.

First, what is requirements analysis? To us, it means the process of extracting the "needs" of the system—*what* the system must do to satisfy the customer, not *how* the system will be implemented. Requirements analysis usually begins with a textual requirements document, a series of discussions with a client, or both. In any case, the audience includes the end user of the system, the developers of the system, and possibly other interested parties (e.g., auditors, contracting officers, etc.) who may need to understand and agree with the proposed set of requirements. The requirements document should communicate a complete, consistent, and feasible statement of what is needed in the system. It should be manageable both before and after it is produced. Requirements include functional operations and (quantified) operational characteristics such as ease of use, reliability, availability, maintainability, and performance. Requirements also include interfaces with which the software must deal, environments that the software must accommodate, and any applicable design constraints.

The first three approaches to requirements analysis have been discussed and practiced in the systems development profession for a decade or more. We have personally used all three methods on large systems, sometimes with success and sometimes with abject failure. The strengths of these first three methods have their place in specific contexts in the fourth method discussed in this section, OOA. Thus, we feel it is important to emphasize that we are not trying to abolish the older, more established methods. Software methods should be utterly pragmatic, without religious fervor. Analysts need all the help they can get. What we are attempting to do is to incorporate the best ideas of the first three methods in a more comprehensive, all-encompassing method—OOA.

Rather than endlessly arguing about which method is better, we prefer to take a pragmatic view, using whatever combination of approaches helps in a given situation no matter what method it comes from.

Each approach will be defined in the following paragraphs with an equation, for easy recognition of the method. Each approach will be examined in light of large-project experience.

Functional Decomposition

Functional decomposition is readily recognized with its steps and substeps. An equation representation, useful in identifying this method in use, is as follows:

Functional decomposition =
Functions
+ subfunctions
+ functional interfaces

The underlying strategy of functional decomposition consists of selecting the processing steps and substeps anticipated for the new system, using previous experience as a guide. The focus is on *what processing* is required for the new system. The analyst then specifies the processing and the functional interfaces.

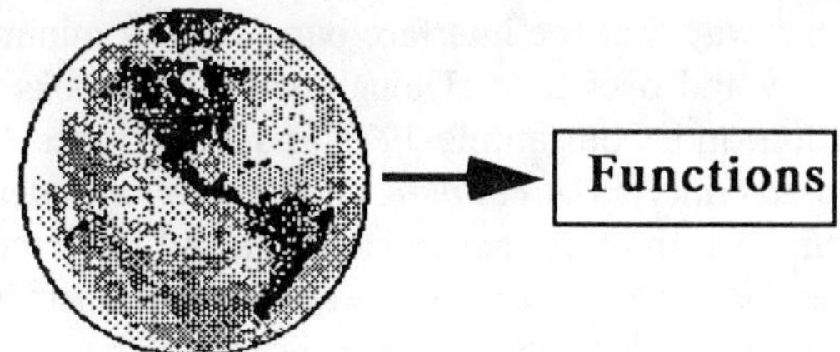

Figure 1: Functional decomposition

Functional decomposition requires humans to map from problem space (e.g., air traffic control) to functions and subfunctions (see Figure 1). The analysts must internalize the subject matter and then write down the corresponding required functions and subfunctions that the system must provide. The resulting specification only *indirectly* maps back to the subject matter. Nothing explicitly maps the functionality back to the subject matter itself. Therefore, it is difficult for the analysts and the users to assess whether the requirements are an accurate statement of what the new system is required to do. With such an approach, problem-space understanding is neither explicitly expressed nor verified for its accuracy; subtle distinctions within the problem space are simply not uncovered.

Is functional decomposition bad? No. Should its use be banned? No. After all, eventually both data and data processing must be specified. In fact, functional decomposition is used in OOA, albeit in a very specific context: defining certain Services (processing) for a specific Object; it may be helpful to break up a large, complicated Service into smaller pieces for convenience in stating what is required. For example, for an aircraft Object, analysts will probably divide a description of the Aircraft Track Service into a number of smaller pieces. They may also use a block diagram or DFD fragment to help guide the reader through the requirements of this Service. But these actions are all done in the context of an Object; the processing steps will not be used as the primary underlying representation during analysis or specification; processing steps are too volatile over time.

Function/subfunction breakdowns are hard to construct (because of the indirect mapping) and highly volatile (because of the continual change of functional capability that can be successfully delivered within budget and schedule constraints). For these reasons, we feel that the overall analysis approach should *not* be based on function/subfunction; a more stable analysis viewpoint and specification organization is needed.

In functional decomposition, analysts end up with system, subsystem, function, and subfunction levels. The big problem lies in choosing the functions and knowing the change volatility of system functionality. Another problem facing the analysts is picking the functions and subfunctions in such a way that the interface bandwidth is minimized, both now and over time. Though earlier textbooks (e.g., [Yourdon and Constantine 1979 and Page-Jones 1988]) have used concepts of *coupling* and *cohension* to describe the composition of system components and the interfaces between those components, many system developers have a difficult time identifying subfunctions so that when a change comes for a little of this processing, a little of that processing, and some added processing, they can capture the new requirements with a minimum of change to the analysis and specification organization.

Data Flow Approach

Another method (and another way to map problem space into a technical representation) is the data flow approach, often described as "structured analysis." One can recognize a data flow approach with this equation:

Data flow approach =
Data (and control) flows
+ Data (and control) transformations
+ Data (and control) stores + Terminators

This is the basic notation. Sometimes information models by various names, (e.g., entity-relationship diagrams) are used too (these will be discussed later in the article).

With this method, the analyst maps from the real world into data flows and bubbles (Figure 2). This mapping requires the analyst (and more significantly, the customer) to follow the flow of data whenever looking at the real world and to map that flow into subsequent analysis and specification. Yet "follow the flow of data" is not one of the basic methods humans use to manage complexity when looking at a problem space; "follow the flow of data" is not one of the basic methods of organization that pervade people's thinking. Considering an event (e.g., a transaction request) and then identifying the processing steps taken in response to that event are quite helpful steps; in fact these steps form one of the secondary strategies in OOA for identifying Services and the steps within a Service. But the flow of steps of processing (using procedural abstraction) is not the flow of data and their gradual refinement (which is a thinking approach that leads to procedural abstraction).

Two major strategies dominate structured analysis. The "old" method [DeMarco, 1978 and Gane and Sarson, 1977] maps the old system to DFDs, then removes the physical idiosyncrasies, then adds new logical requirements and then new physicial considerations.

For the current U.S. air traffic control system, or for many states' registration and title systems, the documentation of end-user requirements of the existing system consists of little more than source code and patched object code from the late 1960s. Studying and modeling such systems is, in effect, studying and modeling a prior mapping of the problem space, rather than the problem space itself. Analysts find it hard to recover from this misplaced focus of study.

The problems with this older strategy became apparent as team after team became ensnared in trying to model the old system, until time, budget, and patience wore out. Analysts just did not know when to stop (and when in doubt, kept adding to the model); as our colleague Steve McMenamin observed, many analysts fell into the "current physical tar-pit," never to emerge.

The "modern" approach first appeared in seminars as early as 1982, in books as early as 1984 (see, for example, [McMenamin and Palmer, 1984]), and more recently in Yourdon's *Modern Structured Analysis* in 1989 [Yourdon, 1989]. The strategy goes like this. Analysts have problems picking bubbles for their DFDs; so to get some help in picking the bubbles, they should first define events. Events are those occurrences in the outside world that a planned-response system must respond to[1]. Then for each event, draw a bubble; for a system with 150 events, draw 150 bubbles. Name each bubble by deciding what the system does in response to the event. Add appropriate input and output flows to each bubble. Place data stores between bubbles that need to communicate with data held over time. Then group the bubbles into page-size bites. Next, draw higher-level summaries, up two or three levels, the highest of which is a "context diagram" in which the entire system is shown as a single bubble. Then for the lower-level bubbles, apply functional decomposition to define even lower levels, as needed.

Additional documentation is needed. The data flows and bottom-level transformations need to be specified with a data dictionary and process specifications, respectively. The upper-level diagrams exist to provide a big picture for the reader; the process-specification content expresses the detail. But much of the lower-level detail must be understood for the graphical summaries to make much sense.

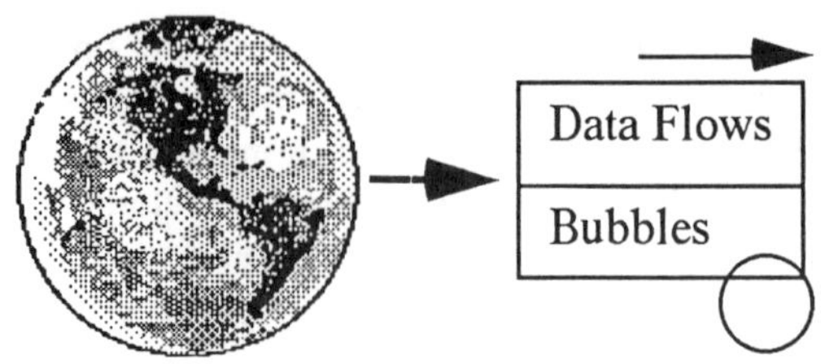

Figure 2: Data flow decomposition

[1] The actual interaction between the user and the system is message based. The event list documented in the "modern" approach to structured analysis is largely a documentation of the individual requests made by human users, so that the event + dataflow correspondence can be expressed. Using a message-based interaction model expresses the correspondence directly.

transition, the radical change in underlying representation causes a major chasm between analysis and design models. As Seidewitz argues, [Seidewitz, unpublished paper] "Functional analysis and specification techniques actually sacrifice closeness to the problem domain in order to allow a smooth transition to functional design methods."

A similar problem plagues those who have tried to follow structured analysis with OOD; this technique seems especially popular with those wrestling with Ada-oriented methods. But if the Object-oriented paradigm is so powerful as an underlying design perspective, why not apply those concepts as a foundation for improving requirements analysis? To do so seems far more natural than many of the transitions we have read about in numerous papers, which in effect say, "The analysts have done their structured analysis. Let's pick the pieces of their results to get a first-cut, Object-oriented view. Then on to the good stuff—design." This even more drastic change in underlying representation causes an even rougher gap between analysis and design models. Such a gap is disastrous over time: requirements documents are ignored, continual changes in requirements are difficult to move into the design, and traceability—a must in government system acquisition—is left with only form and little content.

For many years, analysts have been stymied by the underlying representation shift as they moved from analysis to design. The shift has prevented practitioners from systematically adding design-dependent detail to the results of requirements analysis. Design should consist solely of expanding the requirements model to account for the complexities introduced in selecting a particular implementation—e.g., multiple computational resources this time, particular display devices this time, added Objects to manage other Objects this time, and added Objects to manage external interfaces this time. Problem-space Objects, such as aircraft, continue from analysis into design.

It is a bedrock concept of the OOA approach that the same underlying representation is used in both analysis and design.

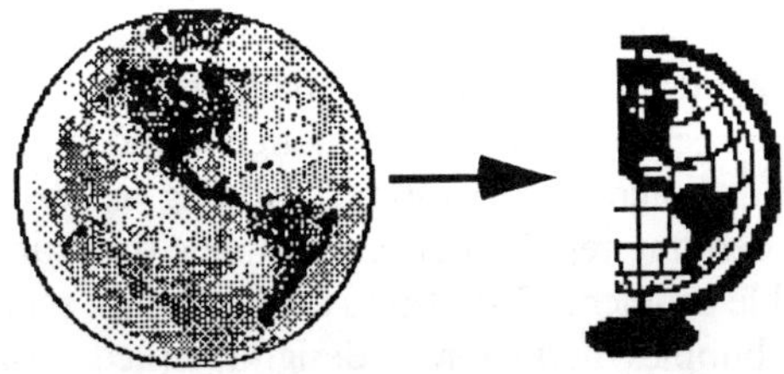

Figure 3: Information modeling decomposition

Information Modeling

Information modeling has evolved over a number of years. The primary modeling tool of information modeling—entity-relationship diagram—has evolved into semantic data models. Modeling the world in data has helped capture problem-space content.

Here's an equation to help identify this method:

Information modeling =
  Objects
  + Attributes
  + Relationships
  + Supertype/Subtypes
  + Associative Objects

The older strategy goes like this. Develop an indented list of Attributes. Then put the Attributes into Object buckets. Add relationships. Refine with supertype/subtypes and associative Objects. Then normalize.

The newer strategy is much the same, except that the initial step is to find Objects in the real world and describe them with Attributes. Otherwise, one proceeds in basically the same fashion.

With the newer strategy, information modeling maps directly from the problem space to Objects in the model. This strategy is a large improvement in mapping, but a more detailed mapping is needed (see Figure 3).

Information modeling is a partial method. It is well presented in several books (e.g., [Shlaer and Mellor, 1988]) and papers (e.g., Loomis, Shaw, and Rumbaugh, 1987]). Here is what's missing:

1. *Services:* the processing requirements for each Object, encapsulated and treated with the Attributes as an intrinsic whole.
2. *Inheritance:* explicit representation of Attribute and Service commonality.
3. *Messages:* a narrow, well-defined interface between Objects.
4. *Structure:* classification structure and assembly structure, as fundamental human methods of organization, are not central issues but should be.

An Observation on Stability versus Volatility

At issue is the impact of additions, extensions, changes, and deletions of feature on the description of system requirements.

Eventually one must address processes and subprocesses (functions and subfunctions). For example, Services will be needed to set up an instance of an object, connect that instance to instances of other objects, and provide on-going

The challenge is in how to pick the bubbles. Event-response partitioning can help. But with too many events the number of bubbles gets out of hand. And little help is given on grouping into higher levels to improve human understandability—the guideline of "group bubbles that deal with common data stores" sounds sensible, but often breaks down in practice. Far too often, organizations fight extended "bubble wars" over which partitioning is the best choice. The upper-level bubbles become such conglomerates that their names can say little more than "Process <noun>."

Another problem with the data flow method is the size of the data dictionary. If there are five levels of diagrams, then hundreds of data flow leveling equations may be required. Moreover, complex interfaces (with other systems, devices, and humans) tend to aggravate the data dictionary equation problem, leading to project data dictionary "explosions" of over 1000 pages of dictionary documentation; the authors have seen a number of large projects with this recurring problem. Yes, CASE tools can help get all the syntax in shape, but the semantics, the underlying meaning, is far beyond what any human reviewer can digest. Communication, most vital in requirements analysis, is greatly weakened. Moreover, interfaces are volatile. The continual change for systems with complex interfaces will only cause even further syntactic and (more significantly) semantic consistency problems.

The data flow approach still has a strong functional emphasis and thus is subject to the same change-resiliency weaknesses that we discussed earlier.

The data flow approach has weak data structure emphasis, and this weakness is one of the greater concerns. The DFD gives weak emphasis to the data store. This weakness is duly acknowledged by many authors describing the data flow method. Many authors have tried to tie information modeling concepts into data flow diagramming to compensate for the weakness. It's an academically pleasing idea (two perspectives, one system under consideration). Yet even in books, the connection is weak—e.g., Yourdon[8] discusses the tie-in, but the leverage attainable in problem-space understanding from data modeling and its influence on a data flow model is all but ignored. And, more important than what a textbook says, *in practice the connection seems virtually nonexistent.* On large projects that we have observed at several defense contractors as well as at a variety of business data processing organizations, the same pattern emerges again and again:

- The analysts (DFD team) rush off to do DFDs.
- After a while, out of synch in time and content, another team (the database team) works on an information model.
- The database team acquires great subject-matter understanding.
- The DFD team likes the insight but resists the massive changes they must make (having grabbed for functionality first).
- The DFD team wins out, and the results of the two teams never get reconciled ("Oh, we'll put it together in design").

Each analyst needs the benefit of both perspectives. *In practice, separate models keep critical issues too disjointed.* Although CASE tool support could help somewhat, the analysts working with DFDs are working primarily with a model that hides the impact of the data structure. Seeing this need again and again spurred us on to develop a single, multilayered notation for OOA; analysts can see the layers they want to see in one model, and they can view Subjects, Objects, Attributes, and Services as a unified whole.

Another concern follows. DFDs are not very helpful for systems or parts of systems that primarily update and retrieve data. Unlike the familar transaction-processing systems of the 1970s and early 1980s, the following pattern appears in most real-world systems today: the diagrams basically show a pair of bubbles, one bubble getting data and writing into a store, and one bubble pulling information out of that store, delivering the data. For example, an air traffic control system for the most part uses one bubble to dump in the data and another bubble to retrieve the data later. Most of the system can be specified in this fashion. The pretty bubble-to-bubble-to-bubble textbook transformations are limited to fairly small aspects of the system, in which the processing is extensive enough to warrant such a refinement of data from one substep to the next to the next—e.g., tracking calculations, in which tracking is an important but rather small part compared to the overall system to be analyzed and specified.

Another major concern about the data flow approach is moving to design: the double burden of shifting the underlying method of organization *and* adding implementation detail. This concept reminds the authors of the cartoon that shows a wide planning chart coming together at one point, with a box reading "and then a miracle happens," followed by a wide path of planning charts emanating out of the box. The transition from analysis to design has been a constant source of aggravation. Many papers have been written; little progress has been made. It is hard enough to add implementation-based design considerations. Adding a substantial shift in underlying representation has made this transition an untenable problem. Data flows are a network representation of bubbles and stores; design-oriented structure charts are a hierarchical representation of modules. No matter how many amusing cartoons are drawn to depict the monitoring. Yet the matters of how much the players (customer, management, and technical staff) decide to automate this time and how sophisticated the Services may be are quite volatile; they are continually subject to the triple constraint of capability, schedule, and budget.

Eventually one must address processes and subprocesses (functions and subfunctions). For example, Services will be needed to set up an instance of an object, connect that instance to instances of other objects, and provide on-going monitoring. Yet the matters of how much the players (customer, management, and technical staff) decide to automate this time and how sophisticated the Services may be are quite volatile; they continually subject to the triple constraint of capability, schedule, and budget.

The external interfaces are next most likely to change. How smart or dumb are the devices? What do the other systems need from the system under consideration? What does this system need from the others? What requests will the human make while using the system?

The next part likely to change is the data Attributes that describe something in the problem space. Yet these changes tend to apply to a single Object, e.g., the aircraft Object and its Attributes, such as call number, serial number, location (latitude, longitude, altitude), and status.

The most stable aspect of the system—that which is least susceptible to potential change—is the Objects in the problem space. For example, whether one specifies a low budget or a sophisticated air traffic control system, one will still have the same basic Objects with which to organize the analysis and ultimately the specification: aircraft, controller, airspace, and the like. The more expensive system will have more Attributes for each Object. The more expensive version will have more elaborate interfaces for monitoring devices and other systems (and additional Objects to model the interfaces). The more expensive system will have more sophisticated Services defined for each Object (e.g., aircraft with an automated tracking Service, Aircraft.Track). The more expensive version may have some additional Objects, too (e.g., a radar Object, with corresponding Attributes, plus Services such as Radar.Interrogate). Yet by and large, the stability of the system (Objects in the problem space) will remain the same across what potentially could be major changes in scope of a software requirements activity.

The approach, however, does not mean that an analyst may not specify Services; Services must be specified regardless of the simplicity or complexity of the system. Rather the approach means that what comes first, predominates. The key lies in deciding what is the primary view, the overall organization, in understanding problem space, communicating that understanding, and ultimately specifying requirements. Underlying OOA is the idea of using information hiding to hide that which is more volatile; with OOA, analysts base the overall organization of their thinking and specification on that which is more stable.

Consequently, as an overall organization in looking at a registration and title system, an analyst looks at owners, vehicles, purchases, titles, registrations, and clerks, and then progressively adds layers of requirements development (Structures, Subjects, Attributes, Services).

Object-Oriented Analysts

"Object-oriented" is a difficult subject, because the term "Object" has come from two different areas of study:

1. from information modeling, meaning a representation of some real-world thing and some number of instances of that thing.
2. from OOP languages, meaning a run-time instance of some processing and values, defined by a static description called a "class."

It has been reported that some conference presentations have been overrun with lengthy discussions over what one really means by the word "Object."

An equation for recognizing an Object-oriented approach would be helpful:

Object-oriented =

Objects
(an encapsulation of Attributes and exclusive Services; an abstraction of the something in the problem space, with some number of instances in the problem space)

+ Classification and inheritance.

One can look at different languages, environments, methods, and books and ask, "Are you really Object-oriented?" Unfortunately, many times the answer is "no"; Object-oriented suffers from being a catchy marketing word, used at times to mean "the good stuff."

Is Ada an Object-oriented language? No. Genericity (i.e., typed parameters) is convenient, but is no substitute for inheritance. In fact, to provide the missing classification and inheritance, one software vendor (Software Productivity Solutions of Melbourne, Florida) markets some tools for Ada.

Is an informtion-modeling approach Object-oriented (e.g., *Object-Oriented Systems Analysis* [Shlaer and Mellor, 1988] a book that would be better titled *Making Semantic Data Modeling Practical)?* No. Services are missing. Classification is missing. Inheritance is missing.

Object-oriented analysis builds on the best concepts from information modeling (entity-relationship diagrams and

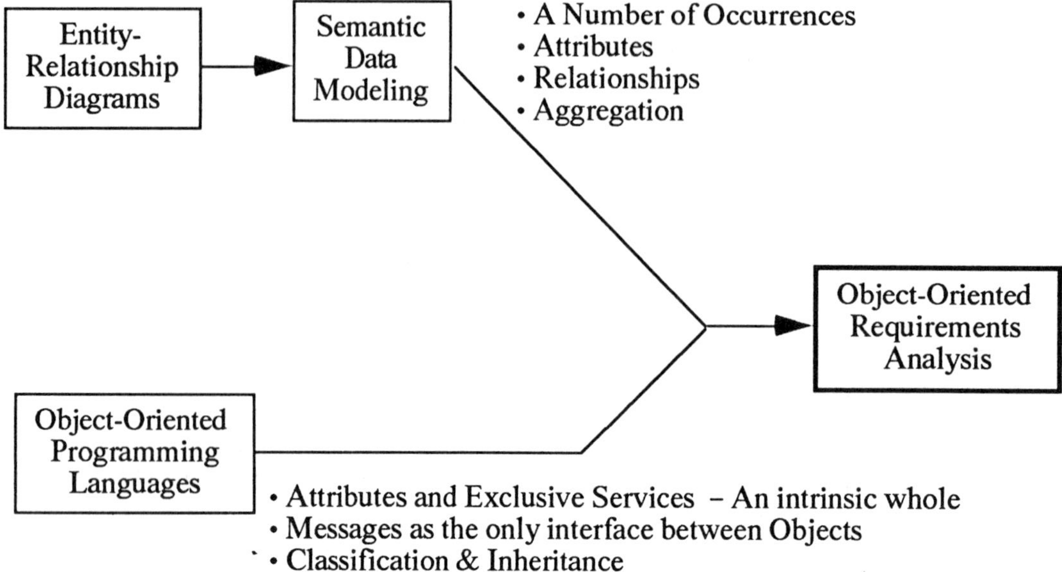

Figure 4: The formulation of OOA

semantic data models) and the best concepts from OOP languages (see Figure 4).

From information modeling comes Attributes, relationships, structure, and an Object that represents some number of instances of something in the problem space.

From OOP languages come encapsulating of Attributes and exclusive Services, treating Attributes and Services as an intrinsic whole, portraying Classification Structure, and explicitly expressing commonality through inheritance.

Instead of an indirect mapping from problem space to function/subfunction or problem space to flows and bubbles, the mapping is direct, from the problem space to the model: aircraft, radar, airspace, and controller Objects; owner, vehicle, purchase, registration, title, and clerk Objects (see Figure 5).

OOA is based on the uniform application of

- pervading methods of organization (the overall framework for both analysis and specification)
- communication with messages (the interaction between the user and the system, and the interaction between instances in the system)
- behavior classification (the overall framework for identifying Services to be provided by each component)

In an overall approach, OOA consists of five major steps:

- Identifying Objects
- Identifying Structures
- Defining Subjects
- Defining Attributes (and Instance Connections)
- Defining Services (and Message Connections)

Yet once the model is built, it is presented and reviewed in five major layers:

- Subject Layer
- Object Layer

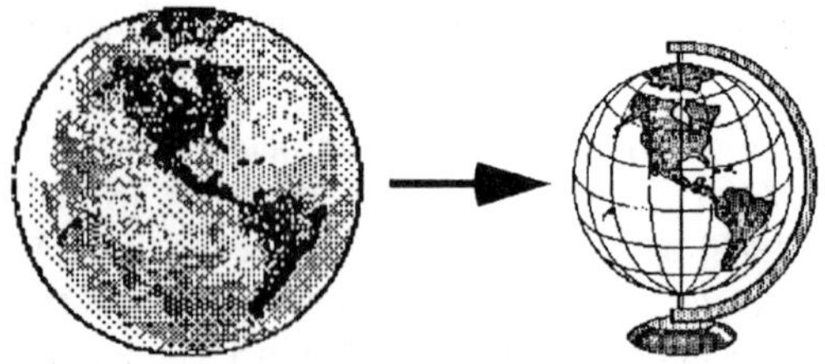

Figure 5: Object oriented organization

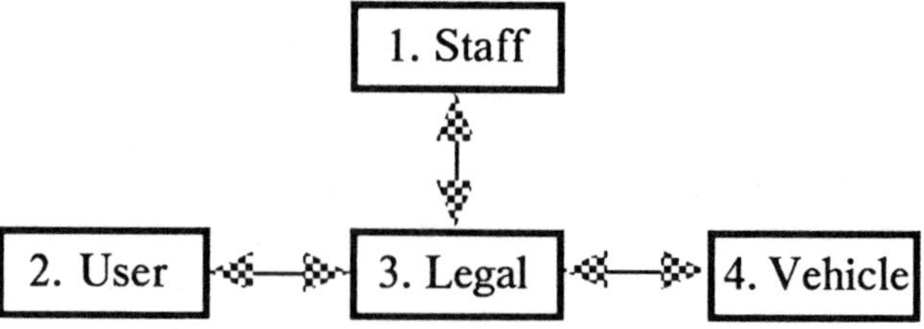

Figure 6: An OOA example Subject layer

- Structure Layer
- Attribute Layer
- Service Layer

Examples of these five *layers* follow:

Subject layer: A Subject is a mechanism for controlling how much of a model a reader considers at one time.

The OOA strategy for the Subject layer is as follows:

1. Add a Subject corresponding to each Structure. Add a Subject corresponding to each Object.
2. If the number of Subjects exceeds or is around seven, then refine the Subjects further: once the connections between Objects and Structures are identified during the Attribute and Service steps, combine tightly coupled Subjects as needed to provide a better overview (roadmap) for the reader to follow.
3. Show Subjects and message connections between Subjects on the Subject layer.
4. Number the Subjects. Show the Subjects on the layer diagrams, to guide the reader from Subject to Subject.

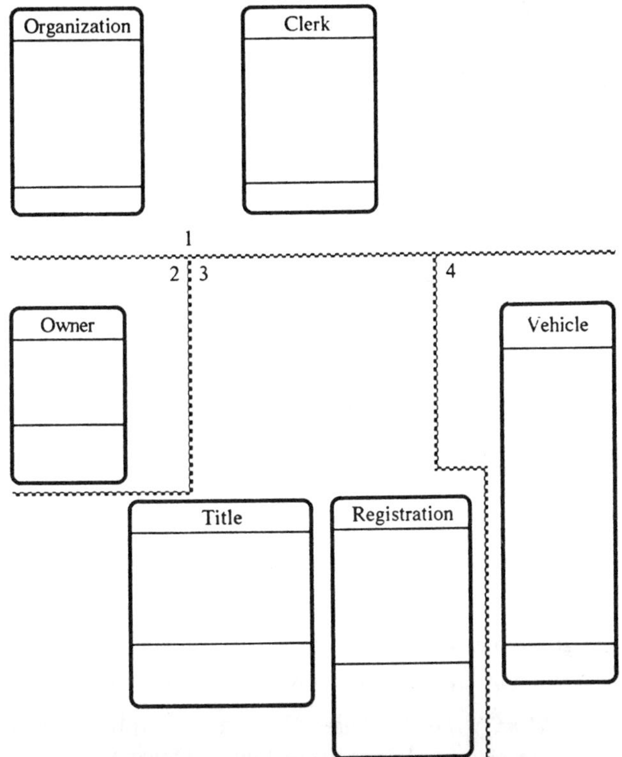

Figure 7: An OOA example of an Object layer

As needed to facilitate communication, each layer may be organized into diagrams separated by Subject.

This model consists of four Subjects (see Figure 6). The Subject layer of abstraction is based on the Structure layer, along with connections identified as part of the Attribute and Service layers.

Object layer: An Object is an abstraction of data and exclusive processing on those data, reflecting the capabilities of a system to keep information about or interact with something in the real world.

The OOA strategy for the Object layer is as follows:

1. Where to look: problem space, text, and pictures.
2. What to look for: structure, other systems, devices, things remembered, role played, locations, organizational units, and descriptive catalogs.
3. What to consider: needed remembrance, needed Services, more than one Attribute, common Attributes, common Services, and essential requirements.
4. What to challenge: unneeded remembrance or Service, single instances, and derived results.
5. How to name: use a singular noun, or an adjective and a noun. Use a name that describes a single instance of an Object. Use the standard subject-matter vocabulary. Use readable names.

The example consists of six Objects—an external system (vehicle), events remembered over time (title, registration), roles displayed by humans (owner, clerk), and an organizational unit (organization) (see Figure 7); the Subject lines are included to guide the reader through sections of large models.

Structure layer: Structure represents complexity in a problem space. Classification Structure portrays class-member organization, reflecting generalization-specialization. Assembly Structure shows aggregation, reflecting whole and component parts.

Structure reflects problem-space complexity, capitalizing on two of the pervading methods of organization used by people. In addition, Classification Structure provides a basis for subsequent inheritance, giving explicit representation of Attribute and Service commonality within such a structure.

The OOA strategy for the structure layer is as follows:

1. *Classification Structure:* consider each Object as a generalization, then as a specialization.
2. *Assembly Structure:* consider each Object as a whole, then as a component part.
3. *Checks:* real-world structure, within the problem space, within scope.

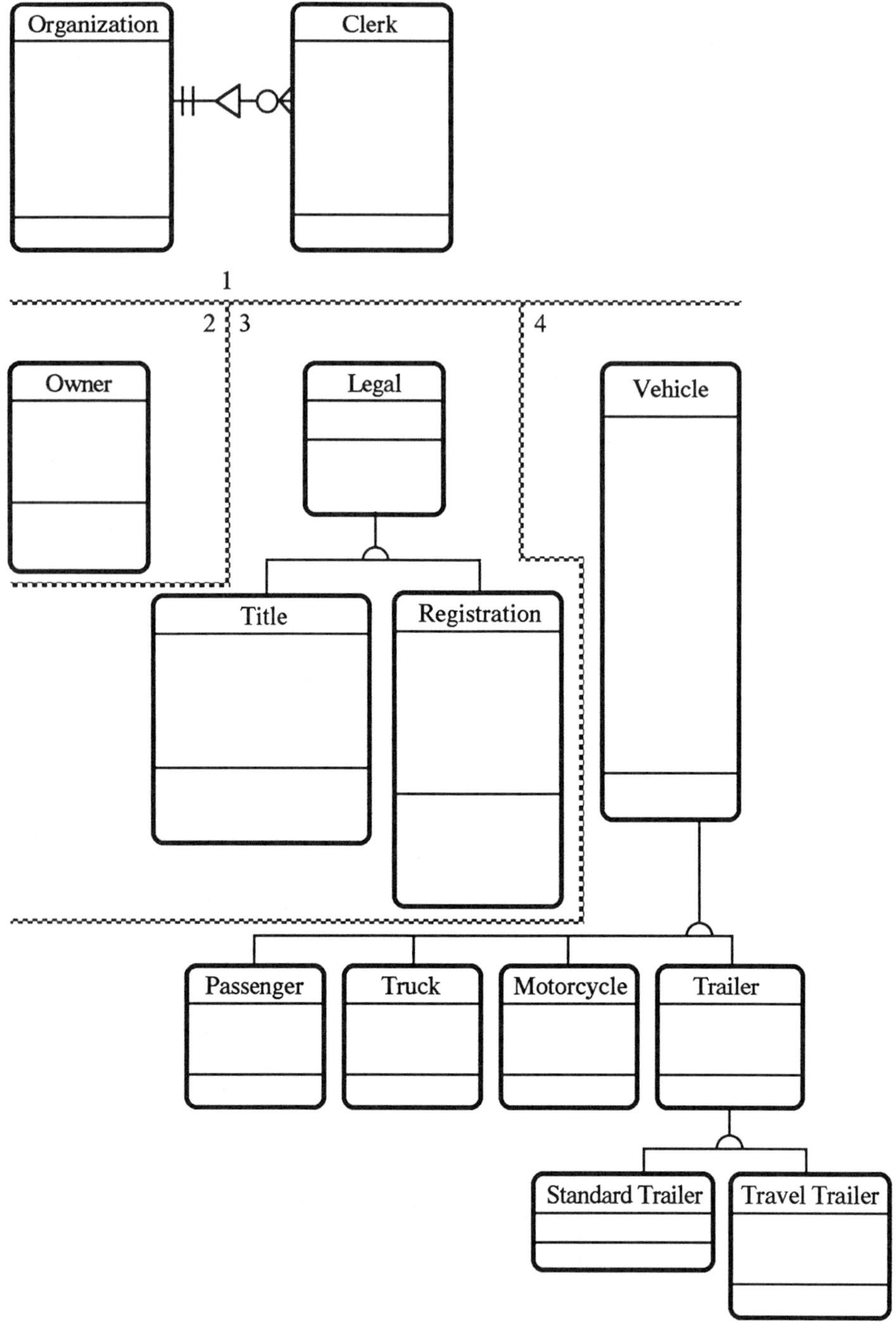

Figure 8: An OOA example of a Structure layer

The model shown in Figure 8, includes two Classification Structures (legal and vehicle). It also includes one Assembly Structure (an organization and its clerks).

Attribute layer: An Attribute is a data element used to describe an instance of an Object or Classification Structure. Attributes are shown on the diagram and specified in the Object repository.

Attributes are listed in the center section of the Object and Structure symbols. Attributes are data elements or logical groupings of data elements.

The OOA strategy for the Attribute layer is as follows:

1. *Identify the Attributes:* Examine the problem space. Attach according to the real-world Object that the Attribute actually describes. Identify at the level of

atomic concept: an individual data element or a natural grouping of closely related data elements.

2. *Position the Attributes:* In Classification Structure, put the common Attributes higher in the Structure and show the specialization below. If an Attribute applies to the majority of specializations, put it in the generalization; then override it for the specializations that do not need it. If an Attribute at times could have the value "not applicable," look closely for an additional Structure.
3. *Identify and define the instance connections:* Add instance connection lines: reflect problem-space mappings; strive for a minimal set of necessary connections; connect with a Classification Structure at the generalization level when the connection applies to all instances, otherwise only at the specific specializations. Define multiplicity: in each direction, establish the connection as a single connection or a collection of connections. Define participation: in each direction, define the connection as optional or mandatory. Check for special cases: connections across three or more Objects or classification structures, many-to-many instance connections, instance connections between instances of same Object, and multiple-instance connections between two Objects.
4. *Revise Objects:* Attributes with "not-applicable" values imply another Classification Structure. Objects with a single Attribute imply that a higher level of abstraction is available, putting that Attribute inside other Objects where it belongs. Repeated Attribute values may signal a new Object; check the Object identification guidelines; check that each resulting Object will have more than one Attribute. Adaptation parameters become Attributes or minimum/maximum parameters for the Attributes.
5. *Specify the Attributes:* Name, description, and (optionally) allowable values, range, limit, unit of measure, and precision. Categorize each Attribute as descriptive, definition, always derivable, or occasionally derivable.
6. *Specify the instance connection constraints:* From the perspective of one instance and its mapping constraints with others. Also specify the mapping constraints due to any assembly connections that an Object participates in as a whole or as a component part.

Note that the Attributes pertaining to all vehicles are defined higher in the Classification Structure and are extended by the specializations (car, truck, and motorcycle) lower in the structure (see Figure 9).

Instance connections represent a mapping of an instance of an Object or Classification Structure with other instance(s); the mapping is shown with a solid line, with markings indicating multiplicity and participation constraints.

Service Layer: A Service is the processing to be performed upon receipt of a message. Services are identified on the diagram and specified on the Object repository.

The Services are listed in the bottom section of the Object and Structure symbols. Services to add, change, delete, and select a Service are implicit to each Object and Structure (and therefore do not appear in the diagram, although such Services are defined in the Object repository). The Object Services show the processing encapsulated with the Attributes.

The OOA strategy for the Service layer is as follows:

1. *Identify Services:* Primary strategy: fundamental Services—occur (add, change, delete, select), calculate, monitor. Secondary strategy 1: Object life history—define the basic sequence, check for variations in each step, add steps; add Services. Secondary strategy 2: State-event-response—define the major system states, list the external events and required responses, expand the Services and message connections.
2. *Identify message connections:* Add message connections for instances already connected by instance connections. Then examine processing needed by one instance from another, looking for additional message connections.
3. *Specify the Services:* Focus on the required externally observable behavior. Use a template. Add diagrams to simplify the specifications. Develop narratives. Put the documentation set together.

The primary strategy focuses on three fundamental Services: occur (add, change, delete, and select and calculate, and monitor. The secondary strategies examine Object life history and state-event response (causation).

Note that the Services pertaining to all vehicles are defined higher in the Classification Structure and are extended by the specializations (car, truck, and motorcycle) lower in the Structure (see Figure 10).

Message connections represent the sending of a message from one Object to another, to get some processing done on behalf of the sending Object; a message connection is shown with a dashed arrow pointing from the sender of the message to the receiver of the message.

Conclusion

The notation and approach of OOA builds on the three constantly employed methods of organization—Objects and Attributes, aggregation, and classification.

OOA is a relatively young method and will continue to evolve. The reader is encouraged to contact Mr. Coad for free updates on the latest advances in OOA.

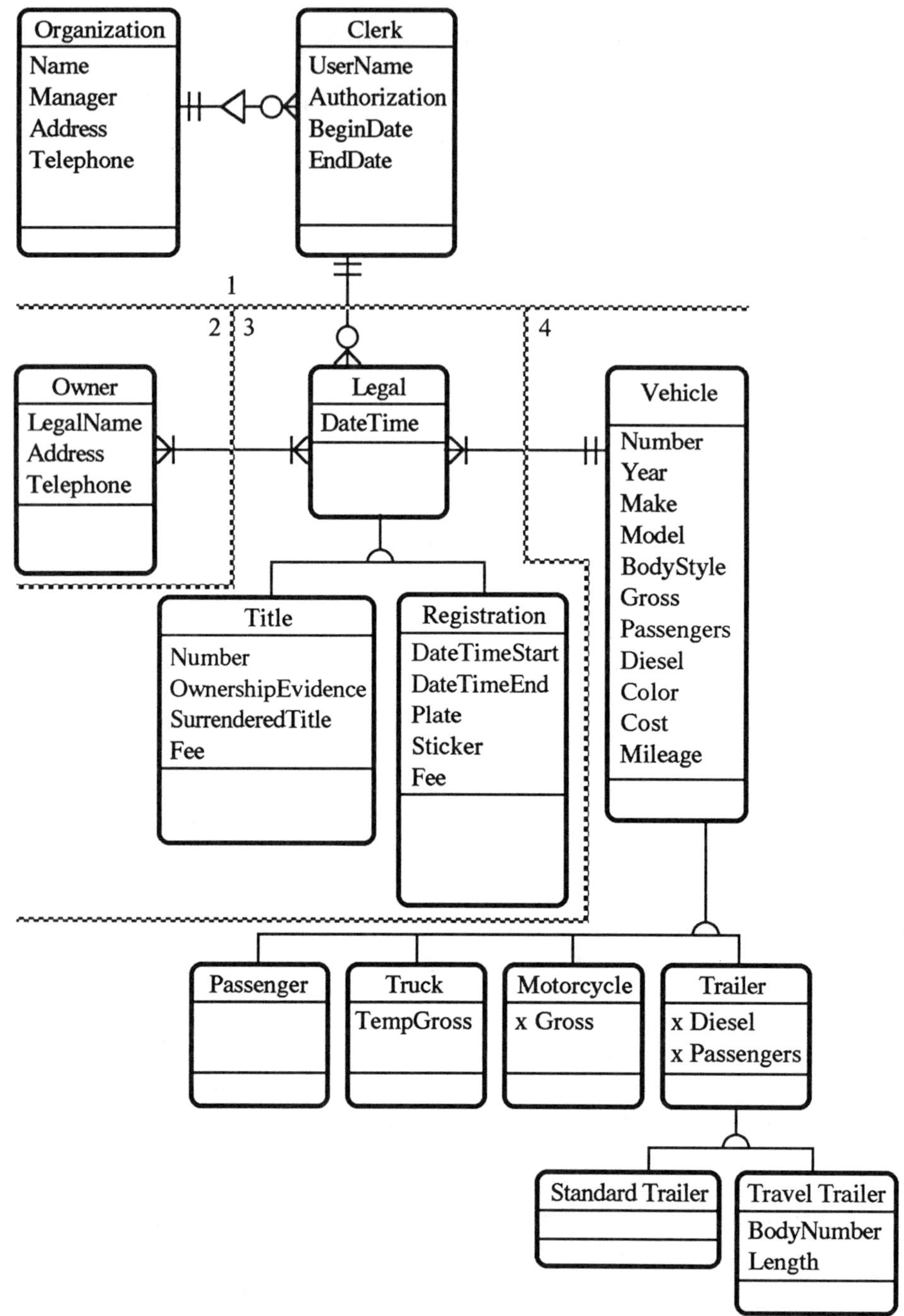

Figure 9: An OOA example of an Attribute layer

Primary Bibliography

Books

[Coad, 1989] Coad, Peter, *Object-Oriented Analysis,* Seminar notes. Object International (Austin, TX), 1989.

[Coad, 1989] Coad, Peter, *Object-Oriented DBMSs.* Seminar notes. Object International (Austin, TX), 1989.

[Coad and Yourdon, 1989] Coad, Peter and Yourdon, Edward, *Object-Oriented Analysis.* Prentice-Hall, 1990 (available 9-89).

[Cox, 1986] Cox, Brad, *Object-Oriented Programming.* Addison-Wesley, 1986.

[Meyer, 1988] Meyer, Bertrand, *Object-Oriented Software Construction.* Prentice Hall, 1988.

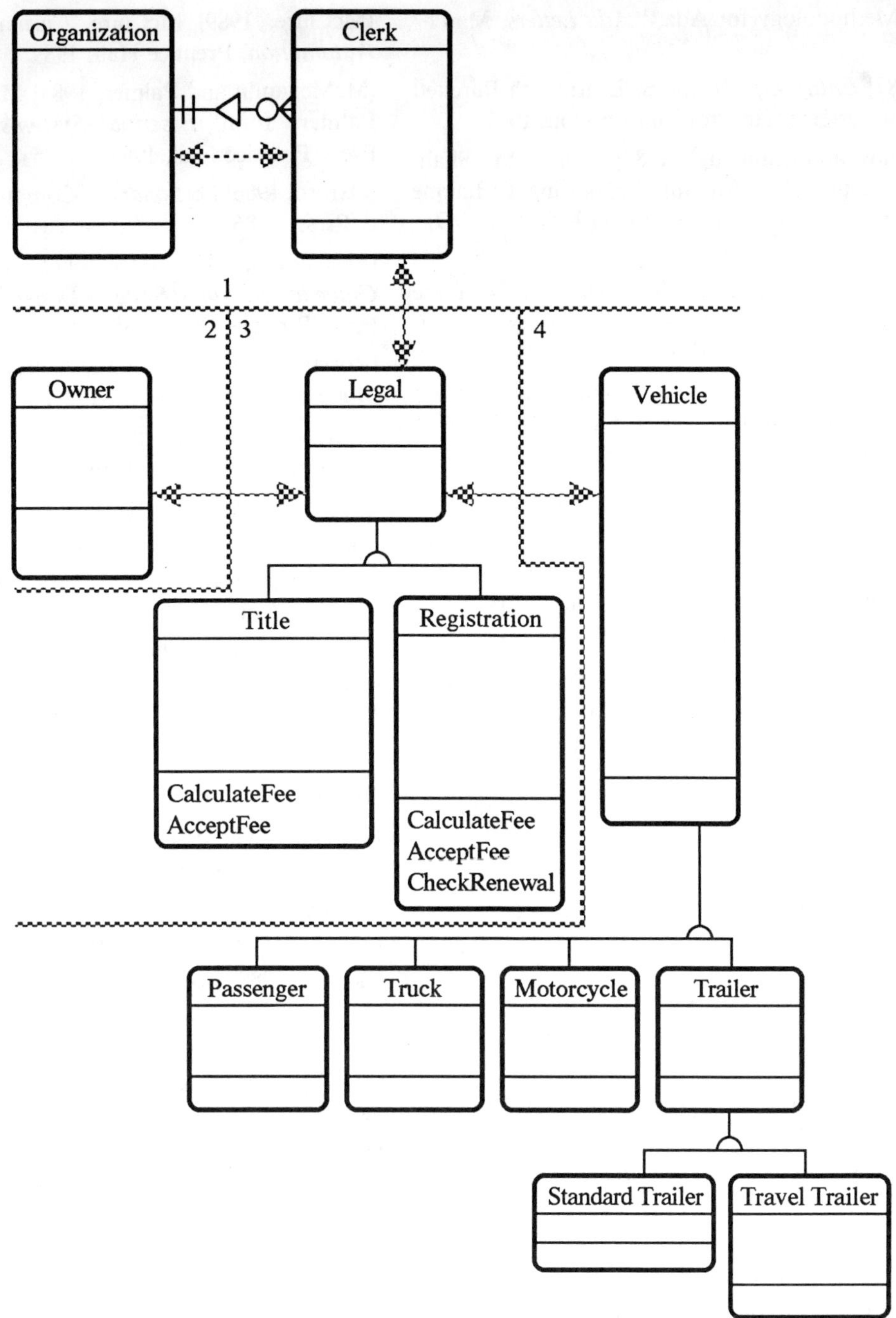

Figure 10: An OOA example of a Service layer

[Shlaer and Mellor, 1988] Shlaer, Sally and Mellor, Steve, *Object-Oriented Systems Analysis.* Prentice-Hall, 1988.

[Smalltalk, 1986] *Smalltalk/V Tutorial and Handbook.* Digitalk, Inc., 1986.

Articles

[Conte, 1987] Conte, Paul, "Understanding Relational Data Bases," *Computer Language,* May 1987.

[Danforth, 1988] Danforth, Scott and Tomlinson, Chris, "Type Theories and Object-Oriented Programming," *ACM Computing Surveys,* March 1988.

[Hull and King, 1987] Hull, Richard and King, Roger, "Semantic Database Modeling: Survey, Applications, and Research Issues," *ACM Computing Surveys,* September 1987.

[Ladden, 1989] Ladden, Richard, "A Survey of Issues to Be Considered in the Development of an Object-Oriented Development Methodology for Ada," *Ada Letters,* March/April 1989.

[LBMS, 1987] *Entity Life Histories,* Learmonth Burchett Management Systems, Houston and London, 1987.

[Loomis, Shaw, and Rumbaugh, 1987] Loomis, M., Shah, A., and Rumbaugh, J., "An Object Modeling Technique for Conceptual Design." *European Conference on OOP,* June 1987.

[Rumbaugh, 1988a] Rumbaugh, J., "Relational Database Design Using an Object-Oriented Methodology," *Communications of the ACM,* April 1988.

[Rumbaugh, 1987] Rumbaugh, J., "Relations as Semantic Constructs in an Object-Oriented Language," *ACM OOPSLA '87 Proceedings,* October 1987.

[Seidewitz and Stark, 1987] Seidewitz, Ed and Stark, Mike, "Towards a General Object-Oriented Software Development Methodology," *Ada Letters,* Volume 7, Number 4.

[Stankovic, 1988] Stankovic, John, "Misconceptions about Real-Time Computing," *IEEE Computer,* October 1988.

[Teorey, 1986] Teorey, T., Yang, D., and Fry, J., "A Logical Design Methodology for Relational Databases Using the Extended Entity-Relationship Model," *ACM Computing Surveys,* June 1986.

[Thomas, 1989] Thomas, Dave, "What's an Object?" *Byte,* March 1989.

Secondary Bibliography

Books

[Berryman, 1984] Berryman, Gregg, *Notes on Graphic Design and Visual Communication.* William Kaufmann, 1984.

[Britannica] "Animal Behaviour," "Classification Theory," "Mood," *Encyclopedia Britannica.*

[Date, 1986] Date, C.J., *An Introduction to Database Systems.* Addison-Wesley, 1986.

[DeMarco, 1978] DeMarco, Tom, *Structured Analysis and System Specification.* Yourdon Press/Prentice Hall, 1978.

[Fisher, 1989] Fisher, Alan S., *CASE: Using Software Development Tools,* John Wiley & Sons, 1988.

[Gane and Sarson, 1979] Gane, Chris and Sarson, Trish, *Structured Systems Analysis: Tools and Techniques,* Prentice-Hall, 1979.

[IEEE, 1983] *IEEE Standard Glossary of Software Engineering Terminology* (Standard 729). IEEE, 1983.

[Jalote, 1989] Jalote, Pankaj, "Functional Refinement and Nested Objects for Object-Oriented Design," *IEEE Transactions on Software Engineering,* March 1989.

[Lanham, 1981] Lanham, Richard A., *Revising Business Prose.* Charles Scribner's Sons, 1981.

[McClure, 1989] McClure, Carma, *CASE Is Software Automation.* Prentice-Hall, 1989.

[McMenamin and Palmer, 1984] McMenamin, Steve and Palmer, John, *Essential Systems Analysis.* Yourdon Press/Prentice-Hall, 1984.

[Oxford, 1986] *Dictionary of Computing.* Oxford University Press, 1986.

[Page-Jones, 1988] Page-Jones, Melliar, *The Practical Guide to Structured Systems Design.* 2nd edition, Yourdon Press/Prentice-Hall, 1988.

[Rosenau, 1981] Rosenau, Milton, *Successful Project Management,* Wadsworth 1981.

[Shertzer, 1986] Shertzer, Margaret, *The Elements of Grammar.* Macmillan, 1986.

[Strunk and White, 1979] Strunk Jr., W. and White, E.B., *The Elements of Style,* Macmillan, 1979.

[Yourdon, 1989] Yourdon, Edward, *Modern Structured Analysis.* Yourdon Press/Prentice Hall, 1989.

[Yourdon and Constantine, 1989] Yourdon, Edward and Constantine, Larry, *Structured Design,* Prentice Hall, 1979.

Articles

[Apple, 1989a] "The Future Belongs to OOP," *Apple Viewpoints,* December 19, 1988.

[Apple, 1989b] "The Power of Object-Oriented Programming," *Apple Direct,* February 1989.

[Boehm, 1988] Boehm, Barry, "Understanding and Controlling Software Costs," *IEEE Transactions on Software Engineering,* October 1988.

[Booch, 1986] Booch, Grady, "Object-Oriented Development," *IEEE Transactions on Software Engineering,* February 1986.

[Bruce, 1988] Bruce, Thomas, "CASE Brought Down to Earth," *Database & Programming Design,* October 1988.

[Chen, 1988] Chen, C. William, "The DBA's Changing Role," *Database Design & Programming,* October 1988.

[Fischer, 1989] Fischer, Gerhard, "Human-Computer Interaction in Software: Lessons Learned, Challenges Ahead," *IEEE Software,* January 1989.

[Ingalls, 1981] Ingalls, David, "Design Principles Behind Smalltalk," *Byte,* August 1981.

[Jacobsen, 1987] Jacobsen, Ivar, "Object-Oriented Development in an Industrial Environment," *ACM OOPSLA '87 Proceedings,* October 1987.

[Kim, Ballou, Chou, Garza, and Woelk, 1988] Kim, Ballou, Chou, Garza, and Woelk, "Integrating an Object-Oriented Programming System with a Database System," *ACM OOPSLA '88 Proceedings,* October 1988.

[Ladden, 1988] Ladden, Richard, "A Survey of Issues... Object-Oriented... and Ada," *ACM Software Engineering Notes,* July 1988.

[Lee, Rissman, D'Ippolito, Plinta, and Scoy, 1987] Lee, Rissman, D'Ippolito, Plinta, and Scoy, "An OOD Paradigm for Flight Simulators," *CMU-SEI Technical Report,* December 1987.

[Liebermann, 1988] Liebermann, Daniel, "Codd's 12 Rules: A Method for DBMS Evaluation," *Database Programming and Design,* December 1988.

[Millikin, 1989] Millikin, Michael, "Object-Orientation: What It Can Do for You," *Computerworld,* March 13, 1989.

[Parnas, 1972] Parnas, David, "On the Criteria for Decomposing Programs into Modules," *Communications of the ACM,* December 1972.

[Potter and Trueblood, 1988] Potter, William and Trueblood, Robert, "Traditional, Semantic, and Hyper-Semantic Approaches to Data Modeling," *IEEE Computer,* June 1988.

[Ramamoorthy, 1988] Ramamoorthy, C.V. and Sheu, Phillip, "Object-Oriented Systems," *IEEE Expert,* Fall 1988.

[Rumbaugh, 1988b] Rumbaugh, Ed, "Controlling Propagation of Operations Using Attributes on Relations," *ACM OOPSLA '88 Proceedings,* October 1988.

[Sanden, 1989a] Sanden, Bo, "An Entity-Life Modeling Approach to the Design for Concurrent Software," *Communications of the ACM,* March 1989.

[Sanden, 1989b] Sanden, Bo, "The Case for Eclectric Design of Real-Time Software," *IEEE Transactions on Software Engineering,* March 1989.

[Seidewitz, 1987] Seidewitz, Ed, "Object-Oriented Programming in Smalltalk and Ada," *ACM OOPSLA '87 Proceedings,* October 1987.

[Seidewitz, 1989] Seidewitz, Ed, "Notes on Object-Oriented Analysis and Specification," Unpublished Notes, December 1988.

[Smith 1988] Smith, Connie, "Applying Synthesis Principles to Create Responsive Software Systems," *IEEE Transactions on Software Engineering,* October 1988.

[Stroustrup, 1988a] Stroustrup, Bjarne, "What Is Object-Oriented Programming?" *IEEE Software,* May 1988.

[Stroustrop 88b] Stroustrup, Bjarne, "A Better C," *Byte,* August 1988.

[Wing and Nixon, 1989] Wing, J.M. and Nixon, M.R., "Extending Ina Jo with Temporal Logic," *IEEE Transactions on Software Engineering,* February 1989. (Ina Jo is a trademark of SDC, now a part of Unisys).

[Wegner, 1987] Wegner, Peter, "Dimensions of Object-Based Language Design," *ACM OOPSLA '87 Proceedings,* October 1987.

Standards

[2167A] *DOD-STD-2167A, Defense System Software Development*. U.S. Department of Defense, February 29, 1988. To request a copy of 2167A and Its Data Item Descriptions, write Naval Publications and Forms Center, 5801 Tabor Ave., Philadelphia, PA 19120 USA. (In the U.S., copies may be requested by calling 215-697-2000).

On-Line Forums

BIX, OOD Conference.

CompuServe, Computer Language Forum.

A COMPARISON OF OBJECT-ORIENTED AND STRUCTURED DEVELOPMENT METHODS

Patrick H. Loy
Loy Consulting, Inc., and
The Johns Hopkins University
3553 Chesterfield Avenue
Baltimore, MD 21213
(301) 483-3532

ABSTRACT

The significance of "object-oriented" as a development method, and the current confusion over the term are addressed. A set of characteristics is proposed as a basis for agreement on a definition of the term. Object-oriented development is compared to the "structured techniques," and work in progress on integrating the two methods is reveiwed. Practical recommendations on assessing the importance of object-oriented development are given.

BIOGRAPHICAL SKETCH

Patrick H. Loy has his own software engineering consulting business, and serves part-time on the faculty of The Johns Hopkins University. His major research interests are in the areas of requirements analysis and design, and he has authored many papers on these topics. He has consulting experience in several software engineering areas, and conducts seminars in the U.S., Canada, and Europe. He also trains software acquisition managers for a U.S. government agency. He has refereed technical manuscripts for the Addison-Wesley Publishing Company, and for professional conferences and journals, including *IEEE Software*. Mr. Loy was formerly a network software analyst for Control Data Corporation's cybernet system. He is a member of the IEEE, ACM, and Computer Professionals for Social Responsibility. Mr. Loy holds the M.S. degree in computer science from The Johns Hopkins University, and the B.S. degree in mathematics from the University of Oregon.

1. INTRODUCTION

It is an undeniable truism that the methods and tools used during software development can have a significant impact on the quality of the final product. Over the past 15 years or so, the "structured techniques" have gained a great deal of acceptance as being methods that can assist the developer in the task of engineering quality into the system as it is being developed. These methods are based on a functional view of the system, with the system being partitioned according to its functional aspects.

Recently a new approach to system modeling has been gaining popularity, and many would say that it is the current state-of-the-art method for system development. This new approach, called "object-oriented," is supported by several programming languages, and several familiar names in the field of computer science endorse it as being the most advanced abstract modeling technique. Moreover, the religious zeal of some proponents of this approach has engendered an expectation that we may be heralding the arrival of the long-awaited "silver bullet" for software development.

Consequently, the subject of object-oriented development (OOD) has generated a great deal of interest among practitioners, with many dp professionals asking the questions, "what exactly is OOD?"; "how does it compare to the structured techniques?"; "is it a partial or complete life cycle method?"; and, "should we adopt it in our organization?"

Unfortunately, these questions have been very difficult to answer. Two areas of confusion lie at the heart of the problem. First, there is no universally agreed upon definition of what constitutes the OOD approach to system modeling. There are some OOD advocates, for example, who, with great conviction, tout Ada as being an object-oriented language, or even as the *premier* object-oriented language. There are others, however, who adamantly dispute that notion, declaring with equal conviction that Ada is decidedly not an object-oriented language.

The second area of confusion, which is closely related to the first, is on the differences between OOD and the structured methods. Some authors have suggested that there is a high degree of compatibility between at least some of the structured techniques and OOD. Others disagree with that notion, claiming that the differences in the modeling perspectives preclude any meaningful compatibility between the methods. Some advocates of OOD claim that it involves a more "natural" way to think than the functional approach. Some proponents of the structured techniques, on the other hand, insist that it is just as "natural" to think about functions as it is to think about objects.

This paper will address itself to the task of cutting through some of the fog surrounding this debate in an attempt to gain some clarity and perspective on the matter.

2. WHY THE ISSUE IS IMPORTANT

Many new software development methods have appeared over the past several years. Consequently, there can be a tendency to view object-oriented development as "just another method" for the developer's toolbox. However, this new approach, as evidenced by its rising popularity and the fact that the concept has matured to the point that it now encompasses a full life cycle approach, represents something more profound. In this author's opinion, OOD embodies a unique, coherent theory of knowledge for system development. As such, it describes a cognitive process for capturing, organizing, and communicating the essential knowledge of the system's "problem space," and, for the model thereby formed, gives guidance on using specific techniques to map this problem space model to a "solution space" model.

The challenge of conceptual models has always been much more than just increasing the number of tools in the developers toolbox. To say "here is a bunch of tools to choose from" is very different from being able to say "here is a coherent theory of knowledge for system development *and* here is a bunch of tools to choose from that can be applied consistent with the theory." The theory gives guidance on what tool is most applicable for a particular situation. Herein lies a danger in the toolbox metaphor: it can be vulgarized to omit the critical need for a corresponding theory of knowledge on the use of the tools. It is nice for the carpenter to have many screwdrivers in the toolbox, but just as important is to *know* when it is appropriate to use the Phillips screwdriver and when to use the standard screwdriver.

Thus, a theory of knowledge is more comprehensive than a particular method for a particular life cycle phase. The work being done on object-oriented analysis (OOA)[1,4] signals the fact that OOD has gone from being a partial to a full life cycle approach, which means that OOD is much broader than just a "method." The emerging OOD paradigm promotes a particular mode of thought, a particular system viewpoint, which has far-reaching implications.

In the context of our discussion, a theory of knowledge for system development must give guidance on how to cope with complexity. Many of today's systems are exceedingly complex, and it is impossible to consider equally all of their attributes. Consequently, to understand such a system an *abstraction* must be used, whereby the most important attributes of the system are illuminated, and the others are suppressed. But, of course, this involves making assumptions about which aspects are more important, and which are less important. OOD is an abstraction that makes different assumptions than structured development (SD) about what to illuminate and what to suppress. Thus, OOD offers a unique and different perspective on what point of view best guides the thinking of the system modeler.

3. TOWARD A DEFINITION OF "OBJECT-ORIENTED"

3.1 Clearing the "Semantic Thicket"

Why is there so much confusion over what "object-oriented" means? To address this question, consider the origins of the term. "Object -oriented programming" emerged as a term associated with the development of Smalltalk, the original object-oriented language, and the one most often regarded as a pure object-oriented language.

Smalltalk drew heavily from Simula, ultimately incorporating the notion of *class* as the sole structural unit, with instances of classes or *objects*, being the concrete units which inhabit the world of the Smalltalk system. To a lesser degree, Smalltalk was influenced by LISP.

Rentsch has provided an interesting history of the origins of object-oriented programming and Smalltalk, and, in 1982, predicted the confusion that would accompany its growing popularity: "My guess is that object oriented programming will be in the 1980's what structured programming was in the 1970's. Everyone will be in favor of it. Every manufacturer will promote his products as supporting it. Every manager will pay lip service to it. Every programmer will practice it (differently). And no one will know just what it is."[2]

To get to the heart of the confusion surrounding OOD, it may be helpful to consider the following points. First, OOD as a development philosophy has its roots in object-oriented *programming*, and evolved bottom up, i.e., from programming to design to requirements analysis. Thus, it is helpful to be familiar with object-oriented programming to grasp the OOD paradigm.

Second, OOD involves an unfamiliar way of thinking to most software developers, and in this respect some confusion is to be expected. Our training has not taught us to think in object-oriented terms. This dynamic can be seen when people are introduced to any new manner of thought. When the structured development techniques were first introduced, they also involved a new way of thinking about software development, and this led inevitably to some confusion. As another example, programmers often state that their first exposure to the simulation language GPSS V "blows their minds" because it involves a way of thinking that is radically different from the procedural languages they are used to.

Beyond these two factors, however, OOD has faced an even deeper problem in being understood. Early on in the history of object-oriented programming, bits and pieces of the concept were supported in various languages, and these languages became erroneously regarded as "object-oriented." Ada is the main example of this. As Ada was taking form in the late 1970's, it was widely understood that it was, in large part, based on features found in Pascal and ALGOL. Later, as Ada became touted as an object-oriented language, people who had experience with Pascal or ALGOL naturally made the connection in their minds that "object-oriented" was somehow a souped up extension of a Pascal-type procedural language. As Cox said, in commenting on the confusion surrounding the object-oriented buzzword, "It is hard to imagine two languages more different than Smalltalk-80 and Ada, yet both are sometimes called object-oriented languages."[3]

In addition, probably due to the heritage of Simula, some modeling techniques that utilize classification have been advertised as being object-oriented. The book by Shlaer and Mellor, *Object-Oriented Systems Analysis*,[4] has been criticized by some as being little more than an approach to semantic data modeling.[5,1] (Interestingly, apart from its title, the term "object-oriented" hardly ever appears in the book.) However, while this author generally agrees with the above cited criticisms as to the incompleteness of the method presented, the book does provide useful guidance for the front-end activities of an object-oriented approach, specifically in the critical task of identifying the "objects," which will be discussed below.

So, object-oriented has become a term that means different things to different people. It is this author's opinion that a uniform definition of object-oriented is possible and desirable, at least in terms of the *characteristics* of an object-oriented approach. Moreover, the literature on the subject is completely adequate in this respect. In coalescing around a definition we should be primarily guided by the original intent of the term, especially in its connection to Smalltalk, and by the development of the theory that has built upon that original meaning, which extended the notion to design and analysis.

3.2 Comparing Development Paradigms

Structured analysis, structured design, and structured programming are collectively known as structured development (SD). The ideas behind these methods are found in the writings of Yourdon and Constantine,[19] Dijkstra,[20] DeMarco,[21] Myers,[22] and many others. Although there are several versions of SD in existence today, all of them are based on a philosophy of system development that analyzes the system from a functional point of view. In describing this viewpoint, Constantine says "the main features of software that are of interest to the analyst, designer, or programmer are the functional aspects: what functions or tasks the software must perform, what subfunctions or subtasks are needed to complete the overall functions, what pieces or component parts will perform various functions, how those functions will be performed."[23] Constantine calls this way of thinking the "functional paradigm." A paradigm is an exemplary model that also constitutes a world view.

Constantine points out that "this focus is so embedded in our thinking about computer programming that we are scarcely aware of it. We do not think of it as constituting a particular way of viewing programs or consider the possibility of alternative views."[23]

Given that this is the current conventional way of thinking, Constantine provides a concise comparison of the functional and object-oriented viewpoints:

> In the functional paradigm, function and procedure are primary, data are only secondary. Functions and related data are either conceived of as independent, or data are associated with or attached to the functional components.
>
> The antithesis of this viewpoint is the object-oriented paradigm. In this paradigm, data are considered primary and procedures are secondary; functions are associated with related data. Problems and applications are looked at as consisting of interrelated classes of real objects characterized by their common attributes, the rules they obey, and the functions or operations defined on them. Software systems consist of structured collections of abstract data structures embodying those object classes that model the interrelated objects of the real-world problem.
>
> From this it should be clear that the object-oriented paradigm is based on a new way of looking at the old dichotomy of procedure and data.[23]

The SD techniques are generally associated with a top-down development strategy, whereas OOD is essentially a bottom-up approach. The "top" of a system structure contains control modules representing the activation of large chunks of the overall capabilities. At the "bottom" are the basic facilities for defining and manipulating the data, and for hiding its structure from the rest of the system. These concepts are embodied in the idea of the "object," as will be discussed later. OOD thus facilitates a natural bottom-up organization of the software.

3.3 Characterizing Object-Oriented Systems

With this overview of the two development paradigms as a framework, below are brief descriptions of the characteristics of object-oriented development. The following discussion is not meant to be a tutorial on the subject, but is presented to help formulate a definition. For more complete discussions of specific object-oriented methods, the reader is referred to the references, especially Coad,[1] Booch,[7] Cox,[3] Rentsch,[2] and Meyer.[26]

Objects
At the heart of OOD is the idea of the "object." An object is an entity defined by a set of common attributes, and the services or operations associated with it. Objects are the major actors, agents, and servers in the problem space of the system, and can be identified by carefully analyzing this domain. Whatever form of system requirements that is provided by the user or client can be used as a starting point for this task. Objects can be found among devices that the system interacts with (e.g., sensors), other systems that interface with the system under study, organizational units (departments, divisions, etc.), things that must be remembered over time (e.g., details about events occuring in the system's environment), physical locations or sites, and specific roles played by humans (clerk, pilot, etc.).

The central problem in OOD turns out to be "finding the objects." As mentioned above, Shlaer and Mellor have made a contribution in this area, providing tools and concepts for enumerating various categories of potential object classes.[4]

In characterizing the object concept it is important to discuss the viewpoint associated with objects. OOD is interested in how an object appears (an outside view), rather than what an object is (an inside view). This shift in viewpoint is critical to the concept of OOD. It enables the system modeler to think not only about objects as classification entities, but also about the intrinsic behavior associated with objects. This intrinsic behavior embodied within an object provides the visibility of the object in relation to other objects.

For example, consider the object called "policeman." The object called "ordinary citizen" is not much interested in exactly what a policeman *is* (inside view) but is *very* interested in the *intrinsic behavior* (outside view) of the object (issues speeding tickets,etc.) Also the ordinary citizen object is interested in what *services* it can invoke from policeman (give directions when lost, etc.), which are also part of the intrinsic behavior of the object.

The term *encapsulation* has come to represent this central notion of OOD, and is based on the concept of *information hiding*, as espoused by David Parnas.[27] Rentsch stresses the importance of this viewpoint for OOD, saying

> The shift in viewpoint from inside to outside is itself an essential part of object oriented programming. In my experience this shift occurs as a quantum leap, the "aha!" that accompanies a flash of insight. In spite of this, I am convinced that the view from outside is the natural one - only my years of training and experience as a programmer conditioned me to "normally" view objects from inside ... The first principle of object oriented programming might be called *intelligence encapsulation:* view objects from outside to provide a natural metaphor of intrinsic behavior.[2]

Nonhierarchic Object Model
Developers accustomed to using structured techniques usually think of the system-structure model as a hierarchy of functions, which maps to a set of nested subroutines. (It should be noted that, at least in the case of structured design, this is a manifestation of the way the method is practiced, not in the method itself. Yourdon and Constantine explicitly allowed for nonhierarchic module collections, as discussed in chapter 18 of their book, *Structured Design*.[19]) The object model, on the other hand, is

a nonhierarchic topology of objects. This topology forms an abstract view of the problem space, whch is meant to map naturally to a nonhierarchic model of the solution space. As Booch says, "a program that implements a model of reality may be viewed as a set of objects that interact with each other."[7]

Processing and Communication

In the OOD model, processing takes place inside objects. "An object, far from being inert matter, is an active, alive, intelligent entity, and is responsible for proviaing its own computational behavior. Thus processing capability is not only inside the object, it is everpresent within and inseparable from the object."[2]

While an object contains processing capability, it is not always self sufficient in this respect, and may need to interact with other objects. The "ordinary citizen" object, for example, can do many things for itself (eat, read, write), but may at times need to invoke the services of the "policeman" object (get directions). Thus communication between objects is needed.

The model being nonhierarchic, objects communicate with other objects by a mechanism of "message passing," which is similar to the concept of "coroutines" as discussed by Yourdon and Constantine.[19] Thus, an invocation of one module by another is not necessarily associated with a hierarchical relationship in the organization of the objects. "Message sending serves as the uniform metaphor for communication in the same way that objects serve as the uniform metaphor for processing capability and synthesis. ... all processing is accomplished by message sending. ... A message serves to initiate processing and request information."[2]

Inheritance

Basic to the idea of OOD is a framework of classing, subclassing, and superclassing, that allows individuals within a collection to *share* common attributes, as needed. This framework is collectively referred to as *inheritance.* If the class "tree," for example, contains the attribute "leafy branches," then members of the tree subclasses (oak, elm, maple, etc.) can inherit this attribute, and it need not be redefined.

Object-Oriented Software Organization

There are several variations of object-oriented methods, all of them being somewhat sketchy. Booch, for example, has offered the skeleton of a step-by-step approach for object-oriented design,[7] and other writers have made similar gestures. Consequently, it is impossible to describe *the* object-oriented method, or to be very specific in discussing exactly what *the* end product of OOD looks like. However, it is possible to discuss a general object-oriented concept that refers to a way of structuring software systems that is language independent.

Object-oriented software organization refers to a structuring approach that makes it possible to organize a system by object-oriented concepts and implement it as a set of "object modules" in conventional procedural languages as well as in object-oriented languages. Constantine has this to say about this concept:

> Object-oriented organization is a form of modular structure in which a program is designed as a structured collection of "object modules" implementing data abstractions. An object module encapsulates the implementation of a class of data structures and their related services, exporting specific services (and sometimes attributes) as features of the "official" external interface of the

module. Object modules are interrelated by their usage of the attributes and services of other modules, just as in conventional functional structures, as well as by feature inheritance. An object module is thus an organizing concept that groups together a collection of functions (services) based on their association with a well-defined class of data structures. Object modules are, in effect, multi-function packages that group functions based on principles of strong association with common data structures, with groups interrelated and defined as classes and subclasses of abstract data. [23]

3.4 Deciding if an Approach is Truly Object-Oriented

The preceeding discussion can be summarized to say that an object-oriented method contains at least these basic ideas: *classification* of data abstractions, *inheritance* of common attributes, and *encapsulation* of attributes, operations and services.
If these characteristics form the basis for a definition of "object-oriented," then it is clear that some languages and methods which are often cited as being object-oriented are something less. According to Peter Coad and Edward Yourdon:

> One can look at different languages, environments, methods, and books and ask "Are you really Object-Oriented?" Unfortunately, many times the answer is "no"; Object-Oriented suffers from being a catchy marketing word, used at times to mean "the good stuff."
>
> Is Ada an Object-Oriented language? No. Genericity, that is, typed parameters, is convenient, but no substitute for inheritance.
>
> Is an information modeling approach Object-Oriented (e.g., Object-Oriented Systems Analysis [Shlaer and Mellor, 1988], a book better titled "making Semantic Data Modeling Practical")? No. Services are missing. Classification is missing. Inheritance is missing. [1]

Coad and Yourdon offer this equation for recognizing an object-oriented approach:

> Object-Oriented =
> Objects
> (an encapsulation of Attributes and exclusive Services;
> an abstraction of the something in the problem space, with
> some number of instances in the problem space)
> + Classification & Inheritance.[1]

The importance of a clear, consistent definition of OOD is that the *essence* of this paradigm for system development not be watered-down, or completely lost in the shuffle, by a loose use of the term. As discussed earlier, OOD represents a theory of knowledge, a mode of thought, that is decidedly unique in its own right. Our use of the term should be directed toward that uniqueness, not toward certain specific *features* of OOD. However, this does not mean that languages or methods that contain certain of those features are of no use. Many of them are, but we should be careful not to characterize them as being "object-oriented," lest we continue to foster the confusion over the term.

4. IS OOD BETTER THAN SD?

A great deal of hopeful enthusiasm has accompanied many of the writings on OOD. According to Cox, "It is time for a revolution in how we build systems ... The revolution is object-oriented programming."[3] From Booch, "[OOD] leads to improved maintainability and understandability of systems."[7] From Danforth and Tomlinson, "[object-oriented programming] represents a positive step toward the design and implementation of complex software systems."[8]

The proponents of OOD usually cite two reasons for their excitement about the approach. One is the claim that the thinking process inherent in OOD is more "natural" than that of SD, i.e., in building an abstract model of reality it is more natural to think in terms of objects than in terms of functions. The other is that the modeling of the problem space maps more directly to the solution space in OOD than it does in SD.

Let us consider the latter argument first. Anyone involved with SD knows that the transition from the analysis model to the design model can be tricky. For example, in moving from a data flow diagram view of the system to creating design structure charts the modeler is forced to make a significant shift in perspective. There are strategies to assist in the matter (transform analysis, transaction analysis, etc.), but it remains a difficult task because the mapping is not truly isomorphic. The proponents of OOD often claim that with OOD the mapping *is* truly isomorphic, or at least far more isomorphic than in SD, which, if true, would offer a great advantage. Coad and Yourdon make this claim, and stress that the singular abstraction medium is a key: "It's a matter of using the same underlying representation in analysis and design. This is a bedrock concept of the [object-oriented analysis] approach."[1]

But is this claim true? Unfortunately, there is little evidence of this in the writings on the subject, a fact which, in part, reflects the relative newness of the field. In fact there are those that refute the notion completely. Constantine says "The mapping from analysis model to design model is every bit as 'not isomorphic' in OOD as in SD <u>once you get beyond textbook and toy examples</u>" (his emphasis).[24] It seems the jury is still out on this question, and the matter will not be resolved until there is some published hard evidence.

Part of the difficulty in resolving this matter is that the overall development environment seems to be largely inadequate to exploit the paradigm fully. Stroustrup has compared several languages in terms of their support for OOD, and points out that if the proper language support is missing the paradigm will be of limited value.[9] And Williams says, "Due to the informality of the approach, lack of adequate language support, and lack of experience with large systems, the potential of the object model in software engineering remains largely unexplored."[6] As might be expected, there is much on-going research in this area.[10] But, the potential emergence of a more isomorphic mapping of problem space to solution space in the OOD paradigm is itself an important reason for software professionals to stay abreast of the developments in the OOD world.

Now to the argument that thinking in terms of objects is more "natural" than thinking in terms of functions. As cited earlier, Rentsch is "convinced that the [OOD] view is the natural one," and as evidence he posits that "children learn Smalltalk very quickly."[2] Coad and Yourdon state that object-oriented analysis "is based upon concepts which we first learned in kindergarten: objects and attributes, classes and members, wholes and parts." They further assert that for today's modern systems "an object-oriented approach... is a more natural way of dealing with such systems."[1]

It is enticing to think that we have stumbled upon a more natural way of thinking after all these years, but does the evidence really support this notion? It is true that kindergarten children readily learn to classify objects, and it may be true that they learn Smalltalk quickly. But they *also* readily ("naturally?") think in terms of functions, and they learn function-oriented procedural languages quickly. Ask a child to tell you about his or her school, and then try to predict if the response will be primarily in functional terms, or in classification terms (but don't bet on it being one or the other). Is one way of thinking really more "natural" than the other?

Constantine doesn't think so, saying, "there are no 'object classes' in the real physical universe, as these are constructs that exist only in the mind of the viewer... 'objects' are no more real or natural than 'functions.'"[23]

Interestingly, this same type of debate exists in other fields of study. In fact some variation of the "form vs. function" controversy is part of every field. In general, it involves how one views the relative importance of the structural vs. the functional aspects of knowledge. In developmental psychology it is the debate between Piaget and the Gestaltists, and then later between Piaget and the new functionalists;[11,12] in epistemology the debate focuses on the relation between the knower and the object known ;[13] in cognitive anthropology the issue revolves around how a grouping of people synthesizes structure and function as they form their own model of reality in pursuing an understanding of the world they live in.

Two Anthropologists, Dr. George Brandon of the University of Maryland, and Dr. Elliot Fratkin of Duke University were interviewed by the author for the purposes of this paper. Both of them were intrigued that such an issue was being argued in the software field, and saw the clear connection to the debate in their own discipline. Both believe it is a manifestation of a universal question, and were decisive in their opinions that the matter is not resolved, and probably never will be resolved.

Obviously, the details of these various debates is beyond the scope of this paper; but the important finding is that there is no final resolution to the matter. The struggle is ongoing. There is very little that you can say with much confidence about a "most natural" way that people think about the realities of their universe. Thus, to say that the object model is a more natural way to think involves a rather sizeable leap of faith.

Undoubtedly, the truth of the matter is that both paradigms are "natural," and that the proper synthesis of the two, in relation to a particular problem, is what should be striven for. In fact, this is part of the challenge for the next period. OOD has helped to crystallize a way of analyzing systems that brings into sharp relief the fact that we have been limited and one-sided in our approach to the matter up to this time. But we must be careful not to throw the baby out with the bath water. Functional partitioning is a very valuable analytical approach. The task ahead is to move the debate to a higher level - not arguing about which is more "natural" - but exploring how we best take advantage of both approaches.

In this author's view, Ward and Mellor were on the right track when they suggested that the system modeler must determine which modeling approach should play a dominant role, based on the particular type of system being modeled.[14] As the methods mature, guidelines need to be developed and refined to help the modeler determine whether the perspective of OOD or SD should dominate in a particular situation.

5. TOWARD AN INTEGRATION OF THE METHODS

Over the past few months, several papers have addressed the synthesis question mentioned above. Ward has recently written a brief tutorial showing that there is no inherent conflict between the two approaches, and that "real-time structured analysis / structured design can, with modest extensions to the notation and to the model-building heuristics, adequately express an object-oriented design."[15] Jalote proposes an "extended object-oriented design methodology," which incorporates a top-down, step-wise refinement approach.[16] Bailin describes a method for combining structured analysis with the object-oriented approach for requirements specifications.[17] Constantine has recently written two papers that address the topic of the integration of the methods.[23,25] In one he stresses that we must get beyond the "madness of methods," and get "back to basics" by agreeing on a set of fundamental principles independent of methods. With sound principles being recognized as more important than specific methods the groundwork will be laid for a coherent integration of the methods. He points out that there are "a number of common principles [that] are revered by almost all the sundry gurus and acolytes," which can form a basis for what he calls "convergent design methods."[25]

This type of work is highly significant on two counts. First, it is useful to begin exploring these areas of compatibility for purely pragmatic reasons: contractual and/or documentation requirements may make it necessary. Second, and more important, it pushes the theory of knowledge for system development to a higher level, and facilitates the evolution of more coherent and useable methods.

6. RECOMMENDATIONS FOR PROJECT LEADERS

Every software development organization should begin figuring out where they stand in relation to OOD and SD. For shops already engaged with the structured methods, this means having a *plan* for assessing if, and how, OOD might be used to advantage. Ideally, such a plan should be part of a technology transfer program of the organization, as proposed by Loy,[18] and should proceed with both bottom-up and town-up activities being done concurrently.

A suggested plan outline is the following:

1. Have at least two, and preferably three or more, senior software engineers start playing around with Smalltalk. If Smalltalk is not an available option, pick another language that incorporates the features mentioned in section 3 above. It is important that some experienced people begin learning the paradigm at the programming level by getting experience with an object-oriented language. This activity can be done part-time in conjunction with other ongoing assignments. But they should keep at it on a regular basis.

2. Concurrent with the above task, start tracking the literature on the subject. Have an organized effort to do this, with different people assigned specific responsibilities in this respect. For example, one person might be assigned to monitor the articles that

appear in one periodical. Much has been written in the past year, especially, and the trend will undoubtedly increase. Continually assess how the experience in other shops relates to your situation. The references cited in section 5 above could be a good starting point.

3. After a few weeks, provide some of the folks involved in the above two tasks with some "formal" OOD training, e.g., a seminar in OOD. This should help to quickly broaden their perspective on the potential of OOD.

4. Get continual, systematic feedback from all people who are involved in the above tasks about their views on OOD. Do they feel it might play a role in your environment? How significant does its value appear to be? How should it be incorporated into your development plans? Their views on these matters may change over time, so it is important that the feedback mechanism be regular and systematic.

5. Based on the results of the above activities, begin to formulate options for integrating OOD into your environment. This will involve considering the whole spectrum of trade-offs specific to your situation.

7. SUMMARY AND CONCLUSIONS

Object-oriented development is bound to have a major influence on the manner in which systems are built. It has matured to where it must be viewed as a theory of knowledge that embodies a unique perspective for capturing, organizing, and communicating the essential features of a system. The OOD paradigm is derived ultimately from object-oriented programming, an understanding of which is helpful to grasp the essence of OOD.

The software engineering community has been sloppy in its use of the term "object-oriented," and there is currently confusion over the meaning of it. The term should refer collectively to the concepts of *classification, encapsulation,* and *inheritance.*

While some contend that OOD involves a more "natural" way to think than does SD, there is little evidence of this. In fact, both approaches are based on modes of thought that might be called "natural." OOD and SD are not incompatible, and much recent work has been devoted to exploring the potential synthesis and integration of the two. Research in this area should help crystallize the contribution of OOD to our field, and push the quest for a theory of knowledge for systems development to a higher level.

Project leaders should have a plan for investigating the worth of OOD to their shops. This plan, a sample of which was offered, should be part of an ongoing technology transfer program.

Acknowledgements

Many people reviewed the first draft of this paper and provided very helpful, constructive criticisms. Many thanks are due, especially, to Larry Constantine, Jack Bond, Merlin Dorfman, Sally Shlaer, Stephen Mellor, and Bruce Blum for their insightful feedback.

REFERENCES

1 Peter Coad and Edward Yourdon, "An Introduction to OOA - Object-Oriented Analysis," (May 30, 1989), *Tutorial: Systems and Software Requirements Engineering,* Vol. 1, edited by Merlin Dorfman and Richard Thayer, IEEE Press, 1989.

2 Tim Rentsch, "Object Oriented Programming," *SIGPLAN Notices,* Vol.17, No. 9, pp. 51-57, 1982.

3 Brad Cox, *Object-Oriented Programming,* Addison-Wesley, 1986.

4 Sally Shlaer and Stephen Mellor, *Object-Oriented Systems Analysis: Modeling the World in Data,* Yourdon Press, 1988.

5 T.L. (Frank) Pappas, "Object-oriented analysis is flawed," *IEEE Software,* January, 1989.

6 Lloyd Williams, *The Object Model in Software Engineering,* Software Engineering Research, 1986.

7 Grady Booch, "Object-Oriented Development," *IEEE Transactions on Software Engineering,* February, 1986.

8 Scott Danforth and Chris Tomlinson, *Type Theories and Object-Oriented Programming,* ACM Computing Surveys, March, 1988.

9 Bjarne Stroustrup, "What is Object-Oriented Programming?", *IEEE Software,* May 1988.

10 *Research Directions in Object-Oriented Programming,* edited by Bruce Shriver and Peter Wegner, MIT Press, 1987.

11 Herbert Ginsburg and Sylvia Opper, *Piaget's Theory of Intellectual Development,* Prentice-Hall, 1969.

12 *New Trends in Conceptual Representation: Chalenges to Piaget's Theory?,* edited by Ellin Kofsky Scholnick, Lawrence Erlbaum Associates, 1983.

13 *Academic American Encyclopedia,* vol. 7, 1981.

14 Paul Ward and Stephen Mellor, *Structured Development for Real-Time Systems,* Yourdon Press, 1985.

15 Paul Ward, "How to Integrate Object Orientation with Structured analysis and Design," *IEEE Software,* March, 1989.

16 Pankaj Jalote, "Functional Refinements and Nested Objects for Object-Oriented Design," *IEEE Transactions on Software Engineering,* March, 1989.

17 Sidney Bailin, "An Object-Oriented Requirements Specification Method," *Communciations of the ACM,* May, 1989.

18 Patrick Loy, "Five Components of a Software Quality Assurance Paradigm", *Proceedings of the Sixth Annual Pacific Northwest Software Quality Conference,* September, 1988.

19 Edward Yourdon and Larry L. Constantine, *Structured Design,* Yourdon Press, 1975.

20 E.W. Dijkstra, *A Discipline of Programming,* Prentice-Hall, 1976.

21 Tom DeMarco, *Structured Analysis and System Specification,* Yourdon Press, 1978.

22 Glenford J. Myers, *Composite/Structured Design,* Van Nostrand Reinhold , 1978.

23 Larry L. Constantine, Object-Oriented and Structured Methods: Toward Integration, *American Programmer,* vol. 2, no. 7/8, August, 1989.

24 Larry L. Constantine, letter to the author (unpublished), July3, 1989.

25 Larry L. Constantine, "Beyond the Madness of Methods: System Structure Modeling and Convergent Design," *Software Development '89: Proceedings,*

Miller-Freeman Publishing Co., 1989.
26 Meyer, Bertrand, *Object-Oriented Software Construction,* Prentice-Hall, 1988.
27 Parnas, David, "On the Criteria to be Used in Decomposing Systems into Modules," *Communications of the ACM,* December, 1972.

CORE - A METHOD FOR CONTROLLED REQUIREMENT SPECIFICATION

G. P. Mullery

Systems Designers Limited

ABSTRACT

Attempts to specify requirements adequately normally fail - sometimes catastrophically. One reason is the lack of a rigorously defined method which directly addresses the needs of requirement specification. CORE, the subject of this paper, is such a method. CORE is the result of several years of practical experiment by the author, using a number of published approaches to specification and design. It is supported by a diagrammatic notation whose key features are a composite of ideas drawn from several widely used notations for expression of requirement or design.

I. INTRODUCTION

It is now widely accepted that there is a cause-effect relationship between poor requirement specification and the final system quality. i.e.:

poor requirement → unsatisfactory system

Three factors are necessary for achievement of the highest quality in computer systems:

- use of standards and procedures
- use of automated aids
- use of consistent methods.

Each factor must be based on consistent, relevant concepts and each concept must be defined as unambiguously as words permit. There is overlap between the factors and so they must be made mutually consistent as well as self-consistent.

This paper describes CORE, a method for COntrolled Requirement Expression. The CORE method has been defined to fit into a set of standards and procedures produced by Systems Designers Limited. A mapping has been defined from the CORE diagrammatic notation into the terminology of the automated aid PSL/PSA (ref.1).

CORE is applicable to description of dynamic aspects of many types of system (i.e. not just computer systems). Current applications include: specifying requirements for a new avionics system; a description of the total project organisation, standards and procedures for the software life-cycle; description of the requirements for an automated aid for system description.

CORE is supported by a diagrammatic notation whose features derive from several widely used specification and design diagrammatic notations. The notation can be applied to the description of both requirement and design. This paper describes its application to requirement.

The more obvious resemblances are between the CORE diagram notation and SofTech's SADT notation (reference 2) and Michael Jackson's Design notation (reference 3). The CORE notation also expresses parallelism which is covered by TRW's SREM notation (RNETS, reference 4). The CORE notation for parallelism is not exactly the same as the RNET notation.

There are close resemblances between some CORE diagrams and those connected with a diagrammatic notation for the Constantine/Myers design method (reference 5).

II. AIMS OF REQUIREMENT SPECIFICATION

The producers of a requirement specification are trying to satisfy three aims:

- define the requirement so that the system can be implemented later and shown to be implemented correctly
- define the requirement so that the customer and end-users of the system can see that it does what they want
- define each part of the requirement so that others involved in defining the requirement can use the information in defining their part.

Satisfying these aims is usually very difficult. The difficulties are often compounded by failure to recognise that what is needed is not one, but several expressions of requirement.

The requirement expression must recognise several views of the system. Major aims must be:

- separation of different viewpoints
- consistency and compatibility of the information in the overlap between viewpoints
- avoidance of unnecessary repetition in producing information common to more than one viewpoint.

Reprinted from *Proceedings of the Fourth International Conference on Software Engineering*, 1979, pages 126-135.

III. CONTENT OF A REQUIREMENT SPECIFICATION

As indicated above, it is necessary to recognise several (possibly overlapping) viewpoints of a system. The CORE method makes wide use of the concept of viewpoint, as will be shown later. Some of the more obvious viewpoints to be considered at or before the time of expression of requirement are:

- a life cycle view (e.g. production plans, information and money flows)
- an environment view (e.g. user interfaces, interfaces with other systems, physical operating conditions such as temperature, power supply, location)
- an operator view (e.g. interfaces between the system and its 'servants' - i.e. people whose jobs exist because the system exists)
- a reliability view (e.g. acceptable failure rates, fault tolerance measures required, recovery and back-up facilities required).

For each valid viewpoint there is a need to identify characteristic information types. Recurring information types can be summarised as:

- actions (e.g. verb-noun phrases, such as 'produce the design', 'transmit a message', 'compute current position', 'restart the system')
- events (e.g. significant instants in time, such as 'phase complete', 'order arrives')
- mechanisms (e.g. agencies for performing actions, such as people, computers, natural forces)
- information (e.g. communications between actions, such as 'estimated position' or 'design end-product)
- media (e.g. the physical realisation of information, such as documents, data highways, storage media).

Full definition of the requirement involves identifying, for the information types of each viewpoint, relationships (e.g. data flow between actions, hierarchies, relative position, temporal order) and attributes (e.g. size, accuracy, frequency, constraints).

Definition of relationships can usually be achieved by either diagrams or words and symbols or by both. Definition of attributes is often most efficiently expressed in words and symbols.

In general it seems that the customer/user community finds diagrammatic expression more acceptable than words and symbols. On the other hand, the development community is more divided, with many preferring to work from words and symbols. A full expression of requirement should thus include words and symbols and diagrams.

IV. CAUSES AND PREVENTION OF FAILURE

The most recurrent causes of failure can be summarised as:

- the complexity of the problem
- poor communication (e.g. between the producers and users of the requirement)
- high volume of information to be handled
- inconsistent, ill-defined approaches to obtaining the necessary information.

Problem complexity results in failures due to infeasibility. Appropriate defences against such failures include use of high quality staff and use of automated assistance, such as simulation.

Poor communication results in ambiguity, inconsistency, incompleteness, untestable requirements and factually incorrect information. Appropriate defences include use of standards and procedures for the expression and checking of information about requirement.

The high volume of information to be handled in many systems results in inconsistent and inadequate production, checking, storage, update and release of information about the requirement. Appropriate defences include the use of automated aids and procedures for their correct integration into project organisation.

Use of inconsistent and ill-defined approaches results in poor presentation (e.g. mixtures of levels of definition, mixtures of viewpoints, ambiguity), inconsistency, incompleteness and general confusion about project status. Appropriate defences include the use of a consistent, well-defined method which is compatible with the use of standards and automated aids.

The various defences against problems must not be applied piecemeal. They must be used as an integrated set of tools, extending to cover the entire system life cycle. This paper discusses a method for requirement specification which has been defined so as to form part of an integrated set of tools.

V. CHARACTERISTICS OF CORE

CORE is founded upon the need to produce a requirement specification whose content reflects the factors mentioned earlier:

- viewpoints (e.g. life-cycle, environment, operator, reliability)
- information types (e.g. actions, events, mechanisms, information, media)
- relationships (e.g. data flows, hierarchies, temporal order)
- attributes (e.g. size, accuracy, frequency, constraints).

CORE defines the steps in production of a requirement specification, with particular emphasis on start-up and the link between steps.

For each step, CORE defines the activities involved and the checks to be applied.

Information collected and the defined CORE checks can be used to detect probable completeness of the requirement. It is not possible to check for genuine completeness.

CORE is supported by a diagrammatic notation which should be used with compatible project standards.

The reader should be clear that the diagrams support the method. They are not a method in themselves. In order to emphasise this distinction, the main diagrammatic rules are defined separately in appendix 1.

The diagrammatic notation is simple and can be applied to many aspects of system description. The next section provides a few introductory remarks on its use for requirement specification.

VI. CORE DIAGRAMS FOR REQUIREMENT SPECIFICATION

For the purposes of requirement specification, CORE diagrams are used to identify the overlapping hierarchic and dynamic relationships arising from the many viewpoints inherent in a complete specification of the known requirement.

CORE diagrams are produced for both actions and data. Actions and data are represented in 'single-thread' diagrams and 'operational' diagrams.

The 'single thread' diagrams represent a form of transaction model as suggested in figure 1, (time flows from left to right).

The model in figure 1 shows that, for a given thread from 'raw materials', to 'approved end-product' and 'rejected end-product' there is a sequence of actions.

Boxes on 'operational' diagrams represent a time-oriented snapshot of the system. They are related to the MASCOT (reference 6) activity. Figure 2 shows a possible operational diagram corresponding to figure 1 (the * indicates iteration). The model in figure 2 shows that 'produce an end product' and 'check an end-product' can be performed in parallel. For example, when one 'end-product' has gone to quality control for checking, another action could be performed by Production Staff while Quality Control performs checks on the first end-product.

CORE is founded partly on the belief that both the 'single thread' and the 'operational' diagrams are necessary to a full understanding of the system requirement.

VII. CORE PRODUCTION PHILOSOPHY

CORE can be looked at in terms of two major roles: the user role and the analyst role. For reasons explained below, the analyst role is always necessary.

The analyst role may be filled by a specially trained user, but cannot be left to untrained users.

A. The User Role

A modern euphemism in the computer industry is the statement that the user is the definitive source of information about the requirement. Unfortunately, in practical terms this is not often true.

In the early stages the user is quite likely to prove a significant block to the availability of information. Quite frequently users have a very imperfect idea of what is required of the system. Those ideas which they do have, they express only partially, considering the missing information to be self-evident.

Users frequently neglect the concepts of reliability and maintenance. Where the concepts are not totally neglected, they are referred to in the vaguest and most untestable terms (e.g. 'the system must be reliable'; 'the system must be flexible').

CORE requires skilled questioning of users. The questioning should be assisted, where possible, by technical experts who have produced similar systems.

Probably the most important function of the user is in establishing the acceptability of the requirement as it is produced.

B. The Analyst Role

CORE requires the production of the requirement specification to proceed in well-defined steps.

Each CORE step consists of three related types of activity. The activities are discussed later.

CORE recognises two basic facts about the production of a requirement specification:

- the sources of information (customer, users, technical experts) neither think nor talk about the system 'top-down'
- there is rarely just one 'top' to a system and at every step in decomposition there are multiple views which contribute to a full understanding of the requirement at that level.

The role of the analyst is to prompt the construction of a requirement specification which expresses all necessary viewpoints and ensures that the views are consistent with each other (i.e. that they can co-exist in the system life cycle).

During start up of requirement specification the analyst must persuade the customer and users to establish the boundary of the system requirement. This normally requires the recognition of the life-cycle viewpoint.

The analyst should attempt to isolate a small number of top level views of the system. For example, the selected views might be those of customer, supplier, maintenance and user organisations.

During subsequent steps of requirement, the analyst role is to prompt customer and users to identify and classify lower levels of viewpoint.

For example the decomposition of 'user organisation' means more than just someone who sits at a terminal keying in commands.

Users might include other systems (possibly including hostile systems - as in the defence environment) or remote suppliers of information or recipients of reports.

The process of viewpoint decomposition forms the basis of each CORE step. At each step the analyst has four aims:

- identify the next appropriate level of viewpoints
- define the viewpoints
- establish the consistency of each viewpoint with the others at the same level and with the previous level of definition
- establish user acceptance of the definitions produced.

VIII. CORE PRODUCTION ACTIVITIES

CORE defines three related production activities. There are related checking activities which are discussed later. The production activities for each step can be summed up under the headings:

- propose relevant viewpoints
- define relevant viewpoints
- confirm relevant viewpoints.

The activities are described below. They occur basically in the order that they are mentioned above, although each successive activity may cause review and alteration of the end-products of its predecessors.

It is highly likely that whole steps up to and including start-up may have to be repeated. CORE aims to reduce the probability of mistakes and omissions, but nothing can guarantee that no problems will occur.

A. Propose Relevant Viewpoints

The aim of this activity is to bound the scope of system description for the current step of requirement specification.

The approach is to determine a small number (two to five) of new relevant viewpoints for the next levels of decomposition.

The method is to discuss previously known information (e.g. premature definitions from earlier steps) and technical advice, if available, with the customer and senior user representatives responsible for the aspect of the system to be decomposed.

If more than five viewpoints are suggested, the process of reduction of viewpoints can be guided by detection of close functional relationship or organisational relationship (indicated by factors such as a viewpoint communicating with only one other of the suggested viewpoints).

B. Define Relevant Viewpoints

The aim of this activity is to define each viewpoint selected by the activity 'propose relevant viewpoints'.

The approach is to prepare a tabular collection of information and a set of CORE diagrams at several levels of decomposition.

For each selected viewpoint, the method is to interview responsible users and technical experts. Each interviewer must be aware of the other viewpoints selected at this step. Relevant prematurely defined information from previous steps must be available.

The tabular information is established first. The table headings are keyed to the information types discussed earlier in this paper. Key factors required are: stimuli and responses (information/media) to this viewpoint; their sources and destinations (mechanisms); the local actions performed by this viewpoint and the actions the proposed system is required to perform for this viewpoint.

The words used above are, of course, just jargon to the user. The interviewer must go prepared with user-oriented examples of the information required.

Using the tabular information and further user comments, the interviewer should construct CORE action and data diagrams showing actions performed by this viewpoint.

Since the diagrams should be agreed by the user and technical expert as a true representation of the selected viewpoint it may be that there will be several interviews over a period of days, or even weeks, before the diagrams are acceptable.

Tabular information which does not appear explicitly on the CORE diagrams should be indicated as belonging to (i.e. being part of a lower level of decomposition of) the names which do appear. Normally each tabular item will belong to only one name on the CORE diagrams.

C. Confirm Relevant Viewpoints

There are two aims for this activity:

- combine the individual viewpoints
- define systematically the reliability requirements at this level.

Combining Viewpoints

The combination of viewpoints results in a set of CORE diagrams showing how the various viewpoints fit together.

In practice the combination of viewpoints leads to identification of new action and data names which are composites of names which existed in the original separate viewpoints.

The new names are referred to as 'cosmetic', since they are necessary only for the combination of views.

Figures 3 and 4 illustrate the use of 'cosmetic' names. Suppose that the production/quality control example earlier were to be changed so that rejected goods were re-directed to production staff for repair.

Figure 3a shows the production single-thread view. Production is followed by either repair or a null activity (for approved end-products).

Figure 3b shows the quality control single-thread view. Inspection is followed by either approval or rejection.

Figure 4 shows that, in combining the single thread views, two 'cosmetic' actions have been introduced because of interactions between production and quality control.

At the top level, figure 4a, the cosmetic action 'enforce quality' is necessary because of an iterative interaction between production staff and quality control (repaired end-products may still be rejected and re-repaired).

At the second level, figure 4b, the cosmetic action 'enforce repair' has been introduced because it is the combination of 'reject an end-product' and 'repair an end product' which forms the alternative to the action 'approve an end-product'. Note that a characteristic of the combined views is that, at its lowest level there is one-to-one correspondence with the lowest level non-null actions of the individual views.

Defining Reliability

Once the individual viewpoints have been completely reconciled the analyst interviews senior user authorities for the current level, using the combined CORE diagrams, to assess the reliability requirements.

Reliability is assessed at each level of the combined diagrams, asking, for each box and each line on the diagram, the following questions:

- what could go wrong?
- can the failure be prevented?
- can the failure be detected?
- can the failure be repaired?
- is it worth trying to prevent/detect/repair at this level?
- what additional actions, mechanisms, media and data are required for reliability at this level?

As an example of the considerations which might arise, in figure 4a, it might be decided that

- Raw materials may be delayed (so keep a spare stock).
- Production staff may be ill (so do not try to operate at 100% capacity).
- Approved end-products may have undetected faults (so set up a customer service facility).
- etc.

The reliability actions and data must be added to the combined diagrams. This will require production of new diagrams and may cause introduction of new 'cosmetic' actions and data names because of interactions between the 'normal' view and the reliability view.

Reliability boxes are distinguished by a line labelled 'reliability' entering the bottom face of the box.

IX. CORE CHECKING ACTIVITIES

CORE checking can be thought of as keyed to the CORE production activities. Failures detected for each activity may lead to a re-cycle of that activity or a review and re-cycle of previous activities.

Some failures will cause re-cycle of entire CORE production steps. The earliest steps are particularly vulnerable to error. The problems in the early stages arise from the unstructured way the information is obtained.

There is no way of making users think or speak about the proposed system in a structured manner. The checks at various stages have the following aims:

At the start
- bound the system by deducing its maximum range of direct influence (e.g. the customers, suppliers, maintainers, users).

At each step
- bound the depth of information to be officially produced
- ensure complete coverage of all prematurely defined information

- ensure consistency of all internal aspects of the current level
- ensure consistency of the current level with the higher level which it purports to represent.

Any premature information which cannot be allocated to a branch of the existing description is an indication that the existing description does not truly bound the system (i.e. there are elements of the system which are not covered).

Similarly, any inconsistency between parts of the existing system is an indication that the system is not bounded or that one of the existing descriptions is wrong.

Completion of requirement can occur only when no further premature information has been recorded and no inconsistencies exist in any current level of system description.

The onset of completion on any one branch of decomposition can be detected by the need at the next level to refer to specific items of equipment (these are design mechanisms) or specific communications media (these are design media).

Finally, for the purposes of adequate understanding at any point in the system description, it is necessary to control the amount of information considered at one time.

CORE guidelines on control of dynamic diagram complexity are similar to those of SADT (reference 2). There should normally be no more than six boxes of any diagram representing flow of time (see Appendix 1). Where more than six boxes can occur, but over-complexity would result, CORE presents guidelines for another form of 'cosmetic' decomposition. The latter guidelines are not discussed further in this paper.

X. CURRENT STATUS OF THE METHOD

A preliminary paper for internal use was produced in February 1979. Systems Designers Limited made small experimental use of the CORE approach prior to that date and are now in process of using it to describe an integrated approach to the software life cycle.

No serious problems have arisen in its use, but this may be because we had already achieved considerable understanding of the problem as a result of our work on standards, procedures and automated aids.

A second, smaller scale, internal use has involved a definition of the requirements for an automated aid for system description. Here too, no serious problems have arisen - probably for the same reasons as already mentioned.

The third use of CORE has been the most instructive and productive. This has consisted of a cooperative project with British Aerospace (Warton Division) in the UK.

A combination seminar and workshop was defined and in April 1979 they were presented to British Aerospace staff. The seminar was fairly successful, but the workshop required further refinement.

Subsequent to the seminar, British Aerospace staff made small experimental use of CORE. In May 1979 British Aerospace started using CORE in conjunction with the automated and PSL/PSA (reference 1) on work connected with a major new avionics project. The combination of CORE and PSL/PSA is referred to by British Aerospace as:

SAFRA - Semi Automated Functional Requirements Analysis

Work on this project is still proceeding, with occasional support from Systems Designers Limited in the use of CORE.

The major benefits from this exercise in relation to the use of CORE have been

- the British Aerospace staff have had relatively little difficulty with use of CORE, even though it was not fully defined at the start of the project
- the difficulties they have reported have illustrated where the seminar and workshop need improvement - the improvements are under development
- the early work shows that the CORE diagrammatic notation is of positive benefit in the process of defining and understanding a requirement specification
- British Aerospace staff have refined the basic questions for tabular information collection to produce a comprehensive user/ technical expert-oriented set of examples for an avionics project.

XI. CONCLUSIONS

CORE is a method which is applicable to the needs of requirement expression. It is supported by a simple diagrammatic notation which can represent many vital viewpoints of the system requirements.

CORE has been used internally by Systems Designers Limited on small experiments and has been used externally by British Aerospace on a larger project connected with a major new avionics system.

Feedback on all practical use has been encouraging. CORE is not perfectly defined and does not represent all information necessary to a requirement. However, CORE has proved usable and useful. It covers much necessary information which is omitted by other single methods applied in isolation. Both the seminar and the workshop on CORE are in process of improvement and should be commercially available by the end of 1979.

Users of any method are reminded that method alone is not sufficient. Standards and automated aids and procedures for their application are vital to achievement and retention of quality throughout the system life cycle.

CORE has been defined in such a way as to fit in with the use of system life-cycle standards and automated aids.

Systems Designers Limited have developed life-cycle standards for software and will shortly integrate CORE use into that set (reference 7).

Systems Designers Limited have mapped the CORE approach onto the terminology of the automated aid PSL/PSA (reference 1) and British Aerospace are evaluating the use of PSL/PSA as an automated check on the consistency of information produced by the CORE approach.

The CORE diagrammatic notation, while of positive benefit, should not be applied without a supporting method. The benefits of such restricted use would be marginal.

XII. ACKNOWLEDGEMENTS

Based on the original ideas of the author CORE is being rigorously defined by a team within Systems Designers Limited Applied Systems and Software Engineering Technology (ASSET) group. The team comprises software engineers with applications experience ranging from commercial D.P. through to high technology real time systems. Acknowledgement is made of their contribution to the development of CORE along with that of the British Aerospace (Warton Division) team applying CORE.

APPENDIX 1

THE CORE DIAGRAMMATIC NOTATION

1. Introduction

CORE diagrams can be separated into two categories:

- dynamic diagrams
- static diagrams

Dynamic diagrams represent flow of time and connections between temporally ordered items.

The highest level of one stream of dynamic diagrams can be thought of as a single box representing the life cycle of the system, with lines representing connections between this system and previous, current or future systems.

All other dynamic diagrams represent part of some level of various hierarchic decompositions of the top box.

Dynamic diagrams have some resemblance to SADT diagrams (reference 2). They should not be interpretted as representing identical concepts to the SADT diagrams.

Static diagrams present the hierarchic structure connecting dynamic diagrams. Each box which appears on a dynamic diagram appears as a box on a static diagram.

Static diagrams have some resemblance to Michael Jackson Design Technique (MJDT) diagrams (reference 3). They should not be interpretted as representing identical concepts to the MJDT diagrams.

The application of the CORE diagrammatic notation to the CORE method for requirement specification involves two streams:

- data decomposition
- action decomposition

The main rules for the CORE dynamic and static diagrams are defined below. Readers should remember that this is not a complete definition.

It may help on first reading to associate dynamic diagram boxes with actions and dynamic diagram lines with data flow.

Dynamic diagrams make use of vertical lines entering a box at its lower face or leaving a box at its upper face. These are not covered in the rules which follow. They are used to indicate viewpoint/mechanism (lower face) or functional equivalence (upper face).

Examples of use of viewpoint lines are shown in figs. 1 to 4 in the main part of this paper.

2. Use of Boxes in Dynamic Diagrams

Figure 5 illustrates the rules.

a) Time flow is represented by left-to-right box ordering left-most boxes occur first, right-most boxes occur last.

b) Mutual exclusion is shown by vertical alignment of the alternative boxes. Mutually exclusive boxes each have a circle in the top right corner.

c) Indeterminate order (and parallelism) is shown by vertical alignment of boxes. No circle is allowed in the top right corner of boxes representing indeterminate order or parallelism.

d) Iteration is shown by an asterisk in the top left corner of the iterated box.

e) Partial overlap of boxes is prohibited.

f) Other rules, not defined here, cover the allowed mixtures of: iteration, mutual exclusion and indeterminate order. Other rules also cover further decomposition of boxes on a diagram.

3. Use of Lines in Dynamic Diagrams

Figure 6 illustrates the rules.

a) A line between two boxes represents a dependence relationship (e.g. data dependence) of the box to the right on the occurrence of the box to the left.

b) A line entering a diagram from the left represents a dependence of the boxes it intersects on the occurrence of one or more external boxes. A line leaving a diagram to the right represents a dependence of one or more external boxes on the occurrence of the boxes it intersects.

c) Subsidiary dependencies can be shown by line branching or joining. Branches representing subsidiary dependence must have different names from each other and from their join.

d) Lines may 'flow' backwards in one of two cases:

- the flow is from an iterated box, back into itself
- the flow is from a box to an iterated box in the same vertical alignment

All other backward flow of lines is prohibited.

e) Lines entering a diagram at the left or leaving a diagram at the right must enter or leave the 'parent' box (i.e. the box that this diagram decomposes) in the same direction.

Rule e) is not illustrated here.

4. Use of Boxes and Lines in Static Diagrams

Figure 7 illustrates the rules.

a) Boxes are arranged in hierarchic order (based on dynamic diagram decomposition). Boxes at a higher level of decomposition appear nearer the top of the page. Boxes at a lower level appear nearer the bottom of the page. Boxes at the same level of decomposition appear horizontally aligned.

b) Hierarchic dependence is shown by lines joining the 'parent' box at its lower face to each 'child' box at its upper face.

c) Box order is related to hierarchic relationship first. The child boxes appear below their parent box.

d) Secondary box order is related to left-to-right appearance on the dynamic diagram of the 'child' boxes. Left-most boxes on the dynamic diagram are also left-most on the static diagram.

e) Dynamic diagram boxes which are vertically aligned appear horizontally aligned on the corresponding static diagram, with the topmost box on the dynamic diagram as the left-most box in the static diagrams.

f) Symbols (* and O) which appear in boxes on dynamic diagrams appear in the same boxes in the corresponding static diagrams.

DOCUMENT REFERENCES

1. D. Teichroew and E.A. Hershey III
PSL/PSA: A Computer-Aided Technique for Structured Documentation and Analysis of Information Processing Systems.
IEEE Trans. on Software Engineering, Vol. SE-3, No.1, January 1977, pp 41-48.

2. D.T. Ross
Structured Analysis (SA): A Language for Communicating Ideas.
IEEE Trans. on Software Engineering, Vol. SE-3, No.1, January 1977, pp 16-34.

3. K. Ratcliff
Data Structure and Structured Design
Conference Notes, Infotech State of the Art Conference on Structured Design, 14-16 Feb 1977, pp 99-115

4. M.Alford
A Requirements Engineering Methodology for Real-Time Processing Requirements
Conference Notes, Infotech State of the Art Conference on Structured Design, 14-16 Feb 1977, pp 31-52

5. R.R. Brown
The Technique and Practice of Structured Design A La Constentine
Conf. Notes, Infotech State of the Art Conf. on Structured Design 14-16 Feb '77, pp 75-97

6. MASCOT Suppliers Association
The Official Handbook of MASCOT (Draft 1)
15 June 1979.

7. G.P. Mullery
Standards for the Production of High Quality Systems
Proceedings of the IFAC Workshop, SAFECOMP: May 1979 (not yet published).

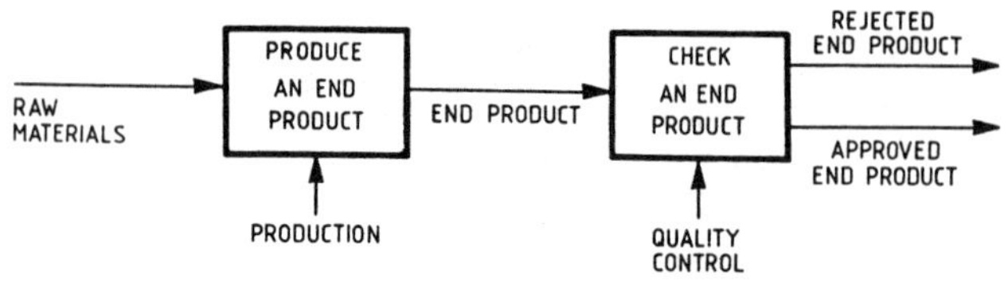

Figure 1 SINGLE THREAD DIAGRAM

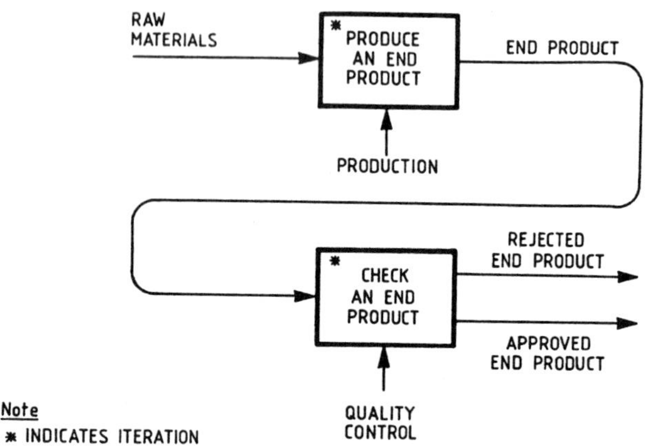

Figure 2 OPERATIONAL DIAGRAM

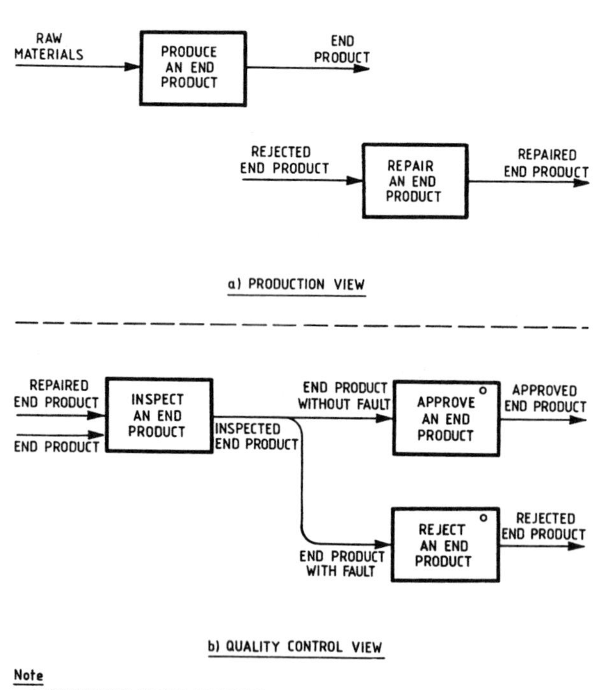

Figure 3 ISOLATED SINGLE THREAD VIEWS

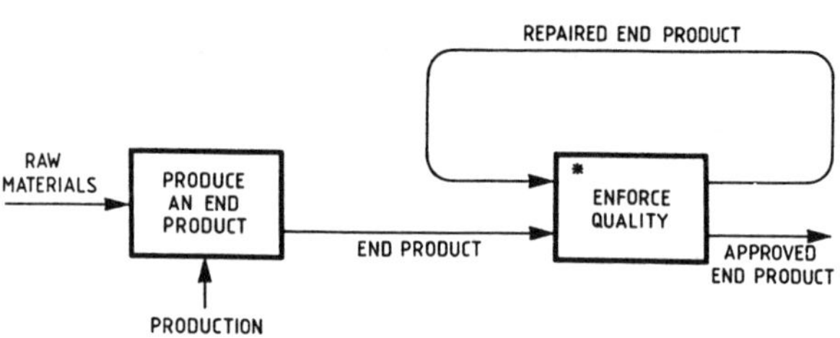

a) FIRST LEVEL COMBINED VIEW

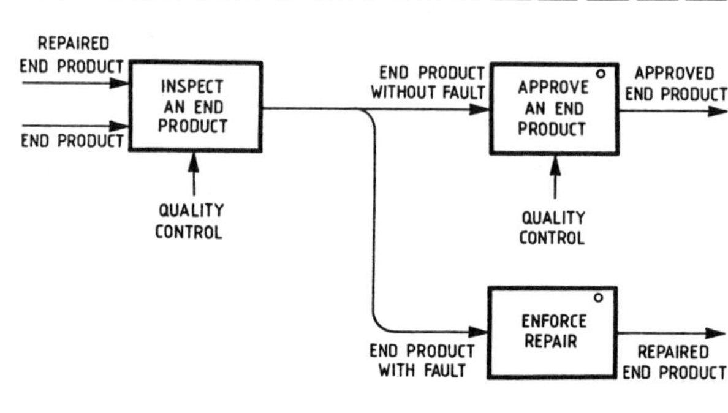

b) DECOMPOSITION OF ENFORCE QUALITY

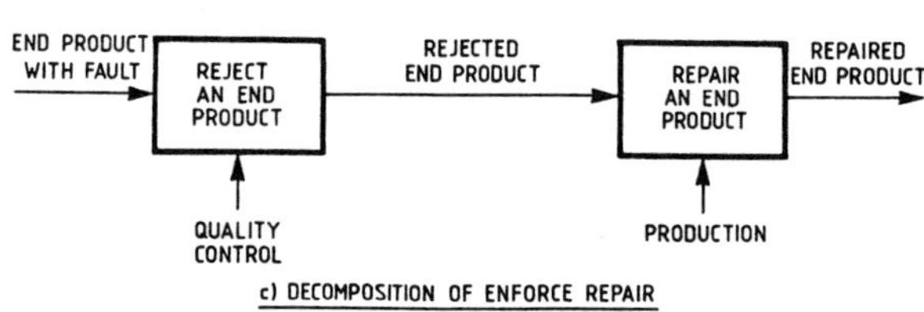

c) DECOMPOSITION OF ENFORCE REPAIR

Figure 4 COMBINED SINGLE THREAD VIEWS

RULE	INTERPRETATION	DIAGRAM
a)	X1, THEN X2, THEN X3	X1 X2 X3
b)	X1, THEN EITHER X2 OR X3, THEN X4	X1 X2° X4 / X3°
c)	X1, THEN BOTH X2 AND X3 (IN ANY ORDER OR IN PARALLEL), THEN X4	X1 X2 X4 / X3
d)	X1, THEN REPEATED INSTANCES OF X2 (POSSIBLY ZERO INSTANCES) THEN X3	X1 *X2 X3
e)	PARTIAL OVERLAP OF BOXES IS PROHIBITED	X1 X2 X3 / X4

Figure 5 ILLUSTRATION OF DYNAMIC BOX NOTATION

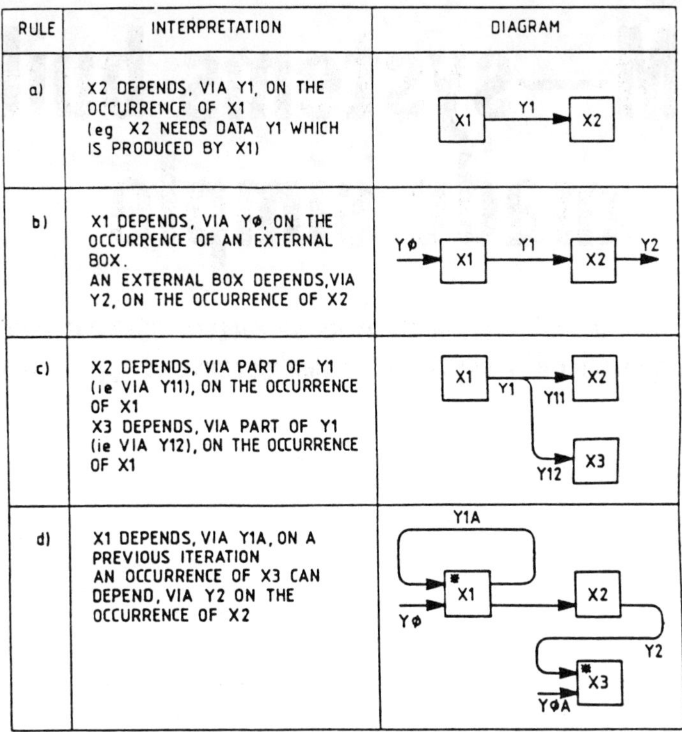

RULE	INTERPRETATION	DIAGRAM
a)	X2 DEPENDS, VIA Y1, ON THE OCCURRENCE OF X1 (eg X2 NEEDS DATA Y1 WHICH IS PRODUCED BY X1)	X1 Y1 X2
b)	X1 DEPENDS, VIA Yφ, ON THE OCCURRENCE OF AN EXTERNAL BOX. AN EXTERNAL BOX DEPENDS, VIA Y2, ON THE OCCURRENCE OF X2	Yφ X1 Y1 X2 Y2
c)	X2 DEPENDS, VIA PART OF Y1 (ie VIA Y11), ON THE OCCURRENCE OF X1 X3 DEPENDS, VIA PART OF Y1 (ie VIA Y12), ON THE OCCURRENCE OF X1	X1 Y1 Y11 X2 Y12 X3
d)	X1 DEPENDS, VIA Y1A, ON A PREVIOUS ITERATION AN OCCURRENCE OF X3 CAN DEPEND, VIA Y2 ON THE OCCURRENCE OF X2	Y1A * X1 X2 Yφ Y2 * X3 YφA

Figure 6 ILLUSTRATION OF DYNAMIC LINE NOTATION

RULE	INTERPRETATION	DIAGRAM
a)	X1 AND X2 ARE AT A HIGHER LEVEL THAN X11, X12, X13, X21, AND X22	X1 X2 X11 X12 X13 X21 X22
b)	X1 IS THE 'PARENT' OF X11, X12 AND X13 X2 IS THE 'PARENT' OF X21, X22	X1 X2 X11 X12 X13 X21 X22
c)	EACH 'CHILD' OF X1 APPEARS BELOW X1 EACH 'CHILD' OF X2 APPEARS BELOW X2	
d) and e)	X1 TO X4 REPRESENT THE STATIC DIAGRAM ORDER CORRESPONDING TO THE DYNAMIC DIAGRAM EXAMPLE IN FIGURE 5b	X1 X2° X3° X4
f)	THE CIRCLE SYMBOLS IN FIGURE 5b APPEAR IN THE CORRESPONDING STATIC DIAGRAM BOXES	

Figure 7 ILLUSTRATING STATIC DIAGRAM BOX AND LINE NOTATION

SSADM—systems building made simple

John Williams shows that, despite the claims of its detractors, SSADM is finding favour with a growing number of analysts in a widening range of applications.

The evolving discipline of software engineering has spawned a wide range of methods, systems and tools and a long series of acronyms to describe them—terms such as CASE, IPSE, PCTE. Behind one of these acronyms, SSADM, is an approach to software engineering in commercial data processing projects that is proving to be one of the more enduring methods.

SSADM—the Structured Systems Analysis and Design Methodology—was originally developed for UK Government development projects by Learmonth and Burchett Management Systems and the Government's computing advisory body, the CCTA.

It looks only at analysis and design, as its name implies, and works by focussing effort on the analysis of data and the ways in which data is used during its life in the system. Any detailed construction, testing and implementation phases of projects and the early: 'What should we be doing anyway;' phases of the project fall outside its scope.

A recent survey of large mainframe installation users indicated that 46% used or planned to use SSADM or one of its variants as the in-house development method. The National Computing Centre, in the UK, which took up the promotion of SSADM to the private sector earlier this year, attracted over 250 companies to seminars on the potential for the method.

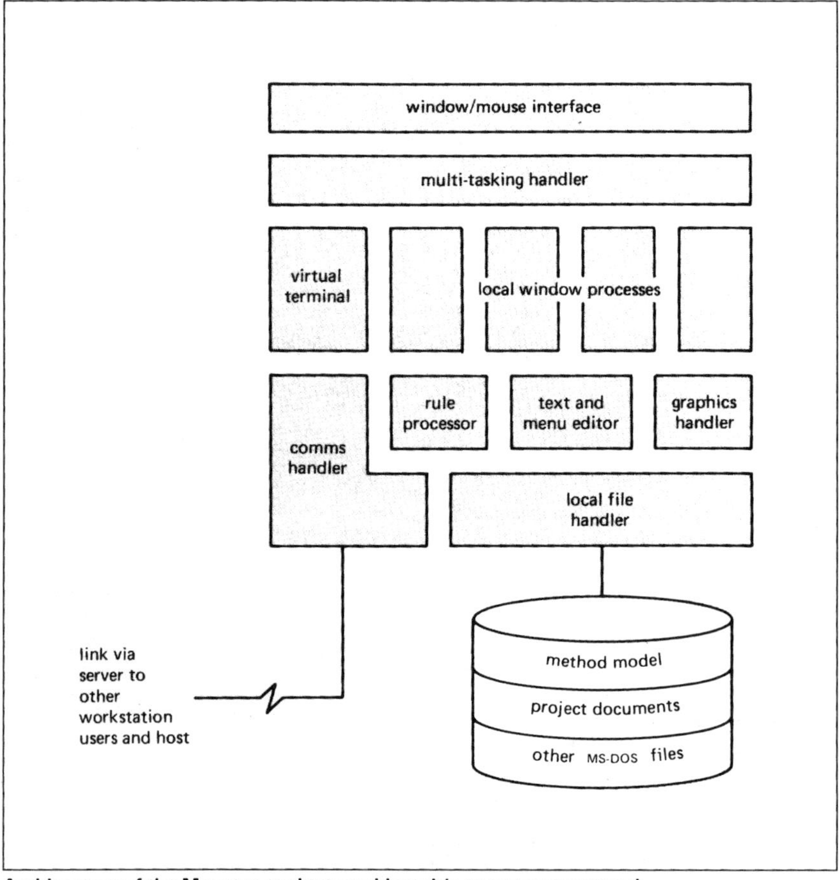

Architecture of the Maestro analyst workbench's SSADM support tool

Yet it is the subject of much debate in the systems engineering field. Its detractors claim it is too bureaucratic and suited mainly to computerising existing applications, rather than originating new approaches to them. Even its adherents would admit that its strengths lie in the former but claim that that is very often where the real problem lies. They can also point out that SSADM, with its spin-offs, is one of the most widely used methodologies.

SSADM supporters put these encouraging figures down to the qualities of the method itself. Comments from users, however, indicate a more pragmatic attitude. According to them, the popularity of SSADM are that it is well documented and supported by training and consultancy from several sources, and that it is supported by an increasing number of tools to put it actually into use.

The documentation and training in the use of the method allow the user to adopt a 'cook-book' approach to its introduction. Because it concentrates on the analysis and design phases, it can be introduced to new projects quite easily, without a need to consider the construction processes and the ultimate run-time environment.

Introducing the tools is even more significant. They make the method easy to implement by automating the tedious parts; by checking the method's validity as the analysis and the design progresses; and by automating information transfer between different parts of the method.

SSADM tools range from plain PC-based analyst workbench products like Excelerator (which provides some SSADM support) and Learmonth and Burchett Management Systems' own Automate and Datamate products, to closely coupled mainframe sub-systems such as ICL's Quickbuild Workbench. There are also complete Integrated Project Support Environments (IPSE), which provide SSADM support facilities integrated into the development

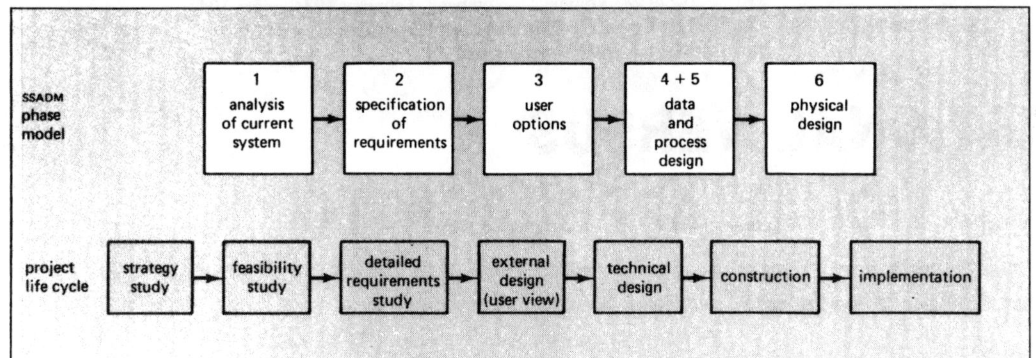

Currently SSADM and its derivatives support only the analysis and design phases fully

process. (These allow several analysts to work as a team and link up with the construction phases of projects.)

Most of the effort in tool support has gone into looking at the SSADM diagrams. Although not the whole of the method, they do represent the techniques most amenable to automation. They are difficult to produce manually and they need to be edited. However, because they collect and present data in a structured manner, they lend themselves to checking and, ultimately, to generating code directly from the information contained within them.

There are three main classes of diagram in SSADM.

First, there is the Logical Data Structure, which provides a way of representing the relationships between data elements in the system. It is eventually expanded into a complete composite logical data design showing structure, data fields, access paths and volumetric information which drives the detailed physical database design.

Then there are Data Flow Diagrams, used to show how data moves around an information system and which processes act upon it. The Entity Life History gives a third view of data showing all events affecting an entity during its life in the system—for example, those that create it, those that modify it in some way, and those that delete it.

Diagramming systems primarily provide a way of picking up the standard symbols and placing them in their correct position in the diagram. For this, the tool products typically use icon/mouse-driven interfaces. SSADM enables symbols to be connected together with the various lines representing the standard types of relationships between items.

It is here that the first benefit of automation arises. The tools can check, for example, that there is some data connected to a process or that data is not only connected to other data.

The second benefit comes from collecting data about the design elements represented by the symbols. This makes it possible to drive large parts of the construction process automatically. This is especially true now that SSADM is being expanded to support the later phases of the development cycle.

An example of the SSADM data flow diagram produced on the Maestro analyst workbench

For example, entries to the mainframe data dictionary, which will ultimately run the system, can be automatically produced once the design is finalised, although it will need further rule-based processing.

Errors in the analysis and design phases are reduced by these techniques too. Data collected about an entity at one point can be reused automatically, ensuring that the entity is handled consistently throughout the system. More importantly though, good tools will support the analysts' natural way of working, allowing them to move from one view of the system to another in the context of the entity they are working on.

Because of this support aspect, SSADM tools allow the analyst to refine the specification downwards, moving from the higher level diagram down through successive, more detailed diagrams until the lowest level is reached. Reaching the next level is usually just a matter of positioning the cursor on the symbol for the required item and selecting an 'Expand' command. This progressive refinement carries with it the context of the definitions in the higher level—dataflows defined at a higher level are automatically included in the lower ones.

All these facilities combine to improve the quality of work and the speed with which the analysis and design process can be carried out and documented. If the tools are integrated into some overall project support system, they can then pass on those benefits to the construction phases of the project.

The introduction of support tools is making SSADM and its derivatives suitable for projects which users would have previously considered too small to warrant its use. With some of its more advanced facilities now becoming available, SSADM wil become increasing relevant for projects, irrespective of the delivery system.

John Williams is software productivity marketing manager at Philips Business Systems, tel: (0206) 575115.

THE OPERATIONAL VERSUS THE CONVENTIONAL APPROACH TO SOFTWARE DEVELOPMENT

The conventional approach to software development is being challenged by new ideas, many of which can be organized into an alternative decision structure called the "operational" approach. The operational approach is explained and compared to the conventional one.

PAMELA ZAVE

For some years there has been a rough consensus on the proper phases of a software development project and on the decisions to be made during those phases. The conventional "software life cycle" has pervaded the field of software engineering, defining the terms we have used and shaping our perceptions of problems and their potential solutions.

More recently there have been complaints about the chronic problems of the conventional life cycle (e.g., [23]). Various new ideas for developing software have been emerging, but these ideas, such as executable specifications and program transformations, have no place in the conventional approach. They can, however, be organized into an alternative strategy called here the "operational approach." A number of current research projects based on the operational approach testify to its growing importance.

DESCRIPTION OF THE TWO APPROACHES

Any software development effort begins with a problem thought to be solvable by a computer system. When computer specialists become involved their first job is to investigate the problem; divergence between the two development approaches arises when those specialists begin to formulate a solution.

Either approach can be described as a sequence of decisions leading to a target system that can be installed and used. In both cases it may be necessary to back up, remake an earlier bad decision, and repeat the subsequent phases. In either case changes in customer needs may cause iteration of the entire sequence. Back-

A NEW APPROACH TO SOFTWARE DEVELOPMENT

Some of the most serious problems of software development were identified years ago but continue to resist practical solutions. Modern programming environments are designed to apply the latest technology to all aspects of software development, but because they do not offer comprehensive solutions to these chronic problems, only modest improvements in productivity can be expected from them.

Meanwhile several research projects, pursued independently, have incorporated an approach to software development so different in its organization of decision-making that unnecessary burdens on developers are eased and some of the usual trouble spots disappear entirely. The fundamental similarities among these projects have been obscured by many differences in style, emphasis, and application area. This article describes the essence of that approach, apart from the details of its instantiations.

The ideas presented here are relatively new and untried, and may not deliver in practice what they promise in theory. But they are interesting in their own right for the new perspective they provide, and if successful will yield substantial gains in software productivity—and cause major changes in the management of the development process.

tracking and iteration will not be considered until we compare the two approaches, however.

The Conventional Approach

The *conventional approach* to software development is pictured in Figure 1.

During the requirements phase, computer specialists formulate a system to solve the problem and define this system in the requirements specification. This specification treats the system as a "black box" describing all required characteristics of its external behavior ("what"), but no characteristics of the internal structure that will generate that behavior ("how"). The specification is almost always written in English, although natural language may be constrained by structure and supplemented by pictures, tables, formulas, etc. [15]. Figure 2 is a requirements specification for a trivial process-control system.

The design phase determines the internal structure of the software system, usually as a decomposition into modules of code. This is a top-down, hierarchical decomposition such that its modules will produce the required functions, be compatible with the hardware and software resources of the runtime environment, encapsulate information likely to change, meet the required performance constraints, and be implementable within the development environment. (For instance, it is often assumed that a module will be assigned to a single programmer.)

Figure 3 (p. 100) is a design for building the trivial process-control system in a runtime environment consisting of a single minicomputer running Pascal. Now the modules are treated as black boxes (only an English description of their externally visible behavior is given), but their interfaces (in this case, through procedure and function calls) are made explicit. A more substantial design might include preliminary allocations of resources and performance to modules, test plans [17], or axiomatic specifications of module behavior.

The implementation phase turns the design into code executable in the runtime environment. This entails defining the internal mechanisms by which each module will meet its behavioral specification (and its performance/resource allocation), and mapping module mechanisms and interface properties into the implementation language. Figure 4 (p. 101) shows parts of a Pascal implementation of the trivial process-control system.

The preceding may seem to be a restrictive and even distorted picture of current software development practice. There are in fact many exceptions (see *Comparison of the Two Approaches*), some of them deliberate improvements to the conventional approach and some of them accidents caused by the deficiencies of the conventional approach. The point is that Figure 1 is the model upon which almost all theorizing and tool-building in software engineering are based. Its central principle is top-down decomposition of black boxes (starting from black-box requirements), from which all structure in Figure 1 devolves.

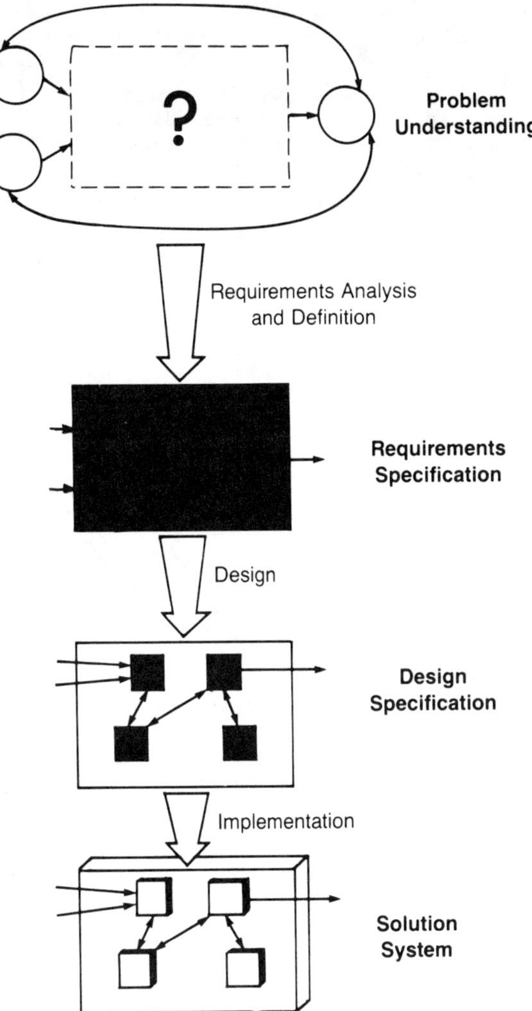

FIGURE 1. The conventional approach to software development is based on the principle of top-down decomposition of black boxes, and all its features can be derived from that philosophy.

The system must read a temperature sensor on each of 10 machines once every second. If a machine is hotter than 125°C, or if its temperature has risen more than 2°C in the last 5 intervals between readings, an alarm must be sounded until the condition ceases. Both the sensor values and the alarm activation flag are accessible as special-purpose hardware registers.

FIGURE 2. A requirements specification is supposed to describe all required characteristics of the external behavior of a system, but say nothing about the internal structure that will generate the behavior. It is almost always written in English (possibly constrained for the purpose or supplemented by graphics and formulas) because there is no suitable formal notation for the whole.

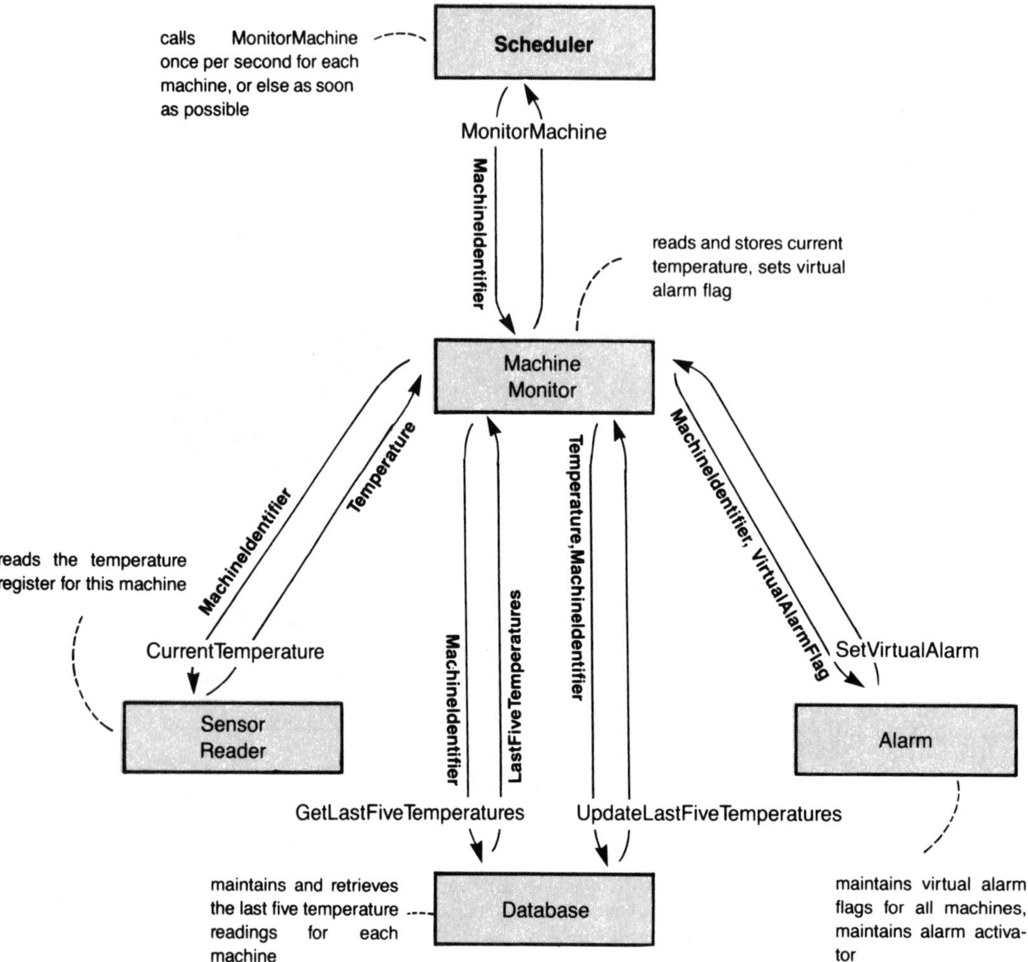

FIGURE 3. A design shows a decomposition of the system into modules of code. Although the interfaces between them are explicitly defined, each module is still a black box. The decomposition must meet functional, performance, resource, modifiability, and developmental requirements simultaneously; this design, for instance, is tailored to a single processor with adequate speed and a centralized memory.

The Operational Approach

The *operational approach* to software development is pictured in Figure 5 (p. 102).

During the specification phase, computer specialists formulate a system to solve the problem and specify this system in terms of implementation-independent structures that generate the behavior of the specified system. The operational specification is executable by a suitable interpreter. Thus external behavior is implicit in the specification (but can be brought out by the interpreter), while internal structure is explicit.

This description may make an operational specification sound like a design, but it is not. First of all the structures provided by an operational specification language are independent of specific resource configurations or resource allocation strategies (and can be implemented by a wide range of them), while designs actually refer to specific runtime environments. For instance, the operational specification[1] of the trivial process-control system sketched in Figure 6 (p. 103) is organized in terms of asynchronously interacting parallel processes, virtual structures that can be implemented in a variety of ways. One way is to multiplex a single physical processor, effecting communication and synchronization through shared memory. Another is to use one physical processor per process, effecting communication and synchronization via messages sent across a data-communication link.

Each *machine-j-monitor* process is responsible for monitoring one machine. It goes through a sequence of discrete states, each of which is a member of the set "LAST-FIVE-TEMPERATURES," i.e., a five-tuple containing the recent history of the machine as known to

[1] The operational treatment of the process-control example will be carried out in PAISLey. For references and a summary of other operational specification languages, see *Some Instances of the Operational Approach*.

```
procedure MonitorMachine(Machine: MachineIdentifier);
     var ReadTemp: Temperature;
     RetrievedLastFiveTemperatures: LastFiveTemperatures;
     ComputedFlag: VirtualAlarmFlag;

     function FiveWayMin
          (TemperatureVector: LastFiveTemperatures): Temperature;
          var Min: Temperature;
          begin
               Min := TemperatureVector[1];
               for i := 2 to 5 do
                    if TemperatureVector[i] < Min
                         then Min := TemperatureVector[i];
               FiveWayMin := Min;
          end;

     begin
          ReadTemp := CurrentTemperature(Machine);
          GetLastFiveTemperatures
               (Machine,RetrievedLastFiveTemperatures);
          ComputedFlag :=
               (ReadTemp >= 125.0)
               or
               ((ReadTemp -
                    FiveWayMin(RetrievedLastFiveTemperatures))
                         >= 2.0);
          SetVirtualAlarm(Machine,ComputedFlag);
          UpdateLastFiveTemperatures(Machine,ReadTemp);
     end;

begin
     while true do
          for i :=1 to 10 do
               begin
                    repeat ; until CurrentTime > Schedule[i];
                    Schedule[i] := Schedule[i] + 1.0;
                    MonitorMachine(i);
               end;
end.
```

FIGURE 4. A solution system consists of code executable in the runtime environment. Here is a fragment of a solution in Pascal. If the solution comes from implementing a design in the conventional approach, the internal mechanisms by which each module meets its behavioral specification are new, and the solution is the first version of the system to be executable. If the solution comes from a transformed specification in the operational approach, no new functions have been added since the specification phase.

the process-control system. The successor to each state is computed by evaluating the mapping:

```
(1)  machine-j-monitor-cycle:
     LAST-FIVE-TEMPERATURES
       → LAST-FIVE-TEMPERATURES,
```

which is defined as:

```
(2)  machine-j-monitor-cycle[hist] =
(3)     process-current-j-temperature
           [(hist,current-j-temperature)];

(4)  current-j-temperature: → TEMPERATURE;

(5)  process-current-j-temperature:
(6)      LAST-FIVE-TEMPERATURES
     × TEMPERATURE
     → LAST-FIVE-TEMPERATURES;
(7)  process-current-j-temperature [(hist,temp)] =
(8)     proj[(1,(maintain-last-five-temperatures
                  [(hist,temp)],
(9)              maintain-virtual-alarm-j-flag
                   [(hist,temp)]
(10)             )
(11)         )];

(12) maintain-last-five-temperatures:
(13)     LAST-FIVE-TEMPERATURES
     × TEMPERATURE
     → LAST-FIVE-TEMPERATURES;

(14) maintain-virtual-alarm-j-flag:
(15)     LAST-FIVE-TEMPERATURES
     × TEMPERATURE
     → FILLER.
```

Lines 1, 4, 5–6, 12–13, and 14–15 are declarations that identify the domains and ranges of their respective mappings. Definitions use a simple functional syntax in which "[]" denotes application of a mapping to its argument and "()" denotes construction of a tuple. (Note that members of the set "$A \times B$" take the form "(a, b).") "proj" is an intrinsic mapping on two arguments, an integer and a tuple; the value of "proj[(i, t)]" is the ith component of the tuple t.

Functional syntax is an operational-specification-language structure that is independent of decisions concerning control and data, and can be implemented by a wide range of them. The two subexpressions whose values contribute the two components of the tuple on lines 8–10 can be evaluated sequentially or in parallel; nothing is said about how or where the values are stored before "proj" is applied to them.

At the end of the process step (after evaluation of "machine-j-monitor-cycle") the old state is *replaced* by the new value just computed. Replacement can later be implemented by modifying the data in place, by constructing a new value in scratch storage and then copying it, or by constructing a new value elsewhere and moving a pointer to refer to it.

Not only are the structures of an operational specification language independent of implementation-oriented decisions, but also the mechanisms (*usages* of the specification-language structures) in an operational specification are derived solely from the problem to be solved. They are chosen for modifiability and human comprehension without regard to any implementation characteristics whatsoever.

For instance, the process structure shown in Figure 6 is essentially a reflection of the real world in which the system will operate: one process per independent, asynchronous object. Each process interacts with and controls or senses only the object to which it corresponds.

For another instance, "maintain-last-five-temperatures" produces an updated value of the temperature history, while "maintain-virtual-alarm-j-flag" decides whether machine-j is cause for an alarm at this time

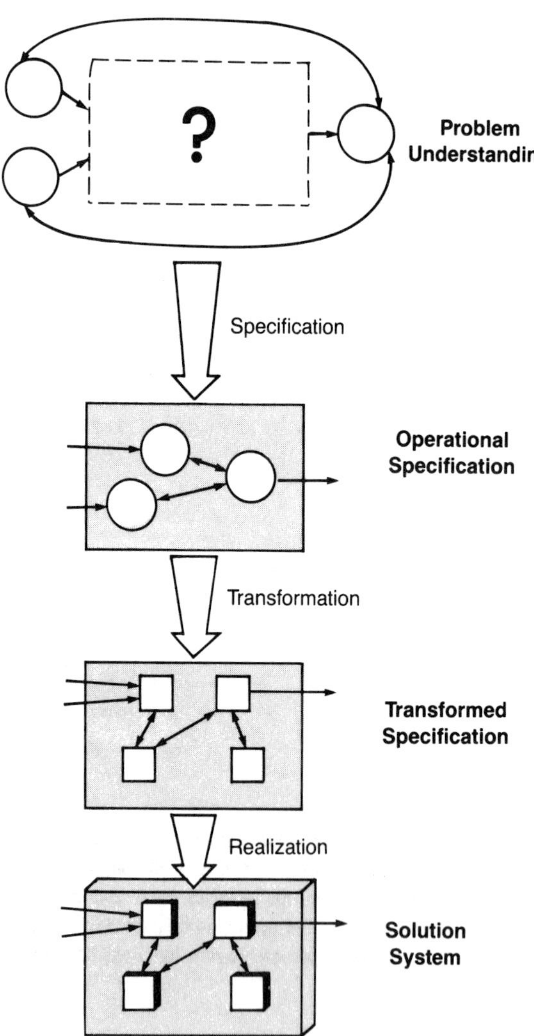

FIGURE 5. The operational approach to software development is based on separation of problem-oriented from implementation-oriented concerns, and all its features can be derived from that philosophy.

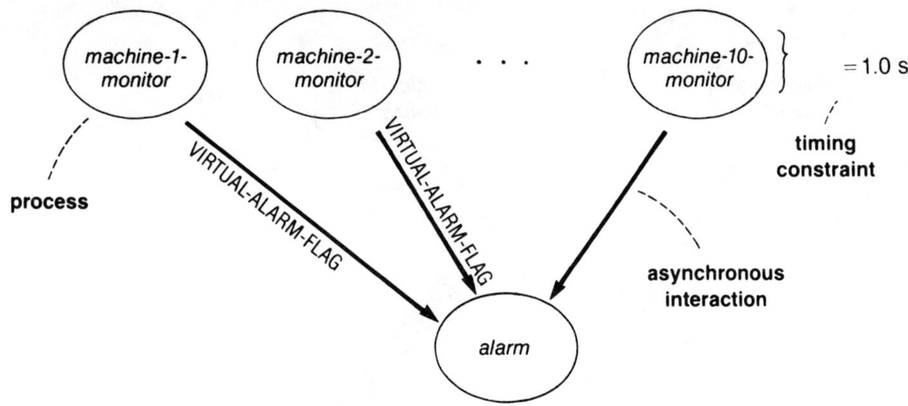

FIGURE 6. An operational specification is a complete and executable representation of the proposed system. It is described in terms of computational structures that are known to have a wide range of possible implementations, and its organization is based as closely as possible on the problem to be solved.

and so informs the *alarm* process ("maintain-virtual-alarm-j-flag" is evaluated only to cause this side effect on another process, so its value is always a place-holding constant). Thus each step of a *machine-j-monitor* process makes and responds fully to one sensor reading. Since the problem is to do this once per second, each step is constrained to take exactly this amount of time.

The principle of problem-oriented specification structure is a universal characteristic of the operational approach, as can be seen in this example from a very different domain:

- An information system should contain a computer-based representation (model) of real-world activities about which it provides information. It must also contain entities (functions) that answer various queries by examining the current state of the model. The model should be separated from the functions in the specification for a variety of reasons: (1) The model should be explicit so that it can serve as a basis for communication with the user. (2) The model defines the terms for the functions and implicitly circumscribes a set of possible functions. (3) The model is more stable than the functions, because the functions can change without the model's changing, but not *vice versa* [10, 22].

The structure of the operational specification is problem-oriented but not implementation-oriented. During the transformation phase the specification is subjected to transformations that preserve its external behavior, but alter or augment the mechanisms by which that behavior is produced, so as to yield an implementation-oriented specification of the same system. The goal of all research efforts in this area is to automate the transformations themselves, although selection of appropriate transformations will remain in human hands for the foreseeable future.

One type of transformation changes the modifiable and comprehensible mechanisms of the operational specification to equivalent ones lying at different points in the trade-off space balancing performance (timing, reliability) and the various implementation resources (processors, memory, communication channels, *etc.*) involved. Some examples of these trade-offs:

- Most people understand (and would specify) Fibonacci numbers in terms of the equation "Fibonacci[n] = Fibonacci[$n - 1$] + Fibonacci[$n - 2$]," but they are far more efficiently computed by storing previous Fibonacci numbers rather than recomputing them.[2]
- If two processes have a producer–consumer relationship, their overall performance can often be improved by introducing buffering between them or even breaking each process into several stages and organizing a pipeline.
- An operational specification based on relational database theory may refer to the state of the database at some particular time in the past (when a given predicate was true). Although such a specification is directly executable, it requires a vast amount of storage, because no state of the database can ever be discarded. A transformation that eliminates this unreasonable use of storage entails noting which items are the subjects of "historical references," and adding extra structures to the database so that all relevant historical information is maintained in its current state [21].

Other transformations are needed so that specification structures can be mapped straightforwardly and efficiently onto a particular configuration of implementation resources. These transformations may introduce explicit representations of implementation resources, or resource allocation mechanisms, that were not present in the original specification.

Figure 7 shows a sequence of transformations on the operational specification of the process-control system. The result is an operational specification with the same structure as the design in Figure 3, because that seems to be the best organization for modules of code running

[2] For a transformation that does this *without* losing the structure of the original definition, see [32].

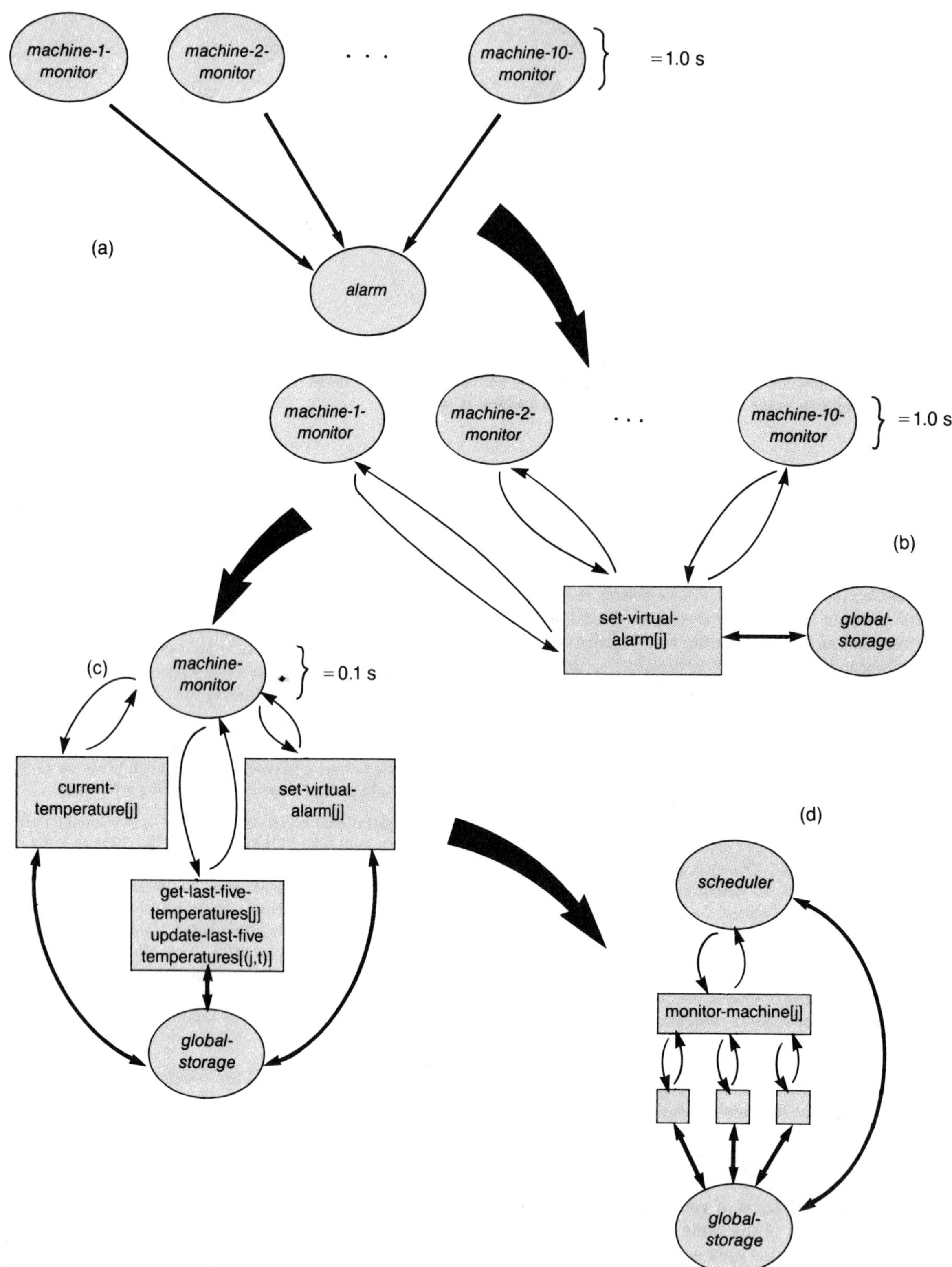

FIGURE 7. The problem-oriented structure of the operational specification must be fitted to a particular configuration of resources and resource-allocation strategies. This is accomplished by applying a series of automated transformations that preserve external behavior, but change the mechanisms producing the behavior.

on a single processor so as to solve this problem. (Note that the transformed specification differs from the design in that its modules are *not* black boxes, but fully specified executable structures.) In this example the same Pascal program will be the result of both development sequences.

Specification (a) has multiple asynchronous processes, each with the power to compute and store information, while the runtime environment has only a single processor and a monolithic memory unit. The transformation from (a) to (b) brings the specification closer to the environment by absorbing the computational role of the *alarm* process into the "machine-j-monitor" processes (as a mapping evaluation), and shifting the storage role of the *alarm* process to a new process representing the physical memory. This transformation preserves behavioral equivalence (because the old *alarm* process was idle except when responding to an interaction), and is a form of "inversion" [18, 19].

Specification (b) still has ten *machine-j-monitor* processes, each of which must take a step every second. The transformation from (b) to (c) reduces these ten processes to one parameterized process capable of monitoring any of the machines (and must cycle ten times a second to catch all of them). The temperature registers and history storage must be parameterized as well. This information is also moved to the *global-storage* process so that the specification will have two processes, one performing all computation but storing no information, the other performing no real computation but storing and retrieving all information.

Specification (c) now fits the physical resources of the runtime environment, but it has a process constrained to cycle once a second and no mechanism for enforcing that constraint. The transformation from (c) to (d) supplies a scheduler which interacts with a real-time clock so as to invoke the monitoring function (evaluate the mapping "monitor-machine") at the proper times.

The language of transformed specifications is basically the same as the language of operational specifications—it may be a subset or superset, but the framework remains. During the realization phase the transformed specification is mapped into the implementation language. The goal of all research efforts in this area is to deal with the challenging problems during specification or transformation, so that the realization step is a straightforward one.

Realization may entail making resource-allocation decisions not directly expressable in the specification language:

- If a specification language is based on relational database theory, and if the implementation language is a procedural one, then all the standard database operations must be implemented.

In other words, the realization creates a virtual machine on which the transformed specification can run.

More routinely, structures of the specification language must be mapped into structures of the implementation language. To go from Figure 7(d) to Figure 4, for instance, the *scheduler* process becomes a nonterminating Pascal program, and the *global-storage* process becomes the global variables in that program. (Note that interactions between the two become memory accesses via a bus but need not be programmed explicitly in Pascal.) Mapping evaluations become Pascal functions and procedures, in the course of which all residual parallelism is removed. Realization may also include programming low-level features that were too commonplace to be bothered with earlier, or translation of some components of the specification to hardware devices.

Just as top-down decomposition of black boxes can be considered the central theme of the conventional approach, the heart of the operational approach is separation of problem-oriented and implementation-oriented concerns via problem-oriented, executable specifications and transformational implementation.

Is There Really a Difference?

It is tempting to draw the picture in Figure 8, and to claim that there is no real difference between the two approaches—that we have merely changed the milestones. This view is incorrect because the four unlabeled boxes in Figure 8 could not exist. Their existence would imply a class of decisions preceding each milestone and another class of decisions following it—while in fact decisions from the two classes are interleaved.

The conventional approach places great emphasis on separating requirements (external behavior) from internal structure, but in the operational approach these are freely interleaved to get the operational specification. This interleaving is necessary to arrive at an executable specification, but it is also an expression of the inevitable coupling between *what* is being done and *how* it is being accomplished.

- Call-processing software in a telephone system must obtain a trunk line between two local exchanges before a long-distance voice connection can be made. If the trunk line is requested as soon as the long-distance number is dialed, the user of an overloaded network (in which there are no free trunk lines) will never hear the audible-ringing sound, nor will the called party's phone ring. If the trunk line is not requested until the called party has answered (on the grounds that trunk lines are scarce and valuable), users may find their calls aborted at this later point. Thus an internal mechanism affects the external behavior of the system.

- Almost any mechanism for processing transactions will impose limits on the sizes of certain input fields. The external behavior of the system includes what action it takes when these limits are exceeded [30].

The operational approach separates the problem-oriented structure of the operational specification from implementation considerations. In the conventional approach the design phase provides the high-level mechanisms that will produce the required behavior, but those structures must also fit the implementation envi-

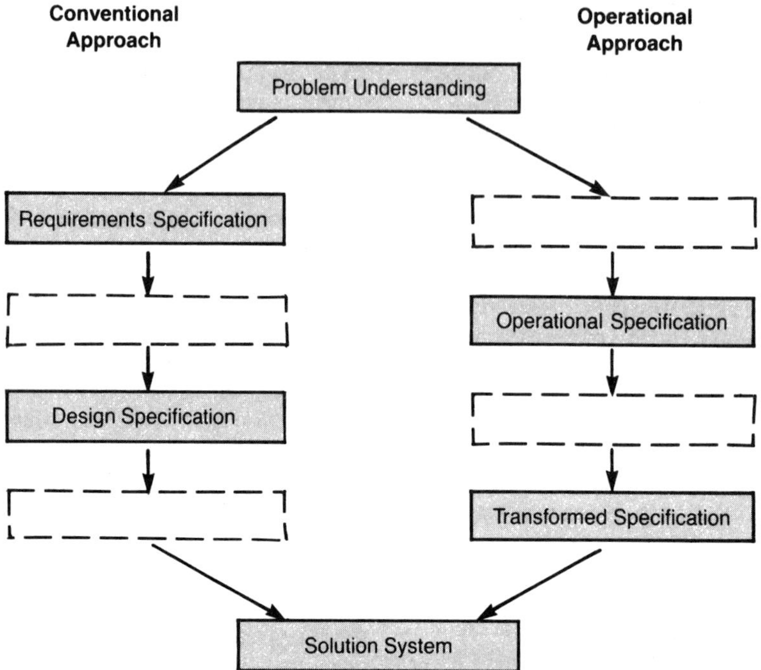

FIGURE 8. An incorrect view. It is tempting to conclude that, as this picture suggests, the two approaches differ only in how the same sequence of decisions is divided and labeled. In fact there are fundamental differences between the two approaches in how decisions are ordered.

roment and meet the performance constraints. Thus designers must consider both problem-oriented and implementation-oriented issues together.

> The designer of a distributed system may wish to decompose into modules on the principle of information hiding [25, 27], but be unable to specify modules that extend across computers. This is because the effects of distribution on performance, reliability, and communication are too pronounced for this property to be left implicit in the design.

The conventional approach separates high-level (intermodule) mechanisms, which are determined during design, from low-level (intramodule) mechanisms, which are determined during implementation. Each mechanism is tailored for performance and resource consumption at the same time it is chosen to carry out a necessary function. In the operational approach all functional mechanisms have been chosen by the time the operational specification is complete, and optimizations of all types of mechanisms may be interleaved during the transformation phase.

Finally, the operational approach separates mechanisms from their realization in terms of the implementation language, while in the conventional approach intramodule mechanisms are interleaved with implementation-language decisions. This is inevitable, since the only way to record these mechanisms is to program them.

Yet another misconception is that an operational specification is no different from a program in a very high-level language (VHLL). A VHLL is a declarative language in which problems within a well-defined domain can be posed. Such a program is an input to an "application generator," which then generates a system to solve the particular problem for a fixed runtime environment. The operational approach is more widely applicable than the VHLL strategy because it requires neither a narrow domain (operational specification languages express solutions, not problems) nor a fixed runtime environment (transformations can be chosen so as to reshape the specification in many different directions).

COMPARISON OF THE TWO APPROACHES

Both approaches are idealizations of what is often a messy aggregation of compromises and retreats. Thus we will evaluate the potential of the two approaches on two separate grounds: (1) how the idealized decision sequence could be exploited if we could achieve it; and (2) how likely it is that the idealized decision sequence can be achieved without extensive backtracking.

How Can The Properties of the Two Approaches Be Exploited?

Validation (Building the Right System) A system development project cannot succeed unless the system really solves the customer's problem. Since the proposed solution (described in the requirements specification or operational specification) is actually formulated by computer specialists, the proposal must be validated by the customer. "The customer" may be a large organization including end users familiar with the application but not with computer systems.

The conventional approach has the advantage that English requirements can be read and approved directly by customers. They can also form the basis of a legal contract. On the other hand, informal requirements are notorious for their incompleteness, inconsistency, and ambiguity. Indeed, these are the problems that first led computer scientists to look for specifications that were formal, and therefore subject to automated checks on their coherence.

Operational specifications are formal, and therefore seem to have the opposite characteristics: machine-processable but inaccessible to end users and other nontechnical people. Once a formal specification has been obtained, however, it is easy to summarize its properties informally in words or pictures. This can be done manually by a computer specialist whose heightened understanding (from dealing with the rigor of formal specification) should facilitate communication on all levels. It can also be done automatically; [29], for instance, describes a project to generate English narrative automatically from an operational specification.

Another important factor in user/analyst communication is the ability of the user to grasp and evaluate the concepts behind any proposal [36]. Experienced systems analysts report that an explicit operational model is much more helpful than black-box requirements, although doing a meticulous job on conventional requirements (e.g., [16]) may help just as much.

Recently the concept of prototyping has added a whole new dimension to the possibilities for user participation in system development. Prototyping is possible under both paradigms, but in substantially different forms.

In the operational approach the specification itself can be used as a prototype, since it is executable. This type of prototype can be produced rapidly [41] and will be produced as an integral part of the ordinary development cycle. It can only be used for demonstrations under tightly controlled "laboratory" conditions, however, because it will probably be missing low-level details, and will certainly lack the packaging, performance, etc., needed for a field trial.

In the conventional approach a prototype is produced by iterating the entire development cycle. This can result in a field-worthy prototype, but the conventional approach gives no particular guidance as to how to produce a prototype more rapidly than a product.

Verification (Building the System Right) Another major problem is to ensure that the delivered system is faithful to its specification. In the conventional approach, this can only be done through testing and/or formal proofs of correctness, each of which has well-known disadvantages. Program proving can only establish consistency between the design specification and the implementation, since the requirements are not formal. Furthermore, it has not been shown that proofs can be constructed by the average programmer in the context of a real development project.

Testing is a more common technique, and can be used to establish consistency between the implementation and the requirements specification (this is the sig-

TABLE I. Advantages of the Conventional and Operational Approaches*

	Conventional	Operational
Validation	Informal requirements can be understood directly by everyone	Formal specifications are rigorous, can be analyzed formally User has a model of the system to internalize and evaluate Operational approach makes rapid prototyping available automatically
Verification		Both testing and program-proving have well-known inadequacies Transformational implementation guarantees correctness
Automation		Transformation and realization are highly automatable
Maintenance		Operational approach addresses directly the structural conflict between efficiency and ease of maintenance
Management	Conventional approach provides organizationally useful milestones Managerial aspects of operational approach unexplored	Executable specification provides early results and accountability

* Assuming that both approaches could be applied successfully to any project, the differing properties of the two approaches would still cause differences in the handling of certain chronic problems. Here advantages of the two approaches are summarized.

nificance of the test plan in [17][3]). Testing is an arduous process, however, and can never prove the absence of errors.

The philosophy of transformational implementation seeks to avoid either testing or verification by deriving the implementation from the specification using only transformations and mappings that have themselves been proven correct, i.e., proven to preserve behavioral equivalence. Compilation is such a transformation. We have little experience in using higher-level transformations (see *Weaknesses of the Operational Approach*), but the idea is so appealing, and the alternatives so inadequate, that it is certainly deserving of some enthusiasm.

Automation The conventional approach has successfully resisted automation for a long time. This is because early (preimplementation) system representations tend to be informal, and because each phase includes decisions about the mechanisms that will generate the required behavior—the automation of which can only be attempted through the techniques of artificial intelligence. Current interest in automated support for the conventional approach centers on integrated programming environments; these environments are useful for the implementation phase only, however, and do not claim to replace the creativity (synthesis) involved in writing a program.

In the operational approach the specification phase is labor-intensive, but its output is a formal object. This means that templates [37] and even components can be reused. This is also a once-promising idea whose luster has dimmed during years of failed attempts, but there is reason to hope that rigorous distinction between problem-oriented mechanisms and optimizations will enable it to work at last [1].

The transformation and realization phases of the operational approach are ripe for automation because all of the behavioral requirements have been translated into computational mechanisms by the time the operational specification is written. From this point on, the system is formally represented, and the decisions yet to be made concern efficiency, computational resource management, and language translation exclusively. The latter subjects can be understood analytically, and this knowledge can be turned into tools which supply everything but judgment.

Maintenance In the structure of software there is an inherent conflict between efficiency and ease of maintenance [3]. Efficiency suggests that information be distributed, while ease of maintenance suggests that it be localized.

- A "demon" is a procedure that is invoked whenever the state of the program satisfies a certain condition. The easily maintained, but inefficient, implementation is one that checks all demon triggering conditions whenever the state changes. The efficient, but hard-to-maintain, implementation is one that distributes knowledge of the demon to all parts of the program where the state could change so as to make that demon's trigger true [21].

In other words, the decomposition suggested by the criteria of comprehensibility and modifiability (fortunately, these two seem to lead to the same decompositions) is not necessarily the same as the decomposition suggested by performance and efficient use of resources.

The conventional approach *per se* does nothing to alleviate this problem, since it supports only one decomposition. The conventional approach can be refined and altered to solve some aspects of it, however—even compilers solve low-level versions of the problem. One approach taken by the A-7 project led by David Parnas at the Naval Research Laboratory [9, 11, 12, 16, 24, 28] is to decompose on the basis of modifiability and then to regroup small logical units into other units, such as processes, chosen for resource-allocation purposes.

The operational approach addresses the structural conflict more directly by dividing development into two major phases exactly on these lines. The operational specification is optimized for maintainability, while the transformations break this structure down in favor of something more efficient.

Since an evolutionary cycle is a redevelopment of the system, the operational approach may promote automation of evolution as well as initial development. If the source of change is the system's required behavior, then the specification is modified, and the previous transformations can simply be reapplied to produce the modified implementation. Speed-ups here will improve responsiveness to changing user requirements [8]. If previous implementation decisions are at fault, then different transformations can be applied to the original specification. In either case the uniform language framework will improve traceability and change control. Note that neither proofs nor tests are robust in the face of change.

Management The conventional approach is well-suited to managerial and organizational needs. The requirements specification defines the interface between users and developers; the design specification defines the interface among the work of many programmers. No one has suggested which organizational structures or work assignments would be appropriate for the operational approach.

All potential advantages of the operational approach for management concern technical and psychological problems. For instance, the conventional approach does not yield executable code until late in development. Since we seldom feel sure of something until we see that it works (and rightly so), this means there is little accountability until it is too late. Nervous people are understandably overeager to produce code, neglecting the analysis and design phases. By prescribing an executable version of the system early in development, the operational approach offers a milestone which is both psychologically satisfying and subject to meaningful evaluation.

[3] It is interesting that one of the problems of conventional testing, namely determining whether the test output is correct, can be solved by the use of an operational specification as an oracle [34].

Can The Recommended Decision Sequences Be Achieved?

Weaknesses of the Conventional Approach The conventional approach stresses that all behavioral decisions should be made before any structural ones. This is an unrealistic and even undesirable expectation, since internal structure inevitably affects such external properties as feasibility, capacity, behavior under stress, and interleaving of independent events. Previous examples have illustrated this, as do the following:

- Ballistic missile-defense systems are at the outer limits of current computer technology. A necessary phase of the development of such systems is "preliminary design" to establish the feasibility of the proposed requirements. These preliminary designs are usually concealed from contractors bidding from the revised requirements.
- Software can be made fault-tolerant only if it has meaningful components whose failure can be detected and whose bad effects can be contained. To the extent that fault tolerance involves user participation, external behavior cannot be analyzed or defined without a virtual structure of components to which fault-tolerant properties can be attached.

Even if we could develop adequate behavioral requirements free of structural bias, there would be considerable difficulty in specifying them formally, since most formalisms introduce internal structure—if only to decompose complexity. Sets of axioms and finite-state machines are among the few representations that do not bias internal structure, but axioms have proven useful only for specifying *components* of complex systems, while finite-state machines (or regular expressions) have proven useful only for specifying very limited properties of complex systems. This problem is undoubtedly part of the reason why most conventional requirements are still written in English.

Another serious problem with the conventional approach is its reliance on a strategy of top–down decomposition for design. Basic methodological principles tell us that implicit decisions should be avoided, that if error-prone decisions must be made early then they should be subjected to early checks, and that individual decisions should be as orthogonal to others as possible. Top–down design leads to decomposition decisions most of whose consequences are implicit, makes the most global decisions earliest yet cannot validate them until the very end, and causes the top-level decisions to affect all properties of the system [10, 22]. It seems that top–down hierarchical decomposition is an excellent way to explain something that is already understood [35], but a poor way to acquire understanding.

- Top-down design allocates both function and performance to modules. During implementation it may be discovered that no implementation of a module's functional requirements can meet its performance requirements, but there was no way to know this earlier.
- Consider the problem of printing, in order, the prime numbers up to 1000. Without prior knowledge of a solution there is no way to decide among these top-level decompositions [10]:

```
(1) "generate table of primes";
    "print table of primes"
(2) for n := 2 step 1 until 1000 do
        if "n is prime" then "print n" fi
(3) n := 2;
    while n < = 1000
        do "print n";
           n := "next prime after n"
        od
```

Note that these criticisms do not apply to verification of the *correctness* of a design decomposition (which can be accomplished top–down (see [26]), nor to TRW's Distributed Computer Design System [31], in which an exploratory "look-ahead" decomposition guides the final decomposition on the level above.

In the operational approach the primary decomposition of complexity is based on problem-oriented vs. implementation-oriented structure rather than hierarchical decomposition. Even within an operational specification, the most prominent structures tend to be discovered by methods other than top–down decomposition. Although it is true that hierarchical abstraction is often used within an operational specification to defer details, these details must be resolved before the specification phase comes to an end.

Weaknesses of the Operational Approach One apparent weakness of the operational approach is the need to reduce external behaviors to internal mechanisms before specifying them. This suggests to many that operational specifications are overconstraining and premature.

There can be no question that this is a danger, but results so far are promising. Particularly noteworthy is

TABLE II. Weaknesses of the Conventional and Operational Approaches*

Conventional	Operational
Conventional approach does not allow for the effect of system structure on system behavior	Operational approach presents a danger of premature design decisions
"Black-box" requirements are very difficult to specify	It may prove difficult to execute specifications with adequate performance
Top–down decomposition is difficult and risky	Transformational implementation is a new and undeveloped technology People may find it hard to guide transformations

* It may not be possible to apply both approaches successfully to any project. Here are the known feasibility problems on each side.

TABLE III. Some Instances of the Operational Approach*

	Jackson System Development Method	PAISLey Project	Gist Project	Applicative Programming
Domain of Origin	Data processing	Real-time systems	AI and database systems	Programming
Special Features	Specific method for obtaining operational specification	Explicit representation and transformation of concurrency and distribution	Very high-level specification language motivated by expressive power of English	Strong mathematical foundations
	Maintainability stressed Operational specification uses implementation language, transformations operate within implementation language	Formal and executable performance constraints Execution of incomplete specifications	Associative retrieval and historical reference Use of constraints to refine nondeterminism (as in common-sense reasoning)	Historical emphasis on efficient execution of the operational specification itself, including special-purpose hardware architectures
Automated Support	Specifications informal, not executable Transformations language-dependent	Complete integrated environment possible and being planned	Complete integrated environment possible and being planned	Specification environments exist Transformations being automated
Current Status	In real-world use	First tools being implemented Methods in research stage	Many tools implemented (including natural-language paraphraser, behavior explainer)	Transformations and special-purpose hardware in research stage, use without them stable
References	[19, 10, 22, 18]	[37–42]	[5, 14, 21, 4]	[2, 32, 13, 33, 6, 7]

* "Domain of Origin" refers to the source of a project's computational model and notational flavor. It does *not* delimit the domain of applicability of a project's techniques. In fact, in all four cases, broad applicability has been shown.

the Jackson System Development (JSD) method (Table III), which is the only instance of the operational approach to have well-developed procedures and guidelines for deriving the operational specification. JSD does not deal adequately with all aspects of system development, but JSD specification techniques are clearly comprehensive and JSD specifications are clearly implementation-independent.

Furthermore, structuring principles discovered by different research efforts do not seem to conflict with one another. We believe that, with further study of operational specifications, we shall arrive at a point where any case in which a behavior appears to have two different specifications will be seen to fall into one of two categories: (1) The two specifications actually produce subtly different behaviors. (2) Of the two specifications, one is clearly superior on solid methodological grounds having to do with the criteria of comprehensibility and modifiability. Thus the other form may be a suitable target for an optimizing transformation.

- An elevator controller receives inputs from request buttons at the various floors and from sensors in the elevator shaft; it controls the elevator motor and signal lights at the various floors. Each of the two functions (motor and lights) needs to know the "state" of the elevator (position, direction, outstanding requests), which can be computed by keeping track of the inputs. It may seem to be an arbitrary choice whether each function performs this computation for itself or whether the results of a single computation are shared by them, but it is not. If the computations are separate they may become somewhat unsynchronized, in which case the elevator's actual behavior may differ from the elevator's "intention" (as indicated by the lights) when race conditions occur. This will be discernable to the user [22].
- Two independent processes in the same system may happen to use some of the same external inputs. The input interface may send the inputs to one of the processes, which will then forward them to the other process. Alternatively, the input interface may replicate the inputs and send them to both processes. The latter is clearly better because it does not violate the original independence of the two processes [37].

The difficult aspect of the implementation-independence problem is that each existing operational specification language seems to be more abstract in some dimensions than in others. If future research fails to change this, however, it may be sufficient to choose a specification language for a particular problem that is implementation-independent and transformable in the properties most critical to the success of the system.

Another potential problem with operational specifications is that they may run too slowly for the kind of testing and demonstration we would like. The technical problems and opportunities here are well-known from the analogy with LISP. Techniques for speeding up LISP execution have ranged from special-purpose hardware to compilation of functions whose definitions have stabilized.

The other major weakness of the operational approach is that transformational implementation is a relatively untried approach, and the necessary theoretical supports are only beginning to be developed. The idea of program transformations has been with us for a long time (they are warmly endorsed in [20]), without noticeable impact.

The actual similarities between transformations of specification and of implementation languages are less than meets the eye, however. Although the line between operational specification languages and high-level implementation languages has grown fuzzy, there is still one clear difference: implementation languages are meant to be compiled automatically into the target code, without human intervention. This means that they *must* allow the programmer some control over use of physical resources, a necessity which complicates the languages and renders them less implementation-independent than specification languages.

> Dynamic structures of all kinds (data structures, processes, *etc.*) are much more difficult to analyze and transform than static ones. The primary reason for using dynamic structures is to conserve storage, a motivation that concerns implementation resources only. Problem-oriented specifications can always declare static structures up to the maximum capacity of the system, and use them as needed.

We conjecture that this inherent complication and implementation-dependence is what makes conventional programming languages difficult to transform. The transformational approach delays resource bindings for as long as possible—until after all necessary adjustments to the behavior-producing mechanisms have been made.

A final problem concerns current plans to have human users choose the transformations to be applied. It is not clear that, after several transformations, the specification will still be comprehensible enough to allow human intervention! Only further research and experience will determine whether or not this is a serious problem.

It may be worth mentioning that even without tools to support transformation, a form of the operational approach is already popular in some circles and has been applied successfully to projects under heavy time pressure. This is the use of shell programming on the UNIX[4] operating system to produce a prototype, followed by expansion and optimization in C.

SOME INSTANCES OF THE OPERATIONAL APPROACH

Despite their common philosophy, the projects summarized in Table III vary widely in style, emphasis, and accomplishments. An operational specification language, for instance, can use as its fundamental model of computation either parallel processes (PAISLey), updates and accesses to an associative database (Gist), or function evaluation (applicative programming). Any of these models can be tailored to a particular application domain by extension, i.e., by predefining structures native to that application.

My viewpoint is inevitably partisan, but the goal of this paper has been to clarify some legitimate and important distinctions. To do this it has been necessary to polarize two sets of ideas that can—and have been—combined in many ways. It has also been necessary to compare what is inherently incommensurate, for the conventional approach is a mature technology whose problems have either been solved or resisted many attempts at solution, while the operational approach is based on technology whose faults have not been filtered in this way. Nevertheless, I hope these means are justified by the ends of promoting general understanding and scientific debate.

Acknowledgments John Cameron will recognize many of our discussions in these pages; Mack Alford, Phil Cannata, Doug Comer, Dennis DeBruler, Peter Denning, Dick Kieburtz, John Manferdelli, Dave Parnas, Jim Weythman, Elaine Weyuker, and Jack Wileden all gave me valuable comments.

[4] Trademark of AT&T Bell Laboratories, Inc.

REFERENCES

1. Alford, M. Software requirements in the 80s: From alchemy to science. *Proc. ACM '80*, Nashville, TN (October 1980).
2. Backus, J. Can programming be liberated from the von Neumann style? A functional style and its algebra of programs. *Commun. ACM 21* (August 1978), 613–641.
3. Balzer, R. Personal communication, April 1982.
4. Balzer, R.M. Goldman, N.M. and Wile, D.S. Operational specification as the basis for rapid prototyping. *ACM SIGSOFT Softw. Eng. Notes 7*, (December 1982), 3–16.
5. Balzer, R. and Goldman, N. Principles of good software specification and their implications for specification language. *Specifications of Reliable Software Conference*, Cambridge, MA (April 1979), 58–67.
6. Bauer, F.L. *et al.* Towards a wide spectrum language to support program specification and program development. *SIGPLAN Notices 13*, (December 1978), 15–24.
7. Bauer, F.L. *et al.* Programming in a wide spectrum language: A collection of examples. *Sci. Comput. Program 1*, (October 1981), 73–114.
8. Blum, B.I. The life cycle—A debate over alternative models. *Softw. Eng. Notes 7* (October 1982), 18–20.
9. Britton, K.H. and Parnas, D.L. A-7E software module guide. *Naval Research Laboratory Memorandum Report* 4702, Washington, D.C. (December 1981).
10. Cameron, J.R. *JSP and JSD: The Jackson Approach to Software Development*, to be published.
11. Clements, P.C. Function specifications for the A-7E function driver module. *Naval Research Laboratory Memorandum Report* 4658, Washington, D.C. (November 1981).
12. Clements, P.C. Interface specifications for the A-7E shared services module. *Naval Research Laboratory Memorandum Report* 4863, Washington, D.C. (September 1982).
13. Darlington, J. An experimental program transformation and synthesis system. *Artif. Intell. 16* (March 1981), 1–46.

14. Goldman, N.M. and Wile, D.S. A relational data base foundation for process specifications. In: *Entity-Relationship Approach to Systems Analysis and Design*, P.P. Chen, ed. Elsevier North-Holland, New York, 1980, 413–432.
15. Heninger, K.L. Specifying software requirements for complex systems: New techniques and their application. *IEEE Trans. Softw. Eng. SE-6* (January 1980), 2–13.
16. Heninger, K.L. *et al.* Software requirements for the A-7E aircraft. *Naval Research Laboratory Memorandum Report. 3876*, Washington, D.C. (November 1978).
17. Hester, S.D., Parnas, D.L. and Utter, D.F. Using documentation as a software design medium. *Bell Sys. Tech. J. 60*, (October 1981), 1941–1977.
18. Jackson, M.A. *Principles of Program Design*, Academic Press, New York, 1975.
19. Jackson, M.A. *System Development*, Prentice-Hall, Englewood Cliffs, NJ, 1982.
20. Knuth, D.E. Structured programming with *go to* statements. *Comput Surv. 6* (December 1974), 261–301.
21. London, P. and Feather, M. Implementing specification freedoms. *Sci. Comput. Program.* 2 (November 1982), 91–131.
22. Michael Jackson Systems Ltd. *Jackson System Development* (course manual), 1982.
23. McCracken, D.D. and Jackson, M.A. A minority dissenting position. *Systems Analysis and Design—A Foundation for the 1980's*, William W. Cotterman *et al.*, eds., Elsevier North-Holland, New York, 1981, 551–553.
24. Parker, R.A. *et al.* Abstract interface specifications for the A-7E device interface module. *Naval Research Laboratory Memorandum Report.* 4385, Washington, D.C. (November 1980).
25. Parnas, D.L. On the criteria to be used in decomposing systems into modules. *Commun. ACM 15* (December 1972), 1053–1058.
26. Parnas, D.L. The use of precise specifications in the development of software. *IFIP Congress*, Toronto, Ontario, August 1977, 861–867.
27. Parnas, D.L. Designing software for ease of extension and contraction. *IEEE Trans. Softw. Eng. SE-5* (March 1979), 128–138.
28. Parnas, D.L. *et al.* Interface specifications for the SCR (A-7E) extended computer module. *Naval Research Laboratory Memorandum Report* 4843, Washington, D.C. (January 1983).
29. Swartout, W. GIST English Generator. *Proc. National Conf. Artif. Intell.*, Pittsburgh, PA (August 1982), 404–409.
30. Swartout, W. and Balzer, R. On the inevitable intertwining of specification and implementation. *Commun. ACM 25* (July 1982), 438–440.
31. TRW Defense and Space Systems Group. Distributed computing design system/DCDS description. *Tech. Rep.* CDRL A004, Huntsville, AB, (August 1981).
32. Turner, D.A. The semantic elegance of applicative languages. *Proc. Conf. Funct. Program. Lang. Comput. Archit.*, Portsmouth, NH, (October 1981), 85–92.
33. Wadler, P. Applicative style programming, program transformation, and list operators. *Proc. Conf. Funct. Program. Lang. Comput. Archit.* Portsmouth, N.H. (October 1981), 25–32.
34. Weyuker, E.J. On testing nontestable programs. *The Comput. J.* 25, 4, (1982), 465–470.
35. Wirth, N. On the composition of well-structured programs. *Comput. Surv.* 6, (December 1974), 247–259.
36. Yeh, R.T. *et al.* Software requirements: New directions and perspectives. *Software Engineering Handbook,* C.V. Ramamoorthy and C.R. Vick, eds., Van Nostrand Reinhold, New York, to appear.
37. Zave, P. The anatomy of a proc136s-control system. Submitted for publication, May 1982.
38. Zave, P. A distributed alternative to finite-state-machine specifications. Submitted for publication, December 1982.
39. Zave, P. An operational approach to requirements specification for embedded systems. *IEEE Trans. Softw. Eng. SE-8* (May 1982), 250–269.
40. Zave, P. Testing incomplete specifications of distributed systems. *ACM/SIGACT-SIGOPS Symp Princ. Distributed Comput.* Ottawa, Canada (August 1982), 42–48.
41. Zave, P. Case study: The PAISLey approach applied to its own software tools. Submitted for publication, June 1983.
42. Zave, P. and Yeh, R.T. Executable requirements for embedded systems. *Fifth Int. Conf. Softw. Eng.* San Diego, California. (March 1981), 295–304.

CR Categories and Subject Descriptors: D.2.1 [**Software Engineering**]: Requirements/Specifications—*methodologies*; D.2.2 [**Software Engineering**]: Tools and Techniques—*top-down programming*; D.2.4 [**Software Engineering**]: Program Verification—*validation*; D.2.9 [**Software Engineering**]: Management—*life cycle, productivity*; D.2.m [**Software Engineering**]: Miscellaneous—*rapid prototyping*
General Terms: Designs, Documentation
Additional Key Words and Phrases: software development methods

Received 1/83; accepted 8/83

Author's Present Address: Pamela Zave, AT&T Bell Laboratories, Room 3D-426, Murray Hill, NJ 07974

The Descartes Specification Language

Joseph E. Urban
Arizona State University
College of Engineering & Applied Sciences
Computer Science Department
Tempe, AZ 85287-5406

Abstract

The Descartes specification language [Urb77, 82, 85] is an executable specification language based on data structuring methods proposed by Hoare. The Descartes language and interpreter provide software developers with the capability to rapidly prototype systems early in the software lifecycle. This paper presents the definition of the Descartes specification language and describes the syntax and semantics of the language. Included in the paper is the motivation for the selection of the data structuring methods and notation. Top-down development of a specification is made possible by the use of modules that are described in this paper. An abstract execution feature, available in the language is presented as an enhancement to the top-down development of specifications for complex software systems.

1: Motivation for the Language Design

Simplicity of rules in the specification language allows for the easy development of a specification. This simplicity in rules can be found in an earlier work by the French mathematician and philosopher, René Descartes [Des37], who developed four rules that he used in the solution of complex problems. The rules are as follows:

> . . . And as a multitude of laws often only hampers justice, so that a state is best governed when, with few laws, these are rigidly administered; in like manner, instead of the great number of precepts of which logic is composed, I believed that the four following would prove perfectly sufficient for me, provided I took the firm and unwavering resolution never in a single instance to fail in observing them.
>
> The first was never to accept anything for true which I did not clearly know to be such; that is to say, carefully to avoid precipitancy and prejudice, and to comprise nothing more in my judgment than what was presented to my mind so clearly and distinctly as to exclude all ground of doubt.
>
> The second, to divide each of the difficulties under examination into as many parts as possible, and as might be necessary for its adequate solution.
>
> The third, to conduct my thoughts in such order that, by commencing with objects the simplest and easiest to know, I might ascend by little and little, and as it were, step by step, to the knowledge of the more complex; assigning in thought a certain order even to those objects which in their own nature do not stand in a relation of antecedence and sequence.
>
> And the last, in every case to make enumerations so complete and reviews so general, that I might be assured that nothing was omitted.

The four rules of solving problems are analogous to the development of a specification in the Descartes specification language. After the first rule is applied, the specifier applies rule two to describe the input expected. An analysis is made of the input based on facts known from applying rule one and bearing in mind the desired output. The output expected is then arrived at by the application of rule three. Hence a synthesis of the solution is developed. Rule four is useful as a verification process to ensure that the specification captures only the desired concept.

The specification language was named Descartes as a result of the above rules.

2: Language Description

2.1: Hoare Trees

In Descartes, the approach to program specification is as follows: define the input and output data and then relate the output data to the input data so that the output data becomes a function of the input data. To describe data, a tree structure is used. The terminal nodes of the tree name actual data

EHO304-6/90/0000/0331$01.00

items and give their type. Each intermediate node of the tree has a meaningful name that describes the data given by all of the terminal nodes of its subtree. Indentation is used to indicate subnodes of nodes in the tree. Each intermediate node structures its subtrees according to one of the data structuring methods (direct product, discriminated union, or sequence) described by Hoare [Hoa72,75]. Therefore, I refer to these trees as "Hoare trees." For example,

```
name
    first
    last
```

shows the node "name" as having two subtrees (indicated by indentation). Hoare uses a cross (×) to indicate a direct product, but in Descartes direct product is the default when a discriminated union or a sequence is not indicated.

The discriminated union is indicated by a plus sign (+) suffixed to the node name. Thus

```
flag+
    on
    off
```

indicates that "flag" is one of the alternatives "on" or "off".

A sequence is indicated by an asterisk (*) suffixed to the node name, so that

```
mail*
    letter
```

indicates that "mail" is a sequence of zero or more elements, each of which is a "letter". The number of elements in the sequence can be any non-negative integer. "Mail" names the entire sequence and individual elements of the sequence are named "mail(1)", and "mail(2)", etc.

2.2: Understanding Hoare Trees

One reason that Hoare trees are used in Descartes is for readability. Programs written in a language supporting record structures that contain large structures usually have the structure in a tree-like notation to enhance readability. Hoare trees provide a simple and natural notation for describing the input and output data of a program. This section extends the notation to that used in Descartes. It is important to note that in this section we are only interested in describing the input and output data. The use of Hoare trees to construct a specification is described in later sections. As an initial step in a software development, we have found it helpful to construct Hoare trees to describe input and output data before constructing the actual specification. During this step, no attempt is made to relate the output data to the input data.

A sequence node, by definition, has one immediate subnode. It is convenient to allow a sequence of a direct product or a sequence of a discriminated union to be written as a single node. Thus

```
×*                 ×*
  y                  y+
    a      or          a
    b                  b
    c                  c
```

can be written as

```
×*             ×*+
  a     or       a
  b              b
  c              c
```

respectively.

Notice that the specifier can include a single subnode under a sequence node (e.g., the "y" node above) and not change the meaning of the Hoare tree.

It is also useful to be able to indicate that the length of a sequence falls within a given range. A Pascal-like range notation is used to indicate a range. A blank is used to indicate that there is no upper bound. Thus, for example,

```
identifier (1..31)
    letter
```

illustrates a lower bound of one and an upper bound of thirty-one and

```
non_null_string(1.. )
    character
```

illustrates a lower bound of one and no upper bound.

When an exact number of elements of a sequence is required, the lower and upper bounds are equal. For example, the sequence node "alpha(175.. 175)" is defined to contain precisely 175 elements.

Sequence nodes that have a range notation can be constructed from direct product, discriminated union, and sequence. The range notation is an aid for the development of clear and concise Hoare trees, (see Figure 1).

```
a                                  a
    b(1.. )   is equivalent to       b
      c                                d
                                           c
                                         e*
                                           c
```

Figure 1

In Descartes, a literal is any string enclosed in single quotes. For example, the name of the language is:

```
language
    'Descartes'
```

In Hoare tree notation, one representation of a fixed-point number is the following:

```
fixed_point_number
    before_decimal(1..)
        digit+
            '0'
            '1'
            '2'
            '3'
            '4'
            '5'
            '6'
            '7'
            '8'
            '9'
    '.'
    after_decimal(1 ..)
        digit+
            '0'
            '1'
            '2'
            '3'
            '4'
            '5'
            '6'
            '7'
            '8'
            '9'
```

Some fixed-point numbers that match the above Hoare tree are:

```
2.0
123.01
0.317
```

while the following do not match the Hoare tree:

```
2
2.
abc.def
.
13.e45
```

Restrictions could have been placed on the upper bound ranges of "before_decimal" and "after_decimal" to satisfy size limitations on the integer and fractional portions, respectively. Having to repeatedly specify the discriminated union "digit" is cumbersome. This irritant and its solution will be discussed later.

2.3: Constructing a Specification

Hoare trees are utilized in Descartes to describe the input data expected, the output produced, and the functional relationship that exists between them. If the input data is considered as a string of characters, then the Hoare tree that describes it can be thought of as a "pattern" that matches the character string, as in a SNOBOL pattern match. The root node of the matching Hoare tree then becomes a name for the entire string, and each intermediate and terminal node becomes a name for the part of the string that it matches. Non-matching subtrees of a discriminated union do not become names of any part of the input. The Hoare tree that describes program output is then composed from nodes used in matching the input. The output from such a node is the character string named by the node as a result of the input match. Thus, the specification method consists of analysis of the input data followed by the synthesis of the output data using the parts discovered on input.

The specification is developed top-downwards into modular units that refine the Hoare trees until no further refinement is desired or possible. Thus a concept can be specified partially by not writing some of the lower-level modules. Modules analyze and synthesize data in the manner described in Subsections 2.3.3 and 2.3.4, respectively. Modules reference data at the abstract level appropriate to the current level of data definition and may reference modules that are to be refined later.

2.3.1: Module Definition

Modules begin with a title (in upper case) that consists of an English phrase describing the function value in terms of the arguments to the function. Those arguments in the title are in upper case and enclosed in parentheses. For example, the title,

```
INTEGER_OF_(FIXED_POINT_NUMBER)
```

has "FIXED_POINT_NUMBER" as the only argument.

Each argument in the title represents input data, which are regarded as a character string, to the module. Arguments can be positioned anywhere in a module title, which is constructed to describe output data. After the title, the module lists analysis and synthesis Hoare trees. These trees analyze the data in a way that will be useful in synthesizing the Hoare tree that describes the value of the function.

The data corresponding to an argument will also be described by a Hoare tree within the "calling" module. The two Hoare tree descriptions of the data must agree exactly in terms of the character string described, but need not analyze the character string in the same way.

The value of a module is usually described by a Hoare tree that is distinguished from the other Hoare trees by the use of "return" as its root node name. Terminal nodes of this tree can be names that define data from the matches found on input, can be literals, or can be module calls. It is sometimes advantageous to describe the value of a module with a "return" as an intermediate node of a Hoare tree. In this case, the value of a module is defined as the value of the "return" subtree and is determined in a similar manner as when "return" is the root node of a Hoare tree.

Module calls may appear as arguments within a module call. When an argument is a module call, this module call must be executed. The value of the module, as described in the previous paragraph, becomes the value of the argument. This allows for arguments to become nested within module calls. Processing of a nested module call requires that the innermost module call be executed first. This processing proceeds outward until the argument of the original module call acquires a value.

2.3.2: Individual Nodes

Match and reference are two types of nodes that can appear in any Hoare tree. A match node must appear in lower case letters. The corresponding reference node must appear in upper case letters. The underscore symbol, " _ ", can be used freely to create meaningful node names. Some examples of match nodes are:

```
record
item
first_character
list
```

Corresponding reference nodes are the following:

```
RECORD
ITEM
FIRST_CHARACTER
LIST
```

A match node is a node that is a possible candidate for acquiring a value as a result of matching. A terminal reference node is a node that is a possible candidate for acquiring a value of a previously matched node with the same name. An intermediate reference node determines whether analysis or synthesis continues past the node. If an intermediate reference node can be associated with a previously matched node with the same name, then processing continues on to the subtree of the reference node. Terminal literal nodes, module title nodes, and module call nodes are also denoted as reference nodes.

Root nodes of Hoare trees that are reference nodes indicate that the Hoare tree is an analysis tree. Root nodes of Hoare trees that are match nodes indicate that the Hoare tree is a synthesis tree. Thus, for example, the arguments from the title (upper case) indicate that the corresponding tree is an analysis tree and that "return" (lower case) indicates a synthesis tree. In general, any number of analysis and synthesis Hoare trees can appear in a specification module. Only a defined "return" match node is used to determine the output of a specification module. A reference node that is an intermediate node is useful in shaping a Hoare tree in which the node occurs. The shaping depends on the corresponding match node.

2.3.3: Matching

All nodes can acquire values during analysis or synthesis, but not every node will necessarily acquire a value. Therefore, any type of node is either defined or undefined. For example, consider the following analysis Hoare tree.

```
INPUT
    letter+
        'a'
        'b'
        'c'
```

with the character "b" as the only character in the input string. After the match is performed, the nodes "'a'" and "'c'" will be undefined literal nodes, whereas "letter" and "'b'" will be defined nodes. The defined nodes will have acquired "b" for a value. Similarly, a synthesis tree for the above could be,

```
return
  LETTER
```

After synthesis of this Hoare tree is performed, "LETTER" and "return" will have acquired "b" for a value. This trivial specification illustrates the presented language features.

Matching of input strings to Hoare trees proceeds as follows. Matching of direct products and discriminated unions is performed as in a SNOBOL pattern match for concatenation and alternation, respectively. Sequence matching can most readily be described as follows. If "a" is the subtree of a sequence "x*", then "X" is matched according to the SNOBOL rules for the following:

```
X+
  end_of_sequence
      NULL
  continuation_of_sequence
      a
      next_x
          X
```

In this Hoare tree, "NULL" is a reference node that is defined as the null string and "X" is a recursive reference node. Sequence ranges other than "*" can be defined in terms of direct product, discriminated union, and "*".

All matches must be anchored at both ends of the string, so that a Hoare tree matches an argument string only if the match covers the entire string. Each node name in the Hoare tree becomes a name for that part of the string that it matches.

2.3.4: *Referencing of Nodes*

Values set from the analysis of input data control the shape of the synthesis tree. Thus, the subtree selected by a discriminated union can be determined as the first subtree having a name that defines some input data. The length of a sequence can be determined in two ways: implicitly, as the same length as determined on input for a (unique) Hoare tree node with the same name; or explicitly, by using the range notation. The number of elements matched in a sequence node can be referenced by the node name (in upper case) and immediately followed by a sharp, "#". Similarly, an individual element matched in a sequence node can be referenced by the node name capitalized and immediately followed by the element reference enclosed in parentheses.

Whenever a non-literal reference node name appears in a specification module, a search attempts to locate the corresponding defined match node. A reference node name can appear as a module call, parameter in a module call, terminal literal node, root node of an analysis Hoare tree, intermediate node, or terminal node. The parameters of the top module in a specification acquire values from the input files that are external input data to the specification. Terminal literal nodes acquire the character string between single quotes as values through analysis or synthesis. Module calls acquire the value that is returned from the invocation of the module. All other reference node names require a search.

The search for a defined match node that corresponds to a reference node involves searching the specification module in which the reference node appears. The two following rules are applied in performing the search: (1) identify the closest reference node that is an antecedent of the reference node that initiated the search and (2) identify the corresponding defined match node of the reference node identified in the first rule. The search is initially limited to the subtree of the match node that is identified in the second rule. If the corresponding match node is not found in the subtree, the search is expanded. The next closest antecedent reference node is used to satisfy the rules and the subtree search is performed. This process is continued until the corresponding match node is found or the entire module has been searched.

The success or failure of locating the corresponding defined match node for an intermediate reference node determines the shape of the Hoare tree as described earlier. If the corresponding defined match node is found for a terminal reference node, then the reference node acquires the value of the match node. Each specification module has a module title that is a reference node. In order to satisfy the rules, we note that a module title has itself as the corresponding match node.

Limiting the search for a match node serves to handle ambiguities. It is possible for the same match node name to occur more than once in a specification. Qualifying a reference node with other reference nodes as antecedents resolves the problem of an ambiguity and makes it easier to construct specifications.

2.4: An Example Specification

A simple sample specification to accept as input a fixed-point number and to output the integer portion is described below. This specification will use the title and input Hoare tree that were presented earlier. The specification is shown in Figure 2.

```
INTEGER_OF_(FIXED_POINT_NUMBER)
    FIXED_POINT_NUMBER
        before_decimal(1 .. )
            digit+
                '0'
                '1'
                '2'
                '3'
                '4'
                '5'
                '6'
                '7'
                '8'
                '9'
        '.'
        after_decimal(1.. )
            digit+
                '0'
                '1'
                '2'
                '3'
                '4'
                '5'
                '6'
                '7'
                '8'
                '9'
    return
        BEFORE_DECIMAL
```

Figure 2

Note that an input of "4.72" would yield "4" as output. A detailed explanation of a larger problem appears in Section 2.7.

2.5: Invoking Submodules

Module invocations can occur in analysis and synthesis trees. A module call is invoked when the node is reached during analysis or synthesis. Modules ease the construction of specifications for complex problems.

A module call is a reference node. The module call acquires a value after return from the called module. As with any module call, arguments may be passed. The number of actual parameters in the module call must match the number of formal parameters in the module title. A parameter must have a corresponding defined match node so that the value of the parameter can be passed to the referenced module. The search for defined match nodes that correspond to the parameters in the module call is performed as described earlier.

It is possible to invoke a module with no arguments. As mentioned earlier, it is cumbersome to continually specify a digit in the fixed-point problem. The problem is alleviated by invoking "DIGIT" as a module. The "DIGIT" must be defined so that it is consistent with all uses of the module. Thus, for example, the fixed-point problem could be specified as follows:

```
INTEGER_OF_(FIXED_POINT_NUMBER)
    FIXED_POINT_NUMBER
        before_decimal(1 ..)
            DIGIT
        '.'
        after_decimal(1.. )
            DIGIT
    return
        BEFORE_DECIMAL
```

The corresponding module for "DIGIT" can be defined as follows:

```
DIGIT
    return+
        '0'
        '1'
        '2'
        '3'
        '4'
        '5'
        '6'
        '7'
        '8'
        '9'
```

Primitive modules exist in Descartes for performing arithmetic, logical, and Boolean operations. Each primitive module expects a fixed number of parameter values. Each actual parameter must be either a reference node that has a corresponding defined match node, a literal, or a module value.

Figure 3 includes all primitive modules that are provided in the language definition.

```
ARITHMETIC PRIMITIVES
    (OPERAND_ONE)_PLUS_(OPERAND_TWO)
    (OPERAND_ONE)_MINUS_(OPERAND_TWO)
    (OPERAND_ONE)_TIMES_(OPERAND_TWO)
    (OPERAND_ONE)_DIVIDED_BY_(OPERAND_TWO)
    (OPERAND_ONE)_RAISED_TO_(OPERAND_TWO)
    where: OPERAND_ONE and OPERAND_TWO are numeric parameters.
LOGICAL PRIMITIVES
    (OPERAND_ONE)_EQUAL_(OPERAND_TWO)
    (OPERAND_ONE)_NOT_EQUAL_(OPERAND_TWO)
    (OPERAND_ONE)_GREATER_THAN_(OPERAND_TWO)
    (OPERAND_ONE)_GREATER_THAN_OR_EQUAL_TO_(OPERAND_TWO)
    (OPERAND_ONE)_LESS_THAN_(OPERAND_TWO)
    (OPERAND_ONE)_LESS_THAN_OR_EQUAL_TO_(OPERAND_TWO)
    where: OPERAND_ONE and OPERAND_TWO can be any string value.
BOOLEAN PRIMITIVES
    (OPERAND_ONE)_AND_(OPERAND_TWO)
    (OPERAND_ONE)_OR_(OPERAND_TWO)
    NOT_(OPERAND_ONE)
    where: OPERAND_ONE and OPERAND_TWO are bit strings.
```

Figure 3

The value returned for arithmetic primitive modules is the result of performing the computation requested in the module title. Arithmetic primitive modules can appear wherever the result of a computation is needed. The other two primitive module groups, logical and Boolean, do not return values. Logical primitive modules evaluate to either true or false. This result determines whether to continue processing down the path of a tree. Boolean primitive modules are used together with logical "values".

The specification of an ordered set of integers can be constructed through the use of an arithmetic primitive module call. The following module is only presented for illustrative purposes. This specification module captures the generation of an infinite set:

```
ENUMERATION _ OF _ (NUMBER)
    NUMBER
        value
            INTEGER
    return
        addition
            (VALUE) _ PLUS _ ('1')
        ' '
        ENUMERATION _ OF _ (ADDITION)
```

If the input parameter is equal to zero, then the output of the specification is the set of positive integers (each integer is separated by a blank). This module does not terminate because the "return" node always initiates another call to the specification module. Specification of a range of ordered integers can be accomplished by using a logical primitive module to limit the generation of integers. The above specification module is modified to output the integers that are greater than the input parameter, up to and including the integer 100. This modification is presented in Figure 4.

Two logical primitive modules are in the above specification module. The ( ) _ EQUAL _ ( ) primitive module ensures that the specification module terminates. A logical primitive module, ( ) _ LESS _ THAN _ ( ), ensures that the input parameter would not cause the specification module to generate integers beyond the range listed in the module call.

2.6: Abstract Execution

Writing specifications in the language is similar to writing programs using top-down structured programming. A user will write the top module consisting of an input Hoare tree, an output Hoare tree, and references to lower-level modules. Each Hoare tree can be partially or completely refined. A partially refined Hoare tree has at least one finite path in the tree that does not terminate with a reference node. A completely refined Hoare tree has every finite path in the tree terminating with a reference node.

The lower-level modules are written in a similar manner until all Hoare trees are completely refined. Because a specification module can be written without completely refining a Hoare tree, some feature is necessary to test modules. Abstract execution serves as a testing feature for specification modules with Hoare trees that are not completely refined. This feature provides the developer with the ability to construct the top module, then test the module. Another advantage is that a module can be tested without a completed sibling submodule. Abstract execution is a feature that must be requested when specification modules are executed on the language processor. Abstract execution allows a terminal match node to match any part of the input string that has its name.

A specification module that contains terminal match nodes is a candidate for abstract execution. Terminal match

```
RANGE _ FROM _ (NUMBER) _ TO _ ONE _ HUNDRED
    NUMBER
        value
            INTEGER
    return +
            (VALUE) _ EQUAL _ ('99')
            (VALUE _ PLUS _ ('1')
            (VALUE) _ LESS _ THAN _ ('99')
            continue
                next
                    (VALUE) _ PLUS _ ('1')
                    ' '
                    RANGE _ FROM _ (NEXT) _ TO _ ONE _ HUNDRED
```

Figure 4

nodes are to be refined at some later time. The specification can be tested throughout the development. This approach allows errors to be caught early in the software lifecycle, rather than later on in the development process.

The specification language allows the user to specify what is to be done rather than how it is to be done. A user need not develop specifications completely. It will be possible to write a top specification module then give this to someone else for completion. This method of constructing specifications is analogous to writing programs in the Chief Programmer Team approach to programming. Writing specifications with this method has positive implications for large projects. The concept of precisely defined subtasks is one of the merits obtained by using the specification language.

The description presented is sufficient for someone to begin writing specifications. The sample specifications presented in the next section provide a closer look at the capabilities of Descartes.

2.7: Telegram Analysis

The following problem to be specified has appeared several times in the literature. Henderson and Snowden [Hen72] presented the "telegram problem" to illustrate the techniques of structured programming. Ledgard [Led74] used the same problem to also illustrate structured programming techniques. Gerhart and Yelowitz [Ger76] have performed an analysis of known errors in the previous two solutions. Noonan [Noo75] also used the problem in his presentation of a specification language. The problem is specified informally as follows (Henderson and Snowden [Hen72]):

> A program is required to process a stream of telegrams. This stream is available as a sequence of letters, digits, and blanks on some device and can be transferred in sections of predetermined size into a buffer area where it is to be processed. The words in the telegrams are separated by sequences of blanks and each telegram is delimited by the word "zzzz". The stream is terminated by the occurrence of the empty telegram, that is a telegram with no words. Each telegram is to be processed to determine the number of chargeable words and to check for occurrences of overlength words. The words "zzzz" and "stop" are not chargeable and words more than twelve letters are considered overlength. The result of the processing is to be a neat listing of the telegrams, each accompanied by the word count and a message indicating the occurrence of an overlength word.

It should be noted that solutions presented in the literature have included the number of overlength words that occurred in a telegram. This count is not what is called for in the informal specification. Only "a message indicating the occurrence of an overlength word" is requested. We can see how easy it is to misinterpret informal specifications. This same misunderstanding has been observed several times by this author while working with students programming the problem from the informal specification.

As mentioned in Subsection 2.2, it is beneficial to use Hoare trees to describe the input and output data format. The telegram problem is complex enough to warrant the use of initial Hoare trees. In the two Hoare trees that follow, notice that there is no attempt to relate output to input.

The format of input data for the telegram problem follows:

```
telegram_stream
    telegram*
        blanks*
            ' '
        word_section*
            word
                CHARACTER
            blanks(1 .. )
                ' '
        'zzzz'
    blanks(1.. )
        ' '
    empty_telegram
        'zzzz'
```

The format of output data for the telegram problem follows:

```
a_listing_of_telegrams_and_charges_from_a_telegram_stream_telegram*
    NEW_PAGE
    text*+
        CHARACTER
        ' '
    NEW_LINE
    overlength_word_message+
        'OVERLENGTH WORDS IN THE TELEGRAM'
        NULL
    NEW_LINE
    NEW_LINE
    'THE NUMBER OF CHARGEABLE WORDS = '
    number_of_chargeable_words
        INTEGER
```

The specification of the telegram problem differs from the specifications presented in the earlier sections. This specification module is presented in several steps as the analysis and synthesis trees are developed top-downwards. Abstract execution, as presented in the previous section, is used in each module with the exception of the final specification module. Using this approach results in the specification of a problem (larger than our earlier specifications) with execution of the specification module occurring early in the development process.

The first approach to the specification is a simple attempt to capture the sequence of telegrams that are in the telegram stream. The simplification is apparent in that only one abstract node, "ok _ or _ overlength", appears in the module. This abstract node will be later refined to analyze telegrams that contain words that are not greater than 12 letters and telegrams that contain at least one word greater than 12 letters. For the moment, it is of little concern as to the structure of individual telegrams. A first attempt at the specification is as shown in Figure 5.

The specification module shown in Figure 5 can be executed by invoking the interpreter with the "-abstract" argument. Literal and abstract (to the appropriate level) input data must be supplied in the input segment. The following abstract input data is an initial test of the specification module:

```
ok _ or _ overlength
zzzz
ok _ or _ overlength
zzzz
ok _ or _ overlength
zzzz zzzz
```

The above input stream was presented over several lines for readability. The actual input is one continuous stream of characters. This convention will be used throughout the rest of this section on the telegram problem. A person executing the specification module may also find the input and output slightly unreadable. This situation could be remedied by allowing a user specified delimiter for abstract "names" that appear in the input stream.

Input consists of three telegrams in the telegram stream. Synthesis depends on two reserved nodes for generating the output. The two nodes are "NEW _ LINE" and "NEW _ PAGE," which are module calls to generate a new line and a

```
A _ LISTING _ OF _ TELEGRAMS _ AND _ CHARGES _ FROM _ A _ (TELEGRAM _ STREAM)
    TELEGRAM _ STREAM
        telegram*
            ok _ or _ overlength
            'zzzz'
        blanks(1.. )
            ' '
        empty _ telegram
            'zzzz'
    return
        TELEGRAM*
            NEW _ PAGE
            OK _ OR _ OVERLENGTH
            NEW _ LINE
            NEW _ LINE
            chargeable _ word _ message
```

Figure 5

```
A _ LISTING _ OF _ TELEGRAMS _ AND _ CHARGES _ FROM _ A _ (TELEGRAM _ STREAM)
    TELEGRAM _ STREAM
        telegram*
            ok _ or _ overlength +
                text _ ok
                text _ overlength
            'zzzz'
        blanks(1.. )
            ' '
        empty _ telegram
            'zzzz'
    return
        TELEGRAM*
            NEW _ PAGE
            OK _ OR _ OVERLENGTH +
                TEXT _ OK
                TEXT _ OVERLENGTH
                    NEW _ LINE
                    'OVERLENGTH WORDS IN THE TELEGRAM'
            NEW _ LINE
            NEW _ LINE
            chargeable _ word _ message
```

Figure 6

new page, respectively. Based on the above input data there are three pages of output generated. Each page consists of the telegram, two new lines, and a message concerning the number of words. The telegram in each case is "ok _ or _ overlength".

The following refinement of the specification module involves the "ok _ or _ overlength" node. This is a simple, but necessary, refinement which shows that a message is generated if a telegram contains an overlength word. Successful completion of this refinement is crucial for any further refinement of the individual telegrams. The specification module appears in Figure 6.

Sample abstract input to the specification module could be as follows:

```
text _ ok
zzzz
text _ overlength
zzzz
text _ ok
zzzz   zzzz
```

The two possibilities for "ok _ or _ overlength" are tested when the specification module is executed with the above input data.

Further refinement of the individual telegrams can continue since the above specification module captures the specification it is supposed to. Refinement will occur for the "text _ ok" node. Results that are obtained in the next step will be used in refining the "text _ overlength" node. A telegram may have extraneous information that occurs before the first word in the text. It is for this reason that an initial word separator is needed before the words appear in the telegram. Each word must be followed by a word separator, including the last word in the telegram. Note that the specification module in Figure 7 is much more concise than the above description.

After refining the "text _ ok" node the specification module is executed with the following abstract input data:

```
initial _ word _ separator
word
word _ separator
word
word _ separator
word
word _ separator
zzzz
text
zzzz
initial _ word _ separator
word
word _ separator
word
word _ separator
zzzz   zzzz
```

```
A _ LISTING _ OF _ TELEGRAMS _ AND _ CHARGES _ FROM _ A _ (TELEGRAM _ STREAM)
    TELEGRAM _ STREAM
        telegram*
            ok _ or _ overlength +
                text _ ok
                    initial _ word _ separator
                    word _ section*
                           word
                           word _ separator
                text _ overlength
                    text
            'zzzz'
        blanks(1.. )
            ' '
        empty _ telegram
            'zzzz'
    return
        TELEGRAM*
            NEW _ PAGE
            OK _ OR _ OVERLENGTH +
                TEXT _ OK
                TEXT _ OVERLENGTH
                    TEXT
                    NEW _ LINE
                    'OVERLENGTH WORDS IN THE TELEGRAM'
            NEW _ LINE
            NEW _ LINE
            chargeable _ word _ message
```

Figure 7

The input data was chosen so that the test exercises the refinement. Notice that the first and last telegrams of the telegram stream test the refinement of the "text _ ok" node.

The final specification that requires abstract execution involves both the "text _ ok" and "text _ overlength" nodes. These nodes include the "word _ section*", thus making it possible to synthesize the number of words in each telegram. The specification module is shown in Figure 8.

The sample abstract input data follows:

```
initial _ word _ separator
character
character
word _ separator
character
character
word _ separator
character
word _ separator
zzzz
initial _ word _ separator
word
word _ separator
word
word _ separator
zzzz
initial _ word _ separator
character
word _ separator
character
character
word _ separator
zzzz  zzzz
```

```
A _ LISTING _ OF _ TELEGRAMS _ AND _ CHARGES _ FROM _ A _ (TELEGRAM _ STREAM)
    TELEGRAM _ STREAM
        telegram*
            ok _ or _ overlength+
                  text _ ok
                      initial _ word _ separator
                      word _ section*
                          word(1..12)
                              character
                          word _ separator
                    text _ overlength
                      text
                          initial _ word _ separator
                          word _ section*
                                 word
                                 word _ separator
            'zzzz'
        blanks(1.. )
            ' '
        empty _ telegram
            'zzzz'
    return
        TELEGRAM*
            NEW _ PAGE
            OK _ OR _ OVERLENGTH+
                TEXT _ OK
                TEXT _ OVERLENGTH
                    TEXT
                    NEW _ LINE
                    'OVERLENGTH WORDS IN THE TELEGRAM'
            NEW _ LINE
            NEW _ LINE
            chargeable _ word _ message
                'THE NUMBER OF CHARGEABLE WORDS = '
                WORD _ SECTION#
```

Figure 8

The above input data tests the refinement of the "text _ ok" node. An outcome of the execution will be a test of the last node, "WORD _ SECTION#". This test will give an indication as to whether the word count is handled properly.

The last specification module in this section is the complete solution to the telegram problem. Abstract execution is not necessary because the terminal nodes of the analysis and synthesis trees are all reference nodes. The main difference between this specification module and the previous one is that the word separator nodes and character nodes are refined as module calls. Figure 9 shows a specification module that captures the concept of the informal specification.

```
A _ LISTING _ OF _ TELEGRAMS _ AND _ CHARGES _ FROM _ A _ (TELEGRAM _ STREAM)
    TELEGRAM _ STREAM
        telegram*
            ok _ or _ overlength+
                text _ ok
                    initial _ word _ separator*
                        DELIMITER
                    word _ section*
                        word(1..12)+
                            LETTER
                            DIGIT
                        word _ separator(1.. )
                            DELIMITER
                text _ overlength
                    text
                        initial _ word _ separator*
                            DELIMITER
                        word _ section*
                            word(1.. )+
                                LETTER
                                DIGIT
                            word _ separator(1.. )
                                DELIMITER
            'zzzz'
        blanks(1.. )
            ' '
        empty _ telegram
            'zzzz'
    return
        TELEGRAM*
            NEW _ PAGE
            OK _ OR _ OVERLENGTH+
                TEXT _ OK
                TEXT _ OVERLENGTH
                    TEXT
                    NEW _ LINE
                    'OVERLENGTH WORDS IN THE TELEGRAM'
            NEW _ LINE
            NEW _ LINE
            chargeable _ word _ message
                'THE NUMBER OF CHARGEABLE WORDS = '
                WORD _ SECTION#
```

Figure 9

There is no sample input data presented for the specification module shown in Figure 9. The interested reader can provide input data and can be convinced that the specification module describes what it is supposed to describe. The reference node, "LETTER" is defined as the discriminated union of the 26 letters of the alphabet. The reference node, "DIGIT," is defined as the discriminated union of the 10 digits, zero through nine. It is possible to define the "DELIMITER" in a manner similar to the reference nodes "LETTER" and "DIGIT". A "DELIMITER" is defined as follows:

```
DELIMITER +
    stop
        ' '
        'stop'
    ' '
```

The top-down development of the specification module was made possible through the refinement of the abstract data structures. This set of specifications was one approach to the solution to the telegram problem. The many simple refinements were presented so as not to sacrifice the thought processes that were illustrated.

5: Conclusions

This paper has provided a definition of the Descartes specification language. The telegram problem was used to illustrate specification development with the abstract execution feature. The Descartes specification language and abstract execution feature are beneficial for rapid development of software through execution of partial specifications. In addition, the refinement of a specification and test data proceed concurrently with the abstract execution feature.

The language processor for Descartes was initially developed in PL/I on the Multics system. Currently, the interpreter is hosted in C on a Sun system. An automated test data generation system for Descartes was implemented on the Multics system and will be hosted on the Sun system. Finally, tool support for a complete specification environment is planned for Descartes.

6. References

[De37] Descartes, R., "Discourse on the Method of Rightly Conducting the Reason and Seeking the Truth in the Sciences," Charles W. Eliot, LL.D., *The Harvard Classics*, Vol. 34, P.F. Collier and Son, New York, 1910, pp. 17-18, anonymously published originally by Jan Maire of Leiden in 1637.

[Ger76] Gerhart, S.L. and Yelowitz, L., "Observations of Fallibility in Applications of Modern Programming Methodologies," *IEEE Trans. on Software Eng.*, Vol. 2, No. 3, Sept. 1976, pp. 195-207.

[Hen72] Henderson, P. and Snowden, R., "An Experiment in Structured Programming," *BIT*, Vol. 12, 1972, pp. 38-53.

[Hoa72] Hoare, C.A.R., "Notes on Data Structuring," *Structured Programming*, Academic Press, Orlando, Fla., 1972, pp. 83-174.

[Hoa75] Hoare, C.A.R., "Data Reliability," *SIGPLAN Notices*, Vol. 10, No. 6, June 1975, pp. 528-533.

[Led74] Ledgard, H., "The Case for Structured Programming," *BIT*, Vol. 14, 1974, pp. 45-57.

[Noo75] Noonan, R.E., "Structured Programming and Formal Specification," *IEEE Trans. on Software Eng.*, Vol. 1, No. 4, Dec. 1975, pp. 421-425.

[Urb77] Urban, J.E., *A Specification Language and Its Processor*, Ph.D. Dissertation, Computer Science Dept. Univ. of SW Louisiana, Dec. 1977.

[Urb82] Urban, J.E., "Software Development with Executable Specifications," *Proc. of the 6th Int. Conf. on Software Eng.*, IEEE Computer Society Press, Wash., D.C., Sept. 1982, pp. 418-419.

[Urb85] Urban, S.D., Urban, J.E., and Dominick, W.D., "Utilizing an Executable Specification Language for an Information System," *IEEE Trans. on Software Eng.*, Vol. SE-11, No. 7, July 1985, pp. 598-605.

STARTS

Software Tools for Application

to Large Real-Time Systems

Z

(a formal specification method)

A Debrief Report, prepared by

M. Norris (British Telecom)

STARTS

Software Tools for Application to large Real-Time Systems

Z
(a formal specification method)

A Debrief Report, prepared by M Norris (British Telecom)

1 INTRODUCTION

Specification methods based on mathematics are currently evolving which satisfy the problems of the increasingly apparent deficiencies of more traditional techniques at the requirements specification stage. As the complexity of systems and the demands for increased functions have grown, so has the need arisen for correct, precise and maintainable specifications. Formal languages like Z are attempting to address themselves to this problem.

Formal specification techniques have recently started to move from academia to the industrial environment, where they are generally being applied to small problems. This is being done to see whether more rigorous specification techniques can produce better quality products which are more easily maintained. The current state of play is that the methods are

First published in 1986 by The National Computing Centre Limited, Oxford Road, Manchester, M1 7ED, England.

emerging from the research stage and are in the process of being assimilated into the armoury of the practicing software engineer. This document is based on several case studies which were aimed at evaluating the likely impact of formalism in an industrial context.

After the management summary we give a brief summary of the background and origins of Z. This is followed by an outline of the language itself and how it can be used as a means of modelling real systems. The following section is concerned with the findings of the case study. It covers the prerequisites to using Z, what types of problem are likely to benefit from it's application and guidelines for presentation and use. A part of one of the case studies is given as an example of the results one might expect

The remainder of the report is concerned with our estimation of the costs and benefits which are likely to accrue in practice from the introduction of Z as a specification standard.

The mathematical notation of Z, the steps involved in proving the specification correct and the process of refinement into code are covered in the detailed appendices to this document.

2 MANAGEMENT SUMMARY

1. This report has been prepared for the STARTS project. It describes experience in using Z at British Telecom Research Laboratories in software development.

2. Z is a rigorous system specification technique. It uses set theory and logic to abstract the essential features of a design. The subsequent analysis and development of the specification can be carried out on well founded mathematical principles.

3. The presentation of the mathematics has received considerable attention and specifications in Z are quite readable. Only a few days training are required to equip an engineer with sufficient knowledge to read a Z specification.

4. It takes time to learn how to use Z as a means of capturing design decisions - probably two weeks intensive study followed by several months practical application. Even then, some of the proof obligations in the analysis and refinement of a specification may require the engineer to be particularly adept in mathematical manipulation.

5. Z is better suited to data oriented problems than to those which are control dominated. This is not to say that Z could not be used in a wide range of application - merely that other methods (e.g. CSP) might be more appropriate.

6. The main benefit of using Z (or any method for that matter) on a project is that it enforces discipline on the design process and guards against the tendency to rush into implementation before ideas are fully formed.

7. There are some tools being developed for Z, although these can only be of limited use. As already stated, the main power of the method is in encouraging better and more rigorous thought in a design. Tools that help with this are a long way off.

8. The benefits of using Z as outlined in this report need to be balanced against the cost of training and the disturbance of existing working practice. The mechanics of using Z will doubtless be eased by the introduction of support tools but the main barrier which must be overcome is one of acceptance, both by engineers and by managers and ensuring that Z is used wisely on appropriate problems.

2.1 Summary Table

Application.	- The specification of sequential data oriented problems.
Characteristics.	- The language notation is based on extended typed set theory. - Structured specifications are achieved via the schema calculus. - A specification can be proved to meet its customer's requirements. - The language provides a true abstraction technique.
Status.	- The notation is still being developed. - The language syntax is constantly changing. - No commercially published book/manual is yet (Autumn 1985) available. - Training courses are run by the Programming Research Group at Oxford University. - Published Case Studies are readily available. - Research into the language for use with concurrent problems is being carried out. - The language is the basis of some current Alvey projects.
Limitations.	- No notation to model concurrency, no account of timing is made. - Not readily integrated with other design techniques, except possibly VDM.
Prospects.	- A toolset is under development under an Alvey funded proposal. - Many large companies are reviewing the language, most notably IBM (U.K), which can only enhance hopes of standards.
Comments.	- Relatively new method based on sound mathematics that is quickly gaining use, but still many years away from full scale commercial use. - There are some application areas which

have not yet been explored and it is therefore too early to make a firm statement of the true use of Z.

Related Approaches.

- VDM. The approaches of Z and VDM are very similar[14]. Both use set theory and logic to create abstract specifications which can be proved correct. The main differences lie in presentation format and degree of standardisation.

3 BACKGROUND TO THE METHOD

The formal language 'Z' has evolved from research work carried out by the Programming Research Group (PRG) at the Oxford University Computing Laboratory. It can be mainly attributed to the work of Abrial [1], Hoare [2], Sufrin [3], Sorensen [4] and Morgan [5].

Over the past three years the language has moved from academia to its application to industrial specification problems. The most notable example is the joint project between PRG and IBM (U.K) Research Laboratories [6], involving the specification of an existing piece of software. Many large industrial research establishments, including BTRL, are now evaluating and applying the language.

The experiences of these industrial applications have been put to good use in improving the way in which specifications are presented. A great deal of effort has been expended in expressing the mathematics of Z in an acceptable way. This is manifest by the definition of the schema language which provides the presentation framework for the mathematical portion of a Z specification.

The mathematical notation itself is based on conventional set theory and predicate calculus with some minor extensions which provide the expressive power to allow the specifier to deal readily with structures which are often encountered during the development of systems.

Data oriented sequential problems are suitable for specification using Z. The definition of control based systems is not readily performed using Z as it cannot readily model concurrency.

The main academic users of Z are the Programming Research Group (PRG) at Oxford University (the developers of the technique) and more recently Surrey University. Both institutions are extending and applying the language together with industry.

The major commercial organisations currently applying Z, are IBM (U.K) Research Labs., STL, ICL, Plessey Research Labs., BP Research Labs., Racal ITD., GEC Research Labs., System Designers and to a smaller extent BTRL. IBM together with PRG have carried out large scale system specification on currently existing software [6], this appears to be the largest commercially oriented specification to date.

4 THE LANGUAGE

4.1 Outline

The reasons for the development of mathematical formal specification techniques and the advantages that they bring have already been outlined, by Norris [13]. In addition to the general attributes of a formal method, Z has the following notable features from a system engineers point of view.

1. The definition of a special notation - Schema language - for the presentation of the mathematics enables readable structured specifications to be readily produced. The addition of explanatory text as shown in the following section further enhances the understandability of a specification in Z.

2. Due to the structured nature of specifications they can be adapted and extended readily to cope with changing customer requirements.

3. The ability to prove theorems about the specification allows test plans for the implementation to be produced.

4. The power of mathematics to abstract the essential elements of a system allows for the prototyping of ideas during its development. At each stage the specification can be proved to be a valid statement of a given set of requirements

5. Data refinement of the specification allows structured code that reflects the specification, and hence the user requirements, to be implemented.

6. The levels of data refinement enables the systems to be implemented in different types of language; i.e. refine to functional language (Lisp) or refine to block structured language (Pascal).

4.2 Constructs To Model Computing

Having outlined the general attributes of the language, we now focus on it's application to the development of software and systems. It is suggested that any reader unfamiliar with formal specification techniques refers to Appendix A for clarification of the following section.

In Z some predefined operators exist that can readily manipulate data types, in a way that is required to model computing problems. Mathematical operators are provided that manipulate data that has been structured into a large data structure, say a relational database, as part of a specification.

In the following example some of these predefined mathematical operators are demonstrated. This guide is not the place to give the syntactic and semantic meaning of the operators, a suitable reference is [4].

The example has been constructed in such a way as to make it easy to demonstrate these operators, and not to give a rigorously defined data model.

Consider a database of company employee records.
A few selected records described in Z would take the form,

```
                      Domain    Range

Employee      : Name <--> Address
Position_held : Name <--> Job_Title
```

The above notation defines two sets of relations, one of employee names and addresses and the other of an employee's position within the company.

These database records are modelled as relations, as opposed to more rigorously typed functions, as it suits the demonstration to be given. However, this would allow an employee to live at more than one address and have more than one job_title, which is unlikely to happen in reality, but this is an unreal problem.

A relation can be broken up into its domain (dom) and range (rng), therefore the dom of Employee is Name and it's rng is Address.

To demonstrate some of the predefined operators the following three tasks will be carried out on the database.

1. A list of the names and addresses of all employees whose name is SMITH.

2. List names and addresses of employees who work as 'cleaners'.

3. A new employee is added to the database.

To express (1) as a predicate we can use the predefined operator, domain restriction ($\lhd$), to restrict the list of pairs of names and addresses to only those with the name SMITH; where list! would take the form list! : Name X Address.

list! = {SMITH} $\lhd$ Employee

The predicate for (2) requires both of the above relations to be considered.

Three operators are used to perform this;

- relational inverse to give the inverse of relation i.e. $Position\_held^{-1}$: Job_Title <--> Name

- relational composition to compose two relations, providing the range of the first is of the same type as the domain of the second, to give the set of pairs of the domain of the first and the range of the second i.e. on the above functions $position\_held^{-1}$; employee gives {Job_Title, Address})

- domain restriction, as already explained.

Putting these together gives the following expression

$$list2! = rng\ ((\{cleaner\} \lhd Position\_held^{-1});\ Employee)$$

To express (3) as predicates, use will be made of the override ($\oplus$) operator (this updates, by overwriting an existing, or adding a new pair of values to a set of relations). To add a new employee to the database input values for Name (n?), Address (a?) and Job_title (j?) required.

For simplicity assume that Name (n?) is unique.

$$Employee' = Employee \oplus \{ n? \mapsto a? \}$$
$$Position\_held' = Position\_held \oplus \{ n? \mapsto j? \}$$

We have tried to show as many operators as possible on a such a small data model. From these examples the reader will see how general computing problems of data structure manipulation (i.e. file access, table updates, list processing etc.) can be modelled in specifications.

5 REQUIREMENTS AND GUIDELINES FOR USE.

The main aims of the work reported here are as follows;

1. To establish what is required before the method can be applied

2. To establish the types of problem to which Z is best suited

3. To establish some guidelines for the development and presentation of specifications in Z

Each of these areas is addressed below, based on our experiences to date.

5.1 Prerequisites

At BT we have found that to become proficient at using Z the following are required

1. an intensive introductory course

2. a comprehensive manual

3. an understanding of the underlying mathematics

4. a set of case studies

5. Probably at least three months practical work to gain experience in applying the technique.

Presently the only institution teaching Z is PRG Oxford, which holds its courses, currently, only a few times a year. There exists no published manual on how to use the language and at BT we have had to use a prelimary draft manual issued by PRG.

It is essential that the engineer attempting to use Z has a firm understanding of the discrete mathematics that forms the foundation of the language, i.e. set theory, predicate calculus, etc. Without a knowledge of this mathematical notation and the consequences of applying it, then there is little hope of being able to understand how to use the method. An introductory text book to this area is Computer Mathematics by Cooke and Bez [7].

There are, fortunately, a large number of papers and case studies on how the language has been applied to problems, for recommended articles see references [4, 5, 6].

5.2 Field Of Application

Z is best suited to data oriented, sequential problems.The architecture of control based systems will not readily described until Z models timing or concurrency. This does not mean that Z cannot be used to conceptually specify real-time or distributed systems, it is more a matter of using the appropriate tool for the job. The choice of programming language for an application is a similar dilemma.

One of the main issues which arises when using Z is the right level of abstraction to adopt in a specification. The higher the level of abstraction the easier it becomes to specify any type of problem. Probably the best strategy, is to take the most simplistic abstract view to model and then use 'data refinement' to produce designs that can be used to implement the system.

A variety of specification case studies have been produced which give an indication of the field of application of the language. A recommended text is 'Specification Case Studies' [9].

There are two applications of Z, other than direct specification, which the language lends itself to. The first is as a thought gathering process and the expression of ideas, it is often convenient to express initial ideas in terms of predicates that can be preserved and reviewed later. The second is the prototyping of ideas that can be proved to meet customer requirements before being developed into the full specification.

5.3 Presenting The Specification

The presentation of a Z specification is a combination of

informal text and formal mathematics. The informal parts act as an introduction to and explanation of the formal parts.

i.e. suggested document layout

```
 ---------------------------------------------------------------|
|                                                               |
|              SPECIFICATION NAME                               |
|                   AUTHOR                                      |
|                                                               |
|     |------------------------------------------------|        |
|     |        Informal Text - Introduction            |        |
|     |                                                |        |
|     |                ---------------------------------        |
|     |               |                                         |
|     |               |   Mathematical Definition               |
|     |               |     - System State                      |
|     |               ---------------------------------         |
|     |                                                |        |
|     |                                                |        |
|     |               ---------------------------------         |
|     |               |                                         |
|     |               |   Mathematical Definition               |
|     |               |       - System Operations               |
|     |               ---------------------------------         |
|     |                                                |        |
|     |                                                |        |
|     |                                                |        |
|     |               ---------------------------------         |
|     |               |                                         |
|     |               |   Theorems                              |
|     |               |    -Proofs of system requirements       |
|     |               ---------------------------------         |
|     |                                                |        |
|     |                                                |        |
|     |                                                |        |
|     |               ---------------------------------         |
|     |               |                                         |
|     |               |    Mathematical Definition              |
|     |               |     - Error conditions etc              |
|     |               ---------------------------------         |
|     |                                                |        |
|     |                                                |        |
|     |------------------------------------------------         |
|---------------------------------------------------------------
```

The document can be divided into three sections;

Introduction - outlines what the specification is about the data involved in the system and any constraints that are to be applied.

System state - the data types in the system and their invarients, also the initial state of the system and proof.

System operations - the set of operations in the system and proof's that they meet their requirements.

5.4 Guidelines For Specification

Knowing where to start with a specification is probably the most difficult thing to get right, especially for the inexperienced user. We have found that the key issue is to get the right level of abstract description for the job in hand without being too vague. Achieving this balance is something which can only come through experience of using the method, but we have compiled a few guidelines from our specification experience.

1. Grouping Entities - model entities of a system as sets, and express the relationships between entities as functions and relations (i.e. model as sets of mapping).

2. Keep It Simple - On initial specification attempts, consider only the most abstract desired features. In reality it may not be possible to implement these highly abstract features, but it enables requirements to be gathered and initial thoughts to be readily expressed.

3. Iterate - The process of producing a draft Z specification should, like any specification developement, be iterative. Adding and refining data can be achieved by the structured notation. However care must be taken when changing or adding data of the mathematical consequences involved.

4. Prove The Obvious Things - The proof of obvious theorems is often omitted, yet when attempted can sometimes lead to difficulties. It is good practice to show all proofs of the requirements of a system.

5. Include Error Conditions - Definitions for error exceptions should be included at an early stage to help high-light system limitations and to enforce concentration on the main issues during data refinement.

6. Use Suggested Specification Layout.

7. Proofs Are Tricky - It should go without saying that care must be taken throughout when proving a specification meets its customer requirements.

6 PRACTICAL APPLICATION

The Advanced System Design Techniques and Tools group at BTRL have evaluated Z, by producing a set of case studies on specification problems. An overview of one of the case studies is presented.

It concerns the specification of the user level interface of an existing high level language code generator (SX1 [10]), that has been in wide spread use at BT and with numerous other companies over the past few years. The input to this code generator is a CCITT SDL diagram or a flowchart and so a specification was produced that modelled the structure for any input chart.

6.1 User Level Specification Of SX1

The user level interface is the logical starting point for any design and so it seemed appropriate to start to specify SX1 from the view the user sees.

The problem with tackling the specification of a system that has already been implemented is knowing where to start. Three attempts had to be made.

Firstly we did not use Z as an abstraction tool but instead applied it to specify SX1 in the way it currently exists, that is, representing the basic functions of the SX1 suite as a series of predicates. This resulted in little more than the replacement of a written outline with rather useless lines of set theory.

In the second attempt Z was used correctly as an abstraction tool. An abstract specification of a flowchart was produced that was not SX1 specific, i.e. it modelled the basic structures in a standard flowchart; sequences, selections and iterations.

Performing this abstraction gives some feel for using Z for the problem without having to worry about the intricate details of the SX1 flowchart structures.

The third and final attempt which is explained in more detail is a conceptual input level to SX1; i.e. an SX1 flowchart.

A few selected schemas are described to explain the input level flowchart structure. These schemas specify an SX1 flowchart that consists only of test and task boxes.

```
-----TEST----------------
|
|  condition : text
|  yes, no   : Label
|
--------------
|
|  yes ≠ no
|
-------------------------
```

This states that a TEST contains a condition, a string of characters, and a pair of distinct labels, yes and no.

Similarly for TASK

```
-----TASK----------------
|
|  operations : text
|  next       : Label
|
-------------------------
```

By using a 'disjoint union' a schema can be built to consist of dissimilar objects.

```
------NODE---------------------------------------------
|                         |                  |            |
|  test <<TEST>>          |  task <<TASK>>   |  <<EXIT>>  |
|                         |                  |            |
-------------------------------------------------------
```

A flowchart can now be represented by a 'graph' consisting of nodes of the various predefined types.

And so we have the structure 'flowchart'.

```
-----FLOWCHART-----------------------
|
|  start       : Label                                   1
|  graph       : Label +-> NODE                          2
|  leads_into  : Label <--> Label                        3
|
--------------
|
|  EXIT ∈ ran graph                                      4
|  ran leads_into = Label - {start}                      5
|
|  Id leads_into ∩ leads_into^+ = {}                     6
|
|  leads_into = U {(l, n) : graph |                      7
|           n ∈ dom test^-1 --> {(l, test^-1(n).yes),
|                                (l, test^-1(n).no)},
|           n ∈ dom task^-1 --> {(l, task^-1(n).next},
|           n = EXIT --> {}
|          }
|
----------------------------------------
```

```
-----FLOWCHART--------------------------
|
| 1. defines the start box in the chart
| 2. each box in the chart has a unique label
| 3. defines the control line between boxes
|
-----------------
|
| 4. there's at least one EXIT box
| 5. there's a unique start box, into which no others lead.
| 6. there are no cycles in the flowchart
| 7. leads_into is made up solely of labels of TEST and TASK nodes and
|    there corresponding 'yes', 'no' and 'next' labels.
|
----------------------------------------
```

This is only a part of the overall problem definition. Now box types can be added relatively easily to give a complete and concise system specification. In this case, the implementation had been carried out, and the specification serves as a reference document.

Other similar case studies have shown the value of taking the conceptual definition through to implementation and this has been successfully achieved in practice.

7 SUPPORT TOOLS

There are currently no tools on the market which make the writing of Z specifications any easier or quicker. There is an Alvey directorate project to create a toolset to support Z but this will not be available for at least another two years, (mid 1988).

In any case, the support tools for Z can only address the problem of record keeping and specification management. They can do nothing to help with the creation of the specification - this is an intellectual effort.

8 CONCLUSIONS

Despite it's undoubted merits we would currently be reticent to adopt Z, or indeed any formal method, as a mainstream design technique. Given the current level of acceptance, careful thought should be given before imposing it as a design standard.

However, the progress of more rigorous methods is inevitable and it is essential that expertise and experience in these techniques is available. In the light of our experience we are now pursuing ways of phasing the introduction of Z (among others) into current working practice.

The cost of retraining teams of software engineers and their management is high. We believe it is only through the teaching of formal specification techniques by universities and polytechnics on computer science degree courses, that significant numbers of software engineers able to competently apply the techniques will become readily available.

The final decision to use Z on a project comes down to whether the benefits outweigh the cost. The information in this report seeks to help in this decision. We summarise our findings below.

8.1 Costs

1. Training - The intensive introductory course (taught by PRG) which would enable you to start using Z for specification is two weeks long.

2. Experience - Having learnt the notation, it probably takes a further two months before any level of competence is achieved. Even then it is important that the user feels at ease with the method. Not everyone has the inclination for this approach to system design.

3. Visibility - A common complaint levelled at formal methods is that they can only be understood by specialists. Z is better than most here and can readily be explained with minimal effort.

4. User resistance - Many people are instantly alienated by mathematical approaches. The reasons for this are many [12] and will not be discussed here. The point is that in order to gain acceptance, the introduction of any formal method must be gradual and related to more familiar methods (e.g structured analysis).

5. Management - The whole idea of Z is to create a full specification before even attempting to implement. This means that progress, especially in the first phases of a project, is hard to measure. A strong management nerve is required to cope with this apparent lack of progress.

8.2 Benefits

1. Clear thought - A notable feature of any mathematical technique is that the specification cannot be formed until the problem is fully understood. In this way inadequate requirements can be picked up very early in the project.

2. Precision - The specification is unambiguous

3. Analysable - The specification can be shown to be a valid statement of requirements: the only problem here is one of identifying the relevant system priorities which should be proved.

4. We like it!. A noticeable improvement in the authors ability to clearly specify a problem has been achieved through the use of the language.

References

[1] J-R. Abrial — The Specification Language Z. Oxford University, Programming Research Group. 1980.

[2] C.A.R Hoare — Notes On Data Structuring Structured Programming, Academic Press.

[3] B. Sufrin, C. Morgan — Notes For A Z handbook Oxford University Computing Laboratory, PRG, Oxford University. 1985.

[4] I.H. Sorensen, B. Flinn — Caviar : A Case Study In Specification Oxford University Computing Laboratory, PRG, Oxford University.

Technical Monograph PRG-48.
June 1985

[5] C. Morgan, B. Sufrin — Specification Of The UNIX File Store. IEEE Transactions On Software Engineering, Vol. 10 NO. 2 March 1984.

[6] I. Hayes — Applying Formal Specification To Software Development In Industry, IEEE Transactions On Software Engineering March 1985.

[7] D. Cooke, H. Bez — Computer Mathematics Cambridge University Press. 1984.

[8] C. Morgan, I. Sorensen — The Schema Language Oxford University Computing Laboratory PRG, Oxford University. 1984.

[9] I. Hayes — Specification Case Studies Oxford Computing Laboratory PRG, Oxford University. Technical Monograph PRG-46. July 1985.

[10] L. Jackson, P.Dell, R.Tinker — Computer Aided Design Of Software Software and Microsystems October 1981.

[11] P. Newman, P.James, M.Norris — Introduction To Mathematics In System Design Journal of the Institute Of British Telecommunication Engineers, January 1986.

[12] Economist Infomatics — Towards formal methods in software engineering Alvey News June 1985 p12

[13] M.Norris — The role of formal methods in system design BT Technical Journal vol3 no4 October 1985

[14] M.Austwick, M.Norris — A guide to the Vienna Development Method STARTS report

APPENDIX A

THE MATHEMATICS BEHIND THE NOTATION

Discrete mathematics (i.e. set theory, predicate calculus) is the basis of Z's mathematical notation, together with the schema language, which enables structured specifications to be produced.

Set theory provides the expressive power from which abstract models of systems can be built, while predicate calculus supplies the logical connectives to manipulate the models. The schema language enables the mathematics to be structured into meaningful entities while also providing a calculus so that a schema can be manipulated in similar ways to predicates. For the reader who is unfamilar with this notation a suitable introductory text is 'Computer Mathematics' [7].

It will be shown how a few of the language constructs can be used to model data, using a simple specification problem of manipulating a collection of integers.

Data objects are defined in terms of sets while operations and constraints on the data as predicates.

Let N represent the set of natural numbers

and so

int : N is the Z type declaration for a 'natural' number. i.e. an integer declaration.

to represent a small set of natural numbers the 'set of' (Powerset), 'P', notation is used.

int_set : P N int_set is a set of integers.

A predicate is placed on this set to constrain the maximum size of integer that can be placed in it.

$$int\_set \quad \{ n: N \mid n \geq 1 \land n \leq 9 \}$$

This predicate states 'int_set' is a subset of the set of integers between 1 and 9. In this particular case the predicate is known as a data type invariant i.e. a statement about the data type 'int_set' that is always true.

The data declaration (known in Z as a signature) of int_set, and its predicate can be packaged into a schema.

```
-----Small_set_of_integers-----------------------------------
|
|    int_set : P N                                SIGNATURE
|
---------------
|
|    int_set ⊆ { n : N | n ≥ 1 ∧ n ≤ 9 }          PREDICATE
|
-------------------------------------------------------------
```

The box structure of the schema has a divider which keeps signatures on one side of it and predicates on the other. All predicates in a schema are logically true statements. Each predicate in the schema is logically 'ANDed' to the next; although this is not shown in the schema; unless specifically 'ORed', the 'OR' symbol being shown.

Only data types declared within a schema or global declarations can be operated upon. If objects in another schema are to be manipulated then these must be declared in the scope of the schema containing the operators.

Small_set_of_integers now becomes an entity that can have operations applied to it, details of the schemas and their calculus can be found in 'The Schema Language' [8] while more general information on Z can be found in 'Notes For A Z Handbook' [3].

A specification for a collection of integers has so far been shown. Now schemas for operations on the data type 'Small_set_of_integers' are presented.

To enable integers to be placed in the set an 'Add' operation is required, likewise a 'Delete' operation to remove integers. A 'decorated Small_set_of_integers' defines the new state of the data type after an operation has been applied.

```
-----Small_set_of_integers'---------------------------------
|
|    int_set' : P N
|
--------------
|
|    int_set' ⊆ { n : N | n ≥ 1 ∧ n ≤ 9 }
|
------------------------------------------------------------
```

The 'Δ' symbol describes all the events before and after an operation.

ΔSmall_set_of_integers = Small_set_of_integers $\wedge$
Small_set_of_integers'

or in full

THE MATHEMATICS BEHIND THE NOTATION

```
-----∆ Small_set_of_integers-----------------------------------
|
|      int_set  : P N
|      int_set' : P N
|
---------------
|
|      int_set  ⊆ { n : N | n ≥ 1 ∧ n ≤ 9 }
|      int_set' ⊆ { n : N | n ≥ 1 ∧ n ≤ 9 }
|
---------------------------------------------------------------
```

Adding an integer to 'int_set' involves taking an input number, checking it is in the allowable integer range (between 1 and 9), and then placing it in the set.

```
-----Add-------------------------------------------------------
|
|    ∆ Small_set_of_integers
|    num? : N
|
---------------
|
|     num? ∈ { n : N | n ≥ 1 ∧ n ≤ 9 }
|     int_set ' = int_set ∪ { num? }
|
---------------------------------------------------------------
```

The '?' symbol identifies input, so 'num?' is the input integer to be placed in the set. The 'set Union' (U) operator performs the addition to the set.

Deleting an integer will be similar in that an input number will be checked and then removed from the set.

```
-----Delete----------------------------------------------------
|
|    ∆ Small_set_of_integers
|    num? : N
|
---------------
|
|    num? ∈ int_set
|    int_set' = int_set − { num? }
|
---------------------------------------------------------------
```

APPENDIX B

THEOREM PROVING

One of the main features of formal methods is the ability to prove that a specification meets its customers requirements. This is achieved by expressing a requirement as a theorem and using a completed specification to prove the theorem true. In Z, a theorem is expressed in terms of predicates and schemas and using a suitable proof method a specification can be shown to meet its requirements.

The proof methods that can be used are :-

Contradiction - for a theorem A
(Note $\vdash$ is the notation for theorem)
(and $\neg$ is the notation for negation)
assume $\neg \vdash$ A and prove false.

Contrapositive - for a theorem $\vdash A \Rightarrow B$
if it can be ascertained $\vdash \neg B \Rightarrow \neg A$
then $\vdash A \Rightarrow B$ can de deduced.

Direct Proof - proving by implication, i.e. that one term implies the next.

Induction - proving a theorem involving natural numbers
first prove, for $\vdash$ A, that $\vdash A(0)$
then prove $n : N \vdash A(n) \Rightarrow A(n + 1)$

Considering the set of integers specification, a trivial proof that can be performed on it is to prove the requirement that if an 'Add' followed by a 'Delete', of the same number, is performed the data structure 'Small_set_of_integers' will effectively be unchanged. However a pre-condition to this proof is that a number cannot be added to the set if it is already in the set.

so Pre_Add $\hat{=}$ [Small_set_of_integers | num? $\notin$ int_set]

SAdd $\hat{=}$ Pre_Add $\fatsemi$ Add

Expressed as a theorem
gives:-

SAdd $\fatsemi$ Delete $\vdash$ set_unchanged

where set_unchanged = Int_set' = Int_set
$\fatsemi$ is the notation for schema composition
This proof will be shown using the 'Direct Proof' method

$SAdd \fatsemi Delete \vdash set\_unchanged$

Schema composition: if we consider an intermediate state that is both the final of the operation SAdd and the initial state of the operation Delete then the composition of SAdd and Delete is the operation which relates the initial state of SAdd to the final state of Delete through the intermediate state. To form the composition of SAdd and Delete we take the state after components of SAdd and the state before components of Delete that have a basename in common, rename both to new variables, take the schema "AND" of the resulting schemas, and hide the new variables.

S is intermediate state

$\exists S : P\ N.\ S = Int\_set \cup \{ num? \} \wedge Int\_set' = S - \{ num? \}$

$= \quad S : P\ N.\ Int\_set' = (Int\_set \cup \{ num? \}) - \{ num? \}$

The $\exists$ can be dropped as S has been substituted for another value.

So $Int\_set' = Int\_set$ i.e. set_unchanged

Although a simple proof, it allows the reader to see how specification proofs are carried out.

APPENDIX C

EXAMPLE SPECIFICATION WITH REFINEMENT

The small integer collection specification will now be shown as an example of document layout.

The Specification Of A Small Integer Collection

Author: Peter James

Introduction

A collection of integer values is defined with operations to add and delete integers to the collection.

Natural numbers are the only base level system data.

[N]

The maximum integer value that can be placed in the collection is nine.

$$\begin{array}{|l} maxint : N \\ \hline maxint \leq 9 \end{array}$$

The State

The integer collection is modelled by a set.

```
-----Small_set_of_integers-----------------------------------
|
|    int_set : P N
|
-------------
|
|    int_set ⊆ { n : N | n ≥ 1 ∧ n ≤ 9 }
|
-------------------------------------------------------------
```

EXAMPLE SPECIFICATION WITH REFINEMENT

The Initial State

Initially the set 'int_set' contains no values.

```
init_small_set_of_integers ≙
                    [small_set_of_integers' | int_set' ={}]
```

There is to exist a small_set_of_integers such that initially the structure contains no value.

```
⊢ ∃ small_set_of_integers'.init_small_set_of_integers
```

The Operations

Integers are to be added to the set by an Add operation and deleted by a Delete. A number is not to be added if it is already in the set.

```
-----Add------------------------------------------------
|
|    Δ Small_set_of_integers
|    num? : N
|
---------------
|
|     num? ∈ { n : N | n ≥ 1 ∧ n ≤ 9 }
|     int_set ' = int_set ∪ { num? }
|
--------------------------------------------------------
```

```
Pre_Add ≙ [Ξ Small_set_of_integers; num? : N | num? ∉ int_set ]
```

So 'set addition' is defined as

```
SAdd ≙ Pre_Add ⨾ Add
```

```
-----Delete---------------------------------------------
|
|    Δ Small_set_of_integers
|    num? : N
|
---------------
|
|    num? ∈ int_set
|    int_set' = int_set − { num? }
|
--------------------------------------------------------
```

The state must be preserved unchanged if an SAdd followed by Delete is performed.

```
SAdd ⨾ Delete ⊢ Set_unchanged
```

From Specification To Implementation

Data refinement is the process by which an abstract specification is refined to a concrete design document. A set of abstract schemas become an implementation document by substituting computable structures for abstract mathematical models. This will be shown by the refinement of the Small Integer Collection specification.

A bit vector is a suitable representation to implement a finite set like 'int_set', a '1' or '0' can be used to identify whether a value is in the set or not. Also a bit vector can readily be implemented as an array in a programming language.

```
-----Bit_vector--------------------------------------------
|
|    v : seq [Bit]                          where Bit = { 1,0 }
|
---------------
|
|    #v = max
|
-----------------------------------------------------------
```

A data type Bit vector exists whose length is equivalent to the maximum value in the set. Therefore element one in 'v' identifies the integer value one, if the Bit value is '1'.

A Retrieve operation will model this relationship.

```
-----Retrieve----------------------------------------------
|
|    Small_set_of_integer
|    Bit_vector
|
-------------
|
|    int_set = dom (v ▷ {1})
|
-----------------------------------------------------------
```

Retrieve identifies the set of integers in 'int_set' by testing the bit vector for bits set to '1'. Concrete designs for Add and Delete are :-

```
-----BV_Add------------------------------------------------
|
|    Δ Bit_vector
|    n? : N
|
----------------
|
|    n? ∈ { n : N | n ≥ 1 ∧ n ≤ 9 }
|    v' = v ⊕ { n?  |-> 1 }
|
-----------------------------------------------------------
```

EXAMPLE SPECIFICATION WITH REFINEMENT

This sets a bit to '1' in the bit vector at the index number 'n?', i.e. conceptually adds an integer to the set.

```
-----BV_Delete------------------------------------------------
|
|       Δ Bit_vector
|       n? : N̄
|
--------------------
|
|       n? ∈ { n : N | n ≥ 1 ∧ n ≤ 9 }
|       v' = v ⊕ { n? |-> 0 }
|
---------------------------------------------------------------
```

BV_Delete sets the appropriate bit to '0'.

To the proof of correctness that the abstract state meets the concrete state, by showing that the concrete BV_Add is a correct design of the abstract Add.

$$BV\_Add \wedge \Delta Retrieve \vdash Add$$

1.	$int\_set = dom\ (v \rhd \{ 1 \})$	Retrieve
2.	$v' = v \oplus \{ n \mapsto 1 \}$	BV_Add
3.	$int\_set' = dom\ (v' \rhd \{ 1 \})$	Retrieve'
4.	$int\_set' = dom\ ((v \oplus \{ n? \mapsto 1 \}) \rhd \{ 1 \})$	2,3
5.	$int\_set' = dom\ (v \rhd \{ 1 \} \oplus \{ n \mapsto 1 \} \rhd \{ 1 \})$	defs.
6.	$int\_set' = dom\ v \rhd \{ 1 \} \cup dom\ \{ n? \mapsto 1 \} \rhd \{ 1 \}$	defs.
7.	$int\_set' = int\_set \cup \{ n? \}$	1, 6

The concrete specification can now be used for the implemention in, for example, Pascal.

```
CONST
     max = 9;

TYPE
     Bit = 0..1;

     Int_range = 1..max;

     Small_set_of_integers = PACKED ARRAY [Int_range] of Bit;

PROCEDURE Add (n : Int_range; var s : Small_set_of_integer);
BEGIN
     s[n] := 1
END;

PROCEDURE Delete (n : Int_range; var s : Small_set_of_integers);
BEGIN
     s[n] := 0
END;
```

Set piece

The system specification activity presents the biggest headache for software developers. Darrel Ince assesses the impact of formal methods and the new MoD defence standard

System specification is the most crucial activity that occurs on the software project. Errors in describing what a system is to do have caused massive overruns, in both budget and project duration; in some cases they have lead to major cancellations. Of all the activities in the software project, it is now the one receiving the most attention.

Developing a complex software product requires the developer to carry out three development activities: system specification, system design and programming. System specification is the process of describing what a system is to do, in user terms. Here, the description of a system will be expressed using words such as enquiry clerk, back order, booking clerk and overdraft, rather than technical terms such as module, synchronous link and subroutine. In order to develop the system specification the developer is provided by the user with an informal statement of requirements.

System design is the process of taking the system specification, and developing an architecture expressed in terms of modules and their interfaces. The stress in system design is to develop a description of how a system is to operate rather, as in system specification, a description of what is required. Finally, programming is the process of translating a system design into program code.

There are a number of reasons for system specification being difficult. The first reason is that the informal statement of requirements given to the developer suffers from a number of deficiencies. In general, such statements are contradictory; incomplete; ambiguous; sometimes over-ambitious, and sometimes under-ambitious. They contain descriptions of functionality at different levels intermixed together. For example, statements about the high-level of the functions of the system will be intermingled with minute descriptions of lower level functions. Although these properties are normally associated with the user's statement of requirements, many of them crop up in system specifications.

The second reason for specification being a difficult task is the nature of the notations that have been used to express system functionality. In the past, this has really meant that English was the medium used. English is an excellent medium for writing poems where ambiguity is regarded as the norm: for expressing a description of a system, its property of ambiguity leads to major problems, where the system designer interprets seemingly innocuous sentences completely differently from the customer's intention.

The third problem with system specification is the size of the documents that are generated. The specification of a simple stock control system for a retailer can occupy hundreds of pages of text, while the specification of a conventional engineered product, say a bridge, might occupy two or three pages of text.

Because system specification occurs at the beginning of a project, an error which remains undetected until the final stages of the project, will be exceptionally serious. Often, such errors require the reworking of the system specification, the modification of the system design, reprogramming, and large scale changes to the system and acceptance tests.

The history of system specification notations starts in the late sixties, when the importance of writing down what a system is to do was recognised. Before then, developers just hacked out programming code. The early specifications were expressed in English and, although this was an improvement over not writing down system functionality, it lead to the problems described above.

The next development in notation occurred in the seventies. A young researcher at IBM, Larry Constantine, became dissatisfied with the techniques and notations used for system specification, and started experimenting with graphical notations. Although graphical flow charts were used for program design at this type. Constantine's early attempts at developing graphical notations were greeted with disdain by mainstream computer scientists.

Except, that is, for one man: Ed Yourdon. Yourdon persuaded

Constantine to help him author a book on graphical notations for system specification and system design. The book, *Structured Design*, has now become a classic; Ed Yourdon founded one of the most successful consulting organisations in the history of computing.

The rest, as they say, is history. Graphical notations for system specification, after a slow start, have now become a major medium on software projects. Notations associated with structured development methods such as Yourdon Structured Design, SSADM, LBMS and SADT are becoming almost the norm for large-scale software development.

The vast majority of these notations are based on data flow diagrams, consisting of bubbles and data flow.

Bubbles represented software processes such as depositing data in a database, displaying an error on a vdu, or scanning a radar for an aircraft signal. Data flows, which are represented by lines joining the bubbles, represent the data that is produced or consumed by the processes represented by the bubbles.

The growth of structured methods during the seventies was quite slow, the main reason for this being that software tools were required. A specifier who had constructed a large data flow diagram, using pencil and paper, often found himself committed to large amounts of redrawing when even small changes to the diagram were required.

The growth of bit-mapped graphics and high resolution computers resulted in a new generation of software tools for manipulating graphics notations. Such case tools are rudimentary, offering only facilities for erasing bubbles, creating bubbles, inserting new data flows etc.

However, at a stroke, they enabled the tedium associated with drawing specification notations to be eliminated and provided the fillip that structured methods required. The development of case technology has meant that structured methods are becoming the most popular way of developing software.

The most extreme end of the spectrum of specification notations is mathematics. It represents a radical change from current approaches. Mathematics has had a mixed impact on software projects, and has the longest history as a specification notation. In 1948 the English computer scientist Alan Turing used logic, the mathematics of true and false statements, to define the action of an assembler code subroutine.

In the late 1960s a large amount of research was carried out into program proving, instigated by the English computer scientist Tony Hoare and the Dutch researcher Edsgar Dijkstra. The aim in program proving was to describe the function of a piece of program code using mathematics, write the program and then prove — without testing — that the program met its mathematical specification.

In the 1960s testing was an even more appalling process than it is now. There were virtually no debuggers, no dynamic analysis tools, and no facilities to store and rerun tests. Consequently, any alternative to testing — particularly one that required no testing effort at all — was treated very seriously.

Unfortunately, a number of problems were discovered. The major one was that the process of proving that a program meets its specification was long and tedious and, more often than not, gave rise to proofs which were textually very much longer than the program itself. In order to overcome this problem researchers attempted to develop automatic program provers: software tools which processed a mathematical specification and a program, and decided, with little human intervention, whether the program was correct.

The search for an efficient program prover became the search for the computing version of the Holy Grail, and in the end the search was unsuccessful.

The failure of program proving lead to a diminution of research into formal methods of software development. However, it was dramatically resuscitated in the early eighties. There were two reasons for this. The first reason was increasing dissatisfaction with development performance on medium to large software projects. The late seventies and eighties saw a large number of projects overrunning, or delivering software which did not match user requirements.

The second reason, and one which was quite artificial, was the Alvey programme. A large part of the software engineering component of the programme was concerned with formal methods of software development. When the first documents from this programme were distributed it was this that caused the most surprise. The Alvey programme was, after all, a response to the Japanese Fifth Generation Project which concentrated on new computer architectures and artificial intelligence.

What the Alvey programme formal methods program indicated was a subtle shift in emphasis. Program proving was concerned with developing a specification and a program independently, and then showing there was a match between them. The formal methods envisaged by the Alvey programme tended to concentrate on the specification first. Once a mathematical specification had been developed the program would be constructed using the specification as a guide. The program development was carried out in small chunks, say a subroutine at a time, so that the complexity associated with program proving would be eliminated.

The two main formal methods of software development currently being used on real software projects are VDM and Z. VDM, which stands for the Vienna Development Method, was originated at the Vienna Laboratories of IBM. It was originally used as a mechanism for accurately defining the structure and meaning of programming languages. However, this original use, has been completely overtaken by its value as a software development method.

The developer who uses VDM first identifies the objects and operations that occur in the application to be computerised. For example, in an air traffic control system typical objects would be planes and radars. Typical operations would be the creation of an aircraft when it came within radar range, the deletion of an aircraft when it landed and the reading of a radar signal from a particular radar installation. Once the objects and operations are identified they are then specified.

Specification in VDM consists of defining the objects using a branch of mathematics called set theory. This is a branch of mathematics which deals with collections of objects. Once the objects have been defined the effect of the operations is clarified. The effect is specified by means of a pre-condition and a post-condition. The former describes what must be true *before* an operation is executed; the latter describes what must be true *after* an operation has been executed. Both these conditions are expressed using logic, to deal with the truth and falseness of statements.

Once the operations have been defined the developer has a specification of his system. The next stage is to carry out design. What he then does is to define a new storage structure based on those available in his programming language and writes down the pre and post conditions for the operations that have been identified. He then validates this design by checking, mathematically, that it is a correct reflection of the specification. The process is continued until the final program code is obtained.

The other formal method popular in this country is Z. Its name arises from the fact that the inventors were confident that it would be the last word in software development methods. Originally it was devised by the French computer scientist Jean Abrial. However, it has been considerably expanded and developed by the Programming Research Group at the University of Oxford.

Z is less a method than a notation. It is semi-graphical in that it consist of mathematics enclosed in boxes known as schemas. Each box describes some stored data and the effect of operations on that stored data. Its advantage, compared with VDM, is that it provides a much more modular description of a system. This enables staff concerned with design, and with requirements analysis, to examine only those parts of the specification that they were concerned with. For example, it enables the designer of the ordering sub-system of a stock control system, to read only those parts of the specification concerned with stock ordering, with little reference to other parts.

The disadvantage of Z compared with VDM is that it lags behind VDM in terms of facilities for transforming the notation into program code. Currently Z is just a specification notation rather than a development method.

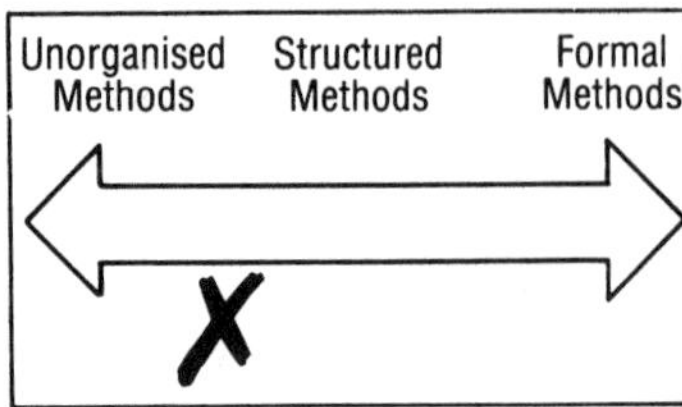

Formal methods such as Z and VDM have impinged little on industrial software projects. It takes a lot of looking to find a real project, unsupported by government or research funding, which uses formal methods. There are a number of reasons for this. First, there is a considerable training problem. The mathematics used – set theory and logic – is not intrinsically difficult. However, few staff have met it before. To become familiar with the mathematics requires weeks of residential training, rather than two or three days normally allowed for a training course. Few companies are willing to commit themselves to such expenditure.

The second reason for the low spread of formal methods is the lack of tools. Carrying out the mathematical proofs required is not difficult. However, the process generates many lines of mathematics and an error can easily be committed. Currently, there are few systems which check the mathematics or provide some degree of automation. The only tools available are structured editors which enable the user to type in a mathematical specification and check it for syntactic correctness. And even these are not commercially supported, being the result of research projects.

The third reason is that it is a major investment decision for a company to move from a structured development method such as SSADM to a formal method. Not only are there considerable training costs, but there are also equally large costs in adjusting the managerial practices of the company, and changing the developmental practices.

One might be tempted to think that formal methods are in decline. However, some recent developments seem to suggest that over the next decade there will be a place for mathematics on the software project. The first development is the increased interest in mathematics of the purveyors of structured methods.

Companies are finding that, although these notations are providing improvements in productivity, there are major problems with the English components of the structured notations that they use. They are now looking to mathematics to supplement weak areas such as the definition of the data in a system.

The second development, and probably the most important, has emanated from the Ministry of Defence. In 1987 the MoD announced its intention to produce a defence standard for safety-critical defence software. When the policy document announced this intention, it contained words and phrases known by software engineering researchers which perplexed the software industry – formal verification, formal method and static analysis.

The MoD was proposing one of the most radical changes in software development to impinge on the information technology industry. They were intending to ask the defence sector to produce software using techniques such as VDM and notations such as Z. Since the vast majority of defence software is safety-critical this would ensure quite a large penetration of formal methods over the next decade.

In a questionnaire, circulated by the Department of Trade and Industry to information technology companies, a third pronounced themselves against the use of mathematics, while a third agreed that a common defence standard was necessary, but doubted the wisdom of using formal methods.

The Ministry of Defence seems to be proceeding with the defence standard. Currently the British software scene can be represented by the spectrum shown on this page, where the cross represents the current state of software development.

If the new defence standard is adopted the cross will have moved much closer to the extreme right hand side of the diagram and will result in the biggest shake up that the British software industry will have experienced.

Darrel Ince is professor of computer science at The Open University.

MARTIN SHALLCROSS

The government is proceeding with the MoD defence standard, despite companies' reluctance to use formal methods

Might is right

RAF: target for MoD's Defence Standard 00-55

Douglas Barrie sees the MoD's adoption of formal methods as a watershed

Defence Standard 00-55 will arrive this year and it already has software developers sitting on the edge of their seats.

Interim Def. Stan. 00-55 as it's known to the cognoscenti marks a watershed in the history of military software development. Its repercussions will also be felt in the commercial sector.

The standard is intended to bring software developers, screaming and kicking if necessary, into the fold of the rigorously defined and designed life-cycle.

The watchword for the standard is reliability. It is aimed at setting down how safety critical software should be developed and validated.

Two engines are driving the Ministry of Defence toward 00-55.

The rapidly escalating costs of both military hardware and software of the human description has led to an increased desire to reduce to a minimum the attrition through systems failure.

Nato airforces collectively lost over 100 aircraft last year through various accidents. At prices running between anything from £10-£25 million a shot the replacement bill was substantial.

Software is beginning to play an increasingly vital role in the frontline fast jet fighters. The advent of fly-by-wire or software-driven aircraft has seen a resultant desire to ensure the reliability and validity of the software to a high degree.

If the MoD is to deploy aircraft and other weapons systems that are reliant on software to carry out their mission — it needs to be confident that they will work.

The other driver behind the MoD's push for the standard is its previously extremely patchy record when it comes to software.

The past decade is littered with projects that have run aground and foundered on the shoals of software development.

Nimrod airborne early warning aircraft and the Cacs 4 shipborne command system met their demise largely due to problems with software. And many of the MoD's current software intensive projects are running late and overbudget.

The MoD set up a steering group for the standard early in 1987 and a draft of the resulting proposals were circulating by September 1988.

By far the most important talking point of the draft standard is its embracing of formal methods.

Peter Froome, a software reliability expert with systems specialist Adelard, was closely involved in the decision to adopt a formal methods approach.

"The really big departure for 00-55," he said, "is making formal methods mandatory."

Formal methods employ formal mathematical techniques of specification to ensure that the spec is logically correct.

This approach will mean considerable upheavals for those firms such as Logica, Sema, SD-Scicon and Software Sciences which carry out sizeable amounts of MoD work. Staff skilled in the use of formal methods are even scarcer than those skilled in programming in Ada.

And a working knowledge of formal methods can't be picked up over night. Firms will have to let staff embark on reasonable lengthy courses either on a full or part time basis.

The MoD already recognises that pushing formal methods will mean sending many software specialists back to the classroom.

A study by Cranfield Information Technology Institute for the MoD confirmed that a formal methods initiative would require a training back-up.

David Youll, a member of CITI, said that familiarisation with the methods would take "several weeks of training," with costs running around £1,000 a week.

As firms will be parting with some of their most profitable software staff and paying for their absence there seems to be little encouragement for firms to take formal methods on-board. Except of course that using formal methods is mandatory.

The general consensus is that the adoption of formal methods will increase the likelihood of software houses getting fixed-priced MoD systems in place without cost overruns being achieved. Parting with a few prime staff and a few thousand pounds is chicken feed to the savings to be made by avoiding cost overruns.

Froome admits at the moment: "There are gaps in formal methods. The interim standard will help to close these and within two years the MoD will introduce a full standard."

A notable omission from 00-55 is the government's standard methodology, SSADM. This hasn't been proposed says Froome because it lacks a sound formal basis.

This will mean a divergence in standards between the civil and military arms of the state. Attempts are being made to resolve this by putting SSADM on a sound formal basis. If this is successful then it may find its way into the full MoD standard.

In terms of programming language 00-55 is also understood to have shyed away from wholeheartedly embracing the Ada military standard language.

Erring on the side of caution because of some lingering doubts over Ada in a real-time environment, the standard is plumping for a choice of both Ada and Pascal subsets.

When the full standards emerge, will Ada proponents convince the doubters?

Chapter 5: Software Requirements Engineering Tools and Techniques

1: Introduction

A *software tool* is a software system or software package used by programmers or software engineers in the performance of their tasks. Examples are software systems used to help develop, test, analyze, or maintain another software system or its documentation, for example, automated design tools, compilers, test tools, maintenance tools, word processors, and so forth [1]. *Software requirements engineering tools,* then, are software tools that help analyze a user's requirements and/or develop a requirements specification.

A special type of software tool is called a computer-aided software engineering (CASE) tool. A CASE tool can assist the software engineer in analyzing, designing, coding, testing, and documenting a software system and in managing a software project.

A *technique* is an approach to performing a required function or job (sometimes called a methodology). In the mid-1980s many of the techniques and methodologies described in Chapter 4 became targets for automation in their own right. Many of these new tools run only on personal computers (PCs) or workstations such as Sun or Apollo or, in a few cases, general purpose machines such as IBM and DEC minicomputers and mainframes. The most common techniques or methodologies automated are realtime and non-realtime structured analysis and design.

The first paper in this chapter examines Software Through Pictures (STP), a typical CASE tool. STP is hosted on workstations, such as Sun and Apollo, but many others run on PCs instead of or in addition to workstations. The second paper discusses Software Requirements Engineering Methodology (SREM), a classic tool hosted on a minicomputer.

The third paper describes Problem Statement Language/Problem Statement Analyzer (PSL/PSA), a tool that has been in use for over 10 years and continues to be modified and upgraded.

The fourth paper discusses Fourth Generation Languages (4GLs), a class of tool with as many implementations as CASE; historically, 4GLs preceded CASE. Other papers examine an automated requirements traceability system and a research tool that utilizes a knowledge-based approach to requirements engineering.

EH0304-6/90/0000/0377$01.00 © 1990 IEEE

2: Description of Papers

The first paper, by A.I. Wasserman and P.A. Pircher, is entitled "A Graphic, Extensible Integrated Environment for Structured Development." This paper describes a workstation-based environment to provide an integrated assembly of graphic tools and analysis and design methods for the development of data systems. These tools are coupled to a project database along with the mechanism for producing declarations, code skeletons, and executable programs. The environment described by the authors is built on an open architecture in which interfaces, tools, and associated files are visible and accessible. The open architecture enables customizing and extending the tool environment to include additional tools. This paper provides an overview of CASE tools and how they can be applied in the small/personal computer environment.

The system described, called Software Through Pictures, automates such tools as structured system analysis, SADT, entity-relationship modeling and structure charts. Software Through Pictures is a family of graphic editors with checking programs. These editors include a dataflow diagram editor, entity-relationship editor, data structure editor, structure chart editor, and transition diagram editor.

The system described, called Software Through Pictures, automates such tools as structured system analysis, SADT™, entity-relationship modeling, and structure charts. Software Through Pictures is a family of graphic editors with checking programs. The editors include a dataflow diagram editor, entity-relationship editor, data structure editor, structure chart editor, and transition diagram editor. The paper describes Software Through Pictures as it existed at the end of 1985. The product has evolved significantly since that time, and many changes have taken place in the individual tools and the overall architecture.

"SREM at the Age of Eight: The Distributed Computing Design System" by Mack Alford, formerly at TRW Huntsville Laboratory, is one of a series of papers [2, 3] Alford has written over the last 12 years on Software Requirements Engineering Methodology (SREM). SREM is an early software requirements methodology and tool. Alford was the principal investigator of the SREM system developed by TRW for the U.S. Army in the mid-1970s. SREM is both a software analysis tool and a representation method primarily for realtime computerized systems. SREM consists of a requirements language (Requirements Statement Language—RSL), a set of tools (Requirements Engineering Validation System—REVS), and a sequence of steps for generating the requirements through use of the language and tools. REVS is used to translate the language, perform automated consistency and completeness analysis, produce documentation, and generate simulations. This paper provides an overview of developments in these areas and summarizes their results. It also describes the origins of SREM, its basic model of requirements, how the model is implemented in RSL, and support software.

The paper describes the first major extension of the SREM concept to address the problems of defining system requirements and allocating them to data-processing subsystems. This new development, called SYSREM, was conducted, designed, and built in 1977-1981 for the U.S. Army.

Finally, the paper describes the new Distributed Computing Design System (DCDS), which is an extension of SREM and SYSREM to all the phases of the lifecycle. DCDS now includes the allocation of system requirements (SYSREM), defining software requirements (SREM), distributed process design, software module design, and integration and test. SREM, while initially public domain, has recently been declared proprietary to the U.S. government and can only be obtained by contractors working on U.S. government contracts that require its use. SREM is included in the tutorial despite its limited use and availability because it was one of the earliest tools to be capable of modeling performance requirements and generating a system simulation. Technology developed by the SREM project has helped to advance the capabilities of many tools for software engineering.

Hasan Sayani has written an up-to-date paper on Problem Statement Language/Problem Statement Analyzer (PSL/PSA). The last overview of PSL/PSA was written in 1977 [4]. Sayani points out that PSL/PSA implemented an entity-relationship approach to system modeling long before that terminology was coined. The PSA database is central to the architecture of PSL/PSA; PSL statements are processed to populate the database. PSA commands cause the database to be analyzed and reports to be generated. A query system permits direct access to the database. Sayani shows examples of PSL statements and PSA reports (textual and graphic). He also provides a history of PSL/PSA and the organizations that developed and maintain it. Finally he shows how PSL/PSA might fit into a full software development environment.

R.H. Cobb's "In Praise of 4GLs," reprinted from *Datamation,* describes what are known as the fourth-generation languages. This paper describes the history of first-, second-, and third-generation languages in which some of the work in programming was transferred from the individual to the machine. The author points out that the first three generations of computer languages were closely tied to the architecture of the computer hardware and that the programmer had two main responsibilities, to find what was to be done and to control the flow of the program. Fourth-generation, or non-procedural, languages alter this approach to programming, as well as the role a program will fill. Non-procedural languages instruct computers by specifying the desired results rather than the action needed to achieve the results. The paper makes a case for the economics of the fourth-generation approach and shows that the use of this technique will reduce the cost of programming.

It should be noted that 4GLs have a limited domain of applicability: systems in which a limited number of types of operation are carried out on a comparatively stable set of data. A spreadsheet is a primitive type of 4GL; it has been notably successful in eliminating the need for trained programmers in generating "programs" for specific applications.

"The Automated Requirements Traceability System (ARTS): An Experience of Eight Years" by Richard Flynn and Merlin Dorfman updates an earlier paper by the same authors. [5] Automated Requirements Traceability System (ARTS) has been in use for eight years, and has been extensively modified during that period. The paper presents the background of requirements traceability and ARTS, the difficulties and benefits of using ARTS, and a more general discussion of the purpose and role of system engineering tools.

The last paper in the chapter presents an ongoing research project rather than a currently available tool. "Towards a Requirements Apprentice" by C. Rich, R.C. Waters, and H.B. Reubenstein describes research being conducted at the Massachusetts Institute of Technology. The Requirements Apprentice is part of a larger research project titled the "Programmer's Apprentice." [6) The Requirements Apprentice is intended to interact with an analyst to help formulate a formal specification of the desired system. The apprentice would accept input in a form close to natural language and would use its knowledge base of the domain (the intended application, such as signal processing or banking) to help structure the requirements. Another part of its knowledge base would contain commonly used elements ("cliches") of the domain for assembly into requirements structures. The human user would review and correct the output of the apprentice.

3: References

[1] Adapted from IEEE *Standard Glossary of Software Engineering Terminology,* ANSI/IEEE Std 729-1983, IEEE, Inc., NY, 1983.

[2] Alford, M.W., "A Requirements Engineering Methodology for Real-Time Processing Requirements," *IEEE Transactions on Software Engineering,* Vol. 3, No. 1, Jan. 1977.

[3] Alford, M.W., "Requirements for Distributed Data Processing Design," *Proceedings of the First International Conference on Distributed Computing Systems,* IEEE Computer Society, Washington, DC, Oct. 1979.

[4] Teichroew, D. and Hershey, E.A., III, "PSL/PSA: A Computer-Aided Technique for Structured Documentation and Analysis of Information Processing Systems," *IEEE Transactions on Software Engineering,* Vol. 3, No. 1, Jan. 1977.

[5] Dorfman, M. and R.F. Flynn, "ARTS: An Automated Requirements Traceability System," *Journal of Systems and Software,* Vol. 4, 1984, pp. 63-74.

[6] Rich, C. and R.C. Waters, "The Programmer's Apprentice: A Research Overview," *Computer,* Nov. 1988, pp. 10-24.

A Graphical, Extensible Integrated Environment for Software Development

Anthony I. Wasserman
Peter A. Pircher

Interactive Development Environments, Inc.
150 Fourth Street, Suite 210
San Francisco, CA 94103

Abstract

Analysis and design are the essential first phases in most software development projects, yet most automated support environments are aimed at the programming phase. This paper describes a workstation-based environment that provides an integrated ensemble of graphical tools for analysis and design coupled to a project database, along with mechanisms for producing declarations, code skeletons, and executable programs. The environment is built on an "open architecture," in which interfaces to the tools and their associated files are visible and accessible. The open architecture supports customization and extensibility of the tool environment, so that it can be effectively linked with traditional programming tools.

1. Goals for an Integrated Design Environment

Many techniques for requirements analysis and software design are graphical. Methods such as Structured Systems Analysis[1,2], SADT™[3], entity-relationship modeling[4], and structure charts[5] rely upon a graphical presentation of information.

Until recently, an obstacle to the widespread acceptance and use of such methods was the lack of automated support. Now that workstations and some personal computers have appropriate hardware to support real-time interactive graphics, analysis and design tools are emerging, typically allowing the user to work with an "intelligent" graphical editor that knows about the notation of the method to produce designs based on the method.[1]

Accordingly, the principal goal of our work was to create an integrated environment that could support software CAD. This software CAD environment, named Software through Pictures™, was aimed primarily at the analysis and design activities, which have been poorly supported in the past. Of course, it was important to provide effective links to the tools that are traditionally found in a programming environment.

1.1. Goals for an Integrated Environment

The key notion underlying the creation of the Software through Pictures tools environment was to bring state of the art hardware and system technology to the software designer[6]. The intended hardware "platform" includes not only a high-performance dedicated processor with a high resolution bit-mapped display, but also distributed file systems, laser printers for documentation support, and necessary operating system support for such hardware.

Another key notion was to produce a "design support environment" that is compatible with extant notions of programming support environments in such a way that they could be combined to form a comprehensive development environment, with appropriate "hooks" in the design environment to connect to the needs of programmers[7].

Subordinate to these notions were numerous goals that were viewed as essential for a powerful environment. The following goals were seen as being particularly important:

- **Customizability**

  Development organizations must be able to adjust tools and their options to conform to local preferences and to local hardware and software configurations.

- **Extensibility**

  Development organizations must be able to integrate their tools (and those acquired elsewhere) into the environment, and to add new tools over time.

- **Usability**

  The tools in the environment should be easy to learn and use, should present a consistent user interface, and should hide the underlying system software from those users who do not wish to see it.

- **Project database**

  The tools in the database should communicate via a general database mechanism so that the database can serve as a repository of project information. This goal further implies that there be a visible linkage between the tools and a specific project and/or system under development, with appropriate version control and configuration management.

- **Checking**

  The design tools must include extensive mechanisms for checking the completeness and consistency of models built with the analysis and design methods. The goal is to aid in detecting errors at the earliest possible stage of the development process.

- **User control**

  The user should be in complete control of the tools, and should be able to set options for tool use, to determine when checking is to be performed (if at all), and to save work in an inconsistent and/or incomplete state.

These goals are independent of the specific functions of the tools in the environment and of the analysis and design methods to be supported.

[1] Of course, many tasks associated with software development are largely textual, and the use of graphics is by no means a panacea, but it is useful to think of "computer-aided design" (CAD) for software in which developers have access to both graphical and textual tools.

"A Graphical, Extensible Integrated Environment for Software Development" by A.I. Wasserman and P.A. Pircher from *SIGPlan Notices*, January 1987, pages 131-142.

1.2. The Analysis and Design Processes

A principal objective of requirements analysis methods is produce a specification of the intended behavior of a system. This process is, of necessity, iterative, as one uses one or more techniques to build a model, possibly executable, of the system. Techniques may include data and/or process modeling, construction of prototypes, and formal mathematical analysis.

In our experience, the early stages of this activity are extremely informal, and become increasingly detailed and formal as the process continues. When using dataflow diagrams, for example, the first diagrams may be little more than sketching, where the objective is to capture the *major* processes, data flows, and data structures, with little attention given to completeness, consistency, types of objects, and low level detail. (Architects often work similarly in sketching out the broad notions of a house or building, without initial concern about room sizes or elevator shafts.)

Much the same can be said for software (including data) design, which aims at producing the structure of a complete system or a component that can be included in a system. In short, both analysis and design are *experimental* processes, in which alternatives are considered and details are filled in.

Automated tools to support analysis and design must therefore respect this process, allowing not only straightforward drawing and modifications to models, but permitting users to explore different models without initially having to supply full details about processes and data and to rectify errors easily.

In the remainder of this paper, we further describe the major aspects of the Software through Pictures environment, emphasizing the ways in which these goals are addressed and met. The "open architecture" approach to building the environment was a key design decision that provided powerful support for achieving these goals.

2. The Software through Pictures graphical editors

2.1. The Family of Editors

A family of graphical editors, with their checking programs, is the most visible piece of the Software through Pictures environment. These editors include:

- Dataflow Diagram Editor (DFE) - supports Structured Systems Analysis, both in the notation used by Gane and Sarson and in the notation used by DeMarco. The associated Control Flow Editor (CFE), State Transition Editor (STE), and table editors support extensions for analysis of real-time systems. One can then perform consistency checking on decomposition of processes and stores information about processes, data elements, data stores, control flows, data flows, etc., in a data dictionary.
- Entity-Relationship Editor (ERE) - supports the entity-relationship data modeling approach, as developed by Chen. One can check for proper declaration of attributes, specification of relationships between entities, and the existence of key attributes for an entity, and generate both a textual form of the entity-relationship schema and a relational database schema.
- Data Structure Editor (DSE) - supports data structure definition following the notation of Michael Jackson[8] and generates a textual form of the data structure, entering the constituent data elements in a data dictionary.
- Structure Chart Editor (SCE) - supports Structured Design, as presented by Yourdon and Constantine, to represent a software architecture, allowing the user to specify the input and output parameters for each module in a system, as well as distinguishing control items (flags) from "pure data." When used in combination with Structured Systems Analysis, it is possible to check the data dictionary for proper use of parameters and consistency.
- Transition Diagram Editor (TDE) - supports the User Software Engineering (USE) methodology for building interactive information systems, allowing the user to draw USE transition diagrams[9] and generate the input to RAPID/USE, a rapid prototyping and application development system. The USE transition diagrams may be animated during the execution of the program.

In many situations, a development group will use all of these tools on a single project. Consider the typical situation of building an information system. The developer begins by identifying the data objects (entities, relationships, and attributes) associated with the application, modeling them in an entity-relationship diagram with ERE. This information will be used in the construction of a set of dataflow diagrams, built with DFE. The dataflows in the dataflow diagrams may then be modeled and defined as data structures and data elements using the Data Structure Editor. In practice, this process proceeds iteratively, with additional information being added to each representation as during analysis.

Analysis of the user interface requirements leads to external design of the system, i.e., the user interface. This interface can be modeled with the USE transition diagrams; the Transition Diagram Editor is used to edit the diagrams and to generate an executable model of the interaction between the user and the system in the RAPID/USE language.

The software architecture emerges from one of these models. In many cases, the architecture results from a transformation of the dataflow diagram, but it may alternatively result from the data structures (as originally proposed by Jackson) or from the executable model of the USE transition diagrams. In any case, the architecture may be represented as one or more structure charts and edited with the Structure Chart Editor.

2.2. Consistent User Interface for Editors

Because all of the editors are often used, it is important that they have a consistent user interface. Each editor uses its own window, where a window has several regions. The large region is the *drawing area*, in which the diagram will be drawn or edited. Directly below the black stripe are two small areas. On the left is the *command indicator*, which shows the current operation. On the right is the *message area*, which shows error messages from the editor and confirmations of reading and writing operations. Below these areas and above the drawing area are the *symbol indicator*, which shows the symbol to be inserted, and the *command panel* (fixed menu),which shows many of the most common commands. (This window is from the Dataflow Diagram Editor.)

All commands are requested by using a three-button mouse. The use of the mouse buttons is consistent. The right button shows the editor commands, using sets of popup or pulldown menus, depending upon the particular machine and window system. Drawing commands are used to create and edit diagrams, while files commands are used to store diagrams in several different formats, A selected command becomes the "current command" and is normally displayed in the "command indicator" region.

Within the drawing area, the left mouse button is used for selecting objects or points in the diagram, as well as for making selections from the fixed menu at the top of the window. The center button is used to undo the previous operation.

As a further consideration in providing a consistent user interface, the editors use the primary window system of the host computer, so that windows used for Software through Pictures behave similarly to other windows on the workstation, and so that users may use other windows concurrently with those used for Software through Pictures.

Figure 1 shows a dataflow diagram created with DFE using the Gane/Sarson form of the notation, as it appears on a Sun

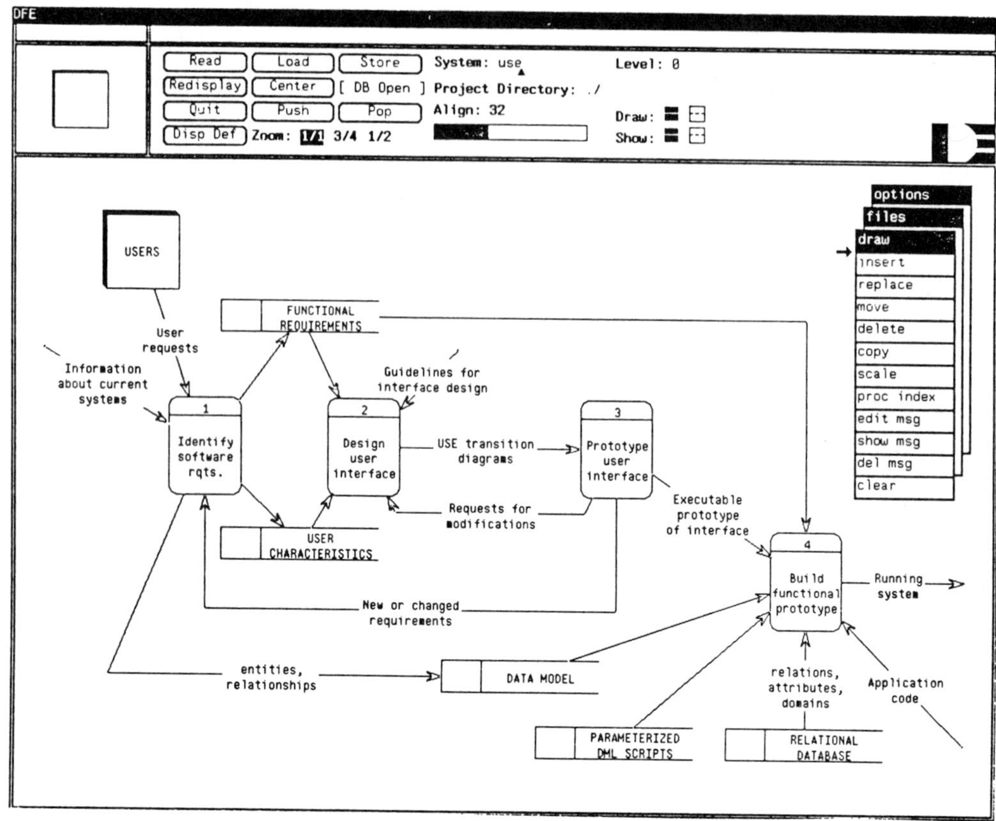

Figure 1 -- A dataflow diagram window using DFE

Workstation. (DFE also supports the DeMarco notation, and diagrams created with one notation are easily converted into the other.) Note that the control panel contains entries for project directory, system name, and level. These entries allow full hierarchical decomposition of the dataflow model, along with integration into the project directory structure described below.

3. Project Database

The notion of a *project database* is well understood, though rarely implemented, in software development environments. The project database serves as a repository in which all of the information associated with a system or project is stored. As described in the software engineering literature, a project database should be used to store everything from requirements to source code and from user documentation to executable programs and program units, replicated as required to support multiple versions of each. Then, in principle, one can make a query against this database to determine the status of the system that it is supporting, or can issue a command that operates upon one or more database objects to modify existing objects and/or to produce new ones. While this goal is not fully attainable with current software technology, a significant subset of that information can be collected and saved in a database.[2]

The Software through Pictures environment is built upon a relational database management system, which is used to support project databases. A project database contains information on the names and definitions of all of the objects used throughout the software development process for a project/system pair. It also contains project history information, references to the diagrams produced with the editors, and locks that support sharing of the diagrams among members of a software development project.

Name management, though, is the most apparent use of the project database, and the part of the database responsible for name management is called the IDE Data Dictionary. The IDE Data Dictionary is built upon the programmer-oriented Troll/USE relational database management system[10, 11].

Relations are defined for all of the major classes of objects that are created with the graphical editors, including the following:

- data_element
- data_structure
- ds_component {components of data structures}
- data_store
- data_flow
- control_flow
- process
- proc_params {input and output parameters of processes}
- message
- externals
- module
- mod_connect {module calling information; caller and callee}
- aliases

(It should be noted that the "process" object is an activity modeled during the analysis phase and that the "module" object is defined during the architectural design phase. The term "process" is used here in the manner of structured analysis methods, not in the manner of operating systems or realtime systems.)

Each of the editors has an option that automatically generates information for the IDE Data Dictionary, modifying the database based on the content of the diagram being edited. The Structure Chart Editor SCE, for example, typically modifies the module, mod_calls, and mod_params relations, while the Dataflow Diagram Editor DFE typically modifies the data_store, data_flow, process, proc_params, and externals relations. If a developer uses all of the graphical editors, then information may be placed in all of these relations.

[2]Database management systems capable of storing large binary objects, such as an executable program, are just now becoming commercially available. Such a capability is needed to achieve the goal of comprehensive database support.

Developers can easily obtain this information, along with cross references and other reports. Such a capability can eliminate ambiguity and can aid in making certain that consistent naming mechanisms are used.

For example, each editor contains a selection item to display the definition of an item in the IDE Data Dictionary. Since the database is shared among all of the editors, the request for information will obtain *all* of the information known about that item.

For example, the request to display the definition of an item ''list_data'' may provide the response shown in Figure 2:

In addition to name management, the IDE Data Dictionary can be used for project information. A history relation keeps track of all of the modifications made to all of the diagrams associated with a system, plus information on the checks made by a user.

Since the project database is simply a set of relations that are created when the user defines a system, it can be easily extended to keep track of additional information. Thus, for example, one could define new attributes or relations to help with some of the project management aspects of system development.

3.1. Project Directory Structure

The project database is placed within a hierarchical project directory structure. For each project, there is one or more ''systems,'' each of which has a substructure to hold the files produced by the graphical editors and the project database. The project database may be shared among two or more systems in a project (or in separate projects, depending on access control) by linking one project database directory into several system substructures.

The program that defines a system is simply a command file (shell script) that builds a directory hierarchy along with the project database. The basic directory structure allows one to create subdirectories for each different type of diagram that can be edited with the Software through Pictures tools. Thus, all of the dataflow diagrams for system *sample* of project *swtools* would be placed in the subdirectory swtools/sample/dfe_files.

In addition to the predefined subdirectories, users may define other subdirectories to hold other information that they may need. Figure 3 shows five user-defined subdirectories: doc, src, obj, bin, and test. Such directories could be used to hold user documentation, source code, object modules, the executable system, and test data, respectively. Such subdirectories could be explicitly created as needed. Alternatively, one could modify the command file that creates the directory structure so that these subdirectories are automatically created each time that a system is defined.

```
Name: list_data
    Defined as Data Structure in DSE Diagram list_user_data
    Type: Sequence
    3 Components:
      list_access_#                        Undefined
      new_list_data                        Undefined
      link_data                            Undefined

    Used in 1 Data Structure
      list_user_data
    Used in 1 Data Flow
     DFE Level  From/To
          0  Offpage Level 0
          Process                         2  maintain_list_database
```

Figure 2 -- Display of data definition from IDE Data Dictionary

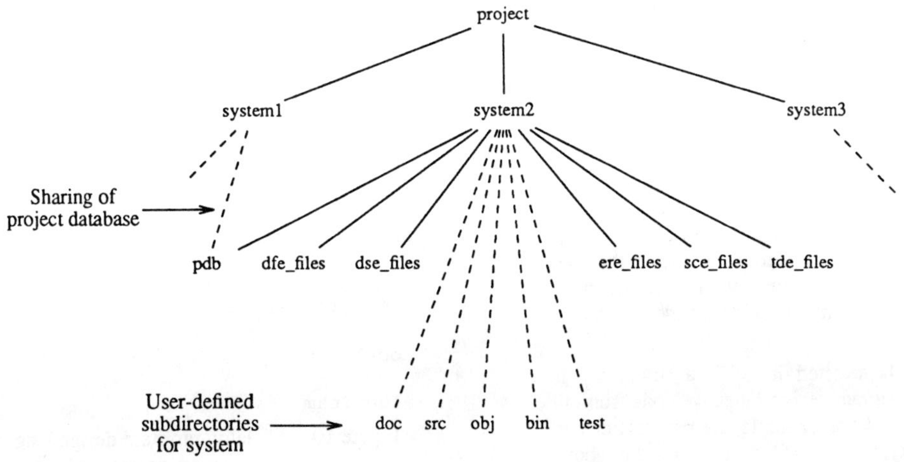

Figure 3 -- Project Directory Structure

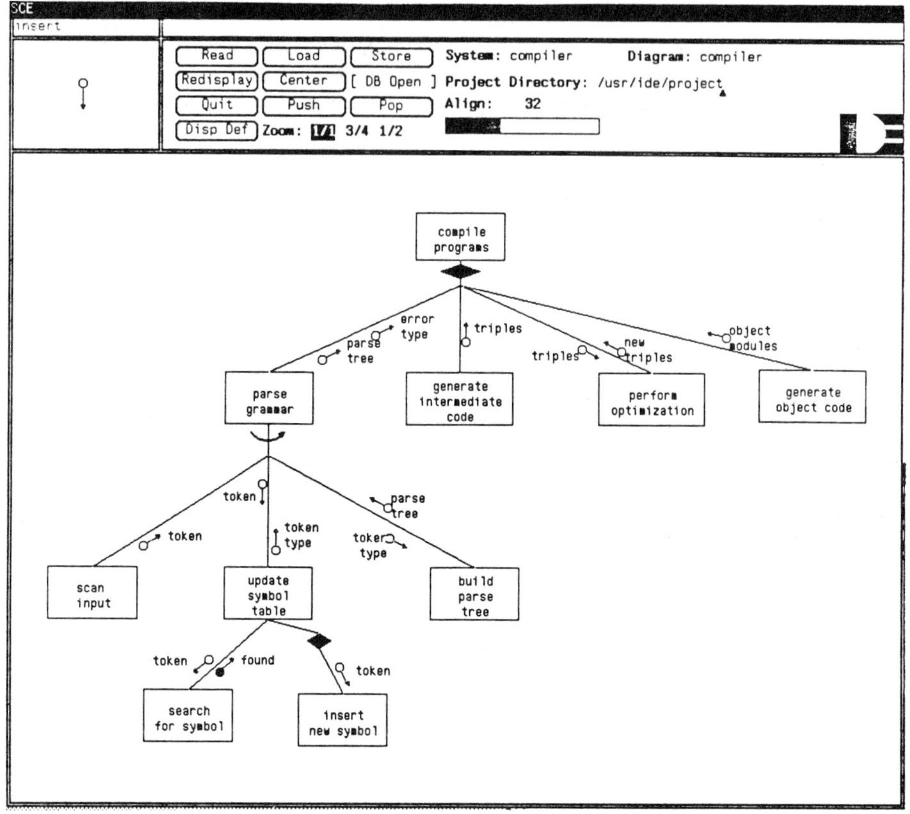

Figure 9 -- Structure chart of hypothetical compiler

represent a calling structure and the small arrows represent the passage of information between modules, with the name of the data item attached to the arrow. An arrow with an open end is a data couple, while an arrow with a filled end is a control couple, such as a flag. The black diamond indicates a conditional call, while the rounded arrow indicates iteration.

Additional text may be associated with a module to provide additional detail on the function or algorithm associated with the module. When the user selects the "edit msg" command in SCE, an editor is invoked, along with the *scpdl* program. The editor operates on either the default version of a "program design language" or, alternatively, on a user-defined language. The *scpdl* program knows about certain key words and is able to make a substitution from the information in the structure chart.

For example, consider the skeleton program design language for a module as shown in Figure 10.

The items within brackets are used by *scpdl* to fill in current values. The user may then edit the resulting file with a text editor. (The user may specify an editor or may use *vi* as a default.) Typically, the skeleton includes the interface information, to which the user adds a textual description of the algorithm and/or data structures local to the module. SCE performs no checking on the text added by the user

When the "pdl" command is selected in SCE, a single file is produced with the collected program design language code from all of the modules in the diagram. As an example, the program design language for the "update symbol table" module of the above structure chart is shown in Figure 11. Notice that it shows the essential information about the calling structure and the input and output data.

```
module      ${name}

Pdl generated
    ${date} at ${time} by ${user}
This module has ${#param} parameters:
    ${@param}

input data params
      ${@indata}
input flags
      ${@inflag}

output data params
      ${@outdata}
output flags
      ${@outflag}

calls
      ${@calls}
called by
      ${@called}

local data

algorithm
```

Figure 10 -- Skeleton program design language showing predefined items

```
module      update_symbol_table

Pdl generated
    18 March 1986 at 23:24:00 by tonyw
This module has 2 parameters:
    token, token_type

input data params
        token
input flags


output data params
        token_type
output flags


calls
        search_for_symbol, insert_new_symbol
called by
        parse_grammar

local data

algorithm
```

Figure 11 -- Program design language skeleton exported from Structure Chart Editor

Instead of using a program design language skeleton, the user could use a code skeleton, using the syntax for a programming language. Then a developer could write code for each module from the initial skeleton, and the "pdl" command would then put out a file with source code for all of the modules thereby edited. Such an approach can work well for small systems, and for top-down implementations, since it is easy to generate the code skeleton for a stub.

4.2. Prototypes of user interfaces

The Transition Diagram Editor supports the User Software Engineering methodology, developed to aid the creation of interactive information systems, systems that provide users with conversational access to data. In such systems, the user interface to the system is critical, and the User Software Engineering approach places a premium on user involvement at the early stages of the software development process. This user involvement is dominated by the ability of the users to participate in the design of the user interface, largely through working with rapidly created and rapidly modifiable versions of the user interface.

An important aspect of the user interface design in User Software Engineering is *dialogue independence*, which means that the dialogue between the user and the system can be designed and implemented independently of the remainder of the system code.

The mechanism for specifying the system is based on augmented state transition diagrams[9]. The Transition Diagram Editor supports the creation of these diagrams, and the *tduse* program generates the executable RAPID/USE language, a textual "nodes-and-arcs" language that provides for describing the state transitions, the output messages associated with each node, the application actions associated with transitions, and the input events that cause a transition to occur. The resulting RAPID/USE program can be compiled and executed, either without actions to produce a prototype system showing only the user interface, or with actions to produce a functioning system.

The *tduse* program can generate RAPID/USE with or without tracing information. With the tracing information, the RAPID/USE program can be compiled in trace mode so that the resulting program can be executed in one window on the workstation while the USE transition diagrams representing the system are concurrently animated in another window. Whenever control is at a given node of a diagram, that node and the previously traversed arc blink. In this way, the developer can visually follow the execution of the program, supplementing the logging information that can also be generated. The diagram tracing is an extremely powerful development and debugging aid.

Much has previously been written about the User Software Engineering methodology and the associated tools for rapid prototyping and application development, and the interested reader is referred to those papers[13, 14].

4.3. Generation of hard copy

In addition to editing diagrams at a workstation, it is essential to be able to produce high quality hard copies of the diagrams, not only for communication among analysts and designers, but also for inclusion in important software documents, such as functional specifications and project proposals. The output should include both the diagram and any text associated with the symbols in the diagram, thereby giving the reader of the hard copy access to all of the information placed in the diagram. Thus, a screen dump, such as those used in this paper, are useful for giving a sense of the editors and the diagrams, but are incomplete. The same statement can be made for any mechanism that uses a raster image of a diagram, since it is much more useful to treat the diagram as a set of objects.

The open architecture approach has again been followed in supporting of hard copy output. We assumed two categories of users: those with a printing device capable of supporting one of the principal output languages for a laser printer, and those without.

For the former category, the graphical editors can generate a description in either the *pic* language of AT&T or PostScript™. The pic output can be used with AT&T's device-independent *troff* program. Most of the available laser printers provide support for one or the other of these languages. Each of the editors has associated programs that can be called to generate the appropriate textual form. For the Dataflow Diagram Editor, these programs are *dfpic* and *dfpost*. These programs are invoked from command files that also include the node messages and other non-pictorial information from the diagram.

For users without a device capable of supporting *pic* or Postscript, it is necessary to use the picture description file produced by the editor. That file is used directly by the editors for loading and storing diagrams. In keeping with the open architecture philospohy, it is an ASCII file with a published format.

5. Customizability and the Tool Information File

There are significant differences among software development environments and among user preferences for tools that are used in those environments. In many instances, it is difficult, if not impossible, to adapt software tools to these different environments. Instead, tools enforce certain built-in assumptions about their location and their use. These assumptions include such things as the location(s) where the executable programs, libraries, and data files must be stored, the options to be given to compilers or loaders, and the format for times and dates.

The IDE Tool Information System allows customization of tools and their environments by users. It is based on the concept of attribute-value pairs, where a value can be associated with some attribute of a software tool or its environment. Management of this system is handled through the IDE Tools library, which allows programs to obtain values for specific attributes at program execution time.

The IDE Tool Information System also allows users to customize tools that they build. These tools can be linked to IDE's other tools, and can use previously defined attributes and values, or can be completely independent of them, relying simply on the IDE Tools library to access the values of newly defined attributes. In this way, the IDE Tool Information System is completely extensible.

The IDE Tool Information System uses a *tool information file* for each machine and, if desired, for each user. Typically, there is a systemwide file that is used by a group of people; however, it is also possible for each user to have an individual file and thereby to customize the tool environment at the personal level.

The IDE Tool Information System can be used for numerous purposes, including the following:

(1) location-independent software -- the value of an attribute may be the location where a tool or a related file is stored

(2) compiler options -- the name of a compiler, along with options, may be stored as the value for an attribute

(3) display information -- the preferred format for dates, times, etc.

(4) user options -- the value of an attribute may be a preference for a particular font or the location of project-dependent files or databases.

Part of a typical ToolInfo file is shown in Figure 12.

This tool information file shows the different uses for the file. The first line, for example, defines the location in the system where the executable version of *troll* is found. Similarly, the entry for troff shows a remote call to the program *ditroff* on machine idesrvr. The entry for *check_dd* shows the optional use of the -v (verbose) flag and the piping of the output to the line printer lw instead of display the output on standard output (the workstation window).

These entries may reference one another. Note that the entry for dfe_print is a call to *dfpic* followed by piping to the program designated by the pic entry and then to the program designated by the troll entry.

The tool information file also makes it easy to work with experimental versions of tools without disrupting other users. The entry for dfps names a program in the IDE development system rather than the "official" release version of the program.

The tool information file also supports the project directory structure in two major ways. First, there are entries for projdir, system, and pdb_enabled so that a user may set a default value for each of these. Those default values are used when an editor is started and may be seen in the control panel for the editor.

Second, the underlying support for the tool information file includes variables, which can be seen in the example here. For example, the variable $s refers to the current system name and $n refers to the -n flag, which is used in the command line for the editors to define whether the database is initially open.

Another feature of the tool information file is its ability to include rules. The RAPID/USE system uses these rules when it encounters a program ending with the suffixes .c, .f, and .o. The .c ending indicates a program written in the C language. The rule is in three parts: what program to invoke on the input file, the name of the resulting output file, and the libraries to use to resolve any undefined names.

Finally, the tool information file is extensible. Users may define new attributes and values, and use the routines of IDE's tools library to reference those attributes and values in new programs.

6. The IDEtool window

It is apparent from the preceding discussion that the IDE tool environment is quite extensive, incorporating nearly 100 executable programs that can work within a project directory system. Furthermore, each of these programs accepts various flags and options and can be called directly by the user if so desired.

```
troll=/usr/local/troll
dateformat=%D %N %Y
timeformat=%h:%.2m:%.2s
weekdays= Sunday Monday Tuesday Wednesday Thursday Friday Saturday
monthnames = Jan Feb Mar Apr May June July Aug Sep Oct Nov Dec
% The editor to call to edit a dfe process node
E_process=/usr/bin/pspec_editor -l $l $%
% IDE tools library for RAPID/USE, Troll/USE and the ToolInfo file
ltoolsup=/usr/local/lib/libtools.a
% C preprocessor flags
ppflags=
% Rules
.c:    cc  ${ppflags} -c -O $<  ;; $@.o ;; -lc
.f:    f77  -c -O $<  ;; $@.o ;; -lF77 -lI77
.o:    ;; $< ;;
% The fonts to use; the ones listed below are the default fonts
small_font=
medium_font=sail.r.6
%large_font=gacha.r.7
dfe_symbols=Gane/Sarson
%PostScript output program from DFE -- experimental version
dfps=/usr/ide/dev/new.editors.src/dfe/tools/dfps
%Pic and Troff programs
pic=/usr/local/pic -Pip
troff=rsh idesrvr ditroff -Pip  -me
projdir=~ide/project
% Print a data flow diagram
dfe_print=dfpic - -h -m -n $p $d | ${pic} | ${troff}
% Check dfe decomposition of this level vs upper level
dfe_decomp=dfe_decomp -v $s $p $d
% Check the entire IDE/DD
check_dd=check_dd -v $f $p $s | lpr -Plw &
dfe_mv_decomp=ideutil $p $s -C 'e dfe' -C 'm ${_fd} ${_td}' -C q
% The program that translates a structure definition to C
dse_c=struct_dd -v -N -C -Ct -d $n $f $p $s $d
% SCE PDL handling
sce_pdl_proto=/usr/local/lib/sce.pdl
```

Figure 12 -- A partial tool information file

While this flexibility and power is extremely useful to knowledgeable users and to sophisticated software development organizations, the range of options can also be overwhelming to a new user seeking only to do Structured Systems Analysis, involving drawing, checking, and printing of a set of diagrams. When such a user is faced not only with IDE's tools, but also with a new underlying operating system, the learning time can be considerable.

Initially, many of the most common options and preferences are set in the tool information file. Since that file is approximately 400 lines long, the novice user is often reluctant to modify it, especially since modification involves use of a text editor that may also be unfamiliar.

Accordingly, we designed IDEtool to serve as an integrating mechanism for the entire software development environment. The user can log in, enter the window environment, type the command

IDEtool

and immediately be presented with a window similar to that shown in Figure 13.

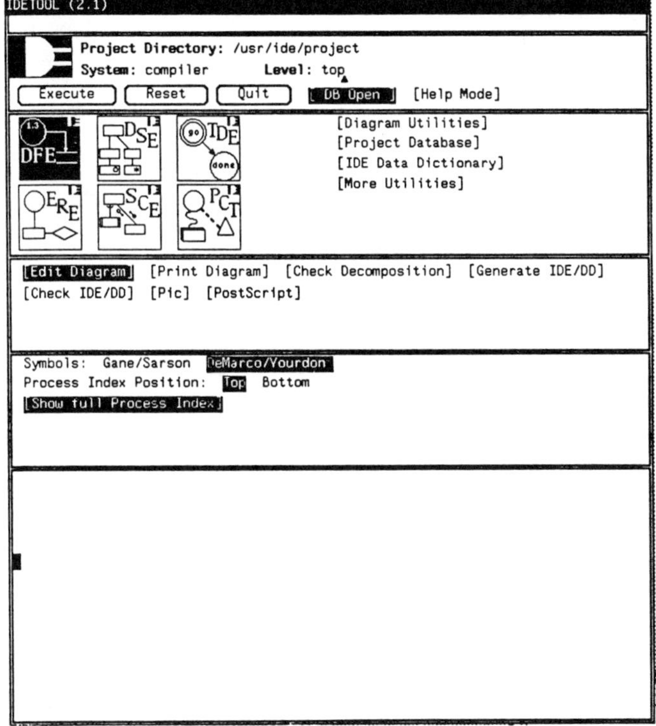

Figure 13 -- The IDEtool window

The IDEtool window contains several different areas, including a control panel, a command area, and an options or argument area. In the figure, the DFE tool has been selected, as shown by the reverse video on the DFE icon. The commands associated with DFE are shown in the next subwindow, and the [Edit Diagram] command is shown as being selected. The options are then shown in a lower subwindow. Various options and commands, plus an integrated help facility, can be accessed through IDEtool without having to learn the syntax and structure of the commands themselves.

The IDEtool window is built dynamically at runtime from a text file that shows the content of the tool, command, and arguments subwindows. An entry such as

/dfe

designates the DFE tool and the characteristics of the selection. An entry such as

//edit

beneath the dfe entry, or, equivalently,

/dfe/edit

is used to indicate the command, help message, and other information associated with one of the aspects of the DFE tool. Various options can be offered, and initial values can be specified for these options to provide the user with a set of default options.

This text file is called the IDEtool specification file; a small portion of such a file is shown in Figure 14.

This approach to the IDEtool specification file is yet another example of the open architecture of the IDE tool environment, and offers numerous advantages, including:

(1) users can modify the file to set their own preferred default values for various options;

(2) users can extend the help messages to provide more extensive online help;

(3) users can translate the file into various languages to support users whose native language is not English;

(4) users can design icons, using the standard icon editing facility, to replace text selection items with icons; note that the IDEtool shows six such icons (which is not consistent with the IDEtool specification file in the figure);

(5) users can extend the IDEtool specification file to link in other tools and commands, including standard commands provided by the host operating system, such as printing and compiling, or tools provided by other vendors. In that way, the user interface to a complete environment, including the IDE tools, can be give a single consistent appearance.

In this way, all of the various tools can be invoked from a single location with a consistent mechanism. We have found that this approach greatly simplifies the user's comprehension of the toolset and sharply reduces the time needed to be able to use the IDE tools.

7. Conclusion and future directions

IDE's Software through Pictures tool environment, currently in use in forty different commercial software development organizations, addresses several important needs of software developers:

(1) access to powerful workstation-based tools for analysis and design;

(2) tool integration through a data dictionary/project database;

(3) extensive checking of dataflow models;

(4) extensibility of the toolset and environment through adherence to an open architecture.

The open software architecture is, in many ways, the most significant contribution of this work, since it shows the feasibility of the open architecture approach when applied to a large set of software tools. The open architecture approach provides users with several mechanisms for extending the IDE toolset *and* for integrating their newly developed tools with IDE's.

(1) The user may extend the database schema.

(2) The user may modify and/or extend the project directory structure.

(3) The user may define a program design language or code skeleton to work with the Structure Chart Editor and thereby generate text files that may be processed by a program design language tool or a language compiler outside the IDE toolset.

(4) The user may build special purpose printing tools to work with the published IDE file formats for diagrams.

(5) The user may extend the tool information file by defining new attributes and values, and by combining those with the initial set in user-developed programs.

(6) The user may modify the IDEtool specification file to change options and modify or add new commands that allow extensibility and customization of the tool set.

This user-modifiability of the directory structure is an example of *open architecture*, in which the structure of the system, along with the files that it produces and uses, are visible to all users.

In keeping with this theme, the definition of the relational database schema is also given in the command file. In that way, the user can add attributes to predefined relations and/or additional relations. The database(s) and the Troll/USE relational DBMS are visible and accessible from outside the software development environment, so that users may extend the environment with their own tools that access or modify the database. (Of course, the users must be careful not to destroy information needed by the graphical editors or the IDE Data Dictionary.)

4. Output from the Graphical Editors

While the graphical editors are valuable simply for their drawing capability and their ability to produce several different types of important software and data models, they also have additional features that serve the overall software development process, including:

(1) generation of declarations, code, and code skeletons;

(2) generation of executable prototypes of user interfaces;

(3) generation of picture description languages so that the pictures produced by the editors may be easily printed on a variety of devices;

The generation of this information is not produced by the editor itself, but rather by one of a set of auxiliary programs called by the editor. The architecture of the IDE toolset is shown in Figure 4. The graphical editors are shown above the dotted line, indicating that they must be executed on a graphical workstation. All of the other tools and the files that they produce are shown below the dotted line, indicating that they are independent of the graphical editors. Thus, those programs may be implemented on a machine without the bit-mapped display and can be used in a network environment with the graphical workstation.

More importantly, these latter programs may be invoked from *outside* the graphical editor, as well as through a menu selection within an editor. This section describes the general functions of these non-graphical programs, although space limitations forbid a complete description.

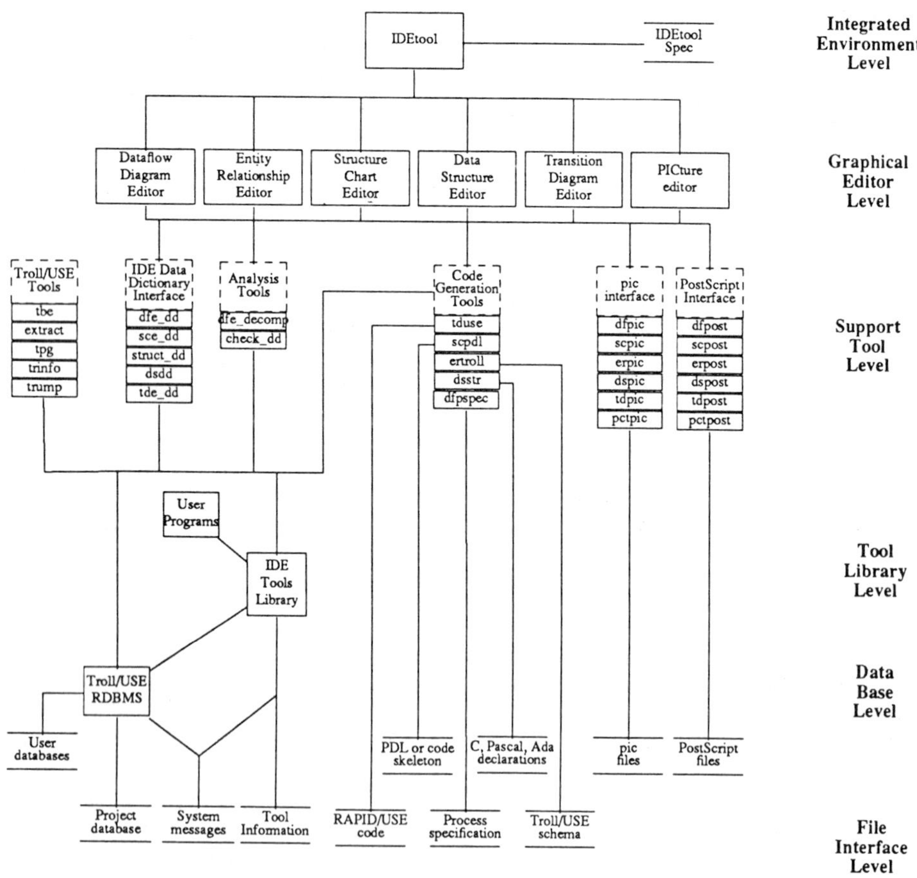

Figure 4 -- Architecture of the IDE toolset

4.1. Generation of declarations and code

Although the IDE tools are primarily aimed at analysis and design, it is recognized that the goal of most projects is the production of one or more executable programs that meet a set of defined requirements. Thus, several of the graphical editors can automatically produce items that are used in subsequent phases of a software development project.

4.1.1. Data Structure Declarations

The Data Structure Editor is intended primarily to support the definition of hierarchical data structures as needed to provide for the decomposition of data through the levels of a set of dataflow diagrams. However, DSE supports the association of type and constraint information with the definition of data items, along with the generation of type and variable declarations in Ada, C, and/or Pascal.

Consider the data structure x shown in Figure 5.

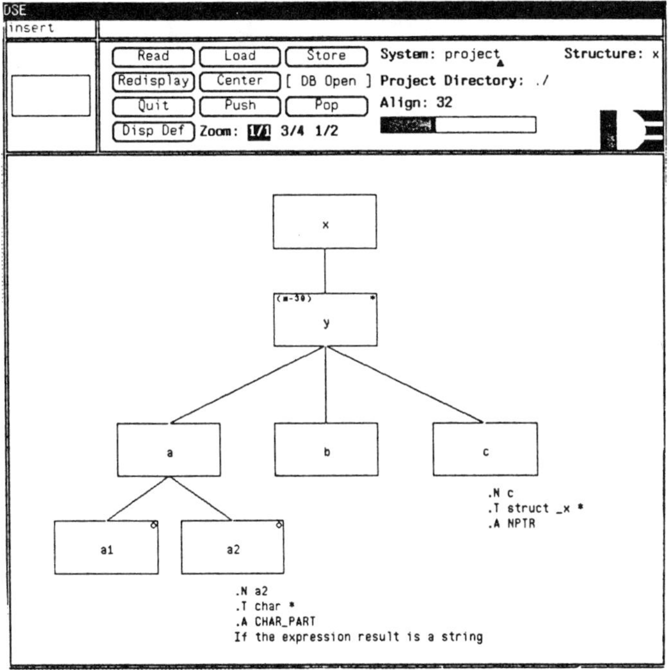

Figure 5 -- Data structure x defined with DSE

The type information associated with a2 and c is shown to the lower right of their boxes in the figure, where the .N stands for name, the .T stands for type, and the .A stands for alias.

When the user requests the generation of C code for x, the program *dsstr* is called to go from the data structure to a structure definition. The structure definition is available in two different forms: one resembling Backus-Naur form, as shown in Figure 6, and the other using Jackson's notation for the structure, as shown in Figure 7.

```
a1 ::= int
a2 ::= char *
a ::= [ a1 | a2 ]
b ::= int
c ::= struct _x *
y ::= a + b + c
x ::= (* - 30) { y }
```

Figure 6 -- BNF for data structure x

```
x ITER (*-30)
    y SEQ
      a SELECT
          a1 ;
      a OR
          a2 ;
      a END
      b ;
      c ;
    y END
x END
```

Figure 7 -- Data structure definition for x using Jackson's notation

The C code is also generated, either as a type definition, or as a structure definition, as shown in Figure 8.

```
# define          A1_field          a1
# define          CHAR_PART         a2
# define          NPTR     c
struct  y {
    union           a {
        int         a1 ;
        char *      a2 ;
    }   a;
    int b ;
    struct  _x * c ;
}           x [30];
```

Figure 8 -- C declaration for structure x

4.1.2. Database schema declarations

The Entity-Relationship Editor is also used for modeling data, and is used to define database schemas. The database schema is drawn with ERE, with the domain (type) and constraint information for the attributes. The user may then select the "schema" command, which calls the program *tosca* to produce a textual entity-relationship schema, and then the "troll" command, which calls the program *ertroll* to produce a relational database definition in the Troll/USE data definition language.

If the user has followed the syntax rules for defining domains and constraints in Troll/USE, then the file produced by *ertroll* can be used as an input file to the Troll/USE relational DBMS to produce a set of relations. In this way, one can rapidly build a database design, examine the resulting relations, and then either modify the graphical version of the E-R model or the relational database schema thereby produced. Such a capability is a powerful form of rapid prototyping, as it allows the ability to produce several variations of the schema in a very short period of time.

4.1.3. Program design languages and code skeletons

The Structure Chart Editor is used to show the architecture of a software system, including modules and the information passed back and forth between modules. Structure charts, as introduced by Constantine *et al.*[12], were intended to be strictly hierarchical, but the Structure Chart Editor supports more general architectures.

The structure chart in Figure 9 shows part of a hypothetical compiler. The rectangles represent program modules, the arcs

```
/dfe
      label [Data Flow Diagrams]
      help  The Dataflow tools contains programs to draw \
            Dataflow Diagrams (DFD's), to generate the IDE Data Dictionary \
            from a diagram, check consistency of decomposed DFD's. \
            Commands to generate various forms of output are also supported.
      tool  DFE
//edit
      label [Edit Diagram]
      msg   Edit Data Flow diagram
      cmd   dfe ${dfe_lindex} ${pindex_pos} ${dfe_symbols} $n $s $p $d
//dfe_decomp
      help  This selection lets you check the decomposition of the \
            current diagram against its parent.
      msg   Check decomposition
      label [Check Decomposition]
      cmd   dfe_decomp ${ext} ${verbose} $s $p $d
///output
      help  Specify output of decomp check
      label Output:
///verbose
      help  Give verbose error messages if on
      label [Verbose]
      switch      "" "-v"
      line  +1
      col   0
///ext
      help  Allow Externals on non context level
      label [Non context Externals]
      switch      "" "-e"
//gen_dd
      help  Generate the IDE Data Dictionary for the current diagram.
      label [Generate IDE/DD]
      msg   Generate IDE/DD
      cmd   dfe_dd  ${verbose} $s $p $d
///output
      help  Filename where output of Generate DD should be written
      label Output:
///verbose
      help  If on, command will tell what it is doing
      label [Verbose]
      switch      "" "-v"
      init  1
      line  +1
      col   0
```

Figure 14 -- Portion of IDE tool specification file for DFE

This range of capabilities extends well beyond what is available to tool users in most settings built from compiled tools, and contrasts sharply to closed environments in which the user must depend on the tool vendor to provide extensions, since there are far fewer "hooks." The closed approach is more often associated with a large monolithic tool intended for a centralized environment, while the open approach is more in keeping with distributed environments such as those found in modern workstations and distributed file systems.

The open architecture is also valuable to tool builders, since the basic IDE tool environment can be easily extended. The software development environment described here is a powerful and practical framework for meeting the growing demands of sophisticated software development organizations.

TM SADT is a trademark of SofTech, Inc. Software through Pictures is a trademark of Interactive Development Environments, Inc. PostScript is a trademark of Adobe Systems, Inc.

8. References

[1] Gane, C. and Sarson, T., *Structured Systems Analysis*, Prentice-Hall, Englewood Cliffs, NJ (1979).

[2] DeMarco, T., *Structured Analysis and System Specification*, Prentice-Hall, Englewood Cliffs, NJ (1979).

[3] Ross, D.T. and Schoman, K.E. Jr., "Structured Analysis for Requirements Definition," *IEEE Transactions on Software Engineering* **SE-3**(1) pp. 6-15 (January, 1977).

[4] Chen, P.P.-S., "The Entity-Relationship Model -- Toward a Unified View of Data," *Transactions on Database Systems* **1**(1) pp. 9-36 (March, 1976).

[5] Yourdon, E. and Constantine, L.L., *Structured Design*, Prentice-Hall, Englewood Cliffs, NJ (1979).

[6] Gutz, S., Wasserman, A.I., and Spier, M.J., "Personal Development Systems for the Professional Programmer," *Computer* **14**(4) pp. 45-53 (April, 1981).

[7] Advanced Projects Research Agency , *Requirements for Ada Programming Support Environments -- "STONEMAN"*, U.S. Department of Defense (February, 1980).

[8] Jackson, M.A., *Principles of Program Design*, Academic Press, London (1975).

[9] Wasserman, A.I., "Extending State Transition Diagrams for the Specification of Human-Computer Interaction," *Transactions on Software Engineering* **SE-11**(8) pp. 699-713 (1985).

[10] Kersten, M.L. and Wasserman, A.I., "The Architecture of the PLAIN Data Base Handler," *Software -- Practice and Experience* **11**(2) pp. 175-186 (February, 1981).

[11] Wasserman, A.I. and Kersten, M.L., *A Troll/USE Tutorial*, Laboratory of Medical Information Science, University of California, San Francisco (1984).

[12] Stevens, W.P., Myers, G.J., and Constantine, L.L., "Structured design," *IBM Systems Journal* **13**(2) pp. 115-139 (1974).

[13] Wasserman, A.I., Pircher, P.A., Shewmake, D.T., and Kersten, M.L., "Developing Interactive Information Systems with the User Software Engineering Methodology," *Transactions on Software Engineering* **SE-12**(2) pp. 326-345 (1986).

[14] Wasserman, A.I. and Shewmake, D.T., "The Role of Prototypes in the User Software Engineering (USE) Methodology," pp. 191-210 in *Advances in Human-Computer Interaction*, ed. H.R. Hartson, Ablex Publishing (1985).

SREM at the Age of Eight; The Distributed Computing Design System

Mack Alford
TRW Huntsville Laboratory

SREM has been extended. Now a requirements-driven model for integrated software engineering environments, SREM has new tools to support its application, the Distributed Computing Design System.

Since its development and initial presentation in 1976, Software Requirements Engineering Methodology, or SREM, technology has evolved in both application and research.[1] The methodology and tools have matured to a point where they are being used on a variety of projects at a number of different locations; the research that led to SREM has been extended to address the problems of specifying system-level requirements and defining a distributed or uniprocessor design that satisfies requirements generated with SREM.

This article overviews developments in these areas and summarizes their results. It also describes the origins of SREM, its basic model of requirements, and how the model is implemented in RSL, the Requirements Statement Language, and supporting software.

An overview of SREM

SREM research was prompted by the observation that the requirements documents produced on a number of projects in the late 1960's did not adequately specify the conditions under which specific actions were to occur. The primary reason for the inadequate specification was determined to be the use of hierarchy-of-functions model for specification of requirements.

As Figure 1a indicates, a hierarchy of functions provides a mechanism for dividing a function into a number of smaller pieces and verifying that the inputs and outputs of the function match those of its decomposition. However, as Figure 1b indicates, the arrival of an input message M1 results in invocation of some sequence of bottom-level functions to process it. The specific sequence of functions selected depends on the values of the message and the current values of program variables; these conditions are usually described in the text of the function's descriptions, not in the model. Because the hierarchy-of-functions model does not explicitly represent the conditions or sequences of processing, requirements generated under it are ambiguous with respect to them. Thus, a great deal of manual effort and interpretation is required to identify the bottom-level functions that should process a specific input message and verify consistency.

The Ballistic Missile Defense Advanced Technology Center, or BM DATC, sponsored SREM research in 1973 in an attempt to formalize and automate techniques for specifying software requirements. The results were a language, RSL,[2] for the statement of software requirements; a set of tools—the Requirements Engineering Validation System, or REVS—to translate the language, perform auto-

Reprinted from *Computer*, Volume 18, Number 4, April 1985, pages 36-46.

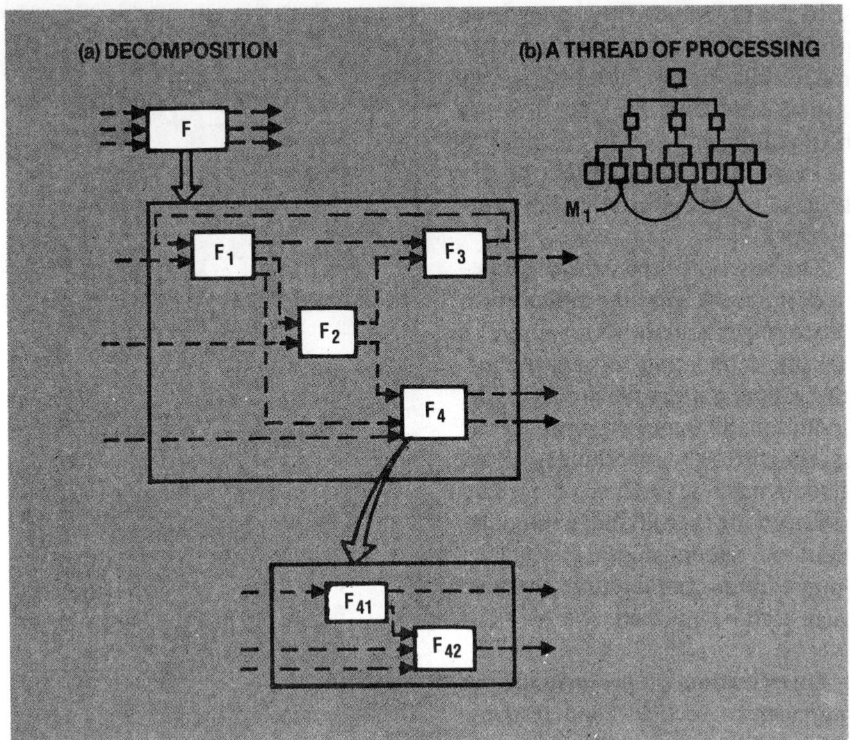

Figure 1. Hierarchy of functions: (a) decomposition, (b) a thread of processing.

and processing. The inputs and outputs are structured into messages that cross interfaces to external subsystems. The state is structured into sets of information about objects the data processor knows; as an object's messages are processed, different types of information about the object are kept. Requirements networks, or R-nets, are used to structure the description of the processing. Each R-net specifies the transformation of a single input message plus current state into some number of output messages plus an updated state. Only one R-net is active at a time, consistent with the state-machine model.

Figure 2 presents the nomenclature of the R-net graph. Each R-net is a graph with nodes representing structural nodes and logic nodes. The R-net includes, at most, one input interface that passes a single input message, some number of output interfaces,

mated consistency and completeness analysis, produce documentation, and generate simulators; and the methodology, SREM, which was expressed as a sequence of steps for generating the requirements through use of the language and tools. These results are described below.

The SREM model of functional requirements. The model of software requirements on which SREM is based is that of a highly structured finite state machine. The state-machine model is used to define processing requirements by specifying a set of inputs and outputs, a set of states, and a function that maps inputs plus current state onto outputs plus updated state. The usual limitation of the state-machine model is its inability to describe complex systems. For example, a state transition diagram can be drawn to represent the state of an elevator that stops at three floors, with buttons as inputs; however, the state transition diagram for 13 elevators that stop at 87 floors is too complex to be represented as a single diagram.

SREM overcomes these difficulties by structuring inputs, outputs, state,

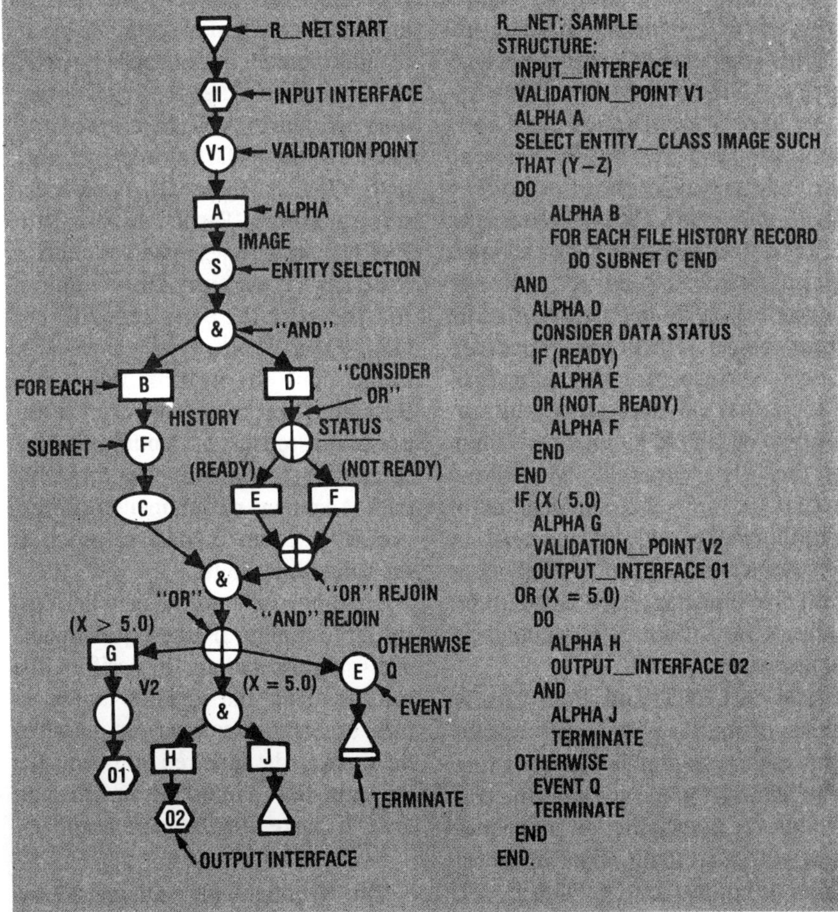

Figure 2. Sample R-net.

some number of ALPHAs specifying transformations, and some number of subnets. The ALPHA, denoted by a rectangle, is used to specify the transformation of an input data set into an output data set, the creation and destruction of state data, and the changing of the kind of state data kept about an object. It can also be used to form a specific output message for an output interface to pass to an external subsystem.

A subnet, represented as an oval, is defined as a processing subgraph with one entrance and one exit point; the subnet is used to show common processing requirements under different conditions and to shorten the length of an R-net.

The graph structure on the R-net uses OR nodes to specify the conditions of processing. Conditions on a path through the graph that leads to an ALPHA imply the conditions under which data are created, accessed, updated, or destroyed. These conditions imply the conditions under which an output message must be produced in response to an input message.

The AND nodes in the graph structure simplify specification of complex processing requirements by representing independent portions of processing. For example, Figure 3 presents an R-net in which processing of an input message can be represented as five independent sets of decisions, each with three choices. The necessary and sufficient condition for this representation is that no data output by any branch of an AND node be input on any other branch. This allows $3 \times 3 \times 3 \times 3 \times 3 = 243$ combinations of output message and state update to be represented in terms of an AND node with five branches, each having three choices, for a total of 15 stimulus-response paths.

The SELECT and FOR_EACH nodes of the R-net are used to select state data to be used in the processing. The SELECT node specifies the conditions for associating an input message with state data about an object called an Entity Class. A FOR_EACH node specifies that each of the elements of a list of data items are to be used for processing. The R-net, thus, provides for explicit specification of the conditions for accessing or updating state data kept about an individual object; thus, it provides the foundation for assuring that no item of data is used before it has been given a value.

The benefits of the structured state-machine model for the statement of processing requirements are several. It lays the foundation for completeness checking (e.g., that the processing has produced all required output messages), consistency checking (e.g., that all data must be produced before it is used), and for specifying the stimulus-response relationships to which response times and accuracy requirements can be attached.

Specification of performance requirements. Accuracy and response-time performance requirements are expressed by means of the concept of a path through the R-nets. A path of processing through an R-net and its associated subnets is specified by attaching named nodes, called *validation points,* onto the R-net graph and then defining the path in terms of a sequence of these validation points (e.g., path V1-V2 in Figure 2). A path can traverse multiple R-nets by using the EVENT node (which enables another R-net) as a connector. The conditions for the path are the sequence of OR_NODE choices that connect its initial point to its terminal point. Response time requirements are expressed in terms of a minimum or maximum response time for a specific path. Accuracy requirements are expressed in terms of data recorded at the validation points.

This approach has the benefit of assuring testability of the requirements and software design; it specifies the measurements that must be taken in order to test the accuracy, and it gives the software designer requirements for the data that should be recorded in order to make the software testable.

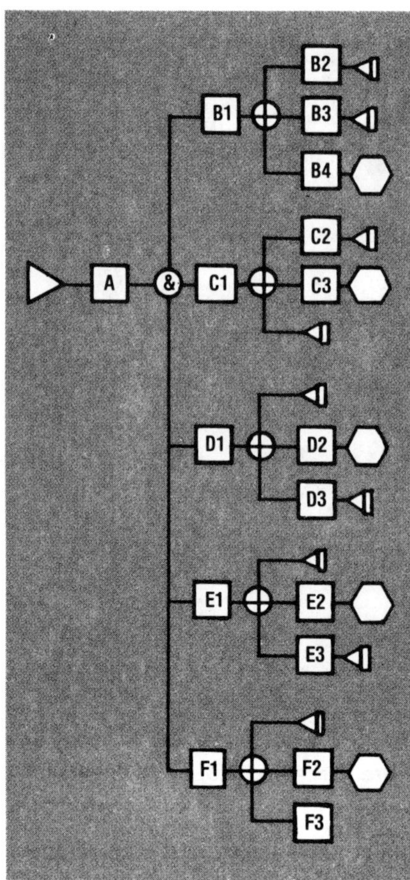

Figure 3. Example of handling complexity.

The Requirements Statement Language. RSL is based on a set of elements, attributes, relationships, and structures. The elements are its nouns, the relationships its verbs, and the attributes its adjectives. The structures describe the graph of processing requirements. RSL uses 21 different kinds of elements, such as the R-nets, ALPHAs, state data, and messages, to represent the features of the requirements model. Each instance of an element has a unique name. A name can have up to 60 characters; this encourages use of self-descriptive names. For example, an ALPHA might be named

DETERMINE_IF_MEASUREMENT_IS_WITHIN_RANGE.

The relationships are expressed in terms of a subject, relationship name, and object; a complementary relationship name links object back to subject. RSL uses 23 relationships to express connections between elements. For example, a specification for an ALPHA to transform one data set into another is expressed by

ALPHA DETERMINE_IF_MEASUREMENT_IS_WITHIN_RANGE. INPUTS DATA MEASURED_POSITION, DATA LIMITS. OUTPUTS DATA WITHIN_RANGE.

The data items that comprise a message are defined by

MESSAGE RADAR_RETURN. MADE BY DATA MEASUREMENT_TIME, DATA MEASURED_RANGE, DATA MEASURED_AZIMUTH, DATA MEASURED_ELEVATION.

The requirement for generation of a specific message at the point when an ALPHA is executed is expressed by

ALPHA A.
FORMS MESSAGE WARNING_MESSAGE.

Whenever the user inputs a relationship to the translator, the complementary relationship is automatically added to the data base as well. This provides automatic cross-referencing capability at the requirements level.

The attributes provide various descriptors of the elements. Every element has an attribute DESCRIPTION, which is used to describe the element; a DATA element might have an additional attribute of UNITS, such as the following:

DATA MEASURED_RANGE.
DESCRIPTION: The range between the radar and the object in track.
UNITS: FEET.

As the above examples show, the syntax of the language is simple. An element is identified, then attribute, relationship, and structure sentences are specified in any order.

RSL provides the R-net and subnet structures for representing the sequences of processing of the SREM graph model. As indicated in Figure 2, the text representation is equivalent to the graphic representation.

RSL is not limited to the specification of processing; it can express other concepts, such as traceability, as well. Additional elements are used to identify source documents, requirements in those source documents, and decisions made in deriving the requirements. A traceability relationship is then used to link these originating requirements and decisions to the lower-level requirements expressed in RSL (e.g., ALPHA, MESSAGE, or SUBNETs). The use of these language constructs provides for automated completeness checking (e.g., that every ORIGINATING_REQUIREMENT traces to some lower-level requirement).

In summary, RSL serves two overall purposes: It provides a checklist of characteristics for requirements specification, and it puts the requirements into a machine-readable form that can be translated into a database for automated consistency and completeness analyses.

Supporting tools. A set of tools, called the Requirements Engineering Validation System, or REVS, was developed to support generation and verification of software requirements using SREM. The tools have six kinds of functions:

(1) *extension* of RSL to tailor it to a specific project,
(2) *translation* of the RSL into an automated database,
(3) *analysis* of the database contents against the consistency and completeness criteria,
(4) *extraction* of information from the database,
(5) *generation* of functional or analytical simulators of the required processing from the requirements specification, and
(6) *generation and display* of graphical descriptions of the R-nets and subnets.

Boehm[3] has recently described the tools' ability to automatically verify requirements.

Methodology description. SREM describes a sequence of steps for defining requirements, expressing them in RSL, and using the tools to check consistency and completeness.

Table 1 gives an overview of the seven phases of SREM, the focus of each phase, and some of the criteria that should be satisfied during each phase. Each phase is broken into a number of lower-level steps. Each step is defined in terms of the subset of RSL generated and the subset of the overall consistency/completeness criteria, which the tools verify. This definition by steps provides a structure for generating the requirements information. For example, Table 1 shows

Table 1. SREM phases and criteria.

	PHASE	FOCUS	CRITERIA
(1)	DEFINE KERNEL	Identify all I/O MESSAGES, R-nets, and ALPHAS.	All input messages processed. All output messages generated.
(2)	ESTABLISH BASELINE	Clean up database. Generate plots of R-nets.	All naming consistent.
(3)	DEFINE DATA	Define data input to and output by each ALPHA.	No data used before given a value.
(4)	ESTABLISH TRACEABILITY	Generate consistent traceability requirements.	All top requirements satisfied.
(5)	SIMULATE FUNCTIONALITY	Simulate DP subsystem functions performed.	Validation that all are processed correctly.
(6)	IDENTIFY PERFORMANCE REQUIREMENTS	Define traceable, testable performance requirements for DP subsystem.	Each path constrained by response time and accuracy.
(7)	DEMONSTRATE FEASIBILITY	Rapid prototype of all critical algorithms.	Accuracy requirements satisfied by prototype algorithms.

that that the R-nets are established before the input-output is finalized and that the traceability from top-level requirements to functional requirements is established before the performance requirements are addressed.

The resulting methodology thus guides the requirements developer through the sequence of steps in which the requirements information should be derived and represented in RSL. As early as possible, the tools should be used to check subsets of the consistency criteria and to provide early detection of errors and some objective management milestones for generating the requirements.

Evolution of SREM. The SREM methodology and tool capabilities are essentially the same today as delivered in 1977. Although the tools were originally developed as proof-of-principle prototypes for use in a batch environment, some of their limitations have been removed. For example, in 1981 the tools were transported to the Vax 11/780, significantly enhancing their utility and availability. In 1983, the database management software was rewritten into Pascal, resulting in a significant increase in their performance on the Vax. Work to enhance the user interface—to, for example, provide an interactive forms-entry capability and improve error diagnostics—is under way.

A working knowledge of SREM is acquired in a standard, two-week training course. The first week consists of lectures with some hands-on experience; the second week concentrates on working through an example with an instructor. As of 1985, over 40 organizations have participated in this type of training course.

Benefits and limitations of SREM. As experience in the application of SREM has grown, a number of its benefits and limitations have emerged. Many of the benefits are direct consequences of SREM's state-machine foundation, including:

- an objective stopping point for requirements specification, which includes definition of all state data and conditions for transforming input messages plus current state into an a set of output messages plus updated state;
- verification of data flow consistency—no item of data is used before it is given a value;
- specification of performance in testable terms (i.e., accuracies of calculation and response time limits of paths of processing); and
- traceability of system-level requirements to processing (software) requirements.

The key concept of SYSREM is that a system function acts over a finite time interval.

Many of the perceived limitations of SREM are also direct consequences of its state-machine foundations:

- SREM forces a requirements engineer to express requirements at a level of detail that conventional development techniques do not usually reach until test planning identifies the stimulus-response threads to be tested. SREM requires more effort during the requirements phase.
- SREM does not specify processing in terms of a hierarchy, which is more familiar than the stimulus-response networks.
- SREM does not directly specify a distributed design because its model assumes that a message is completely processed before the next message is input—although SREM can be used to define requirements for such a design.

These perceived limitations result from a combination of two factors. The first is that SREM specifies a state machine. The second, and more fundamental, factor is that SREM was developed as a stand-alone requirements methodology. It is connected neither to a specific method for specifying system-level requirements and allocating them to a data processor nor to a specific method for translating these requirements into a design. Thus, the relationship between the state-machine level of requirements and the other levels of requirements/design information was not made specific. Subsequent DCDS research addressed these problems.

The systems requirements engineering methodology

The first major extension of the SREM concepts sought to address the problem of defining system requirements and allocating them to the data processing subsystem. The result was called the Systems Requirements Engineering Methodology, or SYSREM. The research leading to SYSREM, conducted from 1977 to 1981, was sponsored by BMDATC. This research extended the SREM state-machine model to represent decomposition and concurrency; it used the same language approach and tools.

Overview of SYSREM. The formal foundation for SYSREM is the graph model of decomposition.[4] System requirements are specified in terms of time functions, their decompositions, and their allocation to system components.

The key concept of SYSREM is that a system function acts over a finite interval of time; this system action is represented as a time function that accepts items arriving during the time interval and transforms them into items that are output during the time interval. An item that the function inputs or outputs can be decomposed into sequences and allowed concurrencies of lower-level items. A time function is thus specified in terms of its input items, output items, invariants of its transformation, completion criteria (anything that causes the system to stop performing a function and switch to some subsequent mode of operation), and performance. Performance is defined in terms of one or more metrics describing the efficiency or accuracy of transformation of the input to the output items.

A decomposition of a function is defined as a graph of lower-level functions that must preserve

- any input and output sequences specified,
- any invariants of the transformation,
- the number and kinds of completion criteria (reasons for exiting the function), and
- performance traceability (the original performance function must be computable from the performance functions of the lower-level functions).

The graph model of decomposition has several unique characteristics, which are illustrated by application to the following patient monitoring problem[1,3]:

A hospital requires a patient monitoring program. An analog device monitors each patient's pulse, temperature, blood-pressure, and skin resistance. The program reads these factors at intervals specified for each patient and stores them in a database. For each patient, safe ranges for each factor are specified—for example, patient X's valid temperature range is 98 to 99.5°F. If a factor falls outside the patient's safe range or if an analog device fails, the system notifies the nurse's station.

The unique features of the SYSREM solution to this problem include the following:

(1) *Both sequences and concurrency are represented.* As illustrated in Figure 4, the function MONITOR PATIENTS is decomposed into a replication of concurrent activities, each of which monitors a single patient. The function MONITOR A PATIENT is then decomposed into a sequence of functions—first, CONNECT PATIENT, then MEASURE AND MONITOR PATIENT, then DISCONNECT PATIENT. Thus, the graph explicitly shows that any patient must be connected before being monitored, but that one patient can be in the process of being connected while another is being disconnected.

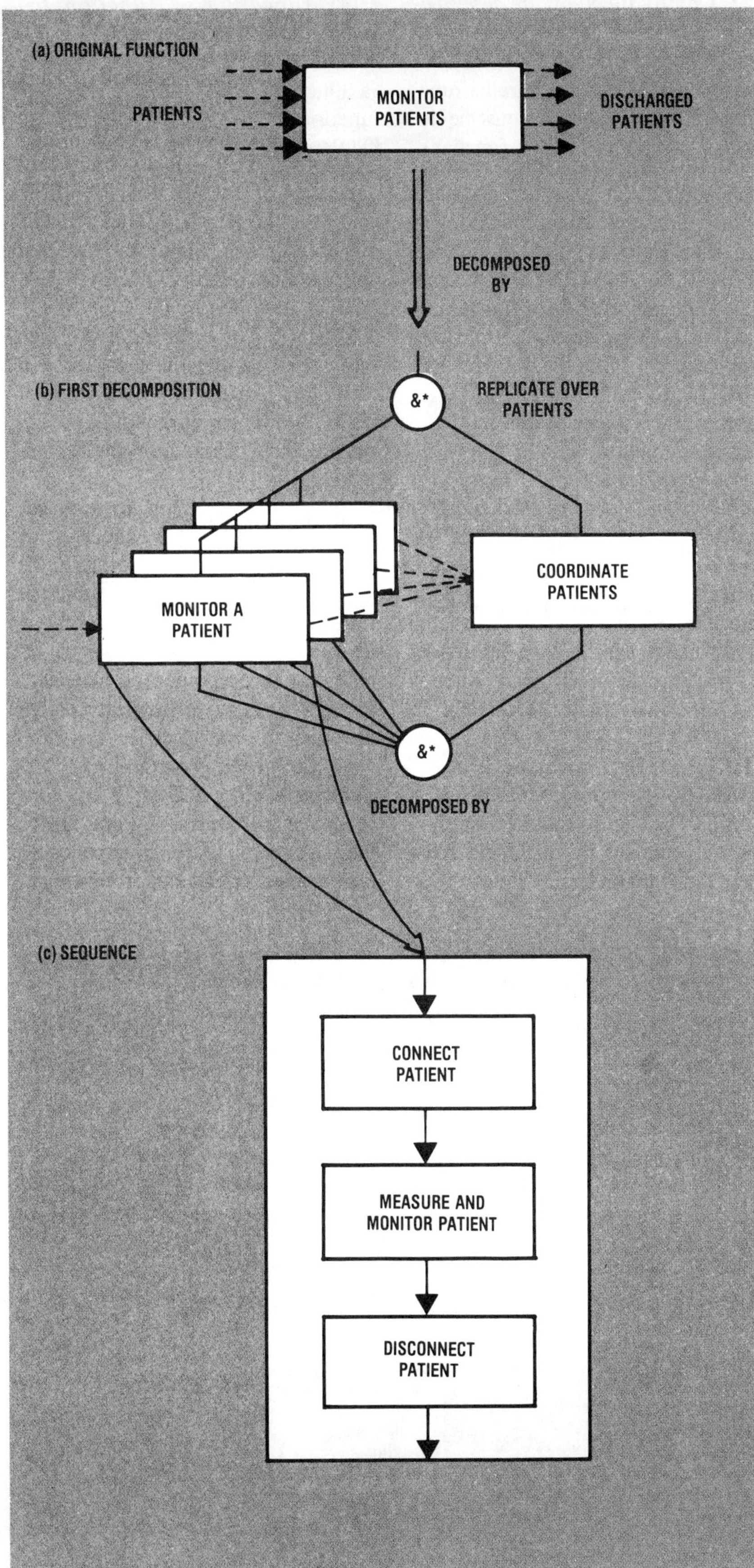

Figure 4. Example SYSREM decompositions: (a) original function, (b) first decomposition, (c) sequence.

(2) *Control functions are derived as an integral part of the decomposition activity.* Whenever a function is decomposed into a set of parallel functions, a control function must be defined to coordinate these functions. This control function accepts status information and issues controls. Figure 4 illustrates this fact: A function MONITOR PATIENTS is decomposed into a replication of functions to monitor each patient and into a control function, COORDINATE PATIENTS, to control conflicts. In this case, conflicts would be due only to resource competition.

(3) *Performance and function are simultaneously decomposed.* Suppose that a performance index of the system is the maximum time it takes to detect and raise an alarm when pulse rate drops for any patient. The overall performance can be decomposed by associating the performance index MAXIMUM TIME TO DETECT AND RAISE AN ALARM FOR THIS PATIENT[3] with each of the lower-level functions MONITOR A PATIENT. The overall maximum response time can be calculated from these individual response times.

(4) *Allocation of function sequences and concurrency to components is another unique feature.* Figure 5a illustrates decomposition of the function MEASURE AND MONITOR PATIENT into concurrent functions of MEASURE PATIENT and MONITOR MEASUREMENTS for each patient. Figure 4 shows that this happens after CONNECT PATIENT and before DISCONNECT PATIENT. These functions are then allocated between the measurement and data processing subsystems. Thus, both concurrency and sequences are required of these components.

(5) *Interface designs are derived.* Figure 5b shows how the allocation of functions to components results in the definition of an interface function that transfers information between subsystems. This interface function is repetitively decomposed and allocated, to yield the layers of interface design necessary to connect the subsystems.

(6) *Exceptions are addressed by defining an additional layer of functions to detect and recover from faults.* Fault detection thus corresponds to taking an exception exit from a function in the standard layer into the layer containing fault-handling functions; fault recovery then corresponds to a transition back to the standard layer.

(7) *The maximum concurrency of the required processing is exposed.* It is exploited later, during the distributed design phase.

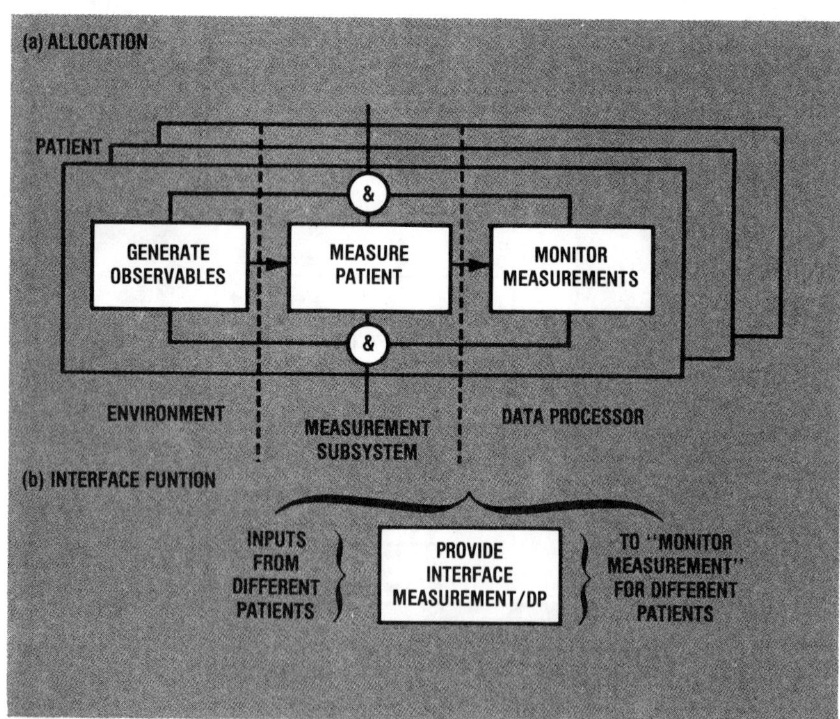

Figure 5. Decomposition of MEASURE AND MONITOR PATIENT; (a) allocation, (b) interface function.

SYSREM/SREM interface. The model used at the system level defines and allocates time functions to a data processing component. These functions are further decomposed to the level at which they accept discrete messages. If the interfaces are serialized (an input must be processed before the next input is addressed), the result is exactly a finite-state machine. These functions can be further decomposed, to the stimulus-response level, by representing them in terms of subnets of RSL, thus yielding the structured state machine of SREM—and providing a smooth transition from system to software requirements. The system specification language was defined to express these concepts.

SSL blends into RSL by relating system-level functions and items to software-level subnets, R-nets, and data. The SSL and RSL languages are thus interlocked and can be viewed as a single language with subsets applying to system and software requirements. Similarly, the methodology steps are interlocked: The end point of SYSREM provides all the information necessary to perform the steps of SREM.

Status. SYSREM is today in a state similar to that of SREM in 1977-78. A SYSREM training course has been developed and used to transfer the technology to several projects.

Distributed computing design system

One of the most significant limitations of SREM was that it left the transition from requirements to design to the ingenuity of the developers. To address this problem, BMDATC in 1981 sponsored research toward a Distributed Computing Design System, or DCDS.

The purpose of this ongoing research is to develop and integrate design languages and tools into the SYSREM/SREM baseline. These languages and tools are to increase reliability and productivity by developing a software engineering environment to record and control the development of requirements, design, code, and tests for a distributed data processing subsystem. Figure 6 presents a conceptual view of the end product: an integrated set of languages, tools, databases, and methods that spans the entire software development cycle.

This research is built on two sets of previous research: the SYSREM/SREM work discussed above, and Mariani and Palmer's[5] approach, also sponsored by BMDATC, to designing distributed processing. A great many published papers have described the results of research on distributed design issues, special problems of communication protocols, distributed database control, distributed failure detection and recovery, etc., but none has demonstrated clear traceability to requirements. The intent of the DCDS is to provide a structure for deriving and considering such problems in a requirements-driven way—and thus eliminate problems of manually translating requirements information into a different representation in order to initiate design. DCDS provides tools to detect and correct errors early and to produce a structure that can be modified and maintained with less effort.

DCDS key concept. The key concept of the DCDS research is the recognition that the SYSREM concepts can be used to define a software design by allocating required processing and state data onto units of code and data structures. The interfaces between these units of code are decomposed and allocated to the level of the functions of the distributed operating system. Fault tolerance is achieved by adding functions to detect and recover from errors, then decomposing and allocating them to units of code assigned to specific processors.

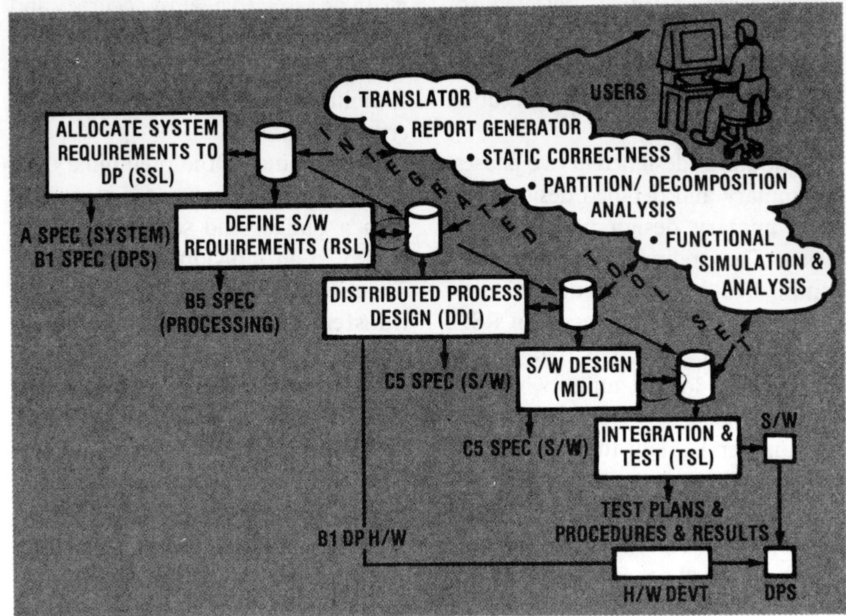

Figure 6. DCDS integrated languages and tools.

A significant result of the research is the recognition that this design model supports separation of the concerns of distributed design from those of algorithm design. Distributed design addresses the problem of selecting the data processor architecture and mapping the required processing onto this architecture to meet the timing and sizing requirements—in other words, it is programming in the large. Module design addresses the problem of constructing the algorithms that accomplish the required transformations and satisfy the overall accuracy requirements; module design is programming in the small. Figure 7 illustrates this approach.

Module design. A module can be viewed as a unit of engineering work in designing and developing an algorithm to accomplish a required transformation. Given no constraints on processor utilization or response time, the first algorithm that satisfies the ac-

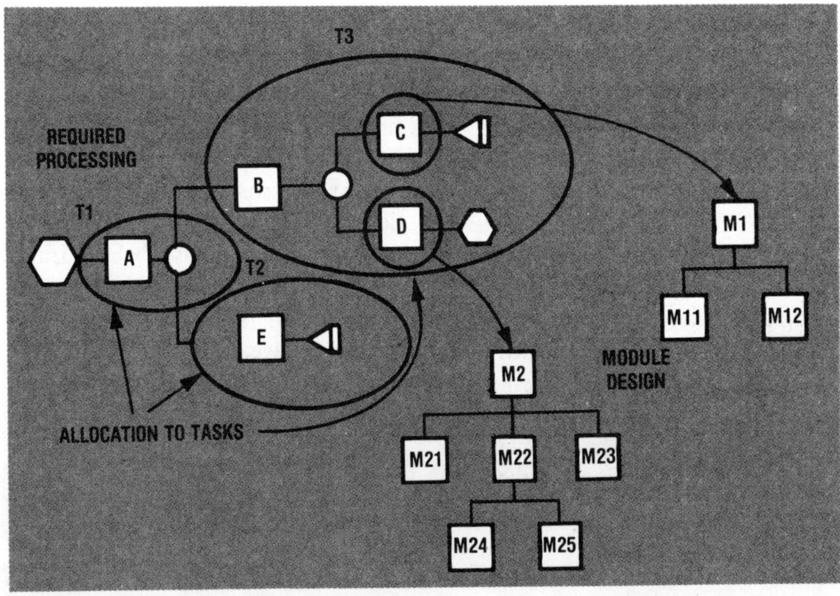

Figure 7. Allocation of required processing to modules and tasks.

curacy requirements is selected for use. Real-time embedded software usually requires more algorithm design effort in order to meet execution time constraints.

A module is designed in two phases, preliminary and detailed design, with a preliminary design review in between. The preliminary design is accomplished by partitioning the required processing, expressed in RSL, into modules. Required data is partitioned into logical units, which are assigned logical types (e.g., an array of real numbers). Algorithms are defined to perform the transformation required of the module; this can result in the definition of lower-level modules and thus a need for further design. In any case, construction preserves the stimulus-response and data-flow properties of the requirements.

The mapping of required processing and data onto modules and data structures is expressed in the Module Design Language; thus, RSL and MDL interlock. For the patient monitoring problem, one might record a design as follows:

```
MODULE COMPARE_LIMITS.
CONSTITUTES ALPHA: COMPARE_ MEASUREMENT_TO_
LIMITS.
INPUTS VARIABLE
V_MEASUREMENT.
OUTPUTS VARIABLE
V_RESULT.
VARIABLE V_RESULT.
REPRESENTS DATA
MEASUREMENT_STATUS.
RANGE: (ALARM, WARNING,
OK).
```

A module design is expressed in terms of a hierarchy of modules; a program design language, or PDL, can be used to express the logic of each module. Several candidate design approaches can be defined in the Module Design Language. The designer estimates sizing and timing for the algorithms and assesses accuracy characteristics. The designer selects an algorithm approach from these candidates before the preliminary design review, so that it can be assessed against accuracy and loading requirements. Tools are used to verify that the design preserves stimulus-response and data flow properties.

By the time of the preliminary design review, each module is associated with a budget and schedule and assigned to an individual programmer. The preliminary design information is transferred to a unit development folder.[6] For each module, an automated unit development folder tool maintains schedule and status, requirements and design descriptions, a PDL description of the design, test plans, code, and test results.

The distributed design methodology can be viewed as having distributed and task design phases.

In summary, the preliminary design of the modules is performed and recorded in a Module Design Language, and the SREM tools are used to check the consistency/completeness criteria. The detailed design, code, and unit testing employs an automated version of the unit development folder to record all intermediate results. This information base becomes invaluable during integration testing, maintenance, and production of the required design documentation.

Distributed design. The distributed design methodology can be viewed as having two major phases: the distributed process design phase, which defines a configuration of processors, allocates required processing and data to the processors, and verifies satisfaction of required response times; and the task design phase, which transforms this logical design into the design of the units of code in a programming language.

The purpose of the distributed process design is to make the design decisions necessary for transforming the requirements on the data processing subsystem, or DPS, into sets of requirements for hardware/software "processes" and their interprocess communication network. In order to address internode design, the decomposition of processes should proceed to the level that permits packaging the requirements for each single processor. The distributed process design defines the system-wide communication protocols, process schedulers, and design standards that affect the multiple nodes of the DPS. The distributed process design must also address DPS-level requirements for reliability, fault tolerance, reconfiguration, growth, and other ". . .ilities."

As Figure 8 indicates, there are four potential levels of a processor distribution: geographical distribution, local network distribution, computer system distribution, and hardware/software distribution. Each level must address a unique set of problems and trade-offs. The constraints, design variables, and objective functions that drive the design activity vary from one level of design to the next.

Allocation of processing to nodes must balance delay time of intranode communication against the nonfunctional requirements for automomy. Allocation of data to geographic nodes must balance the communication delays of remote access of a single copy of data against replication of the data to achieve tolerance to a single-point failure and against the added complexity of maintaining replicated database consistency. A feasible allocation must satisfy several kinds of constraints: response times must be met, execution time and memory size limitations must not be exceeded at any processing node, and communication resources must not be overloaded. Thus, distributed process design follows the same order described in SYSREM: allocation, interface design, resource estimation, and definition of fault-detection and recovery functions.

The Distributed Design Language is used to define the software processes, their allocation to processor nodes, and their relationships to the software requirements-level R-nets, subnets, and data. The DCDS tools are used to verify the completeness of the allocation. The allocation of processing to tasks—that is, scheduled units of

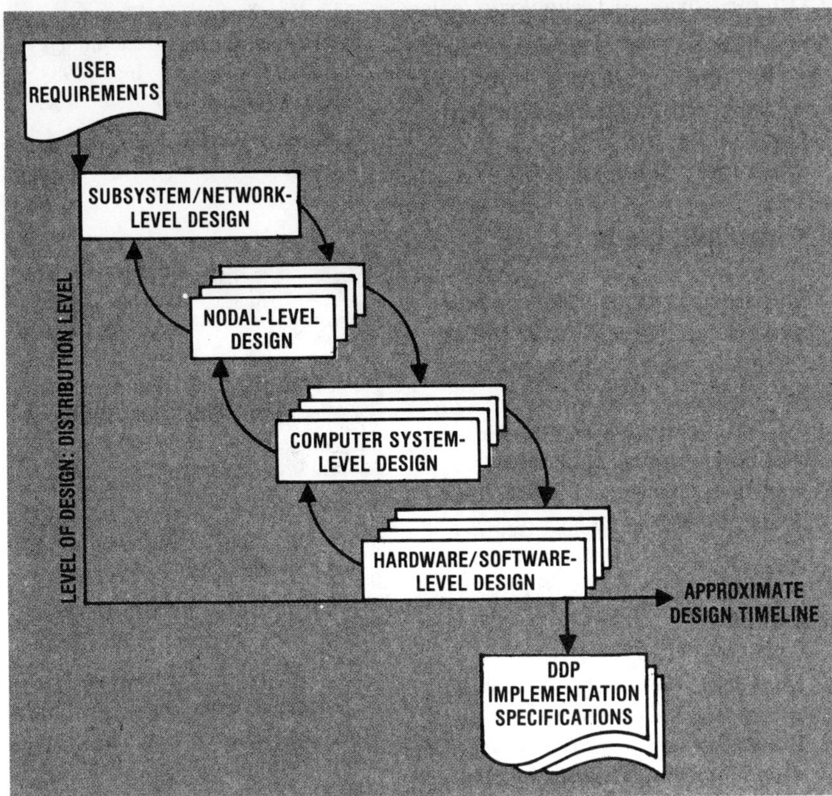

Figure 8. Levels of distributed design.

code—is expressed in a similar fashion. The task read/write relationships to the logical data structures of buffers, messages, and files are recorded. Tools are used to verify that the distributed design preserves the data flow and stimulus-response properties of the requirements. Simulation verifies satisfaction of response times as well as processor and communication constraints.

The process design is complete when the tasks, their scheduling rules, and data structures have been identified and are shown to meet all response times and constraints.

Task design. Task design translates the process design into a design to be coded in a programming language. The logical design phase defines the overall design of the task in terms of a PDL definition of the sequences of reads, writes, and invocations of modules. The physical design then maps this logical design onto data structures and algorithms coded in the selected programming language.

This approach provides for the natural identification of data objects, proposed by Booch[7] and others, for an object-oriented design. The RSL processing requirements define the conditions under which state data is created, selected, accessed, updated, and destroyed. The database is designed by the selection of a data structure and procedures for performing the required data manipulations. The programming language's runtime library or a reusable set of data management utilities can provide these procedures. The data objects can be derived by noting that the allocation of processing between tasks gives rise to the requirement for an interface function between them; this interface function can be decomposed and allocated between a requirement to provide a data object (allocated to the data management system) and requirements for the tasks to use specific read/write mechanisms.

During the physical design phase, the logical data structures are assigned to data structures and declarations, and the logical tasks are coded in the selected programming language. As with the module design, the automated unit development folder tool manages development of the task. A distributed process construction tool uses the DDL definition of design to extract units of code from the AUDF and combine them with operating system code in order to generate the total source code for each node of the distributed processor.

In summary, the Distributed Design Methodology uses a Distributed Design Language to provide traceability from requirements to design and to assure that the stimulus-response and data flow properties of the design are preserved. In addition, the design adds features for detection and recovery from exceptions, thus providing the fault-tolerance features of the design.

Status. An earlier version of the Distributed Design Methodology was successfuly used for the design of a 10-node distributed processing system with software coded in Pascal. TRW in Huntsville is demonstrating the latest version of the methodology and tools with both Pascal and Ada as the target programming languages. Training courses are being developed to initiate transfer of the technology and tools. A Test Specification Language and methodology are also being developed to link the requirements, design, and tests and to verify test coverage completeness.

After eight years of additional research and application, the following conclusion can be made:

(1) SREM demonstrates that it is practical to express processing requirements in terms of a structured finite-state machine. If the effort of test planning and correction of errors discovered during testing are taken into account, SREM appears to require less effort than traditional approaches.

(2) The SREM state-machine model has been extended to address system requirements and designs by representing time sequencing, concurrency, allocation, interface design, fault tolerance, and performance. This ex-

tended model provides a fresh view of the system/software design process.

(3) The sequence of languages—SSL/RSL/MDL/DDL/TSL—is an example of a unified approach to representing intermediate products of software development.

(4) A prototype set of tools sufficient to demonstrate the viability of the approach supports the methodology and languages. Additional productizing of the tools would bring additional benefits to users.

(5) A baseline, requirements-driven methodology that spans the entire life cycle has been developed. It is currently under evaluation to assess its ability to meet its goals of increased reliability and productivity.

During the past eight years, research has been aimed at making SREM evolve into a complete software engineering environment. Considerable growth potential remains, in terms of turning the tools into marketable products, upgrading the technology transfer mechanisms and materials, and extending the DCDS framework to, for example, exploit the state-machine foundations by interfacing with program-proof techniques. □

Acknowledgments

This article presents results of projects sponsored by the Ballistic Missile Defense Advanced Technology Center under contracts DSAS60-78-C-0158 and DASG60-81-C-0059 and by the US Air Force, Rome Air Development Center, under contracts F30602-78-C-0026 and F30602-84-C-0123.

References

1. M. Alford, "A Requirements Engineering Methodology for Real Time Processing Requirements," *IEEE Trans. Software Engineering,* Vol. SE-3, No. 1, Jan. 1977, pp. 60-69.
2. T. E. Bell, D. C. Bixler, and M. E. Dyer, "An Extendable Approach to Computer Aided Software Requirements Engineering," *IEEE Trans., Software Engineering,* Vol. SE-3, No. 1, Jan. 1977, pp. 49-60.
3. B. Boehm, "Verifying and Validating Software Requirements and Design Specifications," *IEEE Software,* Vol. 1, No. 1, Jan. 1984, pp. 75-88.
4. M. Alford. "Requirements for Distributed Data Processing Design," *Proc. First Int'l Conf. Distributed Computing Systems,* Pub. No. CH1445, IEEE Computer Society, Los Alamitos, Calif., Oct. 1979,,pp. 1-14.
5. M. P. Mariani et al., *Tutorial: Distributed System Design,* presented at First Int'l Conf. Distributed Computing Systems, Oct. 1979.
6. B. Boehm, *Software Engineering Economics,* Prentice-Hall, Englewood Cliffs, N.J., 1981, pp. 607-612.
7. G. Booch, *Softwre Engineering with Ada,* The Benjamin/Cummings Publishing Company, Inc., 1983, pp. 220-228.

Mack W. Alford is the chief scientist at TRW's Huntsville Engineering and Software Development Facility. He is also the principle investigator of the Distributed Computing Design System project sponsored by BMDATC. His principal research interest is the integration of various system and software design methods into a single structure spanning the entire software development life cycle.

Alford joined TRW in 1961 and started research into software requirements techniques in 1968. He was the manager of the Requirements Engineering Interface Department on the Site Defense Project in 1972-73. He was responsible for methodology development on the SREM project, developed the SREM training classes. and applied SREM to several projects. He was the project manager of the DCDS project and its predecessors from 1978 until 1983.

Alford attended UCLA and received a BA degree in mathematics in 1962, an MA in 1966, and performed postgraduate work as a TRW fellow during 1970-1973.

Questions concerning this article can be addressed to the author at TRW, 213 Wynn Drive, Huntsville, AL 35805.

PSL/PSA at the Age of Fifteen

Hasan H. Sayani
Advanced Systems Technology Corp. (ASTEC)

1: Introduction

The Problem Statement Language (PSL) and the Problem Statement Analyzer (PSA) were first described in 1971 [1]. PSL™ was introduced in that paper as the equivalent of a blueprinting language for an information systems "factory," and PSA™ as the software to support its usage. This first version (1) was used mainly by the sponsors of the Information Systems Design and Optimization System (ISDOS) project at the University of Michigan. A more widely introduced version, 2.1, was described in an IEEE paper in 1977 [2].

Our goal in this paper is to describe PSL/PSA, to lend a perspective to the changes that have taken place in the PSL/PSA system over 15 years, to examine its acceptance by the information systems community, to portray a scenario of usage, and to comment on the trends in the industry that not only affect PSL/PSA but also similar productivity tools that are now becoming available in the industry.

2: Description of PSL/PSA

2.1: Problem Statement Language

PSL is based on the concept of the Entity-Relationship-Attribute (ERA) model, although at the time of its design the ERA terminology had not been coined. PSL's underpinnings allow up to four Entity-types to participate in a Relationship. Entities may have Attributes and may play roles in a relationship. Because these relationship-roles are not formalized, they cannot have Attributes assigned to them.

The designers of PSL felt that a specification language user must be supplied with constructs appropriate for the task at hand. Therefore, PSL has a set of predefined classes of Entities (e.g., PROCESS, INPUT, ELEMENT, EVENT), Relationships (e.g., EMPLOYS, UPDATES, TRIGGERS), Attributes (e.g., TRACEKEY) and a set of rules (the constructs of the language) which permit only prescribed combinations. One can think of PSL/PSA, therefore, as an application built on top of a generalized Entity Relationship Attribute Management System (ERAMS) with a predefined data definition. However, many of the reports produced by PSA do have semantic knowledge of PSL, e.g., the Contents Reports recognizes Completeness in the context of PSL's data structuring features.

PSL has three levels of formality to describe a system:

- very formal: using only predefined Entity-types and Relationships
- semi-formal: adding user-defined properties
- informal: attaching free form text to entities.

This three-level approach offers users controlled extensibility of the language while still providing the functionality of PSA.

PSL has about 19 Entity-types and about 100 Relationship-types. It helps in understanding PSL to group the types by the "aspect" of system description. Figure 1 summarizes these aspects. Some PSA reports work at the lower granularity of Entities and Relationships while others require the specification of the higher granularity of aspects.

PSL statements are written in free-form and recognized by keywords. Examples of these will be shown later.

2.2: Problem Statement Analyzer

PSA is the software package that manages PSL statements. It can be thought of as a data-based application with the following categories of functionality:

- the *modification* of the database, including the updating and changing of its contents. The database is modified without compromising the integrity of the underlying language
- the *display* of information in the database as predesigned reports; the display feature includes an ad hoc query system
- the *analysis* of information in the database; this analysis focuses on errors of omission and on the production of numeric and cross-referenced summaries
- it permits *control* of the PSA environment

Aspects Applicable to All Principal PSL Objects:
- *Properties and Characteristics*
  - parametric (user extensible) and textual
- *Project Management*
  - provides cross-reference and assignment of definitional responsibilities
- *Requirements Traceability*
  - allocation of requirements to specific components

Information Flow Aspects:
- *System Boundary and Input/Output Flow*
  - shows how the system exchanges data with its environment
- *Data Derivation and Flow*
  - depicts transformation of data within the system
  - allows specification of "right to know"

Architectural Aspects:
- *System Structure*
  - architectural relationships between major components
- *Data Structure*
  - detailed relationships between data objects
  - includes architectural, relational (as in ERA) and security

Behavioral Aspects:
- *System Dynamics*
  - response of system to recognized happenings, changes in situations, and time triggers
- *System Control*
  - shows precedence of Processes and their invocation by others

Performance Aspects:
- *Quantification and Resource Usage*
  - addresses performance and size related specifications

Project Convenience Aspects:
- *Generic Structure*
  - makes it convenient to group, link, or name objects in an ad hoc fashion.

Figure 1: Facets of Systems Development with Appropriate Aspects Provided by PSL

The actual commands, summarized by these categories, are described in Figure 2.

The core architecture of PSL/PSA is summarized in Figure 3.

PSA may be used with varying degrees of interaction. The major modes are:

- *interactive*: PSA commands typed at the terminal and PSA prompts, error messages, and reports received on the terminal
- *batch*: PSA executing commands from a file containing a sequence of commands and without prompting; writing error messages and reports to a file or designated printer
- *monitored*: similar to batch mode but echoing the commands being executed and displaying messages on the terminal

Modification Commands	Analysis Commands
CHANGE NAME	ACCESS RIGHTS ANALYSIS
CHANGE NAME TYPE	ASSERTION CONSISTENCY
COMBINE	CONTENTS ANALYSIS
DELETE NAME	CONTENTS COMPARISON
DELETE TEXT ENTRY	DATA ACTIVITY INTERACTION
INPUT LAYOUT	DYNAMIC INTERACTION
LANGUAGE PROCESSOR	ELEMENT PROCESS ANALYSIS
PROBLEM NAME	ELEMENT PROCESS USAGE
REPLACE TEXT ENTRY	IDENTIFIER ANALYSIS
	RESOURCE CONSUMPTION ANALYSIS
Display Commands	SUBSET ANALYSIS
ACTIVITY FLOW DIAGRAM	UTILIZES ANALYSIS
ATTRIBUTE	
CONTENTS	**Control (of environment) Commands**
DATA DIVISION	COMMAND
DATABASE SUMMARY	DISPLAY
DICTIONARY	EXPAND
EXTENDED PICTURE	HELP
FREQUENCY	LIST
FUNCTION FLOW DATA DIAGRAM	LOOP
KEYWORD IN CONTEXT	MACRO
LAYOUT	SET
LIST CHANGES	STOP
NAME LIST	SYSTEM
NAME SELECTION	
NETWORK	**Modification Commands**
PICTURE	
PROCESS CHAIN	CHANGE NAME
PROCESS SUMMARY	CHANGE NAME TYPE
QUERY SYSTEM	COMBINE
RELATION STRUCTURE	DELETE NAME
SELECTED FORMATTED STATEMENTS	DELETE TEXT ENTRY
STRING SELECTION	INPUT LAYOUT
STRUCTURE	LANGUAGE PROCESSOR
UNIT STRUCTURE	PROBLEM NAME
WRITE TEXT ENTRY	REPLACE TEXT ENTRY

Figure 2: Summary of PSA Commands by Category

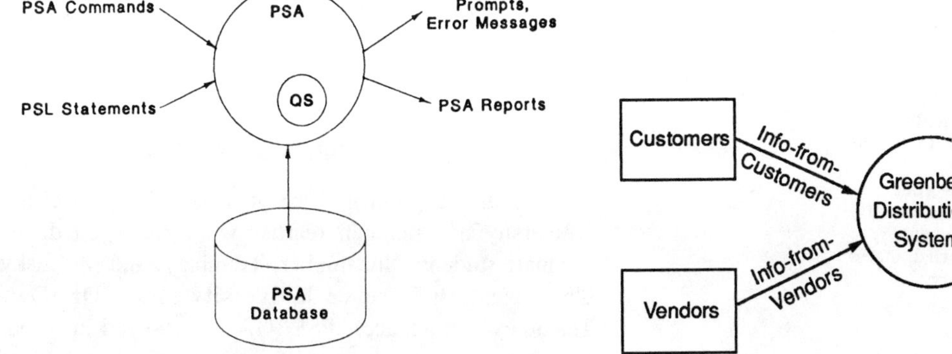

Figure 3: Core Architecture of PSL/PSA

Figure 4: Context Diagram for a System

2.3: Examples of PSL/PSA

Figure 4 shows a context diagram of the type suggested by the Structured Analysis Methodology [3]. This diagram is a graphic specification of the top-level view of a system. The PSL statements in Figure 5 are a linguistic equivalent of the graphic.

PSL Statements for Greenbelt-Distribution System

```
DEFINE PROCESS          Greenbelt-Distribution-System;
      RECEIVES          Info-from-Customers,
                        Info-from-Vendors;
      GENERATES         Info-to-Customers,
                        Info-to-Vendors;

DEFINE INTERFACE        Customers;
      GENERATES         Info-from-Customers;
      RECEIVES          Info-to-Customers;

DEFINE INTERFACE        Vendors;
      GENERATES         Info-from-Vendors;
      RECEIVES          Info-to-Vendors;
```

Figure 5: Context Level View of a System

The three "DEFINE" paragraphs, "sections" in PSL, can be specified in any order; similarly the non-DEFINE statements may be rearranged within a (DEFINE) section. These PSL statements would fit into PSL/PSA's Information Flow aspect of system specification.

Further refinement of the system, the specification of a hierarchy of functions underlying the Greenbelt-Distribution-System, would be part of PSL/PSA's System Structure aspect. The PSA Structure report would depict this as shown in Figure 6. The actual PSA command is shown just before the report output.

If the Data Derivation and Flow aspect had been specified at these lower levels of refinement, it could be displayed as the Activity Flow Diagram of Figure 7.

structure relations=subparts name=Greenbelt-Distribution-System nostatistics - noobject-types norelation-types noline-numbers

```
1       Greenbelt-Distribution-System
 2        accounting
  3         accounts-receivable
   4          prepare-customer-invoices
   4          receive-customer-payments
   4          review-receivables
  3         accounts-payable
   4          receive-vendor-invoices
   4          schedule-payments
   4          send-payments-to-vendors
  3         general-ledger
  3         process-customer-order
   4          evaluate-customer-credit
   4          authorize-shipment
   4          send-letter-to-customers
  3         reconcile-inventory
 2        receiving
 2        stocking
 2        shipping
```

Figure 6: Hierarchy of the System

activity-flow-diagram name=Greenbelt-Distribution-System

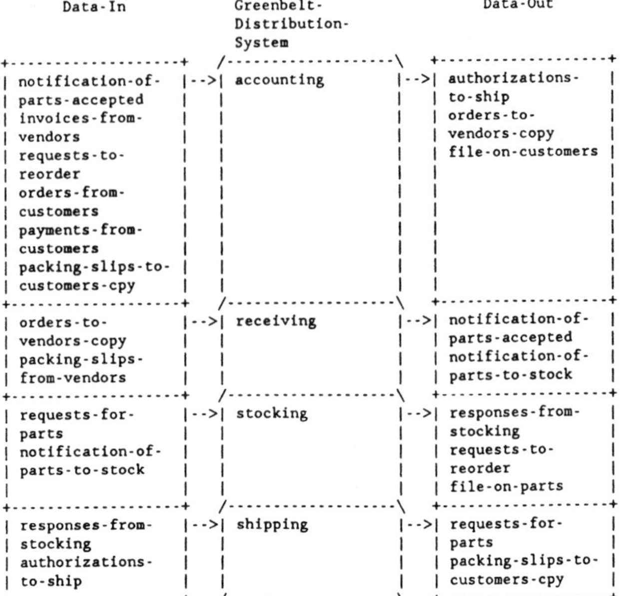

```
        Data-In              Greenbelt-                 Data-Out
                             Distribution-
                             System
+-------------------+   /-------------------\   +-------------------+
| notification-of-  |-->| accounting        |-->| authorizations-   |
| parts-accepted    |   |                   |   | to-ship           |
| invoices-from-    |   |                   |   | orders-to-        |
| vendors           |   |                   |   | vendors-copy      |
| requests-to-      |   |                   |   | file-on-customers |
| reorder           |   |                   |   |                   |
| orders-from-      |   |                   |   |                   |
| customers         |   |                   |   |                   |
| payments-from-    |   |                   |   |                   |
| customers         |   |                   |   |                   |
| packing-slips-to- |   |                   |   |                   |
| customers-cpy     |   |                   |   |                   |
+-------------------+   /-------------------\   +-------------------+
| orders-to-        |-->| receiving         |-->| notification-of-  |
| vendors-copy      |   |                   |   | parts-accepted    |
| packing-slips-    |   |                   |   | notification-of-  |
| from-vendors      |   |                   |   | parts-to-stock    |
+-------------------+   /-------------------\   +-------------------+
| requests-for-     |-->| stocking          |-->| responses-from-   |
| parts             |   |                   |   | stocking          |
| notification-of-  |   |                   |   | requests-to-      |
| parts-to-stock    |   |                   |   | reorder           |
|                   |   |                   |   | file-on-parts     |
+-------------------+   /-------------------\   +-------------------+
| responses-from-   |-->| shipping          |-->| requests-for-     |
| stocking          |   |                   |   | parts             |
| authorizations-   |   |                   |   | packing-slips-to- |
| to-ship           |   |                   |   | customers-cpy     |
+-------------------+   /-------------------\   +-------------------+
```

Figure 7: Hierarchy of Inputs, Outputs and Processes

The structure of data can also be specified, and the System Structures (macro view) and Data Structure (micro view) aspects of the system's specification is portrayed in Figure 8.

The behavior of the system can be described by PSL statements of the System Dynamics aspect. The Process-Chain Report could illustrate these specifications graphically (Figure 9).

Entities described in the database can be selected by user-specified criteria and can be presented in an order specified through the Name Selection command as shown in Figure 10.

An encyclopedic view of any Entity can be obtained with the Selected-Formatted Statements command as shown in the italicized type in Figure 11.

Finally, a Query System permits ad hoc queries about any information in the database. Figure 12 illustrates three queries with the italics indicating the intent of the queries.

In this section we have described the architecture and capabilities of the core PSL/PSA which can play a key role in a larger environment with the addition of ancillary tools and access (bridges) to other tools. To appreciate this larger architecture, we now present a brief history of the evolution of PSL/PSA.

3: Evolution of PSL/PSA

Since its inception in 1968 at the ISDOS project at the University of Michigan (earlier work had been done by graduate students Nunamaker, Tremblay, and McCusky at Case Western Reserve University under Dr. Daniel Teichroew's guidance), PSL/PSA has evolved in response to pressures from the market. Figure 13 shows a quick snapshot of major events.

structure relations=subparts name=info-from-customers nostatistics - noobject-types norelation-types noline-numbers

```
1       info-from-customers
 2          payments-from-customers
 2          orders-from-customers
```

contents name=orders-from-customers

```
 1* (INPUT)      1 orders-from-customers
 1 (GROUP)         2  order-form-num+date-of-order
 2 (ELEMENT)        3    order-form-number
 3 (ELEMENT)        3    date-of-order
 4 (ELEMENT)       2  date-of-order
 5 (GROUP)         2  customer-name
 6 (ELEMENT)        3    first-name
 7 (ELEMENT)        3    middle-name
 8 (ELEMENT)        3    last-name
 9 (GROUP)         2  customer-address
10 (ELEMENT)        3    customer-street-no-and-name
11 (ELEMENT)        3    mail-stop (optional)
12 (ELEMENT)        3    customer-city
13 (ELEMENT)        3    customer-state
14 (ELEMENT)        3    customer-zip
15 (GROUP)         2  order-line (repeats)
16 (ELEMENT)        3    part-number-ordered
17 (ELEMENT)        3    quantity-ordered
18 (ELEMENT)        3    description-of-part-ordered
19 (ELEMENT)        3    total-of-part-ordered
20 (ELEMENT)       2  sub-total-of-this-order
21 (ELEMENT)       2  handling-and-postage
22 (ELEMENT)       2  TOTAL-this-order
23 (GROUP)         2  credit-card-info (may-be-blank)
24 (ELEMENT)        3    type-of-credit-card
25 (ELEMENT)        3    customer-card-number
26 (ELEMENT)        3    date-of-expiration
27 (GROUP)         2  catalog-reference-number
28 (ELEMENT)        3    retail-reference-price
29 (ELEMENT)        3    retail-original-price
30 (ELEMENT)        3    retail-sale-price
31 (ELEMENT)       2  retail-price
```

Figure 8: Macro and Micro View of Selected Input

name-selection selection='match=?customer?' order=alpha

```
 1 customer-address                   GROUP
 2 customer-card-number               ELEMENT
 3 customer-city                      ELEMENT
 4 customer-invoice-number            ELEMENT
 5 customer-name                      GROUP
 6 customer-number                    ELEMENT
 7 customer-order-date                ELEMENT
 8 customer-order-history             GROUP
 9 customer-order-history-ytd         GROUP
10 customer-order-number              ELEMENT
11 customer-orders-initialization     EVENT
12 customer-purchase-order-number     ELEMENT
13 customer-shipment-number           ELEMENT
14 customer-state                     ELEMENT
15 customer-street-no-and-name        ELEMENT
16 customer-zip                       ELEMENT
17 customers                          INTERFACE
18 evaluate-customer-credit           PROCESS
19 file-on-customers                  SET
20 info-about-customers               ENTITY
21 info-from-customers                INPUT
22 info-to-customers                  OUTPUT
23 invoices-to-customers              OUTPUT
24 num-of-customer-shipment           SYSTEM-PARAMETER
25 orders-from-customers              INPUT
26 packing-slips-to-customers         OUTPUT
27 packing-slips-to-customers-cpy     ENTITY
28 payments-from-customers            INPUT
29 prepare-customer-invoices          PROCESS
30 process-customer-order             PROCESS
31 receive-customer-payments          PROCESS
32 send-letter-to-customers           PROCESS
```

Figure 10: All Objects That Deal with "Customer"

process-chain name=customer-orders-initialization nomessage arrows

```
Name=customer-orders-initialization                                   Page 1 of 1

                                                             /--PROCESS--\
                                                             |authorize- |
                                                          ...>| shipment  |
   @---EVENT---@         /--PROCESS--\         ?---COND----?   .  |           |
   | customer- |         | evaluate- |         |   good-   |   .  \TRIG WHEN T/
   |orders-ini-|......>| customer- |......>|credit-risk|....
   |tialization|         |  credit   |         |           |   .
   @-----------@         \-TRIGGERED-/         ?--CHANGED--?   .  /--PROCESS--\
                                                          .  |   send-   |
                                                          ...>|letter-to- |
                                                             | customers |
                                                             \TRIG WHEN F/
```

Figure 9: Behavior of System in Response to Event

selected-formatted-statements name=info-about-customers

```
 1 DEFINE ENTITY                         info-about-customers;
 2      /*  DATE OF LAST CHANGE - Jul 10, 1989, 13:22:21 */
 3      SYNONYMS ARE:  cust-info;
 4      DESCRIPTION;
 5 Contains key customer information and year-to-date order history.
 6 ;
 7      KEYWORDS ARE:  'Marketing Info';
 8      RESPONSIBLE-PROBLEM-DEFINER IS:
 9                'Kaisler Hudson Solomon';
10      SOURCE IS:     'interview with BWT, 8-22-85';
11      COLLECTED IN:  file-on-customers;
12      CONSISTS OF:
13           customer-name,
14           customer-address,
15           customer-number,
16           credit-line,
17           principal-contact,
18           customer-order-history-ytd;
19      IDENTIFIED BY: customer-number;
20      SECURITY IS:   'Organization Security';
21      CARDINALITY IS:
22                300;
23
24 EOF EOF EOF EOF EOF
```

Figure 11: Encyclopedic Report about a Selected Object

Find all Processes that produce data but do not take any in.

Set Name: ** not defined **
Query: PROCESS and ? DERIVES ! and not ? EMPLOYS !
The Number of Objects is: 3
The Objects are:

Object Name	Object Type
prepare-customer-invoices	PROCESS
receive-customer-payments	PROCESS
review-receivables	PROCESS

Find all data Elements that do not have their "type" declared.

Set Name: ** not defined **
Query: ELEMENT and not ? ATTRIBUTE type !
The Number of Objects is: 3
The Objects are:

Object Name	Object Type
customer-invoice-number	ELEMENT
delinquent-account	ELEMENT
valid-account-number	ELEMENT

Find the lowest level (primitive) Processes and find those that do not have Procedures (mini-specs) defined for them.

Set Name: ** not defined **
Query: PROCESS and not ? SUBPARTS ARE ! and not has PROCEDURE
The Number of Objects is: 13
The Objects are:

Object Name	Object Type
authorize-shipment	PROCESS
evaluate-customer-credit	PROCESS
general-ledger	PROCESS
receive-customer-payments	PROCESS
receive-vendor-invoices	PROCESS
receiving	PROCESS
reconcile-inventory	PROCESS
review-receivables	PROCESS
schedule-payments	PROCESS
send-letter-to-customers	PROCESS
send-payments-to-vendors	PROCESS
shipping	PROCESS
stocking	PROCESS

Figure 12: Checking Completeness with ad hoc Queries

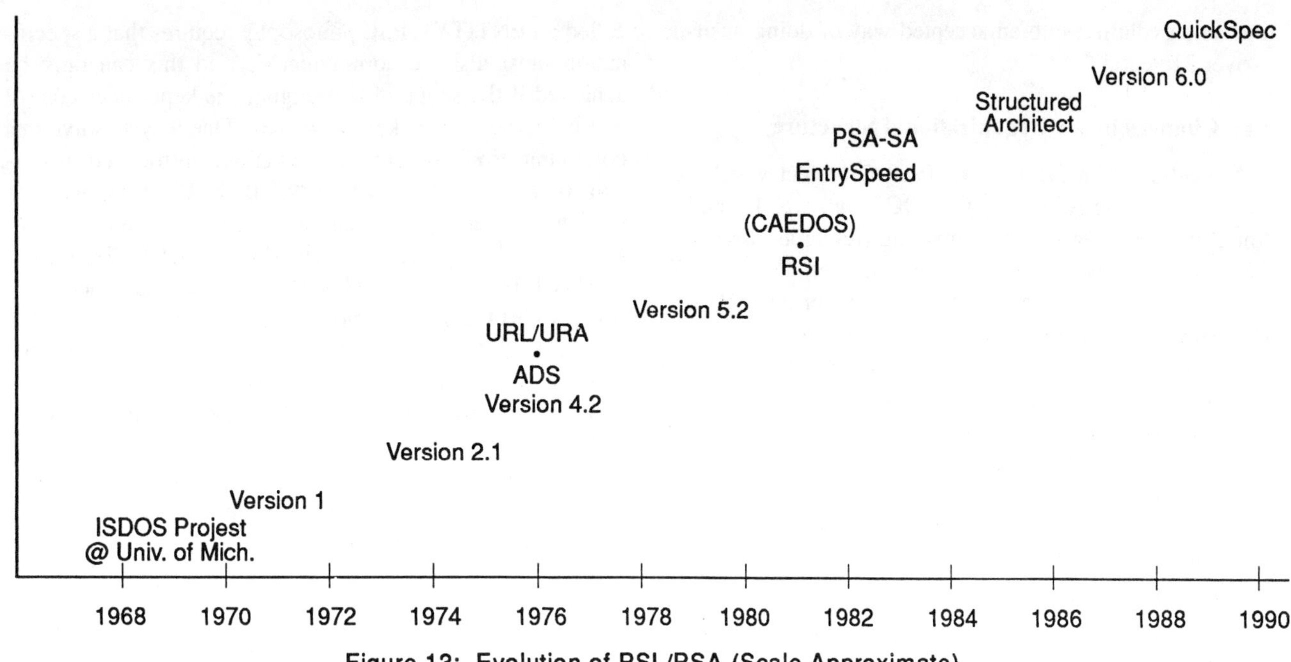

Figure 13: Evolution of PSL/PSA (Scale Approximate)

PSL/PSA was introduced before the acronym "CASE" (Computer-Aided Software Engineering) was coined. The various changes that have affected PSL/PSA are not unique and, in fact, may be a model for the evolution of many such high-technology products. In this section, we give a chronology of the versions, the organizational changes, changes in the language (PSL), the software (PSA), the advent of "add-on" tools, new interfaces to the PSL/PSA system, and the type of support available to its users.

As mentioned earlier, PSL/PSA Version 1 was introduced as a component of automated systems development [1] envisioned by the ISDOS Project. The PSA software was designed along the lines of standard compilers, namely, it had an in-memory symbol table that was populated with appropriate attributes of objects and their relationships to other objects as these were recognized in PSL statements. The ISDOS project's underlying philosophy was that all developments be made available to supporting sponsors, which included Fortune 100 companies and various Government agencies, both civilian and DoD. Thus Version 1 was actually used on real applications. As a result of these "real world" applications, one of the first realizations was that the symbol table concept had to be replaced by a disk-based database management system (dbms). Version 2.0 included an in-house developed network-model dbms called "ADBMS." With some changes, this version of PSL/PSA became known as Version 2.1 and was introduced to a wider audience in 1974.

PSL/PSA was initially designed to capture the logical, or "essential," requirements of an Information System. However, the Electronic Systems Division of the Air Force needed to extend PSL/PSA to address physical, or "allocation," modeling. They contracted for a special version of the PSL/PSA system which in effect would have been Version 3. However, to give it organizational affinity, this version of PSL was called the User Requirements Language (URL) and PSA was called User Requirements Analyzer (URA). Major additions to URL included the concept of "Resources," and the specification of Resource Consumption by Processes. The software (URA) permitted a static analysis of the Resources that would be consumed by the proposed system based on the structure of the system and frequency with which Processes were invoked. The Air Force also needed to produce DoD documentation in approved format from the database, so the software, called the Automated Documentation System (ADS™) [4] was developed to do this. URL/URA also went through some evolution from Version 3.0 through Version 3.3. The acceptance of URL/URA is an interesting story in itself! However, we will not delve into that here.

Concurrent with the URL/URA development, improved Versions of PSL/PSA, 4.0 and later, 4.2, were developed and released around 1976. The enhancements made in the URL/URA Version (including ADS) were incorporated into Version 5.0 of PSL/PSA, which was introduced around 1977. Version 5.0 was followed by Version 5.2 around 1979.

Finally, in 1988, the current version, 6.0, was introduced. It includes changes in both the Language and the Analyzer. These changes will be discussed later. The 1980's also saw the development of auxiliary software designed either to improve the interface to PSL/PSA (e.g., graphic front-end) or to add new functionality (e.g., ability to design a target database from PSL specifications). This too will be described later.

The above evolution is interesting from the perspective of time taken from the germination of an idea, to its introduction, and evolution into an accepted way of doing business —over 21 years!

3.1: Changes in the Organizational Structure

Around 1983, a facet of the ISDOS project was "spun out" as a profit-making entity. ISDOS Inc. was formed in Ann Arbor, Michigan. The remaining (research) aspects of the project at the University were retitled Program for Research in Information Systems Engineering (PRISE). This change was precipitated not only by the University's dual desires of keeping the University work at a research plane and demonstrating that the University could be a good incubator, but also by pressure from users of the PSL/PSA who wanted a commercial level of support. ISDOS Inc. was organized along traditional business lines and sought to make PSL/PSA more of a commercial product than just a research/academic tool.

In 1986 Dr. Teichroew turned over operational control to Dr. Richard Welke, the Canadian distributor of PSL/PSA, who changed the name of the organization to Meta Systems, Ltd. This change brought about further restructuring of the day-to-day operations and a new version of PSL/PSA, Version 6. Special attention was also paid to updating documentation to be more thorough and comprehensive.

In today's environment of venture-funded technology development, it is interesting to note that PSL/PSA has followed a path from university research to a commercial entity without venture funding.

3.2: Changes to the Problem Statement Language (PSL)

Since the chronology of specific changes to PSL is not particularly interesting to other than those intimately involved with PSL/PSA, we will attempt to summarize the changes that have taken place since the last article on PSL/PSA was published in the *IEEE Transactions on Software Engineering* in 1977 [2].

The evolution in the language has amounted to introduction of new Entity-types, removing existing Entity-types, adding new Relationship-types, modifying existing Relationship-types, and similarly altering Attribute-types. These changes have either been requested by users, or have been introduced to support some of the structured methodologies; other changes have been influenced by work done in other phases of the information systems development lifecycle, such as the need to "reverse engineer" program code [5].

The decision as to which demand for language enhancement should be acceded to and which one accommodated by clever modeling has always been a delicate one. The language could range from the simplicity of using very few Entity-types to coming close to natural language (e.g., Structured Analysis uses EXTERNAL, PROCESS, DATA STORE and DATA FLOW, whereas PSL further distinguishes DATA FLOW: EXTERNAL to PROCESS is called an INPUT, PROCESS to EXTERNAL is called an OUTPUT, while a PROCESS to PROCESS DATA FLOW is called an ENTITY). PSL philosophy requires that a specification must also be communicable and this can only be achieved if the scope of the language is kept under control and is limited to few key constructs. One way to solve this communication/simplicity dilemma was introduced in Version 6, allowing the user to "SUBTYPE" instances of a particular Entity-type as another type. For example, PSL Version 6 allows a user to specify that a PROCESS at the top level will be called SYSTEM. The user can also decide to classify PROCESSes at the second level as FUNCTIONs, and those at the third level as TASKs. Hence, while the software thinks of them all as PROCESSes, they are presented to the user with user-defined designations of SYSTEM, FUNCTION, and TASK in the PSA reports. This facility is further enhanced in an interface called QuickSpec™, which will be referred to later in section 3.5.2: Non-graphic Interfaces to PSL/PSA.

This works well up to a point; however, when the usage of PSL needs to be extended beyond its natural domain, the user must distort the usage of the predefined language constructs to suit the situation. It is the equivalent of using a DBMS with a predefined schema to model a situation not designed to be covered by that schema. When such distortions become intolerable, an organization may seek an alternative mechanism for modeling.

3.3: Changes to the Problem Statement Analyzer Software

In this section, we will concentrate on the changes made to PSA itself rather than describe external software that has been developed to either make it easier to use or to provide added functionality.

The utility of most software can be measured in terms of three major non-economic characteristics: functionality, performance and user interface. If these characteristics are paired with the evolution of the usage of the software, an interesting correlation can be discovered. When CASE-type tools were first introduced, the uppermost issue was the functionality. Would they be able to model, say, a real-time system? As the tools were accepted and used on large projects, users demanded sprightly performance. Would they handle 20,000 objects in a reasonable time? Finally, as the tools were put to everyday usage by individuals who were merely doing a job, the ease of use became the issue. It is important to note also that, at any given time, there will be a mix of users, some at each of these three stages of evolution. Hence, the direction of technology evolution depends on the user-mix that the developer is willing to serve (the "market"). Limited resources may therefore be assigned to improve one or more characteristics at the expense of others.

In the last 15 years PSL/PSA has also evolved along this path. While it was housed at the University, emphasis was placed on the functionality. When it was first commercialized, performance became important. Lately, with the competition from other PC-based tools, the interface and "user friendliness" have received considerable attention as described in section 3.5: New Interfaces to PSL/PSA.

3.3.1: Improvement in PSA Functionality

Initially, PSA had a core of simple mechanisms to populate a database, to retrieve information from it, and to present the results in the form of a limited number of reports. As its use began to grow, there was increased demand to retrieve information in many different ways. The retrieval mechanism increased in functionality from the ability to select certain types of Entities, to selecting Entities with certain Attributes, to selecting those participating in certain Relationships. The options for this retrieval mechanism grew in an ad hoc fashion. Finally, realizing that such growth could make the retrieval mechanism very difficult to learn (and support) a generalized Query System (QS™) was added. QS permitted the retrieval of instances of any Entity-type, by any Attribute, or role played in any Relationship(s).

Similarly, the reporting mechanisms also grew. First, there were requests to see the database information in specific new forms. Many of these requests were handled by increasing the functionality of existing reports with additional parameters, and designing some new reports. Next, recognizing that there was a great deal of information in the database, there were requests to perform certain analyses and highlight only that information that was either incomplete or potentially in conflict. Still other reports were requested to support certain methodologies. The number of reports and their parameters began to approach an unmanageable size. This coincided with some work being done on a large Navy Procurement Contract [6] where it was mandated that the Navy requirements be modelled in PSL/PSA for accuracy, then sent out as a Request for Proposal. The traditional batch of PSA reports, or even the scripted output from the Automated Documentation System, was considered inadequate. Hence, a generalized Report Specification Interface (RSI™) was developed. This permitted the user to write a program in the Report Programming Language (RPL), which could algorithmically retrieve, manipulate, and format the results in the desired form. This mechanism allows users to design and write reports that are peculiar to their needs. It also permits users to distort PSL to suit their applications and to produce reports that reflect their view of the model. The functionality of retrieval and reporting is now essentially unlimited.

3.3.2: Improvement in PSA Performance

Because the research into PSL/PSA was being funded by various organizations, the ISDOS project felt obligated to produce software that ran on diverse hardware systems that the sponsors possessed. The result was that there was hardly any medium-to-large computer system to which PSA was not ported. This of course diverted finite resources to the porting and maintenance effort, distracting from improvements in the speed with which PSA could perform.

With the commercialization of PSA, some pragmatic, although not always popular, decisions were made to restrict the porting to targeted hardware systems. Improved quality control and performance were results of this policy. Underlying systems (e.g., ADBMS) were improved by rewriting code in a more modern programming language; access and storage strategies were improved. Commonality among reports was recognized and reports were consolidated, thereby reducing the size of the system and permitting additional focus on the remaining code.

3.4: Added Functionality with External Tools

One of the advantages of having a predefined set of Entities, Relationships, and Attributes that comprise a language such as PSL is that it provides a stable base for both the original developer and for third parties to write additional software, providing functionality not originally present in the software.

An example of added functionality is that of designing a database from the specifications of requirements. Two such packages were developed: one, the View Integration System (VIS™) from Meta Systems, Ltd., and LdbD™ from ASTEC in Maryland. While the two design packages had differences in philosophy, both allowed the user to take the requirements database and produce a third normal form schema to be used in the design phase.

PSL/PSA users matured in their usage of the tool from small projects with limited number of analysts, to larger teams of analysts needing to merge their separate PSA databases describing the target system. PSA has a rather straightforward way of synthesizing the statements made at various times. If the later statements do not contradict the earlier statements, they are accepted and the database enhanced appropriately. If later statements conflict, they are rejected. It is not possible to override the prior statements or to provide rules by which to accept modifications to them. The Structured Architect Integrator (SAI™), introduced by Meta Systems Ltd., has been at the leading edge in solving this dilemma. SAI can play the role of the arbiter between various users and support the data administrator responsible for coordinating the development of the PSA database.

Many developers, tiring of having to develop every system from a blank slate, have wanted to start with an existing system, and to modify or enhance it as dictated by new requirements. Here it is convenient to have existing programs reverse engineered into PSL and to store the programs in a PSA database. REVENGG [5] is such a tool; it can accept COBOL, FORTRAN, some JCL and DBMS statements and can convert them into PSL. The designers can then manipulate this database and use it either to understand the system for maintenance purposes, or as a base for moving to the next evolutionary step in the information system.

3.5: New Interfaces to PSL/PSA

The linguistic input to PSA, PSL statements, can be awkward for some users. Many prefer the pictorial interface provided by graphic tools such as DesignAid® (Nastec) and Excelerator™ (Index Technology). Still other users feel that they want to be "walked through" the input process, as in an interview where a series of questions, posed in the user's terms, would elicit the information needed to produce the required PSL statements. Both of these approaches are available and will be described next.

3.5.1: Graphical Interfaces to PSL/PSA

The PSL/PSA family of tools now includes Structured Architect (SA™), a PC-based drawing tool that models the concepts of Structured Analysis. It also provides a set of local reports that lets the user browse through the system described by using SA. Further, it can produce output that can be synthesized through SAI (which can produce PSL statements), or can be sent directly to PSA as PSL statements.

However, by the time SA was made available, users were requesting functionality beyond its scope, namely, extensions to handle Real-Time systems, and to draw Structure Charts and Entity-Relationship Diagrams. So many users opted for other PC-based graphics packages such as DesignAid or Excelerator (/RTS) even though they recognized the advantage of using PSL/PSA to synthesize the work products of these tools. ASTEC has developed bridges between these front-end tools and PSL/PSA to accommodate these users. Some of these bridges have been one-way (going from the graphic tool to PSL/PSA) and others have been two-way (also going from PSL/PSA back to the graphic tool).

3.5.2: Non-Graphic Interfaces to PSL/PSA

EntrySpeed™ was developed by ASTEC to allow casual users to specify a system by answering queries. Entryspeed questions can follow any of several different methodologies. The user's responses to questions can be re-presented to the user as text, or PSL can be generated from them. By having the user respond to questions posed in a familiar language, any contorted use of PSL/PSA is hidden. This technique also permits the application of a standard "style-sheet" for the usage of PSL/PSA.

Similarly, PSA-SA was developed by (then) ISDOS Inc. It could also produce a packet of reports designed especially for the interface.

Neither of these interfaces is being promoted very aggressively. Nor have users appreciated that such interfaces are particularly suited to the casual user. Although expert users often prefer to write PSL statements directly, users who have been away from PSL for a while could easily re-orient themselves using this interface until they achieve their previous level of proficiency.

QuickSpec, a current product of Meta Systems Ltd., takes advantage of the Windows environment of MS-DOS. It allows the user to import a selected portion of a central PSA database, presented in the user's terms through a filter provided as part of Quickspec. The user can browse, modify, or add information and export data back to the central database.

Finally, reverse engineering output is another non-graphic way to populate PSA databases. With the use of a two-way bridge to a graphic front end, this information may now be examined graphically if desired. An example of a software engineering environment, including the tools described above, is discussed later.

3.6: Support of PSL/PSA Users

In the early days of PSL/PSA in the University of Michigan, the users (sponsors) received enthusiastic if eccentric support from the ISDOS Project. There was one standard course that was essentially a vendor dump of everything that PSL/PSA could do.

When the author cofounded ASTEC in 1978, an extensive set of courses, seminars, and workshops was developed for various audiences at various levels. Instructors have been available as consultants and also undertake to perform contractual services by using the PSL/PSA family of tools, and there is an annual conference sponsored by Meta Systems, Ltd. to discuss new developments, to suggest improvements, and to share experiences in the use of the PSL/PSA family of tools.

4: Acceptance of PSL/PSA

An organization can be said to have accepted a technology when it employs that technology as its normal way of doing business (i.e., all work in that area is performed by using that technology and the loss of this technology would cripple their capability for work). Using this definition of acceptance, the PSL/PSA family of tools has not been widely accepted. There never was a "band wagon" (such as, for example, for Object-Oriented Design) and most users embraced its usage almost reluctantly, often because their clients required it. That is not to say that organizations that geared up to bring PSL/PSA successfully into their organizations did not benefit from it. Indeed, there are several large projects that function productively today because they have the PSL/PSA tool set. The recent RFP for the Reserve Component of the Army (RCAS) [7] was presented to potential bidders in the form of a PSA database.

Most organizations do not appreciate the subtle nuances involved in technology transfer. Typically, there has to be some pressure (often the need to increase productivity) that a technology could alleviate; a receptive climate must be nurtured in the receiving organization. From the perspective of the technology vendor, the opportunity to make the technology known and to be able to aggressively promote it and support its transfer is small. In many ways, PSL/PSA suffered because of its university origins in not being widely marketed when it could have been regarded as a cutting-edge tool. Having lost that initial opportunity, the improved marketing strategies now being brought to bear are chasing after a market distracted by rapidly changing technology and buffeted by organizational myopia. PSL/PSA is being used less by application developers (commercial usage is minuscule) and more by belabored contract monitors in the government who have recognized the potential for its use in the management of various contracts.

Some of the lackluster acceptance can also be laid at the door of an immature information systems industry. For example, while methodologists frequently talk about how to accomplish the tasks of a particular phase in the development life cycle, one hears very little about how to make the transition between one phase and the next, or how to trace back to earlier work, all feasible when using PSL/PSA. Even worse, managers are not even sure what flavor of the development lifecycle they should be following! Since PSL/PSA does not explicitly support any particular lifecycle development method (it expects the users to cast their methodology in PSL/PSA terms), inadequacies are ascribed to PSL/PSA, rather than to the methodologies that lack guidelines for transition between lifecycle phases.

Another roadblock to acceptance is that the use of technology such as PSL/PSA often requires a major cultural shift in the user organization. These shifts can go quite deep, into the very way the analysts and designers think about systems; such change does not occur easily. This problem, along with other distractions discussed below, have impeded the widespread acceptance of PSL/PSA.

4.1: Factors Affecting the Acceptance of PSL/PSA

Various other factors, discussed below, inhibit the acceptance of PSL/PSA, or for that matter, any similar technology.

4.1.1: Support of Methods

During the original design of PSL, there was much discussion as to whether PSL should be made to follow a particular strategy for building systems (e.g., top-down versus bottom-up, outside-in versus inside-out) or whether particular types of information systems should be addressed (e.g., real-time versus administrative versus data-centered). The decision made was to allow the client organization to choose its own methodology and to enable the specification of any type of information system in PSL/PSA. However, the advent of methods such as Structured Analysis has changed that perspective. Whether supporting tools such as PSL/PSA should rigidly enforce methodologies or should allow for local variations is still a subject for debate; and all the debate is delaying the performance of real work.

4.1.2: Influence of Platforms

The blossoming of the PC as a cheap platform (cheaper than, say, that used for CAD/CAM applications) made it feasible for many organizations to provide PCs to their analysts and designers of information systems. However, the mind set that accompanied the PC was often that of a cottage industry instead of a modern automated factory. This type of thinking and the obvious limitations of the PC have caused a great deal of turmoil in the systems departments of organizations. The arrival of "friendly" CASE tools, often no more than toys, also distracted the attention of systems developers. Seduced by the ease of usage of these tools, developers were often blind to the limitations in describing large systems or working as a group. PSL/PSA has been capable of doing both those, but has not been seriously considered, lacking the glittter of color graphics, pop-up menus and a port to the PC. Today, systems departments are struggling with the alternatives of changing from existing PCs to workstations (at a hefty expenditure) or waiting for more powerful PC operating systems. In the meantime, decisions about the selection of technology, methodology, software, etc., are deferred.

4.1.3: PSL Limitations

While PSL presents a good-sized set of the needed constructs in defining information systems, other constructs that are not supported (e.g., the calling sequence in a program) need to be modelled by "creative" use of the language. Hence, PSL is perceived as being a limited, hard-to-use language, although some experience with flexibly definable "cultures" does point out that too much flexibility can result in monstrously unwieldy languages. Some of the limitations in the choice of terms in PSL can be surmounted by constructs in Version 6 (the "SUBTYPE" referred to earlier) and by the use of the interface QuickSpec also described earlier.

Some limitations have more to do with how PSL/PSA has been viewed rather than how it functions. Some organizations, recognizing that PSA plays the role of a higher level (Entity as opposed to Data) management system, instead of actually using PSA, have attempted to emulate it by using tools such as relational database management systems (RDBMS). Most of these organizations have come to the conclusion that such emulations are, at best, cumbersome, very expensive to build on top of the popular RDBMS platform and still unsatisfactory to those who were not party to the development. Such attempts to develop an "emulated PSA" shift focus and resources away from the main objective of building systems. Further, the failure in developing an effective tool and in producing the target system seems to stiffen an organization's resistance to any other new tools in a backlash effect that has been observed to persist for as long as five years.

5: Configuring a Software Engineering Environment with PSL/PSA

An organization planning to use software engineering tools would do well to configure an environment required to perform the tasks. An environment would be most viable if the organization selected methodologies and tools in a top down fashion.

First, a Lifecycle Methodology (LCM) would be picked. This methodology would describe the phases of the development process, the deliverables required of each phase and the traceability (to prior and post phases) that needs to be maintained. Ideally, the LCM would also specify how to move from one phase to the next.

Next the methodologies for individual phases would have to be picked. Here the organization would have to make sure that the products suggested by the phase-methodologies dove-tail into the requirements of the LCM.

Only after having picked the methodologies for the phases should the organization shop for tools to support the selection. This is where the organization may run into problems posed by the immaturity of the information systems industry. Products of individual tools, selected because of specific desirable features, may be difficult to consolidate into one software engineering environment. Hence, the organization should be prepared to "bridge" tools as necessary.

Finally, the organization must set standards and practices for the use of the methodologies and tools that have been chosen. Different roles and responsibilities (e.g., librarian, tool-smith, data administrator) must be defined. Appropriate training and support assistance must be acquired. When all of this is in place, one can claim to have a workable software engineering environment.

5.1: An Example of a Software Engineering Environment (SEE)

Figure 14 shows an example of a SEE with PSL/PSA as a central tool. The figure is best read in layers (rows) from top to bottom. Unshaded boxes represent the Meta System tool set; shaded boxes show some of the tools available from third parties that are usable with PSL/PSA.

The very top row of the diagram shows which methodologies are supported by the tools shown in the boxes in the second row. For example, if the organization was working in the requirements analysis phase and had picked the Structured Analysis method, all but one of the tools would be feasible (the exception being the right-most tool, REVENGG, which expects that a system already has programs written in, say, COBOL or FORTRAN).

If the user wished to use a graphics front-end, SA, DesignAid, or Excelerator (all CASE tools) would support the drawing of data flow diagrams. If the user wanted to use the recent Real-Time extensions to structured analysis, then either DesignAid or Excelerator would be appropriate. (Note: at this time there are over 50 such graphic tools; we are only picking the ones known to have viable bridges to PSL/PSA.)

Assuming that the user had picked, say, Excelerator, and had drawn diagrams on a PC or appropriate workstation, these diagrams could be analyzed, reports produced from them, and checks made for completeness. When the user teams were ready to integrate individual work into a composite, project-wide database supported by PSA, they could use XL-XPRESS to convert their local databases (on the PCs or workstations) to PSL statements.

Had SA been appropriate for the graphic front-end (i.e., no extensions needed for Real-Time), then several analysts could have been assigned portions of the work to be done on their individual workstations. This work could have been synthesized by using SAI. When there were no conflicts, SAI would be asked to generate PSL statements to send to PSA. (Alternatively, and not shown in the figure, SA could also generate PSL statements but then there would be no adjudication of conflicts provided by SAI).

Alternatively, an organization's style may be more linguistic rather than graphic. In this case, they may opt to use a regular text editor and directly type PSL statements. Or, they might prefer to have questions asked (as in an interview) and to supply responses that would then be converted to PSL statements. In this case, they might use a tool such as EntrySpeed.

The PSL statements could be presented to PSA to populate the database. Inconsistencies among individual databases would surface at this point and would be attended to by the individual specifiers, and the translation process repeated (if appropriate) until an "error-free" (i.e., free of conflicts) PSA database was produced.

Now, the project could examine the composite PSA database for errors of omission and for disjoint components in the system specification. The PSA mechanisms that could be used include standard PSA reports, the Query System, or even customized reports by using the Report Specification Interface. An example of such a report produced for use with REVENGG does type-checking of data in calling sequences to supplement compilers that do not enforce strong type-checking. The errors could either be corrected back at the individual databases and the process repeated or the PSA modifier commands could be used to correct the database as necessary.

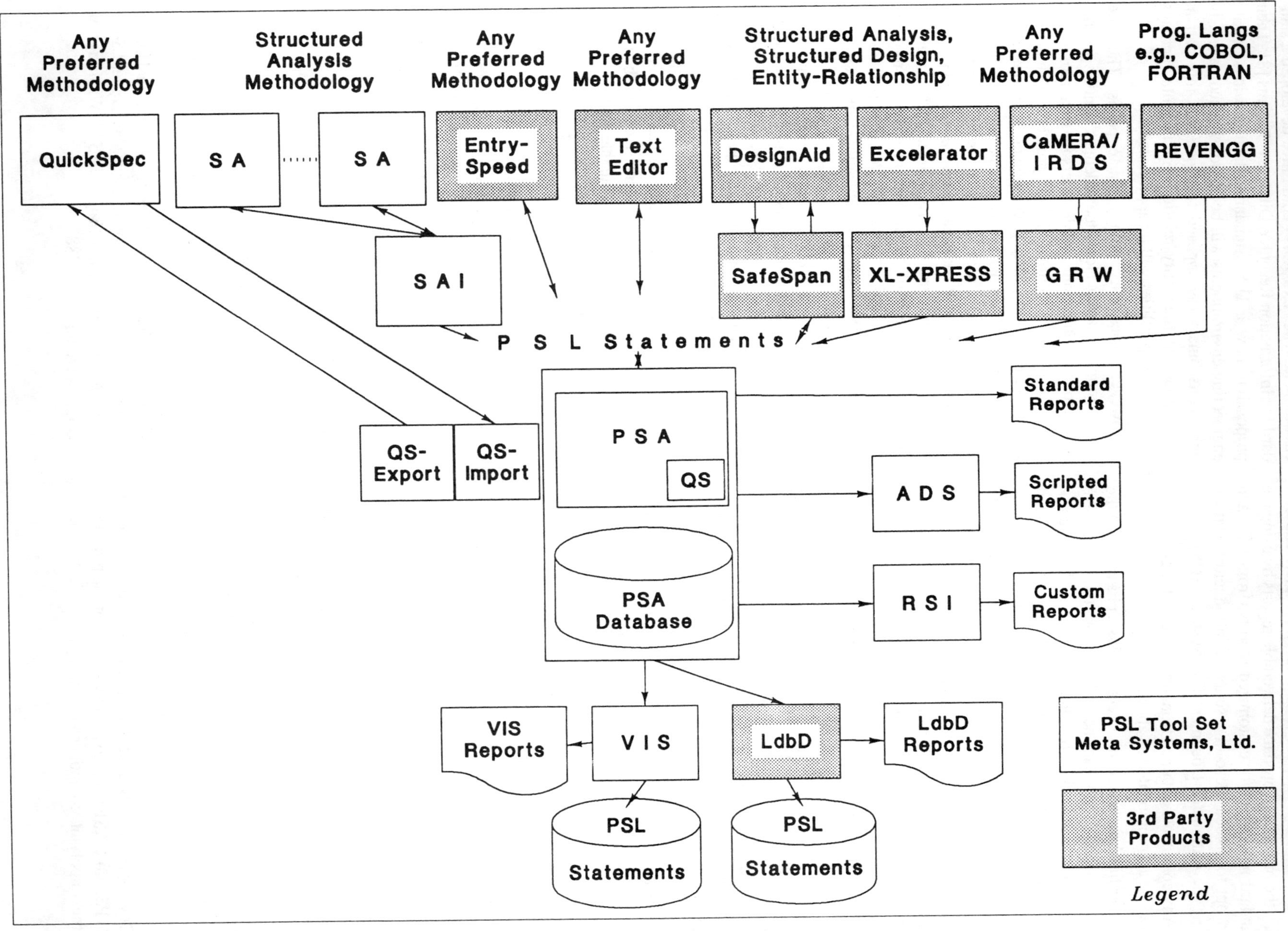

Figure 14: Software Engineering Environment Using PSL/PSA and Auxiliary Tool Set

When the PSA database is certifiably complete and correct, the project can produce deliverable reports by using the standard reports and/or customized reports (from RSI) and can opt to embed these in a script of introductory text by using the Automated Documentation System (ADS).

Any comments obtained from the readers of these reports could be accommodated as above.

After finishing the requirements analysis phase, when the project wished to move to the design phase, they could take advantage of available tools such as VIS or LdbD to automatically generate third normal forms of relevant data found in the requirements analysis phase. The resulting design is produced in the form of PSL statements that could be used to populate the design database. Similarly, the using organization could itself program some algorithms, by using RSI, to automatically convert selected Processes found in the requirements phase to modules in the design phase.

5.2: Variations in the Classic Methodology

If the organization was working with an existing system (say, a suite of FORTRAN programs) and wished to ensure that none of the old functionality was dismissed without examination, it could choose to reverse engineer these programs into PSL statements, by using REVENGG, and could populate a database representing the system as it exists today. This database could be modified to reflect the desired changes and the development could be continued as before.

Or, if the organization were required to use the standard Information Resource Dictionary System (IRDS) [8] for one of its earlier phases and they had used a tool based on an Extended Entity Relationship Attribute model [9], they could use its GRW interface to produce PSL statements.

Often, the methodology used by an organization is dictated by the client. For example, many applications in the Department of Defense require that the 2167A set of documents be produced. These deliverables imply both a lifecycle methodology and a set of phase-specific methodologies. Many of the popular commercial methodologies such as Structured Analysis and Structured Design are acceptable for appropriate phases. The user organization must, nevertheless, develop standards and practices for the use of these methodologies and the tools to produce the deliverables. When the specification is produced in the form of PSL statements, the production of the required documents is relatively simple by using RSI and ADS.

6: Conclusions

Development tools appear to have come full cycle: from PSL/PSA to CASE tools to the recognition of the repository as the important component of the systems development environment. The ANS/X3H4 committee developed a standard for Information Resource Directory Systems [8]. Their proposal is now a U.S. standard. Its usage in software engineering environments will be obviously encouraged. In light of its binary (as opposed to a potential four-part in PSL) model of the entity-relationship-attribute, perhaps PSL/PSA's capabilities will be appreciated.

However, issues of technology transfer persist. There are organizations standing along the sidelines waiting for the perfect tool to come along, while others flit from tool to tool hoping for the same. Neither of these problem-solving techniques promote good system development. And some small organizations do not want to make a "risky" investment until they see a universally accepted tool or some client forces them into a decision. What is needed is a concerted push for pro-active technology transfer. The time and effort required for transferring a technology, such as the PSL/PSA tool set, and institutionalizing that technology, costs as much as the initial purchase of the tools. If organizations fail to approach systems development as an engineering problem and not an art form, and fairly quickly, systems development as we know it will no longer be a viable option for impatient managers. There are several technologies, such as reuse and vertical packaging, emerging to take the place of "stick-built" custom systems.

PSL/PSA is sometimes dismissed as showing its age, although the counter could be that it has matured with experience; it has improved its user interface and there is a great deal of auxiliary software available to use with it. PSL/PSA has obvious potential as a repository and we look forward to widened interest in its use.

7: References

[1] D. Teichroew and H. Sayani, "Automation of System Building," *Datamation*, August 15, 1971, pp. 25-30.

[2] D. Teichroew and E.A. Hershey, III, "PSL/PSA: A Computer-Aided Technique for Structured Documentation and Analysis of Information Processing Systems," *IEEE Transactions on Software Engineering*, Vol. SE-3, No.1, January 1977, pp. 41-48.

[3] E. Yourdon, *Modern Structured Analysis*, Prentice-Hall, Englewood Cliffs, N.J., 1989.

[4] H. Sayani, "The Automated Documentation System" in *Tools for Improved Computing in the 80's*, National Bureau of Standards, Gaithersburg, Md., June 15, 1978, pp. 147-153.

[5] H. Sayani, "Reverse Engineering: An Aid in Understanding" in *Proceedings of the Thirteenth Annual Software Engineering Workshop*, NASA, Washington D.C., November 30, 1988.

[6] *CAEDOS Interactive Graphics Specification: an RFP issued by the Naval Regional Contracting Office*, Long Beach, Calif., September 1981.

[7] *US Army Information Systems Selection and Acquisition Agency, Draft Request for Proposals (DRFP) Describing the Requirements for the Reserve Component Automation System (RCAS) Project*, ATTN: ISSA-ABA (RCAS), 2461 Eisenhower Avenue, Hoffman I, Alexandria, VA 22331-0700, June 1989.

[8] American National Standard for Information Systems: *Information Resource Dictionary System*, (X3, 138-1988) X3 Secretariat/CBEMA, Washington, D.C., July 1988.

[9] H. Sayani: "Enlarging the Base for Case Tools," in *Advance Working Papers, Vol 1., Second International Workshop in Computer-Aided Software Engineering (CASE '88)*, Cambridge, Mass., July 12-15, 1988, pp. 6.35-6.38.

8: Acknowledgments

PSL/PSA is a registered trademark of Meta Systems, Ltd., MI.

QuickSpec, SA, SAI, ADS, RSI, VIS, and QS are Trade Marks of Meta Systems, Ltd., MI.

REVENGG, EntrySpeed, SafeSpan, XL/XPRESS, XL/XPRESS/RTS, LdbD, CaMERA, and GRW are trademarks of Advanced Systems Technology Corp. (ASTEC), MD.

DesignAid is a registered trademark of Nastec Corporation, MI.

Excelerator, Excelerator/RTS are trademarks of Index Technology Corporation (Intech), MA.

Through work in information technology consulting, ASTEC (in Greenbelt Maryland) has supported organizations in exploiting technology to build systems more productively and with improved quality; so we can look at PSL/PSA® from the perspective of someone who has worked with it in several capacities, including training, support, technology transfer, and actual usage on contracts. Also, while a faculty member at the University of Maryland, the author supported its use on the university computer system for students in the Information Systems Management Department

One of the developers of RAMIS II, the first fourth generation language, talks about his favorite way to program.

IN PRAISE OF 4GLS

by Richard H. Cobb

The goal of any language is to communicate, that is, to give and receive information. In the case of computer languages, the goal is communication between people and computers. Traditionally, people have been taught to talk to computers in the language of the computer. Today, however, we are beginning to teach computers to communicate with us in our own language. This did not happen overnight—it evolved through five distinct stages of computer language development: machine, assembler, high-level, nonprocedural, and knowledge-based. Each of these stages has left its mark, helping to spur a dramatic increase in the use of computers.

Early communication between people and computers was based on machine language, the language of the computer hardware itself. Since the computer only understood a well-constructed pattern of zeros and ones, virtually all the effort of programming a computer rested with the user rather than with the computer. In addition, programmers had to deal directly with the physical limitations of hardware instructions and memory size.

Although this early programming was tedious and labor intensive, low programmer productivity was not a serious concern. It was generally thought that only a small number of expensive computers would exist, working on the most difficult problems, with only technical specialists to

communicate with them. This first generation of computer languages is still used by computer builders. But, for the most part, the days of coding in binary are gone.

In the late 1950s, assembler, the second generation of languages, began to emerge. Assemblers were programs that allowed symbols and mnemonics to represent the hardware language of bit patterns. By transferring some of the work of communicating to the computer, assemblers improved communications and extended the use of computing to many more people. They are still used by programmers building some systems software that requires the highest efficiency and direct interaction with computer hardware.

Not long after assemblers were developed, high-level languages began to evolve. During the ensuing years, such well-known procedural languages as COBOL, FORTRAN, BASIC, PL/I, and Pascal emerged. Although they appeared to more nearly approximate the language of humans, they used symbols extensively. These third generation languages are still widely used and have been supplemented with system tools like report writers, database management systems (DBMSs), and application products such as general ledger and material requirements planning systems. Application products like these are written in third generation languages by software vendors, not by in-house programmers. This arrangement has led to significant productivity increases for society, since every company is not reinventing the wheel.

Third generation languages spurred the great increase in information processing that characterized the last 20 years. During that time, the number of mainframes in use increased from hundreds to tens of thousands. Their impact on our society has been enormous. For example, most people agree that many companies could not operate if their computers suddenly just stopped. Expenditures on computing have increased by about 15% per year despite continued dramatic achievements in hardware price/performance, and computer specialists are constantly in short supply.

When third generation languages first appeared, individual application pro-

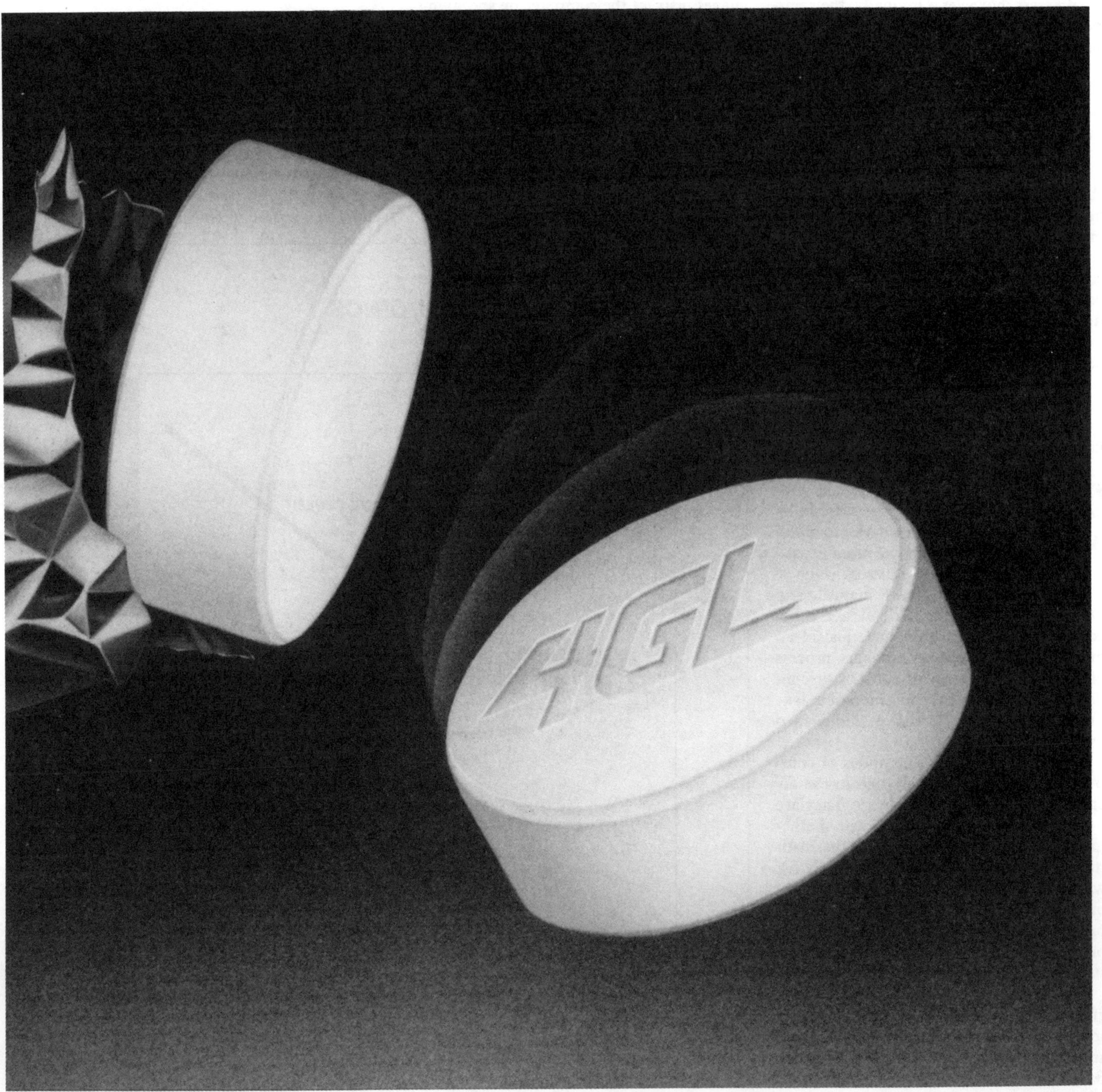

ILLUSTRATION BY BOB ALCORN

The concept behind 4GLs is to transfer the entire concern about program flow from the computer specialist to the computer software.

grams were responsible for establishing, understanding, and using data structures that needed to be accessed. When a change occurred in data structure, the application was very often severely affected. The concept of a DBMS promised a solution to this problem since its data-independent access method gave applications immunity to changes in data structure. This made it easy to develop new applications and reduce environmental maintenance.

Early DBMSs were not without weaknesses, however. Originally, their purpose was to provide insulation between data and programs. Because most early DBMSs were navigational systems with rigidly predefined relationships, applications programmers needed to know a great deal about the structure of the data, bringing the coding of such systems beyond the reach of all but the specialist. As a result, much of the intended objective was sacrificed. Examples of this type of DBMSs include IMS and IDMS.

To eliminate these weaknesses, structure-independent or relational databases were conceived. With a structure-independent database, relationships are defined dynamically—users are not concerned with structure. Moreover, structure-independent databases have become a prerequisite for the successful implementation of nonprocedural or fourth generation languages.

FEW DBMSS PROVIDE ACCESS Only a few systems provide such structure-independent access to data. Some of the more prominent ones are DB2 (IBM), NOMAD2 (Dun & Bradstreet), RAMIS II (Mathematica), and Oracle (Oracle). Although DBMSs are not computer languages, they have played an important role in the evolutionary process of languages. In fact, without structure-independent DBMSs, fourth generation languages would never have come into existence.

The first three generations of computer languages are closely tied to the architecture of computer hardware. They are derivatives of the work of the late mathematician, John von Neumann (of the Institute for Advanced Study, Princeton, N.J.), whose concept of the stored program computer is still embodied in systems that use a program counter. This counter controls program flow by indicating the next instruction to be processed.

With von Neumann-based languages, the programmer has two main responsibilities: to define what is to be done and to control the flow of the program. Based on these responsibilities and the fact that these languages are driven by the characteristics of the machines they run on, von Neumann-based languages are labeled procedural languages.

Fourth generation or nonprocedural languages altered this approach to programming as well as the role of the program counter. The fundamental concept behind a nonprocedural language is to transfer the entire concern about program flow from the computer specialist to the computer software. Nonprocedural languages instruct the computer by specifying the desired result, rather than specifying actions needed to achieve that result.

These 4GLs evolved when it was observed that management of program control could be specified in an algorithmic manner. In this way, the computer software could control the program's flow while permitting the programmer to merely specify the work to be done.

For example, assume that a report is desired showing the total units sold for each product, by customer, in each month and year, with a subtotal for each customer. In addition, each new customer must start on a new page. A 4GL request would look something like this:

```
TABLE FILE SALES SUM UNITS
BY YEAR BY MONTH BY CUSTOMER BY PRODUCT
ON CUSTOMER SUBTOTAL PAGE BREAK
END
```

The logic flow of the same request, using a procedural language like COBOL, would be represented by a flowchart with 58 active procedural blocks and would require 500 to 1,000 lines of coding.

Differences between procedural and nonprocedural languages become clearer when a closer examination of flowcharts is made. In fact, flowcharts were what von Neumann used to define the basis of a

FIG. 1

THIRD GENERATION ECONOMICS

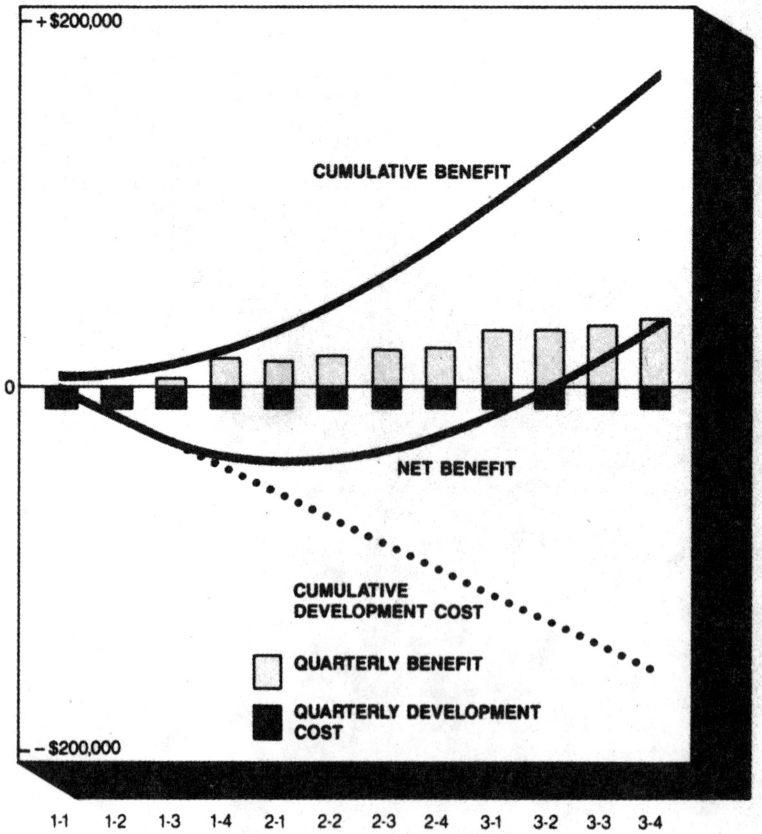

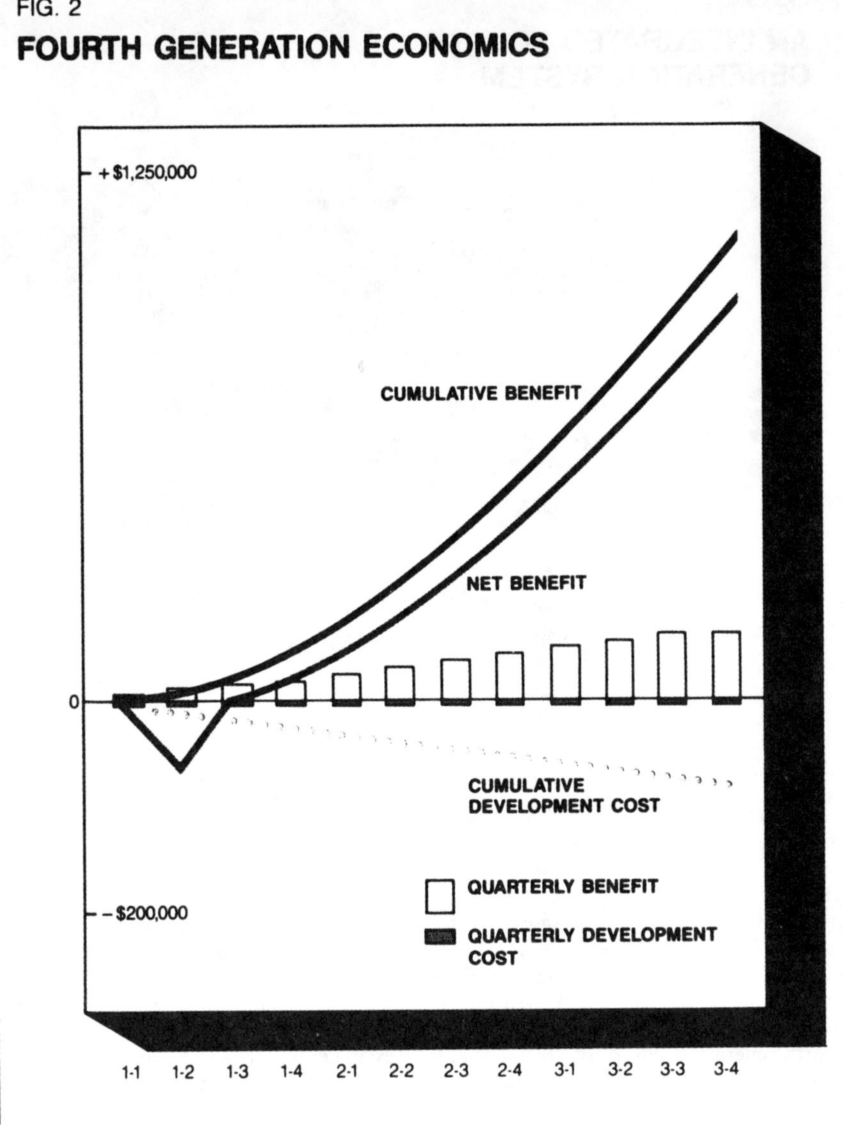

stored computer program. They clearly indicate the reasoning behind all work associated with von Neumann languages.

MANY GAINS TO BE MADE

In the preceding example, only 10 boxes, or 17% of the flowchart, deal with solving the problem. The remainder is concerned with controlling program flow. This is typical of von Neumann languages and indicates why there are so many productivity gains to be made when all effort associated with managing program flow is transferred to the computer, a task it is well equipped to handle. Additionally, because the programmer tends to better understand and concentrate on the desired results, the other 80% or 90% of the program dealing with the program flow would be more likely to contain errors. By eliminating most of this programming, nonprocedural languages tend to improve application reliability by an even larger margin than their program size reduction would suggest.

The nonprocedural approach opened the doors for continuous evolutionary development of the new generation of computer languages. It took about seven years—from 1967 to 1974—to really perfect fourth generation ideas.

4GLs are beneficial because

- they are results oriented;
- they improve productivity by at least 5 to 1, and by as much as 300 to 1 for some activities;
- a large percentage of staff can deal directly with computers without going through intermediaries, since fourth generation languages are designed for both computer specialists and end users;
- they are the ideal tool for the information centers being established by corporations today; and
- they are ideal as applications generators.

Although they have much to offer, acceptance of 4GLs has not been easy for the computer industry. In 1977, few people believed that 4GLs would ever be able to replace third generation languages, like COBOL, by the 1980s. Eight years later, however, as more people have gained experience with 4GLs, many believe the replacement is well on its way.

The large increase in productivity that accompanies the use of fourth generation languages raises interesting economic considerations for potential purchasers of high-level software. For example, compare the use of a fourth generation language, such as RAMIS II, with the typical third generation approach, using COBOL plus a traditional DBMS.

Examine the effect on a single programmer, making the following conservative assumptions:

- The cost of a programmer is $25 per hour.
- A typical application development project takes one programmer eight months to complete.
- The payback period for each project is 12 months.
- Each application has a useful life of two and a half years.

For eight months, the programmer costs money without delivering any benefit until the first application is implemented and starts paying back. The programmer then starts on a second application. At the end of the first year, the programmer has completed one project, which results in four months of savings. The net cost to the company is thus $40,000 at the end of the first year.

After three years, the programmer has completed four projects and has given the company a net benefit of about $24,000, with the break-even point occurring in the tenth quarter. The cumulative results are shown in Fig. 1.

Compare this with a fourth generation language user, assuming a conservative 5-to-1 productivity factor. (A more realistic factor may be over 10 to 1, as reported in a recent—third quarter 1984—product survey by Martin Marietta of 800 users of the RAMIS II 4GL and DBMS.)

With this increased productivity, one person completes seven projects and starts on the eighth in the first year. Thirty-nine project months are saved, giving the company a net benefit of slightly more than $61,000 the first year, with the break-even point occurring in the third quarter. Savings continue to accrue for more than three years, resulting in 40 times more savings (see Fig. 2).

This three-year comparison is illustrated below.

	4GL	3GL
projects completed	22	4
break-even quarter	3	11
total savings	$938,308	$23,889

FIG. 3

AN INTEGRATED FOURTH GENERATION SYSTEM

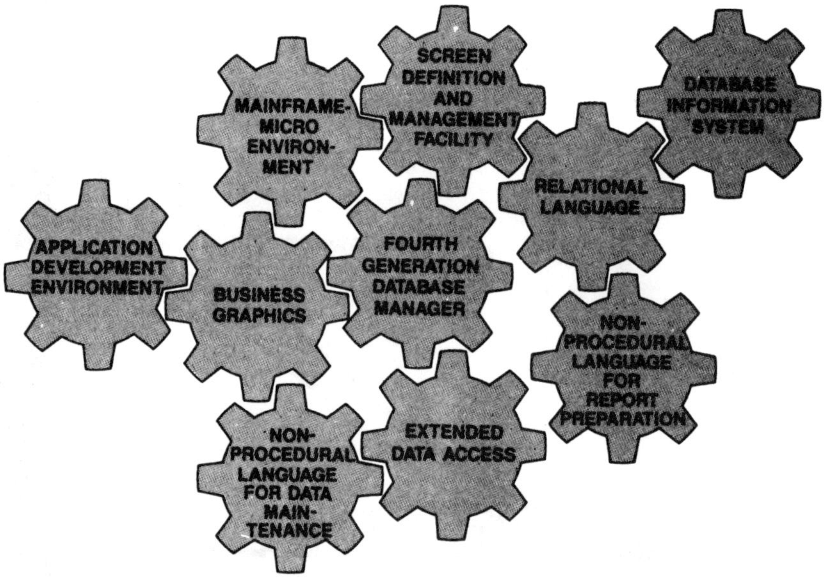

A complete fourth generation system consists of a number of individual elements. In addition to containing fourth generation or nonprocedural languages, a fourth generation system must have other features that make it easy for the user to communicate with the computer, such as

- nonprocedural language for report preparation,
- nonprocedural language for data maintenance,
- screen definition and management facility,
- business graphics,
- spreadsheet analysis,
- fourth generation database manager,
- relational language,
- applications manager,
- extended data access,
- database information system,
- an environment for applications development,
- an environment for information consumers, and
- a micro-to-mainframe environment.

There are two ways to acquire these facilities. One is to obtain each component separately and build bridges between the components. Although a feasible solution, it is difficult to implement since the separate components available are not designed to fit together.

The second solution is to acquire all the functions from one vendor in a single, integrated system containing components that are designed and implemented specifically to work together (Fig. 3). Currently, there are four vendors working toward offering such systems—Mathematica, Princeton, N.J.; Cullinet, Westwood, Mass.; ADR, East Syracuse, N.Y.; and CINCOM, Cincinnati.

One area in which fourth generation systems are often perceived to be lacking is processing efficiency. It seems natural that the dramatic gains in productivity provided by 4GLs should be balanced by significant increases in resource consumption. And, although the performance of fourth generation languages have been found wanting in many instances, it is important to recognize that there is no reason, in principle, why the typical fourth generation language program must be less efficient than its third generation counterpart. In fact, there are good reasons why fourth generation software should be more efficient.

The primary reason for this contention is that a fourth generation system "understands" the programs it processes to a much larger extent than does a third generation compiler. It knows, for instance, that it is producing a report and can try to optimize this process. All a COBOL compiler knows is that it has a large number of statements to process.

The fact is, developers of fourth generation software have concentrated most of their efforts on adding capabilities rather than improving performance. A few vendors, however, are now dramatically increasing their performance-related efforts. Through better software engineering, fourth generation compilers, advanced data structures, and other techniques, fourth generation languages will one day outperform their third generation predecessors. In fact, in many of today's situations, 4GLs outperform even very well written third generation implementations.

Although fourth generation systems are relatively new, current technological developments have moved computer languages into the fifth generation of knowledge-based systems.

At the heart of these systems is the software's ability to make largely correct inferences using an available base of knowledge. This technology, based on research in artificial intelligence, is having a profound impact on our communication with computers and will allow computers to converse with people in their own language. Currently the only knowledge-based system on the market is Mathematica's RAMIS II English. Its knowledge base contains four dictionaries:

- File dictionary—contains information about data in the database files.
- General dictionary—over 4,000 root words and phrases of the English language.
- Dynamic dictionary—accumulates vocabulary as the system is used.
- Application- and user-specific dictionary—incorporates specialized vocabulary.

This type of knowledge-based system permits the user to frame requests in his own jargon or special business terms, putting the power of computing and vast information resources in the hands of information consumers. With such systems, it appears the goal of providing human fluency to computers will be reached within the next 10 years. What will come after that is limited only by our vision of the future.

Fourth generation nonprocedural languages are here to stay. They will soon replace procedural languages as the choice for implementing the vast majority of applications, even applications developed for resale. But even as fourth generation languages are now reaching their potential, the advent of natural language processing and other work in the area of model-driven systems foreshadows their decline. The one thing we can be sure of in information processing is constant change—as one technology is perfected, it is adjusted with an even more powerful technology that one day may replace it. Only organizations that adapt to this rapid pace of advancing technology will survive. ◉

Since 1984, Richard Cobb has been vice president and general manager of the Information Technology Division of Martin Marietta Data Systems, Greenbelt, Md. From 1975 to 1984, Cobb was president of Mathematica Products Group Inc. and senior vp of Mathematica Inc. He was instrumental in developing RAMIS II, the first nonprocedural language. ◉

The Automated Requirements Traceability System (ARTS): An Experience of Eight Years

R.F. Flynn and M. Dorfman
Lockheed Missile and Space Company, Inc.

Abstract

The evolution of the Automated Requirements Traceability System (ARTS) has been an enlightening experience. Requirements management, especially traceability considerations, continues to be of vital interest to those involved with the development of large systems. However, it is still misunderstood and only rarely performed correctly. In this paper, we will discuss our approach to requirements management and traceability. The intent here is to share the eight-year ARTS experience with others who may be building or using requirements management tools. In developing and using ARTS we have come to the conclusion that to be successful you must create flexible tools that can be adapted to fit a particular application environment. You must also thoroughly understand and possibly control the tool's application environment. With these considerations, we have generated a tool-to-task application paradigm that can be used to enhance the development of new software tools and also the application of existing tools to specific functions. We also feel that to improve requirements management tools, requirements definition standards and new tool development efforts are necessary.

Introduction and Overview

A large-scale system development project begins with a concept that is defined during a feasibility study. The customer and possibly several contractors participate in the investigation to determine if the desired capability is possible and practical. Alternative approaches are defined and tradeoffs are evaluated. There is also an attempt to define the system or top-level requirements for the approach selected for the project. The output of that study is a functional baseline defined in a general system specification, a system requirements document, or a request for proposal that serves as the baseline for the new project. The concept is put out to bid and a contractor is selected to create the new capability.

Most projects are developed using a lifecycle model that has traditionally been broken up into several discrete sections. The first element in the lifecycle model and possibly the most difficult for a developer of a new project is analysis or requirements definition.

> As is true for complex hardware systems, the hardest part of the software task is the setting of the exact requirements. . . [1]

Analysis is followed by design, build, test, delivery, and maintenance. A simple graphical depiction of the lifecycle model is shown in Figure 1. Each phase in the cycle is defined by specific documentation and review standards. One phase must be completed before the next is allowed to begin. This is commonly referred to as "baseline management" or the "specify-then-build" approach. The phases of the model all deal with requirements. You are primarily adding many new requirements as the process proceeds or you are changing and deleting existing requirements. Thus, management of this expanding requirements base becomes a very imporant function.

The natural tendency on new projects is to minimize or bypass the analysis phase and immediately begin designing the system by using some perception of the desired concept and experience gained on similar projects. The system specification, if it exists, is usually poorly written and only vaguely defines user desires for the new system. Schedules dictate early baseline definitions along with the creation of supporting documentation before the system is understood and defined. Requirements deficiencies originating in this phase have been identified as one of the major problems in developing large systems.

> In nearly every software project which fails to meet performance and cost goals, requirements inadequacies play a major and expensive role in project failure.[2]

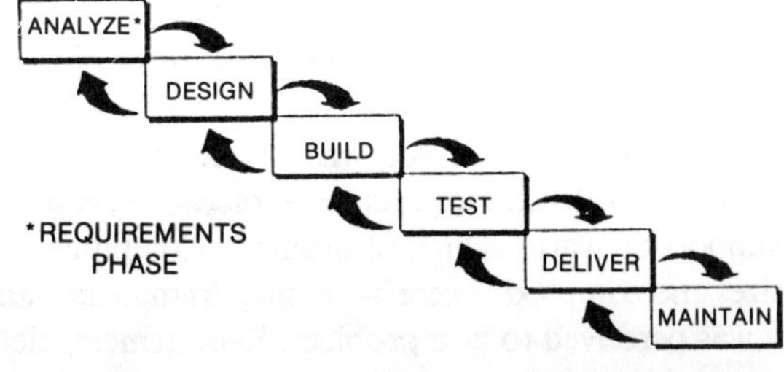

Figure 1: System development life cycle

EH0304-6/90/0000/0423$01.00

Analysis is the phase during which it is least expensive to rectify problems, and yet it is also the phase during which many problems seem to originate.

> Clearly, it pays to invest effort in finding requirements errors early and correcting them in, say, 1 manhour rather than waiting to find the error during operations and having to spend 100 manhours correcting it.[3]

The requirements that were identified in the analysis phase, as well as those added or changed in the later phases, must be traceable. Traceability provides for review of how the system requirements are flowed down to the lower levels and for how lower-level requirements derive from the higher levels. The impact of changes is facilitated and inconsistencies or omissions become apparent.

> The contractor shall document the traceability of the requirements allocated from the system specification. . .[4]

Traceability has traditionally been accomplished by manually linking requirement paragraph number references between documents using very large tables. A given paragraph might contain several requirements, and it was left to the reviewer to determine which specific requirement was being referenced. The process was labor-intensive, prone to errors, and provided little visibility to the process since the links were often made after the documents were generated.

The analysis phase also has the least software tool support. Some tools and techniques that support requirements analysis include Software Requirements Engineering Methodology (SREM), Problem Statement Language/Problem Statement Analyzer (PSL/PSA), N^2 charts, Requirement Networks (R-Nets), Requirement Tracer (RTrace), ARTS, and most of the new Computer-Aided Software Engineering environments. Not all of these tools support requirements traceability, and no traceability standards exist. Requirements tools are either developed and distributed commercially or are created within an organization or project and not made publicly available.The development and use of internal tools is quite common and considered a competitive advantage in the aerospace industry.

The Space Systems Division (SSD) of the Lockheed Missiles and Space Company (LMSC) developed ARTS in 1980 for internal use. The project was initiated as a response to the need for a software requirements traceability capability to support the various lines of business. Computer program sizes and complexity were increasing dramatically and quality was perceived to be a problem. Requirements deficiences were identified as one of the primary causes. It was felt that if a database tool could be built that could store and retrieve the requirements and their linkages in tree formats, the requirements process would be significantly enhanced and customer satisfaction would increase.

ARTS is a database management system into which requirement records can be stored, maintained, and output into reports or formal military standard specifications. Requirements are defined in the database as records made up of fields or attributes that contain information related to the requirement object. One or more of these fields can contain a pointer to the actual requirement's text information that is stored as a module in an external library and is recovered as needed during the requirements manipulation process.

The requirements that ARTS stores are the text-based forms that are normally found in formal specifications. A requirement can be represented as a text statement, a table, or a figure reference. User-selected attributes that relate to the requirements management process are also maintained. No analytical capability is possible with ARTS, but some consistency checking is performed. In a simple context, ARTS is a bookkeeping system for tracking and controlling text-based requirements. It provides visibility during the requirements definition and flowdown process by utilizing the user-specified requirement linkages in either an upward or downward direction to create requirement "trees."

ARTS does more than trace requirements. The impact of changes in top-level requirements or problems with low-level requirements can be easily identified with the use of the ARTS tree reports. ARTS helps with test planning, interface control, and specification preparation. It also provides the vehicle to perform the required status and control functions for the entire requirements management process. This results in a discipline that cannot exist without the tool. The process is speeded up, accuracy is improved, and engineers are freed to concentrate on the actual engineering tasks. All of these requirements management functions, including traceability, must now be performed for most major military or government systems.

General Description of ARTS

ARTS started as an internally funded research and development project in 1980 with a charter to build a requirements traceability system for software engineers. The first tasks were to select a database management system and to add the traceability components. Once these two elements were combined, the system was to be tested, documented, and released.

At approximately the same time that the ARTS database manager search and selection process was proceeding, the Lockheed systems engineering organization was independently formalizing a set of concepts and procedures for the requirements engineering function. That study included the definition of the system hierarchy made up of system elements, system requirements identification, functional decomposition, requirements allocation to component elements in the hierarchy, requirements flowdown into the hierarchy, and requirements traceability. Lockheed chose to use the new ARTS database package on two projects even before the traceability components were completed. This developed a relationship that still exists. The ARTS tool, while originally planned for software requirements traceability, actually became a systems engineering tool that could be used for the entire development project.

Several decisions were made by the ARTS development personnel in both the software and hardware areas very early in the design process. They decided to use a database manager as the core software because of the make-up and quantity of the requirements data. Very few database management systems were available at that time. The developers wanted a system that could be easily delivered at a low cost to its users. That led to the selection of an internally developed package. In the hardware area, the developers wanted to support existing standard computer devices, including terminals and line printers. They also felt that the system should operate on several readily available computers which were at that time a Univac 1100 and a DEC VAX.

The software approach consisted of defining the basic "requirement object" as a single record in the database. From a relational database viewpoint, the requirement occupies one row in a table. The primary key is indexed for faster access and stored in a field or attribute named REQID. This unique REQuirement IDentifier consists of a maximum of eight characters made up of one to four alpha characters and three to five numeric characters with the numeric component incremented by 10 between requirements to allow space to insert additional data (e.g., MST00010, MST00020, SYS0010, or FS0210). The alpha component could represent a unique shortened mnemonic for the "block" or function in the system hierarchy to which the requirement belongs and is usually three or four characters long.

The traceability link is entered into another field called DERIVATION. That entry is the REQID of the parent or source requirement. Multiple entries in a derivation field, representing several parents, are allowed but discouraged. Top-level or system requirements have no derivation but could have a source paragraph number that can be saved in a SOURCE field. Text is accessed with a pointer to a text module stored externally in a library. Other fields could be added as needed and include such items as status, dates, responsible personnel or organizations, keywords, change information, validation method, etc. A representation of the single record structure and the associated pointers is shown in Figure 2.

One unique feature of the selected database management system is the ability to add multiple entries into a single database field. Thus, you can have multiple keywords, derivations, allocations, etc., for a given requirement without building separate tables. These fields can be indexed and the records can be accessed by any of the individual entries. Multiple entries are separated by slashes. The database also provides the capability to select, save, and manipulate sets of requirements.

The requirement records for a program are entered into the database and several report types including tree reports could be generated as needed. Tree output was in the form of tables. Generally they were too large for a graphical output and the original display terminals (e.g., DEC VT100's) could not support graphics.

The development methodology for the ARTS software was based on a combination of rapid prototyping and incremental development. Users existed at the very beginning of the project who expected quick results from the development team. A prototype was initially created and delivered to selected users. As new features were added, they were incorporated by the users, and ideas for new enhancements were fed back to the developers. Once the initial problems were overcome, the system was released to the general user community. Large requirement databases were created, and the prototype became an established tool. The system has been incrementally developed since then, and no major redesign has been done.

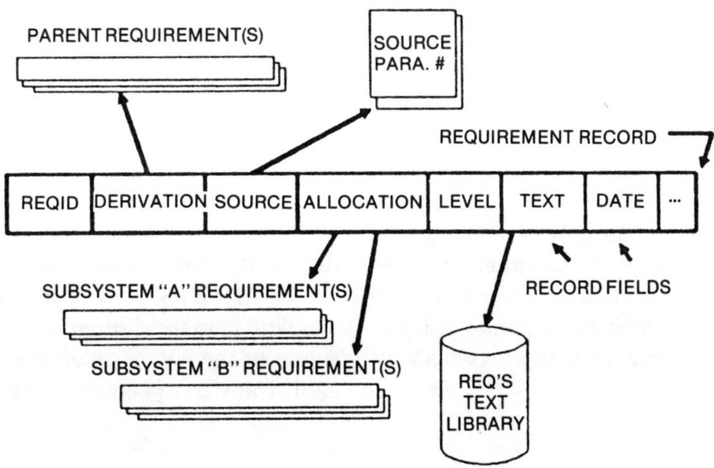

Figure 2: ARTS requirement record structure

The ARTS software was written in the Fortran programming language.The original database code was Fortran IV and the new software was added utilizing Fortran V. The system contains approximately 20K lines of source code. The ARTS tool was not used in its own development and maintenance because of the small size of the project and its incremental development approach.

The Evolution of the ARTS Tool

The ARTS tool has continued to evolve since its creation in 1980. Enhancements and standardization have occurred in both hardware and software areas. A considerable amount of documentation on ARTS has been generated and an ARTS application support group has been formed.

The DEC VAX computer has become the standard minicomputer system at Lockheed because of its low cost, broad software base, and ease of use. Other versions of ARTS were created for the CDC Cyber, IBM mainframes, and Univac 1100s. However, they were rarely used and were difficult to support when a more sophisticated user interface was chosen. Maintenance for these systems was also expensive and, as a result, these versions were eventually abandoned.

The user interface to ARTS was initially considered a problem. Entering and modifying the large number of requirements was very difficult using the command language interface provided with the original database software. The command interface was confusing, inconsistent, and hard to learn.

Several features were added to ARTS to improve the user interface. The command language interface was retained for experienced users, but the commands were renamed based on a new functional grouping and the syntax was made more consistent. A menu interface for new users was also added, along with detailed on-line help information.

An easy method of entering data was a high priority. The requirements data were initially entered into the database from information entered on paper forms that were later keyed to disk files. A batch input and update capability was added to ARTS to manipulate these files and eliminate some of the data entry problems. A forms interface, which allowed the requirement record to be easily added, viewed, or modified, was later designed and built.

To add requirements easily from information stored in specification files, an external processor called SPECIN was built in 1984. It reads a specification stored as an ASCII file, parses the requirement text using keywords, cuts the text to an ARTS text library, and creates a requirements input file that can be added to the database. The initial development of this capability was done as a separate Independent Development project and proved to be a very challenging task.

> Perhaps the most difficult technical problem in providing an effective requirements tracking tool is parsing textual requirements documents to identify and tag individual requirements paragraphs, sentences and keywords.[5]

Improved requirements report writing was also an early priority. The original database program only supported two report formats and none for record treeing. Over the first few years, five tree report formats were added, the original formats were enhanced, and several others were created based on user needs.

Another output format requested was to merge the requirement text and non-requirement text or "boilerplate" text to create a formal specification document. This capability was added and has since become one of the most frequently used capabilities. It has been continually enhanced and currently writes a specification with the following:

- Title page
- Tables of contents
- Tables of figures
- Tables of tables
- Variable page headers and footers with date, page number, and security level inserts
- Page level security monitoring with security markings rolling over to the next page if required
- Alternating page headers for odd and even page numbers
- Minimal white space by "floating" figures/tables to the next page when insufficient space available on the current page
- Repeating table headers when a table spans more than one page
- Page break control
- No split regions on a page
- Controlled blank space on any page
- Controlled merge of boilerplate text and requirement text

Other ARTS software enhancements include internal performance improvements, consistency and completeness checks, automatic field filling, improved screen appearance, a method for controlling system interfaces, many user control options with command level "mode switches," on-line news, status monitoring, REQID renumbering capabilities, and input checking and control. In July 1988, a PC version of ARTS, referred to as PcARTS, was released.[6] It was written in the C programming language and provided a subset of the ARTS capabilities. Requirement data can be easily transferred between the two systems.

Documenting the ARTS system was also a concern. A complete user's manual has been written that includes a system description, "how to" guide, functional description, command details, administration information, training exercises, and much more. Several papers describing ARTS and requirements management have been written and presented.[8, 9, 10, 11] ARTS was included in the NBS Software Development Tools publication,[12] incorporated into the original systems engineering class prepared by Lockheed for the Defense Systems Management College, and is referred to in the Lockheed Space Systems Division Standards and Practices for Software Engineering.[13]

As the ARTS tool and the systems engineering function evolved, the need for people trained in ARTS and requirements analysis grew. To fill that need, a special support group was formed to train and supply personnel to the requesting projects. These people would enter requirements data, maintain and control databases, interface with project engineering, write reports, review documentation, create traceability linkages, and perform other related ARTS and systems engineering tasks. That group's functions now include software development, training, documentation, user support, configuration management, and consulting.

The Use of ARTS

ARTS is a software system that is made up of a set of programs and procedures used to capture, store, maintain, and output requirements information. The complete system, including access to the VAX editor, is shown in Figure 3. There are five programs in ARTS, including the main ARTS database program, the text processor, the SPECIN specification input system, external FORMS, and the text checker TEXTCK. The user interacts with them to read input files, to interface with the database and text library files, and to output reports, including formal specifications.

library files, and to output reports, including formal specifications.

The use of ARTS begins during the analysis or requirements definition phase of a project. A potential user first collects all the requirements for the project from a system specification, request for proposal, statement of work, or any other pertinent sources. They originate with the customer who interfaces with program management. Management works with systems engineers who actually perform most of the requirements managment tasks, which include identifying all the "system" requirements. Data entry or application support personnel performs the physical task of adding or manipulating the data. An ARTS interface description diagram is provided in Figure 4.

Once the top-level or system requirements are collected and a system hierarchy is defined, the ARTS database record storage format is created for the requirements information. The REQID and DERIVATION fields are required. ALLOCATION, LEVEL, SOURCE, TEXT, SUMMARY, DATE, ENGINEER, STATUS, TEST METHOD, PARAGRAPH NUMBER, TEXT PENDING, and KEYWORDS are optional fields that can also be used. An ARTS database is initialized, the storage format is added, and the requirements are entered individually, in batch groups, or from output from the specification input program. These requirements are allocated to lower-level components in the system hierarchy and lower-level requirements are created and added to the database as needed, while maintaining traceability linkages.

The ideal requirements engineering process, as defined by LMSC's System Engineering Organization[14, 15] and supported by ARTS, consists of the steps of identification, allocation, and flowdown. This top-down approach is shown graphically in Figure 5. Once the system hierarchy has been

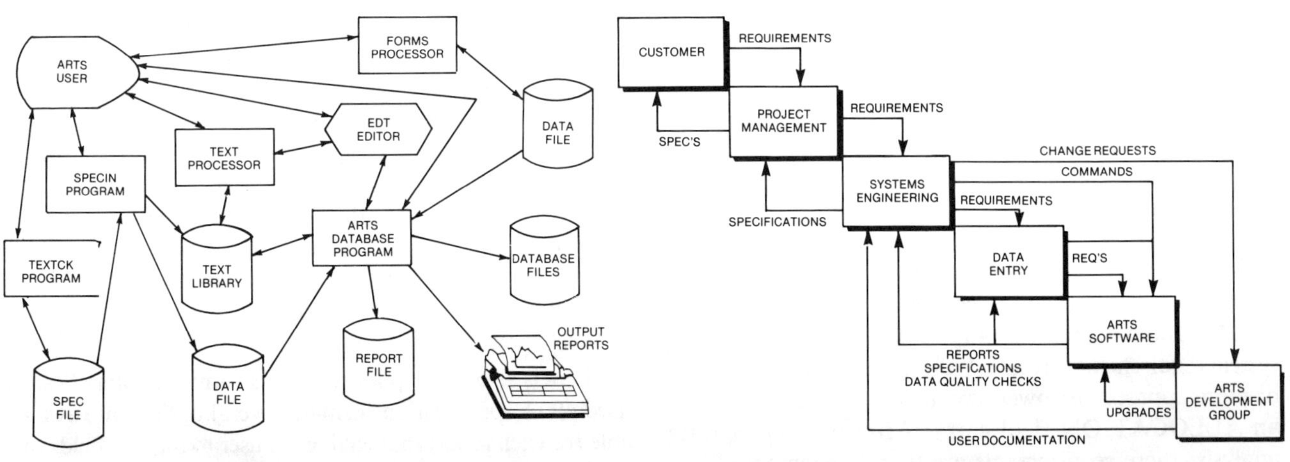

Figure 3: ARTS system flow diagram

Figure 4: ARTS interface description

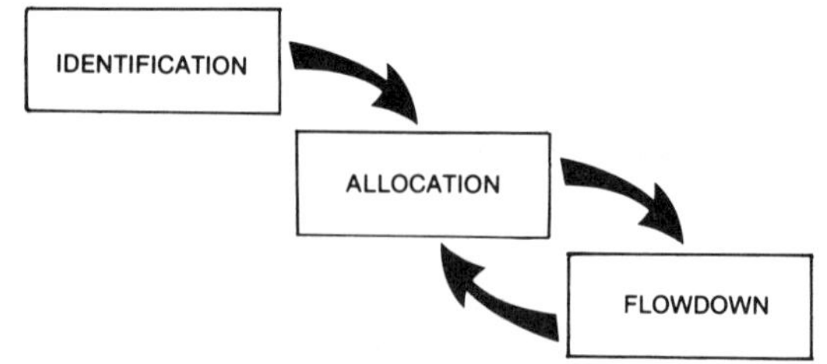

Figure 5: Ideal requirement definition process

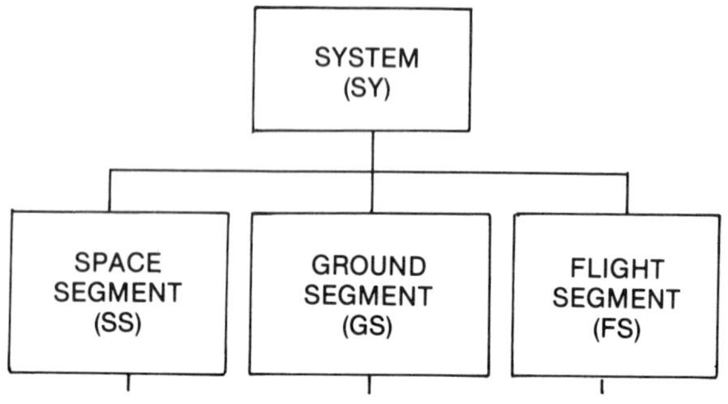

Figure 6: Sample system hierarchy chart

Table 1: Sample requirements field entries

REQUID	LEVEL	ALLOCATION	DERIVATION
SY0010	1	FS/GS	
FS0010	2		SY0010
GS0040	2		SY0010

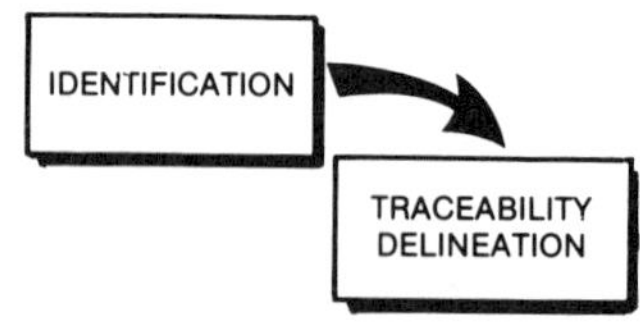

Figure 7: Normal requirement definition process

defined, system requirements are identified first for the top-level "block." After being identified, they are added to the ARTS database in the storage format specified. These system requirements are later "allocated" or pointed to one or more appropriate lower-level blocks through the use of an ALLOCATION field entry. After the appropriate analysis, these requirements are then "decomposed" or "flowed down" into more detailed requirements for each of the lower-level blocks to which the requirement was allocated.

The higher-level requirements are sometimes referred to as "parents" and the more detailed as "children." The lower-level requirements are connected to their parents through the use of a DERIVATION field that contains the REQIDs or identifiers of the parent requirements. Every lower-level requirement must have at least one parent. ARTS allows multiple parents (limited currently to eight) for a requirement. The lower-level requirements are sometimes referred to as "derived requirements."

As an example, a simple system hierarchy is shown in Figure 6. It is composed of a system block in which requirements are allocated and flowed to a space, ground, or flight segment. The resulting requirements for these segments are also allocated and flowed down, which is not shown in this example. A system requirement SY0010 is identified at level 1, and it therefore has no derivation. Requirement SY0010 is later allocated to the flight and ground segments. Requirements FS0010 and GS0040 are then derived at level 2 as children of SY0010, with allocations to be determined later. Examples of the pertinent field entries for these activities are given in Table 1.

If users of ARTS choose not to follow the ideal or recommended approach to requirements management, they can still use the ARTS system. Regrettably, some ARTS users have not integrated the software into the process and still perform the traceability connections after the lower-level document is completed. This is graphically depicted in Figure 7. Such users prefer to record the linkages and use ARTS strictly in an "after-the-fact" bookkeeping mode. While this approach is not recommended, ARTS is flexible enough to be used in this fashion, and all of the traceability reports can still be generated.

The ARTS program will output the records stored in the database in a variety of report formats. There are currently 12 report types of which five are variations of tree reports. Four samples of the most commonly used reports are shown in Table 2, The first example is a tabular report with the field names followed by their entries with the text listed below the text fields. Example 2 is a formatted report with the field information provided in columns. A simple REQID tree report is shown in the third example. The last example is a formatted tree report with the REQID field listed first and indentation of the REQID used to represent levels. The '(U)' in the reports represents a method of identifying security levels for text strings.

There is also an output option to a formal Military Standard 490A specification format. Several options are available for each report that enable the user to include fields of interest and to vary output sizes. Reports can be written either to the screen or to a file for later printing.

Table 2: ARTS report samples

SAMPLE TABULAR REPORT

REQID	AXAF0080
LEVEL	1
DERIVATION	
ALLOCATION	PRD
SOURCE(S)	System Specification (SYS AXAF-001)
SOURCE TITLE	(U) Instrumentation Details
DOCUMENT TITLE	AXAF-101
PARAGRAPH NO	03.02.03
PARAGRAPH TITLE	(U) Initial SI Complement
VERIF PLAN	Demonstration
SUMMARY	The SI shall consist of 3-4 focal plane SI's and 1-2 obj. gratings
STATUS	New
CHANGE PENDING	None

TEXT
The SI (Science Instruments) complement for the intitial launch shall consist of no less than three and up to four focal plane SI's and no less than one and up to two objective gratings.

SAMPLE FORMATTED REPORT

REQID	LEVEL	DERIVATION	ALLOCATION	DOCUMENT TITLE	PARAGRAPH NO	PARAGRAPH TITLE	CHANGE PENDING	TEXT
PRD00610	2	AXAF0080	OBS	PRD (AXAF-201)	03.01.05.06	(U) Objective	Yes	The Observatory shall provide two objective grating mechanisms which shall be located aft of the HRMA.
PRD00615	2	AXAF0080	OBS	PRD (AXAF-201)	03.01.05.06	(U) Grating Positioning on Failure	None	Grating mechanism drives shall provide for a failed configuration which leaves the gratings free and clear from the X-ray beam following two mechanism failures.
PRD00613	2	AXAF0080	OBS	PRD (AXAF-201)	03.01.05.06	(U) Command and Control of Grating Mechanisms	None	The two objective grating mechanisms shall be commandable in and out of the X-ray beam.

SAMPLE REQID TREE REPORT

LEVELS:

1	2	3	4	5	6	7
AXAF0080	PRD00610	OBS0094				
	PRD00613	OBS0094				
		OBS00945				
	PRD00615	OBS00950				
		OBS00955				
	PRD00616					
AXAF0100	PRD00680	OBS00670				
	PRD00690	OBS00680				
	PRD00700	OBS00690				
	PRD00710	OBS00700				
AXAF0120	PRD00020	OBS00050				
		OBS02580				
		OBS02600				
	PRD00080	OBS00150				
		OBS02610				

SAMPLE FORMATTED TREE REPORT

REQID	LEVEL	ALLOCATION	DOCUMENT TITLE	PARAGRAPH NO	PARAGRAPH TITLE	CHANGE PENDING	TEXT
AXAF0080	1	PRD	AXAF-101	03.02.05	(U) Initial SI Complement	None	The SI (Science Instruments) complement for the initial launch shall consist of no less than three and up to four focal plane SI's and no less than one and up to two objective gratings.
PRD00610	2	OBS	PRD (AXAF-201)	03.01.05.06	(U) Objective Grating Locations	Yes	The Observatory shall provide two objective grating mechanisms which shall be located aft of the HRMA.
OBS0094	3		OBS (AXAF-311)	03.02.01.02.1	(U) Transmission Grating Activating	None	The Telescope shall provide two mechanisms capable of moving each of two gratings into and out of the X-ray.

ARTS Today

ARTS was one of the first tools built to perform the requirements management function including traceability. Its unique approach has few competitors. ARTS gives the user visibility to the actual requirements and also control over the requirements management process. In addition to viewing the actual requirement, the user can find the responsible engineer or organization and change status, pending text, revision date or level, test method, test status, keywords, etc. Each requirement can be viewed individually or as a "tree" either up or down.

Many companies have contacted Lockheed in regard to using ARTS, creating an opportunity to market it commercially. However, Lockheed currenty considers ARTS a proprietary product and will not commercially license its use. ARTS has been released to several government contracting agencies and to certain subcontractors.

The ARTS software continues to be fully supported. The current software support consists of program maintenance, problem resolution, upgrades to the existing software, configuration management, conversion of selected capabilities to the PC environment, and software deliveries. User support incorporates telephone and on-site consulting and problem resolution, briefings, demonstrations, documentation, users' meetings, and training classes. Application support includes providing personnel for database administration, data entry and update, report and specification preparation, and assisting the systems engineering functions of requirements identification, allocation, and flowdown.

The use of ARTS and good requirements management techniques are necessary throughout the entire system development lifecycle. This is shown in Figure 8. The requirement process of allocation and flowdown takes place through the design and development phases. New requirements are added and existing requirements are updated or deleted. The process continues through test or verification with the insertion of test-related information for each requirement. During delivery and maintenance phases, the database is used for problem resolution and determining the impact of upgrades.

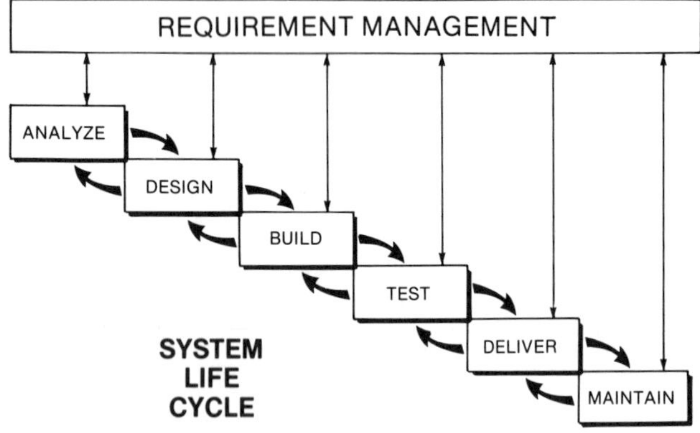

Figure 8:
Requirement management supports the entire system lifecycle

The ARTS system has been available and supported for eight years at Lockheed. The original concept and approach continue to fill a real need, which is to demonstrate good requirements management techniques, including traceability, to Lockheed's customers. That is probably the main reason for the longevity of the tool. ARTS also fulfills an implicit need by contributing to project goals of reduced cost, schedule control, status monitoring, and improved quality.

Another important reason for the ARTS success is the support that is provided to the users. Users know that someone is always available who can answer questions, resolve problems, and provide help or advice. The existence of an application support group from virtually the beginning of the ARTS project helped considerably. The original software developer and the application support group leader also remain with the project to provide the continuity and experience.

ARTS remains a viable tool for several other reasons:

1. The system is flexible and extensible. The user defines the record structure. Only the REQID and DERIVATION fields are required for traceability. However, the user has the power of a database manager.
2. The formal link of the ARTS software with the system hierarchy is optional. The system block's alpha can be used as a part of the REQID, but it is not required.
3. Many input methods facilitate the tedious task of data entry.
4. The requirement storage format can be changed easily. As the project matures, attributes change accordingly. For example, initially a project is interested in completeness and consistency. Later it is concerned with compliance or verification.
5. It is easy to initiate the function. The software, documentation, training, and experienced application personnel are readily available. No software license or cost is necessary.
6. There is no limit to the number of requirements that can be entered. Other software limits, such as the number of fields in a record or the number of characters in a field, do not seem to restrict the usage.
7. The incremental or evolutionary development approach has worked very well. The system is small enough and, with experienced software personnel, changes can be made easily and rapidly.

8. ARTS has finally matured as a software product. The quality of the system, its growth from experience, and resulting in its name recognition have taken a long time and a significant amount of support to attain.

Where ARTS Is Going

Recent internal developments in Lockheed have resulted in the initiation of a study to review the future directions of the ARTS system. One of the key issues is the rehosting of certain existing functions and the creation of several new capabilities utilizing a commercial database management system. Existing users and potential new users are being surveyed about their current and future needs. Lockheed hopes that this interest will result in funding of a completely new version. The contemporary system will take into account the experience gained in supporting ARTS for the last eight years. That decision is expected late in 1989 or early in 1990.

Difficulties with the Use of ARTS

Although ARTS has been successfully used for eight years, some difficulties have emerged. These complications have been grouped into software, application, methodology, and other areas. Each of these sections will be discussed in some detail. The intent of this review is to learn more about the requirements management process and its associated tool needs.

Software complications relate to the difficulties with programming a solution. Sufficient resources in the areas of personnel, budget, time, and hardware are not always available to eliminate or minimize these difficulties. They include the following:

1. The quantity of data involved can be huge. Requirement databases can easily exceed 25,000 records. This results in some very slow database operations.
2. The ARTS database manager does not support multiple users writing to the database simultaneously.
3. The continued development of ARTS has resulted in many options that can be difficult for both new and experienced users to learn and remember.
4. The system has certain limits that affect the process. The most notable is the limit of eight derivations for a given requirement. Structured flowdown ideally results in only one parent, but exceptions are common.
5. There are several obstacles to report generation. The output reports and specifications do not support the full capabilities of new laser printers. The user's documentation now requires special mathematical or Greek characters, superscript or subscript, bold or underline, and graphics that are available with laser printer output. However, the older terminals and the standard line printers for which the original system was designed do not support them.
6. Security constraints require specialized report output. Also, users seem to need to customize their own reports in nonstandard forms.
7. The software and the output devices do not support graphical tree output. Some workstation users now expect output in that form, but hardware costs are high.
8. For specification output, no change page capability exists. This is a very difficult problem to solve since documentation users prefer to work with the formatted page and the ARTS database deals with the information in an unformatted state.

Applications complications arise when users try to do more with the software than it was designed to do, use it in a nonstandard fashion, or just do not use it properly. They include the following:

1. Too much information is included in the REQID field entry. It was only designed to include the alpha associated with the system block and an incrementing number.
2. Requirements are not flowed down in a top-down fashion, resulting in too many derivations. The current ARTS limit is eight.
3. Users try to maintain too many attributes and then do not have the resources to enter or maintain them.
4. Too many fields are keyed in the requirement storage format, which slows operations.
5. Data are changed too often, which results in a high database maintenance effort.
6. Some users skip levels for some requirements, which affects report formatting and consistency checking.
7. There sometimes is too much interest in creating specifications and the traceability is ignored until it is too late to be of real use.
8. Many requirements are only repeated at the next level. No real flowdown is done.
9. The data that are input into the ARTS database are insufficiently reviewed by others in the systems engineering function. In other words, the tool is not completely integrated into the requirements management process.
10. For some projects, a good set of top-level requirements is not created until the project has completed the analysis phase. This makes the top-down approach to traceability very difficult.

Methodology complications arise when a tool does not fit the function for which was it designed. With ARTS, they include the following:

1. Some users have trouble accepting a unique REQID made up of an alpha and numeric component for each requirement. Some applications insist on just the paragraph number reference, even though they do not restrict a paragraph number to include only one requirement, and the same numbers appear in more than one document.
2. It is difficult to determine how many levels of requirements exist in military standard specifications, which generally locate requirements in paragraph 3. There is no agreement as to how the requirements text is detailed in paragraph 3.2 and functionally allocated in paragraph 3.7. A standard specification might contain one or two levels of requirements. A requirement in paragraph 3.7 might be repeated in paragraph 3.2 in the next lower document or considered a new requirement.
3. Many users do not perform allocation before flowdown. The database is only used to store the specification information after the document is completed.
4. Certain generic or support requirements do not decompose as they flow down. They only exist at the system level. An example might be that all software shall be written in Ada or that the system shall have a three-year life span. Safety, logistics, and reliability requirements are a related concern.
5. The requirements management function changes as the using project matures. Changing database formats only partially compensates for this.

ARTS has suffered from several people-related complications over the years. Discussions with individuals at other companies and a review of related articles lead us to the conclusion that these difficulties are not exclusive to Lockheed. The impact of personnel on tool acceptance and use will be discussed in more detail later. The more important people-related difficulties that ARTS has experienced include these:

1. System engineers who try to use ARTS are somewhat fearful of computer-based tools and resent the changes to their methods brought about by the tool.
2. Properly qualified personnel are not assigned to using the ARTS tool. Many have never used a computer.
3. The ARTS tool capabilities were oversold during the early phase of the project. As a result, some disillusionment has carried over to the present, even though the tool has been extensively modified. First perceptions are lasting, especially in an environment where the same systems engineering personnel continue to move between projects.
4. The cost to use the ARTS tool were either not included in the initial quotes by the users or were underestimated, often making their requirements management charges exceed expectations. Users frequently say, "Before we started using ARTS, we could do traceability in a few hours a week. Now it's a full-time job for two people!" The answer is that they really were not doing it before.
5. Some of the ARTS database support functions are best performed by nonengineering personnel. However, these people are sometimes not accepted in the technically oriented systems engineering environment.
6. The users tend to split into two camps: those who love the tool as it is and those who dislike it. There is no middle ground of those who can see the tool for what it is and are willing to assist in making it better.
7. Systems engineering courses are rarely taught in engineering curricula, and few, if any, degrees are available. The courses appear to be staffed by engineers in certain specialized disciplines, such as electronics, who wish to change their career paths. Generally, systems engineering is not well respected in the program structure.

Other complications with ARTS that do not seem to fit any of the previous areas include the following:

1. The name chosen for the tool, Automated Requirements Traceability System, is something of a misnomer. It will automatically display the stored traceability, but the allocation and flowdown are not automated.
2. The hardware base is changing rapidly. Potential users may not possess the standard VAX system that existed when the project was initiated.
3. Viewing data on the screen, even with high-resolution screens, is not as easy as manipulating paper.
4. Knowing when to do quality and consistency checking is difficult. Many users build their databases from the bottom up so checking must be deferred. If the tool is used in a top-down manner, checking can be done when the data are entered.
5. ARTS is a stand-alone tool. The current trend is toward tool environments.

General Tool Considerations

In the review and evaluation of the ARTS tool that we recently completed, it became readily apparent that there are many difficulties associated with successfully inserting a software tool into a project. Many of them have been previously listed. When they were analyzed, we were able to categorize them into four main areas. Further study of these four areas revealed that they encompass the complete environment in which a tool exists. They apply to the development environment, as well as to the application environment. This "complete" environment must be thoroughly reviewed and well understood before a tool can be built, selected, or applied to a particular task. In the rest of this paper, we will concentrate on the application environment associated with requirements management tools.

The tool-to-task paradigm we propose (Figure 9) encompasses four components: situation, computer, people, and data. The situation concerns the internal and external factors affecting the task. The individuals involved represent the people component. They include tool developers, users, project management, and customers. The data component is made up of the objects being manipulated by the people. For our example, it will be requirements. The computer segment has been intentionally separated from the situational aspects because of its unique characteristics, and it represents the fourth aspect of the model. The computer component is made up of hardware and software, with software including operating systems, user interfaces,[16] and support software such as database management systems.

Situation

1. Projects are large in terms of money, people, and tasks.
2. The time frame for the project is long, with many years from concept to delivery. However, the project will be controlled by short-term schedules dictated by baseline management.
3. Several subcontractors will be involved as well as independent validators, probably separated by long distances.
4. The techniques and methods of development projects will change during the life of the project.
5. Financial problems on the project will result in stretch-outs, scope changes, and possibly even cancellation.
6. The project will be reorganized at least once.
7. Security can play a very important role.
8. The organizational structure will be large, with internal competition and politics playing an important role.
9. The project will probably not completely follow the simple lifecycle model and will not be developed in a top-down fashion. Design will start very early.
10. Military standards will play a key role in how the project is developed.

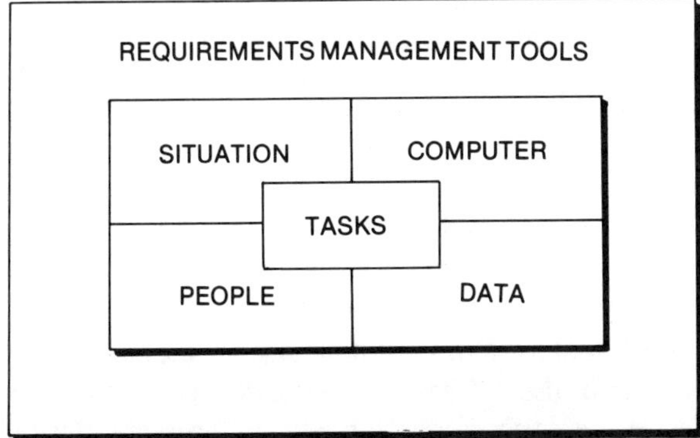

Figure 9: Tool and task interaction

Data

1. There will be a tremendous number of requirements, probably more than 50,000.
2. Requirements are made up of text, graphics, special characters, tables, and related attributes.
3. With full text and related attributes, the databases will be huge, resulting in slow retrieval and update.
4. The data will be extremely volatile, schedule critical, and spread over many locations.
5. No formal definition standards exist for requirements.
6. Requirements are often fragmented and incomplete.
7. The data are extremely visible. Everyone is affected, especially at the beginning of a project.
8. Supporting information is needed to comprehend a given requirement fully. It must be seen in its documentation context.
9. Requirements need unique identifiers with a reference to an output paragraph number.
10. There are different types of requirements, such as performance, support, safety, environmental, logistics, etc.
11. Requirements will be referenced to entire documents. For example, the system shall meet all requirements in document. . .
12. No formal requirements methodology will exist and little training will be provided in systems engineering.
13. Requirements are too explicit at the top and too general at lower levels.
14. Requirements are normally found in documents that are controlled by military standards.
15. Requirement text changes are usually made under formal configuration management.
16. There are military standards for the format of specifications and associated fill-in guides that are used. However, there are no definitive guides for how to write a requirement.

People

1. Requirements management is generally performed by experienced personnel or by new employees just hired out of college.
2. Many of the experienced personnel have not used computers and are somewhat biased against the use of tools.
3. Those who have used computers will be biased towards certain solutions (e.g., Macintosh, dBase, Datatrieve, etc.).
4. People tend to follow fads. They like to use the "in" hardware and software.
5. Many people cannot type or type poorly.
6. Project support and customer personnel turnover on a specific project is high and there will be many personality clashes.
7. The people assigned to requirements management tasks are those who cannot contribute in other engineering tasks.
8. Management is concerned only with the short-term tasks. There will be little long-range planning.
9. Past experience with tools will play an important role. An earlier bad experience may restrict insertion of new tools.
10. Requirements management is not considered important. The function is mostly clerical and considered beneath an engineer.
11. People tend to do only what they have to do and requirements management tasks are not directly written into the contracts.
12. People are more concerned with looks than content. That is reflected in the trend towards desktop publishing for specification output and few tools for evaluating the actual content of the document.
13. The system engineers will disagree among themselves on the need for a system hierarchy and its make-up. They will also have a difficult time with top-level identification, the initial allocation, and the functional decomposition.
14. Requirements management can be boring because of the repetitive nature of the function.

Computer

1. The capability of computers is increasing dramatically.
2. Tools are more tightly coupled with the operating system and with other software packages.
3. More software reuse occurs with the marketing of common libraries, especially in the area of graphical interfaces.
4. Most tools are now being written in the C programming language for speed and portability.
5. Database management systems are proliferating, with a trend toward distributed databases.
6. Networking computers are becoming more popular.
7. Users are moving away from terminals on large mainframe computers toward high-power workstations with enhanced resolution monitors, larger screens, significant amounts of memory, and extremely fast processors.
8. Personal computers and workstations are becoming very similar in capability. However, enough differences that software is not easily ported between systems.
9. There are more brand choices for users with less distinction.
10. Graphical interfaces are gaining support.
11. Desktop publishing is becoming very popular.
12. No single operating system will be used on all systems. UNIX is growing in popularity.
13. Interest in artificial intelligence is growing, especially in the form of expert systems.
14. More training will be required to use the new systems.
15. Computers are getting more powerful, but it will take longer to develop new software because of the increasing complexity of hardware and software.

Observations and Conclusions

When one reviews the environmental characteristics for requirements management tools or for any other type of tool, it is easier to understand why it is so difficult to insert a tool to perform a particular task. This is demonstrated by the small number of requirements tools that exist and the even smaller number that are actually used. For a tool to be successfully inserted, the environment must be well understood. The tool must possess certain attributes that match it to the situation and the data to be manipulated. The proper computer support must exist and the people who will use it must be responsive to the tool.

For a tool to be successful, it must be flexible, since each instance of use will have its own set of special characteristics. However, there is a "flip side" of flexibility. If a tool is too flexible, it may not be applied properly. These are tool attributes that relate to flexibility:

1. The tool must possess active and passive data checking. Not all checks can be made at the time the data are entered. Periodically, consistency must be verified.
2. Batch processing is necessary in addition to the normal interactive interface. The quantities of data are so large that certain functions must be started and completed in a background mode. Data entry is a good candidate for batch operations. True multiple processing is required.
3. It must be easy to add, change, and manipulate the data.
4. Some form of switches or configuration settings must be available to customize the tool to the particular application.
5. The tools must be built on a commercial database manager that supports multiple users and network operations. Distributed databases may be necessary. A good database program will allow more related attributes and even support additional tables defined as needed by the user. It will also supply efficient indexing and sorting.
6. The database structure must be dynamic, since the data attributes will change as the project matures.
7. A programmable user interface may reduce complaints, since the user controls that aspect. Users must have the resources for this task. A programmable report processor is also necessary.

Support for the tool is another important ingredient and must come from management, the development group, an applications group, and the users themselves. For most companies, two management segments are involved. One segment controls the functional organizations responsible for the tool development and applications support groups and the other controls the projects that will be using the tools. Both management groups must be coordinated and willing to support the development, application support, and project groups with hardware, funding, standards, methods, and goals.

The development group's support is also critical. It is responsible for selecting and/or developing tools and methods. Tools are being developed internally, commercially, and by consortiums. The best candidates must be selected and applied to the projects. A single tool or system approach within a company is best, because it eases the transition of employees between projects. Once an approach is selected, the proper training, documentation, demonstrations, and briefings must be made available to users. Feedback from developers to managment is also required in the form of planning, schedules, status, and budgets.

The existence of an applications support group will increase the probability of successfully inserting a tool. An application group will assist users during the early application difficulties and later, as questions or problems arise. It supports the actual use of the tool and performs functions such as data validation, database administration, data entry, data modification, report generation, and status monitoring. These personnel must be fully trained to provide support in situations where the users cannot perform all of the tool tasks themselves. This support can be supplied permanently or on an as-needed basis. One problem with an application support group is funding for training and for retaining staff when they are between assignments. The application group must work closely with the development group to keep current with upgrades and to supply software change requests when needed.

The users of the tools must also have a feedback path to the developers so that modifications can be made as required. They can get questions answered and have any problems resolved. Another user feedback path is to management. Users must supply project status and information as to how the tool is performing and must also supply status and performance information to the application support group. If the tool use is broad enough, users' group can be formed to exchange information.

Certain general observations that can be made about software tools. Tools can make a task easier to perform, but their use will change the process. Any process utilizing computer-based tools can never become totally paperless. Hardcopy output must be provided, and inputs/changes made on paper will serve as inputs. Certain functions can be facilitated by using video projectors along with the tools. An example that has been successfully implemented is an electronic change control board. Documents are projected and the suggested modifications are evaluated by a group. If changes are necessary, they are entered dynamically.

Tools can never be completely automated. A significant amount of human intervention will always be required. Solutions overlap organizational boundaries, so people will have to learn to work together or restructuring will be necessary. A willingness to accept change, to use computers, and to learn new software systems is mandatory.

In the area of requirements management tools, certain specific observations can be made. These tools span the entire system development lifecycle—not just the analysis-phase. Requirements are the glue that binds the cycle. Each of the other phases only adds new requirements at lower levels or fills or modifies the attributes for existing requirements. The system development process is more complicated than most people realize. Tools are designed to help the process, but many other considerations affect it. The complete environment must be considered. Also, inserting a tool into a process changes that process, and change generally causes problems.

Future Directions

The tool-to-task review reveals that the requirements management function on our large projects exists in a complicated environment. This process can be controlled only with the use of computer-based tools. Manually manipulating the large amounts of data is impossible. Support and cooperation among all those concerned are mandatory ingredients to solving the associated problems.

Several improvements to the requirements management process in the future do not involve the tools directly. The first is to develop requirements definition standards.

> There are not even good ways in common use for even stating detailed requirements. . . [1]

As long as we continue to work with the fragmented expressions that are contained in current specifications, we will never make any progress. Clear statements in a consistent format will make allocation and flowdown much easier. That will improve design, which will improve implementation and so on. The first task on a project will then be to restate the system requirements according to these new standards, eliminating the fragmentation. This will be followed by obtaining customer acceptance of the new version before the actual analysis and design begin.

Another task is to define the allocation and flowdown functions in terms of an accepted methodology. Once defined, the new methods and procedures must be included in classes, must be supported by tools and application support groups, and must be used by the projects. The current lifecycle model may have to be revised and baseline management eliminated. Possible alternatives include prototyping and incremental development. The new Military Standard 2167A[4] may need to be revised accordingly. Making these types of changes will not be easy. Our customers must support Lockheed in developing and testing changes in these areas, because they will benefit most from these changes.

Enhancements to the existing requirements management tools are also necessary. Some current developments are very promising for future upgrades and should be included in new research and development projects. They include these:

1. Artificial intelligence in the form of expert systems could be used for allocation and flowdown.
2. Language processors could be developed to evaluate the requirements statements.
3. Hypertext techniques could be used to perform traceability.
4. Object-oriented database managers may prove more appropriate than the current relational models, especially for a more complicated requirement object including text, graphics, and related attributes.
5. Database servers are now being developed that will allow multiple high-speed data access across a network.

The next generation of requirements management tools will either be written in the C programming language, object-oriented C, in a fourth-generation language associated with database managment systems, or in a language embedded structured query language. These tools must be portable and run on PCs, Macintoshes, workstations, and minicomputers. They should support Unix as well as conventional operating systems.

The ARTS tool, as it currently exists, possesses many of the attributes necessary for a tool to be successful. It will continue to be used until a new generation of requirements management tools is developed that takes more consideration of the environmental characteristics alluded to in this paper. The new CASE tools, which include some requirements management capability, must also take these factors into consideration or they will have only limited success in our environment.

It should be recognized that good requirements management techniques are a necessary ingredient for the success of any project. Also, they must be performed throughout the entire lifecycle of the project. Tools will assist the process, but many other factors will come into play. How the tools and these other factors are integrated and controlled is the challenge that we all face.

Glossary

Allocation: The process of partitioning, budgeting, or apportioning a performance or functional requirement to the physical subelements of a system. In this manner, the elements of a system that perform specific requirements or that contribute partially to performing others are identified. In other words, it identifies where a requirement flowdown will occur.

ARTS: Automated Requirements Traceability System, a software database management system for requirements information managment. *ARTS is only available only on a DEC VAX computer system and is considered to be a proprietary product.*

Attribute: A property or description; in the requirements database, something selected by the user to be stored with the requirement text to provide information about the requirement. Used interchangeably with FIELD.

Configuration management: The process that identifies the functional and physical characteristics of an item during its lifecycle, controls changes to those characteristics, and provides information on the status of change actions.[15]

Database manager: The computer processor (software) that controls storing, combining, updating, retrieving, and displaying records. It can also refer to the person who actually controls database access.

Derivation: In a hierarchical structure, the derivation(s) is/are the element(s) at the next higher level that is/are associated with a given element. The lower element is said to be derived from the higher element; not to be confused with a DERIVED REQUIREMENT.

Derived requirement: A requirement at a lower level that is determined to be necessary in order that a top-level requirement can be met. In general, a derived requirement is more specific and is directed toward some sub-element.

Field: A subset of a record with its own characteristics; fields are combined to form a record. Used interchangeably with ATTRIBUTE.

Field entry: A group of characters stored in a field or attribute.

Flowdown: The process of generating lower-level requirements from allocated higher-level requirements. Consists of decomposition of requirements into more detailed statements at lower levels.

Format: The arrangement of fields in a record.

Full text: A text library element or module external to an ARTS database. It is used for requirements information that requires more than a single line of text. Each module or element may contain several paragraphs.

Hierarchy: A type of structure in which each element or block has a level number (1 = highest), and each element is associated with one or more elements at the next higher and lower levels.

Key: A pointer or locator used to retrieve records. A key may be primary or secondary; primary keys are unique, secondary keys may have several occurrences.

Level: Numerical value that represents the relative location of a requirement in a hierarchical structure.

Lower-level requirement: A requirement that is in the hierarchy below top level or below the level of some given requirement.

PcARTS: A verions of the ARTS system that runs on a PC, with a subset of the VAX version's capabilities.

Record: A set of characters that makes up one or more consecutive fields on a related subject. Usually, one record is used per requirement.

REQID: A unique requirement identifier limited by ARTS to eight characters. It is made up of 1-4 alpha characters followed by 2-6 numeric characters (e.g., MST0010 or SYS00010).

Requirement: An authorized and documented need of the customer. A requirement must be sufficiently complete to stand alone; must be verifiable by at least one of the standard methods—test, analysis, demonstration, or inspection; and should cover only a single parameter. A requirement can consist of a block of text, a table, a figure, or any combination thereof. A requirement text phrase usually contains the keyword "shall" (e.g., "The system *shall* transmit collected data in realtime to a remote ground station").

Requirements management: The process of controlling the identification, allocation, and flowdown of requirements from the system level to the module or part level, including interfaces, verification, modifications, and status monitoring.

Storage format: Format into which requirements data records will be stored in the database.

System elements: Those functional groupings of specifiable entities that collectively make up a system, e.g., segment, subsystem, component, unit.

Tree: A hierarchy in which it is expected that an element at a given level has only one parent, i.e., flows from one element at the next higher level. Occasional multiple parents are permitted. Also a graphical representation of such a hierarchy.

Top-level requirement: A requirement that is at level 1 and the hierarchy. It represents a system requirement and has no derivation.

Traceability: Identification and documentation of the derivation path (upward) and allocation/flowdown path (downward) of requirements in the hierarchy. Traceability to and from the design is not explicitly included in this definition.

References

(1) Frederick Brooks et al., *Report of the Defense Science Board Task Force on Military Software,* September 1987.

(2) M.W. Alford and J.T. Lawson, "Software Requirements Engineering Methodology (Development)." *RADC-TR-79-168,* June 1979 (DDC AD A073132).

(3) B.W. Boehm, "Software Engineering," *IEEE Transactions on Computers,* Vol. C-25, No. 12, December 1976.

(4) "Defense System Software Development," *DOD-STD-2167A,* 29 February 1988.

(5) D. Ingram, "Requirements Managment Is Key to Software Quality," *C/A/S/E Outlook,* Vol. 1, No. 5, November 1987.

(6) R.F. Flynn and M.J. Schaefer, *Personal Computer Version of the Automated Requirements Traceability System (PcARTS)—User's Manual Version 2.00,* Lockheed Missile and Space Company, Inc., July 1988.

(7) R.F. Flynn, H.E. Trice, and M.J. Schaefer, *Automated Requirements Traceability System (ARTS) User's Manual—Version 4C,* Lockheed Missile and Space Company, Inc., April 1988.

(8) M. Dorfman and R.F. Flynn, "ARTS—An Automated Requirements Traceability System," *AIAA Computers in Aerospace III Conference,* October 26-28, 1981, San Diego, Calif.

(9) M. Dorfman and R.F. Flynn, "ARTS—An Automated Requirements Traceability System," *The Journal of Systems and Software,* Vol. 4, 1984, pp. 63-74.

(10) D.J. Paul and J.H. Fenton, "Semi-Automated Requirements Analysis for Software and System Engineering," *IIE West Coast Regionalized Conference,* 1983.

(11) D.J. Paul and J.H. Fenton, "Managing Project-Requirements," *Manage,* July 1983.

(12) R.C. Houghton Jr., "Software Development Tools," *NBS Special Publication 500-88,* March 1982.

(13) *SSD Standards and Practices for Software Engineering,"* Code 63, Lockheed Missiles and Space Co., April 1985.

(14) B.S. Blanchard and W.J. Fabrycky, *Systems Engineering and Analysis,"* Prentice-Hall, Inc., Englewood Cliffs, N.J., 1981.

(15) *SSD Systems Engineering Manual,* Code 66, Lockheed Missiles and Space Co., June 1985.

(16) B. Shneiderman, "Designing the User Interface: Strategies for Effective Human-Computer Interaction," Addison-Wesley Publishing Company, Reading, Mass., 1986.

Toward a Requirements Apprentice

Charles Rich – Richard C. Waters – Howard B. Reubenstein

MIT Artificial Intelligence Laboratory
545 Technology Sq.; Cambridge, MA 02139

Abstract

Requirements acquisition is one of the most important and least well supported parts of the software development process. The Requirements Apprentice (RA) will assist a human analyst in the creation and modification of software requirements. Unlike current requirements analysis tools, which assume a formal description language, the focus of the RA is on the boundary between informal and formal specifications. The RA is intended to support the earliest phases of creating a requirement, in which *incompleteness*, *ambiguity*, and *contradiction* are inevitable features.

From an artificial intelligence perspective, the central problem the RA faces is one of *knowledge acquisition*. It has to develop a coherent internal representation from an initial set of disorganized statements. To do so, the RA will rely on a variety of techniques, including dependency-directed reasoning, hybrid knowledge representation, and the reuse of common forms (*clichés*).

1. Introduction

The Programmer's Apprentice project uses the domain of programming as a vehicle for studying (and attempting to duplicate) human problem solving skills. Recognizing that it will be a long time before it is possible to fully duplicate human abilities in this domain, the near-term goal of the project is the development of a system, called the Programmer's Apprentice, which provides intelligent assistance in various phases of the programming task.

Viewed at the highest level, software development is a process that begins with the desires of an end user and ends with a program that can be executed on a machine. The first step of this process is traditionally called requirements acquisition, while the last step is called implementation. Figure 1 shows how the current and proposed demonstration systems in the Programmer's Apprentice project support these activities.

To date, most of the research in the Programmer's Apprentice project has focused on program implementation. This has resulted in the creation of a demonstration Imple-

This report describes research done at the Artificial Intelligence Laboratory of the Massachusetts Institute of Technology. Support for the laboratory's artificial intelligence research has been provided in part by the Advanced Research Projects Agency of the Department of Defense under Office of Naval Research contract N00014-85-K-0124 and in part by IBM.

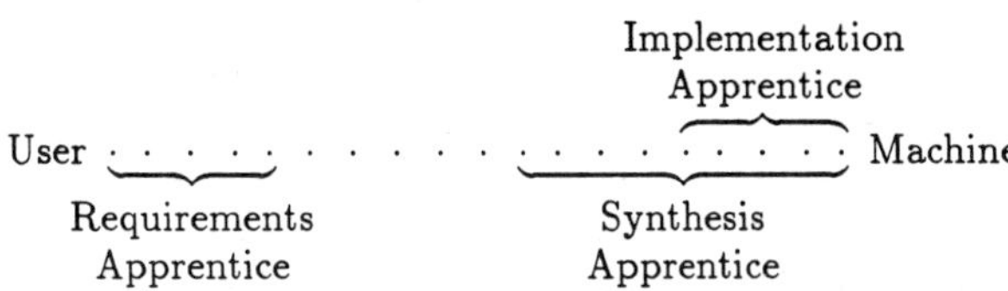

Figure 1: Spectrum of software development activities.

mentation Apprentice called the Knowledge-Based Editor in Emacs (KBEmacs)[25]. The principal benefit of KBEmacs is that it allows a programmer to construct a program rapidly and reliably by combining algorithmic fragments stored in a library. The principal limitations of KBEmacs are that it has a narrow view of the programming process and weak reasoning abilities.

Currently, much of the work on the Programmer's Apprentice is being directed toward the construction of a new demonstration system called the Synthesis Apprentice[22]. This system will have increased reasoning abilities and will therefore be able to assist in a greater portion of the programming process. In particular, the Synthesis Apprentice will be able to detect many kinds of design errors which KBEmacs cannot detect. The Synthesis Apprentice will also be able to deduce implicit design decisions which follow from explicit decisions made by the user.

Work has just begun on a Requirements Apprentice (RA)[21], which will assist an analyst in the creation and modification of software requirements. Research on the RA establishes a second beachhead from which to attack the problem of automating the programming process. The RA will eventually link up with the other parts of the Programmer's Apprentice, which are growing "up" from the implementation end of the spectrum.

2. Focusing the Research

It is useful to distinguish between different phases in the requirements acquisition process. The earliest phase usually takes the form of a "skull session" whose goal is achieving a consensus among a group of users about what they want. The requirements analyst's main role in this phase relies on his personal skills as a facilitator, perhaps with the aid of a team debriefing methodology, such as JAD[8].

The end product of the skull session phase is typically an informal requirement such as the library database requirement that is being used as a benchmark by this workshop.

EH0304-6/90/0000/0439$01.00 © 1987 IEEE

Reprinted from *Proceedings of the Fourth International Workshop on Software Specifications and Design*, 1987, pages 79-86.

Figure 2 (taken from [2]) shows the first few lines of the version of this requirement which was used in the prior two workshops.

```
  Consider a university library database.  There are
two types of users: normal borrowers and users with
library staff status.  The database transactions are:
 (1) Check out a copy of a book.
 (2) Return a copy of a book.
 (3) Add a copy of a book to the library.
 (4) Remove a copy of a book from the library.
 (5) Remove all copies of a book from the library.
  :
```

Figure 2: Informal library requirement © IEEE 1985.

Most current work on software requirements tools (e.g., [5,9,15]) focuses on what is usually called the *validation* phase. The main goal of this part of the process is to increase confidence that a given requirement actually corresponds to the end user's desires. In current research approaches, this is achieved by applying simulation, symbolic execution, and various kinds of analysis to a formal specification. This work does not, however, address the key question of how a formal specification is constructed in the first place. For example, Kemmerer[15] begins by simply exhibiting the translation of the library database requirement into a formal specification. A small portion of his formal specification is shown in Figure 3 (excerpted from [15]).

```
  :
TRANSFORM Return(B:Book) External
 Effect
  (if Checked_Out(B)
   then ∀ B1:Book (N"Checked_Out(B1) =
                  (if B=B1 then False
                   else Checked_Out(B1)))
      & ∀ U1:User (N"Number_Books(U1) =
                  (if U1=Responsible(B)
                   then Number_Books(U1)-1
                   else Number_Books(U1)))
  else NC"(Checked_Out,Number_Books))
  :
```

Figure 3: Formal library requirement © IEEE 1985.

The focus of the RA is on bridging the gap between informal and formal specification—i.e., between Figure 2 and Figure 3. This is a crucial area of weakness in the current state of the art. For example, it was reported at the Second Workshop on Software Specification and Design ([2], p. 107) that some of the greatest problems stemmed from "the process of completing the system analysis work needed to translate the informal specification into the appropriate input for the tools."

A second reason for focusing on the transition from informal to formal is that it brings up fundamental artificial intelligence issues in the area of knowledge acquisition—in particular, *informality* and the process by which informal descriptions evolve into formal ones. In this area, the work on the RA continues in the tradition of the SAFE project[3].

Another key aspect of the RA is that it will contain an extensive library of knowledge about the particular domain of the requirement to be constructed. This is to be contrasted with, for example, a tool for the symbolic execution of a formal requirements language. Such a tool can do a lot to help identify problems with what is in a given requirement. However, it is not in a position to say very much about what might be missing from the requirement. Having specific knowledge about what should be in the requirements associated with a particular domain makes it possible for a tool like the RA to critique what is not in a requirement as well as what is in the requirement.

The current research with goals most similar to the RA is the KATE[11] system. Fickas has proposed an interactive system which will provide assistance over the entire requirements acquisition process. To make this feasible, Fickas intends to rely heavily on exploiting a particular example domain (conference planning).

Interacting with the Apprentice

Figure 4 shows how the RA interacts with other agents involved in the software process. Note that the RA does not interact directly with an end user, but rather acts as an assistant to the requirements analyst. The RA also serves as a bridge between the requirements analyst and the system designer.

End User ⇔ Analyst ⇔ RA ⇔ System Designer

Figure 4: Interacting with the RA.

The main benefit of excluding direct interaction with the end user is that it avoids having to deal with the complexity of natural language input. Natural language understanding is a major research area in its own right, which is, by and large, independent of the central issues in building the RA.

Output of the Apprentice

In current practice, the end product of requirements acquisition is typically a single written document which is produced by the analyst and used both by the end user (for validation) and by the system designer (as the starting point for design). Using the RA, the essential end product of the requirements acquisition process will be a machine-manipulable representation of the requirement inside the RA.. In the long term, this internal representation will be accessed directly by other tools and components of the Programmer's Apprentice. In the short term, this information will be used to answer queries and to generate various documents for the requirements analyst, the end user, and the system designer. An advantage of the RA approach is that different presentations of the information can be produced, tailored to the different needs of the end user, the analyst, and the designer.

The documents generated by the RA could take many forms. They could be textual, diagrammatic, or rendered in a formal specification language. In the near term, effort will focus on the production of more or less traditional textual presentations of requirements. Since many software projects are contractually obligated to provide documents of this form, automatically generating (and re-generating after modification) such documents will be a valuable feature of the RA.

It is important not to focus too early in the development of the RA on designing a new diagrammatic or formal specification language. As with natural language understanding, this is not because these areas are unimportant, but rather because they are largely orthogonal to the key issues underlying the RA, and therefore can be temporarily side-stepped. Experience with other parts of the Programmer's Apprentice has demonstrated the benefits of concentrating first on designing an internal representation that is well suited for automated reasoning and other manipulations. However, in order to demonstrate the semantic adequacy of its internal representation, the RA will support the production of formal specifications in a preexisting specification language such as the one used in Figure 3.

3. Fundamental Issues

Research on the RA brings up two fundamental issues in knowledge acquisition. The first issue is *informality* and the process by which informal descriptions evolve into formal specifications. The second issue is the role, and specific content, of prior knowledge of the common structures (*clichés*) of a domain.

In the area of knowledge acquisition, the work most similar to the RA is concerned with providing automated assistance for acquiring new rules for expert systems. Of particular interest are KLAUS[13] and ROGET[6] which support the acquisition of new concepts and vocabulary, in addition to supporting well-formedness and consistency checking.

Informality

In their work on SAFE[3], Balzer, Goldman, and Wile were the first to argue that informality is an inevitable (and ultimately desirable) feature of the specification process. They began by studying actual natural language software specifications and cataloging the kinds of informality they found. At the end of the project, the SAFE prototype succeeded in demonstrating the production of formal specifications in the language AP2 from pre-parsed, informal, natural language specifications.

The following is a list of general features that characterize informal communication between a speaker (e.g., an end user) and hearer (e.g., an analyst). These features are based on the discussion in [3] and an initial study of the informal requirement in Figure 2.

Abbreviation: Special terms (jargon) are used. The hearer is assumed to have a large amount of specific knowledge which explains the terms.

Ambiguity: Statements can be interpreted in several different ways. The hearer has to disambiguate these statements based on the surrounding context.

Poor Ordering: Statements are presented in the order they occur to the speaker, rather than in an order that would be convenient for the hearer. The hearer needs to hold many questions in abeyance until later statements answer them.

Incompleteness: Aspects of the description are left out. The hearer has to fill in these gaps by using his own knowledge or asking questions.

Contradiction: Statements which are true in the main are liable to be contradictory in detail. This reflects the fact that the speaker has not thought things out completely.

Inaccuracy: For a variety of reasons, some of the statements are simply wrong.

Informality of this kind is not a matter of the speaker being lazy or incompetent. Informality is an essential part of the human thought process. It is part of a powerful *debugging* strategy for dealing with complexity, which shows up in many problem solving domains: start with an almost-right description and then incrementally modify it until it is acceptable (see [23]). Thus, having the RA deal with informality is not just a question of being user friendly—it is a fundamental prerequisite.

One of the goals of research on the RA is to elaborate the initial characterization of informality given above, and to develop strategies and heuristics for removing these features from informal requirements.

The RA will differ from SAFE in several respects. First, the interface to the RA further separates natural language understanding from the essential informality issues. Although parentheses were added manually to the English input to avoid parsing difficulties, SAFE still attempted to deal with a number of other natural language phenomena, such as pronouns, which are better dealt with in other research.

Second, although the SAFE work points to the importance of domain knowledge in resolving informality, it lacks the notion of clichés as a way of representing, organizing, and applying this knowledge. Finally, SAFE is an automatic batch system, whereas the RA is an interactive assistant.

Clichés

Expert engineers rarely construct complex artifacts (e.g., electronic circuits, automobiles, or requirements specifications) by starting from first principles. Rather, they bring to the task their previous experience, in the form of knowledge of the commonly occurring structures (combinations of primitives) in the domain. The term *cliché* is used here to refer to these commonly occurring structures. In normal usage, the word cliché has a pejorative sound that connotes overuse and a lack of creativity. However, in the context of engineering problem solving, this kind of reuse is a positive feature.

Knowledge of the relevant clichés is essential for effective communication on any topic. There is ample evidence that, in general, it is very difficult to acquire new knowledge unless one already has a large amount of relevant old knowledge. Imagine trying to communicate the requirements for an inventory control system to a person who knows nothing about information systems or inventories.

Formally, a cliché consists of a set of *roles* embedded in an underlying *substrate*. The roles of a cliché are the parts which vary from one use of the cliché to the next.

The substrate of the cliché contains both fixed elements of structure (parts that are present in every occurrence) and *constraints*. Constraints are used to check that the parts that fill the roles in a particular occurrence are consistent and to compute parts to fill empty roles in a partially specified occurrence.

Examples of notions similar to clichés in software engineering include the work of Arango and Freeman[1] (domain models) and Lavi[16] (generic models).

Requirements Clichés

A central underpinning of the RA will be an extensive library of clichés in the particular domain of the requirement to be constructed. This emphasis on domain knowledge is a theme which the RA shares with systems such as Φ-NIX[4] and DRACO[18].

As examples of requirements clichés consider the following. A repository is an entity in the physical world. The repository cliché has a number of roles including: the *items* which are stored in the repository, the *place* where the items are stored, the *staff* which manages the repository, and the *users* which utilize the repository.

There are several kinds of repositories. Simple repositories merely take in items and then give them out. A more complex kind of repository supports the lending of items, which are expected to be returned. Another dimension of variation concerns the items themselves. The items may be unrelated or they may be grouped into classes. Example repositories include: storage warehouses (simple repositories for unrelated items) grocery stores (simple repositories for items grouped in classes) and rental car agencies (lending repositories for items grouped in classes)

In contrast to the repository cliché, the information system cliché describes a class of programs rather than a class of physical objects. The intent of the information system cliché is to capture the commonality between programs such as personnel systems, bibliographic databases, and inventory control systems.

The central role of an information system is the *information schema*. This is a meta-description which specifies the logical characteristics of the data to be stored. Other roles of an information system include: a set of *transactions* which can create/modify/delete the data, a set of *reports* which display parts of the data, and *integrity constraints* on the data.

A tracking system is a specialized kind of information system which keeps track of the state of a physical object. The roles of a tracking system are the same as the roles of an information system, with the addition of one new role: the *target* being tracked. The target object is assumed to have a (possibly complex) state and to be subject to various physical operations which can modify this state. The information in the tracking system describes the state of the target object. The transactions modify this information to reflect changes in the target's state.

The main content of the tracking system cliché is a set of constraints which relate roles of the information system part of the cliché to the target role. For example, the constraints can be used to derive the information schema from a description of the possible states of the target.

4. Scenario

As a concrete illustration of the capabilities of the proposed RA, the following presents a scenario showing how the system will interact with a requirements analyst. The scenario, which is excerpted from larger scenarios in [21] and [19], is based on the library database example shown in Figure 2.

Before the scenario begins, it is important to set the scene by describing what the RA is expected to know beforehand. It is assumed that the RA knows nothing about libraries *per se*. The RA does, however, know a considerable amount about the general kinds of systems of which the library database is an instance. In particular, the RA knows about the clichés repository, information system, and tracking system.

In a given situation, the RA could start out with either more or less relevant knowledge. The level of knowledge in this scenario was chosen in order to illustrate a useful middle ground.

Beginning the Requirement

With the commands shown below, an analyst begins the process of using the RA to construct a requirement. Note in the first command that new terms, such as the name LIBDB, are introduced in quotes. The second command gives the overall structure of the desired system. The third and fourth commands define the terms *library* and *copy of a book*.

```
>Begin a requirement for a system called "LIBDB".
>LIBDB is a tracking system which tracks a "library".
>A library is a repository for "copies of books".
>A copy of a book has the properties:
   title - a text string,
   author - a person's name,
   ISBN number - a unique alphanumeric key.
```

Input to the RA will be in terms of some stylized command language. However, the exact command language which will be used has not yet been designed. Therefore, in the scenario, input is shown in simple English sentences.

The net effect of a sequence of commands such as the ones above is to augment the information contained in the RA's internal representation of the evolving requirement. This new information comes from three fundamentally different sources: explicit statements, clichés, and inferences.

After the four commands above, almost all of what the RA knows comes from the combination of the tracking system and repository clichés. In particular, an instance of the tracking system cliché is created with a library (an instance of the repository cliché) in the target role. Since the state of a repository is the collection of items it contains (in this case, copies of books), the constraints in the tracking system cliché are used to derive an information schema that provides fields for the three properties listed above for copies of books.

Note that the new terms LIBDB, library, and copy of a book are far from fully defined at this point. They are both incomplete and ambiguous. They are incomplete because many roles remain to be filled in. They are ambiguous because it is not yet clear which kind of tracking system LIBDB is or which kind of repository a library is. Since incompleteness and ambiguity are inevitable during the early stages of constructing a requirement, the RA refrains from complaining at this point.

Textual Displays

Output from the RA comes in two forms. First there are direct statements to the analyst, for example, describing a contradiction that has been discovered. However, the primary form of output is textual displays generated from parts of the RA's internal representation of the evolving requirement. One kind of display corresponds to viewing sections of a requirements document. Other displays consist of various outlines and summaries.

The default response of the RA to commands from the analyst is to create a textual display which summarizes the major effect of the commands. The analyst can request the generation of other kinds of displays.

Figure 5 shows the RA's default display after the four commands above. The top part of the display shows the table of contents of the requirement as a whole. The bottom part of the display shows the purpose section which would be generated if a requirements document were to be created at this point in the scenario. The bottom of the purpose section summarizes, at an appropriately high level, the main points in the requirement which are currently unresolved.

An important function of the displays is to focus attention. When the RA generates a display, the display naturally focuses the analyst's attention on the information it contains. When the analyst requests a display, the RA can use the context of the display to disambiguate ensuing commands.

The structure of the requirement must vary based on the needs of the organization using the RA. (In Figure 5, it is assumed that the requirement document must conform to the ANSI/IEEE standard[14].) The structure of the requirement also varies based on the top level clichés being used in the requirement. (In Figure 5 the choice of detail sections such as 3.1.1 is dictated by the tracking system cliché.)

Although the first part of the purpose section in Figure 5 is shown in connected English sentences, most of the output generated by the RA is expected to look more like the point-form listing of unresolved issues. As in the case of understanding free-flowing English input, the syntactic aspects of good English are not a key concern here. What is important is deciding *what* to say, for example, choosing the appropriate level of detail (as in [24]).

At one extreme, the RA could assume that the reader has a complete understanding of every cliché. At the other extreme, the RA could describe every cliché used in full detail. The first approach is unwarranted. The second approach would lead to a document which is too large and is likely to be too redundant with what the reader does know. As illustrated here, the RA will attempt to take a middle course, reminding the reader of the various clichés used, but not giving the complete details of each cliché unless asked.

```
                 Table of Contents
1 Introduction
  1.1 Purpose
  1.2 Scope
  1.3 Definitions, Acronyms, and Abbreviations
  1.4 References
  1.5 Overview
2 General Description
  2.1 Product Perspective
  2.2 Product Functions
  2.3 User Characteristics
  2.4 General Constraints
  2.5 Assumptions and Dependencies
3 Specific Requirements
  3.1 Functional Requirements
      3.1.1 Transactions
      3.1.2 Reports
  3.2 External Interface Requirements
  3.3 Performance Requirements
  3.4 Design Constraints
  3.5 Attributes
      3.6.1 Security
      3.6.2 Error handling
-----------------------------------------------------
1.1 Purpose
  The LIBDB system is a tracking system which tracks
a library.  A library is a repository for copies of
books.
  LIBDB records information about the title, author,
and ISBN number of the copies of books in the
library.  Transactions are supported for tracking
what happens to the repository.  Reports are provided
for obtaining information about the copies of books
in the library.
Unresolved issues:
   What kind of tracking system is LIBDB?
   What kind of repository is a library?
   What transactions are supported?
   What reports are generated?
```

Figure 5: Textual display generated by the RA.

Defining Transactions

The next set of commands begin the definition of the transactions to be supported by LIBDB. The analyst first directs the RA's attention to the topic of transactions by moving to the transactions subsection of the document. He then describes the *check out* transaction.

```
>Display the transactions subsection.
>The "check out" transaction tracks the removal of a
 copy of a book.
```

The key term in the second command is *removal*. Removal is one of the standard operations supported by a repository, i.e., taking an item out of the repository and giving it to a user of the repository. Constraints in the tracking system cliché have already generated the expectation of a corresponding transaction. This command gives this transaction a name (check out) and triggers its inclusion in the requirement.

The effect of the two commands above on the display

is illustrated by Figure 6. Most of the information in Figure 6 comes from the repository cliché via the constraints in the tracking system cliché. The bottom of Figure 6 lists a number of issues which still need to be resolved.

```
3.1.1.1 Check Out

  The check out transaction tracks the removal of a
copy of a book from the library.

INPUTS: identifier of a copy of a book (ISBN number).
OUTPUTS: none.
PRECONDITIONS: The input must be in the roster of
   copies of books which are in the library.
EFFECT ON THE INFORMATION STORE: The input is removed
   from the roster of copies of books which are in
   the library.
UNUSUAL EVENTS: If the input is not in the roster of
   copies of books which are in the library, then the
   information system is inconsistent with the state
   of the library.  A notation is made in the error
   log and no other action is taken.
USAGE RESTRICTIONS: none.

Unresolved issues:
   Should historical record keeping be added?
   Should checking of user validity be added?
   Should checking of staff member validity be added?
```

Figure 6: Textual display of the check out transaction.

Fixing an Error

The next two commands continue on the topic of transactions. Note the use of the term *inverse* to define the return transaction. In the repository cliché, the operation of adding an item into the repository is defined to be the inverse of removing an item. Therefore, the first command below triggers the generation of a transaction that tracks the addition of a book.

```
>The "return" transaction is the inverse of check
 out.
>The "add" transaction tracks the addition of a copy
 of a book.

Potential problem:
   The add transaction is exactly the same as the
   return transaction.
```

The command defining the add transaction provokes an immediate complaint from the RA, because it defines adding a copy of a book to be exactly the same as returning a copy of a book. This contradicts the RA's expectation that new terms should not be synonymous with old terms unless explicitly declared to be so. The analyst does not have to deal with this problem immediately—he could go on to other things leaving the problem pending. In this case, however, he decides to deal with the problem right away.

In order to begin the process of tracking down the source of the problem, the analyst asks the RA to present a trace (shown below) of the chain of inference which led to the immediate manifestation of the problem.

Studying this explanation, the analyst realizes that he made an error earlier, in the definition of check out. Checking out a book does not correspond to removing it (permanently) from the repository, but rather to borrowing it (temporarily) from the repository.

```
>Explain the problem.
(1) The add transaction is exactly the same as the
    return transaction.  Because:
  (2) The add transaction tracks the addition of a
      copy of a book.
  (3) The return transaction tracks the addition of
      a copy of a book.  Because:
    (4) The check out transaction tracks the removal
        of a copy of a book.
    (5) The return transaction is the inverse of the
        check out transaction.
    (6) Addition is the inverse of removal.
```

This error may, or may not, appear plausible to a given reader. However, large numbers of errors are made during the creation of a typical requirement (most of which look pretty stupid in retrospect). This error was introduced into the scenario in order to illustrate the ability of the RA to assist in the detection and correction of errors in general.

With the commands below, the analyst corrects the error by redefining the check out transaction. Since statement (5) is not retracted, the return transaction is still the inverse of check out, which implies that the return transaction now tracks the return of a copy of a book. In addition, the RA has inferred that a library is a lending repository, which resolves an outstanding ambiguity.

```
>Retract (4).
>The check out transaction tracks the borrowing of a
 copy of a book.

Note: The return transaction now tracks the return of
   a copy of a book to a lending repository.
```

Fixing a Conceptual Confusion

The scenario continues with the definition of transactions related to removing items from the library.

```
>The "remove" transaction tracks the removal of a
 copy of a book.
>The "remove all" transaction tracks the removal of
 every copy of a book.

Potential problem:
   The term "every" suggests that copies of books are
   members of classes.  If this is not the case, then
   the remove all transaction is exactly the same as
   the remove transaction.
```

The second command above brings to the surface a conceptual confusion which has been buried in the requirement thus far. By using the word *every*, the analyst suggests that the remove all transaction corresponds to removing all instances of a class of items from the library. This is a standard operation on repositories which contain classes of items rather than unrelated items. However, the requirement thus far does not include a class/instance relationship for the library. (As discussed in [2] the informal library requirement is somewhat ambiguous on this issue.)

On seeing the RA's response, the analyst (assumedly in consultation with the end user) thinks a bit more about books and realizes that what were originally defined as the properties of a copy of a book should really be properties of a class called book. A copy of a book is an instance of a particular class of books. Below, he informs the RA of this conceptual change. Among other things, this removes the last element of ambiguity as to what kind of repository a library is.

```
>"Book" is a class with the properties previously
 defined for a copy of a book.
>Redefine a copy of a book to be an instance of a
 book.
>A copy of a book has the property:
  copy number - a number unique within the class.
```

This conceptual reorganization is propagated by the RA throughout the requirement. One effect of the reorganization is to reveal that remove and remove all are indeed distinct transactions. In addition, there are a number of other changes. For example, the input to the check out transaction is changed from an ISBN number to a pair of an ISBN number and a copy number.

Observations On the Scenario

In the interest of brevity, the scenario is truncated at this point. (It continues in [21].) The scenario illustrates that using the RA can improve both productivity and the quality of the requirement produced. These benefits stem from three basic capabilities of the RA: support for clichés, propagation of information, and contradiction detection.

Clichés directly improve productivity by allowing reuse of parts of requirements from project to project. Propagation of information improves productivity by allowing the analyst to provide each piece of information just once, at the point which is most convenient. The RA copies this information to other places where it is relevant.

Contradiction detection improves the quality of the final requirement. This is facilitated by the fact that most errors cause a number of contradictions—the RA only needs to be able to find one of them to recognize that there is an error. The use of clichés contributes to contradiction detection because of the large amount of predefined information which is attached to them. Opportunities for finding contradictions are increased further by the propagation of information from one place in a requirement to another.

5. Accomplishments to Date

Research on the RA is being pursued within the context of the Programmer's Apprentice project. Although many extensions will be necessary, the theoretical work developed as part of the project provides an intellectual platform upon which to build the RA. From the perspective of the RA, the greatest accomplishment to date has been the construction of a hybrid knowledge representation and reasoning system called CAKE[10,20].

Historically, there have been two major approaches to knowledge representation and reasoning. One approach has emphasized the use of predicate calculus and general purpose theorem proving techniques. The other approach, partly in reaction to the difficulty of general purpose theorem proving, has emphasized special purpose representations and reasoning methods tailored to the structure of particular problem domains.

Experience with reasoning about programs and programming suggests that both techniques are needed. Special purpose representations and associated algorithms are essential in order to avoid the uncontrollable combinatorial explosions which often occur in predicate calculus based reasoning systems. On the other hand, predicate calculus reasoning is essential as the "glue" between inferences made in different special purpose representations. Systems, such as CAKE, which combine both types of reasoning are referred to as *hybrid* systems.

CAKE supports several different kinds of special purpose reasoning layered on top of a simple, general purpose, reasoning system based on predicate claculus. Figure 7 shows the layers of the system which are most relevant to the RA.

FRAMES
TYPES
ALGEBRA
EQUALITY
TRUTH MAINTENANCE

Figure 7: The layers of CAKE.

The bottommost layer of CAKE (truth maintenance) is the boolean constraint propagation network from RUP[17]. It provides three principal facilities. First, it acts as a recording medium for dependencies, and thus supports retraction and explanation. (The explanation in the scenario using Because is a presentation of dependency information.) Second, it performs simple "one-step" deductions—specifically, unit propositional resolution. (This will provide the propagation of information illustrated in the scenario.) Third, the truth maintenance layer detects contradictions. Contradictions are represented explicitly in such a way that reasoning can continue with other information not involved in the contradiction. (This allows the RA to let the analyst postpone dealing with problems.)

The equality layer of CAKE provides an incremental congruence closure facility, also taken from RUP. Given any two terms, the equality layer determines whether they can be proved equal by substitution of equals using the set of currently true equalities between terms. (Reasoning about equality between transactions is invoked several times in the scenario to detect potential problems.)

The algebra layer of CAKE consists of special-purpose decision procedures for common algebraic properties of operators, such as commutativity, associativity, transitivity, inverses, and so on. These properties come up everywhere in formal modeling tasks. (In the scenario, the return transaction is defined as the inverse of check out.)

The types layer of CAKE provides a full lattice of subtypes, with intersection, union, and complement types. The notion of types is a basic facility used in all knowledge representation and formal specification systems. (At the end of the scenario, books are defined as types, of which a copy of a book is an instance.)

Finally, the frames layer, which is built using facilities

from many of the layers below, supports the conventional frame notions of slots, instances, and inheritance. These facilities will be used in the RA as the basis for representing clichés and organizing the cliché library.

In the area of applying knowledge representation techniques to software requirements, an important first step was the RML language of Greenspan. Knowledge representation and requirements specification have a shared concern with modeling slices of the real world. Along with Mylopoulos and Borgida[7,12], Greenspan has begun the task of bringing together these two disciplines. The RA can be viewed as continuing this work into inferencing, contradiction detection, and other dynamic issues not yet addressed in RML.

References

[1] G. Arango and P. Freeman, "Modeling Knowledge for Software Development," *Third Int. Workshop on Software Specification and Design*, :63–66, London, August 1985.

[2] R. Babb, *et al.*, "Workshop on Models and Languages for Software Specification and Design," *IEEE Computer*, 18(3):103–108, March 1985.

[3] R. Balzer, N. Goldman, and D. Wile, "Informality in Program Specifications," *IEEE Transactions on Software Engineering*, 4(2):94–103, March 1978.

[4] D.R. Barstow, "Domain-Specific Automatic Programming," *IEEE Transactions on Software Engineering*, 11(11):1321–1336, November 1985.

[5] T. Bell, D. Bixler, and M. Dyer, "An Extendable Approach to Computer-Aided Software Requirements Engineering," *IEEE Transactions on Software Engineering*, 3(1):49–59, January 1977.

[6] J.S. Bennett, "A Knowledge-Based System for Acquiring the Conceptual Structure of a Diagnostic Expert System," *Journal of Automated Reasoning*, 1(1), 1985.

[7] A. Borgida, S. Greenspan, and J. Mylopoulos, "Knowledge Representation as the Basis for Requirements Specifications," *IEEE Computer*, :82-90, April 1985.

[8] A. Crawford, "Joint Application Design: A New Way to Design Systems," in *Guide International Proceedings*, Guide International Corporation, 1982.

[9] M.S. Feather and P.E. London, "Implementing Specification Freedoms," *Science of Computer Programming*, 2:91–131, 1982.

[10] Y.A. Feldman and C. Rich, "Reasoning with Simplifying Assumptions: A Methodology and Example," *AAAI86*, August 1986.

[11] S. Fickas, D. Laursen, and J. Laursen, "A Knowledge-Based Software Specification Environment," *Workshop on Knowledge-Based Design*, Rutgers Univ., 1984.

[12] S. J. Greenspan, Alexander Borgida, and John Mylopoulos, "A Requirements Modeling Language and its Logic," *Information Systems*, 11(1):9–23, Pergammon Press, 1986.

[13] N. Haas and G.G. Hendrix, "An Approach to Acquiring and Applying Knowledge," *AAAI80*, :235-239, August 1980.

[14] *IEEE Guide to Software Requirements Specifications*, ANSI/IEEE Standard 830-1984, July 1984.

[15] R.A. Kemmerer, "Testing Formal Specifications to Detect Design Errors," *IEEE Transactions on Software Engineering*, 11(1), January, 1985.

[16] J.Z. Lavi, "Improving the Embedded Computer Systems Software Process Using a Generic Model," *Third Int. Workshop on Software Specification and Design*, :127–129, London, August 1985.

[17] D.A. McAllester, *Reasoning Utility Package User's Manual*, MIT/AIM-667, April 1982.

[18] J.M. Neighbors, "The Draco Approach to Constructing Software from Reusable Components," *IEEE Transactions on Software Engineering*, 10(5):564–574, September 1984.

[19] H.B. Reubenstein, *A Requirements Analyst's Apprentice: A Proposal*, (Ph.D. Thesis Proposal), MIT/AI/WP-290, September 1986.

[20] C. Rich, "The Layered Architecture of a System for Reasoning about Programs," *IJCAI85*, :540-546, August 1985.

[21] C. Rich and R.C. Waters, *Toward a Requirements Apprentice: On the Boundary Between Informal and Formal Specifications*, MIT/AIM-907, July 1986.

[22] C. Rich and R.C. Waters, *A Scenario Illustrating a Proposed Program Synthesis Apprentice*, MIT/AIM-933, January 1987.

[23] G.J. Sussman, "The Virtuous Nature of Bugs," *Proc. of the Conf. on Artificial Intelligence and the Simulation of Behavior*, Univ. of Sussex, July 1974.

[24] W. Swartout, "The GIST Behavior Explainer," *AAAI83*, :402–407, August 1983.

[25] R.C. Waters, "The Programmer's Apprentice: A Session with KBEmacs," *IEEE Transactions on Software Engineering*, 11(11):1296–1320, November 1985.

Chapter 6: Requirements and Quality Management

1: Introduction

Management is all the activities and tasks undertaken by one or more persons to plan and control the activities of others to achieve an objective or complete an activity that could not be achieved by the others acting independently. *Project management,* in turn, is a system of procedures, practices, technologies, and know-how that provides the planning, organizing, staffing, directing, and controlling necessary to manage an engineering project successfully. *Know-how* in this case means the skill, background, and wisdom to apply knowledge effectively in practice. [1]

The manager is responsible for managing the entire software development. The manager, then, is responsible for such activities as determining whether or not the requirements are complete; deciding whether or not to prototype certain aspects of the requirements; selecting the proper tools and methodologies to use in specifying and representing requirements specifications; and determining when to baseline the system based on the software requirements, when to stop requirements and when to enter into the design phase, and so forth.

Validation is the process of evaluating software at the end of the software development process to ensure compliance with software requirements. [2] The major validation tool is testing. *Testing* is the process of analyzing a system/software item to detect the differences between existing and required conditions and to evaluate the features of the system/software item. [3]

Testing is also the process of exercising or evaluating a system or system component by manual or automated means to verify that it satisfies specified requirements or to identify differences between expected and actual results. Testing cannot be done until the project is complete or almost complete, i.e., there must be code in order to test. However, the later in the lifecycle that requirements errors are found, the more expensive it is to fix them. [4] Therefore, it is important that a software requirements specification be correct and valid before beginning design. This

EHO304-6/90/0000/0447$01.00

determination involves the use of tools, techniques, and procedures independent of testing for the verification of requirements specifications.

Verification is the process of determining whether or not the products of a given phase of the software development cycle fulfill the requirements established during the previous phase. [5] Verification together with validation is called "verification and validation" (V&V), or when accomplished by an organization other than the developer, "independent verification and validation" (IV&V). Some of the major tools of V&V are reviews, inspections, and walkthroughs. A *review* is a formal meeting at which a product or document is presented to the user, customer, or other interested parties for comment and approval. It can be a review of the management and technical progress of the hardware/software development project. [6]

A *walkthrough* is a software engineering review process in which a designer or programmer leads one or more members of the development team through a segment of design or code that he or she has written, while other members ask questions and make comments about technique, style, possible errors, violation of development standards, and other problems. [7] (In recent years, there has been a tendency to call a walkthrough an inspection, although the two are not identical.)

An *inspection* is a semiformal to formal evaluation technique in which software requirements, design, or code are examined in detail by a person or group other than the originator to detect faults, violations of development standards, and other problems. The review members are peers (equals) of the designer or programmer. Error data are collected during inspections for later analysis and to assist in future inspections. The term "peer review" may be used for either a walkthrough or an inspection.

Chapter 6 is concerned with the management of the requirements activity and of the quality of the requirements produced. It contains four papers, one addressing specifically the management aspects of requirements, one addressing configuration management, and two addressing different aspects of requirements quality.

2: Description of Papers

The first paper in the chapter is "Software Requirements—A Management Perspective" by Ray Yeh and Peter Ng. The purpose of the paper is to make management aware of the software requirements problems and process. The paper presents a conceptual framework of the process, attributes, and the contents of the final product, points out possible pitfalls along the way, and offers suggestions to software managers.

In "Elements of Software Configuration Management," a modern classic, Ed Bersoff defines configuration management as the discipline of identifying the configuration of a system at discrete points in time for the purpose of systematically controlling changes to the configuration and maintaining the integrity and traceability of the configuration throughout the system lifecycle. Configuration management keeps track of the various artifacts developed during the lifetime of a software project through identifying, controlling, auditing, and status accounting the various software development products.

Bersoff reminds us that controlling code is not enough: the documentation that enables us to use and operate the code must also be controlled. Among the documents that are controlled are the system and/or software requirements specifications. Bersoff discusses the major problems involved in deciding how to manage the software configuration properly: too much control is cumbersome, too little control invites disaster.

The third paper, by Barry Boehm, is "Verifying and Validating Software Requirements and Design Specifications." Boehm discusses procedures and tools for verifying and validating products during the software lifecycle, with particular attention to software requirements and software design. Boehm's paper describes attributes of a good software requirements specification which should be identified by the verification and validation procedure. The attributes are completeness, consistency, and feasibility (including testability). The paper discusses a taxonomy of a satisfactory software specification. It also discusses verification and validation techniques from the simple manual techniques such as reading, manual cross-referencing, interviews, checklists, and so forth through simple automated techniques such as SREM and PSL/PSA (the subjects of papers elsewhere in this tutorial), detailed manual techniques such as mathematical proofs, and detailed automated techniques such as simulation and prototyping. The paper includes an example of requirements verification and validation using some of the features of SREM.

"Requirement Specification Examinations," by Chuck Hollocker, again concerns the reviews, walkthroughs, and inspections of requirements specifications. Hollocker, who was Chair of the Working Group for Software Reviews and Audits, has prepared this short paper especially for this tutorial on how to review, walk through, and inspect the software requirements specifications.

3: References

[1] Thayer, R.H., "Software Engineering Project Management: A Top-Down View," *Tutorial: Software Engineering Project Management,* edited by R.H. Thayer, IEEE Computer Society, Washington, DC, 1988.

[2] Adapted from *IEEE Standard Glossary of Software Engineering Terminology,* ANSI/IEEE Std 729-1983, IEEE, Inc., NY, 1983.

[3] Adapted from *IEEE Standard Glossary of Software Engineering Terminology,* ANSI/IEEE Std 729-1983, IEEE, Inc., NY, 1983.

[4] Boehm, B.W., *Software Engineering Economics,* Prentice-Hall, Englewood Cliffs, NJ, 1981.

[5] Adapted from *IEEE Standard Glossary of Software Engineering Terminology,* ANSI/IEEE Std 729-1983, IEEE, Inc., NY, 1983.

[6] Adapted from *IEEE Standard Glossary of Software Engineering Terminology,* ANSI/IEEE Std 729-1983, IEEE, Inc., NY, 1983.

[7] Adapted from *IEEE Standard Glossary of Software Engineering Terminology,* ANSI/IEEE Std 729-1983, IEEE, Inc., NY, 1983.

Software Requirements—A Management Perspective

Raymond T. Yeh
Syscorp International
9420 Research Boulevard
Suite 200
Austin, Texas 78759

Peter A. Ng
Institute for Integrated Systems Research
Department of Computer and Information Science
New Jersey Institute of Technology
Newark, New Jersey 07102

Abstract: *The purpose of this paper is to bring about an awareness of the problem of deriving software requirements at the management level. No technical details concerning specific techniques, languages, or methodologies will be discussed. In this paper, a new paradigm for software development is first introduced from the point of an abstraction-based software lifecycle model. It emphasizes requirements, specification, and design rather than coding and incorporates the activities of evaluation and validation into the development process rather than at the completion of the development in each phase of the traditional waterfall model. The presentation primarily provides a conceptual framework for the requirements derivation process, attributes that might go into a requirements document, and management of the requirements derivation process. An objectives analysis is proposed for introduction preceding the process for deriving requirements, thereby allowing for a study of the organization's objectives.*

1. Introduction

The 1970s marked a period of transition in and recognition of the importance of software development. The technological advancements in hardware during the 1960s not only drove the cost of equipment down, but also made possible a new level of software sophistication and a demand for it during the 1970s. In particular, software packages were introduced and distributed to thousands of users; consequently, programmers found themselves not only using programs written by others, but also more frequently, modifying and adapting existing software to suit the requirements of their companies and of the new hardware. (Even today, program maintenance alone continues to make up a significant portion of the total software development cost.) Software in the 1970s was complex, labor-intensive, error-prone, and expensive, a phenomenon known as "software crisis" [Radice 88].

Software was complex because there was no parallel procedure that could handle the rapid growth in the size of applications. As the size of the problem increased, it became completely unmanageable by a single person.

Software was labor-intensive because software development was largely a manual process. Even when only minor changes occurred, programmers had to rework most of a program.

Software was error-prone because of inadequate development and testing methods and because of incomplete documentation. Modification of software usually resulted in altered performance by components that were supposed to be unaffected by such changes. In general, it has been found that "design errors" constituted one-third to three-fourths of the total error count [Thayer 75].

Software was expensive because there were insufficient methods for formulating feasibility analyses of a user's requirements and specifications; by the time the product was finished, it may not have been what the user wanted [Boehm 73, 81]. As a result, cost overruns were the norm rather than the exception.

Finding a solution for the problem of software development became increasingly critical. Thus, the term "software engineering" was introduced at the 1968 North American Treaty Organization (NATO) Conference in Garmisch, Germany [Radice, 88], and a set of techniques for software development was introduced to combat the software crisis. Software was considered an engineering product that required techniques for the phases of plan-

EHO304-6/90/0000/0450$01.00

ning, analysis, design, implementation, testing, and maintenance. The software industry's basic software engineering goals are to improve quality and productivity while reducing costs [Radice 88]. The use of process models, methods, languages, and tools enables the developer to control the process of software development, to improve user satisfaction with software products and to provide the programmer with some guidelines for producing high-quality software.

The 1980s were a period of integration of software technology and of transition from a handicraft approach to an industry approach to software engineering. The industry has replaced many of the labor-intensive development activities with software tools. Therefore, the emphasis during the next decade will be on how to integrate the set of tools further to increase the quality of software, reduce development cost, and improve the programmer's productivity.

In Section 2, we discuss the waterfall model of the software lifecycle, which was introduced to provide a systematic approach to software development. We also present a new paradigm of software development, which concentrates on requirements, specification, and design, rather than coding. In Section 3, we examine several problems in deriving requirements. In Section 4, we discuss techniques for deriving requirements and objectives analyses that can be used to alleviate those problems and we propose adding an objective analysis to precede the requirements analysis. Next, in Section 5, we address what should be included in a requirements document and discuss examples of what might go into a software requirements specification. Finally, we provide certain recommendations to managers pertaining to the process of deriving requirements.

2: An Abstraction-Based Software Lifecycle Model

The traditional waterfall model of the software lifecycle [Royce 70 and Boehm 73] is a phased refinement approach. In general, this approach consists of planning and requirements analysis, architecture, specification, design and implementation, installation and packaging, and maintenance. Verification, validation, and testing are integrated into the appropriate phases. For many reasons, the waterfall model is impractical for large projects. In addition, this approach has been criticized for running high maintenance costs for poorly motivating systems developers to perform abstract tasks in early phases of development, and for complicating systems integration. For example, with the complexity of the problem domains for today's generation of software, some user problems do not admit to "quick" solutions and their respective natures cannot be stated clearly. In these cases, a pilot version of the project may provide solutions. Using existing components and automatic code generators can also lessen the amount of work required of the programmer. But the waterfall model's disadvantages have encouraged researchers to look for new paradigms for software development [Yeh 83, 84] based on an abstraction-based lifecycle model.

An abstract is a description, or specification, of a system that hides certain properties. Abstraction is important because it reduces the complexity of the system. The process model of this paradigm is depicted in Figure 1. It differs from the traditional phased approach in that it concentrates on the hard problems of software, namely, the requirements, specification, and design, rather than on the coding itself. Of equal importance is that evaluation and validation (E&V) are parts of the development process, rather than the completion of the development in each phase.

Central to this approach is the expression of the software system functionality specification in a form can be precisely interpreted and yet does not oversimplify the form of system design implementation. Abstraction can achieve this expression, whereby the functionality specification expresses constraints on the multiple possible embodiments that would achieve different objectives in cost, performance, error tolerance, etc.

Three types of abstractions are essential in characterizing the functional attributes of any software system: function, data, and control. Function abstractions are used to hide certain properties of some algorithms that perform certain transformations, hence allowing a function to be modified without affecting other functions. Data abstractions are used to hide certain properties of the organization of a set of data structures, allowing the interface to be specified independent of its internal representation. Control abstractions are used to hide certain properties of the order of execution of a set of operations, reducing the complexity of a system.

Given a precise statement of functionality, a set of E&V processes can be coupled closely with the design/develop-

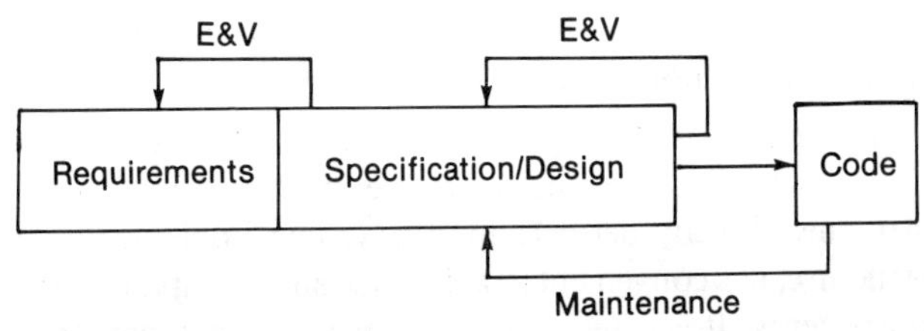

Figure 1: A process model for software evolution

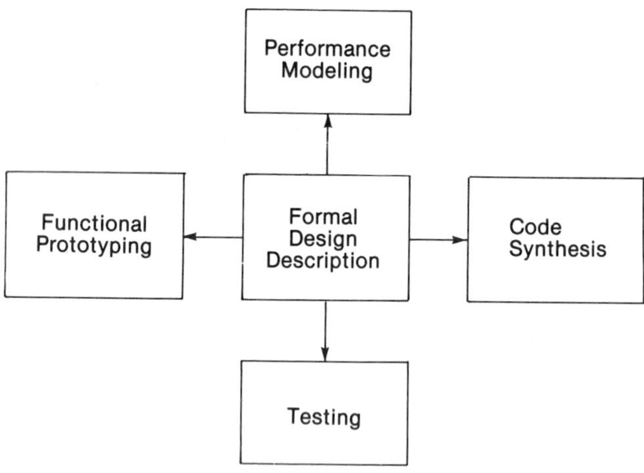

Figure 2: Interactive design steps in the new paradigm

ment process. As shown in Figure 2, rapid functional prototyping, performance modeling, and design testing are all part of this evaluation process. Rapid functional prototyping consists of the direct generation of executable code from the functional statement. This permits early users to review the proposed system's capabilities and also helps them to understand and express their needs. This early evaluation in the development can eliminate many of the causes for later system maintenance. Performance modeling at different stages of the design helps to enforce the performance issues before the system is completed, allowing for an analysis of the different design approaches. Performance evaluation is also used to provide accurate timing analyses and utilization profiles of the proposed system [Baker 89]. Design testing will help rule out poor designs early on by checking interfaces and coupling strength between modules.

The code synthesis arrow in Figure 2 also implies that in this evolutionary paradigm the code is synthesized at the highest level of specification via direct transformation or the use of previously developed components and subsystem designs. It avoids a common barrier for reusing code, namely that even if the functionality is correct, the implementation details might not fit. The reusable component is described in terms of its functionality abstraction; this strategy should make reuse possible.

This paradigm incorporates two kinds of evolution: incremental delivery and maintenance. With the functionality structure directly determining the system implementation structure, it is convenient to add functionality capabilities in increments. It is often valuable to use an implementation of a system with only limited capabilities at early stages of development in order to find specification errors. It also achieves an early pass at system integration, defective design, and interface errors. In brief, this model calls for the design of an executable specification and design language based on abstraction.

3: Problems in Deriving Requirements

A requirement conveys an essential property that the system must satisfy. A complete set of requirements would include a complete, validated specification of the required functions, interfaces, and performances for the software product [Radice 88 and Boehm 81]. Therefore, requirements analysis focuses on studying the interface among hardware, software, and users. It is used to understand the trade-offs between conflicting constraints, to understand the available resources, and to specify the goals of the system. In this section, we discuss several factors that affect the process of requirements derivation.

3.1: Difficulties That Stem from Inherent Complexity

Todays software certainly deals with complex systems. Their complexity comes not only from the size of a system, but mainly from the interactions among its components and the constraints imposed on the system, such as real-time computing, reliability, and geographic distributions of functions and data. Many problems are associated with an inherently complex system. If the system is hard to understand and one-of-a-kind (such as many military systems), difficulties can arise in stating the problem and in deriving its requirements.

3.2: Difficulties in Dealing with Change

In many cases, customers or users do not know precisely what they want or need. As they participate in the process of deriving requirements, they become better aware of the desired system, seek to modify the requirements to fit their new understanding and, consequently, restate the problem.

3.3: Difficulties in Communication

Dealing with change can become more complicated because of difficulties in communication that may arise during the process of deriving requirements. The process requires a great deal of communication between people of diverse backgrounds, levels of expertise, interests, and goals; these people include customers, end-users, analysts, and designers, among others. To determine user requirements, the analyst needs to differentiate carefully between the needs of the end-users themselves and those of users who have some understanding of the users' problems but are not actual end-users.

3.4: Lack of Concern for the Entire Lifecycle

Most of the existing approaches for the traditional waterfall model of the software lifecycle emphasize functional requirements (i.e., what the system is to do). It is our belief that the requirements analysis phase should begin with an objectives analysis. Also, a requirements document should contain information concerning the entire lifecycle. Cost estimates and resource allocations can be initiated from this document and a proper framework for considering design trade-offs in later phases can also be constructed, allowing vital decisions to be made based on complete information. Furthermore, many large software systems go through long lifecycles and evolve through many changes; for maintenance cost control, the ability to evolve must be considered as a major factor in the requirements phase.

4: Techniques for Understanding Requirements

In this section, we first discuss two general techniques, modeling and work breakdown structure (WBS), that can be used to alleviate the problems associated with the process of requirements derivation mentioned in Section 3. These techniques can be incorporated into any requirements methodology in varied forms. We then discuss adding an objectives analysis to precede the requirements analysis [Mittermeir 89].

4.1: Modeling

The most effective way to understand a complex system is to develop a model of that system. The model provides a basis for discussion among those concerned with the requirements derivation.

Different types of models depend on individual applications. In general, the model should include the user's environment so that the analyst who looks at the system from the user's point of view better appreciates the user's needs. This is particularly important because the desired property of an evolving system is that "a small change in the environment should affect a correspondingly small change in the system." This is possible only if both the environment and the system are modeled.

This paper presents two types of models: the conceptual model and the operational model. A conceptual model is constructed at the level at which humans formulate problems. As shown in Figure 3, it describes the interfaces between the proposed system and its environment. For complex problems, a model must be constructed so that it explicitly and formally presents the problems. It can be used by people of different backgrounds, such as users, analysts, and designers, as a basis for discussion of the problems. Therefore, a conceptual model is used to understand large, complex problems.

In many cases, a detailed operational model is required. It can be regarded as an early version of an operational prototype of the system to be developed. The operational model can be used to evaluate whether the proposed system meets the user's needs and to evaluate the feasibility of certain requirements, such as performance or time constraints in an embedded system.

4.2: Work Breakdown Structure

The technique of WBS, which systematically structures the work associated with the entire engineering process, is useful in analyzing complex systems. The purpose of a software WBS can be summarized in two goals, the "process" goal and the "product" goal. The process goal is to keep the various processes that deal with the software components under intellectual control at all times. The product goal is to organize the various software components into a product that others can comprehend.

The basic principle of any WBS is the "separation of concerns" using the mechanisms of simplification, abstraction, partition, and projection.

Simplification allows us to select the most important factors that affect our problems and to solve them. For example, in deriving his laws of motion, Newton first reduced the number of objects concerned from about 10^5 to 10 by selecting mass as the critical criterion. Second, he reduced the number of interactions from 2^{10} to 9 by considering only pair-wise interactions and only those pairs that included the sun.

Abstraction allows us to concentrate on essential properties while suppressing details that are immaterial, at least for the moment. The use of abstractions forms a natural hierarchy for elaborating details in cooperation with the intellectual control of the process.

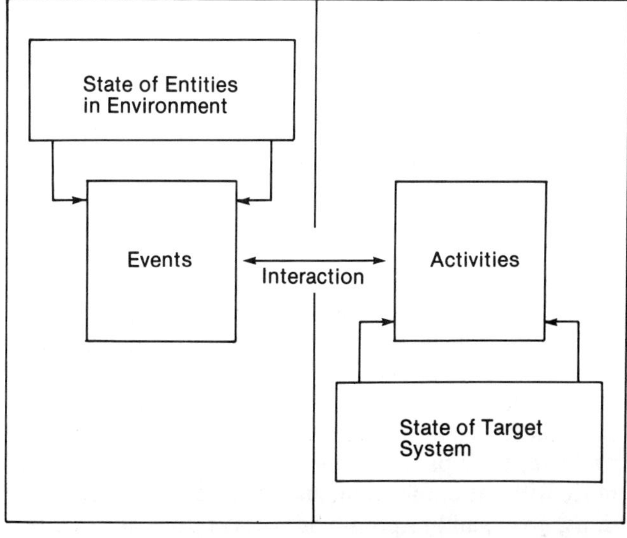

Figure 3: A conceptual model

Partition allows us to concentrate on components of a system one at a time. Partitioning the system lets us form modules; when we use abstraction to refine each partitioned component, we then have both a horizontal and vertical decomposition of the system.

Projection enables us to understand a system from different viewpoints. A projection of a system represents the entire system with respect to only a subset of its properties. The perfect physical analogy is an architectural drawing, which is a two-dimensional view of a three-dimensional building. The notion of a "view" of a database [Astrahan 76] is another example of projection.

All of these mechanisms allow us to separate particular facets of a system from the rest and thereby retain intellectual control.

4.3: Objectives Analysis

The development of software systems should not begin with the requirements analysis. At the requirements analysis phase, a number of unnecessary and possibly restricting assumptions are made because of misconceptions, managerial politics, technical ignorance, mistrust, established practices, personnel resistance, and so forth. Many managerial decisions are made to accommodate personal, rather than organizational, objectives. For the most part, task, process, and personnel assignments are given in the requirements specification without an understanding of their explicit relationships to the organization's objectives. Thus, some unnecessary constraints for the software development may arise. The addition of an objectives analysis phase preceding the requirements analysis allows us to study the organization's objectives (and similarly, the constraints against full achievement of the objectives) and their influences, interactions, and degrees of freedom [Mittermeir 89]. Therefore, an advantage of the objectives analysis is that the new system can be built so that it will accomplish the organization's objectives even when certain modifications of the system are made to account for environmental changes; certainly, modeling the proposed system can be enhanced by the results of the objectives analysis.

Generally, it is important that analysts are not misled by the problems and constraints of the current system. The solution for solving a problem may be different depending on with whom one speaks. The difficulty is that the opinion of the people involved in the daily operations is biased by the level of abstraction from which they conceive the problem, their planning horizon, their detailed acquaintance with the application, and their personal preconceptions, goals, and responsibilities. Therefore, the true picture of "the problem to be solved" can be obtained only by collecting information from all involved parties. Unfortunately, this is a time consuming process. But, the main advantage resulting from this process is that the system can be used effectively by the users because of their participation during the system development [Mumford 81].

4.3.1: Fundamentals of Objectives Analysis

The term "objective" refers to a fundamental, long-lasting, stable purpose of an organization or a human being. The term "goal" means a shorter-term achievement pertinent to a given objective. Thus, an objective contains goals, which in turn contain sub-goals. Goals and sub-goals pertinent to a given objective may interact in positive or negative ways. The goals pertinent to an objective and the associated interactions are called "objective structures."

Assume that an outline always exists for a potential solution to a problem within an organization. The statement that addresses the need of a system and its justification is the point of departure for the analysis effort. It serves to identify the part of the organization that will be affected by the development effort. The major activities of the objectives analysis phase are context analysis, objectives and problem analysis, and problem definition.

Context analysis: The objectives analysis phase begins with determining the preliminary scope of the development effort. This helps the analysts gain some basic understanding of the system and its immediate environment. In other methodologies, similar analysis is undertaken in an investigation phase [Miyamoto 81] or "Ist-Analyses" [Wedekind 76].

In context analysis, the analysts should learn about the basic functions to be performed by the target system, its environment, and the boundaries between the target system and its environment. They must also identify the major quantitative characteristics of the system and its environment [Putnam 78 and Basili 80], such as the number of employees, number of items produced or sold, etc. Combining modeling and context analysis can be an effective approach to understanding complex problems.

When all this information is collected, the persons who are affected by the development effort can be identified. These include the users of the new system, their managers, supervisors, and other personnel. The informants to be questioned during the following activities will be chosen from this list of personnel.

Objectives and problem analysis: A problem can be defined as the difference between an original goal set and the actual goal attained on a certain objectives dimension. For this reason, problems may be good indicators of objective dimensions. However, when solving a problem, it is important to remember those aspects of the organization's goals that have been reached well enough so as not to be mentioned in connection with problems. Since the ultimate solution must continue to accommodate these unstated goals, a simple problem analysis will not yield a complete view of the organization. The major objectives that lead the organization activities must also be considered.

After structuring the obtained objective dimensions into goal/sub-goal relationships, the analysts must determine whether complementary or adversary relationships exist between various goals and/or sub-goals (i.e., the magnitude of intergoal dependencies). The analysts must identify the objectives of adverse groups (e.g., competitors) that could hinder full goal achievement (i.e., the level of current attainment versus the desired attainment). These "negative" objectives will serve as restrictions in later analysis and during the process of selecting the best alternative solutions.

The objectives and problem analysis follows the integration of objectives structures of the different groups within the customer organization by resolving the differences through negotiation and arbitration. Finally, the objectives structure of the organization, which is relevant to the current development effort, should be formally agreed upon and accepted.

Problem definition: Problem definition investigates the definition of the system, its environment, the boundaries between the system and its environment, the problem areas that need to be addressed, and the constraints under which solutions need to be sought.

4.4: Summary

During the process of objectives analysis, the scope of the development effort and the goals of the customer's organization are identified and refined to a point where actual operations and the resources required to perform them have also been identified. As they analyze and refine the objectives, the analysts formulate ways to reach these objectives. Therefore, at the end of the objectives analysis phase, the analysts have identified the goal structure of the customer's organization and a set of alternative solutions, proposed on the basis of their own experience or a detailed study of the problems at hand. The requirements analysis can then continue, including the alternatives evaluation, system requirements analysis, medium definition, and software requirements analysis sub-phases.

5: What Should Be Included in the Requirements Document?

The conceptual model mentioned in the previous section should be a rich, complex information structure; the completeness and precison of conceptually modeling the real world can be enhanced by the process of objectives analysis. Usually there is too much information to be included in the software requirements document (SRD). The SRD can be derived from the conceptual model by filtering and organizing, constantly aiming toward the "best engineered" specification. The SRD can be divided into two major parts: functional requirements and nonfunctional requirements. Here we discuss only examples of what might belong in a software requirements specification. For a complete set of software requirements specifications, see [ANSI/IEEE 84].

5.1: Functional Requirements

Functional requirements describe what the target system does, and these are clearly the heart of the SRD. Section 4 introduced an explicit model of the proposed system's environment as an important tool for requirements analysis, a model that led to the global model shown in Figure 3. From the viewpoint of functional requirements specification, having an explicit model of the environment creates an important advantage: since interactions between the target system and its environment can be explicitly stated, it is easy to specify the interface between system and environment in an accurate, precise, understandable, though modifiable, manner. Thus the task of the functional requirements specification is to find a formal representation for the detailed information needed to fill in Figure 3. In the following paragraphs we discuss several approaches to deriving a functional requirements specification.

5.1.1: Data Models

Data-oriented models concentrate on specifying the states of the conceptual model shown in Figure 3. The state of the target system will always be represented as a data structure, and the state of the environment can be modeled as a data structure that need never be implemented.

A data model must be interfaced with processing aspects of the system. At the very least, a set of primitive data manipulation operations should be enumerated. These operations should be defined in terms of a first-order predicate language and the operations "create," "destroy," and "modify" applied to individuals in the database.

Data-oriented models, which are the heart of requirements analysis and specification, have been very successful in the domains of data processing and business information systems.

References [Yeh 89, Roussopoulos 79, and Mittermeir 80] contain some excellent examples.

5.1.2: Dataflow Processing Models

Dataflow diagrams are the most common models of the processing activities of a system and are used in conjunction with data-oriented models. They simply name the major processing activities of the system and indicate which parts of the data model are the inputs and outputs of each activity. If iterative refinement of the dataflow diagram is supported and activities are defined (usually informally) in terms of data manipulation operations, the diagram will exhibit a level of expressive power sufficient for many data processing systems.

The dataflow approach is central to structured analysis and design technique (SADT) [Ross 77a and Ross 77b], although they also emphasize a methodology for team cooperation. The dataflow approach is supported with automated tools in the problem statement language/problem statement analyzer (PSL/PSA) [Teichroew 77]. It can be extended with control information via Petri nets [Peterson 77] or with resource synchronization [Conner 79].

The deficiencies of the dataflow model for specifying real-time embedded systems are that the global events and activities in these kinds of systems are continuous and are not activated by the appearance of a single input or any simple combination of inputs. At a lower level, they consist of complex combinations of pieces of computation that must occur asynchronously and in parallel. Dataflow as a concept is simply not powerful enough to permit precise specification or effective decomposition of systems, such as embedded ones, in which concurrent and asynchronous operations occur at the requirements level.

5.1.3: The Process Model

The process model, which is better suited for the specification of embedded systems, emphasizes the "events" and "activities" portions of Figure 3. The central concept is the process, an autonomously computational unit that operates in parallel with and interacts asynchronously with other processes. Processes have long been used as abstractions of concurrent activity within multiprogramming systems [Horning 73], and many recent articles have shown that they can be used to model databases, monitors, functional modules, input/output devices, and presumably any other identifiable structure within a computing system (e.g., Hoare 78 and Hansen 78).

Formally, a process is a "state space," or a set of possible states, and a "successor relation" that maps predecessor states onto their possible successors. This simple concept is easily adapted into digital simulation of an object (person, machine, sensors, etc.) in the environment of a computer system.

The result of the generality of processes is that the requirements for a system can be specified by a set of asynchronously interacting processes, some of which represent objects in the environment, and some of which represent objects in the target system. Consequently, a process model with a highly complex overall behavior is easily formed.

Using an executable model that emphasizes the active parts of the required system is the "operational" approach, which was first taken by the software requirements engineering methodology (SREM) system and its requirements specification language RSL [Bell 77, Alford 77, and Davis 77]. In RSL, processing paths from input stimuli to output responses are specified directly and can be simulated for performance purposes. Stimulus-response paths are an important aspect of operational requirements, but are incomplete, since they exclude explicit representations of system states, internal synchronization, or potentially distributed environments.

Process-oriented, applicative, interpretable specification language (PAISLey) [Zave 82 and Zave 81] is another executable language, which in comparison, is more complete than RSL in its inclusion of states, synchronization, and the system's environment. In addition, it shows that the operational approach has three significant advantages for deriving embedded system requirements. The first advantage is that the rigor of having to make a model that "runs" always proves to be a powerful influence against ambiguity and vagueness in requirements. The second advantage of operational specifications is that they provide natural structures to which performance requirements can be attached. This is especially important for embedded systems. References [Zave 79 and Zave 81] show how response time and feedback-loop requirements can be specified formally by attaching timing attributes to functions in specification. A third advantage is that operational specifications make it possible to include resource requirements when necessary. Resource requirements specify the use of a particular resource or a quantity of a resource.

5.2: Nonfunctional Requirements

Most of the literature and methodologies for requirements focus on defining functional capabilities. Nonfunctional requirements, however, have received very little attention and may be an equally important part of the SRD. Since the state of the art is quite far from a comprehensive theory or methodology for these requirements, we present an annotated outline, intended as a checklist of the various topics that should at least be considered, even if not included, in the SRD.

5.2.1: Target System Constraints

Constraints are attributes other than capabilities that restrict the kinds of solutions the designer may consider. Constraints that can be placed on the target system include, but are not limited to, performance, reliability, security, and operating and physical constraints.

Performance: Here, performance includes all factors that describe both the subjective and objective qualities of the target system. Performance is therefore a measurement of "success" of the target system and a constraint below which the system must not be allowed to fall.

Reliability: Reliability can be divided into two basic categories: the availability of the physical equipment and the integrity of the information [Jones 80]. For requirements, the concern is "failures" (noticeable events in which the system violates its specifications), rather than "faults" (mechanical or algorithmic defects that will generate an error) [Zelkowitz 79], since the way the system maintains its specified level of reliability is a concern of the system developers, not those who write requirements. The purpose of defining and classifying the failures is to allow constraints to be placed on the likelihood of such failures.

Security: Much of security is arguably in the realm of design, since it pertains to specific means by which the reliability of the system may be enhanced. However, in two areas security may be an appropriate requirement. The first is physical security, which may include, for example, all military standards for pressurized cable, disconnectable terminals, safes for storing classified tapes and disks, and even the criteria for destroying or reusing storage media. Operational security includes any method that must be used to cipher, modularize, limit transmission, or otherwise affect how or where sensitive information will be available. Note that the physical considerations for reuse of media are in some ways part of the operational category, since it is well known that disks, for example, even when erased or overwritten a dozen times, can be made to reveal their original information with specialized signal differentiating equipment.

Operating constraints: One operating constraint considered here is the frequency and duration of use of a proposed system. Frequency and duration of use are important not only from a staffing and maintenance point of view, but also from the standpoint of available resources. If the computer equipment is, for example, only used as part of the target system for a limited time, it might be used as a general facility at other times. Conversely, an existing facility may be able to support the needs of the target system. In designing a satellite probe, it might be very important to know that a computer module could be connected to a network and used for computational assistance when not operating in its primary capacity.

Control is an important operating constraint in many systems. An unmanned remote facility cannot be restarted by personnel if a failure occurs. Depending on whether personnel can reach the remote site, the equipment may need sophisticated automatic restart or even reconfiguration capabilities. Preventive maintenance may also be impossible in inaccessible locations, such as inside satellites or deep-sea probes. In addition, the location of the remote facility may affect the nature of interactions required, since distant space probes experience significant transmission delays because of speed-of-light limitations.

Physical contraints: The physical constraints requirements should include all factors relating to the physical placement of the equipment. In some applications, even camouflaging the external casing of the hardware itself might be an important physical constraint. Such constraints also include size, weight, power, temperature, humidity, and portability and ruggedness requirements.

System development, evolution, and maintenance: In many organizations, the plan for the development, evolution, and maintenance of a target system is a separate document from the requirements, since the development plan is considered to be a statement of how the requirements will be carried out. On the other hand, in many instances, large computer systems are requested and paid for by one group and developed and delivered by another. Constraints on the magnitude and cost of the development effort may very well be considered requirements by the group paying the bill. In this section, we discuss various development categories relating to the lifecycle plan.

Development strategies: The strategies for developing target systems can be divided into two gross categories: efforts directed toward the single delivery date when the completed operational system will be furnished, and efforts that plan to deliver working subsets of the requirements for evaluation in the field before embarking on a more complete version. The single full-scale effort is often itself iterative [Conn 80], but the early versions of the system are not intended for use by the customer. Prototyping may be required in time-critical situations where delivering any kind of working system will fulfill an immediate need. Similarly, in state-of-the-art projects, careful analysis of a system shell may be needed to evaluate human factors and to clarify the requirements. Most software systems are iterative; for example, operating systems are usually updated on a regular basis throughout their lives.

Scale of effort: The scale of effort is an essential factor in establishing requirements for the development strategies of a target system. In iterative efforts that envision many prototypes or versions, resources should be allocated for personnel, equipment, and overhead associated with the development of each version. When development time is included as a requirement, an evaluation can be made that assesses whether it is possible to complete the stated goals within the proposed time frame. If an extended or advanced development is foreseen for one or more iterations, this information should be incorporated into the requirements. Finally, each version should have a plan for delivery and installation. When equipment is to be installed in aircraft or naval vessels, delivery and installation may be a complex technical endeavor. When many installations are already in the field, the requirements may include special procedures for handling the logistics of updating each installation.

Quality control standards: Control over the quality of the software and hardware product is exercised to guarantee that software and hardware conform to established requirements and perform satisfactorily. Quality control is an important management technique to ensure the success of the project. In general, although the role of quality assurance in software development is vague and software quality measures are still unstandardized, it is reasonable to consider the current ideas on top-down structured, provable, and modularized software as elements of quality control. As a result, many organizations now include standardization enforcement software within their compilers and assemblers.

Milestones and review procedures: Milestones and review procedures evaluate and keep track of partly completed systems. The milestone is an identifiable stage of completion that can be used to determine whether parallel efforts are progressing on time with respect to one another. Developers themselves use review procedures to assess the progress of an effort. The contracting agency may request a feasibility study for implementing a portion of the entire system. In this case, a milestone might reflect the point at which the feasibility has been proven, thus enabling serious subsystem design efforts to begin.

Acceptance criteria: The acceptance criteria identify specific tests and evaluation factors by which the developed system can be judged. Traditionally, the acceptance criteria are the "teeth" in the contract against which disputes are settled. Since a target system can almost never be exhaustively tested, it is critical that the acceptance tests cover every significant combination of functions or activities the system is supposed to perform.

Priority and changeability: Carrying out some requirements may be very important, but other requirements may represent "goldplating." Constraints such as cost, size, training, and development time may make it necessary to delay consideration of some of the less critical requirements. A means for ranking requirements or associating some weighting factors to particular facets of a target system is very useful; these rankings could follow Parnas' modularization based on the likelihood of change [Parnas 72]. If a designer is to be expected to hide system decisions that could easily change in some modular organization, the requirements must give information about what might change. Similarly, if a general requirement can be satisfied by more than one entirely different solution, it may be necessary to include detailed requirements for each of the solutions.

Maintenance: The maintenance category here specifically excludes the evolutionary software activities often classified under "maintenance." The requirements address the system's break down and subsequent return to working condition. For the software, the requirements might specify the staffing needed or a contractual agreement for fixing "bugs." The document might list the kinds of programs or packages that will be supplied to fix "bugs," and the kinds of software to be embedded in the system (such as error logging or path counters) that aid in discovering and tracing errors. As for hardware, it is necessary to know who will perform the preventive maintenance and repairs. The requirements may need to spell out standards for the minimal set of test points at which the repairer can probe and access the operation of the circuit.

5.2.3: Economic Context of System Development

Very few projects are undertaken without considering cost-effectiveness. Even extravagant programs give cost trade-offs serious consideration. Satisfactory economic decisions are much more likely to be made if the cost, goals, and guidelines are spelled out in the requirements documents.

Trade-offs: Requirements for cost trade-offs establish guidelines for determining whether existing equipment and software can be satisfactorily incorporated into the target system or whether a new effort is required. Very often off-the-shelf equipment is not ideal and does not entirely satisfy the requirements. However, cost/trade-off requirements can effectively overrule other requirements, if the sacrifice is not too great. Some criteria are needed to indicate just how important the ready-made requirement is and what might be given up to fulfill that requirement.

Cost of iterative system development: Many projects are developed iteratively, whether or not the customer sees the intervening stages or prototypes; to measure these iterations, almost all projects have milestones or baselines that indicate the achievement of some level of operation or functionality. Without requirements that place cost limitations on these stages, fund allocation to project phases could be unbalanced, starving, for example, later efforts due to disproportionate expenditures at the beginning of the project. In addition, if prototypes are to be delivered to the customer for interim use or evaluation, the requirements should address these costs.

Cost of each instance of the target system: The development effort may be directed at producing many similar or identical target systems. Under these circumstances, the development costs are usually amortized over the entire projected production run. Each instance of the target system will carry costs from materials and from the applicable fraction of development expenses. Any proposed evolutionary change to the target system after delivery will have to take into account the costs of updating each installation.

6: Managing the Requirements Process

In this section, we recommend ways to ensure that the requirements generation process is successful and productive.

6.1: Getting the Needed Information

One concern is how to gain access to information we may need that is hidden somewhere in the environment or in the minds of the users themselves. Another concern is how to broaden the users perspective so that enough subgoals and operational alternatives to accomplish these goals can be found. The information collected in interviews and documents analysis should be prepared so that it can be used as the starting point for refinement through the process of requirements analysis.

6.2: Getting the Users Involved

Requirements do not leap at the system analyst from their problem domain, but evolve through human interaction. Many of the problems that originate early in requirements analysis can be attributed to lack of communication between the user community and software engineers. Some common communication problems are well known: ideas may be expressed vaguely or ambiguously, goals may be contradictory or incompletely formulated, and various users may have differing views of the desired system. Realizing that these difficulties exist leads to the conclusion that good requirements analysis depends on intensive interaction with the user community at all authority levels, as well as on feedback from the software engineers on how they understand the desired system.

6.3: Getting the Baseline Requirements

Requirements will change as the users learn more about the system. Therefore, management should allocate time for changes in the requirements; otherwise, the system delivered may not be what the users desired. Once the frequency of changes settles down, however, a baseline requirement must be obtained before the first software design review. The baseline is intended to interpret mandatory provisions of the requirements specification. The baseline requirement must be "signed off" by the customer and kept firm.

6.4: Concern for Requirements Traceability and Testability

Requirements-tracing uses documentation and specification techniques to establish and maintain bidirectional traceability in two ways from requirements through design and ultimately through coding, and from requirements to validation tests. This tracing maintains awareness of the requirements as design and development activities proceed.

The sequence of events in traceability is relatively easy to establish. Testability of requirements demands much more thought and effort. For example, if there is to be a display that queries a database, then the requirements for response time can be complex. They should include solid reasons for specifying a certain value, or proposed experiments to determine and validate the end user's real needs; the experiments should both verify what the need is and check that the final product meets the need.

6.5: Concern for the Entire Lifecycle Process

This point was stressed earlier; functional requirements are essential to, but are only part of the total requirements.

6.6: Separate the Concerns

Most of the requirements document consists of thick volumes of natural language statements; therefore, traceability and testability are difficult to perform. The document itself should be organized so that each project member can concentrate on a well-defined set of questions. This separation also makes the document easy to change, because it refines the definiton of changes. For example, hardware interfaces should be described without making any assumption about the purpose of the software, so that the hardware section can remain unchanged if the behavior of the software is changed, and vice versa.

6.7: Use Precise Notation

To avoid confusion and minimize the amount of implicit assumptions by the developer, the analyst should avoid narrative and develop a formal system of notation that presents information in a rigorous, consistent, and complete manner.

7: Conclusion

In the new paradigm for evolving software, the abstraction-based software lifecycle model is applied. This model concentrates on the hard problems of software, namely, requirements specification and design, rather than on coding. Evaluation and validation are parts of the development process, rather than the completion of the development in each phase. In this paper, we have examined the conceptual and operational models and WBS as techniques to alleviate problems encountered in the process of deriving requirements. Preceding the requirements analysis, the objectives analysis allows us to study the organization's objectives and the constraints against the full achievement of the objectives, including their influences, interactions, and degrees of freedom.

Material to be included in a software requirements document can be derived from the conceptual model by filtering and organizing, constantly aiming towards the "best-engineered" specification. Only examples of what might go into a software requirements document (functional and nonfunctional requirements) are discussed. For functional requirements, the process model is a better approach than the data-oriented model and dataflow processing model to the precise specification or effective decomposition of embedded systems. Finally, several recommendations are provided for managing the requirements derivation process.

8: References

[Alford 77] Alford, Mack, "A Requirements Engineering Methodology for Real-Time Processing Requirements," *IEEE Transactions on Software Engineering,* SE-3, Jan. 1977, pp. 60-69.

[ANSI/IEEE 84] *IEEE Guide to Software Requirements Specifications,* ANSI/IEEE Standards 830, IEEE, New York, 1984.

[Astrahan 76] Astrahan, M.M., et al., "System R: Relational Approach to Database Management," *ACM Transactions on Database Systems,* June 1976, pp. 97-137.

[Baker 89] Baker, Jerry W., Daniel Chester, and Raymond T. Yeh, "Software Design by Stepwise Evaluation and Refinement," *Modern Software Engineering: Foundations and Current Perspectives,* (eds. P.A. Ng and R.T. Yeh), Van Nostrand Reinhold, New York, Oct. 1989, pp. 239-273.

[Basili 80] Basili, V.R., *Tutorial on Models and Metrics for Software Management and Engineering,* IEEE Computer Society Press, Washington, D.C., 1980.

[Bell 77] Bell, Thomas E., Davis C. Bixler, and Margaret Dyer, "An Extenuable Approach to Computer-Aided Software Requirements Engineering," *IEEE Transactions on Software Engineering,* SE-3, Jan. 1977, pp. 48-59.

[Boehm 73] Boehm, Barry W., "Software and Its Impact: A Quantitative Assessment," *Datamation, 19,* May 1973, pp. 48-60.

[Boehm 81] Boehm, Barry W., *Software Engineering Economics,* Prentice-Hall, Old Tappan, N.J., 1981.

[Conn 80] Conn, Alex Paul, "Maintenance: A Key Element in Computer Requirements Definition," *Proc. COMSPAC,* IEEE Computer Society Press, Washington, D.C., Nov. 1980.

[Conner 79] Conner, M., "Process Synchronization by Behavior Controllers," Ph.D. thesis, Computer Sciences Department, University of Texas at Austin, 1979.

[Davis 77] Davis, Carl C. and Charles R. Vick, "The Software Development System," *IEEE Transactions on Software Engineering,* SE-3, Jan. 1977, pp. 69-84.

[Hansen 78] Hansen, Per Brinch, "Distributed Processes: A Concurrent Programming Concept," *Communications of the ACM, 21,* Nov. 1978, pp. 934-941.

[Hoare 78] Hoare, C.A.R., "Communicating Sequential Processes," *Communications of the ACM, 21,* Aug. 1978, pp. 666-667.

[Horning 73] Horning, J.J. and B. Randell, "Process Structuring," *Computing Survey,* 5, Jan. 1973, pp. 5-29.

[Jones 80] Jones, A.K. and P. Schwarz, "Experience Using Multiprocessor Systems—A Status Report," *Computing Survey,* 12, June 1980, pp. 121-165.

[Mittermeir 80] Mittermeir, Roland, "Requirements Analysis: Top Down or Bottom Up," *TRDA 80/02/02,* Institut fur Digitale Anlagen, Technische Universitat Wein, Vienna, Austria, 1980.

[Mittermeir 89] Mittermeir, Roland, Nicholas Roussopolous, Raymond T. Yeh, and Peter A. Ng, "An Integrated Approach to Requirements Analysis," *Modern Software Engineering: Foundations and Current Perspectives,* (eds. P.A. Ng and R.T. Yeh), Van Nostrand Reinhold, New York, Oct. 1989, pp. 119-164.

[Miyamoto 81] Miyamoto, I. and R.T. Yeh, "A Software Requirements and Definition Methodology for Business Data Processing," *Proc. 1981 Nat'l Computer Conference, AFIPS Conf. Proc. 50,* AFIPS Press, Reston, VA, 1981, pp. 571-581.

[Mumford 81] Mumford, E., "Participative Systems Design: Structure and Method," *Systems, Objectives, Selections 1,* 1981, pp. 5-19.

[Parnas 72] Parnas, D.L., "On the Criteria to Be Used in Decomposing Systems into Modules," *Communications of the ACM,* 15, Dec. 1972, pp. 1053-1059.

[Peterson 77] Peterson, James L., "Petri Nets," *Computing Surveys* 9, Sept. 1977, pp. 227-252.

[Putnam 78] Putnam, L.M., "A General Empirical Solution to the Macro Software Sizing and Estimating Problem." *IEEE Transactions on Software Engineering,* SE-4, July 1978, pp. 345-361.

[Radice 88] Radice, R.A. and R.W. Phillips, *Software Engineering: An Industrial Approach, Vol. I,* Prentice-Hall, N.J., 1988.

[Ross 77a] Ross, Douglas, "Structured Analysis (SA): A Language for Communicating Ideas," *IEEE Transactions on Software Engineering,* SE-3, Jan. 1977, pp. 15-34.

[Ross 77b] Ross, Douglas and Kenneth E. Schoman, Jr., "Structured Analysis for Requirements Definition," *IEEE Transactions on Software Engineering,* SE-3, Jan. 1977, pp. 6-15.

[Roussopoulos 79] Roussopoulos, Nicholas, "CSDL: A Conceptual Scheme Definition Language for the Design of Database Applications," *IEEE Transactions on Software Engineering,* SE-5, Sept. 1979, pp. 481-496.

[Royce 70] Royce., W.W., "Managing the Development of Large Software Systems: Concepts and Techniques," *Proc. WESCON,* IEEE, New York, Aug. 1970.

[Teichroew 77] Teichroew, B. and B.A. Hershey, III, "PSL/PSA: A Computer-Aided Technique for Structured Documentation and Analysis of Information Systems," *IEEE Transactions on Software Engineering,* SE-3, Jan. 1977, pp. 41-48.

[Thayer 75] Thayer, T.A., "Understanding Software through Analysis of Empirical Data," *TRW Software Series,* TRW-SS-75-04, May 1975.

[Wedekind 76] Wedekind, E., "Systemanalyse," Carl Hanser Verlag, Munich, F.R. Germany, 1976.

[Yeh 79] Yeh, Raymond T., "Systematic Derivation of Software Requirements through Structured Analysis," *Computer Science SDBEG-15,* University of Texas at Austin, Sept. 1979.

[Yeh 82] Yeh, Raymond T., "Requirements Analysis—A Management Perspective," *Proc. IEEE Sixth Int'l Computer Software and Applications Conference,* IEEE Computer Society Press, Washington, D.C., 1982, pp. 410-416.

[Yeh 83] Yeh, Raymond T., "Software Engineering," *IEEE Spectrum,* Nov. 1983, pp. 91-94.

[Yeh 89] Yeh, Raymond T., "An Alternative Paradigm for Software Evolution," *Modern Software Engineering: Foundations and Current Perspectives,* (eds. P.A. Ng. and R.T. Yeh), Van Nostrand Reinhold, New York, Oct. 1989, pp. 7-22.

[Yeh 84] Yeh, Raymond T., P. Zave, A.P. Conn, and G.E. Cole, "Software Requirements Analysis—New Directions and Perspectives," *Handbook of Software Engineering* (eds. C. Vick and C.V. Ramamoorthy), Prentice-Hall, Old Tappan, N.J., 1982, pp. 519-543.

[Zave 79] Zave, P., "Formal Specification of Complete and Consistent Performance Requirements," *Proc. Texas Conference on Computing Systems,* IEEE Computer Society Press, Washington, D.C., Nov. 1979, pp. 4B18-4B25.

[Zave 82] Zave, P., "An Operational Approach to Requirements Specification for Embedded Systems," *IEEE Transactions on Software Engineering,* SE-8, May 1982, pp. 250-269.

[Zave 81] Zave, P. and Raymond T. Yeh, "Executable Requirements for Embedded Systems," *Proc. Fifth Int'l. Conference on Software Engineering,* IEEE Computer Society Press, Washington, D.C., 1981, pp. 295-304.

[Zelkowitz 79] Zelkowitz, M.V., A.C. Shaw, and J.D. Gannon, *Principles of Software Engineering and Design,* Prentice-Hall, Old Tappan, N.J., 1979, p. 8.

Elements of Software Configuration Management

EDWARD H. BERSOFF, SENIOR MEMBER, IEEE

Abstract—**Software configuration management (SCM) is one of the disciplines of the 1980's which grew in response to the many failures of the software industry throughout the 1970's. Over the last ten years, computers have been applied to the solution of so many complex problems that our ability to manage these applications has all too frequently failed. This has resulted in the development of a series of "new" disciplines intended to help control the software process.**

This paper will focus on the discipline of SCM by first placing it in its proper context with respect to the rest of the software development process, as well as to the goals of that process. It will examine the constituent components of SCM, dwelling at some length on one of those components, configuration control. It will conclude with a look at what the 1980's might have in store.

Index Terms—**Configuration management, management, product assurance, software.**

Introduction

SOFTWARE configuration management (SCM) is one of the disciplines of the 1980's which grew in response to the many failures of our industry throughout the 1970's. Over the last ten years, computers have been applied to the solution of so many complex problems that our ability to manage these applications in the "traditional" way has all too frequently failed. Of course, tradition in the software business began only 30 years ago or less, but even new habits are difficult to break. In the 1970's we learned the hard way that the tasks involved in managing a software project were not linearly dependent on the number of lines of code produced. The relationship was, in fact, highly exponential. As the decade closed, we looked back on our failures [1], [2] trying to understand what went wrong and how we could correct it. We began to dissect the software development process [3], [4] and to define techniques by which it could be effectively managed [5]-[8]. This self-examination by some of the most talented and experienced members of the software community led to the development of a series of "new" disciplines intended to help control the software process.

While this paper will focus on the particular discipline of SCM, we will first place it in its proper context with respect to the rest of the software development process, as well as to the goals of that process. We will examine the constituent components of SCM, dwelling at some length on one of those components, configuration control. Once we have woven our way through all the trees, we will once again stand back and take a brief look at the forest and see what the 1980's might have in store.

Manuscript received April 15, 1982; revised December 1, 1982 and October 18, 1983.

The author is with BTG, Inc., 1945 Gallows Rd., Vienna, VA 22180.

SCM in Context

It has been said that if you do not know where you are going, any road will get you there. In order to properly understand the role that SCM plays in the software development process, we must first understand what the goal of that process is, i.e., where we are going. For now, and perhaps for some time to come, software developers are people, people who respond to the needs of another set of people creating computer programs designed to satisfy those needs. These computer programs are the tangible output of a thought process—the conversion of a thought process into a product. The goal of the software developer is, or should be, the construction of a product which closely matches the real needs of the set of people for whom the software is developed. We call this goal the achievement of "product integrity." More formally stated, product integrity (depicted in Fig. 1) is defined to be the intrinsic set of attributes that characterize a product [9]:

- that fulfills user functional needs;
- that can easily and completely be traced through its life cycle;
- that meets specified performance criteria;
- whose cost expectations are met;
- whose delivery expectations are met.

The above definition is pragmatically based. It demands that product integrity be a measure of the satisfaction of the real needs and expectations of the software user. It places the burden for achieving the software goal, product integrity, squarely on the shoulders of the developer, for it is he alone who is in control of the development process. While, as we shall see, the user can establish safeguards and checkpoints to gain visibility into the development process, the prime responsibility for software success is the developer's. So our goal is now clear; we want to build software which exhibits all the characteristics of product integrity. Let us make sure that we all understand, however, what this thing called software really is. We have learned in recent times that equating the terms "software" and "computer programs" improperly restricts our view of software. Software is much more. A definition which can be used to focus the discussion in this paper is that software is information that is:

- structured with logical and functional properties;
- created and maintained in various forms and representations during the life cycle;
- tailored for machine processing in its fully developed state.

So by our definition, software is not simply a set of computer programs, but includes the documentation required to define, develop, and maintain these programs. While this notion is not very new, it still frequently escapes the software

Reprinted from *IEEE Transactions on Software Engineering*, Volume SE-10, Number 1, January 1984, pages 79-87.

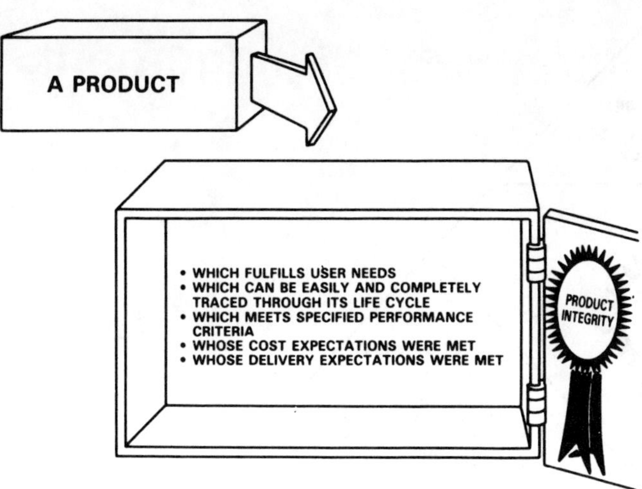

Fig. 1. Product integrity.

development manager who assumes that controlling a software product is the same as controlling computer code.

Now that we more fully appreciate what we are after, i.e., to build a software product with integrity, let us look at the one road which might get us there. We have, until now, used the term "developer" to characterize the organizational unit responsible for converting the software idea into a software product. But developers are, in reality, a complex set of interacting organizational entities. When undertaking a software project, most developers structure themselves into three basic discipline sets which include:

- project management,
- development, and
- product assurance.

Project management disciplines are both inwardly and outwardly directed. They support general management's need to see what is going on in a project and to ensure that the parent or host organization consistently develops products with integrity. At the same time, these disciplines look inside a project in support of the assignment, allocation, and control of all project resources. In that capacity, project management determines the relative allocation of resources to the set of development and product assurance disciplines. It is management's prerogative to specify the extent to which a given discipline will be applied to a given project. Historically, management has often been handicapped when it came to deciding how much of the product assurance disciplines were required. This was a result of both inexperience and organizational immaturity.

The development disciplines represent those traditionally applied to a software project. They include:

- analysis,
- design,
- engineering,
- production (coding),
- test (unit/subsystem),
- installation,
- documentation,
- training, and
- maintenance.

In the broadest sense, these are the disciplines required to take a system concept from its beginning through the development life cycle. It takes a well-structured, rigorous technical approach to system development, along with the right mix of development disciplines to attain product integrity, especially for software. The concept of an ordered, procedurally disciplined approach to system development is fundamental to product integrity. Such an approach provides successive development plateaus, each of which is an identifiable measure of progress which forms a part of the total foundation supporting the final product. Going sequentially from one baseline (plateau) to another with high probability of success, necessitates the use of the right development disciplines at precisely the right time.

The product assurance disciplines which are used by project management to gain visibility into the development process include:

- configuration management,
- quality assurance,
- validation and verification, and
- test and evaluation.

Proper employment of these product assurance disciplines by the project manager is basic to the success of a project since they provide the technical checks and balances over the product being developed. Fig. 2 represents the relationship among the management, development, and product assurance disciplines. Let us look at each of the product assurance disciplines briefly, in turn, before we explore the details of SCM.

Configuration management (CM) is the discipline of identifying the configuration of a system at discrete points in time for the purpose of systematically controlling changes to the configuration and maintaining the integrity and traceability of the configuration throughout the system life cycle. Software configuration management (SCM) is simply configuration management tailored to systems, or portions of systems, that are comprised predominantly of software. Thus, SCM does not differ substantially from the CM of hardware-oriented systems, which is generally well understood and effectively practiced. However, attempts to implement SCM have often failed because the particulars of SCM do not follow by direct analogy from the particulars of hardware CM and because SCM is a less mature discipline than that of hardware CM. We will return to this subject shortly.

Quality assurance (QA) as a discipline is commonly invoked throughout government and industry organizations with reasonable standardization when applied to systems comprised only of hardware. But there is enormous variation in thinking and practice when the QA discipline is invoked for a software development or for a system containing software components. QA has a long history, and much like CM, it has been largely developed and practiced on hardware projects. It is therefore mature, in that sense, as a discipline. Like CM, however, it is relatively immature when applied to software development. We define QA as consisting of the procedures, techniques, and tools applied by professionals to insure that a product meets or exceeds prespecified standards during a product's development cycle; and without specific prescribed standards, QA entails insuring that a product meets or

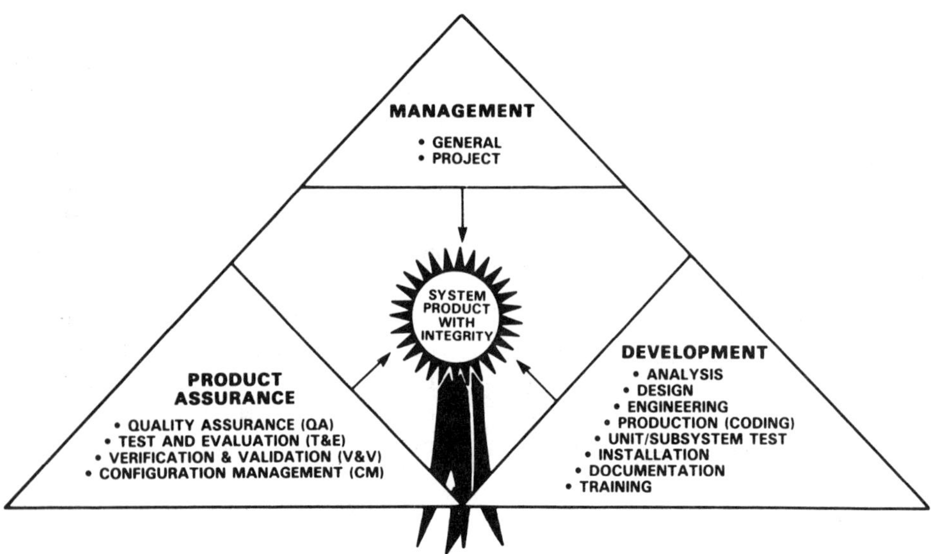

Fig. 2. The discipline triangle.

exceeds a minimum industrial and/or commercially acceptable level of excellence.

The QA discipline has not been uniformly treated, practiced or invoked relative to software development. First, very few organizations have software design and development standards that compare in any way with hardware standards for detail and completeness. Second, it takes a high level of software expertise to assess whether a software product meets prescribed standards. Third, few buyer organizations have provided for or have developed the capability to impose and then monitor software QA endeavors on seller organizations. Finally, few organizations have been concerned over precisely defining the difference between QA and other product assurance disciplines, CM often being subservient to QA or vice versa in a given development organization. Our definition of software given earlier suggests still another reason for the software QA discipline being in the same state as SCM so far as its universal application within the user, buyer, and seller communities. Software, as a form of information, cannot be standardized; only structures for defining/documenting software can be standardized. It follows that software development techniques can only be meaningfully standardized in relation to information structures, not information content.

The third of the four product assurance disciplines is validation and verification (V&V). Unlike CM and QA, V&V has come into being expressly for the purpose of coping with software and its development. Unlike QA, which prinicipally deals with the problem of a product's adherence to preestablished standards, V&V deals with the issue of how well software fulfills functional and performance requirements and the assurance that specified requirements are indeed stated and interpreted correctly. The verification part of V&V assures that a product meets its prescribed goals as defined through baseline documentation. That is, verification is a discipline imposed to ascertain that a product is what it was intended to be relative to its preceding baseline. The validation part of V&V, by contrast, is levied as a discipline to assure that a product not only meets the objectives specified through baseline documentation, but in addition, does the right job. Stated another way, the validation discipline is invoked to insure that the end-user gets the right product. A buyer or seller may have misinterpreted user requirements or, perhaps, requirements have changed, or the user gets to know more about what he needs, or early specifications of requirements were wrong or incomplete or in a state of flux. The validation process serves to assure that such problems do not persist among the user, buyer, and seller. To enhance objectivity, it is often desirable to have an independent organization, from outside the developing organization, perform the V&V function.

The fourth of the product assurance disciplines is test and evaluation (T&E), perhaps the discipline most understood, and yet paradoxically, least practiced with uniformity. T&E is defined as the discipline imposed outside the development project organization to independently assess whether a product fulfills objectives. T&E does this through the execution of a set of test plans and procedures. Specifically in support of the end user, T&E entails evaluating product performance in a live or near-live environment. Frequently, particularly within the miliatry arena, T&E is a major undertaking involving one or more systems which are to operate together, but which have been individually developed and accepted as stand-alone items. Some organizations formally turn over T&E responsibility to a group outside the development project organization after the product reaches a certain stage of development, their philosophy being that developers cannot be objective to the point of fully testing/evaluating what they have produced.

The definitions given for CM, QA, V&V, and T&E suggest some overlap in required skills and functions to be performed in order to invoke these disciplines collectively for product assurance purposes. Depending on many factors, the actual overlap may be significant or little. In fact, there are those who would argue that V&V and T&E are but subset functions of QA. But the contesting argument is that V&V and T&E have come into being as separate disciplines because conventional QA methods and techniques have failed to do an adequate job with respect to providing product assurance, particularly for computer-centered systems with software components. Management must be concerned with minimizing the application of excessive and redundant resources to address the overlap of these disciplines. What is important is that all the functions defined above are performed, not what they are called or who carries them out.

The Elements of SCM

When the need for the discipline of configuration management finally achieved widespread recognition within the software engineering community, the question arose as to how closely the software CM discipline ought to parallel the extant hardware practice of configuration management. Early SCM authors and practitioners [10] wisely chose the path of commonality with the hardware world, at least at the highest level. Of course, hardware engineering is different from software engineering, but broad similarities do exist and terms applied to one segment of the engineering community can easily be applied to another, even if the specific meanings of those terms differ significantly in detail. For that reason, the elements of SCM were chosen to be the same as those for hardware CM. As for hardware, the four components of SCM are:

- identification,
- control,
- auditing, and
- status accounting.

Let us examine each one in turn.

Software Configuration Identification: Effective management of the development of a system requires careful definition of its baseline components; changes to these components also need to be defined since these changes, together with the baselines, specify the system evolution. A system baseline is like a snapshot of the aggregate of system components as they exist at a given point in time; updates to this baseline are like frames in a movie strip of the system life cycle. The role of software configuration identification in the SCM process is to provide labels for these snapshots and the movie strip.

A baseline can be characterized by two labels. One label identifies the baseline itself, while the second label identifies an update to a particular baseline. An update to a baseline represents a baseline plus a set of changes that have been incorporated into it. Each of the baselines established during a software system's life cycle controls subsequent system development. At the time it is first established a software baseline embodies the actual software in its most recent state. When changes are made to the most recently established baseline, then, from the viewpoint of the software configuration manager, this baseline and these changes embody the actual software in its most recent state (although, from the viewpoint of the software developer, the actual software may be in a more advanced state).

The most elementary entity in the software configuration identification labeling mechanism is the software configuration item (SCI). Viewed from an SCM perspective, a software baseline appears as a set of SCI's. The SCI's within a baseline are related to one another via a tree-like hierarchy. As the software system evolves through its life cycle, the number of branches in this hierarchy generally increases; the first baseline may consist of no more than one SCI. The lowest level SCI's in the tree hierarchy may still be under development and not yet under SCM control. These entities are termed design objects or computer program components (see Fig. 3). Each baseline and each member in the associated family of updates will exist in one or more forms, such as a design document, source code on a disk, or executing object code.

In performing the identification function, the software configuration manager is, in effect, taking snapshots of the SCI's. Each baseline and its associated updates collectively represents the evolution of the software during each of its life cycle stages. These stages are staggered with respect to one another. Thus, the collection of life cycle stages looks like a collection of staggered and overlapping sequences of snapshots of SCI trees. Let us now imagine that this collection of snapshot sequences is threaded, in chronological order, onto a strip of movie film as in Fig. 4. Let us further imagine that the strip of movie film is run through a projector. Then we would see a history of the evolution of the software. Consequently, the identification of baselines and updates provides an explicit documentation trail linking all stages of the software life cycle. With the aid of this documentation trail, the software developer can assess the integrity of his product, and the software buyer can assess the integrity of the product he is paying for.

Software Configuration Control: The evolution of a software system is, in the language of SCM, the development of baselines and the incorporation of a series of changes into the baselines. In addition to these changes that explicitly affect existing baselines, there are changes that occur during early stages of the system life cycle that may affect baselines that do not yet exist. For example, some time before software coding begins (i.e., some time prior to the establishment of a design baseline), a contract may be modified to include a software warranty provision such as: system downtime due to software failures shall not exceed 30 minutes per day. This warranty provision will generally affect subsequent baselines but in a manner that cannot be explicitly determined *a priori*. One role of software configuration control is to provide the administrative mechanism for precipitating, preparing, evaluating, and approving or disapproving all change proposals throughout the system life cycle.

We have said that software, for configuration management purposes, is a collection of SCI's that are related to one another in a well-defined way. In early baselines and their associated updates, SCI's are specification documents (one or more volumes of text for each baseline or associated update); in later baselines and their associated updates, each SCI may manifest itself in any or all of the various software representations. Software configuration control focuses on managing changes to SCI's (existing or to be developed) in all of their representations. This process involves three basic ingredients.

1) Documentation (such as administrative forms and supporting technical and administrative material) for formally precipitating and defining a proposed change to a software system.

2) An organizational body for formally evaluating and

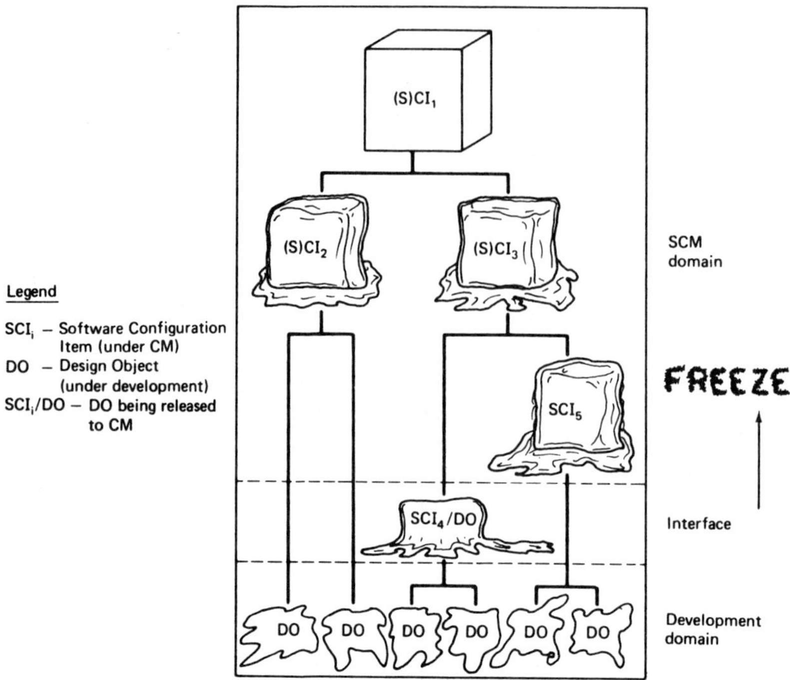

Fig. 3. The development/SCM interface.

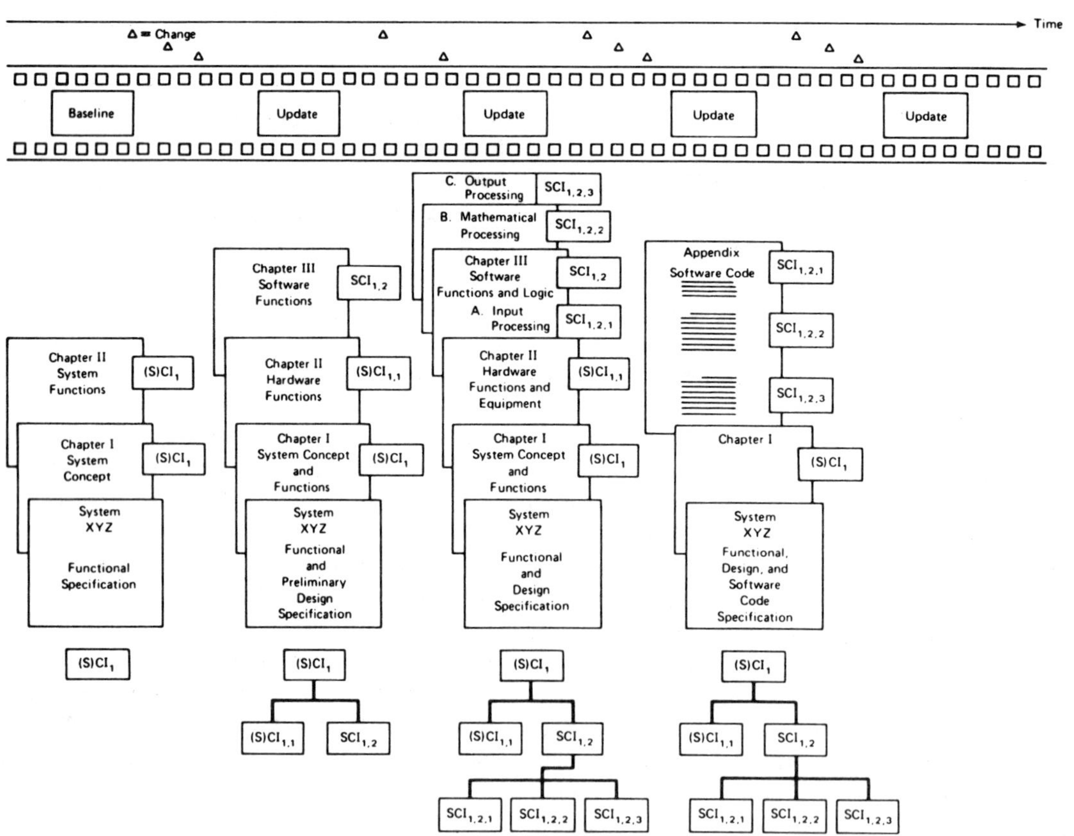

Fig. 4. SCI evolution in a single document.

approving or disapproving a proposed change to a software system (the Configuration Control Board).

3) Procedures for controlling changes to a software system.

The Engineering Change Proposal (ECP), a major control document, contains information such as a description of the proposed change, identification of the originating organization, rationale for the change, identification of affected baselines and SCI's (if appropriate), and specification of cost and schedule impacts. ECP's are reviewed and coordinated by the CCB, which is typically a body representing all organizational units which have a vested interest in proposed changes.

Fig. 5 depicts the software configuration control process.

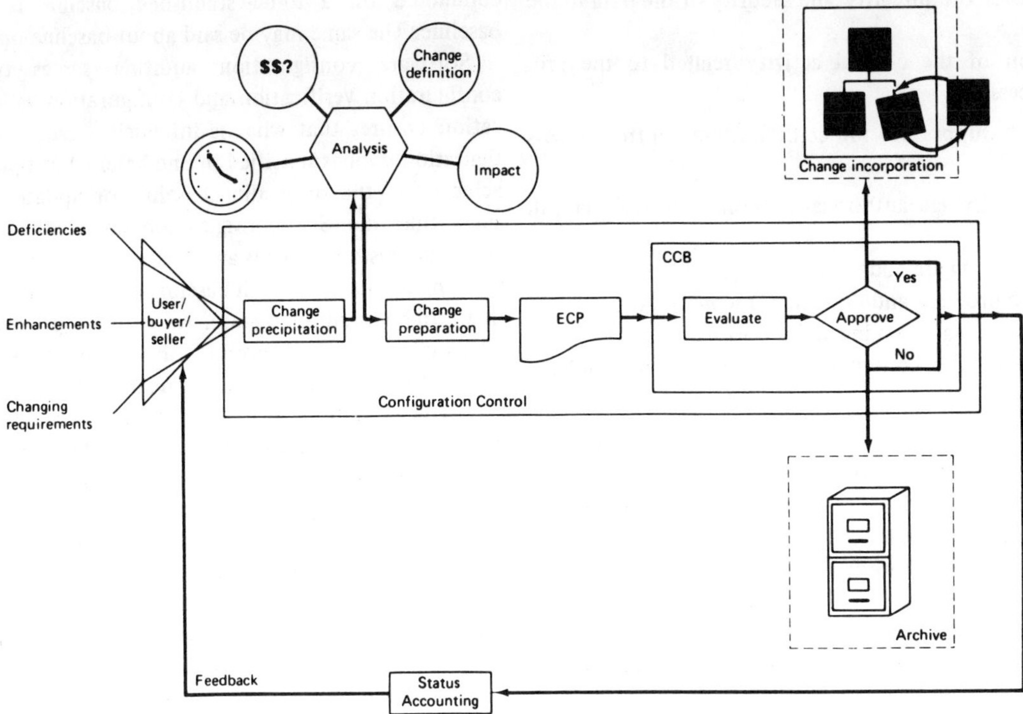

Fig. 5. The control process.

As the figure suggests, change incorporation is not an SCM function, but monitoring the change implementation process resulting in change incorporation is. Fig. 5 also emphasizes that the analysis that may be required to prepare an ECP is also outside the SCM purview. Note also from the figure how ECP's not approved by the CCB are not simply discarded but are archived for possible future reference.

Many automated tools support the control process. The major ones aid in controlling software change once the coding stage has been reached, and are generically referred to as program support libraries (PSL's). The level of support provided by PSL's, however, varies greatly. As a minimum, a PSL should provide a centralized and readily available repository for authoritative versions of each component of a software system. It should contain the data necessary for the orderly development and control of each SCI. Automation of other functions, such as library access control, software and document version maintenance, change recording, and document reconstruction, greatly enhance both the control and maintenance processes. These capabilities are currently available in systems such as SOFTOOL's change and configuration control environment (CCC).

A PSL supports a developmental approach in which project personnel work on a common visible product rather than on independent components. In those PSL's which include access controls, project personnel can be separately assigned read/write access to each software document/component, from programs to lines of code. Thus, all project personnel are assured ready access to the critical interface information necessary for effective software development. At the same time, modifications to various software components, whether sanctioned baselines or modules under development, can be closely controlled.

Under the PSL concept, the programmer operates under a well-defined set of parameters and exercises a narrower span of detailed control. This minimizes the need for explicit communication between analysts and programmers and makes the inclusion of new project personnel less traumatic since interface requirements are well documented. It also minimizes the preparation effort for technical audits.

Responsibility for maintenance of the PSL data varies depending on the level of automation provided. For those systems which provide only a repository for data, a secretary/librarian is usually responsible for maintaining the notebooks which will contain the data developed and used by project personnel and for maintenance of the PSL archives. More advanced PSL systems provide real time, on-line access to data and programs and automatically create the records necessary to fully trace the history of the development. In either case the PSL provides standardization of project recordkeeping, ensures that system documentation corresponds to the current system configuration, and guarantees the existence of adequate documentation of previous versions.

A PSL should support three main activities: code development, software management, and configuration control. Support to the development process includes support to design, coding, testing, documentation, and program maintenance along with associated database schema and subschema. A PSL provides this support through:

- storage and maintenance of software documentation and code,
- support to program compilation/testing,
- support for the generation of program/system documentation.

Support to the management of the software development process involves the storage and output of programming data such as:

- collection and automatic reporting of management data related to program development,

• control over the integrity and security of the data in the PSL,

• separation of the clerical activity related to the programming process.

PSL's provide support to the configuration control process through:

• access and change authorization control for all data in the library,
• control of software code releases,
• automatic program and document reconstruction,
• automatic change tracking and reporting,
• assurance of the consistency between documentation, code, and listings.

A PSL has four major components: internal libraries in machine-readable form, external libraries in hardcopy form, computer procedures, and office procedures. The components of a PSL system are interlocked to establish an exact correspondence between the internal units of code and external versions (such as listings) of the developing systems. This continuous correspondence is the characteristic of a PSL that guarantees ongoing visibility and identification of the developing system.

Different PSL implementations exist for various system environments with the specifics of the implementation dependent upon the hardware, software, user, and operating environment. The fundamental correspondence between the internal and external libraries in each environment, however, is established by the PSL librarian and computer procedures. The office procedures are specified in a project CM Plan so that the format of the external libraries is standard across software projects, and internal and external libraries are easily maintainable.

Newer PSL systems minimize the need for both office and computer procedures through the implementation of extensive management functionality. This functionality provides significant flexibility in controlling the access to data and allocating change authority, while providing a variety of status reporting capabilities. The availability of management information, such as a list of all the software structures changed to solve a particular Software Trouble Report or the details on the latest changes to a particular software document, provides a means for the control function to effectively operate without burdening the development team with cumbersome procedures and administrative paperwork. Current efforts in PSL refinement/development are aimed at linking support of the development environment with that of the configuration control environment. The goal of such systems is to provide an integrated environment where control and management information is generated automatically as a part of a fully supported design and development process.

Software Configuration Auditing: Software configuration auditing provides the mechanism for determining the degree to which the current state of the software system mirrors the software system pictured in baseline and requirements documentation. It also provides the mechanism for formally establishing a baseline. A baseline in its formative stages (for example, a draft specification document that appears prior to the existence of the functional baseline) is referred to as a "to-be-established" baseline; the final state of the auditing process conducted on a to-be-established baseline is a sanctioned baseline. The same may be said about baseline updates.

Software configuration auditing serves two purposes, configuration verification and configuration validation. Verification ensures that what is intended for each software configuration item as specified in one baseline or update is actually achieved in the succeeding baseline or update; validation ensures that the SCI configuration solves the right problem (i.e., that customer needs are satisfied). Software configuration auditing is applied to each baseline (and corresponding update) in its to-be-established state. An auditing process common to all baselines is the determination that an SCI structure exists and that its contents are based on all available information.

Software auditing is intended to increase software visibility and to establish traceability throughout the life cycle of the software product. Of course, this visibility and traceability are not achieved without cost. Software auditing costs time and money. But the judicious investment of time and money, particularly in the early stages of a project, pays dividends in the latter stages. These dividends include the avoidance of costly retrofits resulting from problems such as the sudden appearance of new requirements and the discovery of major design flaws. Conversely, failing to perform auditing, or constraining it to the later stages of the software life cycle, can jeopardize successful software development. Often in such cases, by the time discrepancies are discovered (if they are), the software cannot be easily or economically modified to rectify the discrepancies. The result is often a dissatisfied customer, large cost overruns, slipped schedules, or cancelled projects.

Software auditing makes visible to management the current status of the software in the life cycle product audited. It also reveals whether the project requirements are being satisfied and whether the intent of the preceding baseline has been fulfilled. With this visibility, project management can evaluate the integrity of the software product being developed, resolve issues that may have been raised by the audit, and correct defects in the development process. The visibility afforded by the software audit also provides a basis for the establishment of the audited life cycle product as a new baseline.

Software auditing provides traceability between a software life cycle product and the requirements for that product. Thus, as life cycle products are audited and baselines established, every requirement is traced successively from baseline to baseline. Disconnects are also made visible during the establishment of traceability. These disconnects include requirements not satisfied in the audited product and extraneous features observed in the product (i.e., features for which no stated requirement exists).

With the different point of view made possible by the visibility and traceability achieved in the software audit, management can make better decisions and exercise more incisive control over the software development process. The result of a software audit may be the establishment of a baseline, the redirection of project tasking, or an adjustment of applied project resources.

The responsibility for a successful software development project is shared by the buyer, seller, and user. Software auditing uniquely benefits each of these project participants. Appropriate auditing by each party provides checks and balances over the development effort. The scope and depth of the audits undertaken by the three parties may vary greatly. However, the purposes of these differing forms of software audit remain the same: to provide visibility and to establish traceability of the software life cycle products. An excellent overview of the software audit process, from which some of the above discussion has been extracted, appears in [11].

Software Configuration Status Accounting: A decision to make a change is generally followed by a time delay before the change is actually made, and changes to baselines generally occur over a protracted period of time before they are incorporated into baselines as updates. A mechanism is therefore needed for maintaining a record of how the system has evolved and where the system is at any time relative to what appears in published baseline documentation and written agreements. Software configuration status accounting provides this mechanism. Status accounting is the administrative tracking and reporting of all software items formally identified and controlled. It also involves the maintenance of records to support software configuration auditing. Thus, software configuration status accounting records the activity associated with the other three SCM functions and therefore provides the means by which the history of the software system life cycle can be traced.

Although administrative in nature, status accounting is a function that increases in complexity as the system life cycle progresses because of the multiple software representations that emerge with later baselines. This complexity generally results in large amounts of data to be recorded and reported. In particular, the scope of software configuration status accounting encompasses the recording and reporting of:

1) the time at which each representation of a baseline and update came into being;
2) the time at which each software configuration item came into being;
3) descriptive information about each SCI;
4) engineering change proposal status (approved, disapproved, awaiting action);
5) descriptive information about each ECP;
6) change status;
7) descriptive information about each change;
8) status of technical and administrative documentation associated with a baseline or update (such as a plan prescribing tests to be performed on a baseline for updating purposes);
9) deficiencies in a to-be-established baseline uncovered during a configuration audit.

Software configuration status accounting, because of its large data input and output requirements, is generally supported in part by automated processes such as the PSL described earlier. Data are collected and organized for input to a computer and reports giving the status of entities are compiled and generated by the computer.

The Management Dilemma

As we mentioned at the beginning of this paper, SCM and many of the other product assurance disciplines grew up in the 1970's in response to software failure. The new disciplines were designed to achieve visibility into the software engineering process and thereby exercise some measure of control over that process. Students of mathematical control theory are taught early in their studies a simple example of the control process. Consider being confronted with a cup of hot coffee, filled to the top, which you are expected to carry from the kitchen counter to the kitchen table. It is easily verified that if you watch the cup as you carry it, you are likely to spill more coffee than if you were to keep your head turned away from the cup. The problem with looking at the cup is one of overcompensation. As you observe slight deviations from the straight-and-level, you adjust, but often you adjust too much. To compensate for that overadjustment, you tend to overadjust again, with the result being hot coffee on your floor.

This little diversion from our main topic of SCM has an obvious moral. There is a fundamental propensity on the part of the practitioners of the product assurance disciplines to overadjust, to overcompensate for the failures of the development disciplines. There is one sure way to eliminate failure completely from the software development process, and that is to stop it completely. The software project manager must learn how to apply his resources intelligently. He must achieve visibility and control, but he must not so encumber the developer so as to bring progress to a virtual halt. The product assurers have a virtuous perspective. They strive for perfection and point out when and where perfection has not been achieved. We seem to have a binary attitude about software; it is either correct or it is not. That is perhaps true, but we cannot expect anyone to deliver perfect software in any reasonable time period or for a reasonable sum of money. What we need to develop is software that is good enough. Some of the controls that we have placed on the developer have the deleterious effect of increasing costs and expanding schedules rather than shrinking them.

The dilemma to management is real. We must have the visibility and control that the product assurance disciplines have the capacity to provide. But we must be careful not to overcompensate and overcontrol. This is the fine line which will distinguish the successful software managers of the 1980's from the rest of the software engineering community.

Acknowledgment

The author wishes to acknowledge the contribution of B. J. Gregor to the preparation and critique of the final manuscript.

References

[1] "Contracting for computer software development—Serious problems require management attention to avoid wasting additional millions," General Accounting Office, Rep. FGMSD 80-4, Nov. 9, 1979.

[2] D. M. Weiss, "The MUDD report: A case study of Navy software development practices," Naval Res. Lab., Rep. 7909, May 21, 1975.

[3] B. W. Boehm, "Software engineering," *IEEE Trans. Comput.*, vol. C-25, pp. 1226–1241, Dec. 1976.

[4] *Proc. IEEE* (Special Issue on Software Engineering), vol. 68, Sept. 1980.

[5] E. Bersoff, V. Henderson, and S. Siegel, "Attaining software product integrity," *Tutorial: Software Configuration Management*, W. Bryan, C. Chadbourne, and S. Siegel, Eds., Los Alamitos, CA, IEEE Comput. Soc., Cat. EHO-169-3, 1981.

[6] B. W. Boehm *et al.*, *Characteristics of Software Quality, TRW Series of Software Technology*, vol. 1. New York: North-Holland, 1978.

[7] T. A. Thayer, *et al.*, *Software Reliability, TRW Series of Software Technology*, vol. 2. New York: North-Holland, 1978.

[8] D. J. Reifer, Ed., *Tutorial: Automated Tools for Software Eng.*, Los Alamitos, CA, IEEE Comput. Soc., Cat. EHO-169-3, 1979.

[9] E. Bersoff, V. Henderson, and S. Siegel, *Software Configuration Management*. Englewood Cliffs, NJ: Prentice-Hall, 1980.

[10] ——, "Software configuration management: A tutorial," *Computer*, vol. 12, pp. 6–14, Jan. 1979.

[11] W. Bryan, S. Siegel, and G. Whiteleather, "Auditing throughout the software life cycle: A primer," *Computer*, vol. 15, pp. 56–67, Mar. 1982.

[12] "Software configuration management," Naval Elec. Syst. Command, Software Management Guidebooks, vol. 2, undated.

Edward H. Bersoff (M'75–SM'78) received the A.B., M.S., and Ph.D. degrees in mathematics from New York University, New York.

He is President and Founder of BTG, Inc., a high technology, Washington, DC area based, systems analysis and engineering firm. In addition to his corporate responsibilities, he directs the company's research in software engineering, product assurance, and software management. BTG specializes in the application of modern systems engineering principles to the computer based system development process. At BTG, he has been actively involved in the FAA's Advanced Automation Program where he is focusing on software management and software configuration management issues on this extremely complex program. He also participates in the company's activities within the Naval Intelligence community, providing senior consulting services to a wide variety of system development efforts. He was previously President of CTEC, Inc. where he directed the concept formulation and development of the Navy Command and Control System (NCCS), Ocean Surveillance Information System (OSIS) Baseline now installed at all U.S. Navy Ocean Surveillance Centers. He also served as Experiment Director for the Joint ARPA, Navy, CINCPAC Military Message Experiment. This test was designed to examine the usefulness of secure, automated message processing systems in an operational military environment and to develop design criteria for future military message processing systems. Prior to joining CTEC, Inc., he was Manager of Engineering Operations and Manager of FAA Operations for Logicon, Inc.'s Process Systems Division. He joined Logicon from the NASA Electronics Research Center. He has taught mathematics at universities in Boston, New York, and Washington, DC. His technical contributions to the fields of software requirements and design range from early publications in computer architecture, reliability and programming languages, to more recent publications in software quality and configuration management. A textbook entitled *Software Configuration Management* (Prentice-Hall) represents the product of three years of research in the field by Dr. Bersoff and his colleagues.

Dr. Bersoff is a member of AFCEA, American Management Association, MENSA, and the Young Presidents' Organization.

Reprinted from *IEEE Software*, Volume 1, Number 1, January 1984, pages 75-88.

Verifying and Validating Software Requirements and Design Specifications

Barry W. Boehm, TRW

These recommendations provide a good starting point for identifying and resolving software problems early in the life cycle—when they're still relatively easy to handle.

"Don't worry about that specification paperwork. We'd better hurry up and start coding, because we're going to have a whole lot of debugging to do."

How many projects start out this way and end up with either a total failure or a tremendously expensive self-fulfilling prophecy? There are still far too many, but more and more projects are turning the self-fulfilling prophecy around. By investing more up-front effort in verifying and validating their software requirements and design specifications, these projects are reaping the benefits of reduced integration and test costs, higher software reliability and maintainability, and more user-responsive software. To help increase their number, this article presents the following guideline information on verification and validation, or V&V, of software requirements and design specifications:

- definitions of the terms "verification" and "validation," an explanation of their context in the software life cycle, and a description of the basic sequence of V&V functions;
- an explanation, with examples, of the major software requirements and design V&V criteria: completeness, consistency, feasibility, and testability;
- an evaluation of the relative cost and effectiveness of the major software requirements and design V&V techniques with respect to the major criteria; and
- an example V&V checklist for software system reliability and availability.

Based on the above, we recommend combinations of software requirements and design V&V techniques that are most suitable for small, medium, and large software specifications.

Verification and validation in the software life cycle

Definitions. The recent *IEEE Standard Glossary of Software Engineering Terminology*[1] defines "verification" and "validation" as follows:

- *Verification.* The process of determining whether or not the products of a given phase of the software development cycle fulfill the requirements established during the previous phase.
- *Validation.* The process of evaluating software at the end of the software development process to ensure compliance with software requirements.

In this article we extend the definition of "validation" to include a missing activity at the beginning of the software definition process: determining the fitness or worth of a software product for its operational mission.

Informally, we might define these terms via the following questions:

- *Verification.* "Am I building the product right?"
- *Validation.* "Am I building the right product?"

Objectives. The basic objectives in verification and validation of software requirements and design specifications are to identify and resolve software problems and high-risk issues early in the software life cycle. The main reason for doing this is indicated in Figure 1.[2] It shows that, for large projects, savings of up to 100:1 are possible by finding and fixing problems early in the life cycle. For smaller projects, the savings are more on the order of 4-6:1, but this still provides a great deal of leverage for early investment in V&V activities. Besides the major cost savings, there are also significant payoffs in improved reliability, maintainability, and human engineering of the resulting software product.

Early life-cycle specifications and phases. In general, experience has shown that the software development process proceeds most cost-effectively if software specifications are produced in the following order:

(1) a requirements specification, which states the functions the software must perform, the required level of performance (speed, accuracy, etc.), and the nature of the required interfaces between the software product and its environment;

(2) a product design specification, which describes the overall architecture of the software product and its components; and

(3) a detailed design specification, which identifies the inputs, outputs, control logic, algorithms, and data structures of each individual low-level component of the software product.

The typical software life cycle includes requirements, product design, and detailed design phases that involve the development, verification and validation, approval or disapproval, and baselining of each of these specifications (see Figure 2). However, the nature of the V&V process causes intermingling of the activities associated with each phase. For example, one cannot validate the feasibility of a performance-critical requirement without doing some design and analysis of ways to implement the requirement. Similarly, some design and development of code in a working prototype may be necessary to validate the user-interface requirements.

V&V functions in the early phases. Verification and validation activities produce their best results when performed by a V&V agent who operates independently of the developer or specification agent. The basic sequence of functions performed by the V&V agent, the specification agent (the analyst or software system engineer), the project manager, and the customer are shown in Figure 2.

The key portions of Figure 2 are the iterative loops in which

- the V&V agent analyzes the specifications and issues problem reports to the specification agent;
- The specification agent isolates the source of the problem and develops a solution resulting in an iteration of the specification;
- the project manager and customer approve any proposed iterations that would perceptibly change the requirements baseline; and
- the V&V agent analyzes the iterated specification and issues further problem reports if necessary.

The process continues until the V&V agent completes his planned activities and all problem reports have been either fixed or assigned to a specific agent for resolution within a given time.

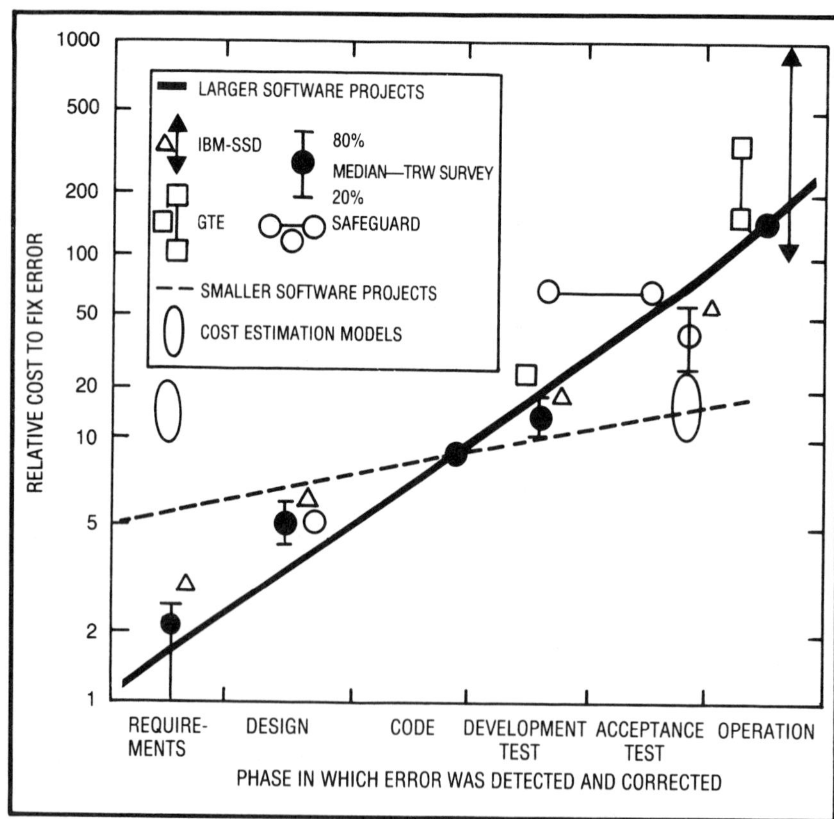

Figure 1. Increase in cost to fix or change software throughout the life cycle.[2]

Verification and validation criteria

The four basic V&V criteria for requirements and design specifications are completeness, consistency, feasibility, and testability. An overall taxonomy of their components is given in Figure 3, and each is discussed in turn below.

Completeness. A specification is *complete* to the extent that all of its parts are present and each part is fully developed. A software specification must exhibit several properties to assure its completeness.

No TBDs. TBDs are places in the specification where decisions have been postponed by writing "To be Determined" or "TBD." For example:

- "The system shall handle a peak load of (TBD) transactions per second."
- "Update records coming from

the personnel information system shall be in the following format: (TBD)."

No nonexistent references. These are references in the specification to functions, inputs, or outputs (including databases) not defined in the specification. For example:

- "Function 3.1.2.3 Output
  3.1.2.3.a Inputs
  1. Output option flags obtained from the User Output Options functions...," which is undefined in the specification.
- "A record of all transactions is retained in the Transaction File," which is undefined.

No missing specification items. These are items that should be present as part of the standard format of the specification, but are not present. For example:

- No verification provisions
- No interface specifications

Note that verification of this property often involves a human judgment call: a small, stand-alone system may have no interfaces to specify.

No missing functions. These are functions that should be part of the software product but are not called for in the specification. For example:

- No backup functions
- No recovery functions

No missing products. These are products that should be part of the delivered software but are not called for in the specification. For example:

- Test tools
- Output postprocessors

The first two properties—"no TBDs" and "no nonexistent references"—form a subset of the completeness properties called closure properties. Closure is distinguished by the fact that it can be verified by mechanical means; the last three properties generally require some human intuition to verify or validate.

Consistency. A specification is *consistent* to the extent that its provisions do not conflict with each other or with governing specifications and objectives. Specifications require consistency in several ways.

Internal consistency. Items within the specification do not conflict with

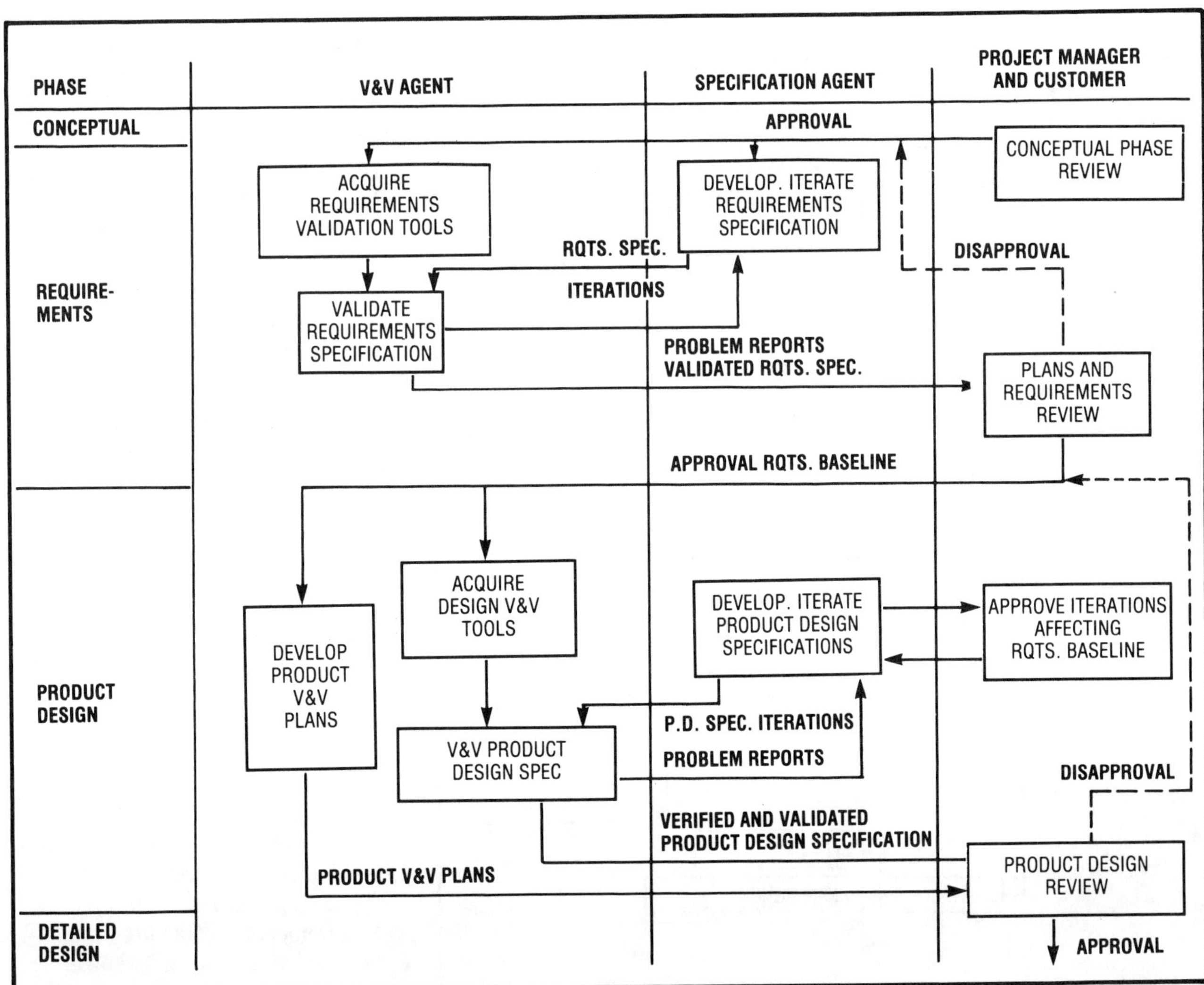

Figure 2. Verification and validation sequences for the requirements and product design phases.

each other, unlike the following counter-examples:

- "Function x
  (1) Inputs: A 4×4 matrix z of reals.
  ⋮
  Function y
  ⋮
  (3) Outputs: A 3×3 matrix z of integers."
- Page 14: "Master real-time control interrupts shall have top priority at all times."
  Page 37: "A critical-level interrupt from the security subsystem shall take precedence over all other processes and interrupts."

External consistency. Items in the specification do not conflict with external specifications or entities, unlike the following counter-example:

- "Spec: All safety parameters are provided by the preprocessor system, as follows: . . ."
  "Preprocessor system spec: The preprocessor initializes all safety parameters except for real-time control safety parameters, which are self-initialized. . ."

Traceability. Items in the specification have clear antecedents in earlier specifications or statements of system objectives. Particularly on large specifications, each item should indicate the item or items in earlier specifications from which it is derived to prevent

- misinterpretations, such as assuming that "on-line" storage implies a requirement for random access storage (a dedicated on-line tape unit might be preferable); and
- embellishments, such as adding exotic displays, natural language processing, or adaptive control features that are not needed for the job to be done (and may not work as reliably as simpler approaches).

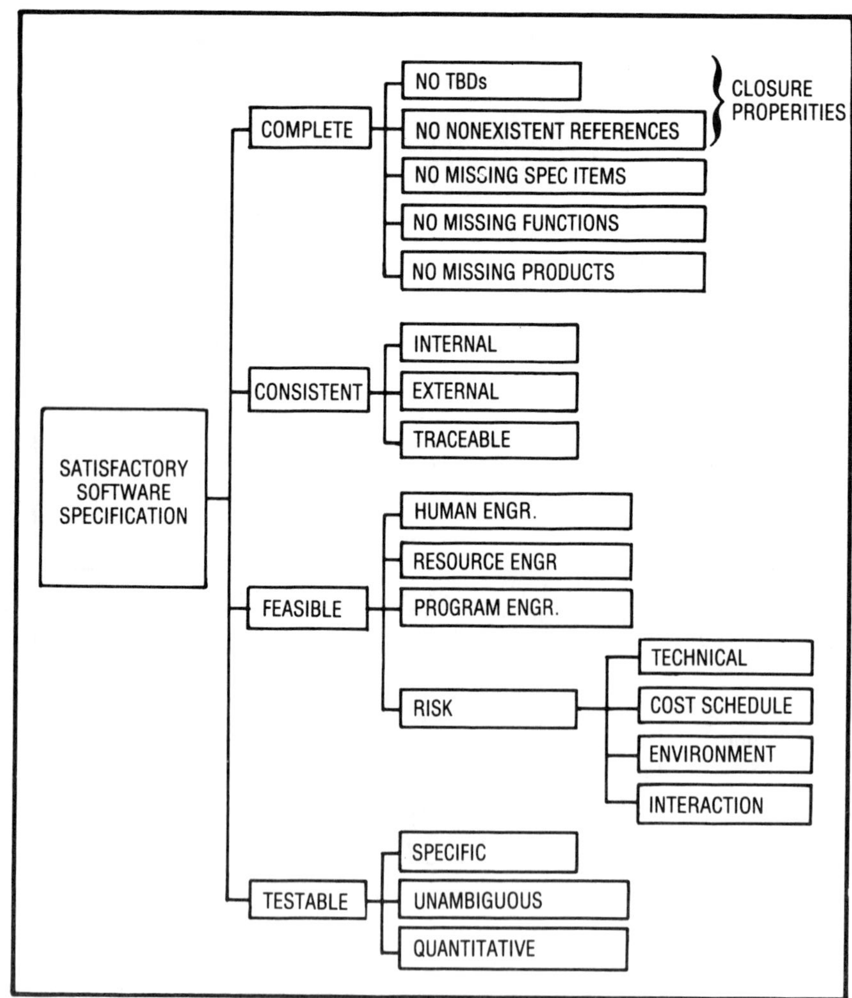

Figure 3. Taxonomy of a satisfactory software specification.

Feasibility. A specification is *feasible* to the extent that the life-cycle benefits of the system specified exceed its life-cycle costs. Thus, feasibility involves more than verifying that a system satisfies functional and performance requirements. It also implies validating that the specified system will be sufficiently maintainable, reliable, and human-engineered to keep a positive life-cycle balance sheet.

Further, and most importantly, feasibility implies identifying and resolving any high-risk issues before committing a large group of people to detailed development.

Human engineering. Verifying and validation feasibility from a human engineering standpoint involves answering the following questions:

- Will the specified system provide a satisfactory way for users to perform their operational functions?
- Will the system satisfy human needs at various levels?
- Will the system help people fulfill their human potential?

Examples of human engineering considerations are given in Shneiderman[3] and in Smith and Aucella.[4]

Resource engineering. This involves the following verification and validation questions:

- Can a system be developed that satisfies the specified requirements (at an acceptable cost in resources)?
- Will the specified system cost-effectively accommodate expected growth in operational requirements over its life-cycle?

Examples of resource engineering considerations are given in Boehm[1] and Ferrari.[5]

Program engineering. This addresses the following questions regarding a specified system:

- Will it be cost-effective to maintain?
- Will it be cost-effective from a portability standpoint?
- Will it have sufficient accuracy, reliability, and availability to cost-effectively satisfy operational needs over its life cycle?

Examples of these program engineering considerations are given in Lipow, White, and Boehm's[6] checklists on maintainability and portability and in the checklist on reliability and availability on p. 87.

Risk. If the life-cycle cost-effectiveness of a specified system is extremely sensitive to some system aspect that is not well-known or understood, there is a high risk involved in the system. If such high-risk issues are not identified and resolved in advance, there is a strong likelihood of disaster if or when this aspect of the system is not realized as expected.

Four major sources of risk in software requirements and design specifications are technical, cost-schedule, environmental, and interaction effects.

Technical risk, for example, can involve

- achievable levels of overhead in a multiprocessor operating system;
- achievable levels of computer security protection;
- achievable speed and accuracy of new algorithms;
- achievable performance in "artifical intelligence" domains (e.g., pattern recognition, natural language processing); and
- achievable levels of man-machine performance (e.g., air traffic control).

Cost-schedule risks include the sensitivity to cost and schedule constraints of such items as

- availability and reliability of the underlying virtual machine (hardware, operating system, database management system, compiler) upon which the specified software will be built;
- stability of the underlying virtual machine;
- availability of key personnel; and
- strain on available main memory and execution time.

Some environmental risk issues are

- expected volume and quality of input data;
- availability and performance of interfacing systems; and
- expected sophistication, flexibility, and degree of cooperation of system users.

A particular concern here is the assessment of second-order effects caused by introduction of the new system. For example, several airline reservation systems experienced overloads because new capabilities stimulated additional customer requests and transactions. Of course, this sort of reaction can't be predicted precisely. The important thing is to determine where system performance is highly sensitive and to concentrate risk-avoidance efforts in those areas.

If the development is high-risk in several areas, the risks tend to interact exponentially. Unless you resolve the high-risk issues in advance, you may find yourself in the company of some of the supreme disasters in the software business.

For example, one large government agency attempted to build a huge real-time inventory control system involving a nationwide network of supercomputers with

- extremely ambitious real-time performance requirements;
- a lack of qualified techniques for the operating system and networking aspects;
- integration of huge, incompatible databases;
- continually changing external interfaces; and
- a lack of qualified development personnel.

Although some of these were pointed out as high-risk items early, they were not resolved in advance. After spending roughly seven years and $250 million, the project failed to provide any significant operational capability and was cut off by Congress.

Testability. A specification is *testable* to the extent that one can identify an economically feasible technique for determining whether or not the developed software will satisfy the specification. To be testable, specifications must be specific, unambiguous, and quantitative wherever possible. Below are some examples of specifications which are *not* testable:

- The software shall provide interfaces with the appropriate subsystems.
- The software shall degrade gracefully under stress.
- The software shall be developed in accordance with good development standards.
- The software shall provide the necessary processing under all modes of operation.
- Computer memory utilization shall be optimized to accommodate future growth.
- The software shall provide a 99.9999 percent assurance of information privacy (or "reliability," "availability," or "human safety," when these terms are undefined).
- The software shall provide accuracy sufficient to support effective flight control.
- The software shall provide real-time response to sales activity queries.

These statements are good as goals and objectives, but they are not precise enough to serve as the basis of a pass-fail acceptance test.

Below are some more testable versions of the last two requirements:

- The software shall compute aircraft position within the following accuracies:
  ± 50 feet in the horizontal;
  ± 20 feet in the vertical.
- The system shall respond to
  Type A queries in $\leqslant 2$ seconds;
  Type B queries in $\leqslant 10$ seconds;

Type C queries in ≤2 minutes; where Type A, B, and C queries are defined in detail in the specification.

In many cases, even these versions will not be sufficiently testable without further definition. For example:

- Do the terms "±50 feet" or "≤2 seconds" refer to root-mean-square performance, 90-percent confidence limits, or never-to-exceed constraints?
- Does "response" time include terminal delays, communications delays, or just the time involved in computer processing?

Thus, it often requires a good deal of added effort to eliminate a specification's vagueness and ambiguity and make it testable. But such effort is generally well worthwhile: It would have to be done eventually for the test phase anyway, and doing it early eliminates a great deal of expense, controversy, and possible bitterness in later stages.

Verification and validation techniques

A number of techniques, outlined in Figure 4 and evaluated below, are effective in performing software requirements and design verification and validation.

Simple manual techniques. Five relatively simple and easily implemented manual techniques—reading, cross-referencing, interviews, checklists, and models—can provide much valuable information for meeting verification and validation criteria.

Simple manual techniques:
- Reading
- Manual cross-referencing
- Interviews
- Checklists
- Manual models
- Simple scenarios

Simple automated techniques:
- Automated cross-referencing
- Simple automated models

Detailed manual techniques:
- Detailed scenarios
- Mathematical proofs

Detailed automated techniques:
- Detailed automated models
- Prototypes

Figure 4. Verification and validation techniques.

Reading. Having someone other than the originator read the specification to identify potential problems is often referred to as "reviewing." Here, however, we call it "reading" and reserve the term "reviewing" for a more formal activity.

Since reading subjects the specification to another point of view, it is very good for picking up any blind spots or misconceptions that the specification developer might have. This is particularly true if the reader is going to be one of the product's testers, users, maintainers, interfacers, or program developers; a tester can, for example, verify that the specification is testable and unambiguous. Another strength of reading is that it requires little preparation. It is also extremely flexible with respect to when, to where, and to what level of detail it is done.

Reading's strong points can turn into weak points if the "little preparation" it does require is not carried out. Readers can waste a lot of time—looking for the wrong things or looking for nothing in paticular—that could have been spent bringing a valuable perspective to focus on a set of significant issues. This is a particular danger on large projects. For detailed designs, the design inspection or walkthrough described by Fagan[7] can be particularly effective. Still, reading is fundamentally limited in the extent to which it can be used to verify a detailed specification's completeness and consistency, or the feasibility of a complex system's performance requirements.

Manual cross-referencing. Cross-referencing goes beyond reading; it involves constructing cross-reference tables and various diagrams—for example, state transition, data flow, control flow, and data structure diagrams—to clarify interactions among specified entities. These entities include functions, databases, and interfacing hardware, software, or personnel.

Manual cross-referencing is effective for the consistency (internal, external, and traceability) and closure properties of a specification, particularly for small to medium specifications. For large specifications, it can be quite cumbersome, leading to the suggested use of automated aids. If these are not available, manual methods are still recommended; the payoff will outweigh the cost and time expended.

Manual cross-referencing will not do much to verify the feasibility of performance requirements or to validate the subjective aspects of human engineering or maintainability provisions.

Interviews. Discussing a specification with its originator will identify potential problems. With minimum effort, you can find out a great deal about its strengths and weaknesses; this will allow you to deploy your V&V resources most effectively by concentrating on the weak points. Interviews are particularly good for identifying potential blind spots, misunderstandings, and high-risk issues. But, like spot-checking, they only identify and scope the specification's major problem areas; the detailed V&V work remains to be done.

Checklists. Specialized lists, based on experience, of significant issues for assuring successful software development can be used effectively with any of the manual methods described above.

Checklists are excellent for catching omissions, such as the missing items, functions, and products discussed under "Completeness." They are also valuable aids in addressing some of the life-cycle feasibility considerations: human engineering, maintainability, reliability and availability, portability, security and privacy, and life-cycle efficiency. But they are not much help in verifying the feasibility of performance requirements or in dealing with detailed consistency and closure questions.

One danger with checklists is that items might be considered absolute requirements rather than suggestions. For example, several features in a portability checklist will not be necessary if the software will never be used on another machine; adding them blindly will just incur unnecessary expense.

Manual models. Mathematical formulas can be used to represent and analyze certain aspects of the system being specified. These manual models are very good for analyzing some life-cycle feasibility issues, particularly accuracy, real-time performance, and life-cycle cost. They are also useful for risk analysis. They are not, however, much help in verifying the details of a specification's consistency and completeness or in assessing subjective factors. Their manual nature makes them inefficient for detailed feasibility analysis of large, complex systems, but they are good for top-level analysis of large systems.

Simple scenarios. Scenarios describe how the system will work once it is in operation. Man-computer dialogues are the most common form of simple scenarios, which are very good for clarifying misunderstandings or mismatches in the specification's human engineering aspects but not for checking completeness and consistency details or for validating performance speed and accuracy.

Simple automated techniques. Automation extends the power of two manual techniques—cross-referencing and simple modeling.

Automated cross-referencing. Automated cross-referencing involves the use of a machine-analyzable specification language—for example, SREM-RSL, Software Requirements Engineering Methodology-Requirements Statement Language;[8,9] PSL/PSA, Problem Statement Language/Problem Statement Analyzer;[10] or PDL, Program Design Language.[11] Once a specification is expressed in such a language, it can be automatically analyzed for consistency, closure properties, or presentation of cross-reference information for manual analysis. Some further automated aids in this category are discussed in the DoD "Methodman" document[12] and its references.

Current automated specification aids have only limited capabilities in addressing accuracy and dynamic performance issues.

Automated cross-referencing is excellent for verifying the detailed consistency and closure properties of both small and large specifications. Using a formatted specification language also eliminates many testability and ambiguity problems because the language forms help prevent ambiguous terms and vague generalities. The automated systems also have less of a problem in checking for additional clerical errors introduced in iterating and retyping a specification.

Current automated specification aids have only limited capabilities in addressing accuracy and dynamic performance issues, and some, particularly SREM-RSL, are not available on many computers. Although their performance on small and medium specifications has improved considerably, they are still somewhat inefficient in performing consistency and completeness checks on very large specifications. Even so, the costs of using them on large specifications are more than repaid by the savings involved in early error detection.

Simple automated models. Mathematical formulas implemented in a small computer program provide more powerful representations than manual models for analyzing such life-cycle feasibility issues as accuracy, real-time performance, and life-cycle costs. Simple automated models are especially good for risk and sensitivity analysis, but, like manual models, are not much help in verifying detailed consistency and completeness, in assessing subjective factors, or in performing detailed feasibility analysis of large, complex systems.

Detailed manual techniques. Detailed scenarios and mathematical proofs are especially effective for clarifying human engineering needs and for verifying finite-mathematics programs, respectively.

Detailed scenarios. Detailed scenarios, which provide more elaborate—and thus more expensive—operational descriptions, are even more effective than simple scenarios in clarifying a system's human engineering aspects.

Mathematical proofs. Mathematical transformation rules can be applied to a set of statements, expressed in a precise mathematical specification language, to prove desired properties of the set of statements. These properties include internal consistency, preservation of "invariant" relations, and equivalence of two alternate sets of statements (e.g., requirements and design specifications). Automated aids to formal specification and verification such as Special/HDM, Gypsy, Affirm, and Ina Jo, are now available and have been compared by Cheheyl et al.[13]

For certain classes of problems—small problems involving the use of finite mathematics—mathematical proofs offer a near-certain guarantee of the properties proved. But mathematical proofs cannot deal with non-formalized inputs (e.g., noisy sensor data, natural language); cannot deal conveniently with "real-variable" calculations or with many issues in synchronizing concurrent processes; and cannot deal efficiently with large specifications.

Detailed automated techniques. Two final techniques—detailed automated models and prototypes—provide the most complete information.

Detailed automated models. Detailed automated models typically involve large event simulations of the system. While more expensive than simple automated models, they are much more effective in analyzing such issues as accuracy, dynamic consistency, real-time performance, and life-cycle cost. The process of generating such models also serves as a good way to catch specification inconsistencies and ambiguities.

Prototypes. In many situations, the feasibility of a specification cannot be conclusively demonstrated without developing some working software. Examples include some accuracy and real-time performance issues, as well as user interface suitability. In such cases, it is often valuable to build a throwaway prototype of key portions of the software: a program that works well enough to resolve the feasibility issues, but lacks the extensive features, error-proofing, and documentation of the final product. The process of building the prototype will also expose and eliminate a number of ambiguities, inconsistencies, blind spots, and misunderstandings incorporated in the specification.

Prototypes can be expensive and do not shed much light on maintainability, but they are often the only way to resolve the critical feasibility issues. (See References 14 and 15 for experiences in prototyping and Chapter 20 of Reference 1 for guidelines on when to prototype.)

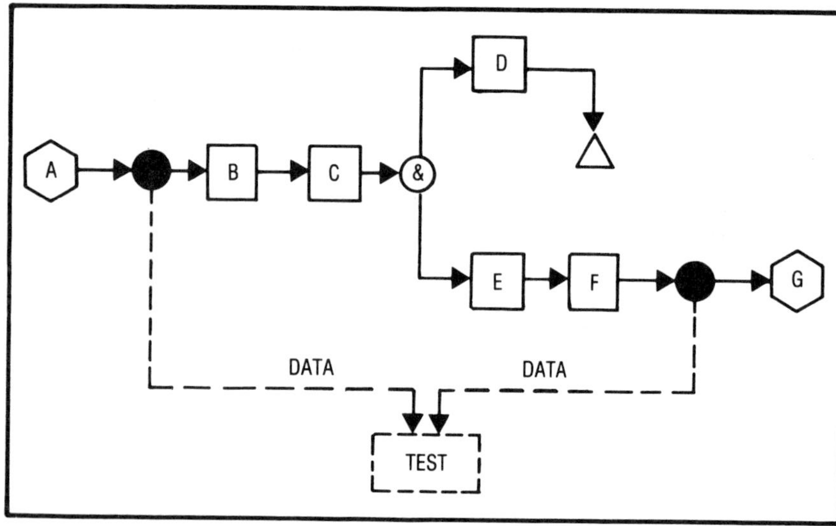

Figure 5. An example of a path analysis structure. Validation points (dark circles) are added to the paths close to the interfaces (hexagons).

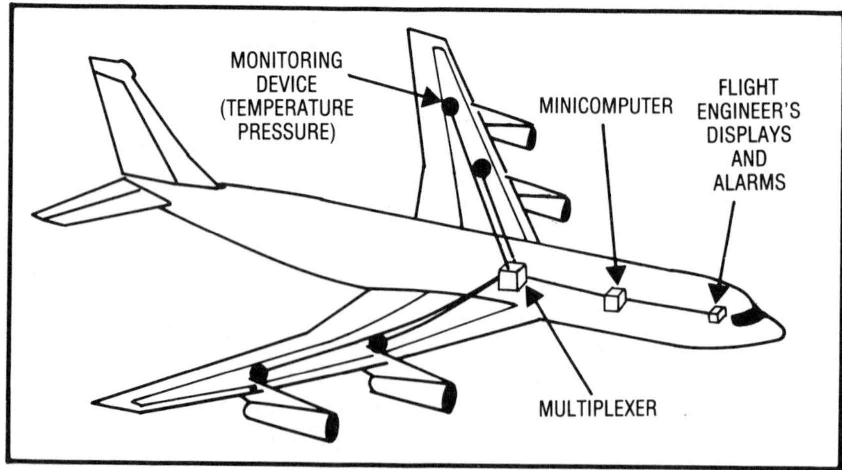

Figure 6. An aircraft engine monitoring system.

An automated aid for requirements V&V

Several available systems—PSL/PSA, SREM, PDL, Special/HDM—provide automated aids to requirements and design verification and validation. To get a feel for what these systems do, let us look at how one of them—the Software Requirements Engineering Methodology, or SREM—handles a simple example, an aircraft engine monitoring system.[16]

Requirements networks. The SREM Requirements Statement Language expresses software requirements in terms of processing paths—that is, the sequences of data processing required to operate on an input stimulus to the software and produce an output response.

The first step in developing an SREM specification is to write it as a description of the processing paths. Thus, if some data is input to a processing path, and a response is required at some other point, we write this in the specification as a fundamental component. To produce several thousand paths for a complex system, a method was developed to integrate simple paths into requirements networks called R_NETS. Thus, all paths initiated by the same input interface are integrated into a common network.

Figure 5 illustrates a network with data coming across an interface (represented by a hexagon). All data coming across the interface have common processing, as indicated by the first two boxes. The AND node is next encountered to indicate a "don't care" parallelism. That is, either branch may be processed first after the AND node. That decision is left as an option for the designer. Validation points (the dark circles) are used to specify performance requirements in an explicitly testable fashion and are added to the paths close to the interfaces. Data is specified that must be available for testing purposes at those points, and an explicit procedure is described for analyzing those data to give a pass/fail relationship.

One advantage of this type of network is that it is integrated from the collection of paths. Therefore, it can be automatically analyzed, using the rules established for R_NETs. Another advantage is that it is similar to classic logic diagrams and flowcharts used by engineers, making it a natural form of communication between engineers. Finally, it possesses natural test points for assuring that the requirement expressed on a path is expressly addressed for testing.

R_NETs, then, are the basic tool used by SREM to define functional requirements unambiguously by showing each path of processing required by the input stimuli to the system.

Engine monitoring system. This simple example for an engine monitoring system, or EMS, will show how the R_NET concept is used in describing requirements.

An airplane with multiple engines has a device that is connected to each engine (see Figure 6). This device measures temperatures, pressure, and the state of two switches. All of the devices are connected to the multiplexer, which is interrogated by an on-board computer. The computer senses when a temperature or pressure goes out of an allowed range and gives an alarm in the cockpit.

A partial system specification for the EMS capabilities might look like this:

(1) Monitor 1 to 10 engines.

(2) Monitor (a) 3 temperatures (0 to 1000°C) (b) 3 pressures (0 to 4000 PSIA), and (c) 2 switches (off, on).

(3) Monitor each engine at a specified rate (1 to 10 times per second).

(4) Output a warning message if any parameter falls outside prescribed limits, and an alarm if outside danger limits.

(5) Record history of each engine.

The R_NET approach (see Figure 7) for defining the EMS functional

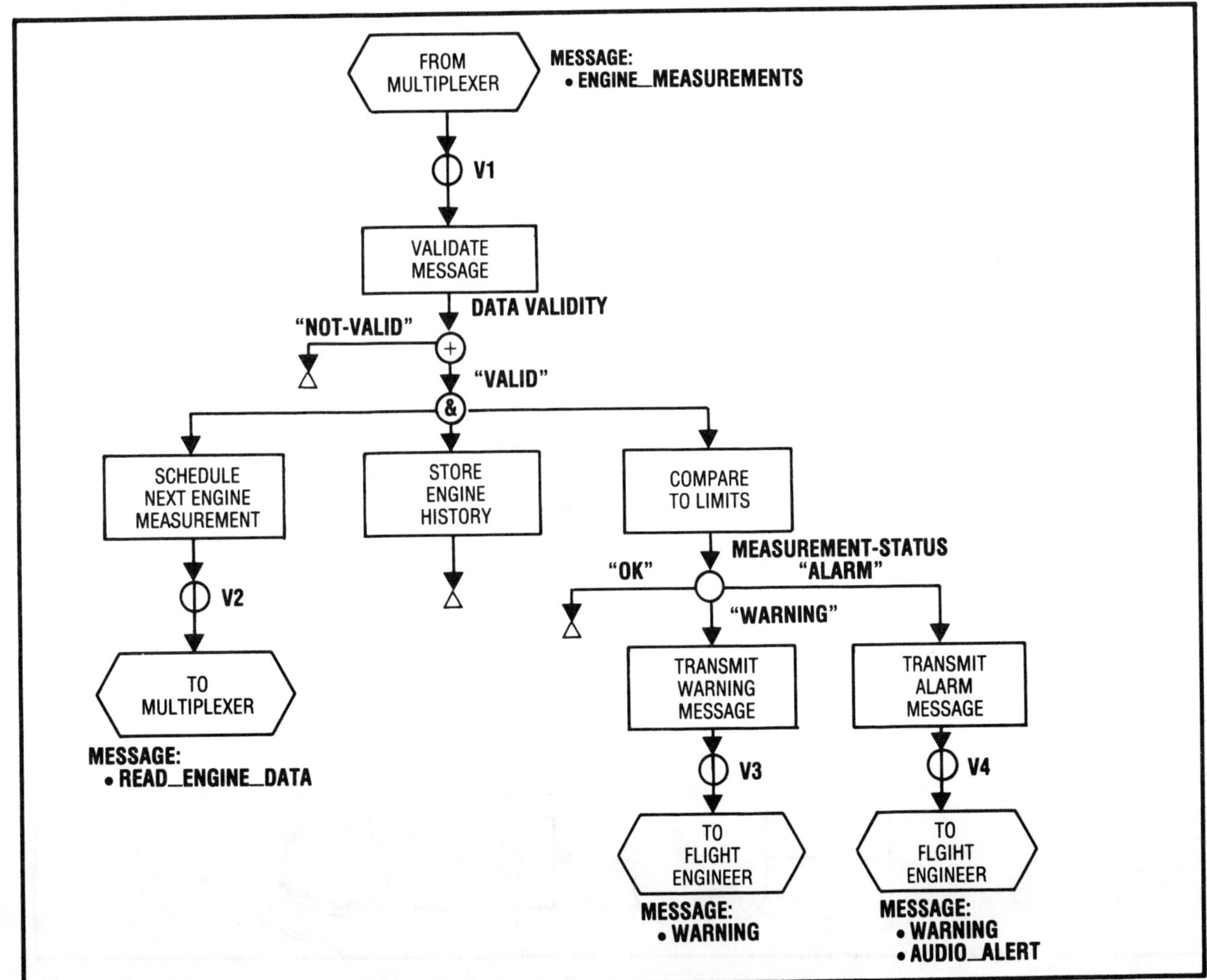

Figure 7. The R_NET approach for the engine monitoring system shown in Figure 6.

requirement presents a clear, unambiguous definition of how each stimulus (called a MESSAGE in SREM terminology) is processed, and where the VALIDATION_POINTs (V1, V2, V3, V4) reside that allow testing of the PERFORMANCE_REQUIREMENTs specified for selected functional processes (paths).

As a result of preparing the R_NET and accomplishing automated error checks, many questions arise. These are typical types of ambiguities resident in system specifications, and the SREM methodology brings them out early and quite clearly. Answers must be attained before completion of the software specification. Examples for the EMS are

(1) Does "output warning" mean each time or just the first time?

(2) How are "prescribed limits" defined?

(3) How quickly must the system output a "warning" or "alarm?"

(4) What does a "warning message" contain?

(5) What is to be done with the history data for each engine?

```
INPUT_INTERFACE : MULTI.
  DESCRIPTION : 3 TEMPERATURES 3 PRESSURES 2 SWITCHES.
  ENABLES : R_NET MONITOR_ENGINES.
  PASSES : MESSAGE ENGINE_DATA.
  DOCUMENTED BY
    SOURCE : TRW_CLASS_NOTES.
  COMPLETENESS : CHANGEABLE.

MESSAGE : ENGINE_DATA.
  MADE BY
    DATA : TEMPERATURE
    DATA : PRESSURES
    DATA : SWITCHES.

DATA : TEMPERATURE.
  INCLUDES
    DATA : INTAKE_TEMP
    DATA : COMPRESSION_TEMP
    DATA : EXHAUST_TEMP.
```

Figure 8. Sample RSL statements related to the R_NET and its data from Figure 7.

Later, we will see how some of these questions were identified by SREM procedures.

Requirements statement language. The SREM approach to attaining explicitness throughout a requirement specification is grounded in the use of the Requirements Statement Language. RSL is a machine-processible, artificial language which overcomes the shortcomings of English in stating requirements. RSL is based on the entity-attribute-relationship model of representing information. Figure 8 illustrates RSL statements related to the R_NET and its data from Figure 7. This figure illustrates the English-like nature of RSL.

Requirements tools and database. The Requirements Engineering and Validation System is an integrated set of tools to support development of the RSL requirements. REVS consists of three segments: a centralized database called ASSM for Abstract System Semantic Model, a translator for the RSL, and a set of automated tools for processing the information in the ASSM. A diagram of the system is shown in Figure 9.

The purpose of the RSL translator is to analyze the RSL statements that are input to it and to make entries in the ASSM corresponding to the

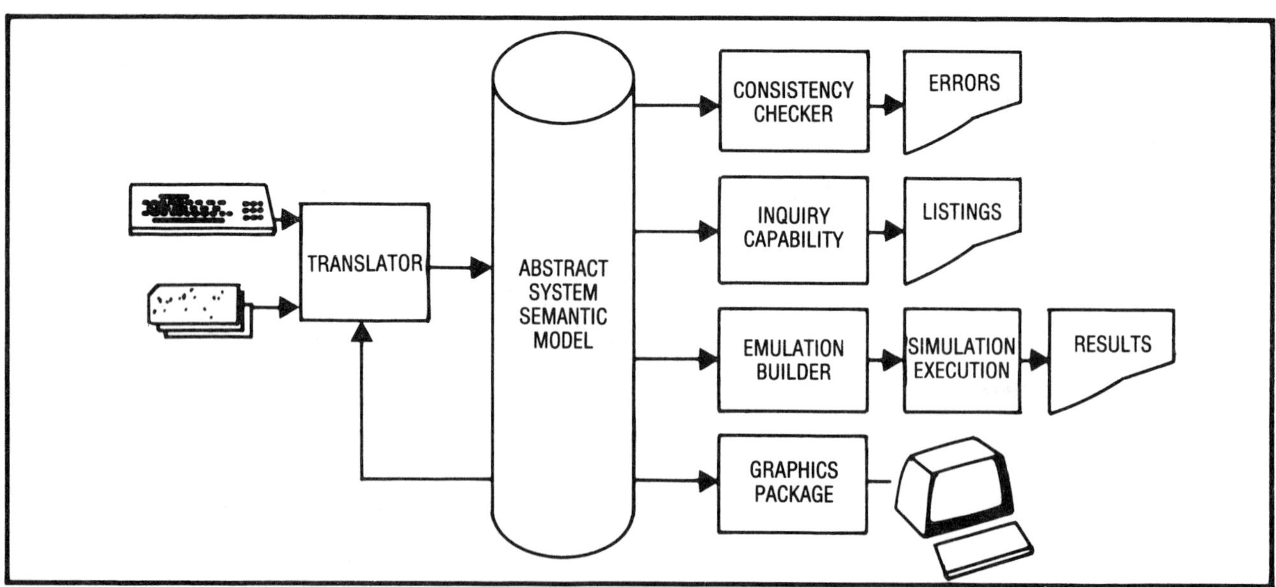

Figure 9. Information flow in the Requirements Engineering and Validation System. REVS is an integrated set of tools that supports the Requirements Statement Language.

meaning of the statements. The translator references the ASSM to do simple consistency checks on the input. This prevents the occurrence of disastrous errors such as the introduction of an element with the same name as a previously existing element or an instance of a relationship that is tied to an illegal type of element. This type of checking catches, at an early stage, some of the simple types of inconsistencies that are often found in requirements specifications.

The information available in the ASSM will support a wide variety of requirements analysis tools. Among these are an interactive graphics package to aid in the specification of the flow paths; static consistency checkers, which check for consistency of information throughout the system; and an automated simulation generator and execution package, which aids in the study of dynamic interactions of the various requirements. Situation-specific reports and analyses, which a particular user or manager may need, are generated through the use of the Requirements Analysis and Data Extraction system. The RADX system is independent of the extensions to RSL so that new concepts added to the language may be included in queries to the database.

A key consideration is that all steps in the SREM approach, including simulations, utilize a common requirements database, which is necessary since many individuals are continually adding, deleting, and changing information about requirements for the data processing system. Centralizaton allows both the requirements engineers and the analysis tools to work from a common baseline and enables implementation of management controls on changes to this baseline.

Automated consistency and completeness checking. Figure 10, a RADX printout for the engine monitoring system, illustrates the RADX query-response capability to test adequacy of engineer inputs to the database.

First, RADX identified that accuracy and response-time limits have not yet been specified. This feature is designed to assure that all appropriate paths are eventually covered by performance requirements.

Next, RADX identified data with no sink—that is, data produced but

```
IRADX COMMAND =
LIST OF_UNSPECIFIED_ACCURACIES

    VALIDATION_PATH : ALARM_RESPONSE.
    VALIDATION_PATH : MULTIPLEXER_CONTROL.
    VALIDATION_PATH : WARNING_RESPONSE.

IRADX COMMAND =
LIST OF_UNSPECIFIED_MAXIMUM TIMES.

    VALIDATION_PATH : ALARM_RESPONSE.
    VALIDATION_PATH : MULTIPLEXER_CONTROL.
    VALIDATION_PATH : WARNING_RESPONSE.

IRADX COMMAND =
LIST OF_UNSPECIFIED_MINIMUM_TIMES.

    VALIDATION_PATH : ALARM_RESPONSE.
    VALIDATION_PATH : WARNING_RESPONSE.

LIST OF_DATA_WITH_NO_SOURCE.

    DATA : ALARM_LIMITS.
    DATA : CHANNEL_NUM.
    DATA : ENGINE_ID.
    DATA : ENGINE_NUMBER.
    DATA : ENGINE_STATUS.
    DATA : LIGHT_ASSIGNMENT.
    DATA : MONITOR_RATE.
    DATA : PARAMETER_LIMITS.
    DATA : P1_ALARM_HI.
    DATA : P1_ALARM_LO.
    DATA : P1_WARN_HI.
    DATA : P1_WARN_LO.
    DATA : P2_ALARM_HI.
    DATA : P2_ALARM_LO.
    DATA : P2_WARN_HI.
    DATA : P2_WARN_LO.

IRADX COMMAND =
LIST OF_MEANINGLESS_VALIDATION_PATHS.

IRADX COMMAND =
LIST OF_USELESS_VALIDATION_POINTS.

IRADX COMMAND =
LIST OF_USELESS_INTERFACES.

IRADX COMMAND =
LIST OF_USELESS_ENTITIES.

IRADX COMMAND =
LIST OF_EMPTY_ENTITIES.
```


Figure 10. Error checks in the Requirements Analysis and Data Extraction system provide immediate, automatic analysis of requirements completeness and consistency.

never used, since it is not input to a processing step and is not contained in an output message. Thus, the engine history that was required to be maintained is never accessed. This probably represents an incompleteness—that is, an overload set of processing requirements.

Finally, there is a set of error categories with no indicated errors of these types in the specifications. When there are no errors of any type remaining, the database will support a good specification for detailed software design and coding.

In sum, this example shows how an automated verification and validation aid can help us avoid and eliminate problems in our requirements and design specifications. This type of aid is particularly good in resolving completeness and consistency problems, but it does not provide much help in resolving user-interface or maintainability issues. This means that we need to employ a mix of techniques to cover our full range of criteria.

Evaluation and recommendations

Evaluation of V&V techniques. Table 1 provides a way to determine the best mix of V&V techniques for a particular project. It evaluates the techniques discussed above with respect to their ability to help verify and validate specifications. The evaluation is done in terms of the basic V&V criteria discussed earlier.

A retrospective analysis indicated that SREM could have caught 63 percent of the requirements problems on one project.

Some quantitative information is also becoming available on the relative effectiveness of those techniques. For example, one retrospective analysis indicated that SREM could have caught 63 percent of the requirements problems on one project. Several studies of design inspections have indicated that they can catch 60 percent of the errors present. Further quantitative information can be found in Chapter 24 of Reference 1.

Small-system V&V. To verify and validate a small specification, the customer and/or project manager should

- outline the specification before opening,
- read the specification for critical issues,
- interview the specification developer(s),
- determine the best allocation of V&V resources, and
- coordinate efforts and resolve conflicts.

The V&V agent should

- read the specification,
- use checklists and manual cross-referencing,
- use simple models if accuracy or real-time performance are critical,

Table 1.
Verification and validation techniques rated according to eight criteria.

	Completeness Small	Completeness Large	Consistency Small	Consistency Large	Traceability Small	Traceability Large	Human Engr.	Resource Engr.	Maint., Relia.	Accuracy	Relative Economics Small	Relative Economics Large
Simple Manual Techniques												
Reading	**	—	**	—	**	—	**	—	**	—	***	*
Manual Cross-Referencing	***	*	***	*	***	*	*	—	*	—	**	*
Interviews	*	*a	*	*a	**	**a	**a	—	**a	—	***	***
Checklists	*	*	—	—	—	—	***	*	***	*	**	*
Manual Models	—	—	—	—	—	—	—	*b	—	*b	**	**
Simple Scenarios	*	—	*	—	**	*	***c	—	—	—	**	**
Simple Automated Techniques												
Automated Cross-Referencing	***	***	***	***	***	***	—	—	—	—	*d	*d
Simple Automated Models	—	—	—	—	—	—	—	**b	—	**b	*	**
Detailed Manual Techniques												
Detailed Scenarios	*	*	*	*	**	**	***	—	—	—	—	*
Mathematical Proofs	***e	—	***e	—	***e	—	—	—	—	—	—	—
Detailed Automated Techniques												
Detailed Automated Models	**	**	**	**	**	**	—	***	—	**	—	*
Prototypes	**	**	**	**	**	**	***	***	*	***	—	*

Ratings:
*** Very strong
** Strong
* Moderate
— Weak

Notes:
a. Interviews are good for identifying potential large-scale problems but not so good for detail.
b. Simple models are good for full analysis of small systems and for top-level analysis of large systems.
c. Simple scenarios are very strong for small-system and strong for large-system user aspects.
d. Economy rating for automated cross-referencing is strong for medium systems.
If the cross-reference tool needs to be developed, reduce the rating to weak.
e. Proofs provide near-certain correctness for the finite-mathematics aspects of software.

- use simple scenarios if the user interface is critical, and
- use mathematical proofs on portions where reliability is extremely critical.

Users should
- read the specification from the user's point of view and
- use a human-engineering checklist.

Maintainers should
- read the specification from the maintainer's point of view,
- use maintainability and reliability/availability checklists, and
- use a portability checklist if portability is a consideration.

Interfacers should
- read the specification, and
- perform manual cross-referencing with respect to the interfaces.

Medium-system V&V. To verify and validate a medium specification, use the same general approach as

Reliability and availability checklist

Rather than being long and exhaustive, this checklist concentrates on high-leverage issues in obtaining a highly reliable and available system.

Reliable input handling

(a) Are input codes engineered for reliable data entry?

Comment: Examples are use of meaningful codes, increasing the "distance" between codes (NMEX, NYRK vs. NEWM, NEWY), and frequency-optimized codes (reducing the number of keystrokes as error sources).

(b) Do inputs include some appropriate redundancy as a basis for error checking?

Comment: Examples are checksums, error-correcting codes, input boundary identifiers (e.g., for synchronization), and check words (e.g., name and employee number).

(c) Will the software properly handle unspecified inputs?

Comment: Options include the use of default values, error responses, and fallback processing options.

(d) Are all off-normal input values properly handled?

Comment: Options are similar to those in (c). "Off-normal" checking may refer not just to the range of values but also to the mode, form, volume, order, or timing of the input.

(e) Are man-machine dialogues easy to understand and use for the expected class of users? Are they hard to misunderstand and misuse?

(f) Are records kept of the inputs for later failure analysis or recovery needs?

Reliable execution

(g) Are there provisions for proper initialization of control options, data values, and peripheral devices?

(h) Are there provisions for protection against singularities?

Comment: Examples are division by zero, singular matrix operations, and proper handling of empty sets.

(i) Are there design standards for internal error checking? Are they being followed?

Comment: These should tell under what conditions the responsibility for checking lies with the producer of outputs, the consumer of inputs, or a separate checking routine.

(j) Are there design standards for synchronization of concurrent processes? Are they being followed?

(k) Are the numerical methods—algorithms, tolerances, tables, constants—sufficiently accurate for operational needs?

(l) Is the data structured to avoid harmful side effects?

Comment: Techniques include "information hiding," minimum essential use of global variables, and use of data cluster (data-procedure-binding) concepts.

(m) Do the programming standards support reliable execution?

Error messages and diagnostics

(n) Are there requirements for clear, helpful error messages?

Comments: These should be correct, understandable by maintenance personnel, expressed in user language, and accompanied by useful information for error isolation.

(o) Are there requirements for diagnostic and debugging aids?

Comment: Examples are labeled, selective traces and dumps, labeled displays for program inputs, special hardware and software diagnostic routines, timers, self-checks, post-processors, and control parameters for easily specifying diagnostic and debugging options.

(p) Are measurement and validation points explicitly identified in the software specifications?

(q) Are database diagnostics specified for checking the consistency, reasonableness, standards compliance, completeness, and access control of the database?

Backup and recovery

(r) Are there adequate provisions for backup and recovery capabilities?

Comment: These include capabilities for archiving programs and data, diagnosing failure conditions, interim fallback operation in degraded mode, timely reconstitution of programs, data, and/or hardware, and operational cutover to the reconstituted system.

(s) Have these provisions been validated by means of a failure modes and effects analysis?

Comment: Potential failure modes include hardware outages and failure conditions (CPUs, memory, peripherals, communications), loss of data (database, pointers, catalogs, input data), and failure of programs (deadlocks, unending loops, nonconvergence of algorithms).

with small systems, with the following differences:

- use automated cross-referencing if a suitable aid is available,
- use simple-to-medium manual and automated models for critical performance analyses,
- use simple-to-medium scenarios for critical user interfaces, and
- prototype high-risk items that cannot be adequately verified and validated by other techniques.

Large-system V&V. Use the same general approach for large specifications as for medium systems, except use simple-to-detailed instead of simple-to-medium models and scenarios.

For special situations, of course, you will have to tailor your own best mix of verification and validation techniques. But in general, these recommendations will provide you with a good starting point for identifying and resolving your software problems while they're still relatively easy to handle. ■

References

1. *IEEE Standard Glossary of Software Engineering Terminology,* IEEE Std. 729-1983, IEEE-CS order no. 729, Los Alamitos, Calif., 1983.
2. B. W. Boehm, *Software Engineering Economics,* Prentice-Hall, Englewood Cliffs, N.J., 1981.
3. B. Shneiderman, *Software Psychology: Human Factors in Computer and Information Systems,* Winthrop Press, Cambridge, Mass., 1980.
4. S. L. Smith and A. F. Aucella, "Design Guidelines for the User Interface to Computer-Based Information Systems," ESD-TR-83-122, USAF Electronic Systems Division, Bedford, Mass., Mar. 1983.
5. D. Ferrari, *Computer Systems Performance Evaluation,* Prentice-Hall, Englewood Cliffs, N.J., 2nd ed., 1983.
6. M. Lipow, B. B. White, and B. W. Boehm, "Software Quality Assurance: An Acquisition Guidebook," TRW-SS-77-07, Nov. 1977.
7. M. E. Fagan, "Design and Code Inspections to Reduce Errors in Program Development," *IBM Systems Journal,* Vol. 15, No. 3, 1976, pp. 182-211.
8. M. W. Alford, "A Requirements Engineering Methodology for Real-Time Processing Requirements," *IEEE Trans. Software Engr.,* Vol. SE-3, No. 1, Jan. 1977, pp. 60-68.
9. T. E. Bell, D. C. Bixler, and M. E. Dyer, "An Extendable Approach to Computer-Aided Software Requirements Engineering," *IEEE Trans. Software Engr.,* Vol. SE-3, No. 1, Jan. 1977, pp. 49-59.
10. D. Teichroew and E. A Hershey III, "PSL/PSA: A Computer-Aided Technique for Structured Documentation and Analysis of Information Processing Systems," *IEEE Trans. Software Engr.,* Vol. SE-3, No. 1, Jan. 1977, pp. 41-48.
11. S. H. Caine and E. K. Gordon, "PDL: A Tool for Software Design," *AFIPS Conf. Proc.,* Vol. 44, 1975 NCC, pp. 272-276.
12. P. Freeman and A. I. Wassermann, "Ada Methodologies: Concepts and Requirements," DoD Ada Joint Program Office, Nov. 1982.
13. M. H. Cheheyl et al., "Verifying Security," *ACM Computing Surveys,* Sept. 1981, pp. 279-340.
14. S. L. Squires, B. Branstad, and M. Zelkowitz, eds., "Special Issue on Rapid Prototyping," *ACM Software Engr. Notes,* Dec. 1982.
15. B. W. Boehm, T. E. Gray, and T. Seewaldt, "Prototyping vs. Specifying: A Multi-Project Experiment," *IEEE Trans. Software Engr.,* 1984 (in publication).
16. M. W. Alford, R. P. Loshbough, and L. R. Marker, "The Software Requirements Engineering Methodology: An Overview," TRW Software Series, TRW-SS-80-03, May 1980.

Barry W. Boehm is a member of the *IEEE Software* Editorial Board. His photo and biography appear on p. 6.

A REVIEW PROCESS MIX

Charles P. Hollocker
Northern Telecom, Inc.
2435 North Central Expy.
Richardson, TX. 75080

Abstract

A multiple examination approach is presented to show how various product review processes can be used in concert. The application cited suggests the following can be done in the requirements phase of critical software development:

- Walkthroughs can be used to achieve a consensus understanding of key requirements.
- A technical review can be held to examine requirements in their entirety for completeness and correctness.
- A software inspection of the requirements specification can be used to verify "fitness-for-use" in guiding the efforts of design, test, and other key functions that depend on the clear and unambiguous communication of requirements..

Introduction

During the course of contributing to the development of the IEEE standard for software reviews and audits (IEEE Std 1028-1988), I had an opportunity to compare notes with a large number of colleagues from different companies. Although the use of formal reviews has become more widespread, it didn't take long before a trend became recognizable. First, the most common company stance on product reviews is to favor one process. Second, rigor (which is welcomed at the program level) tends to be in a state of "trade-off" with flexibility (which is welcomed at the project level), a fact that makes it very difficult to have both. I suggest that the rigor be in the process and the flexibility be in an organization's ability to draw from a family of well defined (i.e., distinct) product review processes. During project planning, available review processes should be mapped to examination needs. Specifically, a different process might be applied to review test plans than was used to review the architecture or details of design. Since distinct processes will vary in their costs and benefits, this view is generally accepted.

A more controversial view, supplied here for evaluation, is that a combination of review processes can be applied against a single project deliverable. The example put together for this tutorial uses

- Walkthroughs to provide early peer approval of critical requirements
- A technical review to examine the requirements set for completeness and correctness
- A software inspection of the requirements specification to verify that it is usable by the people who rely on the specifications for guidance.

To complete this introduction, review process history and motivation are discussed. A sample process description for the multiple examination approach is then provided. The paper ends with some notes on using data analysis to improve the mix of examination processes.

A Brief History of Processes Considered

The walkthrough, according the *IEEE Standard Glossary of Software Engineering Terminology* [1], is

> A software engineering review process in which a designer or programmer leads one or more members of the development team through a segment of design or code that he or she has written, while other members ask questions and make comments about technique, style, possible errors, violation of the development standards, and other problems.

Wide recognition for documenting the walkthrough process goes to Edward Yourdon [2]. Gerald Weinberg [3, 4] is generally credited with furthering the concept of the walkthrough with his "egoless programming" and "egoless technical reviews."

Toward focusing the examination process back to project controls, Michael Fagan has prescribed the software inspection process [5, 6]. Similar to the walkthrough process, inspecting provides several additional benefits at increased overhead. That investment, however, is swiftly returned in the form of improved process control and reduced rework downstream. The key benefits, as summarized by Fagan [5] are that

> ... inspections increase productivity and improve final program quality. Furthermore, improvements in process control and project management are enabled by inspections.

The inspection, according the *IEEE Standard Glossary of Software Engineering Terminology [1], is*

> 1) A formal evaluation technique in which software requirements, design, or code are examined in detail by a person or group other than the originator to detect faults, violation of development standards, and other problems.
> 2) A phase of quality control that by means of examination, observation, or measurement determines the conformance of materials, supplies, components, parts, systems, processes, or structures to predetermined quality requirements.

The latter definition clearly relates to the inspections used in manufacturing, where many like units are produced and a representative sample is examined. If we were to form an analogy with software development, we would see a multitude of distinct units. Units being inspected would have a 100 percent sample rate, because the sample size (1) would be the same as the number produced (1).

Having seen the walkthrough and inspection as two "species" of review, we start to make the transition to defining their "genus." According to the *IEEE Standard Glossary of Software Engineering Terminology* [1], a review is:

> 1) A formal meeting at which a product or document is presented to the user, customer, or other interested parties for comment and approval. It can be a review of the management and technical progress of the hardware/software development project.
> 2) The formal review of an existing or proposed design for the purpose of detection and remedy of design deficiencies that could affect fitness-for-use and environmental aspects of the product, process, or service, and/or for identification of potential improvements of performance, safety, or economic aspects.

Here we see the first definition providing a framework for a genus ("reviews") of examinations. The second definition has a more technical emphasis and suggests an additional "technical review" process of wider application scope than the walkthrough or inspection.

In an effort to promote the application of sound software engineering principles in this area, the IEEE has led the production of a *Standard for Software Reviews and Audits* [7]. Although balloting group membership for this IEEE project was limited to IEEE members, the consensus it represents is much broader, because the standard development team did not require IEEE affiliation. Moreover, progress was reported to the public, thus making drafts available to all interested parties for comment. The standard provides process definition, yet defers application requirements to local project standards.

This paper uses some of the process descriptions established in the IEEE standard, in combination, to show how multiple examinations with different purposes might contribute to the overall requirements specification activity.

Motivation for Applying a Blend of Popular "Review" Processes

The *IEEE Standard for Software Quality Assurance Plans* [8], says the following about the software requirements review (SRR): "The SRR is held to ensure the adequacy of the requirements stated in the Software Requirements Specification."

The *IEEE Standard for Software Quality Assurance Plans* [8] defines critical software as software: "... where failure could impact safety or cause large financial or social losses." For critical software, the need for requirements specification examination, however, can go beyond the application of a single process. Although necessary, the popular objectives of completeness, correctness, and feasibility may not be sufficient to assure predictably high quality in the resulting software. Representation of specifications and the fitness for use of the representation for development, test, and marketing teams could stand additional scrutiny.

Admitting no single (and certainly no consensus) approach for addressing these issues, this paper provides a multiprocess requirements examination approach. Anticipated to be viewed as overkill by many, this approach is intended to show one example of how a one-time, single process, requirements examination might be replaced by a mix of distinct examinations of tighter focus. Clearly tied to the most critical of software applications, this approach is not right for all development efforts. However, the reader is asked to recall that the cost of removing a defect in the requirements phase can easily be as little as 0.5 percent of what that same defect might cost if it were to hit the field.

Although a difference is recognized between a requirement and its form of representation, this paper will refer to a requirements specification document, with the knowledge that other representations are possible.

A Sample Approach

Step 1: The Walkthrough of One or More Requirements

The accepted objective of a walkthrough is to evaluate a software element. Although long associated with code examinations, this process is also applicable to software requirements. The major objectives are to find defects (e.g., omissions, unwanted additions, and contradictions) in the specification and to consider alternative functionality, performance objectives, or representations. Other important objectives of the walkthrough process include exchange of techniques and style variations, and education of the participants.

In this multiprocess examination approach, the walkthrough process can be used to meet the need for peer approval of individual requirements.

During the walkthrough meeting, the author makes an overview presentation of system requirements, architecture, or any other source of direction used in the specification of the requirement(s). This is followed by general discussion and a detailed "walk through". As the walkthrough progresses, defects, suggested changes, and improvements are noted. When the walkthrough is finished, the notes may be consolidated into one report for distribution to participants. It is suggested that a copy of the report be placed in the project file for requirements tracing.

A walkthrough is conducted when the author of the software requirements specification document indicates readiness to present one or more requirements for evaluation.

The minimum input to the walkthrough process includes

- A statement of objectives for the walkthrough
- The draft requirements specification document or its outline
- The requirement to be examined
- Standards that are in effect for the development of the software

The walkthrough process is complete when
- The requirement(s) has been "walked through" in detail
- Deficiencies in functionality and performance have been noted
- Any recommendations have been documented

If a formal output of the walkthrough process is required, then a walkthrough report is issued, listing
- Walkthrough team member names and affiliations
- The software requirement(s) examined
- Objectives that were to be handled during this walkthrough meeting
- Deficiencies, omissions, contradictions, and suggestions
- Recommendations made by the walkthrough team

Step 2: The Technical Review of Requirements Specifications

A technical review is a formal team evaluation of software requirement specifications. It identifies any discrepancies from system specifications and standards and/or provides recommendations after the examination of alternatives. This examination may require more than one meeting and typically has a larger attendance that walkthroughs or inspections. In this multiprocess examination approach, the technical review meets the need for the widespread exposure of requirements to assure correctness, completeness, and feasibility.

The need for conducting a technical review of software requirements is defined by project planning documents. A technical review of requirements is conducted when
- A statement of objectives for the review is established
- The individual(s) responsible for requirements specification indicate readiness for review
- The technical review leader is satisfied that the software element(s) are sufficiently complete for a technical review of the requirements to be worthwhile

The minimum input to the technical review process includes
- A statement of objectives for the technical review
- The software requirements
- Related system specifications, customer requirements, and so on
- Plans, standards, or guidelines against which the requirements are to be examined

Additional applicable reference material can be made available by the individual(s) responsible for software requirements specification.

A technical review is complete when all issues identified in the review "statement of objectives" have been addressed and a technical review report has been issued. The technical review report identifies
- The review team members
- The software requirements reviewed
- Specific inputs to the review
- A list of unresolved deficiencies in the requirements
- A list of management issues
- Action item ownership and status
- Any recommendations made by the review team

Step 3: The Inspection of the Requirements Specification

The objectives of a software inspection are to detect, identify, and describe software element defects. This is a rigorous, though relatively small, peer examination that, for the purpose of this example, verifies that the software requirements specification document is fit for use in driving subsequent development and test activities. Specifically, it verifies that
- The software requirements specification document conforms to applicable standards for format and content
- The document is not ambiguous
- Requirements are stated so as to be testable

Typically, software inspections are performed by three to six peer participants led by a impartial moderator. The moderator is not the author. Defect resolution is mandatory, and rework verification is formal. Both inspection process and product information are recorded.

The software requirements specification document inspection can be triggered by document availability, schedule compliance, or completion of rework required by an earlier inspection. Before scheduling the inspection, it is important that

- Document readiness be verified
- All required supporting information is available
- For a reinspection, all required rework has been verified
- All prior milestones, as identified in the appropriate planning documents, are satisfied.

Inputs to the inspection include

- The software requirements specification document to be inspected
- The approved issue of system requirements or architecture
- Any applicable inspection checklists
- Any standards and guidelines against which the document is to be inspected
- All necessary inspection reporting forms. For a reinspection, the previous inspection defect list is also required

To start the meeting, the moderator introduces the participants and describes their roles. The moderator states the purpose of the inspection and directs the inspectors to focus their efforts toward defect detection, not solution-hunting. The moderator reminds the inspectors to direct their remarks to the reader and to comment only on the product, not the author. It may also be useful to resolve any special procedural questions raised by the inspectors.

The moderator asks for individual preparation times and records the total on the inspection report. It is the moderator's responsibility to reschedule the meeting if the inspectors are not adequately prepared. If homework has not been done, then the meeting should be rescheduled. The moderator reviews the inspection checklist with the team to ensure that the product has been adequately studied before the inspection meeting. That checklist should contain elements to ensure that

- The distribution list identifies the right people, by function
- The signature/approval block is appropriately designed
- The document displays the appropriate proprietary markings
- The document release and issue are clearly designated
- The table of contents reflects the required structure
- References are correct and adequate in coverage
- The "owner" of the post-publication document is clearly identified
- Any assumptions or dependencies are documented
- The requirements are clear, unambiguous, and complete
- Design is appropriately deferred to later stages of development
- Requirement statements are correct and testable.

The reader presents the materials to the inspection team. The inspection team examines the software objectively, and the moderator focuses this part of the meeting on creating the defect list. The recorder enters each defect, location, description, and classification on the defect list. During this time, the author answers any specific questions and contributes to defect detection based on any special understanding of the requirements.

At the end of the inspection meeting, the moderator must have the defect list reviewed with the team to ensure its completeness and accuracy. An exit decision is then made. The purpose of the exit decision is to bring an unambiguous closure to the inspection meeting. The exit decision determines whether the materials meet the inspection exit criteria and prescribes any appropriate rework verification. Specifically, the inspection team identifies the software element(s) disposition as one of the following:

Accept: The software element is accepted "as is" or with only minor rework (e.g., that would require no further verification).

Verify Rework: The software element is to be accepted after the moderator verifies rework.

Reinspect: Schedule a reinspection to verify rework after revision and rework verification.

At a minimum, a reinspection examines the document sections changed to resolve defects identified in the last inspection. During rework, the author revises the materials, addressing all items on the inspection defect list.

A single exit criterion applied to all inspections is that all of the defects that have been detected are resolved. Each project shall develop its own criteria to meet the needs of its specific products and development environment. The moderator will ensure that the materials comply with the exit criteria and that the inspection results have been reported before certifying that the inspection is complete.

Expected output includes a defect listing, summary, and process characterization. The listing identifies the location, description, and category of each defect found. A summary of the number of defects identified in each category is provided. Process characterization is provided by a separate report, frequently called the "inspection report," that identifies

- The number of participants
- The inspection meeting duration
- The size of the materials inspected
- The total preparation time of the inspection team
- The disposition of the software element
- An estimate of the rework effort and rework completion date

Improving Process Mix

Applying a mix of examination processes has the potential of greatly improving product quality and project costs. I would further recommend a program of data analysis and in-process auditing to provide continuous improvement in how a process mix is deployed.

The examinations processes outlined in this paper can provide data for the analysis of the quality of the software requirements and their representation. Further, they can provide information leading to the improved effectiveness of procedures and evaluation process efficiency. To enable these analyses, defects that are identified at the various evaluation meetings can be categorized by defect type, class, and severity.

The defect type identifies a specific attribute of requirements and, for example, may be identified as relating to standards compliance, performance, safety, procedure, interface, representation, etc.

Defect class characterizes evidence of non-conformance and for example, may be categorized as "missing," "wrong," or "extra." Additional defect classes used when examining documents could include "ambiguous" or "inconsistent."

Defects are then ranked by severity, for example, as "major" for defects that would result in failure of the software element(s) or an observable departure from system specification, or as "minor" for defects that would affect only the nonfunctional aspects of the software element.

In addition to counts of defects by type, class, and severity, retained data could contain the identification and disposition of the requirement(s) examined, the date and time of the examination, the moderator, the preparation and meeting times, and the volume of the materials examined.

The management of data requires capabilities for the storage, entry, access, updating, and summary and reporting of the categorized defects. The frequency and types of the analysis reports, and their distribution, are left to the reader.

Once the data collection, analysis, and reporting program is underway, process decisions will be made based on the applicability and accuracy of your data. The most prevalent contributor to invalid data is process variance. The consistency of review process application is critical in warding off efficiency deterioration and allowing continuous improvement: you *must* be measuring what you think you are measuring. Toward controlling this problem, a program of in-process auditing is recommended. Typical program elements include the following:

- Verify the consistency of the product as it evolves through the development process by determining, on a sampling basis, that hardware and software interfaces are consistent with the software requirements specification (SRS).
- Verify the traceability (and maintenance) of the requirements as the project progresses by determining, on a sampling basis, that the design of the product, as the softwaredesign description is evolving, satisfies the functional requirements of the SRS.
- Determine compliance with applicable process standards (e.g., auditing of the inspection process, on a sampling basis, to determine if inspection process rules are being followed).

It may be surprising to learn that software requirements are reviewed without a copy of the system requirements available at the meeting. This would explain why sins of commission are found earlier than sins of omission. Perhaps functions that complain the most about meeting or testing performance requirements were not represented at the examinations; this fact would explain a sudden rash of trouble reports against the requirements specification document. These and many other findings are common.

References

[1] *ANSI/IEEE Standard Glossary of Software Engineering Terminology,* IEEE Std 729-1983. New York, Institute of Electrical and Electronics Engineers, 1983.

[2] Yourdon, Ed. *Structured Walkthroughs.* Yourdon, Inc., New York, 1977.

[3] Weinberg, Gerald M. *The Psychology of Computer Programming.New* York, Van Nostrand Reinhold, 1971.

[4] Weinberg, Gerald M. and Freedman, D. P. "Reviews, Walkthroughs, and Inspections," *IEEE Transactions on Software Engineering*, 10:1, January, 1984, pp. 68-72.

[5] Fagan, M., E. "Design and Code Inspections to Reduce Errors in Program Development," *IBM Systems Journal*, 15:3, July, 1976, pp. 182-211.

[6] Fagan, M., E. "Inspecting Software Design and Code," *Datamation,* October, 1977, pp. 133-144.

[7] *IEEE Standard for Software Reviews and Audits.* IEEE Std 1028-1988. New York, Institute of Electrical and Electronics Engineers, 1988.

[8] *ANSI/IEEE Standard for Software Quality Assurance Plans*. IEEE Std 730-1984. New York, Institute of Electrical and Electronics Engineers, 1984.

Chapter 7: Software System Engineering Process Models

1: Introduction

A *process model* (sometimes called a system or software process model) is a representation of a system/software development process activity intended to explain the behavior of some of its aspects. The process model is less complex or complete than the activity or artifact modeled. There are a number of different process models (approaches, strategies, or paradigms) that can be used by system/software developers to develop their system effectively and efficiently.

This chapter contains six papers concerned with software engineering development strategies. The first paper is an overview of numerous strategies that are available to the software system engineer. The second gives us a new development model, entitled "Dual Life-Cycle Model," which shows the relationship between the management and technical lifecycles. The next four papers each isolate and discuss a strategy: risk analysis, iteration, reusable software, and prototyping as a tool.

2: Description of Papers

The first paper, by A.M. Davis, E.M. Bersoff, and E.R. Comer, discusses a strategy for comparing alternative software development lifecycle models. This paper defines a model of a typical system development that is over budget and behind schedule and never catches up with the user's requirements. The paper also defines such lifecycle metrics as shortfall, lateness, adaptability, longevity, and inappropriateness. The paper goes on to discuss approaches to software development that can reduce problems of lateness, budget, and documentation requirements. These strategies include rapid throwaway prototypes, incremental prototypes, evolutionary prototypes, reusable software, and automated software synthesis. Each of these different software development prototypes is individually discussed and its advantages over the conventional model are shown. The paper provides a number of paradigms that can help the project manager compare and contrast all of the software development lifecycle models in terms of their ability to

satisfy users' needs and to reduce software costs. These five "new models" were compared to the conventional models with respect to their ability to produce software that meets users' needs.

John Manley has initiated and documented a new look at the software development lifecycle—the "Dual Life Cycle Model (DLCM)." This model describes a parallel management and engineering lifecycle, connected by a complex communication system. This DLCM distinguishes between artifacts (tangible work products) produced by managers for engineers, and by engineers for managers, in addition to what managers and engineers produce for their own use. The paper also models a set of management tools that can be used to manage both the management and engineering sides of the DLCM. These are:

- *mission:* vision of leader and direction to travel
- *objectives:* timeless purpose of organizational units
- *goals:* measurable and scheduled milestones
- *action plans:* alternative paths to achieve milestones
- *work packages:* engineering and management supporting activities

The author of this paper, John Manley, coined the term "embedded computer" [1] and was the first person to use the term "CASE" to describe computer-aided software engineering tools. [2, 3]

The third paper is a new classic by Barry Boehm entitled "A Sprial Model of Software Development and Enhancement." An earlier version of this paper was presented by Boehm at a workshop on software requirements in early 1985. This paper describes a revolutionary new view of the software development lifecycle. The spiral model is a more general software development model than those typically in use today and treats as special cases the waterfall and other popular software development paradigms. The primary thrust of the spiral model is to integrate risk analysis and prototyping.

The fourth paper, "Synthesis Process for Software Development" by Art Pyster of the Software Productivity Consortium (SPC), involves a new approach developed at SPC called "Synthesis." Under Synthesis a new system is largely seen as a revision of an old one. Relatively little is built from scratch. There are three main activities during Synthesis:

- create a model that approximates the new application
- map from the application model to a known software model that approximates a valid design
- map from the software design to executable code that approximates a valid implementation

These steps are performed iteratively, adapting the models with each iteration to become ever-better approximations of the desired new system. At each step appropriate verification and assessment are performed.

One of the new paradigms discussed by Davis, Bersoff, and Comer was reusable software. The Grabow and Noble paper on reusable software concepts starts out with the point that the "cost, reliability and timeliness of realtime, embedded computer systems has become a problem. Software reuse is viewed as part of the solution." This paper reviews and presents an evaluation of software development methodologies to determine which methodologies were suitable for producing and maintaining reusable software for realtime embedded computer systems. Nineteen software development methodologies were reviewed, representing a sampling of existing approaches to software development. The methodologies were separated into three categories: research, commercial, and industrial. The paper also includes a discussion of software reuse components, a brief summary of the methodologies review approach, and conclusions based on a Navy study and recommendations for employing reusable software.

The scope of reuse, according to the authors, includes all documentation as well as the actual, executable computer code. The authors believe this broad definition is appropriate because the coding process is a relatively small portion (about 20%) of the total software development effort. As a result, source code reused will provide a relatively small incremental benefit.

The last paper in the chapter, by Hassan Gomaa, is an update and revision of an earlier paper by Gomaa and D.B.H. Scott. [4] Gomaa states that one of the main problems in developing computer applications is specifying the user's requirements such that the requirement specification is correct, complete, and unambiguous. Although prototyping is often considered too expensive, correcting ambiguities and misunderstandings at the specification stage is significantly cheaper than correcting a system after it has gone into production. This paper describes how to prototype and specify the requirements for a computer system to manage and control a semiconductor processing facility. Two approaches to prototyping are described: throwaway prototypes and evolutionary prototypes. Brief examples of the two types are described, and the conditions under which each type might be used are presented. The cost of developing a running prototype should be less than 10 percent of total software development cost.

3: References

[1] Manley, J.H., "Embedded Computers—Software Cost Considerations," *AFIPS Conference Proceedings,* Vol. 43, AFIPS Press, Reston, VA, May 6-10, 1974.

[2] Manley, J.H., "Computer Aided Software Engineering," presented at the 10th Annual Federal DP Expo & Conference, Washington, DC, Convention Center, April 17, 1984.

[3] Manley, J.H., "Computer Aided Software Engineering (CASE): Foundation for Software Factories," *Proceedings IEEE COMPCON '84, Fall Conference on the Small Computer (R)Evolution,* IEEE Computer Society Press, Washington, DC, Sept. 16-20, 1984.

[4] Gomaa, Hassan and D.B.H. Scott, "Prototyping as a Tool in the Specification of User Requirements," *Proceedings of the Fifth International Conference on Software Engineering,* IEEE Computer Society Press, Washington, DC, 1981.

A Strategy for Comparing Alternative Software Development Life Cycle Models

ALAN M. DAVIS, SENIOR MEMBER, IEEE, EDWARD H. BERSOFF, SENIOR MEMBER, IEEE, AND EDWARD R. COMER, MEMBER, IEEE

Abstract—**The classic waterfall model of software engineering is used throughout the production software development community. The escalating costs associated with software development and the unsatisfactory reliability, performance, and functionality of the resulting software have motivated software engineers to develop new alternate models of software development including prototyping, software synthesis, and reusable software. It is difficult to compare and contrast these new models of software development because their disciples often use different terminology, and the models often have little in common except their beginnings (marked by a recognition that a problem exists) and ends (marked by the existence of a software solution). This paper provides a framework which can serve 1) as a basis for analyzing the similarities and differences among alternate life cycle models; 2) as a tool for software engineering researchers to help describe the probable impacts of a new life cycle model; and 3) as a means to help software practitioners decide on an appropriate life cycle model to utilize on a particular project or in a particular application area.**

Index Terms—**Reusable software, software development life cycles, software prototyping, software synthesis, waterfall model.**

INTRODUCTION

THE classic waterfall model (see Fig. 1) was defined as early as 1970 by Royce [1] and later refined by Boehm [2] in 1976 to help cope with the growing complexity of the software projects being tackled. The use of such a model

- encourages one to specify what the system is supposed to do (i.e., to define the requirements) before building the system (i.e., designing);
- encourages one to plan how components are going to interact (i.e., designing) before building the components (i.e., coding);
- enables project managers to track progress more accurately and to uncover possible slippages early;
- demands that the development process generate a series of documents which can later be utilized to test and maintain the system;
- reduces development and maintenance costs due to all of the above reasons; and
- enables the organization that will develop the system to be more structured and manageable.

Manuscript received May 12, 1986; revised November 18, 1986. This work was supported by the Software Productivity Consortium.

A. M. Davis and E. H. Bersoff are with BTG, Inc., Vienna, VA 22180.

E. R. Comer is with Software Productivity Solutions, Inc., Melbourne, FL 32936.

IEEE Log Number 8823075.

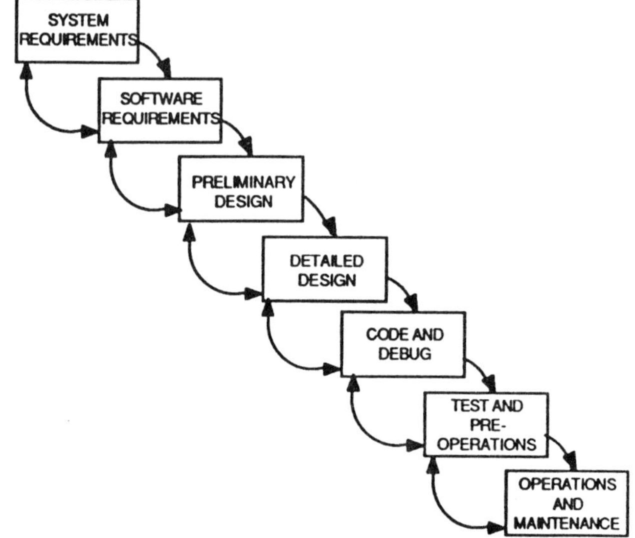

Fig. 1. The waterfall model of software development.

Most "standard" methodologies for commercial corporations, government contractors,[1] and governmental entities[1] follow some basic variation of the waterfall model, although there are a variety of different names for each of the stages. Thus, the requirements stages are often called user needs analysis, system analysis, or specifications; the preliminary design stage is often called high-level design, top-level design, software architectural definition, or specifications; the detailed design stage is often called program design, module design, lower-level design, algorithmic design, or just plain design, etc. For the most part, however, all these methodologies are equivalent.

During the past five to ten years, alternative, radically different methodologies have appeared, including rapid throwaway prototypes, incremental development, evolutionary prototypes, reusable software, and automated software synthesis.

The developers of these techniques had a variety of motivations, but primarily they were looking for ways of rescuing the software industry from what appears to be a dilemma: software is almost always more expensive and

[1]These include, for example, those methodologies derived from DoD-STD-2167, MIL-STD-490, or MIL-STD-1679A.

Reprinted from *IEEE Transactions on Software Engineering*, Volume SE-14, Number 10, October 1988, pages 1453-1461.

delivered later than expected, and to make matters worse, it is often unreliable and fails to meet the ultimate users' needs. Project managers often bypass stages or take shortcuts in order to solve the problem, but these unplanned and extemporaneous alterations of the life cycle just make the software even more expensive, later, and more unreliable.

The *rapid throwaway prototyping* approach (made popular by Gomaa [3]) addresses the issue of ensuring that the software product being proposed really meets the users' needs. The approach is to construct a "quick and dirty" partial implementation of the system prior to (or during) the requirements stage. The potential users utilize this prototype for a period of time and supply feedback to the developers concerning its strengths and weaknesses. This feedback is then used to modify the software requirements specification to reflect the real user needs. At this point, the developers can proceed with the actual system design and implementation with confidence that they are building the "right" system (except in those cases where the user needs evolve). An extension of this approach uses a series of throwaway prototypes [4], culminating in full-scale development.

Incremental development [5] is the process of constructing a partial implementation of a total system and slowly adding increased functionality or performance. This approach reduces the costs incurred before an initial capability is achieved. It also produces an operational system more quickly, and it thus reduces the possibility that the user needs will change during the development process.

In *evolutionary prototyping* (established briefly at the end of [6]), the developers construct a partial implementation of the system which meets known requirements. The prototype is then used by its intended users in order to understand the full requirements better. Whereas incremental development implies that we understand most of our requirements up front and simply choose to implement it in subsets of increasing capability, evolutionary prototyping implies that we do not know up front all of our requirements, but need to experiment with an operational system in order to learn them. Note that in the case of throwaway prototypes we are likely to implement only those aspects of the system that are poorly understood, but that in the case of evolutionary prototypes we are more likely to start with those system aspects that are best understood and thus build upon our strengths. For complex applications, it is not reasonable at this time to expect this application of prototypes to be particularly "rapid" because reliability, adaptability, maintainability, and performance (RAMP) are major forces behind making such system developments expensive and time-consuming. Since the technology is not yet available to *retrofit* RAMP requirements, they would have to be implemented up front, thus forcing software development costs high and schedules to their limit. Evolutionary prototypes will become more practical in the future as techniques for retrofitting RAMP requirements are developed.

Whereas prototyping attempts to reduce development costs through partial implementations, *reusable software* [7] is the discipline of attempting to reduce development costs by incorporating previously proven designs and code in new software products. The software industry is guilty of continuously reinventing the wheel. This is primarily because few tools are available to help reuse software designs or code from previous projects. Clearly, what is needed are techniques to create reusable components, techniques and tools to store and retrieve reusable components, and component specification techniques to help catalog and locate relevant components. The net effect of reusing components would be shorter development schedules (by using wheels rather than reinventing them) and more reliable software (by using components that have been previously "shaken down").

Automated software synthesis is a term used to describe the transformation of requirements or high-level design specifications into operational code. The transformation process may be directed by algorithmic [8] or knowledge-based [9] techniques. As Parnas [10] points out, each generation of software engineering researchers applies the term "software synthesis" to one language "higher" than the one currently used for programming. Thus, when machine language was used, software synthesis referred to the "automatic" translation of assembly language into machine code (now called assembly). Later, it referred to the translation of a high-level language into machine code (now called compilation). Now, it refers to the translation of very-high-level languages (VHLL's) into machine code. Since lines of code produced by person-month are relatively independent of the implementation language, it becomes clear that the higher the programming language used becomes, the more true productivity (as measured by the amount of functionality implemented per person-month) increases.

The purpose of this paper is to describe a paradigm[2] which can be used to compare and contrast each of the above alternative life cycle models with the more conventional waterfall model (and with each other) in the face of constantly evolving user needs.

The Paradigm

For every application beyond the trivial, user needs are constantly evolving. Thus, the system being constructed is always aiming at a moving target. This is a primary reason for delayed schedules (caused by trying to make the software meet a new requirement it was not designed to meet) and software that fails to meet customer expectations (because the developers "froze" the requirements and failed to acknowledge the inevitable changes).

Fig. 2 shows graphically how users' needs evolve over time. It is recognized that the function shown is neither linear nor continuous in reality. Please note that 1) the scale on the x-axis is not shown (the units can be either

[2]The term "paradigm" is used in this paper to mean "metamodel," i.e., a model to describe software life cycle models.

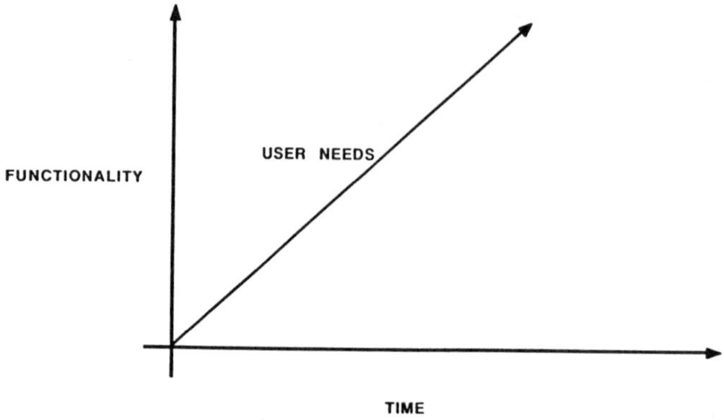

Fig. 2. Constantly evolving user needs.

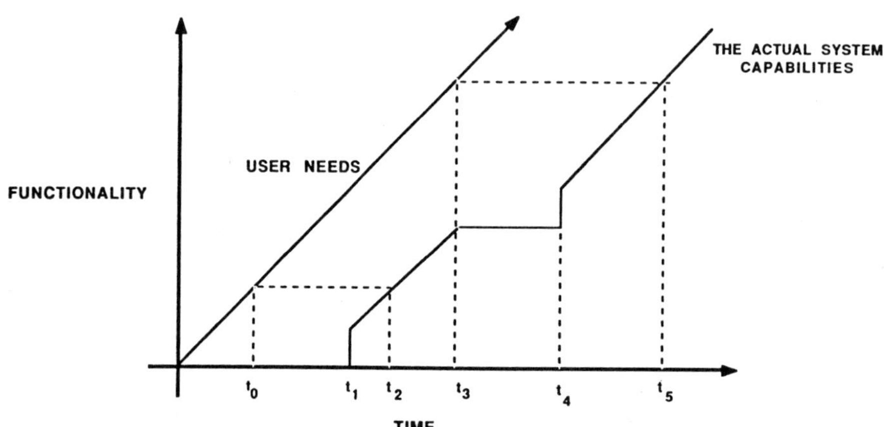

Fig. 3. Software products fall short of meeting all current user needs.

months or years), but could be assumed to be nonuniform, containing areas of compression and decompression, and 2) the units of the scale on the y-axis are not shown, but are assumed to be some measure of the amount of functionality (such as DeMarco's "Bangs for the Buck" [11]). However, none of the observations made in this paper is dependent on either the uniformity of the axes or the linearity or continuity of the curve shown in Fig. 2.

Fig. 3 shows what happens during a conventional software development. At time t_0, a need for a software system is recognized and a development effort commences with relatively incomplete knowledge of the real user needs at time t_0. At time t_1, the development effort has produced an operational product, but not only does it not satisfy the current t_1 needs, it does not even satisfy the old t_0 needs because of a poor understanding of those needs in the first place. The product now undergoes a series of enhancements (between times t_1 and t_3), which eventually enable it to satisfy the original requirements (at t_2) and then some. At some later point in time t_3, the cost of enhancement is so great that the decision is made to build a new system (once again based on poorly understood requirements), development of the product is completed at time t_4, and the cycle repeats itself.

A number of useful metrics can now be defined based on the paradigm defined above. These metrics can later be used to compare and contrast sets of alternative life cycle approaches. These metrics are portrayed graphically in Fig. 4 and are described below.

1) A *shortfall* is a measure of how far the operational system, at any time t, is from meeting the actual requirements at time t. This is the attribute that most people are referring to when they ask "Does this system meet my needs?"

2) *Lateness* is a measure of the time that elapses between the appearance of a new requirement and its satisfaction. Of course, recognizing that new requirements are not necessarily implemented in the order in which they appear, lateness actually measures the time delay associated with achievement of a level of functionality.

3) The *adaptability* is the rate at which the software solution can adapt to new requirements, as measured by the slope of the solution curve.

4) The *longevity* is the time a system solution is adaptable to change and remains viable, i.e., the time from system creation through the time it is replaced.

5) *Inappropriateness* is the shaded area between the user needs and the solution curves in Fig. 5 and thus captures the behavior of shortfall over time. The ultimately "appropriate" model would exhibit a zero area, meaning that new requirements are instantly satisfied.

Each of the alternative life cycle models defined earlier is now analyzed with respect to the paradigm described above.

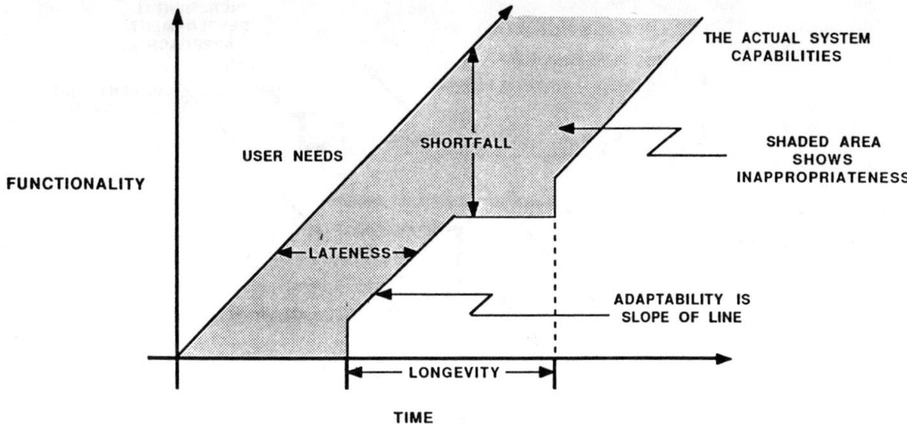

Fig. 4. Software productivity metrics.

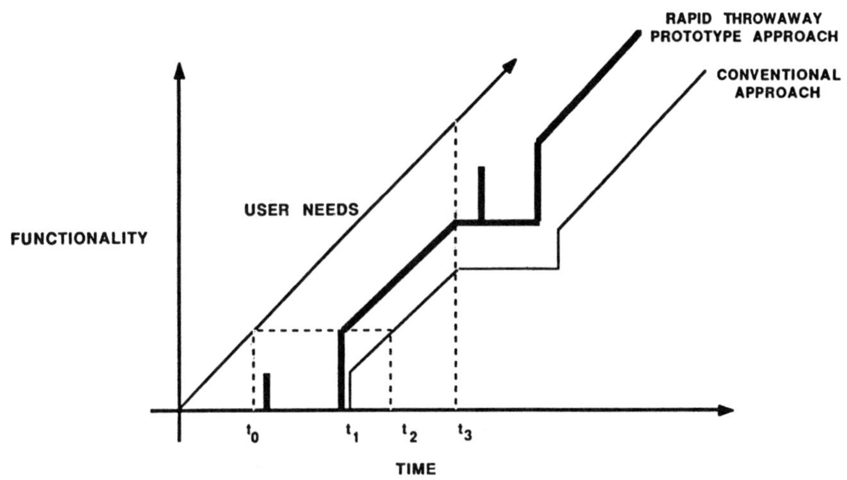

Fig. 5. Rapid prototyping versus conventional.

Rapid Throwaway Prototypes

The use of a rapid throwaway prototype early in the development life cycle increases the likelihood that customers and developers will have a better understanding of the real user needs that existed at time t_0. Thus, its use does not radically affect the life cycle model per se, but does increase the impact of the resulting system. This is shown in Fig. 5, where the vertical line (i.e., the increase in functionality provided by the system upon deployment) at time t_1 is longer than in the conventional approach. Fig. 5 also shows the rapid prototype itself as a short vertical line providing limited and experimental capability soon after time t_0. There is no reason to believe that the length of time during which the product can be efficiently enhanced without replacement is any different than with the conventional approach. Therefore, this period of time for the rapid prototype-based development (i.e., $t_3 - t_1$) is shown in Fig. 5 the same as for the conventionally developed product.

Incremental Development

When using incremental development, software is deliberately built to satisfy fewer requirements initially, but is constructed in such a way as to facilitate the incorporation of new requirements and thus achieve higher adaptability. This approach has two effects: 1) the initial development time is reduced because of the reduced level of functionality, and 2) the software can be enhanced more easily and for a longer period of time. Fig. 6 shows how this approach compares to the conventional approach. Note that the initial development time is less than for the conventional approach, that the initial functionality (A) is less than for the conventional approach (B), and that the increased adaptability is indicated by a higher slope of the curve A–C than for the conventional approach (line B–D). The stair step aspect of the graph indicates a series of well-defined, planned, discrete builds of the system.

Evolutionary Prototypes

This approach is an extension of the incremental development. Here, the number and frequency of operational prototypes increases. The emphasis is on evolving toward a solution in a more continuous fashion, instead of by a discrete number of system builds.

With such an approach, an initial prototype emerges rapidly, presumably demonstrating functionality where the requirements are well understood (in contrast to the throwaway prototypes, where one usually implements the

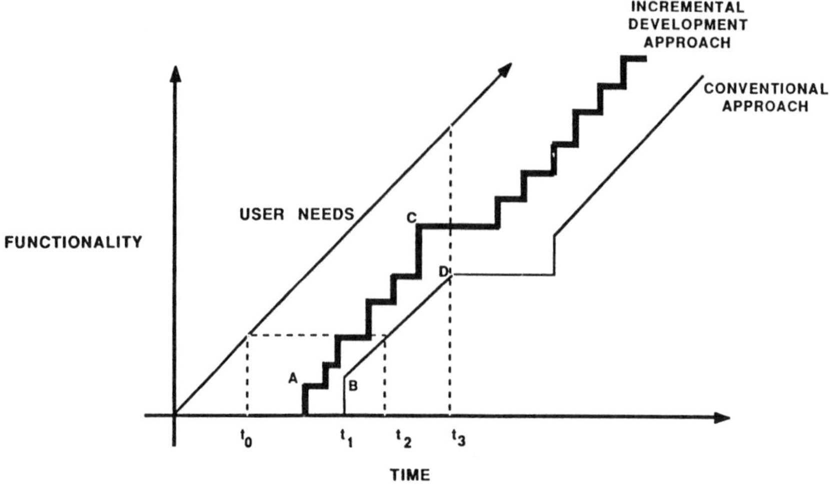

Fig. 6. Incremental development versus conventional.

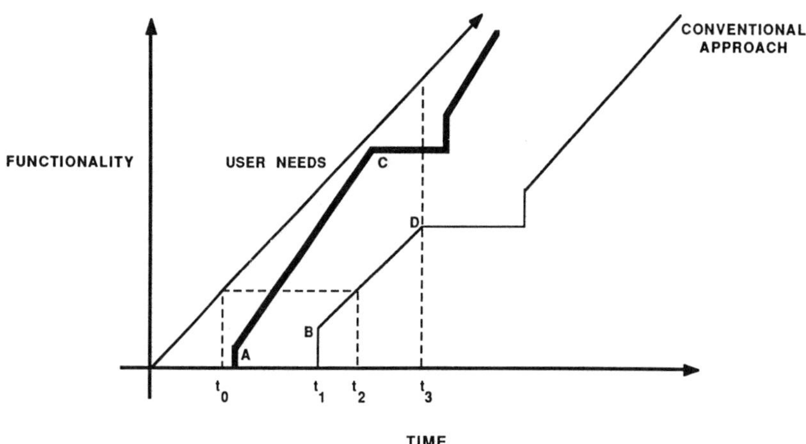

Fig. 7. Evolutionary prototyping versus conventional.

poorly understood aspects first) and providing an overall framework for the software. Each successive prototype explores a new area of user need, while refining the previous functions. As a result, the solution evolves closer and closer to the user needs (see Fig. 7). In time, it too will have to be redone or undergo major restructuring in order to continue to evolve.

As with the incremental development approach, the slope (line A–C) is steeper than in the conventional approach (line B–D) because the evolvable prototype was designed to be far more adaptable. Also, the line A–C in Fig. 7 is not stepped like line A–C in Fig. 6 because of the replacement of well-defined and well-planned system "builds" with a continuous influx of new, and perhaps experimental, functionality.

Reusable Software

Reuse of existing software components has the potential to decrease the initial development time for software significantly. Fig. 8 shows how this approach compares to conventional development. No parameters are changed, except for the development times.

Automated Software Synthesis

In the ultimate application of this approach, as an engineer recognizes the requirements, these are specified in some type of VHLL and the system is automatically synthesized. This approach has two dramatic effects: 1) the development time is greatly reduced, and 2) the development costs are reduced so much that adapting "old" systems is rarely more meritorious than resynthesizing the entire system. Thus, the longevity of any version is low, and the result is a stair-step graph, as shown in Fig. 9, where the horizontal segments represent the time the system is utilized and the time needed to upgrade the requirements. The vertical segments represent the additional functionality offered by each new generation.

Summary

Note that all five approaches reduce the area between the user need graph and actual system functionality graph when compared to conventional development. That is, all five approaches decrease shortfall, lateness, and inappropriateness to varying degrees. It is for this very reason that these alternative life cycle approaches were developed by their inventors.

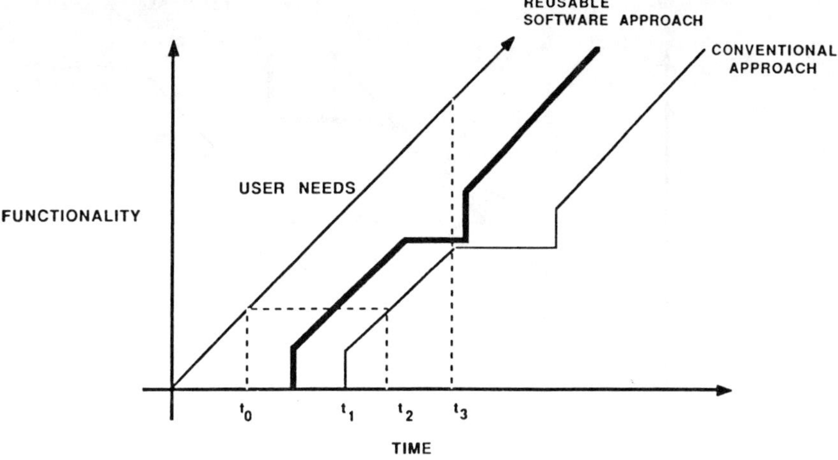

Fig. 8. Reusable software versus conventional.

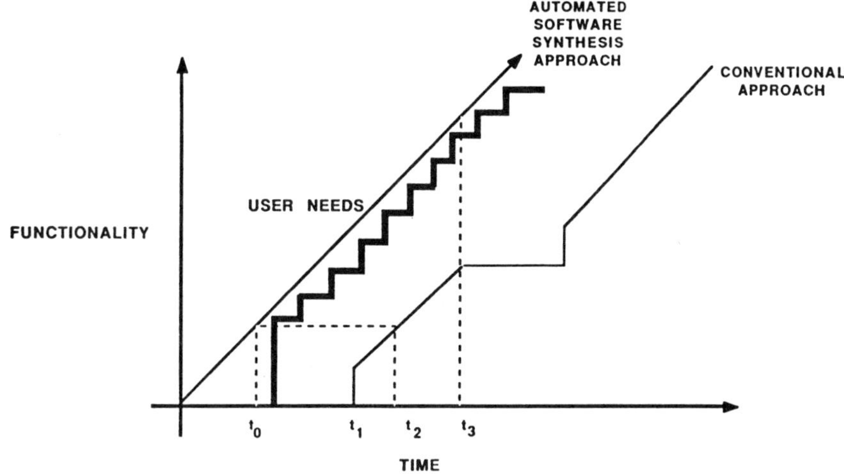

Fig. 9. Automated software synthesis versus conventional.

Other Models

The paradigm discussed in this paper makes it apparent that alternative life cycle models improve product development. It also provides insight into how we might modify the conventional life cycle model to improve our situation. For example, it is apparent by looking at all the models described above that the evolution of requirements is fundamentally ignored during development. In actuality, as important new requirements become apparent, they are reviewed by a configuration control board and either discarded (or perhaps deferred for a later release) or approved [12]. Such an approval may result in relatively expensive modifications to all existing documentation and code under development. If techniques could be developed which would make the intermediate results of the software life cycle (e.g., software requirements specifications, high-level design specifications, detailed design specifications, and code) highly adaptable, then the software development process itself could result in systems that more closely met *current* requirements. If such a scheme were possible, the result would be as shown in Fig. 10. Note that although the development time remains unchanged, the system that appears at time t_1 not only meets all the requirements of time t_0, but most of the additional t_1 requirements as well.

Productivity Analysis

Suppose that at a particular point in time a project manager needed to meet a set of new requirements. He/she could select one of a number of choices:

1) modify the existing program,

2) build a new system from scratch using conventional software development practices, or

3) build a new system from scratch using any of the new alternative approaches.

Currently, many project managers make this selection based on fuzzy perceptions and past experiences. On the other hand, some project managers might analyze the project's aspects which affect the choice. For example, aspects of the application that might affect the selection include

• requirements volatility (i.e., the likelihood that the requirements will change);

• the "shape" of requirements volatility (e.g., discrete leaps, based on brand new threats; or gradual changes, as with a need to do things faster);

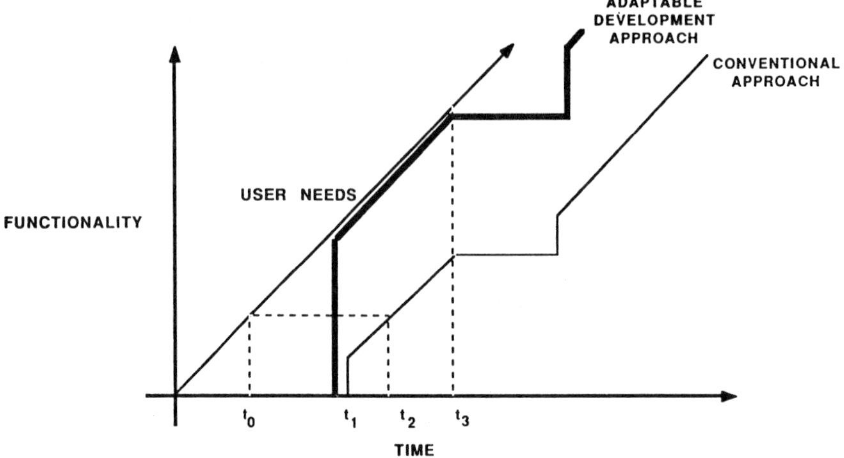

Fig. 10. Adaptable development versus conventional.

• the longevity of the application; and

• the availability of resources to develop or effect changes (i.e., it may be easier to get resources up front than to devote significant resources for enhancements).

Wise project managers must make the appropriate life cycle model selection based not only on maximum functionality in minimum elapsed time at minimum cost, but also on the above four factors. The remainder of this section describes how the paradigm can be used as a potential tool for project managers who wish to consider all the factors in making their life cycle model selections.

Comparisons of life cycle model alternatives based solely on functionality and time can be made using the graphs shown earlier in this paper (i.e., Figs. 5–10). To add cost considerations, a third dimension can be added, as shown in Fig. 11. While the cost over time is certainly projected and tracked today, the cost per unit of functionality is not. Quantifying this three-dimensional model for various development approaches would have three significant outcomes.

1) Comparisons of different life cycle model alternatives could consider not only the functionality needs of the application, but also the funding and funding profile constraints. For example, at a particular point in time, a project manager may need to make a choice between a conventional life cycle and an evolutionary prototype life cycle. He/she could plot the projected costs on a graph like that in Fig. 11 for the two approaches. The resulting plots, shown in Figs. 12 and 13, respectively, graphically show that (for this particular project) the evolutionary prototype approach costs less up front and costs more over the product's life time, but more closely meets user needs than the conventional approach.

2) Future upgrades could be weighed in importance according to the cost impact of the additional functionality.

3) Productivity would be redefined as the functionality provided (i.e., the "bang" per DeMarco [11]) per hour of labor.

Productivity today is usually measured in terms of the characteristics of the solution (e.g., lines of code per hour). This is valid only where the selected characteristic of the solution, for example, lines of code, is a valid reflection of the size and complexity of the problem, which is generally true for manually developed software. This

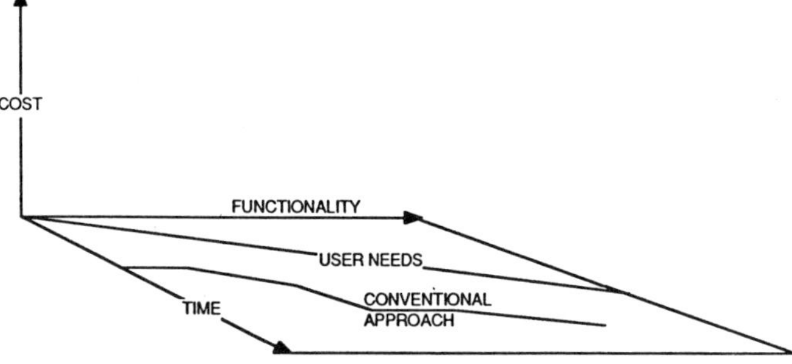

Fig. 11. The cost dimension.

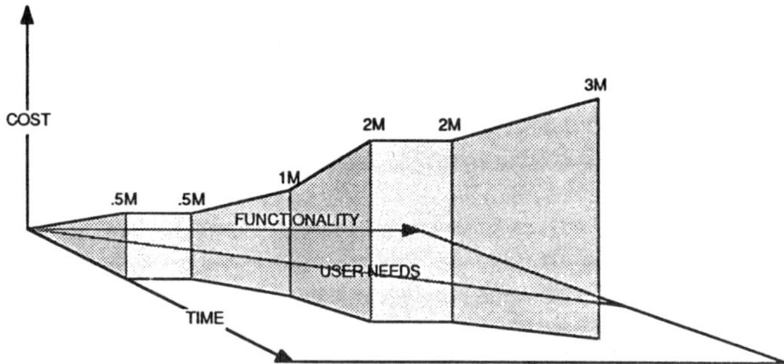

Fig. 12. Possible cost analysis for conventional development.

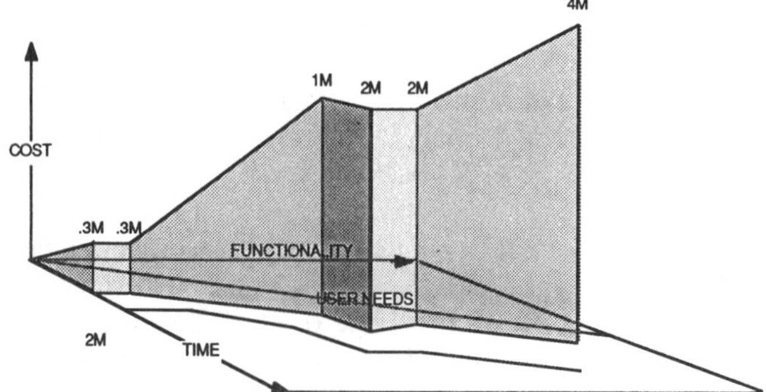

Fig. 13. Possible cost analysis for evolutionary prototype development.

measure of productivity is, however, inappropriate for development models where lines of code are not a valid reflection of the problem space. This is one of the primary reasons that comparison of the various development models is so difficult today.

Future Research

While the paradigm presented in this paper is useful for visualizing conceptual differences between development models, additional research is needed to allow precise tradeoffs to occur. Future research must tackle

- quantifying and measuring the functionality axis (i.e., the bang);
- developing the correct productivity metric in terms of effort per bang;
- understanding and measuring real user needs (in many cases, the gap between the user need and the operational system is an unquantified feeling of dissatisfaction on the user's part); and
- measuring the actual behavior (in terms of functionality, time, and cost) of the solution curves for the various models (i.e., generating techniques to arrive at accurate versions of Figs. 12 and 13 for any particular project).

Based on the paradigm presented in this paper, it follows that the "ultimate" model is one that is predictive of the user needs (i.e., the functionality is available before the user needs it) and exhibits the lowest possible cost. If the user need line could be projected with some degree of accuracy (which requires a mature application domain), then methods could be developed to provide functionality at or ahead of the need.

Summary

A paradigm has been given which helps one compare and contrast alternative software development life cycle models in terms of their abilities to satisfy user needs and reduce life cycle costs. Five "new" models were compared to the conventional model with respect to their abilities to produce software which meets user needs.

Acknowledgement

The authors would like to thank E. Koenke for participating in early discussions on the subject of this paper.

References

[1] W. W. Royce, "Managing the development of large software systems: Concepts and techniques," in *Proc. WESCON*, Aug. 1970.

[2] B. W. Boehm, "Software engineering," *IEEE Trans. Comput.*, vol. C-25, pp. 1226–1241, Dec. 1976.

[3] H. Gomaa and D. Scott, "Prototyping as a tool in the specification of user requirements," in *Proc. 5th IEEE Int. Conf. Software Eng.*, Mar. 1981, pp. 333–342.

[4] B. W. Boehm, "A spiral model of software development and enhancement," *ACM SIGSOFT Software Eng. Notes*, vol. 11, no. 4, pp. 14–24, Aug. 1986; reprinted in *Computer*, vol. 21, no. 5, pp. 61–72, May 1988.

[5] E. Hirsch, "Evolutionary acquisition of command and control systems," *Program Manager*, pp. 18–22, Nov.–Dec. 1985.

[6] D. McCracken and M. Jackson, "Life cycle concept considered harmful," *ACM SIGSOFT Software Eng. Notes*, vol. 7, no. 2, pp. 29–32, Apr. 1982.

[7] T. C. Jones, "Reusability in programming: A survey of the state of the art," *IEEE Trans. Software Eng.*, vol. SE-10, pp. 488–494, Sept. 1984.

[8] H. Partsch and R. Steinbrüggen, "Program transformation systems," *ACM Comput. Surveys*, vol. 15, no. 3, pp. 199–236, Sept. 1983.

[9] D. R. Barstow, *Knowledge-Based Program Construction.* New York: North Holland, 1979.

[10] D. L. Parnas, "Can automatic programming solve the SDI software problem?," in "Software aspects of strategic defense systems," *Amer. Sci.*, vol. 73, pp. 432–440, Sept.–Oct. 1985.

[11] T. DeMarco, *Controlling Software Projects.* New York: Yourdon, 1982.

[12] E. Bersoff, "Elements of software configuration management," *IEEE Trans. Software Eng.*, vol. SE-10, pp. 79–87, Jan. 1984.

Alan M. Davis (M'80–SM'80) received the B.S. degree in mathematics from the State University of New York, Albany, in 1970 and the M.S. and Ph.D. degrees in computer science from the University of Illinois, Champaign-Urbana, in 1973 and 1975, respectively.

He is Vice President and Director of Engineering Services at BTG, Inc., Vienna, VA, where he is responsible for all service-related aspects of BTG's business, including product assurance, SETA, training, and systems analysis. Prior to that, he was Director of Research at BTG, responsible for all aspects of corporate research, and Director of Engineering Technology at BTG, responsible for all software and system engineering consulting and software and system engineering training. Prior to that, he was a Director of Research and Development for GTE Communication Systems, Phoenix, AZ, Director of the Software Technology Center at GTE Laboratories, Inc., Waltham, MA, and an Assistant Professor of Computer Science at the University of Tennessee, Knoxville.

Dr. Davis is the author of numerous papers on software engineering tools and requirements specification techniques and languages. He is currently writing a book entitled *Software Requirements: Analysis and Specifications* (Prentice-Hall).

He is the Chairman of the IEEE Computer Society's Working Group on Software Requirements Standards. He is currently an Associate Editor of *Journal of Systems and Software*, a member of the ACM Computing Practices Advisory Panel, and a past member of the editorial board of *IEEE Software*. He was an IEEE International Distinguished Lecturer in 1983 and in that role toured South America delivering lectures on software requirements specification techniques. He is a member of the Association for Computing Machinery, Sigma Xi, the AFCEA, and the AMA.

Edward H. Bersoff (M'75–SM'78) received the A.B., M.S., and Ph.D. degrees in mathematics from New York University, New York.

He is President and Founder of BTG, Inc., a high-technology systems analysis and engineering firm based in the Washington, DC, area. BTG specializes in the application of modern systems engineering principles to the computer-based system development process. At BTG he has been actively involved in the FAA's Advanced Automation Program, where he is focusing on software management and software configuration management issues in this extremely complex program. He also participates in the company's activities within the naval intelligence community, providing senior consulting services to a wide variety of system development efforts, including the Prototype Ocean Surveillance Terminal (POST), developed by BTG and now deployed worldwide. He was previously President of CTEC, Inc., where he directed the concept formulation and development of the Navy Command and Control System (NCCS) Ocean Surveillance Information System (OSIS) Baseline. He also served as Experiment Director for the Joint ARPA, Navy, and CINCPAC Military Message Experiment. This test was designed to examine the usefulness of secure automated message processing systems in an operational military environment and to develop design criteria for future military message processing systems. Prior to joining CTEC, he was Manager of Engineering Operations and Manager of FAA Operations for the Process Systems Division of Logicon, Inc. He joined Logicon from the NASA Electronics Research Center. He has taught mathematics at universities in Boston, New York, and Washington, DC. His technical contributions to the fields of software requirements and design range from early publications in computer architecture, reliability, and programming languages to more recent publications on software quality and configuration management, including a textbook entitled *Software Configuration Management* (Prentice-Hall).

Dr. Bersoff is a member of the AFCEA, the American Management Association, the Air Traffic Control Association, and Mensa.

Edward R. Comer (M'79) received the B.S. and M.S. degrees in mathematics and the M.S. degree in computer science from the Florida Institute of Technology, Melbourne.

He is President and Founder of Software Productivity Solutions, Inc. (SPS), Melbourne, a software technology company specializing in the development and application of advanced Ada-based methodologies and tools. He has been a primary technical contributor in the development of a number of strategic software technology plans including the research and development plans for the Software Productivity Consortium in the areas of reusable software, software prototyping, and knowledge-based systems for software development; Ada transition plans for a number of corporate clients; and SPS's internal research and development plan for Ada reusability. Prior to founding SPS, he led the Software Technology Section at Harris Government Information Systems, Melbourne. In this role he was responsible for the research, development, and transfer of advanced software techniques and tools for military software. He provided the major technical input and guidance for Harris's integrated software methodology. He was on the original planning group for the Software Technology Project of the Microelectronics and Computer Technology Corporation (MCC). He has developed a number of original techniques for systems requirements definition, Ada software design, interface specification, database design, and structured systems modeling. He also held positions at Harris in modeling and simulation and systems engineering, where he participated in the development of mission-critical systems for command and control, communications, intelligence data handling, avionics, data acquisition, and physical security. He has taught mathematics and computer science at the university level and has taught software and systems engineering courses in a variety of subjects for national seminars and for corporate and government clients.

Mr. Comer has received a Distinguished Engineering Award. He was an author of the first published *Ada Design Language Guide* in industry and participated in the IEEE Ada as a PDL Working Group. He has published numerous papers in database design, Ada design languages, software techniques and environments, communications, and simulation. He was twice the Proceedings Editor of the Annual Simulation Symposium and has served on the program committees of COMSAC 86 and the Ada Applications and Environments Conference. He is a member of the Association for Computing Machinery (SIGAda, SIGSOFT, SIGMOD, and SIGART).

The Dual Life-Cycle Model
An Enterprise Perspective of Software Development[1]

John H. Manley

Professor and Director
Manufacturing Systems Engineering Program
School of Engineering
University of Pittsburgh
Pittsburgh, Pennsylvania 15261
(412) 963-1813

Introduction

Industry and government software professionals continue to debate the relative merits of software product life-cycle models. We urge anyone interested in this question to share our total enterprise perspective of software development as an integrated management-engineering function. This paper reports the results of preliminary research into what all of the players in a large organization do to create large-scale, software-intensive products, with special emphasis on managers.

The broader systems or enterprise-wide view has enabled us to reaffirm the importance of *all* the people who directly affect the software product development process, including not only managers and software engineers, but others, such as facility engineers and accountants. This total enterprise perspective also caused us to gain a deeper appreciation for the incredibly complex web of human relationships and communication paths that affect large-scale software development processes. When we turned our spotlight on what can now be described as the generic communication processes between the hierarchical layers of a software development organization, we found existing software life-cycle models lacking.

This paper reports on an enterprise-wide concept of software development, which is the basis for the large-scale information system birth-to-death life-cycle we are developing. This new integrated, layered, life-cycle conceptual model has been named the **Dual Life-Cycle Model (DLCM).** What is new is that *the DLCM is composed of parallel management and software engineering work product development activities, connected by a defined communications protocol.*

Background

In a recent discussion of software life-cycle models,[1] supporting arguments were presented for yet another in a very long series of candidate models intended to improve the software process. The primary reason for this improved "spiral" model, according to its author Boehm, is that it is risk driven, rather than document or code driven. The latter types have been criticized for years, most recently in a major Department of Defense study published in 1987.[2] Boehm supports his case by providing an excellent chronology of software life-cycle development history, together with reasons why each has been found to be inadequate.

The life-cycle definition problem has also been troublesome to this author for over two decades. As a metallurgical and industrial engineer by formal training, and a software engineer and manager by practice, I have been trying to understand why managers who are responsible for major software development projects frequently have enormous difficulty defining software work packages that can be executed in an orderly manner over the life of a major system development effort. The reason for my frustration is that I have observed that work is planned and executed for large-scale physical systems with complexity comparable to software on a relatively routine basis. When problems arise during a traditional hardware product life cycle, responsible managers and engineers can almost always locate the source of trouble and take prompt corrective action to fix whatever is wrong. Why do we seem to have so much trouble coping with similar software problems, especially those encountered on large-scale information system development projects?

A new perspective on the life-cycle definition problem was gained during the first phase of a major study being performed at the California Institute of Technology's Jet Propulsion Laboratory. The purpose of this continuing

---

[1]The research reported here was supported by the California Institute of Technology's Jet Propulsion Laboratory while the author served as a participant in its Distinguished Visiting Scientist Program.

study, which began in late 1986, is to find ways to reduce the complexity and thereby improve the effectiveness of large-scale information systems engineering and management. To understand the reasons for complexity, we began to examine the following key management and engineering processes:

- Top-level management negotiations with a potential customer for a new product
- Middle-management program and project planning
- Software engineering to include designing, coding, and testing
- System operation and maintenance
- The process of removing a system from service

With respect to the most popular software life-cycle models currently in use, there is general agreement that they are deficient in many ways. The recognized deficiencies are mainly technical or limited to the process. For example, traditional software development models are based largely on a proposed sequence of documentation transformations. It is suspected that these have enabled management to distance itself from significant software problems, since their focus is on the paper product generation and delivery activities, and not on the underlying software product that the paper represents. We have come to recognize that our technical perspective on life-cycle models has been myopic, focusing too intently on the *software* development process life cycle, while ignoring significant precursor activities and influencing factors that occur during *system* concept formulation and feasibility analysis.

Thus, what has been lacking is sufficient consideration of management processes and supporting activities that affect software engineering and especially the information flow between them. With the enterprise view, many significant problems with traditional software life-cycle models become visible, the most important being the abovementioned inadvertent management distance from software, and software professional myopia.

Upon further study, we were surprised to find that the interactions between management and software engineering during the life cycle are not well understood by experienced practitioners and in many ways are actually in conflict. Communications were found to be incomplete, and at best full of distortion and noise. Thus, a follow-on study has been initiated to explore how to connect the software engineering and management processes most efficiently with near noise-free communication channels as practiced on successful projects. To reduce noise we are seeking ways to identify specific information that managers must provide to engineers, and conversely information that engineers must provide to managers. Extraneous information will be targeted for elimination from the process. The goal is to identify a set of *minimum essential information.*

The conceptual model that evolved from this research has become known by the research team as the dual life-cycle model. The new model portrays the conceptual differences between management and software engineering perspectives, as well as the content of communication work products needed to connect management effectively with engineering. A simplified version of the DLCM is shown in Figure 1.

A More Detailed Look at the DLCM

The conceptual dual life-cycle model in Figure 1 draws attention to the communication paths that transfer project information back and forth between the two parallel (dual) life-cycles. Figure 2 represents a more detailed view of the DLCM and illustrates how the specific products produced by software engineers and managers over the complete life of a generic information system product are interrelated.

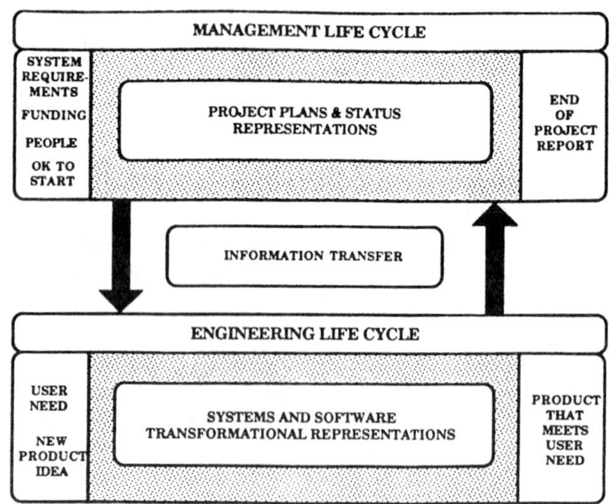

Figure 1: Dual life-cycle model (DLCM) concept

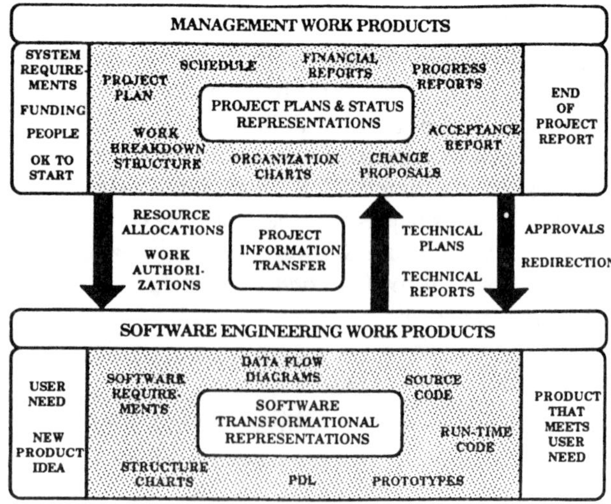

Figure 2: Typical sequence of DLCM work products

Furthermore, all processes within the dual life cycle are initiated by either a user need (technology "pull") or a product idea (technology "push").

To initiate the DLCM, a user need or product idea is transformed into a system concepts document or product specification. This document is used to trigger a series of management actions, which culminate in a formal project approval or rejection to construct and deliver the specified information system product. In addition to approval actions, planning activities delineate project goals, define supporting work packages, and allocate personnel, equipment, and facilities for use on the project.

While management is busy planning, engineers are busy performing technical feasibility studies and conferring with their counterparts in the customer's organization to determine more precisely what will satisfy user needs. At some point, early in the dual life cycle, formal work authorizations are given to the software engineering organization that triggers their participation, along with allocations of resources to carry out their work.

Dual Life-Cycle Artifacts or Work Products

The most important perspective that can be gained from the DLCM concept is the relationship between management and software engineering labor and resulting work products. The primary concern of managers is for project plans and status representations, whereas engineers are primarily concerned with the software product transformation representations shown in Figure 2. This valuable insight, which is obvious from an enterprise perspective, distinguishes the DLCM from the traditional waterfall, acquisition management [3], (2) and variations such as the spiral model.

The dual life-cycle model distinguishes and interrelates four categories of work products that can be represented by an orderly progression of artifacts over the life cycle of any information (or other) system product of interest: (1) communication work products or artifacts produced by managers for engineers, (2) communication artifacts produced by engineers for managers, (3) management artifacts produced by managers for their own use, and (4) technical artifacts produced by engineers for their own use.

In the following paragraphs examples of typical artifacts in each of the above categories are identified in italic type.

Artifacts Produced by Managers for Engineers

Managers are responsible for planning, organizing, staffing, directing, and controlling software engineering activities. They manage engineers by providing them with *authorizations* to begin work and to use specified resources. As projects progress, they monitor and evaluate technical progress by analyzing technical *plans* and *reports*. Managers control work by redirecting specific activities and issuing new *approvals*. Finally, they terminate work by issuing new *task orders* to replace current orders.(3)

Artifacts Produced by Engineers for Managers

Software engineers are responsible for planning, organizing, and carrying out information system development activities. They communicate with management by providing *work plans* for approval and *progress reports* on their accomplishments.

The project information transfer products described above which are exchanged between the two DLCM layers are difficult to prepare, since they involve communication between two quite different cultures. Thus, they are often not the work products of primary interest to the players in either layer who prepare them. Work products of primary interest to most individuals are those pertaining to their own fields of expertise, such as those described below.

Artifacts Produced by Management for Management

Work products created by management for its own use consist of *resource allocation and control documents,* such as work breakdown structures, organization charts, project schedules, financial reports, change proposals, and so forth. These work products are the primary concern of management and make up the only category of products observed in traditional management process descriptions.

Artifacts Produced by Engineers for Engineers

Systems and software engineers are primarily concerned with producing technical *specifications,* software *design representations,* working *prototypes, source code,* and ultimately a run-time product of high quality that satisfies user needs. These work products are the primary concern of software engineers and make up the only category of products observed in traditional software engineering process descriptions.

Work Product Summary

In summary, four categories of work products or artifacts have been identified using the DLCM conceptual model. These are highlighted in Figure 3.

---

(2) A current example of an acquisition management life cycle is that promulgated by the Department of Defense as DOD-STD-2167A [3].

---

(3) Note that these same types of activities are carried out by the higher layers of program, enterprise and customer management, but in less detail the higher the management layer in the hierarchy.

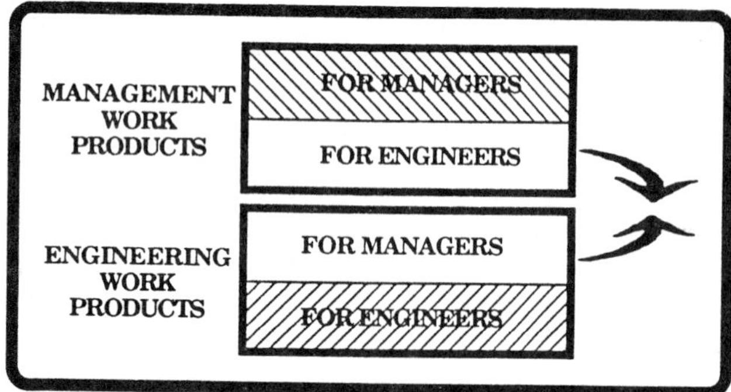

Figure 3: A summary of DLCM work products

An enormous body of literature exists on the best ways to produce management work products that are useful to managers. A smaller but growing body of literature is available on how software engineers should create work products for their own use during the process of developing information systems. Missing from the current literature is a description of the minimum, yet essential, life-cycle information artifacts that should be produced by managers and software engineers for each other noted above. Properly produced and utilized, these essential communication work products can reduce complexity and improve the effectiveness of both management and software engineering process activities.

Understanding information transfer work products, their development, and use is at the heart of the author's current research involving automated manufacturing systems at the University of Pittsburgh. The DLCM and its total enterprise perspective has contributed significantly to our understanding of how large-scale information systems can be developed successfully by effective management and engineering.

Bringing the DLCM to Life in the Real World

Fundamental to actually implementing the DLCM is a mutual understanding by line managers and software engineers of how to make effective use of the total enterprise objectives and goals developed for them by enterprise management. In other words, the personnel in all management and software development layers of the DLCM must clearly understand organizational objectives and must know the specific goals they are trying to achieve as individual members of the team. Without this mutual understanding of each other's roles, complex undertakings face an unnecessary risk of failure.

Therefore, management communication to engineers in the form of management information work products for engineers is critical for success. An organization's statement of "the business we are in" (vision or mission), organizational objectives (timeless purposes), measurable and scheduled goals (milestones), supporting action plans (building-block projects), and specific work packages (well-defined support activities) constitute a hierarchical, linked set of information work products. Taken together, they communicate actions to be taken by subordinates for making things happen in a proactive, constructive, and efficient manner. The model in Figure 4 shows how these management information products conceptually fit together.

Competent managers usually use a goal-setting approach to follow an orderly path to positive results.[4,5] They seldom succumb to the press of unexpected, high-priority interrupts. They stick to the basics. The approach to management communication shown in Figure 4 incorporates these fundamentals and is highly recommended. To help with its implementation and use, the communication work products are defined in more detail as follows:

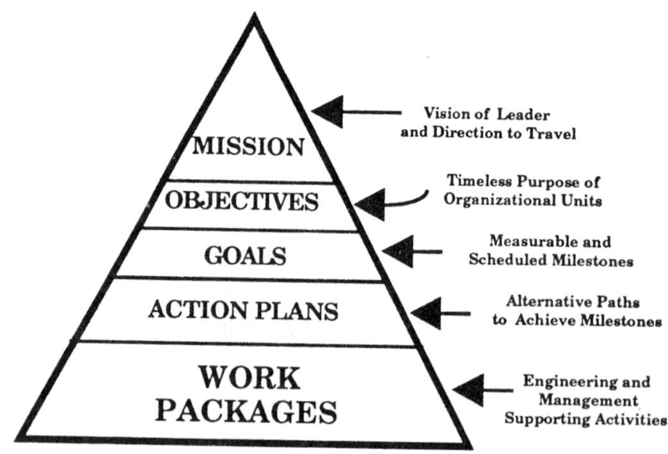

Adapted from King, W. R. and D. I. Cleland, *Strategic Planning and Policy*, Van Nostrand Reinhold Company, New York, 1981, pp. 133-138.

Figure 4: Hierarchy of management communication work products

Mission: A statement describing the well-defined business(es) the organization currently conducts or, alternatively, a visionary statement of what business(es) the organization would like to conduct, in other words, the organization's fundamental reason for existence.

Objective: A timeless, broad-based, generalized statement of intent that supports the organizational mission.

Goal: A statement of specific intent that is quantitatively measurable and bounded by a specific period of time.

Action plan: A work plan detailing measurable steps that focus on achieving a specific goal or, alternatively, one of several work plans required to accomplish a single goal.

Work package: A description of how to perform a supporting activity or task. This can include how to set up a workplace, the major steps involved to accomplish the task, supporting method and tool descriptions, and the criteria or tests required to determine when the task has been satisfactorily completed.

From an enterprise viewpoint, the importance of employing these common-sense management tools to achieve organizational success in an engineering-oriented domain is obvious. They ensure that everyone in an organization shares the same vision of the future and thus understands how their day-to-day tasks help move the organization toward its goal.

When we combine the information products produced by engineers for managers, we have all of the building blocks necessary for effective communications between the DLCM layers. In short, they support a closed-loop process that permits management to define broad objectives, to translate them into specific work packages, and to obtain quantitative feedback on the results.

Defining the DLCM in a Hypothetical Organization

To help understand how the dual life-cycle model can be applied to an actual business enterprise, we will examine Figure 5 to see how a large-scale software system is developed by any organization, government, or commercial company for an external sponsor or customer.[4]

Figure 5 illustrates how an enterprise's top management team can be responsible for approving the scope and con-

[4] It is interesting to note that the same principles apply to any internal information system engineering organization that provides large-scale systems for other units within the same enterprise (for example data processing developing a shop-floor control system for manufacturing), just as software vendors develop systems for their external customers.

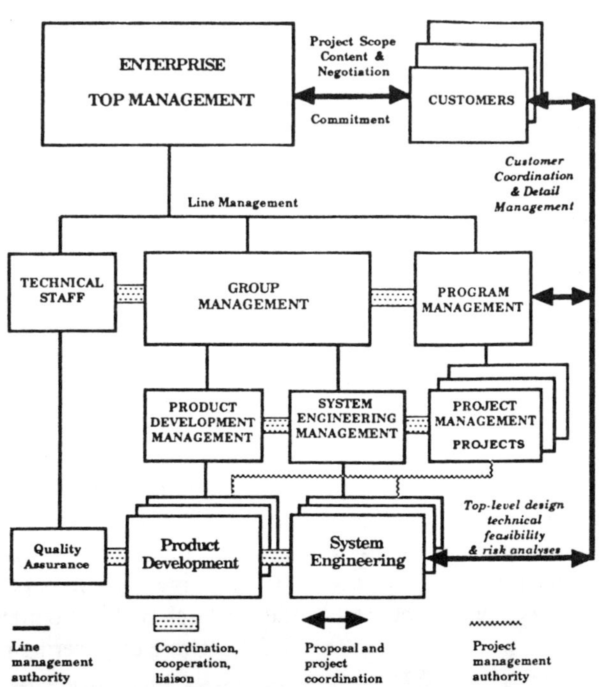

Figure 5: Enterprise perspective of selected management and engineering relationships

tent of new contracts and for formally committing the organization through a contractual process to project acceptance.[5] On the right-hand side of Figure 5 activities that occur during the negotiation phase, at the beginning of the system life cycle, are shown in italics. They include detailed technical feasibility studies, risk analysis, and even some top-level design. This last activity is often performed by software engineers before the company is awarded the contract. Such technical decisions result in constraints on the software development life cycle, discussed more fully later.

Once the contract is signed, a formal project is approved and the management team begins to allocate company resources to carry it out. When multiple projects are already underway, a *program office* is made responsible for rationalizing how the enterprise's project resources will be reallocated to accommodate the new project. For example, when managers are responsible for more than one system development project at a time, they are actually managing a continually changing stream of projects. If a manager is concerned with a single project (or project-like task), then he or she is involved with classical *project management*. To differentiate those higher-level managers having responsibility for more than one project from single-project managers, companies commonly use the terminology *program office management*.

It is important to note the ripple effects that a newly accepted project can have on the existing organization. For example, the impact of program office resource allocation decisions will not only affect the newly awarded project, but personnel and scarce tools, such as high-powered workstations. Even mainframes may be taken away from ongoing projects to satisfy the newly accepted project's requirements. The new project may tip the scales in favor of important investment decisions. For example, an investment in a whole new software engineering environment that will benefit everyone may result. Such consequences stem from cooperative arrangements made in the "matrix management" area shown in Figure 4.

Eventually the project manager receives the required resources and begins detailed work planning on how best to use them to meet the schedule and product performance criteria. Here begins a continuous series of trade-offs that must be made over the entire software product development life cycle with respect to time, cost, and system performance.

In order for program and project managers to respond to the direction of the enterprise's top management team (usually stated in the form of an organizational mission statement reflecting their vision for the future), it is logical to perform a stepwise refinement of the global objectives as expressed by the leadership, using a repeatable process. The goal of the process is to develop building blocks in the form of well-defined, executable activities or work packages. The steps required to implement this process include:

1. Defining the objectives or timeless purposes (subordinate missions) of all organizational units that are independent of individual project requirements
2. Listing the necessary and sufficient, quantitative, and time-bounded goals or specific milestones that will support the project
3. Developing alternative action plans or strategies (sequences of steps and alternative courses of action) to achieve every milestone
4. Defining implementing activities (sets of precedence-related work packages necessary to achieve a specific milestone)
5. Detailing the specific management and engineering activities (work packages) necessary to complete each project

Using the DLCM to Simplify Management Complexity

The research challenge we are undertaking is to rationalize and simplify the complexity of enterprise management. An understandable top layer of the DLCM is the first goal. We will define the most important generic objectives, goals, and work packages considered minimally essential for success. Then, we will define what management needs to provide to engineering for the software engineers to carry out their assigned responsibilities effectively. Finally, we will take existing software product life-cycle models used by major organizations and link them to generic, prescriptive management actions through the *minimum essential information communication network* that is our current research focus.

Requirements Specifications: The Starting Point

The DLCM enterprise perspective of software development leads to the conclusion that the relationship of an information system management process to a software engineering process is considerably more complex than is generally discussed in either the existing management or software engineering literature. The complicated communication structure illustrated in Figure 5 provides just one example to support this assertion. In spite of the formidable complexity associated with this view, we suggest that this larger systems perspective be used as a basis for further research on how to improve the management of large-scale software engineering process activities.

Figure 6 illustrates a first step in using this enterprise DLCM perspective to improve our understanding of management-software engineering relationships. Specifically,

[5] If the project is on behalf of an external customer, the contractual process is a formal legal process.

Figure 6 shows how software and hardware engineering processes are embedded in a system engineering context. Furthermore, it shows how project management for a specific software engineering product development process is a subset of the overall enterprise management system.

Software engineers normally begin formal work on a large-scale information system by analyzing software requirements documentation provided by management and system engineers. This requirements information is represented in Figure 6 by both a technical information vector, Ir, and a management information vector, Ims. Taken together, these vectors provide information to initiate the software engineering process of the engineering layer of the DLCM. Figure 6 also indicates that technical requirements contained in Ir are transformed by software engineering into an output vector I*, representing run-time code embedded in the object information system. The significance of Ir to our research is that it constitutes the generally accepted starting basis for a software product life cycle.

Ir is often a lengthy requirements document that details user technical needs to be satisfied with software. Software requirements documents for large-scale information systems are often developed by multidisciplinary committees. They require considerable additional work to reduce their ambiguity and to complete missing elements before they are useful as an input to software design activities.

It seems reasonable that a detailed analysis of how Ir development is managed during the earliest stages of the total system product life cycle will improve understanding of how to improve this critical first phase of the dual life cycle. In concept, management information passed to engineers engaged in front-end system activities is represented by Ims, with feedback represented by the vector I*ms. The Im and I*m vectors represent management information and feedback affecting the later phases of software engineering activities under the DLCM concept.

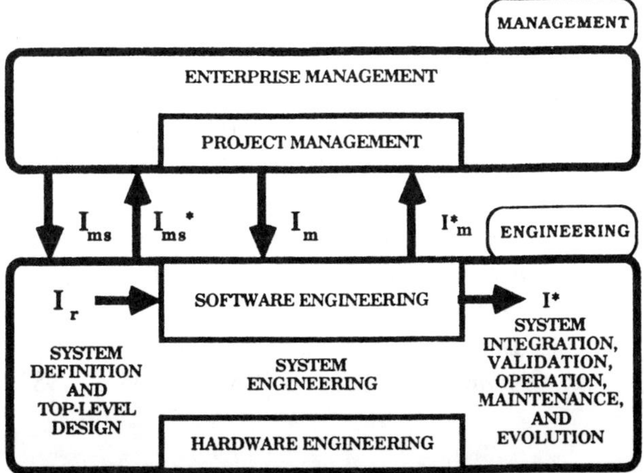

Figure 6: DLCM management and software engineering relationships

In addition to omissons and ambiguities occurring during the front end of the life cycle, we must also take into account the many critical software technical constraints that are often included in the requirements information vector Ir. For example, hardware memory size limitations, programming language preferences, required software development tool chains, and similar elements are often specified as "givens" to software engineers by management as a result of this process.

Current Research Activities

Our current research focuses on the front end of the information system product life cycle. Referring to Figure 6, we are interested in the specific management and system engineering activities that generate the technical information vector Ir. We are analyzing both government and commercial system and software engineering practices to help us identify the minimum essential management information contained in the vector Ims, as well as the technical feedback information from engineering, I*ms. Together, these vectors have an important influence on the software engineering requirements specification vector Ir.[6]

The preliminary work of both management and system engineering results in the development of constraints on the yet-to-be-authorized software development process. Top-level design decisions are being made, as are decisions on the specific personnel to be assigned to the project and the tooling they will be given to carry out their work. The DLCM formalizes this pre-project work and, by doing so, avoids decision failures during the subsequent software engineering activities.

Expected Research Results

We recognize that we are a long way from fully understanding the more important mechanisms involved in the dual life-cycle model. However, we are optimistic that our research will lead to major improvements over current practice.

Three natural results can be derived from this research program. Together, they can significantly improve any organization's ability to build complex, large-scale informa-

[6] Although not shown explicitly in Figure 6, there is also a parallel information vector that provides requirements for the displayed hardware engineering life cycle. We are also examining a small number of related system management and engineering front-end practices for hardware, in the hope that this effort will improve our understanding of the software elements of primary interest.

tion systems. These are not novel, but fit nicely into the context of the organizational management improvement strategy described above. Specific results to be expected are:

1. *Improved product quality:* A better understanding of the specific work packages that make up the software life-cycle process by both managers and software engineers, combined with the elimination of extraneous information requirements, will allow more time for everyone to find ways to do the right jobs better. We expect that the products received by the organization's customers will be of significantly higher quality.
2. *Increased organizational productivity:* A simplified information system life-cycle development process and improved two-way communications between managers and engineers will likely result in a significant increase in overall organizational productivity.
3. *Increased organizational competitiveness:* When productivity and product quality improve, the competitive position of a business in the marketplace is enhanced. Similarly, government organizations, such as the National Aeronautics and Space Administration, in a "race for space" with other countries, will improve their competitive positions.

Attaining these results presupposes that an enterprise's top management levels possess the vision and leadership to support constructive change. We hope that suggested improvements stemming from this research that simplify both work product and process complexities will be welcomed by management at all levels. Management "pull" for improved practices ensures their eventual implementation and, more important moves the state of information system life-cycle practice, especially software development, one step closer to an accepted and respectable engineering profession.

Summary and Conclusions

A brief description of a new software product life-cycle model has been presented. It is composed of parallel management and engineering processes interacting through a complex communication system. The dual life-cycle model distinguishes between artifacts or tangible work products produced by managers for engineers, and those produced by engineers for managers, in addition to what managers and engineers produce for their own use. Each of these four categories of work products can be identified as part of an orderly progression of artifacts over the life cycle of any information (or other) system product of interest.

It has been shown how the DLCM concept can be operationalized using a time-tested and well-organized approach to management. This process produces a closed-loop communication system that is fundamental to sound information system life-cycle practice.

Finally, the purpose of the research program that prompted definition of the DLCM was to seek new ways to reduce complexity and to improve overall effectiveness when engineering large-scale information systems. The DLCM concept provides a basis for these research activities. Much of what is learned from this research effort can be applied to other types of complex, large-scale system engineering product life-cycle processes in industry as well as government organizations. The opportunities appear to be endless!

Acknowledgments

We acknowledge and sincerely appreciate the efforts of many people who are supporting this research at the Jet Propulsion Laboratory and thank them for their contributions. In particular, the original concept of the DLCM is attributed to Arthur I. Zygielbaum, former deputy manager of the Information Systems Division, who originally sponsored this research and is continuing to provide advice and support. Other major contributors who are helping to refine and test DLCM concepts at the Jet Propulsion Laboratory include Charles Beswick, Ed Ng, Thomas Fouser, Chi Lin, Merle McKenzie, and Robert Tauseworthe. I also thank David Baker of the General Electric Corporation for his excellent suggestions for improving both the paper and its underlying models.

References

[1] Boehm, Barry W., "A Spiral Model of Software Development and Enhancement," *Computer,* May 1988, pp. 61-72.

[2] Brooks, F.P., Jr., Chairman, *Defense Science Board Task Force Report on Military Software,* Office of the Under Secretary of Defense for Acquisition, Washington, D.C., September 1987.

[3] Military Standard, Defense Systems Software Development, *DOD-STD 2167A,* Department of Defense, February 29, 1988.

[4] Cleland, David I. and William R. King, *Project Management Handbook,* Van Nostrand Reinhold Company, New York, 1983.

[5] Koenig, Daniel T., *Manufacturing Engineering: Principles for Optimization,* Harper & Row, New York, 1987.

A Spiral Model of Software Development and Enhancement

Barry W. Boehm
TRW Defense Systems Group

1. Introduction

1.1 Overview

The spiral model of software development and enhancement presented here provides a new framework for guiding the software process. Its major distinguishing feature is that it creates a *risk-driven* approach to the software process, rather than a primarily document- driven or code-driven process. It incorporates many of the strengths of other models, while resolving many of their difficulties.

This section presents a short motivational and historical background of software process models and the issues they address. Section 2 summarizes the process steps involved in the spiral model. Section 3 illustrates the application of the spiral model to a software project, using the TRW Software Productivity Project as an example. Section 4 summarizes the primary advantages and implications involved in using the spiral model, and the primary difficulties in using it at its current incomplete level of elaboration. Section 5 presents the resulting conclusions.

1.2 Background

The primary function of a software process model is to determine the *order of the stages* involved in software development and evolution, and to establish the *transition criteria* for progressing from one stage to the next. Thus, a process model addresses the following software project questions:

(1) What shall we do next?

(2) How long shall we continue to do it?

Thus, a process model differs from a software *method* (often called a *methodology*) in that the latter's primary focus is on *how to navigate through each phase* (determining data, control, or "uses" hierarchies; partitioning functions, allocating requirements) and how to represent phase products (structure charts; stimulus-response threads; state transition diagrams).

Why are software process models important? Primarily because they provide guidance on the order in which a project should carry out its major tasks: phases, increments, prototypes, validation tasks, etc.. Many software projects have come to grief because they pursued their various development and evolution phases in the wrong order. The next section illustrates this via a short historical review of software process models.

1.3 Evolution of Process Models

The "Code and Fix" Model

The basic model used in the earliest days of software development contained two steps:

(1) Write some code;

(2) Fix the problems in the code.

The primary difficulties with this model were:

a. After a number of fixes, the code became so poorly structured that subsequent fixes were very expensive. This highlighted the need for a design phase previous to coding.

b. Frequently, even well-designed software was such a poor match to users' needs that it was either rejected outright or expensively redeveloped. This highlighted the need for a requirements phase previous to design.

c. Code was expensive to fix because of poor preparation for testing and modification. This highlighted the need for explicit recognition of these phases, and for test and evolution planning and preparation tasks in the early phases.

The Stagewise Model and the Waterfall Model

Even by 1956, experience on large software systems such as SAGE had led to the recognition of these problems, and to the development of a stagewise model [Benington, 1956][1] to address them. This model stipulated that software be developed in successive stages (operational plan, operational specifications, coding specifications, coding, parameter testing, assembly testing, shakedown, system evaluation).

The original treatment of the *waterfall model* given in [Royce, 1970][2] provided two primary enhancements to the stagewise model:

EH0304-6/90/0000/0513$01.00

Reprinted from *Software Engineering Project Management*, 1987, pages 128-142.

- Recognition of the feedback loops between stages, and a guideline to confine the feedback loops to successive stages, in order to minimize the expensive rework involved in feedback across many stages.
- An initial incorporation of prototyping in the software life-cycle, via a "build it twice" step running in parallel with requirements analysis and design.

The waterfall approach was largely consistent with the *top-down structured programming model* formulated in [Dijkstra, 1970][3] and [Mills, 1971].[4] However, some attempts to apply these versions of the waterfall model ran into the following kinds of difficulties:

- The "build it twice" step was unnecessary in applications where design issues were well-understood (e.g., developing a straightforward payroll system), and subject to such unproductive phenomena as the "second system syndrome" [Brooks, 1975][5], in which the second system is overloaded with baroque embellishments.
- The pure top-down approach needed to be tempered with a "look ahead" step to cover such issues as high-risk, low-level elements and reusable or common software modules.

These considerations resulted in the *risk-management variant* of the waterfall model discussed in [Boehm, 1975][6] and elaborated in [Boehm, 1976].[7] In this variant, each step was expanded to include a validation and verification activity to cover high-risk elements, reuse considerations, and prototyping. Further refinements of the waterfall model covered such practices as incremental development [Distaso, 1980][8], developing program families and organizing software to accommodate change via information hiding [Parnas, 1979][9] and distinguishing pre-specification and post-specification activities via the "two-leg" model [Lehman, 1984].[10]

The successive stages used in the waterfall model helped eliminate many of the difficulties previously encountered on software projects. The waterfall model has become the basis of most software acquisition standards in government and industry. But even with the extensive revisions and refinements of the waterfall model, its basic scheme has encountered significant difficulties, and these have led to the formulation of alternative process models.

The Evolutionary Development Model

A primary source of difficulty with the waterfall model has been its emphasis on fully-elaborated documents as completion criteria for early requirements and design phases. For some classes of software, such as compilers or secure operating systems, this is the most effective way to proceed. But it does not work well for many classes of software, particularly interactive end-user applications. Document-driven standards have pushed many projects to write elaborate specifications of poorly-understood user interfaces and decision-support functions, followed by the design and development of large quantities of unusable code. Further, in areas supported by fourth-generation languages (spread sheet or small business applications), it is clearly unnecessary to write elaborate specifications for one's application before implementing it.

These concerns have led to the formulation of the *evolutionary development* model [McCracken-Jackson, 1982],[11] whose stages consist of expanding increments of an operational software product, with the directions of evolution being determined by operational experience.

The evolutionary development model is ideally matched to a fourth generation language application, and well matched to situations in which users say, "I can't tell you what I want, but I'll know it when I see it." It gives users a rapid initial operational capability, and provides a realistic operational basis for determining subsequent product improvements.

But evolutionary development has its difficulties also. It is generally difficult to distinguish from the old "code and fix" model, whose spaghetti code and lack of planning were the initial motivation for the waterfall model. It is also based on the often-unrealistic assumption that the user's operational system will be flexible enough to accommodate unplanned evolution paths. This assumption is unjustified in three primary situations:

- Situations in which several independently-evolved applications must subsequently be closely integrated;
- "Information-sclerosis" situations in which temporary work-arounds for software deficiencies increasingly solidify into unchangeable constraints on evolution. A typical example is the following comment: "It's nice that you could change those equipment codes to make them more intelligible for us, but the Codes Committee just met and established the current codes as company standards."
- Bridging situations, in which the new software is incrementally replacing a large existing system. If the existing system is poorly modularized, it is difficult to provide a good sequence of "bridges" between the old software and the expanding increments of new software.

The Transform Model

The "spaghetti code" difficulties of the evolutionary development and code-and-fix models can also become a difficulty in various classes of waterfall-model applications, in which code is optimized for performance and becomes increasingly difficult to modify. The transform model [Balzer-Cheatham-Green, 1983][12] has been proposed as a solution to this difficulty.

The transform model assumes the existence of a capability to automatically transform a formal specification of a software product into a program satisfying the specification. The steps then prescribed by the transform model are:

- A formal specification of the best initial understanding of the desired product;
- Automatic transformation of the specification into code;
- An iterative loop if necessary to improve the performance of the resulting code by giving optimization guidance to the transformation system;
- Exercise of the resulting product; and
- An outer iterative loop to adjust the specification based on the resulting operational experience, and to rederive, re-optimize, and exercise the adjusted software product.

The transform model thus avoids the difficulty of having to modify code which has become poorly structured through repeated re-optimizations, since the modifications are made to the specification. It also avoids the extra time and expense involved in the intermediate design, code, and test activities.

But the transform model has various difficulties as well. Automatic transformation capabilities are only available for small products in a few limited areas: spread sheets, small fourth generation language applications, and limited computer-science domains. The transform model also shares some of the difficulties of the evolutionary development model, such as the assumption that users' operational systems will always be flexible enough to support unplanned evolution paths. And it would face a formidable knowledge-base-maintenance problem in dealing with the rapidly increasing and evolving supply of reusable software components and commercial software products.

2. The Spiral Model

The spiral model of the software process has been evolving at TRW for several years, based on experience with various refinements of the waterfall model as applied to large government software projects. The spiral model includes most previous models as special cases, and further provides guidance as to which combination of previous models best fits a given software situation. Its most complete application to date has been to the development of the TRW Software Productivity System; this application will be described in Section 3.

The spiral model is illustrated in Figure 1. The radial dimension in Figure 1 represents the cumulative cost incurred in accomplishing the steps to date; the angular dimension represents the progress made in completing each cycle of the spiral. (The model holds that each cycle involves a progression through the same sequence of steps, for each portion of the product and for each of its levels of elaboration, from an overall concept of operation document down to the coding of each individual program). Note that some artistic license has been taken with the increasing cumulative cost dimension in order to enhance legibility of the steps in Figure 1.

2.1 A Typical Cycle of the Spiral

Each cycle of the spiral begins with the identification of:

- The objectives of the portion of the product being elaborated (performance, functionality, ability to accommodate change, etc).
- The alternative means of implementing this portion of the product (design A, design B, reuse, buy, etc).
- The constraints imposed on the application of the alternatives (cost, schedule, interface, etc.).

The next step is to evaluate the alternatives with respect to the objectives and constraints. Frequently, this process will identify areas of uncertainity which are significant sources of project risk. If so, the next step should involve the formulation of a cost-effective strategy for resolving the sources of risk. This may involve prototyping, simulation, administering user questionnaires, analytic modeling, or combinations of these and other risk-resolution techniques.

Once the risks are evaluated, the next step is determined by the relative risks remaining. If performance or user-interface risks strongly dominate program development or internal interface-control risks, the next step may be an evolutionary development step: a minimal effort to specify the overall nature of the product, a plan for the next level of prototyping, and the development of a more detailed prototype to continue to resolve the major risk issues. If this prototype is operationally useful, and robust enough to serve as a low-risk base for future product evolution, then the subsequent risk-driven steps would be the evolving series of evolutionary prototypes going toward the right in Figure 1.

On the other hand, if previous prototyping efforts have already resolved all of the performance or user-interface risks, and program development or interface-control risks dominate, the next step follows the basic waterfall approach (concept of operation, software requirements, preliminary design, etc. in Figure 1), modified as appropriate to incorporate incremental development. Each level of software specification in Figure 1 is then followed by a validation step and the preparation of plans for the succeeding cycle.

The spiral model also accommodates any appropriate mixture of a specification-oriented, prototype-oriented, simulation-oriented, automatic transformation-oriented, or other approach to software development, where the appropriate mixed strategy is chosen by considering the relative mag-

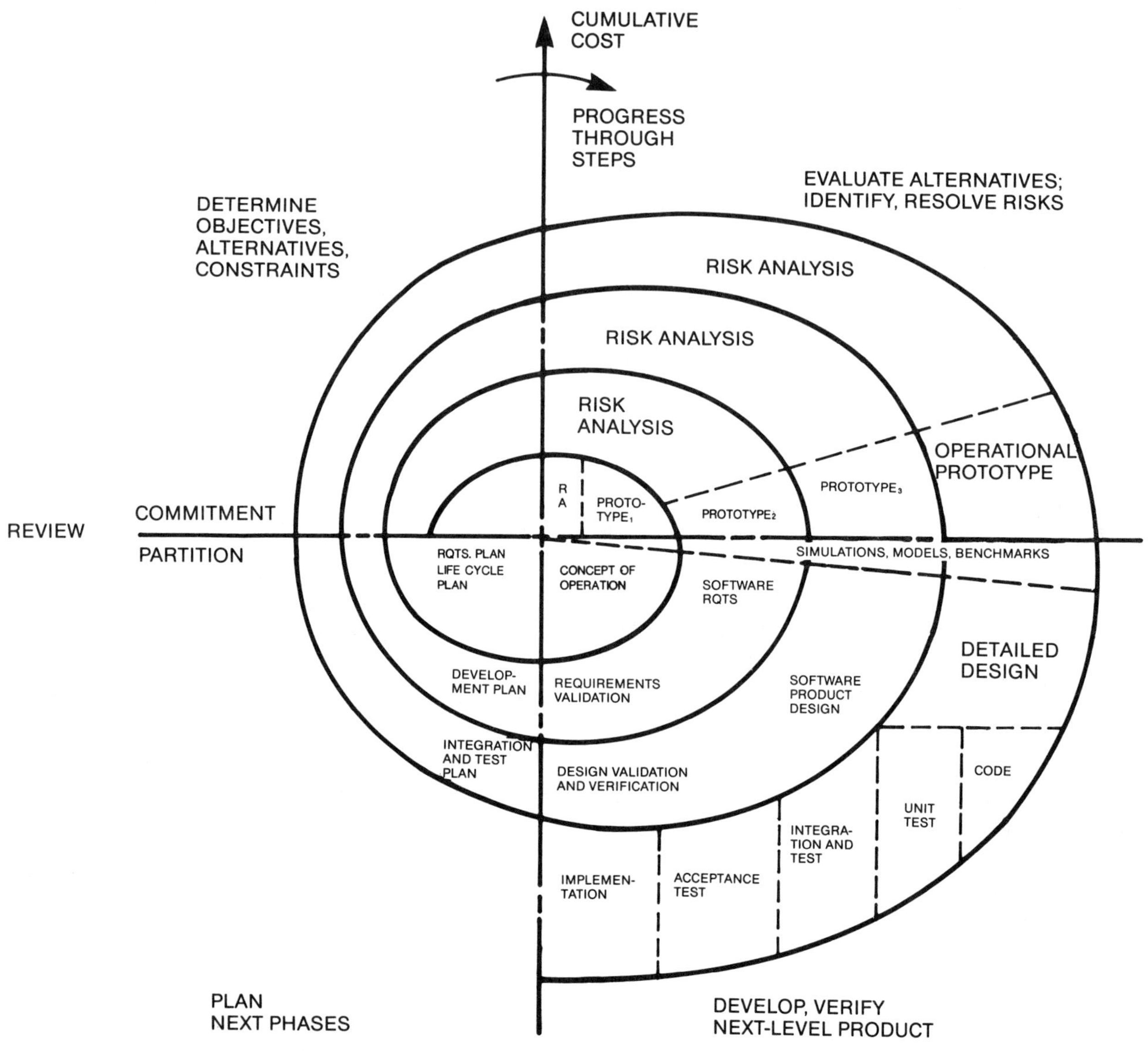

Figure 1: Spiral Model of the Software Process

nitude of the program risks, and the relative effectiveness of the various techniques in resolving the risks. (In a similar way, risk-management considerations determine the amount of time and effort which should be devoted to such other project activities as planning, configuration management, quality assurance, formal verification, or testing).

An important feature of the spiral model is that each cycle is completed by a review involving the primary people or organizations concerned with the product. This review covers all of the products developed during the previous cycle, including the plans for the next cycle and the resources required to carry them out. The major objective of the review is to ensure that all concerned parties are mutually committed to the approach to be taken for the next phase.

The plans for succeeding phases may also include a partition of the product into increments for successive development, or components to be developed by individual organizations or persons. Thus, the review and commitment step may range from an individual walkthrough of the design of a single programmer's component, to a major requirements review involving developer, customer, user, and maintenance organizations.

2.2 Initiating and Terminating the Spiral''

Four fundamental questions arise in considering this presentation of the spiral model:

(1) How does the spiral ever get started?

(2) How do you get off the spiral when it is appropriate to terminate a project early?

(3) Why does the spiral end so abruptly?

(4) What happens to software enhancement (or "maintenance")?

The answer to these questions involves an observation that the spiral model applies equally well to development or enhancement efforts, each of which are initiated by a hypothesis that a particular operational mission (or set of missions) could be improved by a software effort. The spiral process then involves a test of this hypothesis: at any time, if the hypothesis fails the test, the spiral is terminated. Otherwise, it terminates in the installation of the new or modified software, and the hypothesis is tested by observing the effect on the operational mission. Initiation, termination, and iteration of the tasks and products of previous cycles are thus implicitly defined in the spiral model, but not included in Figure 1 in order to simplify its presentation.

Similar spiral-type models have been defined in other fields. [Kolb, 1973][13] defines a four-stage development cycle whose stages are called divergence, assimilation, convergence, and execution. An example of its application to commercial product research and development is given in [Carlsson-Keane-Martin, 1976].[14] The book *Getting to Yes* [Fisher-Ury, 1981][15] defines a four-stage cycle for developing negotiation options; its stages are called problem, analysis, approaches, and action ideas.

3. Using The Spiral Model: The TRW Software Productivity System

The various rounds and activities involved in the spiral model are best understood via an example. This section will show how the spiral model was used in the definition and development of the TRW Software Productivity System (SPS), an integrated software engineering environment described in [Boehm et al., 1984].[16] The initial mission opportunity coincided with a corporate initiative to improve productivity in all appropriate corporate operations, and an initial hypothesis that software engineering was a potentially attractive area to investigate. This initially led to a small, extra "Round 0" circuit of the spiral to determine whether it was feasible to significantly increase software productivity at a reasonable corporate cost. (Very large or complex software projects will frequently precede the "concept of operation" round of the spiral with one or more smaller rounds to establish feasibility and to reduce the range of alternative solutions quickly and inexpensively).

Tables 1, 2, and 3 summarize the application of the spiral model to the first three rounds of defining the SPS. The major features of each round are discussed below, followed by some examples from later rounds such as preliminary and detailed design.

3.1. Round 0: Feasibility Study

This study involved five part-time participants over roughly a 2-3 month time span in 1980. As indicated in Table 1, the objectives and constraints for this round are expressed at a very high level, and in more qualitative terms: "significantly increase," "at reasonable cost," etc.

Round 0 considered a wide number of alternative approaches to significantly improve software productivity at a reasonable cost. Some of these primarily in the "technology" area could lead to the development of a software product, but these were also a number of alternatives in the management, personnel, and facilities areas which could have led to a conclusion not to embark on a software development activity.

The primary risk areas needing resolution were the possibility of situations in which the company would invest a good deal into improving software productivity and find that:

- The resulting productivity gains would not be significant; or that
- Any potentially high-leverage improvements would be incompatible with some aspects of the "TRW culture"

The risk-resolution activities undertaken in Round 0 were primarily surveys and analyses, including structured interviews of software developers and managers; an initial analysis of productivity leverage factors identified by the COCOMO software cost model (see [Boehm, 1981][16], Chapter 33); and an analysis of previous projects at TRW exhibiting high levels of productivity.

The risk analysis results indicated that it was highly likely that significant productivity gains could be achieved at a reasonable cost by pursuing an integrated set of initiatives in the four major areas. However, some candidate solutions, such as a software support environment based on a single, corporate, maxicomputer-based time-sharing system, were found to be in conflict with TRW constraints requiring support of different levels of security-classified projects. Thus, even at a very high level of generality of objectives and constraints, Round 0 was able to answer basic feasibility questions and eliminate significant classes of candidate solutions.

The plan for Round 1 involved a level of commitment on the order of 12 man-months as compared to the 2 man-months invested in Round 0 (During these rounds, all participants were part-time). Round 1 here corresponded fairly well with the initial round of the spiral model shown in Figure 1, in that its intent was to produce a concept of operation and a basic life-cycle plan for implementing whatever preferred alternative emerged.

Table 1: Spiral Model Usage: TRW Software Productivity System, Round 0

Objectives	• Significantly Increase Software Productivity
Constraints	• At Reasonable Cost • Within Context of TRW Culture — Government Contracts, High Tech., People Oriented, Security
Alternatives	• Management : Project Organization, Policies, Planning and Control • Personnel : Staffing, Incentives, Training • Technology : Tools, Workstations, Methods, Reuse • Facilities : Offices, Communications
Risks	• May be no High-Leverage Improvements • Improvements May Violate Constraints
Risk Resolution	• Internal Surveys • Analyze Cost Model • Analyze Exceptional Projects • Literature Search
Risk Resolution Results	• Some Alternatives Infeasible — Single Time Sharing System : Security • Mix of Alternatives Can Produce Significant Gains — Factor of 2 in 5 years • Need Further Study to Determine Best Mix
Plan for Next Phase	• 6-Person Task Force for 6 Months • More Extensive Surveys & Analysis — Internal, External, Economic • Develop Concept of Operation, Economic Rationale
Commitment	• Fund Next Phase

Table 2: Spiral Model Usage: TRW Software Productivity System, Round 1

Objectives	• Double Software Productivity in 5 Years
Constraints	• $10,000 per Person Investment • Within Context of TRW Culture — Government Contracts, High Tech., People Oriented, Security • Preference for TRW Products
Alternatives	• Office : Private/Modular/. . . • Communication : LAN/Star/Concentrators/. . . • Terminals : Private/Shared; Smart/Dumb • Tools : SREM/PSL-PSA/. . .;PDL/SADT/. . . • CPU : IBM/DEC/CDC/. . .
Risks	• May Miss High-Leverage Options • TRW LAN Price/Performance • Workstation Cost
Risk Resolution	• Extensive External Surveys, Visits • TRW LAN Benchmarking • Workstation Price/Performance
Risk Resolution Results	• Ops. Concept : Private Offices, TRW LAN, Personal Terminals, VAX • Begin with Primarily Dumb Terminals; Experiment with Smart Workstations • Defer OS, Tools Selection
Plan for Next Phase	• Partition Effort into SDE, Facilities, Management • Develop First-Cut Prototype SDE — Design-to-Cost : 15 Person Team for 1 Year • Plan for External Usage
Commitment	• Develop Prototype SDE • Commit an Upcoming Project to Use SDE • Commit the SDE to Support the Project • Form Representative Steering Group

3.2. Round 1: Concept of Operations

Table 2 provides a summary of Round 1 of the spiral along the same lines given in Table 1 for Round 0. Rather than simply elaborate on the entries in Table 2, the discussion below focuses on comparing and contrasting the features of Rounds 0 and 1:

- As mentioned above, the level of investment was greater (12 man-months vs. 2).
- The objectives and constraints were more specific ("double software productivity in 5 years at a cost of $l0K/person" vs. "significantly increase productivity at a reasonable cost").
- Additional constraints surfaced, such as the preference for TRW products (particularly, a TRW-developed local area network (LAN) system).
- The alternatives were more detailed ("SREM, PSL/PSA or SADT, as requirements tools etc." vs. "tools"; "private or shared terminals, smart or dumb terminals" vs. "workstations").
- The risk areas identified were more specific ("TRW LAN price-performance within a $10K/person investment constraint" vs. "improvements may violate reasonable-cost constraint").
- The risk-resolution activities were more extensive (including the benchmarking and analysis of a prototype TRW LAN being developed for another project).
- The result was a fairly specific Operational Concept Document, involving private offices tailored to software work patterns, and personal terminals connected to VAX superminis via the TRW LAN. Some choices were specifically deferred to the next round, such as the choice of operating system and specific tools.
- The life-cycle plan and the plan for the next phase involved a a partitioning into separate activities to address management improvements, facilities development, and development of the first increment of a software development environment. (SDE).
- The commitment step involved more than just an agreement with the plan. It added a commitment for an upcoming 100-person software project to be the initial testbed user of the system, and for the environment development to focus on the needs of the testbed project. It also added the formation of a representative steering group to ensure that the separate activities were well-coordinated, and that the environment would not be overly optimized around the testbed project.

Although the plan recommended the development of a prototype environment, it also recommended that the project also employ requirements specifications and design specifications in a risk-driven way. Thus, the development of the environment followed the succeeding rounds of the spiral model.

3.3. Round 2: Top-Level Requirements Specification

Table 3 shows the corresponding steps involved during Round 2 in defining the SPS during early 1981. Since a number of these Round 2 decisions and their rationale are covered in [Boehm et al., 1984],[16] we will not elaborate on them there. Instead, we will summarize two of the highlights dealing with risk management and the use of the spiral model.

- The initial risk-identification activities during Round 2 showed that several system requirements hinged on the decision between a host-target system or a fully portable tool set, and the decision between VMS and Unix as the host operating system. These requirements included the functions required to provide a user-friendly front-end, the operating system to be used by the workstations, and the functions required to support a host-target operation. In order to keep these requirements in synchronization with the other requirements, a special mini-spiral was initiated to address and resolve these issues. The resulting review resulted in a commitment to a host-target operation using Unix on the host system, at a point early enough to work the OS-dependent requirements in a timely fashion.
- Addressing the risks of mismatches to the user-project's needs and priorities resulted in substantial participation of the user-project personnel in the requirements definition activity. This led to several significant redirections of the requirements, particularly toward supporting the early phases of the software life-cycle into which the user project was embarking, such as an adaptation of the Software Requirements Engineering Methodology (SREM) Tools for requirements specification and analysis.

It is also interesting to note that the form of Tables 1, 2, and 3 was originally developed for presentation purposes, but subsequently became a standard "Spiral Model Template" used on later projects. These templates are useful not only for organizing project activities, but also as a residual design-rationale record. Design rationale information is of paramount importance in assessing the potential reusability of software components on future projects.

3.4. Succeeding Rounds of the Spiral"

Within the confines of this paper, it is not possible to discuss each round of the spiral in detail. But it will be useful to illustrate some examples of how the spiral model is used to handle situations arising in the preliminary design and

Table 3: Spiral Model Usage: TRW Software Productivity System, Round 2

Objectives	• User-Friendly System • Integrated Software, Office-Automated Tools • Support All Project Personnel • Support All Life-Cycle Phases
Constraints	• Customer-Deliverable SDE → Portability • Stable, Reliable Services
Alternatives	• OS : VMS/AT&T Unix/Berkeley Unix/ISC • Host-Target/Fully Portable Toolset • Workstations : Zenith/LSI-11/. . .
Risks	• Mismatch to User-Project Needs, Priorities • User-Unfriendly System — 12-Language Syndrome, Experts-Only • Unix Performance, Support • Workstation/Mainframe compatibility
Risk Resolution	• User-Project Surveys, Requirements Participation • Survey of Unix-Using Organizations • Workstation Study
Risk Resolution Results	• Top-Level Requirements Specification • Host-Target with Unix Host • Unix-Based Workstations • Build User-Friendly Front End for Unix • Initial Focus on Tools to Support Early Phases
Plan for Next Phase	• Overall Development Plan — for Tools : SREM, RTT, PDL, OA Tools — for Front End, Support Tools — for LAN, Equipment, Facilities
Commitment	• Proceed with Plans

detailed design of components of the SPS: the preliminary design specification for the Requirements Traceability Tool (RTT), and a detailed design go-back on the Unit Development Folder (UDF) tool.

The RTT Preliminary Design Specification

The Requirements Traceability Tool (RTT) establishes the traceability between itemized software requirements specifications, design elements, code elements, and test cases. It also supports various associated query, analysis, and report generation capabilities. The preliminary design specification for the RTT (and most of the other SPS tools) looked different from the usual preliminary design specification, which tends to show a uniform level of elaboration of all components of the design. Instead, the level of detail of the RTT specification was risk-driven:

- In areas involving a high risk if the design was wrong, the design was carried down to the detailed design level, usually with the aid of rapid prototyping. These areas included working out the implications of various "undo" options, and the effects of various control keys used to escape from various levels of the program.
- In areas involving a moderate risk if the design was wrong, the design was carried down to a preliminary-design level. These areas included the basic command options for the tool, and the schemata for the requirements traceability data base. Here again, the ease of rapid prototyping with Unix shell scripts supported a good deal of user-interface prototyping.
- In areas involving a low risk if the design was wrong, very little design elaboration was done. These areas included details of all of the help message options and all of the report-generation options, once the nature of these options had been established in some example instances.

A Detailed Design Go-Back: The UDF Tool

The Unit Development Folder (UDF) tool collects into an electronic "folder" all of the artifacts involved in the development of a single-programmer software unit (typically 500-1000 instructions): unit requirements, design, code, test cases, test results, and documentation. It also includes a management template for tracking the programmer's scheduled and actual completion of each artifact.

During the detailed design of the Unit Development Folder (UDF) tool, an alternative was considered to reuse portions of the Requirements Traceability Tool (RTT) to provide pointers to the requirements and preliminary design specifications of the unit being developed. This turned out to be an extremely attractive alternative, not only in avoiding duplicate software development, but also in surfacing several issues involving many-to-many mappings between requirements, design, and code which had not been considered in designing the UDF tool. These led to a rethinking of the UDF tool requirements and preliminary design, which avoided a great deal of code rework that would have been necessary if the detailed design of the UDF tool had proceeded in a purely deductive, top-down fashion from the original UDF requirements specification. The resulting go-back led to a significantly different and more capable UDF tool, incorporating the RTT in its "users-hierarchy."

Spiral Model Features Illustrated by the Two Examples

From these two examples, we can see that the spiral approach:

- Fosters the development of specifications that are not necessarily uniform, exhaustive, or formal, in that they defer detailed elaboration of low risk software elements, and avoid unnecessary breakage in their design, until the high-risk elements of the design are stabilized.
- Incorporates prototyping as a risk-reduction option at any stage of development. In fact, prototyping and reuse risk analyses were often used in the process of going from detailed design into code.
- Accommodates go-backs to earlier stages of the spiral as more attractive alternatives are identified or as new risk issues need resolution.

3.5. Results of Using the Spiral Model

The resulting Software Productivity System developed and supported using the spiral model successfully avoided the risks identified, and achieved most of its objectives. The system has grown to include over 300 tools and over 1,300,000 instructions; 93% of the instructions were reused from previous project-developed, TRW-developed, or external software packages. All of the projects using the system have increased their productivity at least 50%; most have indeed doubled their productivity (as compared with cost estimation model predictions of their productivity using traditional methods).

However, one risk area was underestimated—the risk that projects with non-Unix target systems would not accept a Unix-based host system. Some projects accepted the host-target approach, but a good many did not for various reasons (customer constraints, zero-cost target machines). As a result, the system was less widely used on TRW projects than expected. This and other lessons learned have been incorporated into the spiral model approach to developing TRW's next-generation software development environment.

4. Spiral Model Advantages, Difficulties, and Implications

4.1. Spiral Model Advantages

The primary advantage of the spiral model is that its range of options allows it to accommodate the best features of existing software process models, while its risk-driven approach helps it to avoid most of their difficulties. In appropriate situations, the spiral model becomes equivalent to one of the existing process models. In other situations, it provides guidance on the best mix of existing approaches to be applied to a given project. The application of the spiral model to the TRW Software Productivity System discussed in Section 3 provides a good example of a risk-driven mix of specifying, prototyping, and evolutionary development.

The primary conditions under which the spiral model becomes equivalent to other main process models are summarized below.

- If a project has a low risk in such areas as getting the wrong user interface or not meeting stringent performance requirements; and it has a high risk if it loses budget and schedule predictability and control; then these risk considerations drive the spiral model into an equivalence to the waterfall model.
- If a software product's requirements are very stable (implying a low risk of expensive design and code breakage due to requirements changes during development); and if the presence of errors in the software product constitutes a high risk to the mission it serves; then these risk considerations drive the spiral model to resemble the two-leg model of precise specification and formal deductive program development.
- If a project has a low risk in such areas as losing budget and schedule predictability and control, encountering large-system integration problems, or coping with information sclerosis; and it has a high risk in such areas as getting the wrong user interface or user decision support requirements; then these risk considerations drive the spiral model into an equivalence to the evolutionary development model.
- If automated software generation capabilities are available, then the spiral model accommodates them either as options for rapid prototyping or for application of the transform model, depending on the risk considerations involved.
- If the high-risk elements of a project involve a mix of the risk items above, then the spiral approach will reflect an appropriate mix of the process models above. In doing so, its risk-avoidance features will generally avoid the difficulties of the other models.

In addition, the spiral model has a number of further advantages which are summarized below.

- *It accommodates strategies for developing program families, and for the reuse of existing software.* The steps involving the identification and evaluation of alternatives accommodate these options.
- *It accommodates preparation for life-cycle evolution, growth, and changes of the software product.* The major sources of product change are included in the product's objectives, and information-hiding approaches are included in the architectural design alternatives.
- *It provides a mechanism for incorporating software quality objectives into software product development.* This mechanism derives from the emphasis on identifying all types of objectives and constraints during each round of the spiral. The GOALS approach and software engineering goal structure in [Boehm, 1981; Chapter 3][17] provide a process and checklist for incorporating quality objectives.
- *It focuses on eliminating errors and unattractive alternatives early.* The risk-analysis, validation, and commitment steps cover these considerations.
- *It accommodates iterations, go-backs, and early termination of non-viable software projects.* The first two of these aspects were illustrated in the TRW-SPS example. The example also illustrated the overall objective of the spiral approach to start small, keep the spiral as tight as possible, and thus achieve the project's objectives with a minimum resource expenditure.
- *For each of the sources of project activity and resource expenditure, it answers the key question, "how much is enough?"* How much should a project do of requirements analysis, planning, configuration management, quality assurance, testing, formal verification, etc? Using the risk-driven approach, we can see that the answer is not the same for all projects, and that the appropriate level of effort is determined by the level of risk incurred by not doing enough.
- *It can support, and be supported by, advanced software development environments.* The process steps and their associated internal and external products can be treated as data base objects to be handled by an advanced object manager. Also, process and risk-management guidance for software developers can be incorporated into an evolving Knowledge Based Software Assistant or activity coordinator.
- *It does not involve separate approaches for software development and software enhancement (or "maintenance").* This aspect helps avoid the "second class citizen" status frequently associated with software main-

tenance. It also helps avoid many of the problems that currently ensue when high-risk enhancement efforts are approached in the same way as routine maintenance efforts.

- *It provides a viable framework for integrated hardware-software system development.* The focus on risk-management and on eliminating unattractive alternatives early and inexpensively is equally applicable to hardware and software.
- *On the other hand, it avoids forcing software development procedures into hardware development paradigms.* A good example of this is the review called "Critical Design Review," or CDR, which occurs after the detailed design is completed. For a hardware development risk profile, this review is indeed critical: as seen in Figure 2, it is the final review before the project begins to commit the bulk of its resources into producing hardware. From this standpoint, it is indeed critical to invest in an exhaustive, across-the-board review of the detailed design specifications before proceeding. For a software project, however, the risk profile is significantly different. Typically, in order to reduce the crucial factor of software development time, a software project will work out detailed unit interfaces by the Preliminary Design Review (PDR), and then begin to commit the bulk of its resources to large numbers of people doing detailed design and code in parallel (see Figure 2). To interrupt this process with a single, large, across-the-board CDR is not only time-consuming and expensive, but also ineffective, as the inter-unit interface specifications were necessarily verified thoroughly at the PDR. Thus, the critical review for a software project is the PDR; the "detailed design review" function is performed much more cost-effectively by a program of individual design inspections or walkthroughs, followed as appropriate by an overall review of the major issues identified in the walkthroughs.

4.2. Spiral Model Difficulties

Although the full spiral model can be successfully applied in many situations, it still has some difficulties or challenges to address before it can be called a mature, universally applicable model. The three primary spiral model challenges are summarized below.

(1) *The spiral model currently works well on internal software developments like the TRW-SPS, but it needs fur-*

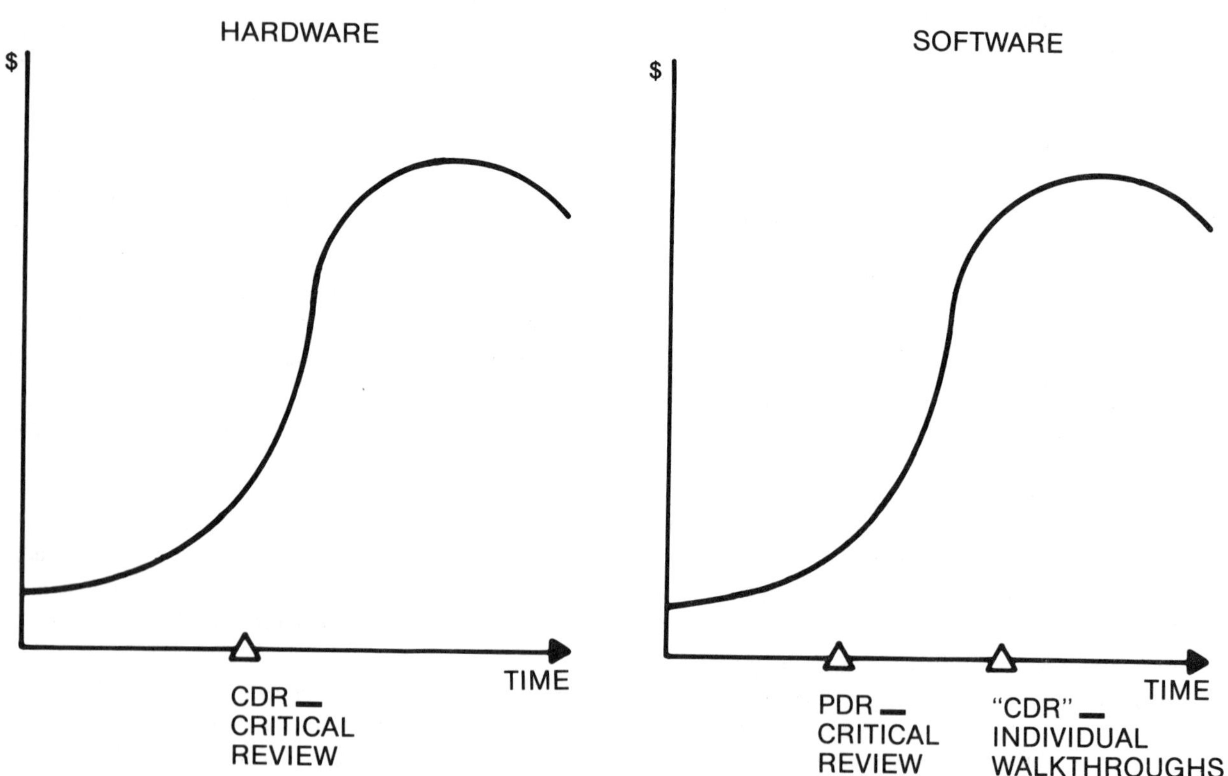

Figure 2: Risk-Oriented Management Refocuses Software Reviews onto Key Software Issues

ther work to match it to the world of contract software acquisition.

Internal software developments have a great deal of flexibility and freedom to accommodate stage-by-stage commitments, to defer commitments to specific options, to establish mini-spirals to resolve critical-path items, to adjust levels of effort, or to accommodate such practices as prototyping, evolutionary development, or design to cost. The world of contract software acquisition has a harder time achieving these degrees of flexibility and freedom without losing accountability and control.

Recently, a good deal of progress has been made in establishing more flexible contract mechanisms, such as the use of competitive front-end contracts for concept definition or prototype fly-offs; the use of level-of effort and award-fee contracts for evolutionary development; and the use of design-to-cost contracts. Although these have been generally successful, the procedures for using them still need to be worked out to the point that acquisition managers feel fully comfortable in using them.

(2) *The spiral model places a great deal of reliance on the ability of software developers to identify and manage sources of project risk.*

A good example is the spiral model's risk-driven specification, which carries high-risk elements down to a great deal of detail, and leaves low-risk elements to be elaborated in later stages, by which time there is less risk of breakage.

However, a team of inexperienced or low-balling developers may also produce a specification with a different pattern of variation in levels of detail: a great elaboration of detail for the well-understood, low-risk elements; and little elaboration of the poorly-understood, high-risk elements. Unless there is an insightful review of such a specification by experienced developer or acquisition personnel, this type of project will proceed to give an illusion of progress during a period in which it is actually heading for disaster.

Another concern is that a risk-driven specification will also be people-dependent. For example, a design may be produced by an expert, but may be implemented by non-experts. In this case, even though the expert does not need a great deal of detailed documentation, it is necessary for him to produce enough additional documentation to ensure that the non-experts will not go astray. Reviewers of the specification must be sensitive to these concerns as well.

With a conventional, document-driven approach, the requirement to carry all aspects of the specification to a uniform level of detail eliminates some potential problems, and creates a situation in which some aspects of reviews can be adequately carried out by inexperienced reviewers. But it also creates a large drain on the time of the scarce experts, who must dig for the critical issues within a large mass of non-critical detail. And further, if the high-risk elements have been glossed over by impressive-sounding references to poorly-understood capabilities (e.g., a new synchronization concept or a commercial DBMS), then there is an even greater risk of the conventional approach giving an illusion of progress in situations which are actually heading for disaster.

(3) *In general, the spiral model process steps need further elaboration to ensure that all of the participants in a software development are operating in a consistent context.*

Some examples are the need for more detailed definitions of the nature of spiral model specifications and milestones, the nature and objectives of spiral model reviews, and the nature of spiral model status indicators and cost-vs-progress tracking procedures. Another need is for guidelines and checklists to be used in identifying the most likely sources of project risk, and the most effective risk-resolution techniques for each source of risk.

It is currently feasible for highly experienced people to successfully use the spiral approach without these elaborations. But for large scale use in situations where people bring widely differing experience bases to the project, added levels of elaboration—such as have been accumulated over the years for document-driven approaches—are important in ensuring consistent interpretation and usage of the spiral approach across the project.

Efforts to apply and refine the spiral model have largely focussed on creating a discipline of software risk management, including techniques for risk identification, risk analysis, risk prioritization, risk management planning, and risk element tracking. An example of the results of this activity is the prioritized top-ten list of software risk items given in Figure 3. Another example is the risk management plan discussed in the next section. Other recent applications and extensions of the spiral model are presented in [Belz, 1986][18] and [Iivari, 1987].[19]

4.3. Spiral Model Implications: The Risk Management Plan

Even if an organization is not fully ready to adopt the entire spiral approach, there is one characteristic spiral model technique which can easily be adapted to any life-cycle model,

Figure 3: A Prioritized Top Ten List of Software Risk Items

Risk Item	Risk Management Techniques
1. Personnel shortfalls	— Staffing with top talent, job matching; teambuilding; morale building, cross-training; pre-scheduling key people.
2. Unrealistic schedules and budgets	— Detailed, multi-source cost and schedule estimation; design to cost; incremental development; software reuse; requirements scrubbing.
3. Developing the wrong software functions	— Organization analysis; mission analysis; ops-concept formulation; user surveys; prototyping; early users' manuals.
4. Developing the wrong user interface	— Task analysis; prototyping; scenarios.
5. Gold plating	— Requirements scrubbing; prototyping; cost-benefit analysis; design to cost.
6. Continuing stream of requirement changes	— High change threshold, information hiding; incremental development (defer changes to later increments).
7. Shortfalls in externally-furnished components	— Benchmarking; inspections; reference checking; compatibility analysis.
8. Shortfalls in externally-performed tasks	— Reference checking; pre-award audits; award-fee contracts; competitive design or prototyping; teambuilding.
9. Real-time performance shortfalls	— Simulation; benchmarking; modeling; prototyping; instrumentation; tuning.
10. Straining computer science capabilities	— Technical analysis; cost-benefit analysis; prototyping; reference checking.

and which can provide many of the benefits of the spiral approach. This is the *Risk Management Plan* summarized in Table 4. The Risk Management Plan basically ensures that each project make an early identification of its top risk items (the number 10 is not an absolute requirement), develop a plan for resolving the risk items, identify and plan to resolve new risk items as they surface, and highlight the project's progress vs. plans in monthly reviews.

The Risk Management Plan has been used successfully at TRW and other organizations, and has ensured an appropriate focus on early prototyping, simulation, benchmarking, key-person staffing measures, and other early risk-resolution techniques which have helped avoid many potential project "show-stoppers." The recent U.S. Department of Defense standard on software management, DoD-STD-2167, requires that developers produce and use risk management plans, as does its counterpart Air Force regulation, AFR 800-14.

Table 4. Software Risk Management Plan

(1) Identify the project's top 10 risk items
(2) Present a plan for resolving each risk item
(3) Update list of top risk items, plan, and results monthly
(4) Highlight risk-item status in monthly project reviews
(5) Initiate appropriate corrective actions

5. Conclusions

(1) The risk-driven nature of the spiral model is more adaptable to the full range of software project situations than are the primarily document-driven approaches such as the waterfall model or the primarily code-driven approaches such as evolutionary development. It is particularly applicable to very large, complex, ambitious software systems.

(2) The spiral model has been quite successful in its largest application to date: the development and enhancement of the TRW SPS. Overall, the spiral approach was highly effective in achieving a high level of software support environment capability in a very short time, and in providing the flexibility necessary to accommodate a high dynamic range of technical alternatives and user objectives.

(3) The spiral model is not yet as fully elaborated as are more established models such as the waterfall model. Thus, although the spiral model can be successfully applied by software-experienced personnel, it needs further elaboration in such areas as contracting, specifications, milestones, reviews, status monitoring, and risk-area identification in order to be fully usable in all situations.

(4) Partial implementations of the spiral model such as the Risk Management Plan are compatible with most current process models, and are highly useful in helping projects to overcome their major sources of project risk.

Acknowledgments

I would like to thank Frank Belz, Lolo Penedo, George Spadaro, Bob Williams, Bob Balzer, Gillian Frewin, Peter Hamer, Manny Lehman, Lee Osterweil, Dave Parnas, Bill Riddle, Steve Squires, and Dick Thayer for their stimulating and insightful comments and discussions of earlier versions of this paper, and Nancy Donato for producing its several versions.

References

(1) H.D. Benington, "Production of Large Computer Programs," *Proc. ONR Symposium on Advanced Programming Methods for Digital Computers*, June 1956, pp. 15-27. Also available in *Annals of the History of Computing*, Oct. 1983, pp.350-361, and *Proceedings, ICSE 9*, IEEE-CS, 1987.

(2) W.W. Royce, "Managing the Development of Large Software Systems: Concepts and Techniques," *Proceedings, WESCON*, August 1970. Also available in *Proceedings, ICSE 9*, IEEE-CS, 1987.

(3) E.W. Dijkstra, "Notes on Structured Programming," Technische Hogeschool Eindhoven, Report No. EWD-248, April 1970. Also in O.J. Dahl, E.W. Dijkstra, and C.A.R. Hoare, *Structured Programming*, Academic Press, 1972.

(4) H.D. Mills, "Top-Down Programming in Large Systems," in *Debugging Techniques in Large Systems*, R. Ruskin (ed), Prentice-Hall, 1971, pp. 41-55.

(5) F.P. Brooks, *The Mythical Man-Month*, Addison-Wesley, 1975.

(6) B.W. Boehm, "Software Design and Structuring" in *Practical Strategies for Developing Large Software Systems*, E. Horowitz (ed), Addison-Wesley, 1975, pp. 103-128.

(7) B.W. Boehm, "Software Engineering," *IEEE Trans. Computers*, December 1976, pp. 1226-1241.

(8) J.R. Distaso, "Software Management—A Survey of the Practice in 1980." *IEEE Proceedings, Sept. 1980, pp. 1103-1119.*

(9) D.L. Parnas, "Designing Software for Ease of Extension and Contraction," IEEE Trans. S/W Engr., March 1979, pp. 128-137.

(10) M.M. Lehman, "A Further Model of Coherent Programming Processes," *Proceedings, Software Process Workshop*, IEEE, Feb. 1984, pp.27-33.

(11) D.D. McCracken and M.A. Jackson, "Life Cycle Concept Considered Harmful," *Software Engineering Notes*, ACM, April 1982, pp. 29-32.

(12) R. Balzer, T.E. Cheatham, and C. Green, "Software Technology in the 1990's: Using a New Paradigm," *Computer*, Nov. 1983, pp. 39-45.

(13) D.A. Kolb, "On Management and the Learning Process," *MIT Sloan School Working Paper 652-73*, Cambridge, MA, 1973.

(14) B. Carlsson, P. Keane, and J.B. Martin, "R&D Organizations as Learning Systems," *Sloan Management Review*, Spring 1976, pp. 1-15.

(15) R. Fisher and W. Ury, *Getting to Yes*, Houghton Mifflin, 1981; Penguin Books, 1983.

(16) B.W. Boehm, M.H. Penedo, E.D. Stuckle, R.D. Williams, and A.B. Pyster, "A Software Development Environment for Improving Productivity," *Computer*, June 1984, pp. 30-44.

(17) B.W. Boehm, *Software Engineering Economics*, Prentice-Hall, 1981.

(18) F.C. Belz, "Applying the Spiral Model: Observations on Developing System Software in Ada," *Proceedings, 1986 Annual Conference on Ada Technology*, Atlanta, GA, 1986, pp. 57-66.

(19) J. Iivari, "A Hierarchical Spiral Model for the Software Process," *ACM Software Engineering Notes*, Jan. 1987, pp. 35-37.

The Synthesis Process for Software Development

Arthur Pyster

Software Productivity Consortium
2214 Rock Hill Road
Herndon, VA 22070 USA

Abstract: *In response to a need for dramatic improvements in the productivity of software developers in the aerospace industry, the Software Productivity Consortium is defining a new process for developing software, called* Synthesis. *Under Synthesis a new system is seen largely as a revision of an old one. Relatively little is built from scratch. There are three main activities during Synthesis: (1) create a model that approximates the new application, (2) map from the application model to a known software model that approximates a valid design, and (3) map from the software design model to executable code that approximates a valid implementation. At each step the focus is on reusing existing models and parts of models to approximate the desired new ones. These steps are performed iteratively, adapting the models with each iteration to become ever-better approximations of the desired new system. At each step, appropriate verification and assessment are performed.*

1: Motivation

The Software Productivity Consortium is chartered by the aerospace companies that own it (called member companies) to improve the productivity of software developers in those companies. The member companies include most of the top DoD contractors, have a combined income of about $100 billion, and are responsible for most of the major U.S. defense programs. Any program to improve the software development productivity of this group of companies must recognize their peculiar needs: (1) large, demanding systems in which the software may exceed one million lines of code, such as the software for the Advanced Tactical Fighter, U.S. space station, and the Strategic Defense Initiative; (2) embedded real-time systems with high reliability and performance requirements such as cruise missile guidance or aircraft flight control; and (3) use of Ada as a programming language.

The member companies currently develop new software through a combination of techniques that include limited prototyping and a "scavenging" approach to software reuse. The Consortium was founded in large part on the premise that dramatic improvements in productivity would be possible if software development processes were revised to accommodate extensive prototyping and systematic reuse. The Consortium has labored for the last 2½ years to test that premise. This paper discusses some of the early results of that effort. Two additional papers that discuss those results in more detail are Nejmeh et al. (1) and Blakemore and Schebella (2).

2: Fundamental Assumptions

The cornerstone of the Consortium program is the ongoing definition of a new process for software development and its subsequent automation. The underlying motivation for the Consortium to define a new software development process is the failure of existing processes to adequately address these two concerns:

1. The hardest parts of developing software are specifying and validating requirements and design.
2. Significant parts of any new software application, including design, are similar to parts of old applications. If located and suitably adapted, those old parts could be reused profitably in the new system.

The process that the Consortium is defining and evolving is called *Synthesis.* When fully developed, Synthesis will cover all development activities, including requirements specification, design, coding, testing, and management. The key differentiator between Synthesis and other processes is its central focus on reuse. Under Synthesis a new system is the result of successively revising approximations of old ones. In a mature Synthesis environment, relatively little would be built from scratch. Even in systems with radically novel requirements or technology, reuse is likely to be applicable to a number of subsystems. Because the new system is built from old parts and often specified in terms of them, much of the verification and validation has already been done. Models of the new system are constructed and validated throughout the devel-

EH0304-6/90/0000/0528$01.00

opment process to ensure that the process converges. Sometimes the models will be executable; i.e., they will be prototypes.

Eleven fundamental assumptions lead the Consortium to propose the Synthesis process for software development:

1. Software should be built iteratively, with each iteration better approximating the ultimately desired solution. If properly managed, change is an ally, not an enemy (3).
2. It is unreasonable to expect fully automated generation of production quality software from high-level specifications, but substantial automated support is possible. Automated generation of executable code is much more reasonable for prototypes in which performance, sizing, and exception-handling requirements are relaxed (4).
3. For each narrow application domain, there are many similarities among systems, even if they are hard to recognize. It is not always easy to recognize the similarities because of cosmetic or arbitrary engineering choices or because the system documentation is poor. In many cases, the similarities are at the subsystem or assembly levels, where they are harder to identify. However, once identified, the similarities can be effective aids in applying reusable technology to construct new systems that are similar to old ones. Similar applications or their implementations are called a *family* (5). The process of identifying commonalities across systems in an application area is called *domain analysis.*
4. The software in each application can be represented as a combination of one or more information-hiding modules the behavior of which is characterized by operational interfaces (6).
5. The design of an application is a specification of the modules that implement the application together with a set of relationships among the modules and the operations they provide. Two generally interesting relationships are *uses* and *composed-of.* There are many others.
6. Members of the same application family can share similar designs and implementations. Differences between the designs and implementations can be characterized precisely enough to aid adaptation and be supported by tools.
7. Developers of new systems can (and should) characterize their new systems in terms of differences from existing ones at all levels of abstraction: requirements, design, and code.
8. If the set of available parts is rich enough, a user should be able to rapidly assemble a prototype that approximates the system that is being sought ultimately.
9. If the set of available parts is rich enough, and the novelty of the system is not too great, the user should be able to evolve the prototype into a usable product. This evolution reflects the iterative nature of development under Synthesis, in which a user builds successively better approximations of the system.
10. The biggest gains in productivity will come from reusing a small number of large parts (such as subsystem designs) rather than from reusing many little parts (such as stack implementations); i.e., productivity improvements are nonlinear with the size of the reused parts, and reusable designs are more valuable than reusable code.
11. A central library of reusable software parts should be available to developers to make reuse effective. Lifecycle objects should be stored in the library, ranging in size from whole systems that have previously been built, down to small packages for performing numerical computation. Domains should range from such purely mathematical and computer science areas as differential equations and symbol tables up to system application areas such as automobile cruise control, aircraft fuel consumption, ship navigation, and weapons targeting. If there are many lifecycle objects, they might be organized into sublibraries or otherwise partitioned to facilitate searching and administration.

3: The Process Steps

The development process based on the assumptions in the previous section is called Synthesis because the new system is synthesized largely by selecting, adapting, and assemblying parts of old systems. New parts are constructed "from scratch" only when nothing in the reuse library is suitable as-is or is adaptable. Most of the Consortium's program focuses on better defining, evolving, and automating Synthesis. The current viewpoint is relatively immature and so is likely to change significantly over the next several years. However, much progress has been made and the rate of progress is likely to accelerate as many fundamental issues are resolved.

Synthesis can be viewed as an evolution from earlier, more traditional development paradigms as shown in Figure 1. The standard development process is the *waterfall* model, which has many variants (7). The most important characteristics of the waterfall process, which serves as the baseline against which to judge other processes, as follows: (1) requirements specification precedes design, which precedes implementation; (2) reuse of existing software is sporadic; and (3) it is primarily the software im-

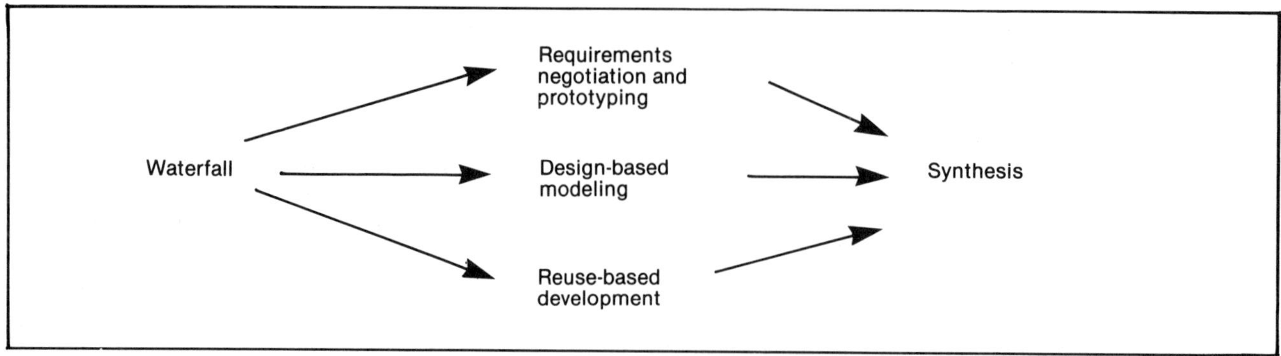

Figure 1: Software development processes

plementation that is iterated and adapted during development rather than the design.

Three new processes are derived from independently varying those fundamental characteristics of the waterfall process. In the *requirements negotiation* process, proposed requirements are weighted against implementation difficulties and costs. Modeling techniques, especially prototyping, are used to calibrate the difficulty of proposed requirements to produce requirements that are optimal relative to the customer's needs and budget and to the available technology. This process dramatically reduces the risk that the system that is ultimately built will not meet user needs either in performance or functionality. In *design-based* modeling, iteration and adaptation are done primarily with the design rather than with the code. The design is assessed, rather than the implementation tested, to answer the question "Is this good enough?" Obviously, design-based modeling requires rich design notations and analysis tools to be effective. This process saves significant time because it is easier to modify compact designs than lengthy implementations of those designs. The *reuse-based* process systematically takes advantage of reusable parts in building new systems. Potentially any lifecycle object can be reused, from requirements to code and test cases. This process saves significant development time by eliminating the need to rebuild lifecycle objects that were built during previous projects. Synthesis combines requirements negotiation, design-based modeling, and reuse-based development.

The three major phases of synthesis are domain analysis, software development, and library population, as shown in Figure 2.

3.1: Domain Analysis

Domain analysis identifies commonalities across applications in a specific business or technology area. This analysis would normally be done by a domain expert who has a deep understanding of applications in the domain. Such an expert probably is a skilled system engineer. Although they use different terminology, Arango (8) and Neighbors (9) identified four steps in domain analysis:

1. Identify the domain components: the objects and operations within the domain and the methods for composing and assessing those objects and operations.
2. Define a method for an application builder to specify the application model in terms of the domain components. The application model is an expression of important aspects of a proposed application; e.g., if the application is an aircraft flight control system, the application model might show the various sensors, actuators, displays, and other aircraft parts from which the application is to be constructed. It might also show the information passed between the parts and the performance characteristics of the individual parts and the system as a whole. The notations of the application builder would likely be domain dependent; e.g., a process control engineer might find it natural to model autopilot behavior partially in terms of differential equations.
3. Identify *canonical* system designs and related software designs that validly implement applications constructed from the components. A canonical design represents the commonalities across the design of many systems. It is a family of designs (i.e., a design in which decisions have been deferred or in which alternative choices have not been made). Depending on how those decisions and choices are made, different behavior will be realized and different implementations will be developed. A design in which the deferred decisions have been made is called *instantiated.* Canonical designs are likely to be obtained by analyzing sample systems in the domain of interest for commonly used approaches. Design components may be extracted directly from existing systems, generalized, and placed in a reusable library. Once the canonical designs have been constructed, they are placed in a reuse library.

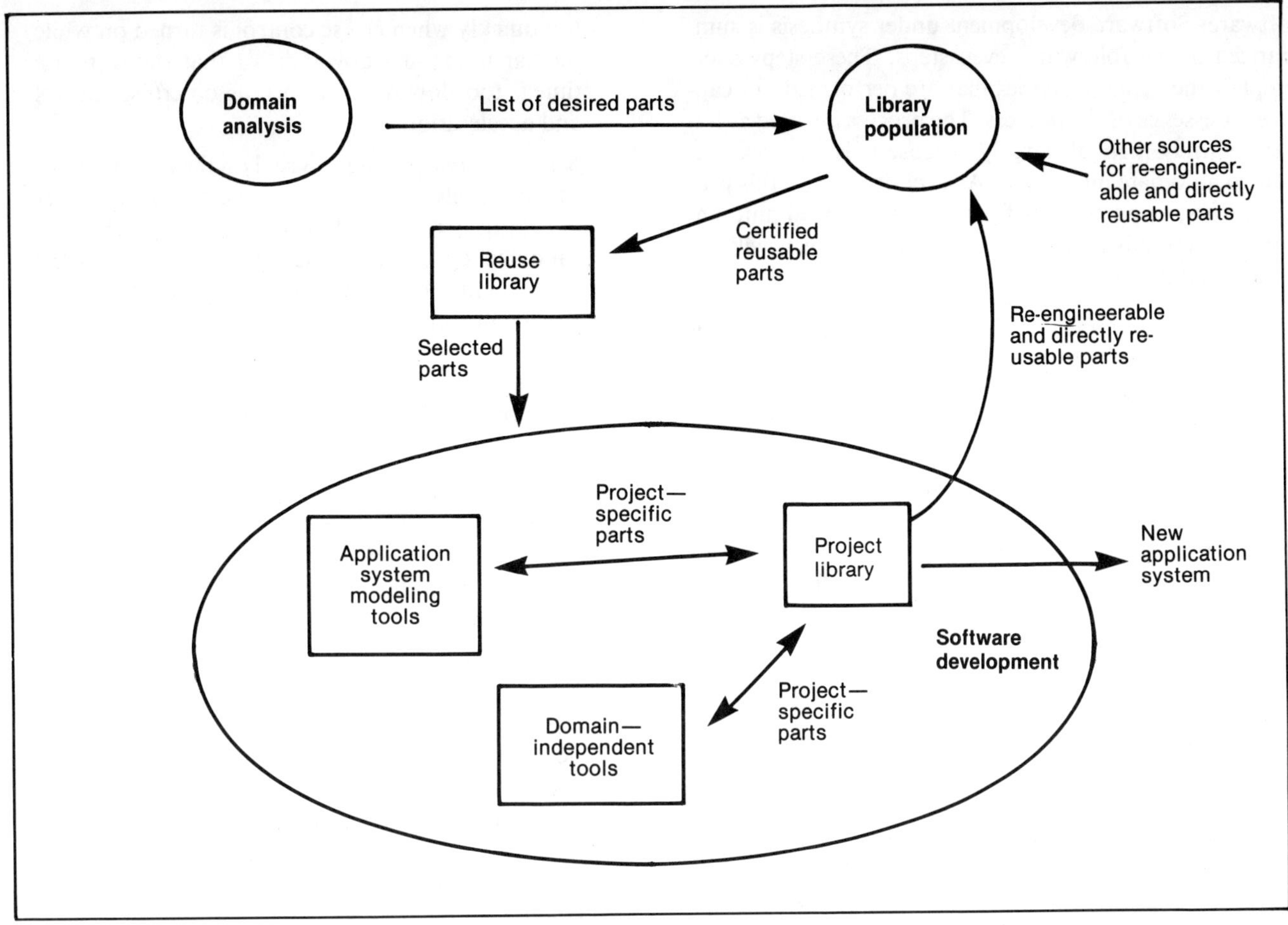

Figure 2: The three major Synthesis phases

4. Indicate how to map from an application model to an appropriate canonical design. The jump from the application arena to that of software is the hardest problem in building a system.

For example, if the domain were cruise missile autopilots, the first step would identify objects such as a sensor, a filter, and an actuator; an operation might be to read a sensor; a composition method might state how to connect a filter to a sensor and under what conditions such a connection is allowed; and an assessor might state the smoothing effect the filter would have on noise in the data passed by the sensor. From the results of this analysis, the second step could be performed. A description of any application in the domain should be expressible in terms of these objects. If the notation for describing the objects is sufficiently rich, an application model can be constructed and analyzed for suitability.

To perform the third and fourth steps requires cooperation between the domain engineer and a software engineer. The latter understands how to structure software domain applications to exploit the commonality inherent in the application model. For example, the software engineer knows how to introduce software objects into the design that can be mapped to objects in the application model.

The domain components themselves are obviously domain dependent. An untested assertion of the Consortium's technical program is that the method for finding and describing those components is largely domain independent. As more domain analyses are performed, the validity of that assertion will be determined.

Of course, domain analysis could be an activity performed in isolation apart from actually building systems from the analysis. On the other hand, it could be an incremental activity in which successive projects build upon previous analysis, enriching that analysis with insights gained from building each new system. It is not yet clear which strategy, if either, is superior.

3.2: Software Development

Once a domain analysis has been performed, the fruits of that analysis can be used to build many software systems without reperforming the analysis or redesigning the software. Software development under synthesis is summarized in the following seven steps. These steps oversimplify the actual activities that are performed but capture the essence of the process. The process is stated as if it were entirely manual, largely because is is not clear yet how to automate much of it. As experience with this process grows, opportunities for near-term partial automation will certainly appear, although some aspects will not be automatable in the foreseeable future.

1. *State requirements:* The system engineer states his requirements as he or she best understands them. These requirements are based on end-user needs and are relatively implementation independent. For example, if the application being developed were an automobile cruise control system, a typical requirement would be a rule requiring that the cruise control system be disabled once the engine is turned off and is not reenabled until the driver explicitly turns it back on. Currently, two styles in which an engineer can state characteristics have been proposed: directly and by analogy.

   In the direct form of specification, the engineer states the requirements largely in terms of a predefined domain-dependent vocabulary and a set of mission attributes. The set of systems that can be described is largely constrained by the vocabulary and attributes to be consistent with the domain for which previous analysis has been performed. An "escape" is provided so that the user can express novel features. For example, the requirement in point 1 may be expressed in a state machine model of cruise control system behavior in which the particular states available to the engineer are predefined for the cruise control system domain. The use of a state machine model for expressing specifications may be common to many domains, but the previous definition of certain states and the meanings for certain transitions would be domain dependent.

   In the analogy form of specification, the engineer states characteristics in terms of differences between those that are needed and those of existing systems in the reuse library. For example, suppose there is a new cruise control system similar to previously built system X except that there is a new constraint: the system will not operate if the car is moving at less than 40 miles per hour. The engineer would simply add a constraint to the transition to state that "on" cannot happen if the current speed is less than 40 miles per hour. This style again constrains the set of systems that can be described.

2. *Construct application model:* Based on the system engineer's input, an application model of the system is constructed and subjected to domain-specific assessment. The model is evolved based on feedback from that assessment. For example, the feedback may indicate that the car could accelerate too quickly when cruise control is turned on while the car is moving downhill, or that the response time is too slow between turning on cruise control and acceleration.

3. *Select canonical design:* Based on the requirements as they evolve from Step 2, the system engineer (working with a software engineer) selects a canonical design from a set of candidate canonical designs; this becomes the instantiated design of either a prototype or of a product when the delayed design choices are finally made. Depending on the choices made, different system designs result. The selection process includes assessments of performance and other criteria of interest.

4a. *Select instantiated design:* There may be an existing instantiated design family member that can fully satisfy the constraints established by the mission requirements. In that case, the software engineer can simply select it.

4b. *Instantiate canonical design:* If the needed design is not available for selection, the engineer may instantiate the canonical design by making the delayed design decisions. For some instantiations, there may be automated support. In the worst case, the engineer would have to instantiate by hand. If the developer of the canonical design anticipated the mission requirements exactly, then instantiation could yield the desired design.

4c. *Modify and invent canonical design:* If selection and instantiation fail, the engineer could modify the canonical design, in effect creating a new design family. This would require making changes to the design not anticipated by the original design developers. Obviously, there is a point of diminishing returns in modifying an existing canonical design versus creating a new canonical design from scratch—or inventing a specific design for the application. The choice would be made case by case.

5. *Implement:* Some of the design modules already have implementations. Others must be implemented. The degree to which modules must be implemented is determined by the richness of the potential set of reusable parts available and novelty of the new system (i.e., how adaptable are the parts and how much of the application domain do they support). Programmers complete the implementation by collecting the appropriate preexisting parts, adapting others that do not quite fit, and as a last resort creating new ones.

6. *Verify:* The new implementation is compiled and ready to be tested. Test data used to assess old systems are modified to reflect the novelties of the new system. Additional test data are generated where modified data are inadequate.

7. *Install:* The completed system is placed in service.

Stating these steps in a simple list creates the illusion that they are performed sequentially. On the contrary, at any point in the construction of a system, the engineer may move freely between steps as required. In fact, it is the ability to move quickly between different levels of system model, from requirements to design to code, that distinguishes this approach from most others. Such an ability comes from having both collections of reusable parts as raw material for rapid assembly of models and from having powerful analysis techniques for evaluating and refining those assembled models. For example, when instantiating the design of a real-time system, allocation of functionality to concurrent processes is one of the most important design decisions. The Consortium has defined a set of quantitative methods to help a designer make those decisions and has constructed a product supporting those methods. These methods are described more in Section 6.5 and in Blakemore and Schebella (2).

Analysis is further enhanced because the system is developed in the context of a *project library,* which is an organized collection of all of lifecycle objects that constitute the system; e.g., documentation, requirements, design, and test cases under configuration management. What distinguishes a project library from a traditional software library is the web of relationships maintained among lifecycle objects and the toolset that supports analysis of those relationships. Using this toolset, an engineer can understand the impact of change as the models evolve. For example, making a seemingly innocent change to a module within a design may affect a host of other objects such as the test plan and test cases used to test that module, documentation on how to use that module, and code that implements the module. Among other uses, the impact analysis toolset is used to identify which lifecycle objects are affected by a change so that the engineer can understand its overall implications.

3.3: Library Population

A gradual increase in the size and quality of its reuse library is essential to improving a company's ability to build new systems from reusable parts. New parts must be *certified* before they are placed in the library; i.e., the library administrator must be assured that they meet standard quality criteria. The new parts will likely come from a periodic systematic analysis of old systems built using Synthesis or other processes. Potentially reusable parts of old systems would be identified, certified, and inserted into the reuse library. Of course, parts may need to be generalized and better verified and characterized before insertion. That is part of certification.

Because of the schedule pressure that all production projects face, it is questionable whether such projects will produce parts and descriptions of them that are certifiable as-is for a reuse library. A separate activity may be necessary to generalize a part so that it is applicable to a range of applications, to characterize it well enough that a potential reuser could understand whether that part applies to the problem at hand, and to verify it well enough that a potential reuser has confidence that the part will work as specified.

4: Aspects of the Process

4.1: Approximations

Inherent in Synthesis is the idea that at any point there are up to three primary models that approximate what the final system must ultimately be: application, design, and implementation. The models are iteratively enhanced until the approximation becomes exact (7). At intermediate points, any or all of the models could be approximations. This is a very flexible approach, allowing for experimentation as required. For example, early in the development, a quick prototype might be needed to validate the user interface of the system. An approximate application, design, and implementation might be suitable for that purpose, assuming the approximations were relatively good with respect to the user interface aspects of the system but poorer with respect to other aspects. As a second case, assume that a software engineer needs to validate the performance aspects of the design of a particular subsystem. The engineer might work from an exact application model and an approximate design model. The design model is postulated to be exact in the subsystem of interest, even though other subsystems are still approximate. There might be no implementation of parts or all of the design. By using dynamics assessment tools that operate on design-level representations, the engineer could analyze the relevant portions of the design and determine the truth of the postulation.

4.2: Ada

Ada is not an inherent aspect of the process but rather a constraint imposed through the federal government on the member companies. Nothing in Synthesis requires the use of Ada, but the Consortium's efforts take Ada into account because the member companies must produce software written in Ada. Unfortunately, prototyping is more difficult when the generated code is in Ada. Ada's strong typing and early binding policies contribute to both its reliability and its run-time efficiency. Unfortunately, these same properties also make compiling Ada time consuming. During prototyping a more flexible language is desirable; this desirability is one of the primary reasons why interpretive languages such as LISP (10) and SMALLTALK (11) are so popular for prototyping. During Synthesis, there can be many mappings from design to code. Some mappings could be to components in more flexible interpretive languages. Rapid construction of prototypes would thereby be allowed in which code parts can be quickly substituted with no lengthy compilation step to complete. If the purpose of prototyping is to experiment with functionality rather than to understand performance or accuracy of the code, generating code in a language other than Ada is potentially valuable. After functionality has been validated, Ada code can be generated and performance and accuracy can be determined.

4.3: Convergence

The Synthesis process is inherently iterative. It is taken on faith that getting valid requirements and design without iteration is too hard for all but the most trivial of problems. Building novel systems requires experimentation.

For iteration to succeed, two things should be true. First, a good starting point for the first iteration must be selected; otherwise a converging evolutionary path is hard to find because the eventual system is so dramatically different from the starting one. Second, there must be a way to guide the creation of iteration $n + l$ so that it is somehow closer to what is required than iteration n is. The starting point for Synthesis is an application or design model that was previously characterized. Its functionality, performance, and other relevant attributes are already known, and the model-validation effort can be focused on just those aspects of the system that are not correctly accounted for by approximation.

Functional and performance-oriented assessment tools are the key to guiding the creation of a new iteration from an old one. The developer must be able to determine quantitatively where the current model falls short, propose a correcting change, and then determine if the new change actually helps. For example, if the design allows multitasking, the Adarts criteria for partitioning modules among tasks could be applied (12), leading to a tasking structure that is quantitatively assessed by means of the dynamics assessment toolset being produced by the Consortium in its first product release. If the tasking performance falls short of what is required, a new tasking structure can be developed and assessed in turn.

4.4: Adaptation

The importance of adaptation is best understood by explaining how Synthesis differs from application generators. As the name implies, an application generator creates running code in a relatively narrow application area from a high-level specification. The process mimics some aspects of Synthesis. An application generator usually contains a single canonical design for a small, well-defined domain. A front end is added through which the user can specify parameter values for the canonical design in a domain-specific way. Finally, a method, often quite simple, to map from the parameterized design to code is provided.

Many successful application generators have been developed in research laboratories and marketed commercially. Fourth-generation languages are largely application generators in such domains as management information systems. The major strength of application generators is that human intervention is not required once the generation process begins. Their major weakness is their lack of adaptability. Not only is human intervention not required when transforming from specification to code, it is not *allowed*. Application generators adopt a "take it or leave it" mentality.

Synthesis explicitly allows the developer to intervene and customize the process by adapting models and model components as the need arises. This ability to intervene compensates for the inability to generate specifications and code automatically and for the inability to fully encode the rules for Synthesis; it introduces intelligence into the process.

Key to the notion of adaptation is the specification of software parts as information-hiding modules, used to form families of programs. An early advocate of this concept was David Parnas (5), who developed it in detail at the Naval Research Laboratory (NRL) (6, 13, 14). Using the NRL method, each module hides one or more "secrets." The behavior of a module is publicly stated in its specification. Those aspects of the implementation of that behavior that are likely to change are called secrets and are hidden from users of that module. Anticipating change in a design and documenting how that anticipated change has been factored into the design are the keys to successful adaptation.

Simple mechanisms for automating adaptation will be considered first. The simplest mechanism is a macroprocessor to support string substitution. Even though this mechanism is relatively simple, it is powerful and is expected to be used heavily.

More complex adaptation mechanisms are possible in which the new part is constructed from a higher-level specification. The Common Ada Missile Packages Project developed the *schema* method for constructing sparse matrix manipulation packages from a higher-level description of the shape of the sparse matrix (15). GRAPHITE is still another approach, in which an Ada package for manipulating graph structures is generated from a high-level specification of the graph (16). Such adaptation mechanisms are really application generators. Generative technology been used largely to create code. An interesting area of exploration will be using this technology to generate designs and other lifecycle objects. For example, the Consortium's Verification Project is now exploring how to generate test cases from grammatical descriptions of program inputs. The most challenging work will be generating pieces of designs and application models.

5: The Hard Problems

The work in Synthesis began in 1988, but not until 1989 has it been understood well enough that most of the Consortium's technical program can be focused around its development. The Consortium believes that a gradual transition to the Synthesis process can be accomplished by its member companies. Figure 1 showed the steps in that evolution. Many hard technical problems stand between the Consortium and a full understanding of both the process and its automation. Technology transfer problems are formidable. Yet the Consortium is addressing these problems incrementally, expecting that partial success can still offer significant improvements in productivity. Some of these problems are posed next as questions; there is no significance to the order in which the questions are posed. This set of questions is expected to remain fairly stable over the next several years and serve as the major guidepost for the Consortium's technical program.

1. Can a systematic approach to domain analysis be identified and documented well enough that it can be captured in a book or a set of technical reports and successfully taught and transferred to engineers in the member companies? Can a toolset be developed that automates a significant portion of domain analysis?
2. Can a domain analysis be performed in most of the major business and technical areas of the member companies?
3. Can one or more application modeling techniques be developed that are rich enough to capture the subtleties of member company applications?
4. Can suitable notations and mechanisms be developed for automating most of the mapping from an application model to an appropriate software design?
5. Can flexible code-generation facilities be developed that map automatically from a design to a prototype implementation? to a product-quality implementation?
6. Can flexible composition methods be defined that allow for automated analysis of the result of composing two or more modules together?
7. Will the volume of information needed to support automated adaptation and composition be small enough or obtained readily enough that providing it for routine software development will be practical?
8. Can the technology for building domain-specific assessment toolsets be generalized to make them efficient to produce for a wide variety of member company domains (e.g., how broadly applicable are stochastic Petri nets and queueing models)?
9. Can parts and relationships stored in a reuse library be described well enough so that the ripple effect of adapting a library part can be bounded? Is it possible to provide similar bounds when the part is developed from scratch in a project library?
10. Can effective measures of productivity for the Synthesis process be defined and implemented and thereby lead to useful feedback from the member companies about the utility of Synthesis?
11. Can an effective transition plan be defined and implemented to move member company projects from a waterfall approach to Synthesis?
12. Can "old" software written with neither reuse nor Synthesis in mind be reused? If it can be reused, does its usefulness justify the effort of cataloging it?
13. Can people be inserted "into the loop" to guide Synthesis in a way in which they can understand the context of the decisions they are asked to make?
14. Can test cases be adapted automatically or semiautomatically to accommodate adaptation of design or code?
15. Are there specific foundation services that are helpful in building many of the tools needed to automate Synthesis?
16. Can designers really anticipate changes that in practice prove to be the needed ones?
17. Which is more economical: (a) building reusable software as part of a larger application-building project, or (b) establishing a project explicitly for building reusable software?
18. Can generative technology be successfully applied to generate designs and other higher-level lifecycle objects?

6: Foundations

The Consortium believes it can make significant contributions to addressing most of the hard problems because of the foundations already laid in the work previously done at the Consortium and elsewhere. These foundations are discussed in this section.

6.1: Naval Research Laboratory (NRL) Methodology

A number of hard problems center on having adequate methods for describing the properties of parts. For example, consider the problem of understanding the behavior of the composition of two modules taken from a reusable library. Obviously, the behavior of the composition is a function of the behavior of the individual modules plus the method of composing them. Even though the composition method is well defined, if the method for describing the behavior of the individual modules is weak, it will be impossible to understand precisely what the composite module does.

As another example, consider the products of a domain analysis: (1) the objects common to the domain, characterized by their properties and by the operations that can be performed on them, (2) the relationships among the objects, and (3) the rules for combining them. Clearly, the quality of the analysis is largely limited by the ability to describe the properties of parts accurately.

The starting point for describing and adapting reusable parts is the NRL methodology mentioned in the previous section. The NRL methodology is object-oriented rather than function-oriented, a fact that the Consortium views as critical to increasing the reusability of designs. The Consortium's view is based on the observation that the most stable parts of a system are the objects that are manipulated, whereas the most volatile parts are the interactions between the parts. A methodology that focuses on objects stresses those aspects that are most stable and therefore most reusable. The methodology states how to describe software parts, providing notations for expressing many, but certainly not all, behavioral characteristics. For example, the methodology states that it is important to express the assumptions on which a module is based; e.g., a processor control program might have a characterizing assumption that it will not be interrupted more than 10 times per second. Guidelines have been written at the Consortium to aid a developer in writing behavioral descriptions (17).

One of the unique features of the NRL methodology that distinguishes it from other object-oriented approaches is a focus on anticipating changes in a design. Such anticipation is the key to adaptation. Anticipated changes are those for which the designer has made explicit allowances in the design choices. Adaptations that fit within anticipated changes should be much easier than those that are not. Guidelines to aid a designer in anticipating changes have been written at the Consortium (18).

The guidebook that describes Synthesis as it is currently understood and practiced within the Consortium is now in its fourth release (17, 18). It is evolving rapidly as a result of feedback from users of the process.

6.2: Reusable Libraries Project

The Reusable Libraries Project has primarily focused on two problems: (1) deciding what information is relevant to a potential reuser of a software part and (2) deciding how to search through a library stocked with parts for which such information is known. The project has completed prototyping a toolset based on its exploration. This toolset will be a product in the Consortiums' first product release.

The project provides a reasonable foundation for proceeding with the Synthesis effort. One of its chief advantages in this regard is the fact that the set of attributes for describing parts is readily extended as exploration reveals new attributes that are important to reuse. Its major drawbacks are that there is still very limited experience using it and it is not well populated yet, drawbacks that will be corrected over time.

6.3: Synthesis 1 Project

The Synthesis 1 Project, which has now been split into several new projects, laid much of the groundwork for the current focus on Synthesis in the Consortium. The project succeeded with its primary goals: (1) to perform a domain analysis of cruise missile autopilots; (2) structure a canonical design for an autopilot based on both the domain analysis and the availability of Ada packages that were developed specifically for that domain; (3) build an application generator that applies mission-level requirements to flesh out the canonical design with appropriate design details; and (4) to emit runnable Ada source code based on the complete design.

However, the impact of those successes was limited for several reasons: (1) a rigorous method for performing and documenting domain analysis did not result from the work, although what was done serves as a foundation for developing that method; (2) only one canonical design was developed, even though it had three kinds of parameters (sensors and commands, control surfaces, and filters); (3) a rigorous method for describing canonical designs did not result from the work, but the work serves as a foundation for developing that method; (4) the synthesizer was truly only an application generator (i.e., the engineer could not guide the selection of a design or code after stating the requirements); (5) the code-generation scheme worked, but it was primitive and not readily generalized. Much of the current and planned effort in the Consortium focuses on eliminating these limitations (e.g., an explicit goal during the next phase of work is to develop a rigorous method for performing and documenting domain analysis).

6.4: Traceability and Impact Analysis

The problem of understanding which lifecycle objects are affected by a proposed change is related to iteration and adaptation. Many relationships interlock the lifecycle objects stored in a reuse library. For example, changes to a design module's interface potentially affect every module that uses the altered module. Test data are associated with code that implements each design module. Changing a design would potentially invalidate some or all of the test data.

Tracking the relationships among lifecycle objects and understanding which of those objects are affected by a proposed change is important to the developer who must update all the affected objects to ensure that the entire system and its supporting documentation are correct. Earlier work in the Consortium focused on tracking relationships among objects (19). The current Impact Analysis Project is now advancing that work by exploring how best to compute the set of objects affected by a potential change and how to automate the creation of relationships. The Consortium's efforts in this area are described in more detail in Nejmeh et al. (1).

6.5: Dynamics Assessment

One of the most important attributes that distinguishes software developed by the aerospace industry from that developed in many other fields is its real-time nature. The description of Synthesis throughout this overview has repeatedly stressed performance assessment as an integral part of the process. For the past eighteen months the Consortium has been developing tools to support dynamics assessment at both the system and software levels, with special emphasis on systems implemented in Ada. A family of very powerful tools has been prototyped (and is now becoming a product) that allow a user to quickly construct a system model based on stochastic Petri nets (SPN) and to generate from that model many interesting facts about performance such as mean throughput, performance bottlenecks, and processor utilization. In addition, a language called Ada Modeling Language (AML) has been defined to allow a software engineer to specify the performance-oriented attributes of a software system written in Ada. A program written in AML looks much like Ada PDL and is therefore familiar to the software engineer. This program is translated into an SPN representation, analysis is performed on the net, and the results are mapped back up to the original AML model. The effect is that a software engineer can take advantage of the powerful SPN model for performance analysis without ever having to write or see an SPN. Analysis is performed in terms of Ada semantics such as the Ada tasking model and rendezvous. This toolset and its proposed evolution are described further in Blakemore and Schebella (2).

6.6: Design

A set of design tools has been prototyped and is now becoming products. These early tools allow an engineer to study the structural properties of systems designed in Ada. The early focus has been on the standard Ada mechanisms for organizing programs: tasks, packages, procedures, etc. This design group has now broadened its focus to look at, among other things, how design modules map into Ada constructs, especially Ada packages, and it anticipates that such a mapping can be largely automated. Of special interest are how to map anticipated changes into Ada structures that accommodate those changes. One of the problems the verification group is looking at is how to map assumptions into executable assertions in Ada that verify that the assumptions are true.

One of the most novel aspects of the early design tools has been their focus on convertibility between different representations. This focus reflects the fact that different models and ways of viewing information are required for different purposes. For example, the design toolset can map automatically between a textual and a graphical representation of Ada. Aside from the obvious benefits for maintaining existing systems, such *reverse engineering* from text to graphical representations is especially important when examining existing systems to identify potentially reusable parts and perform a domain analysis.

7: Early Experiences

Early experiences using pieces of the Synthesis process as it is now understood have been encouraging. The Software Technology Exploration Division of the Consortium is devoted to exploring and prototyping software tools that automate Synthesis. That division successfully prototyped four toolsets that automate some aspect of Synthesis: dynamics assessment, design, reuse libraries, and traceability. These toolsets were explained briefly in the previous section. The division used some aspects of the approaches advocated in the Synthesis process to evolve those prototypes. The results of those efforts are documented in product descriptions which were written by using much of the NRL methodology. Product Set 1, as the first release is called, is commercial-quality implementations of those prototypes. The Software Product Development Division has completed early product releases of two of the toolsets and is now developing the other two. A reuse library has been established in the development division and is being seeded with components that support tool building. A reengineering project has been started to look at the design and code of the first two products for potentially reusable parts.

Unfortunately, there is a chicken-and-egg problem in applying Synthesis. The process in its entirety makes sense only if there is a stock of reusable parts and if developers understand how those parts combine to support applications in a domain. However, to really understand how to describe parts effectively and how to combine those parts, experience is needed in building applications from the parts.

The way to "jump start" the Synthesis process is to build up domain analyses, libraries, composition rules, and applications incrementally as follows. (1) Simple methods are postulated for performing a domain analysis, and for describing parts and composing them. (2) A domain analysis is performed. (3) The library is populated with a small number of parts including at least one canonical design. (4) Based on the domain analysis, composition rules are posited. (5) Several applications are constructed from those parts as appropriate. To the extent the parts, their descriptions, and the composition rules support the building of new applications, the original choices for them were appropriate. Missing parts, inadequate descriptions, and inadequate composition rules point toward areas of needed improvement.

The incremental approach to building up good domain analyses, libraries, and composition rules will allow both the Consortium and the member companies to get the benefits of Synthesis early, allow early validation of Synthesis, and allow smoother evolution of Synthesis concepts, practices, and tools.

Within the Consortium, Synthesis has been used only partially, because the necessary pieces are not yet all in place. To support Synthesis, the Consortium is currently performing a domain analysis of software tool building, identifying and implementing canonical designs appropriate to Consortium tool-building efforts, and constructing new tools by using those designs. A project is also performing a domain analysis on an area of more central concern to the member companies, C^3I, to test and demonstrate the applicability of Synthesis to their business areas.

8: Acknowledgments

Many of the thoughts in this paper have come from inspirational talks with Thomas Durek, David Weiss, and Howard Yudkin. Thoughtful reviews from Mark Dowson, Sam Redwine, and especially David Weiss were helpful in revising earlier drafts.

9: References

1. Brian A. Nejmeh, Thomas E. Dickey, and Steven P. Wartik, "Traceability Technology at the Software Productivity Consortium," *The Proceedings of IFIPS '89,* North-Holland Publishing Co., Amsterdam, The Netherlands, August 1989.
2. Alex Blakemore and Gary Schebella, "Tools for Analyzing the Dynamic Properties of System and Software Designs," *The Proceedings of IFIPS '89,* North Holland Publishing Co., Amsterdam, The Netherlands, August, 1989.
3. Barry W. Boehm, "A Spiral Model of Software Development and Enhancement," *ACM Software Engineering Notes,* August 1986, pp. 14-24.
4. Charles Rich and Richard C. Waters, "Automatic Programming: Myths and Prospects," *IEEE Computer,* August 1988, pp. 40-51.
5. David L. Parnas, "On the Criteria To Be Used in Decomposing Systems into Modules," *Communications of the ACM,* 15, 12, December 1972, pp. 1053-1058.
6. David L. Parnas, Paul C. Clements, and David M. Weiss, "The Modular Structure of Complex Systems," *IEEE Transactions on Software Engineering,* SE-11, 3, March 1985, pp. 259-266.
7. Victor Basili and Alan Turner, "Iterative Enhancement: A Practical Technique for Software Development," *IEEE Transactions on Software Engineering,* SE-1, 4, December 1975, pp. 390-396.
8. Guillermo F. Arango, *Domain Engineering for Software Reuse,* Ph.D. Dissertation, University of California at Irvine, 1988.
9. Jim Neighbors, "The Draco Approach to Constructing Software from Reusable Components," *IEEE Transactions on Software Engineering,* SE-10, September 1984, pp. 564-573.
10. D. Moon, "The Common LISP Object-Oriented Programming Language Standard," in Kim and Lochovsky, *Object-Oriented Programming, Applications, and Databases,* Addison-Wesley Publishing Co., Reading, Mass., 1988.
11. Adelle Goldberg and D. Robson, *Smalltalk 80, The Language and Its Environment,* Addison-Wesley Publishing Co., Reading, Mass., 1983.
12. Hassan Gomaa, "On the Criteria To Be Used for Decomposing Real-Time Systems into Tasks and Modules," *The Proceedings of the 11th International Conference on Software Engineering,* Pittsburgh, Penn., May 1989.
13. David L. Parnas and Paul C. Clements, "A Rational Design Process: How and Why To Fake It," *IEEE Transactions on Software Engineering,* SE-12, 2, February 1986, pp. 251-257.
14. Paul C. Clements, "Using Information-Hiding as a Design Discipline: Techniques and Lessons," *Proceedings of the Structure Development Forum VIII,* Seattle, Wash., August 1986.
15. Dan G. McNicholl, Constance Palmer, et al., *Common Ada Missile Packages (CAMP),* McDonnell Douglas Astronautics Co. AFATL-TR-85-93, May 1986.
16. Lori A. Clarke, Jack C. Wileden, and A.L. Wolf, "GRAPHITE: A Meta-Tool for Ada Environment Development," in *The Proceedings of the IEEE Second International Conference on Ada Applications and Environments,* Miami Beach, Fla., April 1986, pp. 81-90.
17. James Kirby, Jr., "Process for the Production of Reusable Software," in *Software Technology Exploration Guidebook, Volume 2: Technical Guidebook,* August 1988.
18. James Kirby, Jr., "How To Find and Describe Assumptions," in *"Software Technology Exploration Guidebook, Volume 2: Technical Guidebook,* August 1988.
19. Brian Nejmeh, William Cornwell, Thomas Dickey, Haywood Osborne, and Thomas Reid, *Final Prototyping Report for Traceability Project,* SPC-TR-88-20, Version 1.0, Software Productivity Consortium, Herndon, VA, April 1988.

REUSABLE SOFTWARE CONCEPTS AND SOFTWARE DEVELOPMENT METHODOLOGIES

Paul C. Grabow*
The University of Texas
at Arlington

W. B. Noble**
Hughes Aircraft Company
Fullerton, CA

ABSTRACT

Software reuse concepts are discussed based on a review and evaluation of software development methodologies for the Navy. The purpose of the report was to determine which methodologies were suitable for producing and maintaining reusable software for real-time Navy embedded computer systems. A sample of nineteen software development methodologies were reviewed, representing research, commercial, and industrial approaches. Software reuse concepts include the current scope of software reuse, as well as the value and the feasibility of software reuse. The paper aslo gives a brief summary of the methodology review approach, the conclusions from the study, and some recommendations for employing reusable software.

Introduction

The cost, reliability and timeliness of real-time, embedded computer systems has become a problem. Software reuse is viewed as part of the solution. The possible incentives for software reuse include increased reliability, improved development time, and reduced cost [1]. A survey of the state of the art can be found in [2] and [3]. Some of the problems and issues related to software reuse are discussed in [4].

A review and evaluation of software development methodologies was initiated by the Navy [5] to determine which methodologies were suitable for producing and maintaining reusable software for real-time Navy embedded computer systems. The work was a component of the Reusable Software Implementation Program (RSIP) Phase I, an effort to develop reusable software methodology guidelines for Navy embedded computer systems.

In addition to the methodology reviews, the concept of software reuse was discussed in order to (1) understand the wide varieties of reusability that are possible, (2) determine what kinds of software reuse is suitable for a given environment, and (3) uncover problems involved in achieving reusability.

The scope of the study was limited to real-time embedded systems. These include transaction or data-driven systems, such as air traffic control and tactical data systems. Other real-time systems such as interactive (e.g., airline reservation systems) or closed-loop control (e.g., auto pilot) systems were not considered. Embedded systems are dedicated to a single purpose, and cannot be altered in the field (except for maintenance). This is in contrast to a batch processing system, which at any time is dedicated to a single job, but performs substantially different jobs at different times.

Nineteen software development methodologies were reviewed, representing a sampling of existing approaches to software development (rather than a comprehensive review of existing practice). The methodologies were separated into three categories: research, commercial, and industrial. The first relates to approaches that are still in a laboratory environment (usually within a university), the second to those available for purchase on the commercial market, in the public domain, or as government-furnished equipment, and the last to methodologies that are currently in use within large-scale industrial settings.

The rest of this paper includes a discussion of software reuse concepts, a brief summary of the methodology review approach, conclusions based on the Navy study, and recommendations for employing reusable software. The concepts discussed are the current scope of software reuse, source-code libraries, as well as the value and the feasibility of software reuse. The review approach is summarized by giving a definition of a methodology, a list of the methodologies reviewed, and a summary of the framework used to evaluate the methodologies. The conclusions and recommendations are based on the information gained from the methodology reviews and a survey of pertinent articles in the field of software reuse.

---

*Assistant Professor, Computer Science and Engineering
**Member AIAA

Concepts

Scope of Current Software Reuse

Software. In the Navy report, software referred to any product related to producing, operating, or maintaining an executable computer system. This includes all documentation as well as the actual executable computer code. This broad definition is appropriate because the coding process typically represents a relatively small portion (about 15%) of the total software development effort. As a result, source-code reuse would provide a relatively small incremental benefit. Furthermore, source-code reuse poses the greatest hurdles in terms of classification, storage, retrieval, and the need for a precise description of the software's operational characteristics. Therefore, it is fruitful to consider other products which can be more readily reused, and which can provide more benefits (e.g., system requirements and designs).

Software Systems. Three general categories of software systems were considered in the report: 1) application software (the primary product of software development), 2) development software (all of the software used to develop the application software), and 3) field-support software (software used to operate and maintain the application software in the target environments).

Reuse Spectrum. A wide range of software may be reused, on the basis of the above definition. At one end of the reuse spectrum is instruction (statement) reuse. This has been in use since the first programmer saved a segment of an ENIAC pinboard. It has also occurred each time someone reused a few punched cards out of a program deck to save time in repunching the cards. Software reuse at the other end of the spectrum is system reuse. This is represented by a multisite air traffic control system, in which the various sites are provided identical software and hardware, with adaptation data to compensate for site-particular characteristics. Statement reuse is not of particular interest or use, because the size of the reused element is minuscule (and possibly part of the hardware anyway). System reuse, on the other hand, requires that the problem addressed by a new system is identical to that of the old system. The benefit of software reuse lies somewhere between these two extremes.

A Reusable System. An example of a reusable system is a language compiler. Such a system is used on many applications, and by many people, without being changed. It not only exemplifies reusability at the system level, but it provides a vehicle for providing component reusability at a level that is significantly higher than the machine instruction. With a compiler, the basic language components (arithmetic operations, first-order logic constructs, and so on) can be freely reused between programs, so long as the target machine is unchanged, and in a few cases, even across different machine types.

Source-Code Libraries

Software code libraries commonly receive most of the attention when reuse is discussed. There are other issues, however, that must be addressed before libraries can even be considered. For example, the type of software component to be reused must be determined, a method for classifying, storing and retrieving reusable components must be devised, and a methodology for synthesizing existing components to produce new systems must be established. Currently, these issues have not been adequately addressed for large-scale, industrial applications.

A code library is an appealing concept but it is perhaps the most difficult reuse approach to implement. This is especially true for a source-code library that is to be used across organizational boundaries (e.g., between two different companies). At the crux of the problem is a person's inability to precisely describe what a software component does and how it should be used. Truly precise specifications are difficult to write and the information created can easily become unmanageable for large components.

Value of Software Reuse

The value of software reuse is related to its incentives: increased reliability, improved development time, reduced cost, and more efficient use of manpower. However, reuse is only valuable if the effort to locate and reuse the component, plus the effort to catalog the original and design it in a reusable manner, is less than the effort to initially create and verify a component. In many cases, this is related to the size and complexity of the software product. If the component reused is small and simple, the value of reuse is low. On the other hand, if the component to be reused is large and complex, its value is very high.

Feasibility of Software Reuse

Even if the reuse of a software component is valuable, its reuse may not be feasible. Factors that affect feasibility are 1) the size and complexity of the software component, 2) the life-cycle phase which the component represents, 3) the range of applications in which the software will be reused, 4) the organizational distance from the originator of the software to the person attempting to reuse the component, and 5) the variability in interpreting the component.

Size and Complexity. As the size and complexity of the software component goes up, the feasibility usually goes down. Small components are more easily designed, tested, and maintained than large, complex components. In general, this is inversely related to the value of the component.

Life-Cycle Phase. As the life-cycle phase of the component approaches implementation, the feasibility of reuse usually goes down. It is likely easier to reuse a requirements document, for example, than to reuse coded subroutines. Code would have far more assumptions associated with it (e.g., operating system utilities, parameter passing conventions) than would the high-level abstractions used in a requirements document. Also, reusable code implies that all of the documentation associated prior to and during the production of the code are also reusable and very reliable.

Range of Applications. The range of applications in which the software is to be reused determines, to a large extent, how well-defined and how flexible the component must be. If the component is used within a narrow range of applications where terminology and assumptions are well understood, the definition of the component need not be exceptionally rigorous. However, when the range of applications is broad, the component must be very rigorously defined, yet also flexible, since the terminology and assumptions would be more varied and less well-known in a broad range of applications.

Organizational Distance. The organizational distance refers to the number of "organizational layers" that separates the person who reuses a component from the person who initially developed the component. Examples of this distance include "within the same department in a company", "between departments within the same company", "between divisions of the same company", or "between different companies". If the organizational distance is small, the component is more easily reused since the information needed to reuse the component is likely to be available; if the distance is large, this information is often more difficult to obtain. Also, the component need not be as rigorously defined if the organizational distance is small.

Variability. If the variability in interpreting a reusable component is high, its feasibility will be low. For example, the concept of addition, or multiplication, or even complex math functions such as are found in a typical math library, are amenable to simple, concise, and generally accepted definitions, with little potential for misinterpretation. On the other hand, an abstract concept, such as track-to-track correlation or action-entry processing, is subject to a far greater degree of variability in interpretation, performance, and implementation.

Methodology Review Approach

Methodology

In the report, a methodology was defined as a collection of methods, rules, and assumptions used by a discipline (software development) to create a product (software). Stated another way, a methodology should specify three things: "(1) what decisions are to be made, (2) how to make them, and (3) in what order they should be made" [6]. Excluded from the definition are three concepts usually associated with software development methodologies: tools, automation, and integration. However, these are related to the viability of a the methodology, especially in a large-scale, industrial environment; by themselves, they do not constitute a methodology.

A software development methodology to produce and reuse software must have all the properties of a good development methodology plus additional characteristics to handle reuse issues. For example, a good methodology should have a way of clearly specifying the characteristics of a software module. When reuse is desired, though, the level of specification required may be much more formal and detailed.

Methodologies Reviewed

Nineteen software development methodologies were reviewed, representing a sampling of research, industrial, and commercial approaches. (For a more complete reference list see [5].)

Research Methodologies

- Programmer's Apprentice [7-10]
- Harvard Program Development System [11,12],
- System Architect Apprentice (SARA) [13-15],
- Draco [16,17]
- PAISLey [18,19]

Commercial Methodologies

- Software Cost Reduction (SCR) [20-22]
- Restructured Naval Tactical Data System (RNTDS) [5]
- Formal Development Methodology (FDM) [23,24]
- Gypsy Verification Environment (GVE) [25,26]
- Information System Design Optimization System (ISDOS) [27,28]
- Software Requirements Engineering Methodology (SREM) [29,30]
- Higher Order Software (HOS) [31,32]
- Structured Analysis and Design Technique (SADT) [33,34]
- Ada*-oriented Methodologies [35,36]
- Smalltalk [37]
- Raytheon [38]

Industrial Methodologies

- Hughes Aircraft Company [39,40]
- Grumman Aerospace Corporation [41,42]
- Boeing Commercial Aircraft Company [5]

Framework for Methodology Overviews

The following six areas were used as a framework for the review:

Language Technology: Languages to describe a system at each stage in the software development process (e.g., specification languages, design languages, implementation languages, and test languages); based on a simplified software life cycle including specification, high-level design, low-level design, implementation, and testing.

Structuring Methodology: Describes how a software component is defined, classified, stored, identified for reuse, retrieved, and combined with other components to form new systems; includes

breadth of problem domain addressed, life-cycle products reused, level of automated support, level of semantic definition used, and dependence on system archictecture or implementation language.

---

*Ada is a registered trademark of the U.S. Government, Ada Joint Program Office.

The Impact of Prototyping on Software System Engineering

Hassan Gomaa
George Mason University
School of Information Technology and Engineering
Fairfax, VA 22030

Abstract: Traditionally, large-scale software systems have been developed by using the software lifecycle, a phased approach for developing software. However, there are several problems with this approach, particularly for systems whose requirements are not clearly understood. This paper describes how software prototyping may be used to overcome these problems in the development of large-scale software systems and describes two different types of software prototypes: throwaway prototypes and evolutionary prototypes.

1: Introduction

In the last 20 years, the cost of developing software has grown steadily, while the cost of developing and/or purchasing hardware has rapidly decreased (Figure 1). Furthermore, software now typically costs 80 percent of a total project, whereas only 20 years ago the hardware was far more expensive.

Twenty years ago the problems of developing software were not clearly understood. In the late 1960s, it was realized that a software crisis existed. The term software engineering was coined to refer to the management and technical methods, procedures, and tools required to effectively develop a large-scale software system. With the application of software engineering concepts, many large-scale software systems have been developed by using the software lifecycle. This lifecycle, shown in Figure 2, is a phased approach to developing software and is often referred to as the waterfall model. Although certainly a major improvement over the unstructured approach used on early software projects, there remain a number of problems with the "traditional" or conventional software lifecycle:

1. It is somewhat unrealistic because it fails to effectively show iteration between phases, an important factor in any software project.

2. A working system only becomes available late in the lifecycle, typically during system testing. Thus a major problem may go undetected until the system is almost operational, at which time it is usually too late to take effective action.

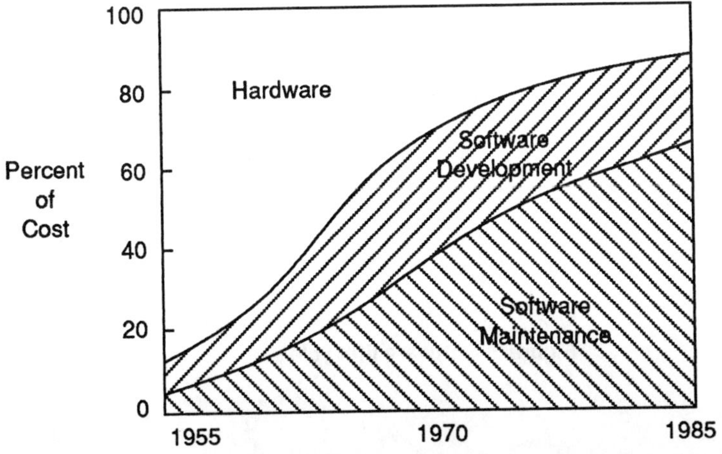

Figure 1: Hardware/software cost trends

3. Software requirements, a key factor in any software development, are not properly tested until a working system is available to demonstrate to the end users.

This paper describes how software prototyping may be used to overcome these problems in the development of large-scale software systems. In particular, it describes two different types of software prototypes: throwaway (also referred to as rapid) prototypes and evolutionary prototypes. The characteristics of these prototypes, tools to assist in their development, and the impact of these prototypes on the software lifecycle are described.

2: Rapid Prototyping of User Requirements

2.1: Problems in Defining User Requirements

The requirements analysis and specification phase of the software lifecycle involves analyzing the user's requirements and then specifying a system to satisfy them.

The procedure usually followed in specifying a new computer system is to write a requirements specification and submit it for the approval of the users. The main problem with this approach is that users find it extremely difficult to visualize how the system will actually function in their own environment just by reading a paper specification. This is particularly the case if the system is to be used by a wide spectrum of users, many of whom have different (sometimes conflicting) requirements and most of whom have no previous computer experience. These users often find a written specification dull to read and difficult to understand. Hence, they are uncertain whether or not the proposed system meets their requirements. It is also very difficult to determine whether a requirements specification is complete, correct, consistent, and unambiguous.

Furthermore, these problems are compounded because experience has shown that errors in requirements specification are usually the last to be detected and the most costly to correct [4]. Many data processing departments spend as much time on the maintenance of existing computer systems as on the development of new ones, and many so-called "maintenance" projects are established to correct errors in the original requirements specification.

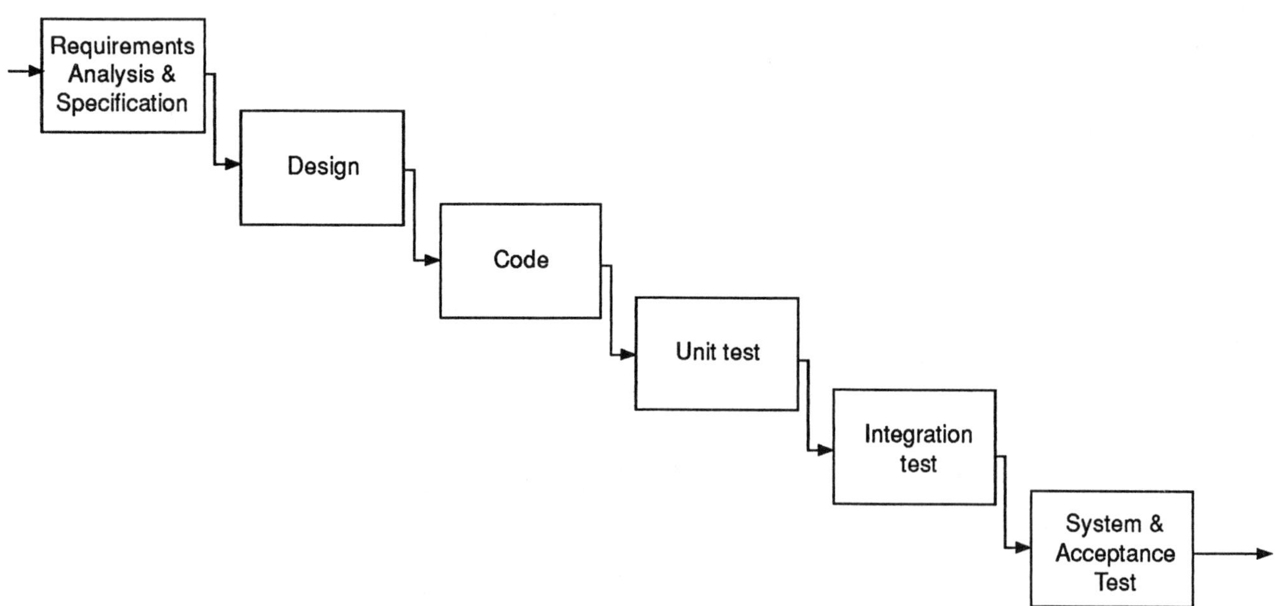

Figure 2: Software lifecycle

Figure 3 shows the types of errors that can be introduced into a software system, and when they are likely to be detected. Figure 3 shows that requirements analysis and specification errors are frequently not detected until system and acceptance test. Worse still, several errors remain undetected until the system is operational Figure 4 shows that the longer an error goes undetected, the costlier it is to correct. Thus the most expensive errors to correct are often errors in requirements analysis and specification.

In recognition of these problems, various methods and tools have been developed to assist the requirements specification process. These tools fall into two main categories, system specification languages [5, 6] and graphical tools [7, 8], or some combination of the two. These tools tend to be of greater value to the developer than to the user. Thus, even with the assistance of these tools, the user is likely to find it difficult to visualize how the system will function in his environment.

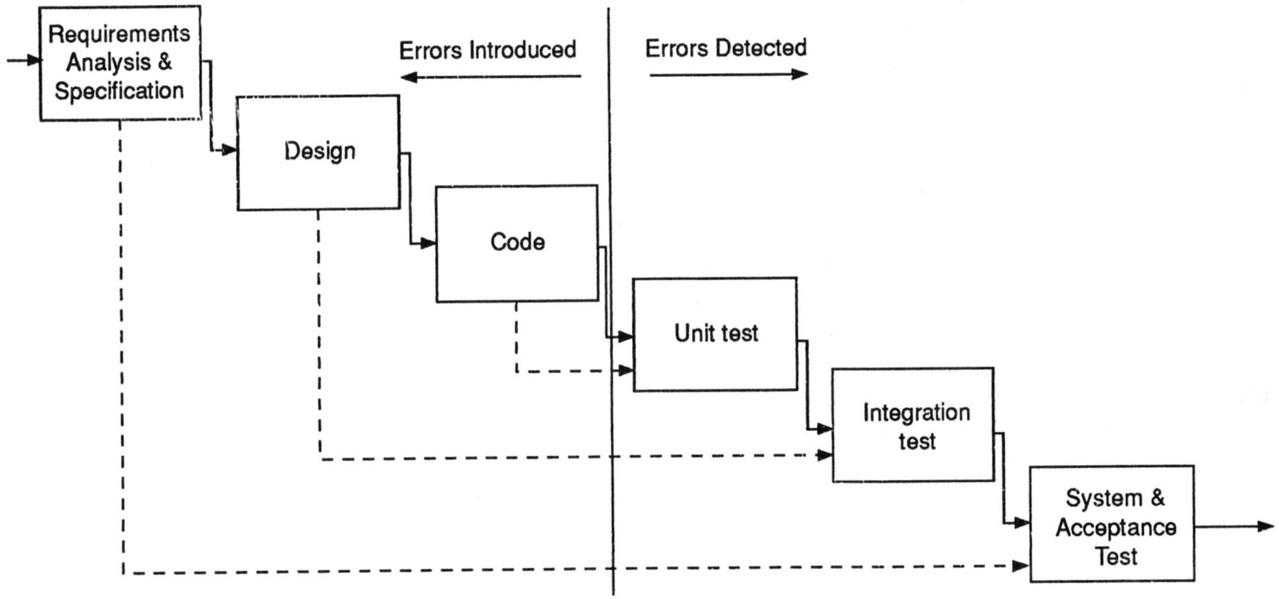

Figure 3: Error detection by phase of lifecycle

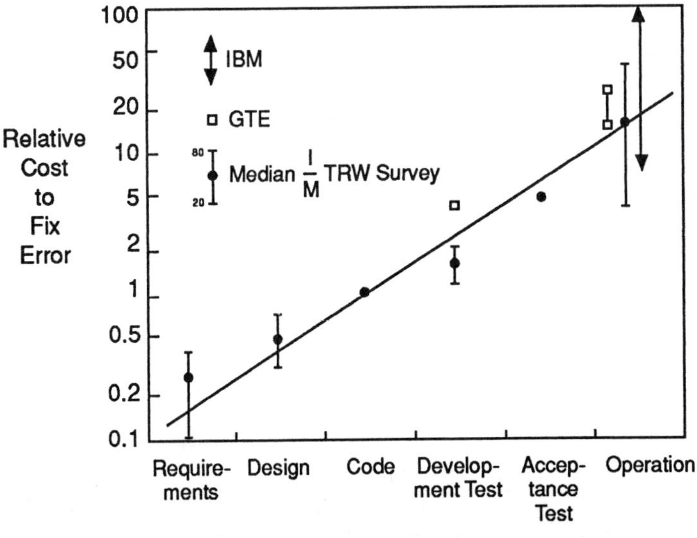

Figure 4: The cost of error correction

2.2: Plan to Throw One Away

In his classical text, "A Mythical Man Month" [9], Brooks advises us to "plan to throw one away; you will, anyhow." He points out that if this advice is not taken, the first version of a production system will in effect turn out to be a prototype. It will be replaced sooner or later by a second system, which corrects the errors in the first.

The best way to avoid these problems and to ensure that the first production system will indeed satisfy the user's requirements is to give the user "hands-on" use of the system. Prototyping is an effective way of providing this "hands-on" experience.

3: Rapid Prototyping

3.1: Nature of a Rapid Prototype

The big advantage that prototyping can bring to the requirements specification process is the capability of bridging the communications gap that exists between the system developer and the user because of their different backgrounds. With a prototype, the user can exercise the system just as though it were already operating in his own environment and thereby can provide vital feedback to the developer on the suitability of the specification.

For a prototype to be an effective tool in assisting the requirements specification process, it must satisfy the following conditions:

1. The prototype must be an actual working system with which one can experiment and from which lessons can be learned to revise the requirements specification.
2. It must be comparatively cheap to develop the prototype (e.g., around 10 percent of the total estimated software development cost). If not, it will be difficult to justify.
3. The prototype must be developed relatively quickly so that it may be evaluated early in the software lifecycle. Because the cost of making changes to a system increases significantly as the development proceeds [4], it is necessary to obtain the user feedback well before the requirements specification is finalized.

4: Rapid Prototyping Approach

4.1: Introduction

The conventional software lifecycle is impacted by the introduction of a prototyping exercise and may be revised accordingly. The phases of the revised lifecycle are as follows:

1. Preliminary analysis and specification of user requirements
2. Design and implementation of a prototype
3. Exercising of a prototype
4. Iterative refinement of a prototype
5. Refinement of the requirements specification
6. Design and implementation of a production system

Figure 5 shows diagrammatically the impact of throwaway prototyping on the software lifecycle.

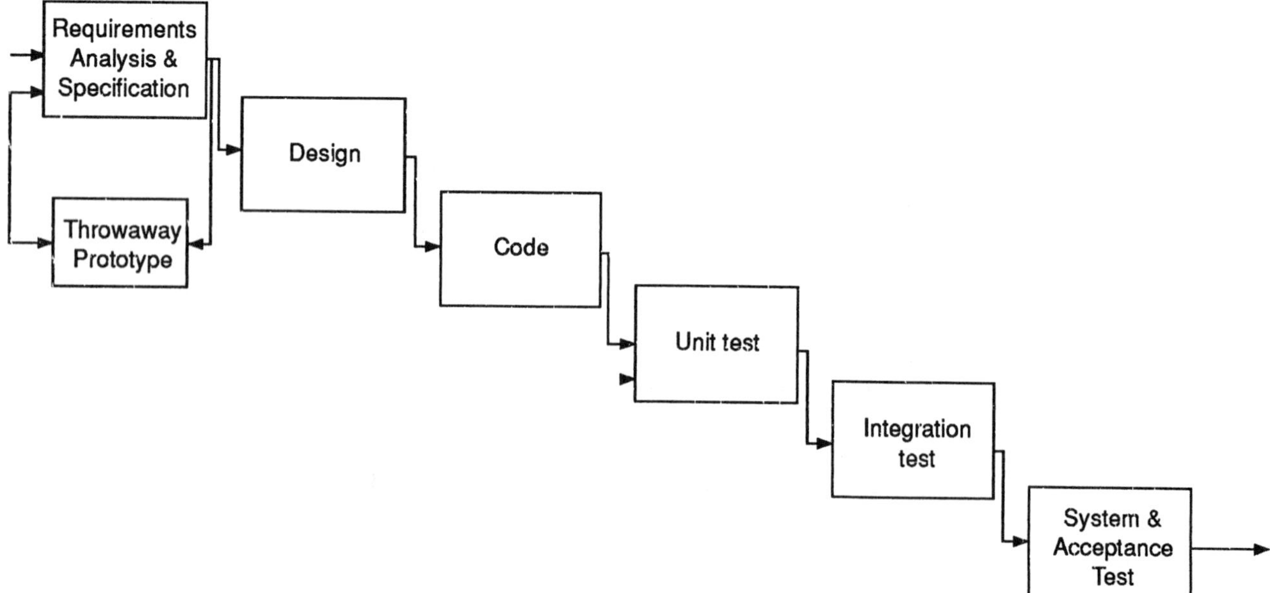

Figure 5: Impact of throwaway prototyping on lifecycle

4.2: Preliminary Analysis and Specification of User Requirements

During this phase, a first attempt is made to analyze the user's needs and to specify a system to satisfy his requirements. This preliminary specification forms the basis from which design and implementation of the prototype may proceed.

It is advantageous to have this preliminary specification to guide the development of the prototype. At this stage, the developer believes he has a reasonable understanding of the user's problem and has completed his first serious attempt at proposing a system to satisfy the user's requirements.

4.3: Design and Implementation of Prototype

The emphasis in developing the prototype is on rapid implementation and low development cost. There are a number of factors that can help achieve these objectives:

1. *Emphasis on user interface:* As the objective of the prototype is to maximize user feedback, the prototype should emphasize the user interface at the expense of lower-level software that is not visible to the user.
2. *Small development team:* Typically, a prototype should be undertaken by a small development team to minimize potential communication problems. The developers should interface closely with the specifiers. Indeed the developers may actually be the specifiers.
3. *Prototype development language:* The developers should use a programming language that helps in the rapid development of the prototype. Emphasis is on reducing development time and is not on the performance of the finished product. An interpretive language is therefore an advantage, because it can lead to rapid detection of programming errors. A language with powerful data manipulation features is also an advantage. One language that satisfies both these criteria is APL.
4. *Tools to help rapid development:* There are a number of tools that can be provided on the host system to help the rapid development of prototypes. In fact, the availability of such tools is an important criterion for the selection of the host system.

A number of languages and tools can help in the development of rapid prototypes; an interpretive language such as APL can be very helpful. The use of reusable code from previous projects is worth considering. However, until recently, effective software reuse has usually been difficult to achieve. One of the most promising class of rapid prototyping tools to emerge in the last few years is that of fourth-generation languages and application generators [15]. These tools are particularly applicable to the application domain of interactive information systems that have a large database component.

Fourth-generation languages and application generators refer to a software development environment that typically includes a database management system (often relational), a non-procedural language used for querying the database, report generation, data manipulation, screen definition, and a graphics capability. Some of these tools are sufficiently user friendly that end users can do their own prototyping.

A good fourth-generation language/application generator provides tools to allow the prototype developer to easily and rapidly:

1. Define the logical data model of the system, that is the overall structure of the database.
2. Define interactive screens that would be used to prompt the end user for data, hence allowing the end user to easily enter data into the database.
3. Provide the capability of defining the range or set of valid values for user-entered data. This capability is then used to validate the data entered by users. If a data item is incorrect, an error message is output and the user is reprompted.
4. Create reports by using the report generation capability to allow users to view data in the database.
5. Use the graphical capability to create bar charts, histograms, pie charts, scatter plots, etc.
6. Provide a query language capability so that end users can interrogate the database.

Fourth-generation languages and application generators have been effectively used to prototype interactive database oriented information systems. They have also been used to develop small to medium size applications. However for large-scale systems, it is more likely that the production system would be developed by using the conventional software lifecycle after the requirements had been prototyped by using the fourth-generation language/application generator.

4.4: Exercising of Prototype

Once the prototype has been developed, it is ready to be exercised by the users. Frequently, a system has many different users with differing requirements. Each user may exercise the prototype from his own viewpoint and may evaluate how well it performs the tasks he requires. Furthermore, use of the prototype may actually influence the user's perception of what he really wants.

The following items should be noted in this phase:

1. Time must be allocated in the software development schedule for users to exercise the prototype and to provide their feedback to the developers.
2. User management commitment must be obtained for time to be made available for users to exercise the pro-

totype. Typically, more users are involved in using the prototype than in assisting with specifying requirements.

3. It is necessary to plan a training course for users to get acquainted with the prototype. Documentation, preferably on line, should be provided for users. This documentation does not need to be as comprehensive as for a production system.
4. Vehicles, such as the provision of an online comment or mailbox mechanism and/or the use of evaluation forms, should be provided to assist in obtaining user feedback.

4.5: Iterative Refinement of Prototype

Based on user feedback, changes are made to the prototype. Depending on user comments, these changes may be minor, such as altering report formats, or they may be major, such as requiring structural modifications to the prototype.

The changes to the prototype should ideally be made quickly and the prototype should then be exercised again by the users. The iterative refinement and experimentation with the prototype continues until it reaches a stage where the benefits of further enhancements to the prototype are outweighed by the time and cost required for these modifications. At this stage, which has to be carefully monitored and evaluated by the user and the developer, further refinement of the prototype stops.

4.6: Refinement of Requirements Specification

A detailed evaluation is now made of the lessons learned through using the prototype. Some of the changes requested by users will have been implemented in the prototype and others may not have been. All user feedback is analyzed and based on this, the requirements specification is revised and forms the basis from which the design and implementation of the production system proceeds.

4.7: Design and Implementation of Production System

The design, coding, and testing of the production system proceeds by following the standard software lifecycle. Developing the prototype will probably provide insights on how the production system should be designed.

In the production system, we place emphasis on the use of software engineering methods and tools such as structured design, structured programming, systematic testing, comprehensive documentation, and walkthroughs. Thus, the primary emphasis should be to provide a maintainable system.

5: Case Study: Process Management and Information System

5.1: Introduction

An illustration of the benefits to be gained by using prototypes to assist in requirements specification is now given. A prototype was used to help specify the requirements of a computer system to manage and control an integrated circuit fabrication facility. The cost of developing and running the prototype was less than 10 percent of the total software development cost.

The system, which was prototyped, is called a process management and information system, (PROMIS) for an integrated circuit fabrication facility [10]. PROMIS was a joint development of I.P. Sharp Associates and the General Electric Company.

This section summarizes the experience gained from developing the prototype. A more detailed description of the prototype is given in [11, 12].

5.2: Overview of the Prototype

PROMIS was planned to be a highly interactive system. The user community is very varied and consists of semiconductor equipment operators, semiconductor process engineers, maintenance engineers, supervisors, and managers. The large majority of users have never used computers before. One major requirements of PROMIS was, therefore, that it should be a "user-friendly" system.

The prototype was designed to concentrate on the user interface. Most user interactions with the system were explicitly prototyped. Users interacted with the prototype through a menu that is implemented as a three-level command tree. Once a function at the lowest level of the tree has been selected, the user is presented with simple English language requests for any required data by that function. Each user input is thoroughly validated and, if an error is detected, meaningful error and information messages are issued.

Development of the prototype started after a preliminary specification of the user's requirements was completed. The prototype was developed in APL by three people over a three month period. The total manpower spent on the prototype was seven man months, which represents about six percent of the total software development effort of 10 man years. In addition, approximately $12,500 was spent in timesharing costs.

5.3: Experience with the Prototype

Users were given a two hour course and a practical demonstration on how to use the prototype. They were then given four weeks to experiment with the prototype.

Two methods were used to obtain the user's feedback: an evaluation form that they were asked to complete and an online mechanism for entering (and reading) user comments. This allowed a user to enter his comments online, while using the prototype, and to review the comments of other users.

The main points revealed by developing and using the prototype were as follows:

1. Misunderstandings between the software developers and users were revealed through use of the prototype. These were clarified.
2. Ambiguities and inconsistencies in the requirements specification were identified, as the prototype was being developed and were subsequently corrected.
3. Omissions in the requirements specification were discovered when users asked for features they considered essential, but that were not available in the prototype.
4. Software errors were discovered in the prototype that were caused by incorrect or missing requirements.
5. Some functions, although implemented, did not provide the user with the information he wanted. These were modified to provide additional or different information.
6. Users were able to give valuable feedback about which features of the system were difficult or confusing to use. Users found certain command names confusing. Certain terminology was also found confusing.
7. In some cases, the user was not sure how he wanted certain functions implemented. Developing the prototype helped him come to a decision on these.

As user feedback was received, some relatively minor modifications, primarily in the areas of report formats and user prompts, were made to the prototype. This enabled users to experience the results of their comments quickly. After five iterations, further development ceased because the primary benefits had been obtained from using the prototype.

A detailed analysis was then made of the user comments. Based on this, the requirements specification was significantly revised. The changes made to the specification were of relatively low cost and would have been considerably more expensive to implement had they been performed later in the software lifecycle.

5.4: Reasons for Low Cost of Prototype

The main reasons why the development cost of the prototype was kept to less than 10 percent of the total software development cost are as follows:

1. *Emphasis of the prototype:* The prototype emphasized the user interface to the system. The objective was to get the most benefit (i.e., user feedback) from the prototype. Consequently, not all aspects of the system were prototyped. In particular, frequently executed user functions were emphasized, not the exception conditions. Data validation, error handling, and logging were not as comprehensive in the prototype as they are in the production system. Certain subsystems, such as system recovery and facility monitoring, were not prototyped at all, because they have little or no interaction with the user and it was felt that their requirements were generally clearly understood. The prototype was a single user system whereas the production system is a multi-user system. Intertask communication and synchronization issues were therefore avoided. Performance considerations were also ignored in the prototype.
2. *Size of the prototype:* The prototype was developed by three people whereas the production system is being developed by a team of 12 people. A much more flexible and less formal development approach was therefore used for the prototype than that required for the production system.
3. *APL language:* APL is an interpretive language with many powerful features for manipulating multidimensional arrays. Consequently, APL programs are often much shorter than programs written in other languages. Because APL is interpretive, APL programmers tend to find it relatively fast to test their programs.
4. *APL system:* The APL system used, SHARP APL [13], has a number of features that assist in program development. It has a file system that is easy to use and a powerful report formatting utility, which facilitates writing and changing of sample reports, a valuable capability in any prototyping exercise. Furthermore, backup and recovery procedures are built into the system.

5.5: Experience with the Production System

The design, coding, and testing of the production system proceeded from the revised requirements specification. The production system was developed on a DEC VAX 11/780 in (structured) Fortran 77, whereas the prototype had been developed on an Amdahl system in APL.

Developing the prototype provided valuable insight to the developers on how the system should be designed, in particular how the system should be structured, how files and data should be structured, which algorithms to use and which not to use.

A more formal software engineering approach was used to develop the production system than was used in the prototype. This included top-down design, information hiding, structured programming, systematic testing, and comprehensive user and system documentation. A software quality assurance program was implemented to ensure the high quality of the software. Emphasis was placed on software usability, reliability, and maintainability.

No significant specification problems were experienced during the subsequent software development and the project was successfully completed on time. User reaction has been very favorable to the system; the most frequent comment has been how easy the system is to use. The major reason for the user friendliness of the system is the experience gained from the prototype.

6: Evolutionary Prototyping by Incremental Development

A different approach to prototyping, one in which the prototype evolves into the final system, is now described. A software development approach that encourages evolutionary prototyping is that of incremental development.

The objective of the evolutionary prototyping approach is to have a subset of the system working early which is then gradually built on. It is advantageous if the first incremental version of the system tests a complete path through the system from external input to external output.

The advantages of the evolutionary prototyping approach are:

1. It provides a good psychological boost to the team and to the management.
2. The incremental versions of the system can be used as prototypes to test certain parts of the system, such as the user interface, or to test certain key algorithms for performance, correctness, or accuracy. With this approach, the prototypes actually evolve into the final system.
3. It can be used to obtain early feedback from users.
4. Some performance measurements can be taken to determine the system response to executing a given transaction.

7: Software Lifecycle for Evolutionary Prototyping

The phases of the software lifecycle for the evolutionary prototyping approach are (see also Figure 6):

1. *Requirement analysis and specification:* This phase involves analyzing the user's requirements and specifying a system to satisfy these requirements.
2. *Architectural design:* During this phase, the system is structured into modules and module interfaces are defined.
3. *Incremental module construction:* This phase involves the complete detailed design of each module to be included in the system increment. It also includes coding and unit testing of the portion of each module to be included in the system increment.
4. *Incremental system integration:* Modules to be included in the system increment are gradually integrated and tested to form subsystems.
5. *Evolutionary construction/integration:* The previous two phases of module construction and system integration are repeated for each system increment. In some cases, the architectural design may need to be updated. The requirements specification may also need to be modified if errors are detected or to accommodate new or changed user requirements.
6. *System testing:* The whole system or major subsystems are tested to determine conformance with the functional specification. To achieve greater objectivi-

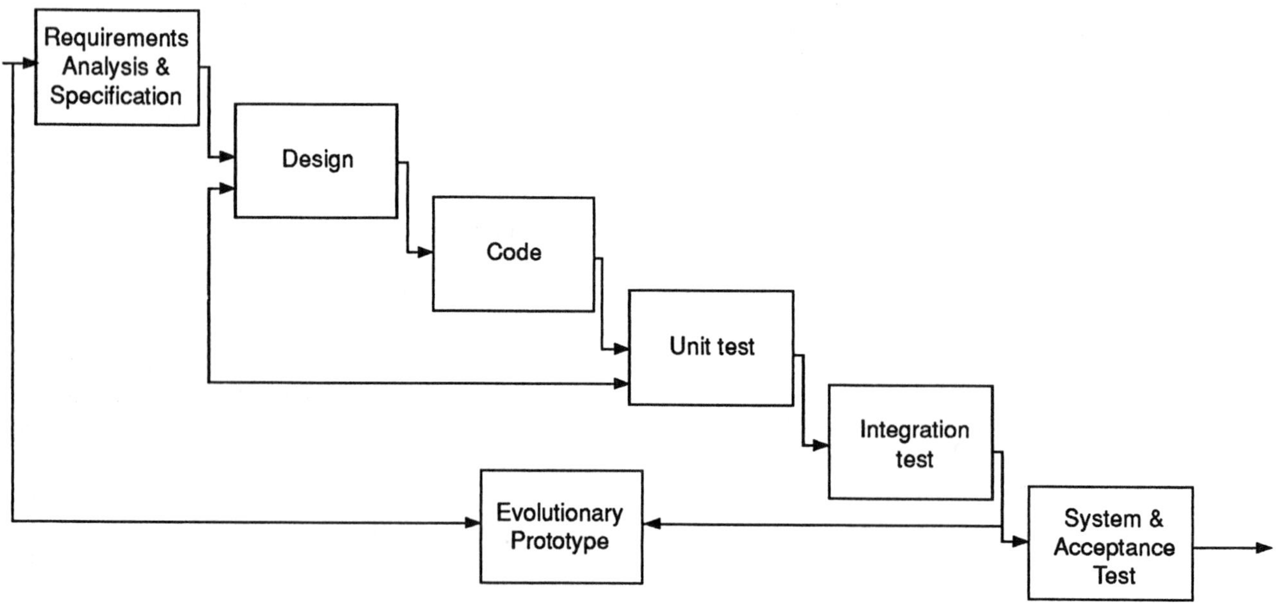

Figure 6: Impact of evolutionary prototyping on lifecycle

ty, it is preferable if system testing is performed by an independent test team.

7. *Acceptance testing:* This is performed by the user.

After the architectural design is complete, the detailed design of each module is carried out. Coding for a given module only commences after the detailed design for that module is complete. However, rather than coding the whole module prior to unit testing, the code may be developed and tested in stages.

As long as the interfaces between modules are fully defined during architectural design, module development may proceed independently. Thus it is not necessary to complete the detailed design of all modules before coding starts. This means that an incremental version of the system may be running before all module designs are completed and some may not even have been started. Thus, for example, the development of error handling modules could be delayed until after an incremental version of the system is operational.

8: Event Sequence Diagrams

A typical software system usually has to deal with a large number of external events. An external event is any external input to the system such as a sensor input or user command. The event sequence diagram is a useful development tool for both design and incremental development. The diagram shows for a group of transforms on a data flow diagram [7, 8], the sequence of actions that are expected to take place when an external event occurs.

The event sequence diagram is based on the data flow diagram. It only shows those transforms in the data flow diagram that are involved in processing the action, typically a subset of all the transforms. It should be noted that whereas a data flow diagram shows data flows and is not concerned with sequencing, the event sequence diagram is at a lower level of detail and is concerned with sequencing actions. Thus it shows the inter-dependence of events. In the event sequence diagram, the actions are numbered sequentially in the order in which they are triggered and the diagram may indeed be labelled with the specific action being performed.

The users of the diagram are to:

1. Provide a better understanding of the dynamic interactions in the system. In this way they may be used as a design tool in the system decomposition process.

   Furthermore by studying the cause-effect relationships, the designer can check whether any necessary steps have been omitted in the design.

2. A tool for deciding on how to stage the incremental software development. Thus to process one external event, features may be required from several transforms. By identifying the group of events to be supported in a given system increment, the functions that need to be provided by the transforms may be determined.

   Initially a relatively small subset of events is selected such that the key elements of the system are exercised. The transforms and hence functions within modules required to support this subset are identified. Thus by classifying groups of external events to be supported, the incremental versions of the system are identified.

3. A vehicle for designing test cases during integration testing. It helps in deciding what inputs should be selected and what output data should be recorded.

9: Example of Evolutionary Prototyping

The evolutionary prototyping approach was used in the development of an industrial robot controller [14]. Event sequence diagrams were used to help identify the system increments.

The objective of the first system increment was to demonstrate that the user could initiate execution of a robot program consisting entirely of motion commands, which would result in motion of the robot arm. Subsequent increments gradually provided greater functionality including more advanced motion commands, sensor/actuator commands, additional robot language and interpreter features, and a more comprehensive user interface.

Using the evolutionary prototyping approach on the industrial controller project resulted in an early version of the system being available. This had a big morale boosting effect on both the team and management. It also had the benefits of validating the system design and of spreading the system integration workload over time.

10: Comparsion of Prototyping Approaches

The first prototyping approach is the throwaway prototype used for prototyping user requirements. Developing a throwaway prototype to assist in specifying user requirements does not eliminate or reduce the need for a comprehensive analysis and specification of user requirements. In fact, prototyping is not likely to reduce the length of the requirements process; it is more likely to increase it. However, it does result in a requirements specification that is more likely to be complete and correct. Hence, further development may proceed with greater confidence, having reduced the chances of unexpected problems arising during development because of omissions, inconsistencies, or errors in the requirements specification. Consequently, it increases the probability of a timely delivery of the product. With the rapid prototyping approach, little emphasis is placed on software quality because the tool is experimental.

The second kind of prototype is the evolutionary prototype that results from using the incremental development approach and is actually an early version of the production system. Since the prototype gradually evolves into the production system, software quality is considered to be of major importance with this prototyping approach. Thus prototype development needs to follow the software lifecycle with requirements specification, system design, and detailed design phases preceding the coding and testing of the prototype. Because the throwaway prototype can be developed much less formally than the evolutionary prototype, it can be developed much more rapidly.

The rapid prototype is considered a throwaway prototype because little emphasis is likely to have been placed on software quality. Maintainability is a much more important consideration in a production system than in a rapid prototype. This type of prototype is of most use when the user requirements are not clearly understood. It significantly reduces the risk of delivering an unappropriate production system to the user.

From a project viewpoint, development of the requirements specification by using a throwaway prototype should be viewed as a project in its own right. Once the prototyping effort has been completed and the revised requirements specification is available, the subsequent software development effort should be treated as a separate project. At this stage, it should be possible to obtain a significantly better estimate of the remaining software development effort required.

On the other hand, with the evolutionary prototype, software quality has to be an important consideration from the start. The incremental development approach may be used effectively on larger projects that can benefit substantially from being staged. In particular, this helps the system integration task by spreading the load over time. It can also be used to verify designs and performance targets at an earlier stage than usual.

11: Conclusions

This paper has described how software prototyping can be used to assist in the development of large-scale software systems. Two different approaches to prototyping have been described, throwaway prototyping and evolutionary prototyping. Examples of their use have also been given.

Rapid throwaway prototypes can be used to help understand user requirements, a major problem in many software projects. Evolutionary prototypes provide an incremental development approach, so that the system may be gradually developed and tested, allowing errors to be revealed and corrected earlier than in the conventional software lifecycle.

12: Acknowledgments

The author is indebted to J.R. DeBolt, R.F. Johnston, and D.B.H. Scott for their major contributions to the requirements specification of PROMIS and the development of both the prototype and the production PROMIS system. The author is also indebted to his colleagues on the industrial controller development project who effectively demonstrated the benefits of the incremental development approach.

12: References

[1] W.P. Dodd, "Prototype Programs," *Computer,* Feb. 1980.

[2] *Proceedings ACM Conference on Rapid Prototyping. ACM Software Engineering Notes,* ACM, Inc., N.Y., Feb. 1983.

[3] B. McNurlin, "Developing Systems by Prototyping," *EDP Analyzer,* Vol. 19, No. 9, 1981.

[4] B. Boehm, "Software Engineering," *IEEE Transactions on Computers,* Dec. 1976.

[5] D. Teichrow and E. Hershey, "PSL/PSA: A Computer Aided Technique for Structured Documentation and Analysis of Information Processing Systems," *IEEE Transactions on Software Engineering,* Jan. 1977.

[6] T. Bell, D. Bixler, and M. Dyer, "An Extendable Approach to Computer Aided Software Requirements Engineering," *IEEE Transactions on Software Engineering,* Jan. 1977.

[7] T. DeMaro, *Structured Analysis and System Specification,* Yourdon Press, N.Y., 1978.

[8] C. Gane and T. Sarson, *Structured Systems Analysis: Tools and Techniques,* Prentice Hall, Englewood Cliffs, N.J., 1979.

[9] F. Brooks, *The Mythical Man-Month,* Addison-Wesley, Reading, Mass., 1975.

[10] J.R. DeBolt, H. Gomaa, and D.B.H. Scott, "PROMIS—A Process Management and Information System for Integrated Circuit Fabrication," *Proc. IEEE Computer Software and Applications Conf.,* IEEE Computer Society Press, Washington, D.C., Nov. 1981.

[11] H. Gomaa and D.B.H. Scott, "An APL Prototype of a Management and Control System for a Semiconductor Fabrication Facility," *Proceedings of the 1980 APL Users Meeting,* Oct. 1980.

[12] H. Gomaa and D.B.H. Scott, "Prototyping as a Tool in the Specification of User Requirements," *Proc. 5th International Conference on Software Engineering,* IEEE Computer Society Press, Washington, D.C., March 1981.

[13] P. Berry, "Sharp APL Reference Manual," I.P. Sharp Associates, 1979.

[14] H. Gomaa, "A Software Design Method for Real-Time Systems," *Communications of ACM,* Sept. 1984.

[15] J. Martin, *Fourth Generation Languages,* Vol. 1, Prentice Hall, Englewood Cliffs, N.J., 1985.

Chapter 8: Case Studies

1: Introduction

The last chapter is devoted to case studies. A *case study* is an illustration or example of the application of a technique or methodology. The case studies here illustrate the methods and techniques from the papers earlier in the tutorial. Several classic requirements case studies that highlight the application of information hiding, formal languages, prototyping, and realtime structured analysis are included.

Finding case studies that are short, concise and elegant is not easy. The papers in this chapter represent the best available. The first paper, by Heninger, implements some of the earlier methods, such as information hiding. The paper by Post is applicable to structured methodologies with a home-grown extension for realtime. The paper by Boehm, Gray, and Seewaldt illustrates the impact of prototyping on software development. The paper by Hayes is an application of formal methods.

2: Description of Papers

"Specifying Software Requirements for Complete Systems: New Techniques and Their Application" by Katherine Heninger describes a software requirements specification developed for the Naval Weapons Center on the redesign and rebuild of the operational flight program of the A-7 aircraft. This paper illustrates the use of new techniques to make a requirements specification concise, unambiguous, and easy to check for completeness and consistency. The techniques are well suited for complex realtime software systems, and they were developed to document the requirements of existing flight software for the Navy's A-7 aircraft. The paper outlines what information belongs in a requirements document and discusses the objectives behind the techniques. Each technique described is illustrated with examples from the A-7 document. This paper introduces documents of the A-7 aircraft as a model of a disciplined approach to requirements specifications; these requirements documents are available to anyone who wishes to see examples of the approach. Copies of the "Software Requirements for the A-7E Aircraft," *NRL Memorandum Report 3876,* can be obtained from the Naval Research Laboratory, Washington, DC 20375, as long as the document is in print.

The techniques used to develop the software for the A-7, as described by Heninger, are modularity and information hiding, formal specifications, abstract interfaces, cooperating sequential processes, process synchronization routines, and resource monitors.

"Application of a Structured Methodology to Real-Time Industrial Systems Development" by Julian Post describes four years of experience with structured analysis and structured design in a medium-size company producing realtime systems. This paper outlines the methods of structured analysis and structured design, as well as walkthroughs, top-down versus bottom-up design, information hiding, and so forth. Included in this paper is a brief assessment of some recent realtime extensions, i.e., how to recognize and handle interrupts from external systems.

"Prototyping vs. Specifying: A Multi-Project Experiment" by B.W. Boehm, T.C. Gray, and T. Seewaldt, reports on an experiment Boehm conducted at the University of California at Los Angeles. In this experiment seven software teams developed versions of the same small (2000-4000 source instructions) applications software products. Four teams used the specifying approach, and three teams used the prototyping approach. The results of the experiment were as follows:

1. prototyping yields products of roughly equivalent performance to specifying, with about 40% less code and 45% less error
2. the prototype products are rated somewhat lower on functionality and robustness, but high on ease of use and ease of learning
3. specifying produces more coherent designs and software that is easier to integrate

"Applied Formal Specifications to Software Development in Industry," by Ian Hayes of the Programming Research Group at Oxford University, relates the experience of using formal methods for an industrial software development. The specification language Z [1] was used in the development of modifications to the application programmer's interface of the IBM Customer Information Control System (CICS). The resulting specification document mixed mathematical and informal statements; the explanatory English made the document readable, while the Z statments made it precise. Hayes found that the formal approach forced the university specification group to learn the applicaton and the industrial group to learn Z. Initially, at least, the specifiers did the majority of the learning.

The experiment in the use of formal methods is regarded as successful. The use of a formal language forced the team to clear up ambiguities in their concept of what the software should do, and some problems with the methods and techniques were uncovered in practice and rectified.

3: References

[1] Norris, M., "Z (a Formal Specification Method)," *A Debrief Report, STARTS,* The National Computing Centre Limited, 1986. Reprinted in *Tutorial: System and Software Requirements Engineering,* edited by R.H. Thayer and M. Dorfman, IEEE Computer Society Press, Washington, DC, 1989.

Specifying Software Requirements for Complex Systems: New Techniques and Their Application

KATHRYN L. HENINGER

Abstract—This paper concerns new techniques for making requirements specifications precise, concise, unambiguous, and easy to check for completeness and consistency. The techniques are well-suited for complex real-time software systems; they were developed to document the requirements of existing flight software for the Navy's A-7 aircraft. The paper outlines the information that belongs in a requirements document and discusses the objectives behind the techniques. Each technique is described and illustrated with examples from the A-7 document. The purpose of the paper is to introduce the A-7 document as a model of a disciplined approach to requirements specification; the document is available to anyone who wishes to see a fully worked-out example of the approach.

Index Terms—Documentation techniques, functional specifications, real-time software, requirements, requirements definition, software requirements, specifications.

I. Introduction

MUCH software is difficult to understand, change, and maintain. Several software engineering techniques have been suggested to ameliorate this situation, among them modularity and information hiding [11], [12], formal specifications [4], [9], [10], [13], [16], [20], abstract interfaces [15], cooperating sequential processes [2], [18], [21], process synchronization routines [2], [8], and resource monitors [1], [6], [7]. System developers are reluctant to use these techniques both because their usefulness has not been proven for programs with stringent resource limitations and because there are no fully worked-out examples of some of them. In order to demonstrate feasibility and to provide a useful model, the Naval Research Laboratory and the Naval Weapons Center are using the techniques listed above to redesign and rebuild the operational flight program for the A-7 aircraft. The new program will undergo the acceptance tests established for the current program, and the two programs will be compared both for resource utilization and for ease of change.

The new program must be functionally identical to the existing program. That is to say, the new program must meet the same requirements as the old program. Unfortunately, when the project started there existed no requirements documentation for the old program; procurement specifications, which were originally sketchy, are now out-of-date. Our first step was to produce a complete description of the A-7 program requirements in a form that would facilitate the development of the new program and that could be updated easily as the requirements continue to change.

Writing down the requirements turned out to be surprisingly difficult in spite of the availability of a working program and experienced maintenance personnel. None of the available documents were entirely accurate; no single person knew the answers to all our questions; some questions were answered differently by different people; and some questions could not be answered without experimentation with the existing system. We found it necessary to develop new techniques based on the same principles as the software design techniques listed above to organize and document software requirements. The techniques suggested questions, uncovered ambiguities, and supported crosschecking for completeness and consistency. The techniques allowed us to present the information relatively concisely, condensing several shelves of documentation into a single, 500-page document.

This paper shares some of the insights we gained from developing and applying these techniques. Our approach can be useful for other projects, both to document unrecorded requirements for existing systems and to guide software procurers as they define requirements for new systems. This paper introduces the techniques and illustrates them with simple examples. We invite anyone interested in more detail to look at the requirements document itself as a complete example of the way the techniques work for a substantial system [5].

First this paper addresses the objectives a requirements document ought to meet. Second it outlines the general design principles that guided us as we developed techniques; the principles helped us achieve the objectives. Finally it presents the specific techniques, showing how they allowed us to achieve completeness, precision, and clarity.

II. A-7 Program Characteristics

The A-7 flight program is an operational Navy program with tight memory and time constraints. The code is about 12 000 assembler language instructions and runs on an IBM System 4 PI model TC-2 computer with 16K bytes of memory. We chose this program because we wanted to demonstrate that the run-time overhead incurred by using software engineering principles is not prohibitive for real-time programs and because

Manuscript received February 12, 1979; revised March 12, 1979.

The author is with the Naval Research Laboratory, Washington, DC 20375.

Reprinted from *IEEE Transactions on Software Engineering*, Volume SE-6, Number 1, January 1980, pages 2-13.

the maintenance personnel feel that the current program is difficult to change.

The A-7 flight program is part of the Navigation/Weapon Delivery System on the A-7 aircraft. It receives input data from sensors, cockpit switches, and a panel with which the pilot keys in data. It controls several display devices in the cockpit and positions several sensors. Twenty-two devices are connected to the computer; examples include an inertial measurement set providing velocity data and a head-up display device. The head-up display projects symbols into the pilot's field of view, so that he sees them overlaying the world ahead of the aircraft. The program calculates navigation information, such as present position, speed, and heading; it also controls weapon delivery, giving the pilot steering cues and calculating when to release weapons.

III. Requirements Document Objectives

For documentation to be useful and coherent, explicit decisions must be made about the purposes it should serve. Decisions about the following questions affect its scope, organization, and style: 1) What kinds of questions should it answer? 2) Who are the readers? 3) How will it be used? 4) What background knowledge does a reader need? Considering these questions, we derived the following six objectives for our requirements document.

1) *Specify external behavior only.* A requirements document should specify only the external behavior of a system, without implying a particular implementation. The user or his representative defines requirements using his knowledge of the application area, in this case aircraft navigation and weapons delivery. The software designer creates the implementation, using his knowledge of software engineering. When requirements are expressed in terms of a possible implementation, they restrict the software designer too much, sometimes preventing him from using the most effective algorithms and data structures. In our project the requirements document must be equally valid for two quite different implementations: the program we build and the current program. For our purposes it serves as a problem statement, outlining what the new program must do to pass acceptance tests. For those maintaining the current program, it fills a serious gap in their documentation: they have no other source that states exactly what the program must do. They have pilot manuals, which supply user-level documentation for the entire avionics system, of which the program is only a small part. Unfortunately, the pilot manuals make it difficult to separate the activities performed by the computer program from those performed by other devices and to distinguish between advice to the pilot and restrictions enforced by the program. The maintainers also have implementation documentation for the current program: mathematical algorithm analyses, flowcharts, and 12 000 lines of sparsely commented assembler code. But the implementation documents do not distinguish between the aspects that are dictated by the requirements and those that the software designer is free to change.

2) *Specify constraints on the implementation.* In addition to defining correct program behavior, the document should describe the constraints placed on the implementation, especially the details of the hardware interfaces. As is usually the case with embedded systems,[1] we are not free to define the interfaces to the system, but must accept them as given for the problem. A complete requirements description should therefore include the facts about the hardware devices that can affect the correctness of the program.

3) *Be easy to change.* Because requirements change, requirements documentation should be easy to change. If the documentation is not maintained during the system life cycle, control is lost over the software evolution; it becomes difficult to coordinate program changes introduced by maintenance personnel.

4) *Serve as a reference tool.* The primary function of the document is to answer specific questions quickly, rather than to explain in general what the program does. We expect the document to serve experienced programmers who already have a general idea about the purpose of the program. Precision and conciseness are valued. Indispensable reference aids include a glossary, detailed table of contents, and various indices. Since tutorial material has different characteristics, such as a narrative style, it should be developed separately if it is needed.

5) *Record forethought about the life cycle of the system.* During the requirements definition stage, we believe it is sensible to exercise forethought about the life cycle of the program. What types of changes are likely to occur [22]? What functions would maintainers like to be able to remove easily [17]? For any software product some changes are easier to make than others; some guidance in the requirements will help the software designer assure that the easy changes correspond to the most likely changes.

6) *Characterize acceptable responses to undesired events.* Undesired events [14], such as hardware failures and user errors, should be anticipated during requirements definition. Since the user knows the application area, he knows more than the software designer about acceptable responses. For example, a pilot knows better than a programmer whether a particular response to a sensor failure will decrease or increase his difficulties. Responses to undesired events should be stated in the requirements document; they should not be left for the programmer to invent.

IV. Requirements Document Design Principles

Our approach to requirements documentation can be summarized by the three principles discussed below. These principles form the basis of all the techniques we developed.

1) *State questions before trying to answer them.* At every stage of writing the requirements, we concentrated first on formulating the questions that should be answered. If this is not done, the available material prejudices the requirements investigation so that only the easily answered questions are asked. First we formulated the table of contents in Fig. 1 in order to characterize the general classes of questions that should be answered. We wrote it before we looked at the A-7

[1] An embedded system functions as a component of a significantly larger system. Parnas [15] has a discussion of embedded system characteristics.

Chapter	Contents
0 Introduction	Organization principles; abstracts for other sections; notation guide
1 Computer Characteristics	If the computer is predetermined, a general description with particular attention to its idiosyncrasies; otherwise a summary of its required characteristics
2 Hardware Interfaces	Concise description of information received or transmitted by the computer
3 Software Functions	What the software must do to meet its requirements, in various situations and in response to various events
4 Timing Constraints	How often and how fast each function must be performed. This section is separate from section 3 since "what" and "when" can change independently.
5 Accuracy Constraints	How close output values must be to ideal values to be acceptable
6 Response to Undesired Events	What the software must do if sensors go down, the pilot keys in invalid data, etc.
7 Subsets	What parts of the program should be easy to remove
8 Fundamental Assumptions	The characteristics of the program that will stay the same, no matter what changes are made
9 Changes	The types of changes that have been made or are expected
10 Glossary	Most documentation is fraught with acronyms and technical terms. At first we prepared this guide for ourselves; as we learned the language, we retained it for newcomers.
11 Sources	Annotated list of documentation and personnel, indicating the types of questions each can answer

Fig. 1. A-7 Requirements table of contents.

at all, basing it on our experience with other software. Then we generated questions for the individual sections. Like any design effort, formulating questions requires iteration: we generated questions from common sense, organized them into forms, generated more questions by trying to fill in the blanks, and revised the forms.

2) *Separate concerns.* We used the principle of "separation of concerns" [3] to organize the document so that each project member could concentrate on a well-defined set of questions. This principle also serves the objective of making the document easy to change, since it causes changes to be well-confined. For example, hardware interfaces are described without making any assumptions about the purpose of the program; the hardware section would remain unchanged if the behavior of the program changed. The software behavior is described without any references to the details of the hardware devices; the software section would remain unchanged if data were received in different formats or over different channels.

3) *Be as formal as possible.* We avoided prose and developed formal ways to present information in order to be precise, concise, consistent, and complete.

The next two sections of the paper show how these principles are applied to describe the hardware interfaces and the software behavior.

V. Techniques for Describing Hardware Interfaces

Organization by Data Item

To organize the hardware interfaces description, we have a separate unit, called a *data item*, for each input or output that changes value independently of other inputs or outputs. Examples of input data items include barometric altitude, radar-measured distance to a point on the ground, the setting of the inertial platform mode switch, and the inertial platform ready signal. Examples of output data items include coordinates for the flight path marker on the head-up display, radar antenna steering commands, and the signal that turns on and off the computer-failed light. The A-7 computer receives 70 input data items and transmits 95 output data items.

In order to have a consistent approach, we designed a form to be completed for each data item. We started with an initial set of questions that occurred to us as we read about the interfaces. How does the program read or write these data? What is the bit representation of the value? Can the computer tell whether a sensor value is valid? As we worked on specific data items, new questions occurred to us. We added these questions to the form, so that they would be addressed for all data items. The form is illustrated in Figs. 2 and 3 at the end of this section.

Symbolic Names for Data Items and Values

The hardware section captures two kinds of information about data items: *arbitrary details* that might change if a device were replaced with a similar device, and *essential characteristics* that would be shared by similar devices. The bit representation of a value is an arbitrary detail; the semantics of the value is an essential characteristic. For example, any barometric altitude sensor provides a reading from which barometric altitude can be calculated–this information is essential. But the resolution, representation, accuracy, and timing might differ between two types of barometric altitude sensors–this information is arbitrary.

Essential information must be expressed in such a way that the rest of the document can use it without referencing the arbitrary details. For example, each data item is given a mnemonic name, so that it can be identified unambiguously in the rest of the document without reference to instruction sequences or channel numbers. If a data item is not numerical and takes on a fixed set of possible values, the values are given mnemonic names so that they can be used without reference to bit encodings. For example, a switch might be able to take the values "on" and "off." The physical representation of the two values is arbitrary information that is not mentioned in the rest of the document in case it changes. The names allow the readers and writers of the rest of the document to ignore the physical details of input and output, and are more visually meaningful than the details they represent.

We bracket every mnemonic name in symbols indicating the item type, for example /input-data-items/, //output-data-items//, and $nonnumeric-values$. These brackets reduce confusion by identifying the item type unambiguously, so that the reader knows where to find the precise definition. Moreover, the brackets facilitate systematic cross referencing, either by people or computers.

Templates for Value Descriptions

The values of the numerical data items belong to a small set of value types, such as angles and distances. At first we described each data item in an ad hoc fashion, usually imitating the descriptions in the documents we referenced. But these documents were not consistent with each other and the descriptions were not always complete. We made great progress when we developed informal templates for the value descriptions, with blanks to be completed for specific data items. For example, the template for angles might read:

> angle (?) is measured from line (?) to line (?) in the (?) direction, looking (?)

For example, <u>magnetic heading</u> is measured from <u>the line from the aircraft to magnetic north</u> to <u>the horizontal component of the aircraft X axis</u>, in the <u>clockwise</u> direction looking <u>down</u>.

Although templates were not used as hard-and-fast rules, their existence made values easier to describe, made the descriptions consistent with each other, and helped us apply the same standards of completeness to all items of the same type.

Input Data Items Described as Resources, Independent of Software Use

When describing input data items, we refrain from mentioning how or when the data is used by the software, to avoid making any assumptions about the software function. Instead, we describe the input data items as if taking inventory of the resources available to solve a problem. We define numerical values in terms of what they measure. For example, the value of the input data item called /RADALT/ is defined as the distance above local terrain as determined by the radar altimeter. Many nonnumerical inputs indicate switch positions; these are described without reference to the response the pilot expects when he changes the switch, since the response is accomplished by the software. For example, when the pilot changes the scale switch on the projected map display, he expects the map scale to change. Since the response is achieved by the software, it is not mentioned in the input data item description, which reads, *"/PMSCAL/ indicates the position of a two-position toggle switch on the projected map panel. This switch has no hardware effect on the projected map display."*

Example of an Input Data Item Description

Fig. 2 shows the completed form for a nonnumerical input data item. The underlined words are the form headings. <u>Value encoding</u> shows how the mnemonic value names used in the rest of the document are mapped into specific bit representations. "Switch nomenclature" indicates the names of the switch positions as seen by the pilot in the cockpit. <u>Instruction sequence</u> gives the TC-2 assembler language instructions that cause the data to be transmitted to or from the computer. We are not usurping the programmer's job by including the instruction sequence because there is no other way to read in this data item–the instruction sequence is not an implementation decision for the programmer. The channel number is a cross reference to the computer chapter where the general characteristics of the eight channels are described. <u>Data representation</u> shows the location of the value in the 16-bit input word. Notice how the <u>Comments</u> section defines the value assumed by the switch while the pilot is changing it. This is an example of a question we asked about all switches, once it had occurred to us about this one.

Output Data Items Described in Terms of Effects on External Hardware

Most output data items are described in terms of their effects on the associated devices. For example, the description of the output data items called //STEERAZ// and //STEEREL// shows how they are used to communicate the direction to point the antenna of the radar. This section does not explain how the software chooses the direction. For other output data items we define the value the peripheral device must receive in order to function correctly. For example, the description of the output data item called //FPANGL// shows that the radar assumes the value will be a certain angle which

Input Data Item: IMS Mode Switch

Acronym: /IMSMODE/

Hardware: Inertial Measurement Set

Description: /IMSMODE/ indicates the position of a six-position rotary switch on the IMS control panel.

Switch nomenclature: OFF; GND ALIGN; NORM; INERTIAL; MAG SL; GRID

Characteristics of Values

Value Encoding:

$Offnone$	(00000)
$Gndal$	(10000)
$Norm$	(01000)
$Iner$	(00100)
$Grid$	(00010)
$Magsl$	(00001)

Instruction Sequence: READ 24 (Channel 0)

Data Representation: Bits 3-7

Comments: /IMSMODE/ = $Offnone$ when the switch is between two positions.

Fig. 2. Completed input data item form.

Output Data Item: Steering Error

Acronym: //STERROR//

Hardware: Attitude Direction Indicator (ADI)

Description: //STERROR// controls the position of the vertical needle on the ADI. A positive value moves the pointer to the right when looking at the display. A value of zero centers the needle.

Characteristics of Values

Unit: Degrees

Range: -2.5 to +2.5

Accuracy: ± .1

Resolution: .00122

Instruction Sequence: WRITE 229 (Channel 7)
Test Carry Bit = 0 for request acknowledged
If not, restart

Data Representation: 11-bit two's complement number, bit 0 and bits 3-12
scale = 512/1.25 = 409.6
offset = 0

( )	Not used		(				INDICATED VALUE				)		
___			___	___	___	___	___	___	___	___	___	___	0	0	0
0	1	2	3	4	5	6	7	8	9	10	11	12	13	14	15

BIT

Timing Characteristics: Digital to DC voltage conversion. See Section 1.5.7.

Comments: The pointer hits a mechanical stop at ± 2.5 degrees.

Fig. 3. Completed output data item form.

it uses to determine the climb or dive angle the aircraft should use during terrain following. We avoid giving any meaning to an output value that is not a characteristic of the hardware.

Example of an Output Data Item Description

Fig. 3 shows the completed form for a numerical output data item. Notice how the value is described in terms of its effect on a needle in a display, rather than in terms of what the needle is supposed to communicate to the pilot. The value is characterized by a standard set of parameters, such as range and resolution, which are used for all numerical data items. For Data representation, we show how the 16-bit output word is constructed, including which bits must be zero, which bits are ignored by the device, and which bits encode the output value. Since the actual output value is not in any standard units of measurement, we also show how it can be derived from a value in standard units, in this case degrees. The relation between output values and values in standard units is given by the equation

output value = scale × (standard value + offset)

Since the same equation is used for all numerical data items, we need only provide the scale and offset values for a particular data item. Thus the output value for the data item //STERROR// in Fig. 3 is derived from a value in degrees by the following expression:

output value = 409.6 × (standard value + 0)

The Timing considerations section contains a pointer to another section; since many output data items have the same timing characteristics, we describe them once, and include cross references. The comment shows a physical limit of the device.

VI. Techniques for Describing Software Functions

Organization by Functions

We describe the software as a set of functions associated with output data items: each function determines the values for one or more output data items and each output data item is given values by exactly one function. Thus every function can be described in terms of externally visible effects. For example, the function calculating values for the output data item //STERROR// is described in terms of its effects on a needle in a display. The meaning conveyed to the pilot by the needle is expressed here.

This approach, identifying functions by working backward from output data items, works well because most A-7 outputs are specialized; most output data items are used for only a small set of purposes. The approach breaks down somewhat for a general-purpose device, such as a terminal, where the same data items are used to express many different types of information. We have one general-purpose device, the computer panel, where the same set of thirteen seven-segment displays can display many types of information, including present position, wind speed, and sensor status. We handled this situation by acting as if each type of information had its own panel, each controlled by a separate function. Thus, we have forty-eight panel functions, each described as if it always controlled a panel, and a set of rules to determine which function controls the real panel at any given moment. This approach, creating ***virtual panels***, allows us to separate decisions about what the values are from decisions about when they are displayed. It also causes the description to be less dependent on the characteristics of the particular panel device than it otherwise would be.

Software functions are classified as either demand or periodic. A *demand function* must be requested by the occurrence of some event every time it is performed. For example, the computer-failed light is turned on by a demand function when a computer malfunction is detected. A *periodic function* is performed repeatedly without being requested each time. For example, the coordinates of symbols on the head-up display are updated by periodic functions. If a periodic function need not be performed all the time, it is started and stopped by specific events. For example, a symbol may be removed from the head-up display when a certain event occurs.

This distinction is useful because different performance and timing information is required for demand and periodic functions. To describe a demand function one must give the events that cause it to occur; an appropriate timing question is ***"What is the maximum delay that can be tolerated between request and action?"*** To describe a periodic function, one must give the events that cause it to start and stop and the conditions that affect how it is performed after it is started; an appropriate timing question is *"What are the minimum and maximum repetition rates for this function?"*

Output Values as Functions of Conditions and Events

Originally we thought we would describe each output as a mathematical function of input values. This turned out to be a naive approach. We found we could seldom describe output values directly in terms of input values; instead we had to define intermediate values that the current program calculated, but that did not correspond to any output values. These in turn had to be described in terms of other intermediate values. By the time we reached input values, we would have described an implementation.

Instead, we expressed requirements by giving output values as functions of aircraft operating conditions. For example, the output data item named //LATGT70// should change value when the aircraft crosses 70° latitude; how the program detects this event is left to the implementation. In order to describe outputs in terms of aircraft operating conditions, we defined a simple language of conditions and events. *Conditions* are predicates that characterize some aspect of the system for a measurable period of time. For example, /IMSMODE/ = $Gndal$ is a condition that is true when the IMS mode switch in the cockpit is set to the GND ALIGN position (see Fig. 2). If a pilot expects a certain display whenever the switch is in this position, the function controlling the display is affected by the value of /IMSMODE/. An *event* occurs when the value of a condition changes from true to false or vice versa. Events therefore specify instants of time, whereas conditions specify intervals of time. Events start and stop periodic functions, and they trigger demand functions. Events provide a convenient way to describe functions where something is done when a button is first pushed, but not if the pilot continues to hold it down. Before we distinguished clearly between events and conditions, situations of this sort were very difficult to describe simply.

Consistent Notation for Aircraft Operating Conditions

Text Macros: To keep the function descriptions concise, we introduced over two hundred terms that serve as text macros. The terms are bracketed in exclamation points and defined in an alphabetical dictionary. A text macro can define a quantity that affects an output value, but that cannot be directly obtained from an input. An example is "!ground track angle!", defined as "the angle measured from the line from the aircraft to true north to !ground track!, measured clockwise looking down." Although the derivation of such values is left to the implementation, text macros provide a consistent, encapsulated means to refer to them while specifying function values.

Text macros also serve as abbreviations for compound conditions that are frequently used or very detailed. For example, !Desig! is a condition that is true when the pilot has performed a sequence of actions that designates a target to the computer. The list of events defining !Desig! appears only in the dictionary; while writing or reading the rest of the document, these events need not be considered. If designation procedures change, only the definition in the dictionary changes. Another example of a text macro for a compound condition is !IMS Reasonable!,[2] which represents the following bulky, specific condition:

> !IMS total velocity! $\leqslant$ 1440 fps AND
> change of !IMS total velocity! from .2 seconds
> ago $\leqslant$ 50 fps

Even though this term is used many times in the function descriptions, only one place in the document need be changed if the reasonableness criteria change for the sensor.

The use of text macros is an application of stepwise refinement: while describing functions, we give names to complicated operating conditions or values, postponing the precise definitions. As the examples above show, we continue introducing new terms in the definitions themselves. This allows us to limit the amount of detail we deal with at one time. Furthermore, like the use of /, //, and $ brackets in the hardware descriptions, the use of ! brackets for text macros indicates to the reader that reference is being made to something that is defined precisely elsewhere. This reduces the risk of ambiguity that usually accompanies prose descriptions (e.g., !Desig! versus designated).

Conditions: We represent these predicates as expressions on input data items, for example, /IMSMODE/=$Gndal$, or expressions on quantities represented by text macros, for example, !ground track angle! = 30°. A condition can also be represented by a text macro, such as !IMS Reasonable!. Compound conditions can be composed by connecting simple conditions with the logical operators AND, OR, and NOT. For example, (!IMS Reasonable! AND /IMSMODE/=$Gndal$) is true only when both the component conditions are true.

Events: We use the notation @T(condition 1) to denote the occurrence of condition 1 becoming *true* and @F(condition 2) to denote the occurrence of condition 2 becoming *false*.

For example, the event @T(!ground track angle! $<$ 30°) occurs when the !ground track angle! value crosses the 30° threshold from a larger value. The event @T(!ground track angle!=30°) occurs when the value reaches the 30° threshold from either direction. The event @T(/IMSMODE/ = $Gndal$) occurs when the pilot moves the switch to the GND ALIGN position. In some cases, an event only occurs if one condition changes when another condition is true, denoted by

> @T(condition 3) WHEN (condition 4).

Thus, @T(/ACAIRB/=Yes) WHEN (/IMSMODE/=$Gndal$) refers to the event of the aircraft becoming airborne while the IMS mode switch is in the GND ALIGN position, while @T(/IMSMODE/=$Gndal$) WHEN (/ACAIRB/=Yes) refers to the event of the IMS mode being switched to GND ALIGN while the airplane is airborne.

[2]This text macro represents the condition that the values read from the inertial measurement set are reasonable; i.e., the magnitude of the aircraft velocity vector, calculated from inertial measurement set inputs, is less than or equal to 1440 feet per second and has changed less than 50 feet per second from the magnitude 0.2 seconds ago.

Using Modes to Organize and Simplify

Although each function is affected by only a small subset of the total set of conditions, we still need to organize conditions into groups in order to keep the function descriptions simple. To do this, we define *modes* or classes of system states. Because the functions differ more between modes than they do within a single mode, a mode-by-mode description is simpler than a general description. For example, by setting three switches, deselecting guns, and keying a single digit on the panel, the pilot can enter what is called the visual navigation update mode. In this mode, several displays and the radar are dedicated to helping him get a new position estimate by sighting off a local landmark. Thus the mode affects the correct behavior of the functions associated with these displays. The use of modes has an additional advantage: if something goes wrong during a flight, the pilot is much more likely when he makes the trouble report to remember the mode than the values of various conditions.

Each mode is given a short mnemonic name enclosed in asterisks, for example, *DIG* for Doppler-inertial-gyrocompassing navigation mode. The mode name is used in the rest of the document as an abbreviation for the conditions that are true whenever the system is in that mode.

The current mode is defined by the history of events that have occurred in the program. The document shows this by giving the initial mode and the set of events that cause transitions between any pair of modes. For example, the transition list includes the entry

> *DIG* TO *DI*
> @T(!latitude! $>$ 70°)
> @(/IMSMODE/=$Iner$) WHEN (!Doppler coupled!)

Thus the system will move from *DIG* mode to Doppler-inertial (*DI*) mode either if the aircraft goes above 70° latitude or if the inertial platform mode switch is changed to INERTIAL while the Doppler Radar is in use.

The table in Fig. 4 summarizes conditions that are true whenever the system is in a particular navigation mode. Thus in *DIG* mode the inertial platform mode switch is set to NORM, the aircraft is airborne, the latitude is less than 70°, and both the Doppler Radar and the inertial platform are functioning correctly. "X" table entries mean the value of that condition does not matter in that mode.

The mode condition tables are redundant because the information can be derived from the mode transition lists. However, the mode condition tables present the information in a more convenient form. Since the mode condition tables do not contain all the mode transition information, they do not uniquely define the current mode.

Special Tables for Precision and Completeness

In an early version of the document, function characteristics were described in prose; this was unsatisfactory because it was difficult to find answers to specific questions and because gaps and inconsistencies did not show up. We invented two types of tables that helped us express information precisely and completely.

MODE	/IMSMODE/	/ACAIRB/	!latitude!	Other
DIG	$Norm$	Yes	<70o	!IMS Up! AND !Doppler Up!
DI	$Norm$ OR $Iner$	Yes	<80o	!IMS Up! AND !Doppler Up! AND !Doppler Coupled!
I	$Iner$	X	<80o	!IMS Up!
IMS fail	X	X	X	!IMS Down!

Fig. 4. Section from the navigation mode condition table.

Condition Table: Magnetic heading (//MAGHDGH//) output values

MODES	CONDITIONS	
DIG, *DI*, *I* *Mag sl*,*Grid*	Always	X
IMS fail	(NOT /IMSMODE/=$Offnone$)	/IMSMODE/=$Offnone$
//MAGHDGH// value	angle defined by /MAGHCOS/ and /MAGHSIN/	0 (North)

Fig. 5. Example of a condition table.

Condition tables are used to define some aspect of an output value that is determined by an active mode and a condition that occurs within that mode. Fig. 5 gives an example of a condition table. Each row corresponds to a group of one or more modes in which this function acts alike. The rows are mutually exclusive; only one mode affects the function at a time. In each row are a set of mutually exclusive conditions; exactly one should be true whenever the program is in the modes denoted by the row. At the bottom of the column is the information appropriate for the interval identified by the mode-condition intersection. Thus to find the information appropriate for a given mode and given condition, first find the row corresponding to the mode, find the condition within the row, and follow that column to the bottom of the table. An "X" instead of a condition indicates that information at the bottom of the column is never appropriate for that mode.

In Fig. 5, the magnetic heading value is 0 when the system is in mode *IMS fail* and the condition (/IMSMODE/=$Offnone$) is true. Whenever the system is in *IMS fail* mode, the following condition is true, showing that the row is complete,

(/IMSMODE/=$Offnone$ OR(NOT /IMSMODE/=$Offnone$))

and the following statement is false, showing the row entries are mutually exclusive.

(/IMSMODE/=$Offnone$ AND(NOT/IMSMODE/=$Offnone$))

Condition tables are used in the descriptions of periodic functions. Periodic functions are performed differently in different time intervals; the appropriate time interval is determined by the prevailing mode and conditions. Each row in the table completely characterizes the intervals within a mode that are meaningful for that function. The conditions must be mutually exclusive, and together they must describe the entire time the program is within the mode. These characteristics ensure that condition tables be complete, that is, all relevant intervals are indicated. They also ensure that condition tables be unambiguous, that is, given the aircraft operating conditions, the correct interval can be determined.

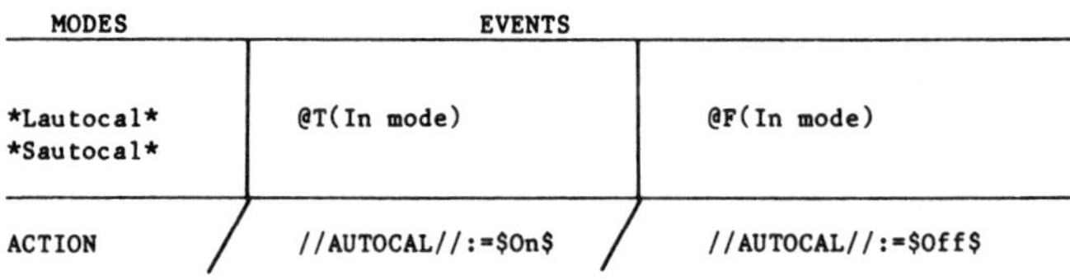

Event table : When AUTOCAL Light Switched on/off

MODES	EVENTS	
Lautocal *Sautocal*	@T(In mode)	@F(In mode)
ACTION	//AUTOCAL//:=On	//AUTOCAL//:=Off

Fig. 6. Example of an event table.

Event tables show when demand functions should be performed or when periodic functions should be started or stopped. Each row in an event table corresponds to a mode or group of modes. Table entries are events that cause an action to be taken when the system is in a mode associated with the row. The action to be taken is given at the bottom of the column.

The event table in Fig. 6 specifies that the autocalibration light controlled by output data item //AUTOCAL// be turned

Demand Function Name: Change scale factor

Modes in which function required:
Lautocal, *Sautocal*, *Landaln*, *SINSaln*, *HUDaln*, *Airaln*

Output data item: //IMSSCAL//

Function Request and Output Description:

Event Table: When the Scale Factor Is Changed

MODES	EVENTS	
Lautocal *Landaln*	@T(In mode) WHEN (//IMSSCAL//=$Coarse$)	X
HUDaln	@T(In mode) WHEN (/IMSMODE/ = $Gndal$ AND //IMSSCAL//=$Coarse$)	@T(In mode) WHEN (NOT (/IMSMODE/=$Gndal$) AND //IMSSCAL//=$Fine$)
Sautocal *SINSaln* *Airaln*	X	@T(In mode) WHEN (//IMSSCAL//=$Fine$)
ACTION	//IMSSCAL//:=$Fine$	//IMSSCAL//:=$Coarse$

Fig. 7. Completed demand function form.

Periodic function name: Update Flight Path Marker coordinates

Modes in which function required:
DIG, *DI*, *I*, *Mag Sl*, *Grid*, *IMS fail*

Output Data Items: //FPMAZ//, //FPMEL//

Initiation and Termination Events:
Start: @T(//HUDVEL// = On)
Stop: @T(//HUDVEL// = Off)

Output description:

The Flight Path Marker (FPM) symbol on the head-up display shows the direction of the aircraft velocity vector. If the aircraft is moving straight ahead from the nose of the aircraft, the FPM is centered on the display. The horizontal displacement from display center shows the lateral velocity component and elevation displacement shows the vertical velocity component.

Although the means for deriving Flight Path Marker position varies as shown in the table below, the position is usually derived from the current !System velocities!. The velocities are first resolved into forward, lateral, and vertical components. Then FPM coordinates are derived in the following manner:

//FPMAZ// shows $\frac{\text{Lateral velocity}}{\text{Forward velocity}}$ //FPMEL// shows $\frac{\text{Vertical velocity}}{\text{Forward velocity}}$

Condition Table: Coordinates of the Flight Path Marker

MODES	CONDITIONS		
DIG, *DI*	X	Always	X
I	/ACAIRB/ = No	/ACAIRB/ = Yes	X
Mag sl, *Grid*	/ACAIRB/=No	!ADC Up! AND /ACAIRB/=Yes	!ADC Down! AND /ACAIRB/=Yes
IMS fail	/ACAIRB/=No	X	/ACAIRB/=Yes
FPM COORDINATES	//FPMAZ//:= 0 //FPMEL//:= 0	based on !System velocities!	//FPMAZ//:= 0 //FPMEL//:=/AOA/

Fig. 8. Completed periodic function form.

on when the two listed modes are entered and off when they are exited. We use the symbol ":=" to denote assignment. The event @T(In mode) occurs when all the conditions represented by the mode become true, i.e., when the mode is entered. @F(In mode) occurs when any one of the conditions represented by the mode becomes false, i.e., when the system changes to a different mode.

Function Description Examples

Figs. 7 and 8 illustrate the forms we created for demand and periodic functions, respectively. All function descriptions indicate the associated output data items, thereby providing a cross reference to the hardware description. The list of modes gives the reader an overview of when the function is performed; the overview is refined in the rest of the description.

The event table in Fig. 7 shows both the events that request the function and the values output by the function at different times. For example, if the //IMSSCAL// value is $Coarse$ when the *Landaln* mode is entered, the function assigns it the value $Fine$. Notice how the table uses the symbolic names introduced in the hardware section for data items and data item values.

In Fig. 8 the initiation and termination section gives the events that cause this periodic function to start and stop. This function starts when another output data item, //HUDVEL//, is assigned the value On, and stops when //HUDVEL// is assigned the value Off. The function positions a symbol on a display device. The position of the symbol usually represents the direction of the aircraft velocity vector, but under some conditions the output data items are given other values. The output description consists of two parts: a brief prose description of the usual meaning of the symbol and a condition table that shows what will happen under different conditions. Notice that every mode in the mode list is accounted for in the table. The relevant conditions for this function are !ADC Up! or !ADC Down!, (the operating status of the air data computer sensor which provides a measurement of true airspeed) and /ACAIRB/= Yes and /ACAIRB/=No (whether the aircraft is airborne). Thus, if the system is in the inertial mode (*I*) and the aircraft is not airborne (/ACAIRB/=No is true), both coordinates of the symbol are set to zero.

VII. Techniques for Specifying Undesired Events

Lists of Undesired Events

In order to characterize the desired response of the system when undesired events occur, we started with a list of undesired events and interviewed pilots and maintenance programmers to find out both what they would like to have happen and what they considered feasible. The key was the list of possible undesired events. To derive this list, we used the classification scheme shown in Fig. 9 as a guide.

For example, in the class "Resource failure–temporary," we include the malfunctioning of each sensor since the sensors tend to resume correct functioning; in the class "Resource failure–permanent," we include the loss of areas of memory.

```
1 Resource Failure
      1.1 Temporary
      1.2 Permanent
2 Incorrect input data
      2.1 Detected by examining input only
      2.2 Detected by comparison with internal data
      2.3 Detected by user realizing he made a mistake
      2.4 Detected by user from incorrect output
3 Incorrect internal data
      3.1 Detected by internal inconsistency
      3.2 Detected by comparison with input data
      3.3 Detected by user from incorrect output
```

Fig. 9. Undesired event classification derived from Parnas [19].

VIII. Techniques for Characterizing Types of Changes

In order to characterize types of changes, we looked through a file of change requests and interviewed the maintainers. To define requirements for a new system, we would have looked at change requests for similar systems. We also made a long list of fundamental assumptions that we thought would always be true about the system, no matter what. In a meeting with several maintenance system engineers and programmers, all but four of the fundamental assumptions were rejected; each rejected assumption was moved to the list of possible changes! For example, the following assumption is true about the current program, but may change in the future: "The computer will perform weapon release calculations for only one target at a time. When a target is designated, the previously designated target is forgotten." By writing two complementary lists–possible changes and fundamental assumptions–we thought about the problem from two directions, and we detected many misunderstandings. Producing a list of fundamental assumptions forced us to voice some implicit assumptions, so that we discovered possible changes we would have omitted otherwise. One reason for the success of this procedure is that it is much easier for a reviewer to recognize an error than an omission.

Listed below are examples of feasible changes.

1) Assignment of devices to channels may be changed.

2) The rate of symbol movement on the display in response to joystick displacement might be changed.

3) New sensors may be added. (This has occurred already in the history of the program.)

4) Future weapons may require computer control after release.

5) Computer self-test might be required in the air (at present it is only required on the ground).

6) It may be necessary to cease certain lower priority functions to free resources for higher priority functions during stress moments. (At present the program halts if it does not have sufficient time to perform all functions, assuming a program error.)

IX. Discussion

We expect the document to be kept up-to-date as the program evolves because it is useful in many ways that are independent of our project. The maintainers of the current program plan to use it to train new maintenance personnel, since it presents the program's purpose in a consistent, systematic way. It is the only complete, up-to-date description of their hardware interfaces. One of the problems they now face when making changes is that they cannot tell easily if there are other places in the code that should be changed to preserve consistency. For example, they changed the code in one place to turn on a display when the target is twenty-two nautical miles away; in another place, the display is still turned on when the target is twenty nautical miles away. The unintended two-nautical-mile difference causes no major problems, but it adds unnecessary complexity for the pilot and the programmer. Inconsistencies such as this show up conspicuously in the function tables in our document. Besides using the document to check the implications of small changes, the maintenance staff want to modify it to document the next version of the program. They expect major benefits as they prepare system tests, since the document provides a description of acceptable program behavior that is independent of the program. In the past, testers have had to infer what the program is supposed to do by looking at the code. Finally they also intend to derive test cases systematically from the tables and mode transition charts.

The usefulness of these ideas is not limited to existing programs. They could be used during the requirements definition phase for a new product in order to record decisions for easy retrieval, to check new decisions for consistency with previously made decisions, and to suggest questions that ought to be considered. However, a requirements document for a new system would not be as specific as our document. We can describe acceptable behavior exactly because all the decisions about the external interfaces have been made. For a new program a requirements document describes a set of possible behaviors, giving the characteristics that distinguish acceptable from unacceptable behavior. The system designer chooses the exact behavior for the new product. The questions are the same for a new system; the answers are less restrictive. For example, where we give a specific number for the accuracy of an input, there might be a range of acceptable accuracy values for a new program.

X. Conclusions

The requirements document for the A-7 program demonstrates that a substantial system can be described in terms of its external stimuli and its externally visible behavior. The techniques discussed in this paper guided us in obtaining information, helped us to control its complexity, and allowed us to avoid dealing with implementation details. The document gives a headstart on the design phase of our project. Many questions are answered precisely that usually would be left to programmers to decide or to discover as they build the code. Since the information is expressed systematically, we can plan for it systematically, instead of working each detail into the program in an ad hoc fashion.

All of the techniques described in this paper are based on three principles: formulate questions before trying to answer them, separate concerns, and use precise notation. From these principles we developed a disciplined approach including the following techniques:

symbolic names for data items and values
special brackets to indicate type of name
templates for value descriptions
standard forms
inputs described as resources
outputs described in terms of effects
demand versus periodic functions
output values given as functions of conditions and events
consistent notation for conditions and events
modes for describing equivalence classes of system states
special tables for consistency and completeness checking
undesired event classification
complementary lists of changes and fundamental assumptions.

This paper is only an introduction to the ideas that are illustrated in the requirements document [5]. The document is a fully worked-out example; no details have been left out to simplify the problem. Developing and applying the techniques required approximately seventeen man-months of effort. The document is available to anyone interested in pursuing the ideas. Most engineering is accomplished by emulating models. We believe that our document is a good model of requirements documentation.

Acknowledgment

The techniques described in this paper were developed by the author together with D. Parnas, J. Shore, and J. Kallander. The author thanks E. Britton, H. S. Elovitz, D. Parnas, J. Shore, and D. Weiss for their careful and constructive reviews of the manuscript.

References

[1] P. Brinch Hansen, *Operating Systems Principles.* Englewood Cliffs, NJ: Prentice-Hall, 1973.
[2] E. W. Dijkstra, "Co-operating sequential processes," in *Programming Languages*, F. Genuys, Ed. New York: Academic, 1968, pp. 43–112.
[3] —, *A Discipline of Programming.* Englewood Cliffs, NJ: Prentice-Hall, 1977.
[4] J. V. Guttag, "Abstract data types and the development of data structures," *Commun. Ass. Comput. Mach.*, vol. 20, pp. 396–404, June 1976.
[5] K. Heninger, J. Kallander, D. L. Parnas, and J. Shore, *Software Requirements for the A-7E Aircraft*, Naval Res. Lab., Washington, DC, Memo Rep. 3876, Nov. 27, 1978.
[6] C. A. R. Hoare, "Monitors: An operating system structuring concept," *Commun. Ass. Comput. Mach.*, vol. 17, pp. 549–557, Oct. 1974.
[7] J. Howard, "Proving monitors," *Commun. Ass. Comput. Mach.*, vol. 19, pp. 273–279, May 1976.
[8] R. Lipton, *On Synchronization Primitive Systems*, Ph.D. dissertation, Carnegie-Mellon Univ., Pittsburgh, PA, 1973.
[9] B. Liskov and S. Zilles, "Specification techniques for data abstractions," *IEEE Trans. Software Eng.*, vol. SE-1, pp. 7–19, Mar. 1975.
[10] B. Liskov and V. Berzins, "An appraisal of program specifications," in *Proc. Conf. on Research Directions in Software Technology*, Oct. 10–12, 1977, pp. 13.1–13.24.
[11] D. L. Parnas, "Information distribution aspects of design methodology," in *Proc. Int. Fed. Inform. Processing Congr.*, Aug. 1971, vol. TA-3.
[12] —, "On the criteria to be used in decomposing systems into modules," *Commun. Ass. Comput. Mach.*, vol. 15, pp. 1053–1058, Dec. 1972.
[13] D. L. Parnas and G. Handzel, *More on Specification Techniques for Software Modules*, Fachbereich Informatik, Technische Hochschule Darmstadt, Darmstadt, W. Germany, 1975.
[14] D. L. Parnas and H. Wurges, "Response to undesired events in software systems," in *Proc. 2nd Int. Conf. Software Eng.*, 1976, pp. 437–446.
[15] D. L. Parnas, *Use of Abstract Interfaces in the Development of Software for Embedded Computer Systems*, Naval Res. Lab., Washington, DC, Rep. 8047, 1977.
[16] —, "The use of precise specifications in the development of software," in *Proc. Int. Fed. Inform. Processing Congr.*, 1977.
[17] —, "Designing software for ease of extension and contraction," in *Proc. 3rd Int. Conf. Software Eng.*, May 1978.
[18] D. L. Parnas and K. Heninger, "Implementing processes in HAS," in *Software Engineering Principles*, Naval Res. Lab., Washington, DC, course notes, 1978, Document HAS.9.

[19] D. L. Parnas, "Desired system behavior in undesired situations," in *Software Engineering Principles*, Naval Res. Lab., Washington, DC, course notes, 1978, Document UE.1.
[20] O. Roubine and L. Robinson, *SPECIAL Reference Manual*, Stanford Res. Inst., Menlo Park, CA, SRI Tech. Rep. CSL-45, SRI project 4828, 3rd ed., 1977.
[21] A. C. Shaw, *The Logical Design of Operating Systems*. Englewood Cliffs, NJ: Prentice-Hall, 1974.
[22] D. M. Weiss, *The MUDD Report: A Case Study of Navy Software Development Practices*, Naval Res. Lab., Washington, DC, Rep. 7909, 1975.

Kathryn L. Heninger received the B.A. degree in English from Stanford University, Stanford, CA, in 1972, the M.S.L.S. degree in library science in 1975 and the M.S. degree in computer science in 1977, both from the University of North Carolina, Chapel Hill.

She is presently a Computer Scientist for the Information Systems Staff at the Naval Research Laboratory, Washington, DC. Her research interests include program design methodologies and parallel processing.

Application of a structured methodology to real-time industrial software development

Reprinted with permission from *Software Engineering Journal*, November 1986, pages 222-235.

by Julian Post

This paper describes four years of experience with the Yourdon diagram-based structured methodology in a medium-sized company producing real-time industrial systems. The methodology is outlined and some of the problems encountered are described along with the substantial benefits gained. There is some discussion of future prospects with Yourdon, including a brief assessment of recent real-time extensions, and of the methodology's ability to take on board automation and more formal methods.

1 Background

The basis of this paper is the experience of GEC Measurements, Leicester Division, with Yourdon structured analysis and design.

The company's software interests are in two main business areas:

- telecontrol systems for the electricity, water, oil and gas industries, which allow an operator at a control centre to monitor and control widely distributed plant
- systems for the control and monitoring of power station plant, particularly turbine governors and data logging systems.

The computers used range from microprocessors to large minicomputers.

Software for individual projects is normally based on standard packages which need customisation for each individual application.

Development and application projects typically employ one to six software engineers over a period of three months to three years, and hence require three man-months to 20 man-years of effort.

Software development is split between several independent sections as prompted by the following natural divisions:

- between market areas
- between small dedicated monitoring and control systems, implemented in firmware, and larger, more flexible systems with sophisticated man-machine interfaces, which are implemented in software
- between application teams working on the current range of equipment and development teams who may be working on an entirely new range of computer hardware.

There are a number of senior personnel, with a variety of backgrounds, to lead these sections and the larger teams within them, as a result of a history of mergers and the natural movement of professional electronic engineers into firmware as microprocessor systems replace hard-wired devices. The independence and individuality of the sections is further increased by the fact that they form part not of a single software department, led by a software manager, but of three engineering departments, led by engineers.

How, then, was there a successful general introduction of a structured methodology?

2 General account of experience with Yourdon

The initial impulse for the introduction of structured analysis and design methods within the company came from a desire to ultilise improved software engineering methods, coupled with the reportedly successful use of the Yourdon methodology in an associated American company.

The first important feature of Yourdon that became apparent was that it could be installed as the company's methodology without a great deal of expenditure, organisation or risk.

A good introduction to Yourdon is obtained from a range of books published by Yourdon Press (Refs. 1–4 and many more), which also provide a substantial body of reference material and advice for when the methodology is being used. Once we satisfied ourselves, through reading and trial usage of the methodology, that selection of Yourdon was appropriate, a one-week in-house Yourdon design course was held for about 20 software designers. The Yourdon lecturers, besides giving the standard course, spent time answering questions prompted by our early experience of applying Yourdon to industrial real-time programming. This course imparted the 'critical mass' of knowledge and confidence needed to introduce Yourdon.

Subsequently, others have normally been introduced to Yourdon by reading the books and by working with someone familiar with the methodology. Walk-throughs have assisted the learning process by ensuring that all software practitioners have their work regularly scrutinised by several others, while they themselves are frequently required to examine others' work. Formal instruction, where given at all, has been limited to a single introductory lecture.

There was clearly little risk that Yourdon would prove unusable, despite the fact that it was, in those days, aimed at data processing rather than industrial real-time systems. This is because the methodology consists of a set of techniques and advice as to how to use them, rather than a rigid, step-by-step 'cook-book' guide to software production. The main techniques advocated are use of data flow diagrams, showing data passed between sections of the software system, and use of structured charts, showing the hierarchical structure within a program. Both these types of diagram are clearly meaningful and useful in any context, including real time (provided a modular style of programming is accepted as a civilised norm).

The supporting techniques of using a data dictionary, giving the breakdown of data areas, and structured English, a precise form of natural language, were also seen as uncontentious and likely to be useful. The advice could clearly be used to a greater or lesser extent, depending on how well it was found to fit the real-time environment.

As anticipated, Yourdon has proved readily adaptable to our work, but how useful has it been?

Unfortunately, it is not possible to give a quantitative answer. Our software tasks are too large and hence relatively too few in number for statistical inferences, especially given the clouding influence of other factors operating in parallel, such as improvements in language and operating system, and of random noise factors, such as the enormous difference in ability between teams.

The most conclusive evidence of the success of Yourdon is that the company has never seriously contemplated changing course. Yourdon continues to be used in all areas except, in general, where software development is based on externally or previously produced non-Yourdon software; and even there some uses of Yourdon have taken place on a 'private initiative' basis.

An undeniable achievement of the methodology is that it has taken root in an establishment containing diverse backgrounds, styles and organisational units and infused it with a common approach to software production and a common form of software documentation. An important implication of this universal adoption is a guarantee that at least the minimum design documentation consistent with following Yourdon is now normally forthcoming at the time when the design work takes place. This is because the methodology specifies that a walkthrough should occur at the completion of each design activity, thereby ensuring that adequate documentation is available at that time.

Such timely production of documentation reduces the problems posed if designers become unavailable during a project or when maintenance or enhancements are required later on, since all such designers' completed designs will have been documented and reviewed.

Rendering the design process visible at an early stage, both to fellow designers and to project management, has another important effect: it minimises the risk that serious design errors, particularly ones arising from misunderstandings between designers, may remain undiscovered until the system test phase of a project. Errors discovered during this phase tend to be expensive, either because thorough eradication of them involves extensive re-design and re-programming or because a quick, cheap inelegant solution leads to difficulties with maintenance or with software extensions later.

The Yourdon design methods lead to division of a system into small modules with well documented interfaces. This provides the basis for thorough, systematic module-by-module testing which, coupled with extensive use of walkthroughs, can lead to high software reliability, as was certainly the case when these techniques were applied to the development of software for the company's microprocessor-based turbine governor product.

The author is confident, despite the absence of statistical evidence, that improvements in the average standard of documentation and of software reliability have actually been achieved for the reasons just discussed. Furthermore, it is believed that, for normal software production, the savings in effort achieved through early discovery of errors and the ability to maintain and amend software efficiently in the absence of the original designer have greatly outweighed the extra effort needed to ensure that proper up-to-date documentation has always been produced and subjected to a walkthrough.

Only for software such as small-scale prototypes and *ad hoc* development aids, where there is no need for team co-ordination and where reliability and ease of maintenance are unimportant, has it paid to neglect the documentation and walkthrough procedures laid down by the Yourdon methodology.

The Yourdon methodology is by no means the only route to the benefits available from comprehensive structured documentation and the use of walkthroughs; but not many other routes appear to be as easy, cheap and safe to follow in the context of industrial real-time software development.

The flexibility of Yourdon, while making it safe to adopt, also makes it capable of use in different ways by different people. This results in controversies over how best to use it. In particular, there have been cases where it has seemed difficult to follow advice given by the methodology, and it has been difficult to decide whether this is because industrial real time is different or because we are too set in our ways. Some of these problems will shortly be discussed; but to put them in context it is necessary first to describe the Yourdon methodology.

3 An outline of the Yourdon methodology

Since the methodology adopted did not include real-time extensions, these are not described here, but they will be covered later, as possible solutions to problems experienced with the standard methodology.

3.1 Analysis

The object of analysis is to provide a complete, unambiguous specification of what a system is to do.

Traditional, English-language analyses tend to be long, unreadable and ambiguous. They are hard to reference and to check out for inconsistencies and omissions.

The Yourdon methodology attacks the problem by use of sets of *data flow diagrams*.

The first diagram constructed is the *context diagram*. This shows the whole system under consideration as a single bubble (or *process*, to use the formal name) with labelled lines, called *data flows*, showing all the data that it is required to input from and output to its environment (Fig. 1A shows the context diagram for an analysis of the telemetry handling sub-system of a telecontrol master station to which autodial facilities are being added).

The process representing the whole system is now expanded out into a *top-level data flow diagram* (Fig. 1B). This shows the functions ascribed by the context diagram to the complete system being achieved by a number of processes (i.e. bubbles) acting in concert. These processes communicate with one another using data flows. They may also use *data stores* to hold data generated for later rather than immediate use (Fig. 1C is an example of a data flow diagram in which a data store, LINE-STATE, is used).

The processes in the top-level diagram may themselves be expanded out into second-level data flow diagrams (such as that of Fig. 1C), in the same way as the context diagram was expanded out to form the top-level diagram. Similarly, processes in second-level diagrams can be expanded out into third-level diagrams, and so on.

However, in each data flow diagram there may be some processes that cannot profitably be broken down further in this way. These are called *primitive processes*. At some level of data flow diagram, it will be decided that none of the processes requires further decomposition — in other words that all processes should be primitive.

All the data flows and data stores shown on the data flow diagram are included in a *data dictionary*. The data dictionary shows a breakdown of each entry into constituent parts (Fig. 1D). Using the dictionary, it is possible to check that the expansions of processes by lower-level data flow diagrams *balance*, which means that the input data flows in the lower-level diagrams add up to those shown arriving at the process in the higher-level diagram, and similarly for the outgoing flows. For example, the data dictionary extract in Fig. 1D shows that data

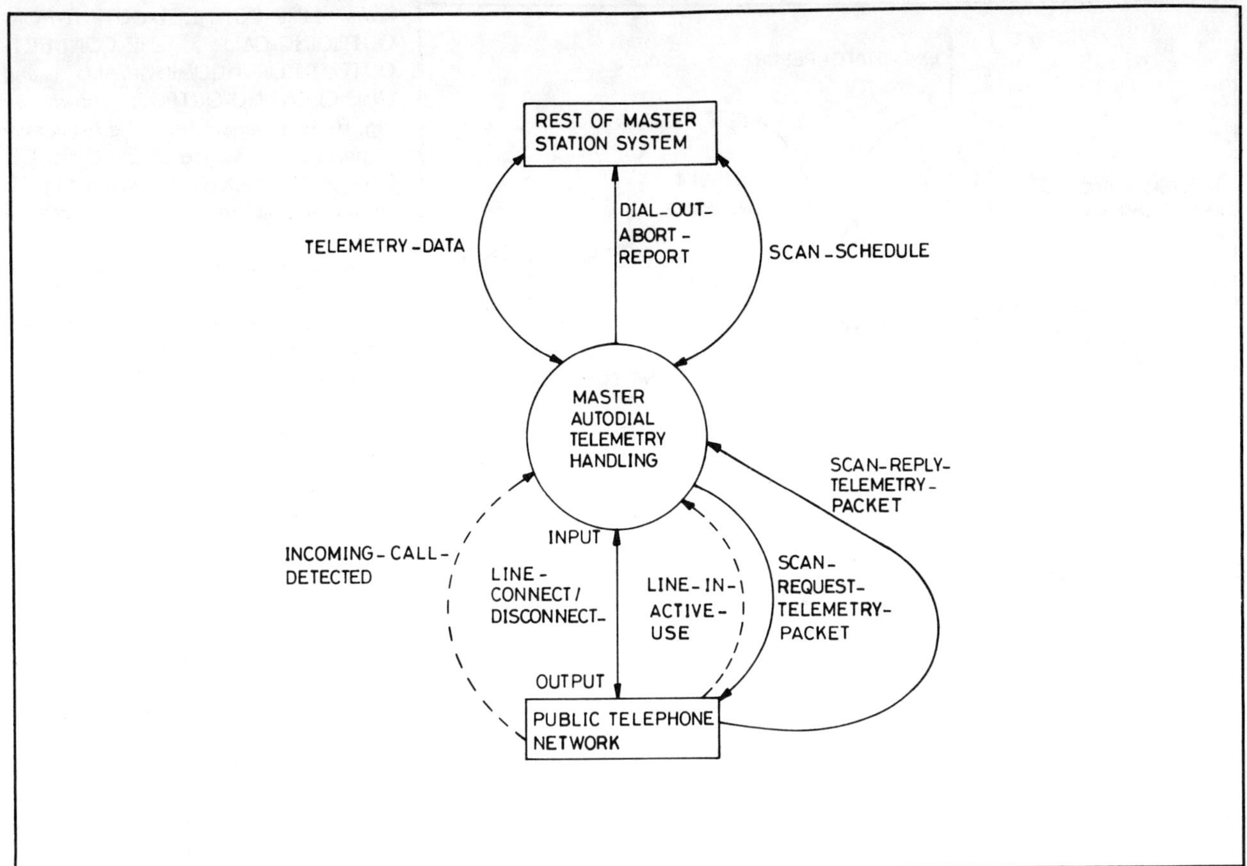

Fig. 1A Structured analysis (master station telemetry handling with autodial): context diagram

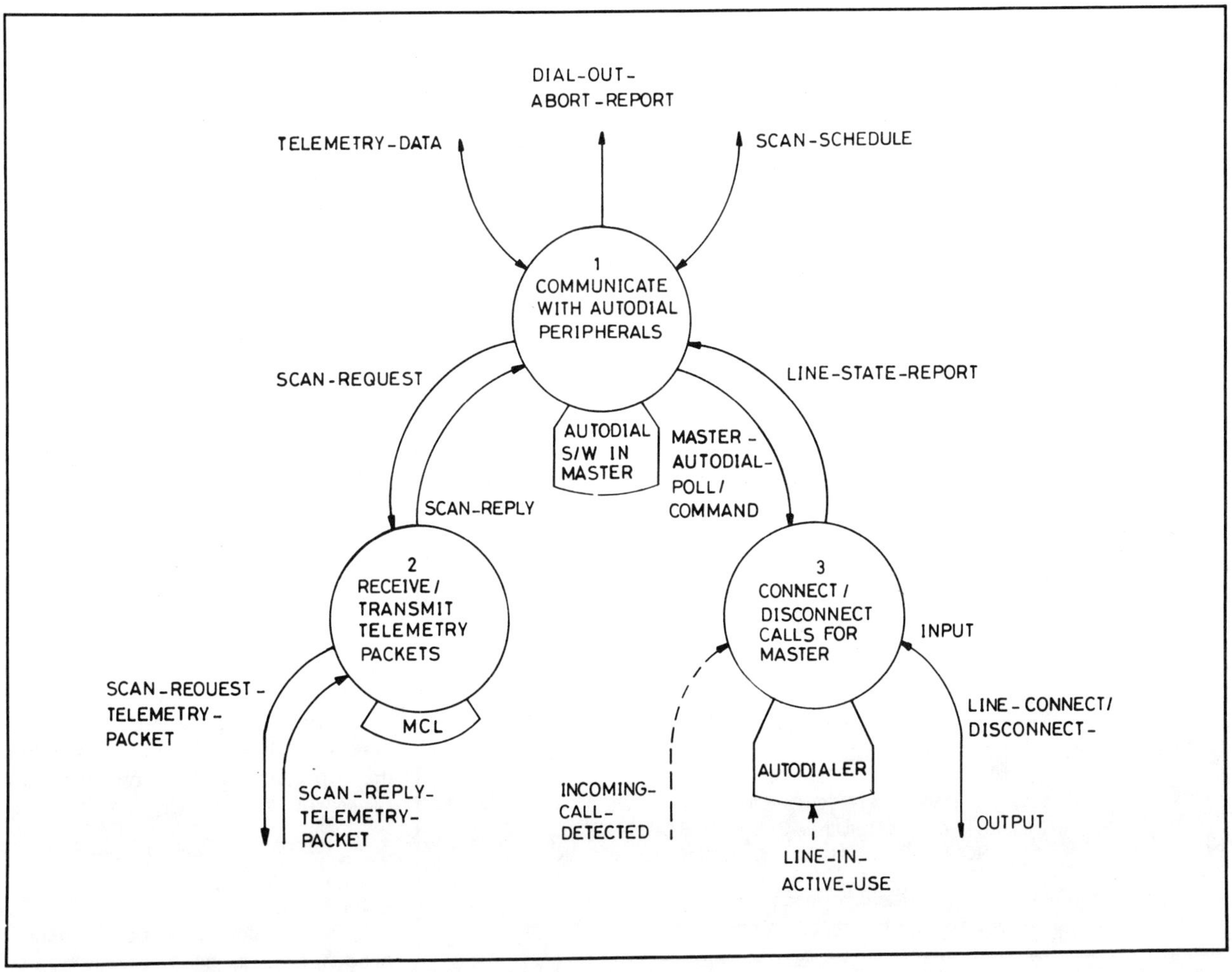

DIAL-OUT-ABORT-REPORT
TELEMETRY-DATA
SCAN-SCHEDULE
1 COMMUNICATE WITH AUTODIAL PERIPHERALS
SCAN-REQUEST
LINE-STATE-REPORT
AUTODIAL S/W IN MASTER
MASTER-AUTODIAL-POLL/COMMAND
SCAN-REPLY
2 RECEIVE/TRANSMIT TELEMETRY PACKETS
3 CONNECT/DISCONNECT CALLS FOR MASTER
INPUT
SCAN-REQUEST-TELEMETRY-PACKET
MCL
LINE-CONNECT/DISCONNECT-
AUTODIALER
SCAN-REPLY-TELEMETRY-PACKET
INCOMING-CALL-DETECTED
OUTPUT
LINE-IN-ACTIVE-USE

Fig. 1B Top-level data flow diagram

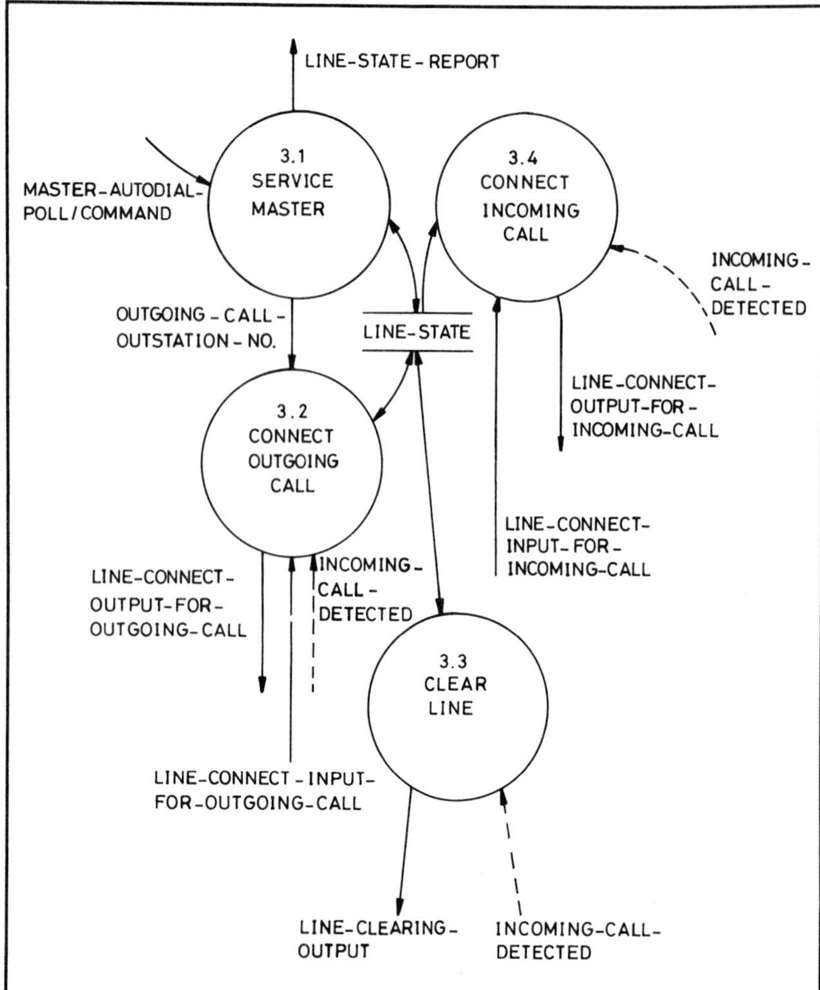

Fig. 1C Expansion data flow for process 3: CONNECT/DISCONNECT CALLS FOR MASTER (AUTODIALER)

```
LINE–CONNECT/DISCONNECT–OUTPUT =LINE–CONNECT–OUTPUT–FOR–OUTGOING–CALL
                               !LINE–CONNECT–OUTPUT–FOR–INCOMING–CALL
                               !LINE–CLEARING–OUTPUT

MASTER–AUTODIAL–POLL/COMMAND = MASTER–AUTODIAL–REQUEST–TYPE
                               + [OUTGOING–CALL–OUTSTATION–NO.]

"NB: OUTGOING–CALL–OUTSTATION–NO. PRESENT ONLY IF
MASTER–STATION–AUTODIAL–REQUEST–TYPE = DIAL–OUT"

MASTER–AUTODIAL–REQUEST–TYPE = 'DIAL–OUT'! 'CLEAR–LINE'! 'POLL'

        Key:  !denotes OR      + denotes AND      [ ] denotes OPTIONAL
```

Fig. 1D Data dictionary extract

```
ON RECEIVING MASTER–AUTODIAL–POLL/COMMAND

1  IF MASTER–AUTODIAL–REQUEST–TYPE IS 'CLEAR–LINE'
   THEN IF LINE–STATE IS 'CONNECTED'
        THEN SET LINE–STATE TO 'BEING CLEARED'

2  IF MASTER–AUTODIAL–REQUEST–TYPE IS 'DIAL–OUT'
   THEN IF LINE–STATE IS 'IDLE'
        THEN
        2.1  SET LINE–STATE TO 'DIALING OUT'
        2.2  EXTRACT OUTGOING–CALL–OUTSTATION–NO.
             FROM MASTER–AUTODIAL–POLL/COMMAND AND ISSUE

3  IF MASTER–AUTODIAL–REQUEST–TYPE IS 'POLL'
   THEN ISSUE LINE–STATE–REPORT CONTAINING LINE–STATE
```

Fig. 1E Minispec for process 3.1: SERVICE MASTER

flows LINE-CONNECT-OUTPUT-FOR-OUTGOING-CALL, LINE-CONNECT-OUTPUT-FOR-INCOMING-CALL and LINE-CLEARING-OUTPUT, shown by Fig. 1C to emanate from the expansion of process 3, balance LINE-CONNECT/DISCONNECT-OUTPUT, which Fig. 1B shows emanating from the process 3 bubble.

Primitive processes are expanded upon using *minispecs* (such as that in Fig. 1E). These are textual specifications explaining what the process does in terms of its incoming and outgoing data flows, as shown in the data flow diagram where the process appears. Accordingly, just as a data flow diagram can be checked to see if it balances with the data flow diagram in which its process appears, so can a minispec. For example, the reader can check from the data dictionary extract that the minispec of process 3.1 in Fig. 1E utilises valid components of incoming flow MASTER-AUTODIAL-POLL / COMMAND shown in Fig. 1C.

The most common medium for the writing of minispecs is *structured English* (as used in Fig. 1E). A structured English minispec consists of a set of notes in a condensed, news-headline/telex style of English, in which all names must be data dictionary entries and where conditional statements and repetitions utilise structured programming constructs such as

IF . . . THEN . . . ELSE . . .
REPEAT . . . UNTIL . . .

Structured English has no fixed syntax. It is up to the writer to produce a concise, precise but comprehensible dialect.

Other forms that minispecs can take include:

- decision trees
- decision tables
- lists of pre-conditions and corresponding post-conditions (both written in structured English).

The analysis, as just described, should be optimised for clarity of expression. Processes must have clear concise names, as must data flows and stores.

When this has been done, the total analysis should be clear, concise and easy to reference compared with an English-language specification. This is due to the superior ability of diagrams to show how components inter-relate ('a picture is worth a thousand words'). The balance checks described above help ensure that the specification is complete and consistent.

3.2 Use of analysis diagrams for top-level design

Once a logical implementation-independent analysis has been carried out, Yourdon prescribes that, for a multi-processor system, system design should commence by adjusting the data flow diagram set so that the top-level diagram shows, as its processes, the activities performed by each processor. Hence this diagram shows the data flows between processors, with data stores representing any shared data storage (Fig. 1B actually represents such a top-level design — the tags MCL and AUTODIALER on processes 2 and 3 are processor names).

Yourdon structured design techniques, which are for the design of sequential programs, can now be applied to design the software in each processor, provided the processor does not employ multi-tasking.

For processors with multi-tasking, it appeared logical to adjust the analysis to fit the implementation architecture in the same way as for multiple processors (real-time Yourdon does now endorse this approach).

In this case, the analysis is modified so that the data flow diagram expansion for the process representing the multi-tasking processor contains one process for each (pseudo-) concurrent task (in a large system some processes may actually represent multi-task sub-systems — their sub-processes, as shown in the next level of data flow diagrams, are arranged to correspond to individual tasks). Each task can now have its program designed using Yourdon structured design.

3.3 Yourdon structured design — use of structure charts

Yourdon handles design of individual sequential programs by top-down decomposition. The 'boss' program module, which organises the performance of the program's function, has defined for it, by the designer, a number of subordinates, each entrusted with a subpart of the function. The designer then divides the work of each subordinate module between a second level of subordinates, and so on. At each level of subordinates, there may be some modules which do not need further subordinates but which can best perform their own simple function on their own. Furthermore, there will be a certain level at which all modules are of this kind.

This hierarchy of a 'boss' module with layers of subordinates is shown on a *structure chart* (such as Fig. 2A), which represents it in the form of a family tree, the same representation as is normally used to show management hierarchies.

All this is the same as for many other structured methodologies. A special feature of the Yourdon structure chart, however, is the showing of all data items (termed *data couples*) and *flags* that are passed between a module and its subordinates. Also, any data stores used for communication between modules are shown on the chart, with flow lines showing which modules access them and which items they access. This inclusion of data flow information helps focus designers' attention on the degree of *coupling* between modules, i.e. the extent of their interaction. In Yourdon structured design, a primary design aim is to minimise coupling.

To help one to do this, the methodology classifies coupling into various types, each assigned its own level of undesirability. For example, 'data coupling', where data items or simple arrays are passed as parameters from a calling module to and from a subordinate, is the least undesirable form of coupling (although it is still to be minimised). 'Stamp' coupling, where two modules send one another a more complex data structure (for example a record), is a slightly less desirable form of coupling, since a change in the data structure format to suit the requirements of one module will affect the design of the other.

The other prime design aim of Yourdon structured design is to give modules *cohesion*, i.e. to ensure that each module, individually, performs a closely associated set of actions. Different types of cohesion are defined and attributed with different levels of strength and hence desirability. For example, a routine to return the square root of a value exhibits the highest form of cohesion, 'functional cohesion', because it performs a single function. A general-purpose initialisation routine exhibits a lower, somewhat inadequate form of cohesion, 'temporal cohesion', if the only connection between its activities is that they are done at initialisation time.

Cohesion is promoted by ensuring that modules have a name which conveys a definite function such as 'compute square root' or 'validate analogue input', rather than either a woolly name such as 'organise initialisation' or, worse still, a code mnemonic such as 'ORIGINI'. A good name usually ensures good cohesion.

If a structured analysis preceded structured design, then there are two related techniques, transform analysis and transaction analysis, for generating a 'first-cut' structure chart from the data flow diagrams. Modules in the design are made to correspond, in general, to processes in the data flow diagram set, so that the meaningful process names employed in the analysis together with the minimisation of data flow should ensure that modules in the design have meaningful names, high cohesion and low coupling.

Another design technique described in Yourdon texts (such as Ref. 1) is the Michael Jackson method, which advocates giving a program a structure matching that of the data being processed. The Yourdon structure chart has the flexibility to accommodate this approach.

3.4 Detailed design of modules

Detailed design consists of producing module header information and pseudo-code.

Module header information typically contains a brief statement of the function of the module (in English) and lists the data that it uses as inputs and the data that it produces as outputs. The header may also state any 'assumptions' made about the incoming data and any 'promises' made about the data produced. For example, a square root routine might assume that the number input to it has been checked to be positive, and it might promise the result to be accurate to within some stated figure.

Pseudo-code is a description of what the module does and how it does it, in a language broadly similar to structured English (an example is given in Fig. 2D).

Since the pseudo-code is implementation-oriented, whereas a minispec's structured English aims not to be, pseudo-code tends to be more detailed and closer to a high-level programming language.

3.5 Code

In the design phase, programs undergo hierarchical decomposition into modules, followed by internal design of each in structured pseudo-code. All that is now required, in order to produce code adhering to the rules of structured programming, is to convert the pseudo-code for each module into code and add the appropriate data declarations. Modularity of code will follow from that of the design. Structured control logic (without GOTOs) in the code will follow naturally from structured control logic in the pseudo-code.

3.6 Testing

Testing is outside the main scope of the methodology. However, Yourdon literature (for example Ref. 1) does recommend a top-down implementation and testing strategy. This involves first coding and testing the 'boss' module, using stubs for its subordinates, and then gradually replacing stubs by the subordinates themselves (now using stubs for their subordinates), and so on, until the complete tested program is in place. In general, the implementation and testing need not progress evenly from the 'boss' module to the lowest tier of subordinates. Testing of some subordinate areas may reach the bottom of the hierarchy before other areas are tested at all. In particular, it is often desirable to get the main input/output facilities of a program tested first and then start adding the rest.

Such an implementation strategy tends to establish the basic soundness of the program architecture first, and then gradually add operational facilities. This gives the user and project management a working skeleton system to see and evaluate at an early stage, followed by a steady increase in available functionality, up until completion time.

3.7 Walkthroughs

Walkthroughs are treated as an essential part of the methodology to the extent that not only are they discussed in general texts (for example Ref. 1), but Yourdon has also produced a book on the subject (Ref. 4).

Walkthroughs should be peer-group reviews. They should locate problems in the material and not try to solve them for the author. Walkthroughs should be formal in the sense that minutes are produced to enable project management to control the correction of any problems revealed.

4 Experience with the analysis set of methods

4.1 Data flow diagrams

Data flow diagrams have proved to be an elegant tool for decomposing a problem into inter-communicating sub-units. They are not only usable for system analysis prior to software design, but can also be used to describe non-computerised procedures such as the software production life cycle itself.

It is easy to recognise a good data flow analysis with its tangle-free layout, its concise, meaningful process names and its few, clearly named data flows.

Reaching this goal, however, does require not only considerable analytic skills but also considerable presentational flair.

Although Yourdon texts and courses provide advice aimed at avoidance of pitfalls, they certainly do not provide a cookbook methodology which, when followed faithfully, guarantees success.

Furthermore, given the specialised nature of the company's application area, it has always been tempting to accept second best in the belief that it is an inevitable consequence of special circumstances. If knowing whether to accept second best for oneself is difficult, knowing whether to accept it for someone else, whose material one is reviewing, is even more so.

4.2 Minispecs

Unfortunately there is a tendency to write minispecs as fairly detailed procedural specifications in a high-level programming-language style of structured English.

Such specifications may be precise, but they are not easy to read, especially for non-programmers. They tend to be solutions rather than specifications of the problem, which violates the principle that an analysis should be implementation independent. If quasi-solutions are produced, it does of course adversely affect the time scale for the analysis phase.

4.3 Data dictionary

The data dictionary is appreciated as being the rigorous back-bone of analysis. It is also its most tangible product, leading directly to the data layouts used in the implementation, whereas the rest of the analysis is, in some degree, superseded at the design phase, when a more precise picture of what the system does emerges.

One problem with the data dictionary on a reasonably large system tends to be the length of names used in order to identify each item meaningfully rather than with mere mnemonics. Long names lead to long, jargon-like minispecs and, later, pseudo-code; they also lead to cluttered data flow diagrams and structure charts.

A large data dictionary tends to be very tedious to finger through when studying and performing balancing checks on the associated data flow diagrams and minispecs (and, later, when studying structure charts and pseudo-code). This problem can be avoided by arranging that each data dictionary name starts off with an indication of its main functional or data area. This ensures that related names are close to one another in the dictionary (which is ordered in the usual alphabetic way).

Such a convention also mitigates another problem, namely that of name clashes when analyses of parts of a system merge their dictionaries. It does, however, further exacerbate the tendency towards long names.

The attention given to the data dictionary has tended to reduce the use of the more diagrammatic representations of data layout employed in the past. These tended to make more digestible reading when well designed. For complicated data structures, such diagrams remain essential and are still used, being included in a data structure dictionary which is referred to by the data dictionary. However, there is a tendency to make do with just the data dictionary, despite its dryness, unless this is clearly unacceptable.

One form of diagram relating to data layout has been introduced as part of the Yourdon real-time extensions, namely the entity relationship diagram. This shows the relationship between classes of object within a system and hence between data stores describing these objects.

4.4 The limited utilisation of the analysis methods

Despite the problems just described, the merits of the analysis methods are well respected. However, the scope of its utilisation within the company does not match up to what the Yourdon methodology intends.

First, a logical (implementation-independent) analysis is seldom done. This is probably because, for most of the systems tackled, the processors and their functions are decided upon for strategic commercial reasons, before analysis commences (for example, the analysis of Fig. 1 is based around re-use of the existing MCL processor, shown as process 2). Furthermore, the architecture in terms of allocation of work to concurrent tasks within a processor is highly influenced by similar systems implemented in the past (it is often actually determined in detail by the architecture of an existing software package which it has been decided to utilise). Where the multi-processor and/or multi-tasking architecture is largely preordained in this way, it is easy and natural to base the top data flow diagram levels on this architecture rather than doing an implementation-independent analysis.

The second frequent breach of Yourdon methodology is not to utilise the analysis methods to model the internal architectures of individual concurrent tasks at all, so that the sole use of the methods is for the design of the relationships between processors and between (pseudo-) concurrent tasks within processors. This, in effect, means that there is no analysis as such, the methods being used solely for top-level design.

For development work, it often makes sense to start designs from a required list of facilities described in fairly broad-brush terms, rather than from a precise analysis. The facilities are very often provided using interpreters of one kind or another, for example ones that interpret VDU format specifications, log formats, plant input scan records or programs in a plant sequencing language. The precise facilities available are best defined, from a user point of view, by descriptions of the syntax, semantics and scope of the interpretive languages supported rather than by a structured analysis.

Furthermore, provision of any description in detail is often best left until the interpreters have been largely designed and hence the precise scope of what can economically be provided has been assessed. Operator interface facilities, such as VDU format editing and display, are best defined in detail only after software prototyping has allowed experimentation to check what might be the best ergonomic approach (experience has shown that a structured analysis of a VDU editor is, anyhow, a particularly obscure means of conveying what is to be provided).

For applications projects, since most customers are not conversant with Yourdon notation, it is usually necessary to produce specifications in English. Communication of precise information tends to be by use of diagrams or tables appropriate to the engineering disciplines involved in the application (such as diagrams showing plant instrumentation and plant input schedules). Where the software supplied includes interpreters, customers may choose to enter their own data for interpretation by the interpreters, after delivery. The company is not then involved in analysis of the detailed functional requirement at all.

It should be noted that, when the design is complete, a specification of the software is provided by the combination of top-level design using data flow diagrams, program structure charts covering each task and the pseudo-code for each module. This specification is fairly similar to that provided by an analysis, since both the analysis and the design normally consist of a hierarchical breakdown with structured English text descriptions for each instance of the smallest sub-division used.

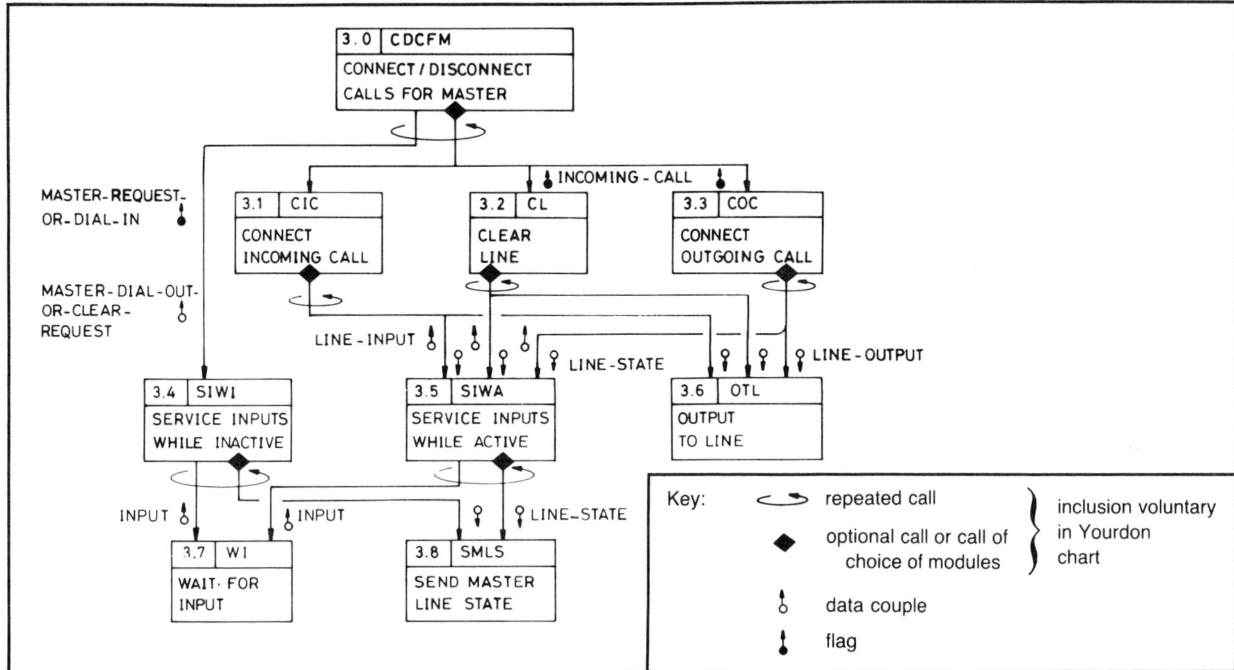

Fig. 2A **Structured design (autodialer): structure chart**

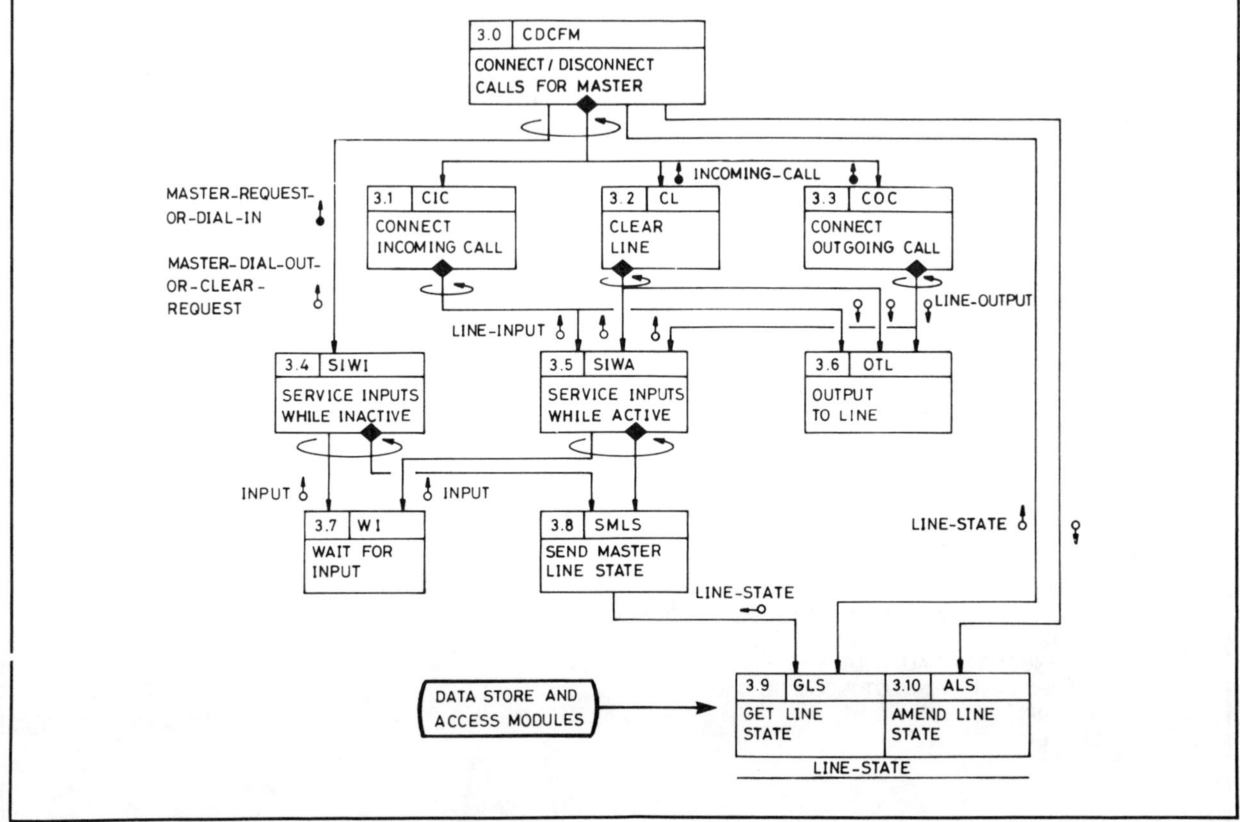

Fig. 2B Structure chart variant with data store and access modules
For key, see Fig. 2A

Even when Yourdon analysis is done, it is the combination of design documentation just described that is normally maintained as the definitive, detailed specification of a software system, not the analysis. This is because the design documentation needs to be kept up to date in any case, for software maintenance reasons.

Production of an analysis must therefore be justified by the need for a fairly rigorous specification, prior to implementation.

4.5 Possible promotion of analysis by Yourdon real-time extensions

One area in which a rigorous early specification is desirable is in defining the interfaces between systems, in cases where early practical experience of interfacing is not possible (for instance because both sides are being designed at once).

The principal graphic tool used for software definition in this type of environment has been the state transition diagram. This diagram is used to show how a system changes its behaviour in response to outside events. Using it has appeared to be more useful than extending the Yourdon analysis below the level where processes represent processors or tasks.

However, the new real-time extensions to the Yourdon methodology incorporate event handling by an extended set of anal-

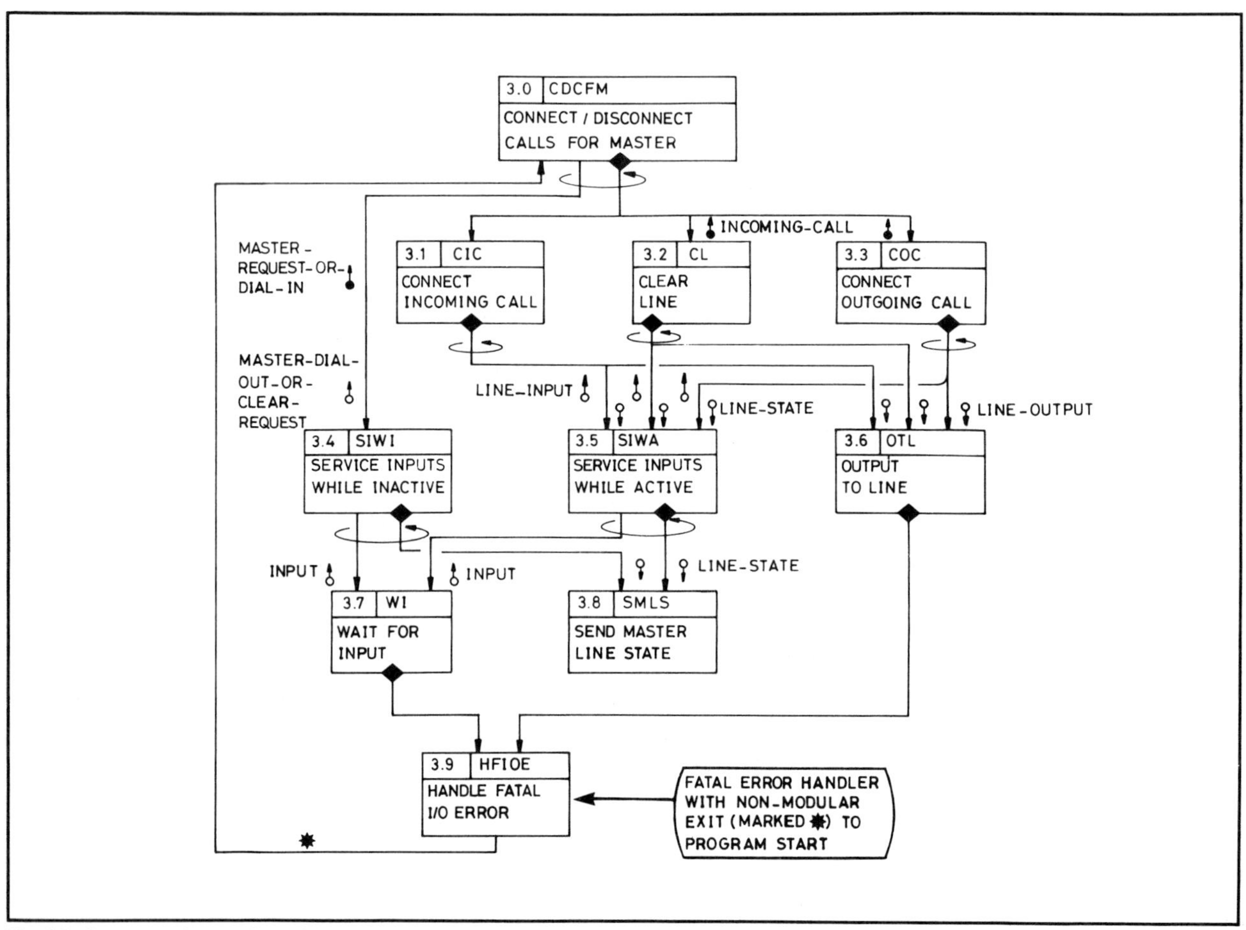

Fig. 2C Structure chart variant with non-modular fatal error handling
For key, see Fig. 2A

```
REPEAT
  CALL 'SERVICE INPUTS WHILE INACTIVE'
       (YIELDING MASTER–REQUEST–OR–DIAL–IN FLAG AND MASTER–DIAL–OUT–OR–CLEAR–REQUEST)
  IF MASTER–REQUEST–OR–DIAL–IN FLAG = 'DIAL IN'
  THEN CALL 'CONNECT INCOMING CALL'
  ELSE
    IF MASTER–AUTODIAL–REQUEST–TYPE IN MASTER–DIAL–OUT–OR–CLEAR–REQUEST = 'DIAL OUT'
    THEN CALL 'CONNECT OUTGOING CALL'
              (YIELDING INCOMING–CALL FLAG)
    ELSE CALL 'CLEAR LINE'
              (YIELDING INCOMING–CALL FLAG)
    (END IF)
    IF INCOMING–CALL = TRUE
    THEN CALL 'CONNECT INCOMING CALL'
  (END IF)
FOREVER
```

Fig. 2D Pseudo-code for process 3.0: CONNECT/DISCONNECT CALLS FOR MASTER (as per Fig. 2A)

ysis diagrams which includes state transition diagrams.

In the revised data flow diagram set, events may arrive directly as signals from outside the system, shown on the context diagram. Alternatively, they may be generated by processes within the system. For example, a process may detect that a value in an incoming data flow has reached a significant level. Events are shown on a data flow diagram as a special (dotted) form of data flow. They are included in the data dictionary and in the balance checks between data flow diagram levels in the same way as ordinary data flows (Figs. 1A and B include event flows and are adequate in the context of real-time Yourdon).

Although ordinary processes (called *data transformations* in real-time Yourdon parlance) may handle events, there is also a new type of process, a *control transformation*, which handles event flows exclusively. A control transformation has the capability of generating special event flows to data transformation processes within the same data flow diagram which trigger or stop their execution, as well as normal event signals to be read by processes inside or outside the system. Hence it arranges changes to the system's behaviour in response to events (Fig. 3A shows a real-time Yourdon data flow diagram expansion for process 3, the autodialer, in Fig. 1B ; a control transformation is included).

Unless it should warrant a data flow diagram expansion (consisting exclusively of control transformations), a control transformation is expanded upon using a state transition diagram rather than a minispec. This diagram shows how the switching on and off of processes and issuing of other event signals is triggered directly or indirectly by external or internal events. It uses boxes containing state names to represent the possible states of the sub-system governed by the control transformation. Connecting lines are used to indicate the possible transitions between states. These transition lines are labelled with the event or events that will cause the transition followed by the actions performed in order to induce the new state (Fig. 3B shows the state transition diagram for the control transformation in Fig. 3A).

Use of control transformations to determine when data transformations run means that the minispecs of primitive data transformations need no longer concern themselves with timing logic. This should tend to make them less procedural in function and hence briefer, neater and less likely to be similar in style and complexity to the pseudo-code produced later on. Furthermore, the use of state transition diagrams makes for a much more satisfactory way of showing timing behaviour than is obtained when timing decisions are distributed around the minispecs of the processes affected.

These features of the real-time Yourdon extensions may result in increased use of the analysis methods in the specification of hardware interfaces, and in the systems and sub-systems that control them.

The company's practical experience of using the real-time Yourdon techniques has so far been limited to an analysis by the author of an autodial unit as an aid to reviewing the unit's English language specification (and a most helpful aid it proved to be!).

The analysis exercise is the source of the Figures in this paper.

Ref. 5 gives a description of the real-time Yourdon methodology.

5 Experience with top-down design using structure charts

5.1 General

The structure chart is the most universally accepted part of the Yourdon methodology. It is recognised as being a good index and overview document for a program. Hence, although some 'old hands' may prefer flowcharts as a design aid, they are prepared to produce structure charts as well.

There is also general compliance with the modular programming principle that each module should always be called at a single start point and should return control to its caller.

This principle ensures that the control hierarchies shown by the structure chart are actually adhered to: a module can only be utilised, directly or indirectly, by those modules indicated by the chart, and conversely it can only pass control to the subordinates shown there.

This enables the structure chart to play an important part in debugging and maintenance, since it defines for each module the parts of the program which any faults in the module or modifications to it might affect.

Hence, as a minimum, the structure chart provides a useful index and a valuable debugging and maintenance aid, even where the designer has not really embraced structured design principles.

However, it must be added that most designers do use top-down structured design principles. They have taken the problem for solution and split it down into sub-problems, each to be solved by a separate module called by the 'boss' module, and they have then split each of these subproblems into smaller sub-problems for solution by lower-level modules, and so on. Furthermore, an attempt is normally made to maximise cohesion and limit coupling. In particular, the undesirability of the vague or complicated module names that go with poor cohesion is well understood. Also, the showing of data flows on the structure chart does discourage excessive coupling.

As with analysis, however, the Yourdon methodology is not a 'cook-book' approach but a set of tools and criteria for optimisation. Although some advice is given by the Yourdon texts, it is still up to the individual designer's skill to produce an elegant solution for the problem in hand.

Again, as with analysis, it has sometimes been difficult to decide whether to accept poor adherence to the methodology as being attributable to the special nature of the application area.

5.2 Problems with workspace areas

One contentious area has been a persistent tendency freely to utilise global workspace areas for communication between program modules, rather than to employ parameter passing more or less exclusively, in order to make inter-module coupling as loose as possible, as Yourdon recommends.

This tendency is believed to stem from three factors:

- the small size of the transactions typically performed by the type of industrial system, where a large number of inputs tend to be subject just to simple monitoring, control, logging and parameter adjustment by the operator
- the fact that the transactions involve little processing using several parameters rather than vice versa
- the real-time nature of the application area.

The small size of a typical transaction may mean that it involves more work in selecting and accessing data than in actively performing operations using this data. Making performance of the operations into a module, which has its data accessed and passed to it by its caller, tends to make the module itself trivial, with the caller doing all the work. Furthermore, the job of passing data as parameters, rather than using it on the spot, is often seen as significant compared with the jobs of accessing the data (usually from arrays or records in memory) and performing the transaction operations themselves, so that parameter passing appears to be prejudicial to system performance. The number of parameters needed is often large enough to be inconvenient to show on the structure chart and to constitute excessive coupling.

A possible solution is for the module performing a transaction to access its own data internally, but to do so by utilising an access module to obtain each item (as done by modules requiring to access LINE-STATE in Fig. 2B). This eliminates the need to pass large numbers of parameters from the module's caller, and it also makes the module independent of the structure of data accessed.

However, the processing overheads involved in using a modular call per parameter access tend to be excessive, even compared with those of passing them from the caller. (An interesting exception to this has been where we have used the language Forth for fast interactive software development. In Forth, all operations, even simple variable accesses and 'add', 'subtract' etc., are performed by routine call; hence explicit use of routines for data access does not impose any significant extra overhead.)

Where data is accessed by modules themselves, directly or by access module call, rather than being passed as parameters, the structure chart must show several modules accessing one data store (directly or indirectly). The lines representing such accesses tend to become numerous and hence tangled, taxing the presentational skills of the designer to produce a clear diagram. The use of access modules, despite improving coupling, makes the structure chart's appearance even worse by cluttering it up with extra boxes (these effects are shown by comparing Fig. 2B with Fig. 2A — note that Fig. 2B would tend to be a tangle of lines if LINE-STATE had to be accessed by modules 3.1, 3.2 and 3.3 as in Fig.2A).

On the other hand, the appearance of a diagram is greatly improved by showing whole data records passed to a module as one parameter (as in Fig. 2A, if LINE-STATE were a record, not just a single item); but this gives poor coupling (if actually reflected in the implementation), since it makes the code of the module dependent on the data store layout. Otherwise (if the individual items are passed separately or accessed by the module directly) it means that the diagram does not show coupling accurately and suffers accordingly, both as an aid to coupling minimisation and as a maintenance reference document.

The combined objectives of minimising coupling and obtaining a clear but complete structure chart have been difficult to achieve, and some kind of compromise and/or a cluttered diagram has tended to be the result.

5.3 Special cases justifying modular programming violations

Another area of contention has been the acceptability of two special-case violations of strict modular programming practice.

One is the use of exits direct to the 'boss' module whenever a module at any structure chart level detects an exception, i.e. an error condition which should cause abortion of the program's current transaction. This avoids the module which finds the error having to pass an error flag back to its caller, which must check the flag and, if it is set, pass an error flag to its own caller, and so on.

The argument against allowing such exits (apart from the 'give an inch and they will take a yard' argument against any concessions) is that maintenance and debugging are easier when a module can only exit to one place after any particular call.

The author takes the view that a well documented exception-handling strategy with non-modular exits is quite acceptable, provided such exits are actually performed by calling an error module which, alone, can perform direct jumps to a single point in the 'boss' module. This means there is only one non-structured control flow, requiring a special indication on the structure chart, namely the return from the error module. A test or debug environment at module, integration or system test can contain a revised version of the error module which performs in any way convenient to the environment. Hence the practical disadvantages from such a well regimented breach of modular rules should be minimal or even non-existent.

Fig. 2C shows how such an arrangement could be used to cater for the auto-dialer re-initialising on fatal input/output errors. Note that the design addition is localised and straightforward.

Another area where there is a case for non-observance of strict modularity is where the same program must be run several times in parallel to perform the same function on several devices or plant areas asynchronously. Such a program may be said to have several *instances*, one for each device or plant area serviced concurrently. For example, a single program logging asynchronously on several printers at once is said to have one instance for each such printer.

The simplest solution for this type of requirement is to use as many copies of the program as necessary, very probably actually using shared code to save memory, if the system operating system and hardware architecture allow this. However, this is not always a practical proposition, typically because of limits on the number of (pseudo-) concurrent tasks or a high store overhead per task.

Hence it may be necessary for a single task to perform all instances of such a program. This is most easily done by arranging that the program runs re-entrantly, in the sense that when one instance reaches a pause point (for example waiting for another character to be typed in the case of a multiple keyboard input program) another instance may resume at the point in the program where it last left off. In general, this requires the program to execute a non-modular jump from where it left off in one instance to where it resumes in another.

However, this can be modelled at the design phase and indeed implemented as a set of separate but identical sub-tasks timesharing in a single task, under control of a mini-executive.

This mini-executive, if regarded as part of the program, does some highly unstructured things, such as record one sub-task's context, which consists of various return links and other private variables, before overwriting these with another sub-task's context — but this is exactly what the main executive hardware or software necessarily gets up to when switching between main tasks.

Each sub-task, individually, is well behaved, resuming after each pause exactly where it left off. The structure chart can be virtually the same as if there were no multiple instances and re-entrancy (for example, Fig.2A could represent an auto-dialer capable of controlling several lines and/or servicing several master stations, provided the module 'WAIT FOR INPUT' were made capable of context switching between master stations and/or lines).

The strictly modular alternative to this arrangement is for control to return to the program 'boss' module whenever an instance of the program requires to pause, a note being made of the current state of the instance, typically in the form of a state number. When an instance becomes active, the 'boss' module typically selects which module to call using the state number. The selected module in turn uses the state number to select a sub-module or sub-section of its code to run, and so on as necessary.

This may lead to a messy and obscure design if pause points do not correspond with changes in functions and hence with natural transitions between sub-modules. In such cases, the author would certainly recommend the 'non-modular' mini-executive approach rather than an ugly, pedantically correct approach, provided such a mini-executive can easily be designed in the implementation environment, and provided that the context information for each sub-task, as saved, is made readily available to and decipherable by a debugger.

5.4 Bottom-up design and information hiding

There are some reservations to be had about top-down methods in a development environment.

Top-down is aimed at breaking down and hence solving a specific problem. In many development projects, most programs are required to solve specific problems and are hence best tackled in this way. For example, the microprocessor-based turbine governing system which was mentioned earlier performs for the most part a fixed set of carefully defined control functions, and so do its constituent programs.

Other developments involve programs of a more general character, for example programs to enable the operator to construct and display diagrammatic VDU displays showing a telemetered system and the current values of variables within it. Such generalised situations tend to lead to a fair measure of bottom-up design. In the case of VDU picture handling, it is likely that bottom-up design, followed by bottom-up implementation, will be used in order to generate a library of routines for handling all relevant facilities provided by the VDU and to explore their ergonomic potential in practice.

Furthermore, a data access package will be produced, enabling all displayable variables to be accessed using reference codes of some kind. The design of the picture builder can now take place, probably top-down, aimed at enabling the operator to use all the useful VDU features supplied in the VDU handling library and to include any variables accessible using the data access package (the reader will note that this is an example of how the functional specification may be developed during implementation, rather than at the previous analysis phase).

Use of bottom-up design packages, such as a data access package, does affect the design in ways other than by altering the order of design and implementation. Such packages tend to keep internal variables hidden from the main program calling them. This involves holding them in private data stores. For example, the data access package may keep a record of what disk-based data is currently in main memory, in order to avoid unnecessary disk transfers. This record is kept privately, since it is not desirable to clutter the design of VDU picture handling software with details about disk-handling strategy, especially as some application systems using the picture-handling software may not utilise disks for holding variables to be displayed.

The general principles of program design using packages that hide information from one another, so that re-designing one for a different environment will not affect the rest, have been laid down by David Parnas (Ref. 6).

Note that data hiding has been behind some of the approaches suggested in previous discussions of design problems. The arrangements for accessing LINE-STATE in Fig.2B means that it is handled only by its trivial access modules, 3.9 and 3.10, and by just two modules, 3.0 and 3.8, that use it. It is hidden from modules 3.1, 3.2, 3.3 and 3.5, which all access it in Fig. 2A. The error-handling technique shown in Fig. 2C1 calises the knowledge that errors exist to modules 3.6, 3.7 and 3.9 and the recommended, re-entrant use of Fig.2A to handle multiple lines or master stations limits knowledge of the multiple usage to module 3.7, WAIT FOR INPUT.

Use of bottom-up design has been brought to the fore in the company by the recent use of Forth. Forth, being an interactive language, encourages such activities as building up libraries of device-handling routines early on, to check that each routine acts as expected and has the anticipated effects on the device.

Furthermore, Forth design methodology, as laid out in Leon Brodie's book 'Thinking Forth' (Ref. 7), encourages the building up of 'lexicons' of Forth words to handle 'components', such as devices and data structures, with which to tackle the main problem more effectively, even for developments where a quite specific problem is to be solved.

5.5 Data-driven software and interpreters

Another interesting aspect of the adoption of Yourdon in conjunction with high-level structured languages has been its effect on the use of interpreters and data-driven techniques.

It has long been general practice to centre standard software packages around data-driven software. Using data-driven packages, an individual system's requirements can very largely be catered for by individually prepared, interpreted data such as VDU formats, log specifications, industrial input processing records and plant control sequences. Such data has in the past been easier to produce and commission than programs to meet the system's special requirements. The interpreted data can also be more compact than the equivalent code (a 1 byte function number in the data typically being equivalent to a routine call sequence in the code, for instance).

However, the interpreter must be designed with care in order to make it flexible enough to meet most likely requirements. It tends to be quite complex and its operation is inherently more abstract and difficult to follow than straightforward code to do a specific job. The Yourdon methodology's promotion of attention to cohesion and coupling does, however, help manage the complexity of the interpreter successfully.

The design produced for the interpreter, as documented by the structure diagram, will of course be that of a general-purpose interpreting engine. For any application, some other documentation will have to show how the engine is harnessed to do the particular job in hand. In cases where a sequencing language or similar is being interpreted, it may well be that the interpreted program requires a second structure chart and a second set of module headers and pseudo-code. Otherwise, special-purpose documentation will normally be needed.

Readable and easily written high-level languages (especially interactive ones such as Forth), the easy-to-follow Yourdon structured design and documentation techniques, and the availability of cheap and plentiful main memory all promote production of a straightforward design for each application, rather than re-use of a general-purpose interpreter with new interpreted data. In the straightforward design, the program structure should be simpler for each system and relate directly to the problem in hand, for ease of understanding and maintenance. Basing one system on the last by adding or replacing modules in a high-level, general-purpose language may be more straightforward than having to learn and understand a special interpreted data language (and maybe then discover that the complex interpreter needs extending). Hence the advantage of the interpreter package is somewhat on the wane.

However, one vital advantage the interpreter does have is its ability to check the data interpreted and thereby avoid program crashes. Hence new data can safely be entered on-line, whereas only in sophisticated (and hence expensive) operating environments is this true for new program code. Therefore, where on-line programming of facilities is required, the interpreter still reigns supreme and its complexities still have to be lived with.

6 Experience with textual design documentation

The need to produce pseudo-code is accepted by most designers under most circumstances. Designers almost always produce module header information. Normally, both these forms of design documentation are eventually incorporated into the code as comments, which helps ensure that they are updated when code changes are made. There are a number of different styles of module description and pseudo-code used, but all styles are easy enough for an outsider to follow; so the differences are not a real embarrassment.

Pseudo-code is sometimes felt to be redundant when a high-level language is used, since it is similar in style to a high-level language itself. This alleged redundancy may be for real; but this is only so if the high-level language compiler can handle the long multi-word data dictionary names, which pseudo-code uses for data, and the long multi-word names, taken from the structure chart, which it uses to refer to other modules called. Furthermore, the compiler must be able to do so without the restriction that only names with differences in the first few characters can be recognised as different.

Most compilers cannot satisfy these requirements, or else give unacceptable performance penalties when long labels are used. In such cases short mnemonics must be used in the code, making it more concise but less readable. The pseudocode is then not redundant after all, unless (as has sometimes been done) the code is copiously annotated with indications of the full names corresponding to the mnemonics.

Another possible excuse for omission of pseudo-code is where factoring is very high, i.e. the program is broken into a large number of very short modules. This has tended to be the case where Forth has been employed, since Forth is designed to be used this way. Where the modules are small enough, the functional description in the module header may be all that is needed in the way of code comments.

The general rule, however, is that pseudo-code comments should be provided; and a case needs to be made before omission can be accepted.

It tends sometimes to be forgotten that production of this Yourdon-specific textual documentation may not be all that is required. Pseudo-code does no more than paraphrase what the module's code actually does in a readable high-level form. Only the module names and the functional description in the module header actually indicate what a module is trying to achieve. For this to be adequate, the program must be structured into quite small simple modules, even by structured design standards.

A program description, over and above that given by the module specification of the 'boss' module, tends to be desirable background and introductory reading for anyone requiring to find out about a program's internal design. If a program uses packages of modules such as the data access package or VDU handling package discussed earlier, then these also require overall introductory descriptions, including a list of entry modules and the facilities they provide. As mentioned before, if data-driven techniques are used, then there will need to be documentation describing the effects of the data being interpreted; design documentation for just the interpreter itself will not be sufficient.

The detailed design documentation, including module headers and pseudocode, has normally been prepared and walked through prior to coding and testing of the code to which it relates. This is done on the basis that effort should not be risked on implementation and testing until the design has been checked and approved.

However, use of an interactive programming environment, such as provided by Forth, may change this situation drastically because of the speed with which code can be tried out. It may well pay to establish quickly that a design works in practice before risking expenditure of effort on documentation and a review. This is especially true of programs (or parts of programs) involving hardware interfaces and/or ergonomics, where practical experience may well 'shoot down' ideas that appeared fine on paper.

7 Experience with coding and testing

Coding has posed few problems. Given structured pseudo-code, the well structured code equivalent is easy to produce in assembler or in any of the high-level languages used, since all either contain structured control constructs such as:

```
IF . . . THEN . . . ELSE . . .
REPEAT . . . UNTIL . . .
```

or can emulate them easily using GOTOs.

Code may be produced before pseudocode when using Forth. This is because it is easy to code up a highly factored design where each module is small. Since Forth only supports structured control constructs, there is no risk of producing unstructured code (unless the programmer wishes to display demoniac ingenuity).

The modularity imposed by structured design enables thorough and systematic testing to be carried out, module by module, each module having its own written and reviewed test specification and recorded test results. As already mentioned, the microprocessor-controlled turbine governor project has shown how such procedures can lead to highly reliable software.

None the less, it needs to be recognised that this type of testing is costly and time consuming. In a product development context, it is often better to have a marketable system ready as early as feasible than to have a completely reliable product at a much later launch date. A well structured product released early can readily be tested thoroughly, if and when market success justifies this. Exhaustive debugging before the market is tested may prove wasteful if the product turns out to be unattractive in its initial form. Note, however, that any control or safety related facilities must be reliable before installation anywhere.

It has already been described (in Section 5.4) how bottom-up implementation and testing have found favour for programs with device interfaces or ergonomic aspects, despite the Yourdon support for top-down techniques.

It should be noted that, whereas bottom-up techniques are sometimes used for new individual program testing, an approach similar in philosophy to top-down program testing is favoured for system testing as a whole. A skeleton system containing the basic operator facilities is first commissioned, and then programs and hence facilities are gradually added to give a steady increase in functionality.

8 Experience with walkthroughs

Walkthroughs are probably the most profound change to the working environment created by adoption of Yourdon. Their most important benefits are that they ensure reasonable documentation and they encourage communication within a team.

Documentation is assured because it has to be provided as the material for a walkthrough. Any gross inadequacies will not just offend documentation standards but will actually annoy the colleagues who have to prepare for the walkthrough by studying the material.

Good communications within a team are achieved provided the correct people are invited to all the walkthroughs and these are held reasonably often. Designers are bound to present their ideas comprehensibly at a walkthrough so that implementors will understand them. The implementor's walkthrough will reveal any misunderstandings that do occur or any unforeseen problems. Designers in neighbouring areas normally detect any misunderstandings about interfaces at each other's walkthroughs, or acquire the knowledge to avoid such misunderstandings in the first place.

Detection of errors at walkthroughs is perhaps not as thorough, in practice, as might have been expected. Simple justification of walkthroughs on the grounds that the time spent by the reviewers is paid for by savings in debugging time may not always be justified. It depends on the relative conscientiousness of the producer and of the reviewers at checking design material.

Code walkthroughs do not have the same communication benefits as design walkthroughs and require greater resistance to boredom on the part of the reviewer. However, especially in the case of code produced by someone unfamiliar with the programming language or environment, a code read-through by someone else is profitable. Possibly establishment of pairs of programmers that perform read-throughs of one another's code is the best solution, as a compromise between full walkthroughs and no checks at all.

Walkthroughs are useful for project control purposes. If an item of design, code, test data or test results has not been

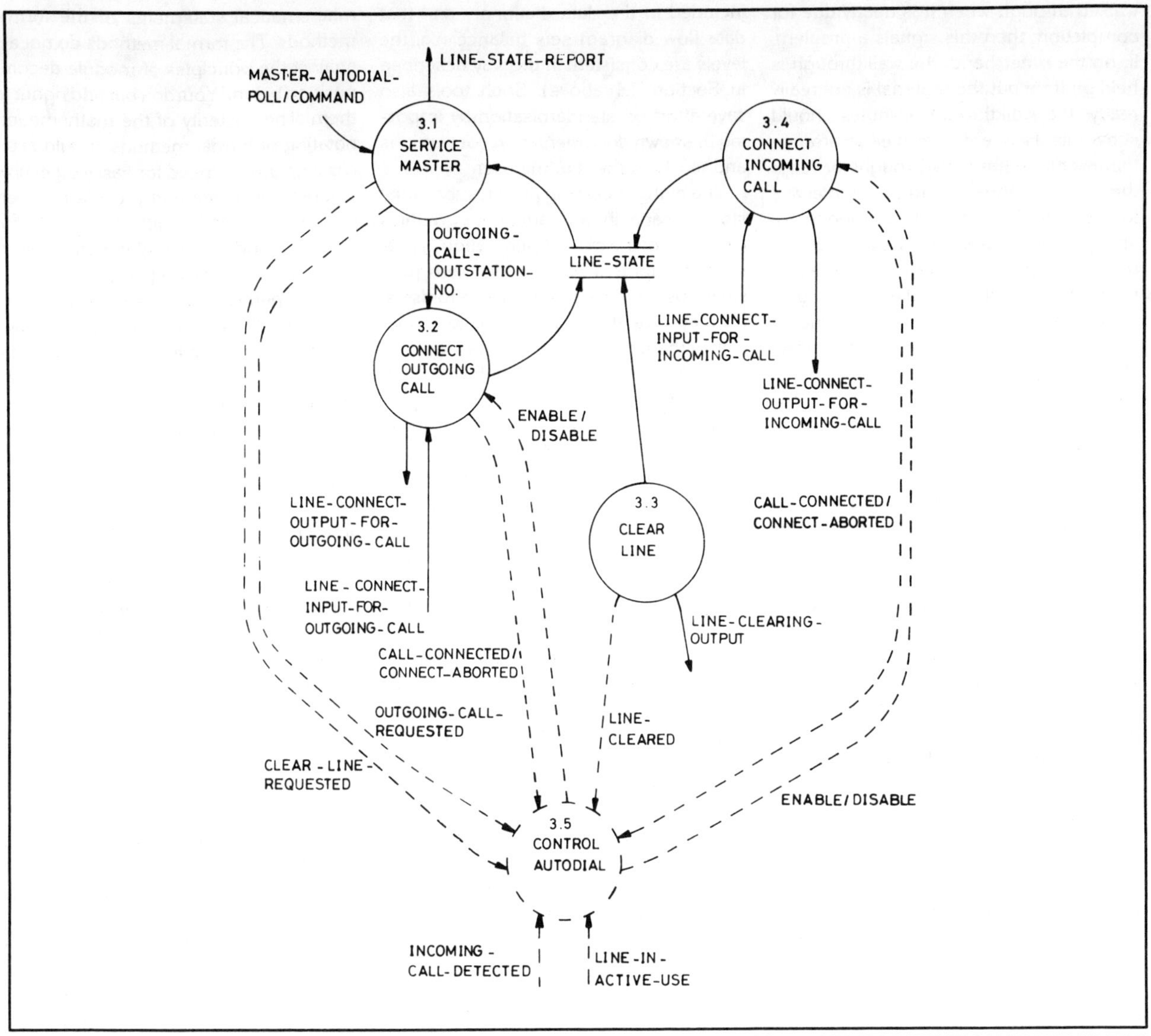

LINE-STATE-REPORT
MASTER-AUTODIAL-POLL/COMMAND
3.1 SERVICE MASTER
3.4 CONNECT INCOMING CALL
OUTGOING-CALL-OUTSTATION-NO.
LINE-STATE
3.2 CONNECT OUTGOING CALL
LINE-CONNECT-INPUT-FOR-INCOMING-CALL
LINE-CONNECT-OUTPUT-FOR-INCOMING-CALL
ENABLE/DISABLE
LINE-CONNECT-OUTPUT-FOR-OUTGOING-CALL
3.3 CLEAR LINE
CALL-CONNECTED/CONNECT-ABORTED
LINE-CONNECT-INPUT-FOR-OUTGOING-CALL
LINE-CLEARING-OUTPUT
CALL-CONNECTED/CONNECT-ABORTED
OUTGOING-CALL-REQUESTED
LINE-CLEARED
CLEAR-LINE-REQUESTED
ENABLE/DISABLE
3.5 CONTROL AUTODIAL
INCOMING-CALL-DETECTED
LINE-IN-ACTIVE-USE

Fig. 3A Real-time Yourdon version of Fig. 1C – expansion data flow diagram for process 3: CONNECT/DISCONNECT CALLS FOR MASTER

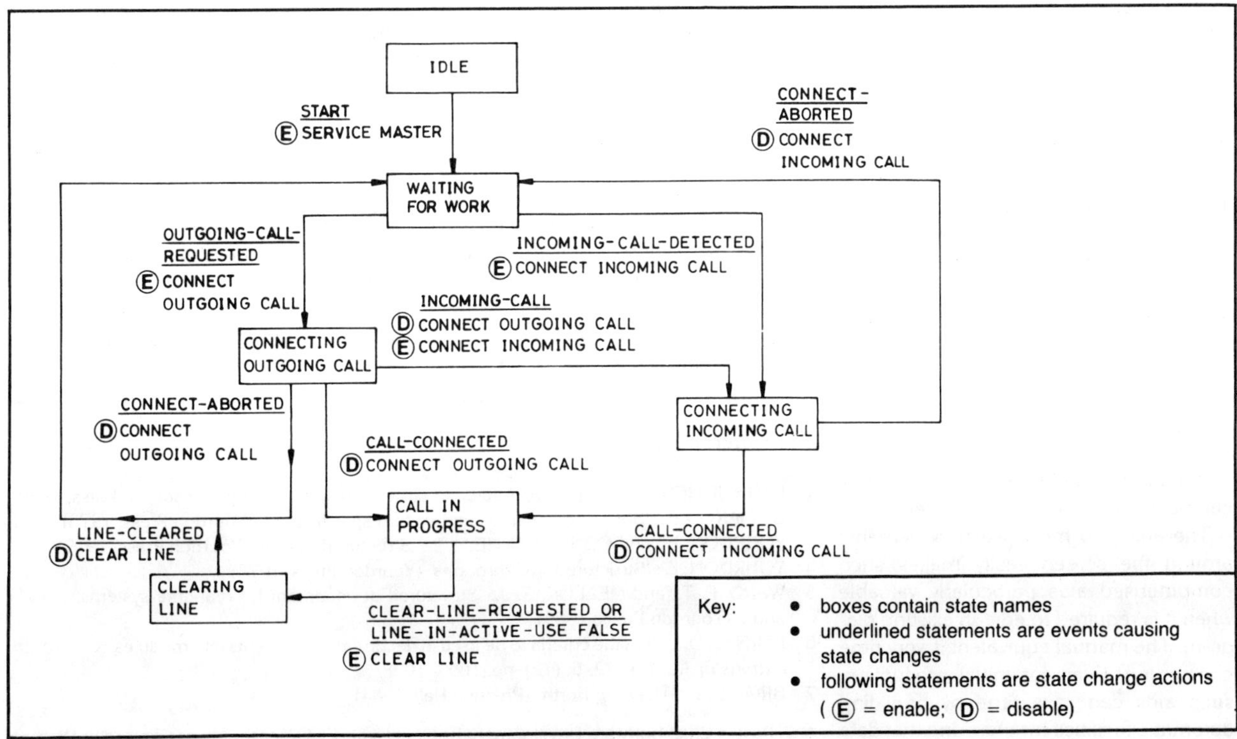

Fig. 3B State transition diagram for process 3.5: CONTROL AUTODIAL

walked through when it is nearly due for completion, then this signals a problem. If, on the other hand, the walkthrough is held on time but the material is not really ready, the walkthrough minutes should show this. Hence it is as well to arrange that everyone has walkthroughs or read-throughs scheduled at frequent intervals to enable their progress to be monitored, and it is mandatory to ensure that the results are minuted, even in the case of read-throughs. If a walkthrough gets delayed significantly, then a meeting to discuss the problems causing the delay should maybe take its place. From personal experience, it is all too easy for a designer to sit on a problem which he is too proud to give up trying to solve privately.

One area where walkthroughs are somewhat problematic is where criticisms of style are involved. Since perfection is hard to achieve, such criticisms are almost always possible and it is difficult to know when to voice them and when not. An individual supervisor can conduct a well planned and tactful campaign, tackling just one or two serious problems at a time, preferably when he can easily justify his criticism by providing a better solution. Walkthroughs tend to generate a sweeping tide of destructive criticism, which may even contain contradictory elements, if members of different schools of Yourdon interpretation are present. Probably questions of style are best raised quickly and simply recorded as 'possible improvements to be considered' in the minutes. The reviewer and his supervisor are then at liberty to give them active consideration sooner, later or not at all.

Walkthrough chairmen have a vital and difficult role to play in ensuring that the material submitted is reviewed in a brisk, friendly and objective manner.

9 Future prospects

This paper indicates that the company is currently basically satisfied with Yourdon; but what of the future?

The author expects that the new real-time methodology may be adopted and may increase the scope of utilisation of the analysis methods in some development situations.

Another expected area of change is the automation of the analysis and design methods so that diagrams as well as text can be entered and edited at a terminal.

The ability to move existing elements around the screen easily makes such computerised aids particularly valuable when it is required to edit an existing diagram. The manual equivalent is very time consuming. Even for initial production, such aids can save time by providing automatic facilities for checking that data items referenced in designs or text are included in the data dictionary and that data flow diagram sets balance (i.e. the levels are consistent in the way described in Section 3.1 above). Such tools also save effort on standardisation by imposing their own documentation conventions and teaching them to the user.

The high processing power, substantial storage capacity and adequate graphics capability of the current generation of personal computers have made them possible hosts for such automated toolsets. Furthermore, their low cost makes provision of them on a one-per-active-designer basis quite a modest capital investment, especially where incorporation of personal computers in the product under development ensures that a pool of them must be made available in any case.

Accordingly, investigations are taking place into the potential of a home-grown toolset and of a number of commercial products, available on personal computers, which support Yourdon analysis and design.

It is necessary, however, to be assured that use of rather complex structure diagrams and long data names can either be curtailed or accommodated successfully on the rather small effective page size of a VDU terminal.

In the future, it is expected that such a toolset will form part of an integrated project support environment (IPSE), along with project management, program generation, program debugging and configuration control tools. Rapid steps are being taken towards assessing requirements in this area.

Another likely area of change is the increasing use of formal methods such as VDM and Z, particularly in fields where high integrity is needed. It is possible that universal usage will follow if their road to high integrity proves cost-effective and universally acceptable, despite the somewhat forbidding mathematical notation currently involved.

The author's opinion is that such methods should supplement rather than replace graphical methods like Yourdon, probably with Yourdon minispecs, module descriptions and pseudo-code being relegated often to the status of explanatory comments by the side of the precise mathematical statements of the formal methods. The formal methods do not act against the principles of module decomposition behind Yourdon but add rigour to them. The austerity of the mathematical notation of formal methods should actually increase the need for easily digestible diagrams to index and provide an overview of the system, both while it is being designed and when maintenance documentation is finally prepared.

What perhaps could supersede Yourdon would be a more prescriptive approach, if one could be invented that worked consistently in the area of real-time industrial software. However, such an approach might well be capable of absorption into Yourdon, just as the Michael Jackson method of program structuring and the use of state transition and entity relationship diagrams have been.

The flexibility of Yourdon makes it likely that it can be married successfully with automation, formal methods and any other advances. The widespread use of Yourdon makes it probable that, where such marriages are possible, they will be brought about.

10 Conclusion

Yourdon is not an easy step-by-step solution to all design problems, nor is it a ready written standards manual for any user. However, it has provided an accepted, common approach to design and a common documentation method. It has also supplied a walkthrough procedure to ensure, at very least, that the documentation is produced. Over and above this, it has encouraged an awareness of criteria for good design and has suggested approaches for meeting these criteria.

The methodology has, particularly in the form of real-time Yourdon, already shown that its flexibility allows it to absorb and be modified by new ideas, and it has already proved able to attract and accommodate successful attempts at automation.

It therefore appears likely that the Yourdon methodology will continue to enjoy its current success.

11 References

1 PAGE-JONES, M.:'The practical guide to structured system design' (Yourdon Press, 1980)
2 De MARCO, T.: 'Structured analysis and system specification' (Yourdon Press, 1978)
3 YOURDON, E., and CONSTANTINE, L. L.: 'Structured design' (Yourdon Press, 1979)
4 YOURDON, E.: 'Structured walkthroughs' (Yourdon Press, 1977)
5 WARD, P. T., and MELLOR, S. J.: 'Structured development for real-time systems'. Vols. 1 and 2 (Yourdon Press, 1985)
6 PARNAS, D. L.: 'On the criteria to be used in decomposing systems into modules', *Communications of ACM*, 1972, **5**, (12), pp. 1053–1058
7 BRODIE, L.: 'Thinking Forth' (Prentice-Hall, 1984)

A. J. Post is Chief Software Development Engineer with GEC Measurements, Leicester Division, New Parks, Leicester LE3 1UF, England.

Reprinted from *IEEE Transactions on Software Engineering*, Volume SE-10, Number 3, May 1984, pages 290-302.

Prototyping Versus Specifying: A Multiproject Experiment

BARRY W. BOEHM, TERENCE E. GRAY, AND THOMAS SEEWALDT

***Abstract*—In this experiment, seven software teams developed versions of the same small-size (2000–4000 source instruction) application software product. Four teams used the Specifying approach. Three teams used the Prototyping approach.**

The main results of the experiment were the following.

1) Prototyping yielded products with roughly equivalent performance, but with about 40 percent less code and 45 percent less effort.

2) The prototyped products rated somewhat lower on functionality and robustness, but higher on ease of use and ease of learning.

3) Specifying produced more coherent designs and software that was easier to integrate.

The paper presents the experimental data supporting these and a number of additional conclusions.

***Index Terms*—Prototypes, requirements analysis, software engineering, software engineering education, software management, software metrics, specifications.**

I. Introduction

A. Motivation

SHOULD the current specification-driven approach to software development be dropped in favor of an approach based on prototyping? There have been several recent proposals of this nature, and a great deal of discussion of the relative merits of the two alternative approaches.

Prototyping offers a number of attractive advantages, such as the early resolution of high-risk issues, and the flexibility to adapt to changing environmental characteristics or perceptions of users' needs. To date, however, there is not much information on whether the prototyping approach retains all of the advantages of the specification-driven approach, such as visibility and control of the software development process, and the ability to manage integration of many small programs into a large product. Nor is there much information on how the nature of a software product developed via prototyping compares with the nature of a product developed via the specification-driven approach.

In order to illuminate these and related issues, we undertook the experiment described in this paper. We had seven teams develop the same software product (a user-interactive software cost estimation model, comprising roughly 3000 Pascal source instructions); four teams used a specification-driven approach, and three used a prototyping approach. The resulting data on the teams' experiences and products provide at least a start toward understanding the relative strengths and weaknesses of the prototyping and specifying approaches, and toward understanding how they may best fit into a next-generation software development methodology.

Manuscript received April 15, 1983; revised January 5, 1984.

B. W. Boehm is with the Software and Information Systems, Division, TRW Defense Systems Group, Redondo Beach, CA 90278 and the University of California, Los Angeles, CA 90024.

T. E. Gray is with the Department of Computer Science, School of Engineering and Applied Science, University of California, Los Angeles, CA 90024.

T. Seewaldt was with the Department of Computer Science, University of California, Los Angeles, CA 90024. He is now with Universitaet Kaiserslautern, Kaiserslautern, West Germany.

B. Background

At the beginning of every software project, the project manager is faced with a critical choice of approach. The primary choices are the following.

1) *Building and Fixing:* Proceed to build the full system with minimal or no specifications. Rework the resulting product as necessary until it satisfies its users.

2) *Specifying:* Develop a requirements specification for the product. Develop a design specification to implement the requirements. Develop the code to implement the design. Again, rework the resulting product as necessary.

3) *Prototyping:* Build prototype versions of parts of the product. Exercise the prototype parts to determine how best to implement the operational product. Proceed to build the operational product, and again rework it as necessary.

There are a number of variations on these three basic approaches, of course, but their essential distinctions are identified reasonably well in the above three options.

Approach 1, Building and Fixing, has been shown to work poorly on most projects of any reasonable size. This is largely because of the highly increased cost of fixing a software product once it is completed and operational [1]. The Specifying approach evolved to avoid the problems encountered in Building and Fixing [2]-[4] and led to the familiar "waterfall" model of software development most frequently seen today.

The Specifying approach has been highly successful in many application areas [5], [6]. However, it encounters difficulties in application areas in which it is hard to specify requirements in advance. This happens most frequently in human-machine interface systems, in which the requirements analyst often has to deal with user responses of the form, "I'm really not sure what I want, but I'll know it when I see it."

In such situations, the Prototyping approach appears attractive. A number of papers have proposed refinements of the waterfall model of the software life-cycle to incorporate prototyping options [7]-[9]. Some authors have gone so far as to suggest that prototyping options make all current life-cycle models completely obsolete and even harmful [10].

C. Open Questions

At this stage, however, not enough is known about the relative merits of specifying and prototyping to summarily reject either approach in favor of the other. The results of recent workshops such as the ACM-IEEE-NBS Workshop on Rapid Prototyping [11] indicate that a number of significant open questions still exist, such as the following.

What characterizes application areas in which prototyping is likely to be more successful than specifying?

What effect does prototyping have on a software project's effort distribution, schedule distribution, and productivity; and on the product's size, quality, maintainability, etc.?

How does prototyping change the mix of skills needed on a software project?

Is there need to adopt a mixed strategy using both specifying and prototyping? If so, when and how?

Clearly, such questions need to be further illuminated via analysis or experimentation before we can formulate definitive recommendations on the critical issue of specifying versus prototyping.

D. The Experiment

The experiment described here was designed to investigate such questions. It involved having seven teams develop their own versions of the same product, four teams using the specifying approach and three teams using the prototyping approach.

The product to be developed was an interactive version of the COCOMO model for software cost estimation [12]. The tables and equations in the model were the same for all projects, and provided an overall definition of the product's requirements. However, each team was to determine and create its own user interface to the model. A previous experiment [13] indicated that the interactive COCOMO model would be a suitable product for such an experiment. It is a reasonably sized job for an experiment, and the user interface constitutes the dominant portion of the product.

The experiment took place in early 1982 as part of a one-quarter first year graduate course in software engineering at UCLA. The four Specifying teams produced a requirements specification, a design specification, and an end product consisting of operational code, a user's manual, and a maintenance manual. The three Prototyping teams produced the same end products, but were required to produce and exercise a prototype by the midpoint of the course, rather than to develop specifications. All of the projects were instrumented to collect data relevant to the open questions above.

E. Outline of Paper

Section II of this paper describes the experimental project in more detail. Section III presents the experimental results. Section IV presents the resulting conclusions. Finally, Appendix A contains the project description given to the students, and Appendix B summarizes the primary lessons learned from an instructional standpoint.

II. The Experimental Project

This section discusses the key aspects of the experiment: the product developed; the project schedule and work environment; the organization into teams; the experimental data collection procedures; and some of the experimental limitations caused by the course schedule and teaching objectives.

A. The Product

Each team was to develop an interactive version of the COCOMO model for estimating the costs of a software product. The model accepts descriptions of the components of the future product in terms of their size, and their ratings with respect to 16 cost-driver attributes (e.g., hardware constraints, database size, personnel experience, use of tools and modern programming practices). It uses these to calculate the amount of time and effort (and resulting dollar cost) required to develop each component and the overall system, and provides a breakdown of the effort into the major development phases and activities.

The model algorithms and tables were provided in [12]; each team was to develop its own file system and user interface (see Appendix A). The user interface for such a product is considerably more extensive than the cost model algorithms. The user interface software must support the selective creation, addition, modification, query, and deletion of the cost-driver parameters describing each component of the software product whose costs are to be estimated. It must support the specification, generation, formatting, and dispatching of desired outputs: overall cost, effort, and schedule estimates, and their breakdown by component, by phase, and by activity. It must detect and provide messages for erroneous inputs, and provide some level of on-line help. There are also a wide variety of further options which may be included, and many alternative ways to accommodate inputs (menus, commands, tables, forms), display outputs, and support user control. Thus, there are a good many issues to be addressed via prototyping or specifying which have a significant influence on the nature of the project and its resulting product.

B. Project Schedule

The major milestones for each type of team were:

Week	Specifying Teams	Prototyping Teams
3	Requirements	
5		Prototype Demo
6	Design Spec Draft User Manual	
10	Acceptance Test User Manual Maintenance Manual	Acceptance Test User Manual Maintenance Manual
11	Project Critique Maintenance Vote	Project Critique Maintenance Vote

The requirements and design specifications were subjected to a thorough review by the instructors. This resulted in a set of Problem Reports returned to the project teams and discussed in a set of Requirements Reviews and Design Reviews. The prototypes were exercised by the instructors, who provided similar feedback on errors, suggested modifications, missing capabilities, etc.

The acceptance test consisted of the instructors' exercising each program to determine whether it performed all of the required capabilities, whether it handled error conditions with useful responses, and whether it exhibited a high degree of user-friendliness. Subsequently, the authors of this paper exercised each product in more detail, and each author rated it on a scale of 0 to 10 with respect to four particular cirteria.

1) *Functionality:* The relative utility of the various computational, user interface, output, and file management functions provided by the product.

2) *Robustness:* The degree to which the user was protected from aborts, crashes, loss of working files, etc.

3) *Ease of Use (Or Lack of Frustration):* The degree of user convenience in performing desired functions, and the avoidance of overconstrained or unexpected program behavior.

4) *Ease of Learning:* The ease with which new users could master the product's workings and get it to do what they wished. This rating covered not only program prompts, help messages, and error messages, but also the user manual and associated job aids or "crib sheets" provided by the teams.

The project critiques were ten-page essays written by each student, addressing the question, "If we were to do the project over again, how could we do it better?" These critiques were analyzed for the degree of consensus among the participants on the most important factors influencing the project results.

The maintenance ballots asked each student to rate each of the other teams' products in the order in which they would prefer to have the product as their product to maintain. The average rating for each product was then calculated as an index of its maintainability. Twenty percent of each person's course grade was based on his product's maintainability rating.

C. Development Environment

The products were developed in UCB Pascal, using a UCLA VAX 11/780 running the Unix (TM: Bell Laboratories) operating system. The Unix environment provided excellent support for both documentation and code development functions. Some difficulties were the overload on the VAX at the end of the quarter combined with poor documentation of the separate compilation facilities in UCB Pascal, which made product integration and test much more complex and time-consuming than expected.

D. Team Organization and Staffing

At the beginning of the course, the students were given a description of the project, and a form to indicate their level of experience with Pascal, with Unix, and with programming; their grade point average; and their preference for which approach to use on the project. The instructors then selected teams based on the students' preferences and on experimental balance.

The 11 students expressing a preference for specifying were divided into four teams (S1-S4). The 7 students expressing a preference for prototyping were divided into three teams (P1-P3). The resulting team characteristics are given in Table I.

TABLE I
EXPERIMENTAL TEAM CHARACTERISTICS

	Specifying					Prototyping			
Team	S1	S2	S3	S4	Avg.	P1	P2	P3	Avg.
No. of people	3	3	2	3	2.75	2	3	2	2.33
Avg. programming experience (mo)	25	47	42	30	36	54	46	60	53
Avg. Pascal exp. (mo)	1	17	7	3	7	30	16	9	18
Avg. Unix exp. (mo)	0	1	12	5	4.5	3	4	0	2.3
Avg. grade point average	3.1	3.6	3.6	3.3	3.37	3.4	3.0	3.3	3.27

Each team was given the freedom to organize in whatever way the members found most appropriate. Most teams used a highly democratic consensus-based organization, with all members performing some design, some programming, some documentation, and some integration and test. Some teams had a single individual develop documents, such as the user's manual.

E. Experimental Limitations

The teaching objectives of the course introduced several experimental limitations which somewhat reduced the sharpness and representativeness of the results.

Technical Leveling: A pure experiment would have isolated the teams to minimize any cross-fertilization of ideas or technical leveling between projects. Here, our teaching objectives caused us to hold every requirements review, design review, and prototype exercise in front of the entire class. Thus, prototypers got some added insights from the specifiers' reviews, and vice versa. However, our impression is that the students did not significantly change their approaches as a result of this information.

Nonrepresentative Reviewing: In order to provide thorough feedback on specifications, and to show the value of early verification and validation, the instructors performed more thorough reviews of specifications than are performed on the typical project. The prototype exercises were also somewhat nonrepresentative in being one-shot exercises by expert users rather than sustained usage by nonexpert users.

Choice of Approach: The Specifying teams were staffed entirely with students who had expressed a preference for the Specifying approach, and similarly for the Prototyping teams. This is largely nonrepresentative of actual projects—although some students' critiques indicated that they would prefer taking the opposite approach if they were to do a similar project again.

Data Collection Procedures: The instructors explained to the students that their grade had nothing to do with the timesheet data they turned in, so there was no reason to falsify data. However, students occasionally exhibit procrastination and lapses in discipline. Thus, it was not too surprising that some of the timesheets were turned in late, with the attendant possibility that some of the data provided were created "from memory."

As stated above, these factors tend to reduce the sharpness and representativeness of the results. However, the net impression from the project critiques is that none of these factors played a critical role in the outcome of the experiment. Thus, the experimental results described below appear to transcend these acknowledged limitations. As a further point of perspective, it is worth noting that many conclusions reached in the software engineering field are still based on sample sizes of one project. Thus, a sample of seven reasonably comparable, moderately representative projects is not too bad.

III. Experimental Results

A. Prototyping Versus Specifying

Product Size and Development Effort: The comparisons of the relative sizes of the products and the relative effort required to develop them produced a striking result: the prototyping teams' products were 40 percent smaller, on the average, and required 45 percent less effort to develop.

The products of the prototyping groups had an average size of 2064 delivered source instructions (DSI), while the products of the specifying groups had an average of 3391 DSI. The average development effort of the prototyping groups was 325 man-hours (MH), and for the specifying groups, 584 MH. Fig. 1 shows the relative results for each project and the averages by type of group.

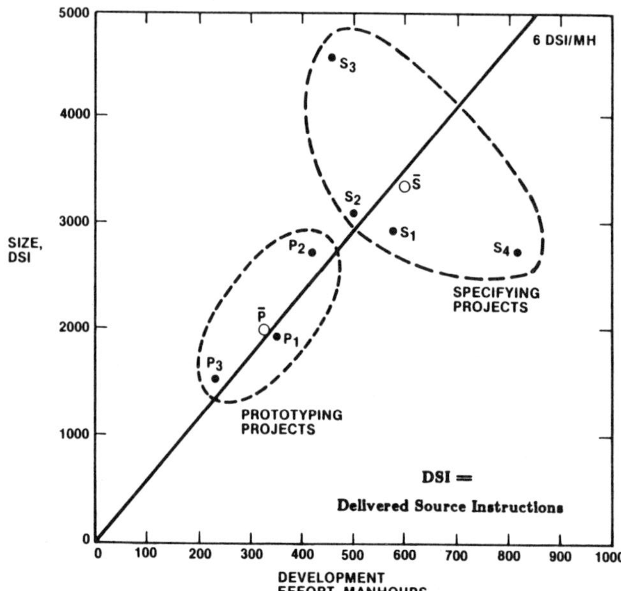

Fig. 1. Prototyping versus specifying: size and effort comparisons.

Both differences might be partly due to the smaller average team size of the prototyping groups (2.33 persons versus 2.75), but comments in the project critiques indicate that the group type most significantly influenced these results. Specifically, the specifying people indicated that it was very easy to overpromise in their specifications. For example, when confronted with a review comment such as, "Some users would like to enter data by rows as well as columns," the specifiers would tend to say, "Sure, that's just another sentence in the spec." When confronted with this sort of comment in their prototype review, prototypers had a better feel for the programming implications, and tended to say, "We'll put that in if we have time."

The range of product sizes was from 1514 DSI to 4606 DSI (Table V below provides data on each project). The second largest product was 3391 DSI, so we consider the 4606 DSI product somewhat anomalous. Even so, the 3:1 range in product sizes in remarkable, considering that each team was developing essentially the same product. This range, and the comparable 3.4:1 range in project effort, tend to corroborate the ranges in [12, ch. 21] on the relative accuracy of early software sizing and costing efforts.

Overall Productivity: One of our hypotheses was that the prototyping projects would have higher "productivity" in terms of delivered source instructions per man-hour (DSI/MH), primarily because the prototyping teams did not have to expend the extra effort to develop requirements and design specifications. This hypothesis was not borne out by the experimental results: both the prototyping and specifying groups averaged roughly 6 DSI/MH, where the number of man-hours includes effort expended for all phases of the project, not just coding. The prototyping groups had an average productivity of 6.3 DSI/MH; the specifying groups, 5.8 DSI/MH.

The range in overall productivity for prototyping groups was from 6 to 6.5 DSI/MH; for specifying groups it was from 3.6 to 10, but with only one group (the same one that produced the largest product) exceeding 6.4 DSI/MH. As shown in Fig. 1, the development effort is generally proportional to the size of the developed product.

Note that the large variation in product size does not invalidate the DSI/MH productivity measure as an indicator of efficiency in producing code. Rather, it illustrates the need for further research into why ostensibly similar products can differ so dramatically in size, and therefore, development cost.

Coding Productivity: An unexpectedly large variation in coding productivity (DSI/programming MH) was observed. The low was 9.7 and the high was 33.8 DSI/MH. While the average for specifying teams (15.7) was 25 percent lower than that of prototyping teams (21), much of this difference is attributable to the pronounced team-size effect discussed in Section III-B.

Product Performance: Since the products of the prototyping groups were smaller and developed with less effort, one might think that they would rate correspondingly lower on performance. However, their overall performance was the same as the performance of the specifying groups (Fig. 2). The prototyped products were rated lower in overall functionality and in their tolerance of erroneous input, but correspondingly higher in their ease of learning and ease of use (i.e., the frustration caused by overconstrained or unexpected program behavior was less for the products of the prototyping groups). There was not a uniform dominance of prototyping or specifying projects on any of the performance ratings. Practically all the ratings were in the range of 3 through 7 (a "5" rating corresponded to an "acceptable" product), but there was considerable variation in ratings within the range in each group.

Maintainability Ratings: At the end of the quarter, students indicated which products they would prefer to maintain and ranked the products accordingly. The maintainability of the prototype group products was rated remarkably higher than the maintainability of the specifying group products. Therefore, the student's subjective evaluations did not confirm the hypothesis that the specifying approach leads to lower main-

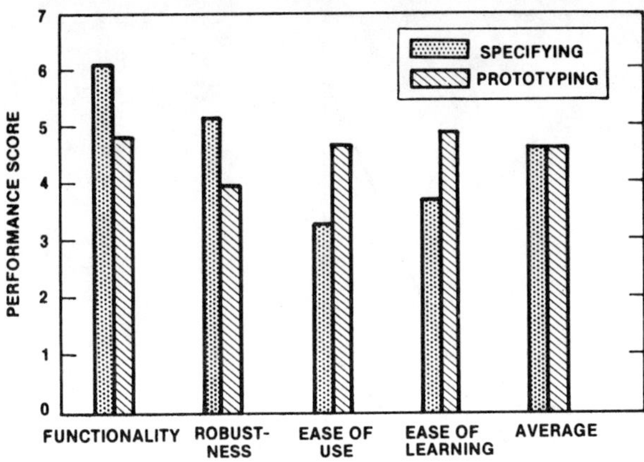

Fig. 2. Specifying versus prototyping: performance comparisons.

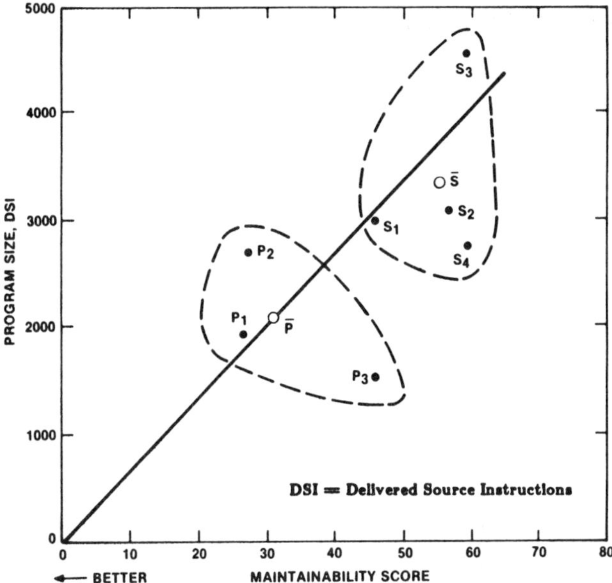

Fig. 3. Maintainability rating versus size.

tenance costs. Somewhat paradoxically, however, the products of the prototype groups were judged worse as a basis for planning add-ons.

In exploring which factors influenced the maintainability rating, we compared the rating to the size of the products (Fig. 3). At first glance, it appears as if the students preferred to maintain smaller products. However, when asked in the follow-up questionnaire what the main criteria for their maintenance rating were, the students ranked the size of the products only third, and size was mentioned only as one factor besides design, programming style and documentation, and performance (see Table II).

Effort Distribution: During the development process, the groups had to meet different deadlines. The specifying groups had to hand in a requirements specification in the third week and a requirements and design specification in the sixth week. The prototype groups had to present their prototype for a prototype exercise in the fifth week. For both groups, the acceptance test took place in the tenth week after project start. Figs. 4 and 5 show the average effort distribution by phase and activity for both group types. While the "deadline

TABLE II
RANKING OF MAINTENANCE RATING CRITERIA

Factor	# Students Citing Factor
design	8
programming style	5
size of the product	4
documentation	3
product performance at acceptance test	2

effect" observed in [13], with major peaks of the total effort before the deadlines, is fairly distinct in the effort distribution of the specifying groups, the effort distribution by phase for the prototyping groups is much smoother. Especially at the end of the quarter, the programming, testing, and fixing effort of the prototyping groups did not peak, as it did for the specifying groups. Instead, the effort-peak for the prototyping groups at the end was mostly due to documentation effort.

Fig. 6 shows the effort distribution by activity in percent of the total effort for both group types. Proportionately, the prototype groups spent less time for designing and programming, more for testing, reviewing, and fixing. The higher effort needed to integrate the prototype products was confirmed by comments in the project critiques.

Going through the whole design process before coding seemed to simplify the integration by forcing developers "to think before coding." On the other hand, building a prototype had the advantage of "always having something that works."

Documentation Productivity: As mentioned already, no difference between the two groups in the overall productivity (DSI/MH) could be observed. However, there appeared to be a significant difference in the documentation productivity. The specifying groups produced, on the average, 2.8 pages per documentation MH, the prototype groups only 1.2 (Table III). An explanation for this effect might be that the members of the specifying groups were more motivated to write documents, for they chose their group type knowing that a lot of documents would have to be produced. In addition, the specifying groups had three deadlines where documents were to be presented, the prototype groups only one. Therefore, the "deadline effect" might have influenced the documentation productivity of the specifying groups more than the documentation productivity of the prototyping groups. Another explanation may be that a good deal of documentation was produced in the process of design; if the design man-hours are added to the documentation man-hours, the difference in pages/MH is reduced to 1.2 versus 0.9.

Retrospective Comments: In the follow-up questionnaire, the students were asked how their project outcome would have differed, if they would have belonged to a different group type. The answers of the students of the specifying groups were not uniform. Some would have expected a better product, some a worse product, if they had been in a prototyping group. On the other hand, the students of the prototyping groups mostly indicated that specifying would have increased the performance of their product and would have resulted in a faster development process. It is interesting that the data of the experiment generally did not confirm this expectation.

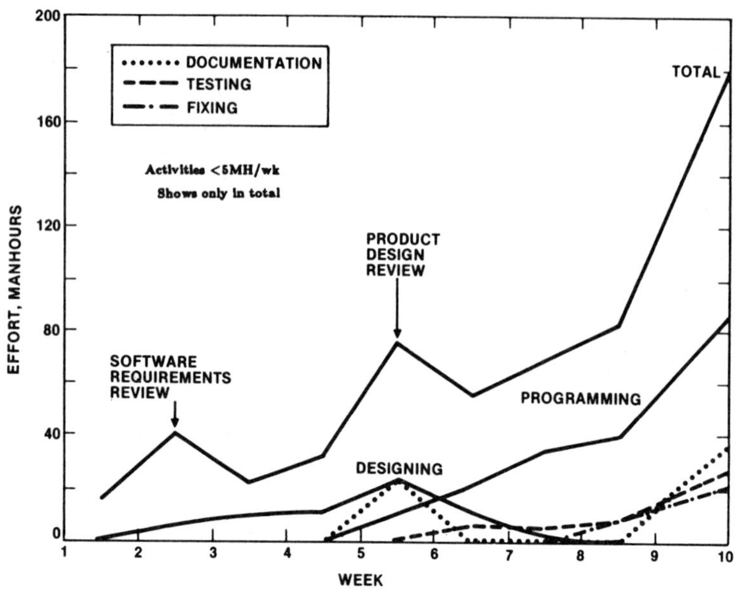

Fig. 4. Effort distribution by phase and activity: specifying groups.

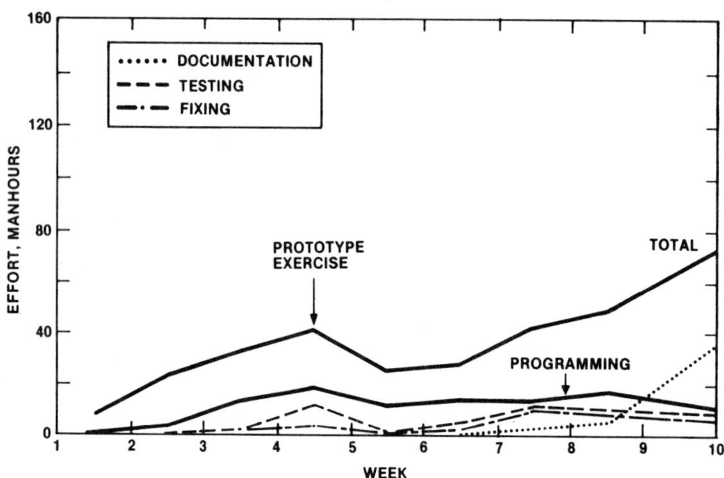

Fig. 5. Effort distribution by phase and activity: prototyping groups.

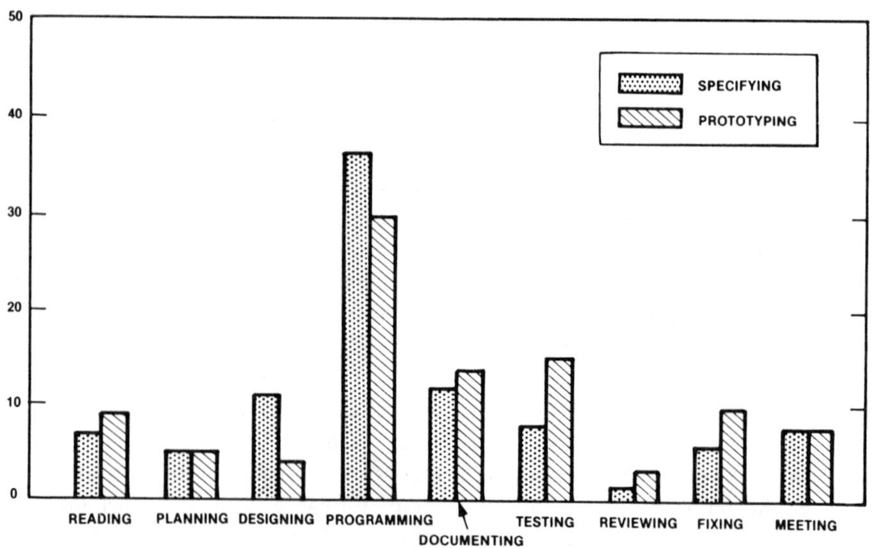

Fig. 6. Distribution of project effort by activity.

TABLE III
COMPARATIVE DOCUMENTATION PRODUCTIVITY

	specifying groups	prototyping groups
pages of documentation	161	54
MH for documentation	69	46
MH for design	67	13
productivity (page/MH)	2.8	1.2
pages/(design + doc. MH)	1.2	0.9

Analysis of Variance: An analysis of variance (ANOVA) was performed to determine the relative levels of statistical significance of the results above. The results are shown in the "Spec/Proto" column of Table V.

In general, a difference between treatment groups is considered significant if its significance score is less than 0.05 (indicated by two asterisks in Table V). A score between 0.05 and 0.10 is considered reasonably significant (indicated by one asterisk in Table V).

Table V thus summarizes the following conclusions about the significance of the differences between the specifying and prototyping groups:

- the differences in documentation size, total man-hours, and maintenance score are significant;
- the differences in program size, functionality, robustness, and ease of learning are reasonably significant;
- the differences in productivity were not significant.

B. Smaller Versus Larger Teams

A second analysis of the data was conducted, investigating the influence of the group size on the product and the development process, independent of the type of team.

Although the smaller teams of both types needed 41 percent less effort to develop their product (338 versus 575 MH), the average size of their products was only 8 percent smaller than the average size of the products of the larger teams (2690 versus 2921 DSI). Therefore, the productivity, as a measure of delivered source instructions per man-hour, was higher for the smaller teams than for the larger teams (7.5 versus 5.4 DSI/MH).

However, the almost equal average product size and the higher productivity might perhaps be due to one exceptional project: one of the two-person teams (*S*3) developed a product which was significantly larger than the products of all the other groups (4606 DSI versus 3164 DSI for the second largest product). The productivity of this group was also by far the highest (10 DSI/MH), due to one extremely prolific programmer. Removing this anomalous case brings the average productivity of smaller teams from 7.5 DSI/MH down to 6.25 DSI/MH and reveals a significant relationship between team size and product size.

The performance of the products of the smaller teams (again, independent of team type) was rated somewhat lower, mainly due to a lower functionality score. It seems that the smaller teams were not that much concerned about providing "fancy" functions, but more about getting their work done. (This may also have been because two of the three smaller teams were prototyping teams.) Due probably also to the lower manpower available, their products were less debugged than the products of the larger teams. On all the other factors—ease of use, ease of learning, and tolerance of erroneous input, the team size had only little correlation.

Comparing the effort the teams spent for different activities, for both prototyping and specifying teams, the smaller teams needed proportionally less time for programming than the larger teams (27 percent of total effort versus 38 percent). As expected, they needed also less time for meetings (5 percent versus 9 percent). Comments in the project critiques and follow-up questionnaires confirm that the larger teams had more communication problems and communication overhead than the smaller teams.

Asked how the product outcome would have changed if they would have been a group of the other group size, people of the larger groups indicated that reducing their team size by one person would have reduced the performance of their products. On the other hand, people of the small teams did not expect an increase in team size to lead to an increase in product performance.

The analysis of variance results comparing the two-person and three-person teams are shown in the "Team Size" column of Table V. Most of the team size differences are not statistically significant; total man-hours and product functionality rating achieve a reasonably significant level. In the other evaluation categories team size does not appear to be a primary driver of the experimental results. However, as noted above, removing the anomalous data of team *S*3 yields a statistically significant ($s = 0.0039$) difference in product size across the groups with different team size. Thus, if we drop project *S*3, team size appears to influence product size more than development style.

C. Characteristics of the Development Process

As shown already in Fig. 6, the dominant activity in the development process of both group types was programming. The specifying groups spent 37 percent of their total effort for programming, the prototyping groups 30 percent. No other activity took more than 20 percent. This result conflicts with one of the results of the earlier experiment reported in [13], in which the percentages of effort for programming (12-17 percent) and documentation (27-32 percent) were reversed. The main reasons were most likely the requirements for more documents (project plans, test plans) and for updating documents, and the larger team sizes in the earlier experiment; and the improved documentation aids provided by Unix in the later experiment.

In the current experiment, due to the tight schedule (only 10 weeks were available for the project), the development documents (requirements specification and design specification) were only written once. After the software requirements review and product design review, they were not corrected to incorporate modifications due to problem reports. Also, they were not updated when changes were made during the development process. Since the team size was relatively small and, therefore, the communication within the groups was good, the lack of up-to-date documents was not critical. However, if up-to-date documents had been required for other reasons, the proportional effort spent for documentation would have increased and, probably, at least reached the programming effort.

TABLE IV
COCOMO ESTIMATES VERSUS PROJECT ACTUALS

Team	Man-Months actual	Man-Months predicted	Actual / Predicted
specifying	3.8	12	0.32
prototyping	2.1	6.6	0.32

In order to investigate whether the COCOMO model can be applied to this kind of class project, the data of the different products were entered in one of the products and a prediction was calculated. The results are shown in Table IV. Even allowing for the 30-40 percent difference due to nonproject activities explained in [12], a significant discrepancy remains. Several factors might have influenced this discrepancy. First, as mentioned above, no final version of the requirements and design specification was written and the documents were not updated. In addition, the fact that seven groups were working on the same kind of project simultaneously and the grade in the course was mostly based on the project outcome might have produced a much more competitive situation than is found in a normal program development environment. Also, the fixed schedule with no possibility for prolongation, imposed by the duration of the quarter, might have contributed to this effect.

Note that the COCOMO prediction offset was independent of the development style. For both specifying and prototyping groups, the model predicted the same percentage of the real effort. The mismatch between model estimates and project actuals is not overly surprising; in general, algorithmic cost models have a difficult time with small projects.

D. Characteristics of Products

Although all groups were given the same task, the product architectures differed significantly. They frequently seemed to be a reflection of the developer personalities (elaborate versus simple displays, terse versus verbose messages, free-form versus directed sequential inputs, etc.).

Most of the groups (6 or 7) developed a menu-driven system. Screen-oriented interaction was preferred to line-oriented interaction. The man-machine interface and the flexibility of the dialogue was very product- and architecture-dependent. In addition, competition stimulated man-machine interface frills.

The distribution of source code by function for products of both group types was almost the same (Fig. 7). Although the main purpose of the product was to calculate a cost, effort, and schedule estimation, the portion of code devoted to this purpose was very small (5-8 percent). The user interface turned out to be the most important part of the system. It took over 50 percent of the code. These results are consistent with the earlier results in [13].

The portion of code devoted to the file management system differs heavily between the products. It comprises anywhere between 5 and 40 percent of the code. Its size depends mostly on the provided capabilities and on how much file management functions of the operating system were used versus implementing a new file management system for the product. (The original directions to the teams said simply "develop a single-user file system for input data.")

In the number of delivered source instructions per person there was only little variation. With one exception (2303 for team S3), they were all in the range of 757-1055 DSI/person. The same is true for the overall performance of the products. With one exception (13.3 points), all products were rated between 17 and 21.3 points.

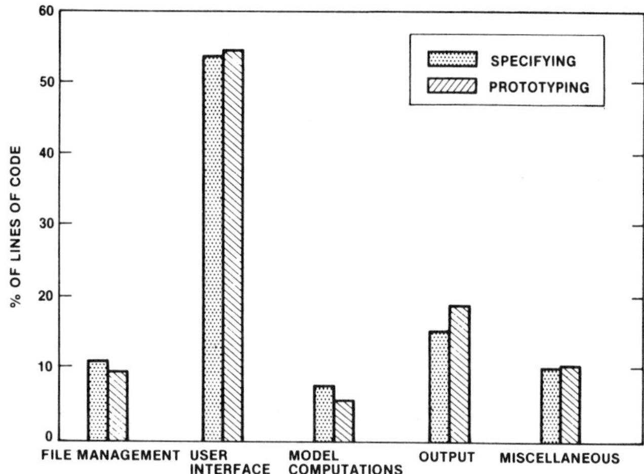

Fig. 7. Distribution of source code by function.

E. Some Other Observations

The organization of the team was left to the individual team members. Since no group leader was explicitly determined, every group followed more or less a democratic approach. Yet, the preferred organization was highly people-dependent. Four students mentioned in their critiques that the democratic approach worked well, while three students would have preferred to have a team leader.

The prototyping strategies were quite consistent over the prototyping groups. After building the prototype, no group started new to build the final product. Rather, 67-95 percent of the prototype code was used in the final product. The size of the prototypes was between 40-60 percent the size of the final product. An overall summary of project results is given in Table V.

IV. CONCLUSIONS

The results of this experiment provide some useful quantitative and qualitative information on the relative effects of the specifying and prototyping approaches on the development of a small applications software product. However, as indicated at several points earlier, initial experiments of this nature are not likely to provide definitive conclusions applicable to all project situations. The experimental results can be sensitive to exceptional individuals' performance or to experimental boundary conditions, or the results may depend on the size and nature of the software application. Therefore, the conclusions below should be considered suggestive rather than definitive. The conclusions are thus presented in project-specific rather than general terms.

A. Conclusions on Specifying Versus Prototyping

Prototyping tended to produce a smaller product, with roughly equivalent performance, using less effort. The prototyped products averaged about 40 percent smaller than the specified products, and required about 45 percent less effort. In performance, they rated somewhat lower on functionality

TABLE V
SUMMARY OF PROJECT RESULTS

	Specifying Teams					Prototyping Teams				ANOVA Significance	
	S1	S2	S3	S4	AVG.	P1	P2	P3	AVG.	Spec/Proto	Team Size
TEAM SIZE	3	3	2	3	2.75	2	3	2	2.33		
PROGRAM SIZE (Deliv. Source Inst.)											
File	64	622	246	714	411	45	356	204	201		
User Interface	1462	1910	2830	1064	1817	1123	1505	815	1148		
Compute	143	62	648	195	262	84	178	70	111		
Output	931	264	267	405	467	349	513	293	385		
Other	385	306	615	331	434	351	174	132	219		
TOTAL	2985	3164	4606	2809	3391	1952	2726	1514	2064	0.0674*	0.7891
Omitting S3 data					2986				2064	0.0668*	0.0039**
DOCUMENTATION (Pages)											
Rqts. Spec.	19	13	11	11	14	-	-	-	-		
Design Spec.	38	123	59	83	76	-	-	-	-		
User Manual	32	45	73	35	46	38	37	30	35		
TOTAL	165	231	181	179	189	58	49	56	54	0.0001**	0.3743
MANHOURS											
thru Rqts.	83	44	44	70	60	-	-	-	-		
thru Design	225	160	144	242	193	-	-	-	-		
thru Prototype	-	-	-	-	102	129	84	105	-		
Reading	29	33	40	72	43	21	24	43	29		
Planning	44	7	30	41	30	22	15	15	17		
Designing	81	46	59	82	67	16	13	12	13		
Programming	276	162	135	289	216	109	147	39	98		
Documenting	48	82	53	92	69	54	50	33	46		
Testing	45	49	55	29	44	27	75	46	49		
Reviewing	2	3	6	20	8	19	3	5	9		
Fixing	27	42	19	48	34	33	39	27	33		
Meeting	30	49	24	80	46	19	44	11	25		
Misc.	7	26	40	37	28	3	13	2	6		
TOTAL	589	498	459	789	584	323	422	232	325	0.0471**	0.0817*
PERFORMANCE											
Functionality	6.33	7	5	6	6.08	5.33	5	4	4.78	0.0799*	0.0799*
Robustness	4.67	5.5	6	4.33	5.13	4.33	4.33	3	3.89	0.0875*	0.7535
Ease of Use	2.33	4	2.67	4	3.25	6	5.33	2.67	4.67	0.2144	0.9133
Ease of Learning	3.67	3.5	4	3.67	3.71	5.67	5.33	3.67	4.89	0.0771*	0.6022
MAINT. SCORE (low is good)	45.5	57	59.5	59	55	21	27.5	45.5	31	0.0217**	0.6968
PRODUCTIVITY (DSI/MH)											
Overall	5.1	6.4	10	3.6	5.8	6	6.5	6.5	6.3	0.9727	0.1737
Coding	10.8	19.5	34.1	9.7	15.7	25	18.5	38.8	21		

and robustness, but somewhat higher on ease of learning and ease of use. Statistically, these differences were at least reasonably significant.

The main reason for this effect appeared to be that prototyping fostered a higher threshold for incorporating marginally useful features into a software product. The process of prototyping gave software developers a more realistic feel for the amount of effort required to add features to a project, and the lack of a definitive specification meant that prototypers were less locked into a set of promises to deliver capabilities than were the specifiers. In the somewhat rueful words of one of the specifiers, remarking on his team's efforts to fulfill the promises in their ambitious specification, "Words are cheap."

Prototyping did not tend to produce higher "productivity" if "productivity" is measured in delivered source instructions per man-hour. However, if "productivity" is measured in equivalent user satisfaction per man-hour, prototyping did tend to be superior. This conclusion reinforces the desire for a better productivity metric than the number of source instructions developed.

Again, this conclusion does not necessarily apply to every project situation. The value-of-information decision guidelines for software projects in [12, ch. 20] identify a number of situations in which the information value of a prototype will not be worth the investment in it. Even for projects similar to the one in this experiment, the specifying approach may be able to produce similarly concise products if the specification reviews are strongly focused on elimination of marginally useful product features.

Prototyping did tend to provide a number of benefits frequently ascribed to it. These included:

- products with better human-machine interfaces;
- always having something that works (at least for "build-upon" if not for throwaway prototypes);
- a reduced deadline effect at the end of the project.

Prototyping led to better maintainability ratings, but the effect was unclear. At the same time, participants' critiques indicated that specifications led to more coherent designs and that prototyping made it harder to plan additions.

Prototyping tended to create several negative effects. These included:

- proportionally less effort planning and designing, and proportionally more testing and fixing;
- more difficult integration due to lack of interface specifications;
- a less coherent design.

These effects become particularly critical on larger products. This suggests that, especially for larger products, prototyping should be followed by a reasonable level of specification of the product and its internal interfaces.

B. Conclusions on Team-Size Effects

Smaller teams produced smaller products with less effort and a higher "productivity" in DSI/man-hour. This conclusion is only statistically significant if the anomalous data for team *S*3 are removed from the analysis. The two-person teams spent smaller percentages of their effort in programming and meeting. Their products were rated somewhat lower on functionality, but about the same on ease of use, ease of learning, and robustness.

Some of this team-size effect may have accounted for some of the differences between the specifying and prototyping results, since the average size of prototyping teams was somewhat smaller (2.33 persons versus 2.75). However, the corroborative evidence from the project critiques indicates that the projects' results were strongly influenced by whether they used a specifying or a prototyping approach.

C. Conclusions on Other Software Engineering Effects

The "deadline effect" observed on a previous project [13] was corroborated. Also, this experiment corroborated the previous observation that most of a product's code is devoted to largely application-independent "housekeeping" functions.

The previous conclusion in [13] that "documentation is the dominant activity during software development" was not corroborated by this experiment. In fact, programming was the dominant activity during this experiment, due most likely to differences in project groundrules and team sizes. This result emphasizes the need for follow-up experiments to confirm conclusions reached during software engineering experiments.

The most effective software project organization in strongly dependent on the nature of the people on the project. Some people's critiques emphasized the need for a strong leader, as in the Chief Programmer Team approach. A larger number of people felt that a more democratic team approach was more effective.

The COCOMO model strongly overestimated the amount of effort required to develop the experimental products. The overestimates were typically by a factor of about 2.5, much larger than could be explained by not counting the typical 30-40 percent of the workday devoted to nonproject activities. Most likely, the extra productivity was a result of exceptional motivation of the people involved, both from the competitive-team aspects and from a Hawthorne effect.

Nothing succeeds like motivation. This was the major cause of both the high team productivity and the very high level of maintainability of their products. The software field in general needs a maintainability motivator similar in power to that of telling students, "20 percent of your course grade will depend on how much others want to maintain your product."

D. Future Research

It is clear that the large number of variables in the present experiment made it impossible to draw unambiguous conclusions. We believe it is equally clear that experiments such as this can make a significant contribution, particularly as others repeat them and thereby increase the sample size.

Subsequent experiments of this type should attempt to reduce the number of variables by:

- making all of the teams the same size (prohibit prime numbers of students per class!);
- more precisely defining the user-interface requirements, so that everyone implements close to the same functionality.

Several different directions for investigation were also suggested by this work.

- Further examinations of the effect of team size on programmer productivity and product size. Use the same development approach and environment, and a precisely defined product definition.
- Further examination of prototyping versus specifying approaches applied to different phases of a development project: definition of functional requirements, design decisions, and implementation decisions. In other words, how does the development approach affect the *nature* of the product, as distinct from the cost of development?

• Examination of the effect of implementation language choice on programmer productivity and product size. A series of class projects should be an excellent way to investigate this question. Of particular interest: comparison of interpreted and compiled languages.

• Examination of factors that influence the style of user-interface chosen by a particular designer, e.g., available development tools, assumptions about user environment, and personality traits of the designer.

• Investigation of the effect of turn-around time on programmer productivity. Is the effect linear or nonlinear? To what extent does it depend upon the programmer's expectations and previous experience?

• Examination of the "user-manual first" approach on product size, quality, and effort expended.

• Investigation of how accurately developers can predict final product size from requirements definitions. Also, how much does the existence of design specs improve accuracy of product size predictions?

• Further investigation of the effect of prototyping versus specifying on maintenance and enhancement costs.

• Further examination of the wide variations observed in coding productivity, with respect to both team size and development approach.

E. Summary

The results of this experiment indicate that both prototyping and specifying have valuable advantages that complement each other. For most large projects, and many small ones, a mix of prototyping and specifying will be preferable to the exclusive use of either by itself. In particular, the results indicate the following.

1) *The current specification-oriented model should not be completely scrapped, particularly on large projects.* The prototypers' experience indicated that interface and design specifications were still particularly valuable in supporting integration and change implementation.

2) *The current model needs to be reoriented to accommodate prototyping,* and such related techniques as incremental development. This involves establishing such new life-cycle milestones as a User Design Review (UDR) to achieve user validation of a prototyped user interface.

3) *Contracting for software acquisition needs to reflect the reoriented model.* This involves the use of competitive front-end prototyping and "fly-offs," and the organization of the development into a series of stabilized increments of functional capability.

4) *The bottom-line driver on selection of the specific mix of prototyping and specifying should be risk management.* Prototyping is not necessary on familiar projects where there is little risk of getting the wrong user interface, requirements, or design. Elaborate specifications are not necessary on smaller projects with good user-developer rapport, where there is little risk of botching the integration process or having an altercation over contract deliverables. Risk management considerations also drive most of the other key management decisions over the software life-cycle (how much to invest in analysis, simulation, new technology, testing, quality assurance, configuration management, etc.), leading to a final implication:

Software projects should develop, maintain, and follow a Risk Management Plan, which identifies potential high-risk issues, establishes plans for resolving them, and highlights risk-item resolution in project status reviews.

As a final note, it is worth reemphasizing the conclusion that the prototyping approach resulted in products that were easier to learn and use. For a field which is searching for ways to make its products more humane, this experiment indicated that the prototyping approach clearly has a great deal to offer.

Appendix A
Project Description Given to Students

Project Objectives

The objectives of this two-quarter project are to develop and maintain a small software product (a version of the COCOMO software cost estimation model) as a team project. The product specifics for each quarter are the following.

Quarter 1 (Winter 1982): Develop an interactive version of the Intermediate COCOMO model, with the following capabilities:

• component-level project effort, schedule and cost estimation (basically, implementing the CLEF procedures in [12, Table 9-1, p. 148]);

• organic-mode projects only, with no adaptation estimation capability (simplification of [12, Table 9-1]);

• effort and schedule distributions by phase;

• single-user file system for storing and retrieving model inputs;

• easy to use by reasonably experienced, somewhat impatient user.

Quarter 2 (Spring 1982): Adapt the product of another team to provide the following additional capabilities:

• all three software development modes (organic, semidetached, embedded);

• adaptation effects;

• maintenance cost and effort estimation;

• effort distribution by activity;

• multiuser file system.

• user-interface enhancements.

Project Approach

Students will develop and maintain the product in three-person teams. Team selection and the types of teams available are covered in the Course Description. Specific schedules for each team's deliverable items are given in the Course Schedule.

Each program will be written in Pascal to run on the UCLA VAX-Unix system.

Product Acceptance

Acceptance tests for all teams' products will be performed on Wednesday, March 17. For preparation, each team shall provide three copies of a users' manual for their product on Monday, March 15.

The acceptance test shall consist of the instructors exercising the team's program to determine whether it:

- handles all cases specified in the objectives above;
- handles off-nominal conditions with useful error responses;
- exhibits a high degree of user-friendliness.

Product Deliverables

Each deliverable item shall be handed in at the classroom in three (3) copies at 4:00 PM of the designated day. Documents shall be page-numbered.

Day	Teams	Deliverable Items
Wed., Jan. 27	S	Requirements specification (see Course Notes for format)
Mon., Feb. 15	S	Requirements/Design spec and Draft Users' Manual (see Course Notes for format)
Mon., Mar. 15	S, P	Users' Manual (see Course Notes for format)
Wed., Mar. 17	S, P	Code and Maintenance Manual (Format TBD)

In addition, "P" Teams will prepare a prototype of their program to be exercised by the instructors on Wednesday, Feb. 10. Finally, each student will hand in two copies of their project critique (see Course Description for details) to either of the instructors by 4:00 PM, Wednesday, March 24.

Choice of Product to Maintain

A copy of each team's deliverable products (code, users' manual, maintenance manual) will be made available for review in (location TBD) during the period March 17-24. Each student is to review each of the other teams' products, and express his preference for which of the other teams' products he would prefer to maintain during the second quarter. A Product Choice form for expressing these preferences is attached; it is to be turned in with your project critique on Wednesday, March 24.

These evaluations will be used to determine:

- which product your team will receive to maintain during the second quarter;
- how well your team's first quarter product is rated for maintainability, as a component of your first quarter grade.

Time Sheets

Every Monday at classtime (4:00 PM), each student is to turn in a filled-out timesheet indicating how many hours during the previous week he spent performing the various project activities (reading, planning. . .). The results will be used for statistical purposes only; your grade will be based on your outputs and not on the number of hours you put in. A blank timesheet is part of this package.

Reviews

The Requirements Specifications produced by the "S" teams on Wednesday, January 27, will undergo a validation process by the instructors, resulting in a set of Design Problem Reports (DPR's) identifying problems found in the spec. (A sample DPR form is part of this package.) Copies of these DPR's will be provided to the "S" teams Monday morning, February 1. During the course period on February 1, a Software Requirements Review (SRR) will be held for each team, to determine the disposition of each DPR (required action, no action, redundant).

A similar process will be carried out for the "S" teams' Product Design specs and Draft Users' Manuals (Spec due Monday, February 15; DPR's returned Wednesday morning, February 17; Product Design Reviews during class February 17).

Appendix B
Instructional Lessons Learned

In this section we identify issues of specific interest to others who might wish to organize a course similar to this one. These comments are based on observations by the instructors as well as student critiques. They highlight a number of areas where we would make changes in any subsequent experiment.

Class Scheduling and Content

The project schedule was too tight for a one-quarter class, with test planning and study of software engineering papers referenced in lectures being the first casualties.

A second class was scheduled for the following quarter in order to examine maintenance and enhancement issues experimentally, but few students continued for the second class due to schedule conflicts.

Optimum scheduling of classroom lectures proved to be impossible: students wanted all lecture material prior to commencing the project.

There was insufficient lecture time for several important topics, e.g., coding and documentation standards, "user-manual first" strategy, and user-interface design issues.

While students considered the course very valuable, they complained that is was too much work, and that there was too much emphasis on the project and not enough on current software engineering literature.

The ideal situation would probably be a required three-course sequence: 1) lecture and reading; 2) product development; and 3) product maintenance.

Project Elements

Implementation of COCOMO cost-estimation equations was straightforward.

The file system was challenging due to lack of familiarity with Unix and the Pascal constructs needed to use operating system services.

The user-interface was challenging because the user-interface requirements were not given to students, and they were unfamiliar with user-interface design principles.

Terminal-independent, full-screen user-interfaces proved difficult due to poor documentation of relevant Unix library routines.

Project Requirements

Requirements definition for the user-interface and file system were too loose for close comparability of projects.

Ambiguity of system requirements led to competition among groups, and consequently overambitious goals. However, tighter requirements definitions for the user-interface might have subverted one of advantages of prototyping—the freedom to try more than one user-interface style.

While constraining the project to a more manageable scope and reducing the number of experimental variables, tighter requirements would also deprive students of useful lessons in system analysis and user-interface design.

Data Collection

The most important point regarding data collection is to insist that the student's timesheets be turned in on time, lest the student be forced to "recreate" the data at the end of the quarter.

It is also important to explain precisely which activities fall into which timesheet categories.

Project critiques were deemed very valuable by instructors, but varied widely in content; therefore, more specific guidelines should have been provided.

Documentation and Coding Standards

While the students were given relevant papers, relatively little emphasis was given to this subject in class. As a result, project results showed little attention to standards. Also, the amount of code documentation (i.e., comments) was highly variable.

We do not believe the lack of standards had any significant impact on experimental results; still, it is clear that more emphasis should be given to this topic in future classes.

Team Size and Experience

Our experience is inconclusive about the optimum team size from an instructional perspective. Small teams had fewer communication problems, but large teams benefited by more debate in design meetings.

The majority of students had less than a year of Pascal or Unix experience, but more important than amount of experience is its distribution. Instructors should survey the students to assist them in creating balanced teams.

Group Projects

Most students valued the group project experience; however, personality conflicts devastated one group.

Students were unsuccessful at inspiring less motivated team members, and they lacked effective methods for resolving conflicts. These problems can lead to unfair evaluation of individual students.

Since students ususally have relatively little experience with group projects, instructors should take pains to warn students that early meetings will be relatively unproductive, as team members try to get to know one another, and that they should make heavy use of electronic mail and design walkthroughs.

Examples of coordination problems that students should be made aware of include simultaneous update of one file by two team members, and two team members picking the same name for a file. Some of these problems can be minimized by using many small source files, combined via INCLUDE statements.

Design Reviews and Product Demonstrations

Letting everyone participate in reviews and demonstrations served our teaching goals very well, although our research goals were slightly compromised by doing this.

Members of both types of teams reported increased appreciation of specification and review techniques after seeing them in action.

Having two instructors review all documents and products provided much better feedback to students.

These sessions provided good opportunities to discuss alternate design decisions.

Development Environment

Use of a severely overloaded VAX 11/780 had an extremely negative impact on project development.

As contention for system resources increased (toward the end of the quarter) insufficient disk space often caused compiles to fail.

The Unix operating system and Berkeley Pascal were reasonable choices, although a more extended Pascal (e.g., one with strings) would have been preferred.

REFERENCES

[1] B. W. Boehm, "Software engineering," *IEEE Trans. Comput.*, pp. 1226–1241, Dec. 1976.

[2] H. D. Benington, "Production of large computer programs," in *Proc. Symp. Advanced Programming Methods for Digital Computers*, ONR, Washington, DC, June 1956, pp. 15–27.

[3] W. A. Hosier, "Pitfalls and safeguards in real-time systems with emphasis on programming," *IRE Trans. Eng. Management*, pp. 99–115, June 1961.

[4] W. W. Royce, "Managing the development of large software systems: Concepts and techniques," in *Proc. WESCON*, Aug. 1970.

[5] R. D. Williams, "Managing the development of large-scale reliable software," in *Proc. 1975 Int. Conf. Reliable Software*, IEEE/ACM, Apr. 1975, pp. 3–8.

[6] R. L. Glass, *Modern Programming Practices: A Report From Industry*. Englewood Cliffs, NJ: Prentice-Hall, 1982.

[7] M. M. Lehman, "Programs, life cycles, and laws of program evolution," *IEEE Spectrum*, Sept. 1980.

[8] P. Kerola and P. Freeman, "A comparison of lifecycle models," in *Proc. 5th Int. Conf. Software Eng.*, IEEE/ACM, Mar. 1981, pp. 90–99.

[9] B. W. Boehm, "Software design and structuring," in *Practical Strategies for Developing Large Software Systems*, E. Horowitz, Ed. Reading, MA: Addison-Wesley, 1975.

[10] D. D. McCracken and M. A. Jackson, "Life cycle concept considered harmful," *ACM SIGSOFT Software Eng. Notes*, pp. 29–32, Apr. 1982.

[11] M. Zelkowitz and M. Branstad, *Proc. ACM SIGSOFT Rapid Prototyping Symp.*, Columbia, MD, Apr. 1982.

[12] B. W. Boehm, *Software Engineering Economics.* Englewood Cliffs, NJ: Prentice-Hall, 1981.

[13] —, "An experiment in small-scale application software engineering," *IEEE Trans. Software Eng.*, pp. 482–493, Sept. 1981.

Applying Formal Specification to Software Development in Industry

IAN J. HAYES

Abstract—This paper reports experience gained in applying formal specification techniques to an existing transaction processing system. The system is the IBM Customer Information Control System (CICS) and the work has concentrated on specifying a number of modules of the CICS application programmer's interface.

The uses of formal specification techniques with particular reference to their application to an existing piece of software are outlined. The specification process itself is described and a sample specification presented. The specifications are written in Z, a specification notation developed at Oxford.

One of the main benefits of applying specification techniques to existing software is the questions that are raised about the system design and documentation during the specification process. Some samples of the problems that were identified by these questions are discussed.

Problems with the specification techniques themselves, that were encountered in applying the techniques to a commercial transaction processing system are outlined.

Index Terms—CICS, formal specification, large scale software.

INTRODUCTION

OXFORD UNIVERSITY and IBM United Kingdom Laboratories Limited are engaged in a joint project to evaluate the applicability of formal specification techniques to industrial scale software. The project is attempting to scale up formal mathematical methods so far used within a research environment to large scale software in an industrial environment. This paper reports the experience gained so far in applying these techniques to describe the application programmer's interface of the IBM Customer Information Control System (CICS).

CICS is widely used to support on-line transaction processing applications such as airline reservations, stock control, and banking. It can support applications involving large numbers of terminals (thousands) and very large databases (gigabytes). The CICS General Information manual [3] gives the following description.

> CICS/VS provides 1) most of the standard functions required by application programs for communication with remote and local terminals and subsystems; 2) control for concurrently running user application programs serving many online users; and 3) database capabilities . . .

CICS is general purpose in the sense that it provides the primitives of transaction processing, and an individual application is implemented by writing a program invoking these primitives. The primitives are similar to operating system calls, but are at a higher level: they also provide such facilities as security checking, logging, and error recovery.

CICS has been in use since 1968, and has undergone continuous development during its lifetime. In the original implementation, the application programmer's interface was at the level of control blocks and assembler macro calls. This is referred to as the *macro* level application programmer's interface. In 1976, a new interface, the *command* level application programmer's interface, was introduced. It provides a cleaner interface which does not require the application programmer to have knowledge of the control blocks used in the implementation of the system. The command level interface is the subject of our work on specification.

CICS is supported on a number of IBM operating systems: DOS/VSE, MVS, and MVS/XA, in such a way that application programs written using the application programmer's interface may be transferred from one environment to another without recoding. In addition, the command level interface supports a number of programming languages: PL/I, Cobol, Assembler, and RPG II. This is achieved by the use of a preprocessor that translates programs containing CICS commands into the appropriate statements in the language being used (usually a call on a CICS module). Hence the application programmer's interface provides a level of abstraction that hides a number of significantly different implementations.

The command level interface is split up into a number of relatively independent modules responsible for controlling various resources of the system. The formal specification work has so far concentrated on specifying individual modules in relative isolation. Of the 16 modules comprising the command level interface three: temporary storage, exceptional condition handling, and interval control, have been specified. Temporary storage provides facilities for setting up named

Manuscript received February 15, 1984; revised May 29, 1984. This work was supported by IBM Corporation.

The author is with the Programming Research Group, Computing Laboratory, Oxford University, Oxford OX1 3QD, England.

Reprinted from *IEEE Transactions on Software Engineering*, Volume SE-11, Number 2, February 1985, pages 169-178.

EHO304-6/90/0000/0594$01.00

temporary storage *queues* that may be used to communicate information between transactions or as temporary storage by a single transaction. Exceptional condition handling provides facilities to handle exceptions raised by calls on CICS commands in a manner similar to PL/I condition handling. Interval control provides facilities to set up timeouts and delays, as well as to start a new transaction at a given time and pass data to it.

With the large number of CICS systems around the world, the usage of the CICS command level application programmer's interface is on a par with many programming languages. As with programming languages, it is important that the interface be clearly specified in a manner independent of a particular implementation.

Uses of Formal Specification

The work reported in this paper deals with specification of parts of an already existing system. Before considering the benefits of specification when applied to *preexisting* software, we will briefly review the benefits of specification in general. (For a more detailed discussion see [8].)

In software development a formal specification can be used by

- designers–to formulate and experiment with the design of the system;
- implementors–as a precise description of the system being built, particularly if there is more than one implementation;
- documentors–as an unambiguous starting point for user manuals; and
- quality control–for the development of suitable testing strategies.

Using a specification, the designer of a system can reason about properties of the system before development starts, and during development, formal verification that an implementation meets its specification can be carried out.

When an existing system is being specified there are both short and long term benefits. In the short term performing the specification

1) uncovers those parts of the existing manuals that are either incomplete or inconsistent, and
2) gives insights into the anomalies of the existing system and can suggest ways in which the system could be improved.

In the longer term the specification can be used

1) for reimplementation of all or part of the system,
2) as a basis for discussing and developing specifications for changes or additions to the system, and
3) to provide a model of the functional behavior of the system suitable for educating new staff.

Reimplementation may involve a new machine architecture, programming language, or operating system, or a restructuring to take advantage of multiprocessor or distributed systems. As the specification is implementation independent, it provides a suitable starting point for each of the above alternatives.

When changes or additions to the system are to be made, new specifications can be developed with reference to the previous specification. This process will give insights into the effect of the changes and their interaction with existing parts of the system.

As the specification is a formal document it provides a more precise description for communication between the designers than natural language descriptions. This should help to reduce misunderstandings between the people involved.

Experimentation with specification provides a much quicker and cheaper method of investigating a number of alternative changes to the system than implementing the changes. On the other than, because the specification is implementation independent, it cannot provide direct answers to questions of how difficult the changes will be to implement, or their impact on the performance of the system. However, as it is at a high level of abstraction it can give a better insight into the interaction of changes with other components of the system; it is just these high level interactions which get lost in the detail of implementation.

While working predominantly at a more abstract level, the specifier must be experienced in implementation and should be aware of the implementation consequences of his decisions. Those parts of the specification for which the implementation consequences are unclear should be further investigated before detailed implementation is begun.

The Specification Process

The starting point for our specification work was the CICS command level application programmer's reference manual [2]. The style of this manual is a combination of formal notation describing the syntax of commands and informal English explanations of the operation of the commands. We developed our initial specification of a module of the system by reference to the corresponding section of the manual. The main goal was to come up with a mathematical model of the module that is consistent with its description in the manual. This involves forming a crude initial model of the module and extending it to cover operations (or facets of operations) not initially dealt with, or refining or redesigning the specification as inconsistencies are discovered between it and the manual.

In attempting the initial specification, questions arose that were not satisfactorily answered by the manual. At this stage a list of questions was prepared and an expert on that module of the system (along with the source code) was consulted to answer the questions according to the current implementation. Questions can arise because

1) the manual is incomplete or vague,
2) the manual is not explicit as to whether possible special cases are treated normally or not,
3) the manual is itself inconsistent, or
4) the chosen mathematical model is inconsistent with the manual in some small way; either the model or the manual is incorrect.

As the system has been in use for some time the answers to the more straightforward questions about its operation have already found their way into the manual. Hence most questions that arose in the specification process were rather subtle and required reference to the source code of the module to be satisfactorily answered. Some of the questions led to inconsistencies being discovered between the manual and the implementation. These inconsistencies could either be errors in the manual or bugs in the implementation. Which way they should be classified depends on the original intent of the designer.

The specification was also given to people experienced in formal specification who gave comments on its internal consistency and style, and they suggested ways in which the specification could be simplified or improved. They were also given a copy of the relevant section of the manual to read *after* they have understood the specification, and were asked to point out any inconsistencies they discovered between it and the specification.

The answers to questions and the review of the specification led to revision of the specification, which led to further questions and further review and so on.

Notation

The specification language Z [1], [6], [7] developed by the Programming Research Group at Oxford University is the primary notation that has been used in this specification work, although this notation is not used within IBM. The formal basis of the notation is elementary set theory. People familiar with set theory from mathematics should have little trouble understanding the specifications. A summary of the notations used within this paper is given in Appendix A.

The style of the specification document is a mixture of formal Z and informal explanatory English. The formal parts of the specification, given in Z, are surrounded in the text by boxes so that they stand apart from the explanatory surrounds and may be more easily found for reference purposes. To make a readable specification, both formal and informal parts are necessary; the formal text can be too terse for easy reading and often its purpose needs to be explained, while the informal natural language explanation can more easily be vague or ambiguous and needs the precision of a formal language to make the intent clear. The formal text provides the link between formality and reality without which the formal text would just be a piece of mathematics. To create a good specification the structuring of the specification and the composition and style of the informal prose are as important as the formal text.

The aim is to provide a specification at a high level of abstraction and thus avoid implementation details. The specification should reveal the operation of the system a small portion at a time. These portions can be progressively combined to give a specification of the whole. This style of presentation is preferred to giving a monolithic specification and trying to explain it; the latter can be rather overwhelming and incomprehensible since there are too many different facets to understand at once. It is hoped that by giving the specification in small portions each piece can be understood and when the pieces are put together the understanding of the parts that has already been gained can lead more easily to an understanding of the whole.

For more complex specifications that are developed via numerous small steps, understanding the whole can be quite difficult, as one needs to remember the function of all the parts and understand the way in which they are combined. In such cases it can be useful to provide both a portion by portion development of the specification and an expanded monolithic specification as well. The latter is more assailable after one has been through a piece by piece development and has an understanding of its various components.

A Sample Specification

As a sample of the type of specification produced we will look in detail at the specification of exceptional condition handling within CICS. The exception check mechanisms of CICS are similar on those provided by PL/I [4]. This module was chosen for exposition because it is one of the smaller modules in the system. The manual entry on which the specification was initially based is given in Appendix B and the formal notation used in this example is described in Appendix A. The specification given here is a final product of a specification process described in the previous section.

Exceptional Conditions Specification

Exceptional conditions may arise during the execution of a CICS command. A transaction may either set up an action to be taken on a condition by using a Handle Condition command, or it may specify that the condition is to be ignored by using an Ignore Condition command. If a condition has been neither handled nor ignored, then the default action for that condition will be used.

For example, to handle *c*ondition x with *a*ction y we can use

Handle Condition$(c = x,\ a = y)$

where the keyword parameter "c=" gives the condition and "a=" gives the action. To ignore condition z we use

Ignore Condition$(c = z)$

We introduce the set CONDITION, which contains all the exceptional conditions that may occur, and also contains two special conditions: *success*—the condition that indicates that a command completed normally, and *error*—a catchall condition that might be used if the exceptional condition that occurred is not handled.

We also introduce the set ACTION which contains all actions that could be taken in response to some exceptional condition. The exact nature of ACTION will not be discussed in detail here. For each programming language supported by CICS it has a slightly different meaning, but for all the languages an action is represented by a label which is given control. There are five special actions used in this specification: *nil*—indicating a normal return (i.e., no action), *abort*—the action that abnormally terminates a transaction, *wait*—indicating that the transaction is to wait until the operation can be completed normally (e.g., wait until space becomes available), *truncate*—indicating that a value too large to fit in a given data area is to be truncated, and *system*—used to simplify the specification of the Handle Condition command.

The State: The state of the exception controlling system can be defined by

Exceptions

$$\text{Handler: CONDITION} \nrightarrow \text{ACTION}$$

$$\text{Handler}(\textit{success}) = \textit{nil}$$

The mapping Handler gives the action to be taken for those conditions that have been set up by either an Ignore Condition or Handle Condition command. The handling action for condition *success* is always *nil* (i.e., return normally). The action for other conditions is determined by some fixed function

$$\text{Default: CONDITION} \rightarrow \text{ACTION}.$$

We state two properties of Default:

$$\text{Default}(\textit{error}) = \textit{abort}$$
$$\textbf{range}(\text{Default}) = \{\textit{nil, abort, wait, truncate}\}$$

The default action for the special condition *error* is to abort and the only default actions are *nil, abort, wait,* and *truncate.*

The initial state of the exception handling system for a transaction is given by

Initial

Exceptions

$$\text{Handler} = \{\textit{success} \mapsto \textit{nil}\}$$

The initial state of the handler is to return normally if the operation completes successfully.

As an example, if starting in the initial state the commands

$$\text{Handle Condition}(c = x,\ a = y)$$
$$\text{Ignore Condition}(c = z)$$

are executed, then the final state will satisfy

$$\text{Handler} = \{x \mapsto y, z \mapsto \textit{nil}, \textit{success} \mapsto \textit{nil}\}$$

The Handle Condition sets up a mapping from condition x to action y and the Ignore Condition maps condition z onto the *nil* action.

The Operations: The two operations, Handle Condition and Ignore Condition, work directly on the above state. We describe a state change using the following schema, which is called "ΔExceptions" (Δ for change).

ΔExceptions

Exceptions
Exceptions′

Exceptions represents the state of the exception handling system before an operation and Exceptions′ the state after. (Appendix A contains an expansion of the above schema.)

The operation Handle Condition is used to set up the action a to be performed on a particular exceptional condition c; it is defined as

Handle Condition

ΔExceptions
c : CONDITION
a : ACTION

$$c \neq \textit{success} \wedge a \notin \{\textit{nil, abort, wait, truncate}\}$$
$$(a = \textit{system}) \rightarrow \text{Handler}' = \text{Handler} \oplus \{c \mapsto \text{Default}(c)\},$$
$$\text{Handler}' = \text{Handler} \oplus \{c \mapsto a\}$$

The first predicate gives the precondition for the operation: the special condition *success* cannot be handled, and the special actions *nil, abort, wait,* and *truncate* cannot be given as handling actions. The second predicate describes the effect of the operation: if the action to be set up is specified as *system*, then instead the default action for the given condition will be set up as the handler for that condition; otherwise the supplied action a will be set up. For example, if the following command is executed in the initial state:

$$\text{Handle Condition}(c = x,\ a = \textit{system})$$

where $\text{Default}(x) = \textit{wait}$, the resulting state will satisfy

$$\text{Handler} = \{x \mapsto \textit{wait}, \textit{success} \mapsto \textit{nil}\}$$

The operation to specify that an exceptional condition is to be ignored is given by

Ignore Condition

ΔExceptions
c : CONDITION

$$c \neq \textit{success}$$
$$\text{Handler}' = \text{Handler} \oplus \{c \mapsto \textit{nil}\}$$

The special condition *success* cannot be specified in an Ignore Condition command. The action to be taken on an ignored condition is to return normally (i.e., *nil*).

Exception Checking: Exception handling can take place on any CICS command except Handle Condition and Ignore Condition themselves. We need to describe the exception checking that takes place on all other commands. The exception checking process determines the action a to be taken on completion of a command. The value of a is dependent on the condition c returned by the command, and the current state of the exception handling mechanism. In addition, any command may specify whether all exceptions are to be handled or not for just the execution of that command. In describing the checking process we will include the Boolean variable handle to indicate this. The following defines the (complex) exception checking mechanism which is included in the definition of each operation (other than Handle Condition and Ignore Condition).

Exception Check	
Exceptions	
handle : Boolean	
c : CONDITION	
a : ACTION	
$\neg$handle	$\rightarrow a = nil$,
$c \in$ **dom** Handler	$\rightarrow a =$ Handler(c),
Default $(c) \neq abort$	$\rightarrow a =$ Default(c),
$error \in$ **dom** Handler	$\rightarrow a =$ Handler$(error)$,
	$a = abort$

If exceptions are not being handled for the command ($\neg$handle) the action is to return normally; otherwise the action is determined from the exception handler. If the condition c has been ignored or handled (including the case where the handle action was specified as *system*) then the corresponding handler action is used. Otherwise, if the default action for the condition is not *abort* the default is used, else if the special condition *error* is handled its handler action is used, otherwise the action will be *abort.*

Questions Raised During Specification

The questions raised about the system during the specification process are an important benefit of the process. They indicate problems either in the documentation of the system or in its logical design, and provide the people responsible for maintaining the system with immediate feedback on problem areas.

In writing a formal specification one is creating a mathematical model of what is being specified, and in creating such a model one is encouraged to be more precise than if one were writing in a natural language. Because of the required precision, questions are raised during the specification process that are not answered by reference to the less formal manual. In fact, the task of formal specification is demanding enough to raise most of the questions about the functional behavior of the system that would be raised by an attempt to implement it. The effort required for a specification, however, is considerably less than that required for an implementation.

We will now discuss some of the questions that were raised during the specification work on CICS modules. It is interesting to note that most of the questions raised required the expert on the module to refer to the source code to give a conclusive answer. We will begin with the questions about exceptional conditions, then a question about interval control, and finally a question about the interaction between temporary storage and exceptional conditions.

Exceptional Conditions

We will first list some questions that were raised during the specification of exceptional condition handling and then examine one of the more interesting questions in detail. All these questions were resolved in producing the specification given in the previous section.

1) What is the range of possible default actions?

2) Is the default action for a particular condition the same for all commands that can raise that condition?

3) Can the special condition *error* be ignored?

4) Is the action for condition *error* only used if the default system action on a condition is *abort*?

5) If executed from the initial state does the sequence

Handle Condition$(c = x,\ a = y)$

. . .

Handle Condition$(c = x,\ a = system)$

return the handler to the initial state?

The reader is invited to try to answer these questions from the manual entry given in Appendix B and then from the specification given in the previous section. We will now look in detail at question 5) above. It shows a subtle operation of the exceptional conditions mechanism that is counter-intuitive.

In an earlier model of the Handle Condition command the following incorrect line was used in the specification.

$$(a = system) \rightarrow \text{Handler}' = \text{Handler} \setminus \{c\}$$

That is, if the action is *system* then the entry for the condition c is removed from the handler ($c \notin$ **dom** Handler$'$). The final model contains the line

$$(a = system) \rightarrow \text{Handler}' = \text{Handler} \oplus \{c \mapsto \text{Default}(c)\}$$

In this version, if the action is *system* the entry in the handler for condition c is set up to be Default(c) (therefore $c \in$ **dom** Handler$'$).

To see the effect of the difference we need to look at the Exception Check mechanism given in the previous section. If we use the second line above then the action when that exception c occurs will be Default(c) (assuming handle is true). In the earlier model, however, the action also depends on whether a handler has been set up for the special condition *error*: the action will be Default(c) unless Default(c) is *abort* and *error* $\in$ **dom** Handler, in which case the action will be Handler$(error)$. The difference between the two versions is subtle and the reader is encouraged to study the definitions of Handle Condition and Exception Check in order to understand the difference.

The exception check mechanism is quite complex. None of the people experienced with CICS who were questioned about exceptional condition handling were aware of the problem detailed above. It is interesting to conjecture why this is so. The most plausible explanation is that the operation of the exception check mechanism is counter-intuitive. For example, the sequence given in question 5)

Handle Condition$(c = x,\ a = y)$

. . .

Handle Condition$(c = x,\ a = system)$

does not leave the exceptional condition handler in its initial state if the default action for condition x is *abort* and a handler has been set up for the special condition *error*; before the above sequence the *error* handler will be used on an occurrence of condition x, but after, the action Default(x) (i.e., *abort*) will be used on an occurrence of x.

If the above sequence did restore the exception condition handler to its initial state, then it could be used to temporarily handle condition x for the duration of the statements between the Handle Condition commands. This form of operation is more what people using the exceptional conditions module expect—hence it is more intuitive.

The Exception Check mechanism is so complex that most readers of either the manual or the specification given in the previous section do not pick up the above subtle operation unless it is explicitly pointed out in some form of warning. This is probably a good argument in favor of revising exception handling to be more intuitive.

The discussion about question 5) above also raises the point that a specification can be incorrect. This case shows one advantage of getting a second opinion on the specification and how it compares to the manual, from a person experienced in formal specification. It is significant that the reviewer reads the specification before reading the manual. The reviewer's mental model of the system is thus based on the mathematical model in the specification. When the reviewer reads the manual looking for inconsistencies with the specification, any questions that arise can be answered by consulting the precise model given in the specification. This contrasts with the person writing the specification who forms a model from the manual and often has to consult other sources to answer questions that arise. Getting a second opinion on the specification and how it compares to the manual is an important ingredient for increasing confidence in the accuracy and readability of the specification.

Interval Control

As another example we will consider one of the problems raised during the specification of the CICS interval control module. Interval control is responsible for operations that deal with the interval timer. The operations provided by interval control can be split logically into two groups: those to do with starting new transactions at specified times, and those to do with timeouts and delays.

In specifying a module of the system we define the state components of the module (in the case of exceptional conditions there was only one state component, Handler). The state components of interval control can be split into two groups that are concerned, respectively, with the two groups of interval control operations. For the most part, operations only refer to or change components of the corresponding state. One exception is the command Start (to start a new transaction) which in some circumstances changes the timeout state components. This can be considered to be a carefully documented anomaly of the current implementation. Both the implementation and documentation could be simplified if the Start command did not destroy the current timeout. More importantly, removal of this interaction would lead to a more useful timeout mechanism, as timeouts would not be affected by a transaction start.

This anomaly is interesting as it points out an unwanted interaction between different parts of a module. In attempting to write the specification this interaction stood out because it involved the Start operation using the timeout state. This form of interaction between parts of modules tends to be pinpointed in the formal specification processes as the offending operations require access to state information other than that of the part to which they belong.

Two further facts reinforce the view that the current operation of the Start command is not the most desirable: if the new transaction is to be started on a different computer system to the one issuing the Start command, or if the start is protected (from the point of view of recovery on system failure) then the start does not destroy the current timeout. Ideally we do not want to have to specify distributed system and recovery effects individually with each operation. We would like to add extra levels of abstraction to describe these effects for the whole system.

Interaction Between Modules

As an example of an interaction between two CICS modules we will consider an interaction between exceptional conditions and temporary storage. When temporary storage runs out of space it can raise the exceptional condition *nospace*. This will be processed in the normal way if it has been explicitly handled; the default action, however, is to wait until space becomes available.

Thus the specification of the temporary storage operations that can lead to a *nospace* exception require access to the exceptional conditions state to determine whether or not the *nospace* exception is handled; if it is handled it can occur, but if it is not, it cannot. These operations would more simply be specified (and implemented) if they had an extra parameter indicating whether or not to wait. It is interesting to note that in the implementation such temporary storage commands are transformed into a call with an additional parameter after the exception handling state has been consulted. It is also interesting that these commands were not correctly implemented if the *nospace* exception were ignored.

Interactions between modules of the system are pinpointed during the formal specification process (just as they would be in an implementation) as an operation from one module will need access to the state components of another. Any such interactions discovered during the specification process should be examined closely as they indicate a breakdown in the modular structure of the system.

Problems with Specification

This section will examine the problems encountered in applying the formal specification techniques themselves, in contrast to the previous section, which examined problems with the system being specified. The problems encountered in applying specification techniques can be split into communication problems between the people involved, the general problem of achieving the "right" level of abstraction in the specification, and more technical problems related to the particular specification technique.

Communication Problems

As specifiers from a university working with a commercial development laboratory, we faced a communications problem. Both parties have their own language: the specifiers use the language of mathematics based on set theory, while the developers use terminology and concepts specific to the system which they are developing. The communication problem is in both directions. This requires education of each party in the language of the other.

In performing a formal specification the specifier needs to understand what is being specified in order to be able to develop a mathematical model of it. To understand the system he needs to read manuals and consult experts, both of which use IBM and CICS terminology. Once a specification is written the specifier would like to get feedback on its suitability from these same experts. This requires that they need to be educated in mathematics to a level at which they can understand a specification. At the current stage of the project the education has been more in the direction of the specifiers learning about the system. In performing a specification of part of a system, the specifier of necessity becomes an expert on the functional behavior of that part (but not on the implementation of the part).

The "Right" Level of Abstraction

In this context "right" means that a piece of specification conveys the primary function of the part of the system it specifies and is not unduly cluttered with details. Most importantly a specification should not be biased towards a particular implementation. However, getting the right specification also involves choosing the most appropriate model and structuring the specification so that the minute details of the component do not hide the primary function.

We can use hierarchical structuring to achieve this. Details of some facet of a component can be specified separately and then that specification can be referenced by the higher level specification. Different cases of an operation (e.g., the normal case and the erroneous case) can be specified independently and combined to give a specification of the whole.

The structure of a good specification may not correspond to the structure one may use to provide an efficient implementation. In specification one is trying to provide a clear logical separation of concerns, while in implementation one may take advantage of the relationships between logically separate parts to provide an efficient implementation of the combined entity. The intellectual ability required of a good specifier is roughly equivalent to that of a good programmer; however, the view taken of the system must be different.

Technical Problems

The technical specification problems discovered in applying formal specification techniques to CICS in particular were

1) putting together the module specifications to provide a specification of the system as a whole,
2) specifying parallelism,
3) specifying recovery on system failures, and
4) specifying distributed systems.

We shall briefly discuss these in turn.

Putting Modules Together: Currently, 3 out of the 16 modules that form the application programmer's interface have been specified and we now feel we have enough insight into the system to consider the problem of putting the specifications of modules together. Each module has state components and a set of operations that work on those state components. Putting the modules together is essentially combining the states together to form the state of the system and extending the operations of the modules to operations on the whole system.

The problems encountered in putting modules together were

1) avoiding name clashes when the modules are combined,
2) specifying the effect on the whole system state of an operation defined within a module of the system, and
3) coping with situations in which an operation of one module refers to state components of another module.

Parallelism: In our current specifications the operations are assumed to be atomic operations acting on the state of the system. We have a sufficient underlying theory to allow one to reason formally about a single sequential transaction. An area for future research is to extend the theory to allow reasoning about the interactions between parallel processes. The current specifications will still be used, but they will need to be augmented with additional specifications which constrain the way in which the parallel processes interact.

Recovery: An important part of a transaction processing system is the mechanism for recovery on failure of the system. The current specifications do not address the problem of recovery. Again, we would like to augment the current specifications so that recovery can be incorporated without requiring the existing part of the specification to be rewritten.

Distributed Systems: A number of CICS systems may cooperate to provide services to users. The main facility provided within CICS to achieve this is the ability to execute certain operations or whole transactions on a remote system. While the individual operation specifications could be augmented to reflect remote system execution, it was thought better to wait until we had a specification of the system and extend that to a distributed system. To reason effectively about a distributed system we need to be able to reason about parallelism.

Conclusions

Formal specification techniques have been successfully applied to modules of an existing system and as an immediate benefit have uncovered a number of problems in the current documentation as well as flaws in the current interface design. In the longer term the formal specifications should provide a good starting point for specifying proposed changes to the system, a more precise description for educating new personnel, and a basis for improved documentation.

In part the reason we have been successful in applying our specification techniques was that the modular structure of CICS is quite good, and we have been able to take advantage of this by concentrating on individual modules in relative isolation.

The questions raised during the specification process are the main benefit in the short term of applying formal specification techniques to existing software. They highlight aspects of the system that are incompletely or ambiguously described in the manual, as well as focusing attention on problems with its structure, for example, undesirable interactions between modules.

In the longer term a formal specification provides a precise description which can be used to communicate between people involved with the system. The specification is less prone to misunderstanding than less formal means of communication, such as natural language or diagrams. It can be used as a basis for a new specification incorporating modifications to the original design, and it provides an excellent starting point for people responsible for improving the documentation. (In another group at Oxford work on incorporating formal specifications into user manuals is being done by Gimson and Morgan [5].)

The time required to specify a module of the system varied from about 4 weeks for Exceptional Conditions to 12 weeks for Interval Control. The time required was related to the size of the module (the number of operations, etc.) and also to the number and severity of problems raised about the behavior of the module. The size of a module specification (in pages) turned out to be roughly comparable to the size of the manual entry for the module. The specification sizes ranged from 4 pages (handwritten) for Exceptional Conditions to 16 pages for Interval Control.

The difficulties encountered with the specification process itself were the language gap between university and industry, and the problem of achieving the "right" level of abstraction. There were also a number of more technical specification problems that arose in applying the techniques: the problem of putting together module specifications to provide a specification of the system as a whole, specifying parallelism, specifying recovery on system failure, and specifying distributed systems. These problems are areas for further research.

APPENDIX A

NOTATION

Schemas

A schema has the general form

```
Name ________________________________
| Declarations
|--------------
| Predicates
|--------------
```

where the variable declarations are of the form

identifier: type

and the predicates give the properties of, and relationships between, the variables.

A schema may be used to describe either a state or an operation. To describe a state the declared variables form the components of the state and the predicates give the invariant properties of the state. For an operation the declarations consist of the initial state components, the final state components, and the inputs and outputs of the operation. As a convention the final state component names are dashed versions of the initial state component names. For an operation the predicate part describes the relation between the inputs, outputs, and initial and final states.

A schema S may be included within another schema T. This has the effect of including all the variables declared in S in the declarations of T and of including all the predicates of S in the predicates of T. A schema name may be decorated (e.g., dashed). This has the effect of decorating in a similar way (e.g., dashing) all the declared variables both in their declaration and their uses within the predicates. For example, the schema ΔExceptions given in the sample specification in the body of the paper is equivalent to

```
ΔExceptions ___________________________
| Handler: CONDITION ⇸ ACTION
| Handler′: CONDITION ⇸ ACTION
|--------------------------------------
| Handler(success) = nil
| Handler′(success) = nil
|______________________________________
```

Logic

Within the predicate part we may use the operators

$\wedge$	and
$\vee$	or
$\neg$	negation
$\Rightarrow$	implication
$=$	equality
$\neq$	inequality
$c \rightarrow x, y$	conditional expression.

For the conditional expression if c is true, the value of the conditional expression is x; otherwise it is y.

Sets

We may construct a set by listing its elements within braces:

$$\{x, y, z\}$$

or by giving some property that only elements of the set have

$$\{x \mid P(x)\}.$$

We may test the following:

- $\in$ membership, e.g., $1 \in \{1, 2, 3\}$
- $\notin$ nonmembership, e.g., $2 \notin \{1, 3, 5\}$
- $\subseteq$ subset, e.g., $\{2, 3\} \subseteq \{2, 3, 4\}$

and perform the following operations on sets:

- $\cup$ set union: $A \cup B = \{x \mid x \in A \vee x \in B\}$
- $\cap$ set intersection: $A \cap B = \{x \mid x \in A \wedge x \in B\}$
- $-$ set difference: $A - B = \{x \mid x \in A \wedge x \notin B\}$.

Functions

We may declare a function f from a set A to a set B by

$$f\colon A \rightarrow B.$$

For each element $x \in A$, $f(x)$ is the value of the function f at $x\,(f(x) \in B)$.

If a function f is not defined for all elements of A (i.e., f is a partial function) then we write

$$f\colon A \nrightarrow B.$$

The domain of definition of f

dom f

is that subset of A (**dom** $f \subseteq A$) for which the function f is defined. The range of f

range f

is that subset of B (**range** $f \subseteq B$) containing exactly those values $b \in B$ such that there exists an $x \in$ **dom** f such that $f(x) = b$. That is

$$\textbf{range } f = \{b \in B \mid \exists x \in A \cdot f(x) = b\}$$

The notation

$$\{x_1 \mapsto y_1, x_2 \mapsto y_2, \cdots, x_n \mapsto y_n\}$$

where each x_i is distinct, defines a function whose domain of definition is the set of x_i's:

$$\textbf{dom } \{x_1 \mapsto y_1, x_2 \mapsto y_2, \cdots, x_n \mapsto y_n\} = \{x_1, x_2, \cdots, x_n\}$$

and the value of the function at x_i is y_i:

$$\{x_1 \mapsto y_1, x_2 \mapsto y_2, \cdots, x_n \mapsto y_n\}(x_i) = y_i.$$

The notation

$$f \oplus g$$

stands for function f overridden by function g (we assume functions f and g are of the same type). The function $f \oplus g$ is defined at a point if either f or g is defined at that point:

$$\textbf{dom } (f \oplus g) = \textbf{dom } f \cup \textbf{dom } g.$$

If g is defined at x then the value of $f \oplus g$ is $g(x)$; otherwise, if f is defined at x the value of $f \oplus g$ is $f(x)$:

$$(f \oplus g)(x) = (x \in \textbf{dom } g \rightarrow g(x), \; f(x))$$

The notation

$$f \backslash s$$

stands for the function f with all elements of its domain that are in the set s removed:

$$\textbf{dom } (f \backslash s) = (\textbf{dom } f) - s$$
$$x \in \textbf{dom } (f \backslash s) \Rightarrow (f \backslash s)(x) = f(x).$$

Appendix B

Exceptional Conditions—Manual Entry

Exceptional conditions may occur during the execution of a CICS/VS command and, unless specified otherwise in the application program by an Ignore Condition or Handle Condition command or by the Nohandle option, a default action for each condition will be taken by CICS/VS. Usually, this default action is to terminate the task abnormally.

However, to prevent abnormal termination, an exceptional condition can be dealt with in the application program by a Handle Condition command. The command must include the name of the condition and, optionally, a label to which control is to be passed if the condition occurs. The Handle Condition command must be executed before the command which may give rise to the associated condition.

The Handle Condition command for a given condition applies only to the program in which it is specified, remaining active until the associated task is terminated, or until another Handle Condition command for the same condition is encountered, in which case the new command overrides the previous one.

When control returns to a program from a program at a lower logical level, the Handle Condition commands that were active in the higher level program before control was transferred from it are reactivated, and those in the lower-level program are deactivated.

Some exceptional conditions can occur during the execution of any one of a number of unrelated commands. For example, IOERR can occur during file-control operations, interval-control operations, and others. If the same action is required for all occurrences, a single Handle Condition IOERR command at the beginning of the program will suffice.

If different actions are required, Handle Condition commands specifying different labels at appropriate points in the program will suffice. The same label can be specified for all commands, and fields EIBFN and EIBRCODE (in the EIB) can be tested to find out which exceptional condition has occurred and in which command.

The Ignore Condition command specifies that no action is to be taken if an exceptional condition occurs. Execution of a command could result in several conditions being raised. CICS/VS checks these in a predetermined order and only the first one that is not ignored (by an Ignore Condition command) will be passed to the application program.

The Nohandle option may be used with any command to specify that no action is to be taken for any condition resulting from the execution of that command. In this way the scope of the Ignore Condition command covers specified conditions for all commands (until a Handle Condition for the condition is executed) and the scope of the Nohandle option covers all conditions for specified commands.

The Error Exceptional Condition

Apart from the exceptional conditions associated with individual commands, there is a general exceptional condition named *error* whose default action also is to terminate the task abnormally. If no Handle Condition command is active for a condition, but one is active for *error*, control will be passed to the label specified for *error*. A Handle Condition command (with or without a label) for a condition overrides the Handle Condition *error* command for that condition.

Commands should not be included in an error routine that may give rise to the same condition that caused the branch to the routine; special care should be taken not to cause a loop on the *error* condition. A loop can be avoided by including a Handle Condition *error* command as the first command in the error routine. The original error action should be reinstated at the end of the error routine by including a second Handle Condition *error* command.

Handle Exceptional Conditions (Handle Condition)

Handle Condition condition [(label)]
[condition [(label)]] . . .

This command is used to specify the label to which control is to be passed if an exceptional condition occurs. It remains in effect until a subsequent Ignore Condition command for the condition is encountered. No more than 12 conditions are allowed in the same command; additional conditions must be specified in further Handle Condition commands. The *error* condition can also be used to specify that other conditions are to cause control to be passed to the same label. If "label" is omitted, the default action for the condition will be taken.

The following example shows the handling of exceptional conditions, such as DUPREC, LENGERR, and so on, that can occur when a *write* command is used to add a record to a data set. DUPREC is to be handled as a special case; system default action (that is, to terminate the task abnormally) is to be taken for LENGERR; and all other conditions are to be handled by the generalized error routine ERRHANDL.

```
EXEC CICS Handle Condition
          ERROR(ERRHANDL)
          DUPREC(DUPRIN)
          LENGERR
```

If the generalized error routine can handle all exceptional conditions except IOERR, for which the default action (that is, to terminate the task abnormally) is required, IOERR (without a label) would be added to the above command.

In an assembler-language application program, a branch to a label caused by an exceptional condition will restore the registers in the application program to their values at the point where the EXEC interface program is invoked.

In a PL/I application program, a branch to a label in an inactive procedure or in an inactive begin block, caused by an exceptional condition, will produce unpredictable results.

Handle Condition Command Option

Condition[(label)]: "Condition" specifies the name of the exceptional condition and "label" specifies the location within the program to be branched to if the condition occurs. If this option is not specified, the default action for the condition is taken, unless the default action is to terminate the task abnormally, in which case the *error* condition occurs. If the option is specified without a label, any Handle Condition command for the condition is deactivated, and the default action taken if the condition occurs.

Ignore Exceptional Conditions (Ignore Condition)

```
Ignore Condition condition
                 [condition] ...
```

This command is used to specify that no action is to be taken if an exceptional condition occurs. It remains in effect until a subsequent Handle Condition command for the condition is encountered. No more than 12 conditions are allowed in the same command; additional conditions must be specified in further Ignore Condition commands. The option "condition" specifies the name of the exceptional condition that is to be ignored.

ACKNOWLEDGMENT

I would like to thank IBM for their permission to publish this paper and reproduce part of one of their manuals as Appendix B. Several members of the IBM Development Laboratory at Winchester, England, assisted the author to understand some parts of CICS; of special note are P. Alderson, P. Collins, and P. Lupton.

This work has benefited from consultations with C. A. R. Hoare, C. B. Jones, and R. Burstall. T. Clement was responsible for the initial specification of temporary storage. P. Fertig, R. Gimsom, J. Nicholls, and B. Sufrin gave useful comments on this paper. Finally, I would like to express my gratitude to C. Morgan and I. Holm Sorensen for their help as reviewers of the specifications, and for their instruction in specification techniques.

REFERENCES

[1] J.-R. Abrial, "The specification language Z: Basic library," Programming Research Group, Oxford Univ., Oxford, England, Internal Rep., 1982.

[2] *CICS/OS/VS Application Programmer's Reference Manual (Command Level)*, IBM Corp., 1980.

[3] *CICS/VS General Information*, IBM Corp., 1980.

[4] *OS PL/I Checkout and Optimising Compilers: Language Reference Manual*, IBM Corp., 1976.

[5] C. C. Morgan, "Using mathematics in user manuals," Programming Research Group, Oxford Univ., Oxford, England, Distributed Computing Project Tech. Rep., 1983.

[6] C. C. Morgan and B. A. Sufrin, "Specification of the Unix filing system," *IEEE Trans. Software Eng.*, vol. SE-10, pp. 128–142, Mar. 1984.

[7] I. H. Sorensen, "A specification language," in *Program Specification* (Lecture Notes in Computer Science, Vol. 134). New York: Springer-Verlag, 1982, pp. 381–401.

[8] J. Staunstrup, *Program Specification: Proceedings of a Workshop, Aarhus, Denmark, August 1981* (Lecture Notes in Computer Science, Vol. 134). New York: Springer-Verlag, 1982.

Ian J. Hayes received the B.Sc. degree in 1972 and the Ph.D. degree in 1983, both in computer science, from the University of New South Wales, Australia.

From 1976 to 1982 he was a Lecturer in Computer Science at the University of New South Wales. Since 1983 he has been a member of the Formalisation of Transaction Processing Project at the Programming Research Group, Oxford University.

Glossary

Richard H. Thayer
Mildred C. Thayer

Scope

This glossary defines the terms used in the field of system and software requirements engineering and supporting disciplines. These definitions have their roots in several management and technical domains: general (mainstream) management, project management, and system and hardware engineering. In addition, there are new definitions and old terms with new meanings. The relationships between these domains and software engineering and software engineering project management can be seen in Figure 1.

The definitions from any domain in Figure 1 usually can be applied to any domain located lower on the hierarchy. For example, a system engineering definition can apply to both system engineering and software engineering, and a project management definition can also apply to software engineering project management. But because of new technologies and meanings a software engineering definition will not necessarily apply to general engineering.

Definitions for hardware and software engineering and system and software system engineering are so similar that

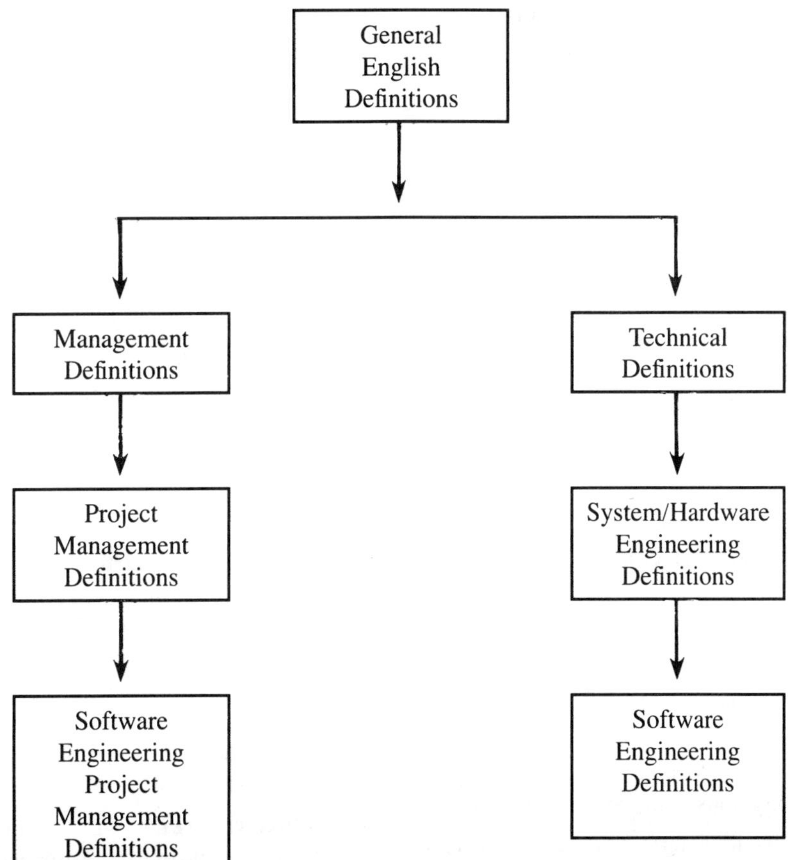

Figure 1. Hierarchical Domains of Software Engineering and Software Engineering Project Management Definitions

the terms *hardware/software* and *system/software* are frequently used to mean applicability in both domains.

The domain of the definition should be understood or identified in the first sentence of the definition. When the definition was taken from another source and the domain of definition was not obvious, the domain was added.

Glossary Structure

Entries in the glossary are arranged alphabetically. An entry may consist of a single word, such as *requirements*; a phrase, such as *requirements engineering*; or an acronym such as *SQA*. Phrases are given in their natural order *(requirements engineering)* rather than reversed *(engineering, requirements)*.

Blanks are taken into account in alphabetizing. They precede all other characters. For example, *ad hoc* precedes *Ada*. Hyphens and slashes follow blanks. Alternative spellings are shown as separate glossary entries with cross-references to the preferred spelling.

No distinction is made between acronyms and abbreviations. Where appropriate, a term that has a common acronym or abbreviation contains the acronym or abbreviation in parenthesis following the term. The abbreviation or acronym might also be a separate entry. The definition is placed with the term or abbreviation, depending on which one has the most usage; and the other will be cross-referenced. For example, *SREM*, an acronym for *Software Requirements Engineering Methodology,* has its definition after *SREM*. In contrast, *SQA*, an acronym for *software quality assurance*, will have its definition after *software quality assurance (SQA)*.

If a term has more than one definition, the definitions are listed with numerical prefixes. This ordering does not imply preference. Where necessary, examples and notes have been added to clarify the definitions.

The following cross-references are used to show a term's relationship to other terms in the glossary:

- *See* refers to a preferred term or to a term whose definition serves to define the term that has been looked up.
- *See also* refers to a related term.
- *Sometime synonymous with* refers to a term that may or may not be synonymous with the defined term, i.e., it is a non-standard usage.
- *Synonymous with* refers to a term that is always or nearly always synonymous with the defined term.
- *Contrast with* refers to a term with an opposite or substantially different meaning.

In a few cases, nonstandard cross-references are used to clarify a particular definition.

Source

In those cases in which a definition is taken or paraphrased from another source or paper, the source is designated in brackets following the definition, for example [Smith 1988]. The use of a source reference does not imply an exact quote, but is an acknowledgement of the source of the definition. A list of all sources used in this glossary are at the end of the glossary.

Acknowledgment

The authors would like to acknowledge the hard work done by Jane Radatz, Chair of the IEEE Computer Dictionary Standards Working Group, who gave us permission to use some of their terms even though the dictionary standard is not finished.

1–2–3–4–5–6–7–8–9–0

4GL — Acronym for fourth-generation language.

a-a-a

A-level specification — A system-level requirements specification generally used to describe very large systems and/or very large subelements, called system segments. [U.S. Department of Defense (DoD) usage] [Military Standard 490A-1985] *Synonymous with system requirements specification. See also B-level specification, B5-level specification, C-level specification.*

abstract execution — A formal computer language-testing feature for specification modules that are partially complete. Machine execution of software specifications is possible with both partial and complete specifications. [Urban et al. 1985] *See also formal language.*

abstract program specification — Formal language specifications, which include: (1) proving the formal correctness of programs, (2) defining and specifying data types, (3) describing the system in levels of abstraction, (4) developing programming languages that facilitate the writing of provable correct programs, and (5) defining the formal semantics of programming languages. [Abbott and Moorhead 1981]

acceptance criteria — In software requirements analysis, the criteria a prospective user will use to determine that the proposed system will meet the software requirements.

acceptance metric — In system/software system engineering, a software metric that can be used as a standard for acceptance of a software product that is produced by a developer for a customer in the context of a contractual agreement. [Keller et al. 1990]

acceptance testing — In a system/software engineering project, formal testing is conducted to determine whether a hardware/software system satisfies its acceptance criteria and enables the customer to determine whether to accept the system. *See also qualification testing, system testing.*

accuracy — In software engineering, a software quality metric that provides: 1. Those characteristics that provide the required precision in calculations and outputs. [RADC TR-85-37 1985] 2. A quantitative assessment of freedom from error. *Contrast with precision.*

accuracy constraint — In hardware/software engineering, the allowable deviation between actual and ideal values. [Heninger 1980]

acquisition — In system development, a method of acquiring systems through the five acquisition phases of concept exploration (CE), demonstration and validation (DEM/VAL), full-scale development (FSD), production, and deployment. This method is primarily used by the U.S. Department of Defense (DoD) for acquiring large systems. *See also concept exploration (CE) phase, demonstration and validation (DEM/VAL) phase, deployment phase, full-scale development (FSD) phase, production phase. See also system development lifecycle.*

acquisition lifecycle — *See system acquisition lifecycle.*

acquisition management — The management and control of the system/software acquisition process through the use of the system acquisition lifecycle.

active guidance — A software requirement analysis tool attribute that provides online support and advice to the users. This tool can determine what errors are contained in the specifications and then can suggest possible solutions to those errors. This tool sometimes is referred to as an "intelligent assistant" [British usage]. [Kramer et al. 1988]

activity chart — A system/software system engineering requirements tool used to display the timing definitions for individual system activities. This is the tool used to define the more detailed timing relationships of the lower level operational tasks performed. The activity chart completes the answer to the "when" questions of system definition. [Lano 1990]

ad hoc development method — A software development methodology that is, in essence, no methodology. However, it is very popular.

Ada — A programming language developed for U.S. Department of Defense (DoD) by a Honeywell-Bull team operating under the direction of Jean D. Ichbiah. The language incorporates software engineering principles such as reliability, portability, and maintainability. Ada is expected to become the dominant language in the 1990s.

Ada-oriented methodology — A software development methodology that is built around the Ada language.

adaptability — 1. In software requirements analysis, a rate at which the software solution can adapt to a new requirement. [Davis et al. 1988] 2. In software engineering, a software quality metric that can be used to assess the ease with which software allows differing system constraints and user needs to be satisfied. [ANSI/IEEE Standard 729–1983]

adaptive maintenance — In software maintenance, consists of any effort that is initiated as a result of changes in the environment in which a software system must operate. [NBS Special Publication 500–106 1983]

adherence metric — In software engineering, a software quality metric that can be used to assess adherence to a well-defined and documented standard, guideline, or principle. The use of adherence metrics provides a technique for measuring deviations, which can be used in a management feedback system to recover to an acceptable level. [Keller et al. 1990]

ADP system — *See computer system.*

AFR — Acronym for Air Force Regulation.

AI — Acronym for artificial intelligence.

algebraic specification — In software engineering (requirements), a formal specification technique that uses algebraic equations and arguments. Algebraic specifications are aimed toward descriptions of abstract data types and stating the operations permitted on them. The algebraic specifications provide a set of axioms that define the behavior of the operation. [STARTS Guide 1987]

algorithm — A finite set of well-defined rules that provides for the solution to a problem in a finite number of steps.

alias — In software engineering (structured analysis methodology), a synonym for the data dictionary name of any dataflow, data element, or file.

allocated requirement — In system/software system engineering, requirements that have been partitioned and allocated (assigned) to a particular hardware/software subsystem for implementation. The allocated requirements form the allocated baseline.

allocation — In system/software system engineering, the assignment or budgeting of top-level functional or nonfunctional requirements among the lower level partitioned functions for accomplishment. In this manner, the elements of a system that perform all or part of specific requirements are identified.

allocation chart — A system/software system engineering requirements tool used to display the correlation and allocation of functions, interfaces, sequences, activities, and organization elements. This tool is used for both external and internal traceability purposes. [Lano 1990]

alpha — A part of the Software Requirements Engineering Methodology (SREM), describes the transformations of each requirements net (R-net) process and identifies input and output data. [Scheffer and Stone 1985] [Alford 1985] [TRW SS-80–03 1980] *See also R-net, SREM.*

ambiguity — A problem in developing software requirements specifications in which requirements statements can be interpreted in several different ways. The receiver has to clarify these statements based on the surrounding context. [Rich et al. 1987]

analog model — A type of model that has similar relations to the object being modeled. For example the electrical representation of a fluid system. *See also model.*

analysis — 1. In system/software engineering, the process of studying a system by partitioning the system into parts (functions or objects) and determining how the parts relate to each other to understand the whole. *Synonymous with software analysis, software requirements analysis, system analysis, system requirements analysis.* 2. In system/software system engineering (validation), analysis is used only for those items for which no reasonable test or demonstration can be defined. A system/software product can be shown to be verified with some analysis based on a combination of data from various levels of tests, along with numerical calculations. *Contrast with demonstration, examination, testing.*

analysis phase — *See software requirements phase.*

animation — A software requirement analysis tool that refers to the process of being able to walkthrough a specific portion of the specification by using certain inputs to determine the behavior of the specifications under different circumstances [British usage]. [Kramer et al. 1988] *See also prototyping.*

annotated requirement — In system/software system engineering, annotation added to the requirements to clarify which requirements are essential and which would be nice to have; which are stable and which might be considered volatile; or which requirements are mandatory, desirable, or optional.

anomaly management — In software engineering, a software quality metric concerned with the continuity of operations of the software under recovery from nonnominal conditions. [RADC TR-85–37 1985]

ANSI — Acronym for American National Standards Institute.

APL — A programming language.

application generator — In software engineering, a mechanism for creating running code in a relatively narrow application from a high-level specification. An application generator usually contains a single canonical design for a small, well-defined domain. Fourth-generation language (4GL) systems are large-application generators in such domains as management information systems.

application software — Software specifically produced for the functional use of a particular application on a computer system; for example, software for a payroll system, gun fire control system, or general accounting ledger. *Sometimes called functional software. Contrast with nonfunctional software, system software.*

apportionment — In system/software system engineering, the allocation of requirements to functional elements also includes the apportionment of overall system requirements to those functional elements. An example of overall system capabilities that would be apportioned is system timing requirements. [Nelsen 1990] *See also allocation.*

appropriateness — In software system engineering (requirements), the ability of a specification to capture, in a manner that is straightforward and free of implementations and considerations, those concepts that are germane to the system's role in the environment for which it is intended. [Roman 1985]

architectural design — In system/software system engineering: 1. The process of defining a collection of hardware and software components and their interfaces to establish a framework for the development of a system/software system. 2. The result of the architectural design process. [ANSI/IEEE Standard 729–1983] *Synonymous with high-level design, internal specification, preliminary design, system design, top-level design.*

architecture — In system/software system engineering, the relationships between the parts of a system. *See also system architecture.*

artificial intelligence (AI) — That part of computer science concerned with designing intelligent computer systems, in other words, systems that exhibit the characteristics associated with intelligence in human behavior: learning, reasoning, understanding, language, solving problems, and so forth. [Burris 1986]

artificial language — *See formal language. See also language.*

ARTS (Automated Requirements Traceability System) — A software requirements tool that enables automated tracking of requirements as they are partitioned and allocated to lower level requirements. ARTS is a software database management system for requirements information management. [Flynn and Dorfman 1990]

assembly language — In software development, a representation of computer instructions and data that usually has a one-to-one correspondence with machine language. Assembly language is more representative of the application procedure than machine language. *Contrast with higher order language, machine language.*

assessment — *See software engineering assessment.*

asynchronous realtime control — In realtime computer-based systems, a method of control where there is no fixed time for each specific event. The completion of one event signals the next event. *Contrast with synchronous realtime control.*

attribute — 1. In system/software engineering (requirements), a property or description, in the requirements database, selected by the user to be stored with the requirement text to provide information about the requirement. [Flynn and Dorfman 1990] 2. In software requirements analysis, qualities of a good software requirements specification. A good software requirements specification is complete, consistent, correct, measurable, modifiable, process free, traceable, and unambiguous. *See also complete, consistent, correct, measurable, modifiable, process free, traceable, unambiguous.* 3. In software engineering (object-oriented methodology), a modifier of an object, a short, informal description of an object. *See also object-oriented method.*

audit — 1. A management review of a hardware/software project for the purpose of assessing compliance with requirements, specifications, baselines, standards, procedures, instructions, codes, and contractual and licensing requirements. 2. In system/software system engineering, an activity to determine through investigation the adequacy of, and adherence to, established procedures, instructions, specifications, codes, and standards or other applicable contractual and licensing requirements, as well as the effectiveness of implementation. [ANSI N45.2.10–1973] *See also code audit, independent audit. See also functional configuration audit, physical configuration audit.*

augmentability — In software engineering, a software quality metric that can be used to measure the ability of the software to expand in both the functions and data. [RADC TR-85–37 1985]

author — In the Structured Analysis and Design Technique (SADT™) methodology (personnel roles), a person who studies requirements and constraints, analyzes system functions, and represents them by models based on SADT diagrams. [Ross and Schoman 1977] *See also SADT™, SADT™ personnel roles.*

automated cross-referencing — In software system engineering (verification and validation techniques), involves the use of a machine and logical specification language that can automatically analyze a specification for consistency, closure properties, or presentation of cross-referencing information for manual analysis. For example, *see SREM, RSL, PSL/PSA, program design language.* [Boehm, *V&V Software Requirements* 1984] *See also verification and validation technique.*

automated documentation support — In software engineering, the generation of software documentation through the use of automated software tools.

Automated Requirements Traceability System — *See ARTS.*

automated software synthesis — A software development strategy for the transformation of requirements or high-level design specification into operational code. This transformation process may be directed by algorithmic or knowledge-based techniques. [Davis et al. 1988]

automated support environment — *See software engineering environment.*

automated technique (detailed) — In software system engineering (verification and validation techniques), methods of verifying and validating a software system, which involves detailed automated models and prototypes that describe the system in detail. Detailed automated models involve large-event simulation, which can be effective in analyzing issues of accuracy, dynamic consistency, realtime performance, and lifecycle costs. The use of a prototype to demonstrate some key portion of the software will often surface numbers of ambiguities, inconsistencies, blind spots, and misunderstandings. [Boehm, *V&V Software Requirements* 1984] *See also verification and validation technique.*

automated technique (simple) — In software system engineering (verification and validation techniques), methods of verifying and validating a software system, which involves automating simple manual techniques such as cross-referencing and building simple automated models. [Boehm, *V&V Software Requirements* 1984] *See also verification and validation technique.*

automated tool — *See software tool.*

automated verification tool — A class of software tools used to evaluate products of the software development process. These tools aid in the verification of such characteristics as correctness, completeness, consistency, traceability, testability, and adherence to standards. [ANSI/IEEE Standard 729–1983] *See also software tool.*

automatic test tool — A software development tool that has the capability of generating test cases, locating potential errors, verifying results, and so forth. These tools include static analysis, dynamic analysis, symbolic execution, and intermediate interface analysis. [Ramamoorthy et al. 1984] *See also software tool.*

autonomy — In software engineering, a software quality metric that can be used to measure the nondependency of the software on interfaces and functions. [RADC TR-85-37 1985]

availability — 1. In software engineering, a software quality metric that can be used to measure the probability that software will be able to perform its designated system function when required for use. 2. The ratio of computer system uptime to total operating time. 3. The ability of a software system to perform its designated function when needed. 4. A software requirement for system operation that involves system reliability, ratio of system uptime to system operating time, and so forth.

axiom — An established rule.

axiomatic specification — In software engineering (requirements), an axiomatic approach to a specification of data types.

b-b-b

B-level specification — A subsystem-level requirements specification generally used to describe subelements of a system or system segments. These subelements are called "configuration items" (CIs). [U.S. Department of Defense (DoD) usage] [Military Standard 490A-1985] *See also A-level specification, B5-level specification, C-level specification, Part I specification.*

B5-level specification — A subsystem-level requirements specification generally used to describe software subelements of a system or system segments. These subelements are called "software configuration items" (SCI). [U.S. Department of Defense (DoD) usage] [Military Standard 490A-1985] *See also A-level specification, B-level specification, C-level specification, software requirements specification.*

Backus-Naur Form (BNF) — In computer science, a metalanguage used to define other languages. Developed by John Backus in 1960 to describe ALGOL (Algorithmic Language), it consists of metalinguistic variables, metalinguistic equivalence symbols, and metalinguistic connectives. [Sammet 1969]

balance — In software engineering (structured analysis methodology), the relationship that exists between "parent-and-child" diagrams in a properly leveled dataflow diagram set; specifically, the equivalence of input and output dataflows portrayed at a given bubble on the parent diagram and the associated child diagram. [DeMarco 1979] *See also Bubble Structured Analysis.*

baseline — 1. A hardware/software work product that has been formally reviewed and agreed upon, which then serves as the basis for further development, and that can be changed only through formal change control procedures. Each baseline must specify items that form the baseline (for example, software requirements, design documentation, and deliverable source code), the review and approval mechanisms, the acceptance criteria associated with the baseline, and the customer and project organization who participated in establishing the baseline. 2. A hardware/software configuration identification document or set of documents formally reviewed and agreed on at a specific time during the system's/software's lifecycle, which completely describes the functional and/or physical characteristics of a hardware/software configuration item. Baselines, plus approved changes to those baselines, constitute the current hardware/software configuration identification of a product.

Examples [U.S. Department of Defense (DoD) usage] of system/software baselines are:

Functional baseline—The initial configuration established at the end of the requirements definition phase.

Allocated baseline—The initial configuration established at the end of either the system design review (large projects) or the preliminary design review (medium or small projects).

Product baseline—The initial configuration established at the end of system testing.

See also configuration management (CM), baseline document, milestone review.

baseline document — System/software documents that establish one of the configuration identifications of a hardware/software configuration item. The system specifications, requirements specifications, and design specifications are examples of baseline identification documents. *See also configuration management (CM), document, engineering document.*

baseline management — A system/software project management concept that employs lifecycle phases, lifecycle phase documents, lifecycle phase reviews, and baselines to manage the project. *See also baseline, baseline document, lifecycle development model, milestone, milestone review, and waterfall model.*

baseline review — *See milestone review, review.*

behavior model — A type of model that is used to represent the response to an input. *See also decision model, descriptive model, normative model.*

black-box testing — A system/software test methodology that is derived from external specifications and requirements of the system. Methods for black-box testing include random testing, testing at boundary values, and a possible error list. It verifies the end results at the system level, but does not check on how the system is implemented. Nor does it assume that all statements in the program are executed. *Contrast with white-box testing. See also functional testing.*

block diagram — In engineering, a diagram of a system, computer, or a device in which the principal parts are represented by suitable annotated geometrical figures showing both the basic functions of the parts and their functional relationships.

blueprint — In the Structured Analysis and Design Technique (SADT™) software requirements methodology, the SADT diagrams are placed on a form that emulates an engineering blueprint. *See also SADT™.*

Boehm, Barry W. — The leading author in the field of software engineering in the U.S. and developer of the COCOMO cost-estimation model.

bottom-up — *See bottom-up synthesis. Contrast with top-down, top-down decomposition.*

bottom-up design — In system/software system engineering, the process of designing a system by identifying low-level components, designing each component separately, then designing structure to integrate the low-level components into larger and larger subsystems until the design is finished. *Contrast with top-down design.*

bottom-up development — In system/software system engineering, pertaining to a system/software system engineering development approach that starts with the lowest level system/software components of a hierarchy and proceeds through progressively higher levels to the top-level component. *See also bottom-up design, bottom-up testing. Contrast with top-down development.*

bottom-up synthesis — To formulate and build an entity or idea by identifying low-level entities, developing each one separately, then integrating the low-level entities into larger and larger subsystems until the total entity or idea is completed. *See also bottom-up design, bottom-up development, bottom-up testing.*

bottom-up testing — In software system engineering (testing), the process of checking out hierarchically organized programs, progressively, from bottom to top, by using software drivers to simulate top-level components. *Contrast with top-down testing.*

boundary condition — *See boundary value.*

boundary value — In software engineering (testing), test data that lies along "boundaries" or extremes of input domain (or output range) classes, data structures, procedure parameters, and so forth. Choices often include maximum and minimum in-range values and minimum out-of-range values.

boundary value analysis — In software engineering (testing), a technique in which test data are chosen to lie along "boundaries" or extremes of input domain (or output range) classes, data structures, procedure parameters, and so forth. Choices often include maximum, minimum, and trivial values or parameters. This technique is often called stress testing. [FIPS Publication 101 1983] *See also stress testing.*

branch testing — In software engineering (testing), a test method satisfying coverage criteria that require, for each decision point, that each possible branch be executed at least once. [FIPS Publication 101 1983]

bubble — In software engineering (structured analysis methodology), a representation of a process. Less formal than the term process or transform. A process drawn on a sheet of paper looks like a circle, thus the term bubble.

bug — In software development, a euphemism for error. The first "bug" originated at Harvard University in the late 1940s. During the hunt for an error on one of the first digital computers, a moth (or bug) was found in the logic circuitry. Since then, all software errors have been called "bugs." *See also debugging, error, fault, unit testing.*

build — In software system engineering, an operational version of a software product incorporating a specified subset of the capabilities that the final product will include. *Sometimes synonymous with version.*

building and fixing software development model — A software development paradigm in which a full system is built with minimum or no specifications and then reworked as necessary to satisfy its users. *See also code and fix process model.*

c-c-c

C-level specification — A subsystem-level design specification generally used by developers for internal design of the configuration item which they are producing. [U.S. Department of Defense (DoD) usage] [Military Standard 490A-1985] *See also A-level specification, B-level specification, C5-level specification, Part II specification.*

C5-level specification — A subsystem-level design specification generally used by software developers for internal design of the software configuration item they are producing. [U.S. Department of Defense (DoD) usage] [Military Standard 490A-1985] *See also A-level specification, B-level specification, C-level specification, software design specification.*

CAD — Acronym for computer-aided design.

CAD/CAM — Acronym for computer-aided design/computer-aided manufacturing.

calculus — A system of mathematical analysis.

CAM — Acronym for computer-aided manufacturing.

canonical design — In software engineering: 1. A design representing the commonalities across the design of many systems. 2. A family of designs. A design in which all design decisions have yet been defined or for which alternative choices have not yet been made. [Pyster 1990]

capacity — In software engineering (requirements), a software metric that can be used to measure the capacity of the system. Examples include the number of simultaneous users and the network requirements. Other capacity metrics are dynamic processing requirements for normal and peak loading, static storage capacity, and spare capacity. [STARTS Guide 1987]

CAPM — Acronym for computer-assisted project management.

CASE — Acronym for computer-aided software engineering.

case study — A documented illustration or example of the application of a technique or methodology to a real world problem.

CASE tool — An automated software engineering development tool that can assist software engineers in analyzing, designing, coding, testing, and documenting a software system and managing a software project. John Manley, University of Pittsburgh, is apparently the first person to use the acronym CASE for *computer-aided software engineering*. [Manley 1984]

CCB — Acronym for configuration control board.

CDR — Acronym for critical design review.

CDRL — Acronym for contract data requirements list.

CE — Acronym for concept exploration.

centre — British spelling of center.

change — In configuration management (CM), a formally recognized revision to a specified and documented program requirement. This may include a change in specification or engineering. *See also configuration control, configuration management (CM), engineering change, engineering change proposal.*

change control — In configuration management (CM), the process by which a change is proposed, evaluated, approved or rejected, scheduled, and tracked [ANSI/IEEE Standard 729-1983]. *See also configuration control, configuration management (CM).*

change status report — In configuration management (CM), details the status of all proposed changes to a hardware/software configuration item for which the developer is responsible and for which existing documentation is listed in the configuration index. The purpose of the report is to provide the customer and the developer with a summary of the current status of all proposed and approved engineering change proposals (ECPs). *See also configuration management (CM).*

changeability — In software engineering, a software quality metric that can be used to measure the ability of the software to accept change. [Boehm, *Spiral Model* 1988]

checking — In computer-aided software engineering (CASE) tools, the ability of the tool to include extensive mechanisms for checking the completeness and consistency of models built with the analysis and design methods. The goal is to aid in detecting errors at the earliest possible stage of the development process. [Wasserman and Pircher 1987]

checklist — In software system engineering (verification and validation techniques), involves specialized lists of necessary activities based on previous successful software development. A checklist can be used effectively with any of the manual verification and validation methods. Checklists are excellent for catching omissions such as missing items, functions, and products. These are valuable aids in addressing some of the lifecycle feasibility considerations, such as human engineering, maintainability, reliability, availability, affordability, security, privacy, and lifecycle efficiency. [Boehm, *V&V Software Requirements* 1984] *See also verification and validation technique.*

chief analyst — In the Structured Analysis and Design Technique (SADT™) methodology (personnel roles), a person fluent in SADT who assists and advises project personnel in the use and application of SADT. *Synonymous with monitor.* [Ross and Schoman 1977] *See also SADT™, SADT™ personnel roles.*

CI — Acronym for configuration item.

classic waterfall model — *See waterfall model.*

cliche — In the Requirements Apprentice, an artificial intelligence system, a prior knowledge of the common structure of a domain. A cliche is a set of rules embedded in an underlying substrata. Cliches directly improve productivity by allowing reuse of parts of the requirements from project to project. Cliches will vary from one use of the cliche to the next. [Rich et al. 1987] *See also reusability, substrata.*

closed-loop process — An engineering process in which the output of the system is fed back to the input. *See also feedback.*

CM — Acronym for configuration management. *See also SCM (software configuration management).*

CM/QA — Acronym for configuration management/quality assurance.

COCOMO software cost-estimation model — A software cost and schedule estimating method that was developed by Barry W. Boehm and documented in *Software Engineering Economics* [Boehm, 1981]. The model is an empirically derived, nonproprietary, cost-estimation model, based on a study by Boehm of 63 software development projects. The model accommodates three categories of software application, has a basic (simple), intermediate, and *detailed* version, and its primary input parameter is the estimated lines of uncommented source code. The intermediate and *detailed* versions of the model contain 15 cost multipliers that recognize differences in the project products and environment. Typically only the intermediate version is used.

code — In data processing: 1. To represent data or a computer program in a symbolic form that can be accepted by a computer. 2. To write a routine. 3. Loosely, one or more computer programs or part of a computer program. [ANSI/IEEE Standard 729–1983] 4. *Synonymous with software.*

code and component testing phase — The period of the system/software lifecycle extending from the completion of design until the system has been coded (implemented) and the components tested. *See also coding, implementation phase, software unit testing.*

code and fix process model — A somewhat antiquated software development approach used in the earlier days of software development. The model contains two steps: (1) write some code, (2) fix the problems in the code. [Boehm, *Spiral Model* 1988] *See also building and fixing software development model.*

code and unit testing — In software engineering, the activity of coding the modules (units) and testing them. Unit testing is normally done by the programmers who coded them. *See also code and component testing phase.*

code audit — In software engineering (verification and validation), an independent review of source code by a person, team, or tool to verify compliance with software design documentation and programming standards. Correctness and efficiency may also be evaluated. [ANSI/IEEE Standard 729-1983] *See also audit, inspection, walkthrough.*

code inspection — *See inspection.*

code skeleton — In software engineering, a means of describing a software module through the use of a "code skeleton" rather than a program design language (PDL). A code skeleton describes the software module through the use of a code syntax. [Wasserman and Pircher 1987]

code walkthrough — *See walkthrough.*

coding — In software engineering, the activity that turns the algorithms defined during the detail design phase into a computer-understandable language.

coding phase — *See implementation phase.*

coding standard — *See standard.*

cohesion — In software engineering (design), the degree to which the tasks performed by a single program module are functionally related. Cohesion is a measure of the strength of association of the elements within a module. *Contrast with coupling.*

command indicator — In computer-aided software engineering (CASE) tools, a specific region of a window in a graphical editor. [Wasserman and Pircher 1987]

command tree — In computer-aided software engineering (CASE) tools, a description of the levels of user commands to implement a system, for example a multilevel menu system.

commenter — In the Structured Analysis and Design Technique (SADT™) methodology (personnel roles), persons (usually authors) who must review and comment in writing on the work of the other authors. [Ross and Schoman 1977] *See also SADT™, SADT™ personnel roles. See also inspection, walkthrough.*

commercial computer environment — A collective term used to include computers, software, people, and facilities that are used to build, operate, and maintain software for business applications. *Contrast with embedded computer system.*

commercial software development methodology — In software engineering, software development methodologies available for purchase on the commercial market, in the public domain, or as government-furnished equipment. [Grabow and Noble 1985]

commissioner — In software acquisition, an organization responsible for obtaining a software system that will satisfy customer or user needs.

common user interface — 1. In a software system, a common set of software, input and output devices, screens, procedures, and dialogue between people and the software system. 2. In a software engineering environment (SEE), a common set of software, input and output devices, screens, procedures, and dialogue between people and the software tools available in the environment.

commonality — In software engineering, a software quality metric that can be used to measure the characteristics of software that provide for the use of interface standards for protocols, routines, and data representations. [RADC TR-85–37 1985]

communication protocol — *See protocol.* [STARTS Guide 1987]

communicativeness — In software engineering, a quality metric that can be used to measure those characteristics of the software that provide useful inputs and outputs that can be assimilated. [RADC TR-83–175 1983]

compatibility — In software engineering, a quality metric that can be used to measure the ability of two or more systems to exchange information. [ANSI/IEEE Standard 729-1983] *See also interoperability.*

complete — A software requirements specification is complete when the following are assured: (1) Everything that the software is supposed to do is included in the software requirements specification. (2) The system responds to all classes of input data (note: it is important to specify the responses to both valid and invalid input). (3) All pages are numbered; all figures and tables are numbered, named, and referenced; all terms and units of measure are provided; and all reference materials are present. (4) No sections are marked "to be determined" (TBD).

completeness — 1. In software engineering, a quality metric that can be used to measure those characteristics of software that provide full implementation of the functions required. 2. In system/software system engineering, a specification is complete to the extent that all parts are present and each part is fully developed.

complexity — In software engineering, a quality metric that can be used to measure the degree of complication of a system or system component, determined by such factors as the number and intricacy of interfaces, the number and intricacy of conditional branches, the degree of nesting, the types of data structures, and other system characteristics. [ANSI/IEEE Standard 729–1983]

component — A basic part of a hardware/software system.

computational accuracy — *See accuracy.*

compute-off — in software acquisition, a means of selecting the best developer for a software and/or hardware system. Several selected developers will build prototypes of their system. Each developer will demonstrate its system under conditions established by the buyer. The "winning" developer will get the final contract. The "compute-off" gets its name from the U.S. Air Force aircraft "fly-off." [U.S. Department of Defense (DoD) usage]

computer — A functional programmable unit that consists of one or more associated processing units and peripheral equipment that is controlled by internally stored programs and that can perform substantial computation, including numerous arithmetic operations or logic operations, without human intervention. [ANSI/IEEE Standard 729–1983]

computer code — *See software.*

computer hardware — The physical portion of a computing system, including the electrical or electronic components, electromechanical components, and mechanical components. *Contrast with software. See also computer.*

computer language — The various codes of letters and numbers the computer uses to enable humans to communicate with computers. *See also artificial language, language, natural language.*

computer program — *See software.*

computer program component (CPC) — A component of a computer program configuration item (CPCI). [U.S. Department of Defense (DoD) usage] *Replaced by computer software component (CSC). See also software component.*

computer program configuration item (CPCI) — *See software configuration item (SCI).* [U.S. Department of Defense (DoD) usage] Department of Defense (DoD) usage] *Replaced by computer software configuration item (CSCI). See also software configuration item (SCI).*

computer program development plan (CPDP) — *See software project management plan.* [U.S. Department of Defense (DoD) usage]

computer program verification — *See verification.*

computer resource — *See resource.*

computer resources integrated support document (CRISD) — Data item description of a lifecycle logistics support plan. [U.S. Department of Defense (DoD) usage] [DoD Standard 2167A 1988]

computer resources integrated support plan (CRISP) — *See computer resources integrated support document (CRISD).* [U.S. Department of Defense (DoD) usage]

computer science — The study of computers, their underlying principles, and use. It comprises such topics as compilers and operating systems; computer networks and interfaces; computer system architecture; hardware design and testing; information structures; programming languages; programming; software engineering; systems analysis and design; theories of information systems and computation; and applications from such disciplines as social sciences, economics, political sciences, engineering, business, and education.

computer software — *See software.*

computer software component (CSC) — A component of a computer software configuration item (CSCI). [U.S. Department of Defense (DoD) usage] *See also software component.*

computer software configuration item (CSCI) — [U.S. Department of Defense (DoD) usage] *See software configuration item (SCI).*

computer software unit — *See software unit.*

computer system — 1. A system composed of a computer(s), peripheral equipment, such as disks, printers, and terminals, and the software necessary to make them operate together. 2. A functional unit, consisting of one or more computers and associated software, that uses common storage for all or part of a program and also for all or part of the data necessary for the execution of the program; executes user-written or user-designated programs; performs user-designated data manipulation, including arithmetic operations and logic operations; and can execute programs that modify themselves during their execution. A computer system may be a standalone unit or may consist of several interconnected units, or it may be embedded in a larger nondata-processing system. [ANSI/IEEE Standard 729–1983] *Synonymous with ADP system, EDP system, embedded computer system. See also computer, software.*

computer system operator's manual (CSOM) — Data item description of operator's manual. [U.S. Department of Defense (DoD) usage]. [DoD Standard 2167A 1988] *See also operator's manual.*

computer-aided design (CAD) — The use of a computer to design a device or a system, display it on a computer monitor or printer, simulate its operation, and provide statistics on its performance. The computer is provided with data concerning the item to be designed, how it is to function, and the rules for the way in which the different components can be joined. *See also computer-aided manufacturing.*

computer-aided manufacturing (CAM) — The use of computers to assist in the manufacturing of products. *See also computer-aided design.*

computer-aided software engineering (CASE) — The use of computers to assist in the design, development, and coding of software.

computer-supported workstation — An input/output device of a digital computer with sufficient development software to support the software engineering development tasks. The device can be a standalone "high-end" workstation (e.g., Sun, Apollo, or IBM workstation) a personal computer (e.g., IBM PC/AT) that can perform some, if not, all of the necessary processing, or a "dumb" terminal that depends on the central processor to perform all necessary processing.

computerized system — A system that has a computer as a major, integral part. The system is dependent on the computer software to function. *Sometimes synonymous with embedded computer system.*

concept analysis — The analysis, simulation, or testing of concept options to determine the expected system performance against the selected criteria.

concept exploration (CE) phase — In system acquisition, the initial period when technical, military, and economic bases for acquisition programs are established through comprehensive studies and experimental hardware/software development and evaluation, resulting in alternative concepts and their characteristics. This phase is generally conducted by a small group to evaluate broad concepts that may be capable of satisfying the user needs. [U.S. Department of Defense (DoD) usage]

concept of operations (CONOPS) document — A system engineering document that: (1) describes the users' environment and process, (2) helps bring to the surface users' views, (3) helps formulate users' expectation, and (4) helps define a user when there is not one. *See also operational concept document* (OCD).

conceptual cleanliness — In software system engineering (requirements), a nonfunctional requirement that pertains to notations such as simplicity, sincerity, and ease of understanding. [Roman 1985] *See also software quality metric.*

conceptual model — In system/software system engineering, a requirements model of the system/software system to be developed, its internal components, and the behavior of both the system and its environment. [Balzer and Goldman 1979] [Roman 1985]

conciseness — In software engineering, a quality metric that can be used to measure those characteristics of software that provide for implementation of a function with a minimum amount of code. [RADC TR-83–175 1983]

configuration — 1. The arrangement of a system or network as defined by the nature, number, and chief characteristics of its functional units. More specifically, the term *configuration* may refer to a hardware configuration or a software configuration. 2. The requirements, design, and implementation that define a particular version of a system or system component. 3. The functional and/or physical characteristics of hardware/software as set forth in technical documentation and achieved in a product. [DoD Standard 480B 1988] *See also configuration management.*

configuration accounting — In configuration management (CM), the act of reporting and documenting changes made to a baseline configuration to establish a hardware/software configuration status. *See also configuration management (CM), configuration status accounting.*

configuration auditing — In configuration management (CM), the process of verifying that all required hardware/software configuration items have been produced, that the current version agrees with specified requirements, that the technical documentation completely and accurately describes the configuration items, and that all change requests have been resolved. [ANSI/IEEE Standard 729–1983] *See also configuration management (CM).*

configuration control — In configuration management: 1. The process of evaluating, approving or disapproving, and coordinating changes to hardware/software configuration items after formal establishment of their configuration identification. 2. The systematic evaluation, coordination, approval or disapproval, and implementation of all approved changes in the configuration of a hardware/software configuration item after formal establishment of its configuration identification. [DoD Standard 480B 1988] *Sometime erroneously used synonymously for configuration management (CM). See also configuration management (CM).*

configuration control board (CCB) — In configuration management (CM), the authority responsible for evaluating and approving or disapproving proposed engineering changes to the hardware/software configuration, and ensuring implementation of the approved changes. [ANSI/IEEE Standard 729–1983] *See also configuration management (CM).*

configuration identification — In configuration management: 1. The process of designating the hardware/software configuration items (CI) in a system and recording their characteristics. 2. The approved documentation that defines a hardware/software CI. 3. The current approved or conditionally approved technical documentation for a hardware/software CI as set forth in specifications, drawings, and associated lists, and documents referenced therein. [DoD Standard 480B 1988] *See also configuration* management (CM).

configuration item (CI) — In configuration management, an aggregation of hardware/software, or any of its discrete portions, that satisfies an end-use function and is designated by the customer for configuration management (CM). CIs may vary widely in complexity, size, and type, from an aircraft, electronic system, or ship system to a test meter, circuit board, or teddy bear. During development and initial production, CIs are only those specification items that are referenced directly in a contract (or equivalent in-house agreement). During the operation and maintenance period, any repairable item designated for separate procurement is a CI. [DoD Directive 5010.19] *See also configuration management.*

configuration management (CM) — In system/software system engineering, the discipline of identifying the configuration of a hardware/software system at discrete points in time with the purpose of systematically controlling changes to the configuration and maintaining the integrity and traceability of the configuration throughout the system lifecycle. *See also change control, change status report, configuration, configuration accounting, configuration auditing, configuration control, configuration control board (CCB), configuration identification, configuration item (CI), configuration management plan, configuration status accounting, software component (SC), software configuration item (SCI).*

configuration management plan — In configuration management (CM), a program for carrying out the project, design, or schedule for hardware/software configuration. *See also configuration management.*

configuration status accounting — In configuration management (CM), the recording and reporting of the information that is needed to manage a hardware/software configuration effectively, including a listing of the approved configuration identification, the status of proposed changes to configuration, and the implementation status of approved changes. [DoD Directive 5010.19] *See also configuration management.*

connection — In software engineering (structured analysis methodology), a reference from one module to a data item or entry point that is defined inside another module. [DeMarco 1979]

CONOPS — Acronym for concept of operations document.

consistency — 1. In software engineering, a quality metric that can be used to measure those characteristics of software that provide for uniform design and implementation techniques and notation. 2. In software engineering (requirements specification), a specification is consistent to the extent that its provisions do not conflict with each other, other specifications, or objectives.

consistent — A software requirements specification is consistent when no set of individual requirements conflict with any other set.

consistent user interface — *See user friendly.*

constraint — A limitation placed on the system. *See also design constraint (requirement).*

context analysis — In the Structured Analysis and Design Technique (SADT™) software requirements methodology, the analysis of the software system in the context of its environment. [Ross and Schoman 1977] *See also SADT™.*

context diagram — In software engineering (structured analysis methodology), a top-level diagram of a leveled set of dataflow diagrams. A dataflow diagram that portrays all the net inputs and outputs of a system, but shows no decomposition. [DeMarco 1979] *See also leveling.*

contract data requirements list (CDRL) — In system acquisition, a listing of all deliverable documentation required and made part of a contract. [U.S. Department of Defense (DoD) usage] *See also deliverable document, documentation, engineering document, interface control document (ICD), management document, software documentation, software maintenance documentation, system documentation, user documentation. See also A-level specification, B-level specification, B5-level specification, C-level specification, C5-level specification.*

contractor — An individual, partnership, company, corporation, or association having a contract with the procuring activity to deliver manufactured products, services, or data. Manufactured products can be hardware/software configuration items.

contractor assessment — *See software engineering assessment.*

contractual requirement — In system/software system engineering, requirements that have been specified in a contractual document.

contradiction — A problem in developing software requirements specifications in that the requirement statements that are true in the main are liable to be contradictory in detail. The reader must then make a decision as to which is correct by using his or her own knowledge or by asking questions. [Rich et al. 1987]

control — *See configuration control, controlling.*

Control Requirement Expression — *See CORE.*

control specification — In software engineering (realtime structured analysis methodology), a control transform description; statement of the process governing the control of data transforms. *Synonymous with CSPEC, state transition diagram (STD).*

control transform — In software engineering (realtime structured analysis methodology), an element of a transformation scheme that represents control of the system.

Control transforms handle event flows. A control transform has the capability of generating special event flows to data transform processes within the same dataflow diagram to trigger or stop their execution. It can also generate normal event signals to be read by processes inside or outside the systems. *Contrast with data transform.*

controlling — All the management activities that ensure that actual work goes according to plan. It measures performance against goals and plans, reveals when and where deviation exists, and, by putting in motion actions to correct deviations, helps ensure the accomplishment of plans.

conventional lifecycle model — *Synonymous with waterfall model.*

CORE (COntrolled Requirement Expression) — 1. A software requirements analysis methodology used primarily in Britain to describe aspects of a system/software system. CORE is supported by diagrammatic notation, whose features derived from several widely used specification and design diagrammatic notations. CORE resembles the diagram notation in Structured Analysis and Design Technique (SADT™) and Michael Jackson's design notations. Notation also expresses parallelism, which is covered by the TRW Software Requirements Engineering Methodology (SREM) notation. 2. A system requirement analysis methodology marketed by British Aerospace and System Designers, Inc. [Mullery 1979]

correct — A software requirement is correct only if every requirement stated there represents something that is required for a system to be built and there is no error that will affect design.

corrective maintenance — In software maintenance, refers to changes necessitated by actual errors (induced or residual "bugs") in a system. [NBS Special Publication 500–106 1983] *See also software maintenance.*

correctness — In software system engineering: 1. A metric that can be used to measure the extent to which software conforms to its specifications and standards. [RADC TR-85–37 1985] 2. The extent to which software is free from design and coding defects, in other words fault free. 3. The extent to which software meets its specified requirements and user objectives.

cost analysis group — In system engineering, a group of people assigned the responsibility of, and trained in, cost analysis. [Sailor 1990]

cost effective — 1. In management, the cost of an item or service is less than the expected return (in dollars) through the use of that item or service. 2. An item or service is more cost effective, when the benefits or payoff, per unit of cost, is highest among alternatives.

cost tradeoff — In system engineering and management, that approach to problem solving that compares and evaluates alternatives (technical) solutions, especially where advantages and costs cannot be accurately measured in numbers, by considering costs of alternatives in comparison with benefits derived.

cost-benefit analysis — In system/software engineering, the comparison of alternative courses of action, or alternative technical solutions, for the purpose of determining which alternative would realize the greatest cost benefit.

coupling — In software engineering (design), a measure of the interdependence among modules in a computer program. Coupling is the amount of information shared between two modules. *Contrast with cohesion.*

CPCI — Acronym for computer program configuration item.

CPU — Acronym for central processing unit of a digital computer.

CRISD — Acronym for computer resources integrated support document.

CRISP — Acronym for computer resources integrated support plan.

critical (detailed) design review (CDR) — In system/software system engineering, a milestone review conducted for each hardware/software configuration item (CI) when the detail design is essentially complete. The purpose of this review will be to: (1) determine that the detail design of the CI under review satisfies the functional and performance requirements of the CI requirement specifications; (2) establish the detail design compatibility among the CI and other items of equipment, facilities, software, and personnel; (3) assess CI risk area (on technical, cost, and schedule basis); and (4) review the detailed design description (specifications). [Military Standard 1521B-1985]. *See also milestone review, review.*

critical software — A software system in which failure could impact safety or cause large financial or social losses.

critical software requirement — In software engineering (requirements), a requirement that contains one or more of the following attributes: (1) a requirement that is essential to the completion of the system's mission; (2) a requirement designated as mandatory by the customer;

(3) a requirement for which successful achievement is considered to be a high-risk item in the development of the system.

cross checking — In computer-aided software engineering (CASE) tools, the ability of the tool to include extensive mechanisms for checking the completeness and consistency of models built with the analysis and design methods. The goal is to aid in detecting errors at the earliest possible stage of the development process.

CRT — Acronym for cathode ray tube.

CSC — Acronym for computer software component.

CSC integration and testing — *See integration and test phase*. [U.S. Department of Defense (DoD) usage] [DoD Standard 2167A 1988]

CSCI — Acronym for computer software configuration items. [U.S. Department of Defense (DoD) usage] *See also software configuration item (SCI).*

CSCI testing — *See testing* [U.S. Department of Defense (DoD) usage] [DoD Standard 2167A 1988]

CSCI-level testing — *See testing*.

CSOM — Acronym for computer system operator's manual.

CSPEC — In software engineering (realtime structured analysis methodology): 1. Acronym for control specification. [Hatley and Pirbhai 1987]. *Synonymous with control specification. Contrast with PSPEC.*

CSU — Acronym for computer software unit.

customer — 1. In system/software system engineering, an individual or organization who specifies the requirements for and formally accepts delivery of a new or modified hardware/software product and its documentation. The customer may be internal or external to the parent organization of the project and does not necessarily imply a financial transaction between customer and developer. 2. The person or persons who pay for the project and usually (but not necessarily) decide the requirements; the customer may or may not be the user. [ANSI/IEEE Standard 830–1984]

customizability — In computer-aided software engineering (CASE) tools: 1. A quality metric that can be used to measure the ability of the CASE tools to adjust to local preferences and local hardware and software configurations. 2. The ability to adjust tools and options to perform to local preferences and local hardware and software configurations and to be able to set options for tool use.

d-d-d

D&F — Acronym for determination and findings.

data — 1. A representation of facts, concepts, or instructions in a formalized manner suitable for communication, interpretation, or processing by human or automatic means. 2. The means for communication of concepts, plans, descriptions, requirements, and instructions relating to technical projects, materials, systems, and services. These may include specifications, standards, engineering drawings, associated lists, manuals, and reports, including scientific and technical reports; they may be in the form of documents, displays, sound records, punched cards, and digital or analog data. 3. In software requirements analysis, data can be categorized as inputs and outputs, stored data, or transitory data (temporary results).

data collection — In software engineering (inspections), the collection of errors and defects found during the inspection process and categorized regarding type class and severity.

data couple — In software engineering (structured design), the data items that pass between a module and its subordinate.

data decomposition — In software engineering (structured analysis methodology), partitioning the data into smaller and smaller pieces to render them more manageable and understandable.

data dictionary — 1. A collection of the names of all data items used in a software system, together with relevant properties of those items; for example, length of data item and representation. 2. In software engineering (structured analysis methodology), a central repository with descriptions of dataflows, data elements, files, databases, and processes referred to in a close-up dataflow diagram set. 3. In software engineering (structured analysis methodology), a technique for showing data definitions and relationships between data elements and dataflows. *See also dataflow diagram (DFD).*

data element — In software engineering (structured analysis methodology), a primitive dataflow, one that is not decomposed into subordinate dataflows. *See also dataflow.*

data item — 1. In software engineering (quality metrics), an item of data necessary in computing a metric value. For example, the number of execution paths is a data item. 2. In system/software engineering, a document identified on the contract data requirements list (CDRL). [U.S. Department of Defense (DoD) usage] [DoD Standard 2167A 1988]

data item description (DID) — A description of the contents of a software document. [U.S. Department of Defense (DoD) usage] [DoD Standard 2167A 1988]

data store — In computer science, a repository of data; a time-delayed dataflow; a file.

data structure diagram (DSD) — In software engineering (structured analysis methodology), a graphic tool to portray relationships between data elements in a file structure. [DeMarco 1979]

Data Structured System Development (DSSD) — A software engineering methodology developed in the early 1970s by Ken Orr. DSSD is based on top-down design and data structures and is based on working backwards to establish the design or requirements. Entity-relationship diagrams define the system contents, and assembly-line diagrams (modified Warnier-Orr diagrams) define the functional flow of the system.

data transform — In software engineering (realtime structured analysis), a part of a dataflow diagram that accepts only data as input and produces data and event flows as output. [Ward and Mellor 1986] *Contrast with control transform.*

data-driven system — In software systems, a type of embedded computer system that receives, processes, and displays a large amount of data (information). Examples are air traffic control and tactical data systems.

data-oriented model — A software requirements analysis technique that concentrates on the system state represented by the data that needs to be maintained.

data-oriented notation (representation) — A software requirement methodology that provides two main types of data-oriented notations: a dataflow notation and a data-structure notation. An example of a dataflow notation is structured analysis, and an example of a data-structure notation is Structured System and Design Methodology (SSADM). [STARTS Guide 1987] *See also notation.*

data-structure design — A software system engineering design methodology used for business applications and other systems with well-understood data structures. It produces a program structure by designing input/output data structures and relies on decomposition based on the higher level nature of these data structures. *Contrast with dataflow design. See also Jackson Structured Design (JSD) Method, Warnier method.*

database — 1. A comprehensive collection of libraries of data normally stored in a computer or on magnetic media. 2. In software engineering (structured analysis), a data store that is accessed in more than one way and that can be modified in format without affecting the programs that accessed it.

database design specification — In software development, a document that describes the content and format of the permanent or semipermanent data necessary for the software to carry out its functions.

database management system (DBMS) — In computer science, a software system that controls storing, combining, updating, retrieving, and displaying records.

dataflow — In software engineering (structured analysis methodology), a graphic representation of the movement of data between processes that act on the data. Used in dataflow diagrams. *See also dataflow diagram (DFD).*

dataflow chart — *See dataflow diagram (DFD).*

dataflow design — A software engineering design methodology for decomposing a program into input modules, transformation modules, and output modules. *Synonymous with structured analysis (SA).*

dataflow diagram (DFD) — 1. In software engineering (structured analysis methodology), a graphic representation (model) of a software system, showing data sources, data sinks, storage, and processes performed on data as nodes, and logical flow of data as links between the nodes. It can also be used to represent hardware/software systems. *Synonymous with dataflow graph, dataflow chart. See also data dictionary, dataflow, leveling, process.* 2. A Structured System Analysis and Design Methodology (SSADM) tool used to show how data moves in an information system and how processes act upon data.

dataflow graph — *See dataflow diagram (DFD).*

dataflow model — A software requirements methodology that makes use of the dataflow diagram (DFD) and its related constructs. *See also dataflow diagram (DFD), SREM.*

DBMS — Acronym for a database management system.

DCDS (Distributed Computing Design System) — A software engineering methodology and tool and a superset of Software Requirements Engineering Methodology (SREM) developed by TRW for the U.S. Army at BMDATC beginning in 1981. DCDS provides tools and methodologies for the entire software development lifecycle. DCDS includes SYSREM (System Engineering Requirements Methodology), SREM, distributed processing design, software module design, and test and integration support. *See also SREM, SYSREM.*

debugging — 1. In software development, the process of correcting syntactic and logical errors detected during coding. With the primary goal of obtaining an executing piece of code, debugging shares with testing certain techniques and strategies but differs in its usual ad hoc application and local scope. [FIPS Publication 101 1983] 2. In software engineering (testing), the process of locating, analyzing, and correcting suspected faults. *Synonymous with unit testing. See also testing.*

decision model — A type of model used to select the most favorable solution from various alternatives. *See also behavior model, descriptive model, normative model.*

decision table — 1. In management, a table of all contingencies being considered in the description of a problem together with the actions to be taken for each set of contingencies. 2. In software engineering (structured analysis methodology), a presentation in either matrix or tabular form of a set of conditions and their corresponding actions. [ANSI/IEEE Standard 729–1983]

decision tree — 1. A tool used in software engineering (structured analysis methodology). 2. A decision table in a tree-like form.

decomposability — In software engineering, a quality metric that can be used to measure the degree of ease with which a software specification can be decomposed into module specifications so that design can be carried out easily.

defect — 1. An accidental condition that causes a functional unit to fail to perform its required function. A manifestation of an error in software. A defect, if encountered, may cause a failure. 2. In hardware/software system engineering, a fault or an error created when the hardware/software system was built. *See also error, fault.*

deficiencies — In system/software system engineering, conditions or characteristics in any hardware/software that are not in compliance with specified configuration.

definition phase — *See software requirements phase.*

deliverable document — In software system engineering, a document that is deliverable to a customer. Examples are users' manual, operator's manual, and programmer's maintenance manual. *See also documentation.*

DEM/VAL — Acronym for demonstration/validation.

DeMarco technique — *Synonymous with structured analysis (SA).*

DeMarco, Tom — The author of the early structured analysis, "standard" and software engineering textbook entitled "Structured Analysis and System Specifications." *See also structured analysis (SA), Structured Analysis and System Specifications.*

demonstration — In system/software engineering (validation), demonstration is used to verify requirements that can not be tested, for example, using an uncontrolled source of stimuli for which the results cannot be entirely predicted. [Nelsen 1990] *Contrast with analysis, examination, similarity, testing.*

demonstration and validation (DEM/VAL) Phase — In system acquisition, the period during which major characteristics are refined through extensive study analysis, hardware and software development, test, and evaluation. The objective of DEM/VAL is to validate the choice of alternatives and to provide the basis for determining whether to proceed into full-scale development.

Department of Defense (DoD) — An institution of the U.S. government responsible for the defense of the country and for carrying out foreign policy.

dependency-corrective reasoning — An artificial intelligence (AI) technique allowing a search method that analyzes dependencies in making decisions. [Rich et al. 1987]

deploy — To place into service or operation, or to place in its operational environment.

deployment — In software system engineering, after final system testing, the software and hardware become operational. [U.S. Department of Defense (DoD) usage]

deployment phase — In system acquisition, the period beginning with the users' acceptance of the first operational unit and extending until the system is phased out of the inventory. The deployment phase is part of production and deployment phase. [U.S. Department of Defense (DoD) usage]

derivation — 1. In a hierarchical structure, the next lower level that is associated with a given element. The lower element is said to be derived from the higher element. 2. In system engineering, the changing or translation of a requirement through analysis into a form that is suitable for low-level analysis or design.

derived requirement — In system/software system engineering (requirements), a lower level requirement that is determined to be necessary for a top-level requirement to be met. When a requirement changes form, it becomes a derived requirement. In general, a derived requirement is more specific and is directed toward some subelement. This usually occurs through the process of analysis, which translates user requirements into parameters that a designer can relate to, such as power and weight.

Descartes — A formal specification language developed at the University of Southwestern Louisiana. Descartes, a specification language, uses data structure methods to analyze program input into constituent parts that are then used to synthesize a description of program output. Descartes is used to specify the functional relationship between the input and output of the system. In the design phase, Descartes' specifications provide precise information about what the system should be designed to do. During the test and maintenance phase, test data can be put to both the specifications and the actual system. The output of specifications and the output of the actual system can then be compared for consistency. [Urban 1990]

descriptive model — A model that describes facts and relationships but does not contain a basis for evaluation of the system. *Contrast with normative model.*

design — *See architectural design, bottom-up design, canonical design, data-structure design, dataflow design, detailed design, external design, functional design, internal specification, low-level design, module design, preliminary design, program design, software design, structured design, system design, top-down design, top-level design, top-level system design, unit design.*

design alternative — In system/software system engineering, the alternative ways that a system can satisfy the system/software requirement—but not with equal cost, time, or risk. [Lavi 1984]

design constraint (requirement) — In software system engineering, any requirement that impacts or constrains the design of a software system or software system component. Examples of design constraints are physical requirements, performance requirements, software development standards, and software quality assurance (QA) standards. [ANSI/IEEE Standard 729–1983] *See also software requirements specification (SRS).*

design inspection — *See inspection.*

design integration — In system/software system engineering, the action taken to ensure that the various subsystems and components of the system meet and operate together as required and expected.

design integration group — In software engineering, the personnel responsible for the design integration. [Sailor 1990]

design optimization — In system/software system engineering, the analysis and decision process leading to improvement and refinement of the selected system architecture.

design phase — The period of time in the software development lifecycle during which the designs for architecture, software components, interfaces, and data are created, documented, and verified to satisfy requirements. *See also detailed design phase, preliminary design phase, software development lifecycle phase.*

design process — *See software design process.*

design review — In system/software system engineering: 1. A review that will be conducted on a periodic basis to assess the degree of completion of technical efforts related to major milestones before proceeding with further technical effort associated with a particular element of the system. The schedule and plan for the conduct of design reviews should be included in the developer's program plan and master schedule. 2. A milestone review at which the preliminary or detailed design of a system is presented to the user, customer, or other interested parties for comment and approval. 3. The formal review of an existing or proposed design for the purpose of: (1) detection and correction of design deficiencies that could affect fitness for use and environmental aspects of the product, process, or service or (2) identification of potential improvements of performance, safety, and economic aspects. [ANSI/ASQC A3–1978] [ANSI/IEEE Standard 729–1983] *See also milestone review, review.*

design specification — In system/software system engineering, a specification that documents the design of a system/software system or system/software component, for example, a system/software configuration item. Typical contents include system or component algorithms, control logic, data structures, data set-use information, input/output formats, and interface descriptions. [ANSI/IEEE Standard 729–1983] *See also design, internal specification, requirements specification.*

design standard — *See standard.*

design trade study — *See trade study.*

design walkthrough — *See walkthrough.*

desirable requirement — In software system engineering (requirements specifications), a degree of necessity implying that these are requirements that would enhance the software products but are not mandatory. [ANSI/IEEE Standard 830–1984] *Contrast with essential requirement, optional requirement. See also requirement, software requirement.*

detailed automated model — In software system engineering (verification and validation techniques), detailed automated models typically involve large event simulation of the system. They are more expensive than simple automated models; however, they are much more effective in analyzing such issues as accuracy, dynamic consistency, realtime performance, and lifecycle costs. [Boehm, *V&V Software Requirements* 1984] *See also verification and validation technique.*

detailed design — 1. In software engineering, the process of refining and expanding the software preliminary design to contain more detailed descriptions of the processing logic, data structures, and data definitions, to the extent that the design is sufficiently complete to be implemented. 2. The result of the detailed design process. [ANSI/IEEE Standard 729–1983] *Synonymous with design, low-level design, module design, program design. Sometimes synonymous with detailed design description, detailed design specification.*

detailed design description (specification) — In software engineering, a document that describes the exact detailed configuration of a computer program. It identifies the input, output, control logic, algorithms, and data structure of each individual low-level component of the software product. In U.S. Department of Defense (DoD) procurements, it is also called computer program product specification, a Type C5-level specification, a Part II specification, or a program design specification. It is the primary product of the detailed design phase. *See also detailed design.*

detailed design phase — The software development lifecycle phase that uses the software system design and software architecture from the previous phase (preliminary design) to produce the detailed logic for each unit such that it is ready for coding. *See also software development lifecycle phase.*

detailed design review — *See critical (detailed) design review.*

detailed design specification — *See detailed design description (specification).*

detailed design stage — *See detailed design phase.*

detailed scenario — In software system engineering (verification and validation techniques), detailed scenarios provide more elaborate and thus more expensive operational descriptions, are even more effective than simple scenarios in clarifying a system's human engineering aspect. [Boehm, *V&V Software Requirements* 1984] *See also verification and validation technique.*

detailed software requirements specification — In software system engineering, a document that contains the following details concerning the delivered software system: functional specifications (functional structure and interrelationships, data specifications and dictionary, overall system operational requirements, functional requirements); constraints (software design constraints, hardware design constraints, user design constraints); user aspects (documentation, component testing and integration testing, configuration and conversion management, support services and maintenance requirements, expansion requirements); installation aspects (hardware installation, conversion, training); deliverables; acceptance requirements; and project management, including quality assurance (QA). [STARTS Guide 1987]

deterministic requirement specification — A system/software requirements specification in which the output of a function is uniquely defined by the input. [Hayes 1986]

developer — In industry, the person or persons who produce a product for a customer. The customer and the developer may be members of the same organization. A developer is sometimes called a supplier. [ANSI/IEEE Standard 830–1984]

development baseline — In system/software system engineering, the informal baseline created when intermediate software products (e.g., subsystem requirement specifications, detailed design documents, users' manual, and test procedures) are completed and placed under local configuration management. *See also configuration management, program librarian, program support library (PSL).*

development lifecycle — *See software development lifecycle, system development lifecycle.*

development phase — *See software requirements phase.*

development specification — *Synonymous with requirements specification.* [U.S. Department of Defense (DoD) usage] [ANSI/IEEE Standard 729–1983] *Synonymous with B-level specification, Part I specification. See also software requirements specification.*

development test and evaluation (DT&E) — In system acquisition, developmental testing and evaluation of individual components, contract items, subsystems and systems at the contractor's facility. Testing focuses on the technological and engineering aspects of the component, contract item, subsystem, or system.

developmental configuration — In a software engineering project, the current configuration of the system under development. The development configuration is less formal than a baseline configuration. *See also configuration management.*

deviation — In system/software system engineering, a specific written authorization, granted before the development of an item, to depart from a particular performance or design requirement of a specification, drawing, or other document for a specific number of units or a specific period of time. A deviation differs from an engineering change in that an approved engineering change requires corresponding revision of the documentation defining the affected item, whereas a deviation does not contemplate revision of the applicable specification or drawing.

DFD — *Acronym for dataflow diagram.*

diagram-based structured methodology — *Synonymous with structured analysis (SA).*

DID — Acronym for data item description. [U.S. Department of Defense (DoD) usage] [DoD Standard 2167A 1988]

Distributed Computing Design System — *See DCDS.*

distributedness — In software engineering, a quality metric that can be used to measure those characteristics of software that determine the degree to which software functions are geographically or logically separated within the system. [RADC TR-85–37 1985]

DMS — Acronym for data management system.

document — 1. A data medium and the data recorded on it. The data generally have permanence and can be read by man or machine. The term *document* is often used to describe human-readable items only, for example, technical documents, design documents, and management documents. 2. To create a document. [ANSI/IEEE Standard 729–1983] *See also deliverable document, documentation, engineering document, management document, milestone document.*

document-driven model — A software development model that emphasizes elaborate documents as completion criteria for early requirement and design phases. It is asserted that document-driven standards require many projects to write elaborate specifications of poorly understood user interfaces and decision support functions. The waterfall model is sometimes called a document driven model. [Boehm, *Spiral Model* 1988]

documentation — 1. A collection of documents on a given subject. 2. The process of generating a document. 3. Any written or pictorial information describing, defining, specifying, reporting, or certifying activities, requirements, procedures, or results. [ANSI N45.2.10–1973] [ANSI/IEEE Standard 729–1983] 4. In software engineering, commonly used to mean users' document, software maintenance document, operator's manual. *See also contract data requirements list (CDRL), deliverable document, document, software documentation, software maintenance documentation, system documentation, user documentation.*

documented — Recorded in writing.

DoD — Acronym for U.S. Department of Defense

DoD Standard 2167A — The identification number assigned to *Military Standard: Defense System Software Development* (February 29, 1988), the premier U.S. Department of Defense (DoD) standard for the development of embedded, realtime, mission-critical software systems.

domain — In mathematics, the domain of a function is the set of values that the independent variable may take on over the range of the independent variable.

domain analysis — In the *Synthesis* software development methodology, the domain analysis identifies commonalities across applications of the specific business or technology area. This analysis would normally be done by domain experts who have a deep understanding within the domain. [Pyster 1990]

driver — In software engineering (testing): 1. Code that sets up an environment and calls a module for testing. [FIPS Publication 101 1983] 2. A dummy program module used to provide top-level test data in the development and testing of a low-level module. *Contrast with stub.*

DSSD — Acronym for Data Structured System Development.

DT&E — Acronym for development test and evaluation.

Dual Life Cycle Model (DLCM) — A software lifecycle model proposed by John Manley. It is composed of parallel management and engineering lifecycles, connected by well-defined communication systems. This software development process distinguishes between artifacts or tangible work products produced by managers for engineers and those produced by engineers for managers, in addition to what managers and engineers produce for their own use. Each of these four categories are work products represented by an orderly progression of artifacts over the lifecycle of any information (or other) system of interest. [Manley 1990]

dual-line projection — A software engineering concept that describes a system from multiple viewpoints. [Davis 1990]

e-e-e

E-R — Acronym for entity-relationship.

ease of learning — In software development, the ease with which new users can master the software product and learn its uses. Ease of learning is facilitated by program prompts, help messages, error messages, users' manuals, and associated job aids.

ease of use — In software development, the degree of user convenience in performing desired functions with the software product, as well as avoidance of overconstrained expected program behavior. *See also usability, user friendly.*

economic constraint — In software system engineering (requirements), a management consideration regarding immediate and long term costs. It may be limited in scope to the development at hand (e.g., development costs); but, most often, an economic constraint involves global marketing and production objectives. [Roman 1985]

EDP system — *See computer system.*

efficiency — In software engineering, a metric that can be used to measure: 1. The relative extent to which a resource is used (i.e., storage, space, processing time, communication time). [RADC TR-85–37 1985] 2. The extent to which software performs its intended functions with a minimum consumption of computing resources. [ANSI/IEEE Standard 729–1983]

electronic development folder (EDF) — *See electronic unit development folder (EUDF)*

Electronic Systems Division (ESD) — A suborganization of the Air Force Systems Command, U.S. Air Force. ESD is responsible for the acquisition and system engineering of the majority of the U.S. Air Force electronic systems.

electronic unit development folder (EUDF) — A software development tool that collects into an electronic "folder" all the entities involved in the development of a single software unit (typically 500 to 1000 lines of code): unit requirements, design, code, test cases, test results, and documentation. It also includes a management template for tracking the programmer's schedule and actual completion of each entity. *See also unit development folder (UDF).*

element — In a set, an element is an object, entity, or concept having the properties that define a set.

elements of a project — System, subsystem, component, or unit.

embedded computer — A computer used in an embedded computer system. Note: John Manley is frequently credited with coining the term "embedded computer." [Manley 1974] *See also embedded computer system.*

embedded computer system — A computer system integral to a larger system whose primary purpose is not computational, for example, a computer system in a weapon, aircraft, automobile, communication network, intelligent point-of-sales system, automatic teller machine, and talking spelling checker for children. *See also computer system.*

embedded software — Software for an embedded computer system. *See also embedded computer system.*

end user — *Synonymous with user.*

engineering — The science concerned with putting scientific knowledge to practical uses. *See also requirements engineering, software engineering, system engineering, system requirements engineering.*

engineering change — In system/software system engineering, an alteration in the configuration of a hardware/software configuration item or items, delivered, to be delivered, or under development, after formal establishment of its configuration identification.

engineering change proposal (ECP) — In system/software system engineering, a term which includes both a proposed engineering change and the documentation by which the change is described and suggested.

engineering document — In system/software system engineering, a document that is prepared as a result of a system/software engineering activity, for example, requirements specification, test document, and design description. *See also documentation, management document.*

engineering environment — *See environment.*

engineering standard — *See standard.*

entity — In an entity-relationship model, the principal object about which information is to be collected, usually denoting a person, place, thing, or event of informational interest. [Chen 1990] *See also entity-relationship model.*

entity life history — A Structured System Analysis and Design Methodology (SSADM) tool which gives a third view of data showing all events affecting the entity during its life in the system. For example, those that create it, those that modify it in some way, and those that delete it. [Williams 1987]

entity type — In an entity-relationship model, a classification of an entity. [Chen 1990] *See also entity, entity-relationship diagram, entity-relationship model.*

entity-relationship diagram (ERD or E-R diagram) — 1. A diagram that depicts a set of data elements and the logical relationships among them. 2. A tool of the structured specification methodology that emphasizes the interfacing of objects to each other. *See also structured analysis (SA).*

entity-relationship model — In software engineering: 1. A model of a software system using entity-relationship diagrams. 2. A tool for communicating between the system analyst, class designer, and end user during the requirements, analysis, and conceptual design phases. [Chen 1990]

environment — In system/software engineering, the conditions under which something is expected to be built or operate. Sometimes synonymous with software engineering environment.

environment interface standard — In software engineering, a standard procedure for describing, designing, building, testing, and maintaining an interface between the environment and the software system. *See also standard.*

environmental characteristic — The attributes or characteristics that make one environment different from another.

environmental requirement — In system engineering, the requirements the system must meet in its relationship with the environment, for example, temperature, altitude, and accessability.

ERD — Acronym for entity-relationship diagram.

error — 1. A discrepancy between a computed, observed, or measured value or condition and the true, specified, or theoretically correct value or condition. [*American National Dictionary for Information Processing Systems* 1982] 2. Human action that results in software containing a fault. Examples include omission or misinterpretation of user requirements in a software specification or incorrect translation or omission of a requirement in the design specification. [ANSI/IEEE Standard 729–1983] *See also bug, failure, fault.*

ESD — Acronym for Electronic Systems Division.

essential model — In software engineering (structured analysis methodology), an ideal software requirements model. Buffers and transformations are idealized; buffers are assumed to have an infinite capacity; and transformation output delays are assumed to be zero. *Sometime synonymous with requirements model.*

essential requirement — In software engineering (requirement specifications), a degree of necessity implying that these are mandatory requirements. The software product will not be accepted without them. *Contrast with desirable requirement, optional requirement. See also requirement, software requirement.*

event — In system/software engineering, an occurrence of an item when the value of the condition changes from true to false or vice versa. An event, therefore, specifies an instance of time, whereas a condition specifies intervals of time. [Heninger 1980]

event list — In software engineering (realtime structured analysis methodology), a list of the external events that cause the system to transform data or change state.

event table — In software engineering (requirements analysis), a table that shows when demand functions should be performed and when periodic functions should be started or stopped. Each row on an event table corresponds to a group or mode. [Heninger 1980]

evolutionary development — In software system engineering, the use of the evolutionary development model.

evolutionary development model — A software development process whose stages consist of expanding increments of an operational software product. The directions of evolution are determined by operational experience. The evolutionary development model gives users a rapid initial operational capability and provides a realistic operational basis for determining subsequent product improvement. [Boehm, *Spiral Model* 1988]

evolutionary prototyping — In software development strategies, the developers construct a partial implementation of the system that meets known requirements. This prototype is then used by its intended user to help understand the full requirements. Incremental development, on the other hand, implies that one understands most requirements up front, but the system is implemented in subsets of increasing capability. Evolutionary prototyping implies a need to experiment with an operational system or to learn the requirements. Note that in the case of throwaway prototypes, only those aspects that are poorly understood may be implemented, but in the case of evolutionary prototypes, those systems aspects that are best understood are more likely to be implemented. *Contrast with incremental development, rapid prototyping.*

examination — 1. In system engineering (validation), examination pertains to verifying the physical attributes such as size, weight, and color. 2. In software system engineering, to verify the physical attributes of a system, such as code, documentation, and storage media. [Nelsen 1990] *Contrast with analysis, demonstration, similarity, testing.*

Excelerator — A computer-aided software engineering (CASE) tool that supports realtime and nonrealtime structured analysis methods.

exception handling — A software requirement specification that concerns system response to error handling, such as to record the error, to respond to it with an error handling routine, or simply to ignore it. [STARTS Guide 1987]

executability — In software engineering (requirements), a factor pertaining to requirement specifications. It describes the extent to which functional simulation and components can be constructed from the requirements specifications before starting the design or implementation. [Roman 1985] *See also requirement specifications language.*

executable language — A computer language that can be directly executable by a computer.

executable program — In software engineering, a computer program written in a language that can be directly executed by a computer. *See also executable language.*

executable program language — *See executable language.*

executable requirements language — In software engineering, an artificial language that is used to represent a software requirement. The resulting formal requirements can be translated directly into an operational application program that implements the requirements. *See also executable requirements specification, formal (verifiable) requirements language, formal language, language.*

executable requirements specification — 1. In software engineering, a software requirement specification that is represented in an executable requirements language. *See also executable requirements language.* 2. A software engineering methodology for translating system requirements into a workable system model that can be understood by both the computers and software engineers. [Urban et al. 1985]

exercise — In a software prototype, the operation of the prototype to obtain answers and to view solutions.

expandability — In software engineering, a quality metric that can be used to measure the relative effort to increase the software capability or performance by enhancing current functions or by adding new functions or data. [RADC TR-85–37 1985]

experiment — An operation carried out under controlled conditions to disclose an unknown effect or law, to test or establish a hypothesis, or to illustrate a known law.

experimental process — *See experiment.*

expert — In the Structured Analysis and Design Technique (SADT™) methodology (personnel roles), a person from whom authors obtain specialized information about requirements and constraints by means of interviews. [Ross and Schoman 1977] *See also SADT™, SADT™ personnel roles.*

explicit requirement — In system/software system engineering, requirements that have been explicitly "spelled out." *Contrast with implicit requirement.*

exploratory prototyping — A software requirements analysis strategy involving the user interface with major system functions used to identify and define user requirements. [STARTS Guide 1987]

Express — A software requirements analysis tool that automates the Structured System Analysis and Design Methodology (SSADM) from the requirements specification stage through logical design. It is DEC VAX hosted and tool-based on the ORACLE database system. [STARTS

Guide 1987] *See also Structured System Analysis and Design Methodology (SSADM).*

extensibility — In computer-aided software engineering (CASE) tools, a metric that can be used to measure the CASE tool's ability to integrate additional tools (and those acquired elsewhere) into the tool environment and to add new tools over time. [Wasserman and Pircher 1987]

external consistency — In software requirement specifications, items within the specifications that do not conflict with external specifications or entities.

external design — *Synonymous with external specification, requirements specification.*

external interface — In system/software system engineering, links (usually in the form of data) between the system and its environment.

external interface requirement — A system/software requirement that specifies a hardware, software, or database element with which a system/software system or system/software component must interface, or that sets forth constraints on formats, timing, or other factors caused by such an interface.

external interface requirements specification — *See Interface control document (ICD).*

external specification — *Synonymous with requirements specification. Contrast with internal specification.*

external system behavior (requirements) — *See requirements specification. Contrast with internal system behavior (design).*

external test data — In software engineering (testing), test data at the extremes, or boundaries, of the domain of an input variable or data that produces results at the boundaries of an output domain. [FIPS Publication 101 1983]

f-f-f

failure — 1. In a system, the termination of the ability of a functional unit to perform its required function. 2. The inability of a system or system component to perform a required function within specified limits. A failure may be produced when a fault is encountered. 3. A departure of program operation from program requirements. *See also error, fault.*

FAR — Acronym for federal acquisition regulation. [DoD Standard 2167A 1988]

fault — In software engineering: 1. An accidental condition that causes a functional unit to fail to perform its required function. [*American National Dictionary for Information Processing Systems* 1982] 2. A manifestation of an error in software. A fault, if encountered, may cause a failure. [ANSI/IEEE Standard 729–1983] 3. *Synonymous with bug. See also error, failure.*

FBD — Acronym for functional block diagram.

FCA — Acronym for functional configuration audit.

feasibility — In software engineering (requirement specifications), a specification is feasible to the extent that the lifecycle benefits of a system specified will exceed lifecycle costs and that the system will satisfy system requirements. It also implies validating that the specified system can be sufficiently maintainable, reliable, and human-engineered to keep a positive lifecycle balance. [Boehm, *V&V Software Requirements* 1984]

feasibility analysis — *See feasibility study.*

feasibility study — In software engineering, a study to determine the benefits and costs, in terms of time, money, and manpower, of a proposed use of a computer to accomplish a given purpose, usually with a recommendation or proposed alternatives.

feedback — 1. In project management, all the management reports that provide information as to whether the project is going according to plan and the degree and cause of any deviation. 2. In electrical circuits, signals or information that is taken from the output stage of a system and is fed back to the input stage of the same system to provide control.

feedback loop — *See feedback.*

FFBD — Acronym for functional flow block diagram.

FFD — Acronym for functional flow diagram.

field — In data processing, a subset of a record with its own characteristics; fields are combined to form a record. *Used interchangeably with attribute.*

field entry — A group of characters that are stored in a field or attribute. [Flynn and Dorfman 1990]

file — 1. In software engineering, *synonymous with data store.* 2. In data processing, an item that contains information on computer system.

final operating capability (FOC) — In acquisition management, the final capability of the system after completion of the development. *Contrast with initial operating capability (IOC).*

finite state grammar — In software engineering (formal requirements specification), a finite state grammar is a restricted form of Backus Naur Form. A finite state grammar is used to specify the requirements for a programming language, a communication protocol, and is a basis for automatic program generation, particularly for generating syntactic analyzers. [STARTS Guide 1987]

finite state machine (FSM) — A hypothetical machine that can only be in one of a given number of states at a specific time. In response to an input, the machine generates an output and changes state. Both the output and new state are purely functions of the current state and the input. A FSM is used to represent the control process in realtime structured analysis. [Davis, *Comparison of Techniques* 1988]

first article — In the full-scale development phase of the acquisition lifecycle, the first item or system built. [Sailor 1990]

first production article — In the production/development phase of the acquisition lifecycle, the first item or system built by using production machines and production procedures. [Sailor 1990]

flag — 1. In software engineering (structured design), the control information that passes between a module and its subordinate. 2. In programming, a variable used to indicate whether a condition has occurred, for example, a flag could be used to indicate that a record was found.

flexibility — In software engineering, a quality metric that can be used to measure the ease of effort for changing the software mission, function, or data to satisfy other requirements. [RADC TR-85–37 1985]

flow — *See dataflow.*

flowdown — A system engineering concept for the systematic decomposition of system requirements into allocated and derived requirements, appropriately assigned to low-level functional components. The flowdown generates a low-level requirements structure from the (system-supplied) top level. (The functional flow block diagram (FFBD) or dataflow diagram (DFD) can be used as a tool for this activity.)

FOC — Acronym for final operating capability.

formal (verifiable) requirements language — An artificial language used to represent a software requirement. The resulting formal requirements can be proven "correct" through proof-of-correctness methods. *See also executable requirements language, formal language, proof of correctness.*

formal analysis — In software engineering, formal analysis uses rigorous mathematical techniques to analyze the algorithms of a solution. The algorithms may be analyzed for numerical properties, efficiency, and correctness. [FIPS Publication 101 1983]

formal design method — In software engineering: 1. A written design specification. 2. Design methods based on mathematical formalism, for example the Vienna Development Method (VDM) and the formal specification language Z developed at the Oxford University Computing Laboratory.

formal design review — *See design review.*

formal language — 1. A language whose rules are explicitly established before its use. *Synonymous with artificial language*. 2. In software development, a computer language that is used to represent a software requirement that can either be proven "correct" through proof-of-correctness methods or can be translated directly into an operational application program that implements the requirements. *See also executable requirements language, formal (verifiable) requirements language, language.*

formal mathematical analysis — A software engineering requirements methodology that uses rigorous mathematical techniques to analyze the problem and to build or produce a specification of the intended behavior of a system.

formal proof-of-correctness — In software development, the act of reviewing, inspecting, testing, checking, auditing, or otherwise establishing and documenting whether or not items, processes, services, or documents conform to specified requirements.

formal qualification review (FQR) — In system engineering, the test, inspection, or analytical process by which hardware/software products at the end-item level are verified to have met specific procuring activities or contractual performance requirements. This review does not apply to requirements verified at functional configuration audit (FCA). [U.S. Department of Defense (DoD) usage] [Military Standard 1521B-1985] *See also functional configuration audit (FCA).*

formal qualification testing — In system/software system engineering, the final qualification testing on the entire contract item. The customer or a designated representative witnesses the formal qualification test, which is a basis for acceptance. [U.S. Department of Defense (DoD) usage] *See also qualification testing.*

formal review — *See review. Contrast with informal review, walkthrough, inspection.*

formal semantic — In software engineering (requirements), a mechanism or method for addressing the semantics of a requirements statement, as well as its syntax. Specification techniques for large-scale systems usually address syntax and inadequately handle semantics. To make use of already developed software components (the concept of reusability), the description of a reusable component must include a semantic description, as well as the syntactic definition of the component's interface. [Grabow and Noble 1985]

formal specification — In software engineering: 1. A specification written and approved in accordance with established standards. 2. A document which primarily uses mathematics to specify system requirements.

formal specification technique — In software system engineering (requirements specifications), a specification method based on mathematics. Formal specification techniques have started to move from academia to the industrial environment where they are generally being applied to small problems. The hope is that more rigorous specification techniques can produce better quality products that are more easily maintained. [Norris 1986]

formal system specification language — In software development, an artificial language that is used to represent software requirement that can be proven "correct" through proof-of-correctness methods.

formal testing — In system/software system engineering, the process of conducting testing activities and reporting results in accordance with an approved test plan.

formal verification — In software system engineering, a process of conducting verification activities and reporting the results.

format — In data processing, the arrangement of fields in a record. [Flynn and Dorfman 1990]

fourth-generation compiler — In computer science, a compiler for a fourth-generation language. [Cobb 1985]

fourth-generation language (4GL) — 1. In software engineering, an application generator in such domains as management information systems. 2. In computer science, a nonprocedural language that tells the computer on which they are used what the specified result is, rather than how to achieve the desired result. *See also formal language, very-high-level language (VHLL).*

FQR — Acronym for formal qualification review.

FQT — Acronym for formal qualification testing.

front-end lifecycle activity — In software engineering (software development lifecycle), the software requirement and (sometimes) preliminary design phase.

front-end process — 1. In system engineering, *synonymous with system engineering process*. 2. In software system engineering, *synonymous with front-end lifecycle activity*.

FSD — Acronym for full-scale development.

FSM — Acronym for firmware support manual. Acronym for finite state machine.

full text — In the Automatic Requirements Traceability System (ARTS), a text library element or module external to an ARTS database. It is used for requirements information that requires more than a single line of text. Each module or element may contain several paragraphs. [Flynn and Dorfman 1990]

full-scale development phase (FSD) — In system acquisition, the period when a system and the major items necessary for its support are designed, fabricated, tested, and evaluated. During the FSD, the system proceeds into the detailed design phase, followed by fabrication, assembly, and test of the first article.

function — 1. In management, a major activity or group of activities that are continuous. For example, the principle functions of management are planning, organizing, staffing, directing, and controlling. 2. In project management, an activity or set of activities that span the entire duration of a software project. Examples of project functions include configuration management, quality assurance (QA), and project cost accounting. 3. In functional analysis, the system or subsystem under study. The function is the activity or behavior of the system, i.e., what it does. 4. In software, a subprogram that is invoked during the evaluation of an expression in which its name appears and that returns a value to the point of invocation.

functional analysis — In system/software engineering: 1. The process of studying a system by partitioning the system into functional parts and determining how the parts relate to each other to understand the whole. *Contrast with object-oriented method.* 2. The process of studying user needs to arrive at a definition of software requirements. *Synonymous with software analysis, software requirements analysis, system analysis, system requirements analysis.*

functional architecture — In the Structured Analysis and Design Technique (SADT™) software requirements methodology, a layout of the activities performed by a system (temporarily disregarding who or what does them) and the things with which those activities interact. The functional architecture description describes the functions and external interfaces. *See also SADT™. See also functional specification, external specification.*

functional baseline — In system/software system engineering, the initial hardware/software configuration identification established at the end of the conceptual phase. This baseline is established by an approved system specification.

functional block diagram (FBD) — *See functional flow block diagram (FFBD).*

functional configuration audit (FCA) — In system/software system engineering, the formal examination of functional characteristics from test data for a hardware/software configuration item, prior to acceptance, to verify that the item has achieved the performance specified in its functional or allocated requirements. [U.S. Department of Defense (DoD) usage] [Military Standard 1521B-1985] *See also formal qualification review (FQR).*

functional decomposition — In software engineering, a method of designing a system by breaking it down into its components in such a way that the components correspond directly to system functions and subfunctions. [ANSI/IEEE Standard 729-1983] *See also hierarchical decomposition.*

functional design — In software engineering, the specification of the working relationships among the parts of a software system. *See also preliminary design.*

functional flow — *See functional flow block diagram* (FFBD).

functional flow block diagram (FFBD) — In system engineering, a technique and method for indicating the sequential relationship of all functions that must be accomplished by a system in performing its activities. The resulting documentation consists of blocks that model functions and connecting edges that model the flow of information. Functional decomposition can be applied to the FFBD to obtain a hierarchy of FFBDs. The FFBD does not indicate the exact time involved in the functional occurrence; a separate timeline analysis is necessary for time-oriented events.

functional flow diagram (FFD) — *See functional flow block diagram (FFBD).*

functional model — In software engineering, a requirements model that provides a mapping from input to output. For example, a finite state machine and Petri nets can help identify and describe various features of the software or can demonstrate the intended operation of the system. [ANSI/IEEE Standard 830–1984]

functional primitive — In software engineering (structured analysis methodology), the lowest level component of a dataflow diagram; a process that is not further decomposed to a subsequent level. [DeMarco 1979]

functional requirement — A system/software requirement that specifies a function that a system/software system or system/software component must be capable of performing. These are software requirements that define behavior of the system, that is, the fundamental process or transformation that software and hardware components of the system perform on inputs to produce outputs. *See also functional requirements specification.*

functional requirements model — In software engineering (requirements specifications), a model that provides a mapping from input to output. Functional models, for example, finite state machines, or Petri nets can help identify and define various features of software or can demonstrate the intended operations of the function. [ANSI/IEEE Standard 830–1984]

functional requirements specification — In system/software system engineering, a specification that sets forth the functional requirements for a system/software system or system/software component. *See also functional requirement.*

functional software — *See application software.*

functional specification — In software system engineering (structured analysis methodology), the classical product of analysis; description of a system to be implemented. [DeMarco 1979] *Synonymous with requirements specification, software requirements specification, system requirements specification. Contrast with nonfunctional specification.*

functional testing — In software system engineering (testing), the testing of the external observed functions of the system. Test cases demonstrate the external observed functions of the system. Test cases demonstrate that software functions are operational, that input is properly accepted and output is correctly produced, and that the integrity of external information is maintained. *Synonymous with black-box testing. Contrast with structural testing.*

functionality — In software engineering (requirements analysis), the relative utility of the various computational, user interface, output, and file manager functions provided by the product.

g-g-g

Gane and Sarson technique — *Synonymous with structured analysis (SA), Structured Systems Analysis (SSA).*

Gane, Chris, and Sarson, Trish — Developers of the *Structured Systems Analysis* technique.

generality — In software engineering, a quality metric that can be used to measure those characteristics of software that provide breadth to the functions performed with respect to the application. [RADC TR-85–37 1985]

GFS — Acronym for government-furnished software

goal — In management, a milestone, which, when accomplished, leads to the attainment of an objective with the desired results or capability.

government-furnished software (GFS) — In acquisition management, software that is furnished to the contractor by the government. [DoD Standard 2167A 1988]

graphical editor — In data processing, a software tool or package that allows the user to create, modify, or delete graphical pictures or data.

graphical tool — *See graphical editor.*

guideline — In system/software engineering, well-documented set of standards and definitions that are used to guide an activity or task. Guidelines are usually not rules or procedures but allow for judgment and flexibility.

h-h-h

Halstead's metric — *See Halstead's software science.*

Halstead's software science — One of the best known and most thoroughly studied measures of software complexity. Software science uses a set of primitive measures that may be derived after code is generated or estimated after design is complete. Halstead uses the primitive measures to develop expressions for the overall program length; potential minimum volume for an algorithm; the actual volume (number of bits required to specify a program); the program level (a measure of software complexity); language level (a constant for a given language); and other features, such as development effort, development time, and even the projected number of faults in the software. [Pressman 1987]

hands-on — 1. A colloquial expression for obtaining practical experience. 2. In training, involving the actual operation of a piece of hardware, such as a terminal.

hardware — The mechanical, magnetic, and electron design, structure, and devices of a computer. *See also computer hardware.*

hardware configuration item (HCI) — In system engineering, a hardware entity which has been established as a configuration item. The hardware configuration item exists where functional allocations have been made which clearly delineate the separation between equipment functions and software functions and the hardware has been established as a configuration item. *Contrast with software configuration item (SCI). See also configuration management (CM).*

hardware interface — In software engineering (requirements specification), includes all kinds of interfaces by hardware systems and equipment to the external world even though, for example, the ultimate interface in a communication system may be another piece of software in another computer. Examples of hardware interfacing include the need to maintain precise timing requirements, take precise analog measurements, and exert precise analog control. [STARTS Guide 1987]

hardware-intensive system — A system that contains a significant amount of hardware in relationship to software and manual procedures. *Contrast with software-intensive system. See also system.*

Hatley, Derek J. — Developer of the Hatley realtime structured analysis (RTSA) methodology and coauthor of the book, *Strategies for Realtime System Specifications* (1987). *See also realtime structured analysis (RTSA).*

HCI — Acronym for hardware configuration item.

heuristic — A procedure that often leads to an expected result, but makes no guarantee to do so. Sometime called a "rule of thumb." [DeMarco 1979]

hierarchic — *See hierarchical decomposition.*

hierarchical decomposition - In software system engineering, a method of designing a system by partitioning it into smaller and smaller pieces through a series of top-down refinements beginning with the top-most component. *See also functional decomposition, modular decomposition, stepwise refinement.*

Hierarchical Design Methodology (HDM) — A software engineering methodology developed at SRI International. It is a collection of program development tools which attempt to formalize a notion of "levels of abstraction" and formally define modules. [Abbott and Moorhead 1981]

hierarchy — 1. A type of structure in which each element or block has a level, and each element is associated with one or more elements at the next higher and lower levels. [Flynn and Dorfman 1990] 2. A structure whose components are ranked into levels of subordination according to a specific set of rules. [ANSI/IEEE Standard 729-1983]

high-level design — *Synonymous with architectural design, internal specification, preliminary design, system design, top-level design.*

high-resolution bit-mapped display — A computer output terminal with a high resolution (a large number of pixels per area).

high-risk issue — In system/software system engineering, a problem or expected problem that either has a high probability of occurring or, if it did occur, will have serious impact in terms of cost, schedule, or delivery of the system.

higher order language — A procedural programming language that usually includes features such as nested expressions, user-defined data types, and parameter passing not normally found in lower order languages; that does not reflect the structure of any one given computer or class of computers; and that can be used to write machine-independent source programs. A single higher order language statement may represent multiple machine operations. [ANSI/IEEE Standard 729–1983] *Contrast with assembly language.*

HIPO (Hierarchy plus Input-Process-Output) — A software engineering methodology developed by IBM Corporation in the early 1970s that is a technique for representing the modules of a system as a hierarchy (the "H" part) and for documenting the insides of each module by defining the input, process, and output for each module (the "IPO" part).

HOL — Acronym for high-order language.

human (manual) procedure — In system/software engineering, a set of procedures that have been allocated to be accomplished manually.

human engineering — In system/software system engineering, a multidisciplinary activity that applies the knowledge, derived from psychology and technology, to specify and design high-quality human-machine interfaces. The human-engineering process encompasses the following steps: activity analysis, semantic analysis and design, syntax and lexical design, user environment design, and prototyping.

human language — *See natural language.*

HWCI — Acronym for hardware configuration item.

hybrid knowledge representation — In an artificial intelligence system called Requirements Apprentice, several different kinds of special-purpose reasoning layered on top of a simple general purpose, reasoning system based on predicate calculus. The layers are: frame, types, algebra, equality, and truth maintenance. [Rich et al. 1987]

i-i-i

IBM — Acronym for International Business Machines Corporation.

ICD — Acronym for interface control document.

identification — *See configuration identification.*

IEEE Guide to Software Requirements Specifications — A software engineering standard developed by the IEEE Computer Society, Software Engineering Standards Subcommittee in 1984, Alan M. Davis, Chair of the working group.

implementation — In software engineering: 1. Converting design to code. 2. Installing and testing the final software product. 3. In data process management, the process of installing a computer system.

Implementation Apprentice — In an artificial intelligence system called Programmer's Apprentice, the Implementation Apprentice allows a programmer to construct a program rapidly and reliability by combining algorithmic fragments stored in a library. [Rich et al. 1987]

implementation language — In software engineering, the computer language used to implement the software design.

implementation model — In software engineering, a real-world software design model subject to real-world limitations. [Ward 1986]

implementation phase — The software development lifecycle phase during which the detailed design is converted into a language that is executable by a computer. The implementation phase can also include unit testing. *Synonymous with coding phase. See also software development lifecycle phase.*

implicit requirement — In software engineering, a requirement that is implied. Implicit requirements require the designer to "know" what the customer wants as well as how to design it. [ANSI/IEEE Standard 830–1984] *Contrast with explicit requirement.*

inappropriateness — In software engineering (requirements analysis), the difference between the user's needs and its solutions. [Davis et al. 1988]

incompleteness — In software engineering (requirements), specifications in which many of the aspects of the requirements are left out. The reader has to fill in these gaps by using his or her own knowledge or by asking questions. [Rich et al. 1987]

incremental development — A software development strategy that involves the process of constructing a partial implementation of a total system by slowly adding increased functionality or performance. The initial system is developed through all the system lifecycle stages, from analysis to implementation. This approach reduces the cost incurred before an initial capability is achieved. It also produces an operational system more quickly and thus reduces the possibility that the user's needs will change during the development process.

incremental testing — In system/software engineering, testing a system or program by parts or sections.

independence — In software engineering, a quality metric that can be used to measure those characteristics of software that determine its nondependency on the software environment (computing system, operating system, utilities, input/output routines, and libraries). [RADC TR-85–37 1985]

independent audit — In software engineering, an independent review of a software project by an outside agency or team that is separate from the organization responsible for the project, for the purpose of assessing compliance with software requirements, specifications, baselines, standards, procedures, instructions, codes, and contractual and licensing requirements. *See also audit, review.*

independent verification and validation (IV&V) — In software system engineering, verification and validation of a software product by an organization that is both technically and managerially separate from the organization responsible for developing the product. The degree of independence must be a function of the importance of the software. [ANSI/IEEE Standard 729–1983] *See also validation, verification and validation, verification.*

industrial software development methodology — In software engineering, those software development methodologies that are currently in use within large-scale industrial settings.

inference — In artificial intelligence: 1. A means of drawing conclusions that follow logically from the given premise. 2. A way to determine whether one formula is implied by another. [Burris 1986]

informal review — In software engineering, a review of an existing or proposed software product and document, typically by the originators' peers, for the purpose of detecting and correcting product and documentation errors. *Contrast with formal review. See also walkthrough, inspection.*

informal specification — *See informal system specification.*

informal system specification — In software engineering (requirements), a term sometimes used to describe a specification that uses natural language to describe system requirements. Note: Informal specifications are easier to read and understand, whereas formal specifications tend to be clearer, precise, unambiguous, and so forth. Whenever there is any doubt about informal specifications, the formal specification should be used to resolve the doubt.

information hiding — A software development technique in which each module's interface reveals as little as possible about the module's inner workings, and other modules are forbidden to use information about the module that is not in the module's interface specification.

information sink — Net receiver of information.

information storage and retrieval — In data processing, the use of a computer system for storing large amounts of related data, items of which can be quickly and easily retrieved and viewed.

information technology — *Synonymous with management information system (MIS)* [British usage].

initial operating capability (IOC) — In acquisition management, the capability of the system when it is first put into service. *Contrast with final operating capability.*

input/output — In data processing, designating the process of entering data into the computer system and receiving the resulting data on a terminal, printer, or other output device.

input/output perspective — *Synonymous with requirements specification.* [Davis 1990]

inspection — In software engineering: 1. A semiformal to formal evaluation technique in which software requirements, design, or code are examined in detail by a person or group other than the originator to detect faults, violations of development standards, and other problems. The review members are peers (equals) of the designer or programmer. Traditional error data is collected during inspections for later analysis and to assist in future inspections. *Sometimes called a walkthrough or peer review. See also inspection moderator, walkthrough.* 2. A phase of quality control that by means of examination, observation, or measurement determines the conformance of materials, supplies, components, parts, systems, processes, or structures to predetermine quality requirements. [ANSI N45.2.10–1973]

inspection leader — *See inspection moderator.*

inspection moderator — In software engineering (inspection), the individual who is trained in the inspection process and who is assigned to monitor the inspection. The moderator ensures that the participants are properly prepared and that the inspection is efficiently and thoroughly conducted. The moderator schedules the inspection, distributes the material being inspected, facilitates the inspection process, and ensures that the errors in the material are recorded and corrected. The moderator is responsible for recording inspection data, making sure that the actions resulting from the inspection are completed, and for conducting reinspections where appropriate. The moderator should not be the producer of the inspected item or the producer's supervisor.

inspection system — In software system engineering, a set of policies, procedures, and methods for performing inspections. *See also inspection.*

instruction (statement) reuse — *See reusability.*

instructor — In the Structured Analysis and Design Technique (SADT™) methodology (personnel roles), a person fluent in SADT, who trains authors and commenters who are using SADT for the first time. [Ross and Schoman 1977] *See also SADT™, SADT™ personnel roles.*

instrumentation — In software engineering (testing), the insertion of additional code into the program to collect information about program behavior during program execution. [FIPS Publication 101 1983]

integrated project support environment (IPSE) — In software engineering, an integrated set of software tools to give automated support to a significant part of the lifecycle of software development project. The purpose of the IPSE is to: (1) support all sizes of projects up to, and including, large projects using large teams and developing large, complex, high quality software, (2) provide controls and facilities to allow projects to be carried out with optimum productivity and quality, (3) integrate all information so that it can be freely exchanged within the project, and (4) provide all users with an appropriate and tailored set of facilities with which to carry out their tasks [British usage]. [STARTS Guide 1987] *See software engineering environment.*

integration and test phase — The software development lifecycle phase that takes the computer code generated during the coding phase, integrates it into the environment, and tests it by using real or simulated input. The output is then analyzed to determine whether the program performed as specified. *See also software development lifecycle phase.*

integration testing — 1. In system engineering, an orderly progression of testing in which software elements or hardware elements or both are combined and tested until the entire system has been integrated. 2. In software system engineering, activity that interconnects sets of previous tested modules to ensure that the sets behave as well as their independently tested module components did. *See also system testing.*

integrity — In software engineering, a quality metric that can be used to measure the extent to which the software will perform without failures caused by unauthorized access to the code or data within a specified time period. [RADC TR-85–37 1985] *See also security.*

interactive system — A computer-based system in which the user gets immediate response to his or her actions or queries.

interface — In system engineering: 1. A shared boundary. An interface might be a hardware component to link two devices or it might be a portion of storage or registers accessed by two or more computer programs. 2. To interact or communicate with another system component or organizational entity.

interface analysis — In system engineering, an approach to identifying and representing functional and physical interfaces between the system and external entities or constraints or between components within the system.

interface constraint — In software system engineering (requirements), *synonymous with external specification.*

interface control document (ICD) — 1. In system/software system engineering, a document that describes the relationship between two components in the system hierarchy. The relationships are usually defined as requirements. 2. In system engineering, that documentation used to define all interface requirements between hardware/software development contractors. 3. A bilateral technical and administrative agreement between affected agencies and contractors. *See also documentation.*

interface control document — *See ICD.*

interface definition chart — A system/software system engineering requirements tool used to display the external and internal system interface. This is the primary tool used to define the functional interfaces and operational relational relationships of the system. The interface definition chart answers the "where" question of system definition. [Lano 1990]

interface requirement — *See external interface requirement.*

interface specification — *See Interface control document.*

internal consistency — In software system engineering (verification and validation techniques), ensuring that items within the same specifications do not conflict with each other. [Boehm, *V&V Software Requirements* 1984]

internal interface — In system/software system engineering, links between the various subunits of the system.

internal specification — *Synonymous with design specification. Contrast with external specification.*

internal system behavior (design) — *See design. Contrast with external system behavior (requirements).*

International Organization for Standards (ISO) — An international standards organization founded in 1947 and headquartered in Geneva, Switzerland. It consists of over 60 countries plus over 20 correspondents, that are countries which do not belong primarily to the standards group but are interested in the results. In 1985, 153 technical committees, 600 subcommittees, and 1150 working groups were under ISO. ANSI is the U.S. member.

International Standards Organization — *See International Organization for Standards (ISO).*

interoperability — In software engineering, a quality metric that can be used to measure: 1. The relative effort to couple the software of one system to the software of another system. [RADC TR-85–37 1985] 2. The ability of two or more systems to exchange information and to mutually use the information that has been exchanged. [ANSI/IEEE Standard 729–1983] *See also compatibility.*

interview — 1. In management (staffing), to evaluate or question a job applicant. 2. In software engineering (verification and validation), a technique which involves discussing a specification with its originator to identify potential problems. Interviews are particularly good for indentifying potential blind spot, misunderstandings, and high-risk issues. [Boehm, *V&V Software Requirements* 1984] *See also verification and validation technique.*

invalid input — In software engineering (testing), test data that lies outside the domain of the program's function. [FIPS Publication 101 1983]

investigative audit — *See audit.*

IOC — Acronym for initial operational capability.

IPSE — Acronym for integrated project support environment.

IRS — Acronym for interface requirements specification.

ISA — Acronym for instruction set architecture.

ISDOS (Information System Design Operation System) — 1. A research project, initiated in 1968 at the University of Michigan under the direction of Dr. Daniel Teichroew, that developed the PSL/PSA system. 2. *Sometimes synonymous with PSL/PSA.*

ISO — Acronym for International Organization for Standards.

iteration — 1. In software engineering, the repeating of a prior step or process as more information become available. In other words, process "n" can be iterated with process "n-1" in which each process "n-1" is reaccomplished in part or whole based on information that was determined during process "n." 2. In programming, the process of repeatedly executing a given sequence of programming language statements until a given condition is met or while a given condition is true. [ANSI/IEEE Standard 729–1983] *See also software development lifecycle phase, software lifecycle phase.*

iterative — *See iteration.*

IV&V — Acronym for independent verification and validation

j-j-j

Jackson Structured Design (JSD) Method — A structured software analysis methodology for the analysis and design of both data processing and realtime systems developed by Michael Jackson Systems Limited. [STARTS Guide 1987]

Jackson System Design (JSD) — *See Jackson Structured Design (JSD) Method.*

k-k-k

Kepner and Tregoe (K-T) analysis technique — A decision analysis technique for objectively choosing between several alternatives. When this technique is used to select the "best" solution, the various possible required characteristics of the final selected solution are separated into a "must" part and a "want" part. Any solution that does not meet every "must" characteristic is eliminated. Each of the "want" characteristics is then scored according to what requirements are met by each alternative solution. These scores are then weighted according to the value given to the characteristic. The alternative solutions are then evaluated, and the best solution is picked. Typically the solution with the highest "want" score is selected. [Sailor 1990]

kitchen sink — A software engineering analysis strategy of throwing everything into a system definition.

knowledge acquisition — In artificial intelligence: 1. Learning new symbolic information coupled with the ability to apply that information in an effective manner. 2. The procedure of extracting knowledge from an expert and encoding it in program form. [Burris 1986]

knowledge representation — In artificial intelligence, the symbolic descriptions that characterize the definition and empirical relationships in a domain.

knowledge structure — In system/software engineering (requirements), a structured collection of concepts and their interrelationship.

l-l-l

language — A systematic means of communicating ideas by the use of conventionalized signs, sounds, gestures, or marks as well as rules for the formation of admissible expressions. [ANSI/IEEE Standard 729–1983] *See also artificial language, computer language, natural language.*

large-scale software development process — *Synonymous with software engineering.*

lateness — In software engineering, a metric that can be used to measure the timelapse between the appearance of the new requirement and its satisfaction. [Davis et al. 1988]

layered requirement — In software engineering (requirements), a drawing or graphical illustration that shows the hierarchy of requirements.

LBMS System Development Methodology — *See LSDM.*

level — In software engineering (requirements), a numerical value that represents the relative location of a requirement in a hierarchical structure. [Flynn and Dorfman 1990]

level of effort — In system acquisition, a contract type in which the developer is to provide a specified number of qualified personnel over a specified period of time to work under the direction of the contracting agency.

leveling — In software engineering (structured analysis methodology), leveling is the decomposition of dataflow diagrams into increasingly detailed diagrams. *See also dataflow diagram (DFD), partitioning.*

leverage — *Sometimes used in place of reusability.*

life cycle — Alternative spelling of lifecycle.

life-cycle — Alternative spelling of lifecycle.

lifecycle — All the steps or phases an item passes through during its useful life. *See also software development lifecycle, software lifecycle, system development lifecycle.*

lifecycle constraint — In software system engineering (requirements), a nonfunctional requirement that pertains to quality of the design that limits the development, maintenance, and enhancement process. [Roman 1985]

lifecycle development model — A model or representation of a software development lifecycle. *See software development lifecycle.*

lifecycle model — A model or representation of a software lifecycle. *See software lifecycle.*

lifecycle phase — A phase of a lifecycle model.

lifecycle requirement — In system/software system engineering, the required activities, tasks, and deliverables for each phase of the lifecycle model.

lifecycle review — *See milestone review.*

LISP — 1. An abbreviation for list processing. 2. An application-oriented language used for list processing. *See also application software.*

Lockheed — Short title for one of the many Lockheed companies, for example, Lockheed Missiles & Space Company, Inc., a large aerospace defense contractor.

Logical Construction of Programs — *Synonymous with Warnier diagram.*

logical data structure — A Structured System Analysis and Design Methodology (SSADM) tool that provides a way of presenting the relationship between data elements in the system. It is eventually expanded into a complete, composite logical data design and structure, data fields, access paths, and volumetric information, which drives the detailed physical database design. [Williams 1987]

logistics — In the system lifecycle, the activity and function of supporting operational systems (systems in use) through the warehousing and furnishing of replacement parts, transportation of people and equipment, establishment and training of maintenance personnel, correcting operational revealed deficiencies, periodic overhaul, and so forth.

longevity — In software engineering (requirements analysis), it is the period of time a system solution remains viable. [Davis et al. 1988]

low-level design — *See detailed design.*

low-level detail — In software engineering (requirements and design), the detail that is provided at the low-level description of the system.

low-level requirement — In software engineering (requirements), a requirement that is in the hierarchy below top-level or below the level of some given requirement.

LSDM (LBMS System Development Methodology) — A software requirements analysis tool developed by Learmonth and Burchett Management Systems (LBMS). It resembles structured analysis in many ways but has some additional extensions. [STARTS Guide 1987]

m-m-m

machine language — In computer science: 1. A stage of computer language development. 2. The instructions (software) that are directly executable by a computer. *Contrast with assembly language, higher order language, very high-level language.*

maintainability — In software engineering, a quality metric that can be used to measure the ease of effort of locating and fixing a software failure within a specified time period. [RADC TR-85–37 1985]

maintenance — *See software maintenance.*

maintenance and enhancement phase — *See operation and maintenance phase.*

maintenance manual — *See software maintenance documentation.*

maintenance phase — *See operation and maintenance phase.*

maintenance project — A software development project described as maintenance to correct errors in the original requirements specification.

man-machine function — *See man-machine interface (MMI).*

man-machine interface (MMI) — In software systems, the shared boundary between the human operator of the system (man) and the software system (machine). Examples of man-machine interfaces that support and enhance human capabilities are user dialogs, graphics, stream formats, and interactive devices.

management — All activities and tasks undertaken by one or more persons to plan and control the activities of others to achieve an objective or complete an activity that could not be achieved by the others acting independently.

management document — A document that is prepared as a result of a management activity, for example, a software project management plan.

management information system (MIS) — The use of computers and computer software specifically to aid in the management of personnel. An automated system designed to provide management with the information required to make basic decisions. [IEEE *Computer Applications Technology Glossary* 1986]

management lifecycle — In project management, all the management actions that take place from the initiation of a project until its completion. This includes determining project goals, planning the project, allocating and leading personnel, defining workpackages, and monitoring progress against plans. [Manley 1990]

management metric — In software system engineering, an indicator that can be used to measure management activities such as budgets spent, value earned, costs overrun, and schedule slippages.

management review — In system/software system engineering, a formal meeting at which the monetary expenditures and schedule are presented to the user, customer, or other interested parties for comment and approval. The monetary expenditures are compared with the budget, and differences between the budget estimates and actual project expenditures are explained. The completion dates are compared with the master schedule, and differences between the scheduled completion dates and actual completion dates are explained.

mandatory requirement — In software engineering (requirements specifications), a degree of necessity that implies that the software will not be acceptable unless these requirements were provided in an agreed manner. [ANSI/IEEE Standard 830–1984]

manual cross-referencing — In software engineering (verification and validation techniques), cross-referencing involves constructing cross-reference tables and various diagrams—for example, state transition, dataflow, and flow and data structure diagrams—to clarify interaction among specified entities. These entities include functions, database, and interfacing hardware, software, or personnel. [Boehm, *V&V Software Requirements* 1984] *See also verification and validation technique.*

manual model — In software engineering (verification and validation techniques), mathematical descriptions of the system that can be used to represent and analyze certain aspects of the system being specified. Manual models are good for analyzing some lifecycle feasibility issues, particularly accuracy, realtime performance, and lifecycle cause. They are also useful for risk analysis. [Boehm, *V&V Software Requirements* 1984] *See also verification and validation technique.*

manual technique (detailed) — In software engineering (verification and validation techniques), detailed manual techniques involve detailed scenarios and mathematical proofs, which are effective for clarifying human engineering aids and for verifying finite mathematics programs. [Boehm, *V&V Software Requirements* 1984] *See also verification and validation technique.*

manual technique (simple) — In software engineering (verification and validation techniques), those techniques that do not involve automation but are easily applied and implemented, such as reading, cross-referencing, interviews, checklists, and models. [Boehm, *V&V Software Requirements* 1984] *See also verification and validation technique.*

market factor — In software engineering tools, nontechnical aspects that will influence the decision to adopt a methodology or tool, including implementation, availability, history, and pricing information. [Grabow and Noble 1985]

master project database (MPDB) repository — *See project database.*

mathematical (logical) foundation — In software engineering, a quality metric that can be used to measure the extent to which the syntax has a sound mathematical model. It is distinct from the precision of the definition of the syntax itself. [STARTS Guide 1987]

mathematical formal specification technique — *See formal specification technique.*

mathematical model — In software engineering, a model of some aspect of a software system using mathematical notations (for example, predicate calculus) to describe system variables and their relationships. *See also mathematical requirements model.*

mathematical notation — In software requirements analysis, notations based on predicate calculus. These express the functionality of a module in terms of preconditions and postconditions. Provided that the precondition is true when the module is entered, requirements are that the module terminate and that the postcondition be true on exit. These conditions are expressed in terms of predicate calculus. [STARTS Guide 1987]

mathematical proof — In software engineering (verification and validation techniques), mathematical transformation rules can be applied to a set of statements, expressed in a precise mathematical specification language, to provide desired properties of the set of statements. These properties include internal consistencies, preservation of "invariant" relationships, and equivalence of two alternative sets of statements (e.g., requirements and desired specifications). Automated aids to formal specifications and verifications such as Special/HDM, Gypsy, Affirm, and Ina Jo are now available. [Boehm, *V&V Software Requirements* 1984] *See also verification and validation technique.*

mathematical requirements model — In software engineering (requirements specifications), a model that uses mathematical relationships to describe the software's behavior. Mathematical models are especially useful for particular application areas, including navigation, linear programming, econometrics, signal processing, and weather analysis. [ANSI/IEEE Standard 830–1984]

mathematical specification language — A software requirements specification language that has semantics based in a proof system. Proofs are used to discover inconsistencies and derived consequences of the specification. Consequences are helpful for validation and checking completeness. [Zave 1984] *See also formal language, proof of correctness.*

McCabe's metric — In software engineering, a metric that can be used to measure the complexity of the program under study.

measurable — A software requirements specification is measurable when some finite process exists to verify that the product meets the requirements.

measurement standard — *See standard.*

Mellor — *See Ward, Paul T. and Mellor, Stephen J.*

MENS — Acronym for mission element need statement. [U.S. Department of Defense (DoD) usage]

menu — In an interactive software system, a list of system commands organized in a hierarchical or tree form. The menu system allow the user to traverse the tree to any level to find the appropriate system command for activation. Menu driven systems are considered to be user friendly.

message — A part of the Software Requirements Engineering Methodology (SREM), message is the name given to the incoming and outgoing data on the requirements net (R-net). [Scheffer and Stone 1985] [Alford 1985] [TRW SS-80–03 1980] *See also R-net, SREM.*

method — In engineering, a detailed approach to solving an engineering problem.

methodology — In engineering, a general approach to solving an engineering problem. *See also software requirements engineering methodology.*

methodology power — In software engineering, a measure of the support that methodology provides is derived by rating its individual capabilities and techniques. It is composed of: (1) formality of notation, (2) complexity of specification produced, (3) rigor of mathematical foundation, and (4) degree of automated support. [Davis and Addleman 1986]

metric — The theory or a system of measurements. *See also software quality metric.*

metric tailoring — In system/software engineering, a means of ensuring that the metric framework meets the characteristics of the project. [Keller et al. 1990]

metrics-guided design — In software engineering (design), the design metric gives the data on which to base a design decision. Design metrics can suggest strategies for testing the design. [Ramamoorthy et al. 1984]

milestone — In project management, a scheduled event that is used to measure progress. Examples of major milestones include the issuance of a specification, completion of system integration, product delivery, and customer or managerial signoff. Minor milestones (called "inch pebbles") might include baselining a software module or completing a chapter of the users' manual. A manager or an individual project member is identified and held accountable for achieving the milestone on time and within budget.

milestone document — A project management document that describes and documents some part of a software development lifecycle. The completion of the document signals the completion of the milestone. For example, the completion of the software requirements specification (SRS) signals the completion of the software requirements analysis phase. *See also milestone, milestone review.*

milestone review — In software engineering: 1. A project management review that is conducted at the completion of each of the hardware/software development lifecycle phases (a milestone)—requirements phase, preliminary design, detailed design phase, implementation phase, test phase, and sometimes installation and checkout phase. For example, a preliminary design review (PDR) is held at the completion of the preliminary design phase. 2. A formal review of the management and technical progress of a hardware/software development project. *See also physical configuration audit (PCA), preliminary design review (PDR), software specification review (SSR), system design review (SDR), system requirements review (SRR), test readiness review (TRR). See also review.*

Mills, Harlan D. — Mathematician and an IBM fellow (retired). Mills was the project manager of the first chief programmer team (New York Times Morgue Project, 1972) which used structured programming.

mini-spec — *Synonymous with process, P-spec.*

mini-spiral — In the spiral process model (by Boehm), a small spiral process initiated to address and resolve the special issues of keeping requirements in synchronization with each other. [Boehm, *Spiral Model* 1988] *See also spiral model.*

Ministry of Defence — The British equivalent of U.S. Department of Defense.

MIS — Acronym for management information system.

missing function — In software engineering, functions that should be part of the software product, but are not called for in the software requirements specifications. [Boehm, *V&V Software Requirements* 1984]

missing product — In system/software engineering, products that should be part of the delivered software, but are not called for in the software requirements specification. [Boehm, *V&V Software Requirements* 1984]

missing specification item — In software engineering, items that should be present as part of a software requirements specification, but are not present. [Boehm, *V&V Software Requirements* 1984] *See missing function, missing product.*

mission — The goals or objectives of an organization or activity. A statement describing the well-defined current businesses of the organization; or alternatively, a visionary statement of what businesses the organization would like to be in, that is, the organization's fundamental reasons for existence. [Manley 1990] Commonly used by the U.S. Department of Defense (DoD).

mission needs statement — *See user needs statement.* [U.S. Department of Defense (DoD) usage]

mission objective — *See mission.*

mission requirement — *See software requirement, system requirement.*

mission statement — *See mission.*

mission timeline — *See timeline, timeline analysis.* [U.S. Department of Defense (DoD) usage]

MM — Acronym for maintenance manual.

MMI — Acronym for man-machine interface.

mockup — In system/software system engineering, a prototype that is developed to simulate the system's response to user actions. This is in contrast to prototypes that actually perform the operation requested by the user. [Dorfman 1990] *See also prototyping.*

model — A representation of an artifact or activity intended to explain the behavior of some aspects of it. The model is less complex or complete than the activity or artifact modeled. A model is considered to be an abstraction of reality. *See also analog model, behavior model, conceptual model, decision model, descriptive model, mathematical model, normative (decision) model, physical model, schematic model.*

moderator — In software engineering (inspection), the participant at a software inspection who focuses the team on defining the defect. *See also inspection.*

modern programming practices (MPP) — *Synonymous with software development methodology.*

modifiable — A software requirements specification is modifiable if the structure and style are such that any necessary changes to the requirements can be made easily, completely, and consistently.

modular — A software system that is modular in design. *See also modular decomposition, modularity, module.*

modular decomposition — A method of designing a software system by breaking it down into modules. [ANSI/IEEE Standard 729–1983] *See also hierarchical decomposition.*

modularity — In software engineering, a quality metric that can be used to measure: 1. Those characteristics of the software which provide a structure of highly cohesive modules with optimum coupling. [RADC TR-85–37 1985] 2. The extent to which software is composed of discrete components such that a change to one component has minimal impact on other components. [ANSI/IEEE Standard 729–1983]

module — In software engineering (design): 1. A program unit that is discrete and identifiable with respect to compiling, combining with other units, and loading; for example, the input to, or output from, an assembler, compiler, linkage editor, or executive routine. 2. A logically separable part of a program. [ANSI/IEEE Standard 729–1983] *Sometimes synonymous with unit.*

module design — *See detailed design.*

monitor — In the Structured Analysis and Design Technique (SADT™) methodology (personnel roles), a person fluent in SADT who assists and advises project personnel in the use and application of SADT. [Ross and Schoman 1977] *Synonymous with chief analyst. See also SADT™, SADT™ personnel roles.*

mouse — A small, hand-held, computer hardware device that is shaped like a stylized mouse with a ball (body), two or three activation buttons (eyes), and connecting cable (tail). The mouse can be moved over the surface of a tablet, causing the cursor to move to a corresponding point in the screen of a monitor (cathode-ray tube). The mouse is used for plotting coordinates in computer graphics or entering commands. Commands can be entered by pointing the mouse at an icon of the command and activating the command by pushing a button.

mouse button — A device located on a mouse that, when pushed, will cause the computer to take action. *See also mouse.*

MPDB — Acronym for master project database (repository).

multilevel menu system — In software engineering (design), a hierarchy of menus.

multitasking — In data processing, refers to procedures in which several separate but interrelated tasks operate under a single program identity.

n-n-n

N² Chart — A system/software system engineering tool and methodology for the tabulation, definition, analysis, and description of functional interactions and interfaces. The N² chart is a fixed-format structure that graphically displays the total bidirectional interrelationships between the individual functions and/or components in a given system or structure. The chart gets its name from the fact that for N functions there are N² intersections or squares on the diagram, each of which may contain a function or function interface. [Lano 1977]

National Aeronautics and Space Administration (NASA) — A U.S. government agency responsible for space exploration and Aeronautical Research.

National Bureau of Standards (NBS) — *See the National Institute of Standards and Technology (NIST).*

National Computing Centre (NCC) — A consortium of British software development corporations that have banded together to improve their software development and to give the United Kingdom (U.K.) an advantage in international competition. NCC directs technical programs, administers national schemes, and develops product services to promote the most effective use of information technology. [STARTS Guide 1987]

National Institute of Standards and Technology (NIST) — A U.S. government organization responsible for providing leadership, technical guidance, and coordination of government effort in the development of technical guidelines and standards in the areas of computers and automatic data processing systems. Note: the National Institute of Standards and Technology (NIST) was formerly called the National Bureau of Standards.

natural language — A language spoken by people, as opposed to a formal language or a language used by computers. *See also artificial language, computer language, formal language, fourth-generation language (4GL).*

nonambiguous — A software requirements specification is nonambiguous only if each requirement stated therein has only one interpretation.

nondeterministic requirement specification — A system/software requirements specification in which the result of the operation does not have to be determined by the output. The properties of the operators are first defined; this definition, in turn, determines the conditions that any output must satisfy. There may be many possible results that will satisfy the given conditions. [Hayes 1986]

nonexistent specification — In software engineering, a reference in the software requirements specification to functions, inputs, or outputs (including databases) not defined in the system specifications.

nonfunctional requirement — In software system engineering, a software requirement that describes not what the software will do, but how the software will do it, for example, software performance requirements, software external interface requirements, software design constraints, and software quality attributes. Nonfunctional requirements are difficult to test; therefore, they are usually evaluated subjectively. *Contrast with functional requirement.*

nonfunctional software — *See system software.*

nonfunctional specification — *See nonfunctional requirement.*

nonphase dependent tool — A software tool that is applicable across all phases of the software development lifecycle, for example, a man-hour tracking tool, a documentation preparation tool, a configuration management tool. *Contrast with a phase-dependent tool.*

nonprocedural language — In computer science, a computer language that instructs the computer by specifying the desired results, rather than the action that is needed to achieve these desired results. An example is a database system used in a relational queries language or a special purpose system. [Cobb 1985]

nonredundant — In system/software system engineering, a piece of information that is reported only once in a software requirements specification. This nonredundancy ensures consistency and easy updating, but does not ensure correctness. [Page-Jones 1988]

normative (decision) model — A model that describes how things ought to be and implies the establishment of standards of correctness or prescription of rules. [Miller and Starr 1969] *Contrast with descriptive model.*

notation — In software engineering, a physical, graphical, or textual means of describing a software requirement design or code [British usage].

O-O-O

object-oriented analysis — In software engineering (requirements), the application of an object-oriented method to software requirements analysis. *Contrast with functional analysis, functional requirement, structured analysis (SA). See also object-oriented design, object-oriented method.*

object-oriented design — In software engineering (design), the application of an object-oriented method to software design. *Contrast with structured design. See also object-oriented analysis, object-oriented method.*

object-oriented method — A software engineering methodology in which the system is viewed as a collection of objects, attributes of the objects, and operations on the objects, with messages passed from object to object. *Contrast with functional analysis, functional requirement, structured analysis (SA), structured design. See also object-oriented analysis, object-oriented design.*

OCD — Acronym for Operational Concept Document.

OCF — Acronym for Operational Concept Formulation.

OM — Acronym for operator's manual.

open architecture — In computer-aided software engineering (CASE) tools, a technique in which interfaces to the tools and their associated files are visible and accessible. [Wasserman and Pircher 1987]

operability — In software engineering, a quality metric that can be used to measure those operational characteristics of the software that provide useful inputs and outputs that can be assimilated. [RADC TR-85–37 1985]

operation and maintenance phase — The software lifecycle phase during which a software product is employed in its operational environment, monitored for satisfactory performance and modified as necessary to correct problems or to respond to changing requirements. [ANSI/IEEE Standard 729–1983] Note: this phase is not a software development lifecycle phase. *See also software lifecycle phase.*

operation phase — *See operation and maintenance phase.*

operational concept document (OCD) — In system/software system engineering, a document normally produced as the first step in the system-definition phase of a given program. The purpose of the OCD is to describe the overall design system characteristics and operational viewpoint. The document is used to coordinate overall nonquantitative system goals for the users, buyers, contractors, and other system-interfacing organizations (e.g., training, facilities, staffing, interfacing, and maintenance elements). The OCD forms the basis for long-range operational planning activities and provides guidance for the development of the subsequent system-definition documents (i.e., functional system specifications, employment plans, long-term budgeting, interface control drawings, etc.). The OCD must satisfy the needs of four types of audiences: users, buyers, builders, and interfacing organizations. [Lano 1990] *See also concept of operations (CONOPS) document.*

operational concept formulation — In system/software system engineering, an activity defining the general system goals, missions, functions, and components and documented in the Operational Concept Document (OCD or CONOPS). This document forms a basis for all subsequent system design, planning, coordination, analysis, definition, and development activities. The effectiveness of the operational concept formulation activity heavily influences the quality of the result of the system performance, schedule, and overall usability parameters. [Lano 1990] *See also operational concept document (OCD).*

operational requirements analysis — In system/software system engineering, the identification of elements and subelements of the operational command mission. This analysis shows which parts of the mission the system intends to support, translates those into system functions, and identifies performance requirements associated with the functions. Requirements refer here to functional and performance characteristics of the projected system, as distinguished from needs that are directed to the command mission. [U.S. Department of Defense (DoD) usage]

operational specification language — A software requirements specification language that has semantics defined in terms of an execution model. The model can be reasoned about, checked for consistency, and validated either by static analysis based on the execution model or by execution. [Zave 1984] *See also formal language, executable language.*

operations planning group — In system engineering, the designated group that prepares the sequence of activities that define how the system will function when it is developed and becomes operational. [Sailor 1990]

operator's manual — A software engineering project deliverable document used by the operators of the system (in contrast to the users) to enable them to support the users and the system. On many systems, particularly modern desktop computers, the operator and the user are the same individual. Under these circumstances the operator's and users' manuals are combined. *Contrast with maintenance manual, users' manual.*

optional requirement — In software engineering (requirements specifications), a degree of necessity that implies a class of function that may or not be worthwhile or necessary. The optional requirement gives its developer the opportunity to propose something that exceeds the software requirements specifications. *Contrast with desirable requirement, essential requirement. See also requirement, software requirement.*

organise — British spelling of organize.

Orr technique — *See Data Structured System Development (DSSD).*

p-p-p

PA — Acronym for Programmer's Apprentice.

PAISLey — 1. A software requirements tool developed by Pamela Zave while at the University of Maryland and later AT&T Bell Laboratories. PAISLey is a language for the requirements specifications of embedded systems using an operational approach. Operational means that the resulting specifications can be executed (or interpreted), and the resulting behavior would mimic the behavior required of the system to be built. 2. Acronym for Process oriented, Applicative Interpretable Specification Language. [Davis, *Comparison of Techniques* 1988]

paradigm — *See software development paradigm.*

Part I specification — A hardware/software requirements specification. [U.S. Department of Defense (DoD) usage] *Synonymous with B-level specification. See also software requirements specification.*

Part II specification — A (detailed) hardware/software design specification. [U.S. Department of Defense (DoD) usage] *Synonymous with C-level specification. See also detailed design specification.*

partitioning — 1. The separation of the whole into its parts. 2. In software engineering, the separation or decomposing of a top-level requirement or design into successively low-level detailed requirements or design. 3. In software engineering, the separation (decomposition) of a system into its logical or physical parts. *Synonymous with decomposition.* 4. A software system engineering concept, used when it is difficult or impossible to describe a problem or a solution any way except in terms of its parts. For example, to understand the problem of defending a nation against ballistic missiles, the parts of the system might be target detection, communication, intelligence gathering and resolution, defense weapon launch, and defense weapon guidance. [Davis 1990]

Pascal — A programming language, named for Blaise Pascal (French mathematician, 1623–1662), designed to support the concepts of software engineering. Pascal is easy to learn and is frequently used as the first programming language taught in school.

path testing — In software engineering (unit testing), a test method satisfying the coverage criteria that each logical path through the program be tested. Often paths through the program are grouped into a finite set of classes; one path from each class is then tested. [FIPS Publication 101 1983]

PCA — Acronym for physical configuration audit.

PcARTS — A subset of the capabilities of the Automated Requirements Traceability System (ARTS) system that runs on a personal computer (PC).

PDL — Acronym for Program Design Language.

PDR — Acronym for preliminary design review.

peer review — In software engineering, *synonymous with walkthrough, inspection.*

perfective maintenance — In software maintenance, includes all changes, insertions, deletions, modifications, extensions, and enhancements that are made to a system to meet the evolving or expanding needs of the user. [NBS Special Publication 500–106 1983]

performance — 1. The ability of a computer system or subsystem to perform its functions. 2. In software engineering, a measure of the ability of a computer system or subsystem to perform its functions; for example, response time, throughput, and number of transactions. [ANSI/IEEE Standard 729–1983] *See also performance requirement.*

performance constraint — In software system engineering (requirements), *synonymous with performance requirement.* [Roman 1985]

performance requirement — A system/software system requirement specifying a performance characteristic that a system/software system or system/software component must possess; for example, speed, accuracy, and frequency.

performance requirements specification — A specification that sets forth the performance requirements for a system/software or system/software component. [ANSI/IEEE Standard 729–1983] *See also functional requirements specification, software requirements specification (SRS).*

performance risk — *See risk.*

performance specification — *See performance requirements specification.*

performance standard — In software engineering, a standard that specifies the quality, quantity, cost, and time to complete a product or activity.

personnel — In management, persons employed in any work, enterprise, service, or establishment.

Petri net — 1. An abstract, formal model of information flow, showing static and dynamic properties of a system. A Petri net is usually represented as a graph having two types of nodes (called places and transitions) connected by arcs, and markings (called tokens) indicating dynamic properties. [ANSI/IEEE Standard 729–1983] 2. A network of related functions in a business operation, in which people are portrayed as nodes, and documents as connections between nodes. [DeMarco 1979] 3. An abstract structured machine with a well-defined behavior that was introduced in 1962 by Petri and later described by Peterson. This machine is used to specify process symmetry during the design phase of time critical applications. 4. A software engineering methodology used to analyze and represent realtime applications.

phase — 1. The stage of development in a product or activity. 2. In software system engineering, one of the stages of the lifecycle model. *See also software development lifecycle phase, software lifecycle phase.*

phase-dependent tool — A software tool that is applicable across one phase (or several phases but less than all phases) of the software development lifecycle, for example, a software cost-estimation tool, a structured analysis and design tool, and a test case generator. *Contrast with nonphase dependent tool.*

physical configuration audit (PCA) — The formal examination of the configuration of a hardware/software configuration item against its technical documentation to establish the product or operational baseline. [Military Standard 1521B-1985] [U.S. Department of Defense (DoD) usage]

physical model — A type of model that uses visual representation, either an enlargement, reduction, or duplicate made to the same scale. *See also model.*

pixel — In computer hardware, a contraction of the term "picture element." Any of the tiny elements that form a digitized picture as on a cathode ray tube (CRT) screen; each represents the degree of brightness and color assigned to that point in the picture.

PM — Acronym for project management, project manager.

PMD — Acronym for program management directive.

PO — Acronym for program office.

point design — In system engineering, the selection of one design that satisfies the requirements without examining other potentially more effective designs.

political constraint — In software system engineering (requirements), a management constraint that deals with policy and legal issues. [Roman 1985]

poor ordering — In software engineering (requirements), a problem in developing software requirements specifications in which the requirement statements are presented in the order of the speaker, rather than in an order that would be convenient to the reader. In poor ordering, the reader must hold many questions in abeyance until later statements answer them. [Rich et al. 1987]

portability — In software system engineering, a quality metric that can be used to measure the relative effort to transport the software for use in another environment or to convert software for use in another operating environment, hardware configuration, or software system environment. [RADC TR-85–37 1985]

PPPI — Acronym for preplanned product improvement. [Sailor 1990]

pragmatic phase — *Synonymous with requirements analysis phase.* [Davis 1990]

precision — A measure of the ability to distinguish between nearly equal values; for example, four-place numerals are less precise than six-place numerals; nevertheless, a properly computed four-place numeral may be more accurate than an improperly computed six-place numeral. [ANSI/IEEE Standard 729–1983]

precision of notation — In software engineering, a software requirements metric that can be used to measure how precisely the syntax of a notation is defined. [STARTS Guide 1987]

predicate calculus — In mathematics, a symbolic logic that uses symbols for qualifiers and for arguments and predicates of propositions, as well as for unanalyzed propositions and logical connectives. A predicate may assume either of two permitted values.

preliminary design — 1. In system/software system engineering, the process of analyzing design alternatives and defining the hardware/software system architecture. 2. In software engineering, preliminary design typically includes definition and structuring of computer program components and data, definition of the interfaces, and preparation of timing and sizing estimates. 3. In system/software system engineering, the result of the preliminary design process. [ANSI/IEEE Standard 729–1983] *Synonymous with architectural design, high-level design, internal specification, system design, top-level design. See also preliminary design description (specification).*

preliminary design description (specification) — A specification that sets forth the preliminary design of the software system. *See also preliminary design.*

preliminary design phase — The software development lifecycle phase that uses the software requirements defined in the previous phase to develop a software architecture and functional flow that will implement those requirements. *See also software development lifecycle phase.*

preliminary design review (PDR) — In system/software system engineering, a milestone review conducted for each hardware/software configuration item (CI) before the detail design process to: (1) evaluate the progress and technical adequacy of the selected top-level design approach, (2) determine its compatibility with the functional and performance requirements of the CI requirements specification, and (3) establish the existence and compatibility of the physical and functional interfaces between the CI and other items of equipment or facilities. [Military Standard 1521B-1985]. *See also milestone review, review.*

preliminary design stage — *Synonymous with preliminary design phase.*

preplanned product improvement (PPPI) — In system/software engineering, future expected improvements to the product are considered during the system/software design and development.

presoftware development — In software engineering, all analysis performed before software requirements analysis is begun.

problem analysis — In system/software engineering, an activity during which one tries to understand fully what the problem is without defining how it will be solved. [Davis 1990] *Synonymous with requirements analysis.*

problem definition — *Synonymous with requirements analysis.*

process — 1. A unique, finite course of events defined by its purpose or by its effect, achieved under given conditions. 2. In data processing, to perform operations on data in a computer. [ANSI/IEEE Standard 830–1984] 3. In software engineering (structured analysis methodology), a description of the process or transform. Used with dataflow diagrams. *See also dataflow diagram. Synonymous with mini-spec.* 4. A transportation or transformation of substances, energy, or information in space or time. 5. In a formal language specification, a process is a set trace.

process free — A software requirements specification is process free when the specification does not contain management or unnecessary design information.

process group — In software engineering, a group of engineers, computer specialists, and other scientists who are concerned with the process used by the development organization for software development. Its typical functions include defining and documenting the process, establishing and defining metrics, gathering data, assisting projects in analyzing data, and advising management on areas requiring further attention. The process group typically conducts quarterly management reviews on process status and may provide review leaders. [Humphrey 1989]

process metric — In software engineering, a metric that can be used to measure characteristics of the methods, techniques, and tools employed in acquiring, developing, verifying, and operating the software. [Keller et al. 1990]

process model — A representation of a system/software development process activity intended to explain the behavior of some aspects of it. The process model is less complex or complete than the activity or artifact modeled. *See also software process model.*

process specification — *Synonymous with design specification.*

process standard — A standard that defines the procedures or operations used in making or achieving a product. *See also standard, product standard.*

process work breakdown structure (WBS) — A work breakdown structure (WBS) for a process, for example, a process WBS for a software project could include at the first level: requirement analysis, design, code, and software testing. *See also product work breakdown structure, work breakdown structure (WBS).*

procurement specification — In engineering projects, a specification that is produced and issued by a procuring agency to obtain a contract for a system development. It is part of a statement of work (SOW). *See also statement of work.*

product assurance — 1. In system/software engineering, the ability to meet reliability and quality levels as required by the contract or requirement specifications. 2. Sometimes (incorrectly) synonymous with quality assurance (QA).

product baseline — The hardware/software configuration identification established at the end of the full-scale-development phase. This baseline is established by an approved "as built" configuration item product specification.

product design specification — In software engineering, a software document that describes the overall architecture of the software product and its components. [Boehm, *V&V Software Requirements* 1984] *See architectural design.*

product development baseline — In system/software system engineering, the informal baseline created when the detailed design specifications are completed and placed under development control. *See also development baseline.*

product external description — *Synonymous with requirements specification.* [Davis 1990]

product improvement phase — The software development lifecycle phase—to improve the product—that begins after the system is employed. *See also operation and maintenance phase.*

product metric — In software engineering, a metric that can be used to measure the characteristics of the delivered documents and software. [Keller et al. 1990]

product space — In system/software engineering, the range of all probable solutions to meet all known constraints. [Davis 1990]

product standard — A standard that defines what constitutes completeness and acceptability of items that are produced as a result of a process. *See also software engineering standard, process standard.*

product work breakdown structure (WBS) — A work breakdown structure (WBS) for a product, for example, a product WBS for a software project could include at the first level: application programs, utility programs, and operating systems. *See also process work breakdown structure, work breakdown structure (WBS).*

production and development phase — In system acquisition, the period beginning with a production readiness review (PRR) until the last system/software system is delivered and accepted. Generally production is initiated at a low rate, and a physical configuration audit (PCA) is held on the first production article to verify that it conforms to specifications and drawings. Production is then built up to a peak rate after it has been determined that changes resulting from initial operational use, testing, production tooling, and manufacturing are incorporated.

production phase — In system acquisition, the period from production approval until the last system or piece of equipment is delivered and accepted. The production phase is part of the production and development phase.

production readiness review (PRR) — In system acquisition, a management milestone review to ensure that the production documentation is ready, the machinery is available, and the workforce is assembled and trained.

program design — *See detailed design.*

program design language (PDL) — In software engineering, the de facto standard for specifying detailed design for software modules. It is written in simple, free-form English with special meanings reserved for certain key words. Sometimes synonymous with structured English, pseudocode. [Davis, *Comparison of Techniques* 1988] *See also Pseudocode Structured English.*

program generator — In data processing, a program that assists users to write their own programs by expanding simple statements into code. *See also fourth-generation language (4GL).*

program librarian — In software engineering, an individual who administers the program support library (PSL). The person responsible for establishing, controlling, and maintaining a software development library. An individual who acts as an administrator, secretary, and librarian for many teams and who maintains and controls all elements of the software configuration, for example, documentation, source listings, and data catalogs, and indexes "reusable" software models. The librarian also assists the team in research, evaluation, and document preparation.

program management directive (PMD) — In acquisition management, the official management directive that provides direction to the implementing and participating organizations. It is used during the entire acquisition cycle to standardize requirements and request studies, as well as initiate, approve, change, transition, modify, or terminate programs. [U.S. Department of Defense (DoD) usage]

program management plan (PMP) — A program management document describing the approach that will be taken for a project. The plan typically describes the work to be done, the resources required, the methods to be used, the configuration management and quality assurance (QA) procedures to be followed, the schedules to be met, and the organization. *See also project management plan, software project management plan.*

program office (PO) — In software engineering management, an organizational structure responsible for monitoring or managing company resources for a multitude of projects. [Manley 1990] [U.S. Department of Defense (DoD) usage] Usually the customer (government) management organization.

program risk — In system engineering, a factor that creates a likelihood that system performance or supportability objectives may not be achieved with an acceptable range of projected program cost and schedules. [Searle 1981]

program support library (PSL) — In software engineering, a centralized and readily available depository with authorized versions of each component of a software system. It contains the necessary development control of each software configuration item. The program support library (PSL) should support three main activities: code development, software management, and configuration control. A PSL has four main components: internal libraries in machine-readable form, external libraries in hardcopy form, computer procedures, and office procedures. [Bersoff 1984] *See also configuration management.*

programme — 1. British spelling of a business program (in contrast to computer program). 2. Archaic British spelling of computer program (software).

Programmer's Apprentice — A knowledge-based system that uses the domain of programming as a vehicle for studying (attempting to duplicate) human problem-solving skills. The Programmer's Apprentice is an intelligent assistant in various phases of the programming task. [Rich et al. 1987]

programming — The coding and unit testing of computer code.

programming phase — *See implementation phase.*

programming support environment — *See software engineering environment (SEE), software support environment (SSE).*

programming tool — *See CASE tool.*

programming-in-the-large — A euphemism for software engineering.

programming-in-the-small — A euphemism for coding.

project — A temporary activity characterized by having a start date, specific objectives and constraints, established responsibilities, a budget and schedule, and a completion date. (If the objective of the project is to develop a software system, then it is sometimes called a software development or software engineering project.)

project database — In system/software engineering, a repository in which all information associated with a system or project is stored. A project database should be used to store everything from requirements to source code and from user documentation to executable programs and program units, replicated as required to support multiple versions of each. [Wasserman and Pircher 1987] *Synonymous with master project database (MPDB) repository.*

project file — *Synonymous with unit development folder (UDF).*

project librarian — In the Structured Analysis and Design Technique (SADT™) methodology (personnel roles), a person who is assigned the responsibility of maintaining a centralized file of all project management documents, making copies, distributing reader kits, and keeping records. [Ross and Schoman 1977] *See also program librarian, SADT™, SADT™ personnel roles.*

project lifecycle — *See software development lifecycle, software lifecycle.*

project management — A system of procedures, practices, technologies, and know-how that provides the planning, organizing, staffing, directing, and controlling necessary to successfully manage an engineering project. Know-how in this case means the skill, background, and wisdom to apply knowledge effectively in practice. *See also software engineering project management.*

project management plan — A project management document describing the approach that will be taken for a project. The plan typically describes the work to be done, the resources required, the methods to be used, the configuration management and quality assurance (QA) procedures to be followed, the schedules to be met, and the project organization. *See also software project management plan.*

project manager — 1. A manager who has responsibility for planning, organizing, staffing, directing, and controlling a project. 2. In software engineering, a manager who has responsibility for planning, organizing, staffing, directing, and controlling a software engineering project. *See also project management, software engineering project management.* 3. In the Structured Analysis and Design Technique (SADT™) methodology (personnel roles), a person who has the final technical responsibility for carrying out the system analysis. [Ross and Schoman 1977] *See also SADT™, SADT™ personnel roles.*

project notebook — In software engineering, a central repository of written material such as memos, plans, technical reports pertaining to a software project. *Loosely synonymous with project file, software development notebook, unit development folder (UDF).*

projection — A software engineering analysis principle that is used to approach some aspects of some problems. Projection describes the system from multiple viewpoints and is analogous to using two-dimensional diagrams to describe an object, that is, to "project" a two-dimensional view of the object. [Davis 1990]

PROLOG — A software specification language based directly on logic. [Abbott and Moorhead 1981]

proof of correctness — In computer science: 1. A formal technique of mathematical logic to infer that a relation between program variables assumed true at program entry implies that another relation between program variables holds at program exit. 2. A program proof that results from applying this technique. *See also formal (verifiable) requirements language, formal language.*

protocol — In software engineering, a set of rules governing the communication and transfer of data between two or more devices in a communication system. The rules define the handling of certain communication problems, such as format, relative timing, error control, and sequence control.

prototype — 1. In engineering, a prototype is a full-scale model and the functional form of a new system or subsystem. (A prototype does not have to be the complete system—only the part of interest.) A prototype is sometimes referred to as a model. 2. In software engineering, a software prototype would be a computer program that implements some part of the system requirements. This prototype can be used to assist in defining requirements or, in this case, to assist in evaluating alternatives. Examples include determining how to obtain the required accuracy in realtime performance issues, as well as user interface suitability. The process of building the prototype will also expose and eliminate a number of the ambiguities, inconsistencies, blind spots, and misunderstandings incorporated in the specifications.

prototyping — 1. A software requirements analysis strategy that includes the idea of building a prototype of a system to give early visibility of the actual functioning and operational behavior to the designer and the customers. Examples of tools used to build prototypes are relational database management systems, fourth-generation languages (4GL), code generation, support writers, query languages, rapid screen design tools, application generators, cultural exercisers, and collections of specialized reusable software components. [STARTS Guide 1987] 2. In system/software engineering, construction of a "quick and dirty" system, beginning with the very minimum of specifications that have been prepared. The purpose of this system is to show the users what they are asking for and to give them a working knowledge of the result that can be achieved by the system they have defined. [Scharer 1981]

prototyping lifecycle model — In system/software engineering, a lifecycle model that incorporates or emphasizes prototyping. *See also lifecycle model, prototyping, software development lifecycle, spiral model, waterfall model.* [Dorfman 1990]

PRR — Acronym for production readiness review.

pseudocode — In software engineering, a general term for structured English or program design language.

PSL — 1. From PSL/PSA, a problem statement language. 2. Acronym for program support library.

PSL/PSA (Problem Statement Language/Problem Statement Analyzer) — In software engineering, one of the earliest requirements analysis tools. PSL/PSA predates the availability of inexpensive graphics terminals. This software engineering development tool was developed by the University of Michigan in the mid-1960s as part of the Information System Design Operation System (ISDOS) project. [Sayani 1990]

PSPEC — In software engineering (realtime structured analysis methodology): 1. Acronym for process specification. [Hatley and Pirbhai 1987] 2.8 *Synonymous with mini-spec, process, process specification. Contrast with CSPEC.*

q-q-q

QA — Acronym for quality assurance.

qualification test — In system/software system engineering, a demonstration of the system/software product.

qualification testing — In system/software system engineering, formal testing, usually conducted by the developer for the customer, to demonstrate that the software meets its specified requirements. *See also acceptance testing, system testing.* [ANSI/IEEE Standard 729-1983]

qualitative and quantitative personnel requirements information (QQPRI) — In system acquisition, this activity consists of developing information relating to numbers and types of personnel needed for field and organizational operations and maintenance, and to project needs for individual and team training. [Searle 1981]

quality — In engineering, the totality of features and characteristics of a product or service that bears on its ability to satisfy given needs. [ANSI/ASQC A3–1978] *See also software quality.*

quality assurance (QA) — In project management, disciplines used by project management to monitor, control, and gain visibility into the development process. Quality assurance includes configuration management, validation and verification, and test and evaluation. [Bersoff 1984] *See also software quality assurance (SQA).*

quality attribute (requirement) — A requirement that specifies the degree of an attribute that affects the quality that the system/software must possess; for example, reliability and maintainability. *See also software quality attribute (requirement).*

quality attribute — *See quality metric.*

quality metric — In software engineering, a metric that verifies complexity, correctness, coupling of modules, degree of dependency of modules, maintainability, modifiability, performance, reliability, reusability, testability, understandability, and verifiability. *See also metric, software performance metric, software quality metric.*

quality tradeoff — *See tradeoff study.*

quantitative metric — In software engineering, a metric that can be used to summarize important information to make distinctions, identify outlying software characteristics, and detect trends. [Keller et al. 1990]

r-r-r

R-net (requirements net) — A part of the Software Requirements Engineering Methodology (SREM), a requirements net (R-net) is a graphical representation of the stimulus-response path of a software system and reflects the processing that must be carried out subsequent to the receipt of each message. The graphical presentation is similar to classic logic diagrams and flowcharts used by engineers. The graph possesses natural test points for assuring that the requirement expressed on a path is expressly addressed for testing. The R-net can be used as a manual tool and representation method or as an input to the Requirements Engineering Validation System (REVS). [Scheffer and Stone 1985] [Alford 1985] [TRW SS-80–03 1980] *See also SREM, REVS.*

RA — Acronym for requirements analysis, Requirements Apprentice.

RADX (Requirements Analysis and Data Extraction) — A part of the Software Requirements Engineering Methodology (SREM). RADX allows analysis of the database to identify requirements that are incomplete, inconsistent, or ambiguous. Examples are identifying response-time limits that have not been specified and data developed but not used. [Scheffer and Stone 1985] [Alford 1985] [TRW SS-80-03 1980] *See also SREM.*

range of reuse — In software engineering (reuse), the range of applications in which the software is to be reused determines how well defined and flexible the system must be. If the component is used within a narrow range of applications where terminology and assumptions are well understood, the definition of the component need not be exceptionally rigorous. When the range of applications is broad however, the component must be rigorously defined; otherwise the terminology and assumptions would be more varied and less well known. [Grabow and Noble 1985]

rapid prototyping — A software engineering strategy that addresses the issue of ensuring that the software product being proposed really meets the user's needs. The approach is to construct a "quick and dirty" partial solution to the system before (or during) the requirement stage. The potential users use this prototype for a period of time and supply feedback to the developer concerning strengths and weaknesses. This feedback is then used to modify the software requirements specification to reflect the user's real needs, and the prototype is discarded. [Davis et al. 1988] *See also prototype.*

rapid throwaway prototyping — See rapid prototyping.

readability — In software engineering (requirements specifications), the ability to read and understand the document. Readability is not associated with correctness or completeness. [Gehani 1982]

reader — In the Structured Analysis and Design Technique (SADT™) methodology (personnel roles), a person who reads SADT diagrams for information, but is not expected to make written comments. [Ross and Schoman 1977] *See also SADT™, SADT™ personnel roles.*

reading — In software engineering (verification and validation techniques), reading involves someone other than the originator reading the specification to identify potential problems. Because reading subjects the specification to another point of view, it pinpoints blind spots or misconceptions that the developer may have. [Boehm, *V&V Software Requirements* 1984] *See also verification and validation technique.*

realtime — In system/software engineering: 1. Pertaining to the processing of data by a computer in connection with another process outside the computer according to time requirements imposed by the outside process. This term is also used to describe systems operating in conversational mode and processes that can be influenced by human intervention while they are in progress. 2. Pertaining to the actual time during which a physical process transpires; for example, the performance of a computation during the actual time that the related physical process transpires, so that results of the computation can be used in guiding the physical process. [ANSI/IEEE Standard 729–1983]

realtime embedded computer system — An embedded computer system used in a realtime environment.

realtime software system — A software system used in a realtime environment.

realtime structured analysis (RTSA) — A software engineering methodology that employs a modified version of structured analysis to accommodate realtime control. The constructs of realtime structured analysis include control transforms, control specifications (usually state-transition diagrams), entity-relationship diagrams, event lists, plus the usual constructs of structured analysis.

realtime Yourdon — *Synonymous with realtime structured analysis (RTSA).*

reasoning — In artificial intelligence, the drawing of inferences or conclusions through the use of reason. It includes the use of predicate calculus and general purpose theorem proving techniques.

reconfigurability — In software engineering, a quality metric that can be used to measure those characteristics of software that provide for continuity of system operation upon the failure of one or more processors, storage units, or communication links. [RADC TR-85-37 1985]

regression testing — In software engineering (maintenance and testing), the rerunning of test cases that a program has previously executed correctly in order to detect errors created during software correction or modification activities. [FIPS Publication 101 1983]

relational composition — A mathematical operation to compose two relationships—providing the range of the first is the same type of domain as the second—to give the set of pairs of the domain of the first the range of the second. [Norris 1986] *See also relational inverse.*

relational database — In computer science, a structure-independent database in which relationships are defined dynamically. Structure-independent databases have become a prerequisite for the successful implementation of nonprocedural or fourth-generation languages. [Cobb 1985]

relational inverse — A mathematical operation to give the inverse of a relation. [Norris 1986] *See also relational composition.*

relationship diagram — *See entity-relationship diagram (ERD or E-R diagram).*

relationship type — In an entity-relationship model, a classification of a relationship type. [Chen 1990] *See also entity, entity-relationship model.*

relative priority — In management, the priority of a task relative to all other tasks.

reliability — In software engineering, a quality metric that can be used to measure the extent to which the software will perform without any failure within a specified time period. [RADC TR-85–37 1985] *See also system reliability.*

reliability growth model — In software engineering, a software development model that is based on the following assumptions: (1) input is selected randomly from the input domain, (2) consecutive inputs have the same disjoint-failure probabilities, (3) all errors have the same disjoint-failure rates, and (4) no new errors are introduced during the error correction. Reliability is then expressed as an exponential function of time and the number of errors. [Ramamoorthy et al. 1984]

reliability model — In software engineering, a means of predicting software reliability from the history of detected errors. [Ramamoorthy et al. 1984]

remedial model — A type of model that describes the actions necessary to be performed to "repair" the system.

report generator — In data processing, a program designed to be run by users and used to prepare reports by giving only a description of the desired content, the format of the output, and certain information concerning the input file. [Grabow and Noble 1985]

report writer — *See report generator.*

request for proposal (RFP) — In system engineering, a request for services, research, or product distributed by a customer to prospective developers with a request that the prospective developers respond with their proposed cost, schedule, and development approach.

requirement — In system/software engineering: 1. A capability needed by a user to solve a problem or achieve an objective. 2. A capability that must be met or possessed by a system or system component to satisfy a contract, standard, specification, or other formally imposed document. 3. The set of all requirements that form the basis for subsequent development of the software or software component. 4. Short description sometimes used in place of the term *software requirements specification. See also software requirement, system requirement. See also requirements specification, software requirements specification, system requirements specification.*

requirement complexity metric — In software engineering, a metric that can be used to measure the complexity of the system as reflected in the requirement specifications.

requirements acquisition — *See requirements analysis.*

requirements allocation — *See allocation.*

requirements allocation sheet (RAS) — In system/software system engineering, a document prepared to facilitate and keep track of the allocation of high-level requirements to low-level components. [Searle 1981] *See also ARTS.*

requirements analysis — In system/software engineering: 1. The process of studying user needs to arrive at a definition of system or software requirements. 2. The verification of system or software requirements. [ANSI/IEEE Standard 729–1983] 3. The systematic process of reasoning about a problem and its constituent parts to understand what is needed or what must be done. Analysis also involves communication with all persons involved with both the requirements and the requirements specifications. [Rzepka and Ohno 1985] *See also software requirements analysis.*

Requirements Analysis and Data Extraction — *See RADX.*

requirements analysis and specification phase — *See software requirements phase.*

requirements analysis phase — *See software requirements phase, system requirements phase.*

Requirements Apprentice (RA) — A knowledge-based system developed at the Massachusetts Institute of Technology by Charles Rich, Richard C. Waters, and H.B. Reubenstein that will assist an analyst in the creation and modification of software requirements. The RA contains an extensive library knowledge about the particular domain of the requirements to be constructed. The focus of the RA is on bridging the gap between informal and formal specifications. The Requirements Apprentice process will be a machine-manipulable representation of the requirements. This information will be used to answer queries and will generate various documentation for the requirements analyst, end user, and the system designer. An advantage of the requirements analysis approach is that different representations of the information can be produced and tailored to the different needs of the end user, the analyst, and the designer. The Requirements Apprentice is part of the Programmer's Apprentice: an intelligent assistant in various phases of the programming task. [Rich et al. 1987] *See also programmer's apprentice.*

requirements definition — *Synonymous with requirements analysis, software analysis, software requirements analysis, system analysis, system requirements analysis.*

requirements definition phase — *See software requirements phase.*

requirements document — *See requirements specification.*

requirements engineering — In system engineering the science and discipline concerned with analyzing and documenting requirements. It comprises needs analysis, requirements analysis, and requirements specifications. *See also requirement.*

requirements engineering environment — In system/software engineering, provides the requirements engineer with appropriate mechanisms to facilitate the analysis, documentation, and checking activities. [Rzepka and Ohno 1985]

requirements flowdown — In system/software system engineering, the systematic decomposition of system requirements into allocated and derived requirements, appropriately assigned to low-level functional components.

requirements inspection — *See inspection.*

requirements isolation — In system/software engineering, the isolation of individual requirements to provide a better method of understanding the individual requirements. The isolation of requirements allows for the grouping of like requirements for allocation to top-level design. [Nelsen 1990]

requirements language — *See executable requirements specification, formal (verifiable) requirements language.*

Requirements Language Processor (RLP) — A software requirements processing system (RPS) developed by GTE Laboratories in Waltham, Massachusetts. [Davis, *Comparison of Techniques* 1988]

requirements management — In system/software system engineering, the process of controlling the identification, allocation, and flowdown of requirements from the system level to the module or part level, including interfaces, verification, modifications, and status monitoring. [Flynn and Dorfman 1990]

requirements management group — In system/software system engineering, a designated group to prepare and maintain the specification tree that identifies all specifications in the system and prepare the system and segment specifications. This group also manages the preparation of all low-level hardware and software specifications and prepares "fill-in" guides for those documents to ensure uniformity of documentation. This group also establishes the traceability of requirements throughout all specifications and maintains the automatic traceability system. A primary function of the group is the operation of the configuration control board (CCB). The group also prepares a design review and audit plan that identifies, schedules, and defines the format for all design reviews and audits to be conducted. [Sailor 1990]

requirements model — In software engineering, a model of some aspect of the system or software requirements. Examples are timing, function, essential capabilities, input, process, and output behavior. *See also timing requirements model.*

requirements network — *See R-net, SREM.*

requirements phase — *See software requirements phase, system requirements phase.*

requirements review — *See software specification review (SSR), system requirements review* (SRR).

requirements review action item — In software engineering project management, an action item that is revealed during a requirements review. *See also review action item, software specification review (SSR), system requirements review (SRR).*

requirements specification — In system/software engineering, a document that states the functions that software must perform, required level of performance (speed, accuracy, etc.), the nature of the required interfaces between the software product and its environment, the type and severity of constraints on design, and the quality of the final product. *Synonymous with external specification. See also software requirements specification, system requirements specification.*

requirements specification documents inspection — In software engineering, the inspecting of software requirements documents to detect, identify, and describe defects of the requirements and the representation. This is a peer examination that: (1) verifies that the document satisfies the system level specification, (2) verifies that the document conforms to applicable standards, (3) verifies deviations from standards and specifications, (4) collects software engineering data (e.g., defect in effort data), (5) does not examine alternative issues. [Hollocker 1990]

requirements specifications language — In software engineering. a machine processable, artificial language, that overcomes the shortcomings of English in stating requirements. [Boehm, *V&V Software Requirements* 1984] *See formal language.*

requirements stage — *See requirements phase.*

requirements statement language — *See requirements specifications language.*

requirements traceability — *See traceability.*

requirements traceability system — In system/software engineering, a mechanism for identifying and documenting the derivation path (upward) and allocation/flowdown path (downward) of requirements in the system development hierarchy. The system development hierarchy starts with system requirements and ends with tested and delivered source code and its supporting documentation.

requirements traceability tool (RTT) — A software development tool that establishes a traceability between itemized software requirements specifications, design elements, code elements, and test cases. It also supports various associated query, analysis, and report generation capabilities. [Boehm, *Spiral Model* 1988] *See also ARTS.*

requirements verification — *See verification.*

research software development methodology — In software engineering, those software development methodologies that are still in a laboratory environment. [Grabow and Noble 1985]

resource — In engineering and management, the people, money, equipment, facilities, transportation, and so forth that are needed or can be used to satisfactorily complete an activity or build a product. Resources can be expendable (money and materials) or nonexpendable (people and machines).

retirement phase — The period of time in the software lifecycle during which support for a software product is terminated. [ANSI/IEEE Standard 729–1983] Note: This phase does not appear in the software development lifecycle. *See also software development lifecycle phase, software lifecycle phase.*

reusability — In software engineering: 1. A bottom-up approach of designing systems from the basic, existing modules and connecting them to form bigger modules eliminating the need to design modules from scratch. [Ramamoorthy et al. 1984] 2. A metric that can be used to measure the relative effort to convert a software component for use in another application.

reusable code — In software engineering, code that can be reused in another application. To be valuable, the reused code must have been tested and used successfully in an application.

reusable library — In software engineering, a central library of reusable software parts that is available to software developers. These reusable parts would range in size from whole systems that have previously been built, down to small packages for performing numerical computations. Domains would range from such purely mathematical and computer science areas as differential equations and simple tables up to system application areas, such as automobile cruise control, aircraft fuel consumption, ship navigation, or weapon targeting. [Pyster 1990]

reusable program generator — In software engineering, a program generator that is highly parameterized to include several possible variations in the application. [Ramamoorthy et al. 1984]

reusable requirement — In software engineering, requirements specifications (verified and used in an application) that can be reused in another application.

reusable software — In software engineering, software that can be reused in another application. To be valuable, the reused software must have been tested and used successfully in an application.

reusable software paradigm — A software development strategy that attempts to reduce development costs by incorporating previously proven designs and code in a new software product. The net effect of reusing components would be shorter development schedules (by reusing software rather than reinventing it) and more reliable software (by using components that have been previously "shaken down"). [Davis et al. 1988]

reuse — In software development, the act of using a software product in a different project.

reverse engineering — A software engineering approach that derives the design or requirements of a system from its code. The design can be represented by a program design language (PDL) or a formal language. By creating a logical view from a physical system, reverse engineering assists in maintaining and enhancing existing systems. [Sayani 1990]

review — 1. In system/software system engineering, a formal meeting at which a product or document is presented to the user, customer, or other interested parties for comment and approval. It can be a review of the management and technical progress of the hardware/software development project. 2. In hardware/software engineering, the formal review of an existing or proposed design for the purpose of detection and remedy of design deficiencies that could affect fitness for use and environmental aspects of the product, process, or service, and for identification of potential improvements of performance, safety, or economic aspects. [ANSI/IEEE Standard 729–1983] 3. In the spiral software development model, the review covers all products developed during the previous cycle, including the plans for the next cycle and the resources required to carry them out. The major objective of the review is to ensure that all concerned parties are mutually committed to the approach to be taken for the next phase. [Boehm, *Spiral Model* 1988] *See also audit, code audit, critical (detailed) design review (CDR), formal qualification review (FQR), functional configuration audit (FCA), independent audit, informal review, milestone review, physical configuration audit (PCA), prelim-*

inary design review (PDR), software specification review (SSR), system design review (SDR), system requirements review (SRR). See also inspection, walkthrough.

review action item — In software engineering project management, an action item that was revealed and assigned during a review.

review leader — In software engineering project management, an individual responsible for a technical review who must identify the review team, establish the schedule, announce the meeting and its location, and distribute input materials to the participants, allowing adequate time for their preparation. [Hollocker 1990]

REVS (Requirements Engineering Validation System) — A part of the Software Requirements Engineering Methodology (SREM), REVS is a set of tools to support generation and verification of software requirements by using SREM. The functions of the tools are: (1) extension of the requirements statement language (RSL) to tailor it to a specific function, (2) translation of the RSL into an automated database, (3) analysis of the database contents against the consistency and completeness criteria, (4) extraction of information from the database, (5) generation of functional or analytical simulators of the required processing from the requirements specification, and (6) generation and display of graphical description of the requirements net (R-net) and subnets. [Scheffer and Stone 1985] [Alford 1985] [TRW SS-80–03 1980] *See also SREM.*

REVS — Acronym for Requirements Engineering Validation System.

RFP — Acronym for request for proposal.

rigor — In software engineering methodologies, a metric that can be used to measure the degree of difficulty in using the software engineering notation.

risk — 1. In system/software system engineering, a potential occurrence that would be detrimental to the project. Risk is measured as the combined effect of the likelihood of the occurrence and a measured or assessed consequence given that occurrence. 2. In software engineering (requirements specifications), if the lifecycle cost effectiveness of a specified system is extremely sensitive to some system aspect and that aspect is not well known or understood, there is a high risk involved in the system. If such high-risk issues are not identified and resolved in advance, then there is strong likelihood of disaster if this risk occurrence is realized. [Boehm, *V&V Software Requirements* 1984]

risk analysis — In system/software system engineering, the methodical process of identifying areas of potential risk, the associated probability of occurrence, and the seriousness of the consequences of the occurrence.

risk management — In system/software system engineering, the integration of risk identification, risk assessment, and risk reduction to optimize the probability of success.

risk management plan — In system/software system engineering project management, a plan that would describe the programmatic aspects of risk identification, risk assessment, risk reduction, and risk management to be performed. The risk management plan should relate the developer's approach for handling risk—avoidance, prevention (control), assumption (retention), transfer, knowledge, and research. A typical risk management plan would: (1) identify the project's top risk items, (2) present a plan for removing each risk item, (3) update monthly lists of top risk items, plans, and results, (4) highlight the risk-item status at monthly project reviews, (5) initiate appropriate corrective actions. [Boehm, *Spiral Model* 1988]

risk reduction — In system/software system engineering, an approach for reducing risk through avoidance, prevention (control), transfer, knowledge, and research.

Rome Air Development Center (RADC) — A U.S. Air Force research and development laboratory concerned with research and development of ground based electronics and computer science.

RSL (Requirements Statement Language) — A part of the Software Requirements Engineering Methodology (SREM). RSL is a machine-processable, artificial language that overcomes the shortcomings of English in stating requirements. RSL is composed of: (1) elements —corresponding roughly to nouns in English, (2) attributes—modifiers of elements, like adjectives in English, (3) relationships—a statement of association of some type between a subject element and object element (verbs in English), (4) structure—the RSL representation of a R-Net. [Scheffer and Stone 1985] [Alford 1985] [TRW SS-80–03 1980] *See also SREM.*

RSL — Acronym for Requirements Statement Language.

RSL translator — In the Software Requirements Engineering Methodology (SREM), a tool for analyzing Requirements Statement Language (RSL) statements. *See also RSL, SREM.*

RTSA — Acronym for realtime structured analysis.

S-S-S

SA — Acronym for structured analysis.

SADT/IDEF — A software requirements specification tool that supports the Structured Analysis and Design Technique (SADT™) methodology. [STARTS Guide 1987] *See also SADT™.*

SADT™ (Structured Analysis and Design Technique) — A proprietary software engineering methodology for analyzing and representing software requirements and design developed in the early 1970s by Douglas Ross of SofTech, Inc. A type of structured analysis methodology, SADT is a framework in which the nouns and verbs of any language can be embedded for the presentation of a hierarchical presentation of an information system. SADT is composed of a graphic language and a method for using it. An SADT model is an organized sequence of diagrams, each with supporting text. SADT also defines the personnel roles in a software project. SADT is a trademark of SofTech, Inc. *See also structured analysis (SA), Structured Analysis and System Specifications. See also SADT™ personnel roles.*

SADT™ personnel roles — The titles and functions of personnel in a software engineering project using the Structured Analysis and Design Technique (SADT™) methodology. *See also commenter, expert, instructor, monitor, project librarian, project manager, reader, technical committee. See also SADT™, SADT/IDEF.*

SAMM — Acronym for Systematic Activity Modeling Method.

SARA — Acronym for System Architect Apprentice.

SAS — Acronym for Structured Analysis Specification.

SC — Acronym for software component.

scenario — 1. A description of a series of events that could be expected to occur simultaneously or sequentially. 2. An account or synopsis of a projected course of events or actions.

schema — 1. In data processing, a set of relationships among data elements in a complex file structure. 2. In software engineering, a diagrammatic presentation [British usage].

schema language — In the formal language Z, the language that provides the presentation framework for the mathematical portion of a Z specification. [Norris 1986]

schematic model — A type of model that uses charts, diagrams, or drawings to describe a state or event. *See also model.*

SCI — Acronym for software configuration items.

SCM — Acronym for software configuration management.

SCN — Acronym for specification change notice.

SDD — Acronym for software design document.

SDF — Acronym for software development file.

SDL — Acronym for software development library.

SDM — A software requirements methodology developed in 1977 by Stewart Madnick at Massachusetts Institute of Technology (MIT).

SDR — Acronym for system design review.

security — In software engineering, the establishment and application of safeguards to protect data, software, and computer hardware from accidental or malicious modification, destruction, or disclosure.

SEE — Acronym for software engineering environment.

segment — 1. In system engineering, a major part of a large hardware/software system. For example, a space system could have a satellite segment, a launch segment, and a ground segment. 2. In software, a self-contained portion of a computer program that may be executed without the entire computer program necessarily being maintained in internal storage at any one time.

SEI — Acronym for Software Engineering Institute.

SEL — Acronym for Software Engineering Laboratory, National Aeronautics and Space Administration (NASA), Goddard Space Flight Center, Greenbelt, Maryland.

semantics — A branch of linguistics that is concerned with the nature, structure, development, and changes in the meaning of words. Semantics is the meaning of a sentence. *Contrast with syntax.*

semiformal process description — In software engineering, a description of a software specification using a subset of the English language with limited syntax and vocabulary. Examples of semiformal process description are structured English and program design language (PDL) [British usage]. [STARTS Guide 1987]

sensitivity analysis — In system/software system engineering, a sensitivity analysis must be performed on all trade studies to determine the value of results to the decision makers. Where the total weighted scores of several alternatives are proximate, a small change in the estimated performance of any alternative against any criteria may change the decision. In these instances, it may be useful to indicate a range of estimated performance values having a known confidence level that can be transformed to the weighted scores. [DoD, *Engineering Management Guide* 1986]

SEPM — Acronym for software engineering project management.

sequence chart — A system/software engineering requirements tool used to display the flow of major system modes and sequences. This is the primary tool used to formally define the basic phases, modes, and sequences of the overall mission. The sequence chart helps answer the "when" questions of system definition. [Lano 1990]

set — In system/software system engineering, groups of records that are created and manipulated during an Automated Requirements Traceability System (ARTS) interactive session. [Flynn and Dorfman 1990]

set theory — In mathematics, a discipline for characterizing groups, sets, and elements. Set theory is the theory of delimiting or combining elements.

shortfall — In software engineering, a metric that can be used to measure how far the operational system is from meeting the actual requirements specifications at a particular time. [Davis et al. 1988]

SID — Acronym for specification increment document.

similarity — In software engineering (verification), a similarity technique compares an item already tested to an item yet to be tested. If there is sufficient similarity between the items and if an analysis of the verification methods indicates that a second test is unlikely to identify additional errors, the second item can be shown to be verified through similarity. *Contrast with analysis, demonstration, examination, testing.*

simple automated model — In software engineering (verification and validation techniques), those techniques that involve the simple manipulation of a mathematical formula by a computer program for analyzing lifecycle feasibility issues such as accuracy, realtime performance, and lifecycle costs. [Boehm, *V&V Software Requirements* 1984] *See also verification and validation technique.*

simple scenario — In software engineering (verification and validation techniques), the scenarios will describe how the system works once it is in operation. Man-computer dialogs are the most common form of simple scenarios, which are effective at clarifying misunderstandings or mismatches in the specification's human engineering aspects, but ineffective at projecting completeness and consistency of details or validating performance, speed, and accuracy. [Boehm, *V&V Software Requirements* 1984] *See also verification and validation technique.*

simplicity — In software engineering, a quality metric that can be used to measure those characteristics of software that provide for the definition and implementation of functions in the most noncomplex and understandable manner. [RADC TR-85-37 1985]

simulation — In system/software system engineering: 1. Physical or mathematical representation of a system to expedite the evaluation of selected system parameters. Simulation is used to explore the effects that alternative system characteristics will have on system performance, without actually producing and testing each alternative system. 2. Use of an executable model to represent the behavior of an object. During testing, the computational hardware, the external environment, and even code segments may be simulated. [FIPS Publication 101 1983] 3. An imitation so that, for example, one program acts like another program.

skull session — In software engineering (software requirement analysis), an activity with the goal of achieving a consensus among a group of users about what they want. In a skull session, the developer's or analyst's main role is as a facilitator to assist the group in arriving at a consensus. [Rich et al. 1987]

Smalltalk — A programming language and environment developed to implement object-oriented design. Smalltalk enables the programmer to define objects that combine a data structure and pointers to a set of operations.

smoking — In system/software system engineering (requirements engineering), a strategy in which the user requests many system features, but wants only one of them.

software — In computer science, data processing, and software engineering, a sequence of instructions suitable for processing by a computer. Processing may include the use of an assembler, a compiler, an interpreter, or a translator to prepare the program for execution, as well as to execute it. [ANSI/IEEE Standard 729–1983] *Synonymous with code, computer code, computer program. Contrast with computer hardware, hardware.*

software acquisition management (SAM) — In system acquisition, the planning, monitoring, and control of a software acquisition.

software analysis — *See analysis.*

software architecture — *See architecture.*

software CAD — *See computer-aided design.*

software code inspection — *See inspection.*

software code walkthrough — *See walkthrough.*

software component (SC) — In software system engineering, a functionally or logically distinct part of a software configuration item (CI) distinguished for purposes of convenience in designing and specifying a complex software CI as an assembly of subordinate elements. Software components may be top level or bottom level. *See also configuration management (CM), software configuration item (SCI).*

software components library — In software engineering, an organized collection of computer programs with a cataloging and indexing capability for locating and retrieving components.

software configuration — *See configuration.*

software configuration auditing — *See configuration auditing.*

software configuration control — *See configuration control.*

software configuration identification — *See configuration identification.*

software configuration item (SCI) — In software system engineering, a software entity that has been established as a configuration item. The software configuration item exists where functional allocations have been made that clearly delineate the separation between equipment functions and software functions and the software has been established as a configuration item. *Contrast with hardware configuration item (HCI). See also configuration management (CM).*

software configuration item testing — *See testing.*

software configuration management (SCM) — *See configuration management.*

software configuration status accounting — *See configuration status accounting.*

software crisis — The term used since the 1960s to describe the recurring system development problem in which software problems cause the system to be late, over cost, and not responsive to the users' or customers' requirements including functionality performance, usability, and maintainability.

software design — In software engineering, the process of defining the software architecture (structure), components, modules, interfaces, test approach, and data for a software system to satisfy specified requirements. [ANSI/IEEE Standard 729–1983]

software design constraint (requirement) — *See design constraint (requirement).*

software design document (SDD) — *See detailed design description (specification).*

software design inspection — *See inspection.*

software design phase — *See design phase.*

software design process — The part of the software engineering process that is concerned with design. *See also software engineering.*

software design specification — *See design specification.*

software design walkthrough — *See walkthrough.*

software detailed design specification — *See detailed design description (specification).*

software development — *See software engineering.*

software development cycle — *See software development lifecycle.*

software development environment — *See software engineering environment (SEE).*

software development file (SDF) — In software engineering, a repository for a collection of material pertinent to the development or support of software. Contents typically include (either directly or by reference) design considerations and constraints, design, documentation and data, schedule and status information, test requirements, test cases, test procedures, and test results. *Sometimes synonymous with unit development folder (UDF).*

software development library — In software engineering, a software library containing computer-readable and human-readable information relevant to a software development effort. [ANSI/IEEE Standard 729-1983] *See also program support library (PSL).*

software development lifecycle — A software development strategy that begins with the decision to develop a software product and ends when the product is delivered. It depicts the relationships among the major milestones, baselines, reviews, and project deliverables that span the life of the project. A project lifecycle model must include project-initiation and project-termination activities. The software development lifecycle typically includes a requirements phase; design phase; implementation (coding) phase; test phase; and, sometimes, installation and checkout phases. *See also software lifecycle.*

software development lifecycle model — *See software development lifecycle.*

software development lifecycle phase — One of the phases of the software development lifecycle. For example: software requirements phase; software design phase; implementation (coding) phase; software test phase; and, sometimes, installation and checkout phases. *See also software development lifecycle.*

software development methodology — In software engineering: (1) an integrated set of software engineering methods, policies, procedures, rules, standards, techniques, tools, languages, and other methodologies for analyzing, designing, implementing, and testing software; and (2) a set of rules for selecting the correct methodology, process, or tools.

software development notebook — In software engineering, a collection of material pertinent to the development of a given software module or subsystem. Contents typically include the requirements, design, technical reports, code listings, test plans, test results, problem reports, schedules, and notes for the module or subsystem. [ANSI/IEEE Standard 729–1983] *See also project notebook, unit development folder (UDF).*

software development paradigm — Software engineering models that can be used as a strategy for developing a software system. Examples are baseline management, top-down development, incremental development, rapid throwaway prototyping, and reusable software.

software development phase — *See software development lifecycle phase.*

software development plan — *See software project management plan.* [U.S. Department of Defense (DoD) usage].

software development process lifecycle — *See software development lifecycle.*

software development project — *See software engineering project.*

software documentation — In software engineering, the technical data or information, including proposals, management plans and documents, requirement specifications, design specifications, computer listings, test documentation, standards, users' manuals, operators manuals, and maintenance manuals that describe or specify the design or details, explain the capabilities, or provide operating instructions to obtain desired results from the system. *See also documentation.*

software engineering — 1. The practical application of computer science, management, and other sciences to the analysis, design, construction, and maintenance of software and its associated documentation. 2. An engineering science that applies the concept of analysis, design, coding, testing, documentation, and management to the successful completion of large, custom-built computer programs. 3. The systematic application of methods, tools, and techniques to achieve a stated requirement or objective for an effective and efficient software system. 4. The application of scientific principles to: (1) the early transformation of a problem into a working software solution and (2) subsequent maintenance of that software until the end of its useful life. [Davis, *Comparison of Techniques* 1988]

software engineering assessment — A Software Engineering Institute (SEI) evaluation of the software engineering capabilities of software developers in order to measure their abilities to develop software in accordance with modern software engineering methods. *See also software engineering assessment instrument, Software Engineering Institute (SEI).*

software engineering assessment instrument — In a software engineering assessment, guidelines and procedures for assessing the ability of software developers to develop software in accordance with modern software engineering methods. The software engineering assessment instrument normally takes the form of a questionnaire and a checklist. *See also software engineering assessment.*

software engineering development model — *See software development lifecycle.*

software engineering environment (SEE) — In software engineering, a system of computers, support software, facilities, procedures, and support personnel that makes the necessary conditions, automatic processes, methodologies, and tools easily available to software developers. A minimum SSE would be a "software tool kit" that provides a set of diverse tools, but with a common interface. A maximum SSE would be a complete "software factory." An SSE architecture allows: (1) the distribution of computing power to all developers, (2) development machines that emulate the characteristics of the target machine, (3) improved human interface, (4) structured processing methodologies for good design and development, (5) improved product testing and analysis, (6) automatic trouble reporting and change control, (7) automatic project planning and scheduling, (8) continuous tracking of project activities, and (9) automatic documentation preparation. *Synonymous with software development environment, software support environment (SSE).*

Software Engineering Institute (SEI) — A U.S. federally funded software engineering laboratory operated by Carnegie Mellon University, Pittsburgh, Pennsylvania, under contract to DoD.

software engineering lifecycle — *See software development lifecycle.*

software engineering notation — In software engineering, the representation method for software requirements and design. [British usage]

software engineering process — The total set of software engineering activities needed to transform a user's requirements into software. [Humphrey 1989] *See also software engineering.*

software engineering project — In software engineering, the set of all activities, functions, and tasks, both technical and managerial, required to satisfy the terms and conditions of the project agreement. A software engineering project is a temporary activity characterized by having a start date, specific objectives and constraints, established responsibilities, a budget and schedule, and a completion date. The project consumes resources and has the goal of producing a product or set of products that satisfies the project requirements, as specified in the project agreement. A software engineering project may be self-contained or may be part of a larger project. In some cases, the project may span only a portion of the software product lifecycle. In other cases, the project may span many years and consist of numerous subprojects, each in itself being a well-defined and self-contained software engineering project. [ANSI/IEEE Standard 1058.1–1987] *Synonymous with software project, software development project.*

software engineering project management — A system of procedures, practices, technologies, and know-how that provides the planning, organizing, staffing, directing, and controlling necessary to successfully manage an software engineering project. Know-how in this case means the skill, background, and wisdom to apply knowledge effectively in practice. *See also project management.*

software engineering project plan — *See software project management plan (SPMP).*

software engineering standard — *See standard.*

software error — *See error.*

software external interface requirement — *See external interface requirement.*

software factory — In software development, an organization, facility, and environment using automated tools suitable for producing software analogous to an automated hardware factory (e.g. automobile, television, electronics). This is in contrast with developing software as a cottage (small, labor intensive) industry (e.g. arts and crafts, oriental rugs).

software failure — *See failure.*

software functional requirement — *See functional requirement.*

software hierarchy — *See hierarchy.*

software interface — In software engineering, a shared boundary. An interface might occur between two software components, between hardware and software components, or between an operator and a software system.

See also common user interface, environment interface standard, and man-machine interface.

software item — In software engineering, source code, object code, job control code, control data, or a collection of these items.

software lifecycle — In software engineering: 1. A model of the phases of a software system that starts when a software product is conceived and ends when the product is no longer available for use. It depicts the relationships among the major milestones, baselines, reviews, and project deliverables that span the life of the system. The software lifecycle typically includes a requirements phase, design phase, implementation (coding) phase, installation and checkout phase, operation and maintenance phase, and, sometimes, retirement phase. *See also software development lifecycle.* 2. A strategy for developing a system that includes the development of requirements, product design, and detailed design that involves the development of verification and validation, approval or disapproval, and baselining of each of these specifications. [Boehm, *V&V Software Requirements* 1984]

software lifecycle model — *See software lifecycle.*

software lifecycle phase — One of the phases of the software lifecycle, for example, software requirements phase; software design phase; implementation (coding) phase; software test phase; installation and checkout phase; operation and maintenance phase; and, sometimes, retirement phase. *See also software lifecycle, software development lifecycle phase.*

software lifecycle review — *See milestone review.*

software maintainability — *See maintainability.*

software maintenance — In software engineering: 1. The performance of activities required to keep a software system operational and responsive after it is accepted and placed into production. [NBS Special Publication 500–106 1983] 2. Modification of a software product after delivery to correct faults, to improve performance or other attributes, or to adapt the product to a changed environment. [ANSI/IEEE Standard 729–1983] *See also adaptive maintenance, corrective maintenance, perfective maintenance. See also software maintenance manual.*

software maintenance documentation — *See software maintenance manual. See also documentation, software maintenance.*

software maintenance manual — A software engineering project deliverable document used by the maintenance personnel of the system (in contrast to the users) to enable them to maintain the system. Maintenance means adaptive maintenance, corrective maintenance, and perfective maintenance. *Contrast with operator's manual, users' manual.*

software management — *See software engineering project management.*

software package — A "preprogrammed" software system used for a particular application, such as a payroll package, an accounting package, or a statistical package. *See also reusable software.*

software performance metric — In software engineering, a metric that can be used to measure the performance of a software system.

software performance requirement — *See performance requirement.*

software preliminary design description — *See preliminary design description (specification).*

software process model — *See software development lifecycle.*

software product evaluation — *See software testing, verification and validation.*

software product specification (SPS) — Data item description of a software detailed design document. [U.S. Department of Defense (DoD) usage] [DoD Standard 2167A 1988]

Software Productivity Consortium (SPC) — An organization chartered by the aerospace companies that own it (called member companies) to improve the productivity of software developers in those companies. Member companies include most of the top U.S. Department of Defense (DoD) contractors, which have a combined income of more than $100 billion and are responsible for major U.S. defense programs. [Pyster 1990]

software program — *See software.*

software program component — *See software component (SC).* [Sailor 1990]

software programmer's manual (SPM) — Data item description of a users' manual. [U.S. Department of Defense (DoD) usage] [DoD Standard 2167A 1988]

software project — *See software engineering project.*

software project management plan (SPMP) — In software engineering project management, the controlling document for managing a software project. A software project management plan defines the technical and managerial functions, activities, and tasks necessary to satisfy the requirements of a software project, as defined in the project agreement. *Synonymous with software development plan, software engineering project plan.*

software prototyping — *See evolutionary prototyping, prototyping, rapid prototyping.*

software purchaser — *Synonymous with customer.* [STARTS Guide 1987]

software quality — In software engineering: 1. The totality of features and characteristics of a software product that bears on its ability to satisfy given needs, for example, to conform to specifications. 2. The degree to which software possesses a desired combination of attributes. 3. The degree to which a customer or user perceives that software meets his or her composite expectations. 4. The composite characteristics of software that determine the degree to which the software in use will meet the expectations of the customer. [ANSI/IEEE Standard 729–1983] 5. Attributes of software that affect its perceived value, for example, correctness, reliability, maintainability, and portability.

software quality assurance (SQA) — In software system engineering, a planned and systematic pattern of all actions necessary to provide adequate confidence that the software and the delivered documentation conforms to established technical requirements. [ANSI/IEEE Standard 729–1983]

software quality attribute (requirement) — In software engineering: 1. A condition or set of conditions defined in terms of software quality metrics that must be satisfied to meet a software need. 2. A requirement that specifies the degree of an attribute that affects quality that the software system must possess, for example, correctness, reliability, maintainability, and portability. *See also software quality metric, software requirements specification (SRS).*

software quality goal — In software engineering (quality metrics), a specific metrics goal that must be achieved, as specified by a metric requirement. [Keller et al. 1990]

software quality metric — In software engineering, a quantitative measure of the degree to which software possesses a given attribute that affects quality. An attribute of software that affects its perceived value for example, correctness, reliability, maintainability, and portability. *See also software quality attribute (requirement).*

software reliability — *See reliability.*

software requirement — In software engineering: 1. A software capability needed by a user to solve a problem to achieve an objective. 2. A software capability that must be met or possessed by a system or system component to satisfy a contract, standard, specification, or other formally imposed document. 3. The set of all software requirements that forms the basis for subsequent development of the software or software component. [ANSI/IEEE Standard 729–1983] 4. Short description sometimes used in place of the term *software requirements specification. See also software requirements analysis, software requirements phase, software requirements specification (SRS).*

Software Requirement Engineering Methodology — *See SREM.*

software requirements analysis — In software engineering, the process of studying user needs to arrive at a definition of software requirements. *Sometimes synonymous with analysis, software analysis, software requirements engineering. See also software requirements specification (SRS).*

software requirements engineering — In software system engineering, the science and discipline concerned with analyzing and documenting software requirements. It involves transforming system requirements into a description of software requirements, performance parameters, and a system configuration through the use of an iterative process of definition, analysis, tradeoff studies, and prototyping. *Sometimes synonymous with software requirements analysis. See also requirement, requirements engineering.*

software requirements generation phase — *See software requirements phase.*

software requirements inspection — *See inspection.*

software requirements phase — The software development lifecycle phase during which the requirements for a software product, such as the functional and performance capabilities, are defined and documented. [ANSI/IEEE Standard 729–1983] *See also software lifecycle phase.*

software requirements review (SRR) — *Synonymous with software specification review (SSR).*

software requirements specification (SRS) — 1. In software system engineering, a document that clearly and precisely describes each of the essential requirements (functions, performance, design constraints, and quality attributes) of the software and the external interfaces. Each requirement is defined in such a way that its achievement can be objectively verified by a prescribed method, for example, inspection, demonstration, analysis, or test. [ANSI/IEEE Standard 830–1984] 2. Data item description of a software requirements specification. [U.S. Department of Defense (DoD) usage] [DoD Standard 2167A 1988] *See also detailed design description (specification), preliminary design description (specification), software design constraint (requirement), software external interface requirement, software functional requirement, software performance requirement, software quality attribute (requirement), software requirements analysis, version description document (VDD).*

software reusability paradigm — 1. A software development strategy that incorporates the reuse of existing software components. The reusable components are contained in a software library. The possible incentives for software reuse include increased reliability, improved development time, and reduced cost. 2. *See reusability.*

software reuse — In software engineering, the reuse of already completed and tested software components (e.g., code, design, and requirements specifications).

software reuse methodology — *See software reusability paradigm.*

software science — *See Halstead's software science.*

software size — In software engineering: 1. The actual or estimated size of the software system built or to be built. Software size normally is measured in terms of delivered lines of source code. 2. A metric that can be used to measure the amount of software. Examples are source lines of code, numbers of modules.

software specification — *See software requirements specification.*

software specification review (SSR) — In software system engineering, a milestone review conducted to finalize software configuration item (SCI) requirements so that the software developer can initiate preliminary software design. The SSR is conducted when SCI requirements have been sufficiently defined to evaluate the developer's responsiveness to and interpretation of the system/segment level technical requirements. A successful SSR is predicated on the developer's determination that the software requirements specification and interface specifications form a satisfactory basis for proceeding into the preliminary design phase. [Military Standard 1521B-1985] *See also milestone review, review.*

software support environment (SSE) — *See software engineering environment.*

software system — In system engineering, a collection of related software that allows the accomplishment of some system engineering requirement.

software system engineer — An engineer who practices software system engineering. *See also software system engineering.*

software system engineering — 1. A technical and management process. The technical process is the analytical effort necessary to transform an operational need into a software design of the proper size and configuration, and its documentation in requirements specifications. The management process involves assessing the risk and cost, integrating the engineering specialties and design groups, maintaining configuration control, and continuously auditing the effort to ensure that cost, schedule, and technical performance objectives are satisfied to meet the original operational need. [adapted from Sailor 1990] Software system engineering has the same relationship to software engineering as system engineering has to hardware engineering (all types). 2. A special case of system engineering.

software system library — In software engineering, a controlled collection of system-resident software that can be accessed for use or incorporated into other programs by reference, for example, a group of routines that a linkage editor can incorporate into a program as required. [ANSI/IEEE Standard 729–1983] *See also software development library.*

software system specification language — *See requirements specification language.*

software system synthesis phase — *See software requirements phase.*

software system testing phase — *See software testing phase.*

Software Technology for Application to Large Realtime Systems — *See STARTS.*

software technology transfer — In engineering, the awareness, convincing, selling, motivating, collaboration, and special effort required to encourage industry, companies, organizations, and software engineering projects to make good use of new software development methodologies and technology products. *See also technology transfer, technology transfer gap.*

software test and evaluation master plan (STEMP) — *See test and evaluation master plan (TEMP).*

software test and integration — In software system engineering, that part of software engineering concerned with the testing and integration of the software system.

software test description (STD) — Data item description of software test documents. [U.S. Department of Defense (DoD) usage] [DoD Standard 2167A 1988]

software test plan (STP) — Data item description of a software test plan. [U.S. Department of Defense (DoD) usage] [DoD Standard 2167A 1988]

software testing — *See testing. See also black-box testing, white-box testing.*

software testing phase — The software development lifecycle phase during which the software system is tested against the requirements. *See also test document, testing.*

Software through Pictures — A computer-aided software engineering (CASE) tool/environment developed and marketed by Interactive Development Environments. Software through Pictures includes the following editors: Control Flow Editor, Control Specification Editor, Data Structure Editor, IDEtool Window, Transition Diagram Editor, State Transition Editor, and Structure Chart Editor. [Wasserman and Pircher 1987]

software tool — A software system or software package used by programmers or software engineers in the performance of their tasks. Software systems used to help develop, test, analyze, or maintain another software system or its documentation. Examples of these tools are automated design tools, compilers, test tools, maintenance tools, and word processors. [ANSI/IEEE Standard 729–1983] *See also CASE tool.*

software unit — In a software system, the lowest element of a software hierarchy that contains one or more of the following characteristics: (1) a unit comprising one or more logical functional entities, (2) an element specified in the design of a computer software component (CSC) that is separately testable [DoD Standard 2167A 1988], (3) the lowest level to which software requirements can be traced, and (4) the design and coding of any unit can be accomplished by a single individual within the assigned schedule. *Sometimes synonymous with module.*

software unit testing — *See unit testing.*

software user's manual (SUM) — Data item description of a users' manual. [U.S. Department of Defense (DoD) usage] [DoD Standard 2167A 1988]

software utility — In data processing, a software system or tool to support other software systems or tools. *See also software tool.*

software-intensive system — A system that contains a significant amount of software in relationship to hardware and manual procedures. [Dorfman 1990] *Contrast with hardware-intensive system. See also system.*

source-code library — In software engineering (reuse), the physical or logical location of reusable software components. A source-code librarian is responsible for classifying, storing, and retrieving reusable components. [Grabow and Noble 1985]

source-code reuse — In software engineering, the reuse of source code previously developed in a current development. Source-code reuse poses the greatest hurdle in terms of classification, storage, retrieval, and the need for precise description of the software's operational characteristics. [Grabow and Noble 1985]

Space Systems Division (SSD) — A suborganization of the Air Force Systems Command, U.S. Air Force. The SSD is responsible for the acquisition and system engineering of space and missile systems

SPC — Acronym for Software Productivity Consortium.

special test data — In software engineering (testing). test data based on input values likely to require special handling by the program. [FIPS Publication 101 1983]

specification — In engineering: 1. A document that prescribes, in a complete, precise, verifiable manner, the requirements, design, behavior, or other characteristics of a hardware/software system or hardware/software system component. 2. The process of developing a specification. 3. A concise statement of a set of requirements to be satisfied by a product, material, or process. The specification indicates, whenever appropriate, the procedure used to determine whether the requirements given are satisfied. [ANSI N45.2.10–1973] [ANSI/IEEE Standard 729–1983] *See also software requirements specification (SRS), system requirements specification. See also design specification, engineering document, formal specification, functional specification, interface specification, performance specification, requirements specification, software requirements specification.*

specification addendum — In system/software system engineering, a new specification for a new hardware/software configuration item, created from the specification for an existing configuration item by "add" or "delete" notations. This is accomplished by writing the new specification by direct reference to the existing specification on a paragraph-by-paragraph basis.

Specification and Description Language (SDL) — A software requirements technique that was developed in the late 1970s by the Consultative Committee International Telephone and Telegraph (CCITT). The language is widely used (in Europe) in the design and specification of event-based software, such as telecommunication switching systems. A system described in the Specification and Description Language (SDL) consists of a number of concurrent communicating processes. Each process is described as a finite number of states and any amount of data manipulation between states. The results of the data manipulation between states may influence state transitions. [Rockstrom and Sarraco 1982]

specification change notice (SCN) — In system/software system engineering, a contract change notice involving specifications. [U.S. Department of Defense (DoD) usage]

specification increment — 1. In software engineering (structured analysis methodology), description of a proposed change of requirement in a format (e.g., dataflow diagrams, data dictionary, structured English, and data structure diagrams) that facilitates integration into the structured specification. 2. A specification increment document (SID). [DeMarco 1979]

specification language — A software requirements language with one or more of the following properties: (1) Simplifies the process of delivering system specifications and information from informal user requirements. A specification language should assume an appropriate model for software structure that simplifies the development with specifications from informal requirements. (2) Permits the specification to be analyzed for internal consistency, precision, and completeness. (3) Facilitates the validation that specifications really meet the user's requirements. [Ramamoorthy et al. 1984] *See also formal language.*

specification phase — *See software requirements phase, system requirements phase.*

specification tool — In software engineering, a software tool that can assist the engineer in determining and representing the requirements specifications. *See also CASE tool.*

specification tree — In system/software system engineering, a set of specifications arranged in a treelike order. *See also traceability.*

specification-driven approach — *Synonymous with waterfall model.*

specificity — In software engineering, a quality metric that can be used to measure those characteristics of software that provide for singularity in the definition and implementation of functions. [RADC TR-83–175 1983]

spiral model — 1. A software development strategy developed by Barry W. Boehm that creates a risk-driven approach to the software process in contrast to a document-driven or code-driven process. The spiral model holds that each cycle involves a progression through the same sequence of steps, for each portion of the product, and for each of its levels of elaboration, from an overall concept of operations document down to the coding of individual programs. [Boehm, *Spiral Model* 1988] 2. A software development process model that represents combinations of the conventional (baseline management), prototyping, and incremental models to be used for various portions of a development. It shifts the management emphasis from development of products to risk analysis and avoidance and explicitly calls for evaluation concerning whether a project should be terminated. [Dorfman 1990] *See also process model, waterfall model.*

SPM — Acronym for software programmer's manual.

SPMP — Acronym for software project management plan.

SPS — Acronym for software product specification.

SQA — Acronym for software quality assurance.

SREM (Software Requirement Engineering Methodology) — A software requirements engineering methodology developed by TRW in 1973–1978 for the Army Ballistic Missile Division/Advanced Technology Center. SREM consists of a Requirements Statement Language (RSL); a set of tools, Requirements Engineering Validation System (REVS), to translate the language, perform automatic consistency and completeness analysis, produce documentation, and generate simulations; and the methodology, SREM, which is expressed as a sequence of steps for generating the requirements through use of the language and tools and assists in producing a software requirement specification. [Scheffer and Stone 1985] [Alford 1985] [TRW SS-80–03 1980] *See also alpha, DCDS, message, R-net, RADX, REVS, RSL, stimulus-response path, subnet, SYSREM, validation point.*

SRR — Acronym for software requirements review, system requirements review.

SRS — Acronym for software requirements specification, system requirements specification.

SSADM (Structured System Analysis and Design Methodology) — A structured system analysis methodology developed for the United Kingdom (U.K.) government software development projects by Learmonth and Burchett Management Systems (LBMS). Three main classes of diagrams are used in SSADM: logical data structures, which represent the relationship between data elements within the system; dataflow diagrams, which show how data moves around an information system and which processes act upon; and the entity life history, which gives a third view of data showing all events affecting the entity during the life of the system. An entity life history, for example, includes those who created it, those who modified it in some way, and those who deleted it. [Williams 1987]

SSDD — Acronym for system/segment design document.

SSDS — Acronym for system/segment design specification.

SSE — Acronym for software support environment.

SSR — Acronym for software specification review.

SSS — Acronym for system/segment specification

stable requirement — In software engineering (requirements specifications), a requirement may be considered stable if the needs it addresses will not change in the expected life of the software. [ANSI/IEEE Standard 830–1984] *Contrast with volatile requirement.*

stagewise model — A software productivity model developed in 1956 by H.D. Benington [1956] on large software systems such as the Semi-Automatic Ground Environment (SAGE) system. This model led to the recognition of software problems and the development of the stagewise model. This effort specifically states that the software should be developed in stages (operational plan, operational specifications, coding specifications, coding, parameter testing, assembly testing, shakedown, system evaluation). [Boehm, *Spiral Model* 1988]

standard — 1. A standard is an approved, documented, and available set of criteria used to determine the adequacy of an action or object. 2. A document that sets forth the standards and procedures to be followed on a given project or by a given organization. 3. A software engineering standard is a set of: (1) procedures that define the processes for and (2) descriptions that define the quantity and quality of a product from a software engineering project. *See also process standard, product standard.*

STARTS (Software Technology for Application to Large Realtime Systems) — A realtime development program designed to stimulate the development, understanding, and application of software engineering methods and tools in the construction of large, realtime systems. STARTS was initially developed to allow numerous United Kingdom (U.K.) companies to combine their assets to evaluate modern software engineering tools and techniques.

STARTS Guide — An excellent reference manual produced by the National Computing Centre, United Kingdom (U.K.).

state chart — A software requirements analysis methodology that is an extension to the finite state machine. The extension provides a notation and set of conventions to facilitate the hierarchical decomposition of finite state machines and a mechanism for communicating between concurrent finite state machines. [Davis, *Comparison of Techniques* 1988]

state diagram — *See state transition diagram (STD).*

state machine — *See state chart, state transition diagram (STD).*

state transition diagram (STD) — In software engineering (realtime structured analysis methodology), a representation of how the external events cause the system to change from performing one set of transforms to another. *See also state transition matrix (STM).*

state transition matrix (STM) — In software engineering (realtime structured analysis methodology), a representation of how the external events cause the system to change from performing one set of transforms to another. *See also state transition diagram (STD).*

state-of-the-art — In engineering, the current (latest) technology, but not necessarily in use. *Contrast with state-of-the-practice.*

state-of-the-art technique — 1. The highest level of development, in a technique, device, or scientific field, achieved at any particular time. 2. In engineering, those technologies and methodologies that are the most effective and efficient available.

state-of-the-practice — In engineering, the current (latest) technology in use. *Contrast with state-of-the-art.*

statement of operational need (SON) — *Synonymous with user needs statement.*

statement of requirement — *Synonymous with statement of work (SOW).*

statement of work (SOW) — In system/software projects, a description of all the work required to complete a project. The statement of work (SOW) is normally part of a contract and is written by the customer or procuring agency. It may or may not include a procurement specification.

static analysis — In software engineering (verification and validation techniques), direct analysis of the form and structure of a product without executing the product. It may be applied to the requirements, design, or code. [FIPS Publication 101 1983]

STD — Acronym for software test description, state transition diagram.

STEMP — Acronym for software test and evaluation master plan.

step-sequenced N^2 chart — *See time-sequenced N^2 chart.* [Lano 1977]

stepwise refinement — A system/software development methodology in which data definitions and processing steps are defined broadly at first and then with increasing detail. [ANSI/IEEE Standard 729–1983] *See also hierarchical decomposition, modular decomposition, top-down development.*

stimulus-response path — A software requirements technique used with the Software Requirements Engineering Methodology (SREM) that decomposes the requirements with respect to the processing that must be carried out subsequent to the receipt of each stimulus. [Roman 1985] *See also R-net, SREM.*

STM — Acronym for state transition matrix.

STP — Acronym for software test plan.

STR — Acronym for software test report.

stress testing — *See boundary value analysis.*

structural testing — In software engineering (testing), the testing of the internal structure of the system. Logical paths through the software are tested by providing test cases that exercise specific sets of conditions or loops. *Synonymous with white-box testing. Contrast with functional testing.*

structure chart — In software engineering (structured methodology), a treelike representation of a program structure. It is used to represent the organization (usually hierarchical) of program components (modules), the hierarchy of control, and the flow of data and control. A structure chart is used in structured design. *See also structured design.*

structured — In software engineering, a term that means the artifact or methodology is logical in nature and is documented and implemented in a consistent manner throughout all levels of the system. [Nelsen 1990]

structured analysis (SA) — In software engineering (methodology), a state-of-the-art software analysis technique that uses dataflow diagrams (DFDs), data dictionaries, and processes descriptions to analyze and represent a software requirement. The technique supports both nonrealtime and realtime systems. *See also dataflow, dataflow diagram (DFD), data dictionary, leveling, process.*

Structured Analysis and Design Techniques (SADT™) — *See SADT™ (structured analysis and design technique).*

Structured Analysis and System Specification (SASS) — A software development method developed by Tom DeMarco. It is a spinoff of the earlier structured analysis work of Douglas Ross and is closely related to the design work of Constantine and Yourdon. The SASS is a pure top-down technique in which the analyst starts with a single process showing all system inputs and outputs and then repeatedly decomposes the process to show greater and greater detail.

structured analysis requirements model — In software engineering, a representation of a system using dataflow diagrams, data dictionary, process specifications, and data structure diagrams.

structured analysis/realtime — *See realtime structured analysis (RTSA).*

Structured Architect — A PSL/PSA computer-aided software engineering (CASE) tool that allows analysts to work independently on personal computers (PCs) to create dataflow diagrams, data dictionary entries, and process specifications according to the rules and procedures of the structured analysis methodology.

structured coding — *See structured programming.*

structured design — 1. In software engineering, a design technique that involves hierarchical partitioning of a modular structure in a top-down fashion, with emphasis on reduced coupling and strong cohesion. [DeMarco 1979] 2. A disciplined approach to software design that adheres to a specified set of rules based on principles such as top-down design, stepwise refinement, and dataflow analysis. [ANSI/IEEE Standard 729–1983]

structured design chart — *See structure chart.*

structured documentation — In software engineering, a disciplined approach to the creation of software documentation.

structured English — In software engineering (structured analysis methodology), a subset of the English language with limited syntax, limited vocabulary, and an indentation convention to call attention to logical blocking; a metalanguage for process specification. [DeMarco 1979] Structured English uses imperative English verbs without adjectives and adverbs, terms from the data dictionary, and reserved words to denote logic. Its "programming language" syntax consists of simple sentences, closed-end decisions, closed-end repetition, and combinations of these three.

structured program — A computer program (software) consisting of a basic set of control structures, each one having one entry point and one exit point. The set of control structures typically includes sequences of two or more instructions, conditional selection of one of two or more instructions or sequences of instructions, and repetition of an instruction or a sequence of instructions. [ANSI/IEEE Standard 729–1983] *See also structure chart, structured programming.*

structured programming — 1. In software engineering, designing, building, and testing structured programs. *See also structured program.* 2. In the mid-1970s, *synonymous with software engineering.*

Structured Requirements Definition (SRD) — A software requirements methodology developed and described by Ken Orr in his book, *Structured Requirements Definition* [1981].

structured specification — In system/software engineering, a software requirements analysis methodology and representation method that consists of the following tools: dataflow diagram (DFD), data dictionary, and tools that specify processes (structured English, state-transition diagram, decision trees, and decision tables).

structured specification methodology — A software engineering methodology based on the structured analysis requirements model.

Structured System Analysis and Design Methodology — *See SSADM.*

Structured Systems Analysis (SSA) — A structured system analysis methodology that was developed by C.P. Gane and T. Sarson and documented in their book, *Structured System Analysis: Tools and Techniques*, 1979. It is a spinoff of the earlier structured analysis work of Ross and is closely related to the design work of Constantine and Yourdon. SSA is a pure top-down technique in which the analyst starts with a single process showing all system inputs and outputs then repeatedly decomposes the process to show greater and greater detail. The textbook by the same name [1979] is well illustrated and easy to read. [Gane and Sarson 1979]

stub — In software development (testing), a low-level, dummy program module used to receive and respond to test data produced during the development and testing of a high-level module. 2. In software development, a program statement substituting for the body of a program unit and indicating that the unit is or will be defined elsewhere. [ANSI/IEEE Standard 729–1983] *Contrast with driver.*

stub unit — *See stub.*

subcontractor — In engineering, an individual, partnership, corporation, or association, that contracts with another contractor (the prime contractor) to design, develop, or manufacture items.

subnet — A part of the Software Requirements Engineering Methodology (SREM), it is a name given to the requirements net (R-net) that acts like a library routine in that it has a set of processes common to many systems. *See also R-net, SREM.*

subschema — 1. Portion of a schema. 2. In data processing, description of a private model of a file structure, as conceived by a single user. [DeMarco 1979]

substrata — In artificial intelligence, the substrata of a cliche contains both the fixed elements of structure (parts that are present in every occurrence) and constraints. Constraints are used to check that the parts that fill the roles in a particular occurrence are consistent and to complete parts (to fill empty roles) in a partially specified occurrence. [Rich et al. 1987]

subsystem — In engineering, a group of assemblies or components or both combined to perform a single function. [ANSI/IEEE Standard 729-1983]

SUM — Acronym for software user's manual.

supplier — In software engineering, *synonymous with developer*. [STARTS Guide 1987]

survivability — In software engineering, a quality metric that can be used to measure the extent to which the software will perform and support critical functions without failures, within a specified time period when a portion of the system is inoperable. [RADC TR-85–37 1985]

sustaining engineering — *Synonymous with software maintenance* [NASA usage].

SwSE — Acronym for software system engineering.

symbolic execution — In software engineering (testing), an analysis technique that derives a symbolic expression for each program path. [FIPS Publication 101 1983]

synchronous realtime control — In a realtime computer-based system, a method of control in which there is a fixed time for each specific event. The events are all initiated by a signal from a clock. *Contrast with asynchronous realtime control.*

syntax — A branch of linguistics that is concerned with the arrangements of words or elements in a sentence and to their relationships with each other. Syntax is the relationships of word groups, phrases, clauses, and sentences, that is, sentence structure. *Contrast with semantics.*

syntax checker — In computer science, software that tests for the correct structure of expressions in a language.

Synthesis — A software development strategy developed by the Software Productivity Consortium (SPC) that involves three main activities: (1) creating a model that approximates the application, (2) mapping from the application model to a known software model that approximates a valid design, (3) mapping the software design model to executable code that approximates a valuable implementation. These steps are performed iteratively, adapting the models with each iteration to become even better approximations of the desired new system. At each step, approximate verification and assessments are performed. Under Synthesis, a new system is seen as a revision of an old one. Relatively little is built from scratch. [Pyster 1990]

Synthesis Apprentice — In an artificial intelligence (AI) system called Programmer's Apprentice, a special purpose AI system that is able to detect many kinds of design errors.

synthesis tree — In computer science, a method of producing the output of a specification by combining analyzed strings, literals, and calls to modules.

SYSREM (System Requirements Engineering Methodology) — An early modification of the SREM methodology. System requirements are specified in terms of time functions, their decomposition, and their allocation to system components. In SYSREM: (1) both sequence and concurrency are represented, (2) control functions are defined as an integral part of the decomposition activity, (3) performance and function are simultaneously decomposed, (4) function sequences and concurrency are allocated to components, (5) interface designs are derived, (6) exceptions are addressed by defining an additional layer of functions to detect and recover from faults, and (7) the maximum concurrency of the required processing is exposed. [Scheffer and Stone 1985] [Alford 1985] [TRW SS-80–03 1980] *See also SREM.*

system — 1. A collection of hardware, software, people, facilities, and procedures organized to accomplish some common objectives. 2. In system engineering, a set of software programs that provides the cohesiveness and control of data that enables the system to solve problems.

system accessibility — In software engineering, a quality metric that can be used to measure those characteristics of software that can provide for control and audit of access to the software and data. [RADC TR-85–37 1985]

system acquisition lifecycle — A model of a hardware/software system development program that begins with the decision to develop a system and ends when the system is delivered. The acquisition lifecycle has the five acquisition phases of concept exploration (CE), demonstration and validation (DEM/VAL), full-scale development (FSD), production, and deployment. Primarily used by the U.S. Department of Defense (DoD) for acquiring large systems. *See also concept exploration (CE) phase, demonstration and validation (DEM/VAL) phase, deployment phase, full-scale development phase (FSD), production phase. See also system development lifecycle.*

system acquisition lifecycle phase — One of the phases of the software acquisition lifecycle. For example: concept exploration (CE) phase, demonstration and validation phase (DEM/VAL), full-scale development (FSD) phase, deployment phase, production phase. *See also system development lifecycle* phase.

system analysis — *See analysis. See also system requirements engineering.*

system analysis group — In system engineering, a designated group of individuals responsible for all simulations and fundamentals analysis done at the systems level. [Sailor 1990]

System Architect Apprentice (SARA) — A realtime design methodology developed at the University of California at Los Angeles (UCLA) by Gerald Estrin, which provides a language and graphical convention for the representation of concurrency and a simulator for design validation. [Estrin 1978]

system architecture — In system engineering, the structure and relationship among the components of a system. The system architecture may also include the system's interface with its operational environment. [ANSI/IEEE Standard 729–1983]

system boundary — In system engineering, a special means to say that an entity belongs to the system and that another entity belongs to the environment. [Davis 1990]

system clarity — In software engineering, a quality metric that can be used to measure those characteristics of software that provide for clear description of program structure in the simplest and most understandable manner. [RADC TR-85–37 1985]

system compatibility — In software engineering, a quality metric that can be used to measure those characteristics of software that provide for the hardware, software, and communication compatibility of two systems. [RADC TR-85–37 1985]

system configuration — *See configuration.*

system decomposition — *See decomposability.*

system definition — In system engineering, describes the overall goals and limitations of the system.

system design — In system/software system engineering: 1. A lifecycle phase during which the major hardware or software subsystem in the interrelationship is defined. 2. The process of defining the hardware and software architectures, components, modules, interfaces, and data for a system to satisfy specified system requirements. 3. The result of the system design process. *Sometimes synonymous with architectural design, high-level design, internal specification, preliminary design, top-level design. Sometimes synonymous with requirements specification, software specification, software requirements specification, system specification, system requirements specification. See also software design.*

system design description — *See system design.*

system design phase — The period of time in the system lifecycle (contrast to software lifecycle) during which the system architectural design and detailed designs are defined and documented. *See also system requirements phase.*

system design review (SDR) — In system/software system engineering, a system milestone review conducted when the definition effort has proceeded to the point where system requirements and the design approach are defined. Alternative design approaches and corresponding test requirements have been considered and the developer has defined and selected the required equipment, logistic support, personnel, procedural data, and facilities. This normally is late in the definition phase. This review is conducted in sufficient detail to ensure a technical understanding between the system developer and the customer. The system segments are identified in the system design specification, and the hardware/software configuration items are identified in the requirements specifications. *See also milestone reviews, reviews.*

system developer — In system/software engineering, a person or organization who develops systems/software systems.

system development — *See system engineering.*

system development lifecycle — A model of a hardware/software (system) project that begins with the decision to develop an engineering or hardware/software system and ends when the product is delivered. It depicts the relationships among the major milestones, baselines, reviews, and project deliverables that span the life of the project. A project lifecycle model must include project-initiation and project-termination activities. The system development lifecycle typically includes a system requirements phase, system architectural design phase, design and development phase (normally done at the hardware/software segment/subsystem-level), test phase, and sometimes installation and checkout phase. *See also software development lifecycle phase, acquisition lifecycle, system design phase, system requirements phase.*

system development lifecycle phase — One of the phases of the software development lifecycle. For example: system requirements phase, system architectural design phase, design and development phase (normally done at the hardware/software segment/subsystem-level), test phase, and sometimes installation and checkout phase. *See also software development lifecycle, system acquisition lifecycle.*

system documentation — In system engineering, technical data or information, including specifications, standards, engineering drawings, associated lists, manuals, computer listings, and printouts that describe or specify the design or details, explain the capabilities, or provide operating instructions to obtain desired results from the system. *See also documentation.*

system effectiveness group — In system engineering, a designated group of individuals consisting of specialists from reliability, maintainability, logistics, human factors, safety, productivity, electromagnetic compatibility (EMC), and other engineering specialities for the purpose of incorporating their knowledge into the system requirements. [Sailor 1990]

system effectiveness model — A model that examines items considered most critical to the development of a system, such as cost, schedule, availability, performance, and produceability, to establish a measure of the total system effectiveness. [Sailor 1990]

system element — In system/software system engineering, those functional groupings of specifiable entities that collectively make up a system, for example, segment, subsystem, component, and unit. [Flynn and Dorfman 1990]

system engineer — An engineer who practices system engineering. *See also system engineering.*

system engineering — The application of scientific and engineering efforts to: (1) transform an operational need into a description of system performance parameters and a system configuration through the use of an iterative process of definition, synthesis, analysis, design, test, and evaluation; (2) integrate related technical parameters and ensure compatibility of all related, functional, and program interfaces in a manner that optimizes the total system definition and design; (3) integrate reliability, maintainability, safety, survivability, human, and other such factors into the total engineering effort to meet cost, schedule, and technical performance objectives. [Military Standard 499A 1974]

system engineering design team — In a system engineering project, a designated group of people responsible for developing the design and allocating the requirements to low-level subsystems of a hardware-software system.

system engineering manager — *See system engineering project manager.*

system engineering organization — In a system engineering project, a selected group of engineers responsible for conducting certain aspects of system engineering. Not all system engineering activities are done in the system engineering organization; and not all engineers in a system engineering organization are system engineers. *See also cost analysis group, design integration group, operations planning group, requirements management group, system analysis group, system effectiveness group, system verification group.* [Sailor 1990]

system engineering process — In engineering, the multidisciplinary activity that begins with function analysis and arrives at a total system design through a process that considers and evaluates a spectrum of user requirements and economic and technical variables that are relevant to candidate approaches. [Searle 1981]

system engineering project — The set of all activities, functions, and tasks, both technical and managerial, required to satisfy the terms and conditions of the project agreement. A system engineering project is a temporary activity that is characterized by having a start date, specific objectives and constraints, established responsibilities, a budget and schedule, and a completion date. A system engineering project consumes resources and has the goal of producing a product or set of products that satisfies the project requirements, as specified in the project agreement. In some cases, a system engineering project may span many years and consist of numerous subprojects, each being a well-defined and self-contained system engineering project. *See also software engineering project.*

system engineering project manager — In system engineering, a manager who has responsibility for planning, organizing, staffing, directing, and controlling an engineering project. *See also project management, project manager, software engineering project management.*

system hierarchy — *See hierarchy. See also component, element, segment, software component (SC), software program, subsystem, system.*

system integration — In system/software system engineering, the action to ensure that the various segments and elements of the total system can operate together and interface with the external environment as required and expected.

system integration and testing — *See integration and test phase.*

system management model — In system engineering management, consists of a predetermined scenario of management actions and events to keep a system of lifecycle phases in a standard sequence.

system program office — In system engineering management, the organization that manages the acquisition of specific products being developed by contractors. [U.S. Department of Defense (DoD) usage]

system reliability — In system engineering, a quality metric that can be used to measure the probability that a system, including all hardware and software subsystems, will perform a required task or mission for a specified time in a specified environment. [ANSI/IEEE Standard 729–1983] *See also reliability.*

system requirement — In system engineering: 1. A system capability needed by a user to solve a problem or to achieve an objective. 2. A system capability that must be met or possessed by a system or system component to satisfy a contract, standard, specification, or other formally imposed document. 3. The set of all system requirements that forms the basis for subsequent development of the system or system component. [ANSI/IEEE Standard 729–1983] *See also system requirements specification (SRS), system requirements phase, software requirement.*

system requirements analysis and design — *See system engineering.*

system requirements analysis — The process of studying user needs to arrive at a definition of system requirements. *Sometimes synonymous with analysis, system requirements engineering.*

system requirements engineering — The science and discipline concerned with analyzing and documenting system requirements. It involves transforming an operational need into a system description, with system performance parameters and a system configuration, through the use of an iterative process of definition, analysis, tradeoff studies, and prototyping. *See also requirement.*

system requirements phase — The period of time in the system lifecycle (contrast to software lifecycle) during which the requirements for a system product, such as the functional and performance capabilities, are defined and documented. *See also system design phase.*

system requirements review (SRR) — In system engineering, a system milestone review that ascertains the adequacy of the system developer's efforts in defining system requirements. It will be conducted when a significant portion of the system functional and performance requirements has been established, normally in the definition phase (or equivalent effort). *See also milestone review, review.*

system requirements specification (SRS) — In system engineering. a specification that sets forth the requirements for a system or system segment. Typically included are functional requirements, performance requirements, interface requirements, design requirements, and development standards. *Synonymous with system specification.*

system reuse — *See reuse.*

system segment specification — *Synonymous with requirements specification, software specification, software requirements specification, system specification, system requirements specification, system/segment specification.* [Davis 1990]

system software — Software designed for a specific computer system or family of computer systems to facilitate the operation and maintenance of the computer system and associated programs, for example, operating systems, compilers, utilities. [ANSI/IEEE Standard 729–1983] *Sometime called nonfunctional software. Contrast with application software.*

system specification — *See system requirements specification (SRS).*

system technology — *See technology.*

system testing — 1. In system engineering, the process of testing an integrated hardware and software system to verify that the system meets its specified requirements. [ANSI/IEEE Standard 729–1983] *See also acceptance testing, qualification testing.* 2. In software system engineering, the activity of checking that the entire software system is fully integrated in its actual hardware environment according to the requirements specification.

system trade — *See trade study.* [Sailor 1990]

system validation — *See validation.*

system verification — *See verification.*

system verification group — In system engineering, a designated group of people responsible for conducting a system verification. [Sailor 1990]

system/segment design description (SSDD) — Data item description of a system design specification. [U.S. Department of Defense (DoD) usage] [DoD Standard 2167A 1988]

system/segment specification (SSS) — Data item description of a system requirements specification. [U.S. Department of Defense (DoD) usage] [DoD Standard 2167A 1988] The system/segment specification becomes the functional baseline for the system or segment.

Systematic Activity Modeling Method (SAMM) — A software development methodology originated and refined by the Boeing Company in the 1970s. Systematic Activity Modeling Method (SAMM) is a data-flow oriented method in that separate activities can be identified and are related to each other by means of a data flow. SAMM was designed to be used in the system definition, requirement analysis, and design phase.

t-t-t

target document — In software engineering (structured analysis methodology), the end product of analysis. The description of a system to be implemented. To be characterized a target document, the description should include all of the criteria for project success. [DeMarco 1979]

TBD — Acronym for "to be determined" or "to be done."

TBR — Acronym for "to be resolved."

TBS — Acronym for "to be supplied."

technical committee — In the Structured Analysis and Design Technique (SADT™) methodology (personnel roles), a group of senior technical personnel assigned to review the analysis at every major level of decomposition. This group either resolves technical issues or recommends a decision to the project management. [Ross and Schoman 1977] *See also SADT™, SADT™ personnel roles.*

technical feasibility analysis — *See feasibility analysis.*

technical feasibility study — *See feasibility analysis.*

technical process — In software system engineering, the analytical effort necessary to transform an operational need into a description of a software system; a software design of the proper size, configuration, and quality; its documentation in requirements and design specifications; and the procedures necessary to test, verify, and accept the finished product.

technical review — In software system engineering, a formal team evaluation of software requirements specification. This review identifies any discrepancies from system specifications and standards and provides recommendations after the examination of alternatives. This examination may require more than one meeting and typically has a larger audience than walkthroughs and inspections. In this mid-process examination approach, the technical review meets the need for widespread exposure of requirements to assure correctness, completeness, and feasibility. [Hollocker 1990] *See also review.*

technology — A collective term for a group of practices, tools, techniques, and/or methods.

technology insertion — *Synonymous with technology transfer.*

technology transfer — The awareness, convincing, selling, motivating, collaboration, and special effort required to encourage industry, companies, organizations, and projects to make good use of new technology products. *Synonymous with technology insertion. See also software technology transfer, technology transfer gap.*

technology transfer gap — The time interval (measured in years) between the development of a new product, tool, or technique and its use by the consumers of that product, tool, or technique. *See also software technology transfer, technology transfer.*

technology transition — *See technology transfer.*

TEMP — Acronym for test and evaluation master plan.

termination — In a software process model, the ending of the software development lifecycle.

test — In software engineering: 1. A set of one or more test cases. 2. A set of one or more test procedures. 3. A set of one or more test cases and procedures. [ANSI/IEEE Standard 829–1983] *See also test, test case, test case specification, test data, test design specification, test document, test phase, test plan, test procedure specification, test readiness review (TRR), testing.*

test and evaluation master plan (TEMP) — In system/software system engineering, a planning document for identifying all testing to be performed on the system/software system. The plan includes scope, tasks, costs, schedule, and assigned responsibilities.

test bed — In software engineering (testing): 1. A test environment containing the hardware, instrumentation, tools, simulators, and other support software necessary for testing a system or system component. 2. The repertoire of test cases necessary for testing a system or system component. [ANSI/IEEE Standard 830–1984] *See also test, testing.*

test case — In software engineering (testing), a specific set of test data and associated procedures developed for a particular objective, such as to exercise a particular program path or to verify compliance with a specific requirement. [ANSI/IEEE Standard 729–1983] *See also test, testing.*

test case design — *See test case, test coverage.*

test case specification — In software engineering (testing), a document specifying inputs, predicted results, and a set of execution conditions for a test item. [ANSI/IEEE Standard 829–1983] *See also test, testing.*

test coverage — In software engineering (testing): 1. The selection of test cases so that all statements are executed at least once. 2. In software engineering (metrics), the ratio of executed code to potential code during the test process. Metrics to measure test coverage include the percentage of the total statements executed (statement coverage), the percentage of the total branches taken (decision or branch coverage), and the percentage of the total conditions in all decisions in the system covered (path or condition coverage). Test coverage is typically embodied in standards describing metrics, test procedures, and test reports. [Ramamoorthy et al. 1984] *See also software testing, testing.*

test data — In software engineering (testing), data developed to test a system or system component. [ANSI/IEEE Standard 729–1983] *See also test, test case, testing.*

test data review — *See review, test data.*

test data set — In software engineering (testing), the set of input elements used in the testing process. [FIPS Publication 101 1983]

test design specification — In software engineering (testing), a document specifying the details of the test approach for a software feature or combination of software features and identifying the associated tests. [ANSI/IEEE Standard 829–1983] *See also test, testing.*

test document — *See test case specification, test design specification, test plan, test procedure specification.*

test driver — In software engineering (testing), a program that directs the execution of another program against a collection of test data sets. Usually, the test driver records and organizes the output generated as the tests are run. [FIPS Publication 101 1983]

test environment — *See test bed.*

test harness — *See test driver.* [FIPS Publication 101 1983]

test phase — In software system engineering (testing), the period of time in the system/software development lifecycle during which the components of a system/software product are integrated, and the software product is evaluated to determine whether or not requirements have been satisfied. [ANSI/IEEE Standard 729–1983] *See also software development lifecycle phase, test, testing.*

test plan — In software engineering (testing), a document describing the scope, approach, resources, and schedule of intended testing activities. The test plan identifies test items, the features to be tested, the testing tasks, who will do each task, and any risks requiring contingency planning. [ANSI/IEEE Standard 829-1983] *See also test, testing.*

test procedure specification — In software system engineering (testing), a document specifying a sequence of actions for the execution of a test. [ANSI/IEEE Standard 829–1983] *See also test, testing.*

test readiness review (TRR) — In software system engineering, a milestone review to determine that the software test procedures are complete and to ensure that the software developer is prepared for formal software performance testing. The results of informal testing also are reviewed. [Military Standard 1521B-1985]. *See also milestone review, review, test, testing.*

testability — 1. In software engineering, a software quality metric that can be used to measure those characteristics that provide for testing. 2. In software engineering (requirements specifications), the extent that one can identify an economically feasible technique for determining whether the developed software will satisfy this specification. To be testable, specifications must be specific, unambiguous, and quantitative wherever possible. [Boehm, *V&V Software Requirements* 1984]

testing — In software system engineering: 1. A verification method that applies a controlled set of conditions and stimuli for the purpose of finding errors. This is the most desirable method of verifying the functional and performance requirements. Tests results are documented proof that the requirements were met and can be repeated. The resulting data can be reviewed by all concerned for confirmation of capabilities. *Contrast with analysis, demonstration, examination, and similarity.* 2. The process of analyzing a system/software item to detect the differences between existing and required conditions and to evaluate the features of the system/software item. [ANSI/IEEE Standard 729–1983] 3. The process of exercising or evaluating a system or system component by manual or automated means to verify that it satisfies specified requirements or to identify differences between expected and actual results. *Compare with debugging.*

The STARTS Guide — *See STARTS Guide.*

theorem proving technique — In formal languages, procedures for proving theorems or assertions. *See also formal language, proof of correctness.*

time-critical function — In software engineering (requirements), those requirements that affect reaction time, down time, or availability.

time-sequenced N² chart — An N² chart that was developed to present system operational sequencing definitions and their relationship to the system components. [Lano 1977]

timeline — In system engineering, the two-dimensional sequential display of system functions (Y-axis) against an analog time base (X-axis).

timeline analysis — In system/software system engineering, a method that depicts the concurrency, overlap, and sequential relationship of functions and related tasks and identifies time-critical functions. Time-critical functions are those that affect reaction time, down time, or availability. Timeline analysis can be used to support trade studies, which in turn support decision making at the system level.

timing constraint — In software engineering (requirements), a design constraint on system development.

timing requirements model — In software engineering (requirements specifications), a model that has been augmented with timing constraints. [ANSI/IEEE Standard 729–1983]

to be determined (TBD) — In system/software system engineering, a term (normally written "TBD") that is placed in the system/software requirements specifications where decisions have been postponed for a later time. Each TBD entry should be annotated with the following: (1) the reason for the TBD, (2) who is responsible for removing the TBD, (3) the expected date of removal of the TBD, and (4) under what conditions the TBD can be removed. [Boehm, *V&V Software Requirements* 1984]

to be supplied (TBS) — In system/software engineering (requirements), a term that means that the system item identified in the requirements specification will be supplied to the developer.

tool — In system/software engineering, a step-by-step formalized, manual, or automated process for solving an engineering problem. *See also CASE tool, software tool.*

top-down — *See top-down decomposition. Contrast with bottom-up, bottom-up synthesis.*

top-down analysis — A system/software engineering methodology that means requirements are allocated and decomposed from the top, or system level, down through subsystems, hardware components, and software programs in an orderly fashion. [Nelsen 1990]

top-down decomposition — A software engineering concept that means going from abstract view to physical entity; from general description to detailed description; from broad viewpoint to a detailed viewpoint. *See also top-down analysis, top-down design, top-down development, top-down testing.*

top-down design — In system/software engineering, the process of designing a system by identifying its major components, by decomposing them into their low-level components, and by iterating until the desired level of detail is achieved. *Contrast with bottom-up design.*

top-down development — In system/software engineering, pertaining to an approach that starts with the highest-level system/software component of a hierarchy and proceeds through progressively lower levels; for example, top-down analysis, top-down design, top-down programming, and top-down testing.

top-down testing — In software engineering (testing), the process of checking out hierarchically organized programs, progressively, from top to bottom, of using simulations of low-level components (called stubs). [ANSI/IEEE Standard 729–1983] *Contrast with bottom-up testing.*

top-level dataflow diagram — In software engineering (structured analysis methodology), the highest level of dataflow diagrams.

top-level design — *See architectural design, preliminary design.*

top-level requirement — In system/software system engineering, a requirement that is at level number one in the hierarchy. It represents a system requirement and has no derivation.

top-level requirements specification — *See top-level requirement.*

top-level system design — *See architectural design.*

trace — In formal language notation, a set of events, hence, a relationship between time and action. [Norris 1986] *See also formal language.*

traceability — 1. In software engineering, a quality metric that can be used to measure those characteristics of software that provide a thread of origin from the implementation to the requirements, with respect to the specific development envelope and operational environment. [RADC TR-85–37 1985] 2. In software engineering (requirement specifications), identification and documentation of the derivation path (upward) and allocation/flowdown path (downward) of requirements in the hierarchy.

traceable — A software requirements specification is traceable if the origin of each of the requirements is clear and if it facilitates the referencing of each requirement in future development or enhancement documents.

tracing — In software engineering: 1. To track the implementation of each software requirement into tested code. 2. A procedure for providing an auditable track from the requirements, through design, to the completed and tested product, and back.

trade study — In system/software system engineering, consists of comparing two or more candidate designs with respect to all the characteristics that are important to the intended applications. Characteristics to be considered include not only the identified performance, but also factors of cost, availability, and development times. The factors include affordability, maintainability, growth potential, safety, impact on interfacing, or support to the system, and flexibility with respect to low-level design solutions. [Searle 1981]

trade tree — In system/software system engineering, a visual means of depicting the tradeoff decisions in a treelike manner.

tradeoff study — *See trade study.*

transaction analysis — In software engineering (structured analysis methodology): 1. A design strategy for the derivation of a modular structure from a dataflow diagram (DFD) describing the process. 2. A design strategy that is applicable to portions of the DFD where there is parallel flow of similar data items by type. [DeMarco 1979]

transaction-driven system — *See structured analysis (SA).*

transaction-oriented system — *See structured analysis (SA).*

transform description — In software engineering (structured analysis methodology), a statement describing the logical procedures that govern transformation of input dataflows into output dataflows at a given functional primitive. [DeMarco 1979] *See also bubble, mini-spec, process, PSPEC.*

transform model — A software engineering development strategy that prescribes the following steps: (1) informal specification of the best initial understanding of the desired product; (2) automatic transformation of the specification into code; (3) an iterative loop, if necessary, to improve the performance of the resulting code by giving optimization guidance to the transformed system; (4) exercise of the resulting product; (5) repetition of the iterative loop to adjust to the specification based on resulting operational experience, and (6) rederiving, reoptimizing, and exercising the adjusted software product. The transform model assumes existence of a capability to automatically transform a formal specification of a software product to a program satisfying the specification. [Boehm, *Spiral Model* 1988]

transformation — In software engineering (structured analysis methodology), the transformation of the input by a process (mini-spec, PSPEC) into the output.

transition diagram — *See state transition diagram.*

tree — In a software engineering (methodology), a hierarchy in which it is expected that an element at a given level has only one derivation, that is, flows from one element at a given level to the next higher level. Occasional multiple derivations are permitted. A tree is a graphical representation of such a hierarchy. [Flynn and Dorfman 1990]

TRR — Acronym for test readiness review.

turnaround time — In software engineering, the time from when a programmer submits a program to the computer operations personnel until it is run and the results of the run are returned.

Type A specification — *See A-level specification.*

Type B specification — *See B-level specification.*

Type B5 specification — *See B5-level specification.*

Type C specifications — *See C-level specification.*

Type C5 specification — *See C5-level specification.*

u-u-u

U.K. — Acronym for United Kingdom. The United Kingdom includes England, Scotland, Wales, and Northern Ireland.

UDF — Acronym for unit development folder.

unambiguous — A software requirement specification is unambiguous if the requirement stated has only one semantic interpretation.

unambiguous language — A language in which there is only one interpretation. [Gomaa and Scott 1981]

uncertainty — In management (planning), a state of knowledge in which the decision maker is not knowledgeable about all the data and information necessary for accurate decisions or possible outcomes of an action.

unit — *See software unit. See also module.*

unit code inspection — *See inspection.*

unit design — The design of a software unit. *See also software design.*

unit design inspection — *See inspection.*

unit development folder (UDF) — In software engineering project management, a central depository for recording the progress that has been made toward a "unit's" objectives. A UDF is used by project management for monitoring software work accomplished. A unit can be a single project member or project team. Initial development credited to Frank Ingrassia. *Sometime synonymous with software development file.*

unit testing — In software engineering (testing), the process of ensuring that the unit executes as intended. This usually involves testing all statements and branch possibilities. *Sometimes synonymous with debugging.*

UNIX — In computer science, a modern operating system developed at Bell Laboratories.

untestable requirement — In system/software engineering, requirements that cannot be tested. For example, some realtime, critical defense systems cannot be tested because actual inputs are not available. Other requirement attributes that sometimes cannot be tested properly are constraints and nonfunctional requirements, such as flexibility and evolvability. [Ramamoorthy et al. 1984]

usability — 1. In software engineering, a metric that can be used to measure the relative effort for using software (training and operation), for example, familiarization, input preparation, execution, and output interpretation. [RADC TR-85–37 1985] 2. A metric used with computer-aided software engineering (CASE) tools that can be used to measure the ease in which the tool can be learned and used. Usability includes a consistent-use interface and should hide the underlying system software from those users who do not wish to see it. [Wasserman and Pircher 1987]

user — 1. One who uses the services of a computer system. [IEEE *Computer Applications Technology Glossary* 1986] 2. The person or persons who operate or interact directly with the computer system. The user and the customer are often the same individuals or entities. *Synonymous with end user. See also customer.*

user control — In computer-aided software engineering (CASE) tools, the ability of the user to be in complete control of the tools, to be able to set options for tool use, to be able to determine when checking is to be performed (if at all), and to work in a inconsistent and/or incomplete state. [Wasserman and Pircher 1987]

user documentation — *See users' manual.*

user environment — In system/software system engineering (requirements analysis), the environment of a user that has an impact on the software requirements.

user friendly — 1. In software development, the capability for a consistent user interface, default parameter settings, the use of icons and windows, self-explanatory commands, and online help messages. A user-friendly system should hide the underlying system software from those users who do not wish to see it. 2. Pertaining to a computer system, device, program, or document designed with ease of use as a primary design objective. [IEEE *Computer Applications Technology Glossary*

1986] 3. A software system that has been designed for use by inexperienced people and includes one or more helpful features to assist the user. *Synonymous with user oriented.*

user interface — In software engineering, the software, input and output devices, screens, procedures, and dialogue between people and the software system. *See also interface.*

user interface requirement — In software engineering, the specified requirements for the user interface. *See also user interface.*

user needs statement — In system/software system engineering, a statement from the expected user of the system to: (1) identify the user, (2) describe the user's environment and process, (3) establish the user's views on the system, and (4) assist in formulating the user's expectation.

user oriented — *See user friendly.*

user requirement — *Synonymous with software requirement* [British usage].

users' guide — *See users' manual.*

users' manual — In software engineering projects, a manual used to provide a computer system user or customer personnel with the necessary instructions concerning usage of a software system and instructions on how it is to be operated. The manual content and format is specifically designed to meet the needs of the intended user. *Contrast with maintenance manual, operator's manual.*

V-V-V

V&V — Acronym for verification and validation.

validation — In software engineering, determination of the correctness of the final program or software produced from a development project with respect to the user's needs and requirements. Validation answers the question, "Am I building the right product?" [Boehm, *V&V Software Requirements* 1984]

validation method — In software engineering, a method of validating systems/software requirements using tests, demonstrations, analysis, similarity, and examinations. [Nelsen 1990] *See also analysis, demonstration, examination, similarity, testing.*

validation point — A part of the Software Requirements Engineering Methodology (SREM). A validation point forms the link between the functional processing requirements and performance required for the processing. Validation points come in pairs, and performance criteria must be identified for each pair. [Scheffer and Stone 1985] [Alford 1985] [TRW SS-80–03 1980] *See also R-net, SREM.*

VDD — Acronym for version description document

VDM (Vienna Definition Method) — A software requirements methodology. VDM is a formal method for software development based on work carried out at IBM's laboratory in Vienna, Austria. It is a formal specification language that uses set theory and logic to create abstract specifications that can be proved correct. Data and associated operations are presented in a mathematical language. VDM is useful for specifying functional behavior and derives a correct design from the specification. VDM cannot express nonfunctional requirements. [STARTS Guide 1987]

vendor — A company or firm that manufactures and sells goods. A software vendor (sometimes called a software house) develops and sells software and software packages.

verifiability — 1. In software engineering, a metric that can be used to measure the relative effort to verify the specified software operation and performance. [RADC TR-85–37 1985] 2. In software requirements analysis, a software requirements specification is verifiable only if every requirement stated therein is verifiable. A requirement is verifiable only if there exists some finite cost-effective process with which a person or machine can check that the actual, as-built software product meets the requirement.

verification — In software engineering: 1. The process of determining whether the products of a given phase of the software development cycle fulfill the requirements established during the previous phase. Verification answers the question, "Am I building the product right?" *See also validation.* 2. The act of reviewing, inspecting, testing, checking, auditing, comparing, or otherwise establishing and documenting whether items, processes, services, or documents conform to specified requirements. 3. Formal proof of program correctness. *See also formal (verifiable) requirements language.* 4. In system/software system engineering, a generalized term that can mean: test (using precision instrumentation), demonstration (a functional test), analysis (or simulation), or examination (or documentation). [Sailor 1990]

verification and validation (V&V) — In software engineering, a software quality assurance (SQA) procedure that includes both verification and validation. The basic objectives in verification and validation of software requirements and design specifications are to identify and resolve software problems and high-risk issues early in the software cycle. [Boehm, *V&V Software Requirements* 1984] *See also independent verification and validation, validation, verification.*

verification and validation technique — In software systems engineering, a methodology for performing software requirements and design verification and validation. *See also automated cross-referencing, automated technique (detailed), automated technique (simple), checklist, detailed automated model, detailed scenario, interview, manual cross-referencing, manual model, manual technique (detailed), manual technique (simple), mathe-*

matical proof, prototype, reading, simple automated model, simple scenario. [Boehm, *V&V Software Requirements* 1984]

verification criteria — In software systems engineering, criteria for requirements and design specifications to determine that they are complete, consistent, usable, and testable. [Boehm, *V&V Software Requirements* 1984]

version — In a software system, an operational software product that differs from other like products as to capability, environmental requirements, and configuration. *Sometimes synonymous with build. See also configuration management.*

version description document (VDD) — In system/software system engineering, a specification that sets forth the exact version of a hardware/software configuration item and its interim changes. It is used to identify the current version and, accordingly, accompanies each version of a hardware/software configuration item and each release of an interim version change to a configuration item. [U.S. Department of Defense (DoD) usage] [DoD Standard 2167A 1988]

very-high-level language (VHLL) — In software development: 1. A type of programming language in which the instructions to the computer closely reflect the natural language of the problem. This approach emphasizes the use of languages that are expressive and simple to use for writing program functions. 2. An executable language can sometimes be automatically transformed to code. Its purpose is to accept certain parameters and to generate an application program. *Sometime synonymous with formal languages, fourth-generation language (4GL).*

virtuality — In software engineering, a quality metric that can be used to measure those characteristics of software that present a system that does not require user knowledge of the physical, logical, or topological characteristics. [RADC TR-85-37 1985]

visibility — In software engineering, a quality metric that can be used to measure those characteristics of software that can be used to provide visibility and insight to decision makers. [Keller et al. 1990]

volatile requirement — In software engineering (requirements specifications), a requirement may be considered volatile when it is thought that the requirements will change (sometimes rapidly) during the expected life of the software. [ANSI/IEEE Standard 830–1984] *Contrast with stable requirement.*

W-W-W

walkthrough — In software engineering, a software inspection process, conducted by the peers of the software developer, to evaluate a software element. Although usually associated with code examination, this process is also applicable to the software requirements and software design. The major objectives of the walkthrough are to find defects (e.g., omissions, unwanted additions, and contradictions) in a specification or other product and to consider alternative functionality, performance objectives, or representations. [Hollocker 1990] *See also inspection.*

walkthru — Alternative spelling for walkthrough.

wants-needs evaluation technique — *See Kepner and Tregoe (K-T) analysis technique.*

Ward, Paul T. and Mellor, Stephen J. — Developers of the Ward and Mellor realtime structured analysis methodology and coauthors of the book, *Structured Development for Realtime Systems* [1986]. *See also realtime structured analysis (RTSA).*

Warnier diagram — *See Warnier-Orr charts (diagram).*

Warnier method — A software engineering methodology based on the data structure developed by Jean Warnier in the early 1970s. Similar to Jackson's JSD method, it assumes that the data structure is the key to a successful software design effort. The logical construction of programs approach employs four different design representation schemes: data organization diagrams, logical sequence diagrams, instruction lists, and pseudocode.

Warnier-Orr charts (diagram) — In software engineering, a software design tool and representation method developed by Warnier and modified by Orr that enables the analyst to represent the software system in a hierarchical manner.

Warnier-Orr methodology — *See Data Structured System Development (DSSD).*

waterfall — *See waterfall model.*

waterfall chart — *See waterfall model.*

waterfall model — A software development lifecycle strategy first developed by Winston W. Royce [1970], that partitions the project into manageable phases—requirements, design, implementation, and test—and establishes milestones, documents, and reviews at the end of each phase. In the model, the successful completion of one lifecycle phase in the waterfall chart corresponds to the achievement of the counterpart goal in the sequence of software engineering goals for the software process. The waterfall model recognizes the iteration between phases.

waterfall software development lifecycle model — *See waterfall model.*

WBS — Acronym for work breakdown structure.

WBS directory — *See work breakdown structure (WBS).*

white-box testing — In software engineering (testing), a software test methodology at the module level in which test cases are derived from the internal structure of the program. It may execute all the statements or branches in the program to check on how the system is implemented. Some methods of white-box testing are statement coverage, branch coverage, and path coverage. [Ramamoorthy et al. 1984] *Contrast with black-box testing, functional testing. See also structural testing.*

work breakdown structure (WBS) — In project management, a method of representing in a hierarchical manner the parts of a product or process. A WBS can be used to represent a process (requirement analysis, design, code, or software test) or a product (application programs, utility programs, or operating systems). *See also process work breakdown structure, product work breakdown structure.*

workstation-based environment — In computer-aided software engineering (CASE) tools, an integrated assembly of graphical tools for analysis and design coupled to a project database, along with mechanisms for producing declarations, code skeletons, and executable programs. [Wasserman and Pircher 1987]

x-x-x

y-y-y

Yourdon methodology — *Synonymous with structured analysis (SA) and structured design.*

Yourdon Software Engineering Workbench — A computer-aided software engineering (CASE) tool to support Yourdon structured analysis method. It runs on an IBM personal computer (PC). [STARTS Guide 1987]

Yourdon Structured Analysis for Realtime Systems — A computer-aided software engineering (CASE) tool to support Yourdon realtime structured analysis method. It runs on an IBM personal computer (PC). [STARTS Guide 1987]

Yourdon technique — *Synonymous with structured analysis (SA) and structured design.*

Yourdon, Edward J. — The individual who made the concept of structured analysis and structured design popular. Author of *Modern Structured Analysis* [1989] the new structured analysis standard.

z-z-z

Z — A formal software requirements language (pronounced "ZED") that evolved from research work carried out by the Programming Research Group at the Oxford University Computing Laboratory. Z uses a mathematical-notation-based conventional set theory and predicate calculus with some minor extensions. Note: Z cannot easily model concurrency, nor is it integrated with other software engineering techniques. [Norris 1986]

References for Glossary

[Abbott and Moorhead 1981] Abbott, R.J., and D.K. Moorhead, "Software Requirements and Specifications: A Survey of Needs and Languages," *The Journal of Systems and Software,* Vol. 2, No. 4, 1981, pp. 297–316.

[Alford 1985] Alford, M.W., "SREM at the Age of Eight: The Distributed Computing Design System," IEEE *Computer*, Vol. 18, No. 4, April 1985, pp. 36–46. Reprinted in R.H. Thayer and M. Dorfman (eds.), *Tutorial: System and Software Requirements Engineering,* IEEE Computer Society Press, Washington, DC, 1990.

[*American National Dictionary for Information Processing Systems* 1982] *American National Dictionary for Information Processing Systems*, Information Processing Systems Technical Report, X3/TR-1–82, American National Standards Committee X3, Information Processing Systems, X3 Secretariat, Computer and Business Equipment Manufacturers Association (CBEMA), 1982.

[ANSI N45.2.10–1973] ANSI N45.2.10–1973, *Quality Assurance Terms and Definitions*, American National Standards Institute, NY, 1973.

[ANSI/ASQC A3–1978] ANSI/ASQC A3–1978, *Quality Systems Terminology,* American National Standards Institute, NY, 1978.

[ANSI/IEEE Standard 1058.1–1987] ANSI/IEEE Standard 1058.1-1987, *IEEE Standard for Software Project Management Plans,* The Institute of Electrical and Electronics Engineers, Inc., NY, approved by American National Standards Institute October 6, 1988.

[ANSI/IEEE Standard 729–1983] ANSI/IEEE Standard 729–1983, *IEEE Standard Glossary of Software Engineering Terminology,* The Institute of Electrical and Electronics Engineers, Inc., NY, approved by American National Standards Institute August 9, 1983.

[ANSI/IEEE Standard 829–1983] ANSI/IEEE Standard 829–1983, *IEEE Standard for Software Test Documents,* The Institute of Electrical and Electronics Engineers, Inc., NY, approved by American National Standards Institute August 19, 1983.

[ANSI/IEEE Standard 830–1984] ANSI/IEEE Standard 830–1984, *IEEE Guide for Software Requirements Specifications*, The Institute of Electrical and Electronics Engineers, Inc., NY, approved by American National Standards Institute July 20, 1984.

[Balzer and Goldman 1979] Balzer, R., and N. Goldman, "Principles of Good Software Specification and Their Implications for Specification Languages," *Proceedings of the Specifications of Reliable Software Conference* (Cambridge, MA, April 3–5, 1979), pp. 58–67.

[Benington 1956] Benington, H.D., "Production of Large Computer Programs," *Proceedings of the ONR Symposium on Advanced Methods for Digital Computers* (June 1956), Office of Naval Research, Washinton, DC, 1956, pp. 15–27. Available in *Annals of the History of Computing,* Vol. 5, No. 4 AFIPS Press, October 1983, pp. 350–361, and *Proceedings of the 9th International Conference on Software Engineering* (Monterey, CA, March 30-April 2, 1987), IEEE Computer Society Press, Washington, DC, 1987, pp. 299–310.

[Bersoff 1984] Bersoff, E.H., "Elements of Software Configuration Management," *IEEE Transactions on Software Engineering,* Vol. SE-10, No. 1, January 1984, pp. 79–87. Reprinted in R.H. Thayer and M. Dorfman (eds.), *Tutorial: System and Software Requirements Engineering,* IEEE Computer Society Press, Washington, DC, 1990.

[Boehm, *Software Engineering Economics* 1981] Boehm, B.W., *Software Engineering Economics,* Prentice-Hall, Inc., Englewood Cliffs, NJ, 1981.

[Boehm, *Spiral Model* 1988] Boehm, B.W., "A Spiral Model of Software Development and Enhancement," in R.H. Thayer (ed.), *Tutorial: Software Engineering Project Management,* IEEE Computer Society Press, Washington, DC, 1988. Also published in IEEE *Computer*, Vol. 21, No. 4, April 1988, pp. 61–72.

[Boehm, *V&V Software Requirements* 1984] Boehm, B.W., "Verifying and Validating Software Requirements and Design Specifications," *IEEE Software,* Vol. 1, No. 1, January 1984, pp. 75–88. Reprinted in R.H. Thayer and M. Dorfman (eds.), *Tutorial: System and Software Requirements Engineering,* IEEE Computer Society Press, Washington, DC, 1990.

[British usage] Either the term is unique to the United Kingdom or the definition is different from that used in the U.S.

[Burris 1986] Burris, L.B., "Definition of AI and Other Interesting Terms," unpublished paper, 1986.

[Chen 1990] Chen, P.P., "Entity-Relationship Approach to Data Modeling," in R.H. Thayer and M. Dorfman (eds.), *Tutorial: System and Software Requirements Engineering,* IEEE Computer Society Press, Washington, DC, 1990.

[Cobb 1985] Cobb, R.H., "In Praise of 4GLs," *Datamation*, July 15, 1985, pp. 90–96. Reprinted in R.H. Thayer and M. Dorfman (eds.), *Tutorial: System and Software Requirements Engineering,* IEEE Computer Society Press, Washington, DC, 1990.

[Davis 1990] Davis, A.M., "The Analysis and Specification of System and Software Requirements," in R.H. Thayer and M. Dorfman (eds.), *Tutorial: System and Software Requirements Engineering,* IEEE Computer Society Press, Washington, DC, 1990.

[Davis and Addleman 1986] Davis, M.J., and D.R. Addleman, "Practical Approach to Specification Technology Selection," *The Journal of Systems and Software,* Vol. 6, No. 3, 1986, pp. 285–294.

[Davis et al. 1988] Davis, A.M., E.H. Bersoff, and E.R. Comer, "A Strategy for Comparing Alternate Software Development Life Cycle Models," *IEEE Transactions on Software Engineering,* Vol. SE-14, No. 10, October 1988, pp. 1453–1461. Reprinted in R.H. Thayer and M. Dorfman (eds.), *Tutorial: System and Software Requirements Engineering,* IEEE Computer Society Press, Washington, DC, 1990.

[Davis, *Comparison of Techniques* 1988] Davis, A.M., "A Comparison of Techniques for the Specification of External System Behavior," *Communications of the ACM,* Vol. 31, No. 9, September 1988, pp. 1098–1115. Reprinted in R.H. Thayer and M. Dorfman (eds.), *Tutorial: System and Software Requirements Engineering,* IEEE Computer Society Press, Washington, DC, 1990.

[DeMarco 1979] DeMarco, T., *Structured Analysis and System Specification,* Prentice-Hall, Inc., Englewood Cliffs, NJ, 1979.

[DOD Directive 5010.19] DoD Directive 5010.19, *Configuration Management,* U.S. Department of Defense, October 28, 1987.

[DoD Standard 2167A 1988] DoD Standard 2167A, *Defense System Software Development,* U.S. Department of Defense, February 29, 1988.

[DoD Standard 480B 1988] DOD Standard 480B, *Configuration Control—Engineering Changes, Deviation and Waivers,* U.S. Department of Defense, July 15, 1988.

[DoD, *Engineering Management Guide* 1986] Technical Management Department, Defense Systems Management College (DSMC), *System Engineering Management Guide,* 2nd edition, DSMC, Fort Belvoir, VA, 1986.

[Dorfman 1990] Dorfman, M., "System and Software Requirements Engineering," in R.H. Thayer and M. Dorfman (eds.), *Tutorial: System and Software Engineering Requirements,* IEEE Computer Society Press, Washington, DC, 1990.

[Estrin 1978] Estrin, G., "SARA Aides Design for Software for Concurrent Systems," *Proceedings of the National Computer Conference* (Anaheim, CA, June 5–8, 1978), AFIPS Press, 1978, pp. 325–336.

[FIPS Publication 101 1983] FIPS Publication 101, *Guideline for Lifecycle Validation, Verification, and Testing of Computer Software,* Federal Information Processing Standards Publication 101, Institute for Computer Science and Technology, National Bureau of Standards, Gaithersburg, MD, 1983.

[Flynn and Dorfman 1990] Flynn, R.F., and M. Dorfman, "The Automated Requirements Traceability System (ARTS): An Experience of 8 Years," in R.H. Thayer and M. Dorfman (eds.), *Tutorial: System and Software Requirements Engineering,* IEEE Computer Society Press, Washington, DC, 1990.

[Gane and Sarson 1979] Gane, C.P., and T. Sarson, *Structured Systems Analysis: Tools and Techniques,* Prentice-Hall, Inc., Englewood Cliffs, NJ, 1979.

[Gehani 1982] Gehani, N., "Specifications: Formal and Informal—A case Study," *Software Practice and Experience,* Vol. 12, 1982, pp. 433–444.

[Gomaa and Scott 1981] Gomaa, H., and D.B.H. Scott, "Prototyping as a Tool in the Specifications of User Requirements," *Proceedings of the 5th International Conference on Software Engineering* (San Diego, CA, March 9-12, 1981), 1981.

[Grabow and Noble 1985] Grabow, P.C., and W.B. Noble, "Reusable Software Concepts and Software Development Methodology," *Proceedings of the AIAA Computers in Aerospace V Conference* (Long Beach, CA, October 21–23, 1985), American Institute of Aeronautics and Astronautics, NY, 1985, pp. 140-147. Reprinted in R.H. Thayer and M. Dorfman (eds.), *Tutorial: System and Software Requirements Engineering,* IEEE Computer Society Press, Washington, DC, 1990.

[Hatley and Pirbhai 1987] Hatley, D.J., and I.M. Pirbhai, *Strategies for Real-Time System Specifications*, Dorset House Publishing, NY, 1987.

[Hayes 1986] Hayes, I.J., "Using Mathematics to Specify Software," *Proceedings of the First Australian Software Engineering Conference* (Camberra, Australia, May 14–16, 1986), The Institution of Radio and Electronics Engineers, Australia, 1986, pp. 67–71.

[Heninger 1980] Heninger, K.L., "Specifying Software requirements for Complex Systems: New Techniques and Their Application," *IEEE Transactions on Software Engineering,* Vol. SE-6, No. 1, January 1980, pp. 2–13. Reprinted in R.H. Thayer and M. Dorfman (eds.), *Tutorial: System and Software Requirements Engineering,* IEEE Computer Society Press, 1990.

[Hollocker 1990] Hollocker, C.P., "Requirement Specification Examinations," in R.H. Thayer and M. Dorfman (eds.), in *Tutorial: System and Software Engineering Requirements,* IEEE Computer Society Press, Washington, DC, 1990.

[Humphrey 1989] Humphrey, W.S., *Managing the Software Process*, Addison-Wesley Publishing Co., Inc., Reading, MA, 1989.

[IEEE *Computer Applications Technology Glossary* 1986] *IEEE Glossary of Computer Applications Terminology (Draft),* IEEE, Inc., NY, 1986.

[Keller et al. 1990] Keller, S.E., L.G. Kahn, and R.B. Panara, "Specifying Software Quality Requirements With Metrics," in R.H. Thayer and M. Dorfman (eds.), *Tutorial: System and Software Requirements Engineering,* IEEE Computer Society Press, Washington, DC, 1990.

[Kramer et al. 1988] Kramer, J., K. Ng, C. Potts and K. Whitehead, "Tool Support for Requirements Analysis," *Software Engineering Journal,* May 1988, pp. 86–96.

[Lano 1977] Lano, R.J., "The N^2 Chart," TRW-SS-77–04, TRW Defense and Space Systems Group, Redondo Beach, CA, 1977. Republished as *A Technique for Software and Systems Design*, Vol. 3, North-Holland Publishing Co, NY, 1979. Extract published in R.H. Thayer and M. Dorfman (eds.), *Tutorial: System and Software Requirements Engineering,* IEEE Computer Society Press, Washington, DC, 1990.

[Lano 1990] Lano, R.J., "A Structured Approach for Operational Concept Formulation," in R.H. Thayer and M. Dorfman (eds.), *Tutorial: System and Software Requirements Engineering,* IEEE Computer Society Press, Washington, DC, 1990.

[Lavi 1984] Lavi (Loeb), J.Z., "A Systems Engineering Approach to Software Engineering," *Proceedings of the Software Process Workshop* (Egham, England, February 6–8, 1984), IEEE Computer Society Press, Washington, DC, 1984, 1-21.

[Manley 1974] Manley, J.H., "Embedded Computers—Software Cost Considerations," *Proceedings of the National Computer Conference* (Chicago, IL, May 6–10, 1974), Vol. 43, AFIPS Press, Reston, VA, 1974.

[Manley 1984] Manley, J.H., "Computer Aided Software Engineering," *Selected Conference Papers, 10th Annual Federal DP Expo & Conference* (Washington, DC, April 17–19, 1984), Interface Control Group, Inc., Vienna, VA, 1984.

[Manley 1990] Manley, J.H., "The Dual Life Cycle Model: An Enterprise Perspective of Software Development," in R.H. Thayer and M. Dorfman (eds.), *Tutorial: System and Software Requirements Engineering,* IEEE Computer Society Press, Washington, DC, 1990.

[Military Standard 1521B-1985] Military Standard 1521B (USAF), *Technical Reviews and Audits for Systems, Equipment, and Computer Programs,* U.S. Department of Defense, 1985.

[Military Standard 490A-1985] Military Standard 490A, *Specification Practices,* U.S. Department of Defense, 1985.

[Military Standard 499A-1974] Military Standard 499A, *Engineering Management (USAF),* U.S. Department of Defense, May 1, 1974.

[Miller and Starr 1969] Miller, D.W., and M.K. Starr, *Executive Decisions and Operations Research,* Prentice-Hall, Inc., Englewood Cliffs, NJ, 1969.

[Mullery 1979] Mullery, G.P., "CORE - A Method For Controlled Requirement Specification," *Proceedings of the th International Conference on Software Engineering* (Munich, September 17–19, 1979), IEEE Computer Society Press, Washington, DC, 1979, pp. 126–135. Reprinted in R.H. Thayer and M. Dorfman (eds.), *Tutorial: System and Software Requirements Engineering,* IEEE Computer Society Press, Washington, DC, 1990.

[NBS Special Publication 500–106 1983] Martin, R.J., and W.M. Osborne, *Guidance on Software Maintenance,* NBS Special Publication 500–106, Institute for Computer

Science and Technology, National Bureau of Standards, Gaithersburg, MD, 1983.

[Nelsen 1990] Nelsen, E.D., "System Engineering and Requirement Allocation," in R.H. Thayer and M. Dorfman (eds,) *Tutorial: System and Software Engineering Requirements,* IEEE Computer Society Press, Washington, DC, 1990.

[Norris 1986] Norris, M., "Z (A Formal Specification Method): A Debrief Report," The National Computing Centre Ltd., Manchester, England, 1986. Reprinted in R.H. Thayer and M. Dorfman (eds.), *Tutorial: System and Software Requirements Engineering,* IEEE Computer Society Press, Washington, DC, 1990.

[Orr 1981] Orr, K.T., *Structured Requirements Definition,* Ken Orr and Associates, Topeka, KS, 1981.

[Page-Jones 1988] Page-Jones, M., *The Practical Guide to Structured Systems Design,* 2nd edition, Prentice-Hall, Inc., Englewood Cliffs, NJ, 1988.

[Pressman 1987] Pressman R.S., *Software Engineering: A Practitioner's Approach,* 2nd edition, McGraw-Hill Book Co., NY, 1987.

[Pyster 1990] Pyster, A., "The Synthesis Process for Software Development," in R.H. Thayer and M. Dorfman (eds.), *Tutorial: System and Software Requirements Engineering,* IEEE Computer Society Press, Washington, DC, 1990.

[RADC TR-83–175 1983] Bowen, T.P., J.V. Post, J.T. Tsai, P.E. Presson, and R.L. Schmidt, *Software Quality Measurement for Distributed Systems:* Vol. 1, *Final Report;* Vol. 2, *Guidebook for Software Quality Measurement;* Vol. 3, *Distributed Computing Systems: Impact on Software Quality;* RADC TR-83-175, prepared by Boeing Aerospace Company for Rome Air Development Center, Griffiss AFB, NY, 1983.

[RADC TR-85–37 1985] Bowen, T.P., G.B. Wigle, and J.T. Tsai, *Specification of Software Quality Attributes:* Vol. 1, *Final Technical Report;* Vol. 2, *Software Quality Specifications Guidebook;* Vol. 3, *Software Quality Evaluation Guidebook;* RADC TR-85–37, prepared by Boeing Aerospace Company for Rome Air Development Center, Griffiss AFB, NY, February 1985.

[Ramamoorthy et al. 1984] Ramamoorthy, C.V., A. Prakash, W. Tsai, and Y. Usuda, "Software Engineering: Problems and Perspectives," IEEE *Computer*, Vol. 17, No. 10, October 1984, pp. 191–209. Corrected copy reprinted in R.H. Thayer (ed.), *Tutorial: Software Engineering Project Management,* IEEE Computer Society Press, Washington, DC, 1988.

[Rich et al. 1987] Rich, C., R.C. Waters, and H.B. Reubenstein, "Toward a Requirements Apprentice," *Proceedings of the 4th International Workshop on Software Specifications and Design* (Monterey, CA, April 3–4, 1987), IEEE Computer Society Press, Washington, DC, 1987, pp. 79–86. Reprinted in R.H. Thayer and M. Dorfman (eds.), *Tutorial: System and Software Requirements Engineering,* IEEE Computer Society Press, Washington, DC, 1990.

[Rockstrom and Sarraco 1982] Rockstrom, A., and R. Saracco, "SDL — CCITT Specification and Description Language," *IEEE Transactions on Communications,* Vol. COM-30, No. 6, June 1982, pp. 1310–1317.

[Roman 1985] Roman, G-C., "A Taxonomy of Current Issues in Requirements Engineering," IEEE *Computer,* Vol. 18, No. 4, April 1985, pp. 14–22. Reprinted in R.H. Thayer and M. Dorfman (eds.), *Tutorial: System and Software Requirements Engineering,* IEEE Computer Society Press, Washington, DC, 1990.

[Ross and Schoman 1977] Ross, D.T., and K.E. Schoman, Jr., "Structured Analysis for Requirements Definition," *IEEE Transactions on Software Engineering,* Vol. SE-3, No. 1, January, 1977, pp. 6–15.

[Royce 1970] Royce, W.W., "Managing the Development of Large Software Systems," *Proceedings of the IEEE WESCON* (Los Angles, CA, August 25–28, 1970), IEEE Press, NY, pp. 1–9. Reprinted in R.H. Thayer (ed.), *Tutorial: Software Engineering Project Management,* IEEE Computer Society Press, Washington, DC, 1988.

[Rzepka and Ohno 1985] Rzepka, W., and Y. Ohno, "Requirements Engineering Environments: Software Tools for Modeling User Needs," Guest Editors' Introduction, IEEE *Computer,* Vol. 18, No. 4, April 1985, pp. 9–12.

[Sailor 1990] Sailor, J.D., "System Engineering Overview," in R.H. Thayer and M. Dorfman (eds.), *Tutorial: System and Software Requirements Engineering,* IEEE Computer Society Press, Washington, DC, 1990.

[Sammet 1969] Sammet, J.E., *Programming Languages: History and Fundamentals,* Prentice-Hall, Inc., Englewood Cliffs, NJ, 1986.

[Sayani 1990] Sayani, H.H., "PSL/PSA at the Age of Fifteen," in R.H. Thayer and M. Dorfman (eds.), *Tutorial: System and Software Requirements Engineering,* IEEE Computer Society Press, Washington, DC, 1990.

[Scharer 1981] Scharer, L., "Pinpointing Requirements," *Datamation,* April 1981, pp. 139–151. Reprinted in R.H. Thayer and M. Dorfman (eds.), *Tutorial: System and Software Requirements Engineering,* IEEE Computer Society Press, Washington, DC, 1990.

[Scheffer and Stone 1985] Scheffer, P.A., and A.H. Stone III, "A Case Study of SREM," IEEE *Computer,* Vol. 18, No. 4, April 1985, pp. 47–54.

[Searle 1981] Searle, L.V., *An Air Force Guide to System Specification,* ESD TR-81–128, Electronic Systems Division, Hanscom AFB, MA, 1981.

[STARTS Guide 1987] National Computing Centre, The, *STARTS Guide,* 2nd edition, 2 vols., The National Computing Centre, Ltd., Manchester, England, 1987.

[TRW SS-80-03 1980] Alford, M.W., R.P. Loshbough, and L.R. Marker, "The Software Requirements Engineering Methodology: An Overview," TRW SS-80-03, TRW Defense and Space Systems Group, Redondo Beach, CA, May 1980.

[U.S. Department of Defense (DoD) usage] The term is primarly use by the U.S. Department of Defence and the aerospace industry.

[Urban 1990] Urban, J.E., "The Descartes Specification Language," in R.H. Thayer and M. Dorfman (eds.), *Tutorial: System and Software Requirements Engineering,* IEEE Computer Society Press, Washington, DC, 1990.

[Urban et al. 1985] Urban, S.D., J.E. Urban and W.D. Dominick, "Utilizing an Executable Specification Language for an Information System," *IEEE Transactions on Software Engineering,* Vol. SE-11, No. 7, July 1985, pp. 598–605.

[Ward 1986] Ward, P.T., "The Transformation Schema: An Extension of the Data Flow Diagram to Represent Control and Timing," *IEEE Transactions on Software Engineering,* Vol. SE-12, No. 2, February 1986, pp. 198–210.

[Ward and Mellor 1986] Ward, P.T., and S.J. Mellor, *Structured Development for Real-Time Systems:* Vol. 1, *Introduction & Tools;* Vol. 2, *Essential Modeling Techniques;* Vol. 3, *Implementation Modeling Techniques;* Yourdon Press, NY, 1986. (Note: the principal (first) author for Vol. 3 is S.J. Mellor.)

[Wasserman and Pircher 1987] Wasserman, A.I., and P.A. Pircher, "A Graphic, Extensible Integrated Environment for Software Development," *Proceedings Second ACM SIGSOFT/SIGPLAN Software Engineering Symposium on Practical Software Development Environment* (Palo Alto, CA, December 9–11, 1986), ACM Press, NY, 1986. Published in ACM *SIGPLAN Notices,* Vol. 22, No. 1, January 1987, pp. 131–142. Reprinted in R.H. Thayer and M. Dorfman (eds.), *Tutorial: System and Software Requirements Engineering,* IEEE Computer Society Press, Washington, DC, 1990.

[Williams 1987] Williams, J., "SSADM—System Building Made simple," *Systems International,* November 1987, pp. 91–92. Reprinted in R.H. Thayer and M. Dorfman (eds.), *Tutorial: System and Software Requirements Engineering,* IEEE Computer Society Press, Washington, DC, 1990.

[Yourdon 1989] Yourdon, E., *Modern Structured Analysis,* Yourdon Press Computing Series, Prentice-Hall, Inc., Englewood Cliffs, NJ, 1989.

[Zave 1984] Zave, P., "The Operational Versus the Conventional Approach to Software Development," *Communications of the ACM,* Vol. 27, No. 2, February 1984, pp. 104–118. Reprinted in R.H. Thayer and M. Dorfman (eds.), *Tutorial: System and Software Requirements Engineering,* IEEE Computer Society Press, Washington, DC, 1990.

Annotated Bibliography

The following is an annotated list of books and publicly available reports on system and software requirements engineering. Although the place of publication shown may be in the U.S., the book may actually be published or available in other international cities (e.g., Brisbane, London, Manchester, Melbourne, and Singapore). When the background or viewpoint of the author is non-USA, it is noted.

Abbott, R.J., *An Integrated Approach to Software Development,* John Wiley and Sons, Inc., NY, 1986, 359 pages.
This reference is useful in the development of requirements and software design documents. Its format is organized around a collection of annotated outlines for technical documents relevant to the development and maintenance of software. The annotations explain why the documents are organized as they are and why their contents are as shown.

Beizer, B., *Software System Testing and Quality Assurance,* Van Nostrand Reinhold Co., NY, 1984, 380 pages.
An overview of testing and quality assurance methods for software development. It also covers all types of testing procedures, configuration management, and verification and validation.

Bergstra, J.A., J. Heering, and P. Klint, *Algebraic Specification,* Addison-Wesley Publishing Co., Inc., Ridgely, MD, 1989, 416 pages.
This book is one of the ACM Press Frontier Series which uses examples and case studies to show how the algebraic specification techniques can be applied to the rapid prototyping of software. The book uses a practical approach, to show how the formal approach to the specification of software can provide gains in programmer productivity.

Boehm, B.W., *Software Engineering Economics,* Prentice Hall, Inc., Englewood Cliffs, NJ, 1981, 775 pages.
This book tells you all you will ever want to know about software economics and software development cost estimating. This is the most referenced book in software engineering today. Every project manager should have a copy on the bookshelf.

Boehm, B.W., *Tutorial: Software Risk Management,* IEEE Computer Society Press, Washington, DC, June 1989, 512 pages.
The book focuses on identifying the major sources of risk on a software project; understanding the essential concepts and techniques involved in software risk assessment and control; and applying these concepts and techniques to practice day-to-day software project situations.

Booch, B., *Software Engineering with Ada,* The Benjamin/Cummings Publishing Co., Inc., Menlo Park, CA, 1983, 504 pages.
This book treats Ada as a design tool and not as just another programming language. There are special flags indicating sections of special interest for managers and programmers.

Bowen, T.P., G.B. Wigle, and J.T. Tsai, Specification of Software Quality Attributes, Vol. 1, *Final Technical Report,* 108 pages; Vol. 2, *Software Quality Specifications Guidebook,* 142 pages; Vol. 3, *Software Quality Evaluation Guidebook,* 303 pages; RADC-TR-85-37, prepared by Boeing Aerospace Company for Rome Air Development Center, Griffiss AFB, NY, February 1985.
The most extensive and comprehensive information on software quality metrics available.

Brooks, F.P., Jr., *The Mythical Man-Month: Essays on Software Engineering,* Addison-Wesley Publishing Co., Inc., Reading, MA, 1975, 206 pages.
The software engineering project management best-seller. This classic written by Fred Brooks is a series of essays dealing with the management of computer programming projects. The essays are drawn from the author's experience as project manager for the IBM System/360 and for its OS/360 operating system. They blend software engineering facts with insights from the author and other builders of complete computer systems. Don't miss reading it.

Bruce, P. and S.M. Pederson, *The Software Development Project: Planning and Management,* John Wiley and Sons, Inc., Inc., NY, 1982, 234 pages.
This volume offers project managers a coherent framework for implementing and controlling a software development project from definition and analysis of requirements through the actual operation of a software system. All information is applicable to commercial and scientific projects in both public and private sectors. The techniques described provide a structured approach to planning, costing, and scheduling a software development effort and to organizing and managing the project team. The book is augmented with a set of tear-out charts suitable for quick reference or presentation material.

Buckley, F.J., *Implementing Software Engineering Practices,* John Wiley and Sons, Inc., NY, 1989, 208 pages.

This book by Fletcher Buckley shows you how to implement cost-effective software engineering practices in an industrial and/or commercial organization. The guidance provided is practical rather than theoretical and uses an easy-to-follow, how-to-implement style. The author has spent more than ten years in the design, building, and use of software engineering standards. He was the first chair of the IEEE Computer Society Software Engineering Standards Subcommittee and chaired the first working group to develop a guide for software quality assurance planning. The book provides a set of procedures and standards that apply to a software development project as it passes through the software development lifecycle process. Each phases is discussed in detail with a view toward the standards that must be in position in order to implement these activities.

Bullinger, H.J. and R. Gunzenhauser, *Software Ergonomics Advances and Applications,* John Wiley and Sons, Inc., NY, 1988, 186 pages.
Software ergonomics is a new field that bridges the gap between technical and human-factors approaches to software development. This book presents recent scientific advances from the point of view of the user, offering practical guidelines for designing dialogue-based user interfaces.

Cameron, J., *Monograph: JSP & JSD–The Jackson Approach to Software Development,* 2nd Edition, IEEE Computer Society Press, Washington, DC, May 1989, 400 pages.
The book covers introductory material and detailed explanations of topics in thc arca of Jackson Structured Programming and Jackson Software Development. It is geared primarily for system analysts, designers, programmers, software engineers, and academics teaching courses in these areas.

Candullo, C., Jr., *System Development Standards,* McGraw-Hill Book Co., Inc., NY, 1985, 766 pages.
This is a practical book with guidelines on how to develop and deliver a system. The book generally follows the requirements-design-implementation-test lifecycle and is hardware/software independent. The first part contains the principles of system development, followed by a description of the methodology, required documentation, and forms necessary to be applied during the systems development lifecycle. The last half of the book contains blank forms that could be tailored for the reader's own project. The books is mainly applicable to a commercial data processing project.

Chikofsky, E.J., *Technology Series: Software Development–Computer Aided Software Engineering,* IEEE Computer Society Press, Washington, DC, 1988, 132 pages.
This book discusses the CASE environments that provide a mechanism for systems analysts to document and model an information system from its inception as user requirements through its design and implementation. The book discusses analytic tools to ensure consistency, completeness, and conformance to standards.

Chow, T.S., *Tutorial: Software Quality Assurance: A Practical Approach,* IEEE Computer Society Press, Washington, DC, 1985, 506 pages.
This tutorial provides the reader with a comprehensive view of software quality issues, the various components of a software quality assurance plan, and ways of implementing quality assurance.

Coad, P. and E. Yourdon, *OORA–Object-Oriented Requirements Analysis,* Prentice Hall, Inc., Englewood Cliffs, NJ, 1989.
An early book on object-oriented requirements analysis. Worth reading.

Davis, A.M., *Software Requirements: Analysis and Specification,* Prentice Hall, Englewood Cliffs, NJ, 1989.
This new book of software requirements analysis and specification presents an all-encompassing discussion on system and software engineering. Davis is the chair of the IEEE working group for the "Guide to Software Requirements Specifications."

DeMarco, T., *Structured Analysis and System Specification,* Yourdon Press, NY, 1978, 366 pages.
This is the benchmark book and standard for structured software analysis and structured requirement specifications, to the extent that structured analysis is sometimes called the "DeMarco technique." This book should bc read by all designers and managers who hope to use structured analysis on their software development systems.

Deutsch, M.S. and R.R. Willis, *Software Quality Engineering–A Total Technical and Management Approach,* Prentice Hall, Inc., Englewood Cliffs, NJ, 1988, 330 pages.
This short but compact book gives specific details about software quality assurance and the techniques and tools that are used to ensure software quality. There is an excellent chapter on understanding software quality and specifying software quality requirements. The book includes information on conducting design reviews, walkthroughs, and inspections. The book goes into managing the aspects of software quality design, including such topics as what is required for quality engineering and who is responsible for doing software quality engineering. This book is an excellent and complimentary text to complete a software engineer's bookshelf.

Evans, M.W., *The Software Factory–A Fourth Generation Software Engineering Environment,* John Wiley and Sons, Inc., NY, 1989, 336 pages.

This book discusses the software development process and presents the concept of the software factory—an integrated software engineering environment for the development and support of software. The book uses dozens of case studies and exercises, discusses the implementation of the software factory, and focuses on large-scale DOD software environments.

Fairley, R.E., *Software Engineering Concepts,* McGraw-Hill Book Co., NY, 1985, 376 pages.
This excellent text presents a thorough overview of software engineering. It includes two excellent chapters on project management with emphasis on project planning and lifecycle cost models. This general overview provides top-level information on software requirements, design, and verification and validation techniques. Also covered is a discussion on modern programming-language features.

Fisher, A.S., *CASE: Using Software Development Tools,* John Wiley and Sons, Inc., NY, 1988, 287 pages.
This book describes the various types of CASE tools and practices and how they can reduce a software development project's cost, schedule, and risk. The book includes the Yourdon/DeMarco structured analysis, data modeling, and user interface design.

Freedman, D.P. and G.M. Weinberg, *Handbook of Walkthroughs, Inspections, and Technical Reviews: Evaluating Programs, Projects, and Products,* 3rd Edition, Little, Brown and Co., Boston, MA, 1982, 450 pages.
The third edition of this handbook uses a question-and-answer format to explain how and why technical reviews are conducted. The authors discuss both formal and informal reviews. This is a very practical book on the author's personal experience in conducting formal technical reviews, walkthroughs, and inspections. The book covers how to conduct a review, reporting the results of the review, types of reviews, and types of materials reviewed.

Freeman, P., *Tutorial: Software Reusability,* IEEE Computer Society Press, Washington, DC, 1987, 304 pages.
Provides a variety of original and reprinted materials relevant to reusability in the process of creating software-intensive systems. The topics discussed range from concepts to case studies and from specific techniques to research explorations that may never be practical. The focus, however, is on what is currently possible for actual usage.

Gane, C.P. and T. Sarson, *Structured Systems Analysis: Tools and Techniques,* Prentice Hall, Inc., Englewood Cliffs, NJ, 1979, 253 pages.
This book describes the somewhat classic structured software requirements system entitled "structured systems analysis." The book provides marvelous illustrations and examples of how to apply structured analysis methods and manual tools to analyze a software system. It is a clearly written book and explains structured analysis at the management level.

Gehani, N. and A. McGettrick (eds.), *Software Specification Techniques,* Addison-Wesley Publishing Co., Inc., Reading, MA, 1989, 477 pages.
This book brings under one cover 21 recent papers on critical papers on critical problems of software specification. These papers, grouped into four sections, cover topics such as the principles and properties of good specification, various specification methods, the use of specifications to specify software systems, and systems that check specifications for correctness and execute them to provide a correct prototype.

Glass, R.L., *Modern Programming Practices: A Report from Industry,* Prentice Hall, Inc., Englewood Cliffs, NJ, 1982, 311 pages.
In 1977, Rome Air Development Center contracted with six U.S. aerospace firms to discern which software development methodologies were the most effective. Bob Glass did us all a favor when he reduced this seven-inch-thick stack of documentation into an excellent summary.

Hatley, D.J. and I.A. Pirbhai, *Strategies for Real-Time System Specifications,* Dorset House Publishing, NY, 1987, 436 pages.
This is one of two reference books on realtime extensions to structured analysis (see Ward and Mellor for the other one). The book explains in great detail how to build data-flow diagrams and control flow diagrams along with their accompanying descriptions and data dictionaries. The Hatley Method, as it is called, is supported by many of the emerging CASE tools.

Hekmatpour, S. and D. Ince, *Software Prototyping, Formal Methods and VDM,* Addison-Wesley Publishing Co., Inc., Reading, MA, 1989, 222 pages.
This book provides insight to rapid prototyping using formal methodology; it includes in-depth coverage of the EPROS prototyping system as well as case studies on the use of VDM for formal specification and system development.

Humphrey, W., *Managing the Software Process,* Addison-Wesley Publishing Co., Inc., Reading, MA, 1989, 450 pages.
This text is an outgrowth of the author's experience in software management at IBM. This text examines the current state of software development and covers the basic principles of software process management for both small and large-scale projects, and suggest improvements in software management and evaluation.

IEEE Software Engineering Standards, 3rd Edition, IEEE, Inc., NY, 1988.

This is a collection of currently available Institute of Electrical and Electronic Engineers, Inc. (IEEE) software engineering standards.

Jensen, R.W. and C.C. Tonies, *Software Engineering,* Prentice Hall, Inc., Englewood Cliffs, NJ, 1979, 591 pages.
This early book on software engineering provides an excellent review of software engineering as it pertains to systems. The chapters on project management fundamentals and software design are excellent.

Kowal, J.A., *Analyzing Systems,* Prentice Hall, Inc., Englewood Cliffs, NJ, 1988, 461 pages.
This book is about the techniques of software development, particularly techniques that can be applied in the software requirements design phases of the software development lifecycle. This book provides excellent descriptions of probably all of the most used software development techniques in the USA today. This includes dataflow diagrams, minispecifications, and hierarchical relationship diagrams. In addition, it has a detailed description of the more recent realtime modeling techniques along with an excellent example using an auto rental system to illustrate both logical and physical analysis.

Lano, R.J., *A Technique for Software and Systems Design,* North-Holland Publishing Co., NY, 1979, 131 pages.
This reference provides a comprehensive treatment of the types and uses of N^2 charts. Many illustrative examples are presented and discussed. This is the only comprehensive treatment of N^2 charts in existence.

Martin, J. and C. McClure, *Diagraming Techniques for Analysts and Programmers,* Prentice Hall, Inc., Englewood Cliffs, NJ, 1985, 412 pages.
This is a complete, easy-to-read description of many of the modern software development methodologies and techniques. It makes an excellent reference for project managers who need to know more about the new methodologies of developing software systems.

Mellor, S.J. and P.T. Ward, *Structured Development for Real-Time Systems:* Vol. 3, *Implementation Modeling Techniques,* Yourdon Press, NY, 1986.
See entry after Ward, P.T. and S.J. Mellor.

Orr, K.T., *Structured Systems Development,* Yourdon Press, NY, 1977, 192 pages.
This book presents a detailed discussion of the data structure approach to software design as developed by Warnier's "logical construction of programs" (LCP) method.

Page-Jones, M., *Practical Guide to Structured Systems Design,* 2nd Edition, Prentice Hall, Inc., Englewood Cliffs, NJ, 1988, 384 pages.
This is a second edition of the benchmark book and standard on how to write structured design. This book provides an outline of the tools of structured analysis and shows how to use them for analysis and designing tasks. It is extremely readable, full of interesting anecdotes and examples, and it can be read and understood in a short time.

Peters, L., *Advanced Structured Analysis and Design,* Prentice Hall, Inc., Englewood Cliffs, NJ, 1987, 295 pages.
This book discusses structured analysis and design from an advanced viewpoint. By "advanced" the author means that the topics that are normally treated separately are now treated as one continuous process—structured analysis, structured design, and information modeling. The text discusses how to establish and write software analysis using the structured analysis method; how to make the transition to using it for design and then how to write a structured chart to complete the design. It also includes allied techniques such as work breakdown structure, evaluating and improving modular interaction, and evaluating and improving modules and event diagrams.

Pressman, R.S., *Software Engineering: A Practitioner's Approach,* 2nd Edition, McGraw-Hill Book Co., NY, 1987, 587 pages.
This second edition is greatly expanded and improved. All aspects of software engineering are covered. The book contains new chapters on object-oriented and real-time design and additional emphasis on software quality assurance and configuration management, and it virtually ignores coding (as it should). The book devotes a chapter to system and requirements engineering.

Shatz, S. and J.P. Wang, *Tutorial: Distributed-Software Engineering,* IEEE Computer Society Press, Washington, DC, January 1989, 294 pages.
This tutorial considers each of the key problems involved in disturbed-software analysis, design, implementation, and testing. Focuses on developing correct and reliable software—the most significant problem in developing distributed computing systems.

Shneiderman, B., *Designing the User Interface,* Addison-Wesley Publishing Co., Inc., Ridgely, MD, 1987, 448 pages.
This book surveys human factors that must be considered in designing interactive systems. The purpose of the book is to help the reader design systems that are both easy to learn and easy to use, i.e., systems that are both effective and successful. The book contains detailed discussions and practical advice on topics like commands, menus, direct manipulation, keyboards, screens, documentation, on-line help, and training.

Slayer, S. and S.J. Miller, *Object-Oriented Systems Analysis, Modeling the World in Data,* Yourdon Press Com-

puting Series, Prentice Hall, Inc., Englewood Cliffs, NJ, 1988, 156 pages.
This book is a simple book that provides the groundwork for an object-oriented approach to system development through information modeling. The approach proposed by the author focuses on identification, formalization, and verification of expert knowledge from diverse businesses and technical disciplines to determine the information requirements of the system. The book emphasizes how to collect information and knowledge about the problems at hand; how to transform the knowledge into objects, attributes, and relationships; and how to fully incorporate the resulting information into a software development process. The book uses a picture-book style to illustrate the concept of objects, attributes, and relationships.

Sommerville, I., *Software Engineering,* 3rd Edition, Addison-Wesley Publishing Co., Inc., Reading, MA, 1989, 672 pages.
Ian Sommerville's third edition continues with the excellent coverage of software engineering that he exhibited in edition two (don't buy edition one). New topics covered are object-oriented design and formal specification languages (including algebraic specifications). Sommerville discusses software management issues such as project planning, configuration management, and quality assurance. The book is divided into five major parts with numerous small chapters, each chapter covering only a selected part of software engineering. The book, however, gives short coverage of traditional U.S. type techniques such as functional requirements specifications and structured analysis and design. This book has a U.K. slant.

STARTS Guide—See The STARTS Guide.

Thayer, R.H., *Tutorial: Software Engineering Project Management,* IEEE Computer Society Press, Washington, DC, 1988, 499 pages.
This tutorial presents a "top-down view" of software engineering project management and assembles under one cover a sufficient body of knowledge about managing successful software engineering projects. The tutorial is comprised of reprints and original papers from some of the most prominent software engineers in this country, e.g., Boehm, Buckley, Fairley, and Yourdon. Thayer's paper, entitled "Software Engineering Project Management: A Top-down View," summarizes the functions and activities necessary to successfully manage a software development project.

The STARTS Guide, The National Computing Centre Limited, 2 volumes, Manchester, England, 1987, 606 pages.
This guide was developed as part of the Software Technology for Application to Large Real-Time Systems (STARTS) initiative at the National Computer Center, Manchester, England. It is a very detailed set of procedures, applicable in many cases to software development in the U.K., but with a few exceptions applicable to software development in the USA. It covers such topics as project management; configuration management; project infrastructure and support environment; requirements definition and design; and verification, validation, and testing. The book is extremely easy to read, and it discusses in great detail and integrates the use of modern CASE tools. The various available CASE tools available in the U.K. are assessed and evaluated for appropriateness for various types of project applications. Volume 2 contains a one or two page description of each available software CASE tool available in the U.K. along with a price, assessment of the tool's capability, and source. This is one of the most valuable books available in Europe and even has a great deal of value in the U.S. (British viewpoint.)

Tracz, W., *Tutorial: Software Reuse–Emerging Technology,* IEEE Computer Society Press, Washington, DC, 1988, 400 pages.
This tutorial provides an overview of the basic issues concerning software reuse and discusses the reasons why software is, is not, and should be reused. The book also focuses on the mental and supplemental tools that support software reuse including components, software libraries, methodologies, Ada reuse experience, and object-oriented computing.

Ward, P.T. and S.J. Mellor, *Structured Development for Real-Time Systems,* Vol. 1, *Introduction and Tools,* 166 pages; Vol. 2, *Essential Modeling Techniques,* 172 pages, Vol. 3, *Implementation Modeling Techniques,* 194 pages, Yourdon Press, NY, 1986. (Note: the principal author for Volume 3 is S.J. Mellor.)
These three small volumes update structured analysis and structured design. Written primarily for realtime applications, they also update the structured techniques and terminology and therefore should be read by both realtime and non-realtime professionals. Vol. 1 is an introduction to the structured techniques. Vol. 2 describes realtime structured analysis, and Vol. 3 describes realtime structured design.

Weinberg, G.M., *The Psychology of Computer Programming,* Van Nostrand Reinhold Co., NY, 1971.
Despite the apparent age of this book the information is still current. The psychology of programming is presented in an attempt to provide a better understanding of how people work together in a software development environment. Weinberg presents his concept of "egoless" programming and egoless technical reviews (called walkthroughs) as a means of reducing programming errors.

Yourdon, E., *Managing the Structured Techniques,* Yourdon Press Computing Series, Prentice Hall, Inc., Englewood Cliffs, NJ, 1989, 224 pages.
This is Ed Yourdon's fourth edition of his book on how to manage the structured techniques. The primary purpose of this book is not to show how the technical aspects of these methods work, but rather to help the reader manage the various structured techniques. The discussion of CASE tools has been updated to reflect current developments. A chapter has been entered on chief program techniques, structured walkthroughs choosing which technique to implement first, choosing a pilot project, and developing standards for the structured technique. The bibliography, which has been enlarged and brought up to date, now lists a basic library for the system developer and manager.

Yourdon, E., *Modern Structured Analysis,* Yourdon Press Computing Series, Prentice Hall, Inc., Englewood Cliffs, NJ, 1989, 688 pages.
This new book on structured analysis updates the classic material and has become the new standard. The book includes the older, non-realtime (batch) systems and the newer realtime techniques. Much of the terminology also is updated (the term mini-spec has been dropped in favor of the more professional sounding "process specification"). Modern concepts of data modeling, prototyping, and fourth generation languages are included. Basic analysis issues are discussed, such as interviewing techniques, cost benefit studies, and estimating techniques, as well as advanced techniques of dataflow diagrams and entity-relationship diagrams. Also included are the use of state-transition diagrams and ways of integrating them with dataflow diagrams for realtime application. The book emphasizes the modeling of the expected system and deemphasizes the modeling of current physical systems. Nearly 1,000 illustrations are included as well as two comprehensive case studies illustrating the various tools and techniques discussed in the book. An excellent set of references is included at the end of each chapter as well as a series of questions and exercises. The book is easier to read and keeps up with Yourdon's clear writing style.

Yourdon, E., *Structured Walkthroughs,* 4th Edition, Yourdon Press Computing Series, Prentice Hall, Inc., Englewood Cliffs, NJ, 1989, 192 pages.
This book updates the original edition which was first published in 1977. The book is intended to assist readers in understanding the structured walkthrough and to implement it in their companies. The walkthrough, which is similar in approach and technique to the IBM inspection system, has been rated by many companies as being the equal of unit testing in finding errors in units of code. The book highlights the work of system analysts, reduces the emphasis placed on programmers, and focuses on the increased role of users in the system development process.

Yourdon, E., *Techniques of Program Structure and Design,* Prentice Hall, Inc., NY, 1975, 363 pages.
This book is a well-formatted and easy-to-understand text on using top-down design, structured programming, chief programmer teams, and testing. Yourdon provides lots of examples.

Selected References and Other Readings

Richard H. Thayer
Merlin Dorfman

This is a partial list of the most important references in system and software requirements engineering. Many of these references were cited in the papers in this tutorial. The sources of terms used in the "Glossary" plus the references used in the various chapter introductions can also be found there.

To obtain documents, see list of publishers and professional societies in "How and Where to Find it: Sources of System and Software Engineering Requirements Information" in *Standards, Guidelines, and Examples: System and Software Requirements Engineering*, edited by Merlin Dorfman and Richard H. Thayer and published by the IEEE Computer Society Press, Washington, DC, 1990.

References

a-a-a

Abbott, R.J., *An Integrated Approach to Software Development*, John Wiley and Sons, Inc., NY, 1987.

Abbott, R.J., and D.K. Moorhead, "Software Requirements and Specifications: A Survey of Needs and Languages," *The Journal of Systems and Software*, Vol. 2, No. 4, 1981, pp. 297–316.

Addleman, D.R., M.J. Davis, and P.E. Presson, *Specification Technology Guidebook*, RADC TR-85–13, prepared by Boeing Aerospace Company for Rome Air Development Center, Griffiss AFB, NY, 1985.

Adrion, W.R., M.A. Brandstad, and J.C. Cherniavsky, "Validation, Verification, and Testing of Computer Software," *Computing Surveys*, Vol. 14, No. 2, June 1982, pp. 160–192. Also published as NBS Special Publication 500–75, Institute for Computer Science and Technology, National Bureau of Standards, Gaithersburg, MD, 1981.

AFR 800–14, *Lifecycle Management of Computer Resources in Systems,* U.S. Air Force, September 14, 1987.

Alford, M.W., "A Requirements Engineering Methodology for Real-Time Processing Requirements," *Proceedings of the 2nd International Conference on Software Engineering* (San Francisco, CA, October 13–15, 1976), IEEE Computer Society Press, Washington, DC, 1976, p. 69. Also published in *IEEE Transactions on Software Engineering*, Vol. SE-3, No. 1, January 1977, pp. 60–69.

Alford, M.W., "SREM at the Age of Eight: The Distributed Computing Design System," IEEE *Computer*, Vol. 18, No. 4, April 1985, pp. 36–46. Reprinted in R.H. Thayer and M. Dorfman (eds.), *Tutorial: System and Software Requirements Engineering*, IEEE Computer Society Press, Washington, DC, 1990.

Alford, M.W., and J.T. Lawson, "Software Requirements Engineering Methodology (Development)," RADC TR-79–168, prepared by TRW Defense and Space Systems Group, Huntsville, AL, for Rome Air Development Center, Griffiss AFB, NY, 1979.

Alford, M.W., R.P. Loshbough, and L.R. Marker, "The Software Requirements Engineering Methodology: An Overview," TRW SS-80–03, TRW Defense and Space Systems Group, Redondo Beach, CA, May 1980.

American National Dictionary for Information Processing Systems, Information Processing Systems Technical Report, X3/TR-1–82, American National Standards Committee X3, Information Processing Systems, X3 Secretariat, Computer and Business Equipment Manufacturers Association (CBEMA), 1982.

ANSI N45.2.10–1973, *Quality Assurance Terms and Definitions*, American National Standards Institute, NY, 1973.

ANSI/ASQC A3–1978, *Quality Systems Terminology*, American National Standards Institute, NY, 1978.

ANSI/IEEE Standard 1012–1986, *IEEE Standard for Software Verification and Validation Plans*, The Institute of Electrical and Electronics Engineers, Inc., NY, approved by American National Standards Institute February 10, 1987.

ANSI/IEEE Standard 1042–1987, *IEEE Guide to Software Configuration Management*, The Institute of Electrical and Electronics Engineers, Inc., NY, approved by American National Standards Institute March 10, 1988.

ANSI/IEEE Standard 1058.1–1987, *IEEE Standard for Software Project Management Plans*, The Institute of Electrical and Electronics Engineers, Inc., NY, approved by American National Standards Institute October 6, 1988.

ANSI/IEEE Standard 1063–1987, *IEEE Standard for Software User Documentation*, The Institute of Electrical and Electronics Engineers, Inc., NY, approved by American National Standards Institute February 2, 1989.

ANSI/IEEE Standard 729–1983, *IEEE Standard Glossary of Software Engineering Terminology*, The Institute of Electrical and Electronics Engineers, Inc., NY, approved by American National Standards Institute Aug 9, 1983.

ANSI/IEEE Standard 730–1984, *IEEE Standard for Software Quality Assurance Plans*, The Institute of Electrical and Electronics Engineers, Inc., NY, approved by American National Standards Institute December 17, 1984.

ANSI/IEEE Standard 828–1983, *IEEE Standard for Software Configuration Management Plans*, The Institute of Electrical and Electronics Engineers, Inc., NY, approved by American National Standards Institute December 17, 1984.

ANSI/IEEE Standard 829–1983, *IEEE Standard for Software Test Documents*, The Institute of Electrical and Electronics Engineers, Inc., NY, 1987, approved by American National Standards Institute August 19, 1983.

ANSI/IEEE Standard 830–1984, *IEEE Guide for Software Requirements Specifications*, The Institute of Electrical and Electronics Engineers, Inc., NY, approved by American National Standards Institute July 20, 1984.

ANSI/IEEE Standard 983–1986, *IEEE Guide for Software Quality Assurance Planning*, The Institute of Electrical and Electronics Engineers, Inc., NY, approved by American National Standards Institute February 20, 1986.

Arthur, L.J., *Programmer Productivity: Myths, Methods, & Murphology*, John Wiley and Sons, Inc., NY, 1983.

Augustine, N.R., *Augustine's Laws*, Penguin Books, Inc., NY, 1987.

Austwick, M., and M. Norris, "VDM: A Debrief Report," *STARTS* Debrief Reports, The National Computing Centre Ltd., Manchester, England, 1986. *See also STARTS Debrief Reports for reports on other software tools and methods.*

b-b-b

Babich, W.A., *Software Configuration Management: Coordination for Team Productivity*, Addison-Wesley Publishing Co., Inc., Reading, MA, 1986.

Baker, J.W., D. Chester, and R.T. Yeh, "Software Design by Stepwise Evaluation and Refinement," in R.T. Yeh and P.A. Ng (eds.), *Handbook of Computer Aided Software Engineering*, Van Nostrand Reinhold Co., NY, 1989.

Balzer, R., and N. Goldman, "Principles of Good Software Specification and Their Implications for Specification Languages," *Proceedings of the Specifications of Reliable Software Conference* (Cambridge, MA, April 3–5, 1979), IEEE Computer Society Press, Washington, DC, pp. 58–67.

Basili, V., and D. Weiss, "Evaluation of A Software Requirements Document by Analysis of Change Data," *Proceedings of the 5th International Conference on Software Engineering* (San Diego, CA, March 9–12, 1981), IEEE Computer Society Press, Washington DC, 1981, pp. 314–323.

Beizer, B., *Software System Testing and Quality Assurance*, Van Nostrand Reinhold Co., NY, 1984.

Beizer, B., *Software Testing Techniques*, Van Nostrand Reinhold Co., NY, 1983.

Benington, H.D., "Production of Large Computer Programs," *Proceedings of the ONR Symposium on Advanced Methods for Digital Computers* (June 1956), Office of Naval Research, Washington, DC, 1956, pp. 15–27. Available in *Annals of the History of Computing*, Vol. 5, No. 4, AFIPS Press, Reston, VA, October 1983, pp. 350–361, and *Proceedings of the 9th International Conference on Software Engineering*, (Monterey,CA, March 30-April 2, 1987), IEEE Computer Society Press, Washington, DC, 1987, pp. 299–310.

Bergstra, J.A., J. Heering, and P. Klint, *Algebraic Specification*, Addison-Wesley Publishing Co., Inc., Ridgely, MD, 1989.

Berliner, E., and P. Zave, "An Experiment in Technology Transfer: PAISLey Specification of Requirements for an Undersea Lightwave Cable System," *Proceedings of the 9th International Conference on Software Engineering* (Monterey, CA, March 30-April 2, 1987), IEEE Computer Society Press, Washington, DC, 1987, pp. 42–50.

Bersoff, E.H., "Elements of Software Configuration Management," *IEEE Transactions on Software Engineering*, Vol. SE-10, No. 1, January 1984, pp. 79–87. Reprinted in R.H. Thayer and M. Dorfman (eds.), *Tutorial: System and Software Requirements Engineering*, IEEE Computer Society Press, Washington, DC, 1990.

Bersoff, E.H., V.D. Henderson, and S.G. Siegel, *Software Configuration Management: An Investment in Productivity Integrity*, Prentice-Hall, Inc., Englewood Cliffs, NJ, 1980.

Berzins, V., and M. Gray, "Analysis and Design in MSG 84: Formalizing Functional Specifications," *IEEE Transactions on Software Engineering*, Vol. SE-11, No. 8, August 1985, pp. 657–670.

Bjoerner, D., "On the Use of Formal Methods in Software Development," *Proceedings of the 9th International Conference on Software Engineering* (Monterey, CA, March 30-April 2, 1987), IEEE Computer Society Press, Washington, DC, 1987, pp. 17–29.

Boar, B.H., *Application Prototyping: A Requirements Definition Strategy for the 80s*, John Wiley and Sons, Inc., NY, 1984.

Boehm, B.W., "A Spiral Model of Software Development and Enhancement," in R.H. Thayer (ed.), *Tutorial: Software Engineering Project Management*, IEEE Computer

Society Press, Washington, DC, 1988. Also published in IEEE *Computer*, Vol. 21, No. 5, May 1988, pp. 61–72.

Boehm, B.W., "Improving Software Productivity," IEEE *Computer*, Vol. 20, No. 9, September 1987, pp. 43–57. Reprinted in R.H. Thayer (ed.), *Tutorial: Software Engineering Project Management*, IEEE Computer Society Press, Washington, DC, 1988.

Boehm, B.W., "Seven Basic Principles of Software Engineering," *The Journal of Systems and Software*, Vol. 3, No. 1, 1983, pp. 3–24.

Boehm, B.W., "Software and Its Impact: A Quantitative Assessment," *Datamation*, May 1973, pp. 48–60.

Boehm, B.W. and P.N. Papaccio, "Understanding and Controlling Software Costs." *IEEE Transactions on Software Engineering*, Vol. SE-14, No. 10, October 1988, pp. 1462–1477.

Boehm, B.W., "Verifying and Validating Software Requirements and Design Specifications," *IEEE Software*, Vol. 1, No. 1, January 1984, pp. 75–88. Reprinted in R.H. Thayer and M. Dorfman (eds.), *Tutorial: System and Software Requirements Engineering*, IEEE Computer Society Press, Washington, DC, 1990.

Boehm, B.W., M.H. Penedo, E.D. Stuckle, R.D. Williams, and A.B. Pyster, "A Software Development Environment for Improving Productivity," IEEE *Computer*, Vol. 17, No. 6, June 1984, pp. 30–44.

Boehm, B.W., *Software Engineering Economics*, Prentice-Hall, Inc., Englewood Cliffs, NJ, 1981.

Boehm, B.W., *Tutorial: Software Risk Management*, IEEE Computer Society Press, Washington, DC, 1989.

Booch, E.G., "Object-Oriented Development," *IEEE Transactions on Software Engineering*, Vol. SE-12, No. 2, February 1986, pp. 211–221.

Bowen, T.P., G.B. Wigle, and J.T. Tsai, *Specification of Software Quality Attributes:* Vol. 1, *Final Technical Report;* Vol. 2, *Software Quality Specifications Guidebook;* Vol. 3, *Software Quality Evaluation Guidebook;* RADC TR-85–37, prepared by Boeing Aerospace Company for Rome Air Development Center, Griffiss AFB, NY, February 1985.

Bowen, T.P., J.V. Post, J.T. Tsai, P.E. Presson, and R.L. Schmidt, *Software Quality Measurement for Distributed Systems:* Vol. 1, *Final Report;* Vol. 2, *Guidebook for Software Quality Measurement;* Vol. 3, *Distributed Computing Systems: Impact on Software Quality*, RADC TR-83–175, prepared by Boeing Aerospace Company for Rome Air Development Center, Griffiss AFB, NY, 1983.

Branstad, M., J. Cherniavsky, and W. Adrion, "Validation, Verification, and Testing for the Individual Programmer," NBS Special Publication 500–56, Institute for Computer Science and Technology, National Bureau of Standards, Gaithersburg, MD, 1980.

Brooks, F.P. Jr., (chairman), "Report of the Defense Science Board Task Force on Military Software," Office of the Undersecretary of Defense for Acquisition, U.S. Department of Defense, Washington, DC, September 1987.

Brooks, F.P. Jr., *The Mythical Man-Month: Essays on Software Engineering*, Addison-Wesley Publishing Co., Reading, MA, 1975.

Brooks, F.P. Jr.,"No Silver Bullet: Essence and Accidents of Software Engineering," IEEE *Computer*, Vol. 20, No. 4, April 1987, pp. 10–19.

Bruce, P., and S.M. Pederson, *The Software Development Project: Planning and Management*, John Wiley and Sons, Inc., NY, 1982.

Bruyn, W., R. Jensen, D. Keskar, and P. Ward, "An Extended System Modeling Language (ESML)," ACM *SIGSOFT Software Engineering Notes*, Vol. 13, No. 1, January 1988.

Buckley, F.J., "Establishing Software Engineering Standards in an Industrial Organization," in R.H. Thayer (ed.), *Tutorial: Software Engineering Project Management*, IEEE Computer Society Press, Washington, DC, 1988.

Buckley, F.J., *Implementing Software Engineering Standards*, John Wiley and Sons, Inc., NY, 1989.

Burris, L.B., "Definition of AI and Other Interesting Terms," unpublished paper, 1986.

Buxton, J.N., P. Naur, and B. Randell (eds.), *Software Engineering Concepts and Techniques*, Petrocelli/Charter, NY, 1976.

c-c-c

Caine, S.H., and E.K. Gordon, "PDL—A Tool for Software Design," *Proceedings of the 1975 National Computer Conference* (Anaheim, CA, May 19–22, 1975), Vol. 44, AFIPS Press, Reston, VA, 1975, pp. 271–276.

Cameron, J.R., "An Overview of JSD," *IEEE Transactions on Software Engineering*, Vol. SE-12, No. 2, February 1986.

Cameron, J.R., *Monograph: JSP & JSD—The Jackson Approach to Software Development*, 2nd edition, IEEE Computer Society Press, Washington, DC, May 1989.

Candullo, C. Jr., *System Development Standards*, McGraw-Hill Book Co., Inc., NY, 1985.

Card, D.N., F.E. McGarry, and G. Page, "Evaluating Software Engineering Techniques," *Proceedings of the Eight Annual Software Engineering Workshop* (NASA/Goddard Space Flight Center, November 3, 1983), NASA/SEL-83–007, NASA/Software Engineering Laboratory, Greenbelt, MD, November 1983.

Charette, R., *Software Engineering Environments*, McGraw-Hill Book Co., NY, 1986.

Chen, P.P., "Entity-Relationship Approach to Data Modeling," in R.H. Thayer and M. Dorfman (eds.), *Tutorial: System and Software Requirements Engineering*, IEEE Computer Society Press, Washington, DC, 1990.

Chen, P.P., "The Entity-Relationship Model—Toward a Unified View of Data," *ACM Transactions on Database Systems*, Vol. 1, No. 1, March, 1976, pp. 9–36.

Chow, T.S., *Tutorial: Software Quality Assurance: A Practical Approach*, IEEE Computer Society Press, Washington, DC, 1988.

Cleland, D.I., and W.R. King, *Management: A Systems Approach*, McGraw-Hill Book Company, NY, 1972.

Clements, P.C., "Using Information-Hiding as a Design Discipline: Techniques and Lessons," *Proceedings of the Structured Development Forum VIII* (Seattle, WA, August 1986).

CMU/SEI 87-TR-23 — *See Software Engineering Institute, 1987.*

Coad, P., and E. Yourdon, *OOA—Object-Oriented Analysis*, Prentice-Hall, Inc., Englewood Cliffs, NJ, 1989.

Cobb, R.H., "In Praise of 4GLs," *Datamation*, July 15, 1985, pp. 90–96. Reprinted in R.H. Thayer and M. Dorfman (eds.), *Tutorial: System and Software Requirements Engineering*, IEEE Computer Society Press, Washington, DC, 1990.

Cox, B.J., "Message/Object Programming: An Evolutionary Change in Programming Technology," *IEEE Software*, Vol. 1, No. 1, January 1984, pp. 50–61.

Cox, B.J., *Object-Oriented Programming: An Evolutionary Approach,* Addison-Wesley Publishing Co., Inc., Ridgely, MD, 1986.

d-d-d

Dart, S.A., R.J. Ellison, P.H. Feiler, and A.N. Habermann, "Software Development Environments," IEEE *Computer*, Vol. 20, No. 11, November 1987, pp. 18–28.

Davis, A.M., "A Comparison of Techniques for the Specification of External System Behavior," *Communications of the ACM*, Vol. 31, No. 9, September 1988, pp. 1098–1115. Reprinted in R.H. Thayer and M. Dorfman (eds.), *Tutorial: System and Software Requirements Engineering*, IEEE Computer Society Press, Washington, DC, 1990.

Davis, A.M., "A Taxonomy for the Early Stages of the Software Development Life Cycle," *The Journal of Systems and Software*, Vol. 8, No. 4, 1988, pp. 297–311.

Davis, A.M., "Automating the Requirements Phase: Benefits to Later Phases of the Software Life-Cycle," *Proceedings of IEEE COMPSAC* '80 (Chicago, IL, October 27–31, 1980), IEEE Computer Science Press, Washington, DC, 1980, pp. 42–48.

Davis, A.M., "Rapid Prototyping Using Executable Requirements Specifications," ACM *SIGSOFT Software Engineering Notes*, Vol. 7, No. 5, December 1982, pp. 39–44.

Davis, A.M., "The Analysis and Specification of System and Software Requirements," in R.H. Thayer and M. Dorfman (eds.), *Tutorial: System and Software Requirements Engineering*, IEEE Computer Society Press, Washington, DC, 1990.

Davis, A.M., "The Design of a Family of Applications-Oriented Requirements Languages," IEEE *Computer*, Vol. 15, No. 5, May 1982, pp. 21–28.

Davis, A.M., E.H. Bersoff, and E.R. Comer, "A Strategy for Comparing Alternative Software Development Life Cycle Models," *IEEE Transactions on Software Engineering,* Vol. SE-14, No. 10, October 1988, pp. 1453–1461. Reprinted in R.H. Thayer and M. Dorfman (eds.), *Tutorial: System and Software Requirements Engineering,* IEEE Computer Society Press, Washington, DC, 1990.

Davis, A.M., *Software Requirements: Analysis and Specification,* Prentice-Hall, Inc., Englewood Cliffs, NJ, 1989.

Davis, M.J., and D.R. Addleman, "Practical Approach to Specification Technology Selection," *The Journal of Systems and Software*, Vol. 6, No. 3, 1986, pp. 285–294.

DeMarco, T., *Structured Analysis and System Specification*, Prentice-Hall, Inc., Englewood Cliffs, NJ, 1979.

Deutsch, M.S., "Focusing Real-Time Systems Analysis on User Operations," *IEEE Software*, Vol. 5, No. 5, September 1988.

DoD Directive 5010.19, *Configuration Management* U.S. Department of Defense, October 28, 1987.

DoD Standard 2167A, *Defense System Software Development*, U.S. Department of Defense, February 29, 1988.

DoD Standard 480B, *Configuration Control—Engineering Changes, Deviation and Waivers,* U.S. Department of Defense, July 15, 1988.

DoD Standard 7935A, *DoD Automated Information Systems (AIS) Documentation Standards,* U.S. Department of Defense, October 31, 1988.

DoD, Engineering Management Guide — *See Technical Management Department, Defense Systems Management College (DSMC), 1986. See also Sailor, 1983.*

Donaldson, H., *A Guide to the Successful Management of Computer Projects,* John Wiley and Sons, Inc., NY, 1978.

Donelson, W.S., "Project Planning and Control," *Datamation*, June 1976.

Dorfman, M., "System and Software Requirements Engineering," in R.H. Thayer and M. Dorfman (eds.), *Tutorial: System and Software Requirements Engineering,* IEEE Computer Society Press, Washington, DC, 1990.

Dorfman, M., and R.H. Thayer (eds.), *Standards, Guidelines, and Examples:* System and Software Requirements Engineering, IEEE Computer Society Press, Washington, DC, 1990.

Dorfman, M., and R.F. Flynn, "ARTS - An Automated Requirements Traceability System," *Proceedings AIAA Computers in Aerospace III Conference* (San Diego, CA,

October 26–28, 1981), American Institute of Aeronautics and Astronautics, NY, 1981.

Dorfman, M., and R.F. Flynn, "ARTS—an Automated Requirements Traceability System," *The Journal of Systems and Software,* Vol. 4, No. 1, 1984, pp. 63–74.

e-e-e

ESD TR-81-128 — *See Searle, 1981.*

ESD TR-87-136 — *See Humphrey and Sweet, 1987.*

ESD TR-88-001 — *See Schultz, 1988.*

Estrin, G., "SARA Aides Design for Software for Concurrent Systems," *Proceedings of the National Computer Conference* (Anaheim, CA, June 5–8, 1978), AFIPS Press, Reston, VA, 1978, pp. 325–336.

Evans, M.W., *The Software Factory: A Fourth Generation Software Engineering Environment,* John Wiley and Sons, Inc., NY, 1989.

f-f-f

Fagan, M.E., "Design and Code Inspections to Reduce Errors in Program Development," *IBM Systems Journal,* Vol. 15, No. 3, 1976, pp. 182–211.

Fagan, M.E., "Inspecting Software Design and Code," *Datamation*, Vol. 23, No. 10, October 1977, pp. 133–144.

Fayol, H., *General and Industrial Management*, Sir Isaac Pitman & Sons, Ltd., London, 1949.

FIPS Publication 101, *Guideline for Lifecycle Validation, Verification, and Testing of Computer Software,* Federal Information Processing Standards Publication 101, Institute for Computer Science and Technology, National Bureau of Standards, Gaithersburg, MD, 1983.

FIPS Publication 11–2, *Guidelines, American National Dictionary for Information Processing Systems,* Federal Information Processing Standards Publication 11–2, Institute for Computer Science and Technology, National Bureau of Standards, Gaithersburg, MD, 1982.

FIPS Publication 38, *Guidelines for Documentation of Computer Programs and Automated Data Systems,* Federal Information Processing Standards Publication 38, Institute for Computer Science and Technology, National Bureau of Standards, Gaithersburg, MD, 1976.

Flynn, R.F., and M. Dorfman, "The Automated Requirements Traceability System (ARTS): An Experience of 8 Years," in R.H. Thayer and M. Dorfman (eds.), *Tutorial: System and Software Requirements Engineering,* IEEE Computer Society Press, Washington, DC, 1990.

Freeman, P., and A.I. Wasserman, *Tutorial: Software Design Techniques,* 4th edition, IEEE Computer Society Press, Washington, DC, 1983.

Freeman, P., *Tutorial: Software Reusability,* IEEE Computer Society Press, Washington, DC, 1987.

Furia, N., "A Comparative Evaluation of RSL/REVS and PSL/PSA Applied to a Digital Flight Control System," *Proceedings of the AIAA 2nd Computers in Aerospace Conference* (Los Angeles, CA, October 22–24, 1979), American Institute of Aeronautics and Astronautics, NY, 1979, pp. 330–337.

g-g-g

Gane, C.P., "Data Design in Structured Systems Analysis," *Infotech State of the Art Report on Data Design,* 1980.

Gane, C.P., and T. Sarson, *Structured Systems Analysis: Tools and Techniques,* Prentice-Hall, Inc., Englewood Cliffs, NJ, 1979.

Gehani, N., "Specifications: Formal and Informal—A case Study," *Software—Practice and Experiences,* Vol. 12, 1982, pp. 433–444.

Gehani, N., and A. McGettrick (eds.), *Software Specification Techniques,* Addison-Wesley Publishing Co., Inc., Reading, MA, 1985.

Goldberg, R., "Software Engineering: An Emerging Discipline," *IBM System Journal,* Vol. 25, Nos. 3/4, 1986, pp. 334–353.

Gomaa, H,. "The Impact of Prototyping on Software System Engineering," in R.H. Thayer and M. Dorfman (eds.), *Tutorial: System and Software Requirement Engineering,* IEEE Computer Society Press, Washington, DC, 1990.

Gomaa, H., "A Software Design Method for Real-Time Systems," *Communications of the ACM,* Vol. 27, No. 9, September 1984.

Gomaa, H., and D.B.H. Scott, "Prototyping as a Tool in the Specifications of User Requirements," *Proceedings of the 5th International Conference on Software Engineering* (San Diego, CA, March 9–12, 1981), IEEE Computer Society Press, Washington, DC, 1981.

Grabow, P.C., and W.B. Noble, "Reusable Software Concepts and Software Development Methodology," *Proceedings of the AIAA Computers in Aerospace V Conference* (Long Beach, CA, October 21–23, 1985), American Institute of Aeronautics and Astronautics, NY, 1985, pp. 140–147. Reprinted in R.H. Thayer and M. Dorfman (eds.), *Tutorial: System and Software Requirements Engineering,* IEEE Computer Society Press, Washington, DC, 1990.

h-h-h

Harel, D., "Statecharts: A Visual Formalism for Complex Systems," *Science of Computer Programming,* Vol. 8, 1987.

Harel, D., H. Lachover, A. Naamad, A. Pnueli, M. Politi, R. Sherman, and A. Shtul-Trauring, "STATEMATE1: A Working Environment for the Development of Complex Reactive Systems," *Proceedings of the 10th International Conference on Software Engineering* (Singapore, April 11–15, 1988), IEEE Computer Society Press, Washington, DC, 1988, pp. 396–406.

Hatley, D., "The Use of Structured Methods in the Development of Large Software-Based Avionics Systems," *Proceedings of the AIAA/IEEE 6th Digital Avionics Systems Conference* (Baltimore, MD, December 3–6, 1984), IEEE Press, Washington, DC, 1984, pp. 6–15.

Hatley, D.J., and I.M. Pirbhai, *Strategies for Real-Time System Specification,* Dorset House Publishing, NY, 1987.

Hayes, I.J., "Applying Formal Specification to Software Development in Industry," *IEEE Transactions on Software Engineering,* Vol. SE-11, No. 2, February 1985, pp. 169–178.

Hayes, I.J., "Using Mathematics to Specify Software," *Proceedings of the First Australian Software Engineering Conference* (Canberra, Australia, May 14–16, 1986), The Institution of Radio and Electronics Engineers, Australia, 1986, pp. 67–71.

Heninger, K.L., "Specifying Software requirements for Complex Systems: New Techniques and Their Application," *IEEE Transactions on Software Engineering,* Vol. SE-6, No. 1, January 1980, pp. 2–13. Reprinted in R.H. Thayer and M. Dorfman (eds.), *Tutorial: Systems and Software Requirement Engineering,* IEEE Computer Society Press, Washington, DC, 1990.

Hoare, C.A.R., "Data Reliability," *ACM SIGPLAN Notices,* Vol. 10, No. 6, June 1975, pp. 528–533.

Hoare, C.A.R., "Notes on Data Structuring," in J. Dahl, E.W. Dijkstra, and C.A.R. Hoare, *Structured Programming,* Academic Press, NY, 1972, pp. 83–174.

Hollocker, C.P., "Requirement Specification Examinations," in R.H. Thayer and M. Dorfman (eds.), *Tutorial: System and Software Requirements Engineering,* IEEE Computer Society Press, Washington, DC, 1990.

Houghton, R.C., Jr., "Software Development Tools," NBS Special Publication 500–88, Institute for Computer Science and Technology, National Bureau of Standards, Gaithersburg, MD, 1982.

Howden, W.E., "Life-Cycle Software Validation," IEEE *Computer,* Vol. 15, No. 2, February 1982, pp. 71–78.

Howes, N.R., "On Using the Users' Manual as the Requirements Specification II," in R.H. Thayer and M. Dorfman (eds.), *Tutorial: System and Software Requirements Engineering,*IEEE Computer Society Press, Washington, DC, 1990.

Howes, N.R., "On Using the Users' Manual as the Requirements Specification," in R.H. Thayer (ed.), *Tutorial: Software Engineering Project Management,* IEEE Computer Society Press, Washington, DC, 1988.

Hull, R., and R. King, "Semantic Database Modeling: Survey, Applications, and Research Issues," *ACM Computing Surveys,* Vol. 19, No. 3, September 1987.

Humphrey, W.S., and W.L. Sweet, "A Method for Assessing the Software Engineering Capability of Contractors, Preliminary Version," Software Engineering Institute Report CMU/SEI-87-TR-23 and U.S. Air Force Electronic Systems Division Report ESD TR-87–136, September 1987.

Humphrey, W.S., *Managing the Software Process,* Addison-Wesley Publishing Co., Inc., Reading, MA, 1989.

i-i-i

IBM, "HIPO - A Design Aid and Documentation Technique" IBM GC20–1851–0, International Business Machines Corporation, Armonk, NY.

IEEE Glossary of Computer Applications Terminology (Draft), The Institute of Electrical and Electronics Engineers, Inc., NY, 1986.

IEEE Software Engineering Standards, Hardbound Edition of Software Engineering Standards, 3rd edition, The Institute of Electrical and Electronic Engineers, Inc, NY, 1989.

IEEE Standard 1028–1988. *IEEE Standard for Software Reviews and Audits,* The Institute of Electrical and Electronics Engineers, NY, approved by IEEE Standards Board June 9, 1988.

Ingram, D., "Requirements Management Is Key to Software Quality," *CASE Outlook,* Vol. 1, No. 5, November 1987.

Ingrassia, F.S., "The Unit Development Folder (UDF): A Ten-Year Perspective," in R.H. Thayer (ed.), *Tutorial: Software Engineering Project Management,* IEEE Computer Society Press, Washington, DC, 1988.

Institute of Electrical and Electronic Engineers, Inc. — *See IEEE. See also ANSI/IEEE.*

j-j-j

Jackson, M.A., *Principles of Program Design,* Academic Press, London, 1975.

Jensen, R.W., and C.C. Tonies, *Software Engineering,* Prentice-Hall, Inc., Englewood Cliffs, NJ, 1979.

Jones, T.C., "Reusability in Programming: A Survey of the State of the Art," *IEEE Transactions on Software Engineering,* Vol. SE-10, No. 9, September 1984, pp. 488–494.

k-k-k

Keller, S.E., L.G. Kahn, and R.B. Panara, "Specifying Software Quality Requirements With Metrics," in R.H. Thayer and M. Dorfman (eds.), *Tutorial: System and Software Requirements Engineering,* IEEE Computer Society Press, Washington, DC, 1990.

Kepner, C.H., and B.B. Tregoe, *The Rational Manager,* McGraw-Hill Book Co., NY, 1965.

Kerola, P., and P. Freeman, "A Comparison of Life Cycle Models," *Proceedings of the 5th International Conference on Software Engineering* (San Diego, CA, March 9–12, 1981), IEEE Computer Society Press, Washington, DC, 1981, pp. 90–99.

Koontz H., and C. O'Donnell, *Principles of Management: An Analysis of Managerial Functions,* 5th ed., McGraw-Hill Book Company, NY, 1972.

Koontz, H., C. O'Donnell, and H. Weihrich, *Management,* 7th ed., McGraw-Hill Book Co., NY, 1980.

Kowal, J.A., *Analyzing Systems,* Prentice-Hall, Inc., Englewood Cliffs, NJ, 1988.

Kramer, J., K. Ng, C. Potts, and K. Whitehead, "Tool Support for Requirements Analysis," *Software Engineering Journal,* May 1988, pp. 86–96.

l-l-l

Lano, R.J., "A Structured Approach for Operational Concept Formulation," TRW SS-80–02, TRW Defense and Space Systems Group, Redondo Beach, CA, 1980.

Lano, R.J., "A Structured Approach for Operational Concept Formulation," in R.H. Thayer and M. Dorfman (eds.), *Tutorial: System and Software Requirements Engineering,* IEEE Computer Society Press, Washington, DC, 1990.

Lano, R.J., "The N^2 Chart," TRW-SS-77–04, TRW Defense and Space Systems Group, Redondo Beach, CA, 1977. Republished as *A Technique for Software and Systems Design,* Vol. 3, North-Holland Publishing Co, NY, 1979. Extract published in R.H. Thayer and M. Dorfman (eds.), *Tutorial: System and Software Requirements Engineering,* IEEE Computer Society Press, Washington, DC, 1990.

Lavi (Loeb), J.Z., "A Systems Engineering Approach to Software Engineering," *Proceedings of the Software Process Workshop* (Egham, England, February 6–8, 1984), IEEE Computer Society Press, Washington, DC, 1984, 1–21.

Lehman, M.M., "Programs, Life Cycles, and Laws of Program Evolution," IEEE *Spectrum,* September 1980.

Loy, P.H., "Design Documentation Retrofitting: An Approach for Retrieving Reusable Code," *Proceedings of the Fifth Annual Pacific Northwest Software Quality Conference* (Portland, OR, October 19–20, 1987), c/o Lawrence and Craig, Inc., P.O. Box 40244, Portland, OR 97204, pp. 156–173.

m-m-m

Manley, J.H., "Computer Aided Software Engineering (CASE): Foundation for Software Factories," *Proceedings of IEEE COMPCON '84 Fall Computer Conference on the Small Computer (R)Evolution* (Arlington, VA, September 16–20, 1984), IEEE Computer Society Press, Washington, DC, 1984, pp. 84–91.

Manley, J.H., "Computer Aided Software Engineering," Presented at the 10th Annual Federal DP Expo & Conference (Washington, DC, April 17, 1984).

Manley, J.H., "Embedded Computers—Software Cost Considerations," *Proceedings of the National Computer Conference* (Chicago, IL, May 6–10, 1974), Vol. 43, AFIPS Press, Reston, VA, 1974.

Manley, J.H., "The Dual Life Cycle Model: An Enterprise Perspective of Software Development," in R.H. Thayer and M. Dorfman (eds.), *Tutorial: System and Software Requirements Engineering,* IEEE Computer Society Press, Washington, DC, 1990.

Mantei, M., "The Effect of Programming Team Structures on Programming Tasks," *Communications of the ACM,* Vol. 24, No. 3, March 1981, pp. 106–113.

Martin, J., and C. McClure, *Diagramming Techniques for Analysts and Programmers,* Prentice-Hall, Inc., Englewood Cliffs, NJ, 1985.

Martin, R.J., and W.M. Osborne, *Guidance on Software Maintenance,* NBS Special Publication 500–106, Institute for Computer Science and Technology, National Bureau of Standards, Gaithersburg, MD, 1983.

MASCOT Handbook, 1987 — *See The Official Handbook of MASCOT.*

McCabe, T.J., *Structured Testing: A Software Testing Methodology Using the Cyclomatic Complexity Metric,* NBS Special Publication 500–99, Institute for Computer Science and Technology, National Bureau of Standards, Gaithersburg, MD, 1982.

McCracken, D., and M. Jackson, "Life Cycle Concept Considered Harmful," ACM *SIGSOFT Software Engineering Notes,* Vol. 7, No. 2, April 1982, pp. 29–32.

Metzger, P.W., *Managing a Programming Project,* 2nd edition, Prentice-Hall, Inc., Englewood Cliffs, NJ, 1981.

Meyer, B., "On Formalism in Specifications," *IEEE Software,* Vol. 2, No. 1, January 1985.

Meyer, B., *Object-Oriented Software Construction*, Prentice-Hall, Inc., Englewood Cliffs, NJ, 1988.

Military Standard 1521B (USAF), *Technical Reviews and Audits for Systems, Equipment, and Computer Programs*, U.S. Department of Defense, 1985.

Military Standard 481B, *Configuration Control (Short Form), Engineering Changes, Deviations, and Waivers*, U.S. Department of Defense, July 15, 1988.

Military Standard 490A, *Specification Practices*, U.S. Department of Defense, June 4, 1985.

Military Standard 499A, *Engineering Management (USAF)*, U.S. Department of Defense, May 1, 1974.

Miller, D.W., and M.K. Starr, *Executive Decisions and Operations Research*, Prentice-Hall, Inc., Englewood Cliffs, NJ, 1969.

Mills, H.D., "Software Engineering Education," *Proceedings of the IEEE*, Vol. 68, No. 9, September 1980, pp. 1158–1162.

Mills, H.D., "Stepwise Refinement and Verification in Box-Structured Systems, IEEE *Computer*, Vol. 21, No. 6, June 1988, pp. 23–36.

Misra, S.K., and P.J. Jalics, "Third Generation vs. Fourth Generation Software Development," *IEEE Software*, Vol. 5, No. 4, July 1988.

Mullery, G.P., "CORE - A Method for Controlled Requirement Specification," *Proceedings of the 4th International Conference on Software Engineering* (Munich, September 17–19, 1979), IEEE Computer Society Press, Washington, DC, 1979, pp. 126–135. Reprinted in R.H. Thayer and M. Dorfman (eds.), *Tutorial: System and Software Requirements Engineering*, IEEE Computer Society Press, Washington, DC, 1990.

Musa, J.D., "Software Reliability," in *Handbook of Software Engineering*, C. Vick and C.V. Ramamoorthy (eds.), Van Nostrand Reinhold Co., NY, 1984, pp. 392–412.

Musa, J.D., "Software Engineering: the Future of a Profession," *IEEE Software*, Vol. 2, No. 1, January 1985, pp. 55–62.

Myers, G.J., *Composite/Structured Design*, Van Nostrand Reinhold Co., NY, 1978.

n-n-n

Nassi, I., and B. Shneiderman, "Flow Chart Techniques of Structured Programming," ACM *SIGPLAN Notices*, Vol. 8, No. 8, August 1973.

National Computing Centre, *The STARTS (Software Tools for Application to Large Real-Time Systems) Debrief Reports*, The National Computing Centre Ltd., Manchester, England. *See separate entries under STARTS Debrief Reports*.

National Computing Centre, *The STARTS Guide*, 2nd edition, 2 vols., The National Computing Centre, Ltd., Manchester, England, 1987.

Naur, P., and B. Randell (eds.), *Software Engineering: Report on a Conference Sponsored by the NATO Science Commission* (Garmisch, Germany, October 7–11, 1968), NATO Scientific Affairs Division, Brussels, January 1969.

NBS (NIST) Special Publication 500–165, 1989 — *See Wallace and Fujii, 1989*.

NBS Special Publication 500–106, 1983 — *See Martin and Osborne, 1983*.

NBS Special Publication 500–56, 1980 — *See Branstad et al., 1980*.

NBS Special Publication 500–75, 1981 — *See Adrion et al., 1981*.

NBS Special Publication 500–88, 1982 — *See Houghton, 1982*.

NBS Special Publication 500–99, 1982 — *See McCabe, 1982*.

Neighbors, J.M., "The Draco Approach to Constructing Software from Reusable Components," *IEEE Transactions on Software Engineering*, Vol. SE-10, No. 9, September 1984, pp. 564–574.

Nelsen, E.D., "System Engineering and Requirement Allocation," in R.H. Thayer and M. Dorfman (eds,) *Tutorial: System and Software Requirements Engineering*, IEEE Computer Society Press, Washington, DC, 1989.

Newport, J.P., Jr., "A Growing Gap in Software," *Fortune*, April 28, 1986, pp. 132–142.

NIST Special Publication 500–165, 1989 — *See Wallace and Fujii, 1989*.

Norris, M., "Z (A Formal Specification Method): A Debrief Report," The National Computing Centre Ltd., Manchester, England, 1986. Reprinted in R.H. Thayer and M. Dorfman (eds.), *Tutorial: System and Software Requirements Engineering*, IEEE Computer Society Press, Washington, DC, 1990. *See also STARTS Debrief Reports for reports on other software tools and methods*.

NRL Report 7909 — *See Weiss, 1975*.

o-o-o

Orr, K.T., *Structured Requirements Definition*, Ken Orr and Associates, Topeka, KS, 1981.

Orr, K.T., *Structured Systems Development*, Yourdon Press, 1977.

Ouchi, W.G., *Theory Z: How American Business Can Meet the Japanese Challenge*, Addison-Wesley, Reading, MA, 1981.

p-p-p

Page-Jones, M., *The Practical Guide to Structured Systems Design,* 2nd edition, Prentice-Hall, Inc., Englewood Cliffs, NJ, 1988.

Parnas, D.L., "On the Criteria to Be Used in Decomposing Systems into Modules," *Communications of the ACM,* Vol. 15, No. 12, December 1972, pp. 1053–1058.

Parnas, D.L., "Software Aspects of Strategic Defense Systems," *American Scientist,* Vol. 73, September-October 1985, pp. 432–440.

Parnas, D.L., and P.C. Clements, "A Rational Design Process: How and Why to Fake It," *IEEE Transactions on Software Engineering,* Vol. SE-12, No. 2, February 1986, pp. 251–257.

Partridge, D., *Artificial Intelligence,* John Wiley and Sons, Inc., NY, 1986.

Peters, L.J., *Advanced Structured Analysis and Design,* Prentice-Hall, Inc., Englewood Cliffs, NJ, 1987.

Peterson, J.L., *Petri Net Theory and the Modeling of Systems,* Prentice-Hall, Inc., Englewood Cliffs, NJ, 1981.

Pirnia, S., and M.J. Hayek, "Requirements Definition Approach for an Automated Requirements Traceability Tool," *Proceedings of the IEEE 1981 National Aerospace and Electronics Conference* (Dayton, OH, May 19–21, 1981), Vol. 1, IEEE Computer Society Press, Washington, DC, 1981, pp. 389–394.

Poston, R.M., and M.W. Bruen, "Counting Down to Zero Software Failures," *IEEE Software,* Vol. 4, No. 5, September 1987.

Powers, M.J., D.R. Adams, and H.D. Mills, *Computer Information Systems Development: Analysis and Design,* South-Western Publishing Co., Palo Alto, CA, 1984.

Pressman, R.S., *Software Engineering: A Practitioner's Approach,* 2nd edition, McGraw-Hill Book Co., NY, 1987.

Pyster, A., "The Synthesis Process for Software Development," in R.H. Thayer and M. Dorfman (eds.), *Tutorial: System and Software Requirements Engineering,* IEEE Computer Society Press, Washington, DC, 1990.

q-q-q

r-r-r

RADC TR-79–168 — *See Alford and Lawson, 1979.*

RADC TR-83–175 — *See Bowen, Post, Tsai, Presson, and Schmidt, 1983.*

RADC TR-85–135 — *See Addleman, Davis, and Presson, 1985.*

RADC TR-85–37 — *See Bowen, Wigle, and Tsai, 1985.*

Ramamoorthy, C.V., A. Prakash, W. Tsai, and Y. Usuda, "Software Engineering: Problems and Perspectives," IEEE *Computer,* Vol. 17, No. 10, October 1984, pp. 191–209. Corrected copy reprinted in R.H. Thayer (ed.), *Tutorial: Software Engineering Project Management,* IEEE Computer Society Press, Washington, DC, 1988.

Ramamoorthy, C.V., and P. Sheu, "Object-Oriented Systems." *IEEE Expert,* Fall 1988.

Rich, C., and R.C. Waters, "Automatic Programming: Myths and Prospects," IEEE *Computer,* Vol. 21, No. 8, August 1988, pp. 40–51.

Rich, C., and R.C. Waters, "The Programmer's Apprentice: A Research Overview," IEEE *Computer,* Vol. 21, No. 11, November 1988, pp. 10–24.

Rich, C., R.C. Waters, and H.B. Reubenstein, "Toward a Requirements Apprentice," *Proceedings of the 4th International Workshop on Software Specifications and Design* (Monterey, CA, April 3–4, 1987), IEEE Computer Society Press, Washington, DC, 1987, pp. 79–86. Reprinted in R.H. Thayer and M. Dorfman (eds.), *Tutorial: System and Software Requirements Engineering,* IEEE Computer Society Press, Washington, DC, 1990.

Riddle, W.E., and J.C. Wileden, *Tutorial: Software System Design—Description and Analysis,* IEEE Computer Society Press, Washington, DC, 1980.

Rockstrom, A., and R. Saracco, "SDL — CCITT Specification and Description Language," *IEEE Transactions on Communications,* Vol. COM-30, No. 6, June 1982, pp. 1310–1317.

Roman, G-C., "A Taxonomy of Current Issues in Requirements Engineering," IEEE *Computer,* Vol. 18, No. 4, April 1985, pp. 14–22. Reprinted in R.H. Thayer and M. Dorfman (eds.), *Tutorial: System and Software Requirements Engineering,* IEEE Computer Society Press, Washington, DC, 1990.

Roman, G-C., M.J. Stucki, W.E. Ball, and W.D. Gillett, "A Total System Design Framework," IEEE *Computer,* Vol. 17, No. 5, May 1984, pp. 15–26.

Ross, D.T., "Applications and Extensions of SADT," IEEE *Computer,* Vol. 18, No. 4, April 1985, pp. 25–34.

Ross, D.T., "Structured Analysis (SA): A Language for Communicating Ideas," *IEEE Transactions on Software Engineering,* Vol. SE-3, No. 1, January 1977, pp. 16–34.

Ross, D.T., and J.W. Brackett, "An Approach to Structured Analysis," *Computer Decisions,* Vol. 8, No. 9, September 1976, pp. 40–44.

Ross, D.T., and K.E. Schoman, Jr., "Structured Analysis for Requirements Definition," *IEEE Transactions on Software Engineering,* Vol. SE-3, No. 1, January 1977, pp. 6–15.

Royce, W.W., "Managing the Development of Large Software Systems," *Proceedings of the IEEE WESCON* (Los Angeles, CA, August 25–28, 1970), IEEE Press, NY, pp. 1–9. Reprinted in R.H. Thayer (ed.), *Tutorial: Software Engineering Project Management,* IEEE Computer Society Press, Washington, DC, 1988.

Rzepka, W., and Y. Ohno (eds.), Special Issue "Requirements Engineering Environments," IEEE *Computer,* Vol. 18, No. 4, April 1985.

Rzepka, W., and Y. Ohno, "Requirements Engineering Environments: Software Tools for Modeling User Needs," Guest Editors' Introduction, IEEE *Computer,* Vol. 18, No. 4, April 1985, pp. 9–12.

S-S-S

Sailor, J.D., "System Engineering Overview," in R.H. Thayer and M. Dorfman (eds.), *Tutorial: System and Software Requirements Engineering,* IEEE Computer Society Press, Washington, DC, 1990.

Sailor, J.D., *System Engineering Management Guide,* Defense Systems Management College, 1983. (The second [1986] edition of this book can be obtained from the Superintendent of Documents, U.S. Government Printing Office, Washington, DC).

Sammet, J.E., *Programming Languages: History and Fundamentals,* Prentice-Hall, Inc., Englewood Cliffs, NJ, 1969.

Sayani, H.H., "PSL/PSA at the Age of Fifteen," in R.H. Thayer and M. Dorfman (eds.), *Tutorial: System and Software Requirements Engineering,* IEEE Computer Society Press, Washington, DC, 1990.

Scharer, L., "Pinpointing Requirements," *Datamation,* April 1981, pp. 139–151. Reprinted in R.H. Thayer and M. Dorfman (eds.), *Tutorial: System and Software Requirements Engineering,* IEEE Computer Society Press, Washington, DC, 1990.

Scheffer, P.A., and A.H. Stone III, "A Case Study of SREM," IEEE *Computer,* Vol. 18, No. 4, April 1985, pp. 47–54.

Schell, W., and P. Zave, "Salient Features of an Executable Specification Language and Its Environment," *IEEE Transactions on Software Engineering,* Vol. SE-12, No. 2, February 1986, pp. 312–325.

Schulmeyer, G.G., and J.I. McManus, *Handbook of Software Quality Assurance,* Van Nostrand Reinhold Co., NY, 1987.

Schultz, H.P., *Software Management Metrics,* ESD TR-88–001, prepared by The MITRE Corporation for the Electronic Systems Division, Hanscom AFB, MA, 1988.

Sciortino, J., and D. Dunning, "Software Traceability, Requirements Testability, and Auditing Model," AIAA Paper 84-2633, *Proceedings of the AIAA/IEEE Digital Avionics Systems Conference* (Baltimore, MD, December 3–6, 1984), American Institute of Aeronautics and Astronautics, NY, 1984, pp. 159–166.

Searle, L.V., *An Air Force Guide to System Specification,* ESD TR-81–128, Electronic Systems Division, Hanscom AFB, MA, 1981.

Seidewitz, E., and M. Stark, "Towards a General Object-Oriented Software Development Methodology," ACM *Special Interest Group on Ada (SIGAda) Letters,* Vol. 7, No. 4, July-August 1987, pp. 4–54 to 4–67.

Shlaer, S., and S.J. Mellor, *Object-Oriented Systems Analysis: Modeling the World in Data,* Yourdon Press, Prentice-Hall, Inc., Englewood Cliffs, NJ, 1988.

Shneiderman, B., *Designing the User Interface: Strategies for Effective Human Computer Interaction,* Addison-Wesley Publishing Co., Inc., Ridgely, MD, 1987.

Software Engineering Institute (SEI), — *See Humphrey and Sweet.*

Sommerville, I., *Software Engineering,* 3rd edition, Addison-Wesley Publishing Co, Workingham, England, 1989.

Squires, S.L., B. Branstad, and M. Zelkowitz (eds.), "Special Issue on Rapid Prototyping," ACM *SIGSOFT Software Engineering Notes,* Vol. 7, No. 5, December 1982.

STARTS Debrief Report, "ARTEMIS: A Debrief Report," The National Computing Centre Ltd., Manchester, England, 1986.

STARTS Debrief Report, "CORE: A Debrief Report," The National Computing Centre Ltd., Manchester, England, 1986.

STARTS Debrief Report, "J S D (Jackson System Development): A Debrief Report," The National Computing Centre Ltd., Manchester, England, 1986.

STARTS Debrief Report, "PRICE S: A Debrief Report," The National Computing Centre Ltd., Manchester, England, 1986.

STARTS Debrief Report, "SAFRA: A Debrief Report," The National Computing Centre Ltd., Manchester, England, 1986.

STARTS Debrief Report, "SDL: A Debrief Report," The National Computing Centre Ltd., Manchester, England, 1986.

STARTS Debrief Report, "SLIM: A Debrief Report," The National Computing Centre Ltd., Manchester, England, 1986.

STARTS Debrief Report, Austwick, M., and M. Norris, "VDM: A Debrief Report," The National Computing Centre Ltd., Manchester, England, 1986.

STARTS Debrief Report, Norris, M., "Z (A Formal Specification Method): A Debrief Report," The National Computing Centre Ltd., Manchester, England, 1986.

STARTS Guide, 1987 — *See National Computing Centre, The.*

Stay, J.F., "HIPO and Integrated Program Design," *IBM Systems Journal,* Vol. 15, No. 2, 1976, pp. 143–154.

Stevens, W.P., G.J. Myers, and L.L. Constantine, "Structured Design," *IBM Systems Journal,* Vol. 13, No. 2, 1974, pp. 115–139.

Svoboda, C.P., "Structured Analysis: A Tutorial," R.H. Thayer and M. Dorfman (eds.), *Tutorial: System and Software Requirements Engineering,* IEEE Computer Society Press, Washington, DC, 1990.

Swartout, W., and R. Balzer, "On the Inevitable Intertwining of Specification and Implementation," *Communications of the ACM,* Vol. 2, No. 7, July 1982, pp. 438–440.

System Engineering Management Guide, 1986 — *See Technical Management Department, Defense Systems Management College (DSMC). See also Sailor, 1983.*

t-t-t

Tausworthe, R.C., "The Work Breakdown Structure in Software Project Management," *The Journal of Systems and Software,* Vol. 1, No. 3, 1980, pp. 181–186. Reprinted in R.H. Thayer (ed.), *Tutorial: Software Engineering Project Management,* IEEE Computer Society Press, Washington, DC, 1988.

Technical Management Department, Defense Systems Management College (DSMC), *System Engineering Management Guide,* 2nd edition, DSMC, Fort Belvoir, VA, 1986.

Teichroew, D.T., and E.A. Hershey III, "PSL/PSA: A Computer-Aided Technique for Structured Documentation and Analysis of Information Processing Systems," *IEEE Transactions on Software Engineering,* January 1977, pp. 41–48.

Teorey, T., D. Yang, and J. Fry, "A Logical Design Methodology for Relational Databases Using the Extended Entity-Relationship Model," *ACM Computing Surveys,* Vol. 18, No. 2, June 1986.

Thayer, R.H. (ed.), *Tutorial: Software Engineering Project Management,* IEEE Computer Society Press, Washington, DC, 1988.

Thayer, R.H., "Software Engineering Project Management: A Top-Down View," in R.H. Thayer (ed.), *Tutorial: Software Engineering Project Management,* IEEE Computer Society Press, Washington, DC, 1988.

Thayer, R.H., A.B. Pyster, and R C. Wood, "Major Issues in Software Engineering Project Management," *IEEE Transactions on Software Engineering,* Vol. SE-7, No. 4, July 1981, pp. 333–342.

Thayer, R.H., and A.B. Pyster, "Guest Editorial: Software Engineering Project Management," *IEEE Transactions on Software Engineering,* Vol. SE-10, No. 1, January 1984, pp. 2–3.

Thayer, R.H., and M. Dorfman (eds.), *Tutorial: System and Software Requirements Engineering,* IEEE Computer Society Press, Washington, DC, 1990.

Thayer, R.H., and W.W. Royce, "Software System Engineering," in R.H. Thayer and M. Dorfman (eds.), *Tutorial: System and Software Requirement Engineering,* IEEE Computer Society Press, Washington, DC, 1990.

The Institute of Electrical and Electronics Engineers — *See IEEE, Institute of Electrical and Electronics Engineers, Inc.*

The Official Handbook of MASCOT, Joint IECCA & MUF Committee on Mascot, Royal Signals and Radar Establishment, Malvern, Worcestershire, England, June 1987.

The STARTS Guide — See National Computing Centre, The.

Tracz, W., Tutorial: *Software Reuse—Emerging Technology,* IEEE Computer Society Press, Washington, DC, 1988.

TRW SS-73–07 — *See TRW Systems Group, 1973.*

TRW SS-77–04 — *See Lano, 1977.*

TRW SS-80–02 — *See Lano, 1980.*

TRW SS-80–03 — *See Alford, et al., 1980.*

TRW Systems Group, *TRW Software Development and Configuration Management Manual,* TRW SS-73–07, TRW Defense and Space Systems Group, Redondo Beach, CA, 1973.

TRW, Inc., *Distributed Computing Design System/DCDS Description,* Technical Report CDRL A004, TRW, Inc., Huntsville, AL, August 1981.

u-u-u

U.S. Air Force — *See Military. See also DoD.*

U.S. Department of Defense — *See DoD. See also Military.*

Urban, J.E., "The Descartes Specification Language," in R.H. Thayer and M. Dorfman (eds.), *Tutorial: System and Software Requirements Engineering,* IEEE Computer Society Press, Washington, DC, 1990.

Urban, S.D., J.E. Urban, and W.D. Dominick, "Utilizing an Executable Specification Language for an Information System," *IEEE Transactions on Software Engineering,* Vol. SE-11, No. 7, July 1985, pp. 598–605.

Urban, S.D., J.E. Urban, and W.D. Dominick, "Utilizing an Executable Specification Language for an Information System," *IEEE Transactions on Software Engineering*, Vol. SE-11, No. 7, July 1985, pp. 598–605.

v-v-v

w-w-w

Wallace, D.R., and R.U. Fujii, "Software Verification and Validation: Its Role in Computer Assurance and Its Relationship with Software Project Management Standards," NIST Special Publication 500–165, National Computer Systems Laboratory, National Institute of Standards and Technology, Gaithersburg, MD, 1989

Ward, P.T., "The Transformation Schema: An Extension of the Data Flow Diagram to Represent Control and Timing," *IEEE Transactions on Software Engineering*, Vol. SE-12, No. 2, February 1986, pp. 198–210.

Ward, P.T., and S.J. Mellor, *Structured Development for Real-Time Systems:* Vol. 1, *Introduction & Tools:* Vol. 2, *Essential Modeling Techniques;* Vol. 3, *Implementation Modeling Techniques,* Yourdon Press, NY, 1986. (Note: the principal (first) author for Vol. 3 is S.J. Mellor.)

Warnier, J-D., *Logical Construction of Programs,* 3rd edition, translated by B. Flanagan, Van Nostrand Reinhold Co., NY, 1976.

Wasserman, A.I., "Extending State Transition Diagrams for the Specification of Human-Computer Interaction," *IEEE Transactions on Software Engineering,* Vol. SE-11, No. 8, August 1985, pp. 699–713.

Wasserman, A.I., "User Software Engineering and the Design of Interactive Systems," *Proceedings of the 5th International Conference on Software Engineering* (San Diego, CA, March 9–12, 1981), IEEE Computer Society Press, Washington, DC, pp. 387–393.

Wasserman, A.I., and L.A. Belady, "Software Engineering: The Turning Point," IEEE *Computer,* Vol. 11, No. 9, September 1978, pp. 30–41.

Wasserman, A.I., and P.A. Pircher, "A Graphic, Extensible Integrated Environment for Software Development," *Proceedings Second ACM SIGSOFT/SIGPLAN Software Engineering Symposium on Practical Software Development Environment* (Palo Alto, CA, December 9–11, 1986), ACM Press, NY, 1986. Published in ACM *SIGPLAN Notices*, Vol. 22, No. 1, January 1987, pp. 131–142. Reprinted in R.H. Thayer and M. Dorfman (eds.), *Tutorial: System and Software Requirements Engineering,* IEEE Computer Society Press, Washington, DC, 1990.

Waters, R.C., "The Programmer's Apprentice: A Session with KBEmacs," *IEEE Transactions on Software Engineering,* Vol. SE-11, No. 11, November 1985, pp. 1296–1320.

Wegner, P., "Capital-Intensive Software Technology," *IEEE Software,* Vol. 1, No. 3, July 1984, pp. 7–45.

Weinberg, G.M., and D.P. Freedman, "Reviews, Walkthroughs, and Inspections," *IEEE Transactions on Software Engineering,* Vol. SE-10, No. 1, January 1984, pp. 68–72. Reprinted in R.H. Thayer (ed.), *Tutorial: Software Engineering Project Management,* IEEE Computer Society Press, Washington, DC, 1988.

Weinberg, G.M., *The Psychology of Computer Programming,* Van Nostrand Reinhold Co., NY, 1971.

Weiss, D.M., "The MUDD Report: A Case Study of Navy Software Development Practices," NRL Report 7909, Naval Research Laboratory, Washington, DC, May 21, 1975.

Weyuker, E., "On Testing Nontestable Programs," *The Computer Journal,* Vol. 25, No. 4, 1982, pp. 465–470.

Williams, J., "SSADM—System Building Made simple," *Systems International,* November 1987, pp. 91–92. Reprinted in R.H. Thayer and M. Dorfman (eds.), *Tutorial: System and Software Requirements Engineering,* IEEE Computer Society Press, Washington, DC, 1990.

x-x-x

y-y-y

Yau, S.S., and J.P. Tsai, "A Survey of Software Design Techniques," *IEEE Transactions on Software Engineering,* Vol. SE-12, No. 6, June 1986, pp. 713–721.

Yeh, R.T., "Requirements Analysis—A Management Perspective," *Proceedings of IEEE Computer Society's Sixth International Computer Software and Applications Conference* (COMPSAC 82) (Chicago, IL, November 8–12, 1982), IEEE Computer Society Press, Washington, DC, 1982, pp. 410–416.

Yeh, R.T., "Software Engineering," *IEEE Spectrum,* November 1983, pp. 91–94.

Yeh, R.T., P. Zave, A.P. Conn, and G.E. Cole, Jr., "Software Requirements: New Directions and Perspectives;" in C.R. Vick and C.V. Ramamoorthy, (eds.), *Handbook of Software Engineering,* Van Nostrand Reinhold Co., 1984, pp. 519–543. Reprinted in R.H. Thayer (ed.), *Tutorial: Software Engineering Project Management,* IEEE Computer Society Press, Washington, DC, 1988.

Yourdon, E., "What Ever Happened to Structured Analysis?" *Datamation,* June 1, 1986, pp. 133–138.

Yourdon, E., and L.L. Constantine, *Structured Design: Fundamentals of a Discipline of Computer Program and System Design,* 2nd edition, Yourdon Press, NY, 1979.

Yourdon, E., *Managing the Structured Techniques,* 4th edition, Yourdon Press Computing Series, Prentice-Hall, Inc., Englewood Cliffs, NJ, 1989.

Yourdon, E., *Managing the System Life Cycle* 2nd edition, Yourdon Press, NY, 1988.

Yourdon, E., *Modern Structured Analysis,* Yourdon Press Computing Series, Prentice-Hall, Inc., Englewood Cliffs, NJ, 1989.

Yourdon, E., *Structured Walkthroughs,* 4th edition, Yourdon Press Computing Series, Prentice-Hall, Inc., Englewood Cliffs, NJ, 1988.

Yourdon, E., *Techniques of Program Structure and Design,* Prentice-Hall, Inc., Englewood Cliffs, NJ, 1976.

Z-Z-Z

Zave, P., "An Operational Approach to Requirements Specification for Embedded Systems," *IEEE Transactions on Software Engineering,* Vol. 8, No. 3, May 1982, pp. 250–269.

Zave, P., "The Operational Versus the Conventional Approach to Software Development," *Communications of the ACM,* Vol. 27, No. 2, February 1984, pp. 104–118. Reprinted in R.H. Thayer and M. Dorfman (eds.), *Tutorial: System and Software Requirements Engineering,* IEEE Computer Society Press, Washington, DC, 1990.

Zave, P., and R. Yeh, "Executable Requirements for Embedded Systems," *Proceedings of the 5th International Conference on Software Engineering* (San Diego, CA, March 9–12, 1981), IEEE Computer Society Press, Washington, DC, 1981, pp. 295–304.

Zave, P., and W. Shell, "Salient Features of an Executable Specification Language and Its Environment," *IEEE Transactions on Software Engineering,* Vol. 12, No. 2, February 1986, pp. 312–325.

INDEX

This is a combined index for both of the following companion tutorials:

R.H. Thayer and M. Dorfman (eds.), *System and Software Requirements Engineering*, IEEE Computer Society Press, Washington, DC, 1990.

M. Dorfman and R.H. Thayer (eds.), *Standards, Guidelines, and Examples on System and Software Requirements Engineering*, IEEE Computer Society Press, Washington, DC, 1990.

The pages printed with ordinary (nonbold) text can be found in *System and Software Requirements Engineering*. The pages printed with **bold** text can be found in *Standards, Guidelines, and Examples on System and Software Requirements Engineering*.

About the Authors

Merlin Dorfman, PhD, is a technical consultant in the Data Systems Engineering Organization, Space Systems Division, Lockheed Missiles & Space Company, Sunnyvale, California. He specializes in system engineeing for software-intensive systems (requirements analysis, top-level architecture, and performance evaluation) and in algorithm development for data processing systems. He has performed concept exploration, system implementation, and operations and maintenance of data systems; he has worked on proposal teams and company-funded technology projects as well as on development contracts. He was in charge of the development of ARTS (Automated Requirements Traceability System).

He is the author of a four-day course, "Software Requirements and Design Specifications," for Learning Tree International (formerly Integrated Computer Systems) of Los Angeles, California. He has been a guest lecturer on software system engineering in the course "Management of Software Acquisition" at the Defense Systems Management College.

Dr. Dorfman is an associate fellow of the American Institute of Aeronautics and Astronautics (AIAA), co-chair of its Technical Committee on Software Systems, and a past chairman of the AIAA San Francisco section. He is co-editor of a volume, *Progress in Aeronautics and Astronautics: Aerospace Software Engineering,* scheduled for publication by AIAA in 1990. Dr. Dorfman represents the Lockheed Corporation on the Embedded Computer Software Committee of the Aerospace Industries Association. He is an affiliate member of the IEEE Computer Society and is a registered Professional Engineer in the states of California and Colorado.

He has BS and MS degrees from the Massachusetts Institute of Technology and a PhD from Stanford University, all in aeronautics and astronautics. He is a member of the Tau Beta Pi and Sigma Gamma Tau honorary societies.

Richard H. Thayer, PhD, is a professor in computer science at the California State University, Sacramento. He is a national and international consultant and lecturer in software requirements, software engineering, system engineering, and project management. Since 1981, Dr. Thayer has given his seminar, "Systems and Software Requirements Engineering," to a worldwide audience of engineers and managers in 15 countries in Europe, the Middle and Far East, and the Americas.

Prior to this, he served more than 20 years in the U.S. Air Force as a senior officer in a variety of positions associated with engineering, programming, research, teaching, and management in computer science and data processing. His numerous positions included six years as a supervisor and technical leader of scientific programming groups, four years with the U.S. Air Force R&D program in computer science, and six years of managing large data processing organizations.

Dr. Thayer is a senior member of the IEEE Computer Society and the IEEE Software Engineering Standards Subcommittee. He was chairperson of the working group that developed the IEEE's *Standard for Software Project Management Plans.* He is an associate fellow of the American Institute of Aeronautics and Astronautics where he served on the AIAA Technical Committee on Computer Systems, and a member of the Association for Computing Machinery. He is also a registered professional engineer.

He has a BSEE and an MS degree from the University of Illinois at Urbana and a PhD from the University of California at Santa Barbara; all are in electrical engineering.

He is the editor of the IEEE *Tutorial: Software Engineering Project Management,* 1988. He is also the author of more than 30 technical papers and reports on software project management, software engineering, and software engineering standards and is an invited speaker at many national and international software engineering conferences and workshops.

IEEE COMPUTER SOCIETY

A member society of the Institute of Electrical and Electronics Engineers, Inc.

Policies of the IEEE Computer Society

Headquarters Office

1730 Massachusetts Avenue, N.W.
Washington, DC 20036-1903
Phone: (202) 371-1012
Telex: 7108250437 IEEE COMPSO

Publications Office

10662 Los Vaqueros Circle
Los Alamitos, CA 90720
Membership and General Information: (714) 821-8380
Publications Orders: (800) 272-6657

European Office

13, Avenue de l'Aquilon
B-1200 Brussels, Belgium
Phone: 32 (2) 770-21-98
Telex: 25387 AWALB

Asian Office

Ooshima Building
2-19-1 Minami-Aoyama, Minato-ku
Tokyo 107, Japan

IEEE Computer Society Press Publications

Monographs: A monograph is a collection of original material assembled as a coherent package. It is typically a treatise on a small area of learning and may include the collection of knowledge gathered over the lifetime of the authors.

Tutorials: A tutorial is a collection of original materials prepared by the editors and reprints of the best articles published in a subject area. They must contain at least five percent original materials (15 to 20 percent original materials is recommended).

Reprint Books: A reprint book is a collection of reprints that are divided into sections with a preface, table of contents, and section introductions that discuss the reprints and why they were selected. It contains less than five percent original material.

Technology Series: The technology series is a collection of anthologies of reprints each with a narrow focus of a subset on a particular discipline.

Submission of proposals: For guidelines on preparing CS Press Books, write Editor-in-Chief, IEEE Computer Society, 1730 Massachusetts Avenue, N.W., Washington, DC 20036-1903 (telephone 202-371-1012).

Purpose

The IEEE Computer Society advances the theory and practice of computer science and engineering, promotes the exchange of technical information among 97,000 members worldwide, and provides a wide range of services to members and nonmembers.

Membership

Members receive the acclaimed monthly magazine *Computer*, discounts, and opportunities to serve (all activities are led by volunteer members). Membership is open to all IEEE members, affiliate society members, and others seriously interested in the computer field.

Publications and Activities

Computer. An authoritative, easy-to-read magazine containing tutorial and in-depth articles on topics across the computerfield, plus news, conferences, calendar, interviews, and new products.

Periodicals. The society publishes six magazines and four research transactions. Refer to membership application or request information as noted above.

Conference Proceedings, Tutorial Texts, Standards Documents. The Computer Society Press publishes more than 100 titles every year.

Standards Working Groups. Over 100 of these groups produce IEEE standards used throughout the industrial world.

Technical Committees. Over 30 TCs publish newsletters, provide interaction with peers in specialty areas, and directly influence standards, conferences, and education.

Conferences/Education. The society holds about 100 conferences each year and sponsors many educational activities, including computing and science accreditation.

Chapters. Regular and student chapters worldwide provide the opportunity to interact with colleagues, hear technical experts, and serve the local professional community.

Ombudsman

Members experiencing problems—magazine delivery, membership status, or unresolved complaints—may write to the ombudsman at the Publications Office.

Other IEEE Computer Society Press Texts

Monographs

Integrating Design and Test: Using CAE Tools for ATE Programming:
Written by K.P. Parker
(ISBN 0-8186-8788-6 (case)); 160 pages

JSP and JSD: The Jackson Approach to Software Development (Second Edition)
Written by J.R. Cameron
(ISBN 0-8186-8858-0 (case)); 560 pages

National Computer Policies
Written by Ben G. Matley and Thomas A. McDannold
(ISBN 0-8186-8784-3 (case)); 192 pages

Physical Level Interfaces and Protocols
Written by Uyless Black
(ISBN 0-8186-8824-6 (case)); 240 pages

Protecting Your Proprietary Rights in the Computer and High Technology Industries
Written by Tobey B. Marzouk, Esq.
(ISBN 0-8186-8754-1 (case)); 224 pages

Tutorials

Ada Programming Language
Edited by S.H. Saib and R.E. Fritz
(ISBN 0-8186-0456-5); 548 pages

Advanced Computer Architecture
Edited by D.P. Agrawal
(ISBN 0-8186-0667-3); 400 pages

Advanced Microprocessors and High-Level Language Computer Architectures
Edited by V. Milutinovic
(ISBN 0-8186-0623-1); 608 pages

Communication and Networking Protocols
Edited by S.S. Lam
(ISBN 0-8186-0582-0); 500 pages

Computer Architecture
Edited by D.D. Gajski, V.M. Milutinovic, H.J. Siegel, and B.P. Furht
(ISBN 0-8186-0704-1); 602 pages

Computer Communications: Architectures, Protocols and Standards (Second Edition)
Edited by William Stallings
(ISBN 0-8186-0790-4); 448 pages

Computer Grahics (2nd Edition)
Edited by J.C. Beatty and K.S. Booth
(ISBN 0-8186-0425-5); 576 pages

Computer Graphics Hardware: Image Generation and Display
Edited by H.K. Reghbati and A.Y.C. Lee
(ISBN 0-8186-0753-X); 384 pages

Computer Grahics: Image Synthesis
Edited by Kenneth Joy, Max Nelson, Charles Grant, and Lansing Hatfield
(ISBN 0-8186-8854-8 (case)); 384 pages

Computer and Network Security
Edited by M.D. Abrams and H.J. Podell
(ISBN 0-8186-0756-4); 448 pages

Computer Networks (4th Edition)
Edited by M.D. Abrams and I.W. Cotton
(ISBN 0-8186-0568-5); 512 pages

Computer Text Recognition and Error Correction
Edited by S.N. Srihari
(ISBN 0-8186-0579-0); 364 pages

Computers for Artificial Intelligence Applications
Edited by B. Wah and G.-J. Li
(ISBN 0-8186-0706-8); 656 pages

Database Management
Edited by J.A. Larson
(ISBN 0-8186-0714-9); 448 pages

Digital Image Processing and Analysis: Volume 1: Digital Image Processing
Edited by R. Chellappa and A.A. Sawchuk
(ISBN 0-8186-0665-7); 736 pages

Digital Image Processing and Analysis: Volume 2: Digital Image Analysis
Edited by R. Chellappa and A.A. Sawchuk
(ISBN 0-8186-0666-5); 670 pages

Digital Private Branch Exchanges (PBXs)
Edited by E.R. Coover
(ISBN 0-8186-0829-3); 400 pages

Distributed Control (2nd Edition)
Edited by R.E. Larson, P.L. McEntire, and J.G. O'Reilly
(ISBN 0-8186-0451-4); 382 pages

Distributed Database Management
Edited by J.A. Larson and S. Rahimi
(ISBN 0-8186-0575-8); 580 pages

Distributed-Software Engineering
Edited by S.M. Shatz and J.-P. Wang
(ISBN 0-8186-8856-4 (case)); 304 pages

DSP-Based Testing of Analog and Mixed-Signal Circuits
Edited by M. Mahoney
(ISBN 0-8186-0785-8); 272 pages

End User Facilities in the 1980's
Edited by J.A. Larson
(ISBN 0-8186-0449-2); 526 pages

Fault-Tolerant Computing
Edited by V.P. Nelson and B.D. Carroll
(ISBN 0-8186-0677-0 (paper) 0-8186-8667-4 (case)); 432 pages

Gallium Arsenide Computer Design
Edited by V.M. Milutinovic and D.A. Fura
(ISBN 0-8184-0795-5); 368 pages

Human Factors in Software Development (Second Edition)
Edited by B. Curtis
(ISBN 0-8186-0577-4); 736 pages

Integrated Services Digital Networks (ISDN) (Second Edition)
Edited by W. Stallings
(ISBN 0-8186-0823-4); 404 pages

For Further Information:

IEEE Computer Society, 10662 Los Vaqueros Circle, Los Alamitos, CA 90720

IEEE Computer Society, 13, Avenue de l'Aquilon, 2, B-1200 Brussels, BELGIUM

IEEE Computer Society, Ooshima Building, 2-19-1 Minami-Aoyama, Minato-ku, Tokyo 107, JAPAN

Interconnection Networks for Parallel and Distributed Processing
Edited by C.-l. Wu and T.-y. Feng
(ISBN 0-8186-0574-X); 500 pages

Local Network Equipment
Edited by H.A. Freeman and K.J. Thurber
(ISBN 0-8186-0605-3); 384 pages

Local Network Technology (3rd Edition)
Edited by W. Stallings
(ISBN 0-8186-0825-0); 512 pages

Microprogramming and Firmware Engineering
Edited by V. Milutinovic
(ISBN 0-8186-0839-0); 416 pages

Modern Design and Analysis of Discrete-Event Computer Simulations
Edited by E.J. Dudewicz and Z. Karian
(ISBN 0-8186-0597-9); 486 pages

New Paradigms for Software Development
Edited by William Agresti
(ISBN 0-8186-0707-6); 304 pages

Object-Oriented Computing—Volume 1: Concepts
Edited by Gerald E. Peterson
(ISBN 0-8186-0821-8); 214 pages

Object-Oriented Computing—Volume 2: Implementations
Edited by Gerald E. Peterson
(ISBN 0-8186-0822-6); 324 pages

Office Automation Systems (Second Edition)
Edited by H.A. Freeman and K.J. Thurber
(ISBN 0-8186-0711-4); 320 pages

Parallel Architectures for Database Systems
Edited by A.R. Hurson, L.L. Miller, and S.H. Pakzad
(ISBN 0-8186-8838-6 (case)); 478 pages

Programming Productivity: Issues for the Eighties (Second Edition)
Edited by C. Jones
(ISBN 0-8186-0681-9); 472 pages

Recent Advances in Distributed Data Base Management
Edited by C. Mohan
(ISBN 0-8186-0571-5); 500 pages

Reduced Instruction Set Computers
Edited by W. Stallings
(ISBN 0-8186-0713-0); 384 pages

Reliable Distributed System Software
Edited by J.A. Stankovic
(ISBN 0-8186-0570-7); 400 pages

Robotics Tutorial (2nd Edition)
Edited by C.S.G. Lee, R.C. Gonzalez, and K.S. Fu
(ISBN 0-8186-0658-4); 630 pages

Software Design Techniques (4th Edition)
Edited by P. Freeman and A.I. Wasserman
(ISBN 0-8186-0514-0); 736 pages

Software Engineering Project Management
Edited by R. Thayer
(ISBN 0-8186-0751-3); 512 pages

Software Maintenance
Edited by G. Parikh and N. Zvegintzov
(ISBN 0-8186-0002-0); 360 pages

Software Management (3rd Edition)
Edited by D.J. Reifer
(ISBN 0-8186-0678-9); 526 pages

Software-Oriented Computer Architecture
Edited by E. Fernandez and T. Lang
(ISBN 0-8186-0708-4); 376 pages

Software Quality Assurance: A Practical Approach
Edited by T.S. Chow
(ISBN 0-8186-0569-3); 506 pages

Software Restructuring
Edited by R.S. Arnold
(ISBN 0-8186-0680-0); 376 pages

Software Reusability
Edited by Peter Freeman
(ISBN 0-8186-0750-5); 304 pages—

Software Reuse: Emerging Technology
Edited by Will Tracz
(ISBN 0-8186-0846-3); 392 pages

Structured Testing
Edited by T.J. McCabe
(ISBN 0-8186-0452-2); 160 pages

Test Generation for VLSI Chips
Edited by V.D. Agrawal and S.C. Seth
(ISBN 0-8186-8786-X (case)); 416 pages

VLSI Technologies: Through the 80s and Beyond
Edited by D.J. McGreivy and K.A. Pickar
(ISBN 0-8186-0424-7); 346 pages

Reprint Collections

Selected Reprints: Dataflow and Reduction Architectures
Edited by S.S. Thakkar
(ISBN 0-8186-0759-9); 460 pages

Selected Reprints on Logic Design for Testability
Edited by C.C. Timoc
(ISBN 0-8186-0573-1); 324 pages

Selected Reprints: Microprocessors and Microcomputers (3rd Edition)
Edited by J.T. Cain
(ISBN 0-8186-0585-5); 386 pages

Selected Reprints in Software (3rd Edition)
Edited by M.V. Zelkowitz
(ISBN 0-8186-0789-0); 400 pages

Selected Reprints on VLSI Technologies and Computer Graphics
Edited by H. Fuchs
(ISBN 0-8186-0491-3); 490 pages

Technology Series

Artificial Neural Networks: Theoretical Concepts
Edited by V. Vemuri
(ISBN 0-8186-0855-2); 160 pages

Computer-Aided Software Engineering (CASE)
Edited by E.J. Chikofsky
(ISBN 0-8186-1917-1); 132 pages